COOL HOTELS

BEST OF EUROPE

teNeues

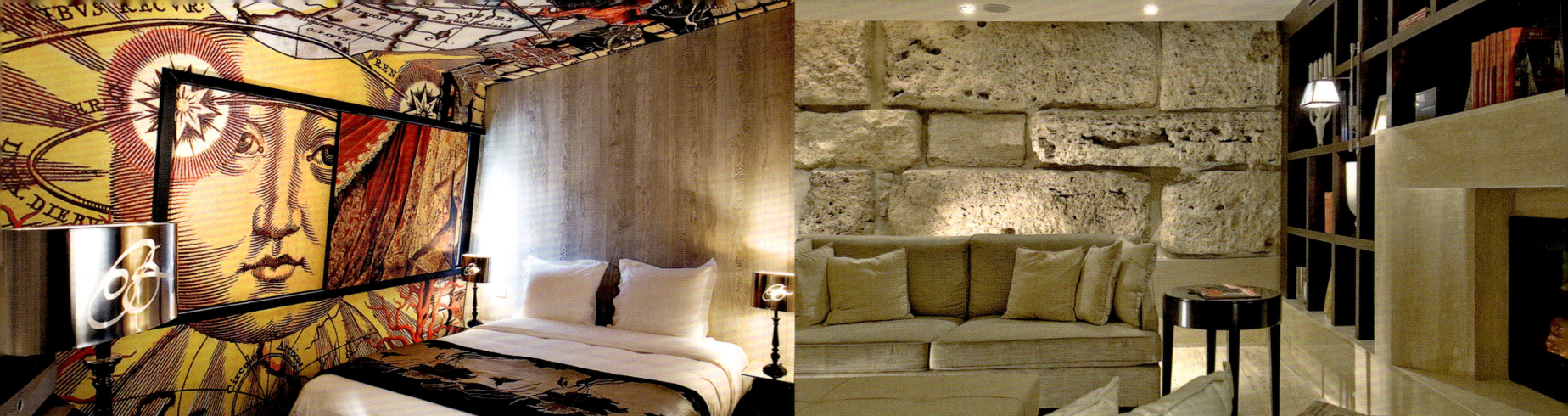

COOL HOTELS

BEST OF EUROPE

	Introduction	6

Russia
Moscow	Ararat Park Hyatt Moscow	16
Moscow	Swissôtel Krasnye Holmy	20

Estonia
Tallinn	The Three Sisters Hotel	22

Sweden
Stockholm	Berns Hotel	26
Stockholm	Hotel J	28

Denmark
Copenhagen	Fox	32
Copenhagen	First Hotel Skt. Petri	36

Ireland
Galway	g Hotel	40
Dublin	Dylan	44
Navan	Bellinter House	48

United Kingdom
Brighton	Hotel Pelirocco	52
Chandler's Cross	The Grove	54
Malmesbury	Whatley Manor	58
Cotswolds	Cowley Manor	64

London	The Berkeley	68
London	B+B Belgravia	72
London	Blakes Hotel	74
London	Claridge's	80
London	Haymarket Hotel	84
Leeds	42 The Calls	88
Edinburgh	The Glasshouse	92

Netherlands
Amsterdam	Hotel de Filosoof	94
Amsterdam	misc eatdrinksleep	98
Amsterdam	Lloyd Hotel	100
Rotterdam	Stroom	104
Maastricht	Eden Designhotel Maastricht	106
Maastricht	Kruisherenhotel	110

Belgium
Antwerp	Hotel Julien	116
Brussels	Monty Small Design Hotel	120
Brussels	Royal Windsor	124

Germany
Berlin	Adlon Kempinski	128
Berlin	Lux Eleven	132
Berlin	Q!	136
Hamburg	SIDE	140

Frankfurt	Goldman 25hours Hotel	142
Frankfurt	Villa Kennedy	146
Cologne	Chelsea	150
Lohmar	Schloss Auel	152
Stuttgart	Der Zauberlehrling	156
Munich	Hotel La Maison	160
Munich	Bayerischer Hof	164

Czech Republic
Prague	andel's Hotel & Suites Prague	170
Prague	Hotel Josef	174
Prague	Maximilian	178

Hungary
Budapest	Lánchíd 19	182

Austria
Kitzbühel	Ski & Golfresort Kitzhof	186
Salzburg	Hotel Schloss Fuschl	190
Vienna	Palais Coburg Residenz	194

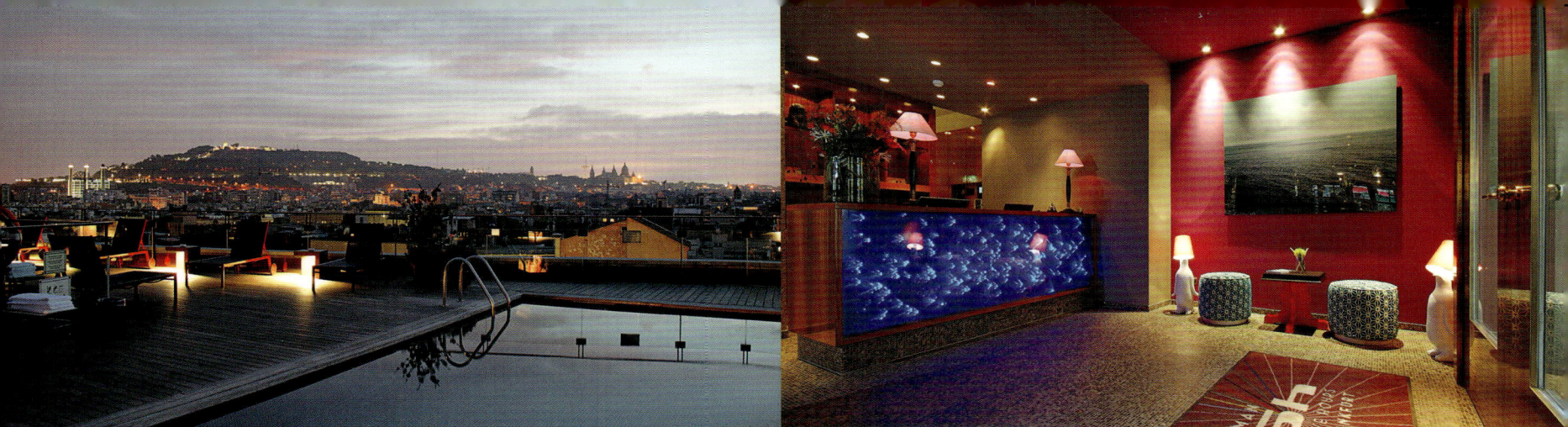

Switzerland

Arosa	Tschuggen Grand Hotel	198
Interlaken	Victoria-Jungfrau Grand Hotel & Spa	202
St. Moritz	Badrutt's Palace Hotel	206
Zurich	Greulich	210
Zurich	Widder Hotel	214

France & Monaco

Corsica	Casadelmar	218
Monaco	Columbus Monaco	222
Avignon	Hôtel Cloître Saint Louis	226
Grasse	Bastide Saint Mathieu	230
Ménerbes	La Bastide de Marie	234
Nice	Negresco	238
Saint-Tropez	Pastis Hotel St Tropez	242
Cap Ferrat	Royal Riviera	246
Paris	Hotel Le Bellechasse	250
Paris	Sofitel Trocadéro Dokhan's	254
Paris	Hotel Keppler	258
Paris	Hotel LUMEN Paris Louvre	262

Italy

Florence	Continentale	266
Florence	Granducato	270
Gargnano	Grand Hotel a Villa Feltrinelli	274
Milan	Town House Galleria	278
Turin	Le Méridien Turin Art+Tech	282
Perugia	Brufani Palace	284
Venice	Bauer il Palazzo	288
Verona	Byblos Art Hotel Villa Amista	292
Rome	Casa della Palma	296
Rome	St George Roma	300

Spain

Mallorca	Hotel hm jaime III	304
Mallorca	Tres	308
Barcelona	987 Barcelona Hotel	312
Barcelona	Casa Fuster	314
Barcelona	H1898	318
Barcelona	Market Hotel	322
Barcelona	Hotel Soho Barcelona	326
Granada	Palacio de los Patos	330
Madrid	Hotel de las Letras H&R	334
Madrid	Hotel Puerta América	336
Madrid	Hotel Urban	342

Portugal

| Porto | Porto Palacio Hotel | 346 |
| Lisbon | Jerónimos 8 | 350 |

Greece

Athens	Fresh Hotel	354
Athens	Semiramis	358
Mykonos	Mykonos Grace Hotel	364
Santorini	Perivolas	368

Turkey

| Istanbul | Ajia Hotel | 372 |
| Istanbul | Sumahan | 378 |

Index	384
Photo Credits	395
Imprint	396

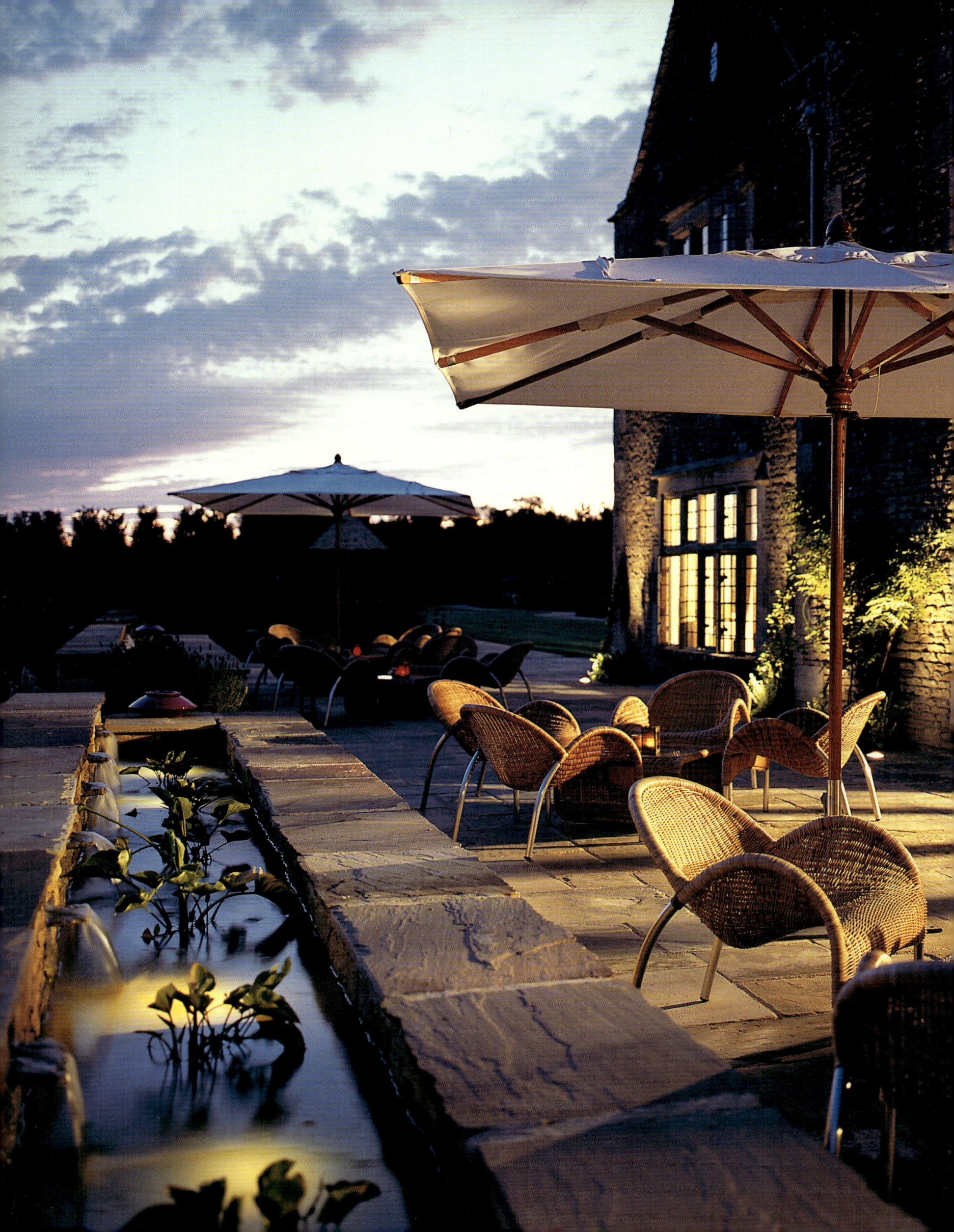

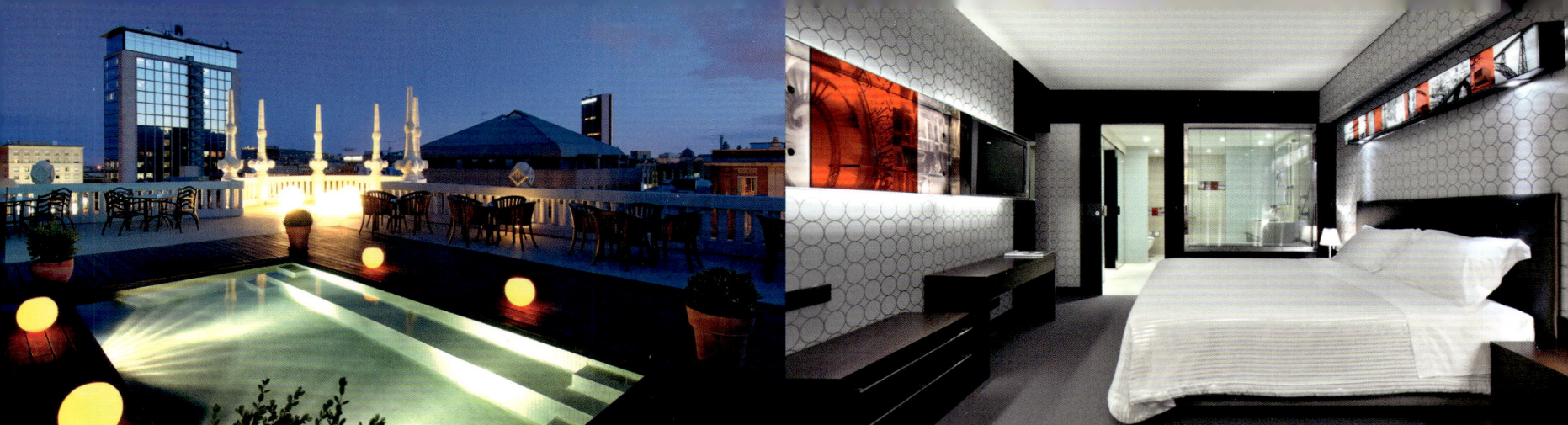

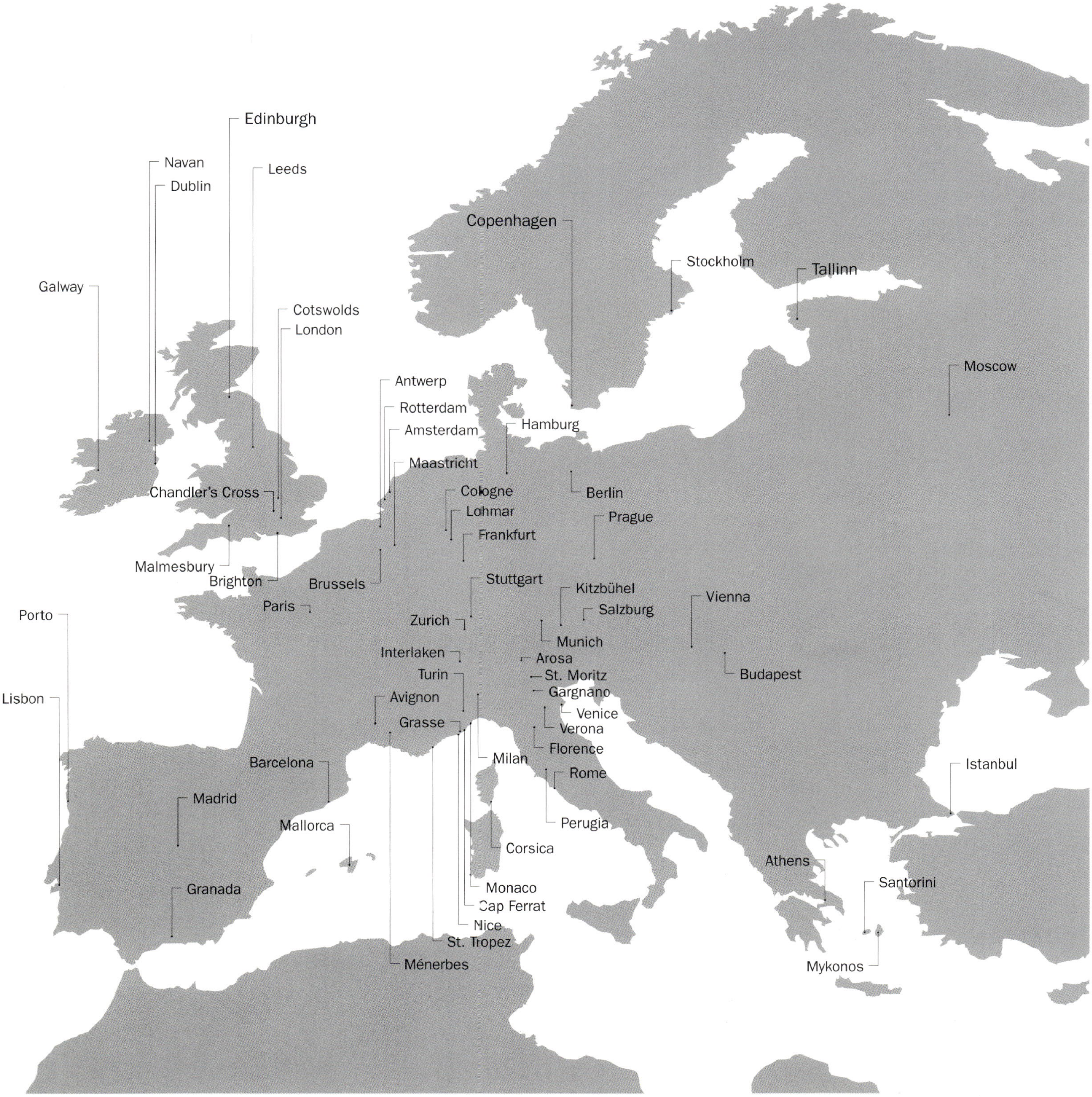

Edinburgh

Navan
Dublin

Leeds

Copenhagen

Stockholm

Tallinn

Galway

Moscow

Cotswolds
London

Antwerp

Rotterdam

Amsterdam

Hamburg

Maastricht

Chandler's Cross

Cologne

Berlin

Lohmar

Prague

Frankfurt

Malmesbury

Brighton

Brussels

Stuttgart

Kitzbühel

Vienna

Paris

Zurich

Salzburg

Porto

Munich

Interlaken

Arosa

Budapest

Turin

St. Moritz

Lisbon

Avignon

Gargnano

Grasse

Venice

Verona

Barcelona

Milan

Florence

Istanbul

Madrid

Rome

Mallorca

Perugia

Corsica

Granada

Athens

Monaco

Santorini

Cap Ferrat

Nice

St. Tropez

Mykonos

Ménerbes

It was the suite in a mansard in Saint-Germain-des-Prés that made the weekend in the city perfect. Forever chic designed in light grey tones with high mirror walls that make the small bath twice as big and a bed where dreams come true. A bottle of red wine and some cheese were standing on the table waiting to greet us, a small library offered the classics of French literature, and from two tiny balconies we could see the tip of the Eiffel Tower that was lit up in the evenings like New Year's fireworks. It was heaven over Paris.

Such travel descriptions, such portraits can be drawn for more and more hotels in Europe. Whether in a metropolis or in the middle of nowhere, provided with 18 or 180 rooms, offering casual luxury or only the best of basics, everyone of them has its personal signature and tells its individual story. Perhaps it is one of an eccentric hat maker and bohemian who discovered his passion as hotelier on Ireland's coast, perhaps a visionary who brought a futuristic flair into the Swiss Alps with sails of glass and steel, or a former Bond Girl who seduces London society instead of 007 with exotic interiors matching any film scene.

There are hotels that take up the style of their surroundings and carry on with them consequently though not dogmatically. Then there are others that take the principles of opposites to extremes and amuse, irritate or knowingly provoke you with contrasts. Anyone who has ever spent the night in the boudoir of a British sex bomb or in the surreal fantasy world of a French fashion designer knows what I am talking about. More common, but no less exciting, is the combination of different epochs as well as the mixture of old and new. Clean chic behind the facade of a Spanish palace of the 19th century, American lodge style in the European Alps or modern interpretation of art deco in a traditional grand hotel—it is such breaches of style that make up coolness.

The creative heads behind these hotels are now and then still unknown architects and designers looking for a playground or stepping stone—but also the famous figures in the branch open their sketch books more and more to draft facades, suites or sculptures. Even for stars like Lord Norman Foster, Zaha Hadid or David Chipperfield, hotels are still prestige projects. And for the respective owners great names not only mean rising numbers of guests, but also professionally fulfilled guest wishes. These wishes have fundamentally changed in the last few years. Travelers who are more often away for short periods look for hotels they could undyingly fall in love with at first sight , that oscillate between relaxation and experience, which also inspire and stick in one's mind. In brief: Hotels that are not just a place to sleep but also a place to live.

Such hotels are not created just as any chain hotel along the feeder to the city center, and not with the word "design" in the catalogue, black-and-white pictures in the lobby or colorful bed clothes. Such hotels need a concept thought out individually, intelligently and detailed, but also a concept that seems completely natural, utterly casual and self-evident. They have to understand the trends of tomorrow as well as the latest technology and psychology to profit. Europe offers the perfect framework for such works of art with its openness and multiplicity, for houses that awaken passion for a landscape or insight into a city's soul. Such hotels open new horizons—not just the heaven over Paris.

Anna Streubert

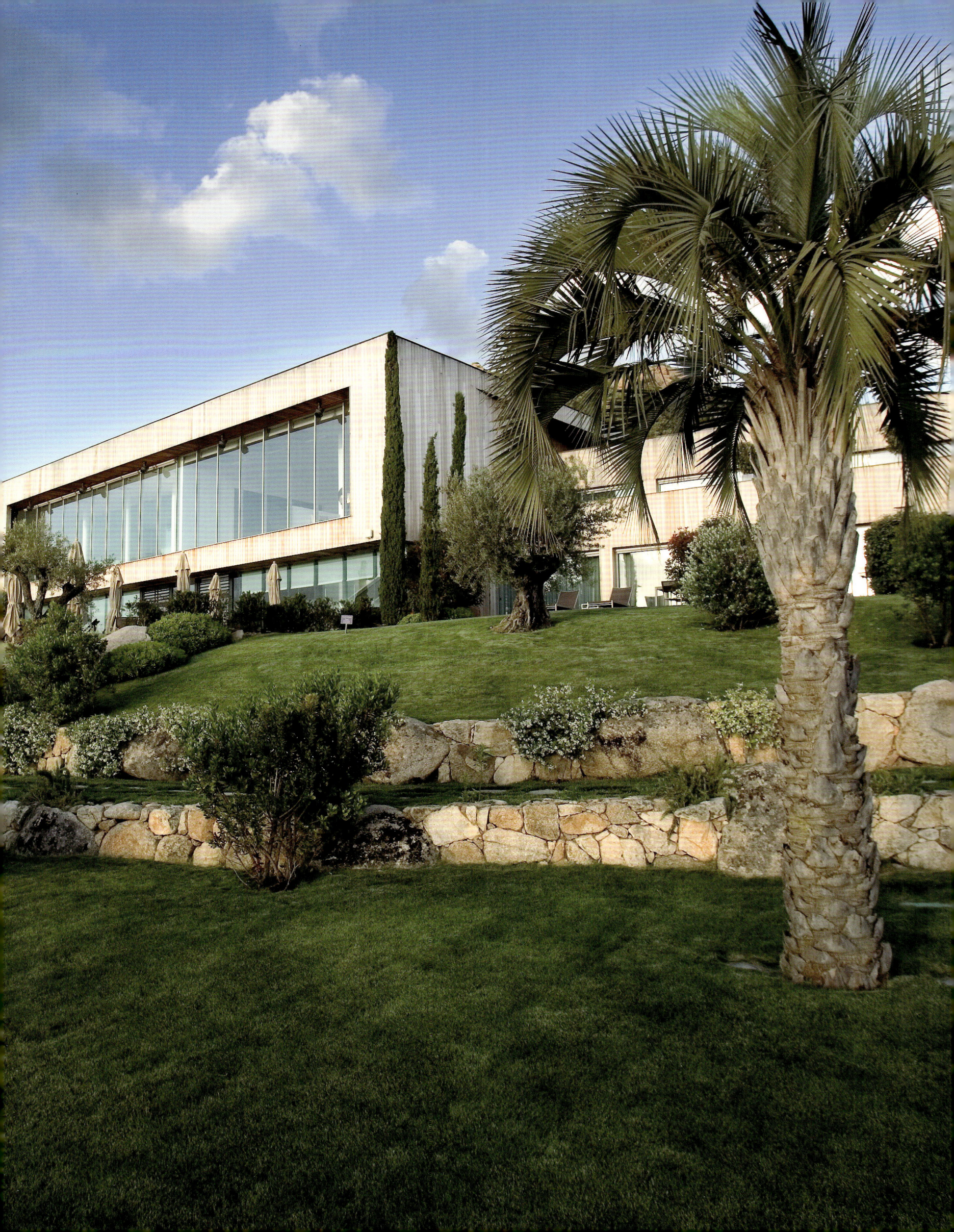

Es war die Suite in einer Mansarde in Saint-Germain-des-Prés, die das Wochenende in der Stadt perfekt machte. In hellen Grautönen zeitlos chic gestaltet, mit hohen Spiegelwänden, die dem kleinen Bad doppelte Größe verliehen, und einem Bett, das Träume wahr werden ließ. Zur Begrüßung standen eine Flasche Rotwein und Käse auf dem Tisch, eine kleine Bibliothek bot Klassiker der französischen Literatur, und von zwei winzigen Balkonen aus konnte man bis zur Spitze des Eiffelturms sehen, die abends wie ein Silvesterfeuerwerk funkelte. Es war der Himmel über Paris.

Solche Reiseskizzen, solche Portraits lassen sich für immer mehr Hotels in Europa zeichnen. In Metropolen oder mitten im Nirgendwo gelegen, mit 18 oder 180 Zimmern ausgestattet, legeren Luxus oder nur „Best of Basics" bietend zeigt jedes von ihnen eine persönliche Handschrift und erzählt eine individuelle Geschichte. Vielleicht die eines exzentrischen Hutmachers und Bohemiens, der an Irlands Küste seine Leidenschaft als Hotelier entdeckte, vielleicht die eines Visionärs, der mit Segeln aus Glas und Stahl futuristisches Flair in die beschauliche Schweizer Bergwelt brachte, oder die eines ehemaligen Bond Girls, das heute statt 007 die Londoner Society mit exotischen Interieurs verführt.

Es gibt dabei Hotels, die den Stil ihrer Umgebung aufgreifen und diesen konsequent aber entspannt weiterführen, und wiederum andere, die das Prinzip der Gegensätze auf die Spitze treiben und mit Kontrasten amüsieren, irritieren oder bewusst provozieren. Wer einmal eine Nacht im Boudoir einer britischen Sexbombe oder in der surrealen Fantasiewelt eines französischen Modeschöpfers verbracht hat, weiß, wovon die Rede ist. Etwas gängiger, aber nicht weniger spannend sind die Kombination unterschiedlicher Epochen sowie der Mix von Alt und Neu. Clean Chic hinter einer spanischen Palastfassade aus dem 19. Jahrhundert, amerikanischer Lodge-Stil in den europäischen Alpen oder modern interpretierter Art déco in einem traditionellen Grand Hotel – es sind solche Stilbrüche, die Coolness ausmachen.

Die kreativen Köpfe hinter diesen Hotels sind bisweilen noch unbekannte Architekten und Designer, die eine Spielwiese oder ein Sprungbrett suchen – immer häufiger öffnen aber auch die Berühmten der Branche ihre Skizzenbücher und entwerfen Fassaden, Suiten oder Skulpturen. Selbst für Stars wie Lord Norman Foster, Zaha Hadid oder David Chipperfield sind Hotels noch Prestigeprojekte. Und für die jeweiligen Bauherren bedeuten große Namen nicht nur steigende Gästezahlen, sondern auch professionell erfüllte Gästewünsche. Denn diese haben sich in den vergangenen Jahren grundlegend geändert: Reisende, die immer häufiger und immer kürzer unterwegs sind, suchen Hotels, in die sie sich auf den ersten Blick und unsterblich verlieben können, die zwischen Entspannung und Erlebnis oszillieren, die inspirieren und nachwirken – kurz: Hotels, die nicht nur Plätze zum Schlafen, sondern Orte zum Leben sind.

Solche Hotels schafft man nicht mit einem x-beliebigen Kettenhotel an der Zubringerstraße zum Zentrum, und nicht mit dem Wörtchen „Design" im Katalog, Schwarz-Weiß-Bildern in der Lobby oder bunten Bettüberwürfen. Solche Hotels brauchen ein individuelles, intelligentes und bis ins Detail durchdachtes Konzept, das aber vollkommen natürlich, ungezwungen und selbstverständlich wirkt. Sie müssen von den Trends von morgen so viel verstehen wie von jüngster Technik, und von Psychologie so viel wie von Profit. Europa bietet mit seiner Offenheit und Vielfältigkeit den perfekten Rahmen für solche Kunstwerke, für Häuser, welche die Leidenschaft für eine Landschaft wecken oder Einblick in die Seele einer Stadt geben. Solche Hotels eröffnen neue Horizonte – nicht nur den Himmel über Paris.

Anna Streubert

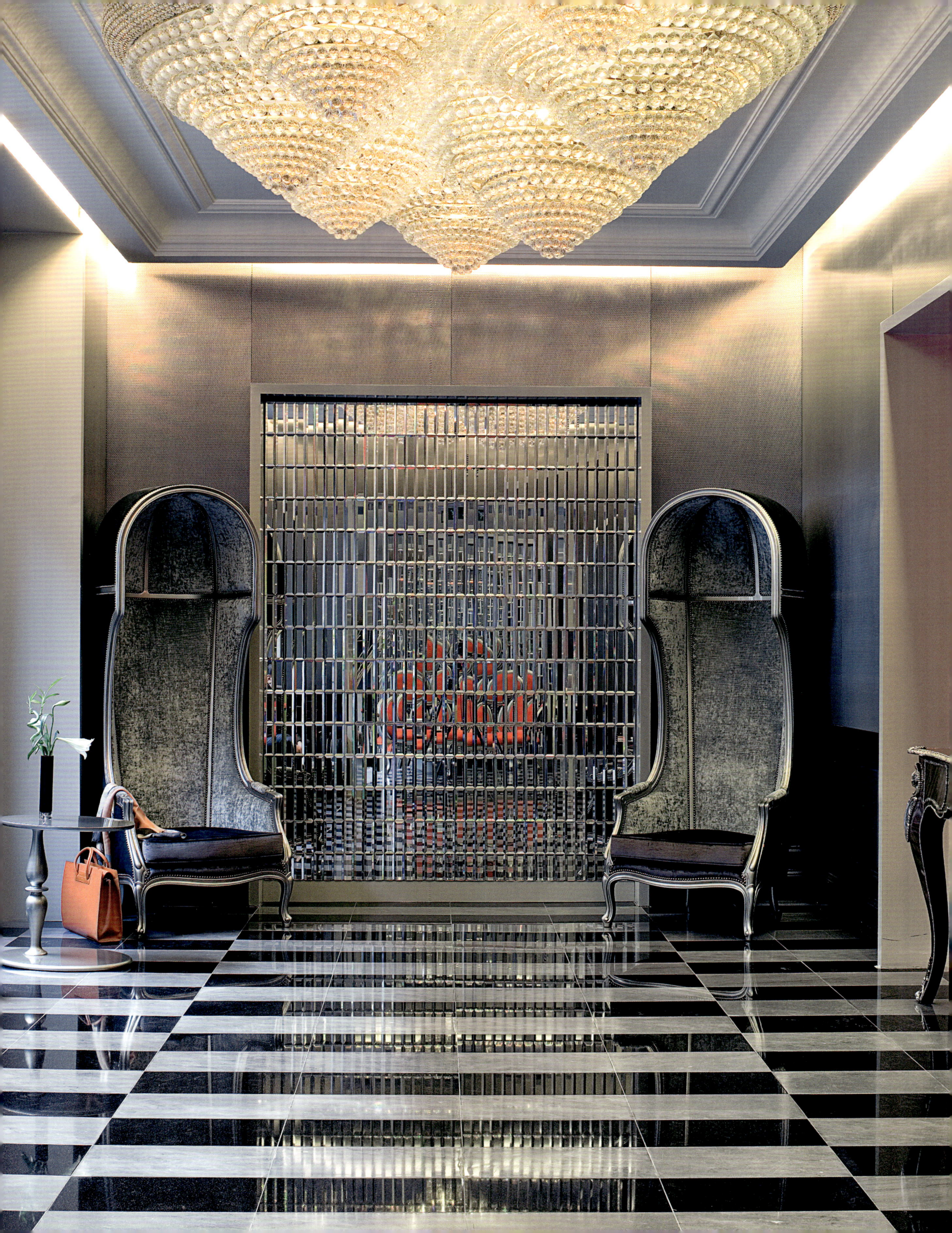

Des Endroits Parfaits

C'était la suite sous les toits de Saint-Germain-des-Prés qui avait rendu ce weekend en ville parfait. D'une élégance intemporelle, elle avait des tons gris clairs, de grands miroirs sur les murs qui faisaient paraître la salle de bain deux fois plus grande, et un lit dans lequel tous les rêves pouvaient se réaliser. En signe de bienvenue, une bouteille de vin rouge et du fromage étaient posés sur la table, une petite bibliothèque proposait des classiques de la littérature française et depuis les deux petits balcons on pouvait voir jusqu'à la tour Eiffel, qui s'illuminait le soir comme un feu d'artifice. C'était le ciel de Paris.

De tels souvenirs de voyages, de telles descriptions correspondent à de plus en plus d'hôtels en Europe. Situés dans des métropoles ou au milieu de nulle part, disposant de 18 ou 180 chambres, proposant un luxe discret ou simplement le meilleur des basiques, tous affichent un style personnel et racontent une histoire particulière. Peut-être celle d'un chapelier excentrique, qui a découvert sa passion pour les hôtels de la côte irlandaise, peut-être celle d'un visionnaire, qui avec des voiles de verre et d'acier, a créé une atmosphère futuriste dans les montagnes de Suisse, ou celle d'une ancienne James Bond girl qui a préféré séduire la société londonienne plutôt que 007 avec une décoration intérieure exotique.

Il y a des hôtels qui captent le style de leur environnement, et le transcende sans dogmatisme, il y en a d'autres qui poussent le principe des opposés à l'extrême et amusent, irritent ou provoquent avec leurs contrastes. Qui a passé une nuit dans le boudoir d'une vamp anglaise ou dans le monde fantastique d'un créateur de mode français sait ce que cela signifie. Plus répandus, mais non moins passionnants, les mélanges de différentes époques, ou de l'ancien et du moderne. Du « clean chic » derrière le mur d'un palais espagnol du XIXème siècle, un chalet de style américain dans les Alpes européennes ou de l'art déco réinterprété de manière moderne dans un grand hôtel traditionnel : ces ruptures de style peuvent être le sommet du cool.

Les têtes créatives derrière ces hôtels sont souvent des architectes et designers encore inconnus, qui cherchent un terrain de jeu ou un palier dans leur carrière. Cependant, de plus en plus souvent, les célébrités du métier ouvrent leurs carnets d'esquisses pour dessiner des façades, des suites ou des sculptures. Même des stars comme Lord Norman Foster, Zaha Hadid ou David Chipperfield considèrent encore les hôtels comme des projets prestigieux. Et pour les propriétaires des hôtels, ces grands noms ne représentent pas seulement une augmentation du nombre de leurs clients, mais aussi une manière de répondre aux désirs de ces derniers, désirs qui ont considérablement changé au cours des dernières années. Les voyageurs, qui partent souvent pour des périodes plus courtes, cherchent des hôtels pour lesquels ils peuvent avoir le coup de foudre, qui oscillent entre relaxation et aventure, qui les inspirent et leur laissent des souvenirs. Pour résumer, des hôtels qui ne soient pas seulement des lieux où dormir, mais des lieux où vivre.

On ne crée pas de tels hôtels en reprenant les formules de n'importe quelle chaîne hôtelière de centre ville, ou en faisant figurer le mot « design » à toutes les pages du catalogue, ou encore en se contentant de mettre des photos noir et blanc à la réception ou des couvre-lits colorés dans les chambres. De tels hôtels nécessitent un concept personnalisé, intelligent et bien pensé jusque dans les détails, pour paraître entièrement simples, naturels et évidents. Ils doivent comprendre les tendances de demain tout comme les dernières techniques, la psychologie au-delà du profit. Avec son ouverture d'esprit et ses multiples facettes, l'Europe constitue le décor idéal pour de telles œuvres d'art, qui éveillent votre passion pour un décor ou vous font découvrir l'âme d'une ville. De tels hôtels ouvrent de nouveaux horizons, et pas seulement le ciel de Paris.

Anna Streubert

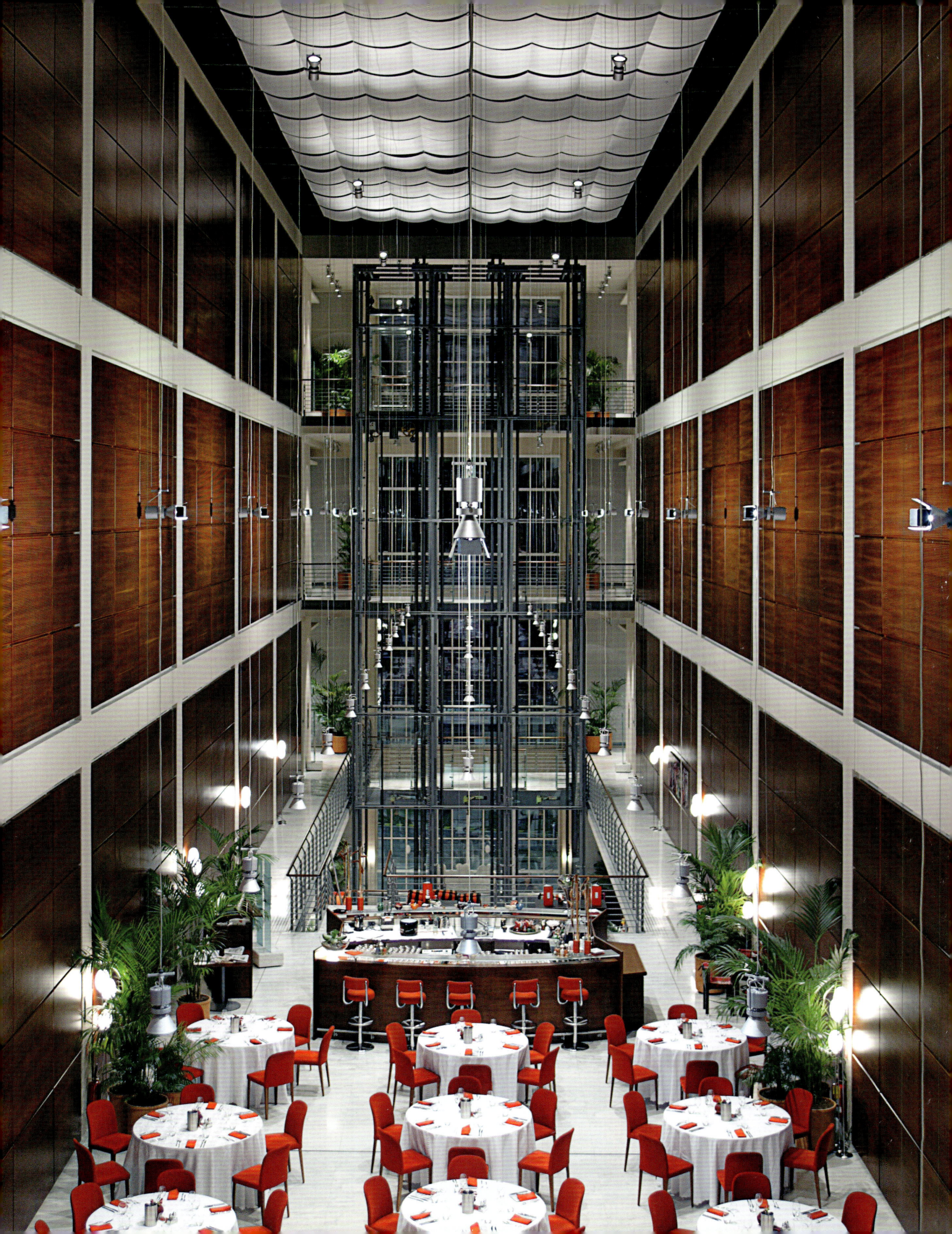

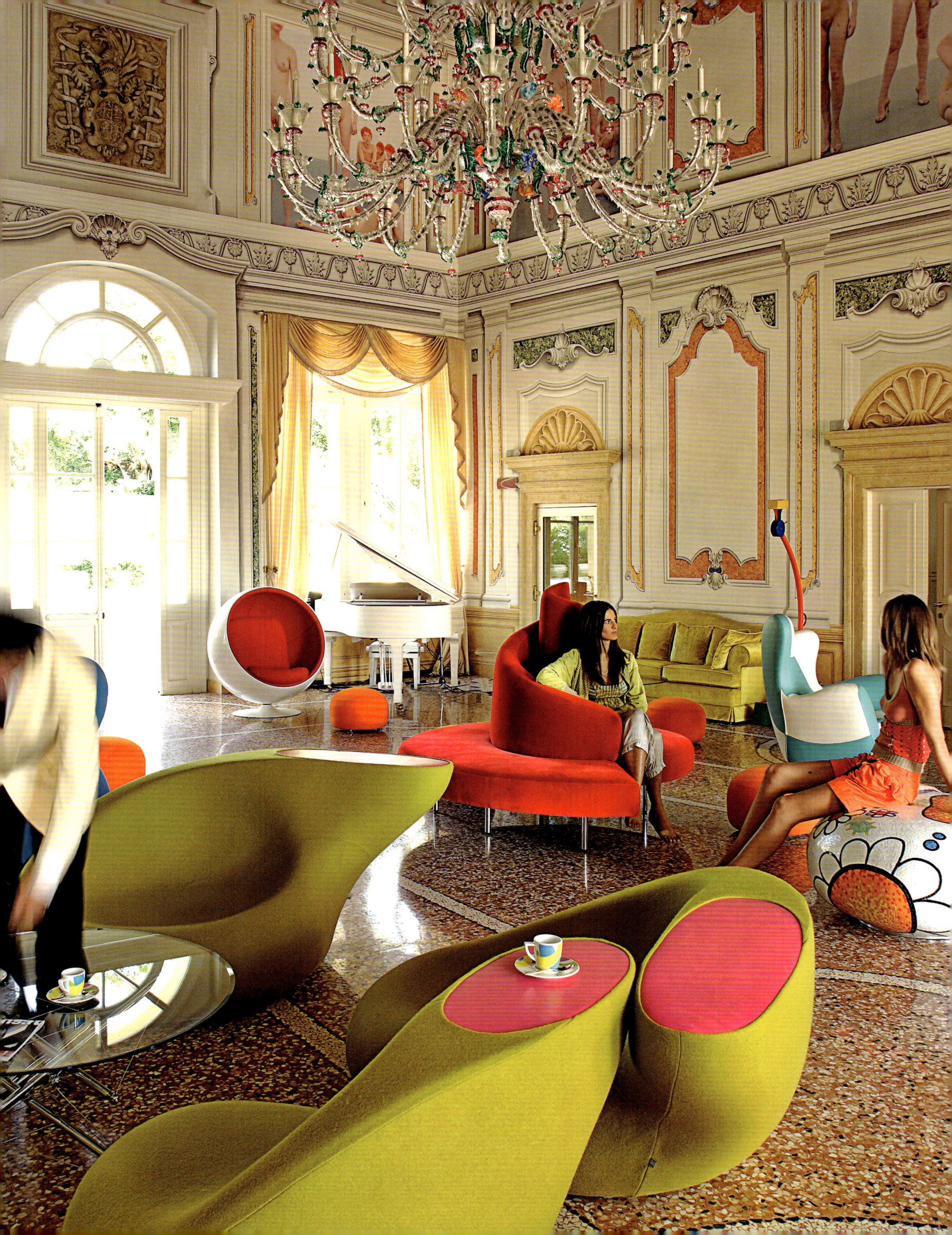

La suite abuhardillada en Saint-Germain-des-Prés aseguró la perfección de la escapada de fin semana en la ciudad. La combinación de distintas tonalidades de gris claro de una elegancia a prueba del tiempo, las altas paredes de espejos, que conferían una sensación de amplitud al cuarto de baño, y una cama que transformaba los sueños en realidad. A modo de bienvenida, una botella de vino tinto y queso en la mesa. Una pequeña biblioteca ofrecía clásicos de la literatura francesa y desde dos minúsculos balcones se podía observar la cúspide de la Torre Eiffel, que brillaba como un haz de fuegos artificiales en una noche de fin de año. Era el cielo sobre París.

Estas escenas de viaje se ven dibujadas por cada vez más hoteles en Europa. En las metrópolis o en mitad de la nada, con 18 o 180 habitaciones, de un lujo desenfadado o simplemente ofreciendo "lo mejor de lo básico", cada uno de estos hoteles muestra su carácter personal y cuenta una historia individual. Quizás la historia de un sombrerero excéntrico y bohemio que descubrió en la costa de Irlanda su vocación de hostelero; quizás la de un visionario que, con velas de cristal y de hierro, añadió un toque futurista al bucólico entorno montañoso de Suiza; o quizás la historia de una de las primeras chicas Bond, quien hoy no seduce al agente 007, sino a la sociedad de Londres con interiores exóticos.

Hay hoteles que asimilan el estilo de su entorno y lo desarrollan de manera consecuente pero distendida y los hay que llevan al límite el principio de las contraposiciones y divierten, confunden o provocan deliberadamente a base de contrastes. Quien haya pasado una noche en el boudoir de una diva británica o en el mundo fantástico y surrealista de un modisto francés sabrá de qué se trata. Un tanto más corriente pero no menos intrigante es la combinación de diferentes épocas, así como la mezcla de lo antiguo con lo moderno. El estilo minimalista tras la fachada de un palacio español del siglo XIX, el estilo Lodge americano en los Alpes o una interpretación vanguardista del art-déco en un Grand Hotel tradicional son ejemplos de propuestas de estilo transgresoras que crean espacios extraordinarios.

Las mentes creativas detrás de estos hoteles son, en su mayoría, arquitectos o diseñadores todavía desconocidos que buscan un proyecto donde aplicar toda su fantasía o un trampolín para su carrera. Aún así, cada vez son más las personalidades de esta industria que abren sus cuadernos para diseñar fachadas, suites o esculturas. Incluso para famosos como Lord Norman Foster, Zaha Hadid o David Chipperfield, los hoteles son proyectos que pueden otorgar un gran prestigio. Para los respectivos constructores, los nombres célebres no sólo se traducen en una elevada cifra de huéspedes, sino también en una respuesta profesional a las exigencias de los clientes. Y las exigencias han cambiado mucho durante los últimos años, con viajeros que están de camino cada vez más y por períodos más cortos y que buscan hoteles de los que poder enamorarse a primera vista y para siempre. Hoteles que ofrezcan tanto relax como aventura, que inspiren y dejen huella; en pocas palabras: hoteles que no sólo sean lugares dónde dormir sino también espacios para vivir.

El elemento común entre estos hoteles no es su pertenencia a una cadena cualquiera, ni que estén situados en una vía de acceso al centro de la ciudad, tampoco que la mera palabra "diseño" figure en sus catálogos, que exhiban cuadros en blanco y negro en el vestíbulo o que sus camas estén cubiertas por colchas multicolores Tras estos hoteles se esconde un concepto individual, inteligente y pensado hasta el último detalle que, no obstante, se manifiesta de una forma completamente espontánea, desenfadada y natural. Para lograrlo hay que saber tanto de futuras tendencias como de últimas tecnologías y tanto de psicología como de generación de beneficios. Por su carácter abierto y su gran diversidad, Europa constituye el lugar idóneo para estas obras de arte, para los inmuebles que despiertan la pasión por un paisaje o que permiten conocer el alma misma de una ciudad. Estos hoteles abren nuevos horizontes –y no sólo el cielo sobre París.

Anna Streubert

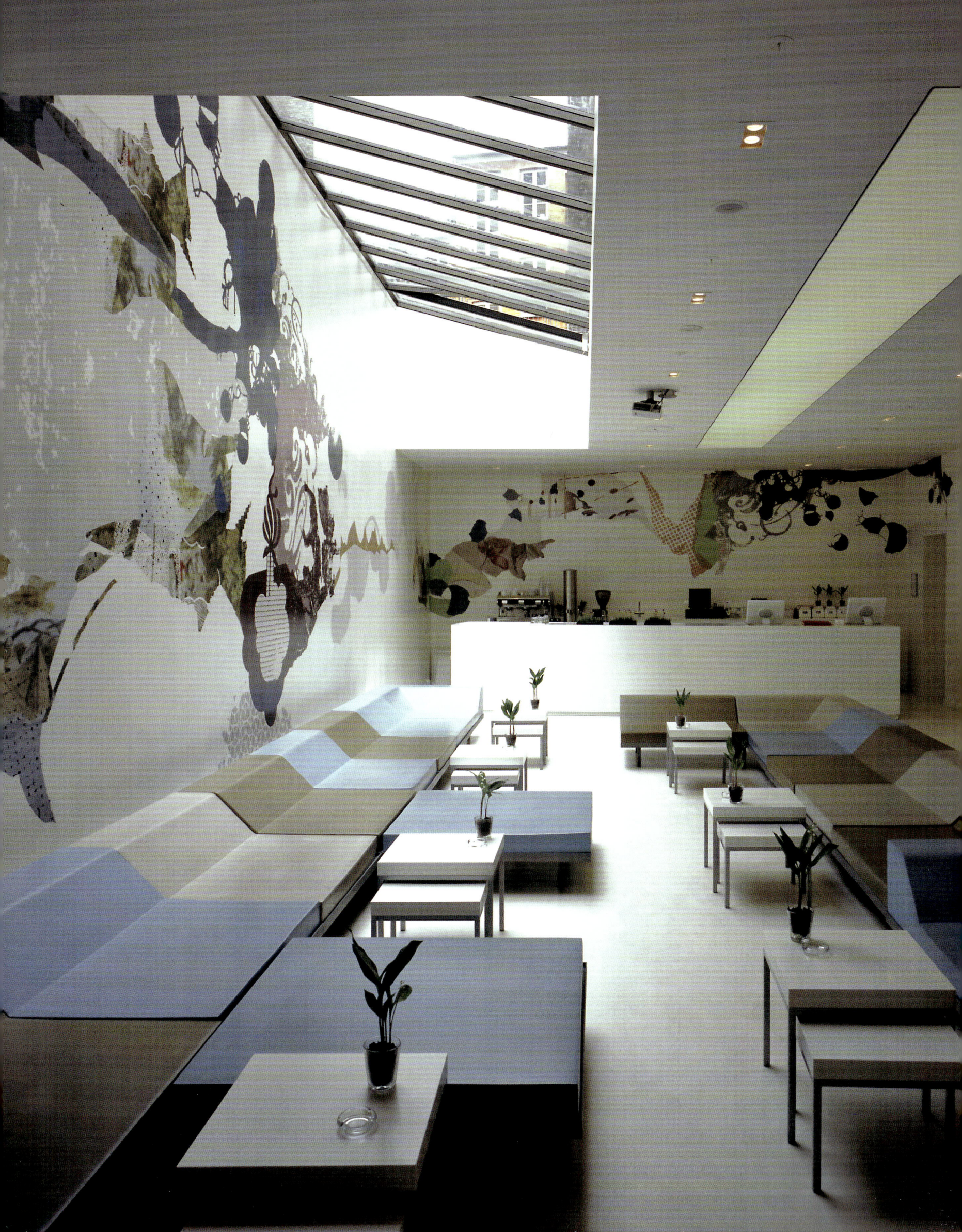

Fu la suite in una mansarda del quartiere di Saint-Germain-des-Prés a rendere perfetto il fine settimana in città. Una suite dal fascino senza tempo decorata nelle tonalità del grigio chiaro, con alte pareti a specchio che facevano apparire il piccolo bagno due volte più grande e un letto che trasformava i sogni in realtà. In omaggio agli ospiti, sul tavolo c'erano una bottiglia di vino rosso e del formaggio, una piccola biblioteca proponeva classici della letteratura francese, e da due minuscoli balconi si apriva una vista che spaziava fino alla cima della Torre Eiffel, che la sera luccicava come uno spettacolo di fuochi d'artificio per l'ultimo dell'anno. Era il cielo sopra Parigi.

Scorci di viaggio, quadretti come questi in Europa vengono offerti da un numero sempre più grande di alberghi. Situati in grandi città o in mezzo al nulla, provvisti di 18 o 180 camere, in grado di offrire lusso in maniera informale o semplicemente il "best of basics", tutti questi hotel hanno una propria personalità e una storia tutta loro. Forse quella di un eccentrico cappellaio e tipo bohémien che ha scoperto la sua passione di albergatore sulla costa dell'Irlanda, forse quella di un visionario che con delle vele in vetro e acciaio ha arricchito il tranquillo paesaggio montano della Svizzera con un tocco di atmosfera futuristica, oppure quella di una ex Bond girl che oggi, anziché 007, seduce la società londinese con un albergo dall'interno esotico.

Ci sono hotel che si adeguano allo stile del paesaggio che li circonda, completandolo in maniera armonica ed equilibrata, e altri che spingono all'estremo il principio delle contrapposizioni, e con i loro contrasti divertono, confondono o volontariamente provocano. Chi ha trascorso una notte nel salottino di una diva britannica o nel surreale mondo della fantasia di uno stilista francese, sa di che cosa stiamo parlando. Un po' più conosciuta, ma non per questo meno accattivante, è la combinazione di epoche diverse e il mix di antico e moderno. "Puramente chic" dietro una facciata spagnola del XIX secolo, in stile "lodge" americano tra le alpi europee o art déco in chiave moderna all'interno di un tradizionale Grand Hotel – sono queste discontinuità di stile che rendono un albergo "cool".

Le menti creative che stanno dietro questi alberghi sono architetti e designer ancora sconosciuti in cerca di una palestra o un trampolino di lancio – sempre più spesso, però, anche i famosi del settore aprono il quaderno degli schizzi e disegnano facciate, suite o sculture. Persino per architetti famosi come Lord Norman Foster, Zaha Hadid o David Chipperfield, progettare un albergo è ancora un lavoro di prestigio. E per i committenti, grossi nomi non significano solo aumento del numero degli ospiti, bensì anche possibilità di soddisfare i loro desideri in modo professionale. Perché negli ultimi anni gli stessi ospiti degli alberghi sono cambiati radicalmente: intraprendono viaggi sempre più frequenti e sempre più brevi e cercano alberghi in cui innamorarsi irresistibilmente a prima vista, alberghi che oscillino tra il relax e l'avventura, che incantino e lascino il segno – in poche parole, hotel che non siano solo posti dove dormire, bensì posti da vivere.

Alberghi di questo tipo non sono hotel appartenenti a una qualsiasi catena e situati lungo la strada che porta in centro, e non basta la parolina "design" stampata sul catalogo, foto in bianco e nero nella lobby o copriletto colorati. Alberghi di questo tipo hanno bisogno di un progetto realizzato su misura, con sapienza e cura nel dettaglio, ma che risulti assolutamente naturale, spontaneo e per nulla forzato. Devono avere un occhio tanto per le tendenze del domani quanto per le tecnologie più moderne, la psicologia e gli affari. Grazie alla sua naturalezza e varietà, l'Europa offre il perfetto scenario per tali opere d'arte, per strutture che suscitano passione per un determinato paesaggio o gettano uno sguardo nell'anima di una città. Alberghi di questo tipo aprono nuovi orizzonti – non solo il cielo sopra Parigi.

Anna Streubert

Ararat Park Hyatt Moscow

Moscow, Russia

Neglinnaya Street 4
Moscow 109012
Russia
Phone: +74 9 57 83 12 34
Fax: +74 9 57 83 12 35
www.moscow.park.hyatt.com

Price category: €€€€
Rooms: 220 including 17 suites
Facilities: Café, restaurant, bar with panoramic views over the city, spa, library
Services: Business services, WiFi, 24 h room service
Located: Close to Bolshoi Theater, few minutes walk from the Kremlin and Red Square
Public transportation: Metro Sokolnicheskaya, Lubyanka, Tagansko-Krasnopresnenskaya, Kuznetskiy Most
Style: Timeless, world-class, residential-style hotel

The luxury hotel in the heart of Moscow was built on a marble foundation and high columns. Across from Red Square, glass elevators transport the guests from the atrium to the modern suites with velvet sofas, leather armchairs and, of course, the newest high-tech functions for working with a laptop. The "Conservatory Café" is a bright glasshouse above the city roofs with terrace furniture and white cushions to sit on while dining and enjoying the view. Under a baldachin in the "Ararat Café," named after the famous artists' meeting place of the '60s, a waiter will serve you Armenian specialties.

Auf einem Marmorfundament und riesigen Säulen ist das Luxushotel im Herzen Moskaus erbaut worden. Gegenüber vom Roten Platz transportieren gläserne Fahrstühle die Gäste vom Atrium in die modernen Suiten mit samtenen Sofas, Ledersesseln und, natürlich, den neuesten Hightech-Funktionen für die Arbeit am Laptop. Auf Terrassenmöbeln mit weißen Polstern speist man im „Conservatory Café", einem lichten Wintergarten über den Dächern der Stadt. Armenische Spezialitäten servieren Kellner unter einem Seiden-Baldachin im „Ararat Café", benannt nach dem berühmten Künstlertreff der 60er Jahre.

Construit sur des fondations de marbres et de larges piliers, cet hôtel de luxe a été érigé au cœur de Moscou. En face de la Place Rouge, des ascenseurs de verres transportent les clients de l'atrium jusqu'à leurs suites dotées de canapés de velours, de fauteuils en cuir et bien sûr, des derniers équipements high-tech nécessaires pour travailler sur un ordinateur portable. Les repas se prennent en terrasse sur des coussins blancs au « Conservatory Café », un jardin d'hiver très lumineux au-dessus des toits de la ville. L'« Ararat Café », nommé d'après la célèbre rencontre d'artistes des années 60, sert des spécialités arméniennes sous un baldaquin de soie.

Sobre una base de mármol y con pilares gigantes se construyó este hotel de lujo en el corazón de Moscú. Frente a la Plaza Roja, unos ascensores de cristal transportan a los huéspedes desde el atrio hasta las modernas suites, que están equipadas con sofás de terciopelo, sillones de cuero y, por supuesto, las últimas tecnologías para trabajar con el portátil. En el "Conservatory Café", un jardín de invierno luminoso sobre los techos de la ciudad, se come sentado en muebles de terraza cubiertos con cojines blancos. En el "Ararat Café", cuyo nombre proviene del famoso lugar de encuentro de artistas en los años 60, los camareros sirven especialidades de la cocina armenia bajo un baldaquín de seda.

Questo albergo di lusso nel cuore di Mosca è stato costruito su una base di marmo ed enormi colonne. Di fronte alla Piazza Rossa, gli ascensori con pareti di vetro conducono gli ospiti dall'atrio dell'albergo a moderne suite con divani di velluto, poltrone in pelle e, naturalmente, le più moderne funzioni high-tech per lavorare con il portatile. Nel "Conservatory Café", un luminoso giardino d'inverno che sovrasta i tetti della città, si mangia su sedie da giardino con cuscini chiari. E nell'"Ararat Café", che prende il nome dal famoso punto di incontro di artisti negli anni '60, vi verranno servite specialità armene sotto un baldacchino di seta.

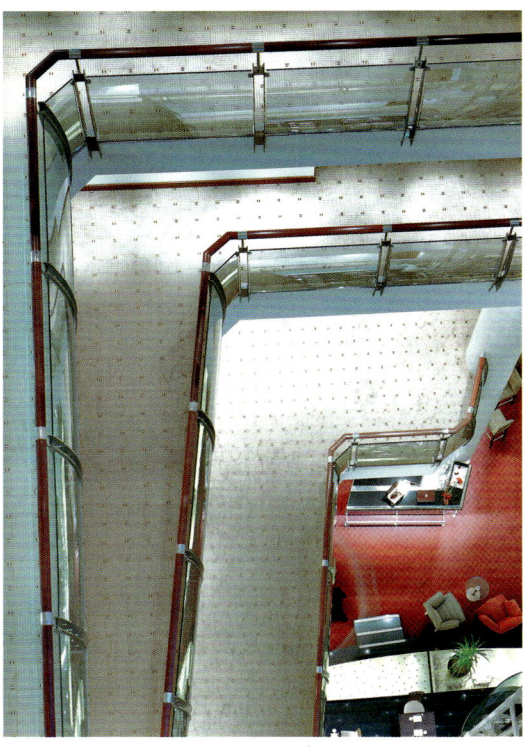
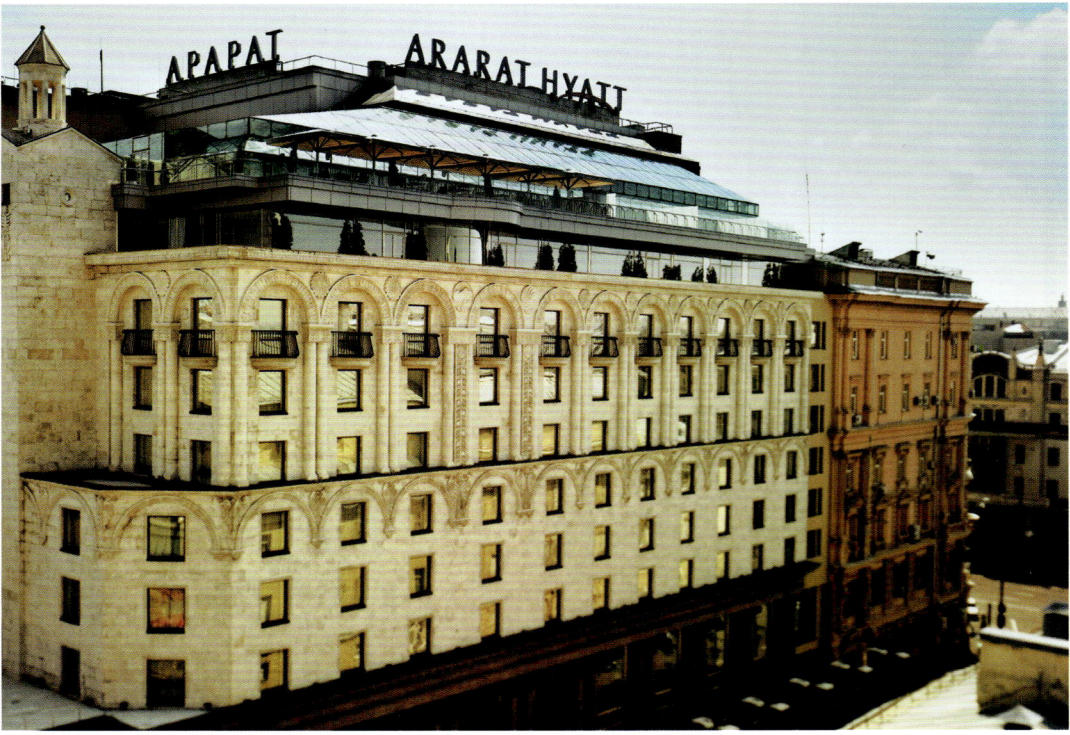

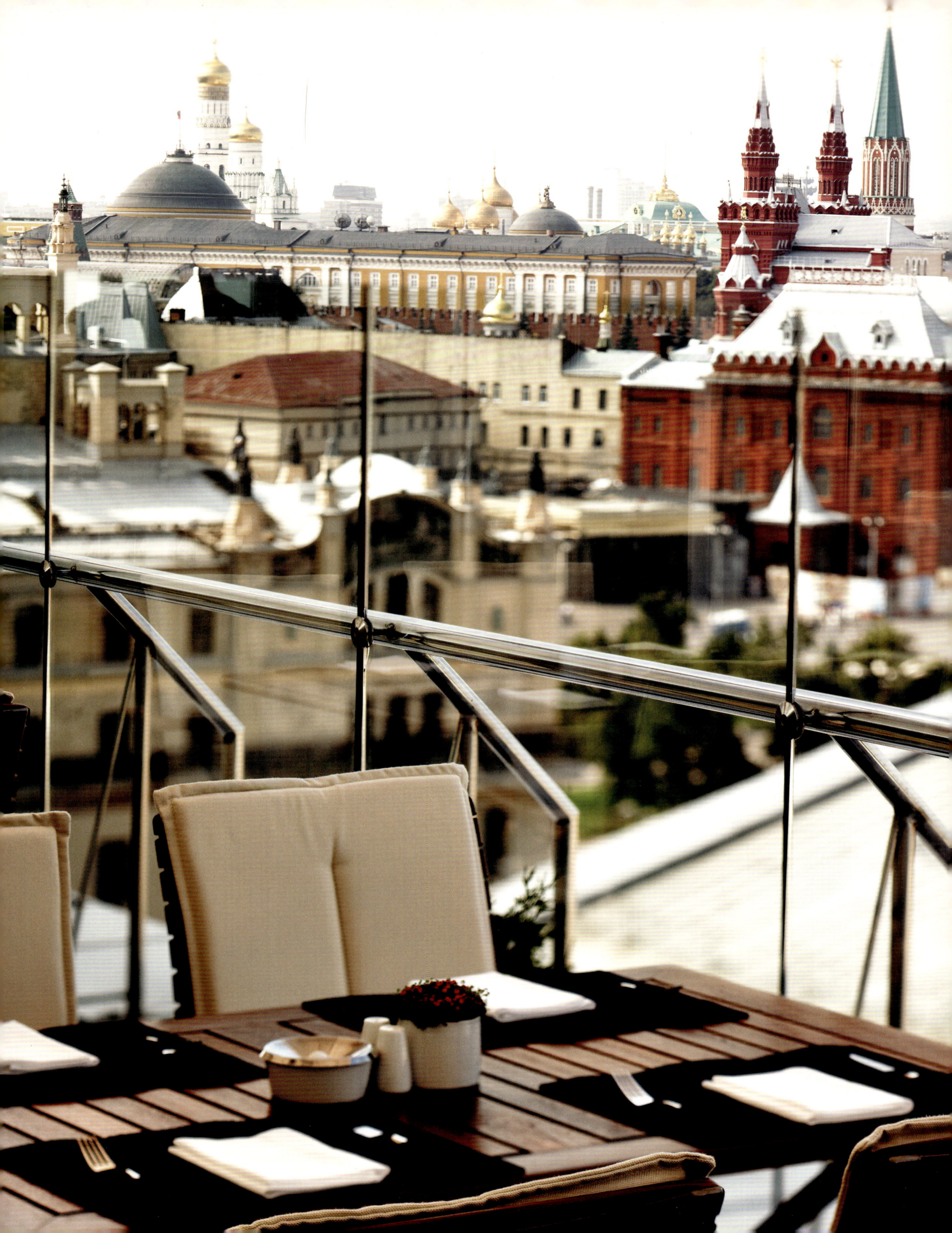

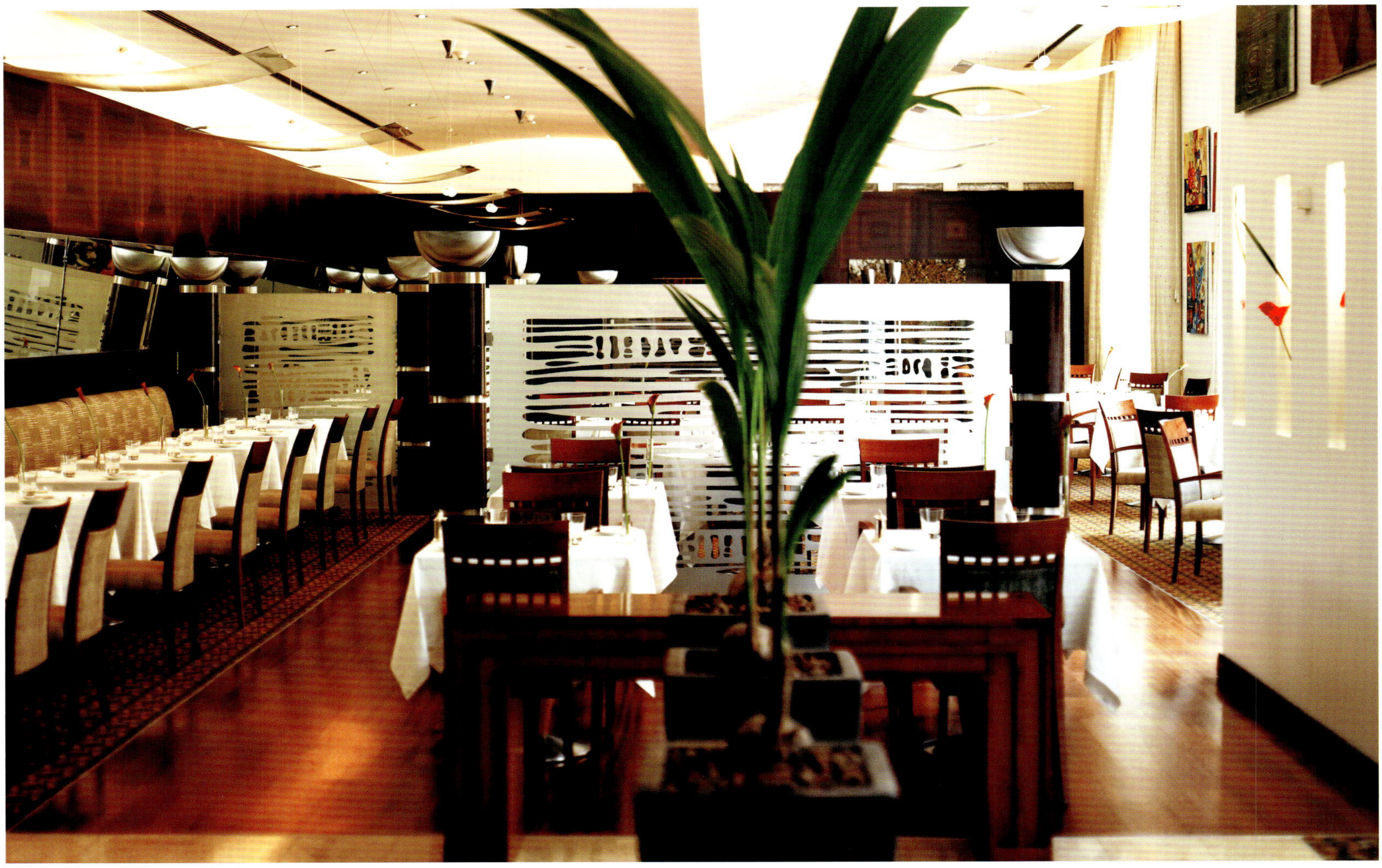

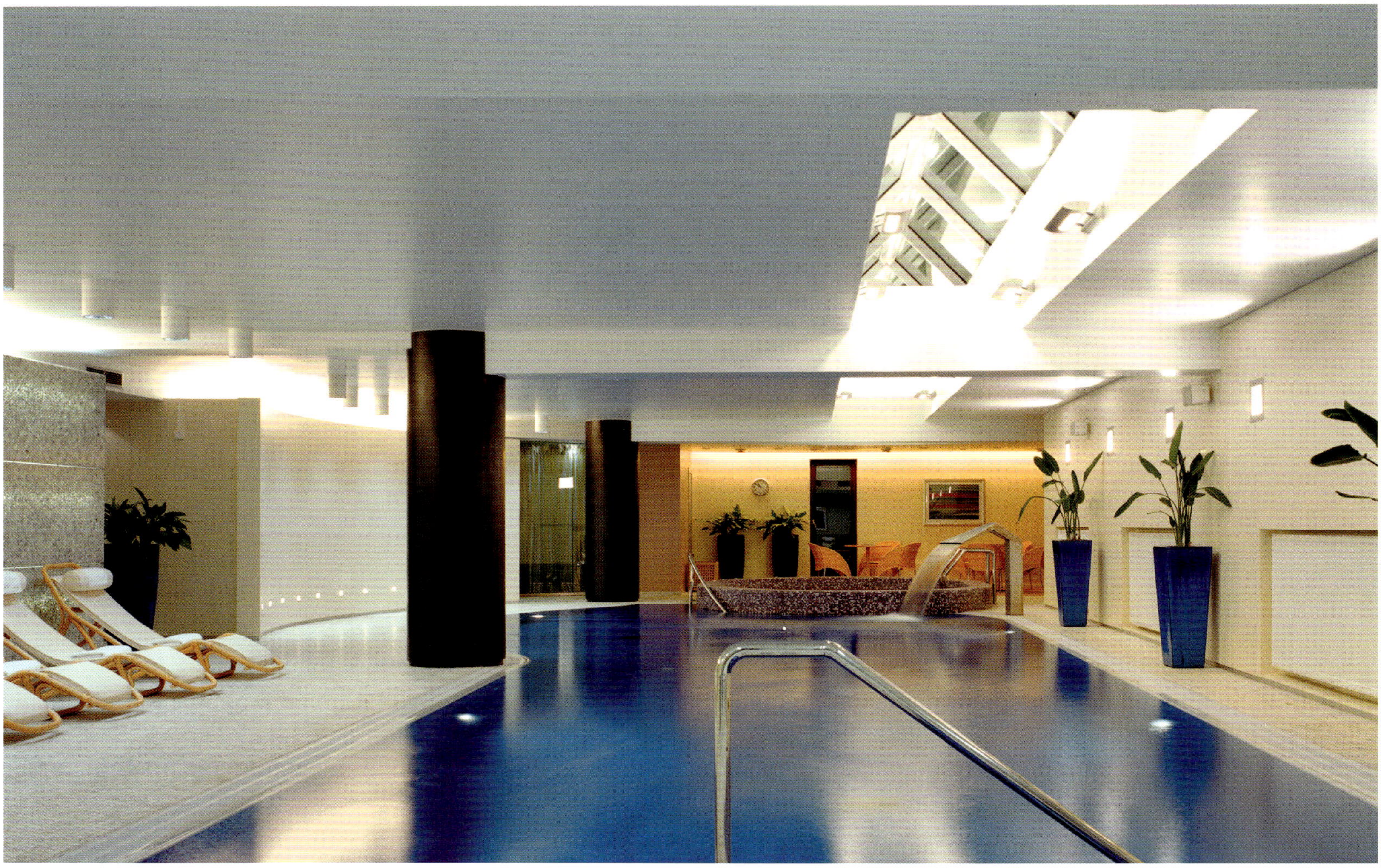

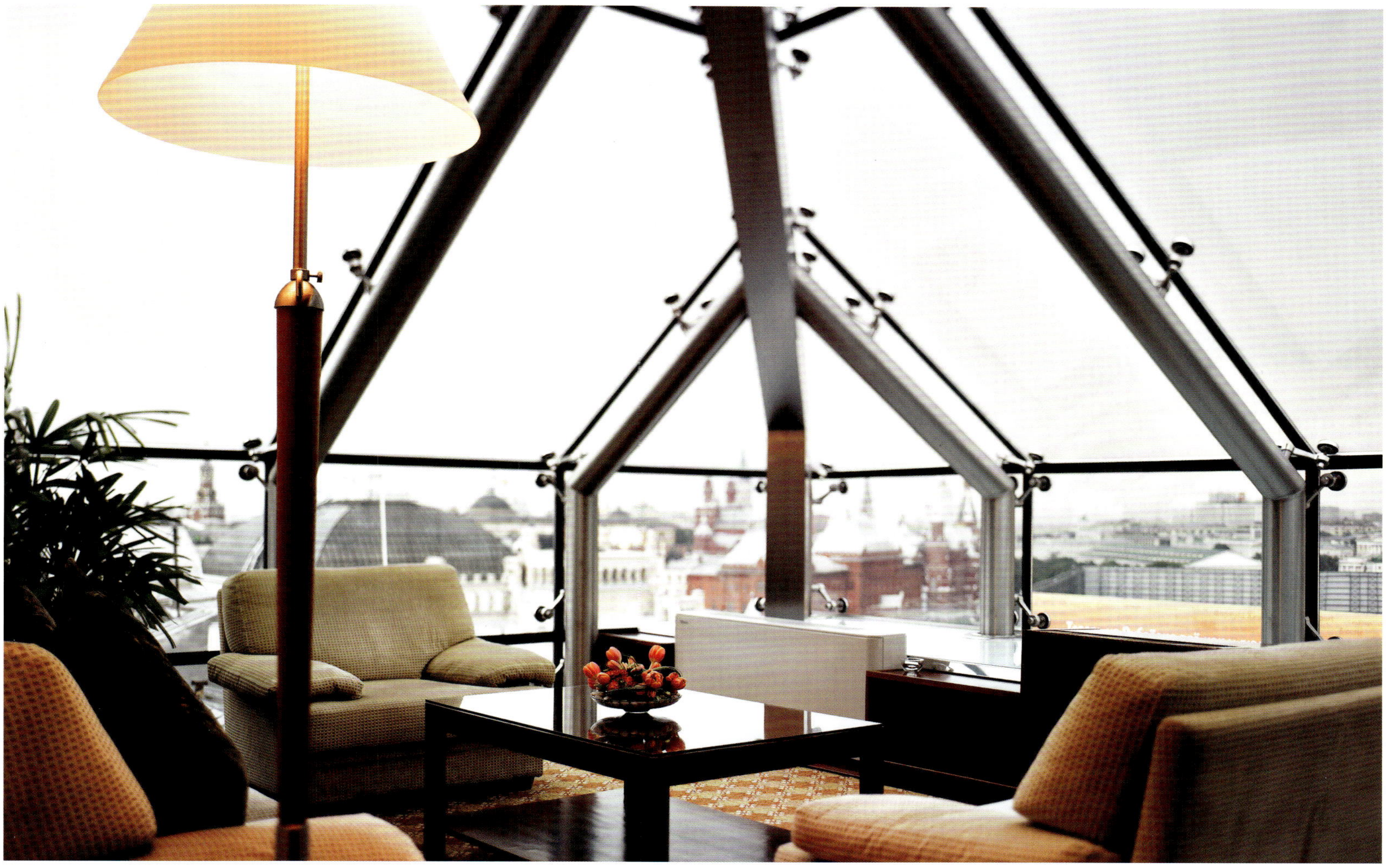

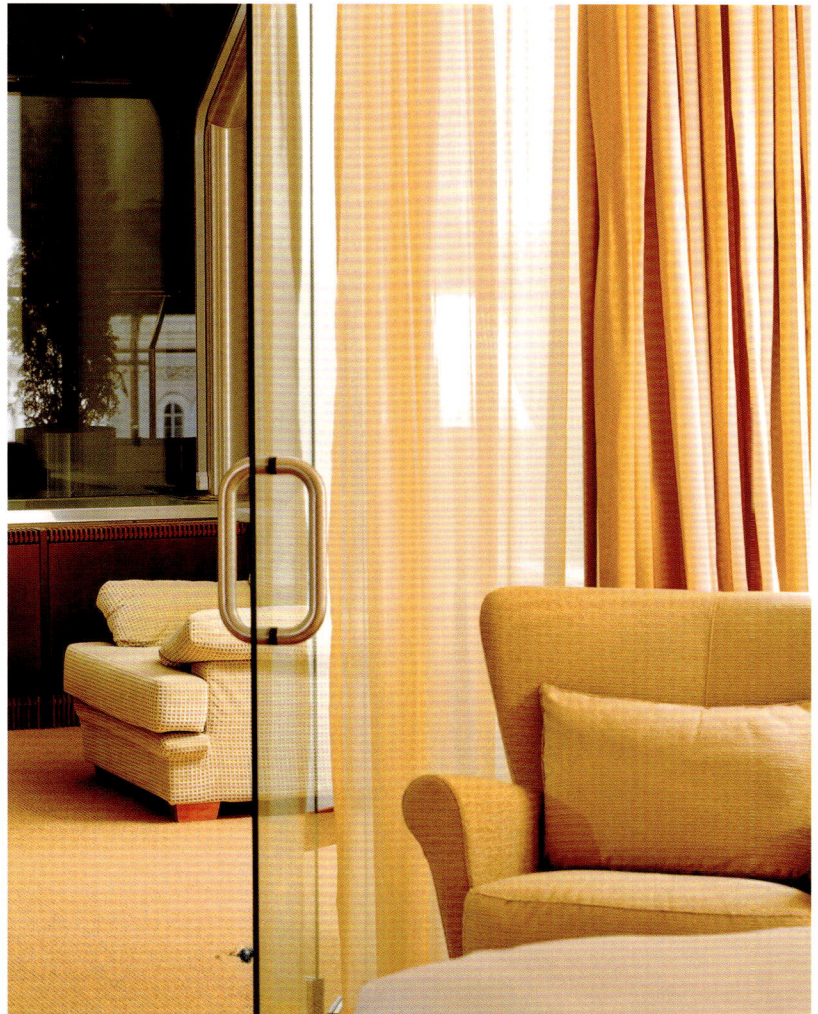

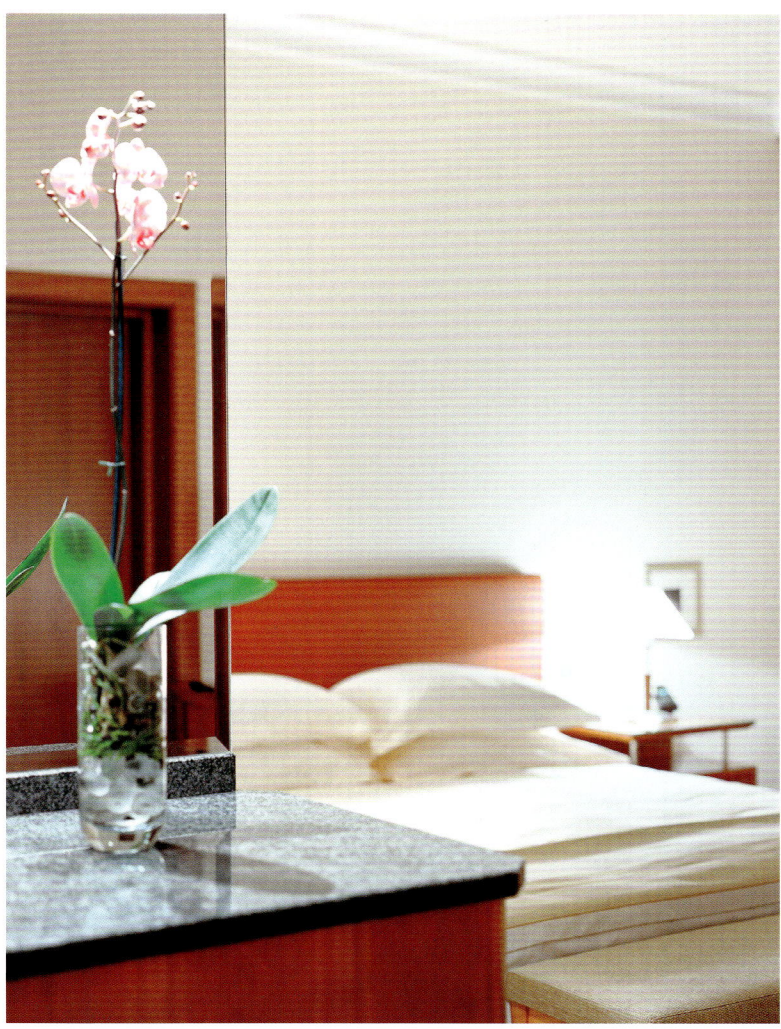

Swissôtel Krasnye Holmy

Moscow, Russia

Kosmodamianskaya Embankment.
52, Bld. 6
Moscow 115054
Russia
Phone: +74 9 57 87 98 00
Fax: +74 9 57 87 98 98
www.swissotel.com/moscow

Price category: €€€€
Rooms: 233 rooms including 27 suites with the latest state-of-the-art technology
Facilities: 2 restaurants, 3 bars, 11 conference rooms, spa
Services: Parking, concierge, business center
Located: In business district within a short distance from the Kremlin
Public transportation: Few minutes away from Paveletskaya metro and train station (express train to Domodedovo International Airport)
Style: Modern, dynamic and contemporary style

On the island between the Moskva and the Vodootvodny Canal the Swissôtel Krasnye Holmy rises above the most expensive metropolis in the world. One highlight in the truest sense of the word is the spectacular panoramic view of the churches, fortresses and palaces of the city, whether from the comfortable chaise longue in one of the suites with ceiling-high windows or from the round "City Space Bar & Lounge" on the 34th floor. A nice idea for waking up after long nights: there are espresso machines in each of the 233 rooms.

Auf der Insel zwischen der Moskva und dem Wodootwodny-Kanal überragt das Swissôtel Krasnye Holmy die teuerste Metropole der Welt. Ein Highlight im wahrsten Sinne des Wortes sind die spektakulären Panorama-Ausblicke auf die Kirchen, Festungen und Paläste der Stadt, ob von der komfortablen Chaiselongue in einer der Suiten mit deckenhohen Fenstern aus oder von der runden „City Space Bar & Lounge" auf der 34. Etage. Schöne Idee zum Wachwerden nach langen Nächten: die Espressomaschine auf jedem der 233 Zimmer.

Situé sur une île entre la Moskova et le Canal de Vodootvodny, le Swissôtel Krasnye Holmy s'élève au-dessus de la métropole la plus chère du monde. La vue panoramique sur les églises, les forteresses et les palais de la ville est un véritable joyau, que ce soit depuis une confortable chaise longue dans une des suites dotée de hautes baies vitrées, ou depuis le 34ème étage et son « City Space Bar & Lounge » circulaire. Dans chacune des 233 chambres, un percolateur à espresso permet de mieux se réveiller après une longue nuit.

Situado en la isla entre el canal Vodootvodny y el Moskva, el Swissôtel Krasnye Holmy sobresale en una de las metrópolis más caras del mundo. Tanto desde el confortable diván de una de las suites de grandes cristaleras que llegan hasta el techo, como en el redondo bar panorámico "City Space Bar & Lounge" en la planta 34 del hotel, se le ofrece al huésped una espectacular vista de las iglesias, fortalezas y palacios de la ciudad. Y una buena ocurrencia para despejarse tras una noche larga: máquinas de expreso en cada una de las 233 habitaciones.

Dall'isola situata tra il fiume Moskva e il canale Vodootvodny, il Swissôtel Krasnye Holmy domina la metropoli più cara del mondo. Che le ammiriate dalle confortevoli chaise longue delle suite con finestre alte quanto le pareti o dal rotondo "City Space Bar & Lounge" del 34° piano, le spettacolari vedute panoramiche sulle chiese, le fortezze e i palazzi della città sono un highlight nel senso letterale del termine. Le macchine per espresso disponibili in ciascuna delle 233 stanze sono una bella trovata per il risveglio dopo notti interminabili.

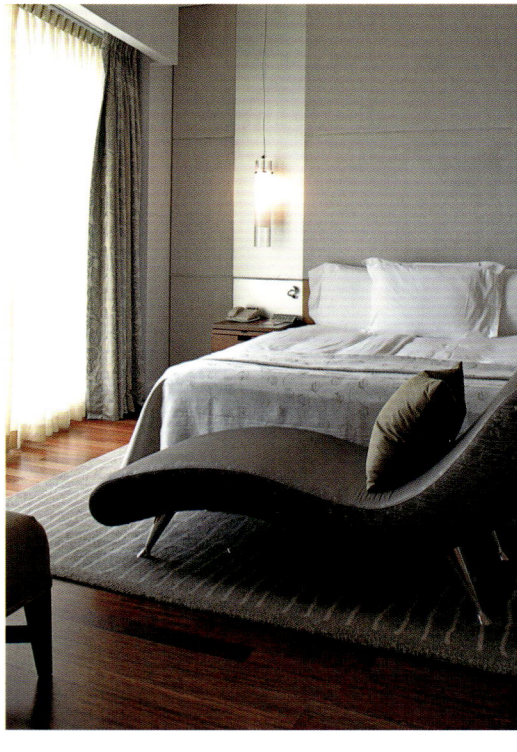
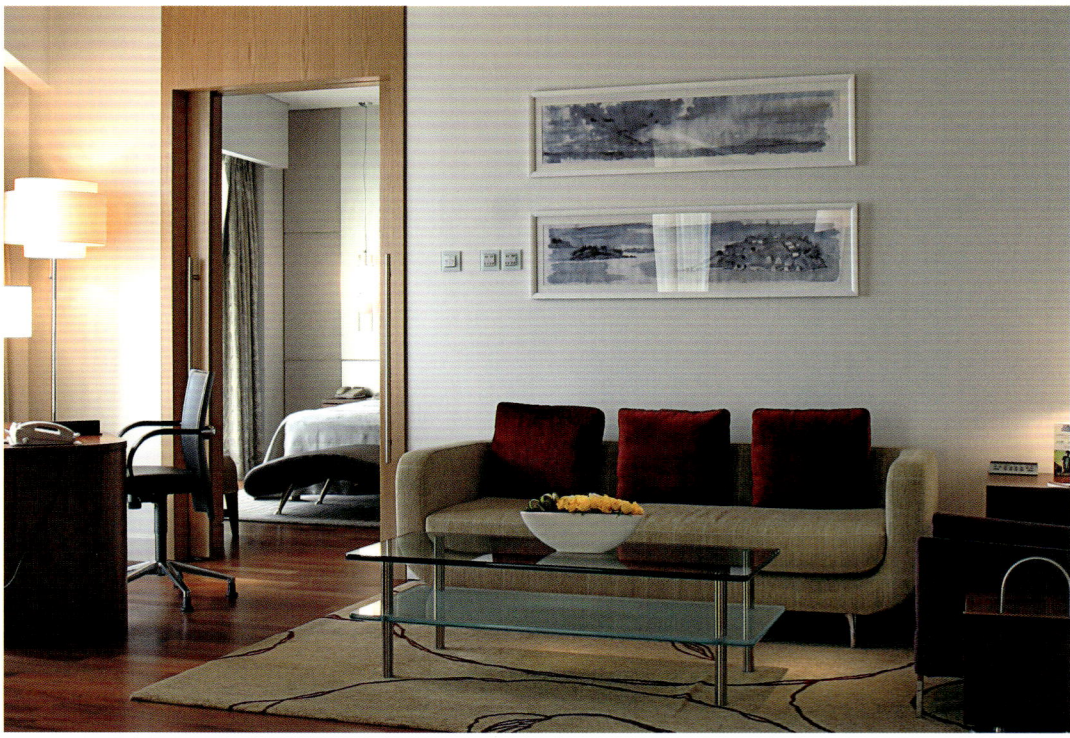

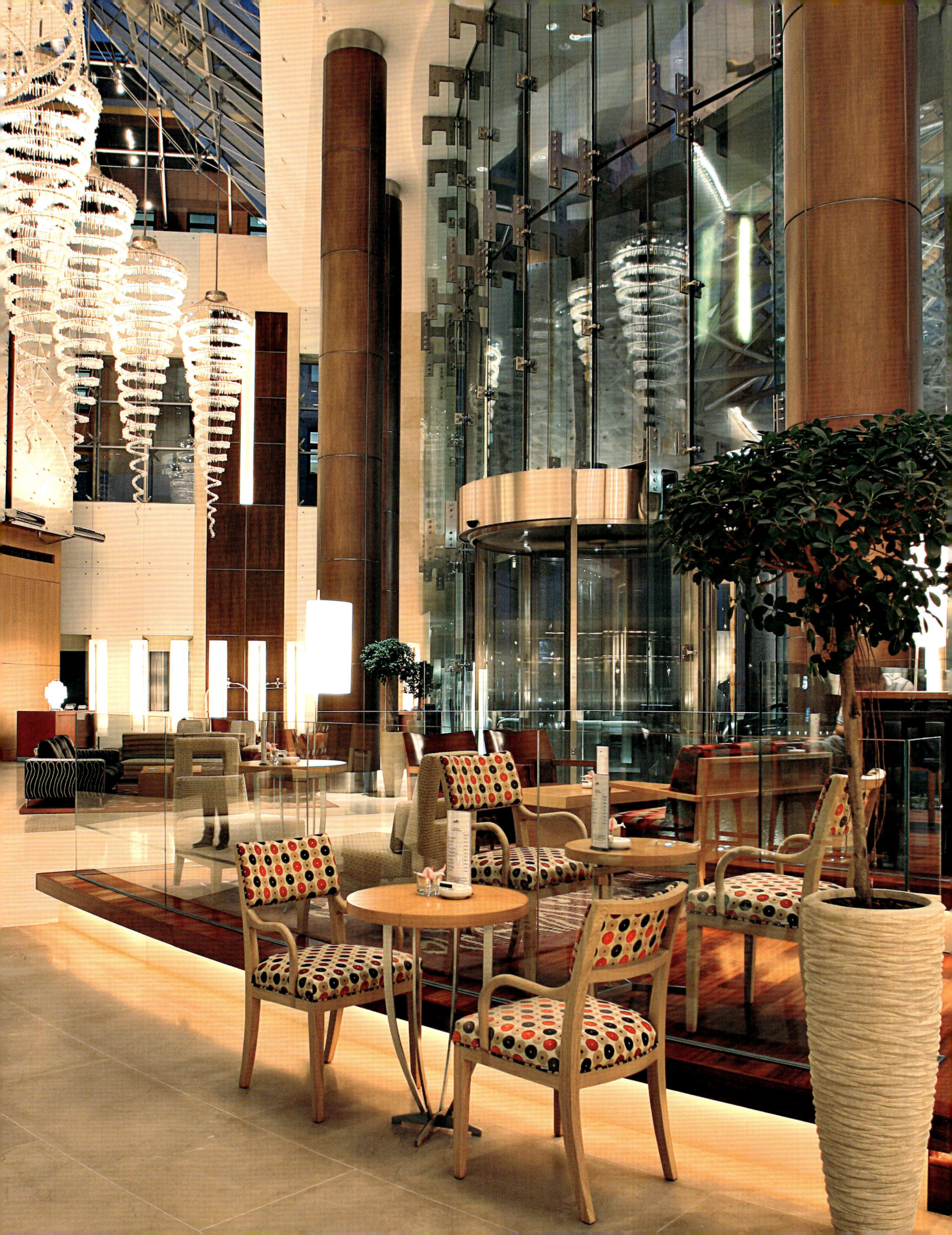

10123 Tallinn
Estonia
Phone: +372 630 6300
Fax: +372 630 6301
www.threesistershotel.com

Rooms: 23 rooms and suites
Facilities: Restaurant, wine bar, summer wine garden, conference rooms for private events
Services: Free airport shuttle on request, 24 h room service, complimentary newspapers, daily laundry and dry cleaning, free WiFi in public areas
Located: In the old town center of Tallinn, just a few steps away from Town Hall Square
Public transportation: Bus and tram stops 500 m from the hotel
Style: Historical boutique hotel with modern flavor

The guests of this exceptional hotel trio check in for travel through time. In the 14th century, respected merchants and ministers used to live in the merchant houses with pointed gables on the famous Pikk Street of Tallin's old city. Today, this historical ensemble has been carefully restored, you can discover Le Corbusier classics among oak beams, fireplaces, fantastic frescos and hidden stairways. The Carte Blanche Dinner is a highlight on the menu: the cook takes the freshest ingredients in the kitchen to perform magic at the guest's behest.

Gäste dieses außergewöhnlichen Hotel-Trios begeben sich auf eine Zeitreise: in den spitzgiebeligen Kaufmannshäusern an der bekannten Pikk Straße in Tallins Altstadt residierten bereits im 14. Jahrhundert angesehene Händler und Minister. Inzwischen wurde das historische Ensemble behutsam restauriert. Zwischen Eichenbalken, Kaminen, fantastischen Fresken und versteckten Treppen entdeckt man heute Le-Corbusier-Klassiker. Ein Highlight auf der Speisekarte ist das Carte-Blanche-Menü: Der Koch zaubert sechs Gänge aus den frischesten Zutaten der Küche, ganz nach Geschmack.

Les clients de cet étonnant trio d'hôtel font un vrai voyage dans le temps : au XIVème siècle vivaient déjà grands marchands et ministres dans les maisons de commerçants à pignons de la fameuse rue Pikk, dans la vieille ville de Tallin. Entre temps, cet ensemble historique a été soigneusement rénové. Entre les poutres de chêne, les cheminées, les fantastiques fresques et les escaliers cachés, on peut découvrir aujourd'hui les classiques de Le Corbusier. Le Menu Carte Blanche est le joyau de la carte du restaurant : le chef utilise des ingrédients de la première fraîcheur et laisse faire la magie, selon les goûts de chacun.

A su llegada los huéspedes de esta extraordinaria tríada hotelera inician un viaje en el tiempo: las casas de puntiagudos pináculos de la famosa calle Pikk en el centro antiguo de Tallín estaban habitadas, ya en el siglo XIV, por mercaderes y distinguidos ministros. Actualmente, este conjunto histórico se muestra cuidadosamente restaurado. Entre vigas de roble, chimeneas, maravillosos frescos y escaleras escondidas, el visitante puede descubrir hoy los clásicos de Le Corbusier. En el restaurante, el verdadero broche de oro lo ponen los menús Carte Blanche: el cocinero crea un magnífico menú de seis platos a base de los ingredientes más frescos de la cocina, y todo acorde al gusto de cada uno.

Gli ospiti di questo straordinario trio di alberghi siano pronti a partire per un viaggio nel tempo: nelle case dai tetti aguzzi lungo la famosa via Pikk del centro storico di Tallinn vivevano commercianti e ministri già nel XIV secolo. Da allora questo storico complesso di edifici è stato restaurato con grande cura. Fra travi di legno di quercia, caminetti, fantastici affreschi e scale nascoste si scoprono oggi famosi pezzi di Le Corbusier. La proposta più allettante del ristorante è il menu carte-blanche: utilizzando i freschi ingredienti della cucina, lo chef mette insieme come per magia un menu di sei portate a completa scelta degli ospiti.

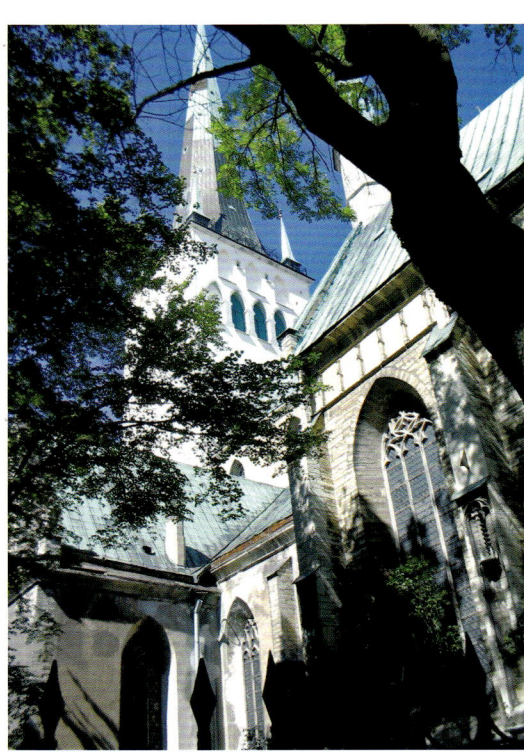

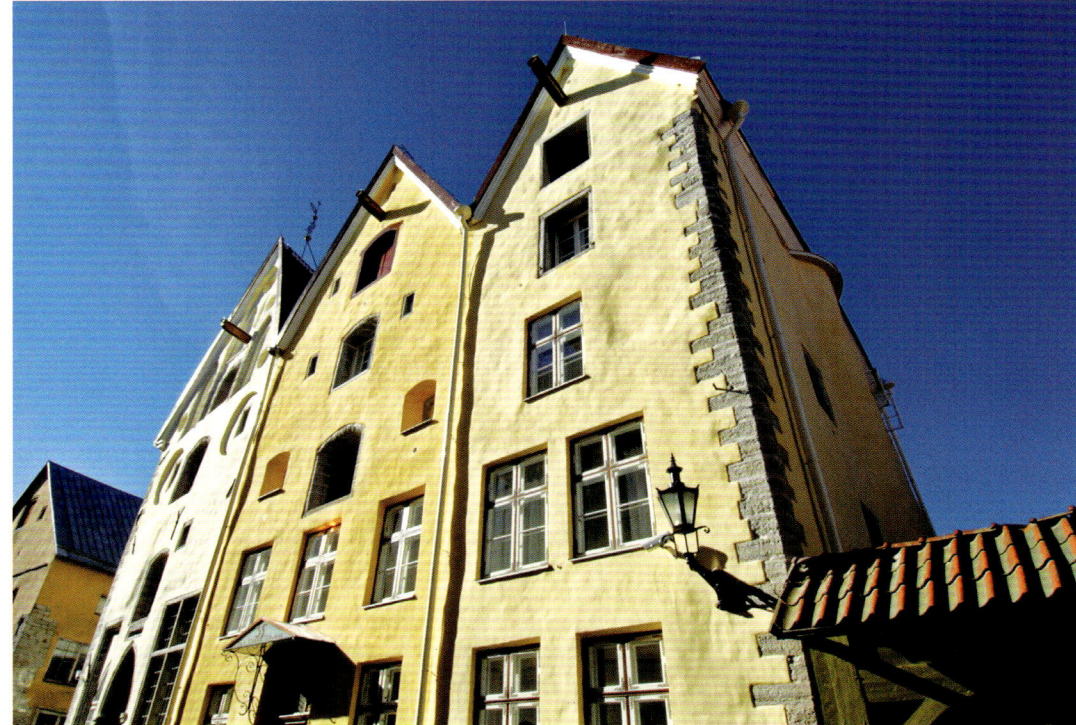

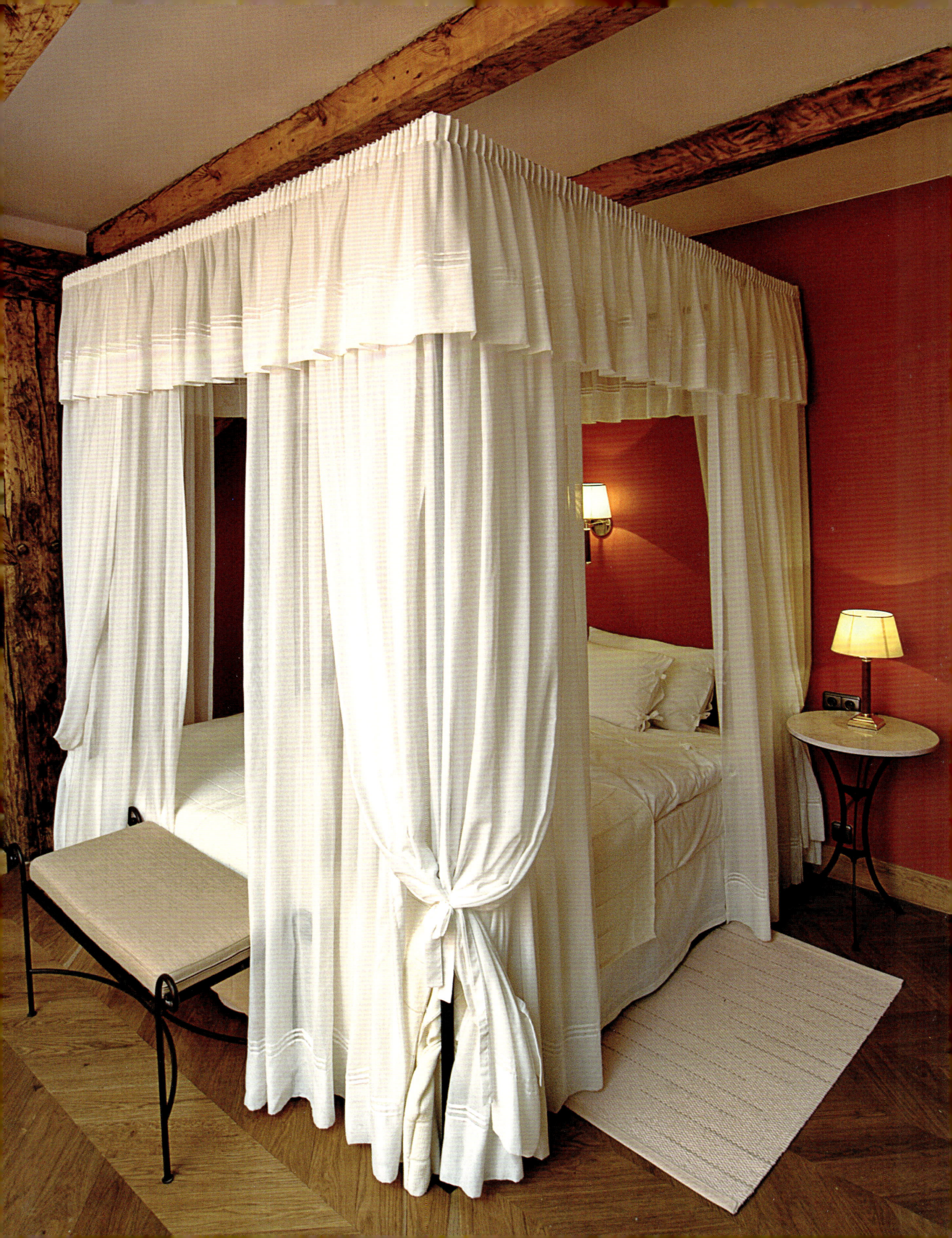

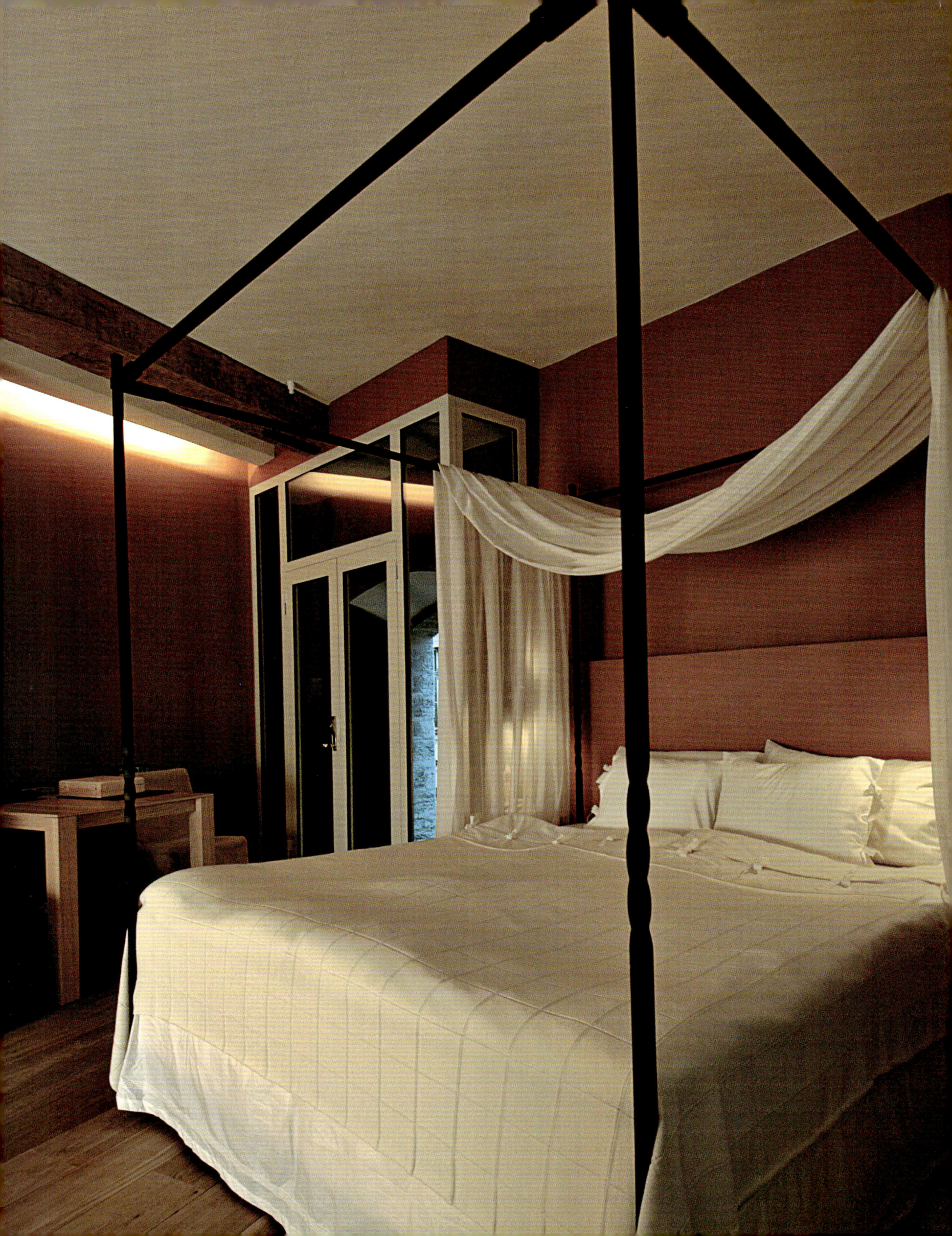

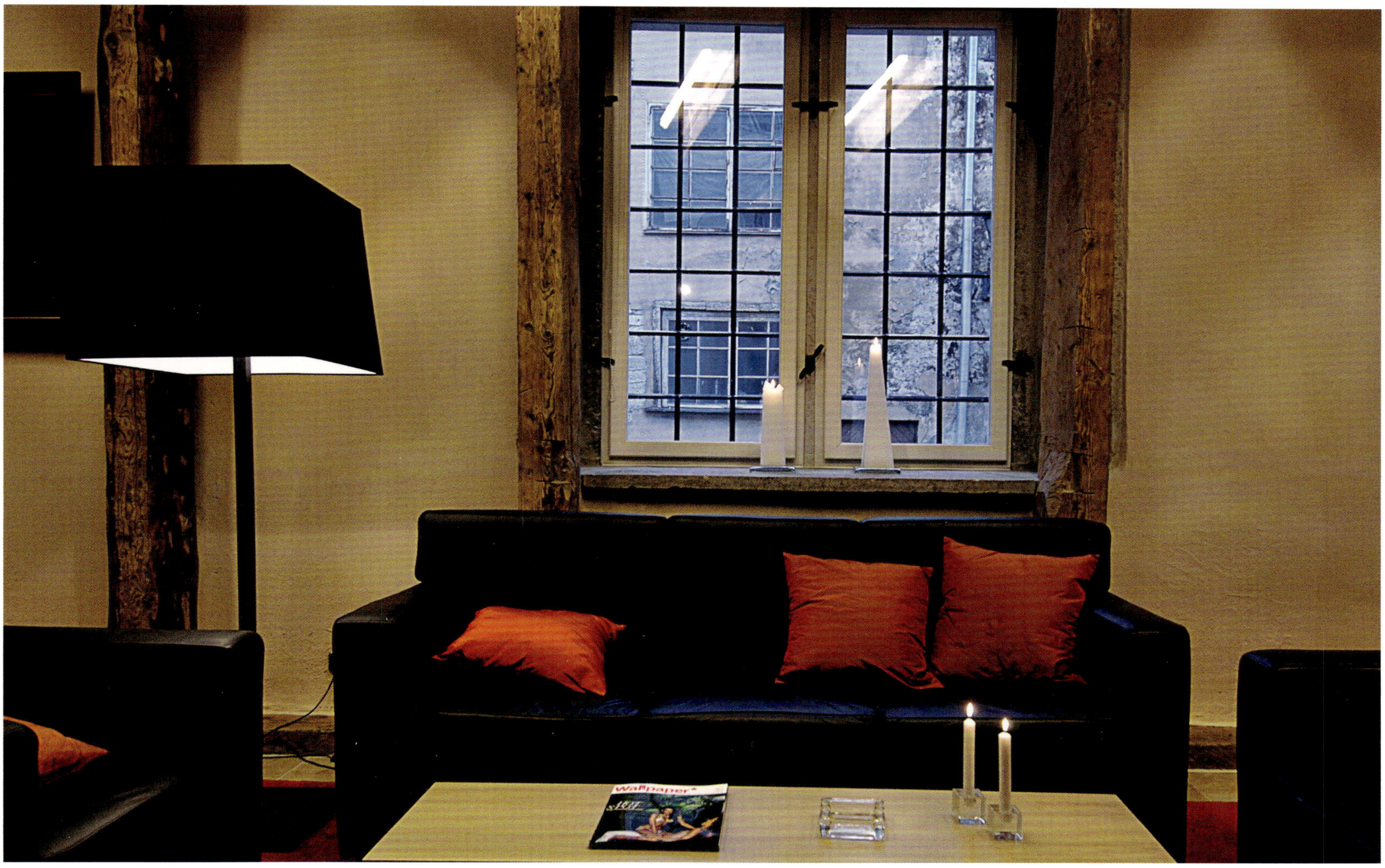

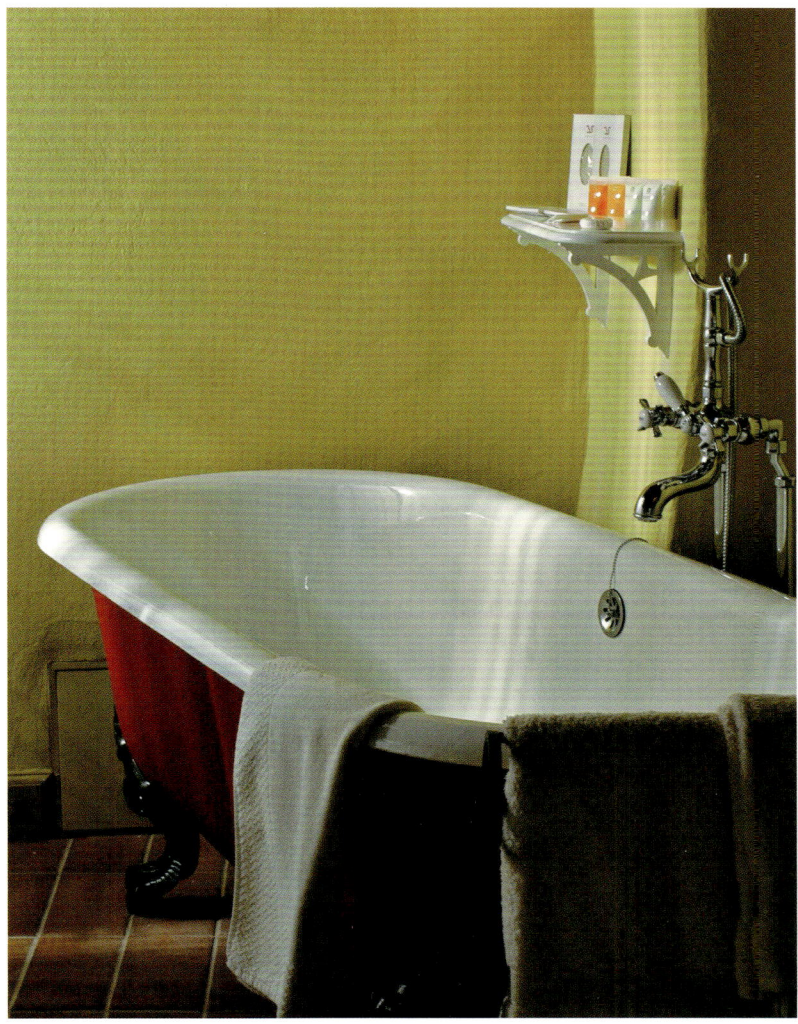

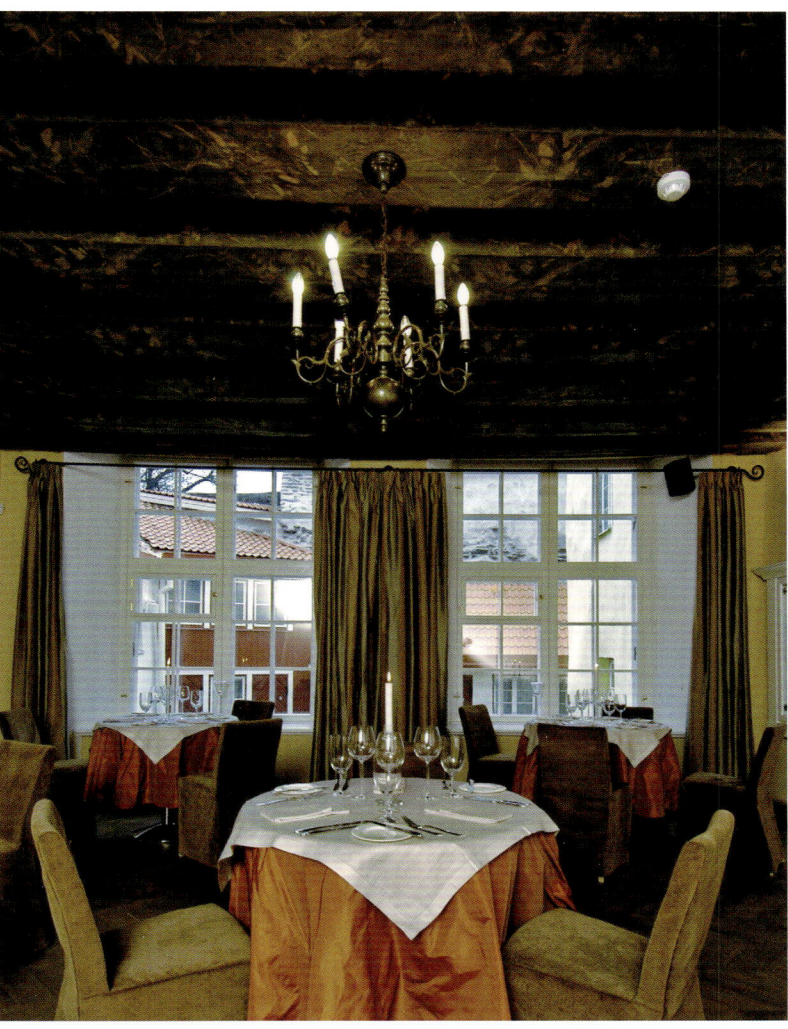

Berns Hotel

Stockholm, Sweden

Näckströmsgatan 8
Stockholm 11147
Sweden
Phone: +46 8 566 322 00
Fax: +46 8 566 322 01
www.berns.se

Price category: €€
Rooms: 65 rooms
Facilities: Bar, 2 restaurants, nightclub, theater, concert hall
Services: Extensive concierge service, room service
Located: In the heart of the city, next to Norrmalmstorg and Berzelii Park
Public transportation: Underground Red line Östermalmstorg, Blue line Kungsträdgården; bus Norrmalmstorg
Style: Boutique hotel

Behind the impressive facade dating back to 1863, there are 65 rooms and suites in sizes from "Extra Small" to "Extra Large" and sophisticatedly furnished with cherry wood, precious materials and designer lamps. Marlene Dietrich once freshened up her lipstick in suite 431 before going on stage. Besides featuring a concert hall, there are a theater and a gallery in the hotel making the Berns the perfect address for art, music and culture fans. One highlight is the bar with its breathtaking ceiling height and chandeliers.

Hinter der eindrucksvollen Fassade aus dem Jahr 1863 warten 65 Zimmer und Suiten – in den Größen „Extra Small" bis „Extra Large" und sehr sophisticated mit Kirschholz, edlen Stoffen und Designerlampen eingerichtet. In der Suite 431 zog sich einst Marlene Dietrich die Lippen nach, ehe sie auf die Bühne ging – neben einem Konzertsaal gehören ein Theater sowie eine Galerie zum Haus und machen das Berns zur perfekten Adresse für Kunst-, Musik- und Kulturfans. Ein Highlight ist die Bar mit ihrer atemberaubenden Deckenhöhe und ihren Lüstern.

Derrière la façade impressionnante datant de 1863 se cachent 65 chambres et suites qui prolongent la première impression, avec des tailles allant d'« Extra Small » à « Extra large », et une décoration très sophistiquée avec du merisier, des matériaux précieux et des lampes de designer. Marlene Dietrich s'est repoudré le nez dans la suite 431 avant de monter sur scène – outre la salle de concert, l'hôtel comporte en effet un théâtre et une galerie, ce qui fait du Berns l'adresse parfaite pour les amateurs d'art et de culture. Un de ses points forts est le bar avec sa hauteur sous plafond époustouflante.

Detrás de la impresionante fachada de 1863 aguardan 65 habitaciones y suites de todos los tamaños, desde las pequeñas "Extra Small" hasta las enormes "Extra Large", todas muy sofisticadas y decoradas con maderas de cerezo, materiales de lujo y lámparas de diseño. En la suite 431, Marlene Dietrich repasó antaño el contorno de sus labios antes de salir a escena. El hotel dispone de una sala de conciertos, un teatro y una galería de arte, lo que hace de él un lugar perfecto para los amantes del arte, de la musica y de la cultura. Uno de sus puntos fuertes es el bar, con un techo de una altura que simplemente quita el aliento y estupendas arañas de cristal.

Dietro alla notevole facciata datata 1863 vi aspettano 65 camere e suite – da quelle "extra small" alle "extra large", arredate in modo molto sofisticato con legno di ciliegio, stoffe raffinate e lampade di design. Nella suite 431 Marlene Dietrich si ritoccò il rossetto prima di salire sul palcoscenico – oltre a una sala concerti, la struttura comprende anche un teatro e una galleria d'arte, che fanno del Berns l'indirizzo ideale per appassionati di arte, musica e cultura. Da non perdere il bar con il suo alto soffitto e i suoi lampadari da capogiro.

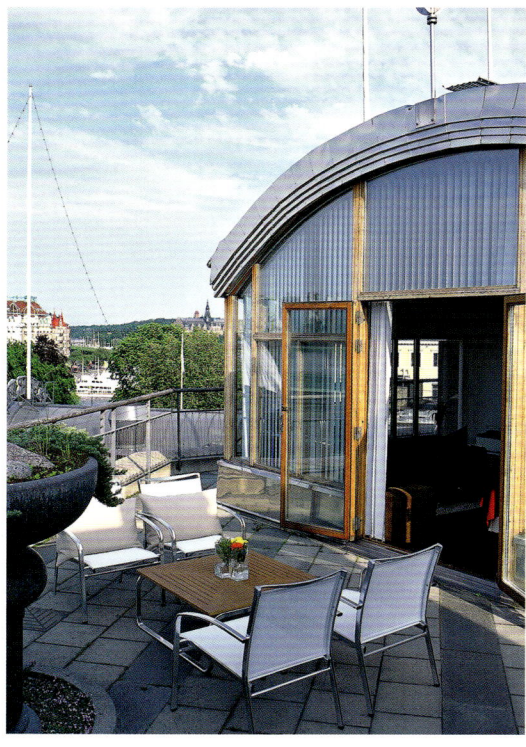 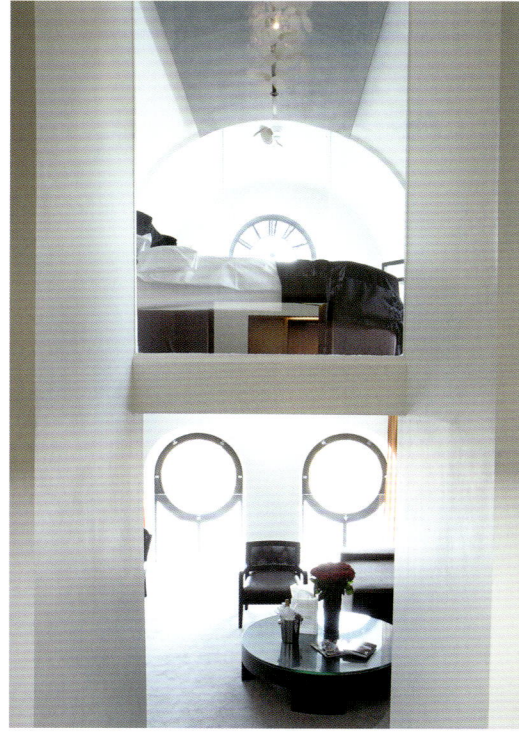 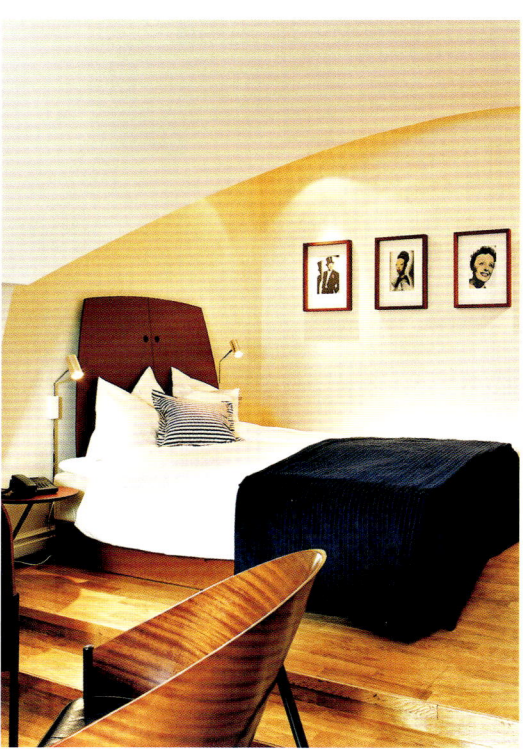

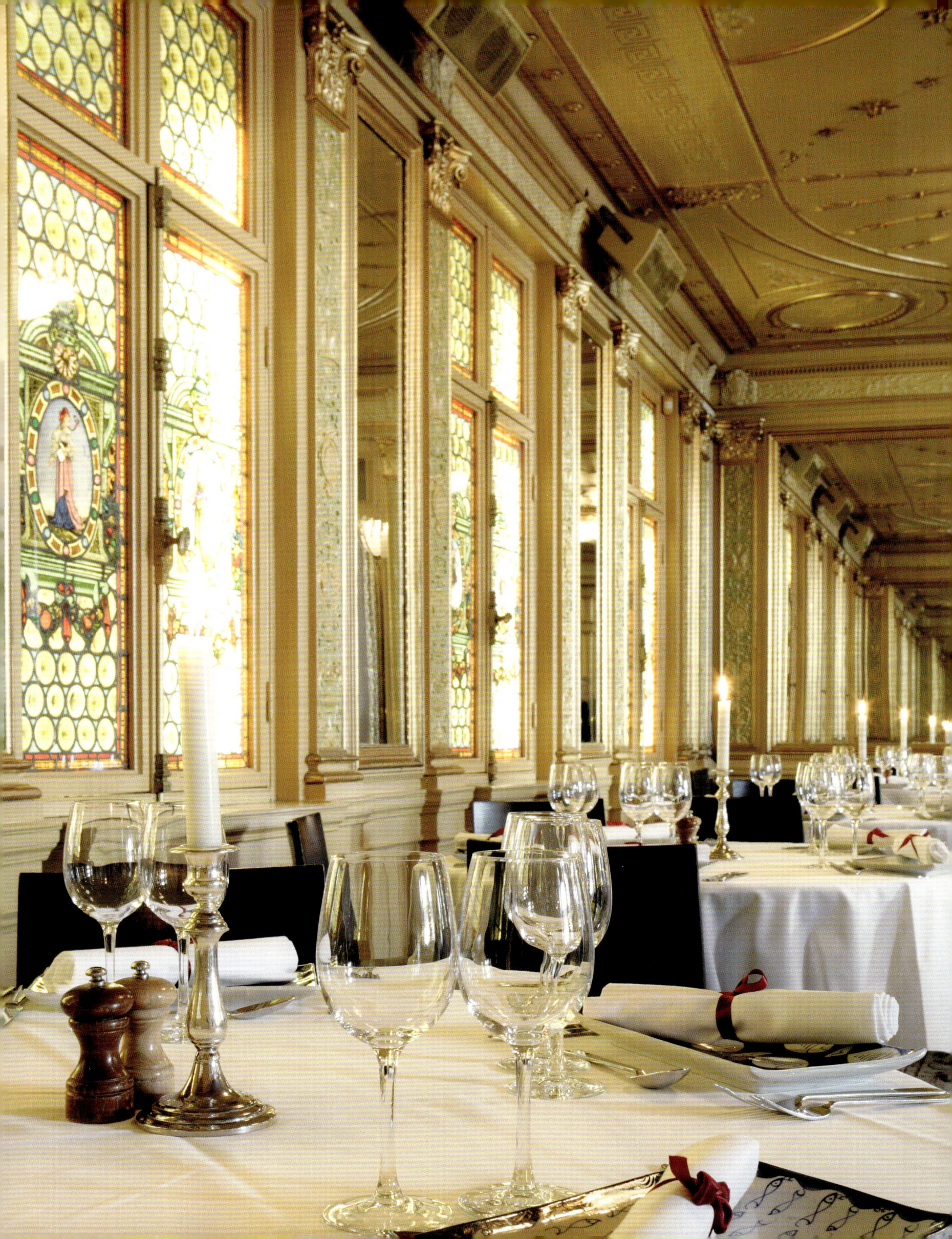

Stockholm 13127
Sweden
Phone: +46 8 601 300 0
Fax: +46 8 601 300 9
www.hotelj.com

Rooms: 45 rooms including 5 suites
Facilities: Seafood restaurant, bar/lounge, sauna, boutique, drugstore, convention center
Services: Concierge, 24 h room service, dry cleaning, babysitting, massage service
Located: On the waterside at Nacka Strand, 15 min by boat from the city center
Public transportation: Boat M/S Ballerina; bus 443, 465 Nacka Strand
Style: Contemporary marine

Casual Newport-chic is cultivated in the 45-room hotel situated on Nacka beach only a 20-minute drive from Stockholm. The proper arrival is, however, by boat since the J in the name is from the legendary '30s sailing class in the America's Cup. Dark wooden floors, stained white-beamed ceilings and ship lanterns underscore the maritime orientation. In the summer you can breakfast in the garden with a view to the harbor and the Djurgarden island. When the north wind freshens the air, the fireplace in the lobby is lit.

Lässigen Newport-Chic kultiviert das knapp 20 Autominuten von Stockholm direkt am Nacka Strand gelegene 45-Zimmer-Hotel. Stilecht reist man allerdings mit dem Boot an, schließlich spielt das J im Namen auf die legendäre 30er-Jahre-Segelklasse beim America's Cup an. Dunkle Holzböden, weißlasierte Balkendecken und Schiffslampen unterstreichen das maritime Ambiente. Im Sommer kann man im Garten mit Blick auf den Hafen und die Insel Djurgarden frühstücken. Wenn der Nordwind auffrischt, werden in der Lobby die Kaminfeuer entzündet.

Cet hôtel au chic Newport très étudié, avec ses 45 chambres, est situé à moins de 20 minutes en voiture de Stockholm, directement sur la plage de Nacka. Dans le plus pur style traditionnel, on y arrive par bateau et d'ailleurs l'Hotel J a choisi son nom en hommage aux légendaires bateaux des années 30 concourant lors de l'America's Cup. Des sols de bois sombre, des plafonds à poutres blanches apparentes et des lampes de bateaux soulignent l'atmosphère marine. Pendant l'été, on peut prendre le petit-déjeuner dans le jardin, avec vue sur le port et l'île de Djurgarden. Quand le vent du nord se fait plus incisif, les cheminées du hall sont allumées.

El hotel de 45 habitaciones, situado en la playa de Nacía a unos 20 minutos en coche de Estocolmo, se caracteriza por su desenfadado estilo chic Newport. Pero es con el barco como realmente se llega a él con clase; después de todo, la J del nombre hace referencia a la legendaria clase de embarcaciones que participó en la Copa América en los años 30. El ambiente es marcadamente marinero, con suelos de maderas oscuras, cubiertas con vigas barnizadas en blanco y lámparas de barco. En verano se puede desayunar en el jardín contemplando el puerto y la isla Djurgarden. Cuando sopla el viento del norte se encienden las chimeneas en el vestíbulo.

Un rilassato stile newport chic per questo albergo da 45 stanze, situato direttamente sulla spiaggia di Nacka, a 20 minuti scarsi da Stoccolma. La J del nome è un riferimento alla leggendaria classe "J" delle regate dell'America's Cup degli anni '30: volendo mantenere piena fedeltà al suo stile, si dovrebbe arrivare in barca. Pavimenti in legno scuro, soffitto a travi verniciate in bianco e luci da nave accentuano l'atmosfera marinaresca degli ambienti. In estate è possibile fare colazione in giardino, godendo così di una splendida vista sul porto e sull'isola Djurgarden. Quando il vento del nord rinfresca l'aria, nel caminetto della lobby viene acceso il fuoco.

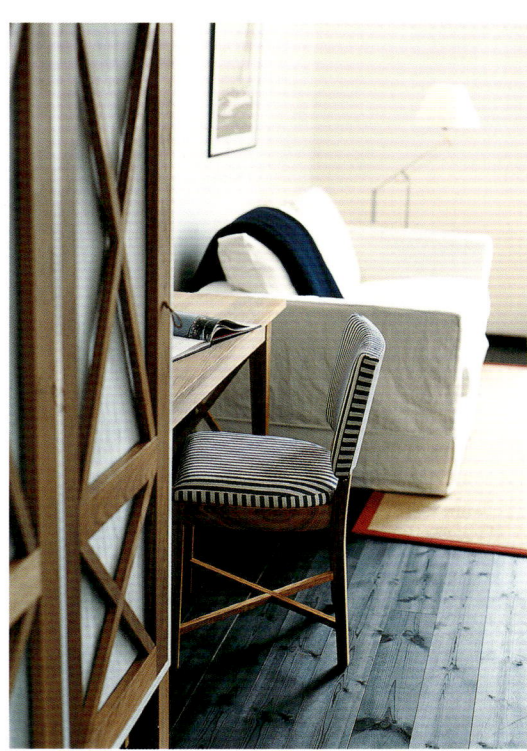
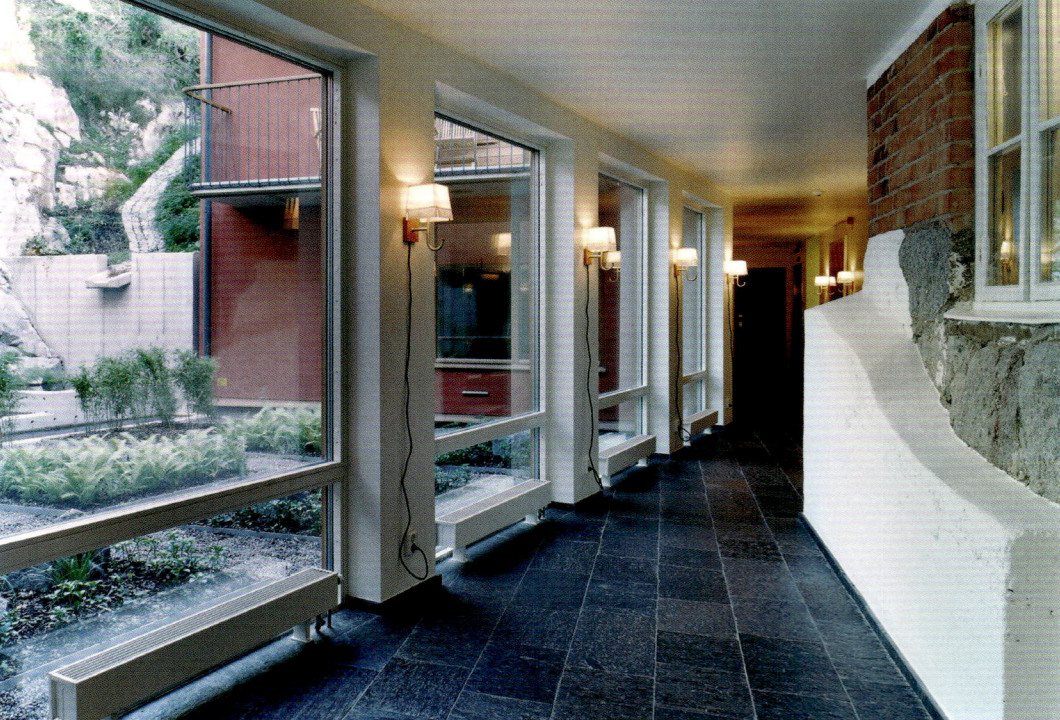

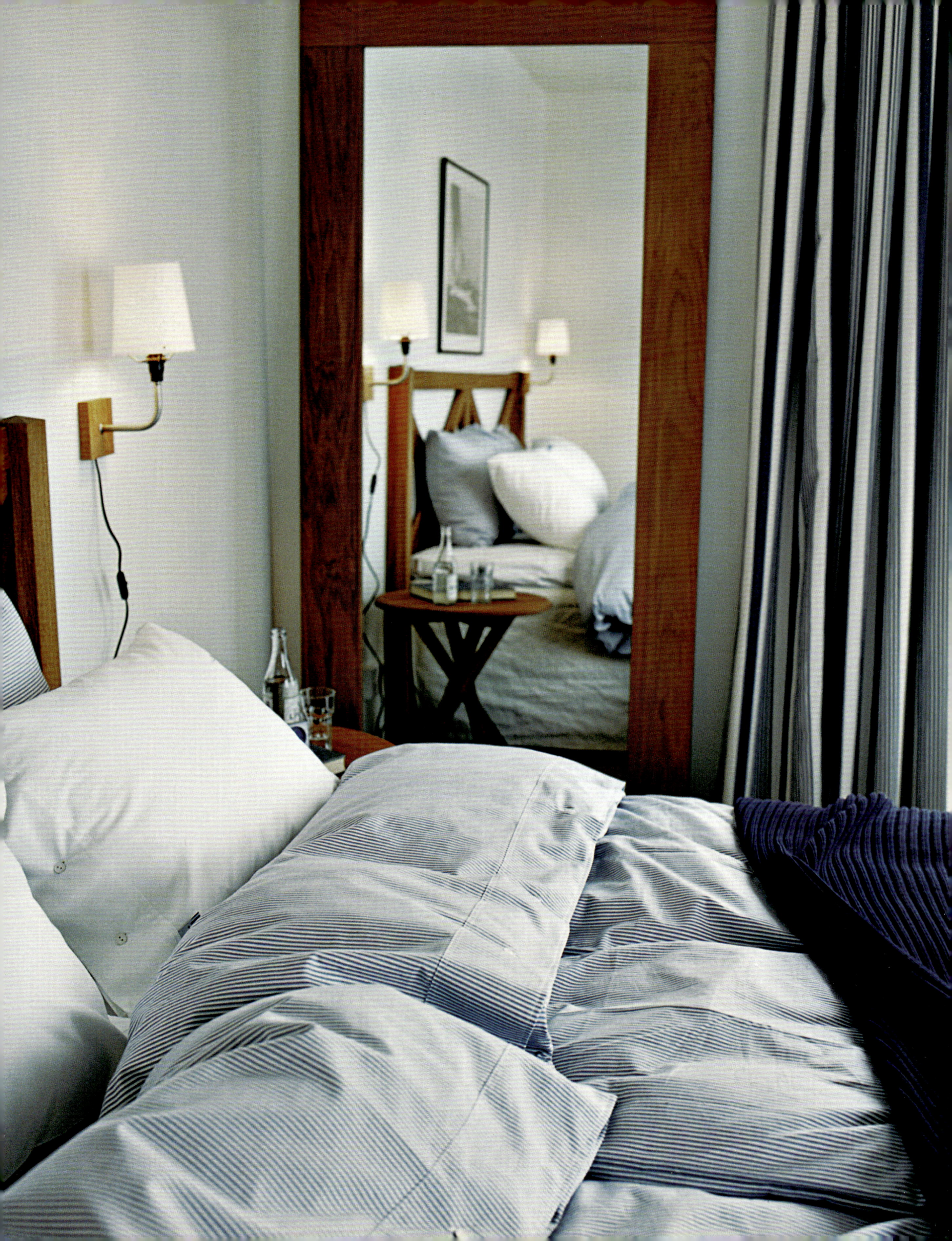

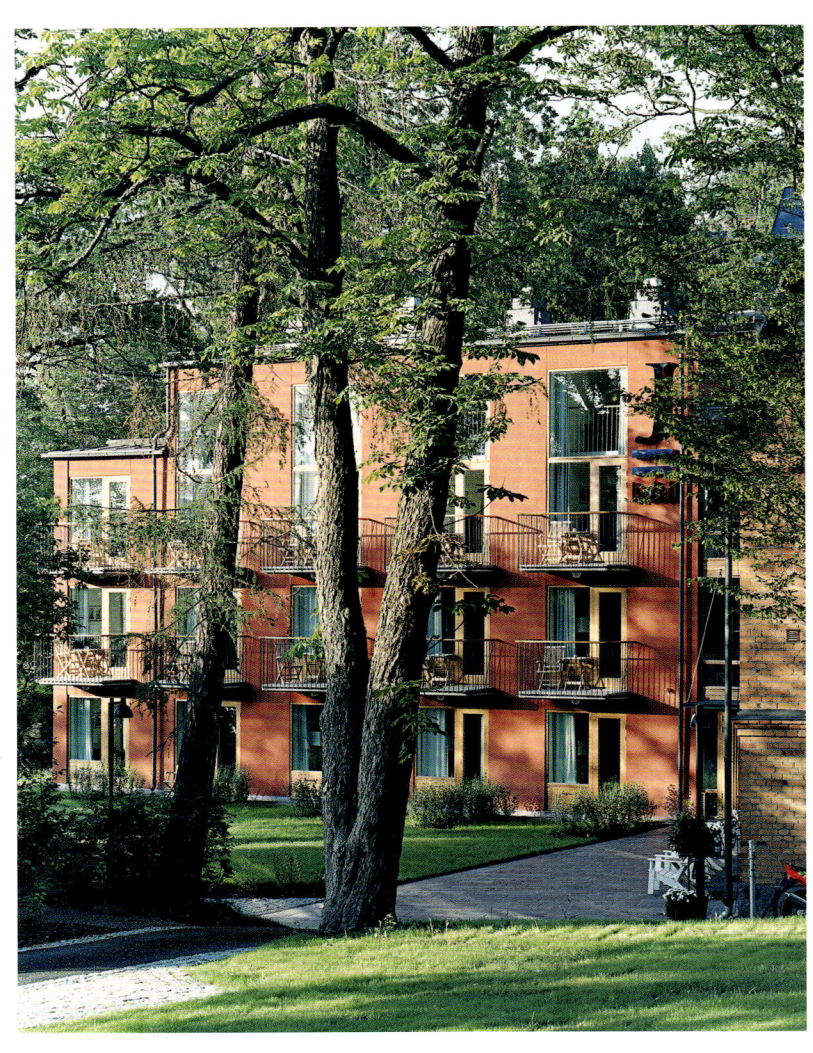
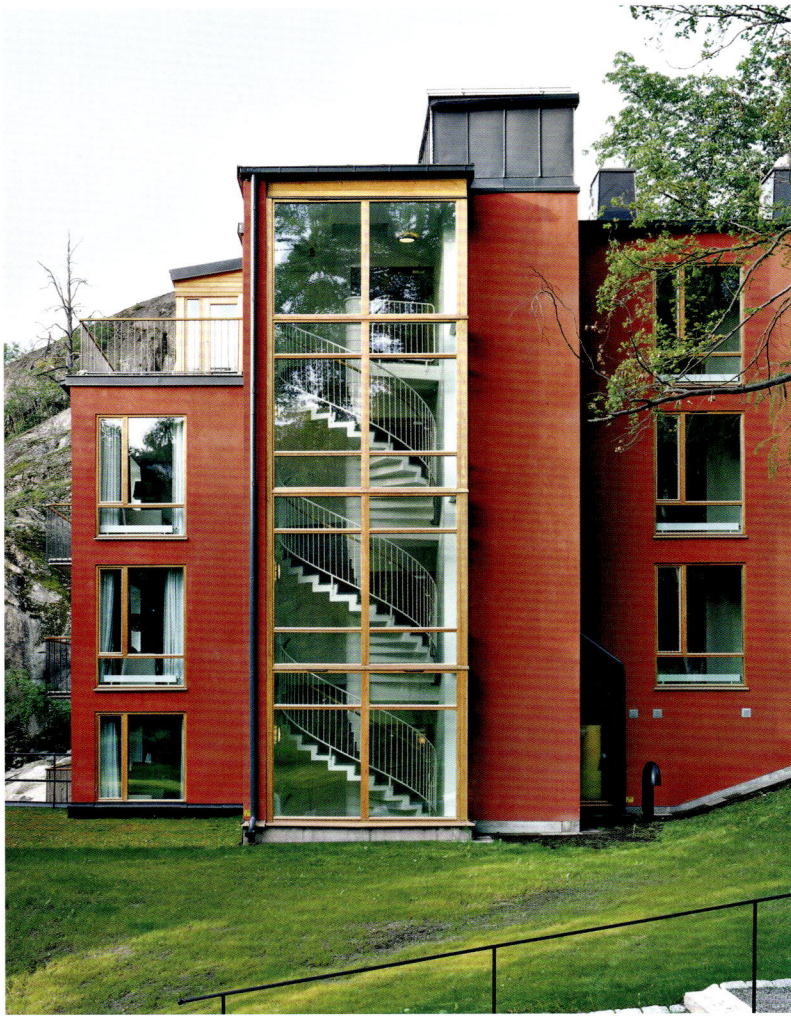

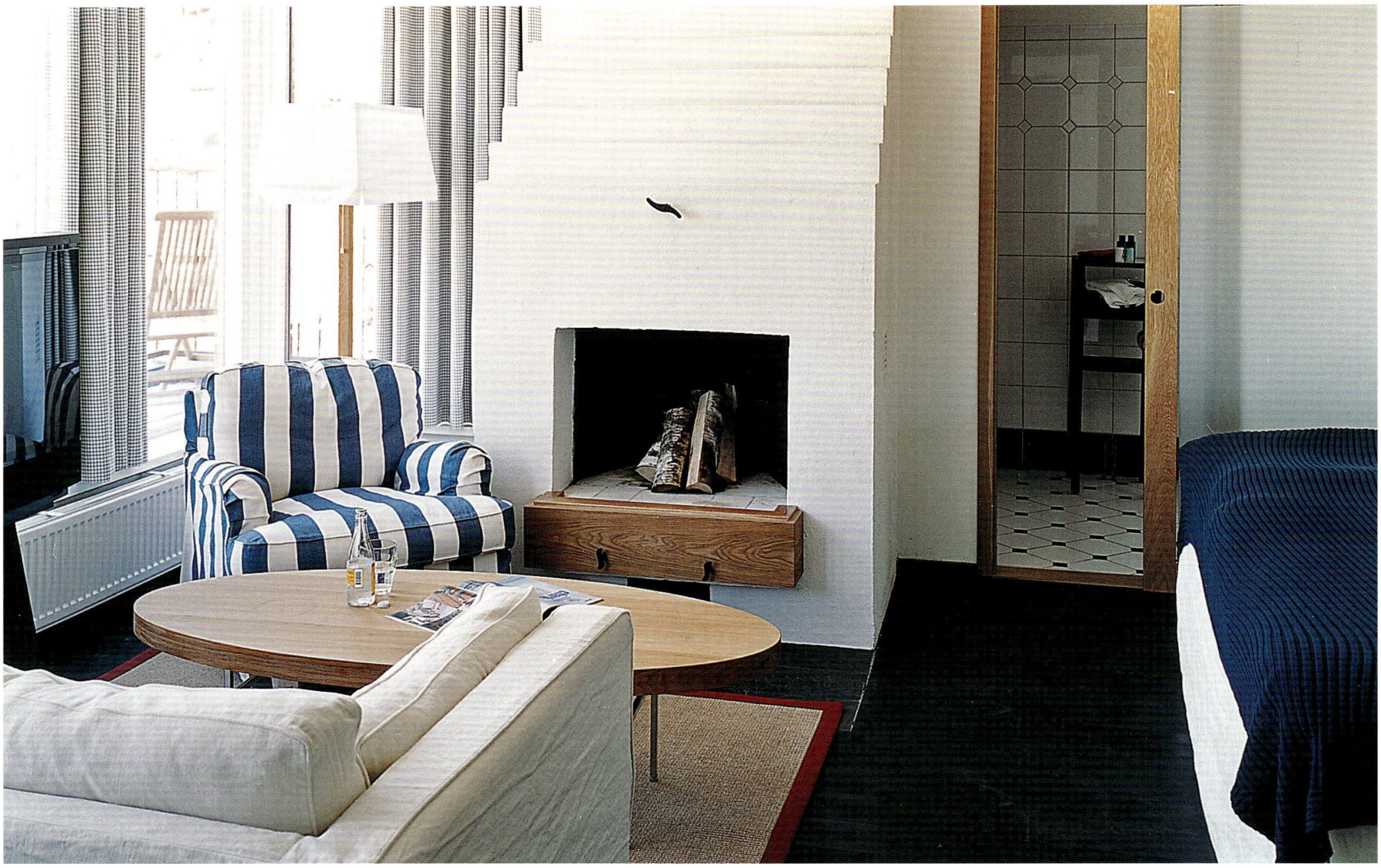

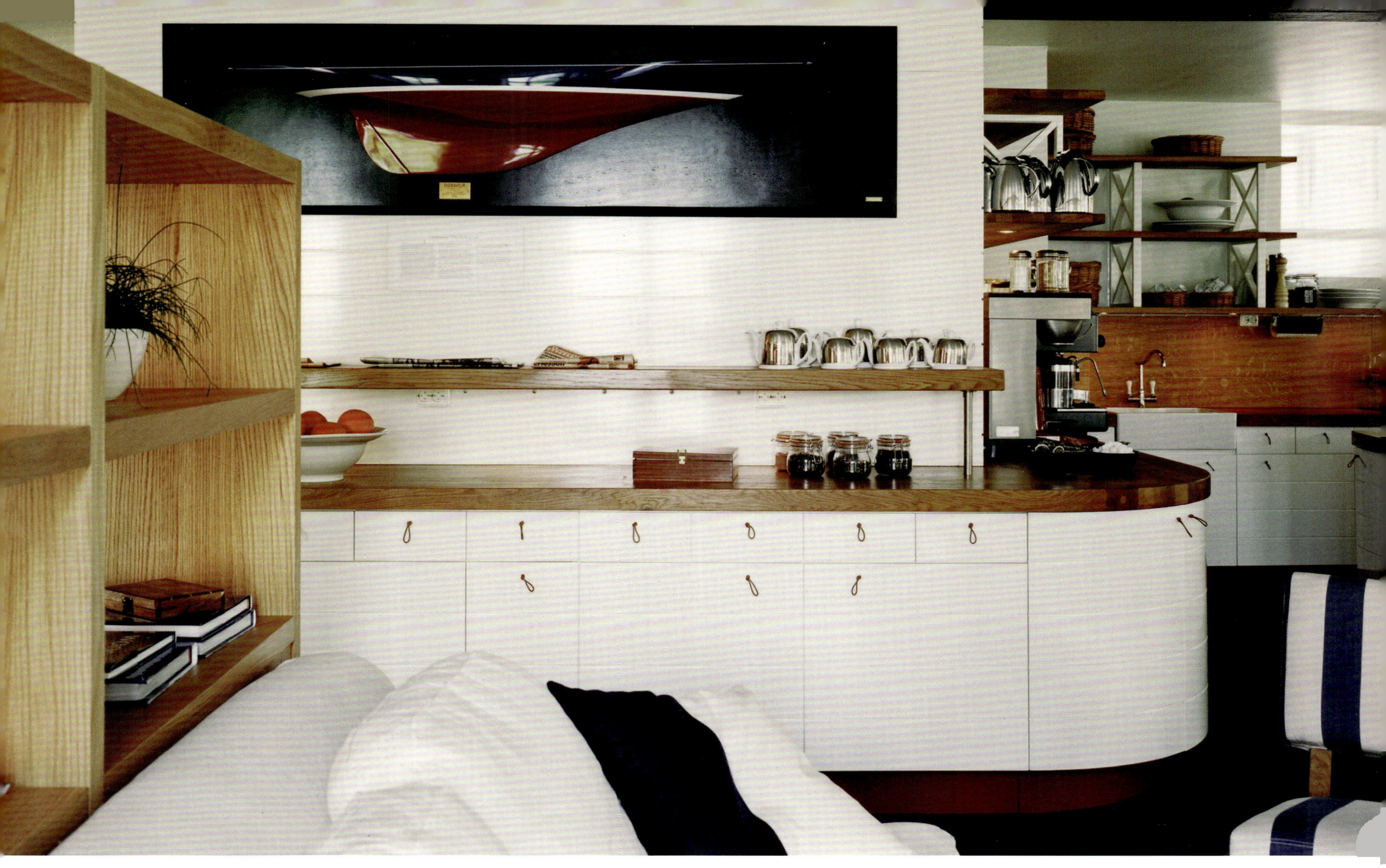

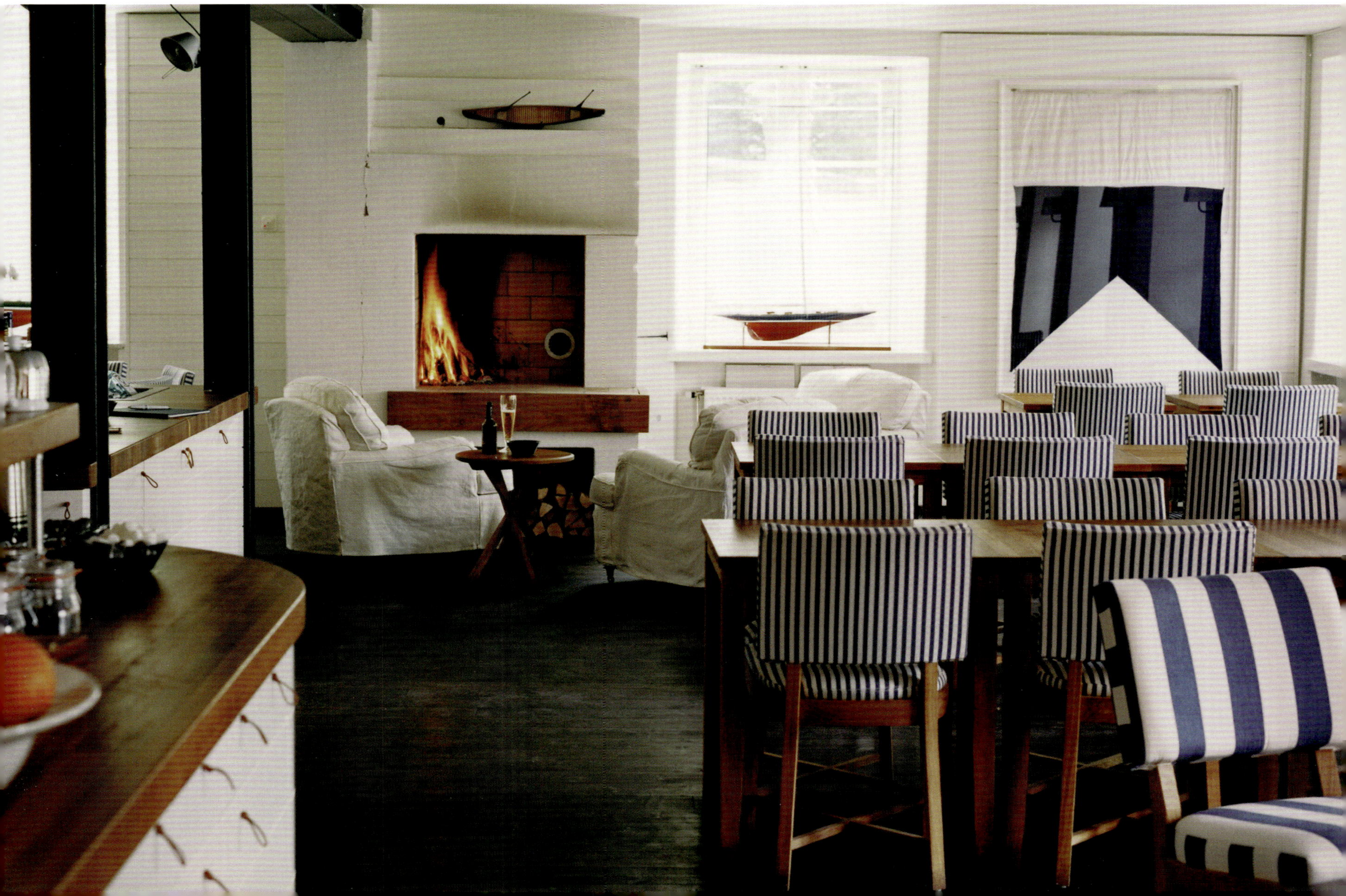

1551 Copenhagen
Denmark
Phone: +45 33 13 30 00
Fax: +45 33 14 30 33
www.hotelfox.dk

Rooms: 61 rooms
Facilities: Bar and restaurant Intoxica, Tiki bar, roof terrace
Services: Free WiFi, flatscreen TVs, international newspapers and magazines, room service
Located: In the center by the City Hall Square and the shopping district
Public transportation: Most buses stop by the City Hall Square
Style: Creative, art

What happens when you let 21 international artists loose on the design of a hotel? Behind each of the 61 doors to the room lurks a surprise: Maybe an oversized monkey is on the wall ordering "Sleep!", or an entirely red boudoir. A Heidi landscape of the Alps or a zen-influenced concentration room. Whoever leaves this creative brain pool reaches the Stroget, Copenhagen's bustling fashion mile, after only a few steps away. Breakfast here is a culture vulture's dream with felt-warmed pots emitting the unmistakable aroma of coffee and freshly prepared smörgasbröd peeping from paper bags.

Was geschieht, wenn man 21 internationalen Künstlern die Gestaltung eines Hotels überlässt? Hinter jeder der 61 Zimmertüren wartet eine Überraschung: ein überlebensgroßer Affe an der Wand, der „Sleep!" befiehlt, ein ganz in rot gehaltenes Boudoir, eine alpine Heidi-Landschaft, ein Zen-beeinflusster Konzentrationsraum. Wer diesen kreativen Brainpool verlässt, gelangt nach wenigen Schritten auf die Stroget, Kopenhagens quirlige und modische Einkaufsmeile. Auch das Frühstück hat hier Kultcharakter, mit Kaffee in Filzwärmekannen und frisch zubereitetem Smörgasbröd in Papiertüten.

Qu'arrive-t-il quand vous permettez à 21 artistes internationaux de concevoir un hôtel ? Une surprise vous attend derrière la porte de chacune des 61 chambres : un singe plus grand que nature sur le mur qui vous ordonne de dormir « Sleep! », un boudoir complètement rouge, un paysage alpin digne d'Heidi, une chambre méditative inspirée par le zen. Lorsqu'on quitte ce bouillon de culture créative, on n'est qu'à quelques pas de la Stroget, la rue commerciale tendance et animée de Copenhague. Même le petit-déjeuner a un côté culte ici, avec des cafetières couvertes de feutre et des smörgasbröd frais dépassant de sacs en papier.

¿Qué ocurre cuando se deja el diseño de un hotel en manos de 21 artistas internacionales? Detrás de cada una de las puertas de las 61 habitaciones espera una sorpresa. Un mono de tamaño natural en la pared que nos manda a la cama con un enorme "Sleep!", un boudoir completamente en rojo, un paisaje alpino sacado del cuento de Heidi, una habitación de meditación inspirada en la filosofía zen. A muy pocos pasos de este laboratorio de creatividad se encuentra la Stroget, la bulliciosa y moderna zona de tiendas de Copenhague. Aquí el desayuno también tiene carácter de culto, con cafeteras térmicas de fieltro y pan Smörga recién hecho en bolsitas de papel.

Che cosa può succedere se 21 artisti internazionali vengono incaricati di progettare un solo albergo? Succede che dietro la porta di ognuna delle 61 stanze dell'hotel l'ospite può attendersi una sorpresa: una enorme scimmia dipinta sulla parete, che ordina "Sleep!", un boudoir realizzato esclusivamente in rosso, un paesaggio alpino in cui quasi ci si aspetta di veder comparire Heidi, una stanza in stile zen per stimolare la concentrazione. E allontanandosi da questo crogiolo di creatività artistica si arriva, dopo soli pochi passi, sullo Stroget, la via pedonale più vivace e alla moda di Copenhagen. Qui la prima colazione è un vero e proprio rito, con il caffè caldo servito in bricchi rivestiti di feltro e le Smörgasbröd, fresche tartine svedesi presentate in cartocci di carta.

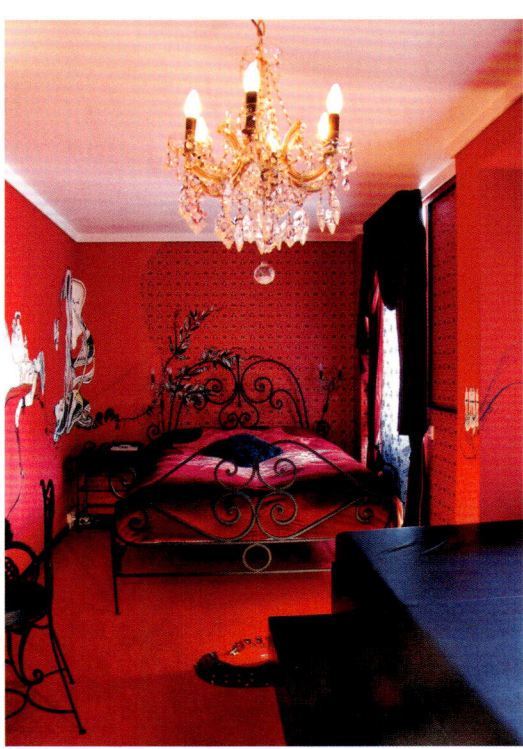
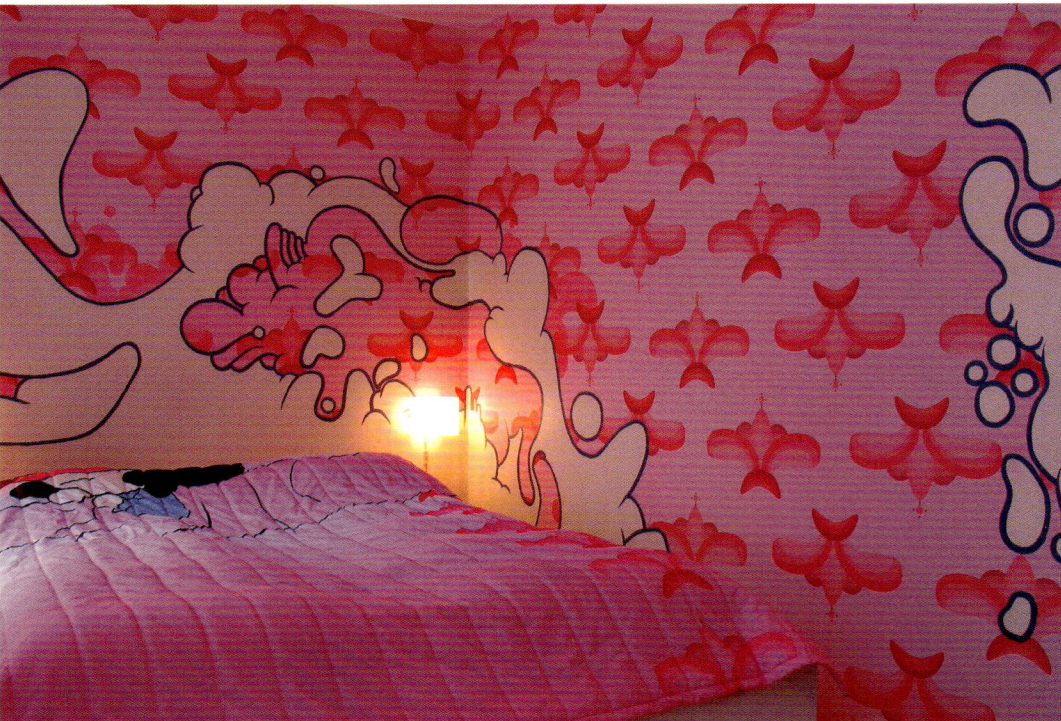

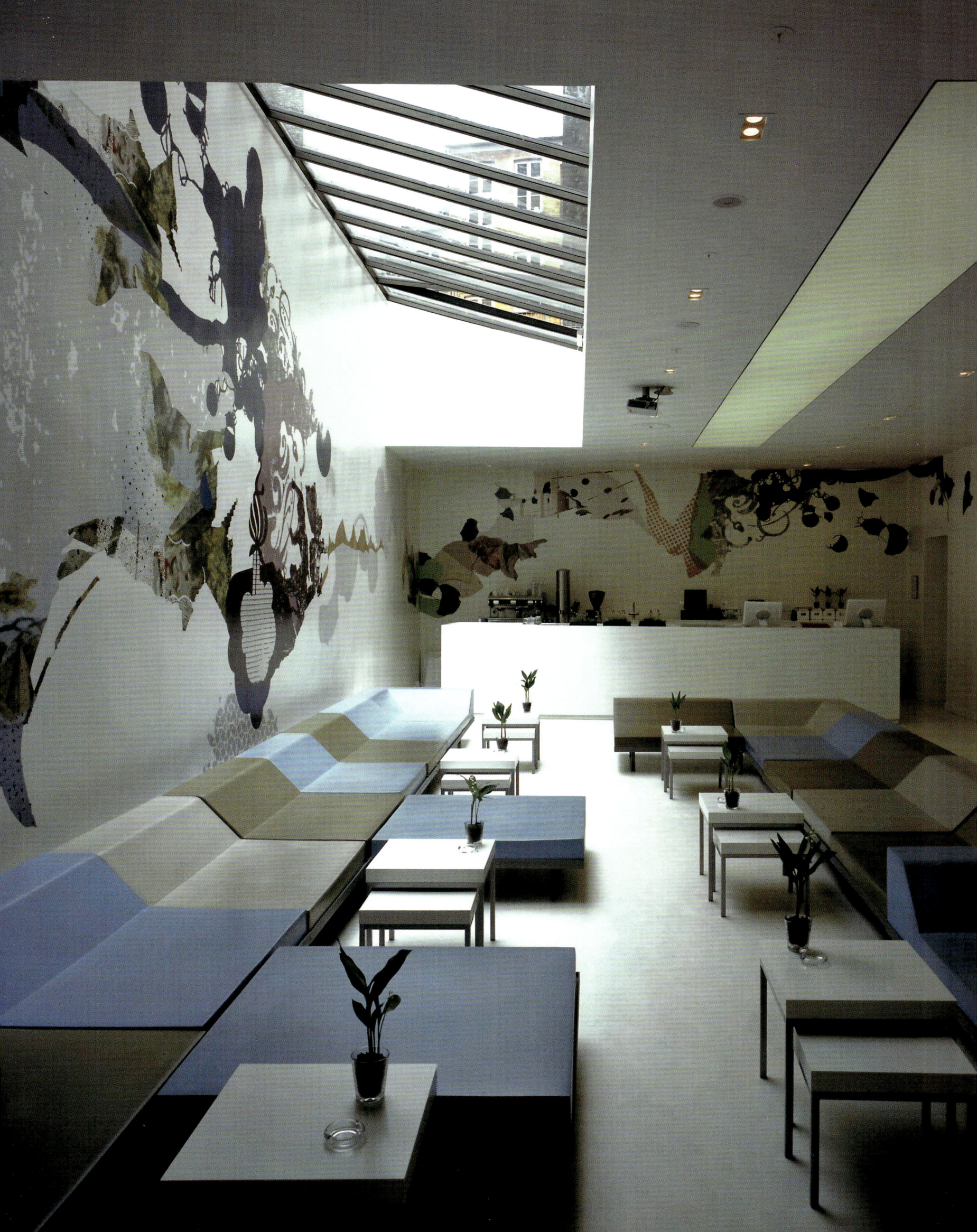

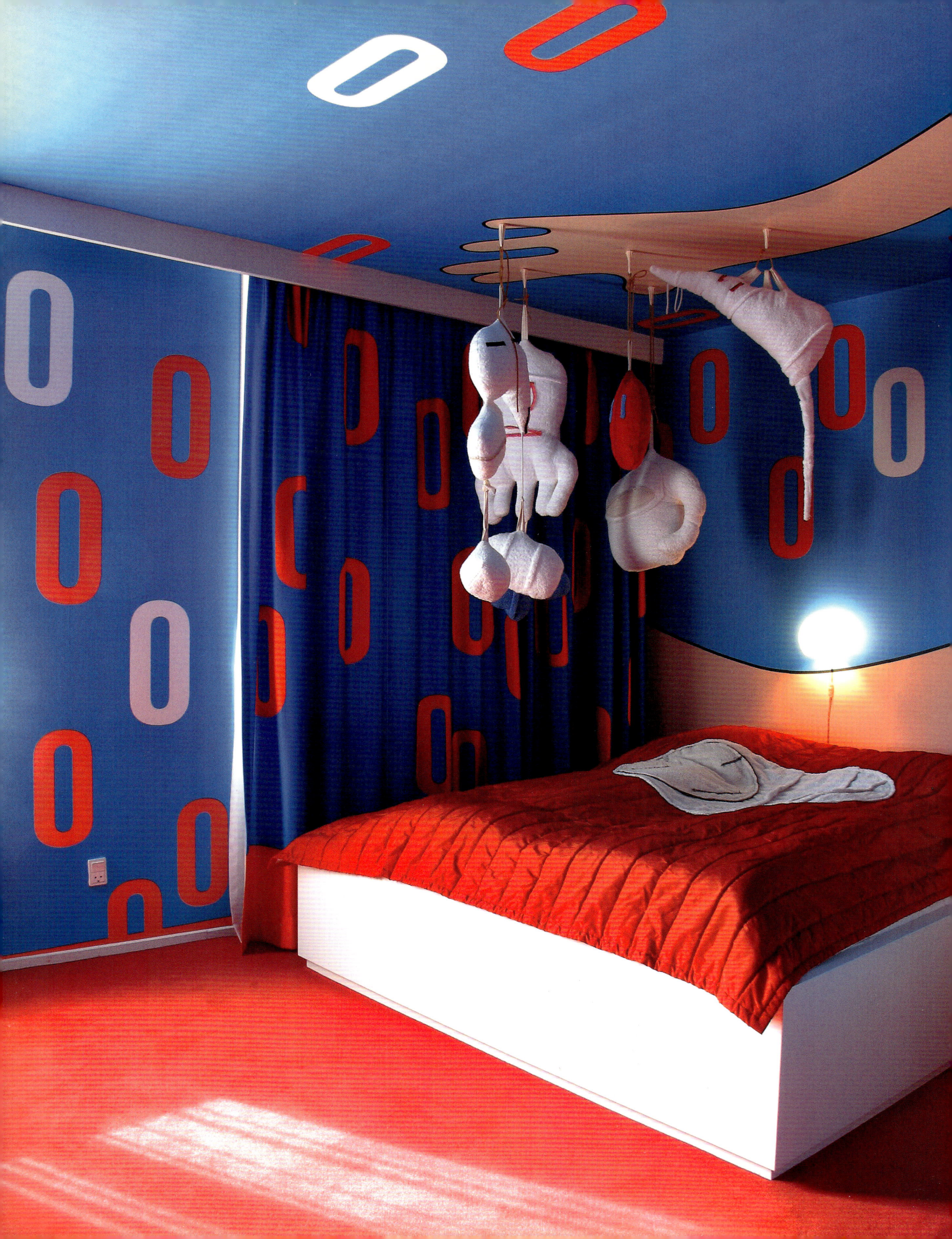

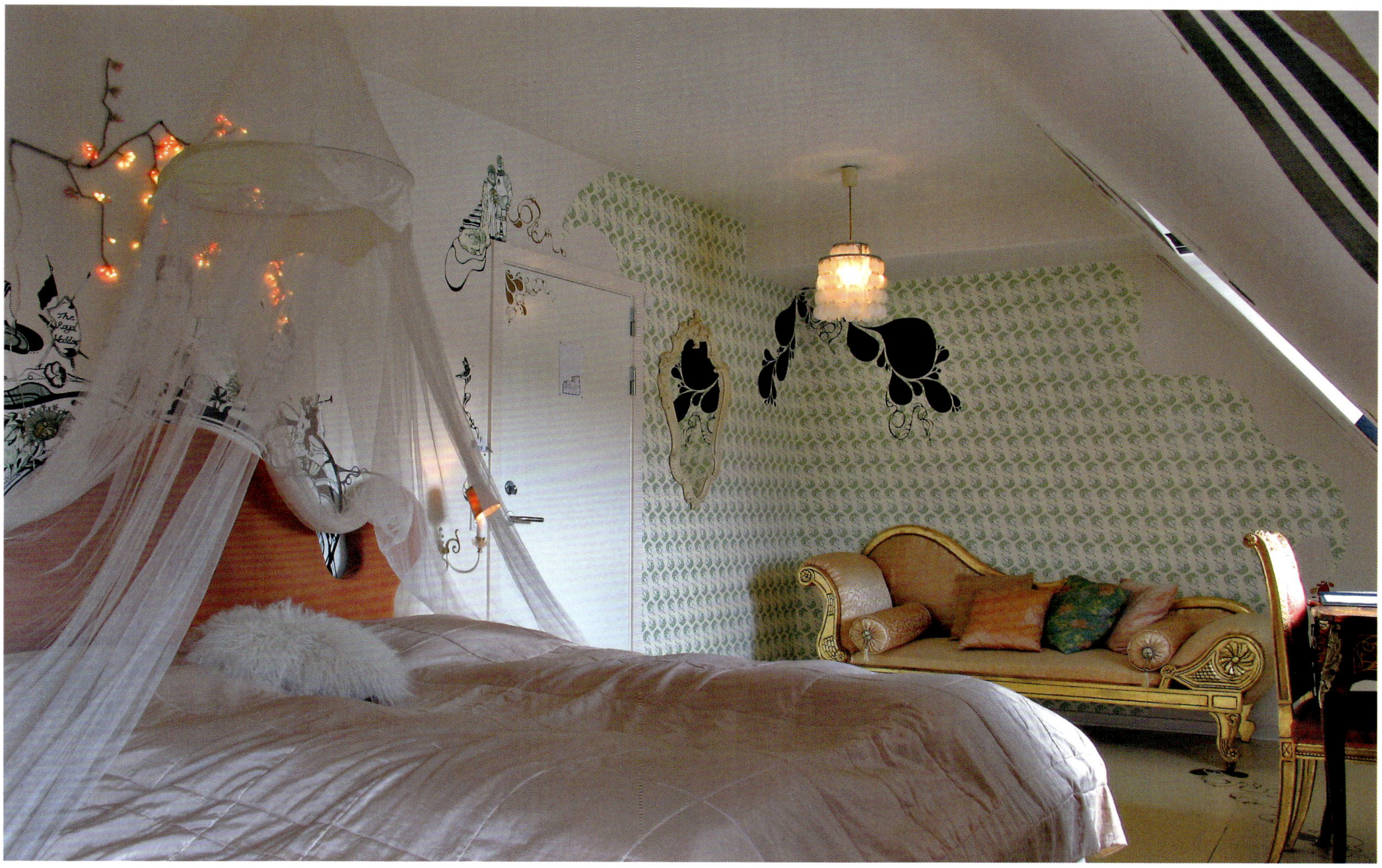

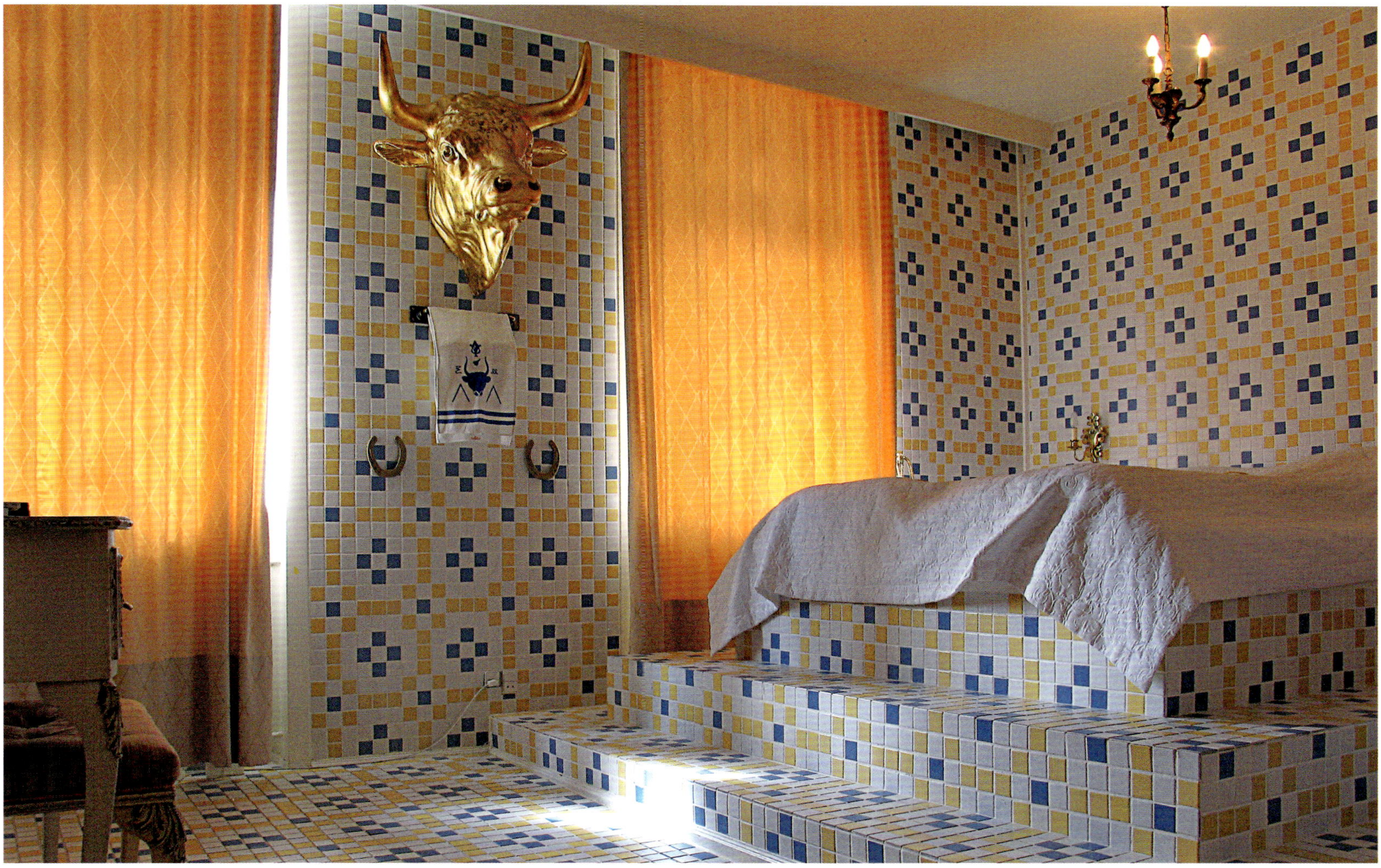

First Hotel Skt. Petri

Copenhagen, Denmark

Krystalgade 22
1172 Copenhagen
Denmark
Phone: +45 33 45 91 00
Fax: +45 33 45 91 10
www.hotelsktpetri.com

Price category: €€
Rooms: 268 rooms and suites including 1 penthouse
Facilities: Bar, restaurant, café, fitness suite, courtyard terrace
Services: Concierge, valet parking, massage, private yoga, 24 h roomservice, air-conditioning, broadband internet access, a two-lined telephone, TV, minibar, safe
Located: In the heart of the old Latin Quarter of Copenhagen
Public transportation: A 2 min walk from train and metro connections
Style: Modern Scandinavian

2003 saw the transformation of a department store from the '30s to Copenhagen's hippest hotel. The 268 rooms and suites bear witness to the quality of Scandinavian design: functionality, timeless modernity and reduction to essentials. Situated in a quiet corner of the old city, a grand view opens out over the roofs of the Nordic metropolis on the upper floors. The color concept was made by the Danish artist Per Arnoldi, whose credo is that colors are an intensive form of communication.

Ein Warenhaus aus den 30er Jahren wurde 2003 zu Kopenhagens hippstem Hotel umgebaut. Die 268 Zimmer und Suiten zeigen, was die Qualität skandinavischen Designs ausmacht: die Funktionalität, die zeitlose Modernität, die Reduktion auf das Wesentliche. In einer ruhigen Ecke der Altstadt gelegen, eröffnet sich von den oberen Stockwerken ein grandioser Blick auf die Dachlandschaft der nordischen Metropole. Der dänische Künstler Per Arnoldi, dessen Credo ist, dass Farben eine intensive Form der Kommunikation sind, entwarf das Farbkonzept.

2003 a vu la transformation d'un grand magasin des années 30 en l'hôtel le plus branché de Copenhague. Les 268 chambres et suites témoignent de la qualité du design scandinave, de sa fonctionnalité, sa modernité intemporelle et sa réduction à l'essentiel. Situé dans un coin tranquille de la vieille ville, il offre une large vue sur les toits de la métropole nordique depuis les étages supérieurs. Le concept couleur a été créé par l'artiste danois Per Arnoldi, pour qui les couleurs sont une forme intense de communication.

En 2003, unos grandes almacenes de los años 30 fueron transformados en el hotel más chic de Copenhaguen. Sus 268 habitaciones y suites son testimonio de la calidad del diseño danés: en la funcionalidad, en la modernidad atemporal y en la reducción a lo esencial. El hotel se encuentra en un rincón tranquilo del casco antiguo y, desde sus pisos superiores, se puede disfrutar de un grandioso panorama de los tejados de la metrópolis nórdica. Todos los colores del hotel forman parte del concepto ideado por el artista danés Per Arnoldi, quien cree firmemente en el cromatismo como intensa forma de comunicación.

Nel 2003, un department store degli anni 30 è stato ristrutturato per dare vita all'hotel più alla moda di Kopenhagen. Le 268 camere e suite sono testimonianza della qualità del design scandinavo: la funzionalità, la modernità senza tempo, la riduzione all'essenziale. Situato in una tranquilla zona del centro storico, dai piani superiori offre una vista grandiosa sui tetti della metropoli nordica. La scelta cromatica si deve all'artista danese Per Arnoldi, il cui credo è che i colori siano un'intensa forma di comunicazione.

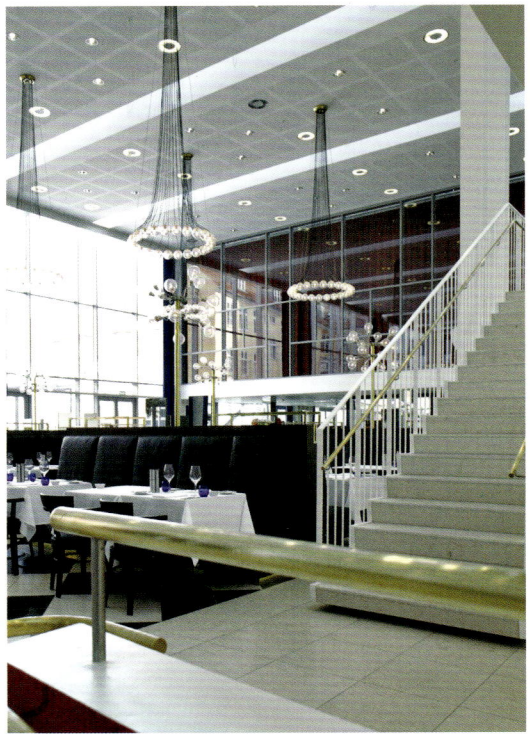
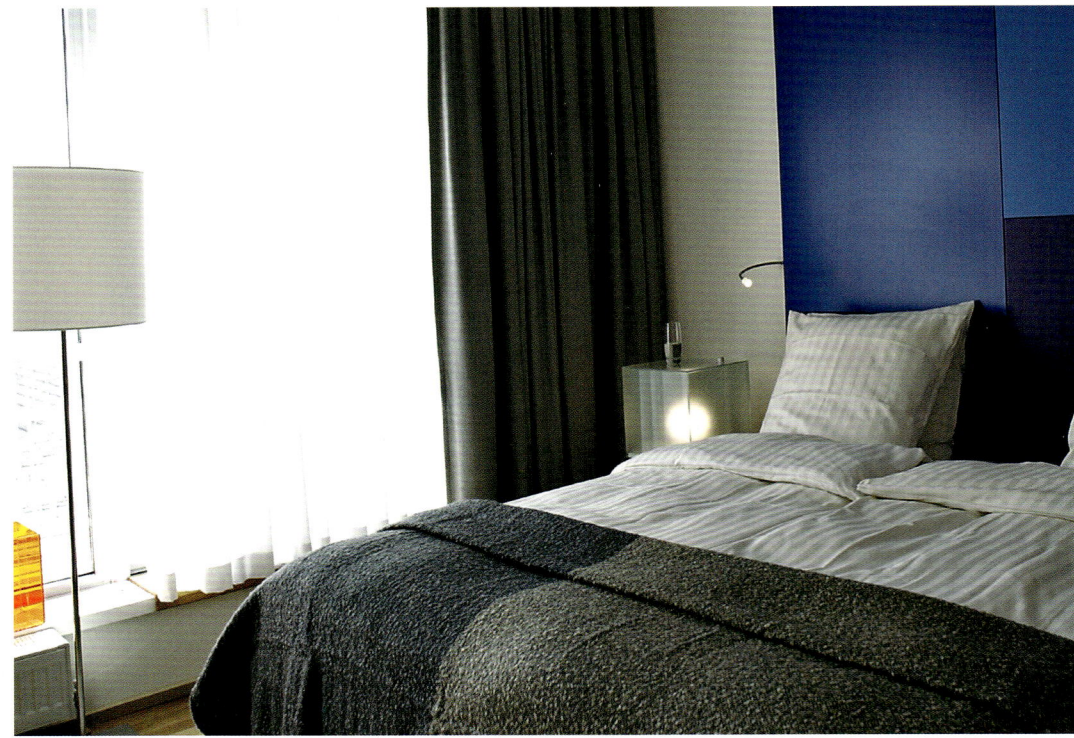

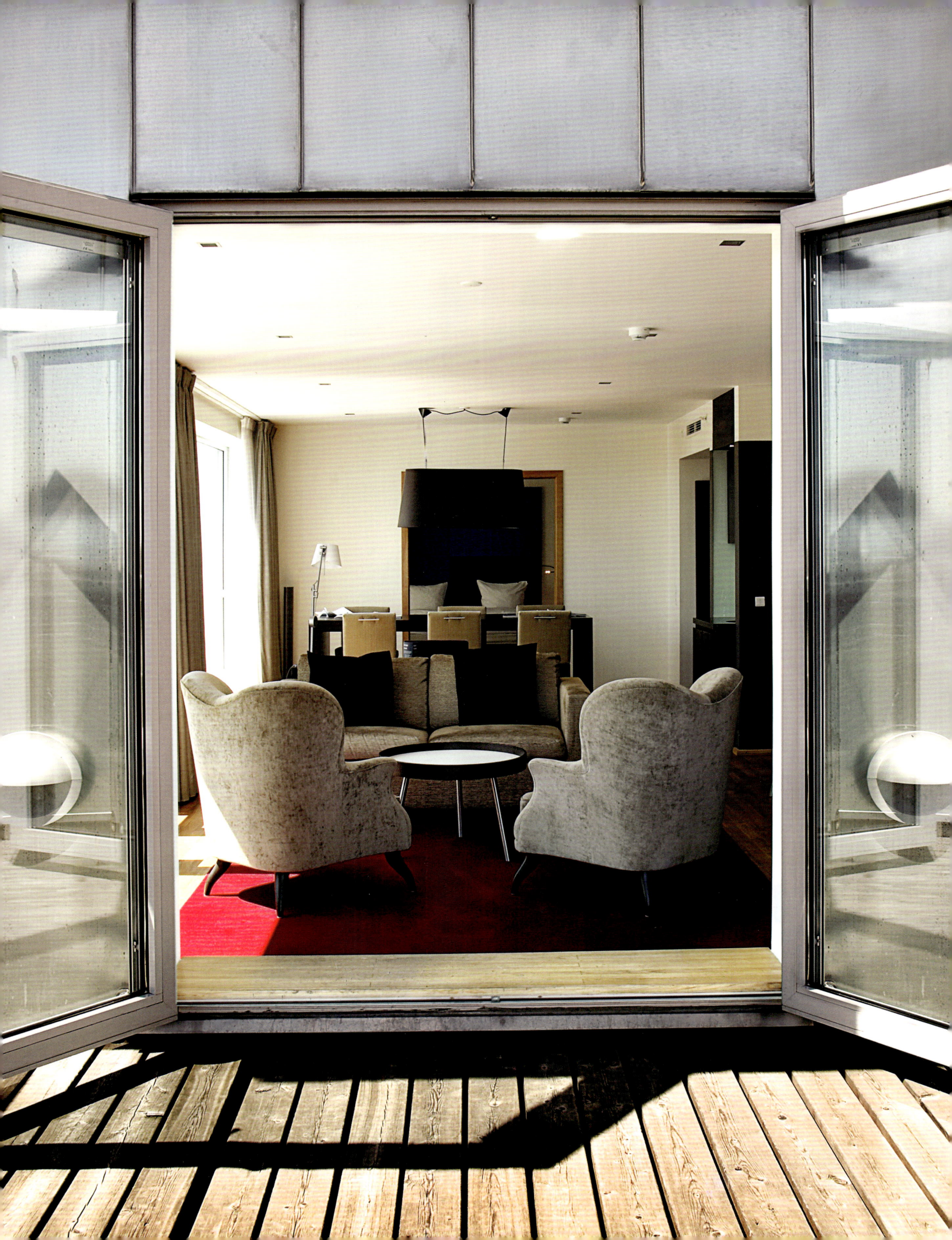

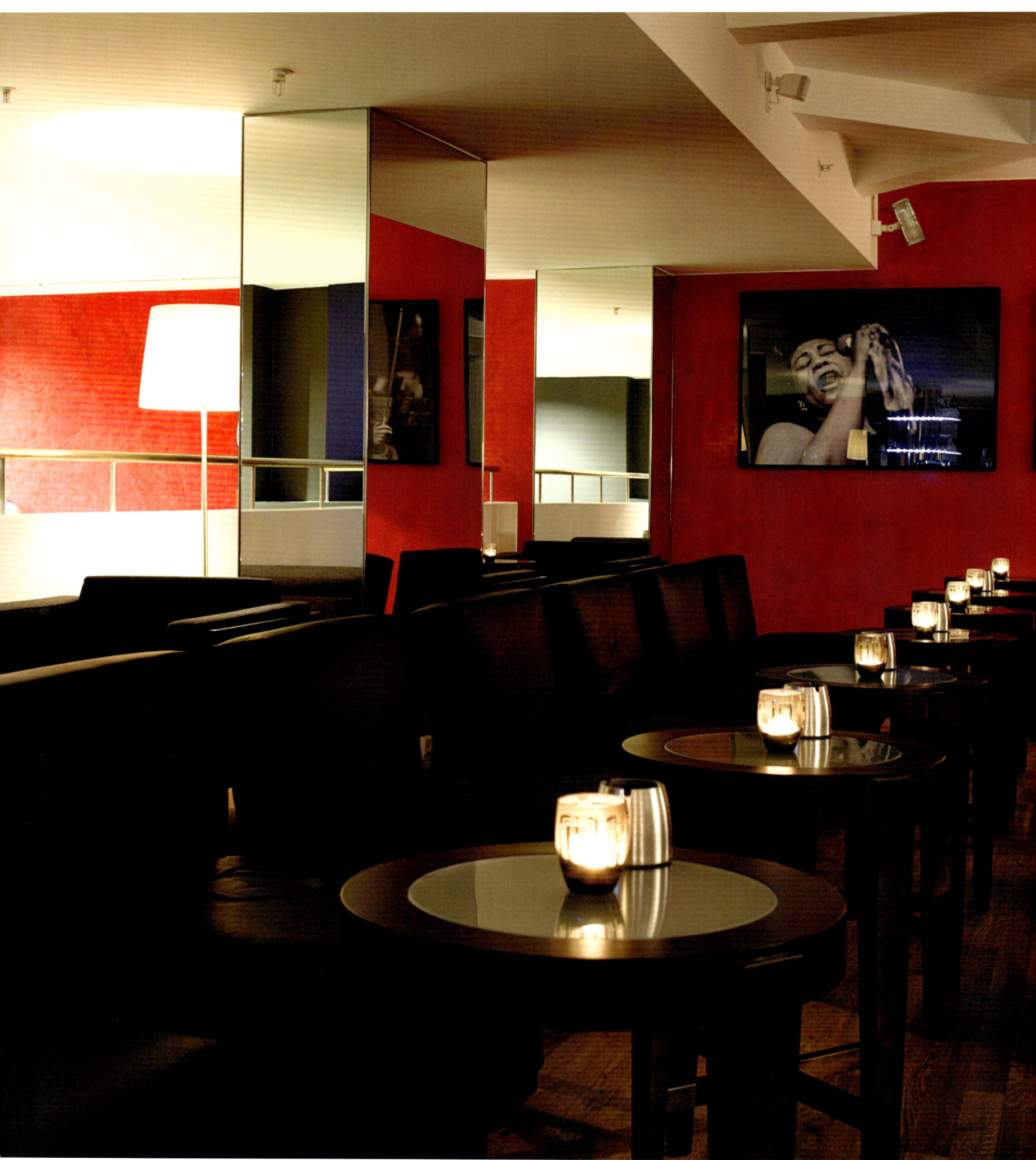

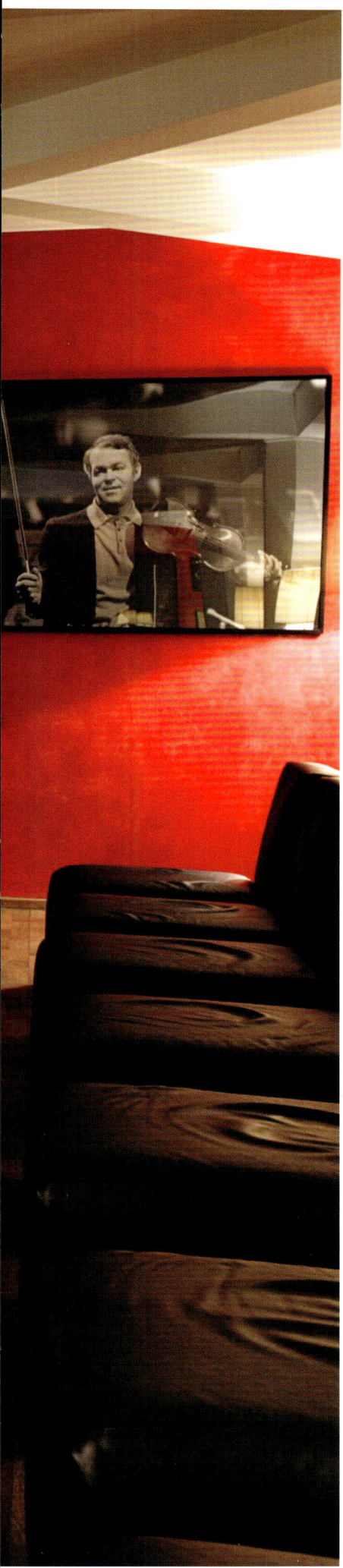

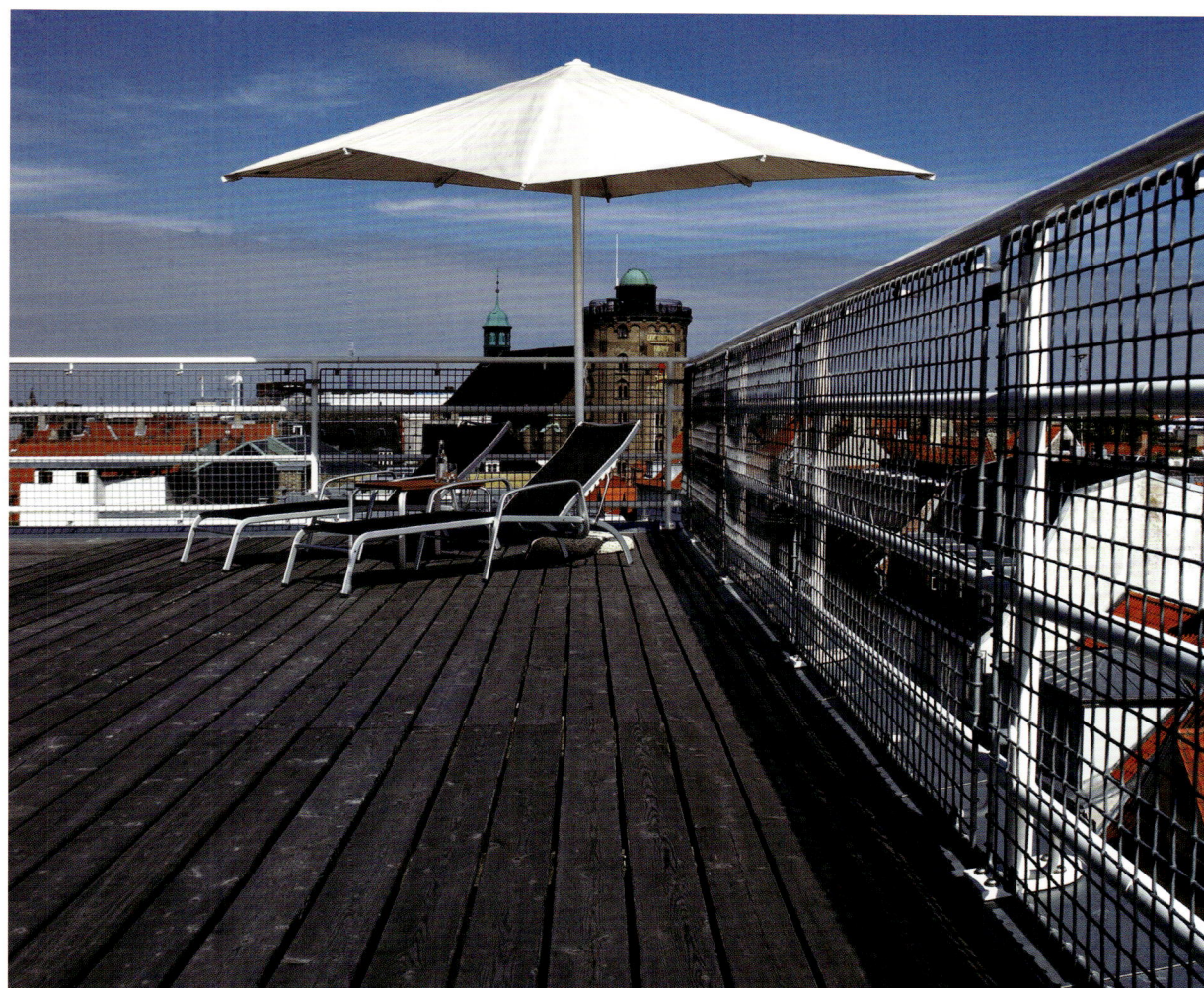

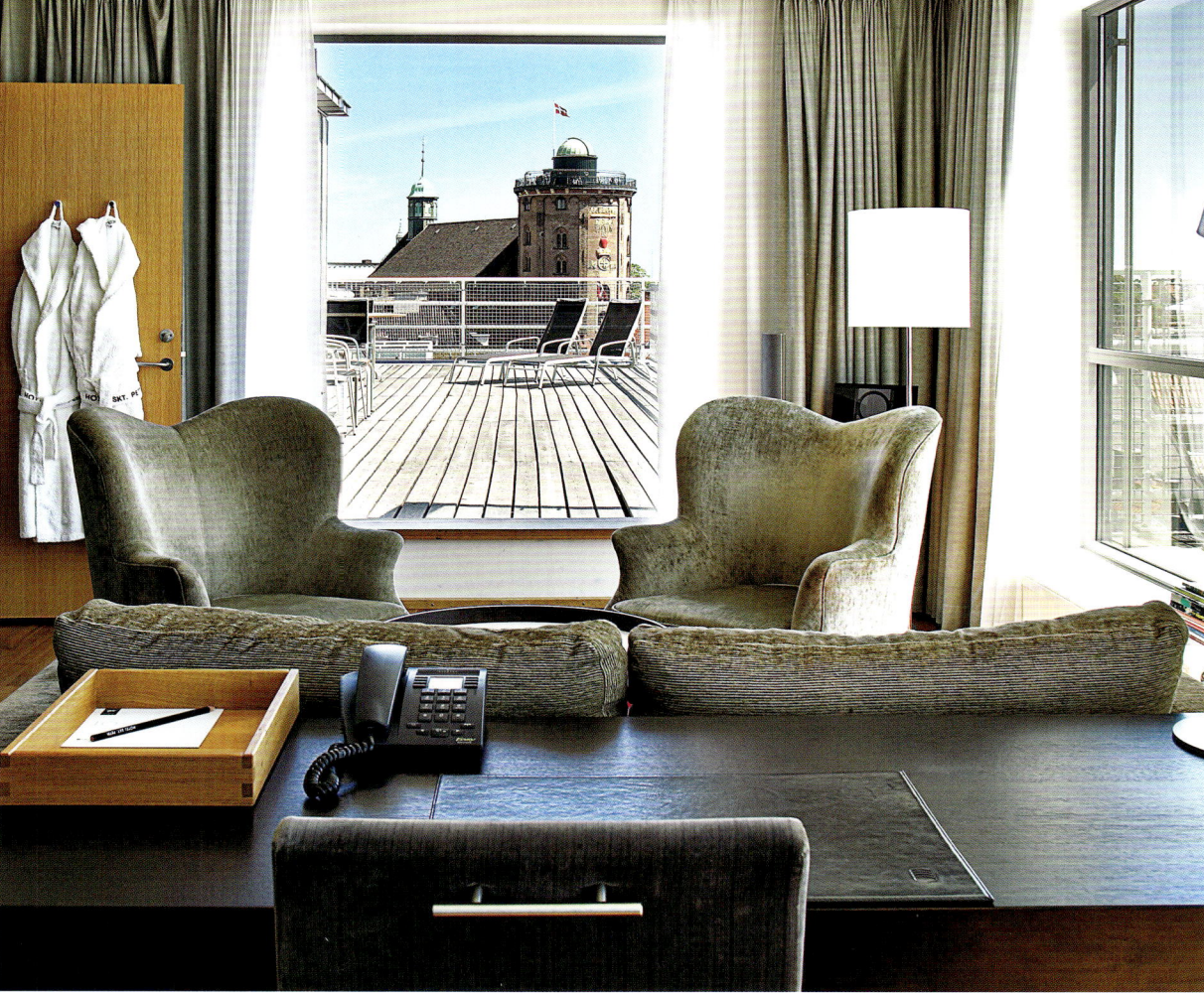

Galway
Ireland
Phone: +353 91 865 200
Fax: +353 91 865 203
www.theghotel.ie

Rooms: 101 rooms including 2 Speciality Suites and the Presidential Suite
Facilities: Designed lounger areas, ESPA at the g
Services: Complimentary valet parking, babysitting, Eye Cinema next door
Located: 10–15 min walk to the city
Public transportation: 5 min to train station, bus stop in front of the hotel
Style: Hollywood glamour

His hats are high fashion and his hotel is Hollywood: Philip Treacy has instilled the glamour of the dream factory on the shores of his native Ireland in the g combining two worlds that are otherwise as different as fire and water. Truly bohemian and eccentric is your sojourn in a lobby walled with black glass, in the Pink Salon with a carpet that will dizzy you, or at the bar set with thousands of red Swarovski stones. The 101 rooms are sensuously done in shades of oyster and gold as well as shell motifs to pay homage to the landscape around Galway.

Seine Hüte sind Haute Couture, sein Hotel ist Hollywood: Philip Treacy bringt mit dem g den Glamour der Traumfabrik an die Küste seiner Heimat Irland – und verbindet zwei Welten, die sonst so unterschiedlich wie Feuer und Wasser sind. In der Lobby mit Wänden aus schwarzem Glas, im Pink Salon mit schwindelerregendem Teppich oder in der Bar mit tausenden roten Swarovski-Steinen regieren Boheme und Exzentrik. Die 101 Zimmer geben sich sinnlich – Austern- und Goldnuancen sowie Muschelmotive sind eine Hommage an die Landschaft rund um Galway.

Ses chapeaux sont haute-couture, son hôtel est hollywoodien : avec le g, Philip Treacy importe l'usine à rêve pour apporter une touche de glamour sur la côte de son pays, l'Irlande, et mêle ainsi deux mondes, normalement aussi incompatibles que l'eau et le feu. Votre séjour sera marqué par l'esprit bohème et excentricité, dans un hall de réception aux murs de verre noir ou dans le salon rose au tapis vertigineux, ou encore au bar serti de milliers de cristaux Swarovski. Les 101 chambres ont des teintes nacrées et dorées et des motifs de coquillage, hommage sensuel au paysage irlandais entourant Galway.

Sus sombreros son de alta costura y su hotel es el mismo Hollywood. Con su hotel g, Philip Treacy lleva el glamour de la "fábrica de sueños" a la costa de su Irlanda natal. Con ello logra unir dos mundos que suelen ser tan diferentes como la noche y el día. La vida bohemia y el excentricismo reinan en el vestíbulo de paredes de cristal negro, en el Pink Salon con su alfombra vertiginosa o en el bar decorado con miles de cristales rojos de Swarovski. Las 101 habitaciones irradian sensualidad: los matices de ostra y dorado, así como los motivos de conchas, hacen homenaje al paisaje de los alrededores de Galway.

I suoi cappelli sono d'alta moda, il suo hotel da film: con il g Philip Treacy porta il glamour di Hollywood sulla costa dell'Irlanda, sua patria – e unisce così due mondi altrimenti opposti come l'acqua e il fuoco. Nella lobby con pareti in vetro nero, nel Pink Salon con il suo vorticoso tappeto e nel bar dai mille cristalli rossi di Swarovski regnano atmosfera bohéme ed eccentricità. Le 101 camere hanno un piglio sensuale – le tonalità ostrica e oro e i motivi ispirati alle conchiglie sono un omaggio al paesaggio che circonda Galway.

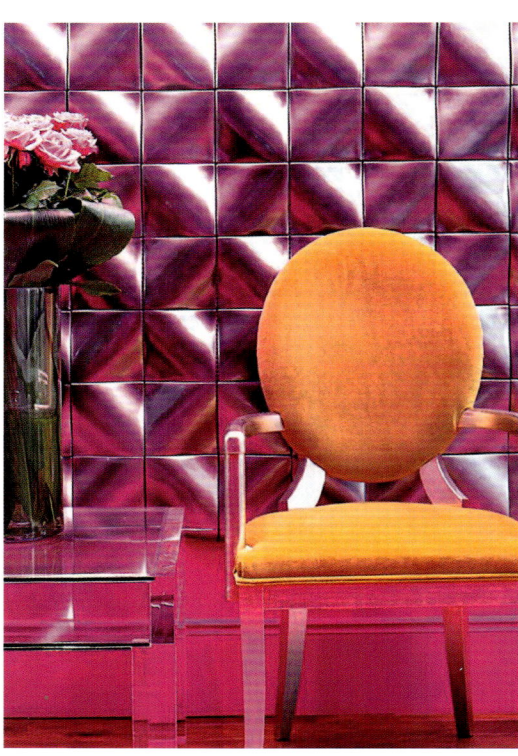
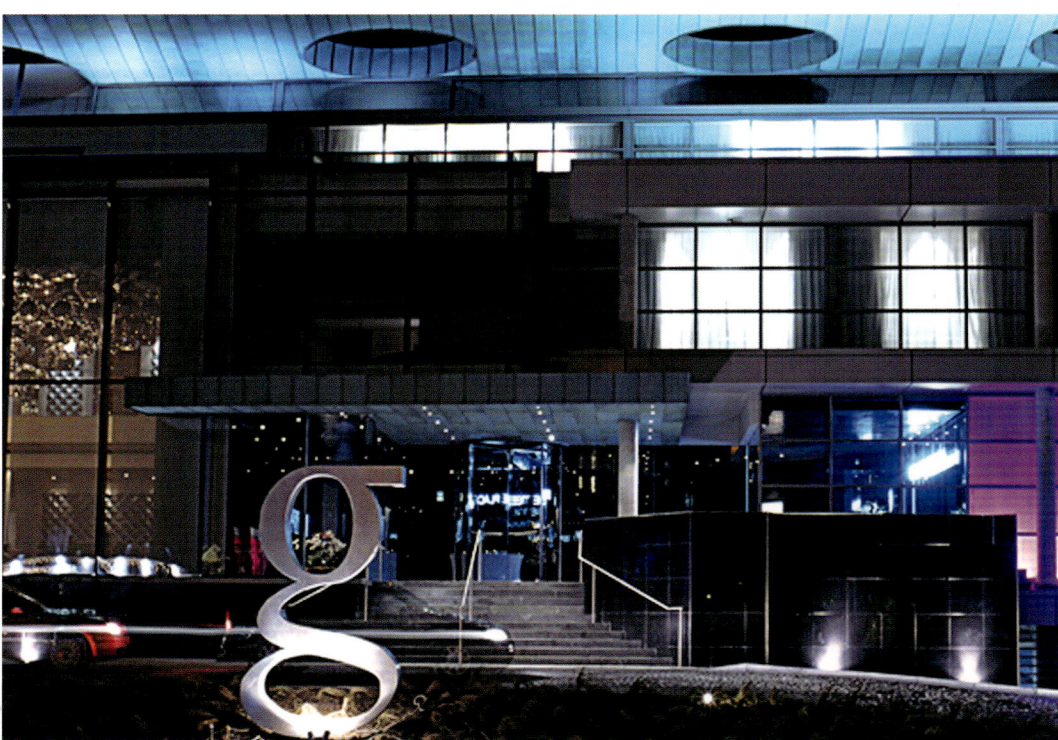

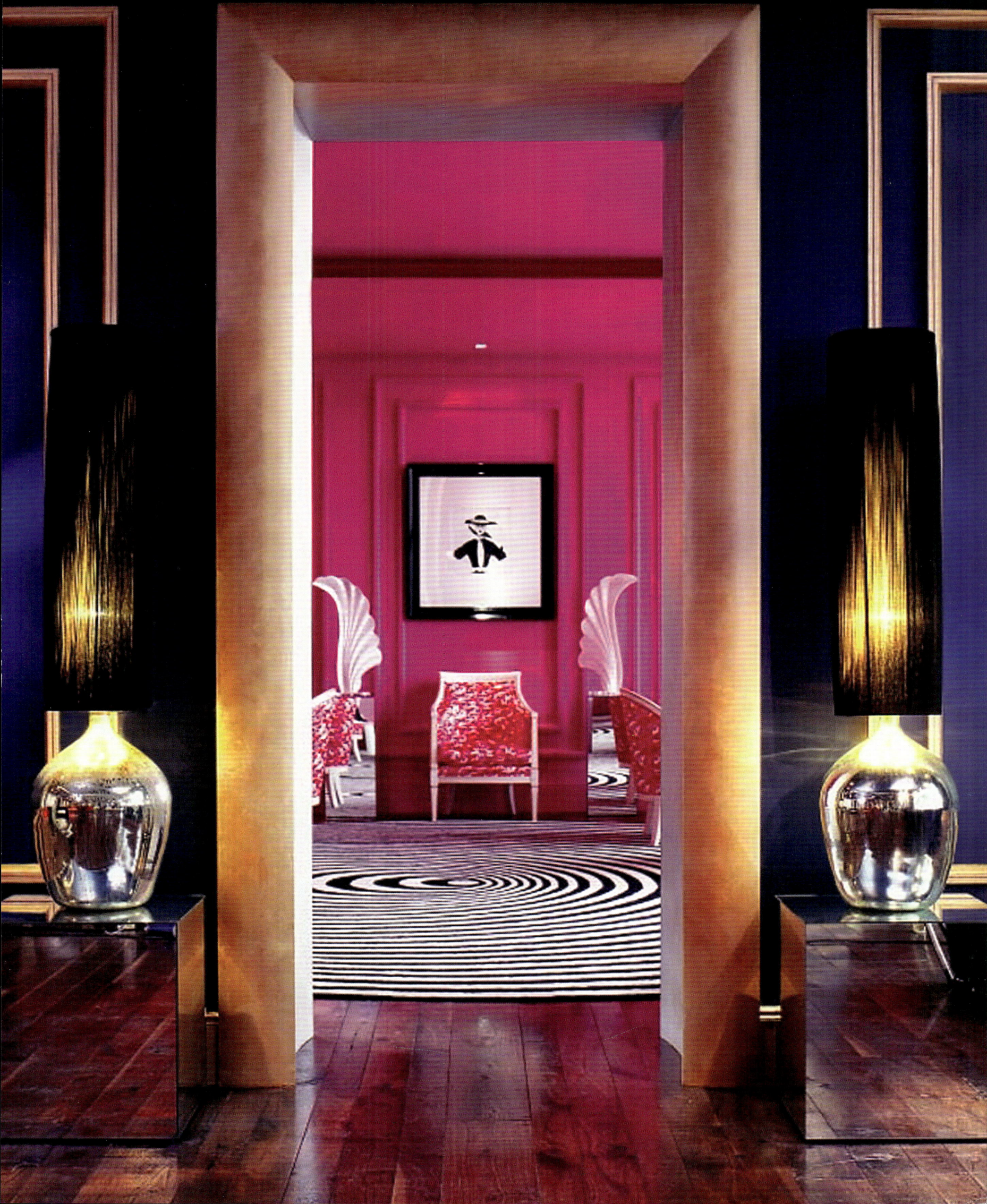

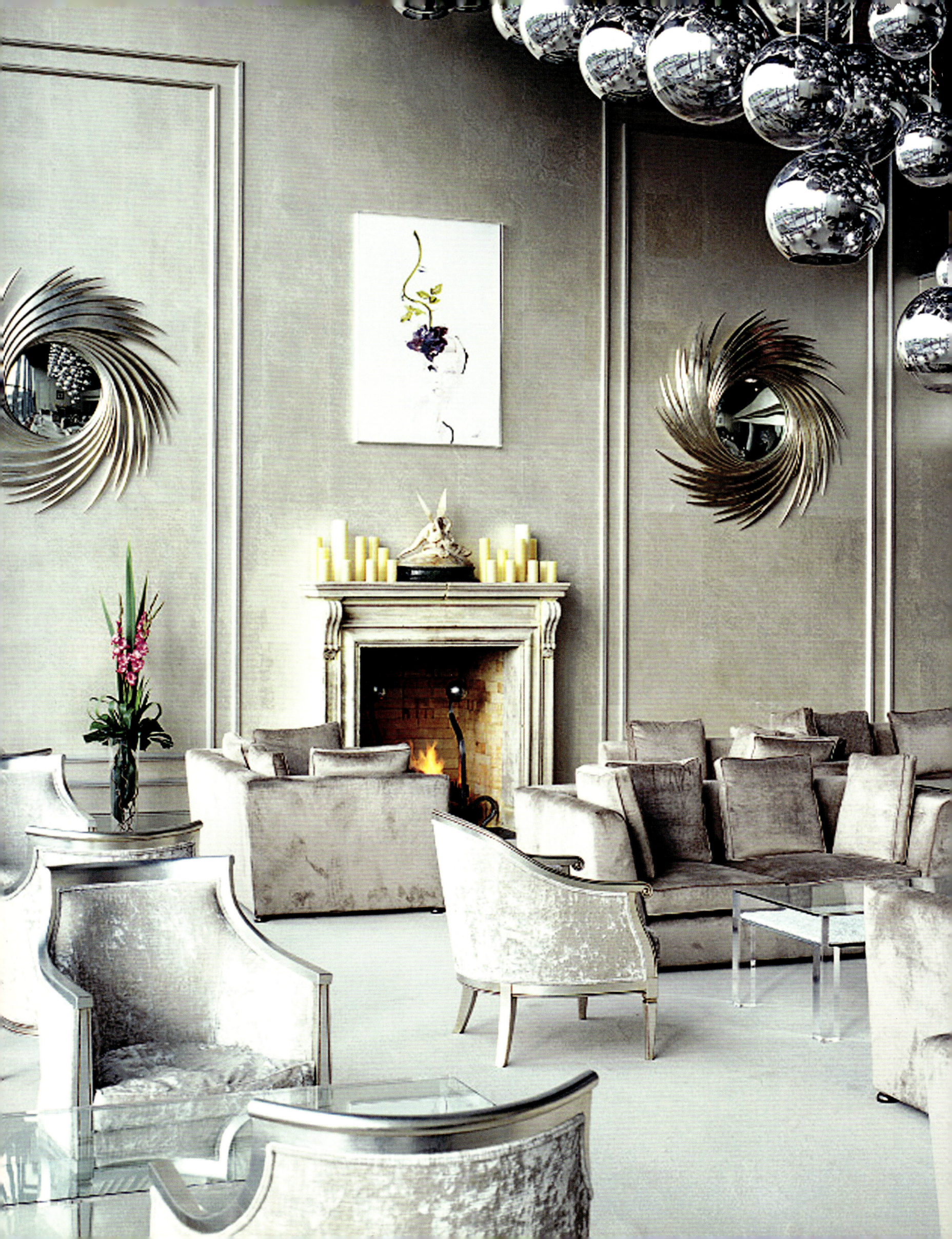

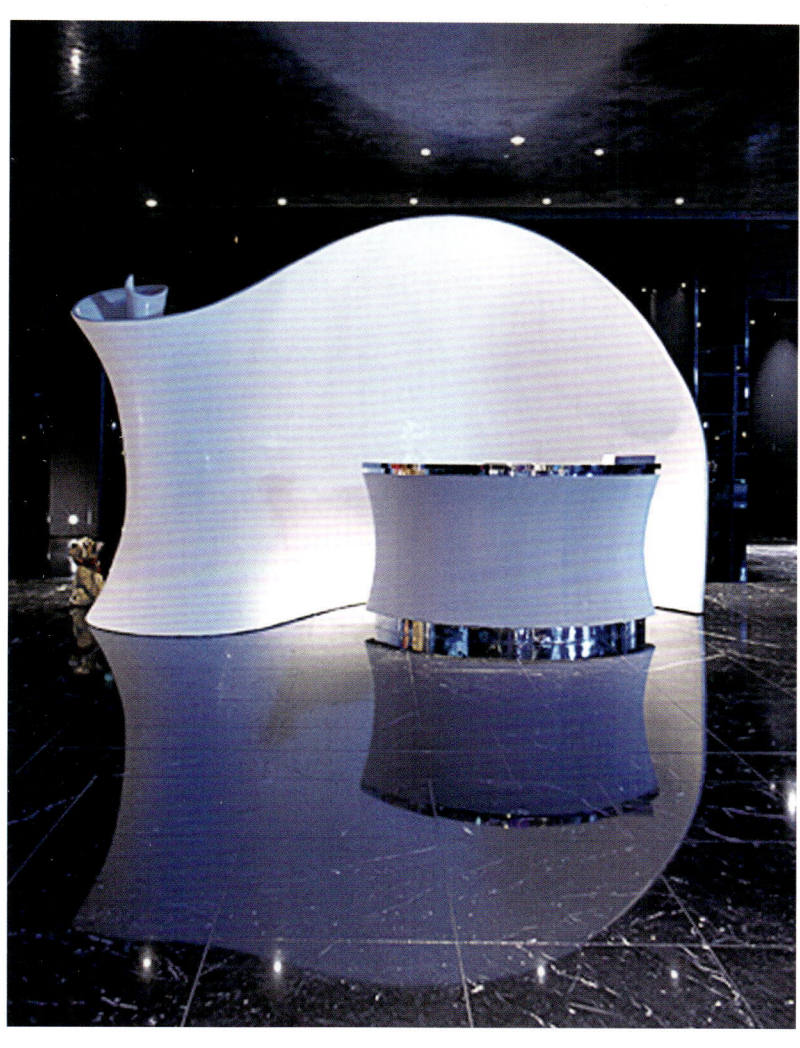
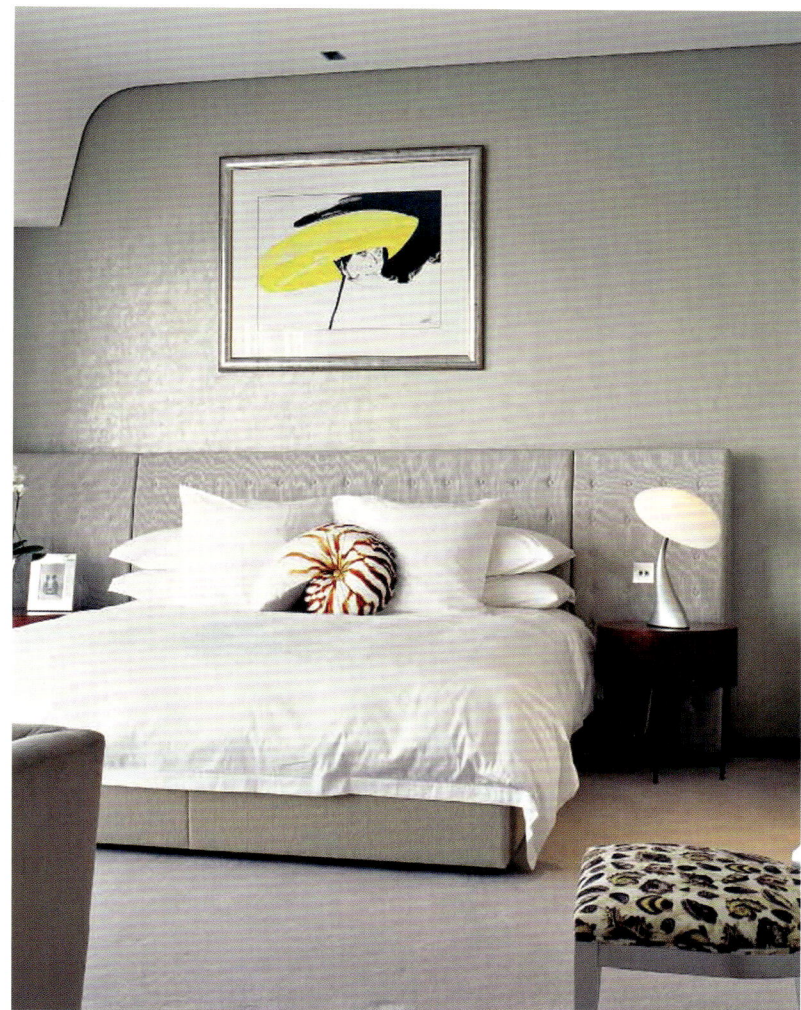
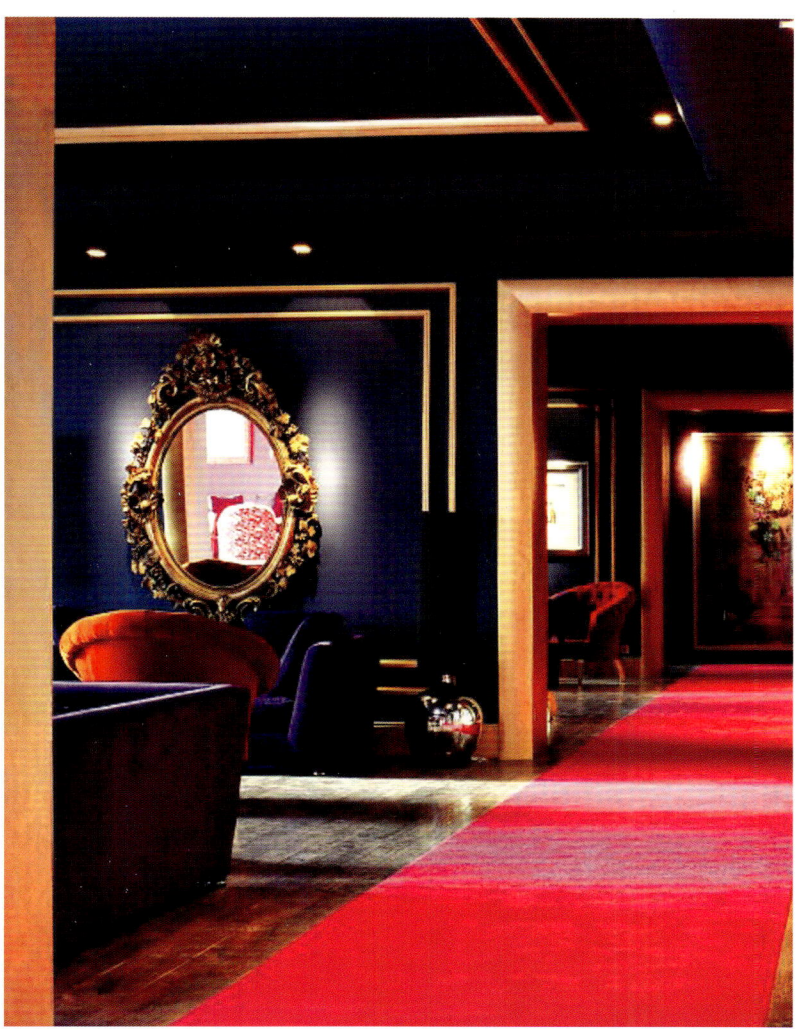
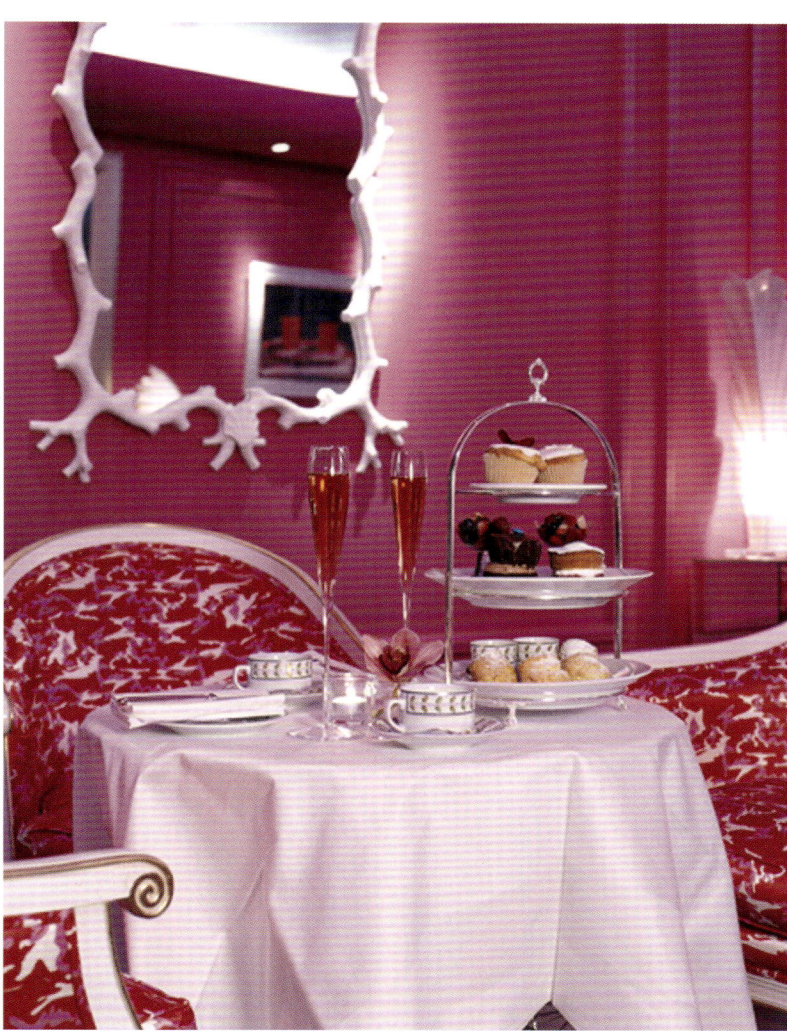

Dublin 4
Ireland
Phone: +353 1 660 3000
Fax: +353 1 660 3005
www.dylan.ie

Rooms: 44 rooms including 5 suites
Facilities: Dylanbar, Still Restaurant, The Library, private dining room
Services: Concierge, 24 h room service, valet parking
Located: In the city center, just a 10 min walk from St. Stephens Green
Public transportation: Bus
Style: Relaxing haven with breathtaking views

With 44 individually furnished rooms, this boutique hotel offers comfort of the highest quality in style and personality. The mix of ultra-modern designer furniture and carefully mixed in antiques makes up its exceptional atmosphere. The contemporary technological equipment includes plasma TVs, Internet access, cordless telephones, iPod stations, as well as floor heating in the puristic styled baths. The house's own restaurant "Still" offers modern Irish cuisine, the "Dylanbar" is also patronized by local residents.

Mit 44 individuell eingerichteten Zimmern verbindet dieses Boutique-Hotel Komfort auf höchstem Niveau mit Stil und Persönlichkeit. Der Mix aus ultramodernen Designermöbeln und geschickt eingestreuten Antiquitäten ergibt ein außergewöhnliches Ambiente. Zur zeitgemäßen technologischen Ausstattung zählen Plasma-Fernseher, Internetzugang, schnurlose Telefone, iPod-Stationen sowie Fußbodenheizungen in den puristisch gestylten Bädern. Das hauseigene Restaurant „Still" bietet moderne irische Küche, die „Dylanbar" schätzen auch Hauptstadtbewohner.

Avec 44 chambres décorées différemment, cet hôtel-boutique combine le plus haut niveau de confort avec du style et de la personnalité. Le mélange de meubles ultramodernes et d'antiquités intelligemment disposées crée une atmosphère inhabituelle. Téléviseurs écran plasma, accès internet, téléphone sans fil, stations d'accueil iPod ainsi que chauffage par le sol dans les salles de bains épurées, font partie de son équipement technologique contemporain. Le restaurant de l'établissement, « Still », offre de la cuisine irlandaise moderne, et les locaux apprécient le « Dylanbar ».

Este hotel boutique aúna en sus 44 habitaciones de diseño individual confort al máximo nivel con estilo y personalidad. La mezcla de muebles de diseño ultramoderno y algunas antigüedades colocadas con gran gusto y habilidad genera un ambiente muy especial. Dentro del moderno equipamiento tecnológico se encuentran televisores de plasma, acceso a Internet, teléfonos inalámbricos, estaciones de iPod y suelos radiantes en los baños de estilo purista. El restaurante propio "Still" ofrece cocina moderna irlandesa y el "Dylanbar" es apreciado también por los habitantes de la capital.

Le 44 camere di questo boutique hotel, arredate ciascuna in maniera originale, sanno conciliare stile e personalità con un comfort di altissimo livello. Il suo peculiare mix di mobili dal design ultramoderno e pezzi d'antiquariato accuratamente inseriti nel contesto dà origine a un'atmosfera di grande originalità. La dotazione tecnologica delle stanze, di ultima generazione, comprende televisore al plasma, accesso a Internet, telefoni cordless, stazioni iPod e, nei bagni dallo stile essenziale, il riscaldamento a pavimento. Il ristorante della casa "Still" offre moderna cucina irlandese, ed il "Dylanbar" è non a caso molto apprezzato anche dai dublinesi DOC.

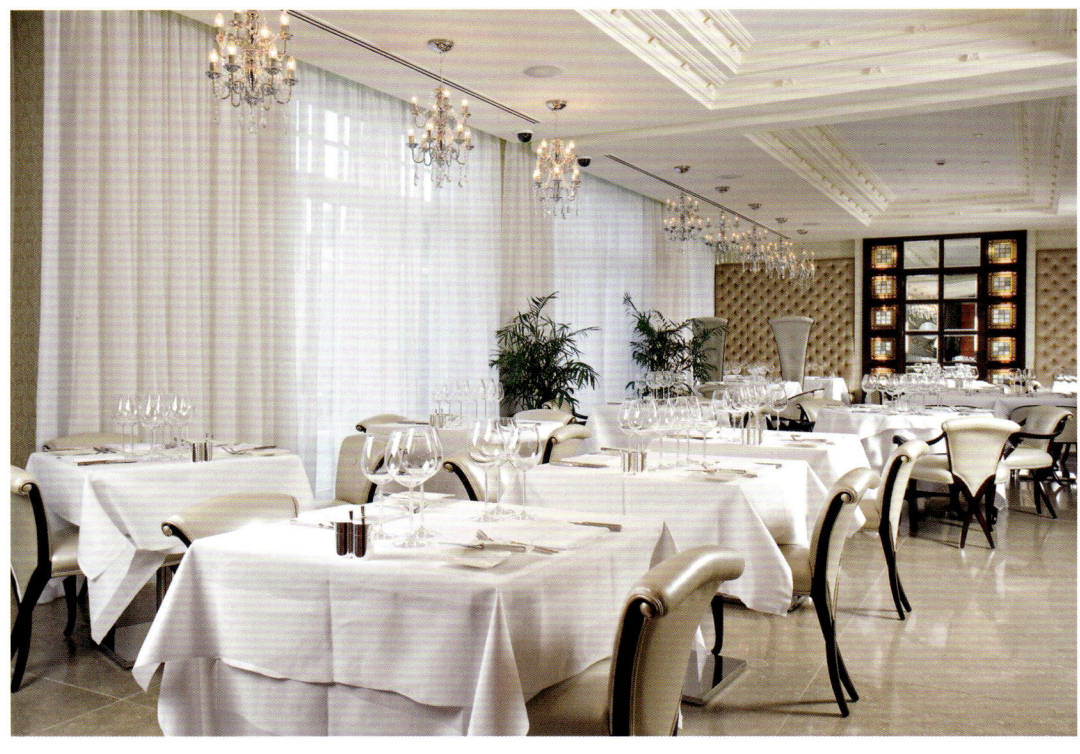
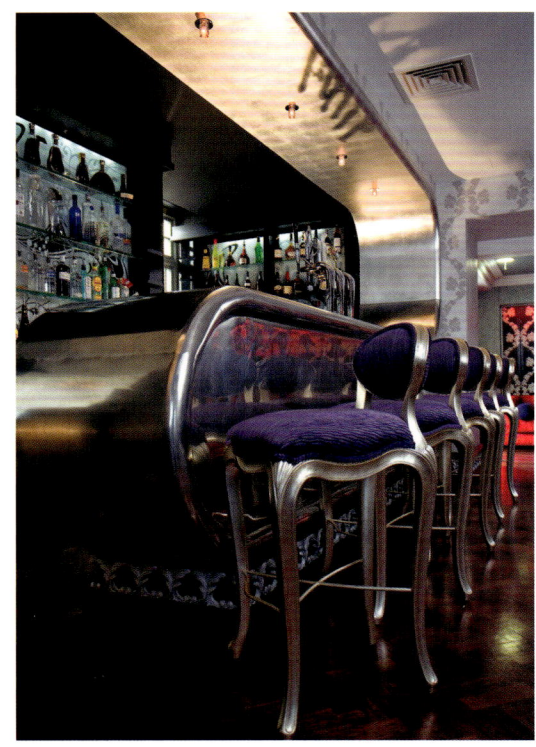

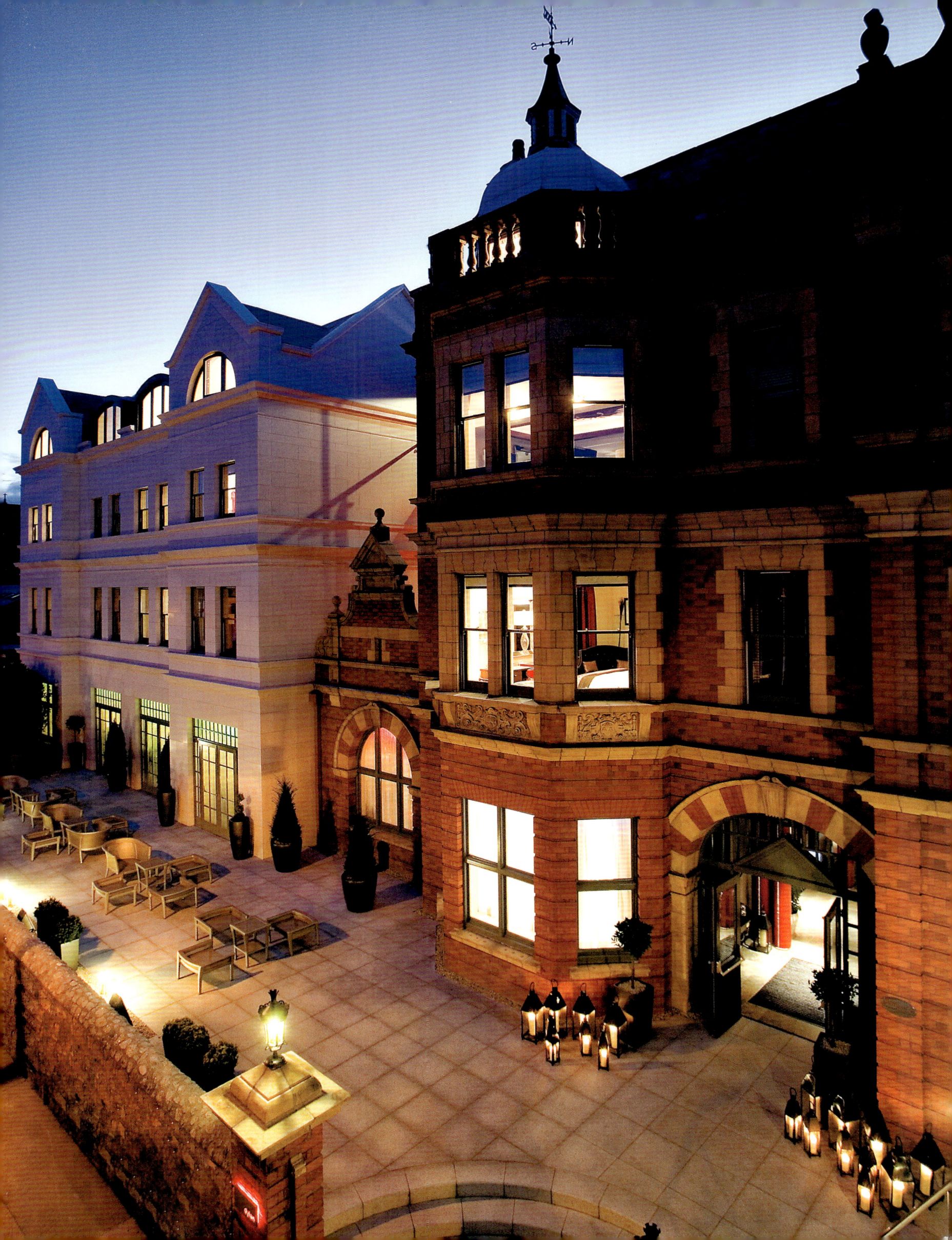

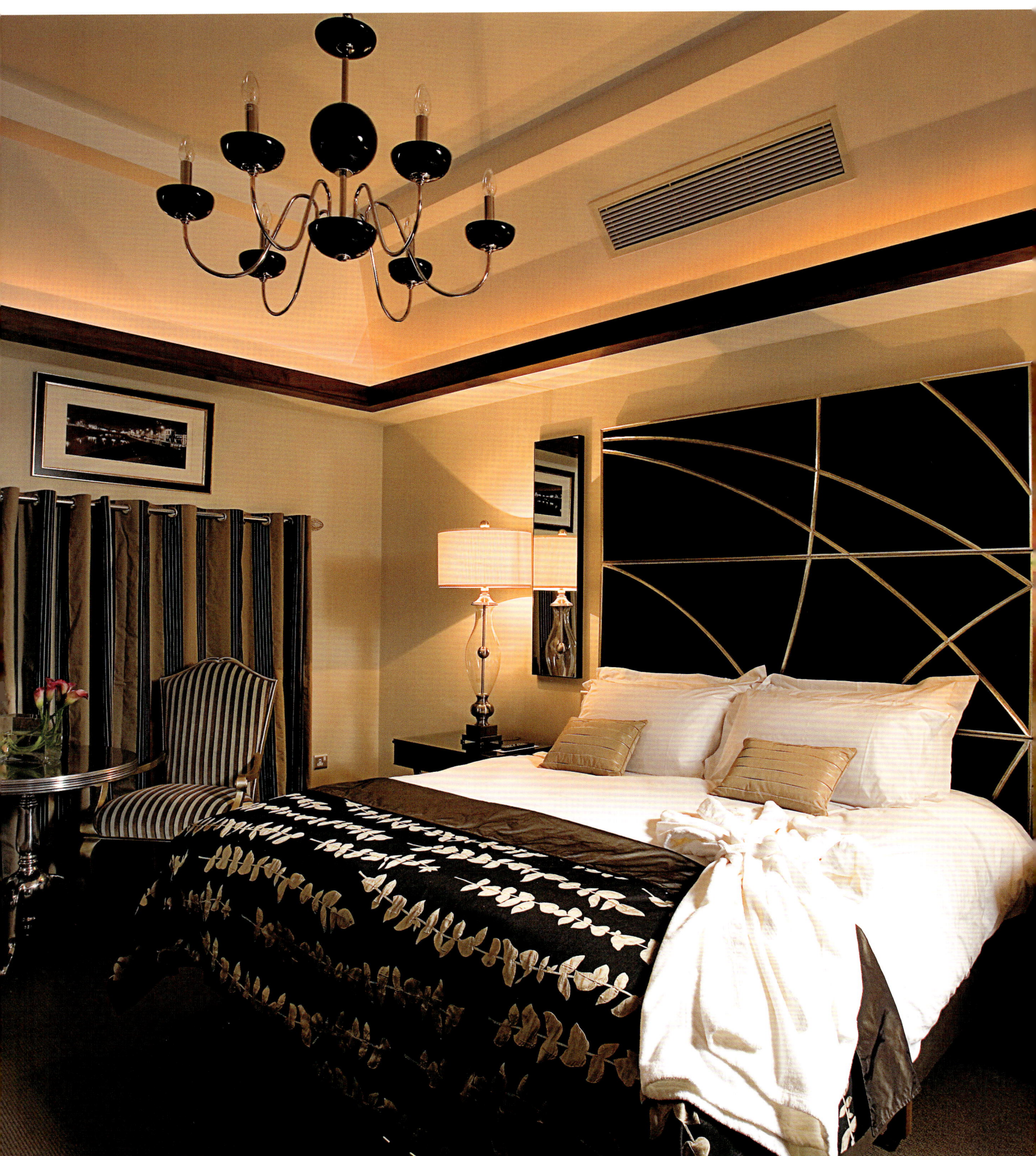

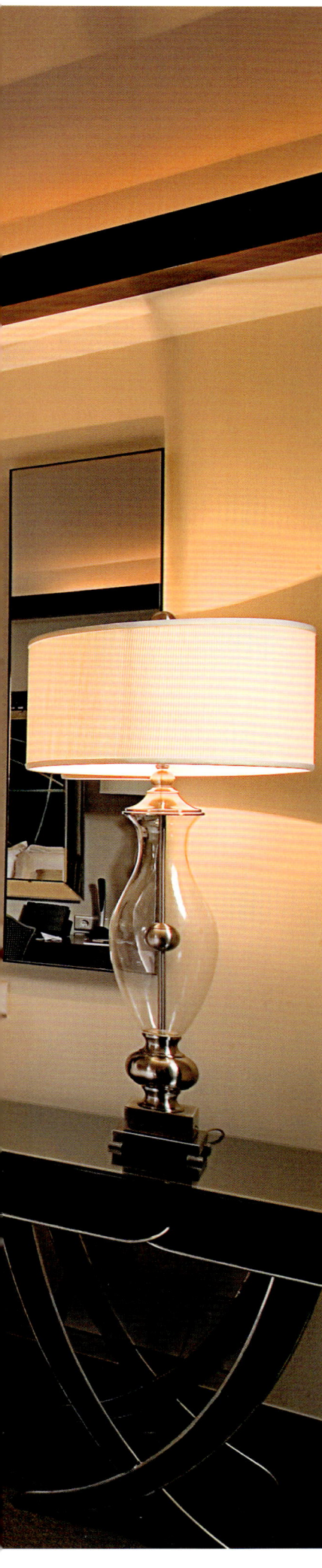

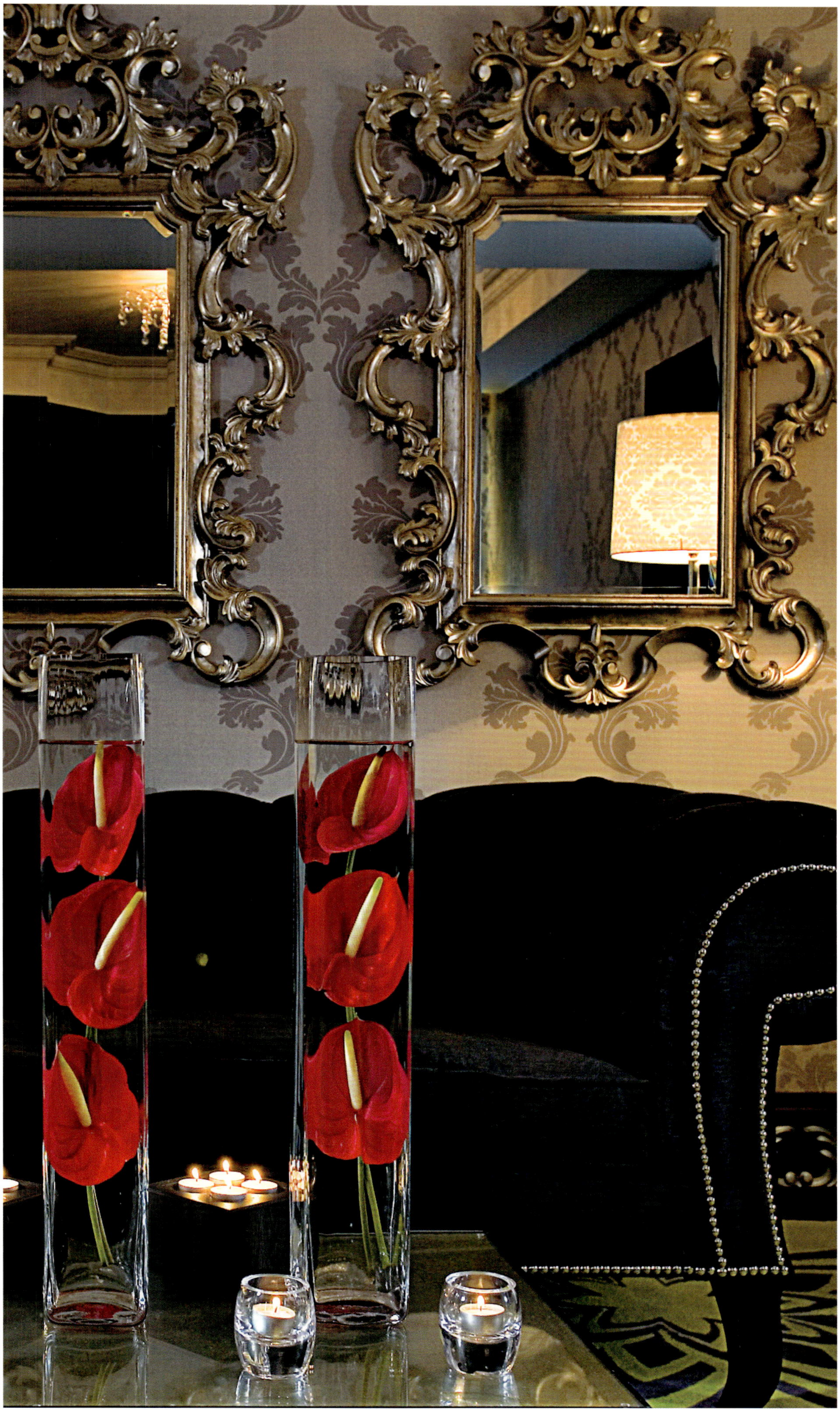

Ireland
Phone: +353 46 903 0900
Fax: +353 46 903 1367
www.bellinterhouse.com

Rooms: 34 rooms
Facilities: Bar, restaurant, spa, leisure facilities
Services: Babysitting, room service, on property fishing
Located: In the lush green countryside
Style: Classic contemporary

This manor house built in 1750 is situated on the banks of the Boyne River in County Meath. It has 34 individually styled bedrooms. All rooms have great big beds with goose down pillows, handcrafted furniture, Internet access as well as plasma TVs with DVD players. The drawing room with its ceiling-high windows and open fireplace is warm and inviting, while the library and games rooms are a retreat for both young and old. The spa and the infinity pool are perfect for relaxation.

Am Ufer des Flusses Boyne in der Grafschaft Meath liegt dieses 1750 erbaute Herrenhaus. Es verfügt über 34 individuell ausgestattete Zimmer. Allen Zimmern gemeinsam sind übergroße Betten, mit Gänsedaunen gefüllte Kissen, handgefertigte Möbel, Internetzugang sowie Plasma-Fernseher mit DVD-Spielern. Der Drawing Room mit seinen raumhohen Fenstern und offenen Kaminen ist behaglich und einladend, während die Bibliothek und die Spielzimmer ideale Rückzugsorte für Jung und Alt bieten. Spa und Infinity-Pool sorgen für perfekte Entspannung.

Sur la berge de la Boyne, dans le comté de Meath, ce manoir construit en 1750, propose 34 chambres toutes décorées différemment. Toutes les chambres ont des lits géants avec des oreillers en plume d'oie, des meubles faits mains, un accès internet et un téléviseur écran plasma avec lecteur de DVD. La salle de dessin avec ses hautes fenêtres et ses cheminées ouvertes, est très agréable et accueillante, pendant que la bibliothèque et les salles de jeux sont des refuges idéal pour les petits et les grands. Pour la détente l'hôtel offre un spa et une piscine à débordement.

A orillas del río Boyne, en el condado de Meath, se levanta esta casa señorial construida en 1750. Sus 34 habitaciones de diseño individual tienen enormes camas, cojines rellenos de plumas de ganso, muebles artesanales, acceso a Internet y televisores de plasma con reproductores de DVD. La sala de estar Drawing Room con sus enormes ventanales cubriendo toda la pared y sus chimeneas es acogedora y agradable. Para entretenerse hay una biblioteca y una sala de juegos con mesas de billar, para relajarse un spa y una piscina cuyo borde se funde con el horizonte.

Questa residenza signorile edificata nel 1750 sorge sulle rive del fiume Boyne, nella contea di Meath. Le sue 34 stanze, arredate ciascuna in maniera originale, offrono letti di grandezza superiore alla media, con cuscini di piuma d'oca, mobili realizzati a mano, accesso a Internet e televisori al plasma con lettori DVD. Il salone, con le sue finestre che arrivano al soffitto e il caminetto con fuoco a vista è accogliente e invitante. La biblioteca, biliardo e sala giochi sono il posto ideale per il tempo libero di grandi e piccini, lo spa e la infinity pool sono perfetti per i vostri momenti di relax.

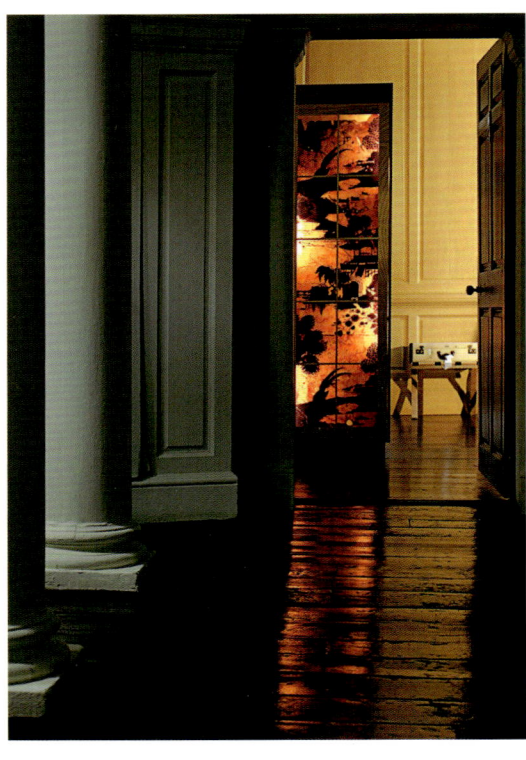
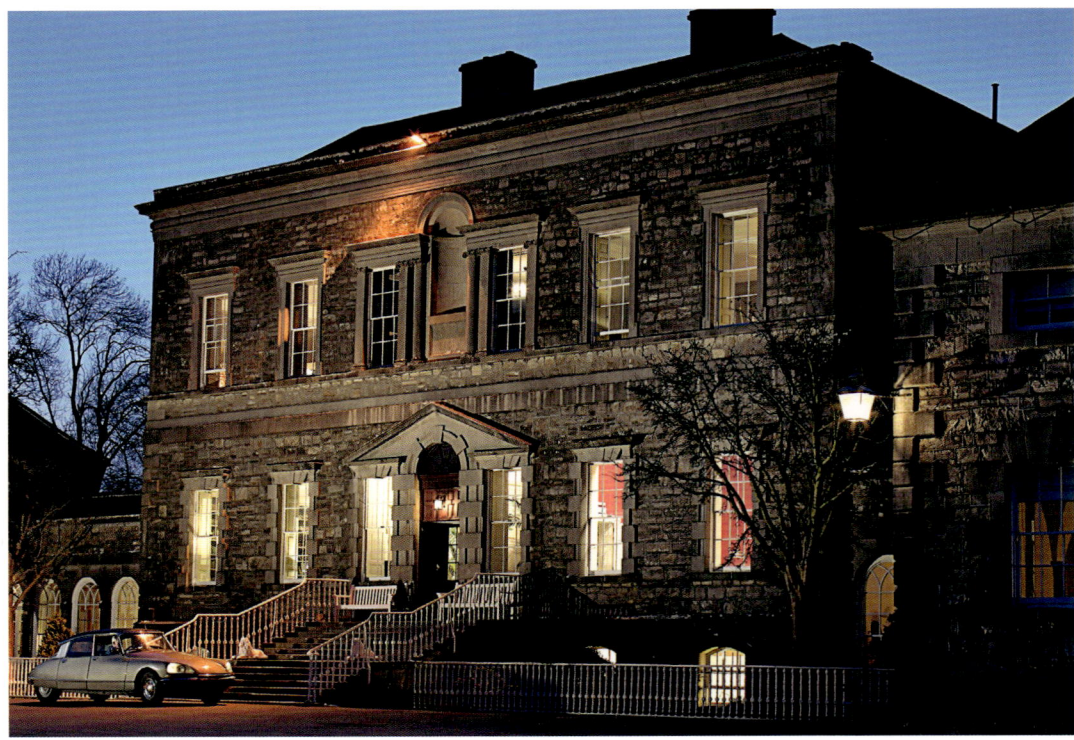

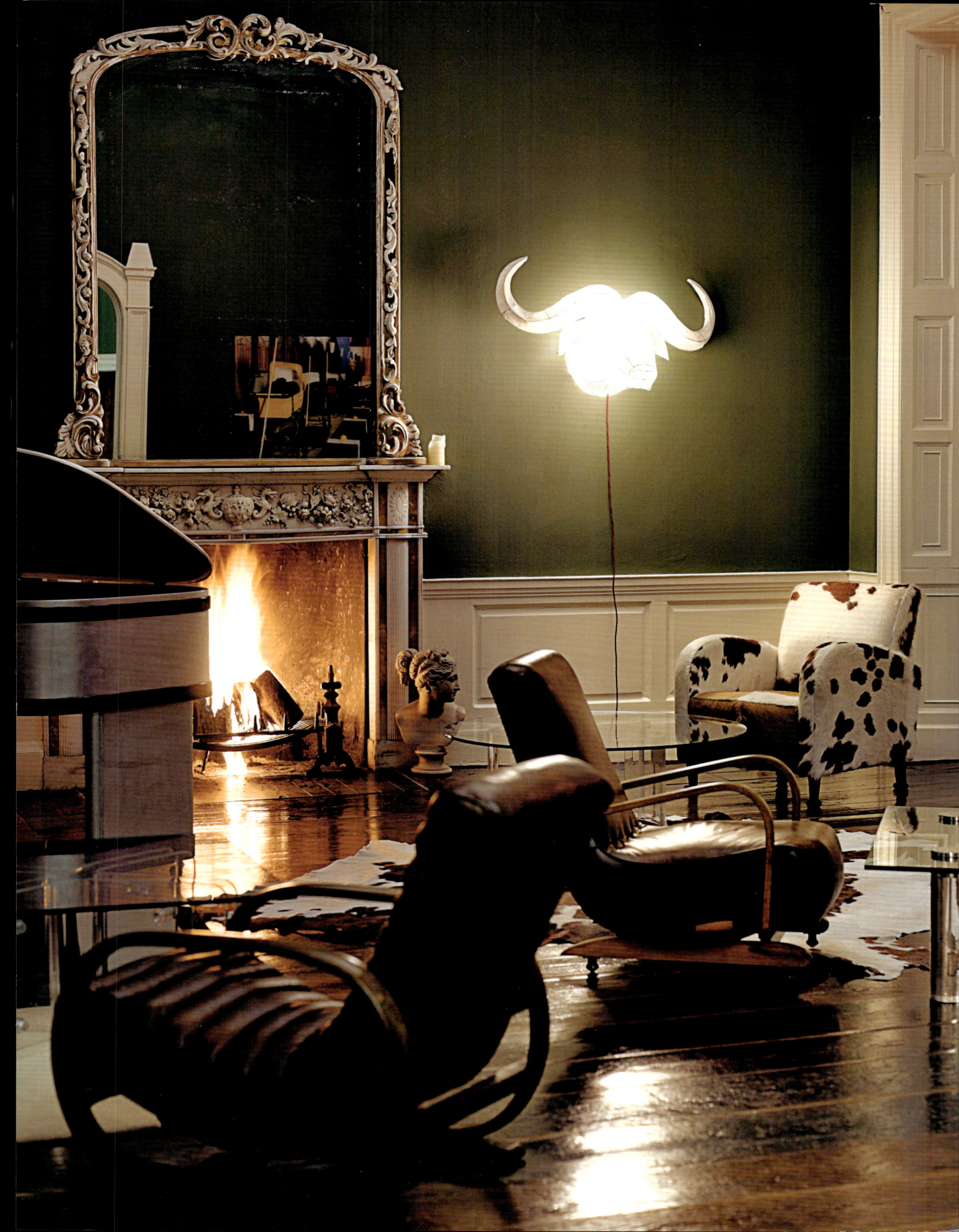

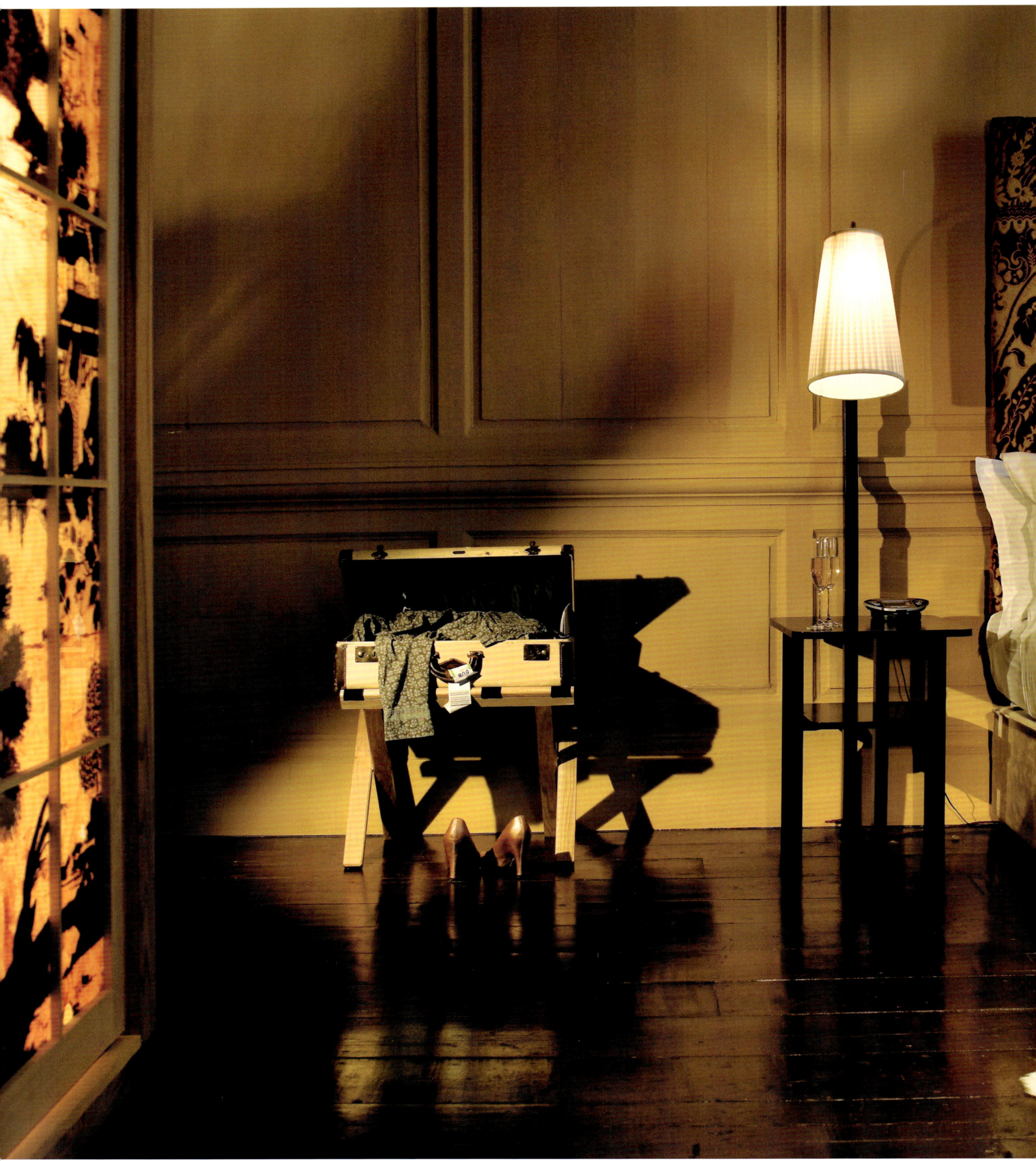

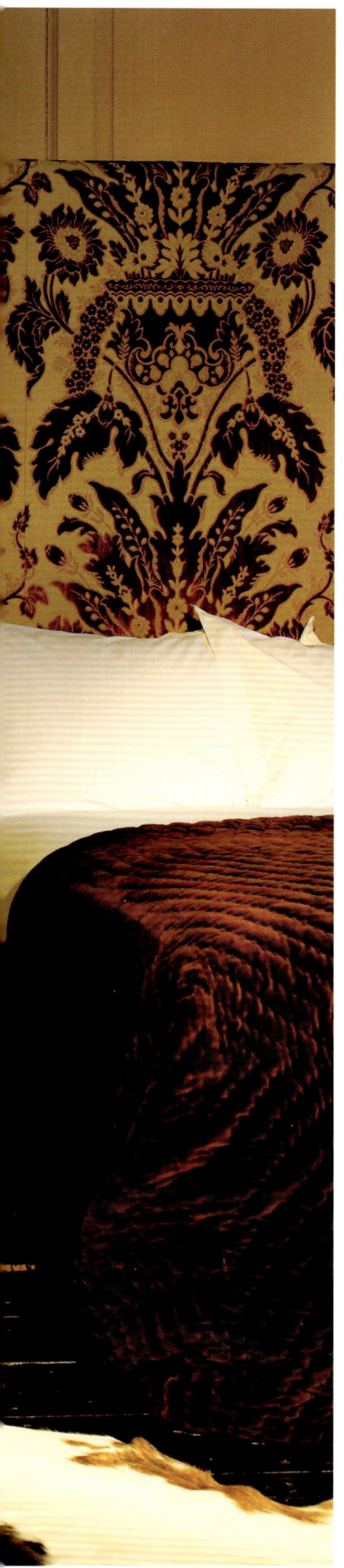

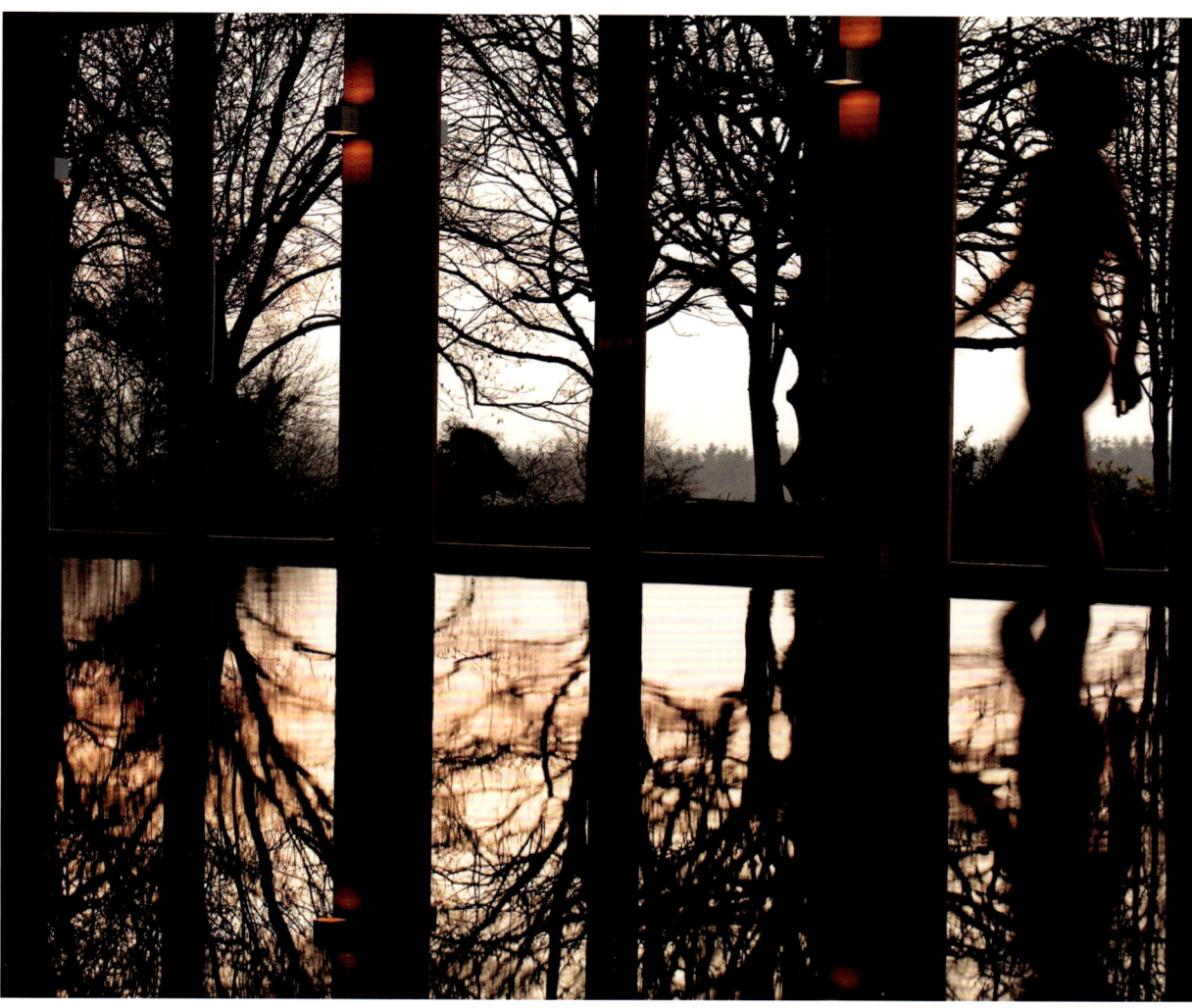

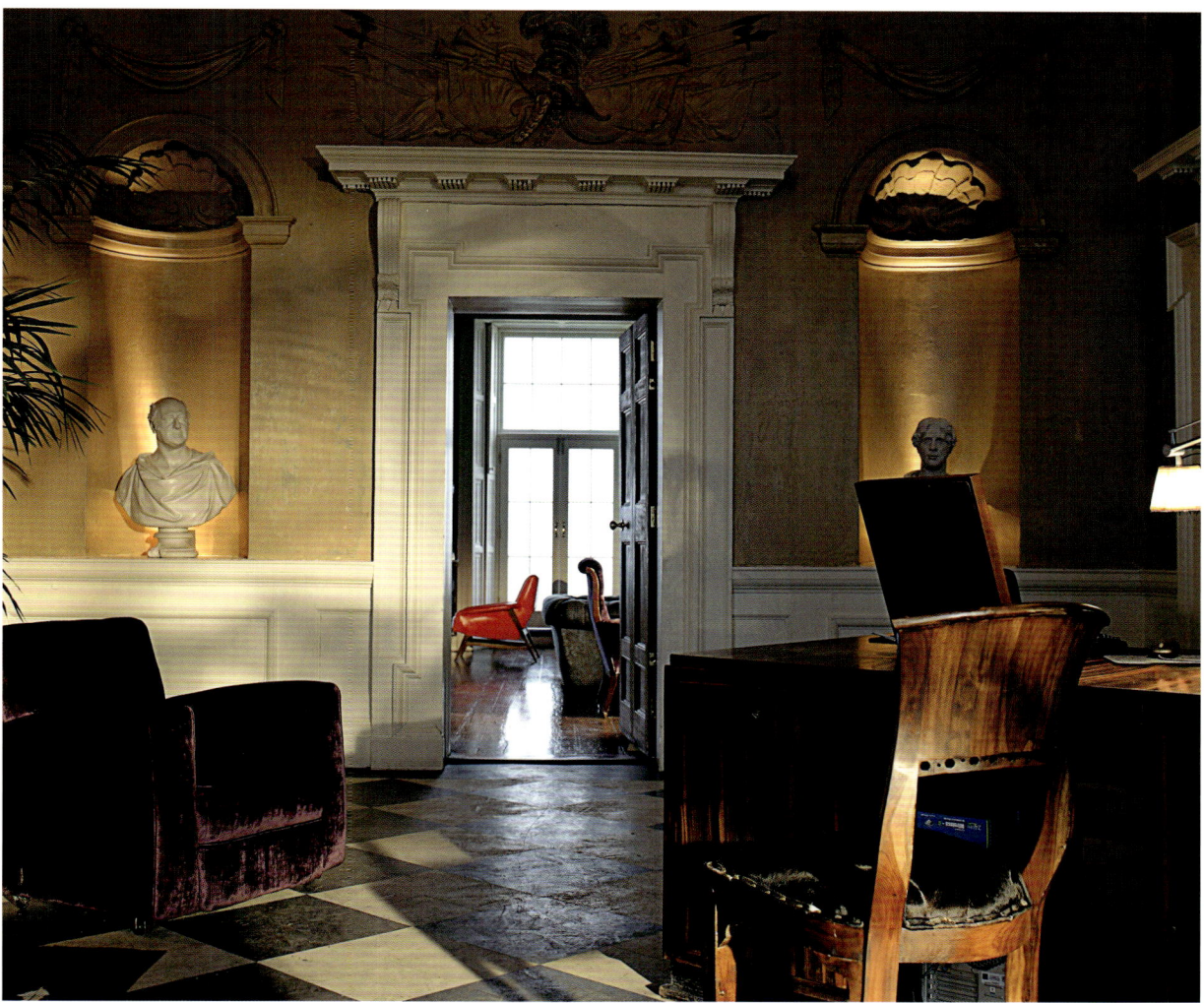

Brighton BN1 2FG
United Kingdom
Phone: +44 1273 327 055
Fax: +44 1273 733 845
www.hotelpelirocco.co.uk

Rooms: 19 rooms
Facilities: PlayStation bar, ever changing photographic and art gallery, 14 people conference room
Services: PlayStation in every room, Durex Play Time room service menu offering sexy goodies
Located: On Regency Square on the seafront in the center of Brighton
Public transportation: Bus, taxi
Style: Art deco

The average looking facade is deceiving: the Pelirocco is no hotel for softies in search of summer freshness in Brighton. A reservation here gets you a kaleidoscope of British eccentricity, pop culture and boudoir kitsch. The 19 rooms in "England's best rock 'n' roll hangout" (*Evening Standard*) are designed as unique as they are oblique—they are inspired by pin-up girls and musicans, street style and aerospace. Even in the bar you can beam yourself into other dimensions propelled by PlayStations and cult cocktails.

Die Durchschnittsfassade täuscht: Das Pelirocco ist kein Hotel für sanfte Seelen auf der Suche nach Sommerfrische in Brighton. Wer hier reserviert, findet sich in einem Kaleidoskop aus britischer Exzentrik, Popkultur und Boudoir-Kitsch wieder. Die 19 Zimmer in „Englands bestem Rock-'n'-Roll-Hangout" (*Evening Standard*) sind so individuell wie schräg designt – inspiriert von Pin-up-Girls oder Musikern, vom Streetstyle oder Weltraum. Selbst in der Bar kann man sich in andere Dimensionen beamen: mit Hilfe von PlayStation und Kult-Cocktails.

La façade d'allure très commune déçoit : le Pelirocco n'est pas un hôtel pour les midinettes en quête de fraîcheur estivale à Brighton. Celui qui réserve ici se retrouvera dans un kaléidoscope d'excentricité britannique, de culture pop et de trash boudoir. Les 19 chambres du « Meilleur Repaire Rock'n'Roll d'Angleterre », selon l'*Evening Standard*, sont à la fois personnalisées et décorées de manières détonante, inspirée à la fois par les pinups ou les musiciens de la scène internationale, le style urbain ou l'espace. Même au bar, on peut se projeter dans d'autres dimensions, grâce à PlayStation ou des cocktails culte.

Su corriente fachada engaña, pero el Pelirocco no es un hotel para los espíritus calmos que tan sólo busquen la fresca brisa del verano de Brighton. El huésped que reserve una habitación aquí se encontrará con un caleidoscopio de excentricismo británico, movida pop y el kitsch de un boudoir francés. Las 19 habitaciones del que se considera "el mejor lugar de encuentro para los roqueros" (según la publicación *Evening Standard*) están diseñadas de manera tan individual como atrevida y se inspiran en motivos que van desde las chicas "pin-up" a artistas de la música, desde el estilo urbano al espacio cósmico. Incluso en su bar se puede viajar a otras dimensiones, ya sea con la ayuda de la PlayStation o de un buen cóctel.

Non lasciatevi ingannare dalla sua ordinaria facciata: il Pelirocco non è un albergo per romanticoni in villeggiatura a Brighton. Chi prenota in questo hotel si ritrova in un caleidoscopio in cui si mescolano eccentricità britannica, cultura pop e gusto kitsch stile boudoir. Le 19 camere del "miglior posto rock'n'roll d'Inghilterra" (secondo il quotidiano *Evening Standard*) sfoggiano design personalizzati e coraggiosi – ispirati alle pin-up girls o a musicisti, allo street style o all'universo. Persino nel bar ci si può proiettare in altre dimensioni: con l'aiuto di PlayStation e cocktail assolutamente venerabili.

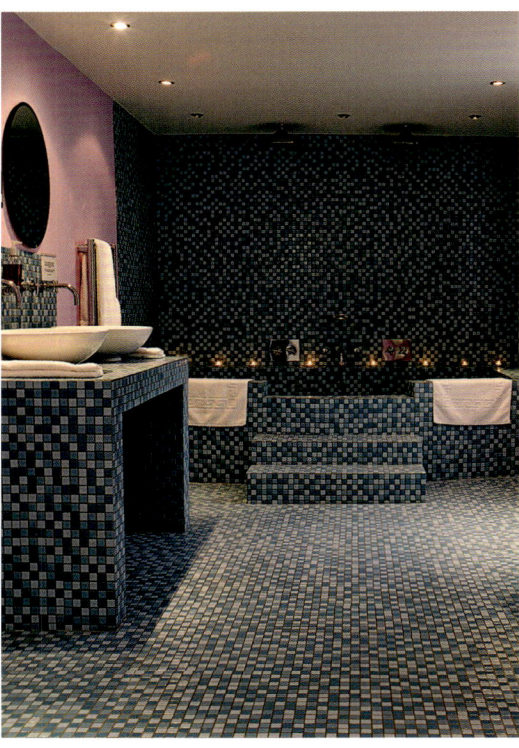
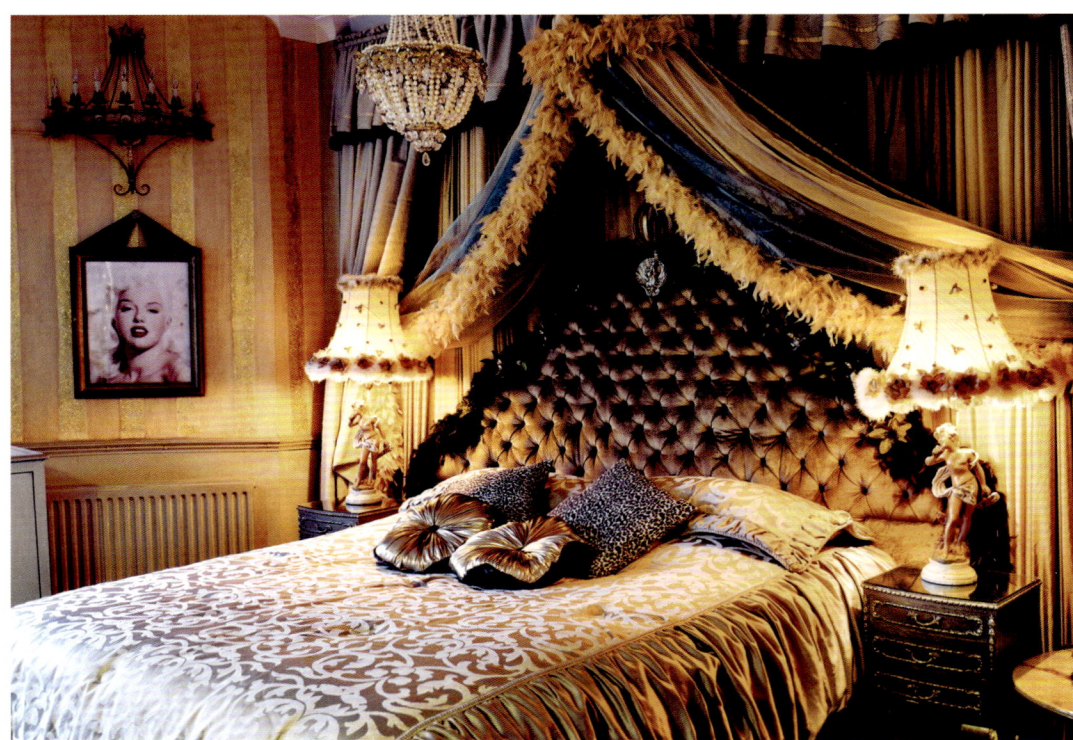

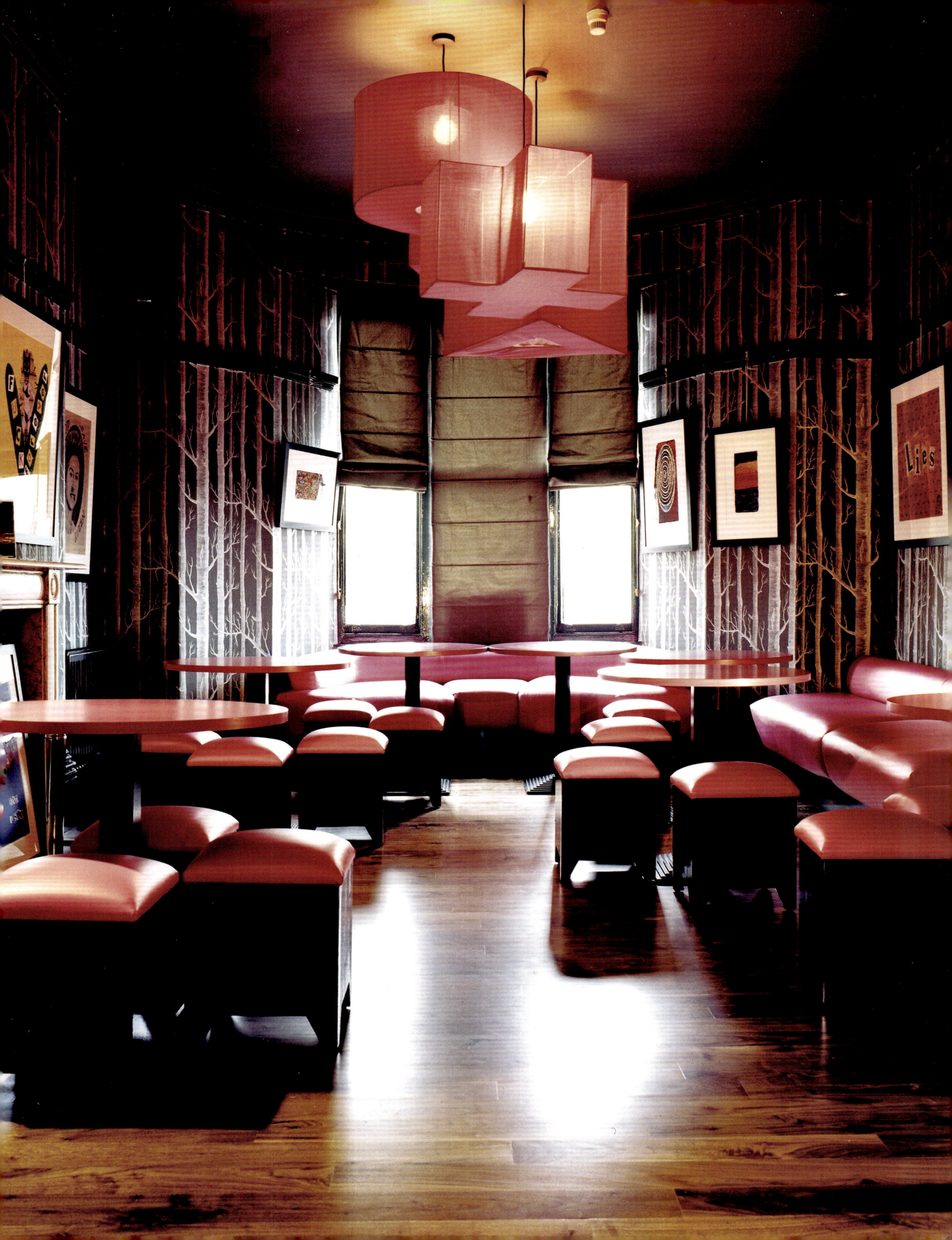

The Grove

Chandler's Cross, United Kingdom

Chandler's Cross
Hertfordshire WD3 4TG
United Kingdom
Phone: +44 1923 807 807
Fax: +44 1923 221 008
www.thegrove.co.uk

Price category: €€€
Rooms: 227 rooms and suites
Facilities: 3 restaurants, 2 bars, 4 drawing rooms, spa, 18-hole golf course, kids club, park and woodland, urban beach, private dining facilities
Services: Babysitting, room service, dry cleaning, concierge, valet parking, helipad
Located: 29 km from Central London and 30 min from Heathrow airport
Public transportation: Watford Junction train station
Style: Groovy Grand

In the 18th century the Earls of Clarendon invented "weekending" at The Grove, a favorite pastime of the English to spend weekends away from the hustle and bustle of the big city and retreat to the countryside. Today this luxurious country estate counts as one of the most beautiful weekend retreats for Londoners, just 18 miles from the city itself. Stress and cares disappear amongst 300 acres of pristine English countryside, luxurious bedrooms, delicious food and wine, an unmistakably indulgent spa and world-class golf course.

Im 18. Jahrhundert hat der Earl of Clarendon auf The Grove das „Weekending" erfunden – jene Lieblingsbeschäftigung der Briten, ihr Wochenende fern der Hektik der Großstadt im Grünen zu verbringen. Der Luxus-Landsitz, nur 30 Kilometer außerhalb der Stadt, gehört heute zu den schönsten Wochenendrefugien der Londoner. Stress und Sorgen verschwinden inmitten der 120 Hektar großen unberührten englischen Landschaft: hier werden luxuriöse Schlafzimmer, köstliches Essen und wohlschmeckende Weine, ein unverkennbar entspannendes Spa und ein Weltklasse-Golfplatz geboten.

Au XVIIIème siècle, le Comte de Clarendon a inventé le « weekend » au The Grove – le passe-temps favori des Anglais étant de passer le week-end à la campagne, loin de la bousulade de la grande ville. Aujourd'hui, cette gentilhommière luxueuse à 30 kilomètres hors la ville compte comme l'un des plus beaux refuges pour le weekend des Londoniens. Au sein de ce paysage anglais vierge de 120 hectares le stress et les soucis disparaissent : des chambres luxueuse, des plat délicieux et des vin savoureux, une salle de bien-être évidament relaxante et un terrain de golf de classe internationale sont à la disposition des hôtes.

En el siglo XVIII, el Conde de Clarendon inventó en la mansión The Grove una de las actividades favoritas de los británicos: el weekending, o lo que es lo mismo, pasar los fines de semana en un retiro natural lejos del bullicio de la gran ciudad. Esta mansión rural de lujo sigue siendo uno de los refugios más bonitos elegidos por los londinenses para pasar los fines de semanas a tan solo 30 kilómetros de Londres. El estrés y las preocupaciones desaparecerán en las 120 hectáreas de virgen campaña Inglesa: habitaciones de lujo, comida y vinos deliciosos, el spa sin dudas ..., y el curso de primera clase de Golf.

Si dice che fu presso il The Grove che il conte di Clarendon, nel XVIII secolo, inventò il "weekending" – il passatempo preferito degli inglesi, cioè quello di trascorrere il fine settimana nel verde, lontano dall'andirivieni della grande città. Questa lussuosa villa di campagna è ancora oggi per i londinesi uno dei più bei rifugi per il weekend a soli 30 kilometri da Londra. Stress e preoccupazioni scompaiono nei 120 ettari di incontaminata campagna Inglese: stanze lussuose, cibo e vini deliziosi, una senza dubbio indulgente spa ed un corso di Golf di prima classe.

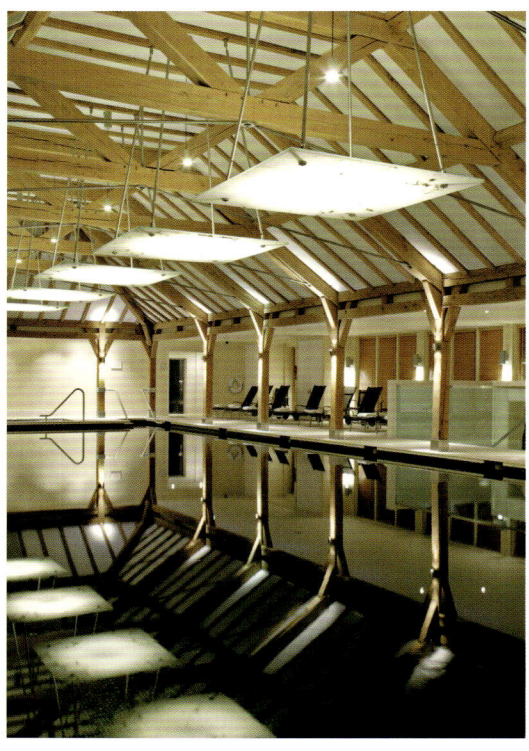
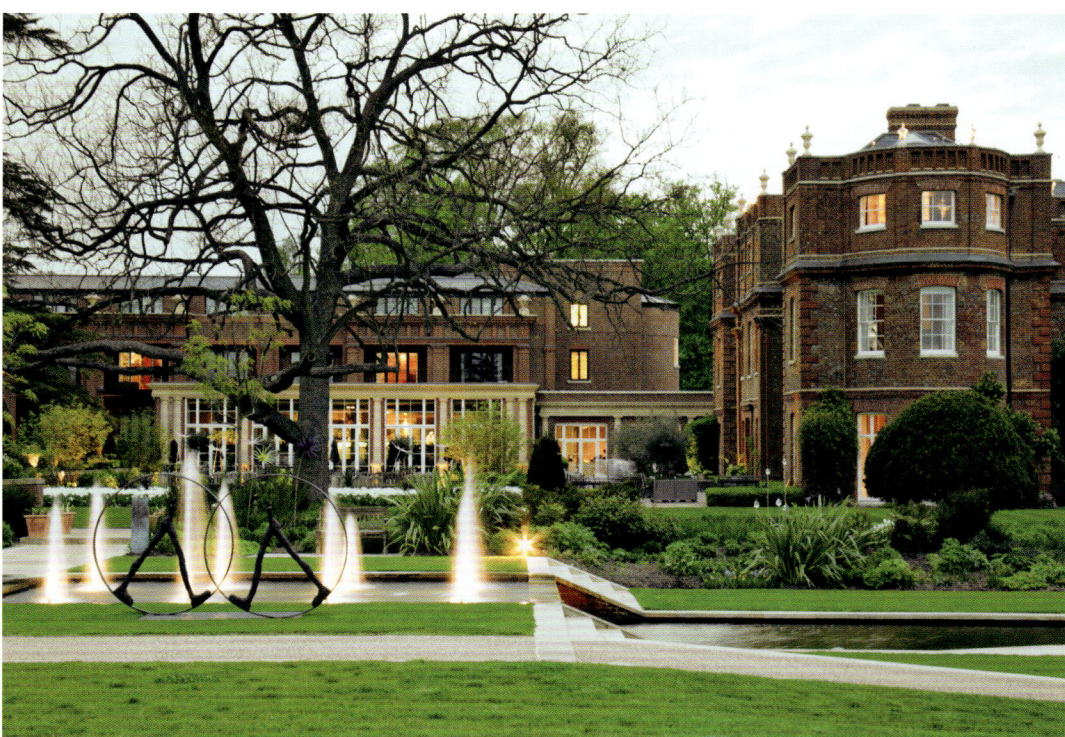

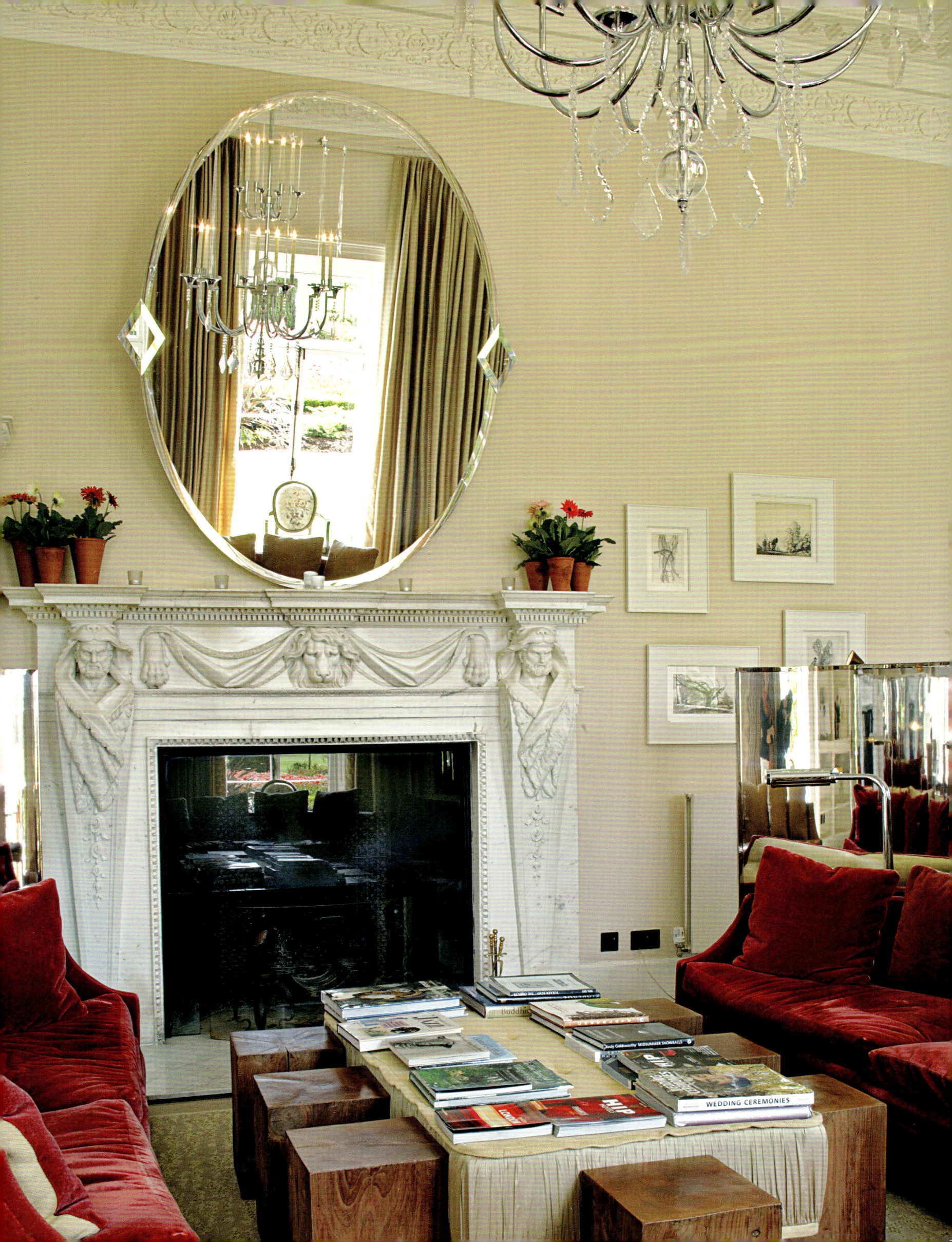

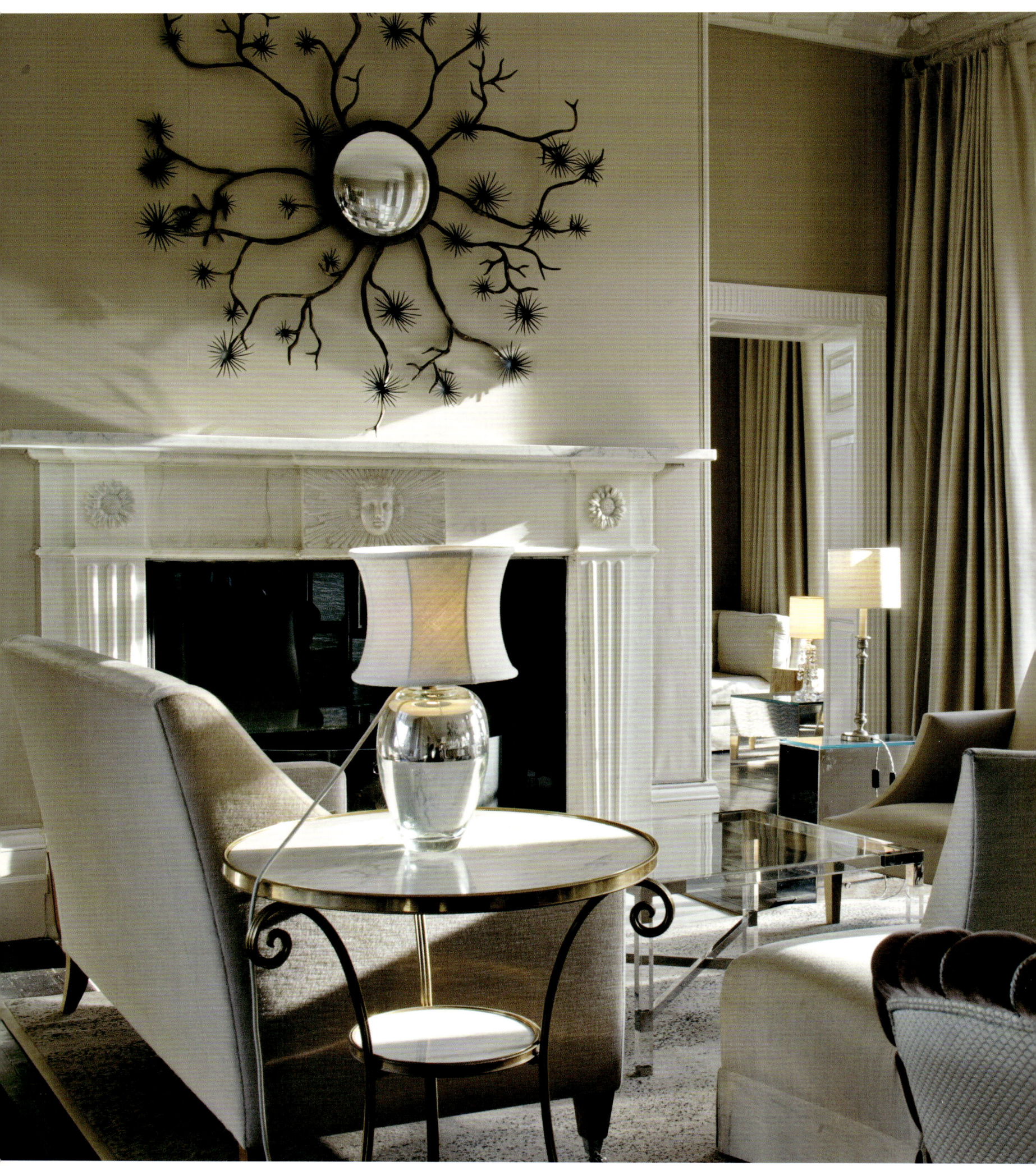

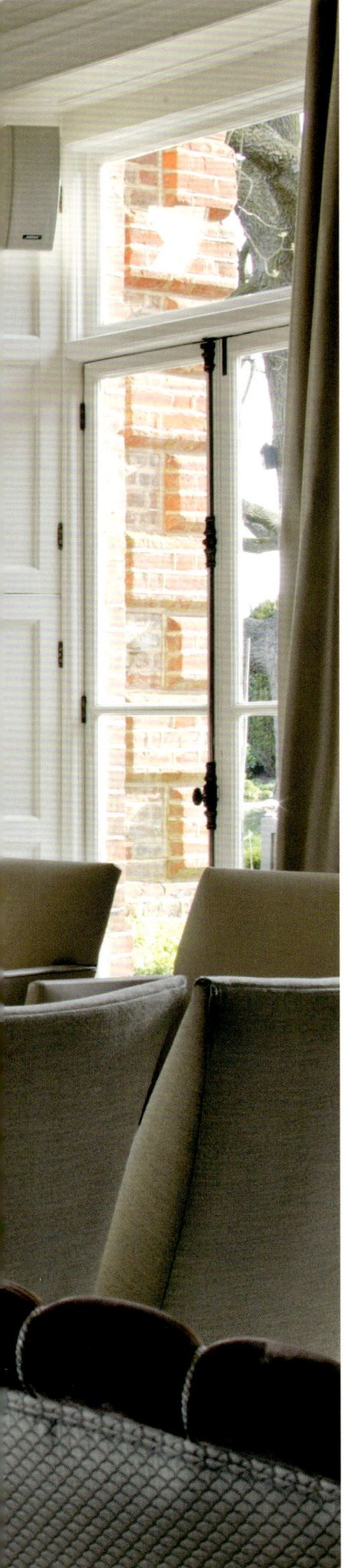

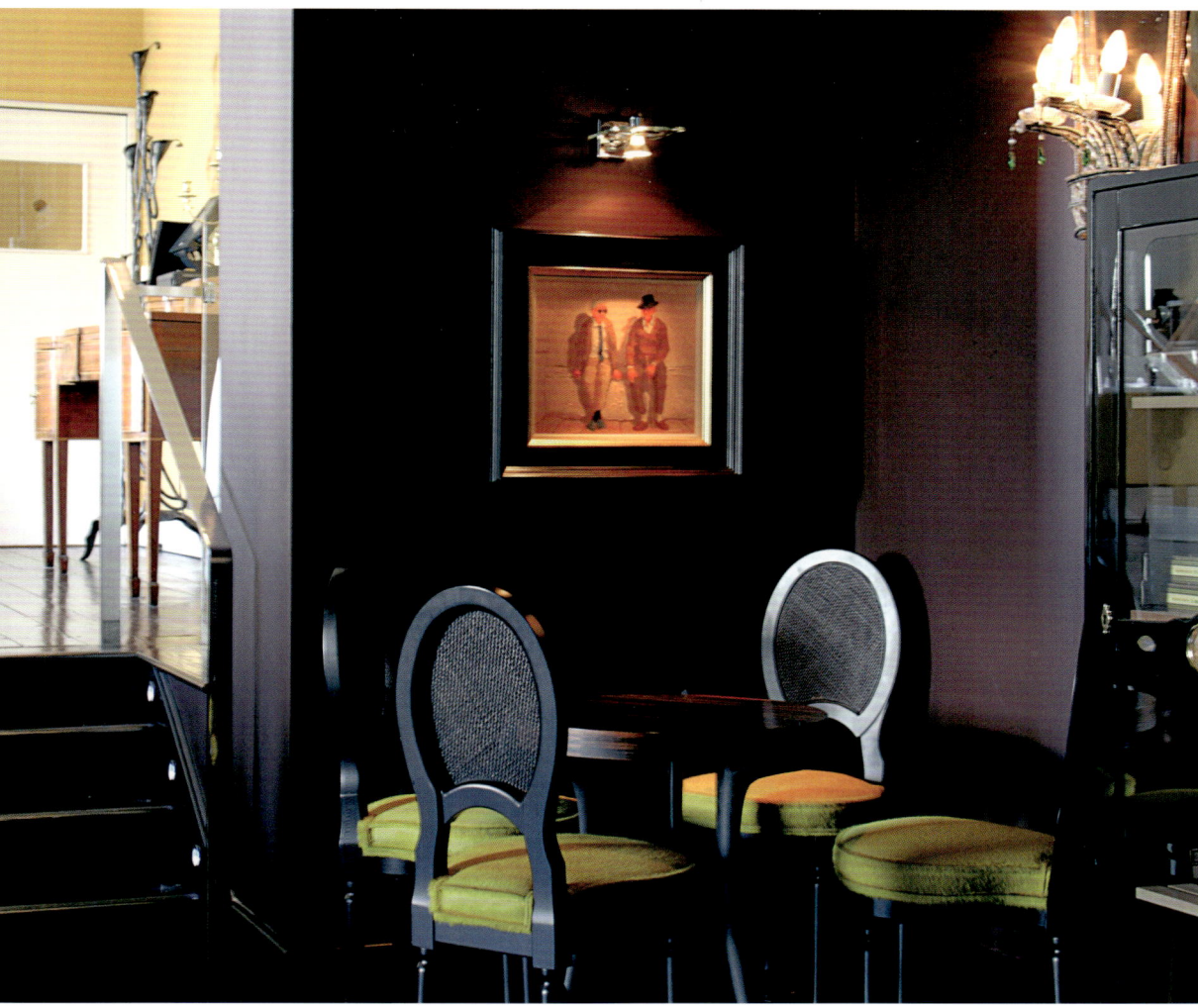

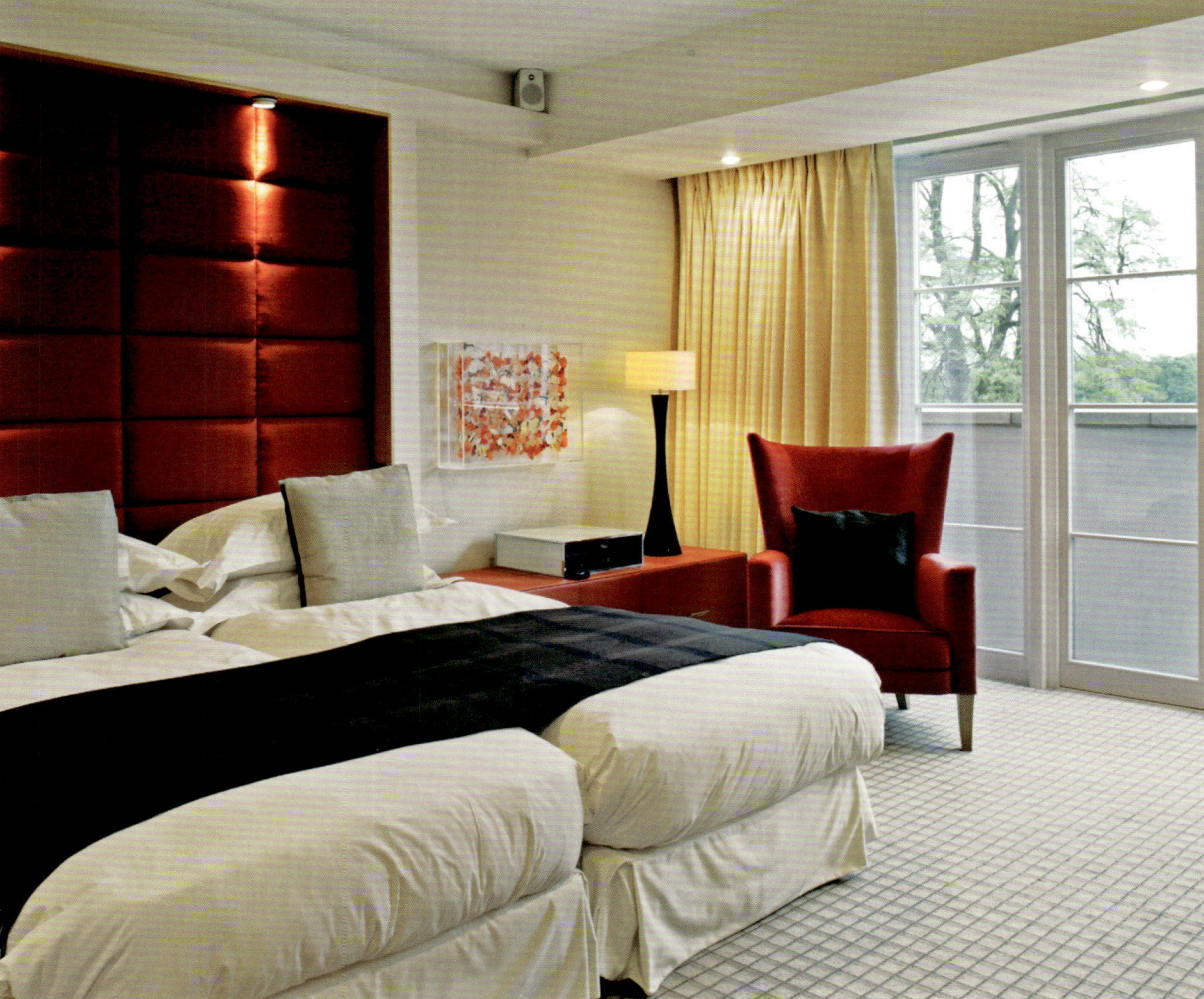

Easton Grey
Malmesbury SN16 0RB
Wiltshire
United Kingdom
Phone: +44 1666 822 888
Fax: +44 1666 826 120
www.whatleymanor.com

Price category: €€€
Rooms: 23 rooms including 8 suites
Facilities: Michelin star restaurant The Dining Room, the brasserie Le Mazot, Aquarias spa, La Prairie "Art of Beauty" center, conference suite, cinema for guests
Services: 24 h room service, valet parking, spa treatments (exclusive use available)
Located: In the open Wiltshire countryside
Public transportation: Train from London Paddington to Chippenham
Style: Traditional with a contemporary theme

In the '20s this building of typical Cotswolds' sandstone served as a hunting lodge. In 2003 the manor house was remodeled into an elegant contemporary country hotel. The 15 rooms and eight suites are done in warm and earthy colors and have been furnished with heavy, expensive fabrics and valuable antiques. The craft of English gardening can be fully admired in the 26 gardens of different layouts. Only La Prairie products are used in the modern spa—a slight reminiscence of the Swiss owners.

In den 20er Jahren diente das mit dem typischen Sandstein der Cotswolds gebaute Anwesen als Jagdsitz. 2003 wurde das Herrenhaus zu einem eleganten, zeitgemäßen Landhotel umgebaut. Die 15 Zimmer und acht Suiten sind in warmen, erdigen Farben gehalten und wurden mit schweren, aufwendigen Stoffen und wertvollen Antiquitäten bestückt. In 26 unterschiedlich angelegten Gärten lässt sich bewundern, was englische Gartenkunst vermag. Im modernen Spa wird mit La-Prairie-Produkten gearbeitet – eine kleine Reminiszenz an die Schweizer Besitzerfamilie.

Pendant les années 20, cette résidence typique en grès de Cotswold a servi de pavillon de chasse. En 2003, le manoir a été converti en un élégant hôtel contemporain. Les quinze chambres et les huit suites ont des couleurs chaudes, terriennes, sont meublées dans des tissus lourds et élaborés, et décorées d'antiquités précieuses. Dans les 26 jardins aménagés différents, on peut admirer la beauté du paysagisme anglais. Les produits de soin La Prairie sont utilisés dans le spa moderne, petit rappel des origines suisses des propriétaires.

En los años 20, esta propiedad construida con la típica piedra arenisca de la región de los Cotswolds era una casa de cazadores. En 2003 fue renovada y transformada en un elegante y moderno hotel rural. En las 15 habitaciones y las ocho suites se han mantenido los cálidos colores térreos y se han añadido pesados tejidos muy elaborados y antigüedades de gran valor. En sus 26 jardines diferentes se puede admirar el arte de la jardinería inglesa. En el moderno spa se emplean solo productos La Prairie, una pequeña reminiscencia a la familia de propietarios suiza.

Questa tenuta, costruita negli anni '20 usando la tipica arenaria delle Cotswolds, era originariamente adibita a residenza di caccia. Nel 2003 la casa signorile è stata trasformata in un hotel di campagna elegante e adeguato ai moderni standard di qualità. Per l'arredamento delle 15 camere e delle otto suite sono stati scelti colori caldi e terrosi, stoffe pesanti e raffinate, e preziosi pezzi d'antiquariato. Nei 26 giardini che compongono la tenuta, ognuno diverso dagli altri, è possibile gettare uno sguardo d'insieme sui migliori risultati dell'arte del giardino inglese. Nel moderno spa vengono impiegati i prodotti della linea La Prairie – un piccolo omaggio alle radici svizzere della famiglia dei proprietari.

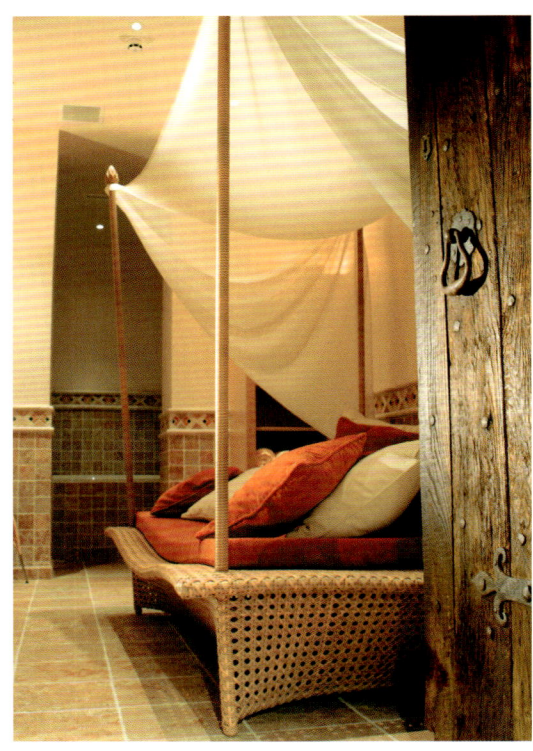
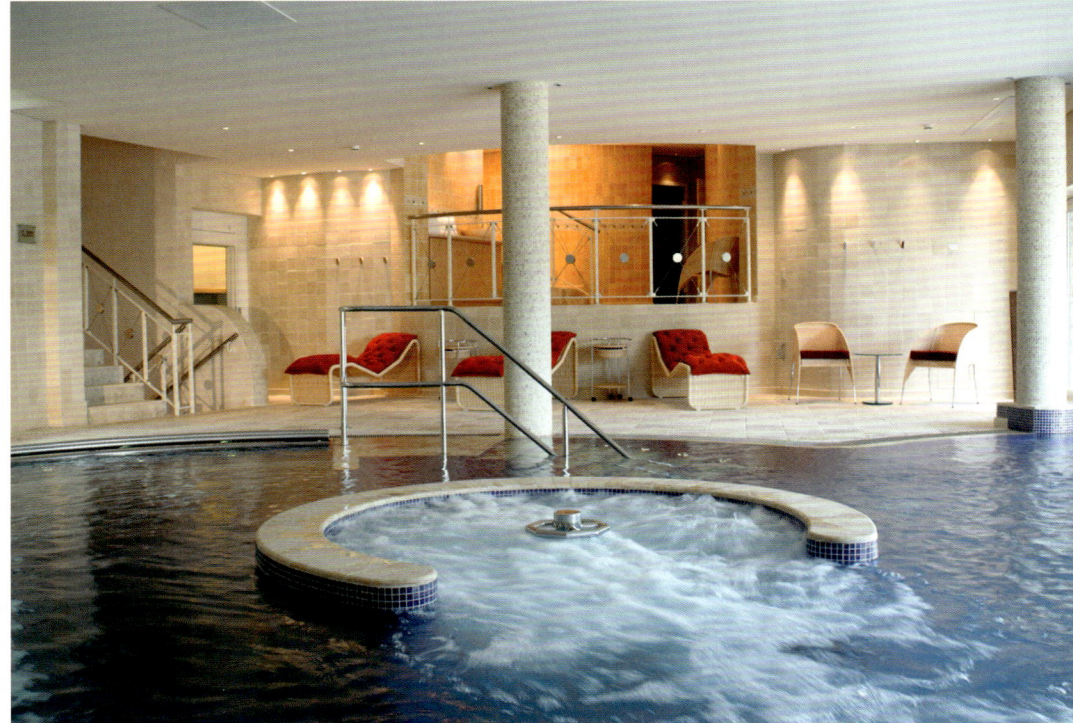

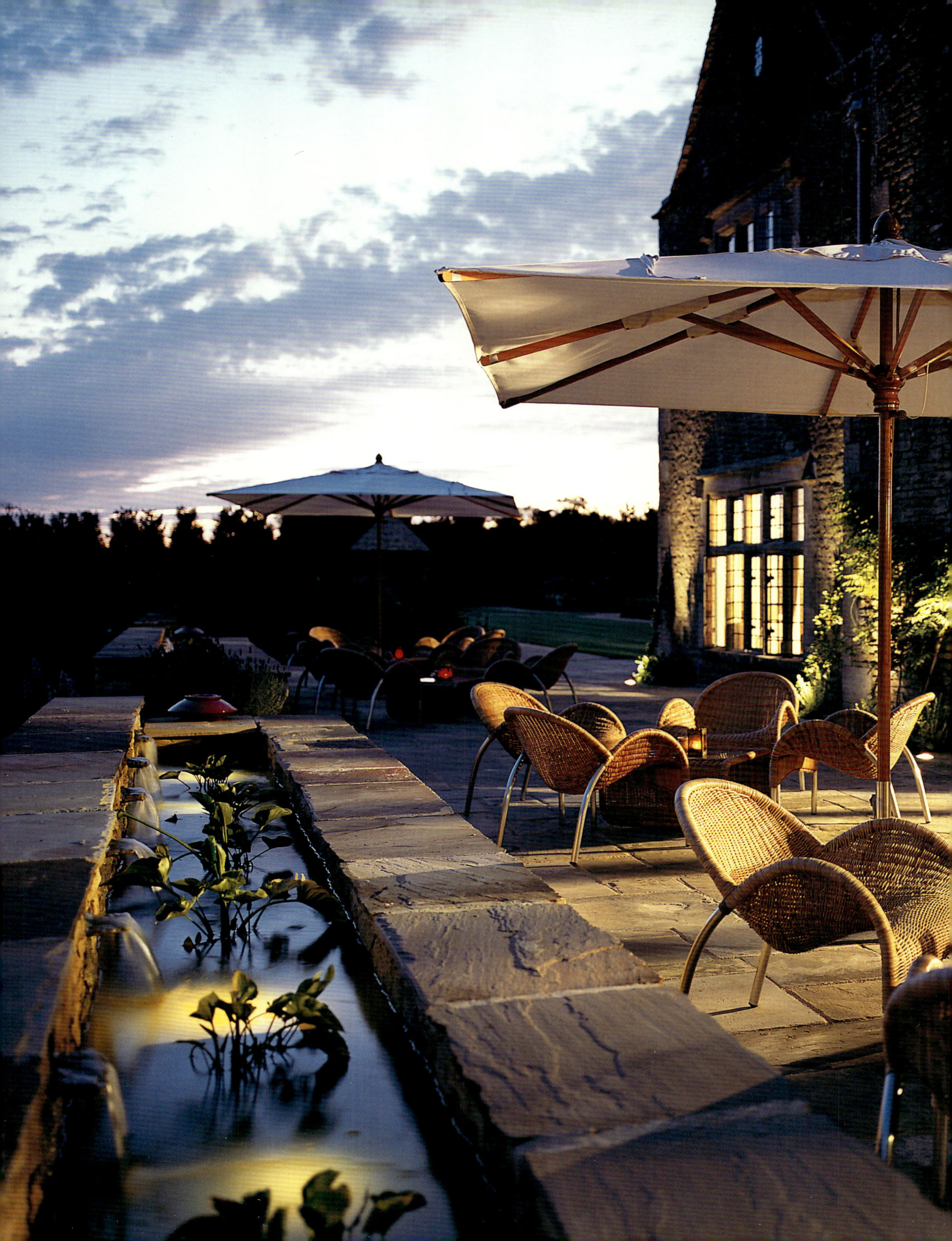

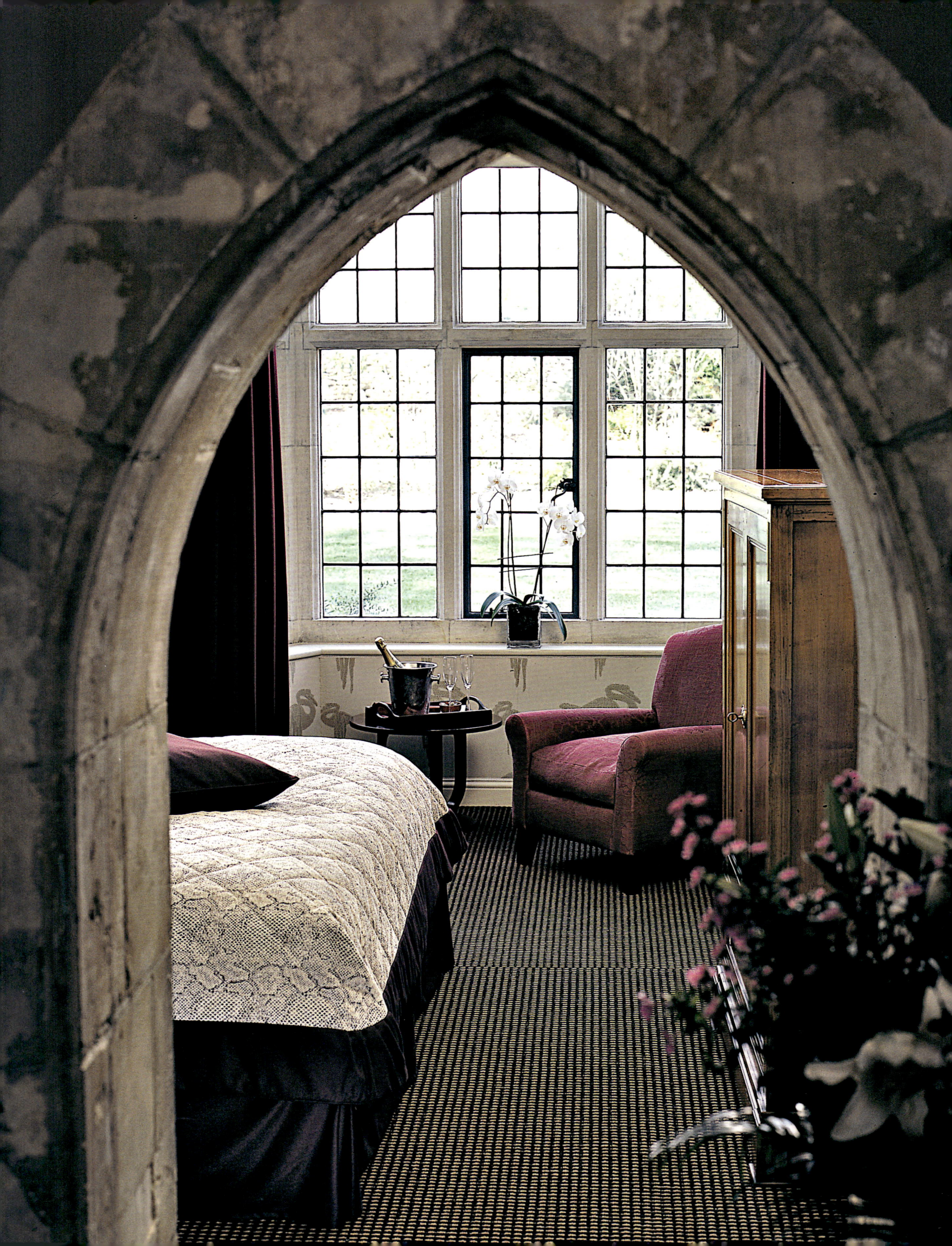

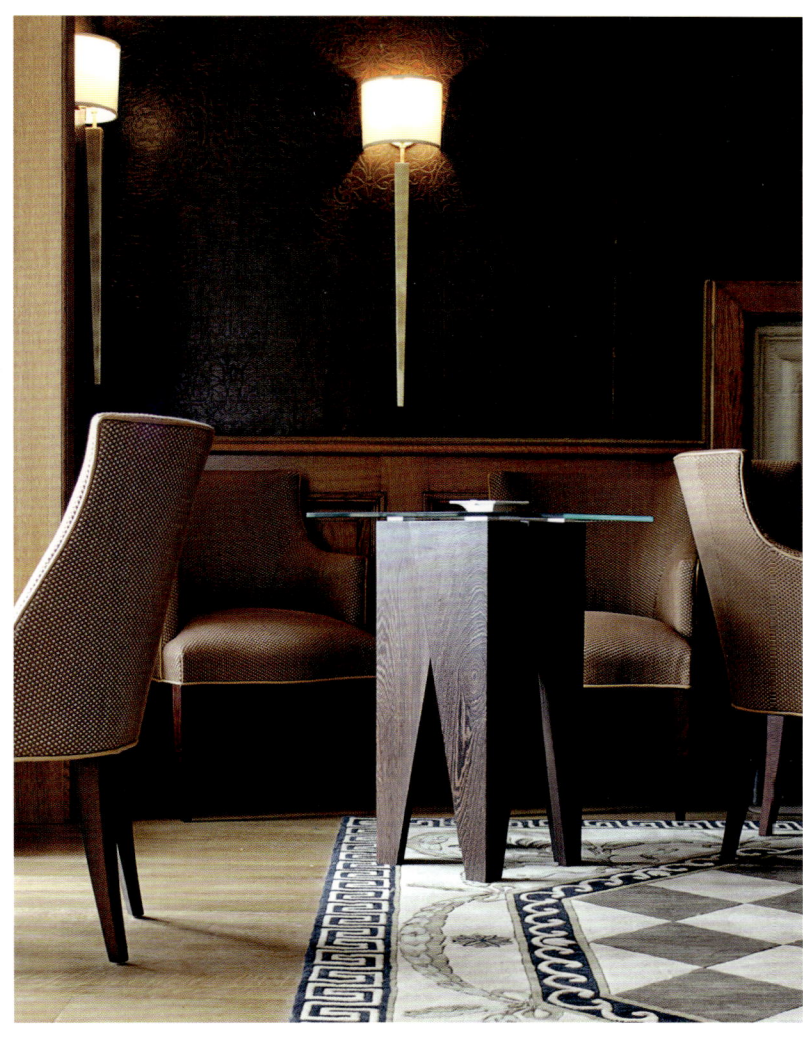
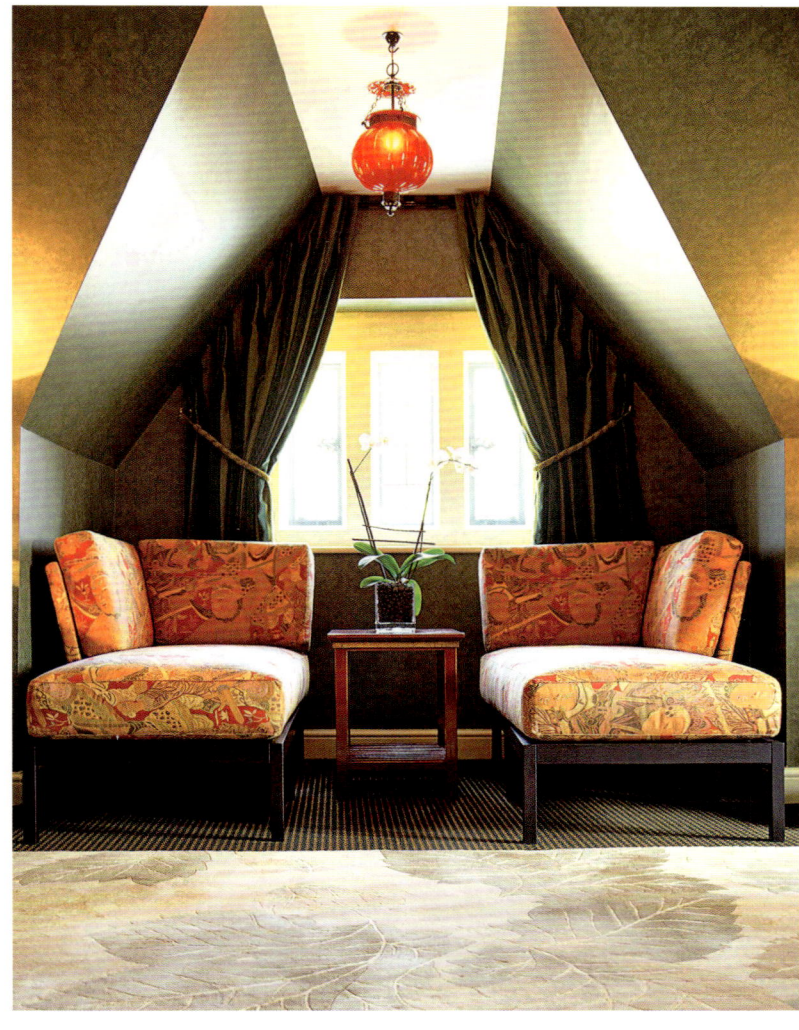
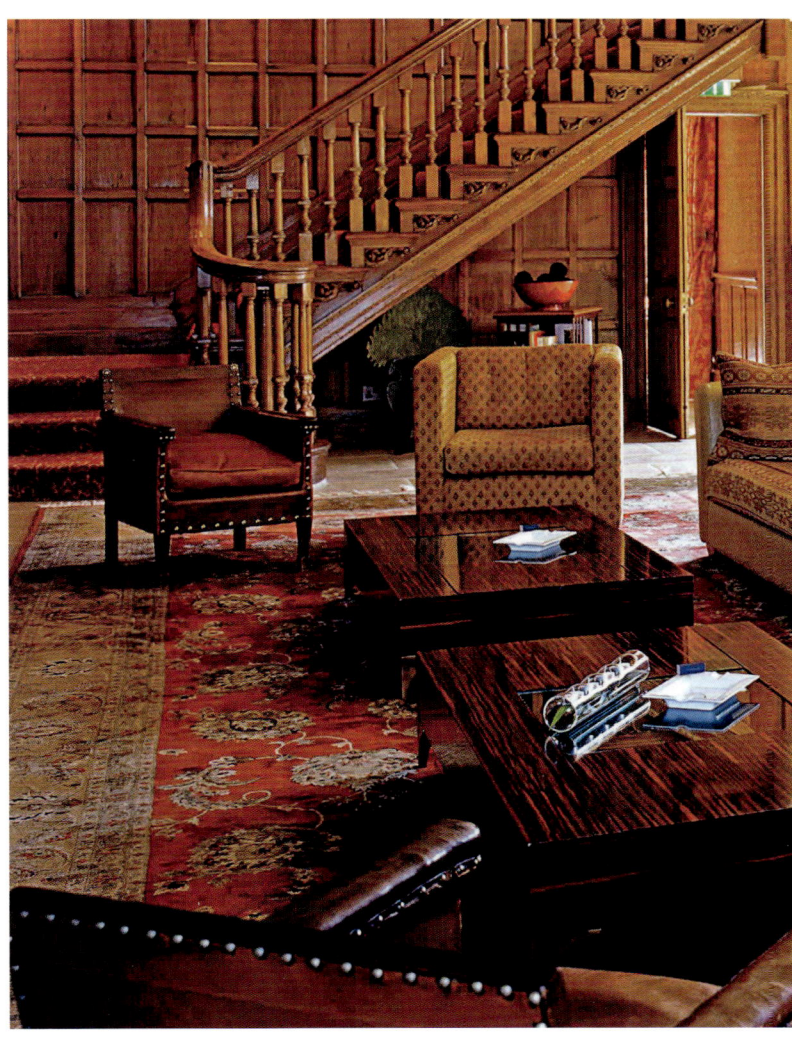
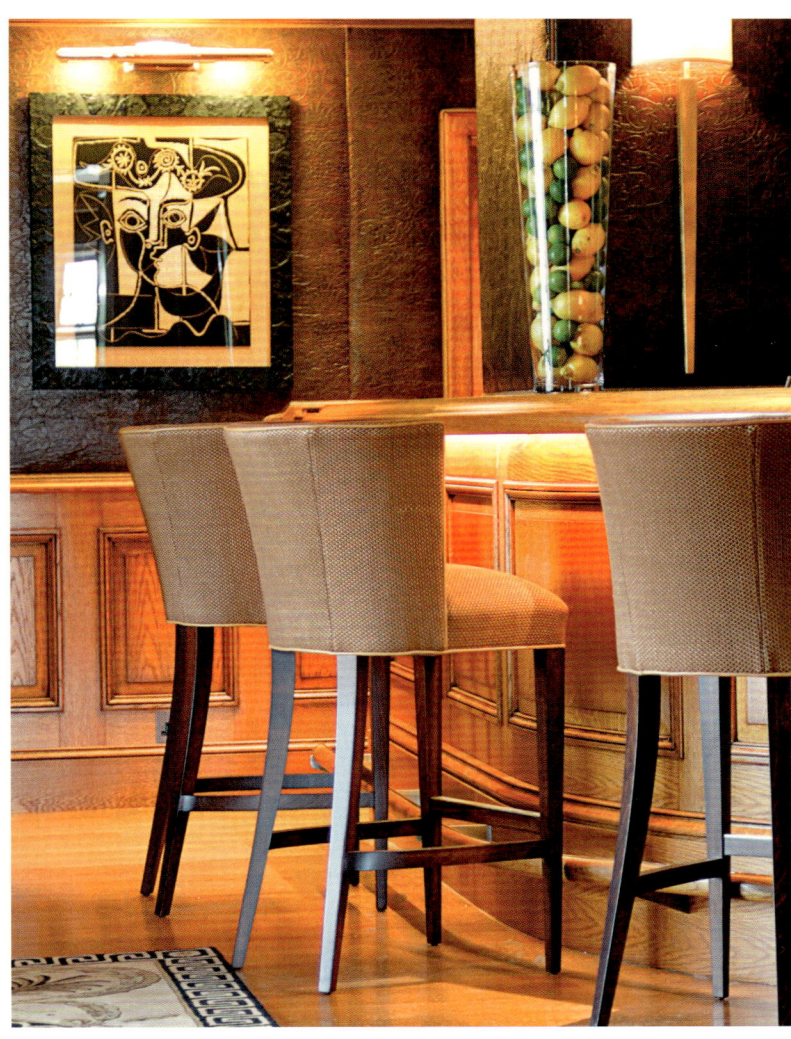

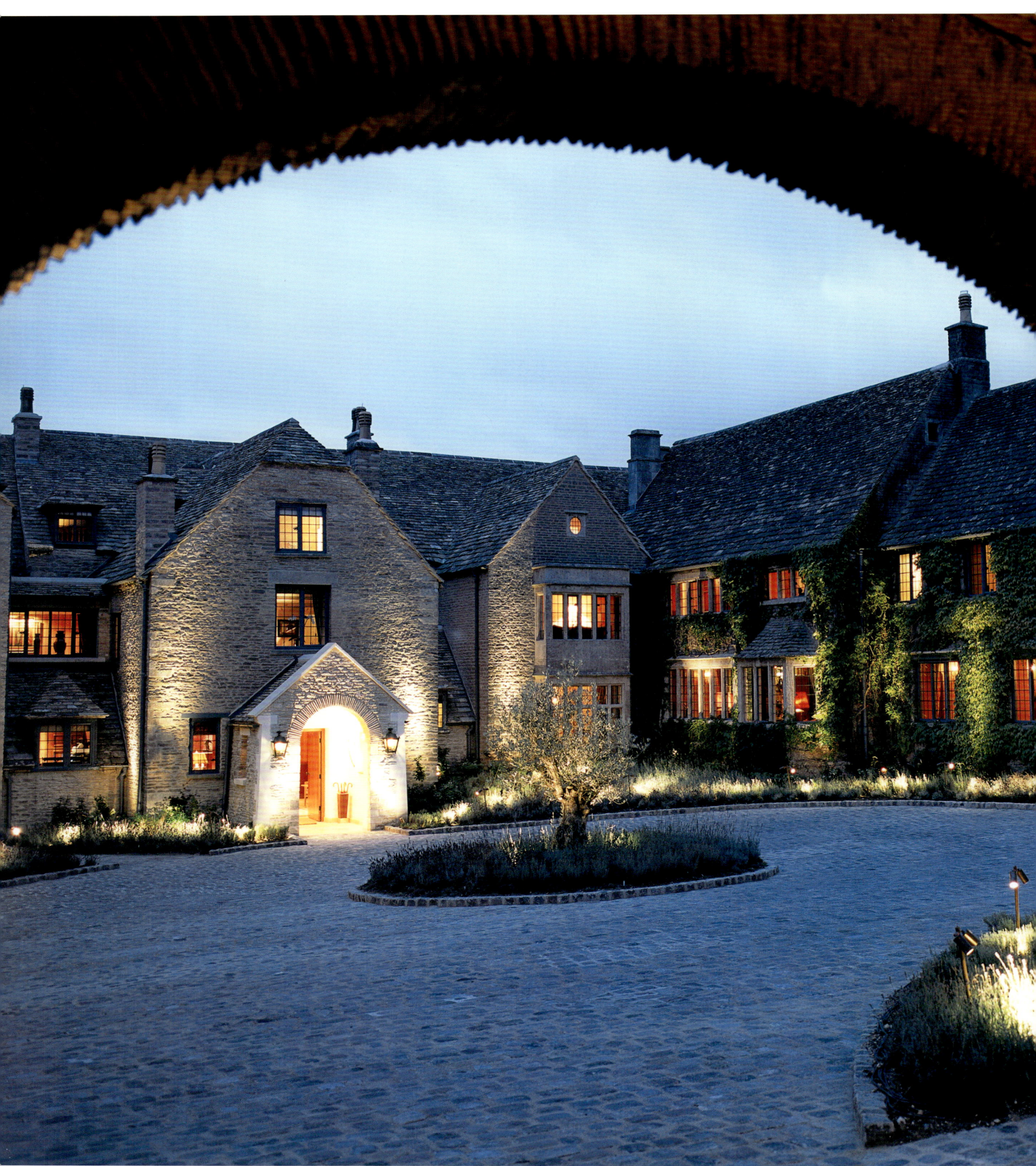

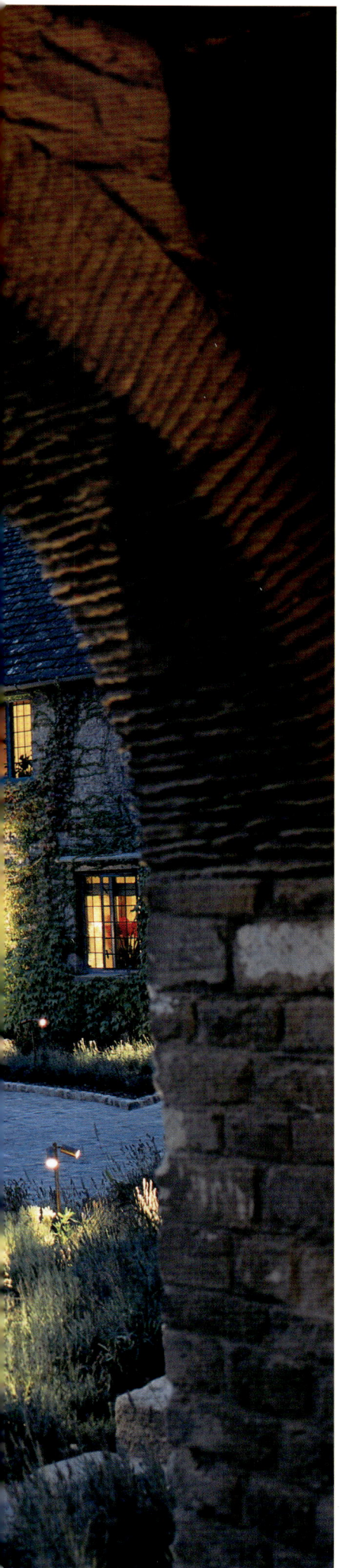

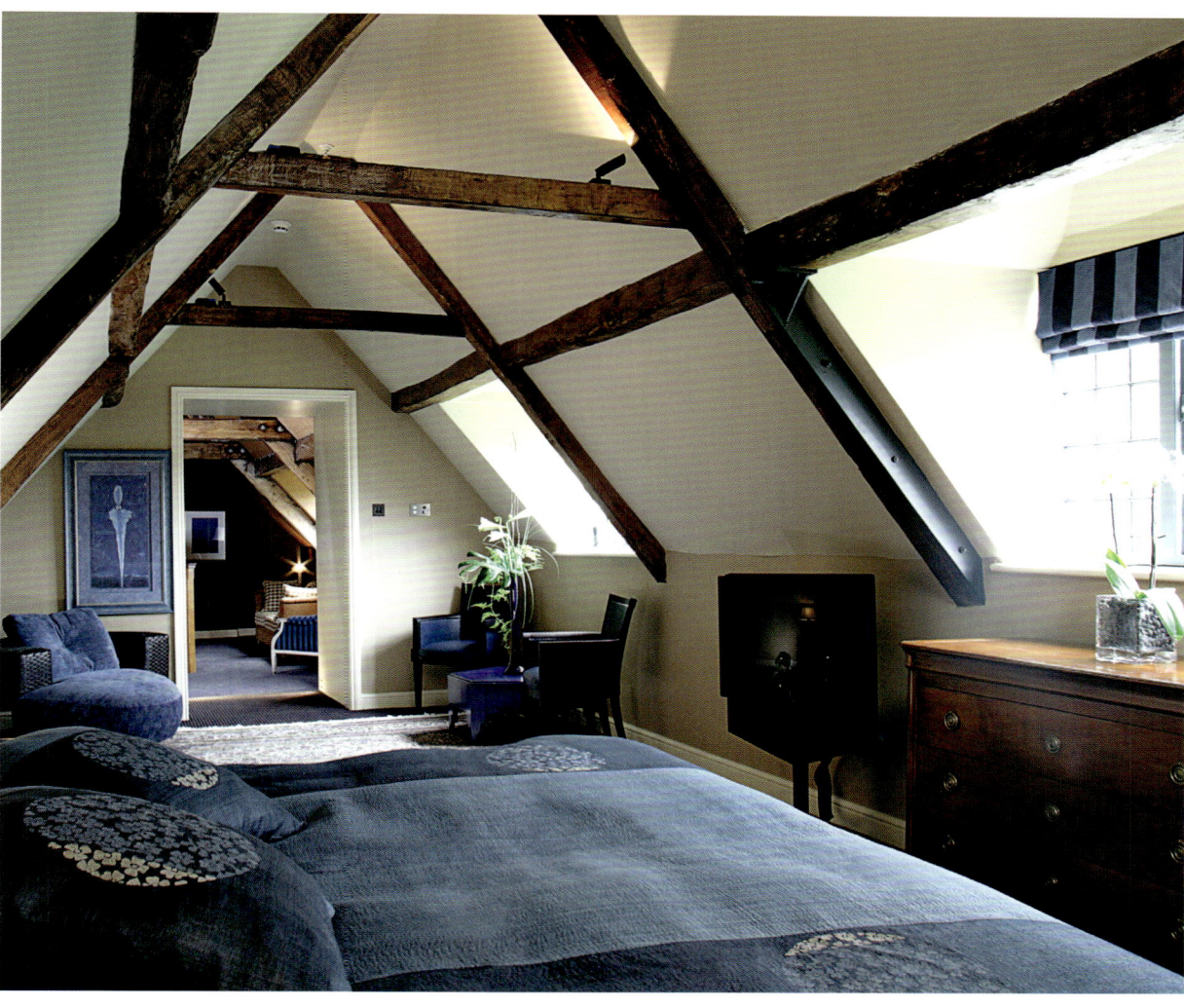

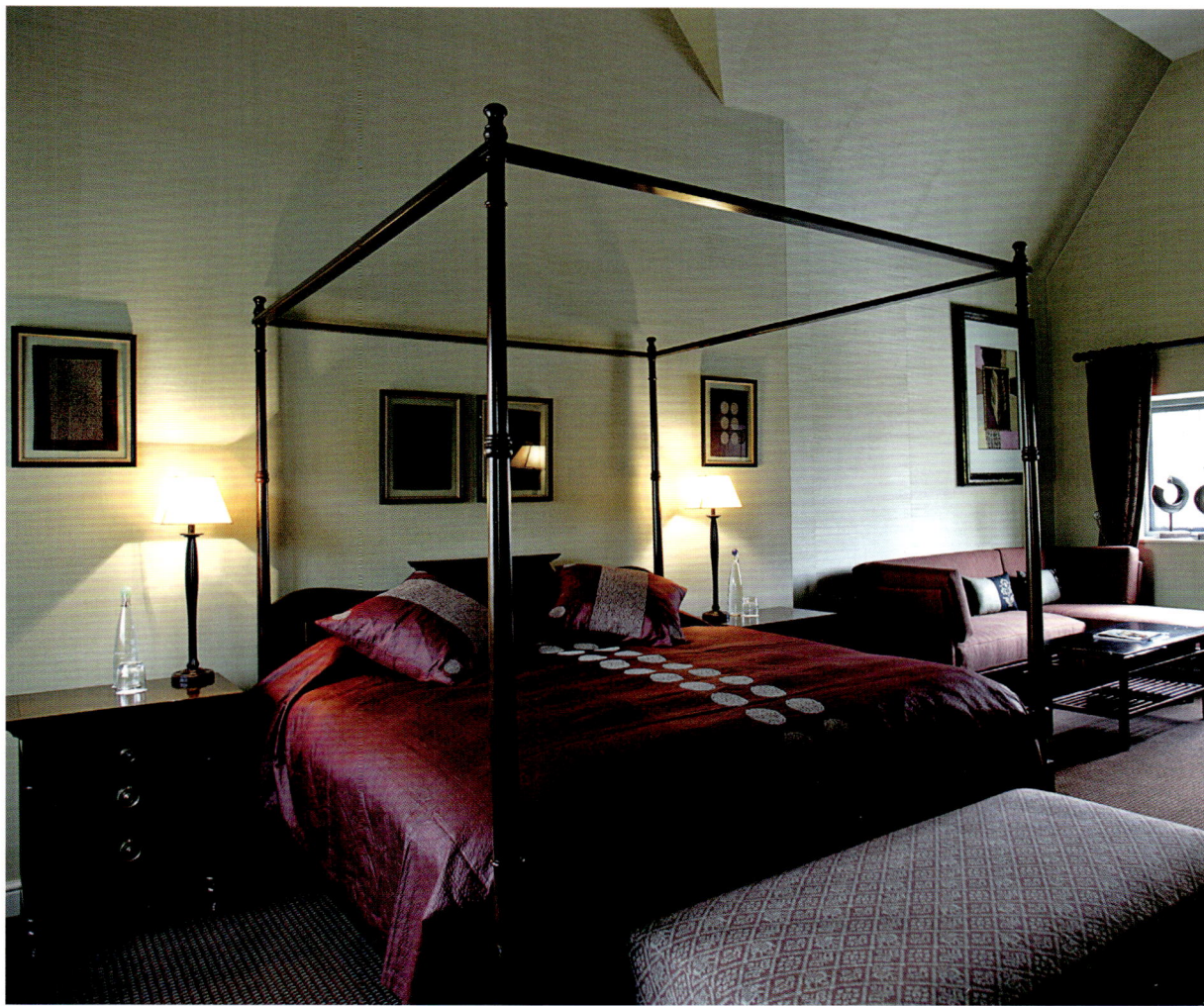

Cowley Manor

Cotswolds, United Kingdom

Cowley
Gloucestershire GL53 9NL
United Kingdom
Phone: +44 1242 870 900
Fax: +44 1242 870 901
www.cowleymanor.com

Price category: €€
Rooms: 30 suites
Facilities: Restaurant, terrace and indoor dining, bar, spa, 55 acres of private gardens
Services: 24 h room service, babysitting available, horse riding, winery visits
Located: In the Cotswolds, renowned for its historical villages, near the shopping hub of Cheltenham
Public transportation: Cheltenham Spa and Kemble train stations, transfer to airports
Style: Contemporary chic

The country house hotel near Cheltenham brought a kind of coolness you usually only know from London to the gentle hilly landscape of the Cotswolds. Modern but hardly minimalistic was the owners' order to the architects of De Matos Storey Ryan for the conception. There is not a single antique in the splendid late 19th-century Italian-influenced manor house but unbelievably large and luxurious baths with free-standing tubs. The modern spa that is almost sunk into the ground is considered a highlight of modern architecture.

Das Country-House-Hotel nahe Cheltenham brachte eine Coolness, wie man sie sonst nur von London kennt, in die sanfte Hügellandschaft der Cotswolds. Modern, aber nicht minimalistisch, so lautete die Vorgabe des Besitzerpaares an die Architekten von De Matos Storey Ryan für das Konzept. Keine einzige Antiquität findet sich in dem italienisch inspirierten Prachtbau aus dem späten 19. Jahrhundert. Dafür unglaublich großzügige und luxuriöse Bäder mit freistehenden Wannen. Der fast in die Erde versenkte moderne Spa gilt als Highlight moderner Architektur.

Cet hôtel-maison de campagne près de Cheltenham a apporté une touche de cool qu'on ne trouvait autrefois qu'à Londres dans le paysage vallonné de Cotswold. Un concept moderne, mais pas minimaliste, voilà les consignes données par le couple de propriétaires à l'architecte De Matos Storey Ryan. On ne trouvera pas une seule antiquité dans ce magnifique bâtiment d'inspiration italienne de la fin du XIXème siècle. A la place, il y a des salles de bains immenses et luxueuses avec des baignoires sur pieds. Le spa, qui est quasiment immergé dans le sol, est considéré comme un joyau d'architecture moderne.

El hotel rural cercano a Cheltenham añadió a este apacible paisaje de suaves colinas de la región de los Cotswolds un toque de movida urbana típico de Londres. Moderno pero no minimalista, ese era el concepto que la pareja de propietarios expuso a los arquitectos del estudio De Matos Storey Ryan. En el majestuoso edificio de inspiración italiana de finales del siglo XIX no se puede encontrar una sola antigüedad; en su lugar, lujosos baños de tamaño asombrosamente grande con bañeras libres. El moderno spa semisubterráneo es considerado un destacado ejemplo de la arquitectura moderna.

Questa casa in stile country nei dintorni di Cheltenham è riuscita a dare al morbido paesaggio collinare delle Cotswolds un tocco "British" che si crederebbe di poter trovare solo a Londra. Moderno ma non minimalista: queste le indicazioni date dalla coppia di proprietari agli architetto De Matos Storey Ryan. Nello splendido edificio del tardo XIX secolo, ispirato allo stile italiano, non si trova un singolo pezzo d'antiquariato; al suo posto bagni incredibilmente lussuosi dotati di vasche libere. Il moderno spa, quasi incastonato nel terreno, è considerato un eccellente esempio di architettura moderna.

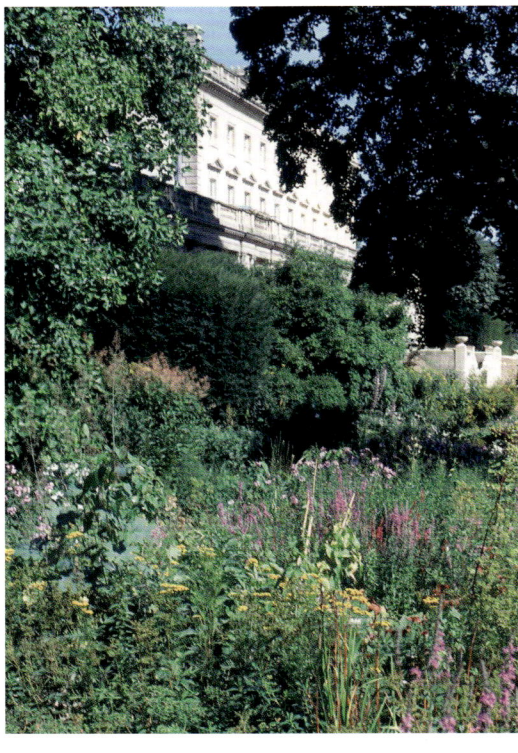
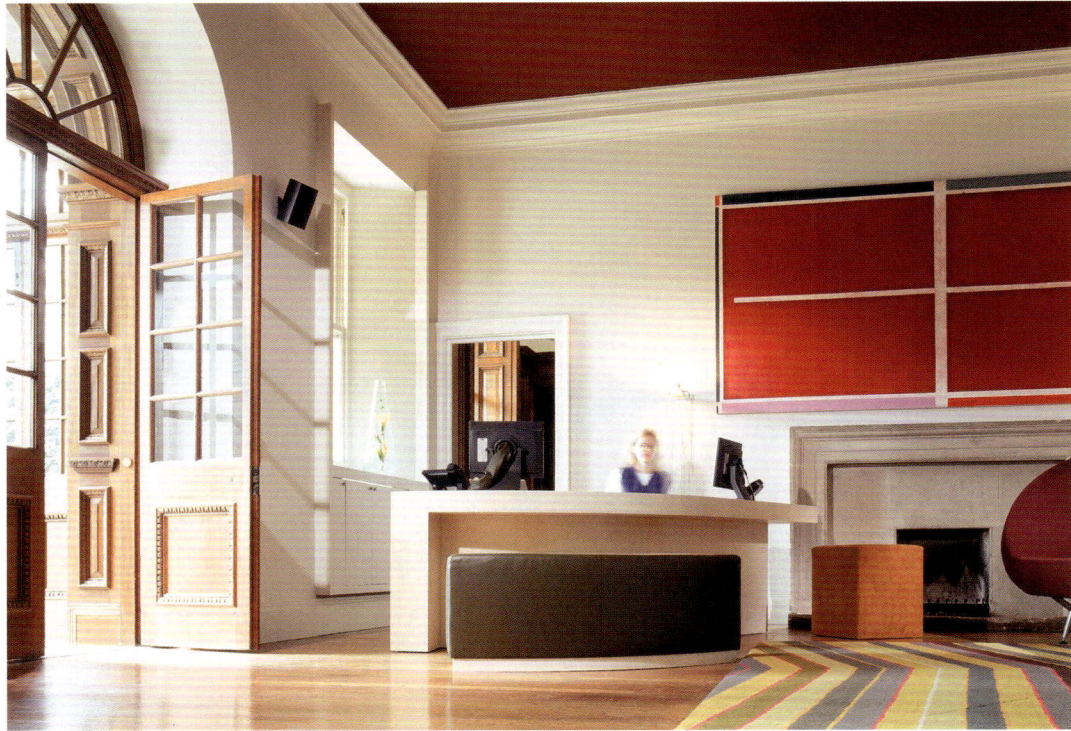

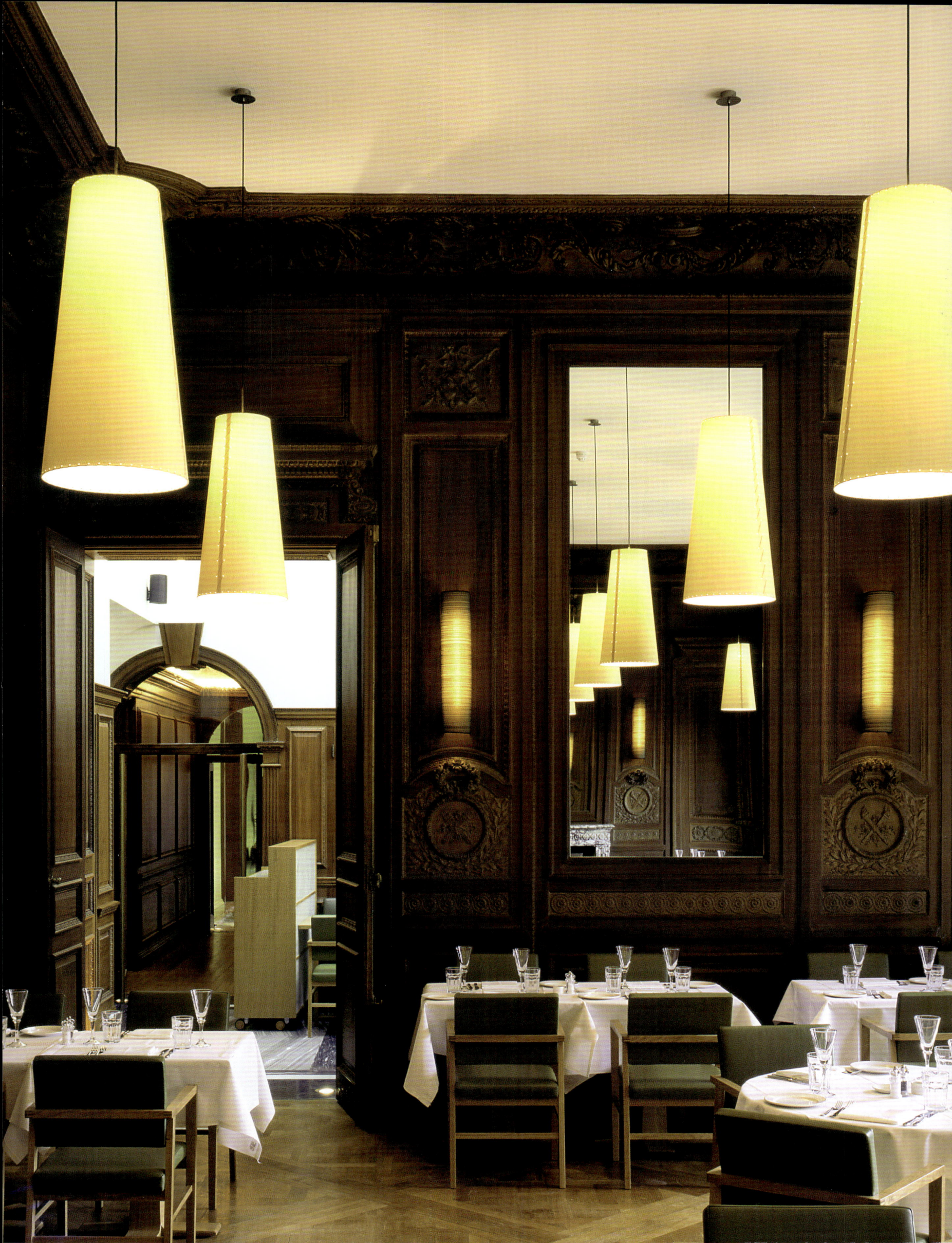

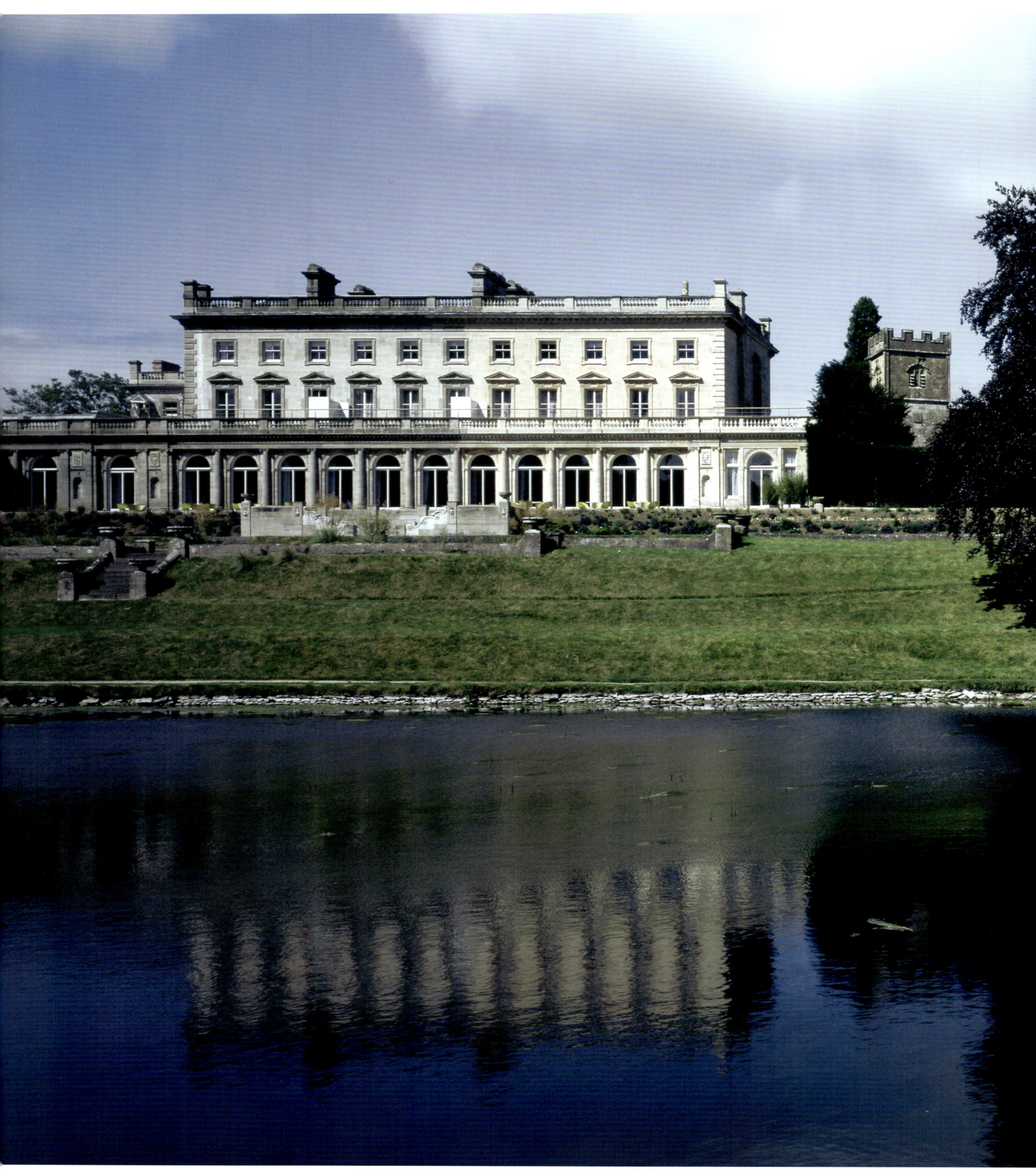

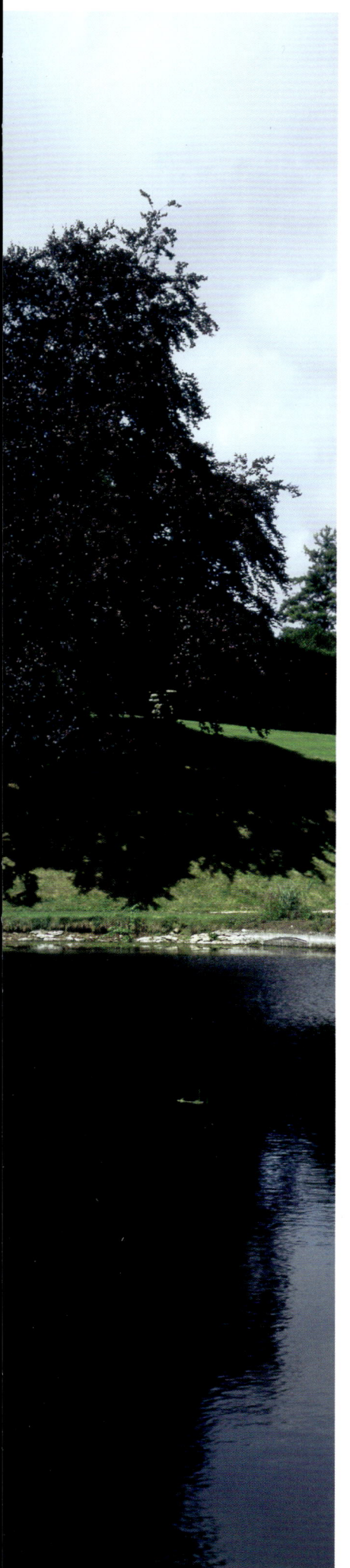

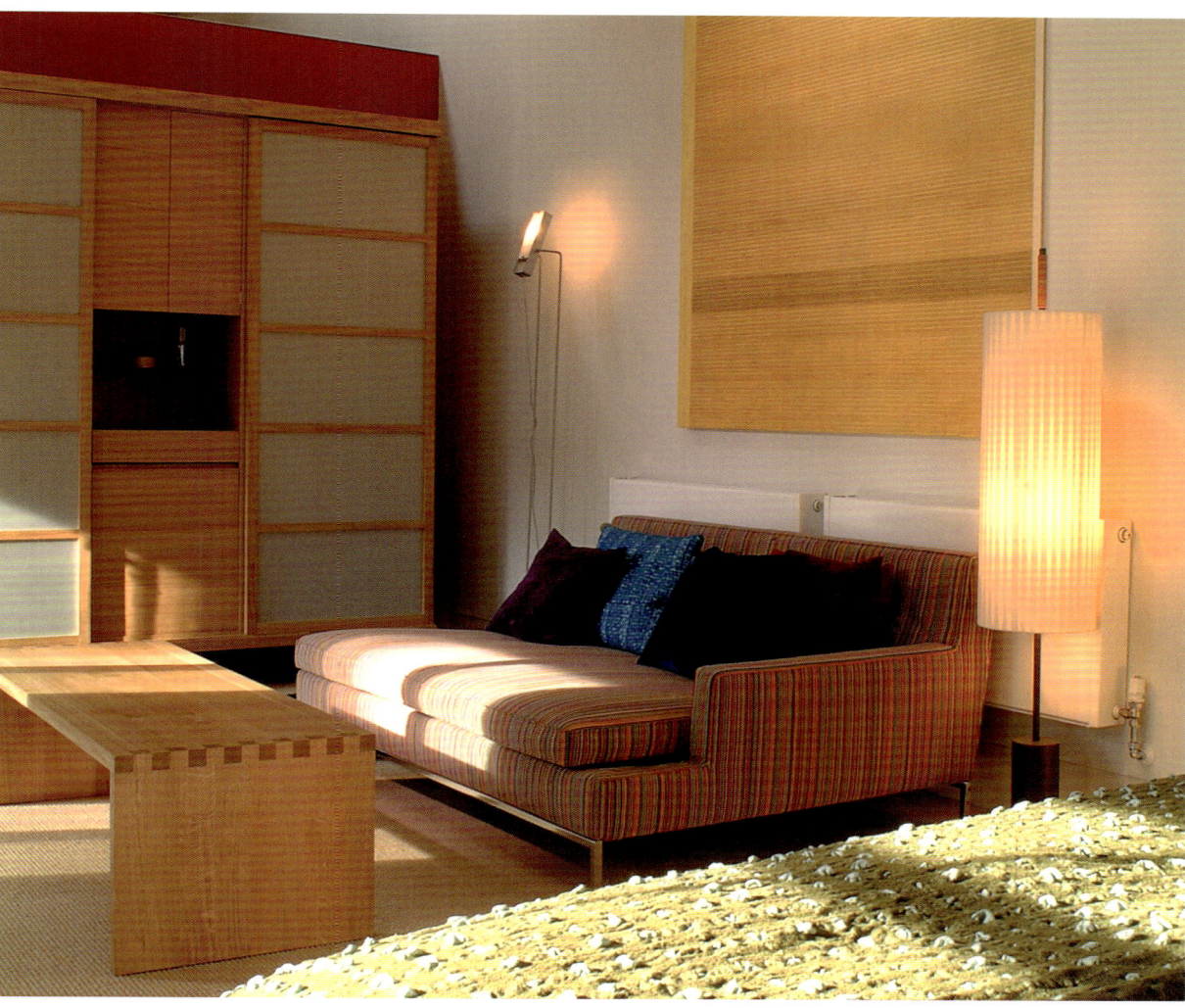

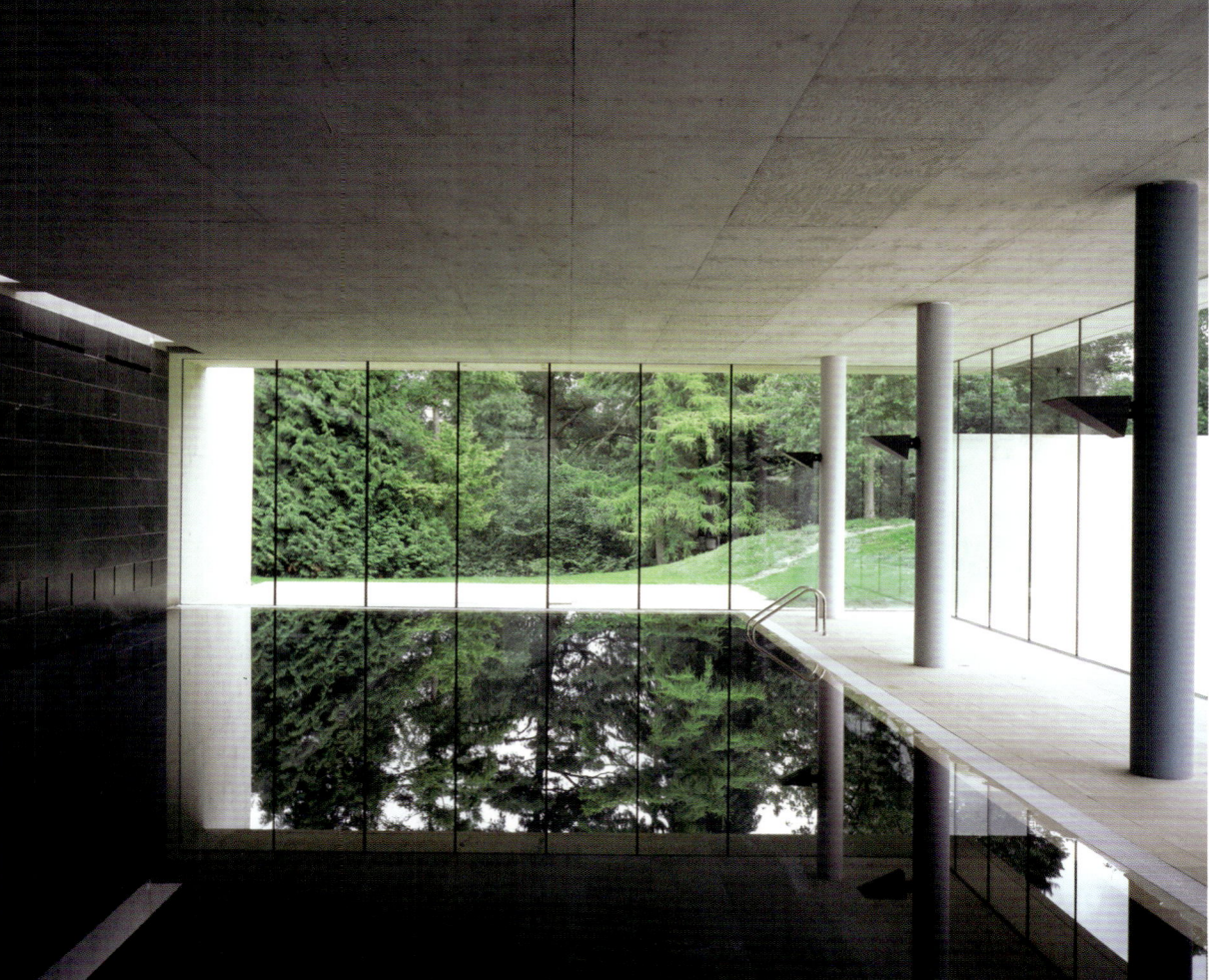

London SW1X 7RL
United Kingdom
Phone: +44 20 7235 6000
Fax: +44 20 7235 4330
www.the-berkeley.com

Rooms: 214 rooms including 65 suites
Facilities: The Blue Bar, Marcus Wareing's 2 Michelin stars Pétrus restaurant, Gordon Ramsay's Boxwood Café, rooftop swimming pool and spa
Services: Babysitting, concierge, spa, personal shoppers
Located: In the heart of Knightsbridge
Public transportation: Underground Hyde Park Corner, Knightsbridge; Victoria train station
Style: Contemporary Chic

It was once located in Berkeley Street, but in 1972 the hotel moved to Hyde Park where it freshens up traditional London luxury with the "latest lifestyle." "The Blue Bar," designed by David Collins, is considered to be the best place to meet. The two Michelin-starred restaurant "Pétrus" also bears Collins' handwriting and Gordon Ramsay's "Boxwood Café" blesses the hotel with another culinary highlight. Some of the 214 rooms lure with their own conservatory terraces, other have saunas or balconies. The new Berkeley Suites are the most elegant.

Einst an der Berkeley Street gelegen, zog das Hotel 1972 an den Hyde Park, wo es traditionellen Londoner Luxus mit „Latest Lifestyle" auffrischt: So gilt die von David Collins gestaltete „The Blue Bar" als Szenetreff. Auch das mit zwei Michelin-Sternen prämierte Restaurant „Pétrus" zeigt Collins Handschrift und mit Gordon Ramsay's „Boxwood Café" besitzt das Haus ein weiteres kulinarisches Highlight. Einige der 214 Zimmer locken mit eigenen Wintergartenterrassen, andere haben Saunen oder Balkons. Am elegantesten sind die neuen Berkeley Suites.

A l'origine situé sur Berkeley Street, l'hôtel a déménagé à Hyde Park en 1972, où il a donné une deuxième jeunesse au luxe traditionnel de Londres avec son style branché. « The Blue Bar » conçu par David Collins est un lieu de rencontre apprécié. Le restaurant étoilé au Michelin, le « Pétrus », porte aussi la signature de Collins, et avec le « Boxwood Café » de Gordon Ramsay, l'établissement offre un autre joyau culinaire. Certaines des 214 chambres profitent de leur propre terrasse et d'autres possèdent des saunas ou des balcons. Les plus élégantes d'entre elles sont les nouvelles Berkeley suites.

Antiguamente ubicado en la calle Berkeley este hotel se mudó, en 1972, al parque Hyde Park, donde refresca el tradicional lujo londinense con el estilo de vida más actual. Por esta razón, el bar "The Blue Bar", diseñado por David Collins, constituye un punto de encuentro en la escena local. El restaurante "Pétrus", premiado por la guía Michelín, lleva también la firma de Collins. Además, el hotel cuenta con otra atracción culinaria, el "Boxwood Café" de Gordon Ramsey. Algunas de las 214 habitaciones atraen con sus propias terrazas con jardines de invierno, otras tienen saunas o balcones. Las más elegantes son las nuevas Berkeley suites.

Situato un tempo in Berkeley Street, nel 1972 il albergo si è trasferito a Hyde Park, innestando su un lusso londinese tradizionale le ultime tendenze in materia di lifestyle: "The Blue Bar", arredato da David Collins, si è affermato così come punto d'incontro alla moda. Sia con il ristorante "Pétrus", anch'esso firmato da Collins e premiato dalla Guida Michelin, sia con il "Boxwood Café" di Gordon Ramsay la casa dispone di due straordinarie attrattive gastronomiche. Alcune delle 214 camere invogliano gli ospiti con un elegante giardino d'inverno, altre ancora dispongono di sauna o balcone. Il culmine dell'eleganza è raggiunto dalle nuove Berkeley suite.

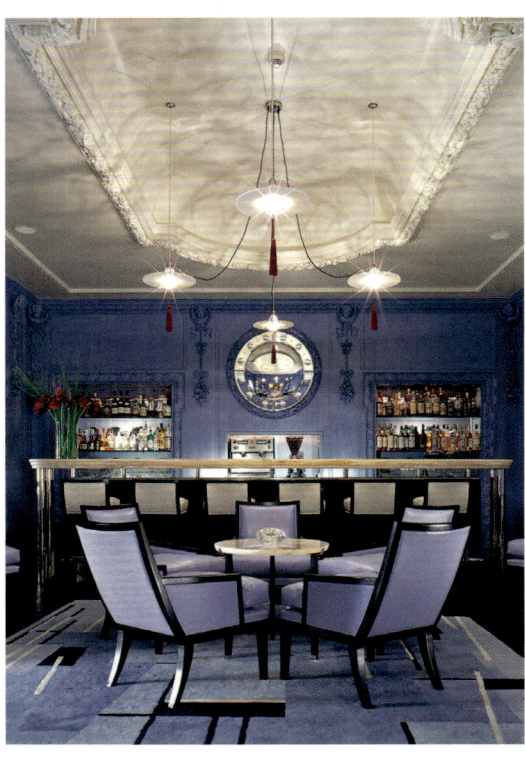

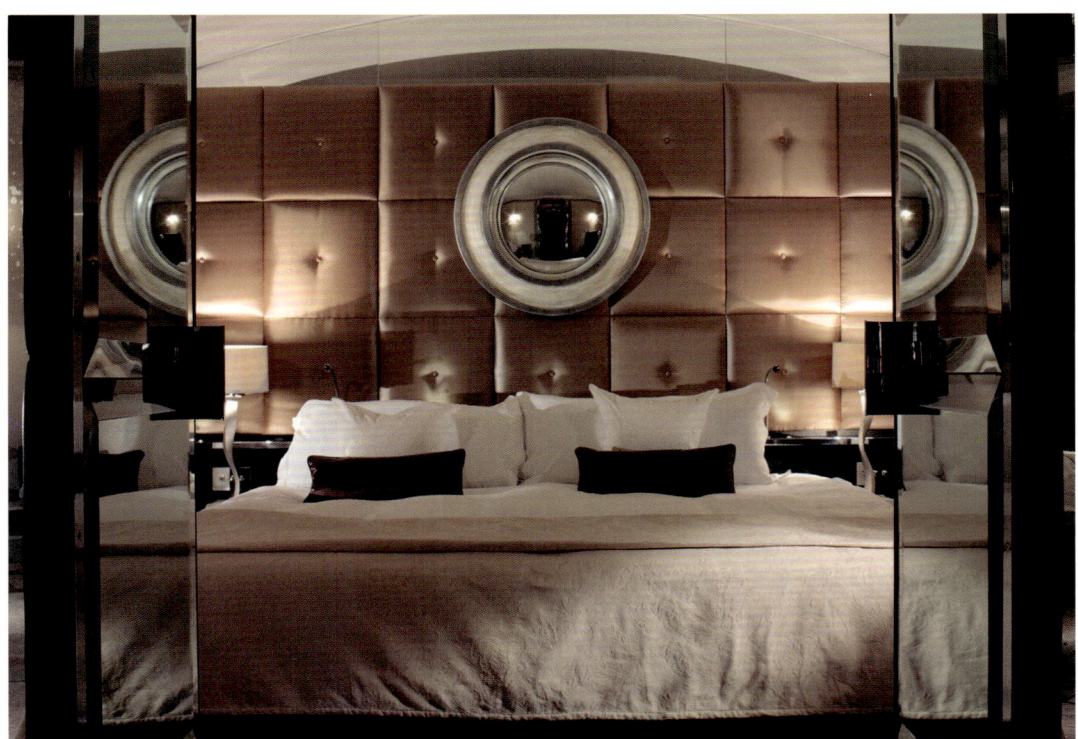

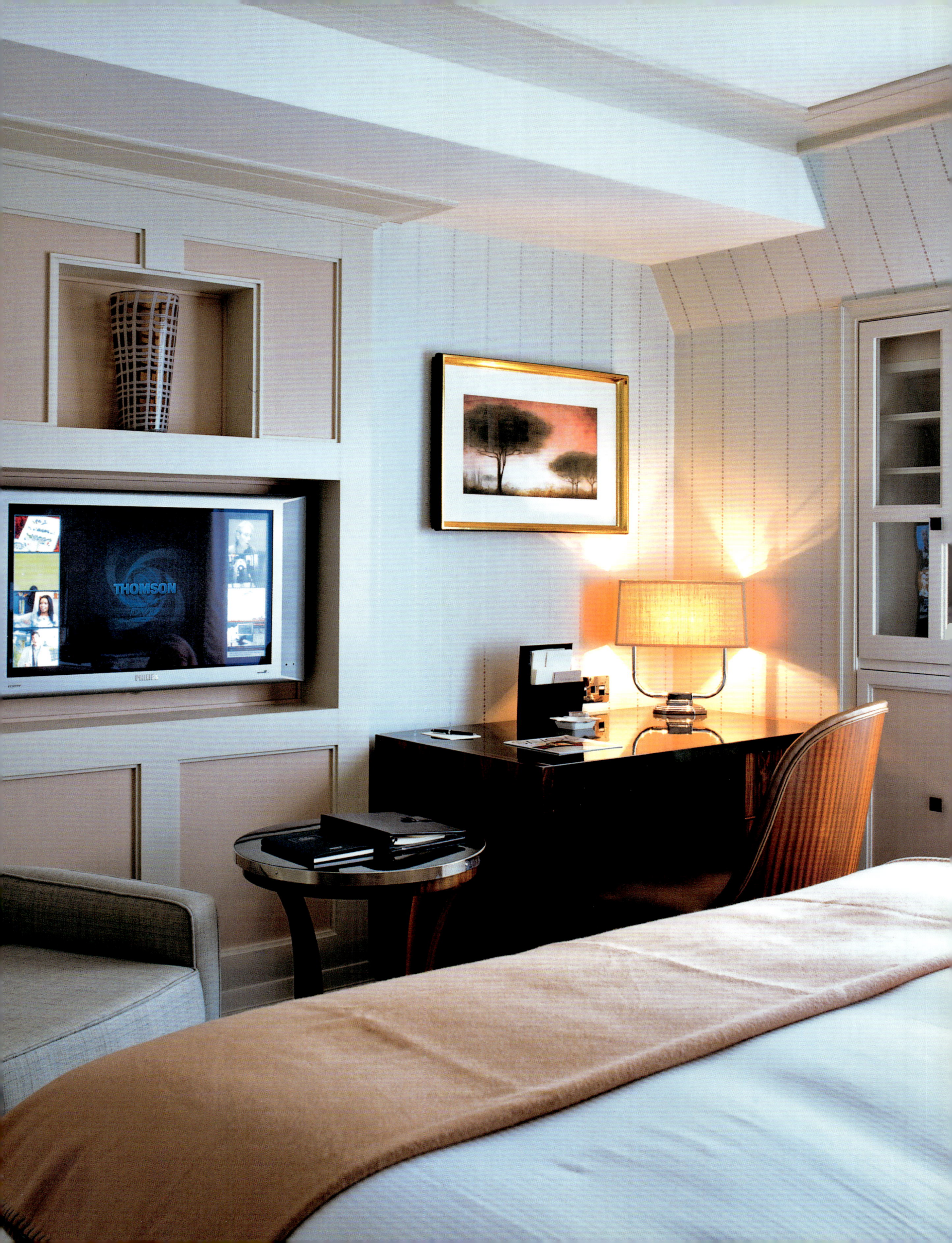

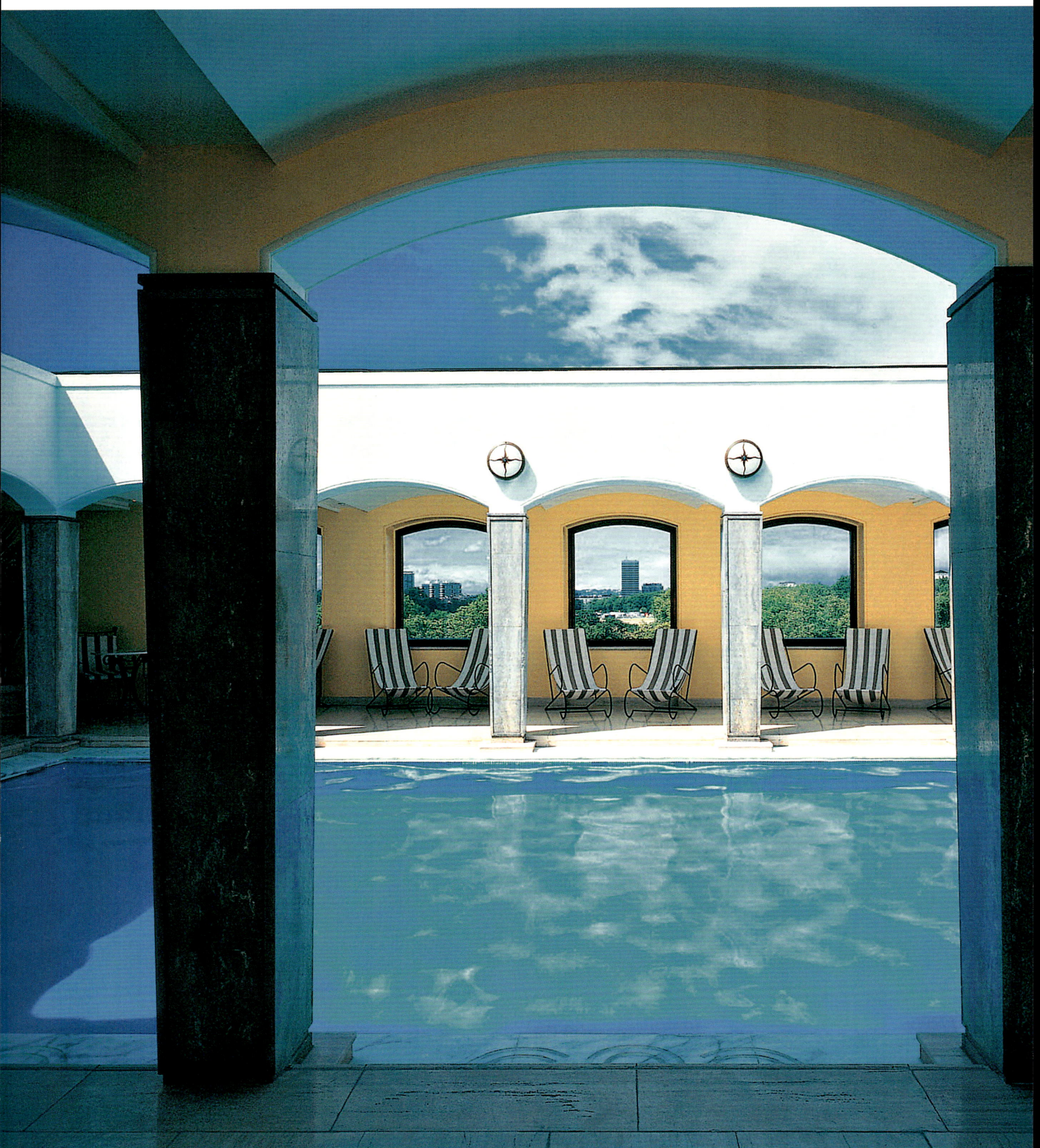

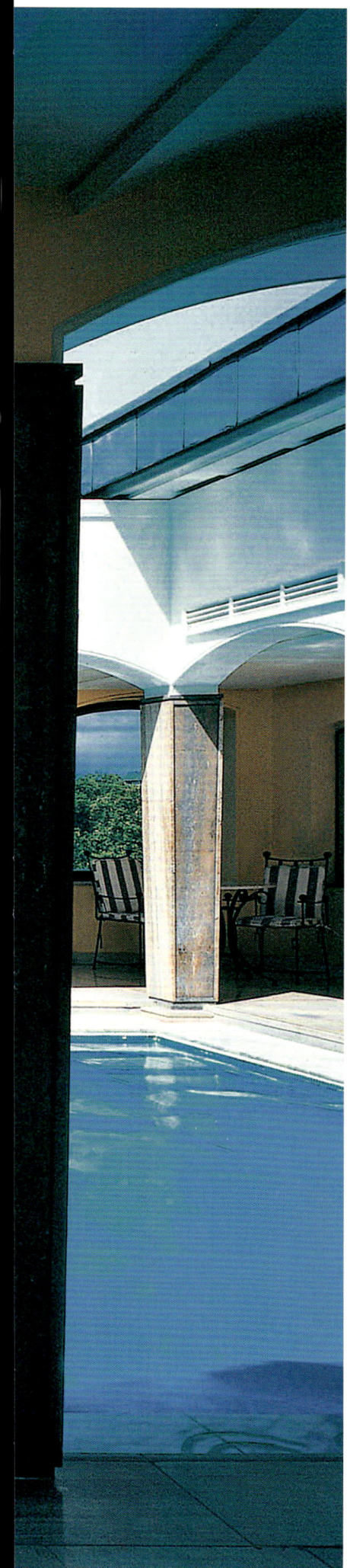

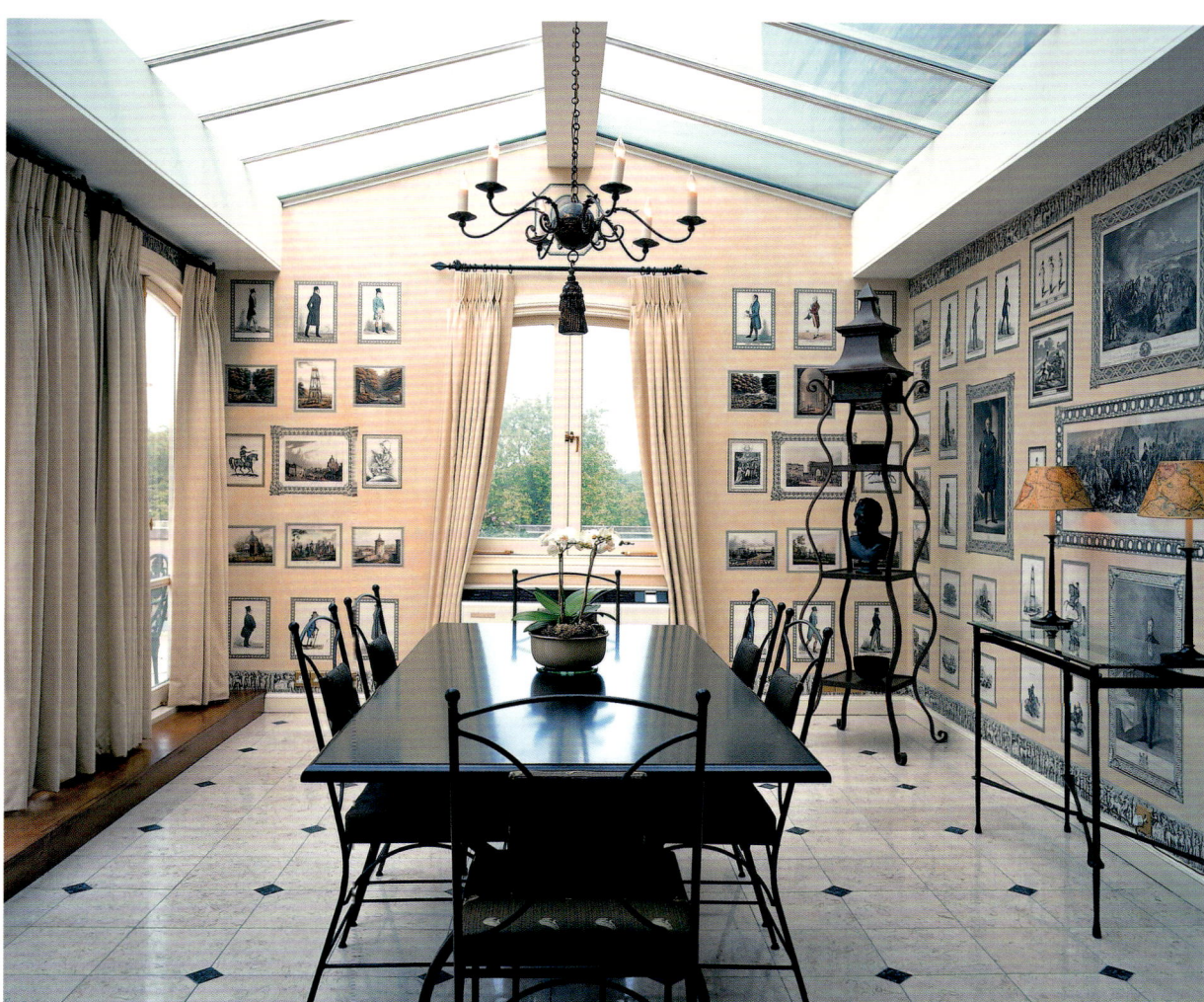

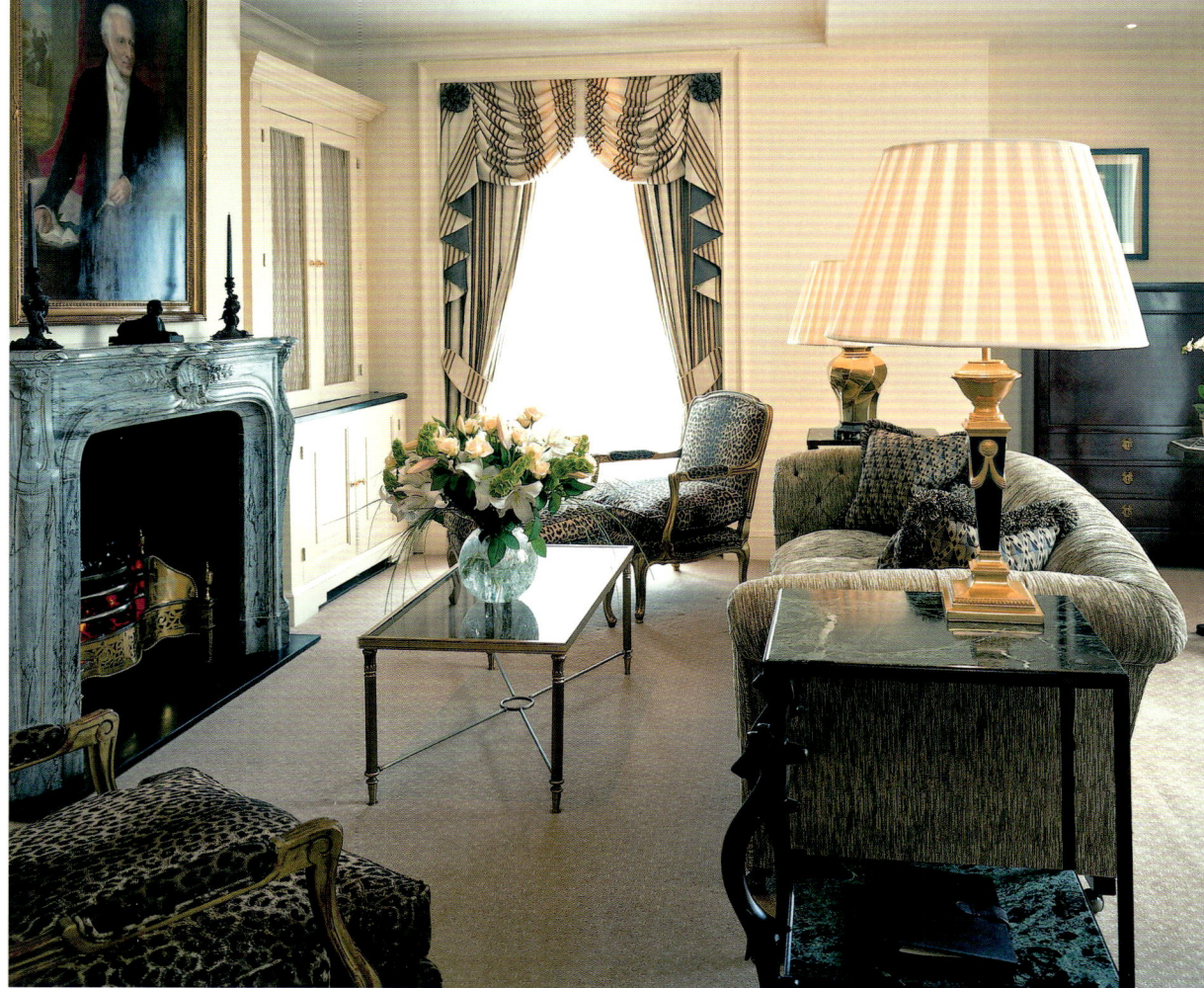

London SW1W 9QD
United Kingdom
Phone: +44 20 7259 8570
Fax: +44 20 7259 8591
www.bb-belgravia.com

Rooms: 17 rooms including 2 family rooms
Facilities: Guest lounge, breakfast room, private garden
Services: Concierge guest service
Located: In the residential neighborhood of Belgravia
Public transportation: 10 min walk from Victoria train, underground, coach station and Gatwick Express
Style: Cool and contemporary

You cannot live more nobly in London than in Belgravia. The large embassies reside here and Russian oligarchs are driving the real estate prices sky-high. Here of all places in these somewhat snobby surroundings, a group of British hotel owners decided to open a B&B that puts a new twist on the idea of a room with breakfast. The interior is stylish; the high-tech equipment includes flat screen TVs and free internet access. And, of course, the breakfast is included at a price that is moderate for London.

Nobler als in Belgravia kann man in London nicht wohnen. Die großen Botschaften residieren hier, russische Oligarchen treiben die Immobilienpreise in schwindeler-regende Höhen. Ausgerechnet in dieser leicht snobistischen Umgebung hat eine Gruppe britischer Hoteliers ein Bed and Breakfast eröffnet, das der Idee vom Zimmer mit Frühstück einen neuen Dreh gibt. Das Interieur ist stylisch, das technische Equipment mit Flatscreens und freiem Internetzugang auf dem neuesten Stand. Und selbstverständlich ist das Frühstück im für Londoner Verhältnisse moderaten Preis inbegriffen.

Nulle part ailleurs à Londres, on ne peut vivre aussi noblement qu'au Belgravia. Les grandes ambassades sont dans le quartier, les oligarques russes font monter les prix de l'immobilier à des hauteurs vertigineuses, et c'est ici, dans cet environnement quelque peu snob, qu'un groupe d'hôteliers a ouvert un « Bed and Break-fast », qui donne au concept de chambre et de petit-déjeuner une toute nouvelle signification. L'intérieur est élégant, l'équipement technique avec écrans plats et accès internet gratuit est conforme aux standards les plus récents. Et bien sûr le petit-déjeuner est inclus, à un prix modéré pour Londres.

En Londres no hay otro lugar donde se viva de manera más elegante que en la zona de Belgravia. Las grandes embajadas se encuentran aquí y los oligarcas rusos hacen subir los precios de los inmuebles hasta niveles de vértigo. Ha sido precisamente en esta zona de ambiente esnob, donde un grupo de hoteleros ha abierto un bed and breakfast que da una nueva vuelta de tuerca a la idea convencional de cama y desayuno. El interior se viste con las nuevas tendencias, el equipamiento técnico, con pantallas planas y conexión a Internet, está a la última. Por supuesto, el desayuno está incluido. Bastante asequible para los precios de Londres.

A Londra è impossibile trovare un quartiere più raffinato di quello di Belgravia; qui risiedono i grandi ambasciatori, e qui gli oligarchi russi spingono ad altezze ver-tiginose i prezzi immobiliari. È proprio in questo contesto leggermente snob che un gruppo di albergatori britannici ha deciso di aprire un bed & breakfast capace di dare una svolta all'idea tradizionale della camera con colazione. Gli interni sono di gran classe, gli accessori tecnologici di ultima generazione (televisori a schermo piatto e accesso libero a Internet). Naturalmente, la colazione è compresa nel prezzo, che è modesto, se rapportato alla zona di Londra in cui ci troviamo.

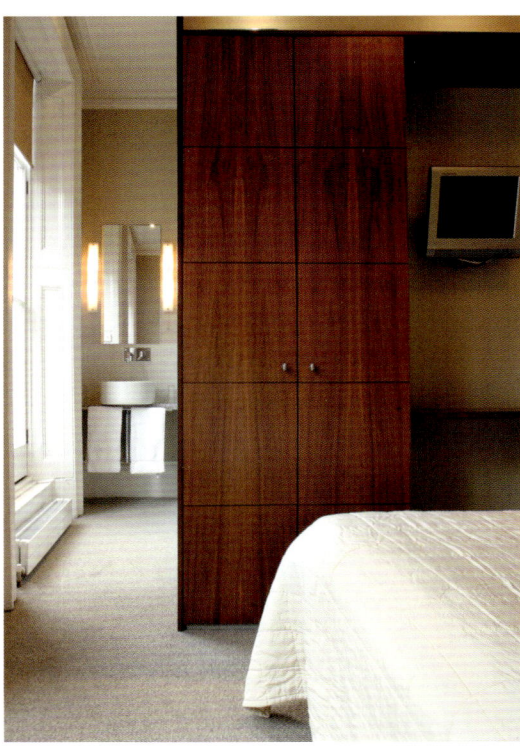
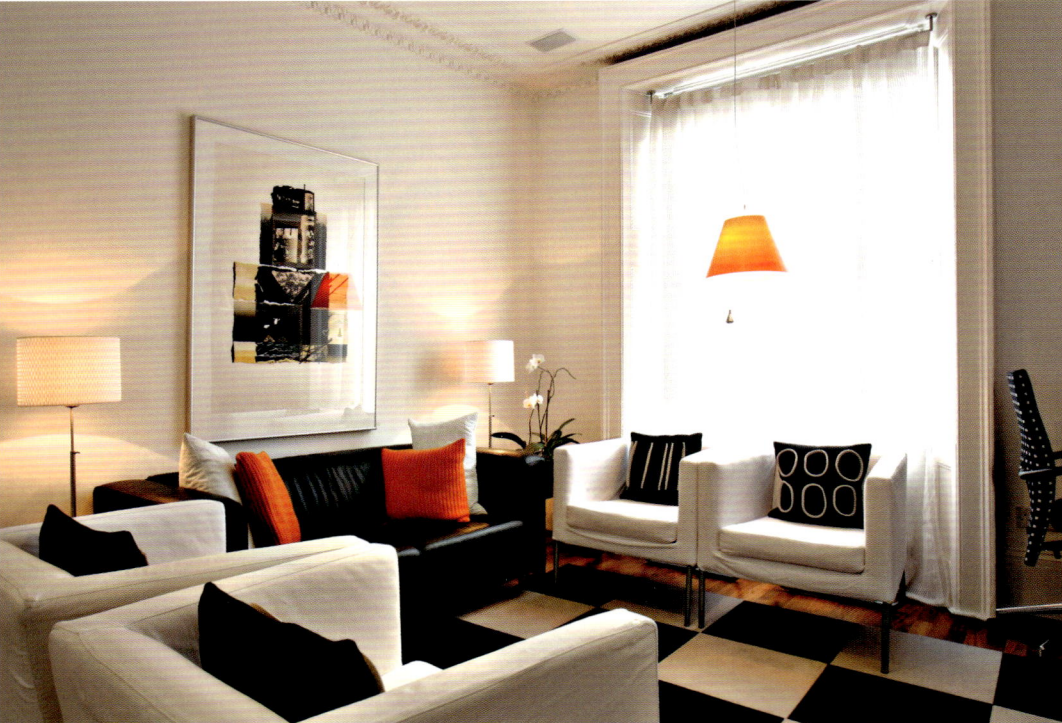

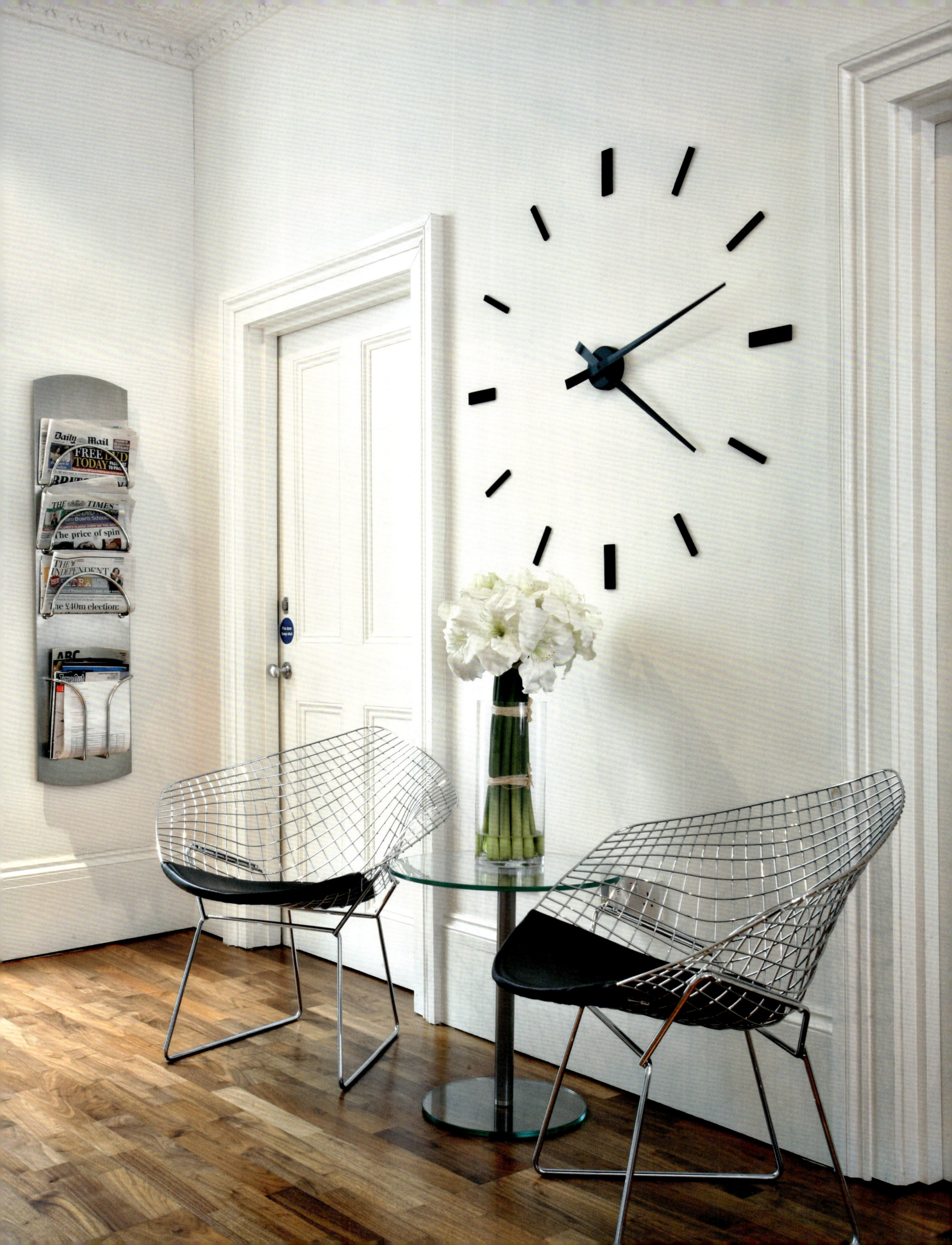

London SW3PF
United Kingdom
Phone: +44 20 7370 6701
Fax: +44 20 7373 0442
www.anouskahempeldesign.com

Rooms: 50 rooms and suites
Facilities: Restaurant, health club, conference rooms
Services: 24 h room service, concierge service, babysitting, laundry, car rental
Located: In South Kensington and Chelsea area
Public transportation: Underground South Kensington, Gloucester Road
Style: Sophisticated and contemporary

Checking in here is not the end of your journey, it is just the beginning of a grand sojourn: the luggage and colonial furnishings in the lobby point the way to Provence or Venice, to Napoleon's era, the Empire of the Chinese Dragon or the Arms of James Bond—suite 007 has been dedicated by designer Anouska Hempel to her own career as Bond girl (*In Her Majesty's Secret Service*). Good to note: Stars appreciate the boutique hotel for their unlimited No Paparazzi Policy as well as for extras like oxygen in the minibar.

Wer hier eincheckt, ist nicht am Ende seiner Reise, sondern am Anfang: Die Koffer und Kolonialmöbel in der Lobby weisen den Weg in die Provence oder nach Venedig, in die Ära Napoleons, ins Reich des chinesischen Drachens oder in die Arme von James Bond – die Suite 007 hat Designerin Anouska Hempel ihrer eigenen Karriere als Bondgirl gewidmet (*Im Geheimdienst Ihrer Majestät*). Ein gutes Stichwort: Stars schätzen das Boutiquehotel für seine uneingeschränkte No-Paparazzi-Politik ebenso wie für Extras wie Sauerstoff in der Minibar.

S'enregistrer ici, ce n'est pas la fin du voyage, mais le début d'un grand séjour : les valises et les meubles coloniaux dans le hall montrent le chemin vers la Provence ou Venise, l'ère napoléonienne, l'empire des dragons chinois ou les bras de James Bond. Anouska Hempel, l'architecte d'intérieur, s'est dédié la Suite 007 en mémoire de sa carrière en tant que James Bond girl dans le film *Au service secret de Sa Majesté*. Point essentiel, les stars apprécient cet hôtel-boutique pour sa politique anti-paparazzi absolue, ainsi que pour ses extras, comme l'oxygène dans le minibar.

Quien llegue a este hotel seguramente no se encuentra al final de su viaje, sino más bien al principio. Las maletas y los muebles de estilo colonial en el vestíbulo nos señalan el camino hacia la Provenza o Venecia, hacia la época de Napoleón, la del imperio del dragón chino o incluso hacía los brazos de James Bond. La diseñadora Anouska Hempel dedicó la suite 007 a su propia carrera como chica Bond (*Al servicio secreto de su majestad británica*). Este es un hotel boutique que los famosos valoran tanto por su política de "cero paparazzis", como por sus "extras" –empezando por el oxígeno en el minibar.

Entrare in questo albergo non segna la fine del proprio viaggio, ma appena l'inizio: i bauli e i mobili coloniali della lobby conducono gli ospiti nella Provenza o a Venezia, all'epoca di Napoleone, nel regno del drago cinese o tra le braccia di James Bond – la suite 007 è stata dedicata dalla designer Anouska Hempel alla propria carriera in qualità di Bond girl in *Al servizio di Sua Maestà*. Un altro punto a favore del Blakes: le star apprezzano questo boutique hotel per la sua incondizionata politica anti-paparazzi – e per gli extra come l'ossigeno nel minibar.

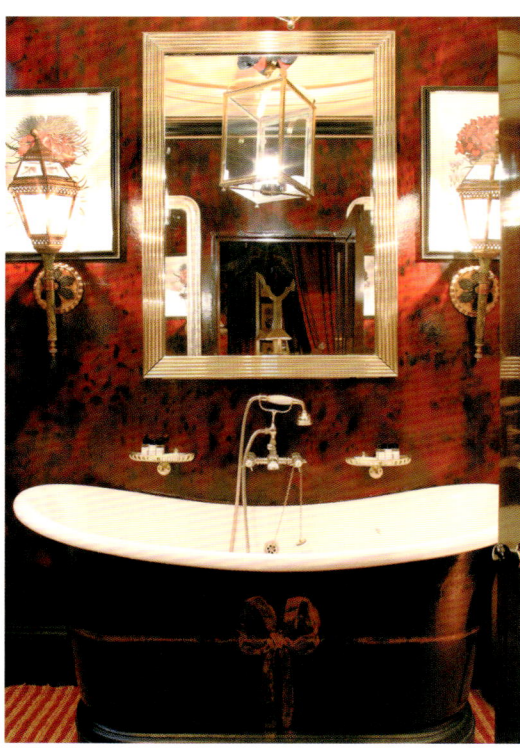
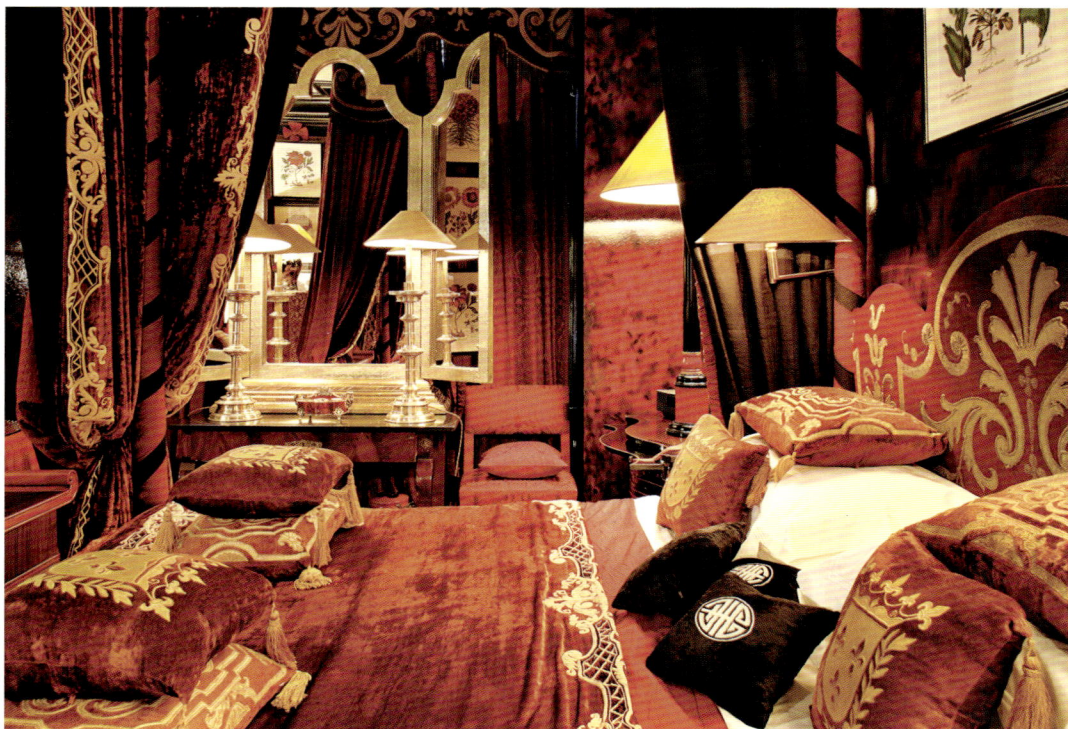

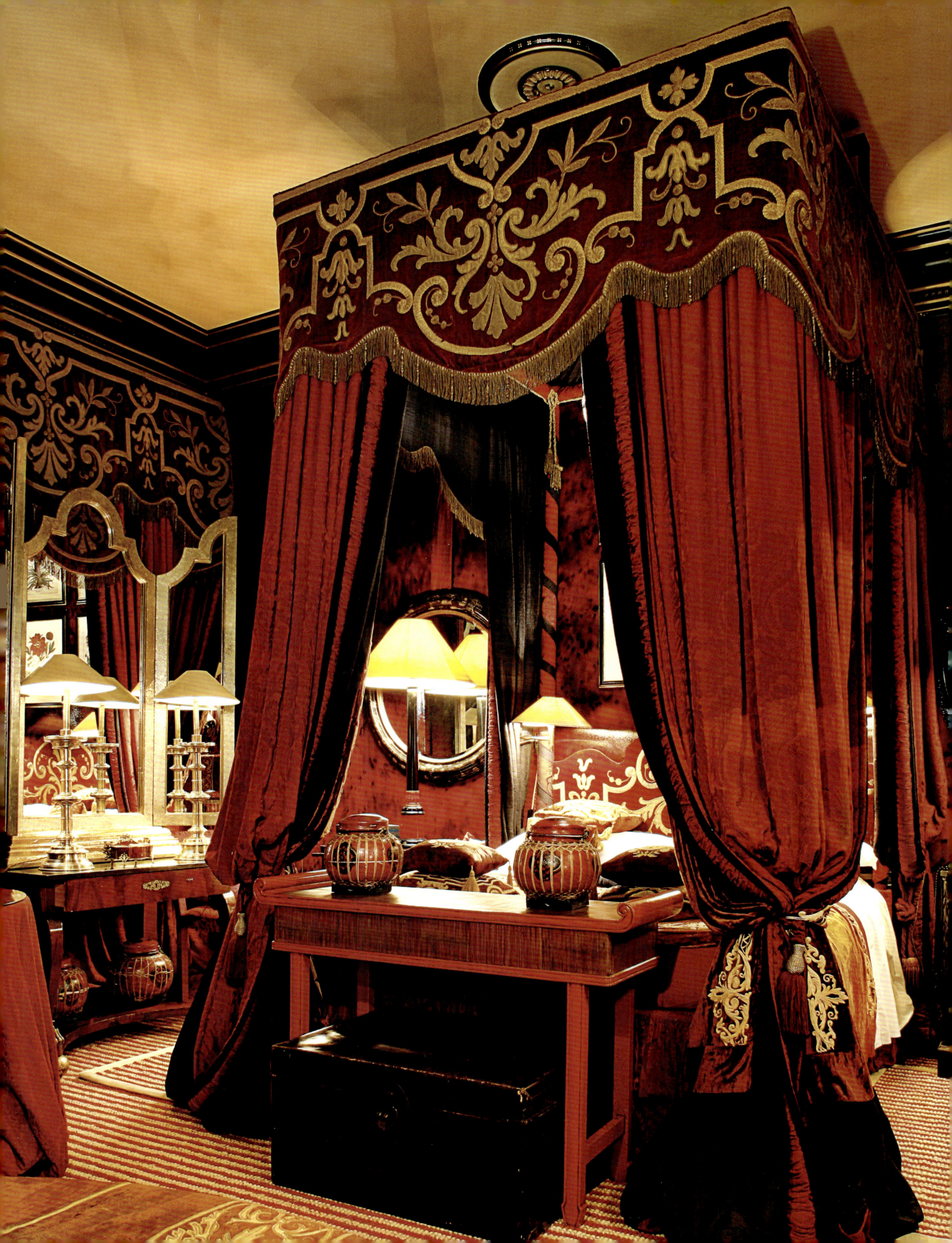

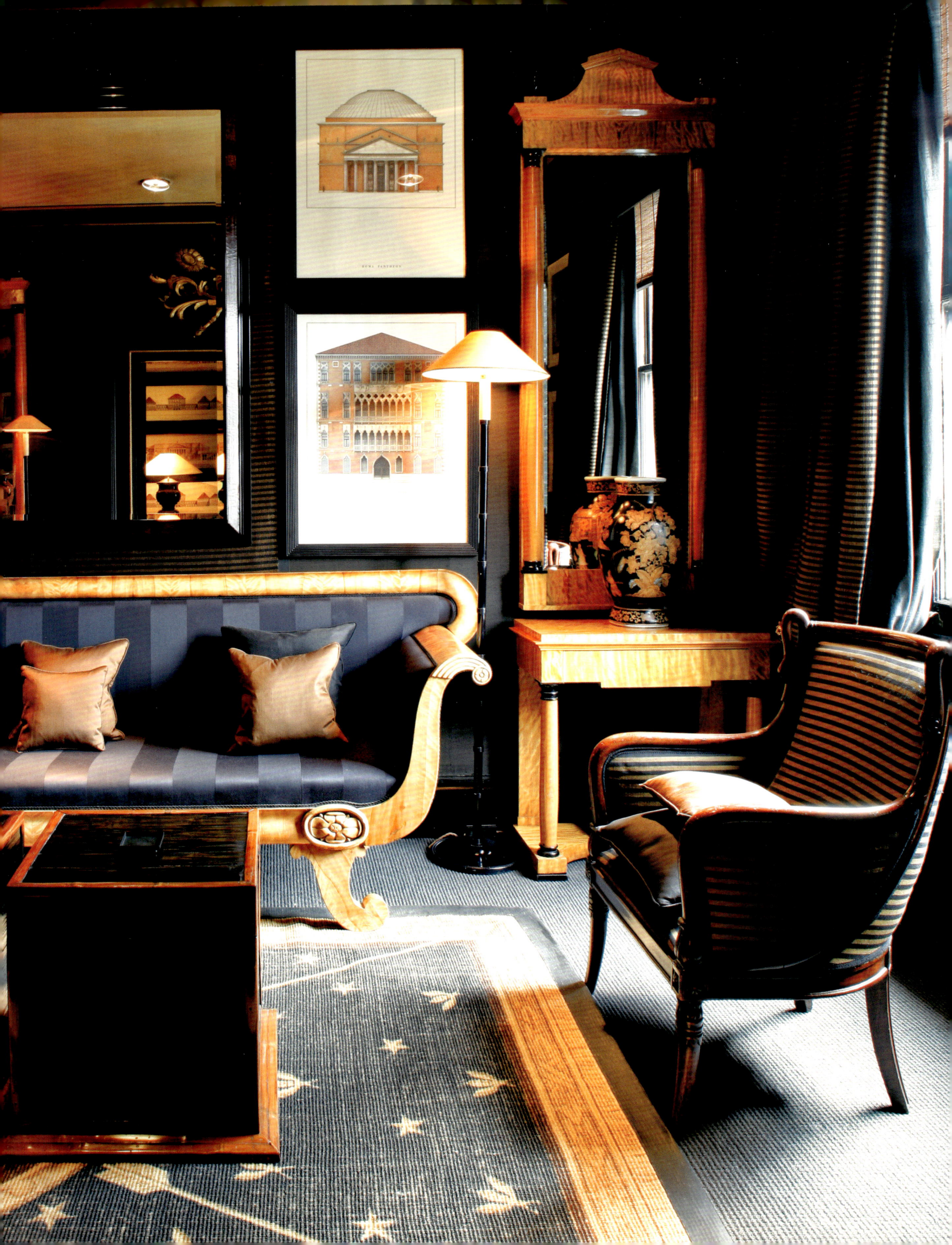

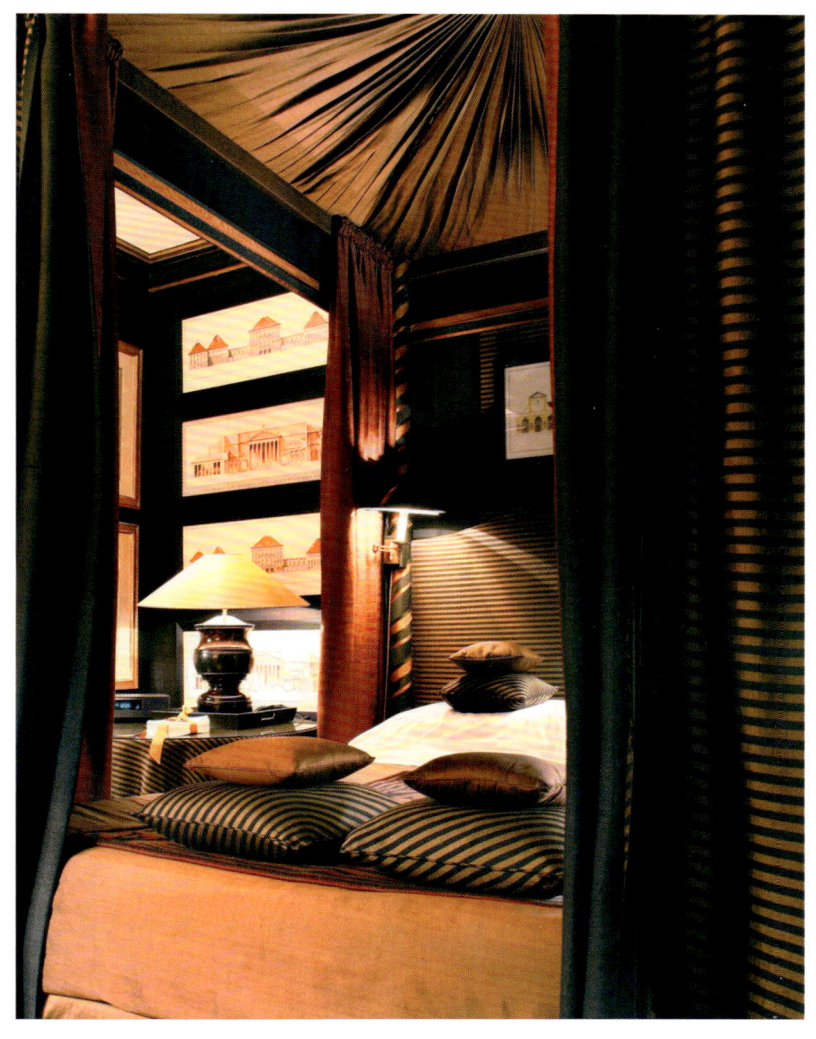
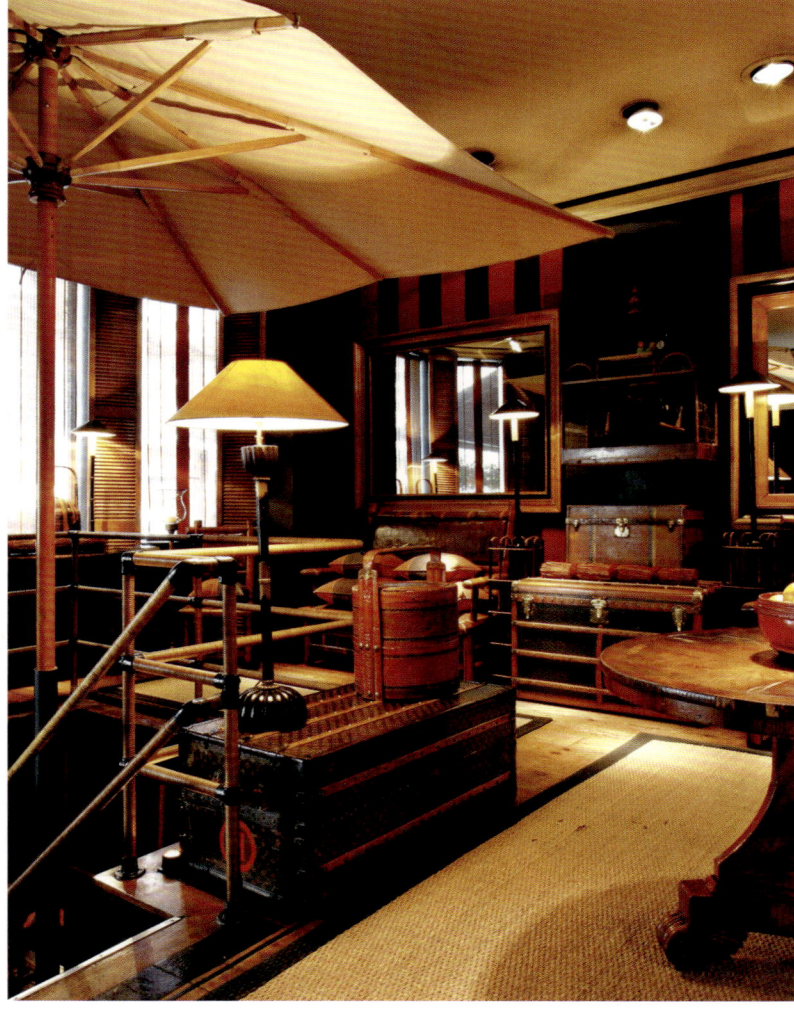
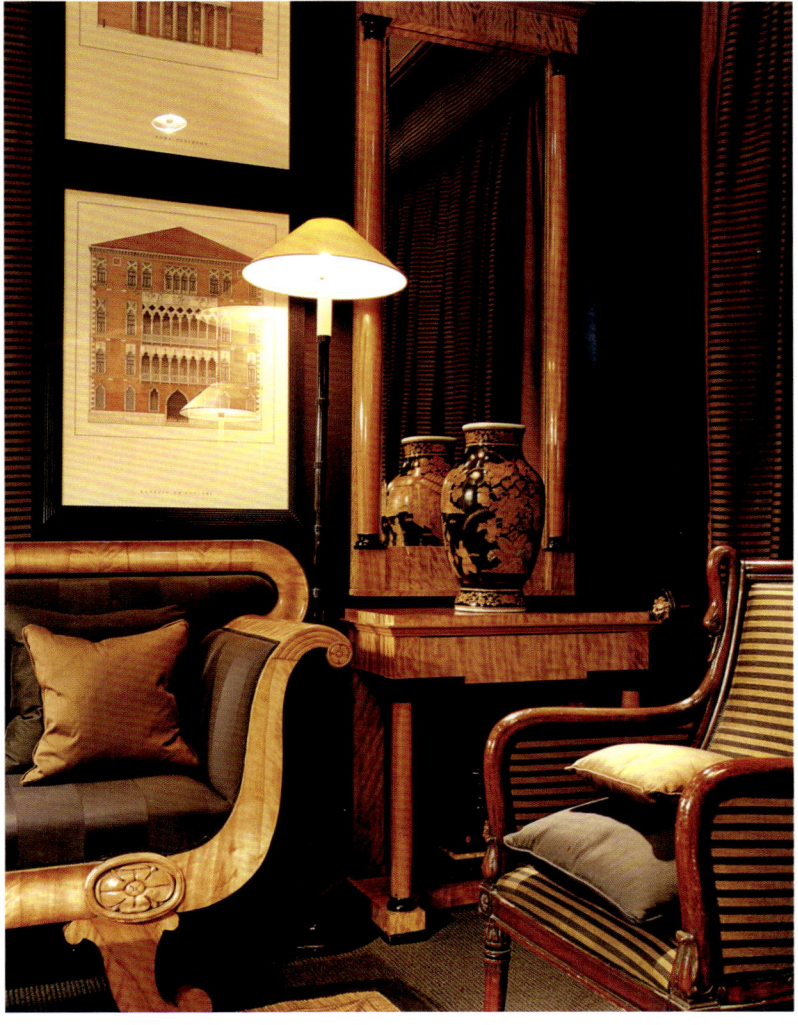
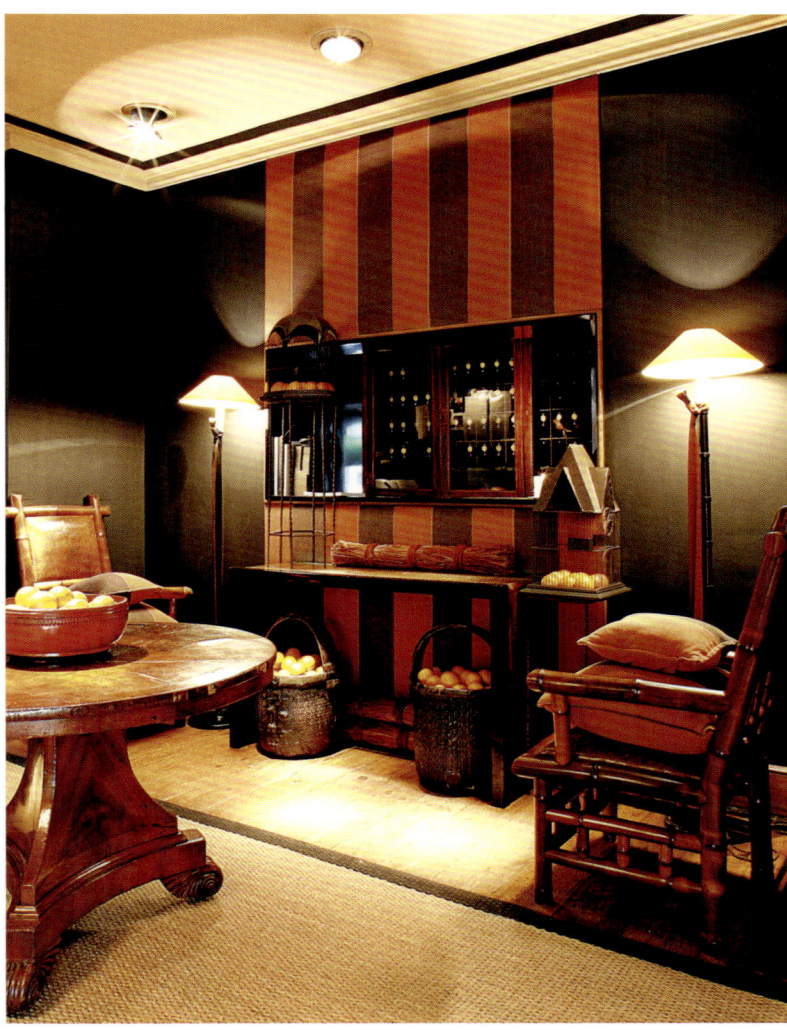

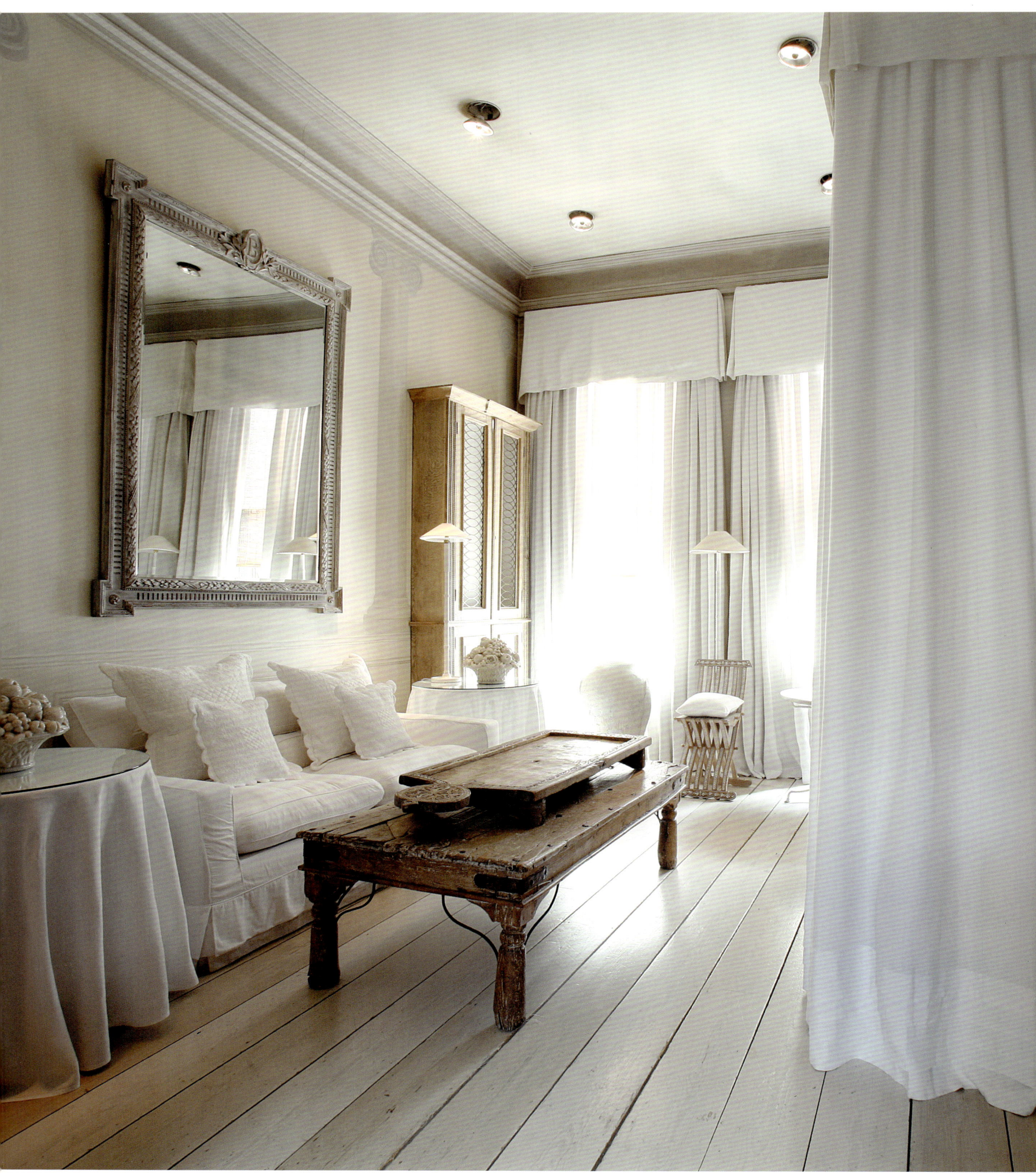

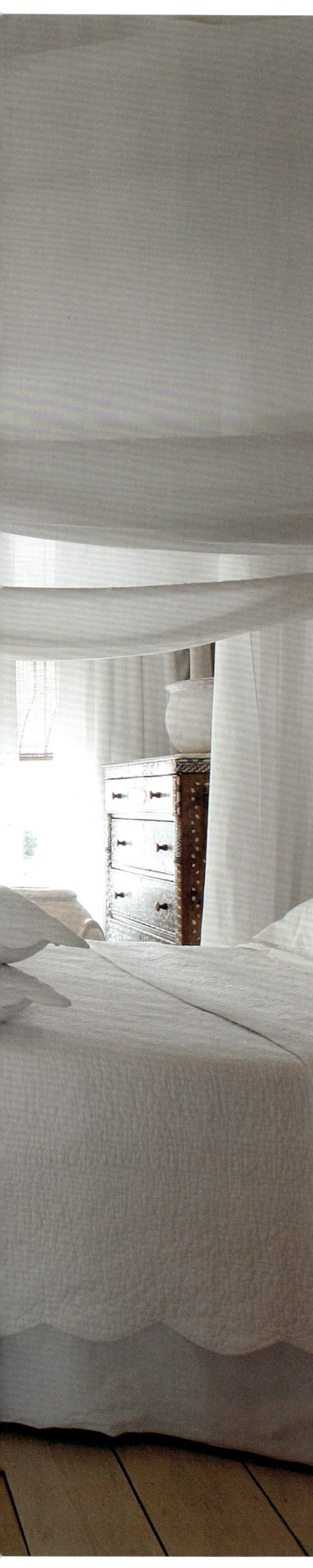

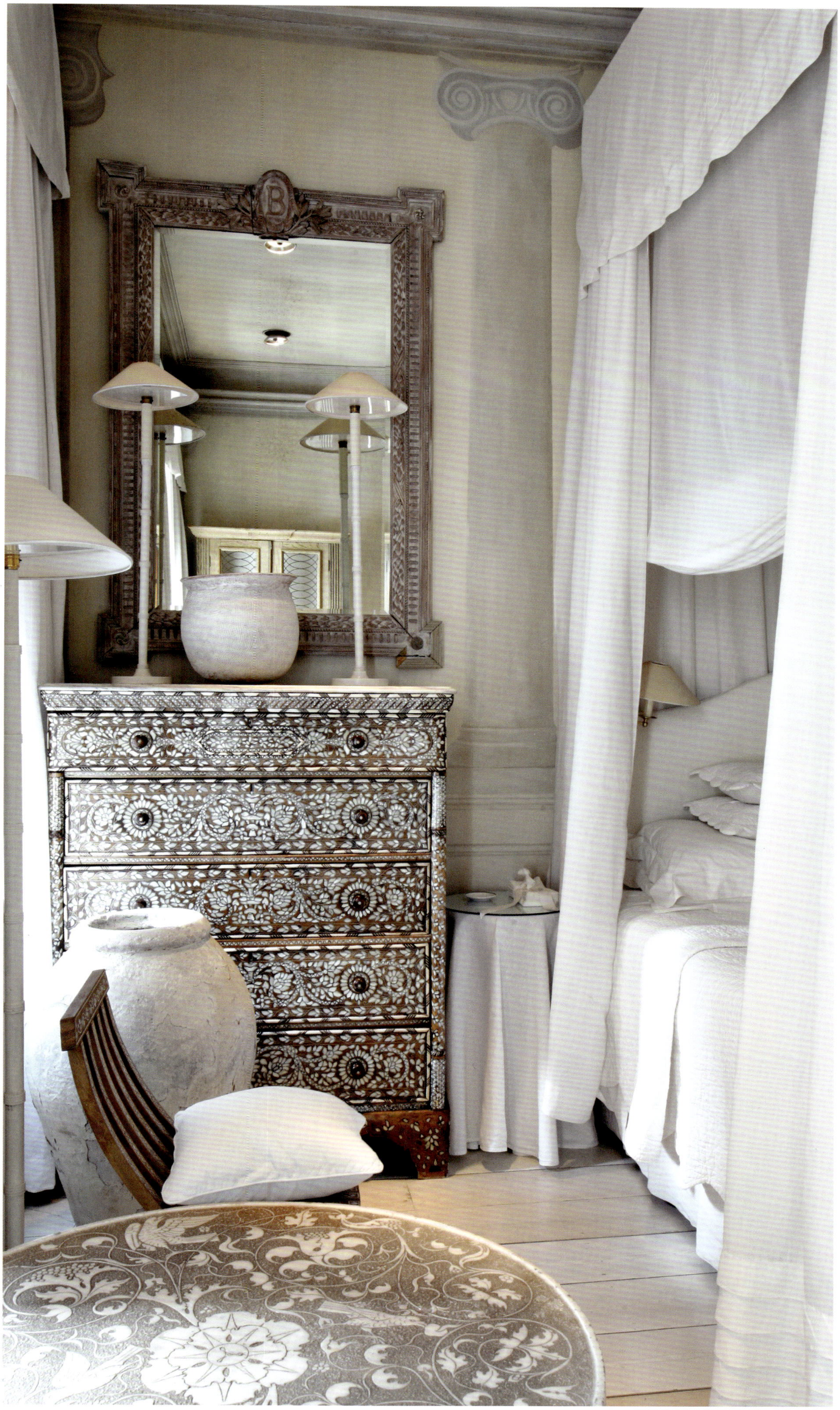

Claridge's

London, United Kingdom

Brook Street, Mayfair
London W1K 4HR
United Kingdom
Phone: +44 20 7629 8860
Fax: +44 20 7499 2210
www.claridges.co.uk

Price category: €€€€
Rooms: 203 rooms
Facilities: Claridge's Bar, The Fumoir, Gordon Ramsay at Claridge's, The Foyer and The Reading Room Restaurant, Claridge's Beauty and Fitness
Services: 24 h room service, concierge, babysitting upon request
Located: In the heart of Mayfair
Public transportation: Underground Bond Street, Green Park and Oxford Circus
Style: Traditional

The guest book at Claridge's reads like a Who's Who of nobility and politics: Here is where Queen Victoria met Empress Eugénie in 1860. Here is where Churchill declared a suite to be Yugoslavian territory during the World War II in order to support King Peter of Yugoslavia in exile. Here the Queen has been received for numerous banquets. Each of the 203 rooms draws a line between history and the present—the new ones and 970 square-foot Linley Suites are the best art deco revival that London has to offer.

Das Gästebuch des Claridge's liest sich ein Who is Who des Adels und der Politik: Hier trafen sich 1860 Königin Victoria und Kaiserin Eugénie, hier erklärte Churchill während des Zweiten Weltkriegs eine Suite zum jugoslawischen Staatsgebiet, um König Peter von Jugoslawien im Exil zu unterstützen, und hier wurde die Queen bereits zu diversen Banketten empfangen. Jedes der 203 Zimmer zieht eine Linie zwischen Geschichte und Gegenwart – die neuen und 90 Quadratmeter großen Linley Suiten sind das beste Art-déco-Revival, das London zu bieten hat.

Le registre des clients du Claridge se lit comme le Who's Who de la noblesse et de la politique : en 1860 la Reine Victoria et l'Impératrice Eugénie s'y sont rencontrées, c'est ici, pendant la Seconde Guerre Mondiale, que Churchill a déclaré une suite territoire yougoslave afin de soutenir le roi exilé Pierre de Yougoslavie, et la Reine y a assisté à de nombreux banquets. Chacune des 203 chambres relie l'histoire au présent : les nouvelles suites Linley de 90 mètres carré offrent le meilleur du revival art déco londonien.

El libro de visitas del Claridge's se presenta como un quién es quién del mundo de la aristocracia y la política. Fue aquí donde, en 1860, se reunieron la reina Victoria y la emperatriz Eugenia, donde Churchill, durante la segunda Guerra Mundial, declaró una suite territorio yugoslavo para respaldar al exiliado rey Pedro de Yugoslavia y donde se ha recibido ya, en varios banquetes, a su majestad la reina de Inglaterra. Cada una de las 203 habitaciones establece un nexo entre la historia y el presente, y las suites Linley de 90 metros cuadrados son la mejor evocación del estilo art-déco que Londres pueda ofrecer.

Il registro degli ospiti del Claridge's sembra un'enciclopedia dedicata ai personaggi più famosi dell'aristocrazia e della politica. Qui nel 1860 s'incontrarono la regina Vittoria e l'imperatrice Eugénie, qui durante la seconda guerra mondiale Churchill dichiarò una suite territorio yugoslavo per offrire sostegno a re Pietro di Yugoslavia in esilio, e sempre qui la regina d'Inghilterra ha già partecipato a diverse cerimonie. Ciascuna delle 203 stanze dell'albergo traccia un confine tra storia e presente – le nuove suite Linley, con i loro 90 metri quadrati, sono il più bel revival dell'art déco che possa offrire Londra.

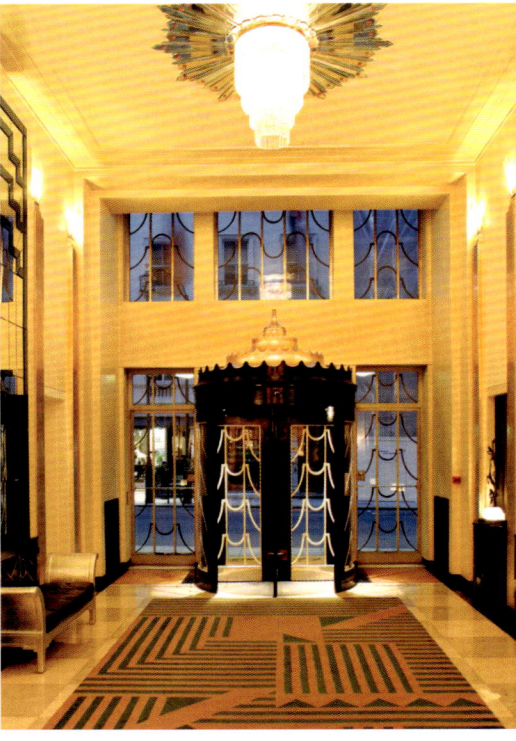
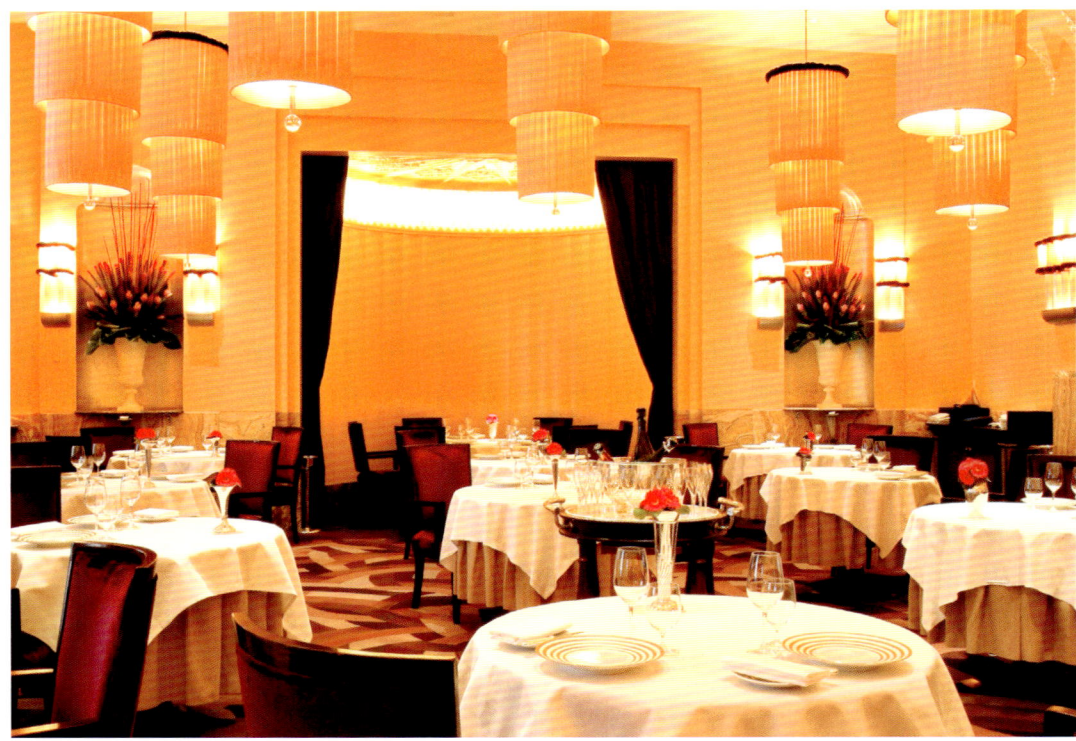

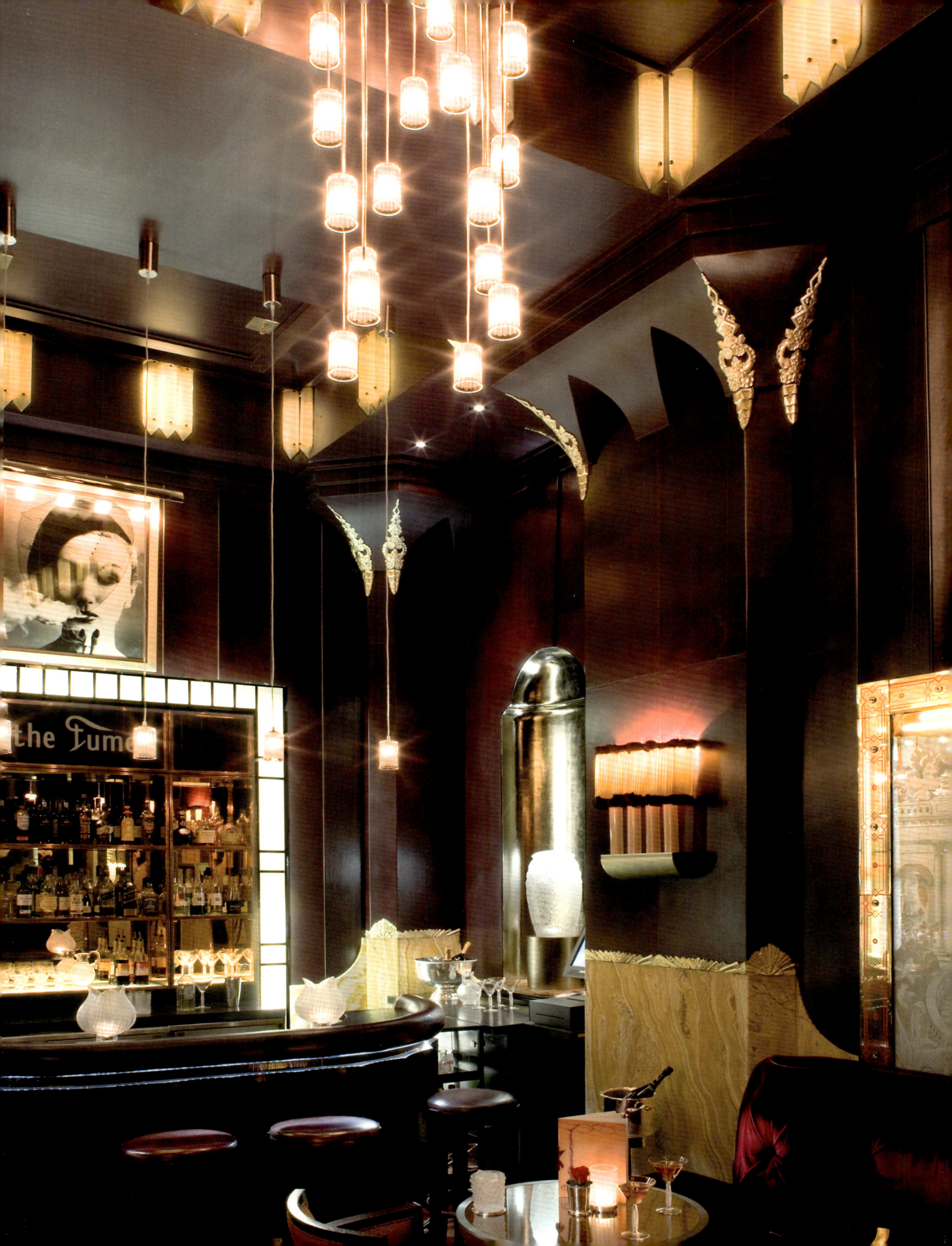

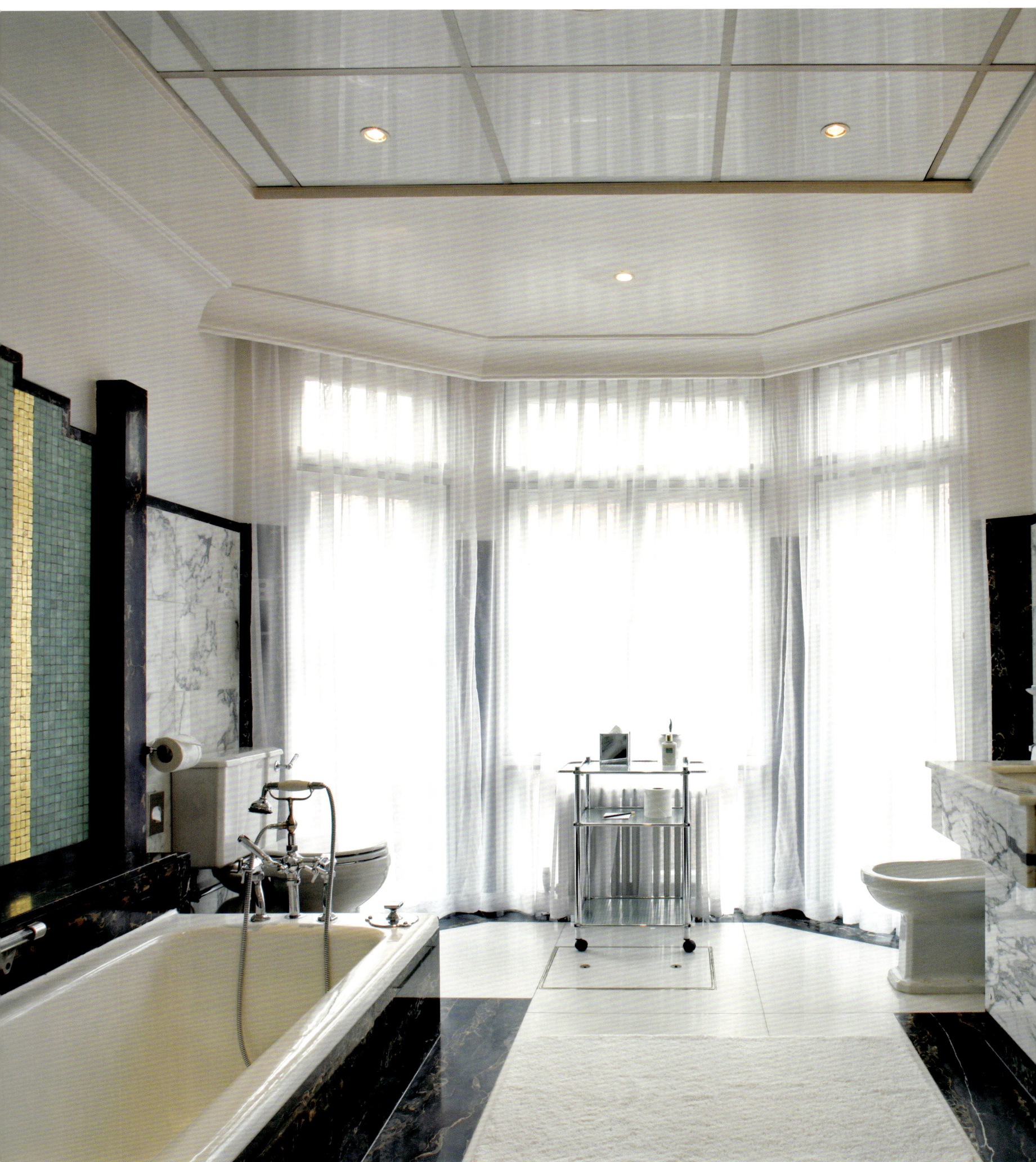

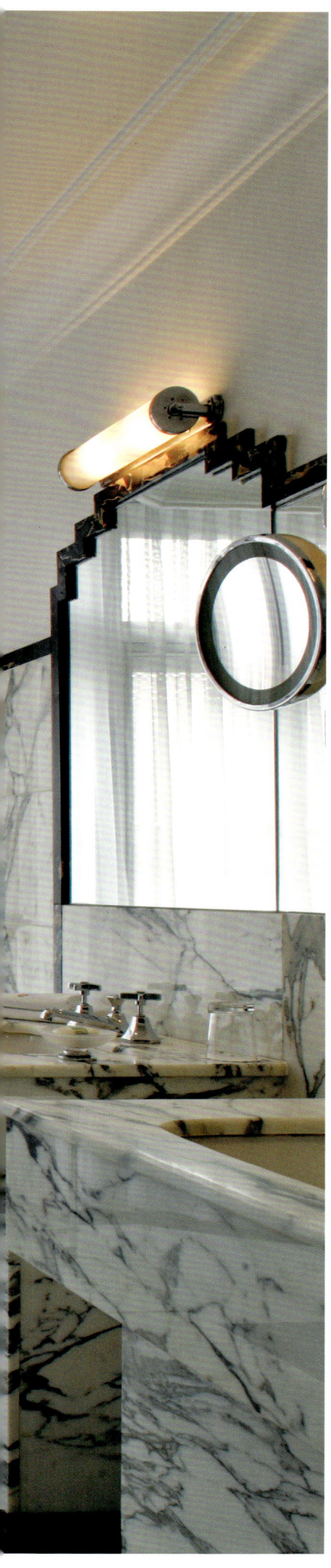

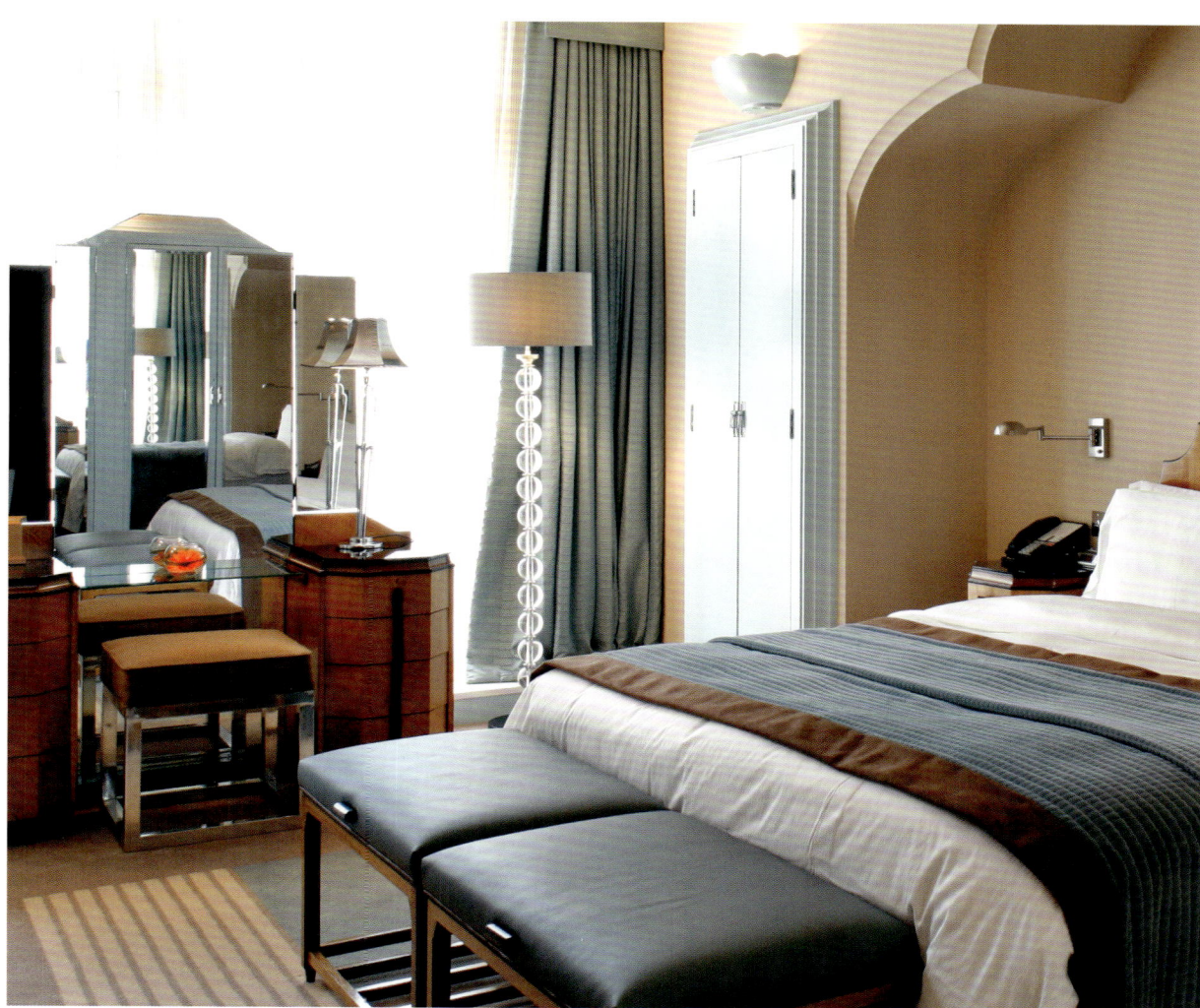

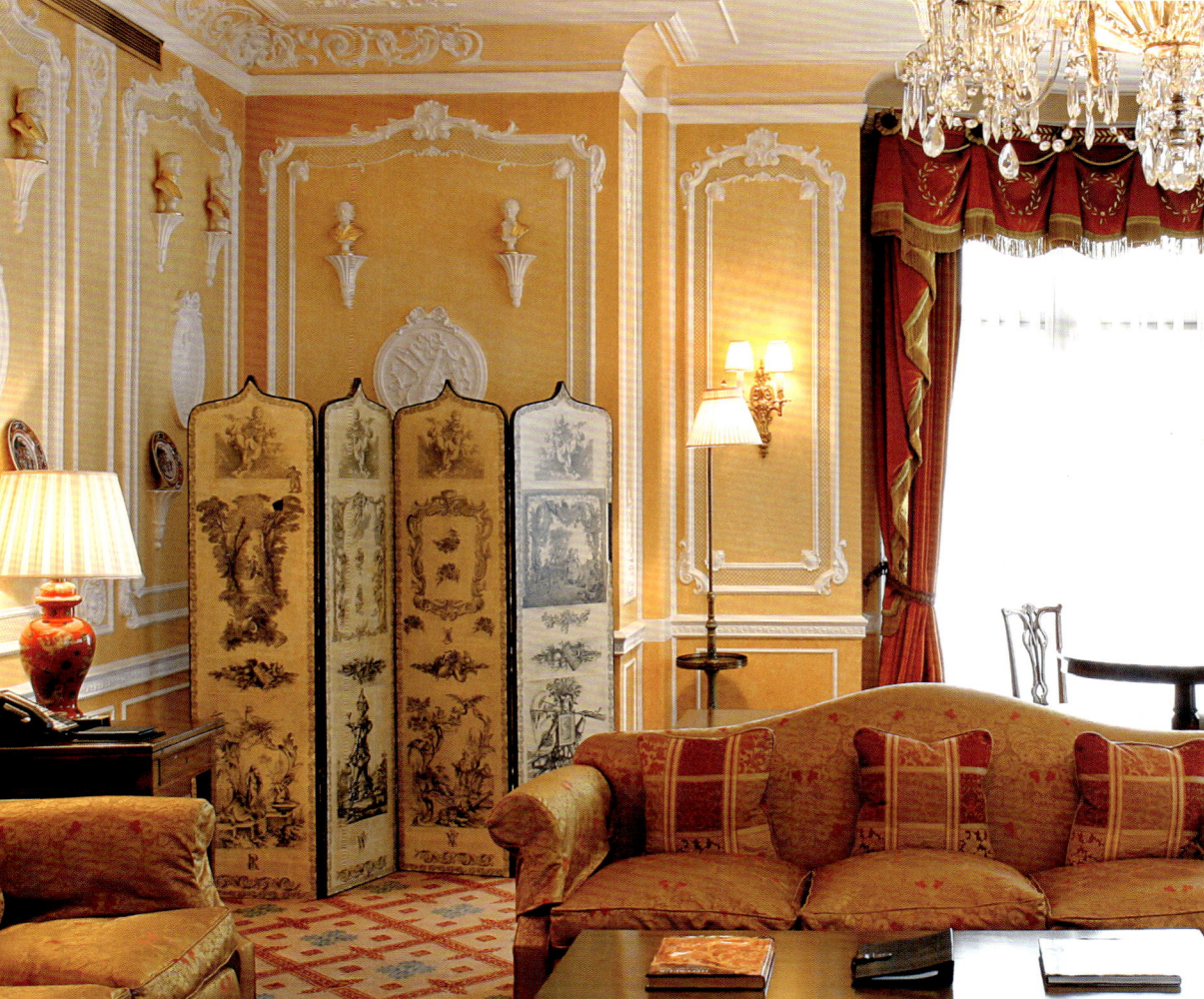

Haymarket Hotel

London, United Kingdom

1 Suffolk Place
London SW1Y 4BP
United Kingdom
Phone: +44 20 7470 4000
Fax: +44 20 7470 4004
www.firmdale.com

Price category: €€€
Rooms: 50 rooms and suites
Facilities: Brumus Bar & Restaurant, exclusive 2–5 bedroom townhouse, conservatory, library, 18-m indoor swimming pool, several private event spaces
Services: Concierge
Located: In the heart of London's theater district
Public transportation: Underground Piccadilly Circus
Style: Interiors by Kit Kemp

In the heart of London's theater district and direct neighbor of the famous Theatre Royal Haymarket, this hotel offers the finest English luxury that even evokes an "Encore!" call from those other than stage friends. Its 50 spacious rooms and suites are individually furnished in contemporary English style with antiques and modern art. The dramatically lighted large pool area with bar can be rented for private parties, as can the exclusive "Shooting Gallery." In the "Brumus Bar" they offer the finest seasonal cuisine with special emphasis on organic produce.

Im Herzen von Londons Theaterbezirk und in unmittelbarer Nachbarschaft des berühmten Theatre Royal Haymarket gelegen, bietet dieses Hotel feinsten englischen Luxus nicht nur für die Freunde der Bühne. Seine 50 großzügig geschnittenen Zimmer und Suiten sind individuell in zeitgenössischem Englischen Stil mit Antiquitäten und moderner Kunst ausgestattet. Ein dramatisch beleuchteter großer Poolbereich mit Bar kann für private Veranstaltungen gemietet werden, ebenso wie die exklusive „Shooting Gallery". In der „Brumus Bar" wird gehobene saisonale Küche geboten, die besonderen Wert auf Bioprodukte legt.

Au cœur du quartier des théâtres de Londres et tout près du célèbre Théâtre Royal de Haymarket, cet hôtel est l'incarnation du luxe anglais le plus fin, qui ne fait pas plaisir seulement aux amateurs de théâtre. Ses 50 chambres et suites spacieuses sont toutes meublées différemment dans un style anglais contemporain, combiné avec des antiquités et de l'art moderne. L'espace piscine à l'éclairage théâtral, avec bar, peut être loué pour des soirées privées, tout comme la splendide « Shooting Gallery ». Au « Brumus Bar », la meilleure cuisine saisonnière est servie, avec un accent mis sur les produits bios.

Ubicado en el corazón del barrio de Londres famoso por sus espectáculos, y justo al lado del Theatre Royal Haymarket, este hotel ofrece el más refinado lujo inglés; y no sólo para los amantes de los escenarios. Sus 50 espaciosas habitaciones y suites están decoradas individualmente con antigüedades y arte moderno, siguiendo el estilo inglés contemporáneo. La zona de la piscina, con su propio bar y una iluminación propia de un teatro, puede ser reservada para organizar eventos privados, como también la "Shooting Gallery", una exclusiva habitación ideal para cenas o reuniones íntimas. La carta del "Brumus Bar" ofrece exquisitos platos de temporada y otorga un papel especial a los ingredientes biológicos.

Situato nel cuore del quartiere dei teatri di Londra e nelle immediate vicinanze del famoso Theatre Royal Haymarket, quest'albergo offre agli amici del palcoscenico (ma non solo a loro) lusso inglese di prima classe. Le sue 50 camere e suite, di dimensioni piuttosto grandi e ognuna diversa dall'altra, sono arredate in stile inglese contemporaneo con oggetti d'antiquariato e opere d'arte moderna. La grande zona piscina, con bar e illuminazione da sogno, può essere affittata per eventi privati, come pure l'esclusiva "Shooting Gallery". Nel "Brumus Bar" vengono servite specialità di stagione preparate principalmente con prodotti biologici.

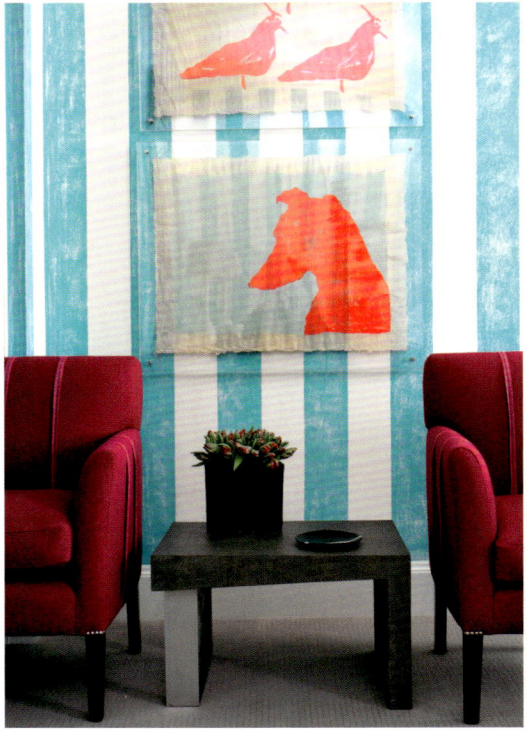
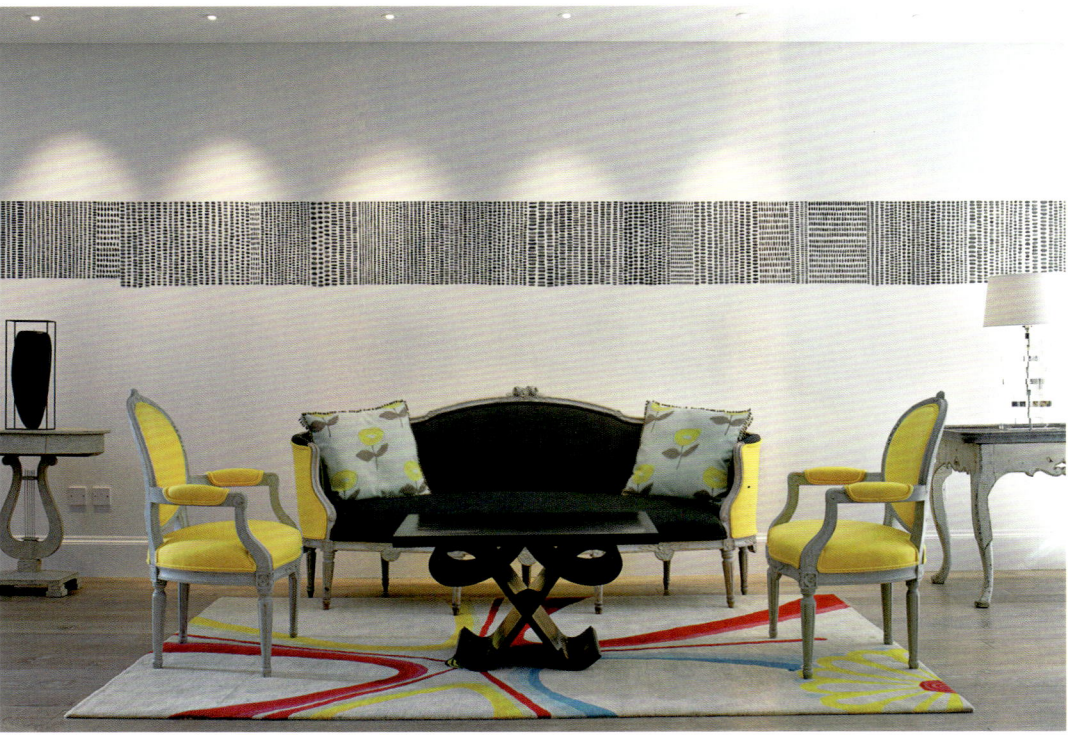

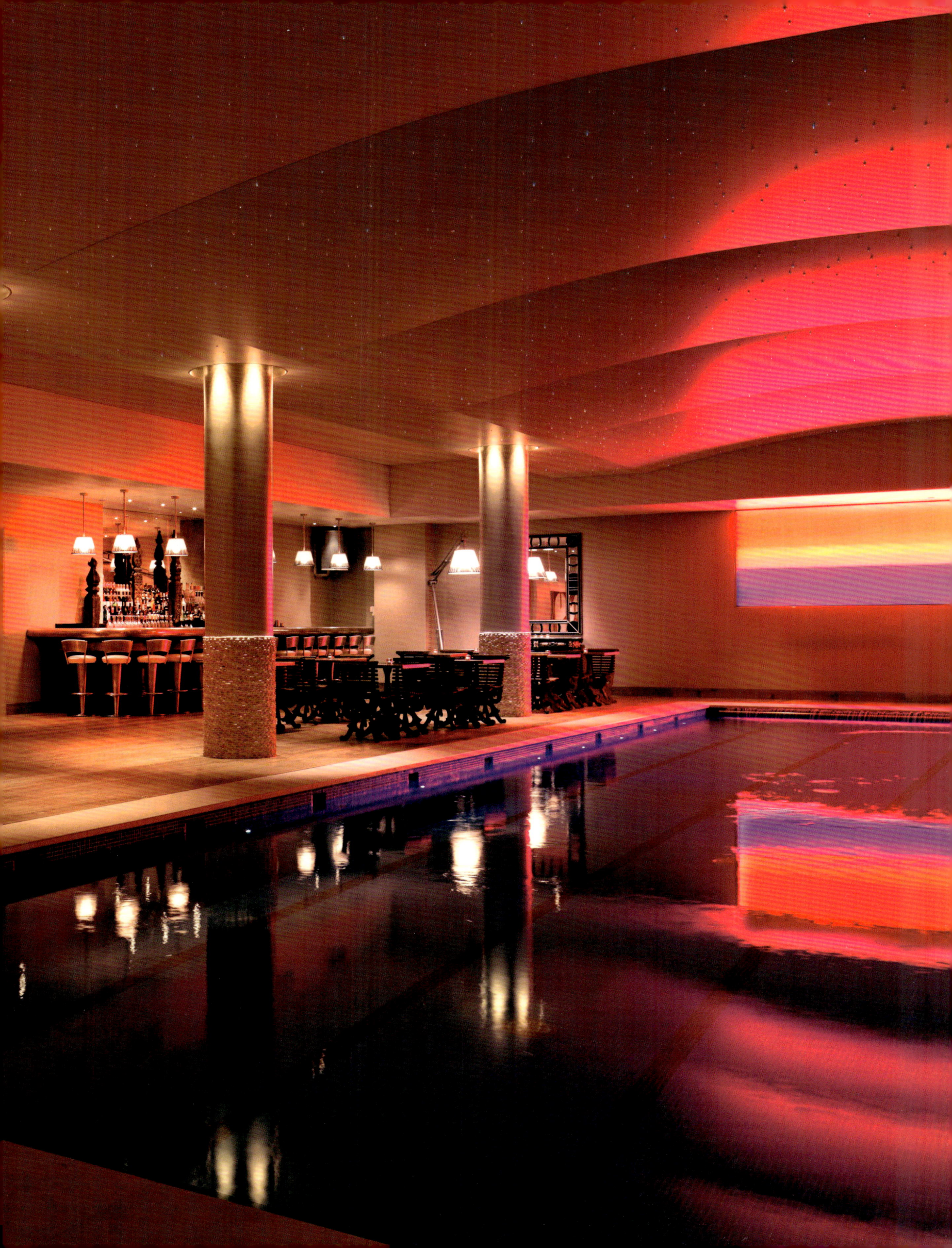

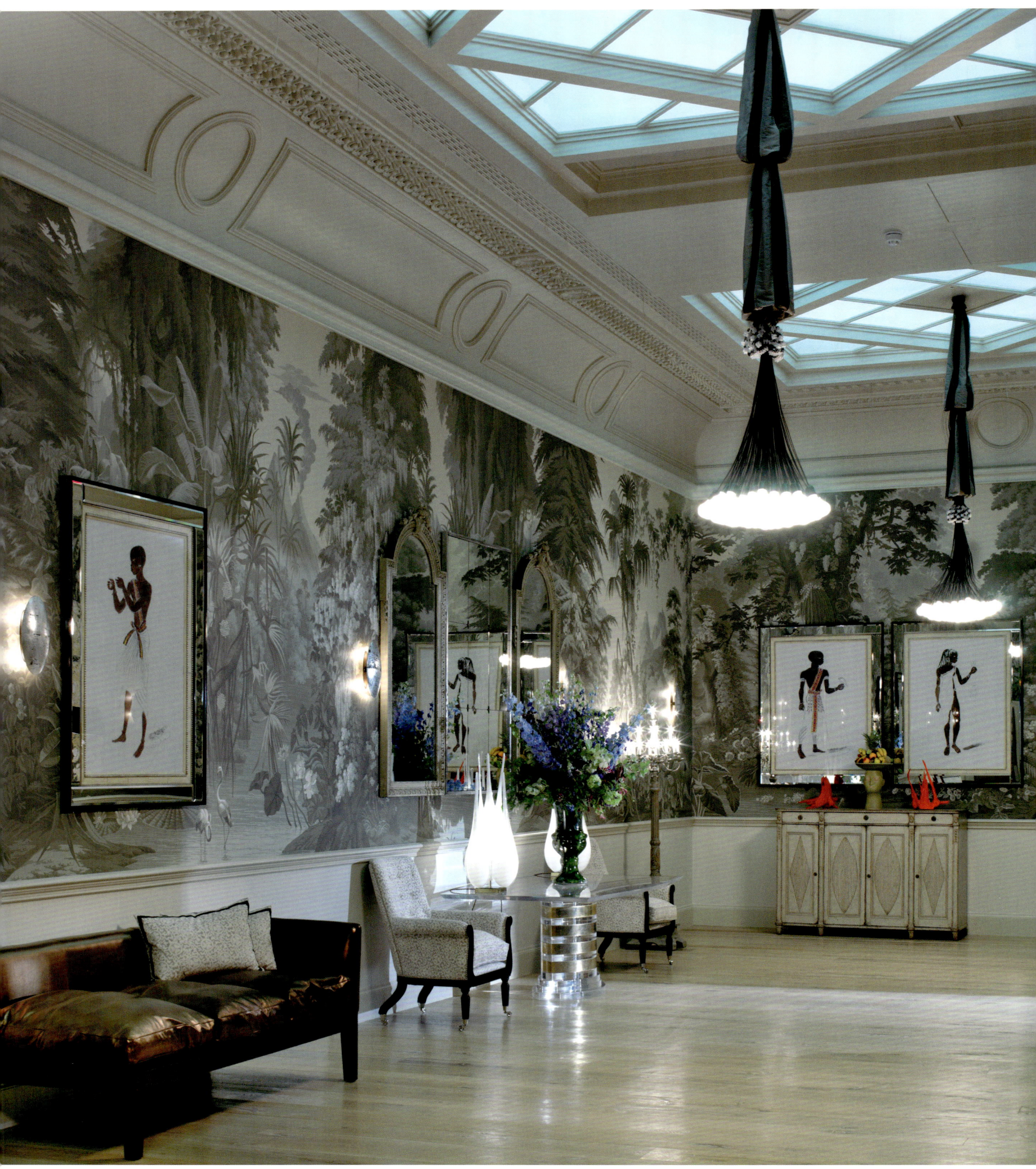

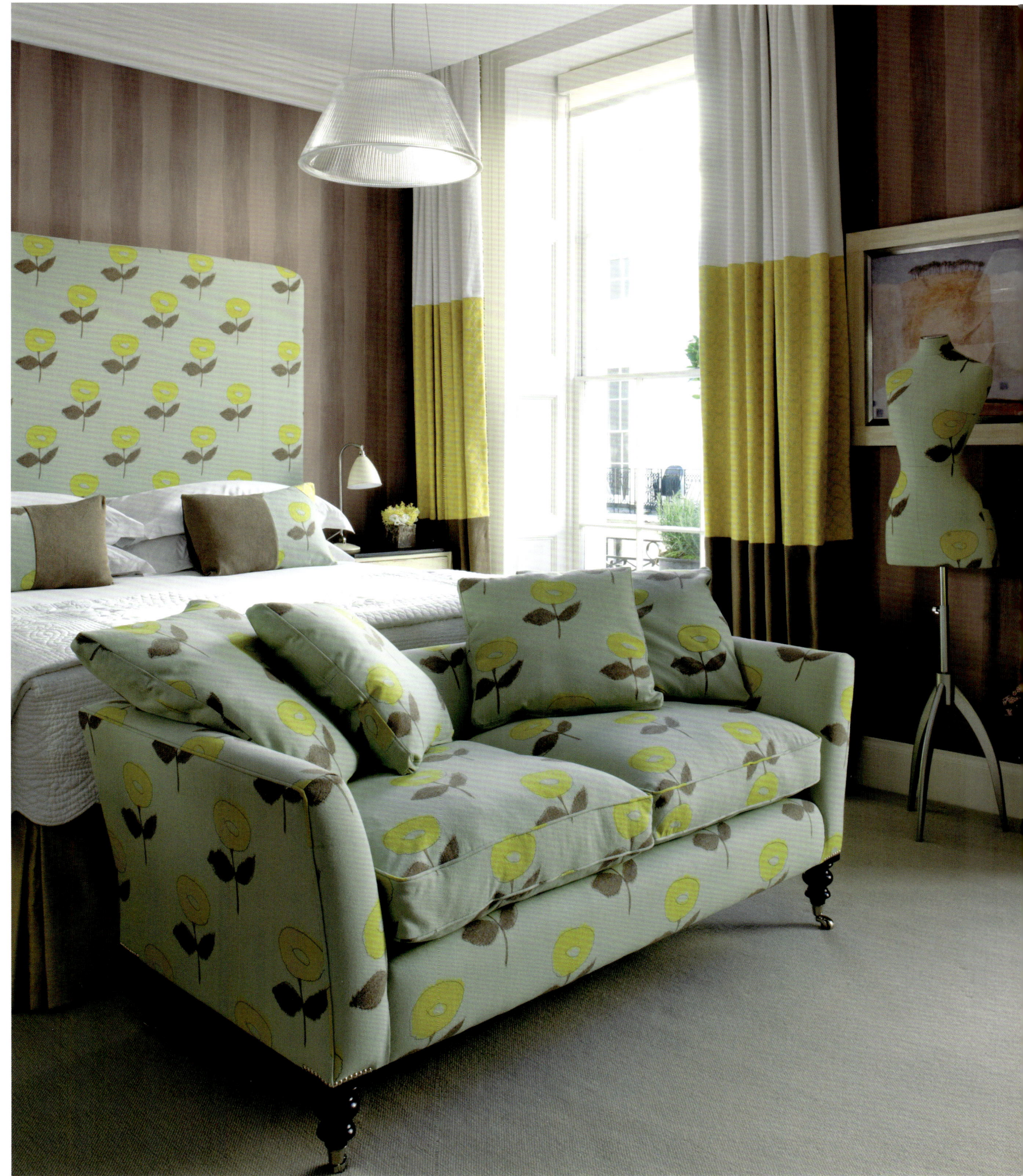

42 The Calls

Leeds, United Kingdom

42 The Calls
Leeds LS2 7EW
United Kingdom
Phone: +44 113 244 0099
Fax: +44 113 234 4100
www.42thecalls.co.uk

Price category: €€
Rooms: 41 rooms and suites
Facilities: Brasserie 44 (next door)
Services: 24 h room service, fishing rods in rooms overlooking the river, WiFi, private bar, Molton Brown toiletries, plasma TVs with satellite channels
Located: Overlooking the River Aire
Public transportation: A short walk from Leeds City Station
Style: Designed in a 18th-century corn mill

The Calls is a cobblestone street drawn along the River Aire and number 42 is an old mill that has been transformed into a hotel in 1991. The past still lives here: many of the 41 rooms have high windows and rough walls, or stretch out over the water. The Penthouse Suite is situated under a pointed roof with timbers. Besides the brasserie, the room service is also recommendable and very discrete—the dinners are served through a service hatch next to the bedroom door.

The Calls ist eine kopfsteingepflasterte Straße, die sich am Fluss Aire entlang zieht – und das Gebäude mit der Nummer 42 eine alte Mühle, die 1991 in ein Hotel verwandelt wurde. Hier ist die Vergangenheit noch immer lebendig: Viele der 41 Zimmer besitzen hohe Fenster und rohe Wände oder reichen übers Wasser hinaus; die Penthouse Suite liegt unter einem Spitzdach mit dicken Balken. Neben der Brasserie ist auch der Room Service empfehlenswert und sehr diskret – die Menüs werden durch eine Luke neben der Tür serviert.

The Calls est une rue pavée qui s'étend le long de l'Aire, et l'établissement situé au numéro 42 est un vieux moulin converti en hôtel en 1991. Le passé y est resté très vivant : la plupart des 41 chambres ont de hautes fenêtres et des murs nus ou s'étendent le long de l'eau. La suite penthouse repose sous la charpente d'un toit pointu. Outre la brasserie, le room service est aussi d'excellente qualité et très discret : les repas sont servis à travers une trappe dans la porte.

The Calls es una calle de piedra adoquinada que se extiende a lo largo de la orilla del río Aire. El edificio en el número 42 es un antiguo molino que, en 1991, fue reconvertido en hotel. En este edificio el pasado no se ha esfumado. Muchas de las 41 habitaciones tienen ventanas altas y paredes de enlucido rústico, y algunas reposan directamente sobre las aguas del río. Debajo de un techo abuhardillado sujeto por gruesas vigas se encuentra la suite del ático. Sin duda recomendable es también su brasserie y el muy discreto servicio de habitaciones –los menús se sirven a través de una ventanilla colocada junto a la puerta de la habitación.

The Calls è una strada acciottolata che si estende lungo il fiume Aire – e l'edificio al numero 42 un vecchio mulino che nel 1991 è stato trasformato in un albergo. Qui il passato è ancora vivo: molte delle 41 camere hanno finestre alte e pareti grezze, oppure danno sul fiume. La Penthouse Suite si trova sotto un tetto a punta con massicce travi a vista. Oltre alla brasserie merita provare anche il servizio in camera, offerto in maniera molto discreta – i piatti vengono serviti attraverso una finestrella situata vicino alla porta della camera.

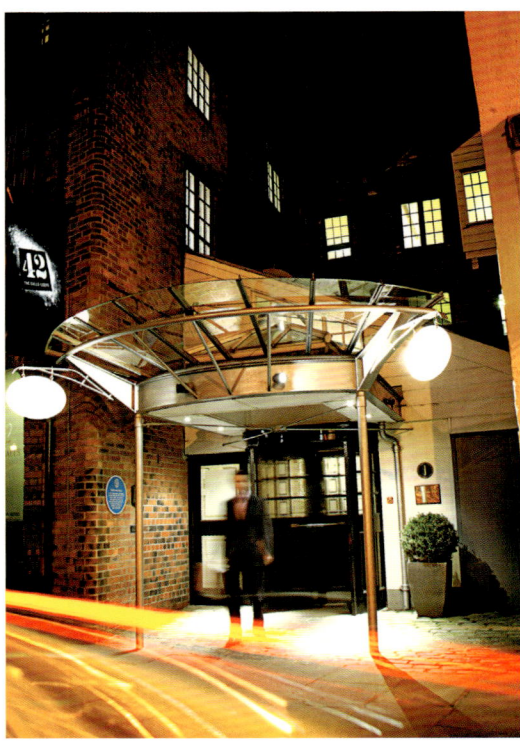
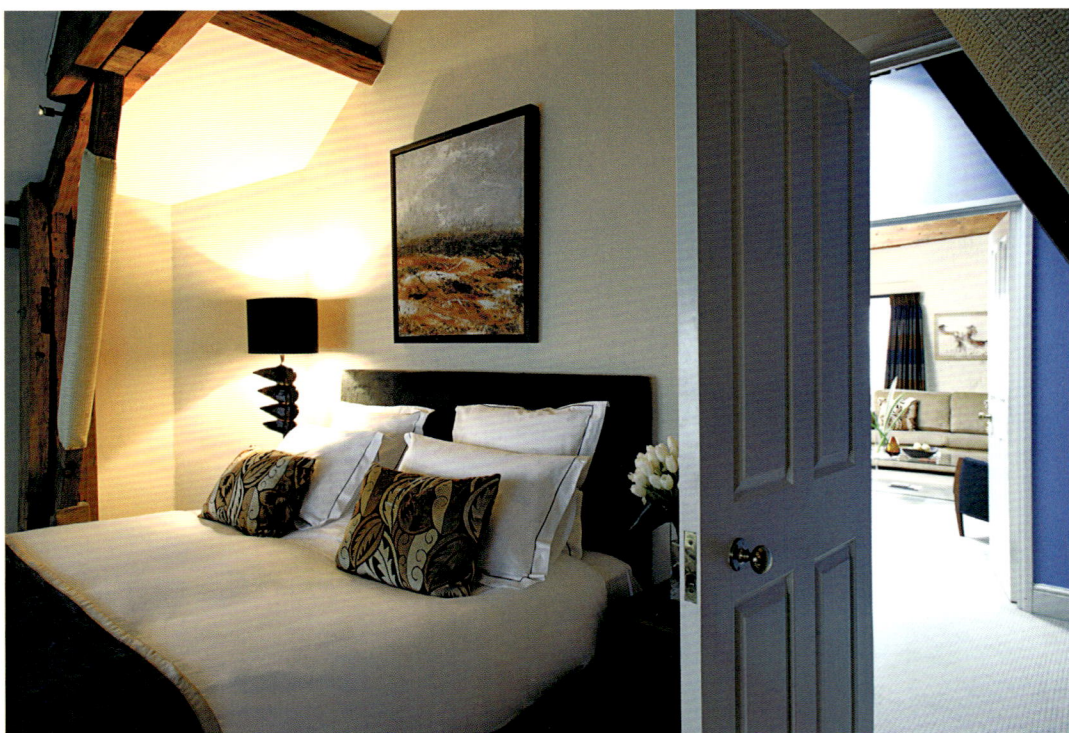

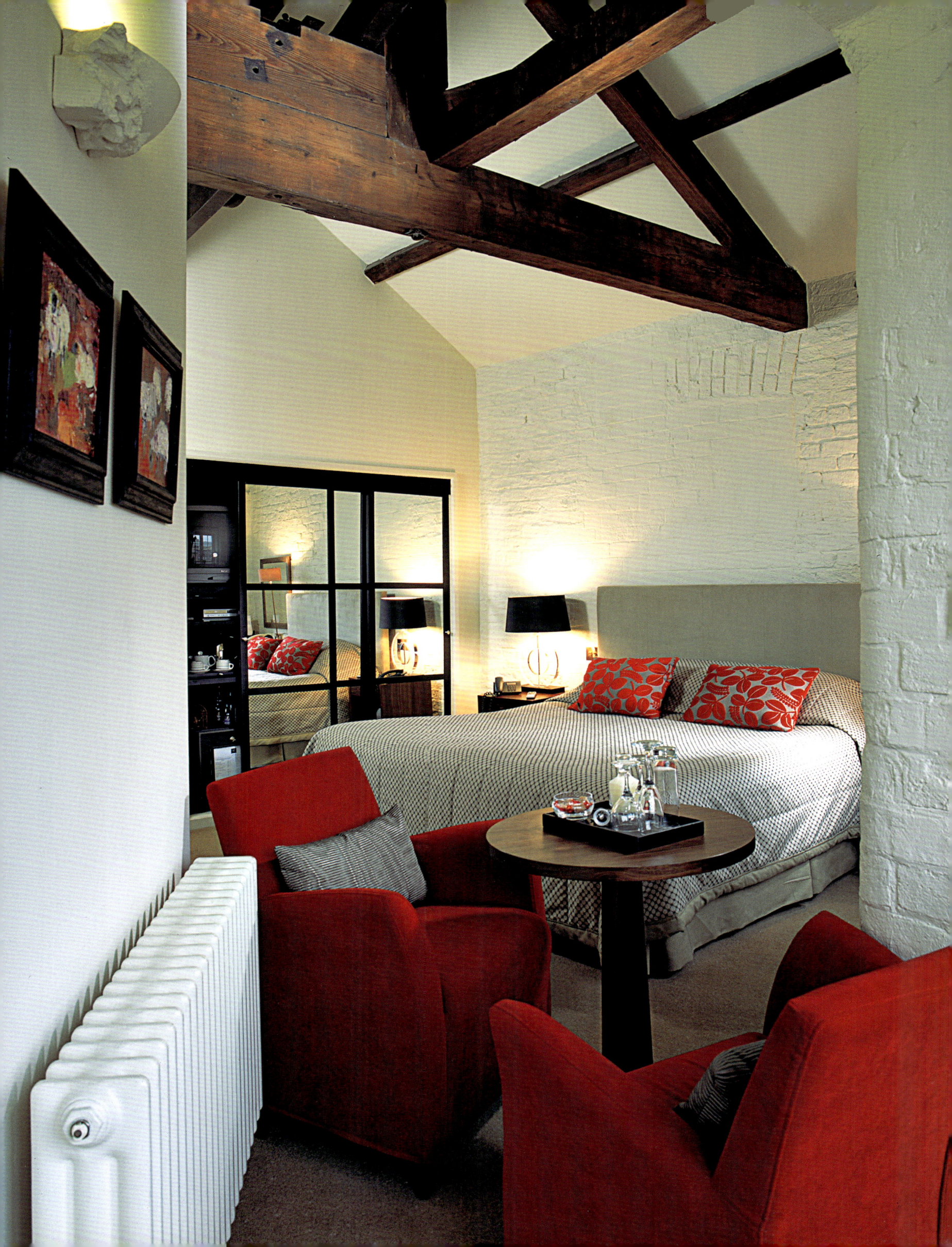

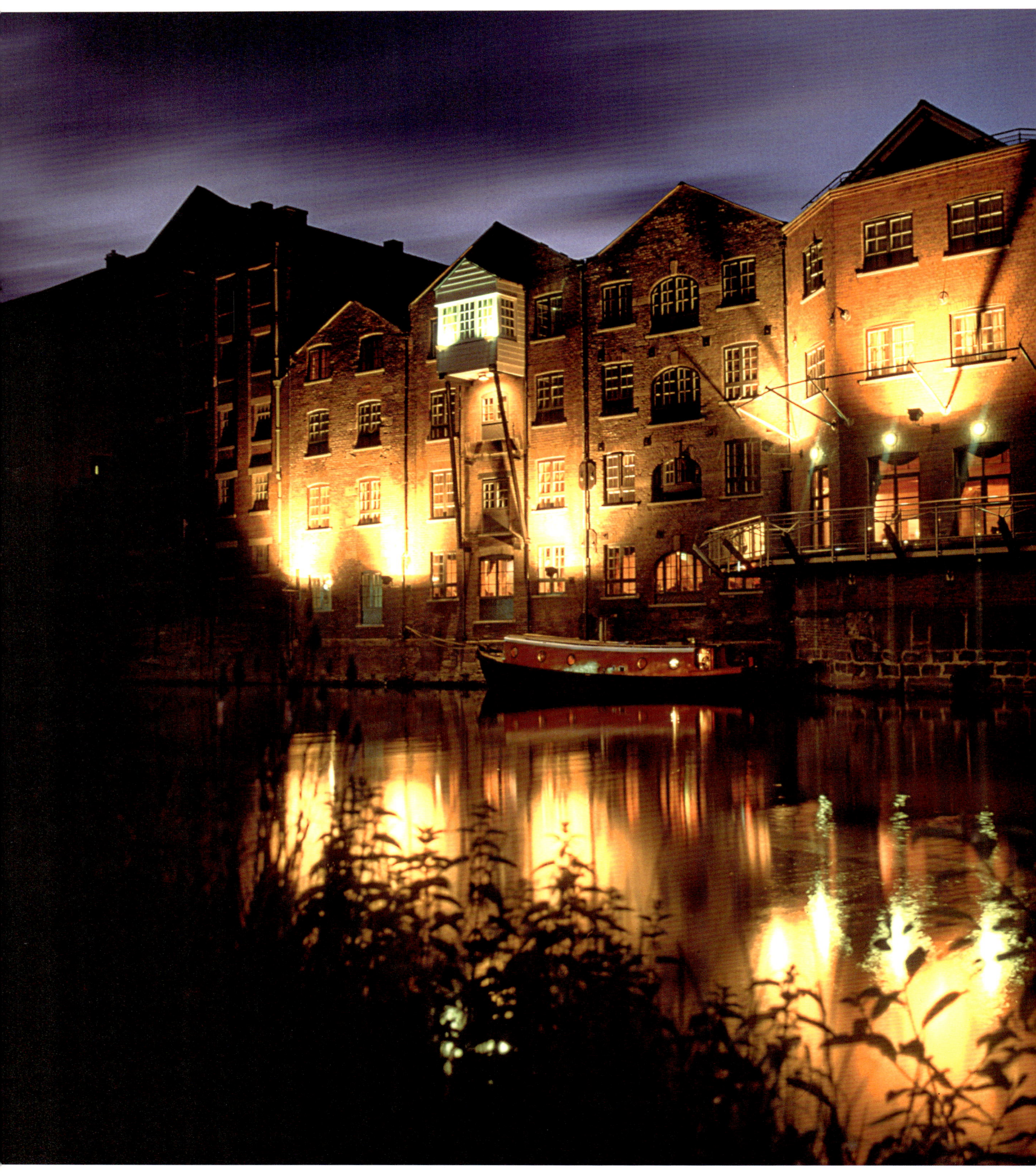

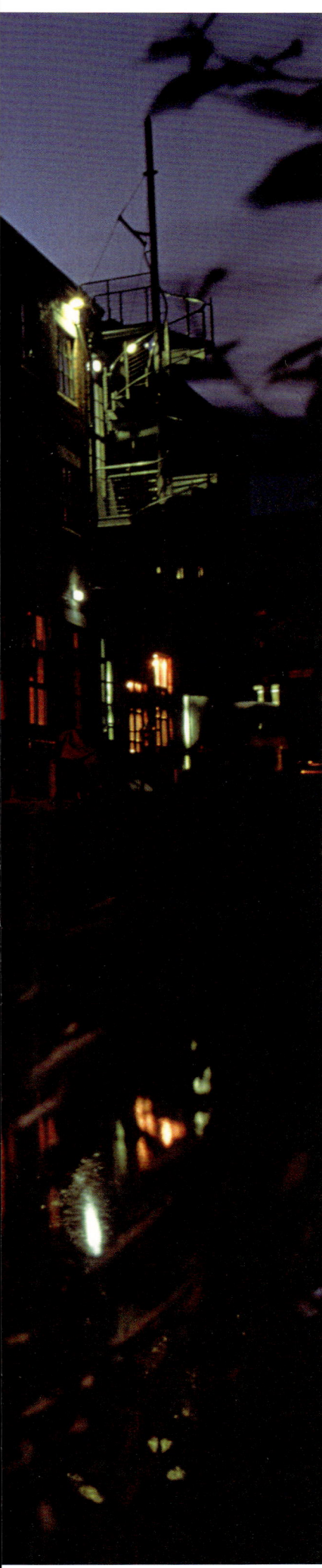

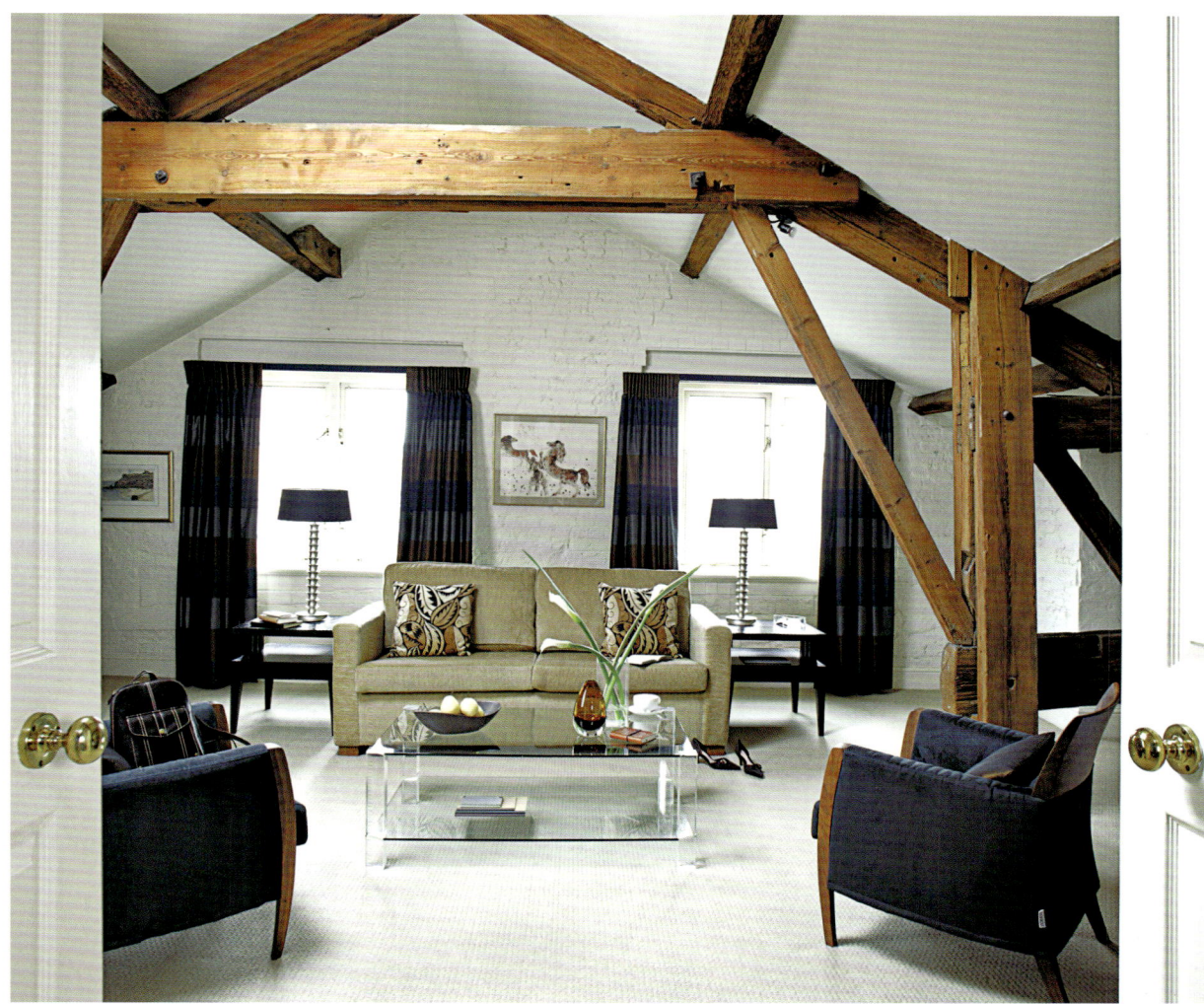

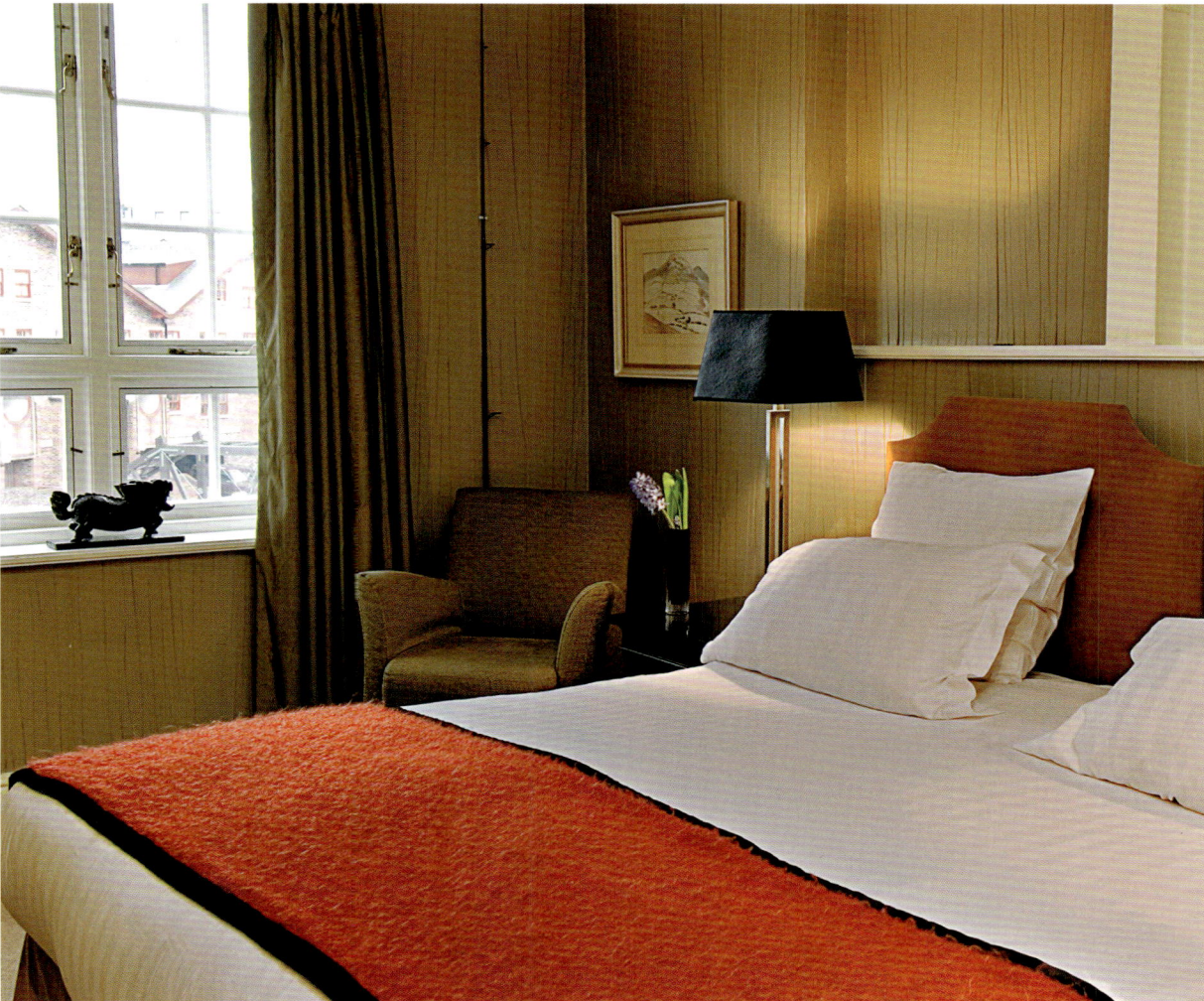

The Glasshouse

Edinburgh, United Kingdom

2 Greenside Place
Edinburgh EH1 3AA
United Kingdom
Phone: +44 131 525 8200
Fax: +44 131 525 8205
www.theetoncollection.com/
glasshouse

Price category: €€
Rooms: 47 rooms and 18 suites
Facilities: Rooftop garden, The Snug honesty bar
Services: 24 h room service, 24 h concierge, babysitting, in-room spa treatment, WiFi
Located: In the center of Edinburgh, a short stroll from Waverley train station and Princess Street, close to Edinburgh Castle
Public transportation: A 5 min walk from Waverley train station
Style: Contemporary boutique hotel

Your arrival is awaited by personal calling cards, a taster of whiskey is provided in the suites, Korres skincare line in the bathroom—these are the details that make The Glasshouse one of the most stylish addresses in Edinburgh, just as the contrasts between the 150-year old facade of Lady Glenorchy Church and the 65 rooms with high windows bringing the best light upon the clear design. There are views worthy of any film from any of the suites' terraces and the unbeatable concierge will give you the best sightseeing tips.

Bei der Ankunft liegen persönliche Visitenkarten bereit, in den Suiten stehen Whiskey bereit und im Bad die Pflegelinie von Korres – es sind diese Details, die The Glasshouse zu einer der stilvollsten Adressen Edinburghs machen. Ebenso wie die Gegensätze zwischen der 150 Jahre alten Fassade der Lady Glenorchy Church und den 65 Zimmern, deren hohe Fenster das klare Design ins beste Licht setzen. Von den Terrassen der Suiten eröffnen sich kinotaugliche Aussichten – die besten Tipps fürs Sightseeing verrät der unschlagbare Concierge.

Votre arrivée est saluée par des cartes de visites personnelles, du whisky posé sur la table des suites et des produits de soin Korres dans la salle de bain : ce sont les détails qui font de The Glasshouse l'une des adresses les plus distinguées d'Edinbourg. Tout comme le contraste entre la façade vieille de 150 ans de l'église Lady Glenorchy et les 165 chambres dont les hautes fenêtres confèrent le meilleur éclairage possible aux lignes claires du design. Depuis les terrasses des chambres, une vue cinématographique s'ouvre à vous, et le concierge est imbattable lorsqu'il s'agit de donner les meilleures astuces pour profiter de la ville.

En su habitación, al huésped le esperan sus propias tarjetas de visita personalizadas, una botella de whisky en la suite y en el cuarto de baño, productos cosméticos de la marca Korres. Son precisamente estos detalles los que convierten el hotel The Glasshouse en una de las posadas con más estilo de Edimburgo. También a ello contribuye sin duda el marcado contraste entre la fachada de la iglesia Lady Glenchory, de 150 años de antigüedad, y las 65 habitaciones inundadas por la luz que penetra a través de sus altos ventanales y que resalta un diseño bien definido. Desde las terrazas de las suites se abre una vista de película y el imbatible conserje ofrece al huésped los mejores consejos para visitar esta ciudad.

Al vostro arrivo troverete biglietti da visita, personalizzati, una bottiglia di whisky nella suite, e nel bagno la linea di cosmetici Korres – sono questi dettagli a fare del Glasshouse uno degli alberghi più raffinati di Edimburgo. Proprio come il contrasto tra la facciata della Lady Glenorchy Church, risalente a 150 anni fa, e le 65 camere, dotate di alte finestre che mettono in perfetta luce il design dalle linee semplici. Dalle terrazze delle suite si aprono vedute da set cinematografico e l'imbattibile portiere vi darà consigli per la visita alla città.

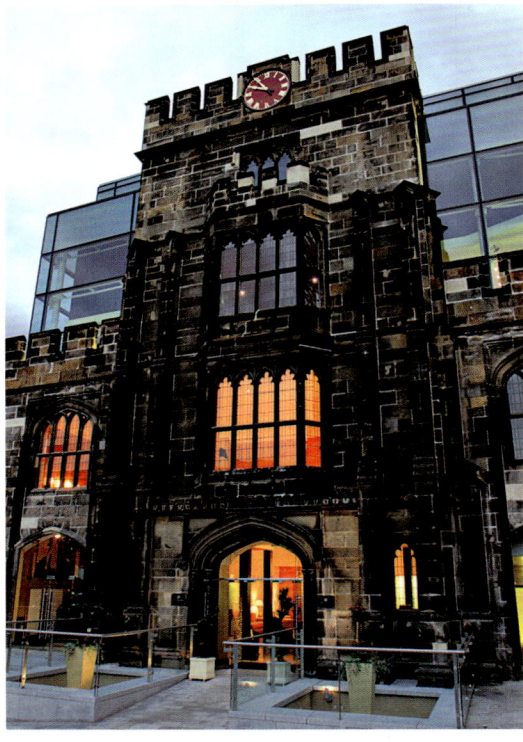
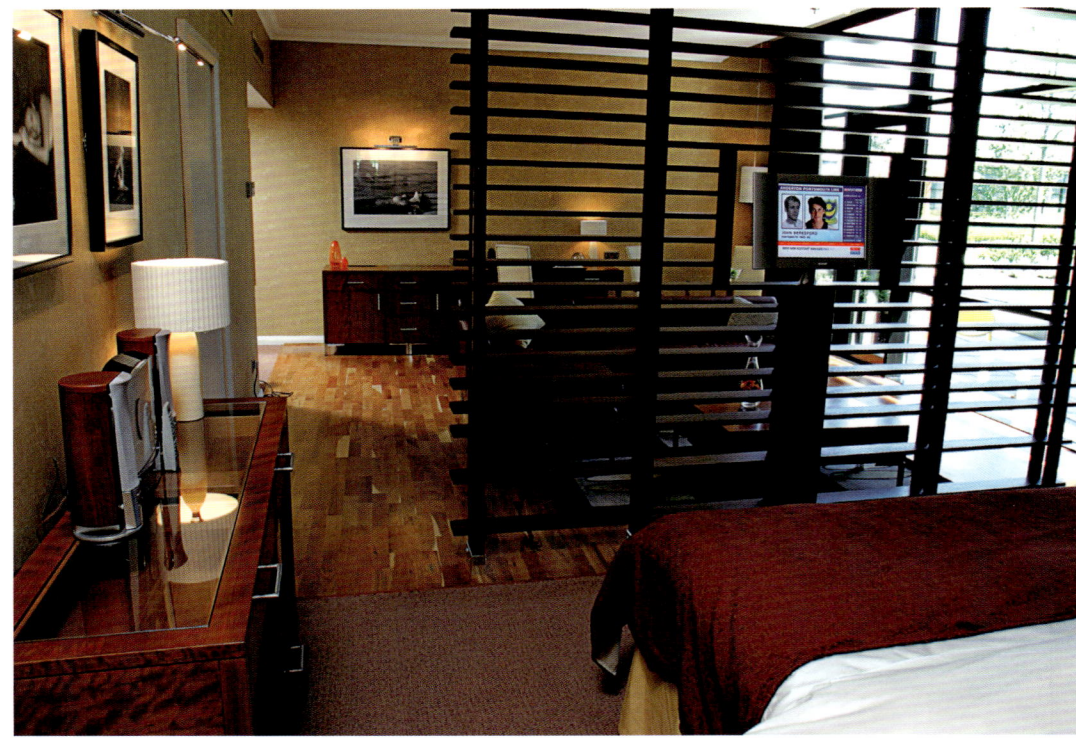

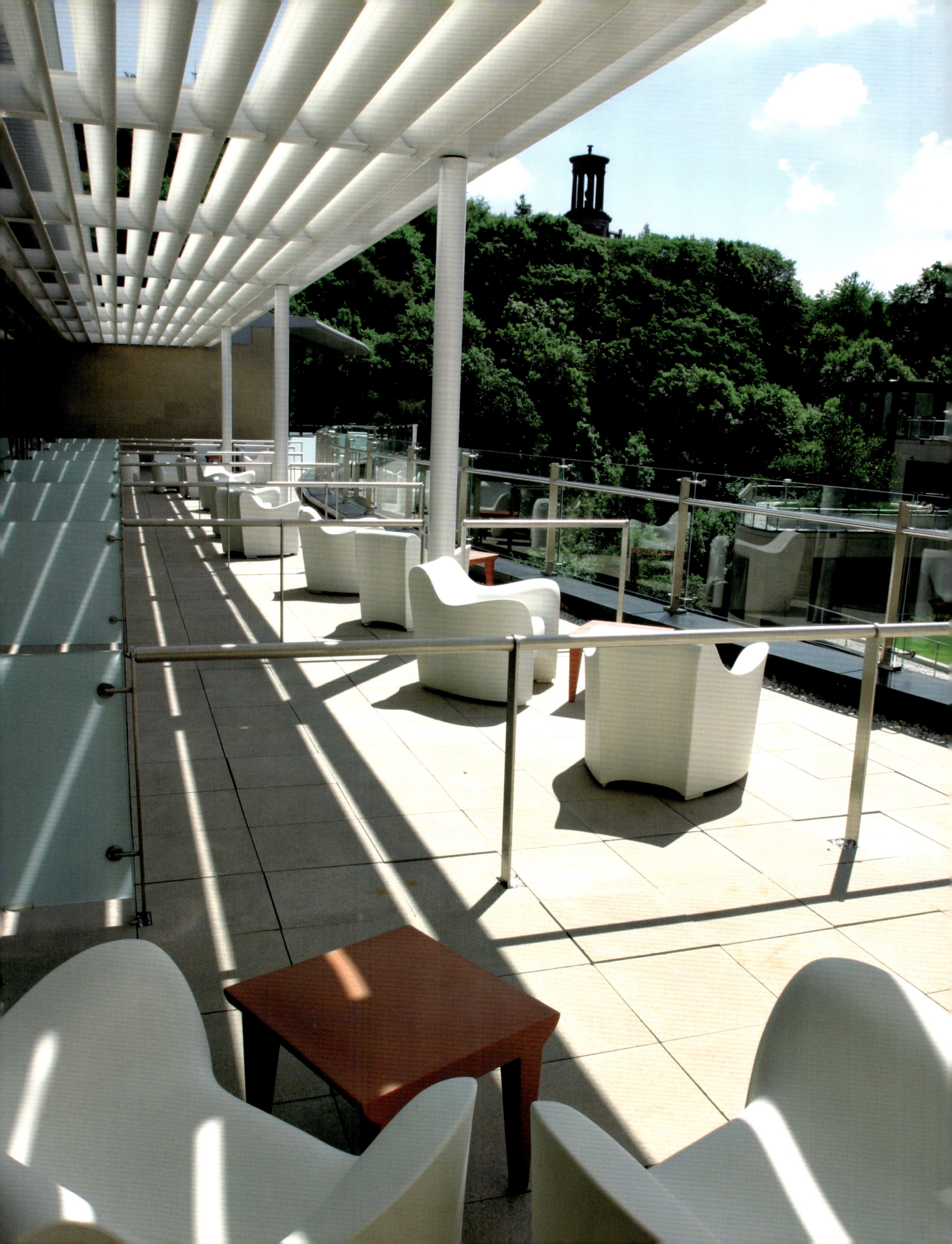

Netherlands
Phone: +31 20 683 3013
Fax: +31 20 685 3750
www.hoteldefilosoof.nl

Facilities: Bar Symposium, meeting rooms, health club
Services: Parking, personal computer, WiFi, free newspapers
Located: In the city center
Public transportation: Tram 1 Jan Pieter Heijestraat
Style: Modern-art

Famous philosophers inspired the designers of the hotel while working on the 38 rooms. In the Passion Suite guests are immersed in the world of the French theorist Georges Bataille and, on rose linens under a gold ceiling, they can contemplate how close passion and fear are. They dedicated a room with a tranquil deep blue interior to the Chinese thinkers Confucius and Lao Tse. Anyone wanting to let his thoughts fly is granted enough space in the enchanting hotel garden or in the neighboring beautiful Vondelpark.

Berühmte Philosophen inspirierten die Designer des Hotels beim Gestalten der 38 Räume. In der Passion Suite tauchen Gäste in die Welt des Französischen Theoretikers Georges Bataille ein und sinnieren auf Rosenbettwäsche unter einer goldenen Decke, wie nah sich Leidenschaften und Ängste sind. Den chinesischen Denkern Konfuzius und Lao-Tse widmeten sie ein Zimmer mit beruhigendem, tiefblauem Interieur. Wer seinen Gedanken lieber fliegen lässt, dem bietet der bezaubernde Hotelgarten ausreichend Platz – oder der schöne Vondelpark nebenan.

Des grands philosophes ont inspiré la conception des 38 chambres de cet hôtel. Dans la « Passion Suite », les clients se plongent dans l'univers du théoricien français Georges Bataille et réfléchissent sous un plafond doré, dans une literie décorée de roses, sur la relation étroite entre passion et peur. Une chambre à l'intérieur bleu, très apaisante, est dédiée aux penseurs chinois Confucius et Lao-tseu. Pour ceux qui préfèrent laisser voler librement leurs pensées, l'hôtel dispose d'un vaste jardin, et le très beau parc Vondel est tout prêt.

Para esbozar sus 38 estancias, los diseñadores del hotel se dejaron inspirar por célebres filósofos. Los huéspedes de la Passion Suite pueden sumergirse en el mundo del teórico francés Georges Bataille y reflexionar, sobre sábanas de rosas y bajo un techo dorado, sobre la delgada línea que separa la pasión del miedo. La habitación con un relajante interior de color azul intenso fue dedicada a los pensadores chinos Confucio y Lao-Tse. Y el visitante que prefiera dejar fluir sus pensamientos al aire libre encontrará sitio de sobra para ello en el encantador y espacioso jardín del hotel –o, tampoco lejos de allí, en el sugestivo Vondelpark.

Musa ispiratrice per la realizzazione delle 38 camere di questo hotel sono stati alcuni famosi filosofi. Nella Passion Suite gli ospiti si immergono nel mondo del teorico francese Georges Bataille, e tra lenzuola di rose e coperte dorate riflettono su dove stia il confine tra passione e paura. Ai pensatori cinesi Confucio e Lao-Tse è dedicata una camera dal rilassante interno blu notte. Chi volesse fare volare i propri pensieri troverà abbastanza spazio nell'incantevole giardino dell'albergo – o nel suggestivo Vondelpark situato accanto.

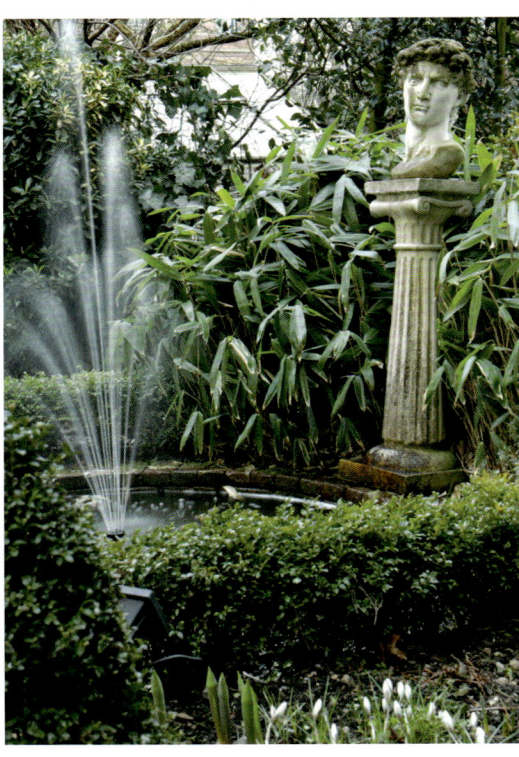
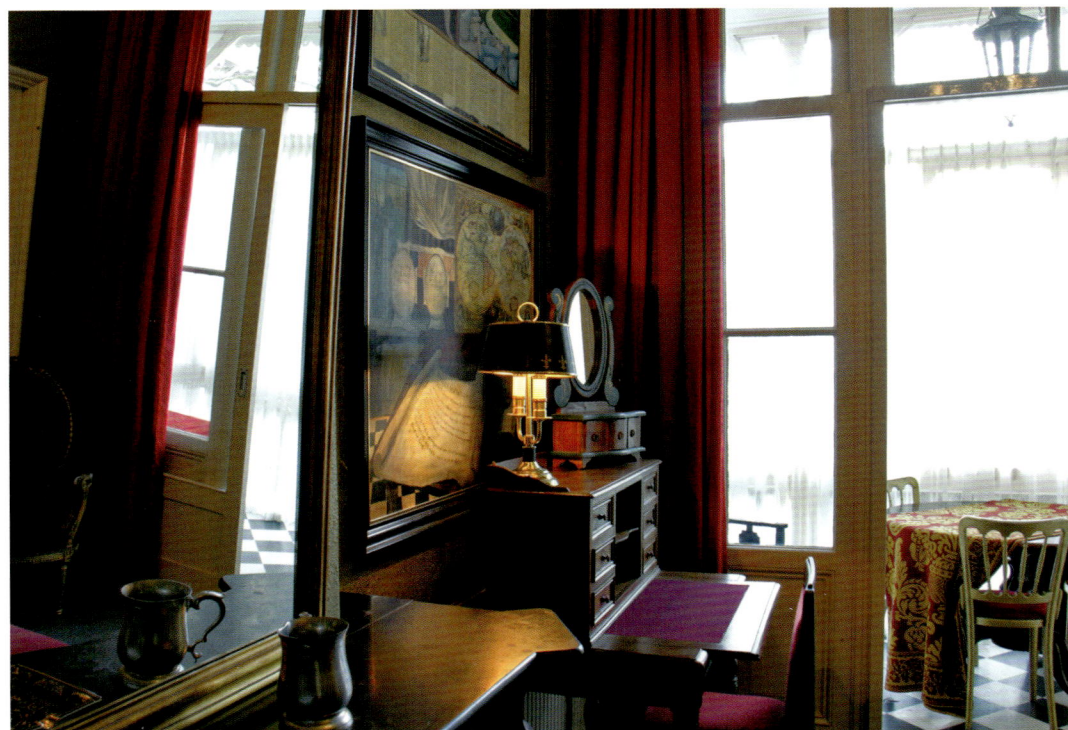

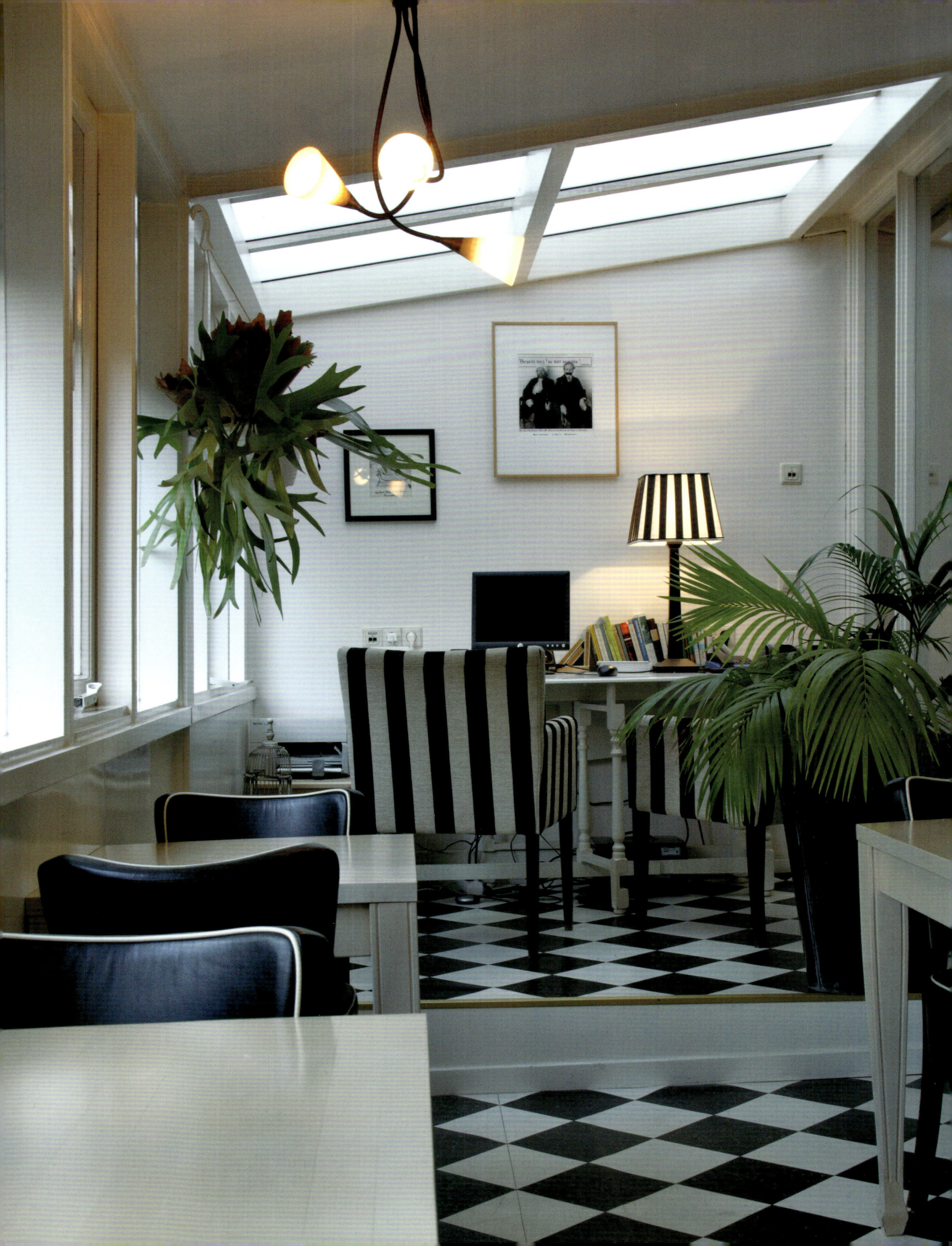

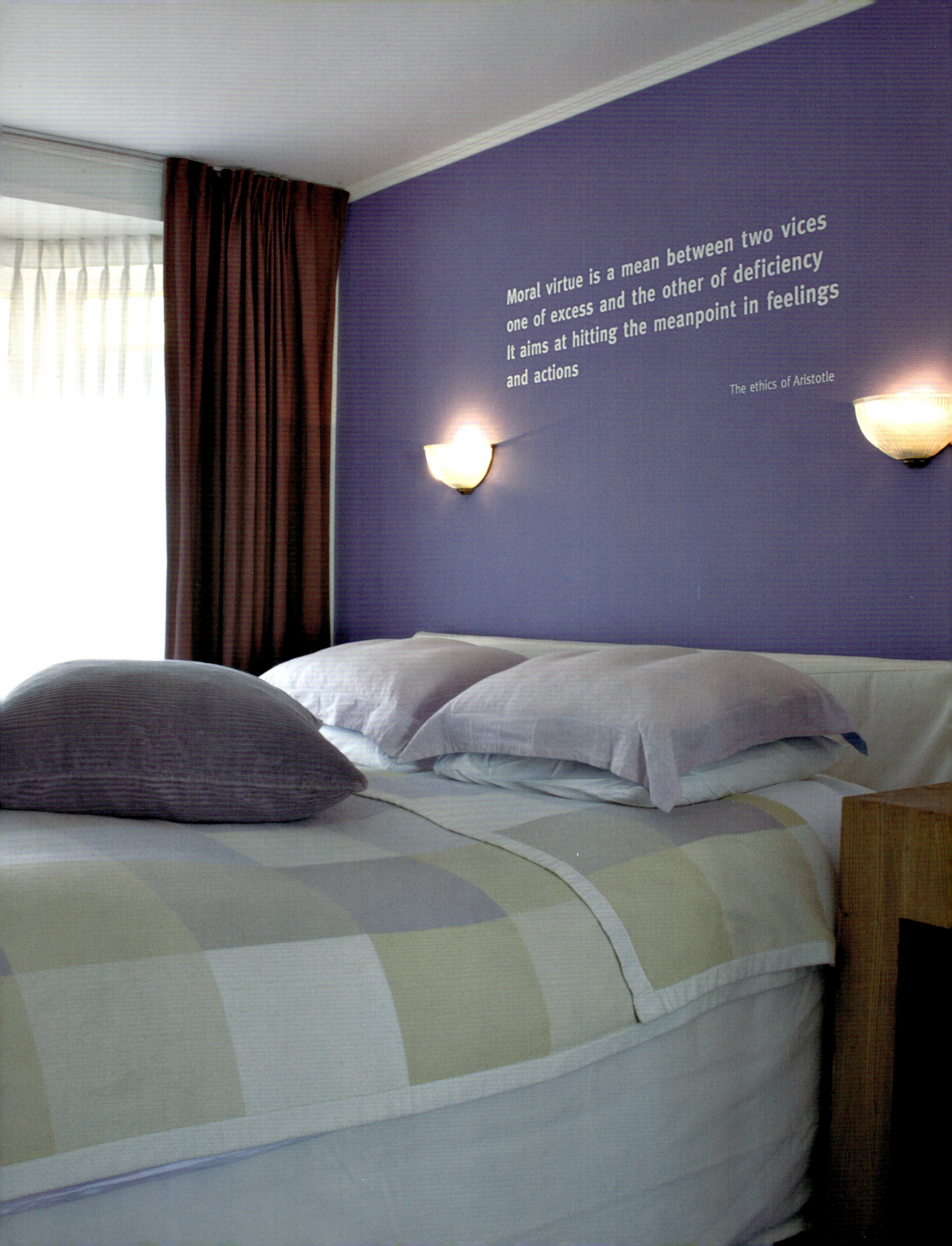

Moral virtue is a mean between two vices one of excess and the other of deficiency It aims at hitting the meanpoint in feelings and actions

The ethics of Aristotle

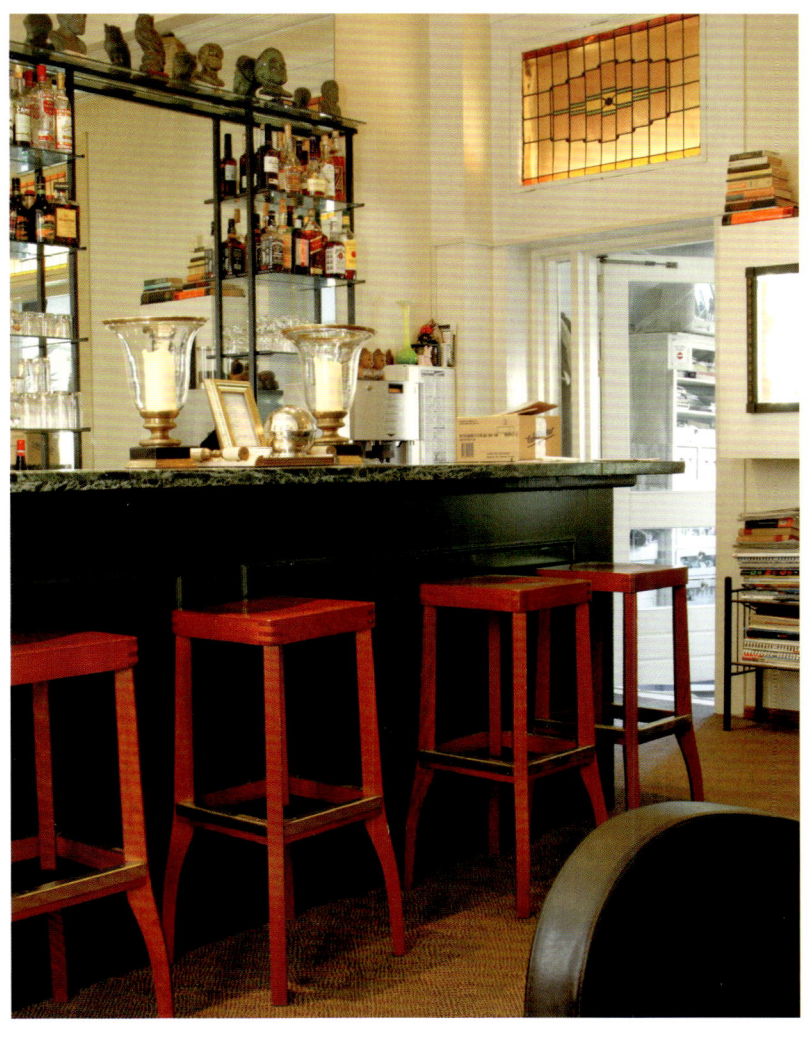

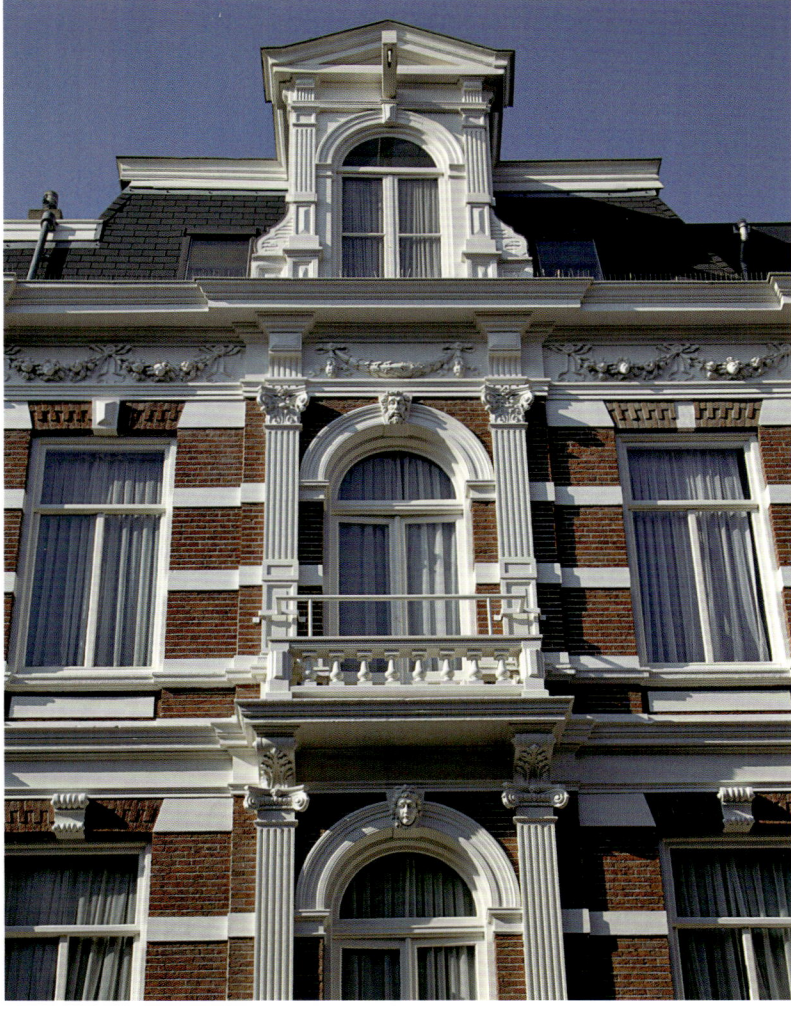

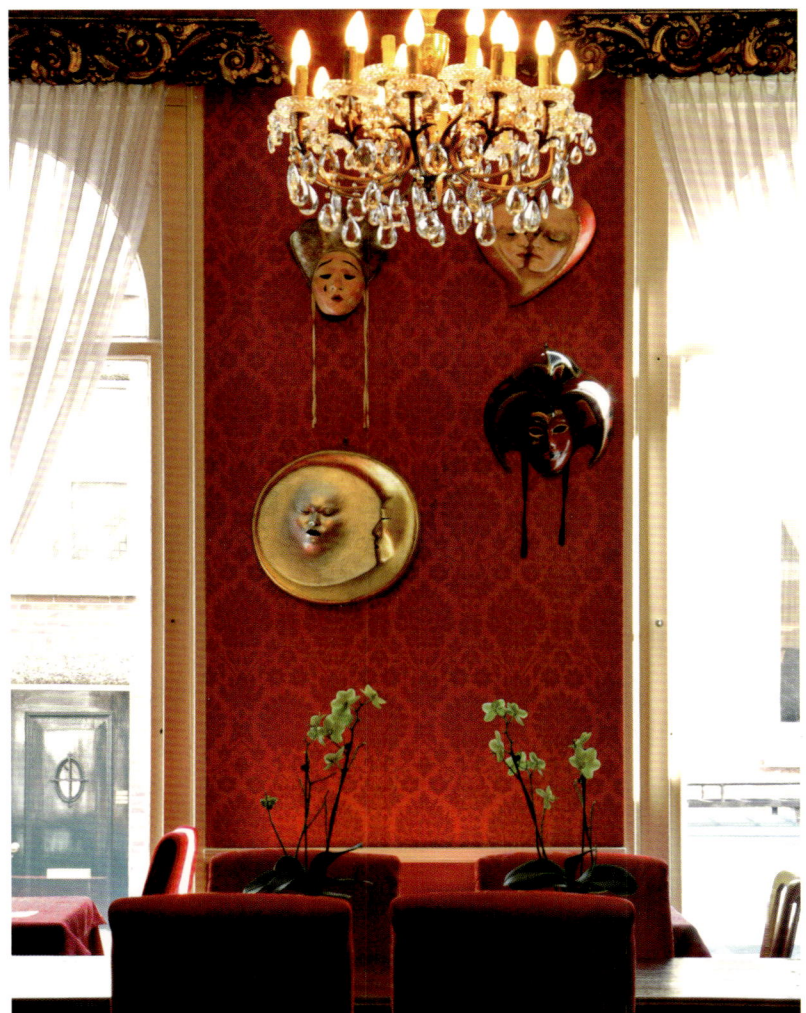

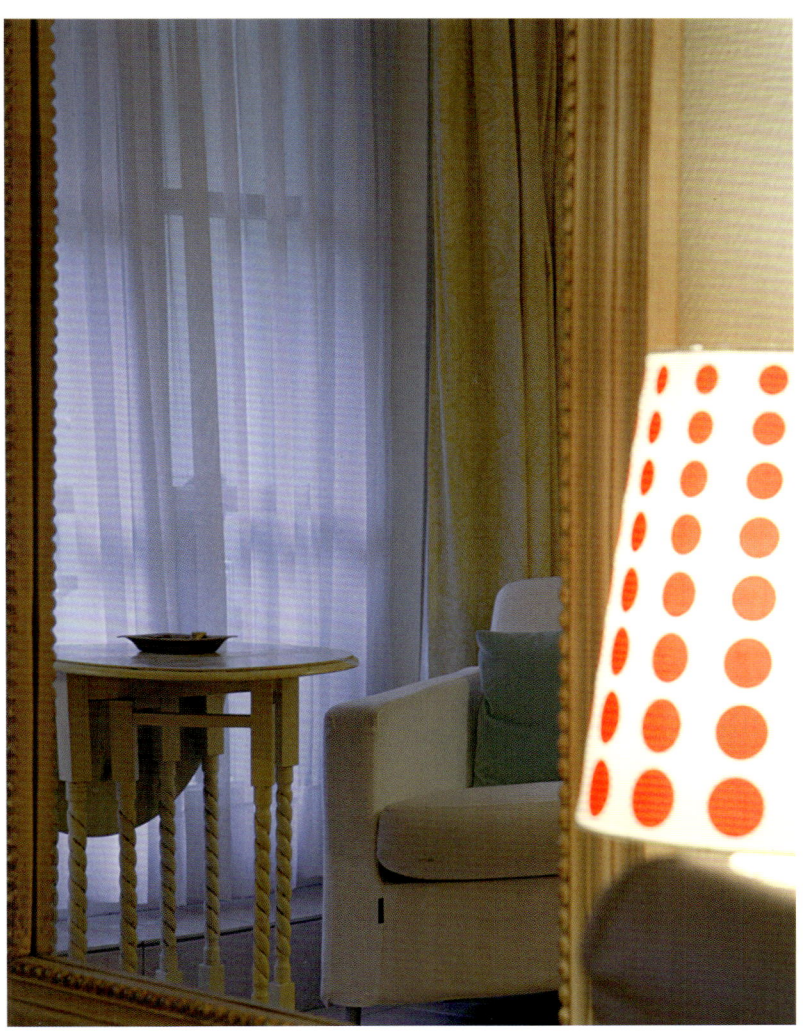

misc eatdrinksleep

Amsterdam, Netherlands

Kloveniersburgwal 20
1012 CV Amsterdam
Netherlands
Phone: +31 20 330 6241
Fax: +31 20 330 6242
www.misceatdrinksleep.com

Price category: €
Rooms: 6 rooms
Facilities: Bar, restaurant
Services: Boat tour, taxi service, concierge, complimentary non-alcoholic drink & snack bar
Located: Next to the picturesque Nieuwmarkt square, in the heart of the historic center
Public transportation: Tram Dam; Metro Nieuwmarkt
Style: Boutique hotel

Next to the Nieuwmarkt in the historical center of Amsterdam, a cyclist metropolis, you will find this privately run boutique hotel. The six individually designed rooms in this 17th-century canal house all look out over one of this city's oldest canals or over an enchanting garden. Young designer Thijs Bakker found self realization in the Design room and the Baroque room celebrates the revival of new opulence. There is also proof of Amsterdam's hospitality: the minibar is free.

Neben dem Nieuwmarkt, im historischen Zentrum der Radfahrer-Metropole, liegt dieses privat geführte Boutique-Hotel. Die sechs individuell gestalteten Räume in dem alten Grachtenhaus aus dem 17. Jahrhundert zeigen alle auf einen der ältesten Kanäle der Stadt oder auf einen bezaubernden Garten. Im Design-Raum haben sich Jungdesigner wie Tijhs Bakker verwirklicht und der Barock-Raum feiert das Revival der neuen Opulenz. Dazu gibt es noch einen Beweis Amsterdamer Gastfreundschaft: Die Minibar ist kostenlos.

Près du Nieuwmarket, dans le centre historique de la capitale de la bicyclette, se trouve ce boutique hôtel dans un bâtiment du 17ème siècle. Les six chambres au design différent donnent toutes sur l'un des canal des plus anciens de la ville ou un magnifique jardin. Dans la chambre design, le jeune designer Thijs Bakker ont pu se réaliser et la chambre baroque célèbre la renaissance d'une nouvelle opulence. Preuve supplémentaire du sens de l'hospitalité d'Amsterdam : le minibar est gratuit.

Junto a la plaza de Nieuwmarkt, en el centro histórico de Amsterdam, la metrópolis de los ciclistas, se encuentra este boutique hotel de gestión privada. Las seis habitaciones de diseño individual de esta mansión del siglo XVII dan a uno de los más antiguos canales y a un encantador jardín. En la estancia Design el joven diseñador Tijhs Bakker hace gala de su talento y la habitación Baroque celebra el resurgimiento de la opulencia moderna. A todo esto se añade una muestra de la gran hospitalidad de los autóctonos: el huésped puede servirse del minibar a expensas del hotel.

Questo boutique hotel gestito da privati si trova vicino al Nieuwmarkt, nel centro storico di Amsterdam, la metropoli dei ciclisti. Le sei camere arredate in modo personalizzato e ospitate in una casa del XVII secolo danno su uno dei più antichi canali e su un incantevole giardino. Nella stanza Design si sono realizzati giovani talenti come Tijhs Bakker e la suite Barocco celebra il revival della nuova opulenza. A ciò si aggiunge una dimostrazione dell'ospitalità che contraddistingue Amsterdam: il minibar è gratuito.

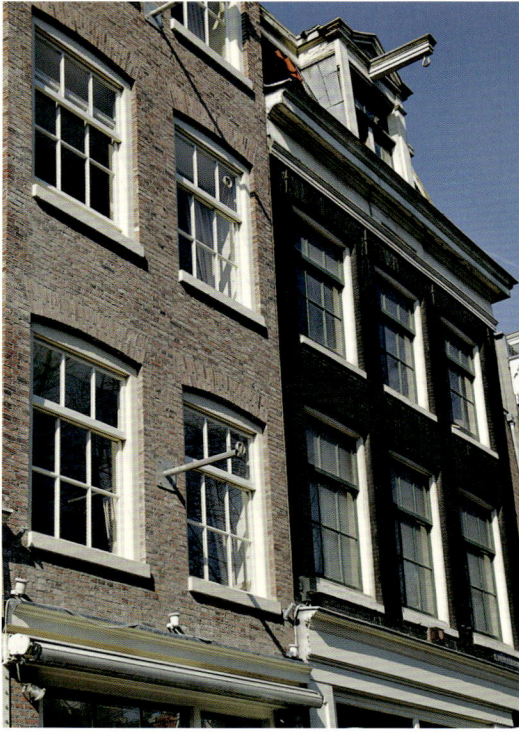
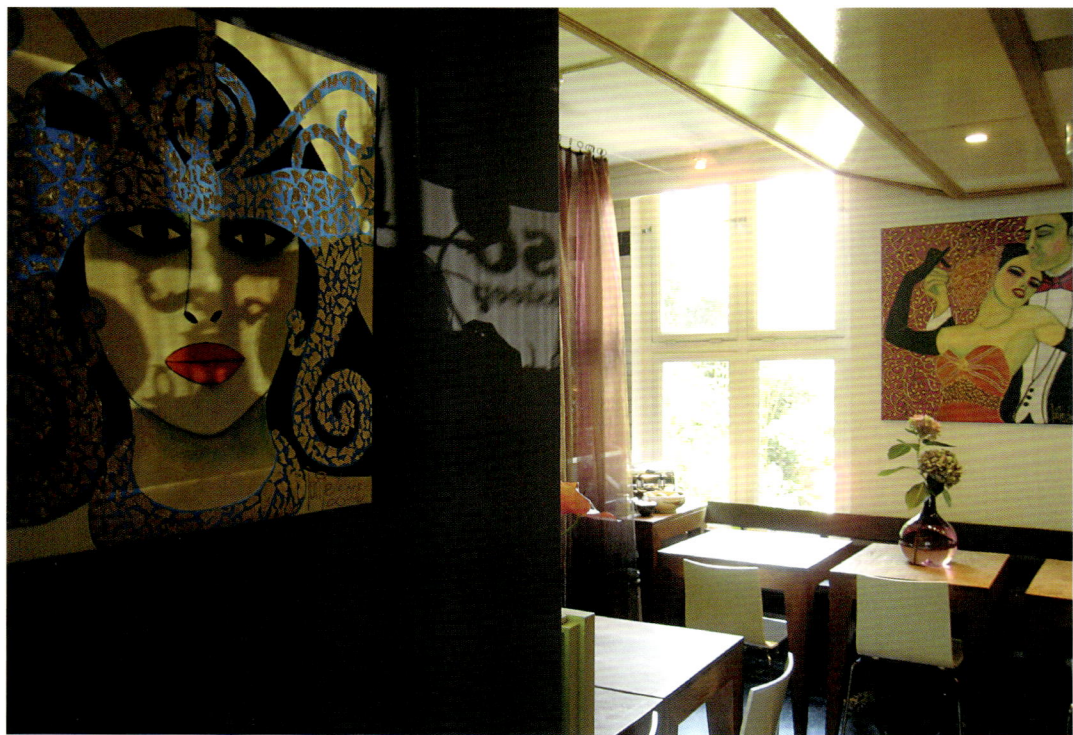

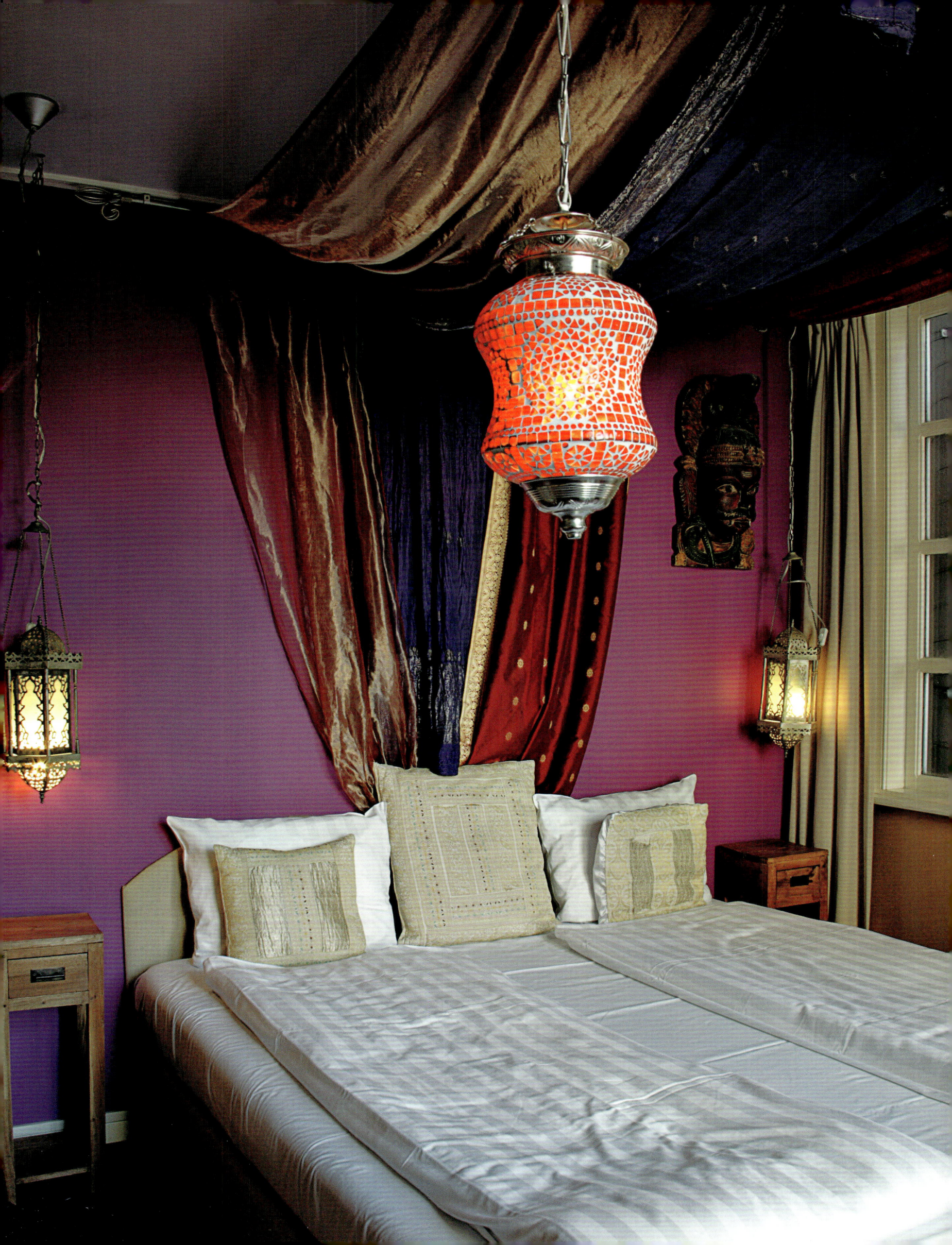

1019 BN Amsterdam
Netherlands
Phone: +31 20 561 3636
Fax: +31 20 561 3600
www.lloydhotel.com

Rooms: 117 rooms
Facilities: Bar, restaurant, library, shop, "Cultural Embassy"
Services: Lloyd Time on Mondays, 24 h room service, WiFi
Located: Centrally, in the fashionable heart of Eastern Docklands area
Public transportation: Tram 26 Rietlandpark
Style: Urban, quirky and boho-chic

The Dutch architects' office MVRDV managed a stroke of genius while replanning the Lloyd Hotel in the dock area of East Amsterdam. They got totally into the core of the monumental 1921 brick building that used to serve as an emigrant hotel. They cut open the middle to make an atrium and put in open flights of stairs and galleries. Holland's top designers, above all the Droog Group, gave their fantasies free reign for the five to one star rooms.

Mit der Umplanung des Lloyd Hotels in den Docklands im Osten Amsterdams, ist dem holländischen Architekturbüro MVRDV ein Geniestreich geglückt: Sie rückten dem monumentalen Ziegelbau von 1921 mit frischen Ideen auf den behäbigen Leib, der einstmals als Emigrantenhotel diente. Den Mittelteil öffneten sie zu einem Atrium und zogen Freitreppen und Galerien ein. Für die Fünf- bis Ein-Sterne-Zimmer haben Hollands Top-Designer ihre Fantasie spielen lassen – allen voran die Gruppe Droog.

Avec la rénovation architecturale de l'hôtel Lloyd dans le quartier du port, à l'est d'Amsterdam, les architectes MVRDV ont réussi un coup de génie. Avec leurs idées nouvelles, ils se sont totalement emparés de ce monumental immeuble de briques datant de 1921, qui abritait autrefois un hôtel accueillant des immigrés. La partie centrale a été ouverte pour créer un atrium et dotée de perrons et de couloirs. Pour les chambres classées de une à cinq étoiles, les plus grands designers hollandais, et avant tout le Groupe Droog, ont laissé courir leur imagination.

Los arquitectos del estudio MVRDV reformaron de manera genial el hotel Lloyd en la zona del barrio portuario al este de Ámsterdam. Su receta: aplicar al monumental edificio de ladrillos de 1921 y antiguo hotel de emigrantes una gran dosis de ideas innovadoras. En la parte central se abrió un atrio y se introdujeron escalinatas y galerías. Las habitaciones, con categorías que oscilan de una a cinco estrellas, fueron concebidas con una gran imaginación por los diseñadores más prestigiosos de los Países Bajos y, principalmente, por el grupo Droog.

Con la completa ristrutturazione del Lloyd Hotel, nei bacini portuali della parte orientale di Amsterdam, lo studio di architettura olandese MVRDV ha messo a punto un vero e proprio colpo di genio: con fresche idee è riuscito infatti ad alleggerire il pesante corpo di questa monumentale costruzione in mattoni del 1921 che un tempo fungeva da albergo per emigrati. La parte centrale dell'edificio è stata aperta a formare un atrio e sono state aggiunte scalinate e gallerie. Per la realizzazione delle camere, da cinque a una stella, hanno dato sfogo alla propria fantasia i più grandi designer dell'Olanda – primo fra tutti il gruppo Doog.

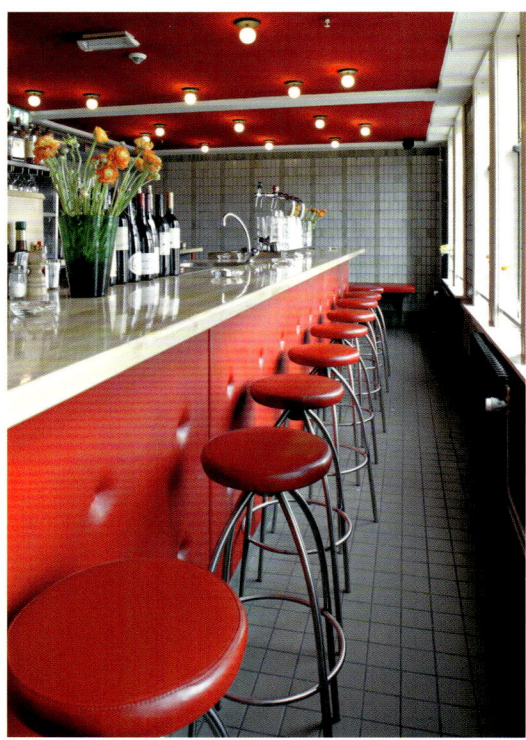
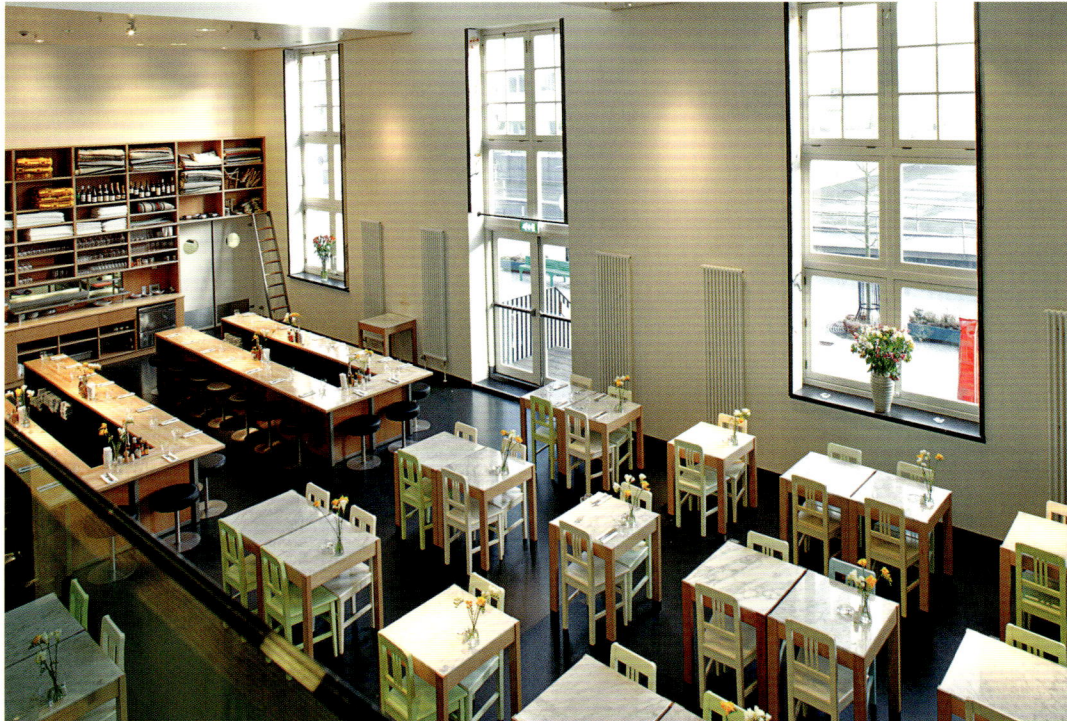

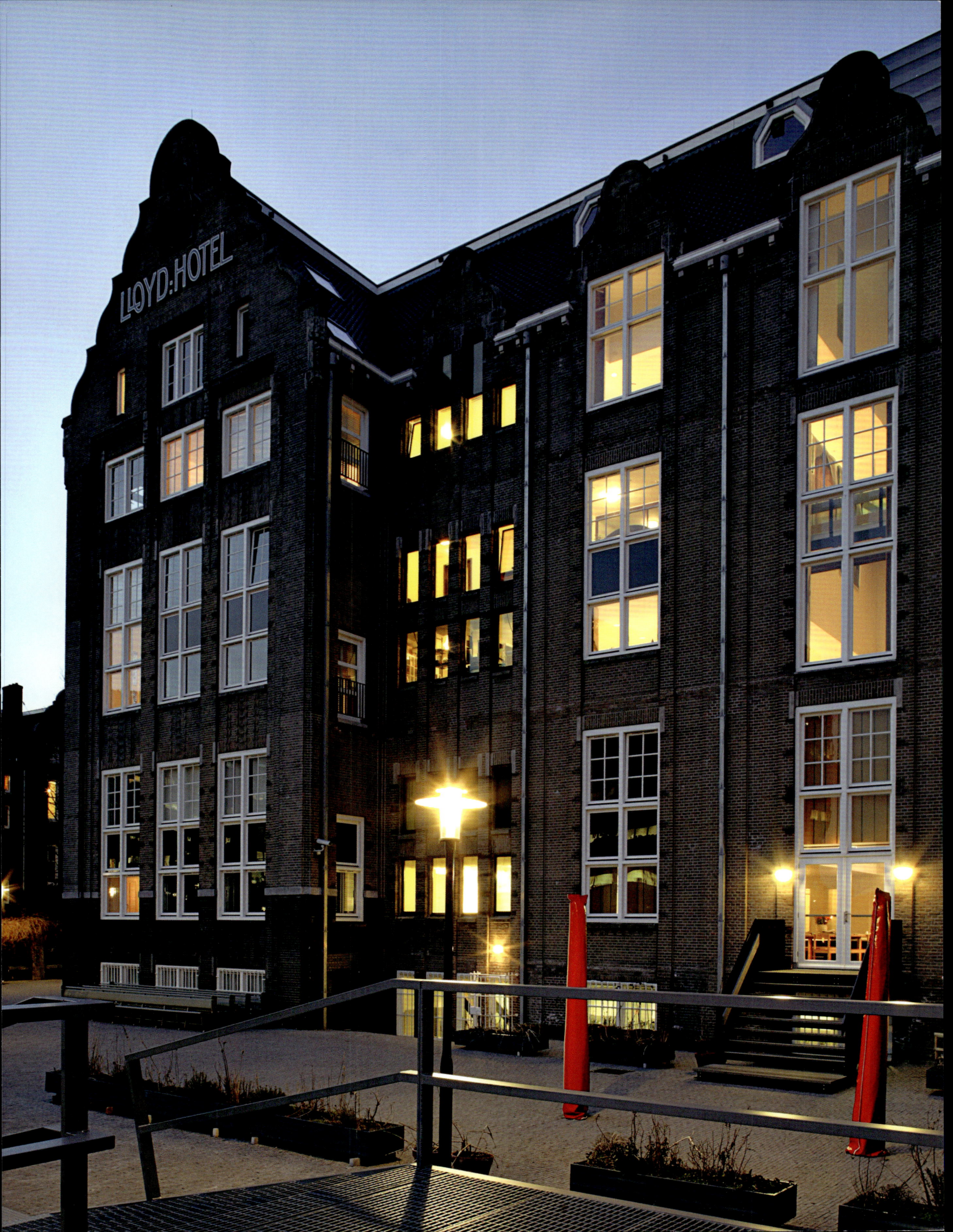

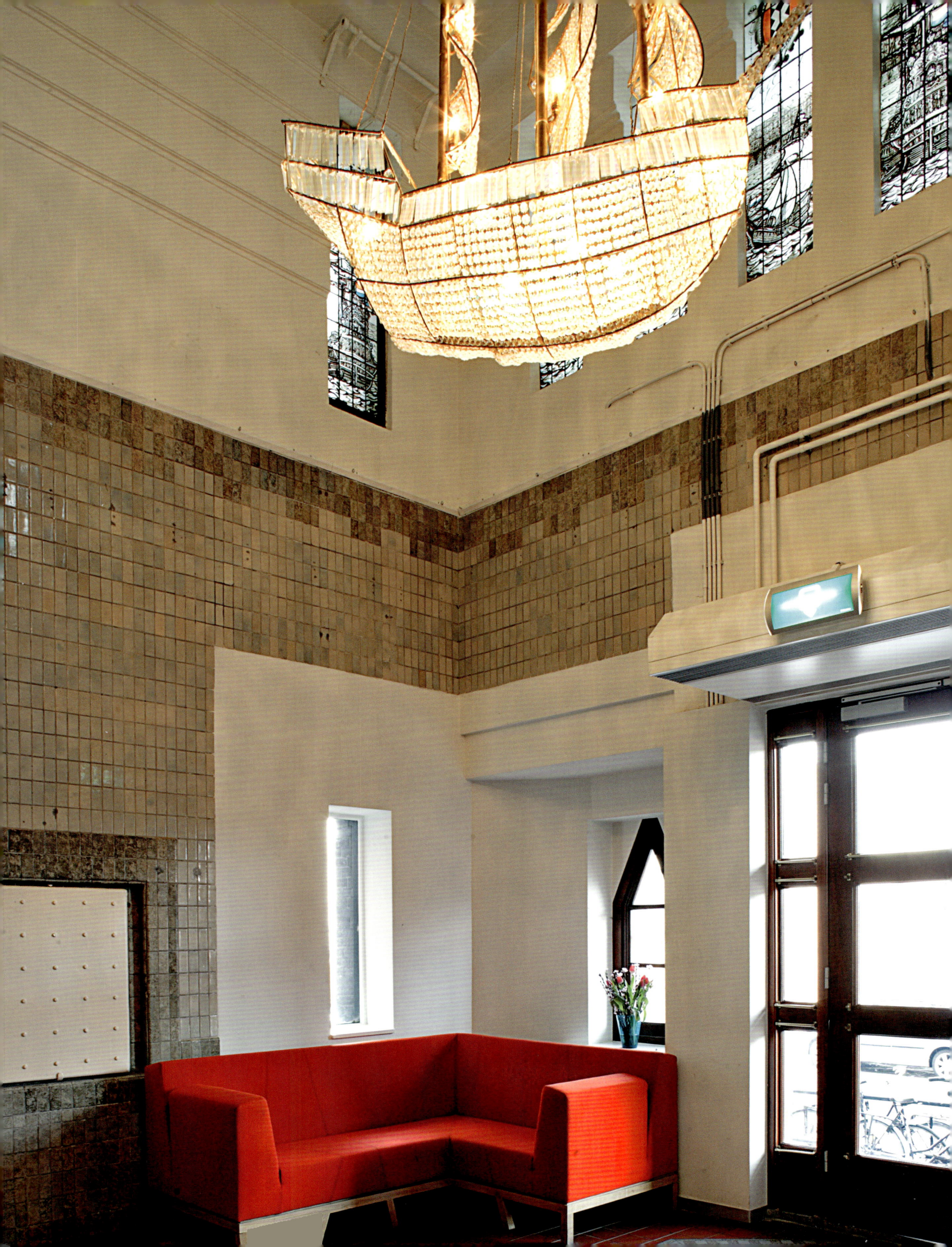

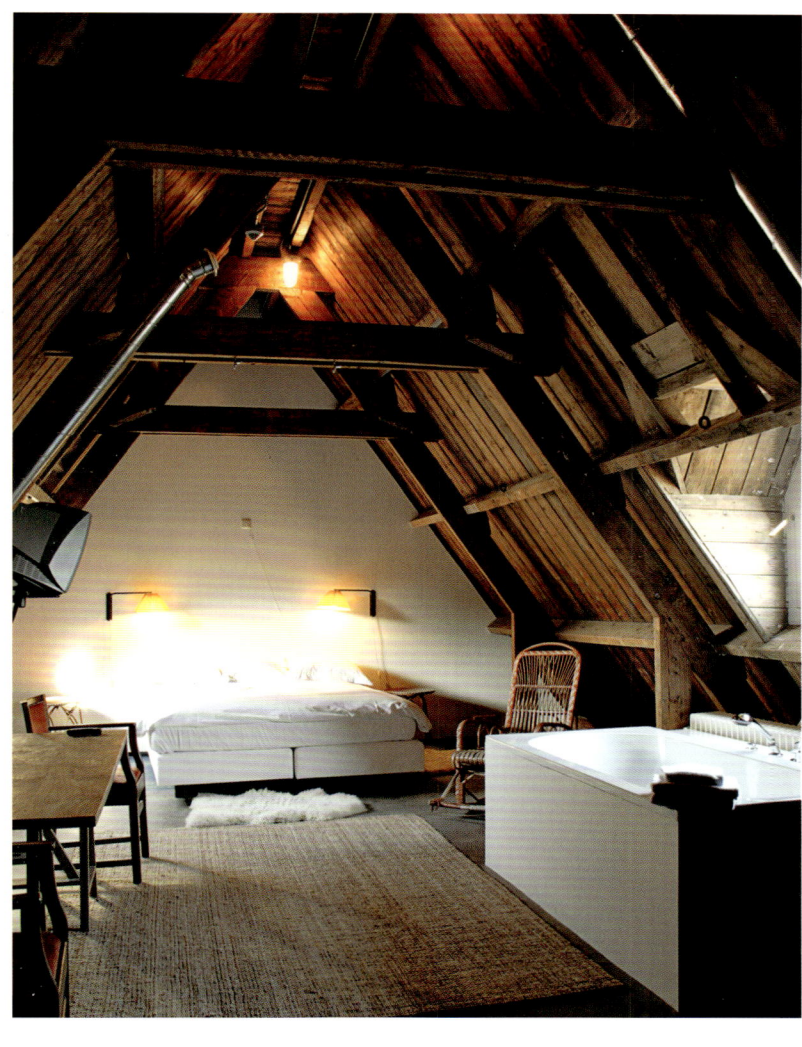

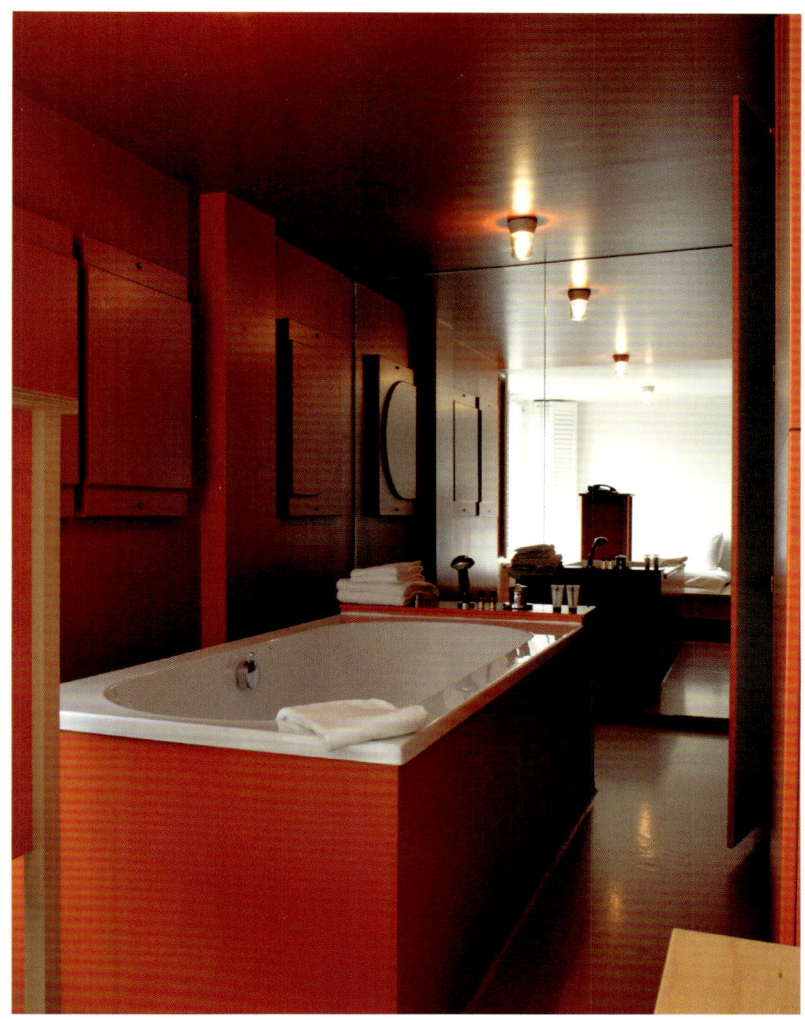

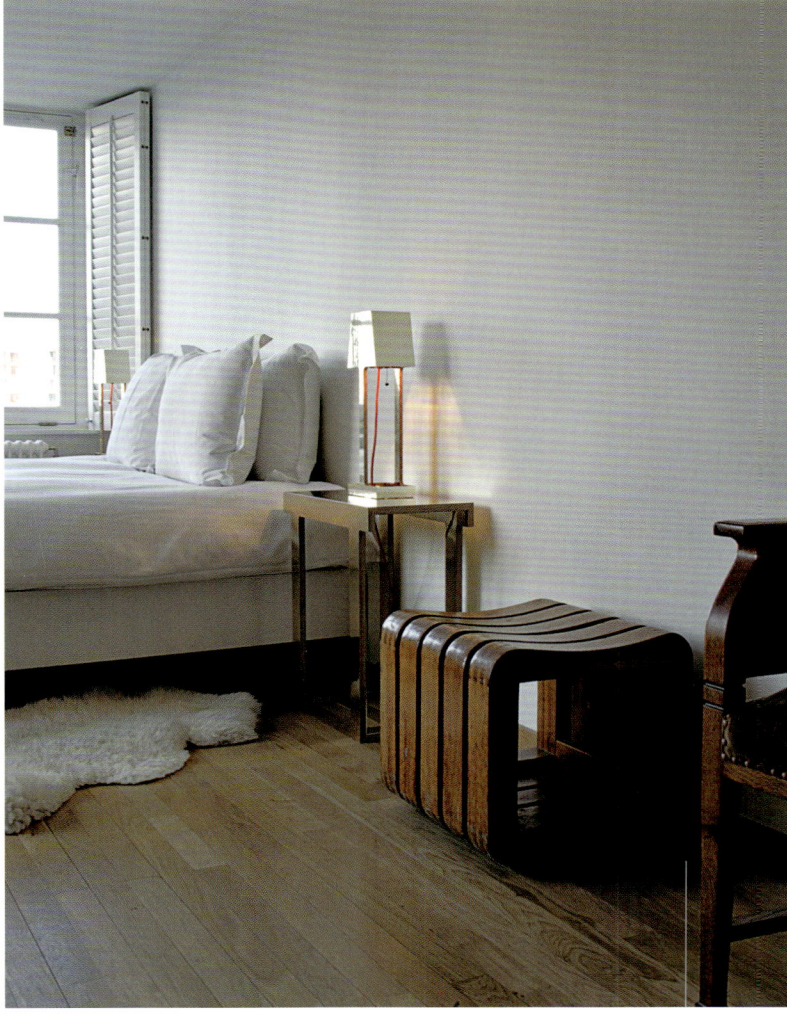

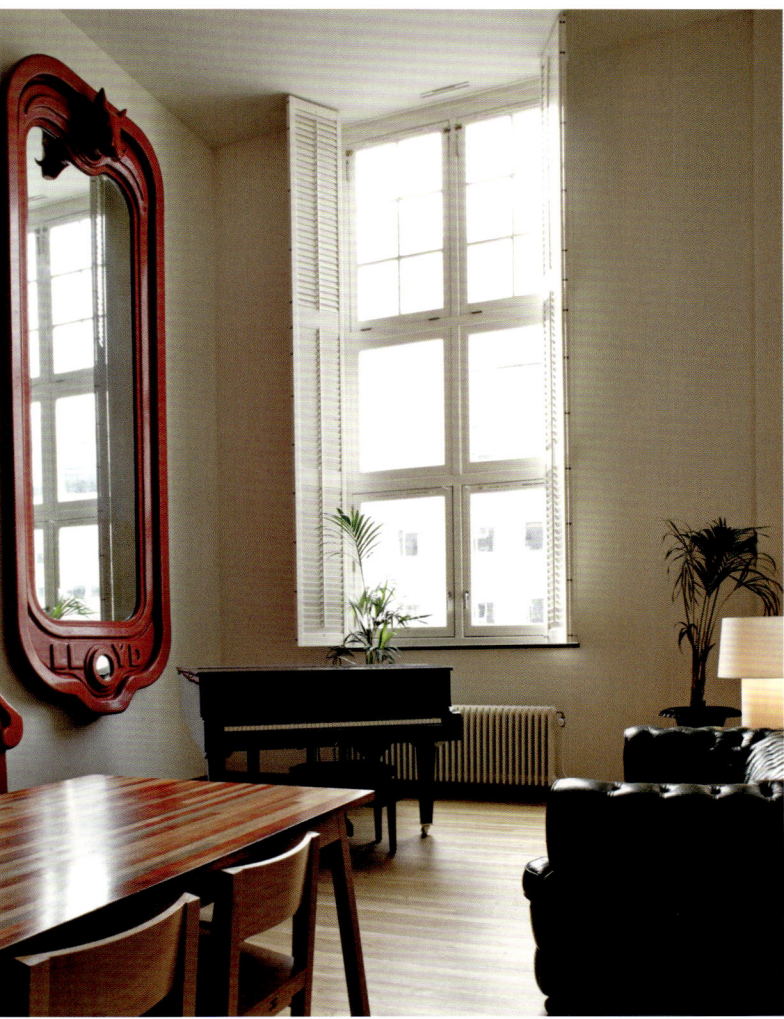

3024 EA Rotterdam
Netherlands
Phone: +31 10 221 4060
Fax: +31 10 221 4061
www.stroomrotterdam.nl

Rooms: 18 studios
Facilities: Bar, restaurant, 3 meeting rooms, VIP zone
Services: Free internet
Located: Near the Euromast and Musea, 10 min from the city center
Public transportation: Tram 8 Pieter de Hooghweg; Metro Coolhaven
Style: Design hotel

Water and wellness play the leading role at Rotterdam's Stroom. This is recognized as soon as you go through the doors to the studios and see the opulent bathing lounges. Those in need of recovery can submerge in a double bath on holiday. Late sleepers can plug in for breakfast any time of day, even on the roof terrace of the former powerhouse without shocking anyone. The flat screen monitors in the colorful restaurant let anyone look into the cooks' pots who wants to be sure what he is getting. And taking a seat at the long tables like at home in the kitchen, let you make acquaintances quickly.

Wasser und Wellness spielen im Rotterdamer Stroom die Hauptrolle. Das zeigt sich schon darin, dass hinter den Eingangstüren zu den Studios gleich die großzügigen Badelounges liegen. Erholungsbedürftige können in Doppelbadewanne in den Urlaub abtauchen. Frühstück für Langschläfer gibt es den ganzen Tag, auf Wunsch auch auf der Dachterrasse des ehemaligen Elektrizitätswerks. Im farbenfrohen Restaurant lassen sich die Köche über einen Flachbildschirm in die Töpfe schauen. Und weil man an den langen Tischen sitzt wie zu Hause in der Küche, sind auch Bekanntschaften schnell gemacht.

L'eau et le bien-être jouent le premier rôle au Stroom, à Rotterdam. Cela se manifeste dès qu'on franchit la porte d'entrée des studios, où se trouvent de spacieuses salles de bains. Ceux qui ont besoin de vacances peuvent se plonger dans des baignoires doubles. Pour les amateurs de grasse matinée, le petit-déjeuner est disponible toute la journée, et peut aussi sur demande être servi sur la terrasse du toit de cette ancienne centrale électrique. Le restaurant coloré dispose d'écrans plats qui permettent aux convives de jeter un œil sur le travail du chef. Et s'asseoir à une longue table en cuisine, comme chez soi, permet de nouer facilement des contacts.

Los protagonistas del hotel Stroom en Róterdam son el agua y el wellness, un hecho que se refleja a primera vista en la ubicación de los espaciosos salones de piscinas justo frente a las puertas de entrada de los estudios. Los sedientos de relax pueden sumergirse en bañeras dobles. Para complacer a los más dormilones, el desayuno se sirve a lo largo de todo el día y, a petición, también en la azotea de esta antigua central eléctrica. En el colorido restaurante, los cocineros consienten a sus huéspedes echar una ojeada a sus cazuelas a través de un monitor de plasma. Y puesto que en las largas mesas uno se siente como en casa, las nuevas amistades se hacen al vuelo.

Acqua e benessere sono gli ingredienti principali dello Stroom di Rotterdam. Lo si capisce già dal fatto che gli ampi "bagni salotto" si trovano subito dietro le porte d'ingresso dei monolocali. Chi ha bisogno di rilassarsi può tuffarsi nella vacanza immergendosi in vasche da bagno doppie. Per i dormiglioni la colazione viene servita tutto il giorno, su richiesta anche sulla terrazza del tetto della ex centrale elettrica. Nel ristorante dai colori vivaci, si può vedere su uno schermo piatto che cosa bolle nelle pentole dei cuochi. E seduti ai lunghi tavoli, quasi si fosse nella cucina di casa propria, nascono presto nuove amicizie.

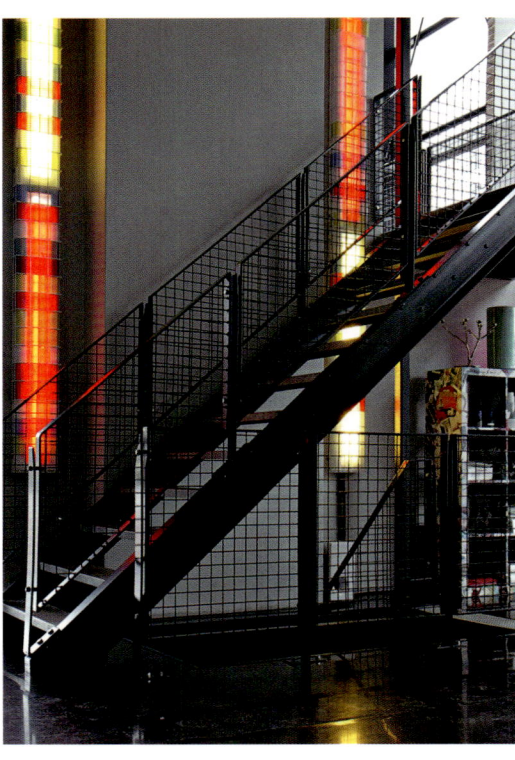 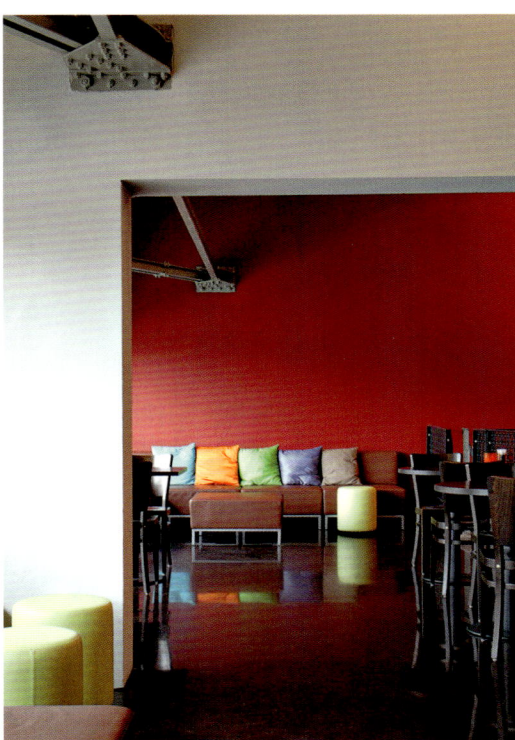 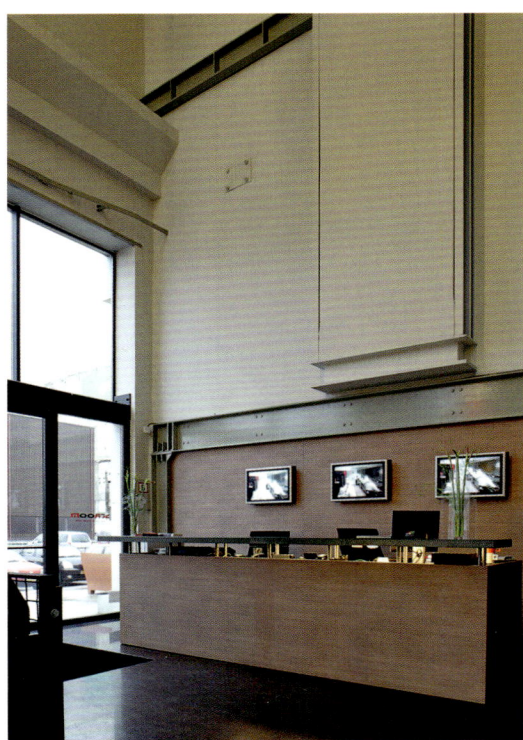

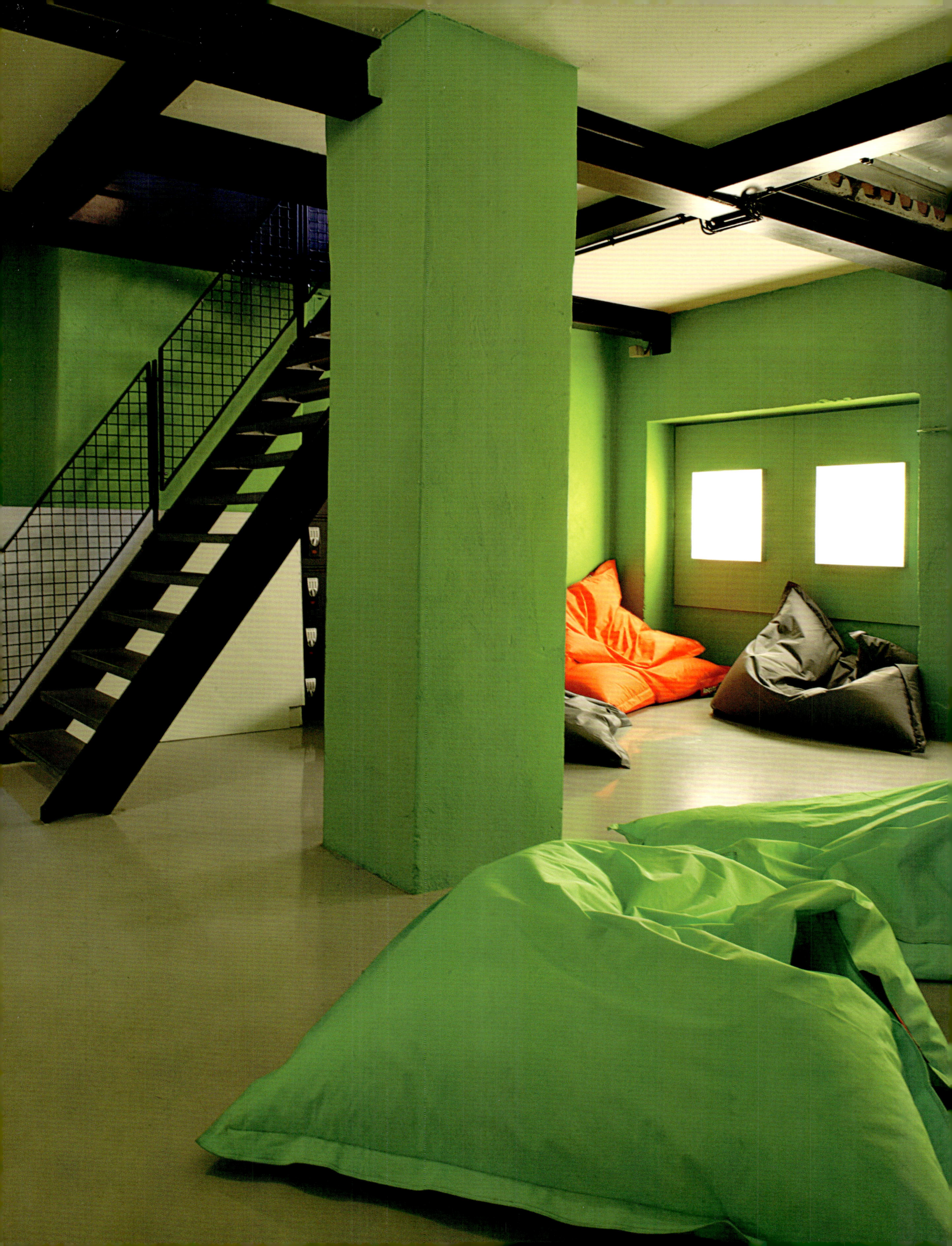

Eden Designhotel Maastricht

Maastricht, Netherlands

Stationsstraat 40
6221 BR Maastricht
Netherlands
Phone: +31 43 328 2525
Fax: +31 43 328 2526
www.edencityhotels.com

Price category: €
Rooms: 73 rooms
Facilities: Cocktail bar, trendy sandwich bar Simply Bread, beauty lounge, fitness room
Services: Room service, free newspapers and magazines, WiFi
Located: In the city center, in the hip Wyck quarter
Public transportation: Close to central train and bus station
Style: Design

The Eden Designhotel in the lively Wyck quarter of Maastricht was formerly known as La Bergère. Its 100 year old facade conceals a surprise of reduced design, graphic lines and cool materials like metal and Plexiglas behind it. A pinch of eccentricity is sprinkled in with the velvet rose pillows and colorful diced carpet. Room 305 is very elegantly furnished with creations of the Italian Minotti brand. Workaholics can have a workstation with computer, printer and fax rolled into the room. After work you can look through a newspaper in the pleasant reading lounge "La Byb."

Hinter der 100-jährigen Fassade des Eden Designhotels, früher bekannt unter dem Namen La Bergère, im lebendigen Wyck-Viertel von Maastricht überraschen reduziertes Design, grafische Linien und kühle Materialien wie Metal und Plexiglas. Eine Prise Exzentrik streuen die samtenen Rosenkissen und kunterbunt gewürfelten Teppiche ein. Raum 305 ist hochelegant mit Kreationen der italienischen Möbelmarke Minotti bestückt. Wer an den Laptop muss, dem wird eine Workstation mit Computer, Drucker und Fax ins Zimmer gerollt. Nach getaner Arbeit empfiehlt sich die Zeitungslektüre im „La Byb", der behaglichen Leselounge.

Derrière la façade centenaire du Eden Designhotel, autrefois connu sous le nom La Bergère, dans le quartier très animé de Wyck à Maastricht, le design minimaliste surprend, avec ses lignes graphiques et ses matériaux froids comme le métal et le plexiglas. Une pincée d'excentricité se répand sur les coussins en velours et les tapis multicolores. La chambre 305 est très élégamment meublée de créations de la marque italienne Minotti. Si vous avez besoin de matériel informatique, une station de travail complète est apportée dans votre chambre, avec ordinateur, imprimante et fax. Après une rude journée de travail, la lecture d'un journal est recommandée dans le confortable salon de lecture « La Byb ».

El Eden Designhotel era antes conocido como La Bergère. Detrás de su fachada centenaria en el bullicioso barrio Wyck de Maastricht, sorprenden el diseño reducido, las líneas gráficas y los materiales fríos como el metal o el plexiglás. Los aterciopelados cojines de rosas y las moquetas multicolores añaden un toque de excentricismo. La elegantísima habitación 305 está amueblada con creaciones de la casa italiana Minotti. Y quien necesite encender el portátil puede pedir una pequeña oficina sobre ruedas, completada con ordenador, impresora y fax. Y para cuando el huésped haya terminado su trabajo, se recomienda la lectura del periódico en el confortable salón "La Byb".

L'Eden Designhotel, era prima conosciuto come La Bergère. Dietro la sua secolare facciata del, nell'animato quartiere di Wyck, a Maastricht, verrete piacevolmente sorpresi da design essenziali, linee ben definite e materiali freddi come metallo e plexiglas. I cuscini di velluto a forma di rosa e i variopinti tappeti a quadri aggiungono un pizzico di eccentricità. L'elegantissima stanza 305 è arredata con pezzi della marca di mobili italiana Minotti. A chi deve usare il portatile viene allestita in camera una workstation provvista di computer, stampante e fax. Una volta finito il lavoro, non c'è niente di meglio di un giornale da leggere nel "La Byb", il confortevole salotto adibito alla lettura.

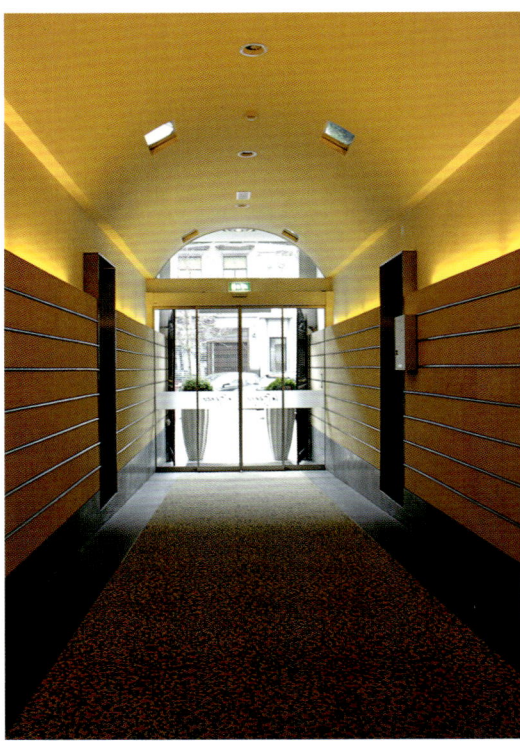 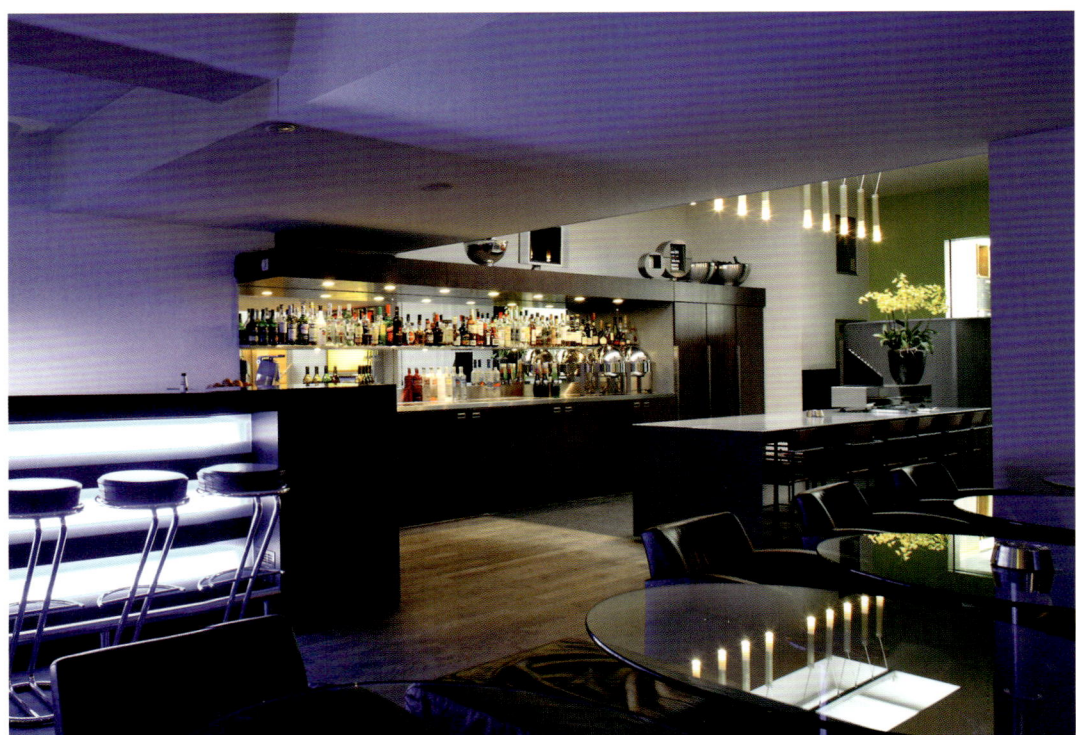

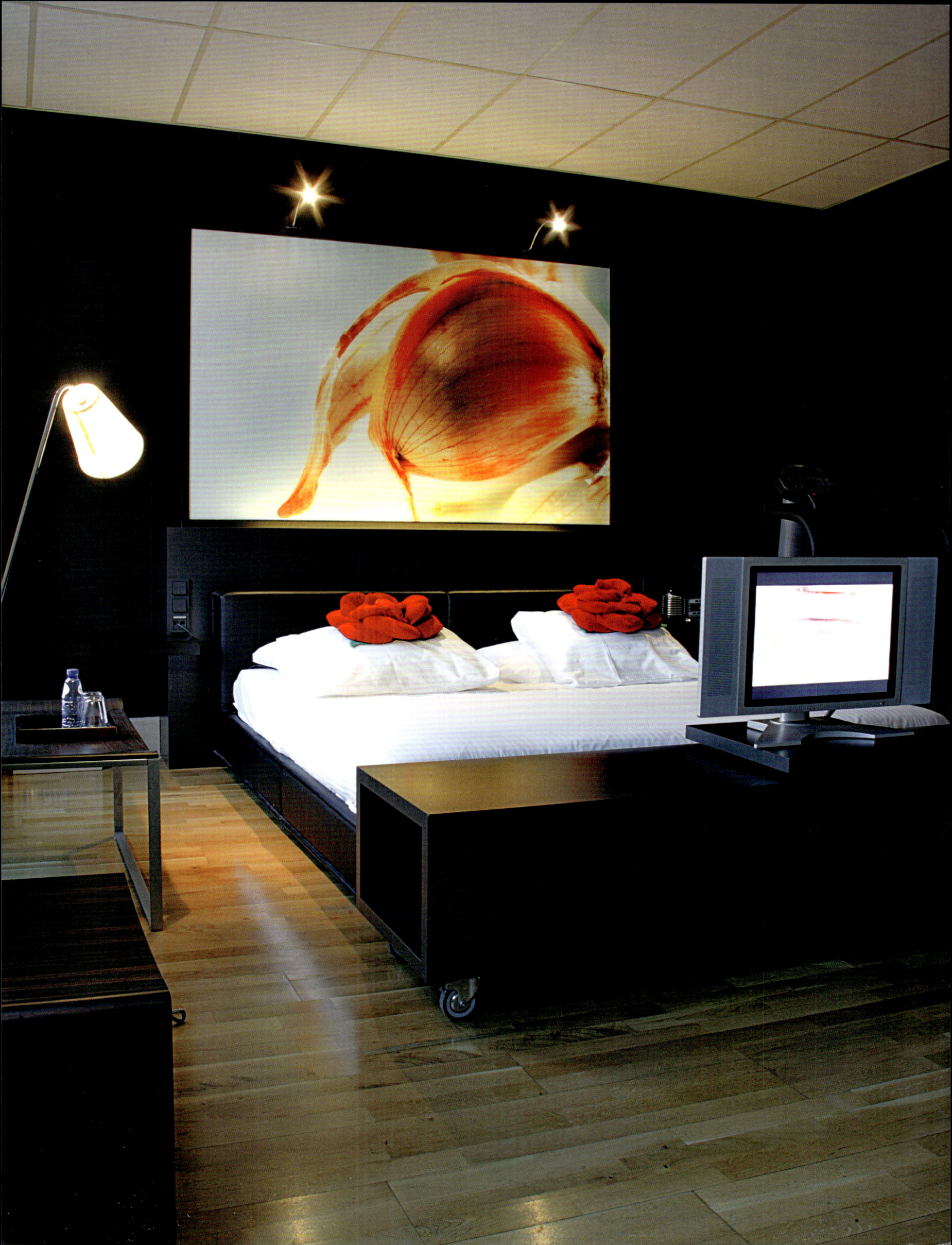

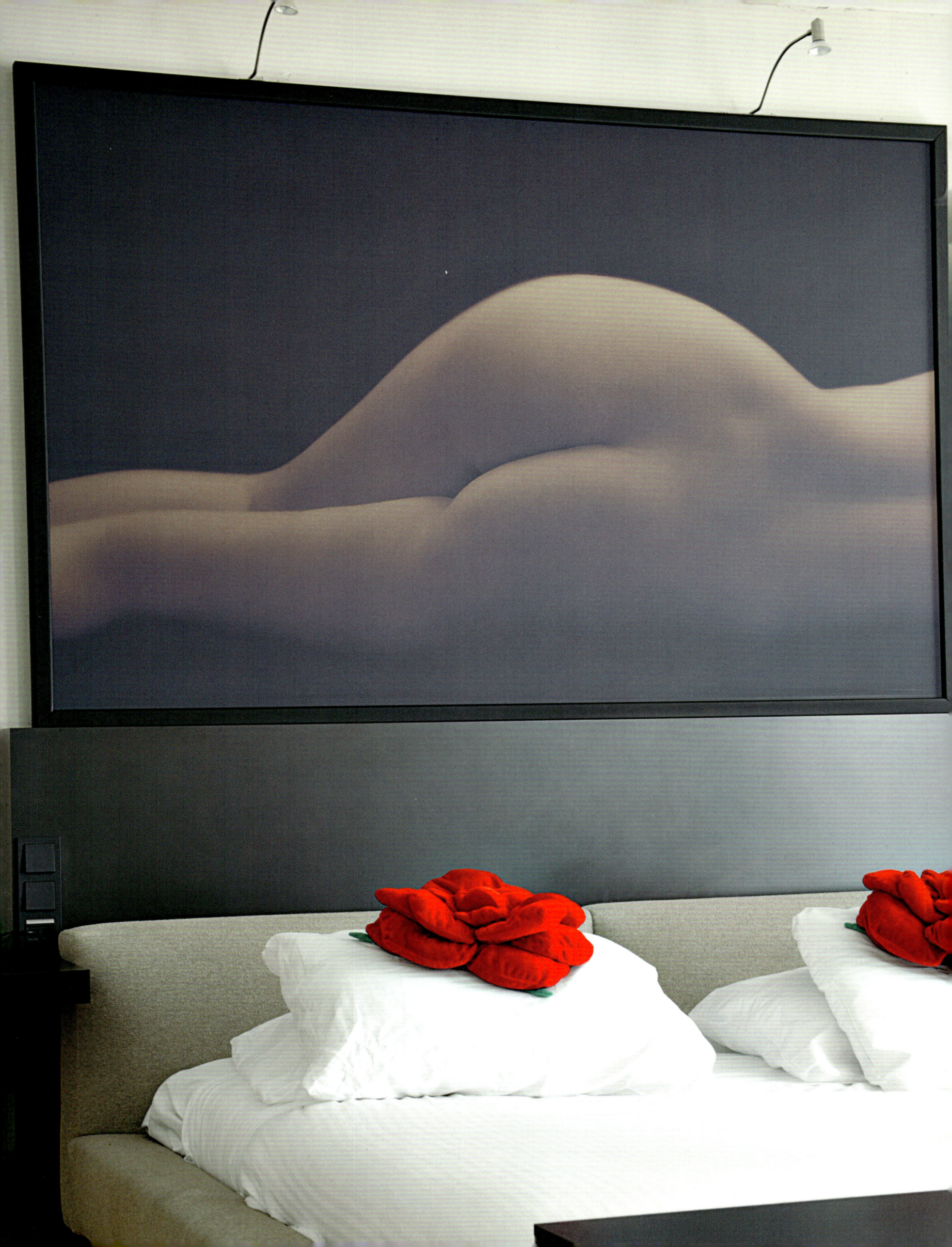

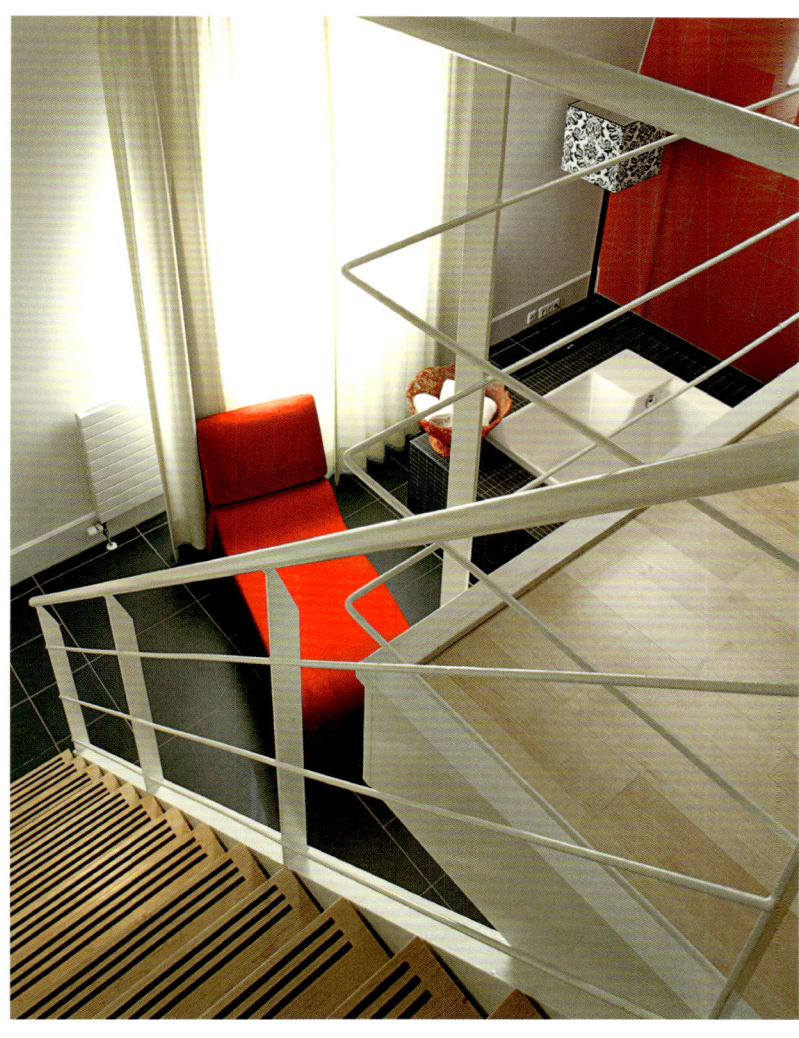

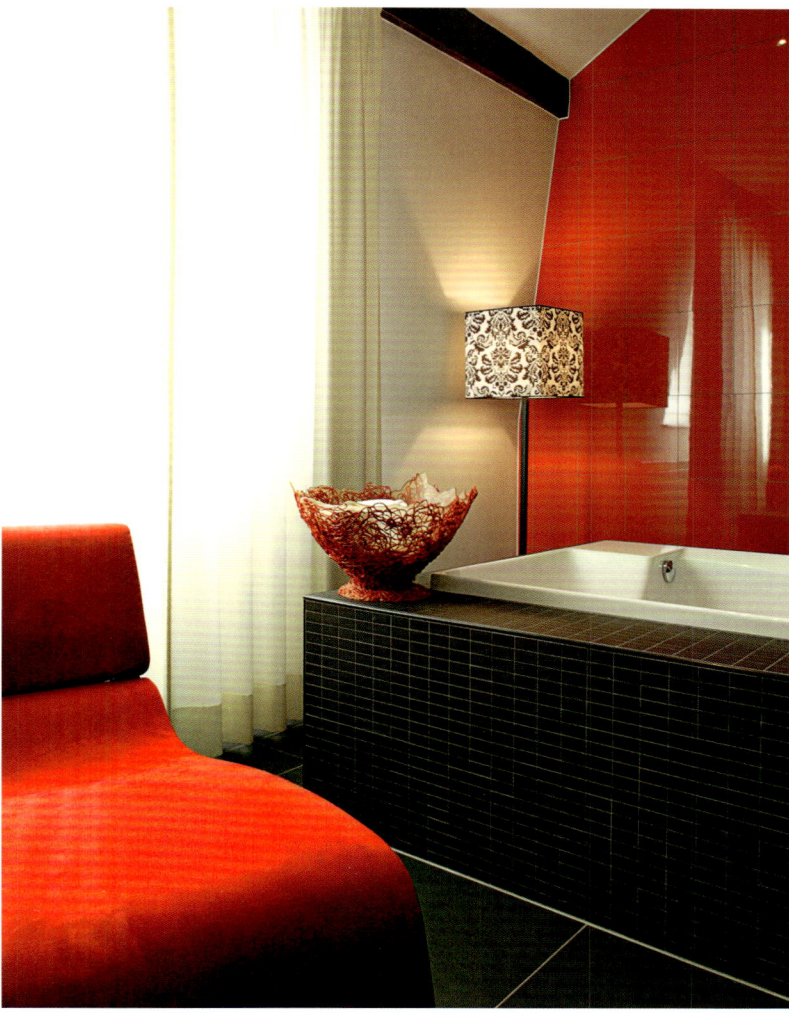

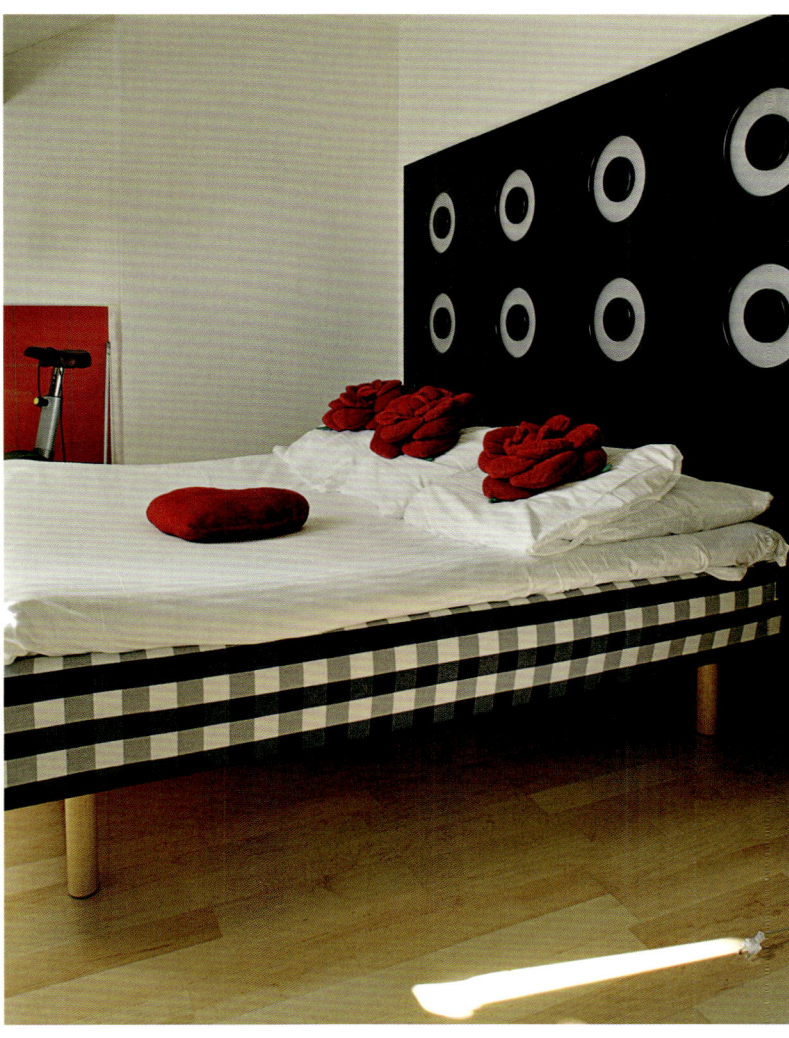

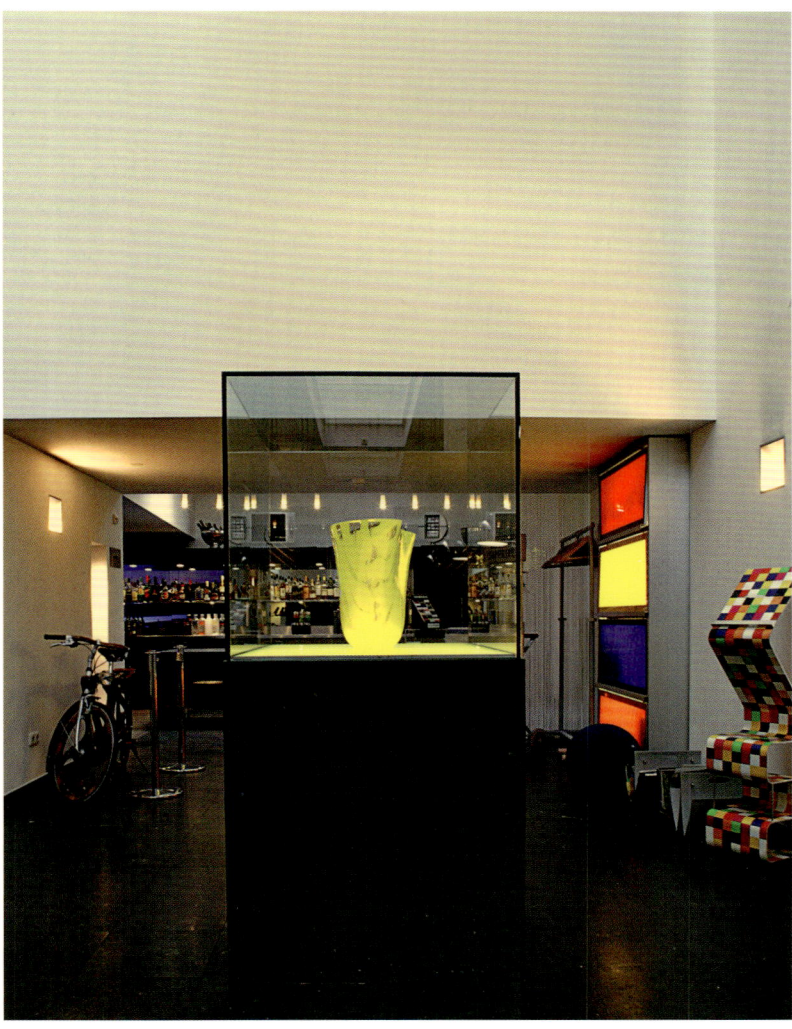

Kruisherenhotel Maastricht

Maastricht, Netherlands

Kruisherengang 19–23
6211 NW Maastricht
Netherlands
Phone: +31 43 329 2020
Fax: +31 43 323 3030
www.chateauhotels.nl

Price category: €€
Rooms: 32 rooms and 28 suites
Facilities: Winebar Rouge & Blanc, Kruisherenrestaurant, lounge corners, library, garden
Services: 24 h room service, laundry service, shoe shine, limousine service, valet parking, babysitting, dog walking, bicycles and Vespas available
Located: In the city center
Public transportation: Bus 3 Wolder, Kommelplein
Style: Design hotel

Whoever opens his eyes in this hotel is likely to believe in a hallucination at first. Instead of looking at white walls, many a guest looks through ancient Gothic stained-glass windows. The 15th-century monastery with an idyllic garden underwent state of the art renovations and is certain to transfer a traveler into another dimension. Design classics, wall paintings and the lighting magician Ingo Maurer's conception round off the artistic ensemble. Breakfast is served in the gallery with a breathtaking view of Maastricht.

Wer in diesem Prachthotel die Augen aufschlägt, glaubt im ersten Moment an eine Sinnestäuschung: Statt auf weiße Wände blickt mancher Gast durch uralte Buntglasmosaike gotischer Kirchenfenster. Das nach allen Regeln der Kunst renovierte Kloster aus dem 15. Jahrhundert mit idyllischem Garten versetzt Reisende augenblicklich in eine andere Dimension. Designklassiker, Wandmalereien und ein Beleuchtungskonzept von Lichtmagier Ingo Maurer runden das kürstlerische Ensemble ab. Frühstück wird auf der Empore serviert, mit atemberaubenden Ausblicken auf Maastricht.

Lorsque l'on voit pour la première fois ce magnifique hôtel, on croit être victime d'hallucination : au lieu des murs blancs, l'hôte regarde à travers les hauts vitraux colorés d'église gothique dans certaines chambres. Ce monastère du XVème siècle, rénové en employant les dernières techniques, et ses jardins idylliques transportent immédiatement les voyageurs dans une dimension totalement différente. Des classiques du design, des peintures murales et un concept d'éclairage élaboré par le magicien des lumières Ingo Maurer complètent cet ensemble artistique. Le petit-déjeuner est servi sur la galerie, avec une vue imprenable sur Maastricht.

Aquel que abra los ojos en este lujoso hotel tardará en dar crédito a lo que ve, en lugar de paredes blancas advertirá antiquísimas vidrieras de mosaicos góticos. Este antiguo monasterio de jardines idílicos, que data del siglo XV, fue renovado respetando cada una de las reglas del arte. Este lugar es capaz de transportar a otra dimensión y en un solo instante a aquel que lo visita. Los clásicos del diseño, las pinturas murales y el concepto de iluminación concebido por el mago de las luces, Ingo Maurer, crean un conjunto armónico. El desayuno se sirve en una galería alta con vistas maravillosas sobre Maastricht.

Chi apre gli occhi in questo magnifico albergo, per un attimo pensa a un'illusione ottica: al posto di pareti bianche ci sono antichissimi mosaici di vetro colorato provenienti da finestre di chiese gotiche. Questo monastero del XV secolo, rinnovato a regola d'arte e provvisto di un giardino idilliaco, trasporta i viaggiatori per un attimo in un'altra dimensione. Classici pezzi di design, pitture murali e un'illuminazione ideata dal mago della luce Ingo Maurer completano questo artistico ensemble. La colazione viene servita nel matroneo, con vedute mozzafiato su Maastricht.

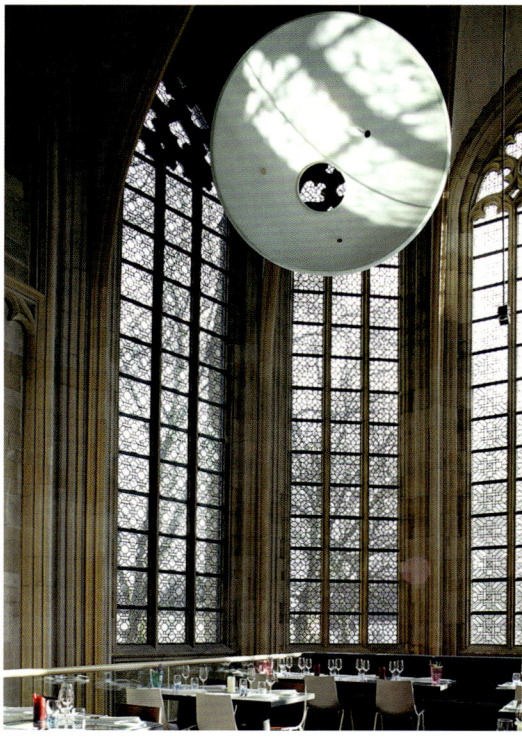

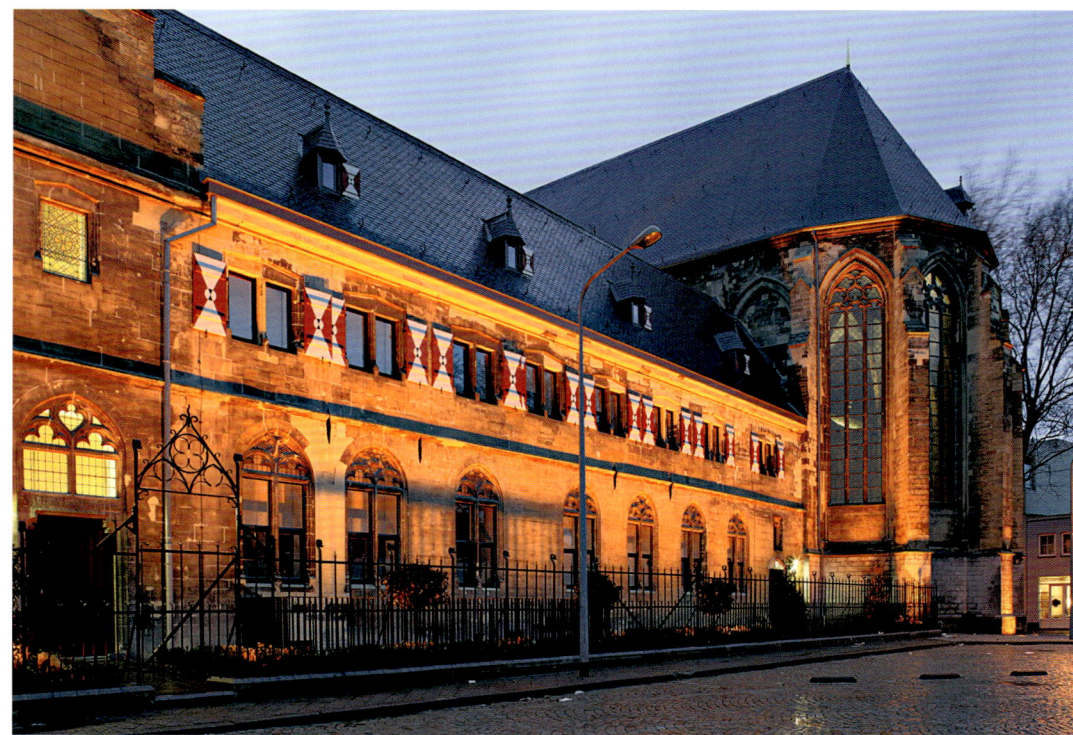

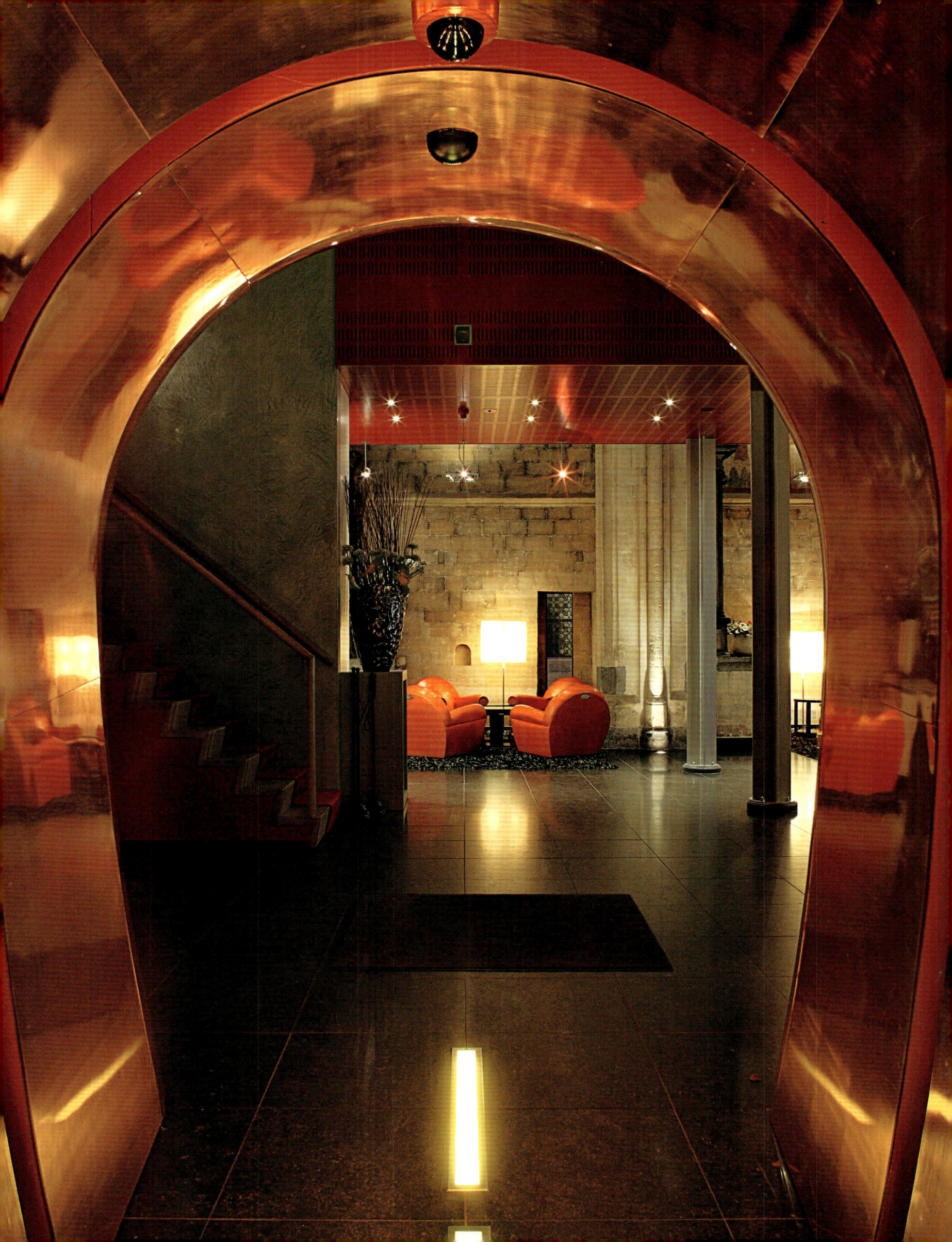

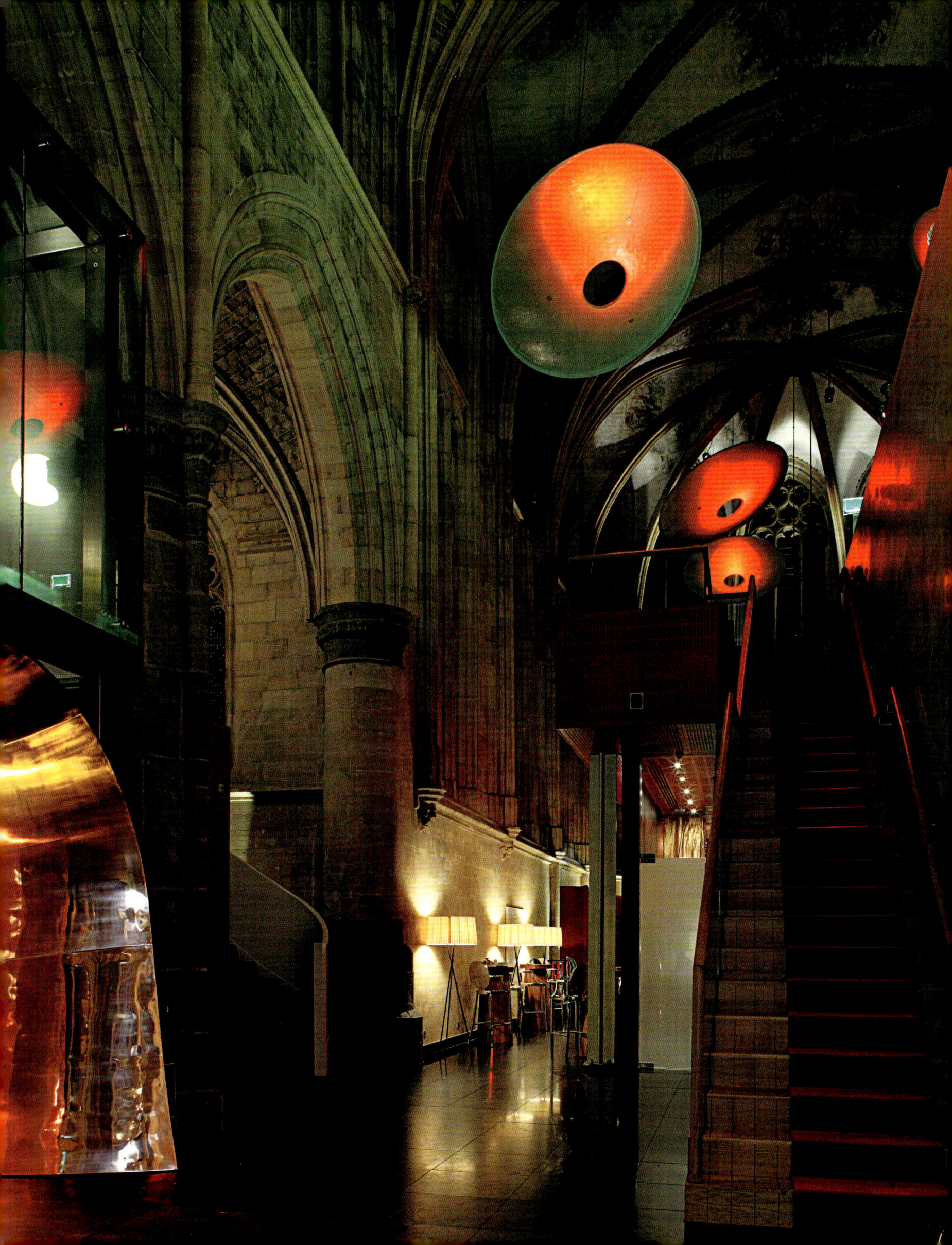

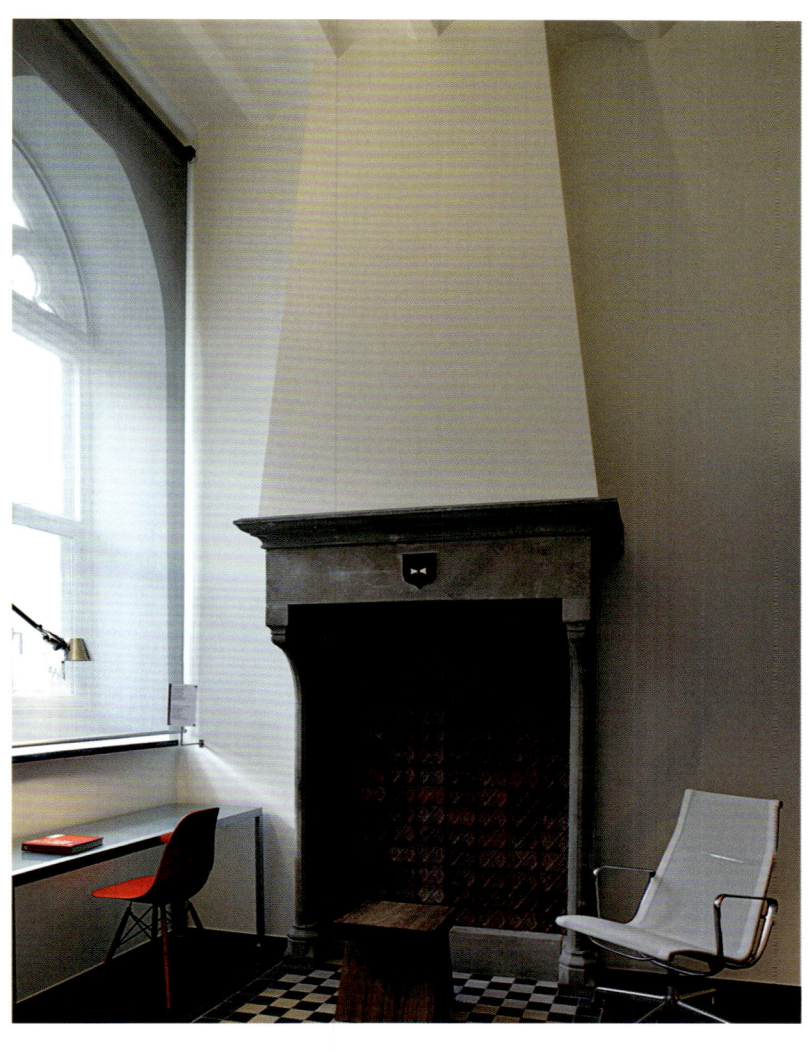
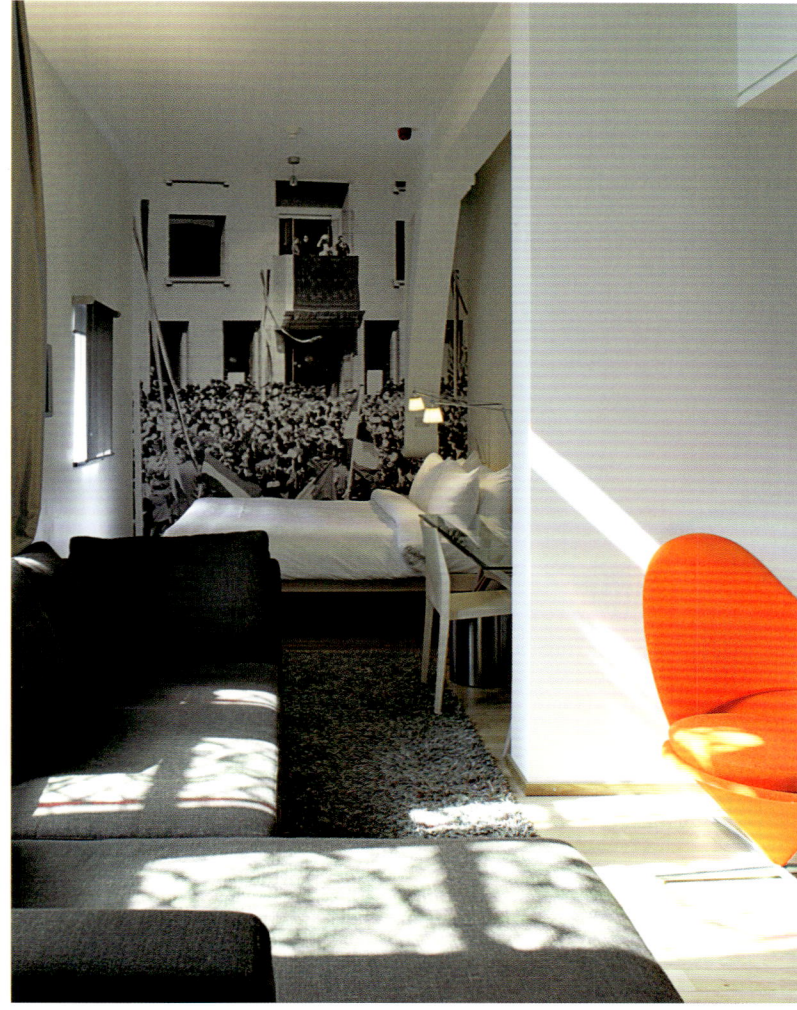
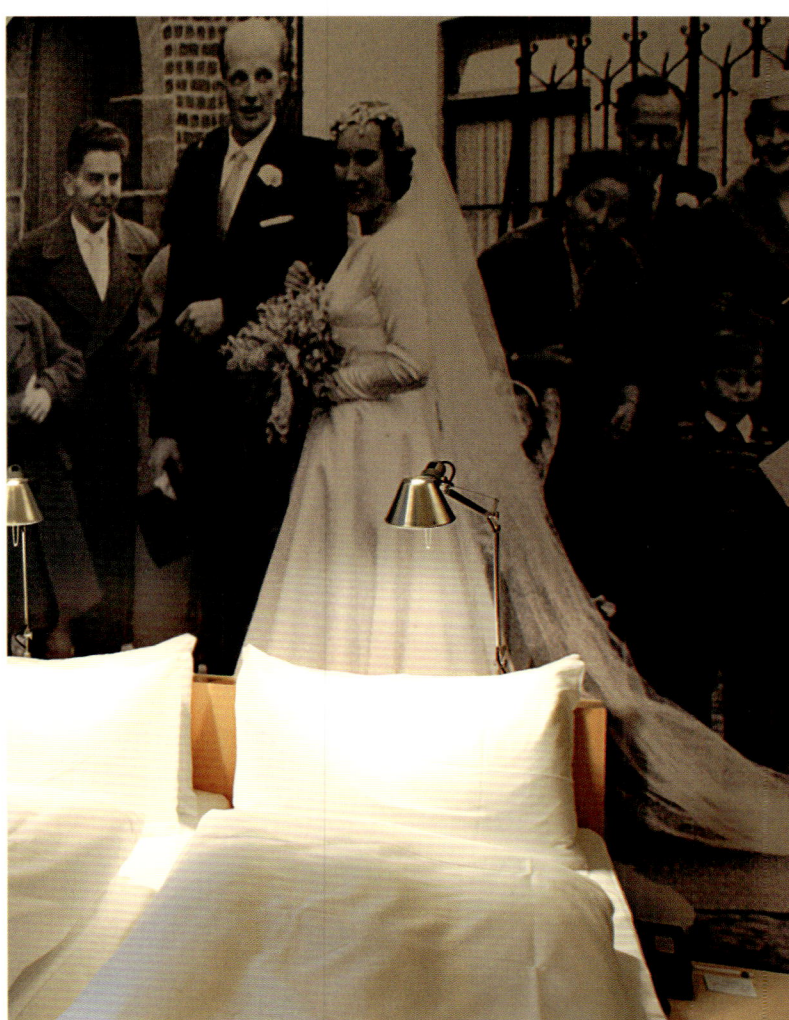
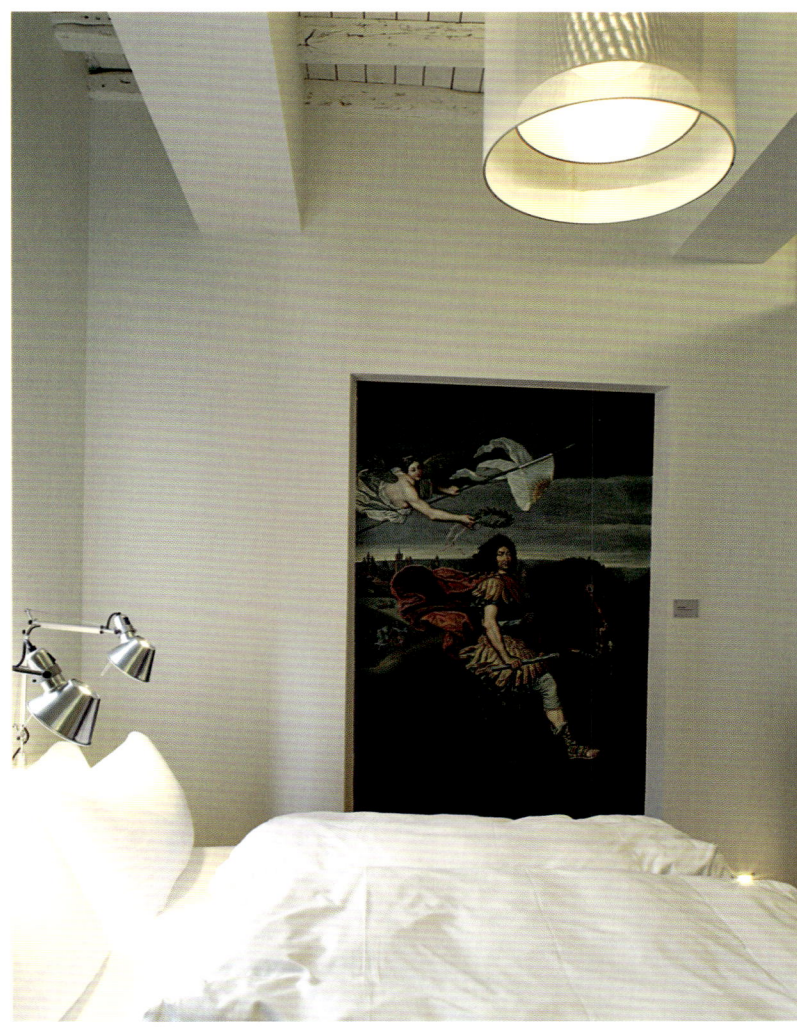

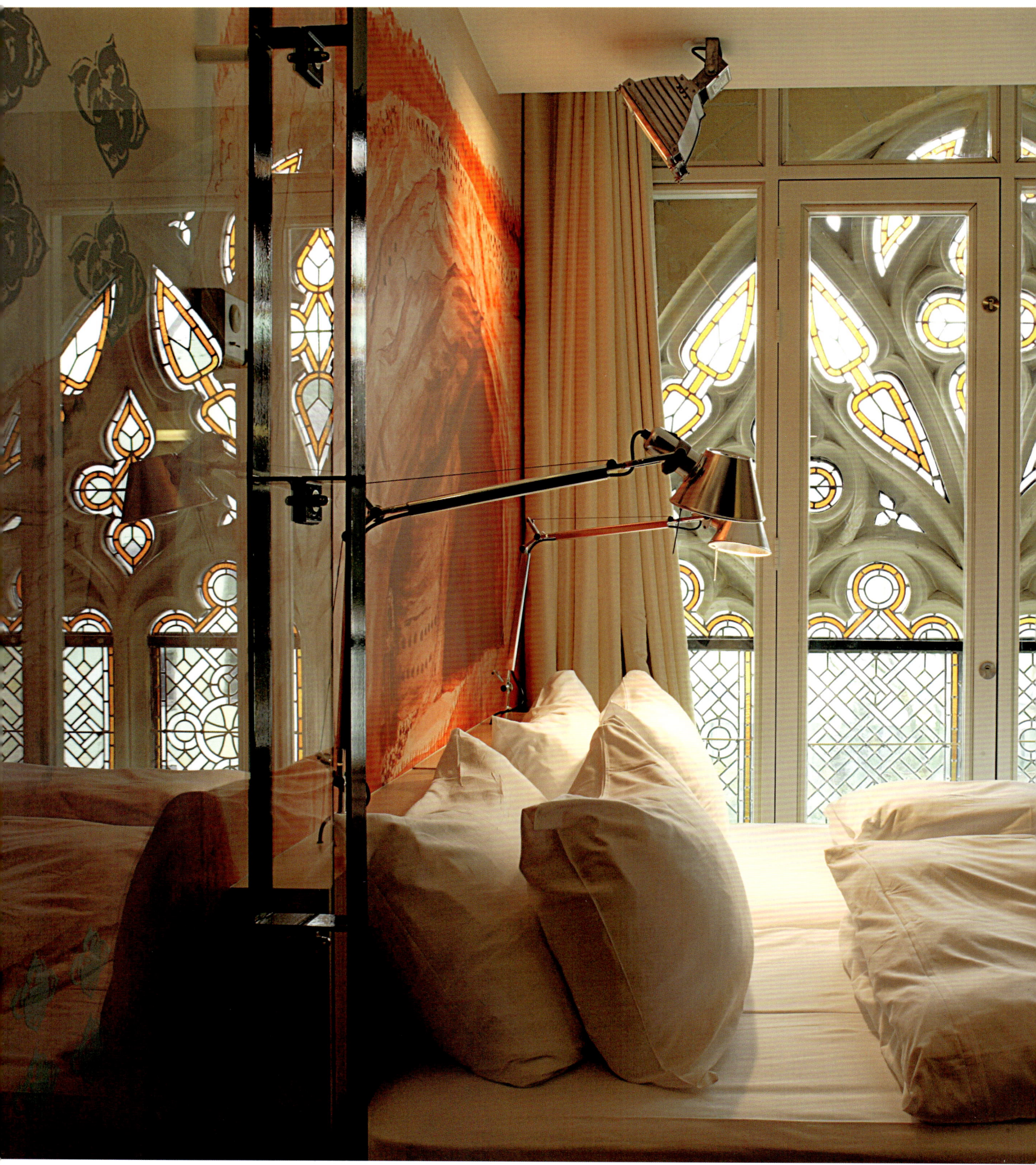

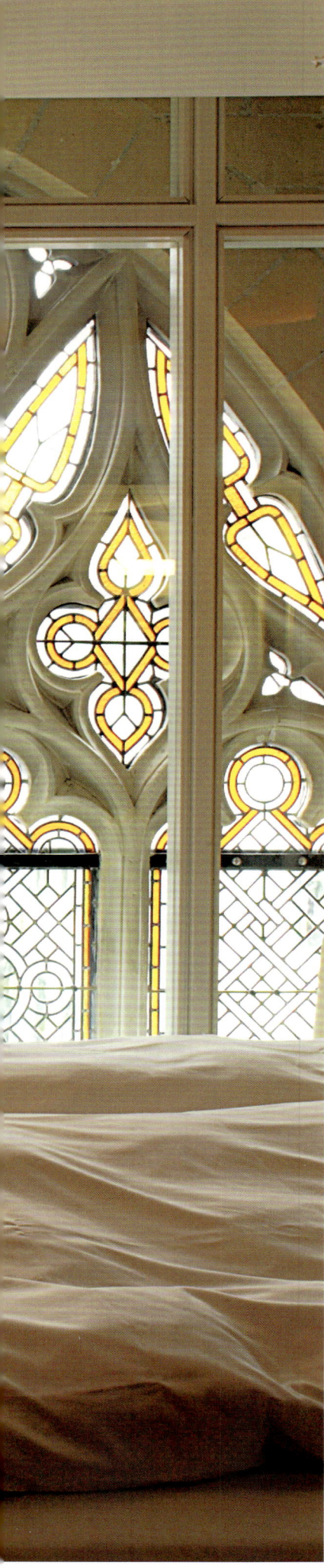

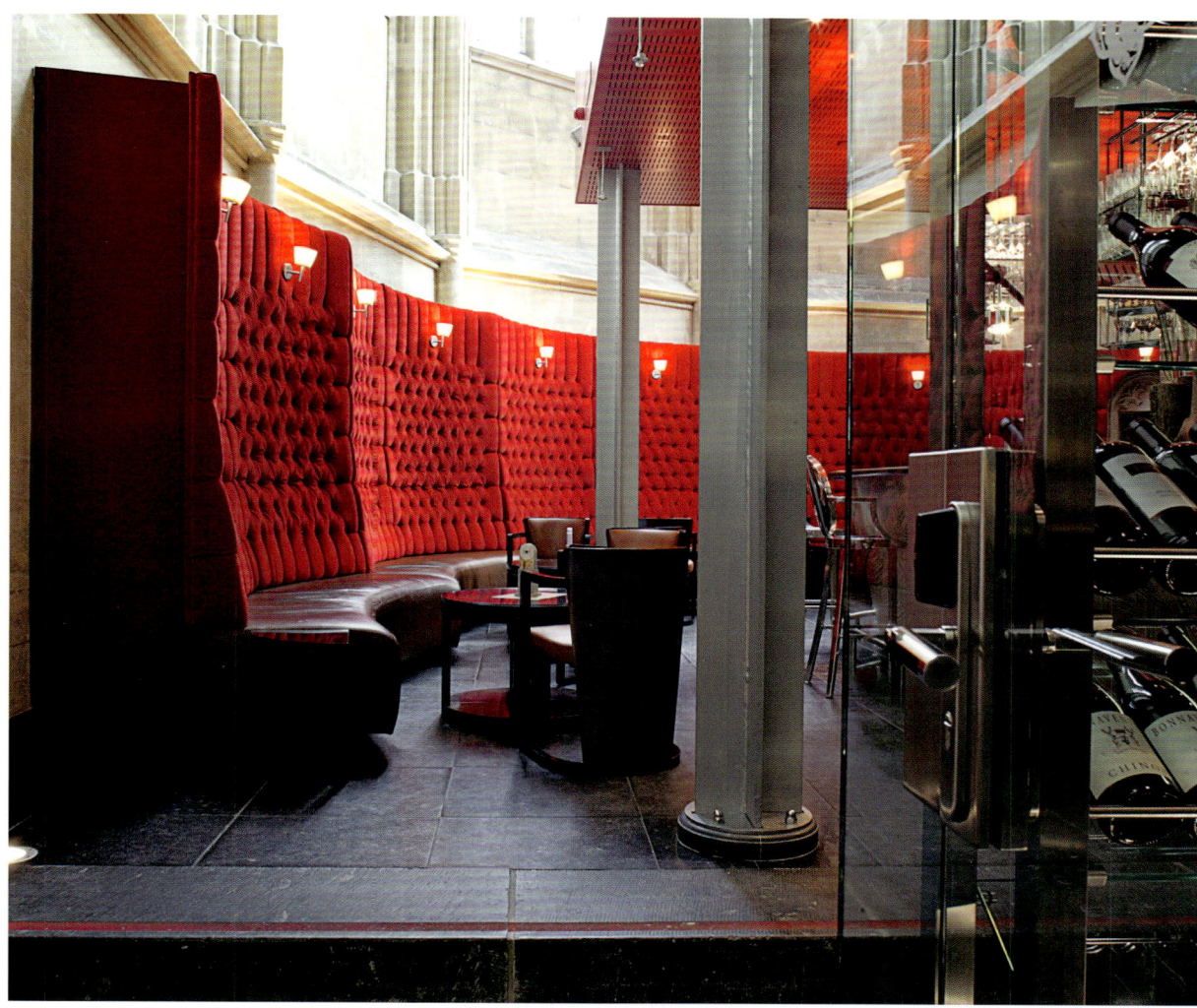

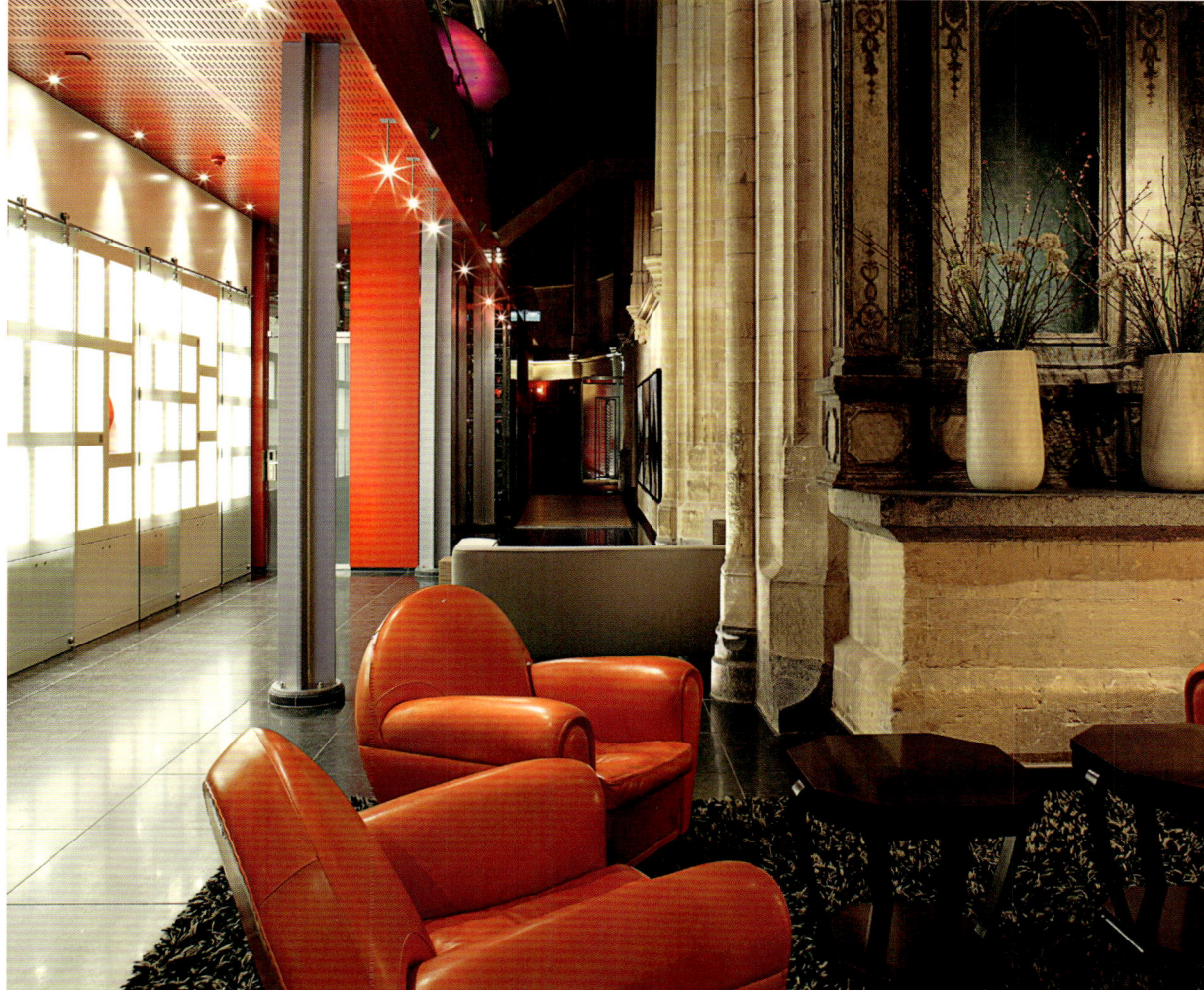

Hotel Julien

Antwerp, Belgium

Korte Nieuwstraat 24
2000 Antwerp
Belgium
Phone: +32 3 229 06 00
Fax: +32 3 233 35 70
www.hotel-julien.com

Price category: €€
Rooms: 11 rooms
Facilities: Breakfast room, library, lounge/bar, special designed porcelain for Hotel Julien
Services: Free WiFi, laundry and dry cleaning, babysitting, DVD and CD library, 24 h front desk, non-smoking rooms, choice of newspapers and magazines
Located: In the old city center
Public transportation: Tram 10, 11; Underground 2, 15
Style: Contemporary design

Two of the typical narrow 16th-century buildings in Antwerp house the wonderful small hotel in the heart of the trendy Belgian metropolis. Its eleven rooms are grouped around a green inner court that makes a city oasis out of the hotel. Classical modern furniture largely by Ray and Charles Eames are combined with light materials to make up the friendly atmosphere. The lounge fitted with elaborate wood carvings and the open fireplace invites you to come in and relax. The famous fashion designers Dries van Noten and Martin Margiela have their studios nearby.

Zwei der typischen schmalbrüstigen Antwerpener Häuser aus dem 16. Jahrhundert beherbergen das kleine, feine Hotel im Herzen der belgischen Trendmetropole. Seine elf Zimmer gruppieren sich um einen grünen Innenhof, der das Hotel zur Stadtoase werden lässt. Möbel der Klassischen Moderne, viele von Ray und Charles Eames, kombiniert mit hellen Stoffen, prägen das Ambiente. Im Salon mit seinen aufwendigen Holzschnitzereien lädt ein offener Kamin zum Entspannen ein. Und die berühmten Modedesigner Dries van Noten und Martin Margiela haben ihre Ateliers in unmittelbarer Nähe.

A Anvers, deux petites maisons typiques du XVIème siècle abritent un petit hôtel luxueux au cœur de la métropole belge. Ses onze chambres sont regroupées autour d'une cour intérieure verte, qui transforme l'hôtel en oasis urbaine. Des meubles classiques modernes, dont on doit un grand nombre à Ray et Charles Eames, mariés à des tissus légers, créent une atmosphère conviviale. Le salon, avec ses sculptures de bois tortueuses et sa cheminée ouverte, invite à la relaxation. Et les célèbres créateurs de mode Dries van Noten et Martin Margiela ont leur atelier tout près.

Este pequeño y refinado hotel, albergado en dos de las típicas casas amberinas de estrechas fachadas del siglo XVI, se encuentra en el corazón de la metrópolis de la moda belga. Sus once habitaciones se agrupan en torno a un patio interior lleno de vegetación, que hace del hotel un oasis en plena ciudad. El ambiente está marcado por muebles de la modernidad clásica, muchos de ellos de Ray y Charles Eames, combinados con tejidos claros. En el salón, con sus laboriosas tallas en madera, una chimenea invita a relajarse. Además, los famosos diseñadores Dries van Noten y Martin Margiela tienen sus estudios a dos pasos del hotel.

Situato nel cuore di una delle città più alla moda del Belgio, questo albergo piccolo ed elegante è ospitato da due case nel tipico stile di Antwerpen, risalenti al XVI secolo e riconoscibili per la stretta facciata. Le sue undici stanze sono raggruppate attorno a un verde cortile interno, che rende l'hotel quasi un'oasi nella città. L'ambiente è caratterizzato dalla presenza di mobili di modernariato, molti dei quali di Ray e Charles Eames, combinati con stoffe dai colori chiari. Nel salone, elaborate sculture in legno e un camino con fuoco a vista invitano gli ospiti ad abbandonarsi al relax. E nelle immediate vicinanze si trovano gli atelier dei famosi stilisti Dries van Noten e Martin Margiela.

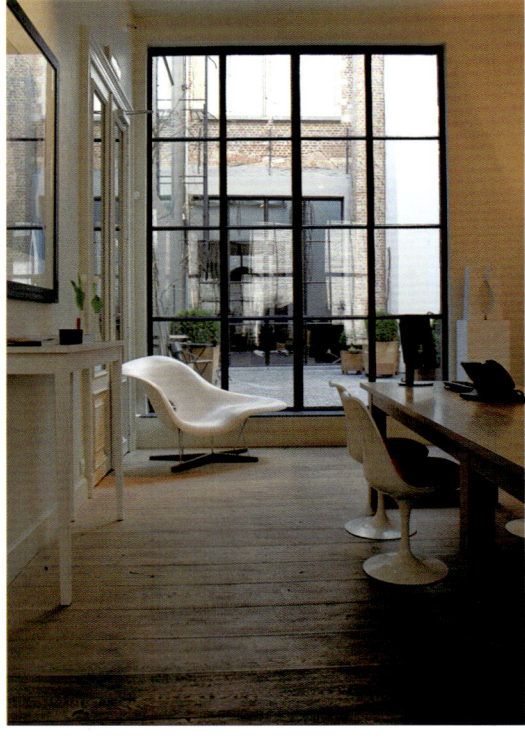 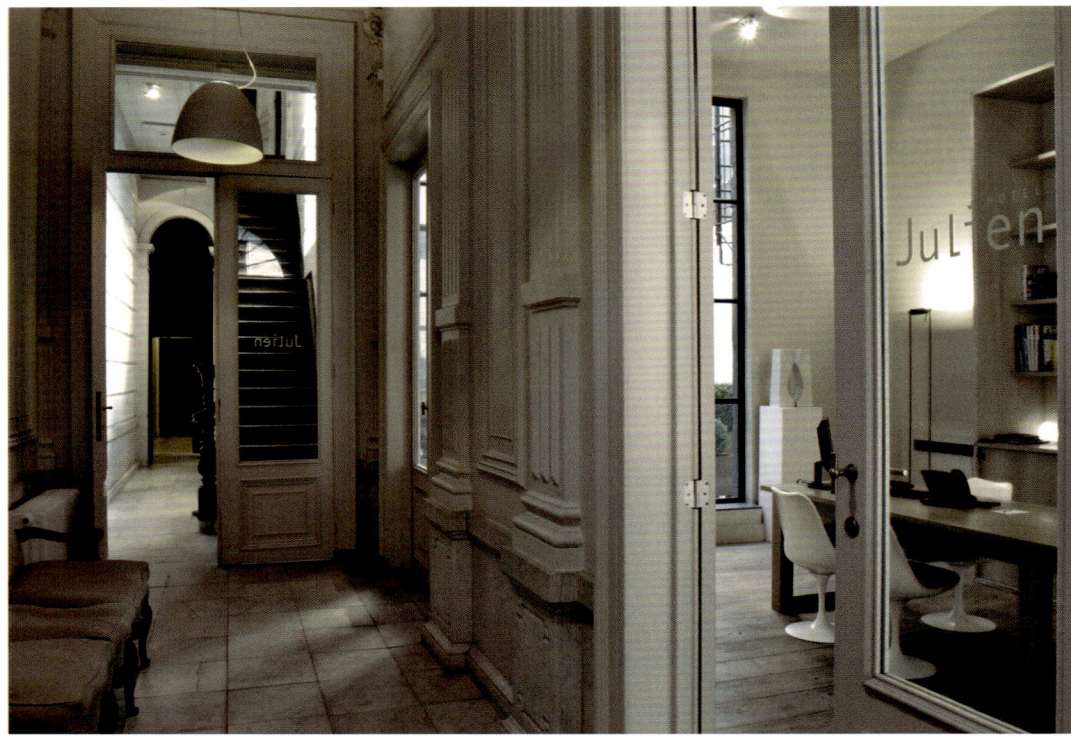

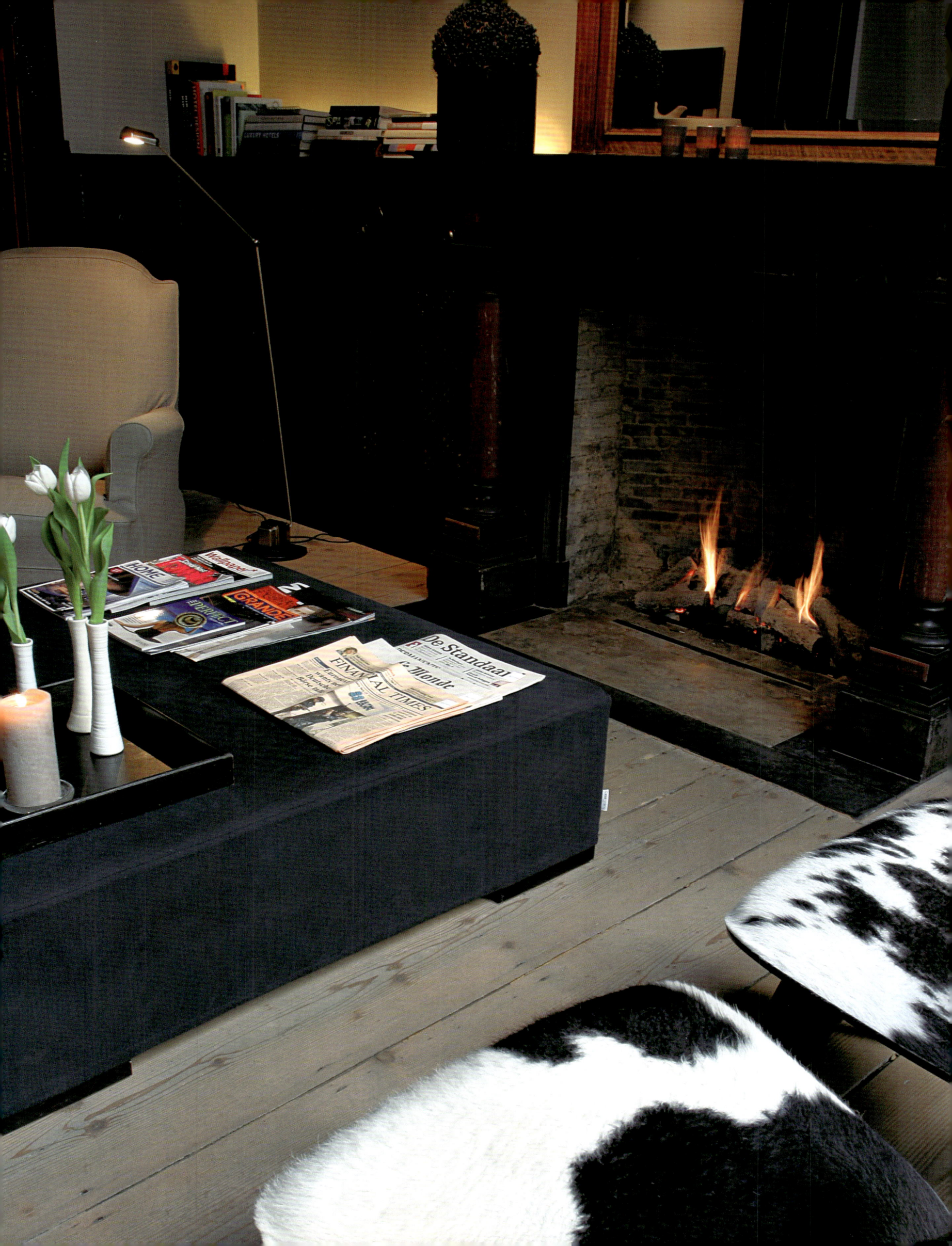

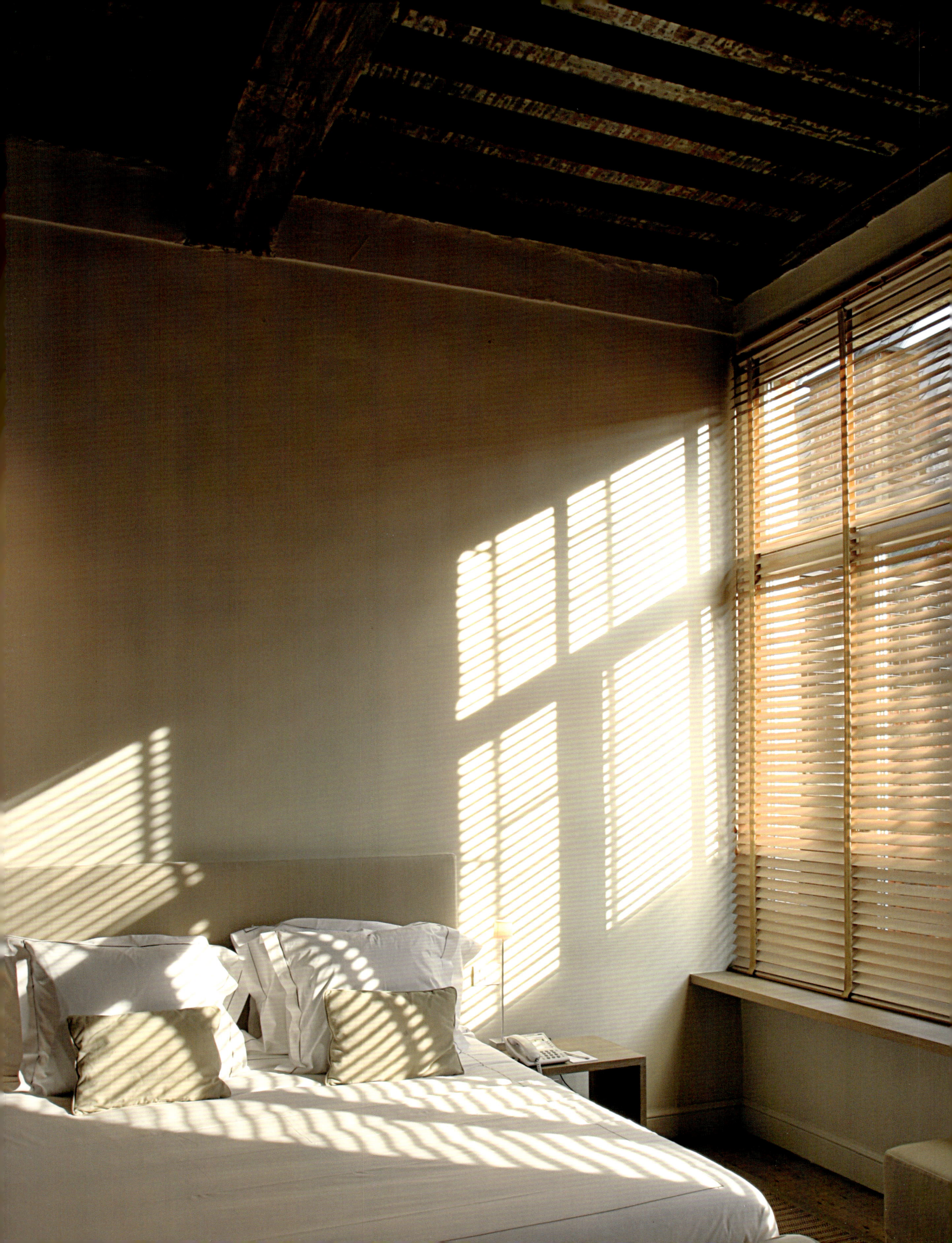

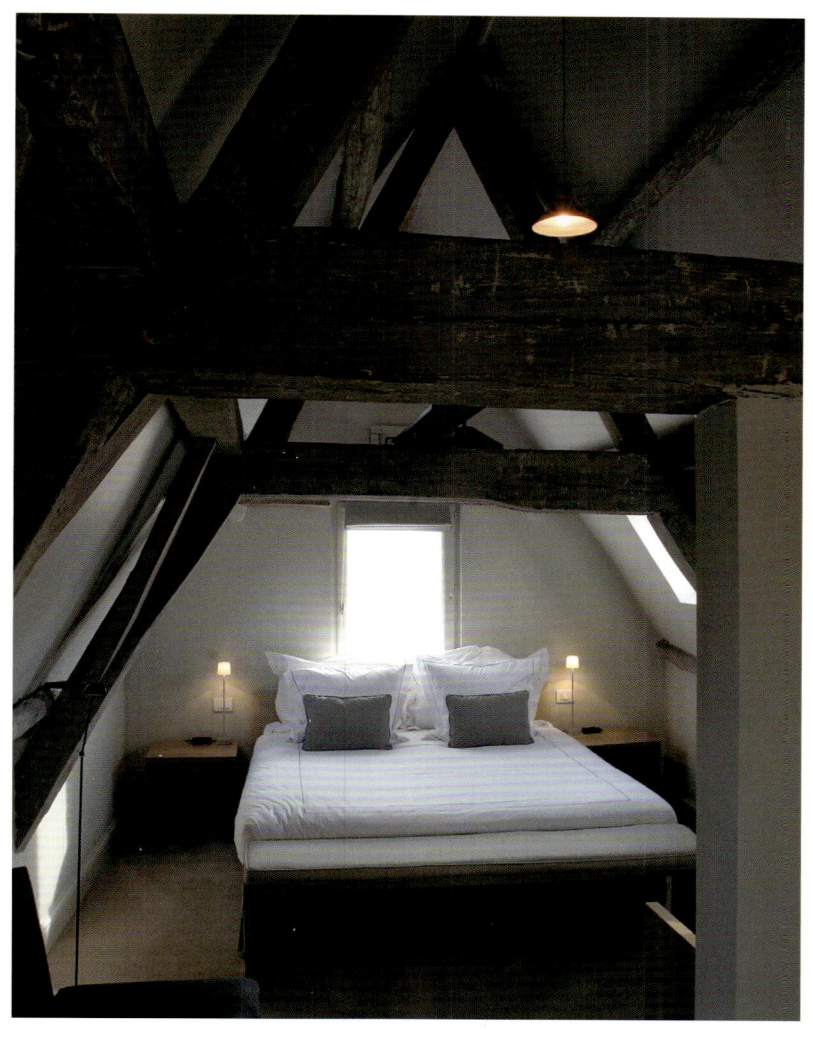
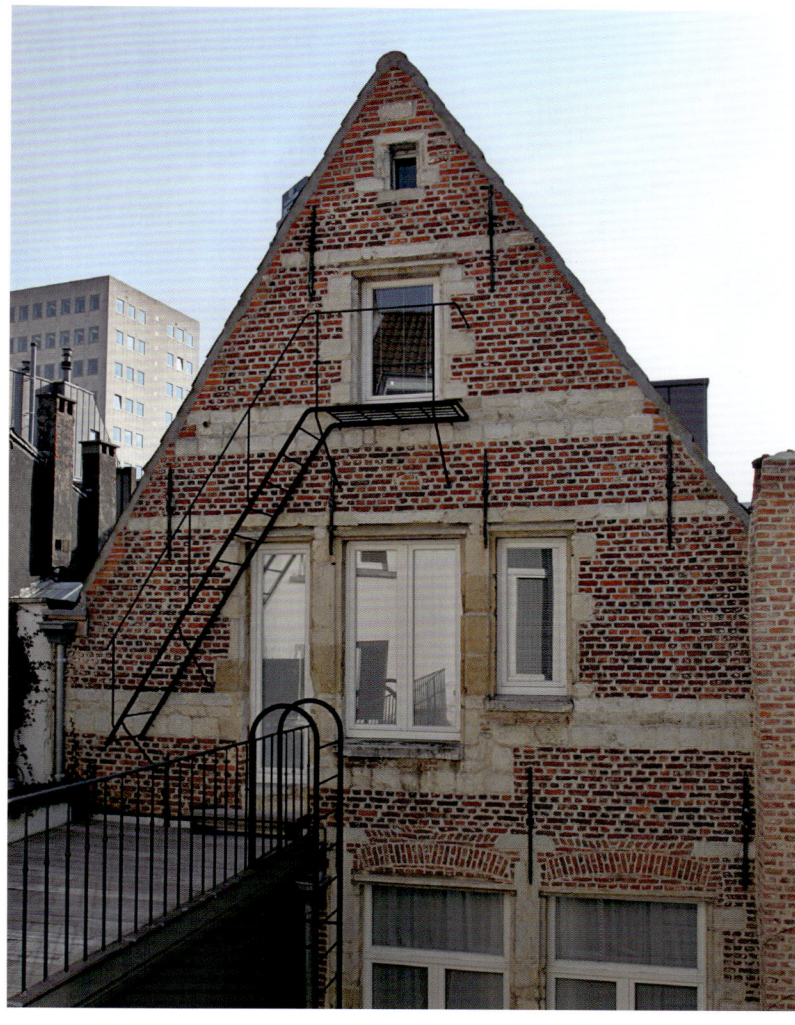
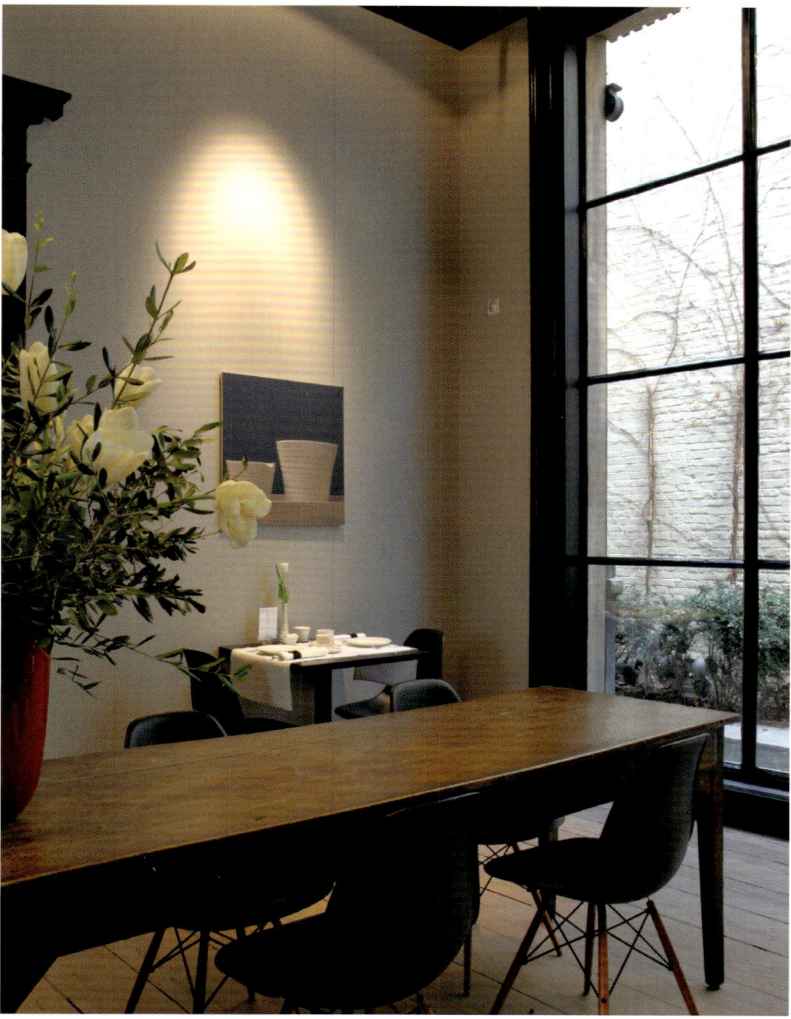
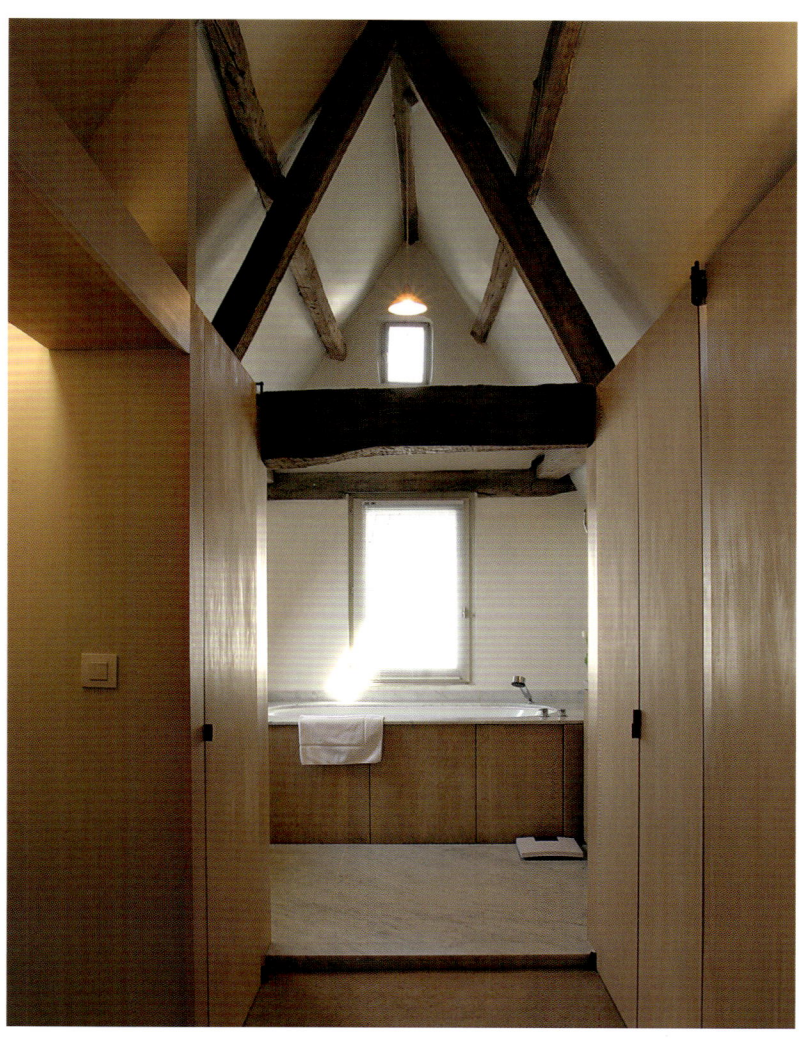

Hotel Julien | Antwerp, Belgium **119**

1200 Brussels
Belgium
Phone: +32 2 734 56 36
Fax: +32 2 734 50 05
www.monty-hotel.be

Rooms: 18 rooms
Facilities: Bar, table d'hotes breakfast, business desk, garden
Services: Babysitting, free WiFi, bicycle rental, 24 h reception, luggage storage
Located: In the Montgomery area
Public transportation: Underground, tram, bus
Style: Design and contemporary

Despite the many museums in Brussels there is no design museum. This made the owner of the Monty decide to make a showroom for contemporary design out of her 18 room hotel near the seat of the EU. It is worthwhile for guest to go on a discovery trip to see where Charles Eames' Rocking Chair is, which room is lighted by Ingo Maurer's Holonski, and where you can relax in Ron Arad's club chair Size Ten. The atmosphere is quite personal, almost familiar. You will have your breakfast together with the other guests on the *table d'hôte*, one big dining table.

Trotz der Museumsvielfalt in Brüssel gibt es kein Design-Museum. Das brachte die Besitzer des Monty auf die Idee, ihr 18-Zimmer-Hotel in der Nähe des EU-Sitzes zu einem Showroom für zeitgenössisches Design zu machen. Es lohnt sich für Gäste auf Entdeckungsreise zu gehen, zu schauen, wo Charles Eames Rocking Chair steht, welches Zimmer Ingo Maurers Holonski beleuchtet, wo man in Ron Arads Clubsessel Size Ten relaxen kann. Die Atmosphäre ist persönlich, fast familiär. Gefrühstückt wird gemeinsam an einer Table d'hôte, einem großen Esstisch.

Même s'il existe une grande variété de musées à Bruxelles, il n'y a pas de Musée du Design. Cela a donné l'idée à la propriétaire du Monty de convertir son hôtel de 18 chambres, situé près du siège de l'UE, à une salle d'exposition du design moderne. Les clients peuvent faire une petite expédition pour découvrir où se trouve la Rocking Chair de Charles Eames, quelle chambre est éclairée par une Holonski d'Ingo Maurer, et où l'on peut se reposer dans le fauteuil club Size Ten de Ron Arad. L'atmosphère est personnelle, presque familiale. Le petit-déjeuner se prend en commun autour d'une vaste table d'hôte.

A pesar de la gran cantidad de museos existentes en Bruselas, ninguno está dedicado al diseño. Esto les dio a los dueños del Monty la idea de hacer de su hotel de 18 habitaciones, situado en las proximidades de la sede de la UE, una sala de exposición de diseño contemporáneo. Vale la pena hacer una pequeña expedición por el hotel y descubrir dónde se encuentran la mecedora Rocking Chair de Charles Eames, qué habitación está iluminada por Holonski de Ingo Maurer o dónde puede uno relajarse en el butacón Size Ten de Ron Arad. El ambiente es muy íntimo, casi familiar. El desayuno se sirve en una *table d'hôte*, una gran mesa de comedor.

Nonostante la ricchezza di musei della città, a Bruxelles manca un museo del design. È stata proprio questa lacuna a dare ai proprietari del Monty l'idea di fare del loro albergo da 18 camere, posto nelle vicinanze della sede dell'UE, uno spazio espositivo del design contemporaneo. Gli ospiti possono dedicarsi all'esplorazione della casa e scoprire, per esempio, dove si trova la Rocking Chair di Charles Eames, quale stanza è illuminata dalla Holonski di Ingo Maurer, dove ci si può rilassare nella poltrona club Size Ten di Ron Arad. L'atmosfera è raccolta, quasi familiare. La colazione viene servita a una *table d'hôte*, una spaziosa tavola dove gli ospiti mangiano assieme.

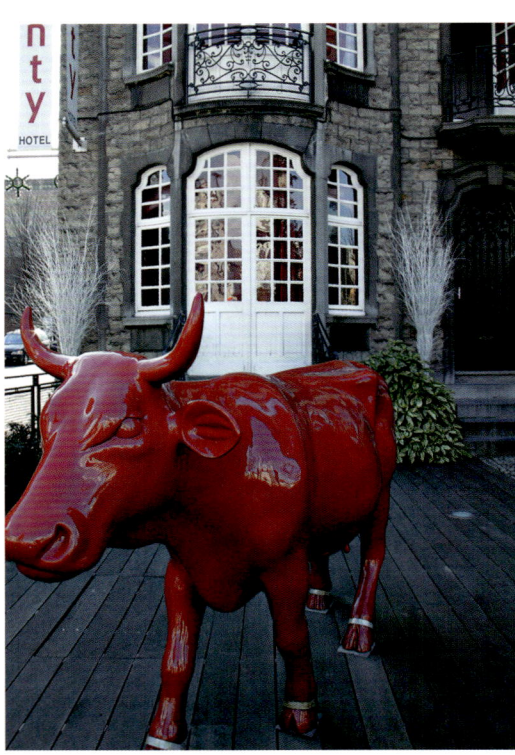

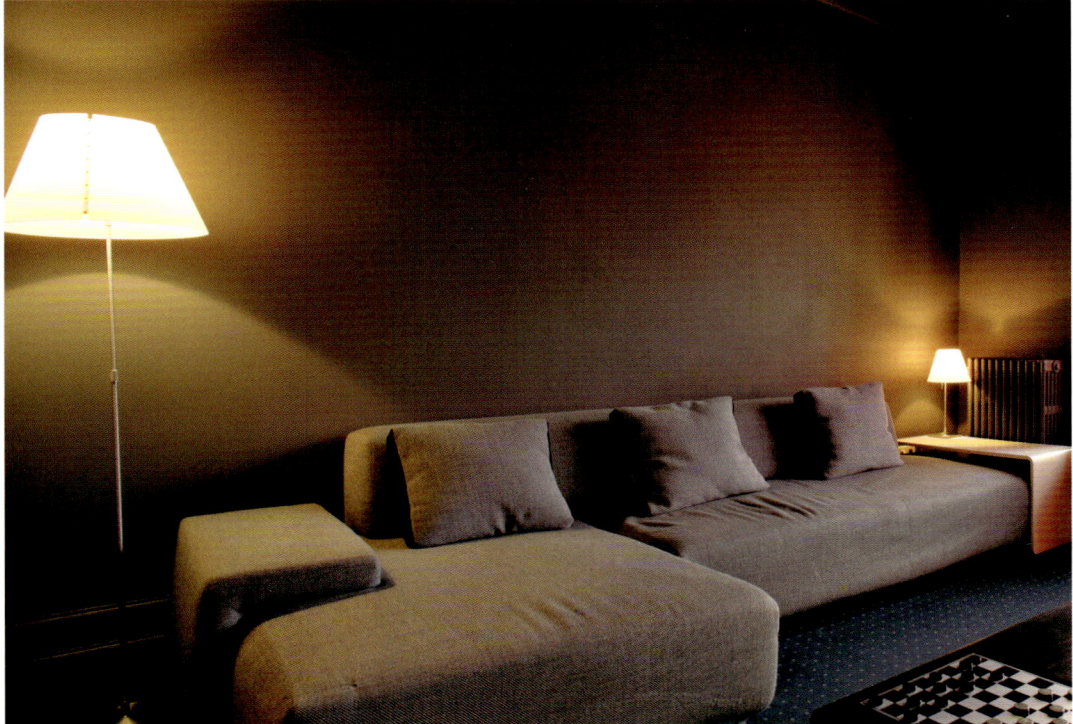

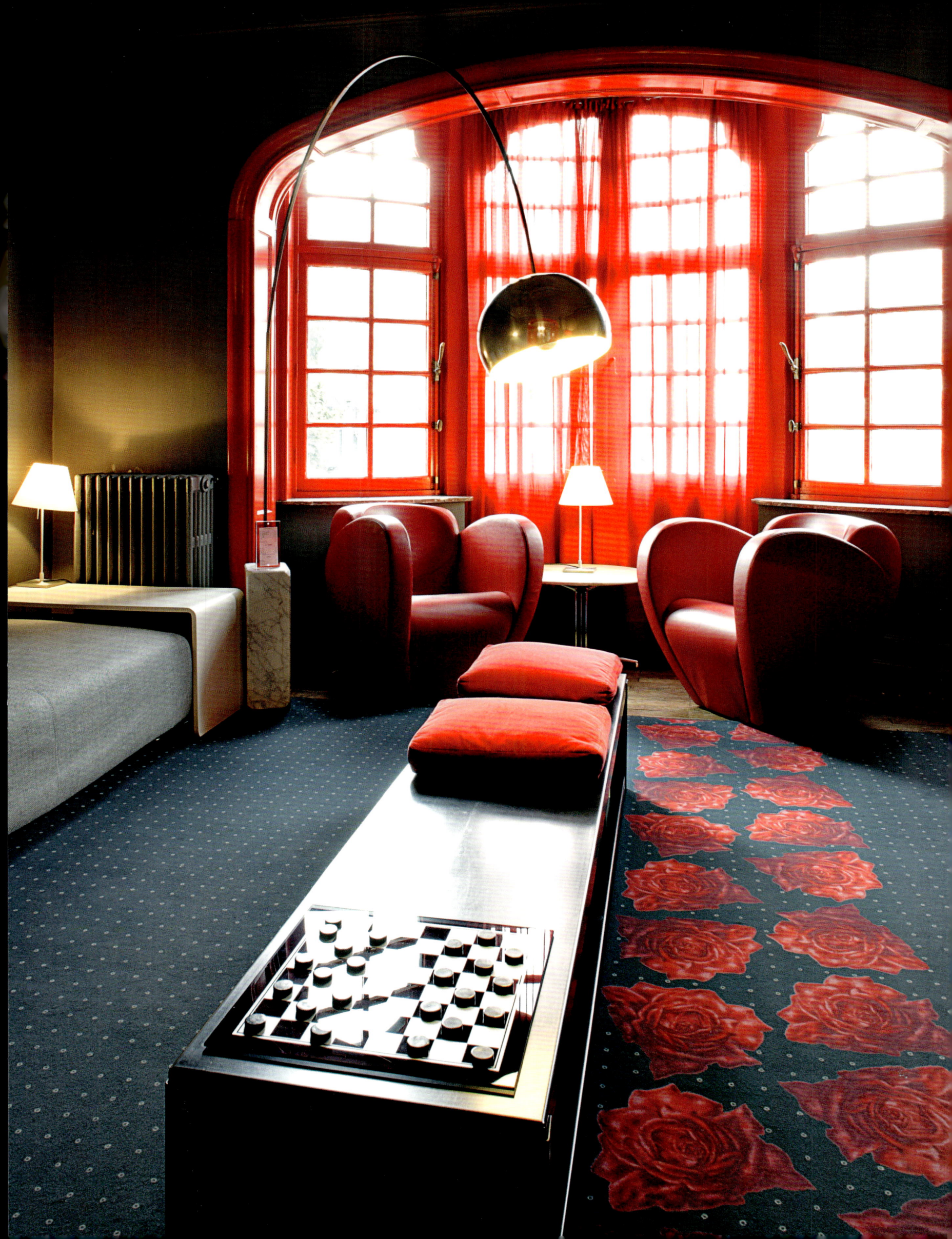

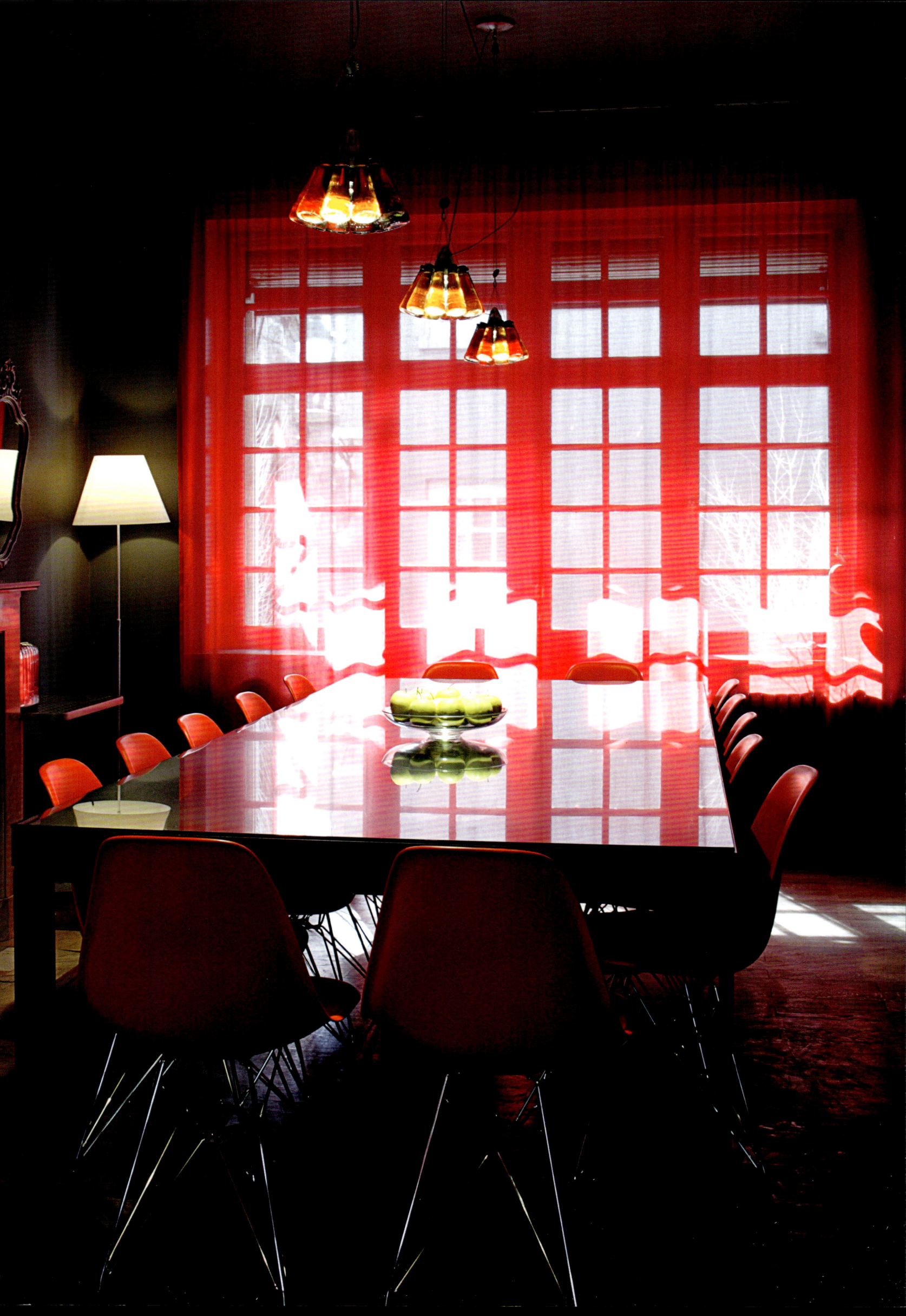

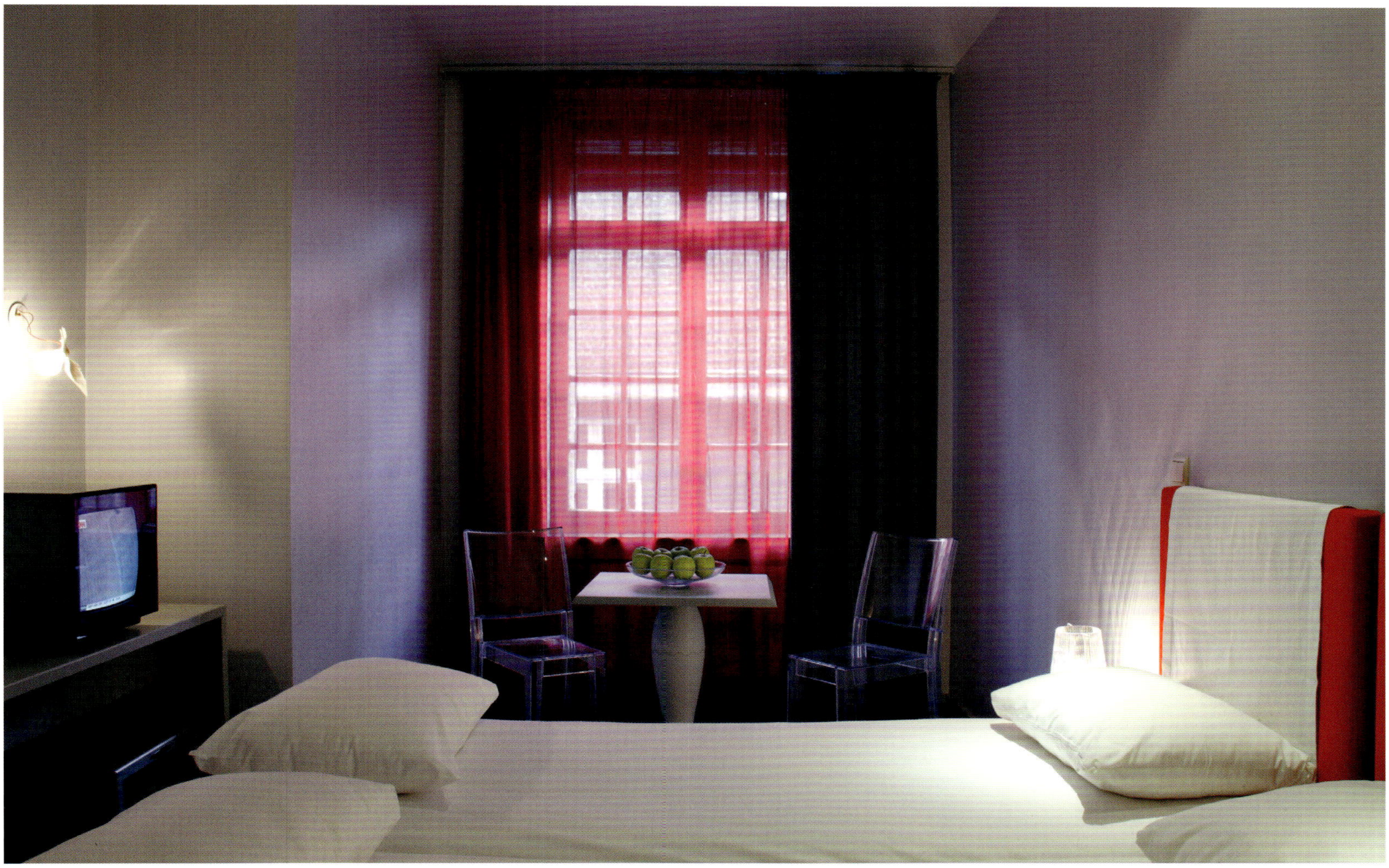

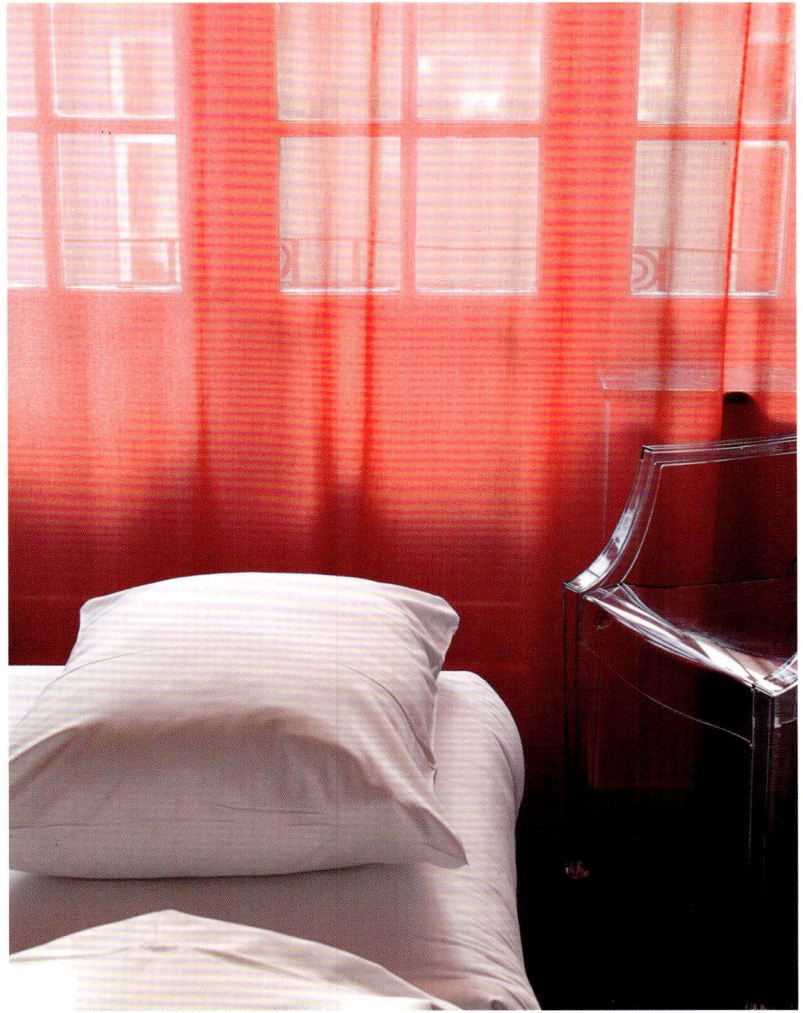

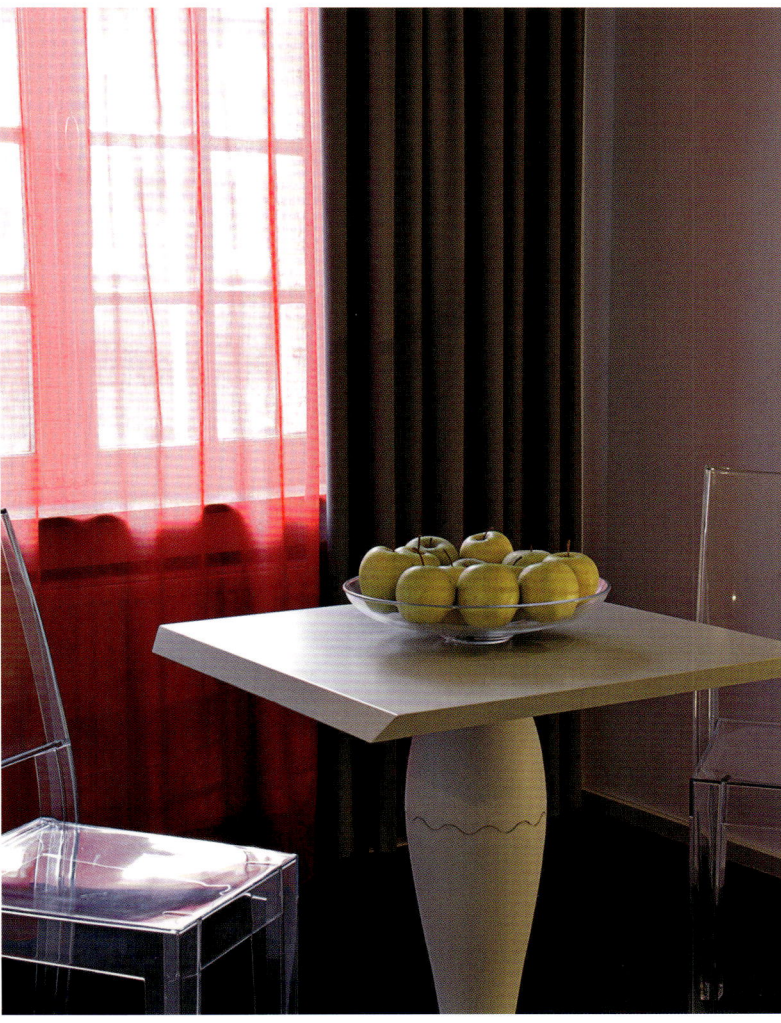

1000 Brussels
Belgium
Phone: +32 2 505 55 55
Fax: +32 2 505 55 00
www.royalwindsorbrussels.com

Rooms: 266 rooms including 16 suites and 1 Royal Suite
Facilities: Chutney's Bar and Restaurant, nightclub, free fitness center and sauna, business center with internet access
Services: Babysitting on request, laundry and dry-cleaning
Located: Just off the world-famous Grand Place and in front of the Grand Casino Brussels
Public transportation: Walking distance from Brussels' Central Station
Style: Elegant and sophisticated

No interior designer, but rather twelve fashion designers took part in the creation of some of the 266 freshly renovated rooms of the five star hotel. In the otherwise classically elegant style of the hotel, the Fashion Rooms each seem like an artist's enclave, from the purists Zen Suite with bamboo furniture by Jean-Paul Knott to the futuristic New Millenium Wonderland by Marina Yee to the oriental boudoir by Mademoiselle Lucien. The antique market in the Sablon, the Royal Gardens and the famous Grand Place are all just a short walk away.

Kein Interieurdesigner, sondern zwölf Modedesigner haben einige der 266 frisch renovierten Zimmer des Fünf-Sterne-Hotels gestaltet. In dem sonst elegant-klassisch gestylten Hotel wirken die Fashion Rooms wie künstlerische Enklaven: von der puristischen Zen-Suite mit Bambusmöbeln von Jean-Paul Knott über das futuristische New Millenium Wunderland von Marina Yee bis zum orientalischen Boudoir von Mademoiselle Lucien. Der Antikmarkt in der Sablon, die Königlichen Gärten und der berühmte Grand Place, sind nur einen kurzen Spaziergang entfernt.

Aucun architecteur d'intérieur, mais douze créateurs de mode ont pris part à la création de certaines des 266 chambres récemment rénovées de cet hôtel cinq étoiles. Par contraste avec le style élégamment classique de l'hôtel, les Fashion Rooms ressemblent toutes à une enclave artistique, de la suite Zen puriste avec ses meubles en bambou de Jean-Paul Knott, à la futuriste New Millenium Wonderland de Marina Yee, en passant par le boudoir oriental de Mademoiselle Lucien. Le marché des antiquaires du Sablon, les Jardins Royaux et la célèbre Grand Place ne sont qu'à quelques pas. Et si vous avez besoin de trois connexions téléphoniques dans votre chambre, il n'y a qu'ici que vous pourrez les avoir.

No fueron interioristas, sino doce diseñadores de moda, los que decoraron algunas de las 266 habitaciones, recientemente renovadas, de este hotel de cinco estrellas. Estas habitaciones, llamadas Fashion Rooms, son como enclaves artísticos dentro del hotel, donde predomina la elegancia clásica. Algunos ejemplos son la purista suite Zen de Jean-Paul Knott, con sus muebles de bambú, la habitación futurista New Millenium Wonderland de Marina Yee o el boudoir oriental de Madmoiselle Lucien. El mercado de antigüedades en el distrito Sablon, los Jardines Reales y el famoso Grand Place están a pocos pasos del hotel.

Non fu un designer d'interni, bensì dodici stilisti ad arredare alcune delle appena rinnovate 266 camere di questo albergo a cinque stelle. In mezzo a uno stile classico ed elegante, le fashion rooms appaiono come delle enclavi artistiche: dalla purista Zen Suite, con mobili in bambù di Jean-Paul Knott, al futuristico New Millenium Wonderland di Marina Yee fino al boudoir orientale di mademoiselle Lucien. Il mercato dell'antiquariato presso il Sablon, i giardini reali e la famosa Grand Place si possono raggiungere con una breve passeggiata.

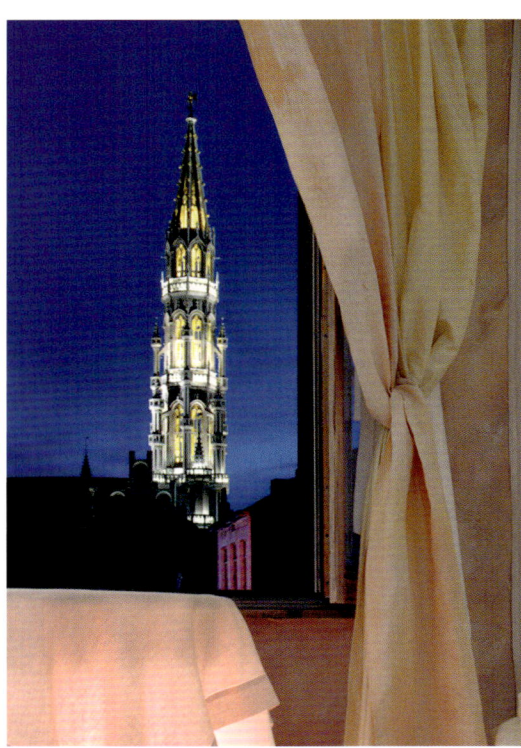
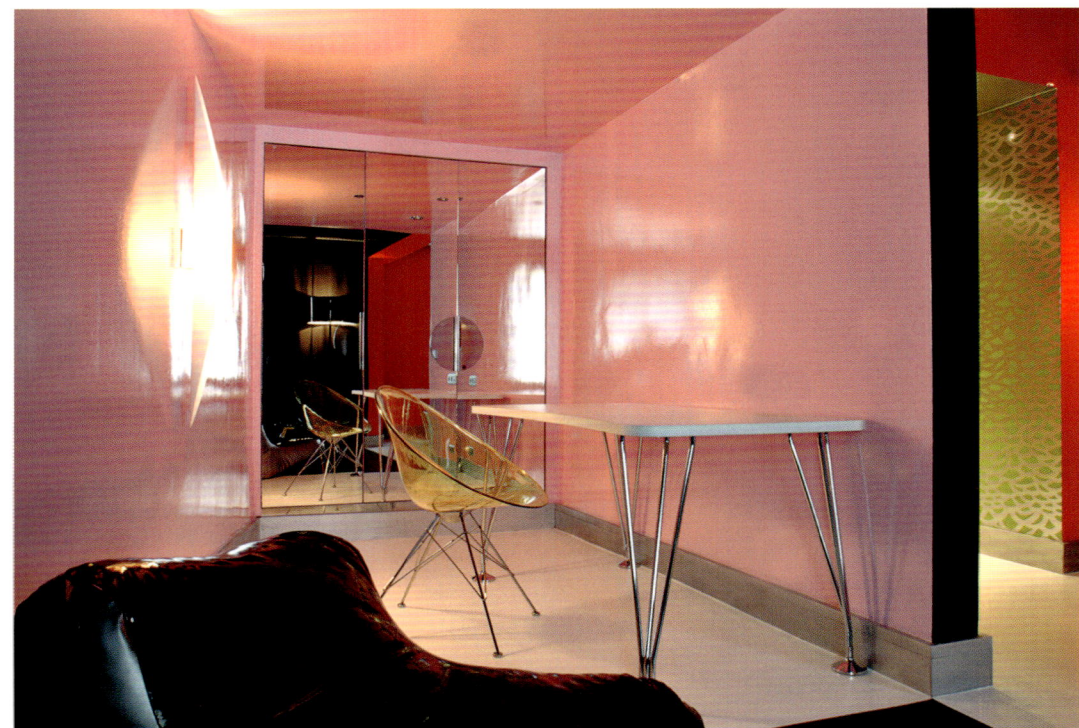

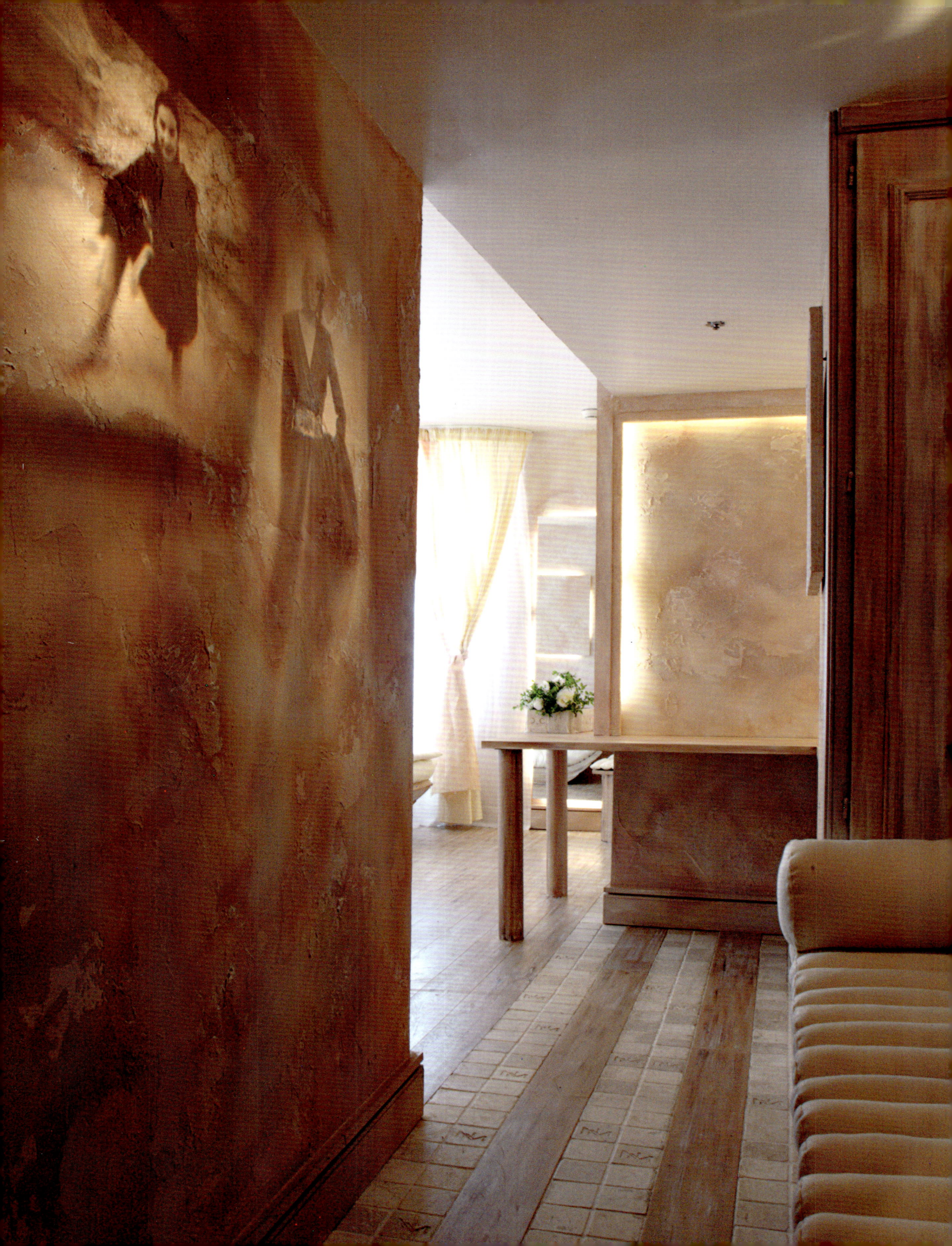

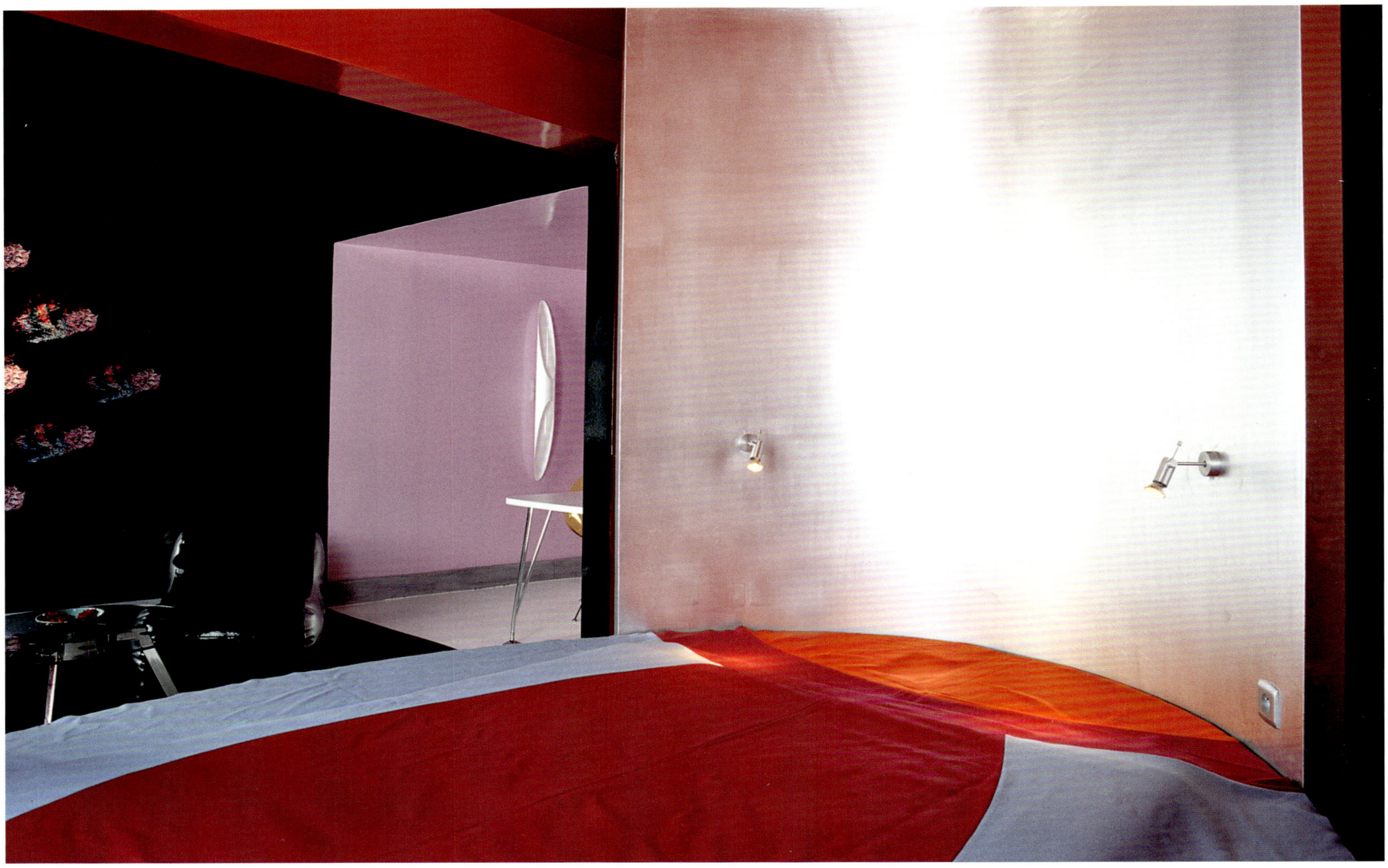

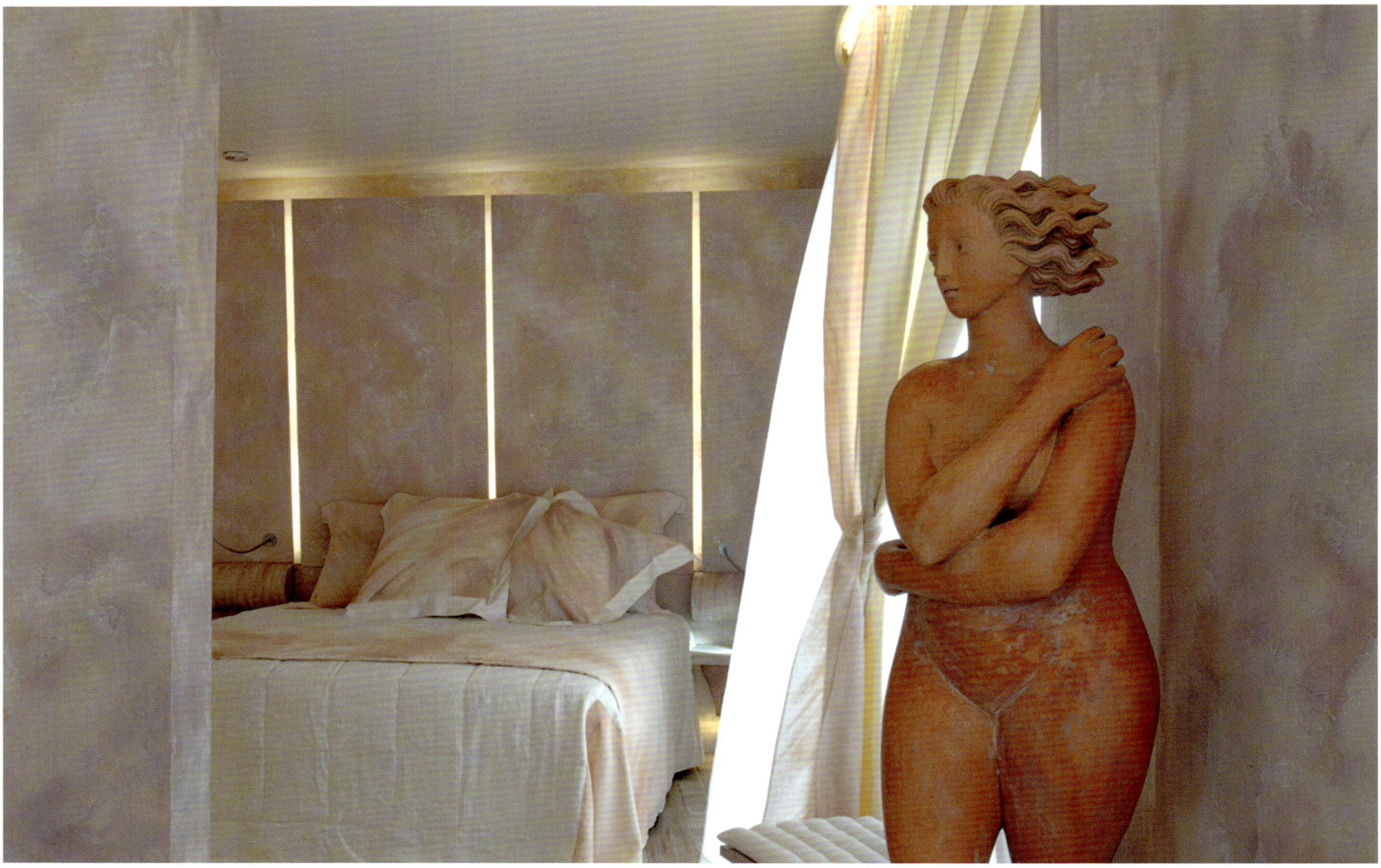

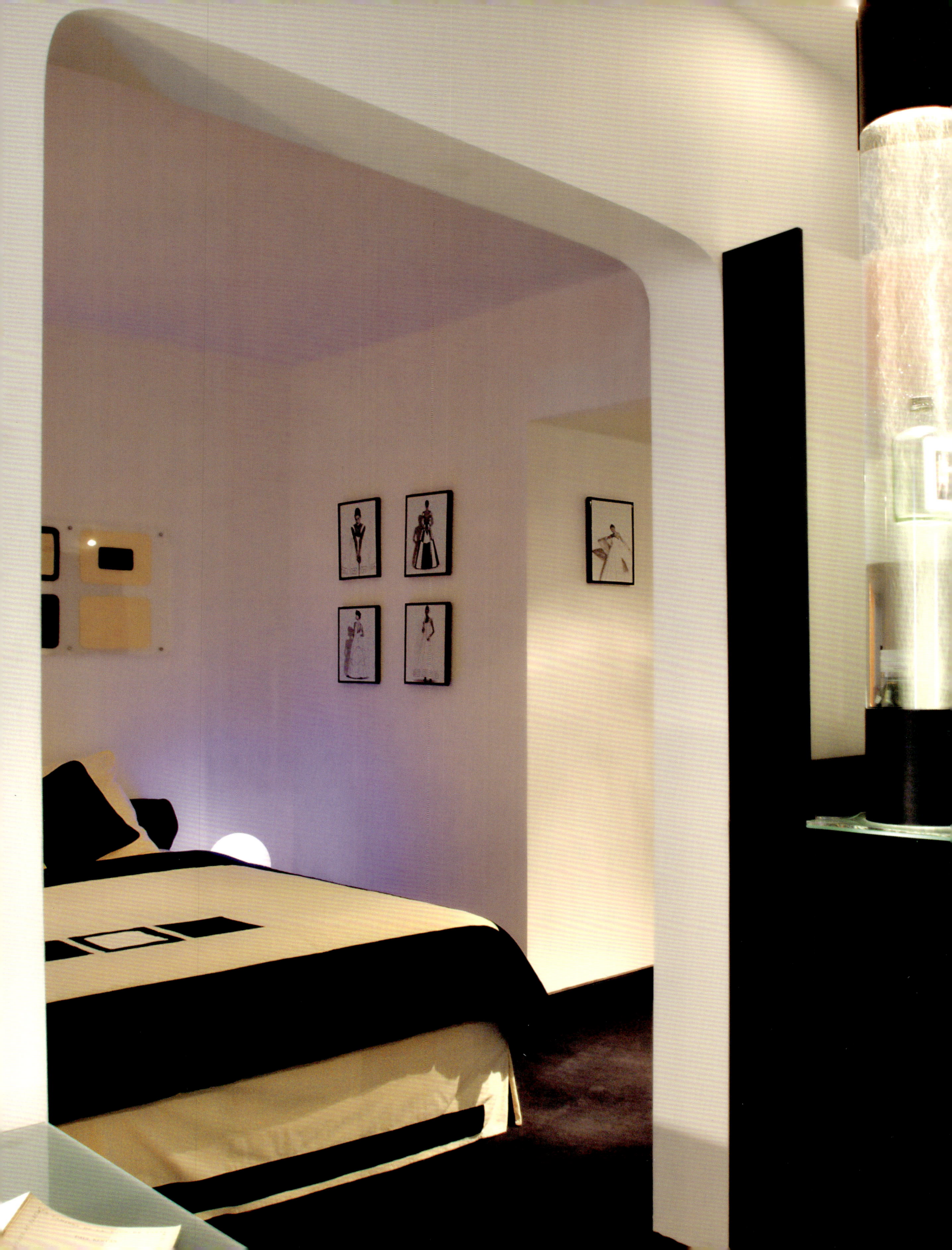

Unter den Linden 77
10117 Berlin
Germany
Phone: +49 30 22 61 0
Fax: +49 30 22 61 22 22
www.hotel-adlon.de

Price category: €€€
Rooms: 304 rooms and 78 suites
Facilities: Bar, 2 restaurants, terrace, spa
Services: Concierge, limousine service, butler, WiFi
Located: In the center, directly at the Pariser Platz and Brandenburg Gate
Public transportation: S-Bahn Unter den Linden
Style: Classic-elegant

No hotel in Germany is more deeply interwoven in German history than the Adlon at Brandenburg Gate, which celebrated its 100th anniversary in 2007. After reconstruction in 1997, the luxury hotel was able to take up its glamorous past again. Crowned heads of state and high state visitors put up again at Pariser Platz. The newest accomplishment is an Asian-inspired day spa with 16 treatment rooms. With Tim Raue, the grand hotel also features one of the most experimenta cooks of the German gourmet scene.

Kein Hotel in Deutschland ist so eng mit der deutschen Geschichte verwoben, wie das Adlon am Brandenburger Tor, das 2007 seinen 100 Geburtstag feierte. Nach der Wiedererrichtung 1997 konnte das Luxushotel an seine glamouröse Vergangenheit anknüpfen. Gekrönte Häupter und hohe Staatsgäste steigen auch heute wieder am Pariser Platz ab. Neueste Errungenschaft ist ein asiatisch inspirierter Dayspa mit 16 Treatment-Räumen. Und mit Tim Raue leistet sich die große Hoteldame einen der experimentierfreudigsten Köche der deutschen Gourmetszene.

Aucun autre hôtel d'Allemagne n'est aussi lié à l'histoire allemande que l'Adlon, situé à la Porte de Brandebourg, et qui a célébré son centième anniversaire en 2007. Suite à sa reconstruction en 1997, l'hôtel a pu se rattacher à nouveau à son passé glamour. Les têtes couronnées et les prestigieux invités d'Etat séjournent à nouveau sur la Pariser Platz. Les derniers ajouts sont le spa de jour, d'inspiration asiatique avec 16 salles de soin. Et en la personne de Tim Raue, ce grand hôtel s'offre le chef le plus expérimental de la scène gastronomique allemande.

En Alemania no hay otro hotel que esté tan ligado a la historia del país como el Adlon. En 2007, el establecimiento situado al lado de la puerta de Brandenburgo celebró su primer centenario. Tras su reconstrucción en 1997, el hotel retomó su glamoroso pasado. Reyes y dignatarios vuelven a hospedarse en la Pariser Platz. La nueva perla del hotel es un day spa de inspiración asiática, con 16 salas de tratamiento. Otro de los puntos fuertes de esta casa tradicional es Tim Raue, uno de los cocineros más innovadores de la escena gastronómica alemana.

Nessun altro albergo tedesco è così profondamente legato con la storia della Germania come l'Adlon, situato presso la Porta di Brandeburgo; nel 2007 la casa ha festeggiato il suo centesimo anniversario. Dopo la ricostruzione, avvenuta nel 1997, questo lussuoso hotel ha saputo preservare i legami con il suo passato ricco di glamour. Così, ancora oggi, teste coronate e alte personalità politiche scelgono di dimorare in questo albergo sulla Pariser Platz. Tra le sue più recenti acquisizioni c'è un day spa in stile asiatico, con 16 stanze per trattamenti. E in Tim Raue gli ospiti più attenti alla buona tavola troveranno uno dei cuochi più innovativi della scena gastronomica tedesca.

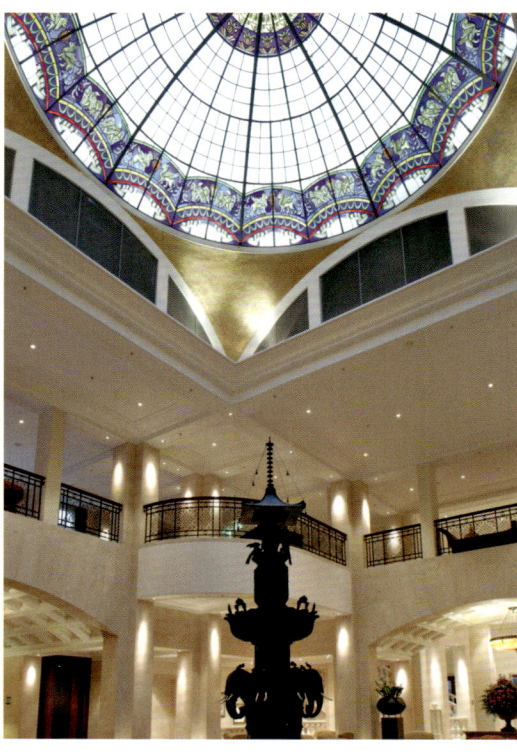
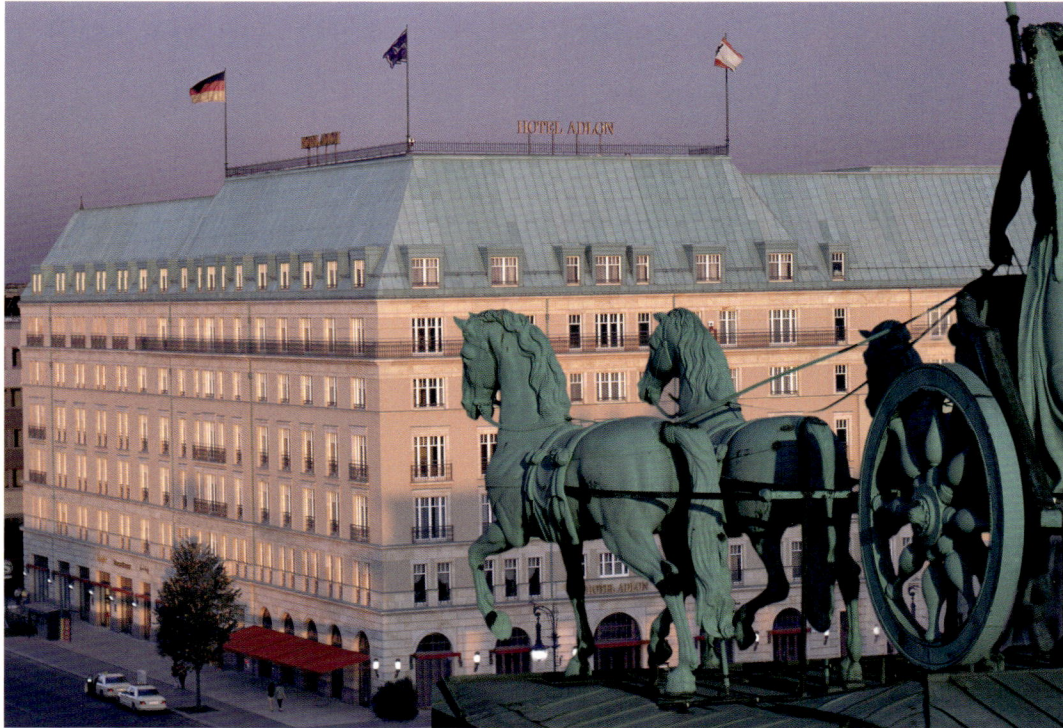

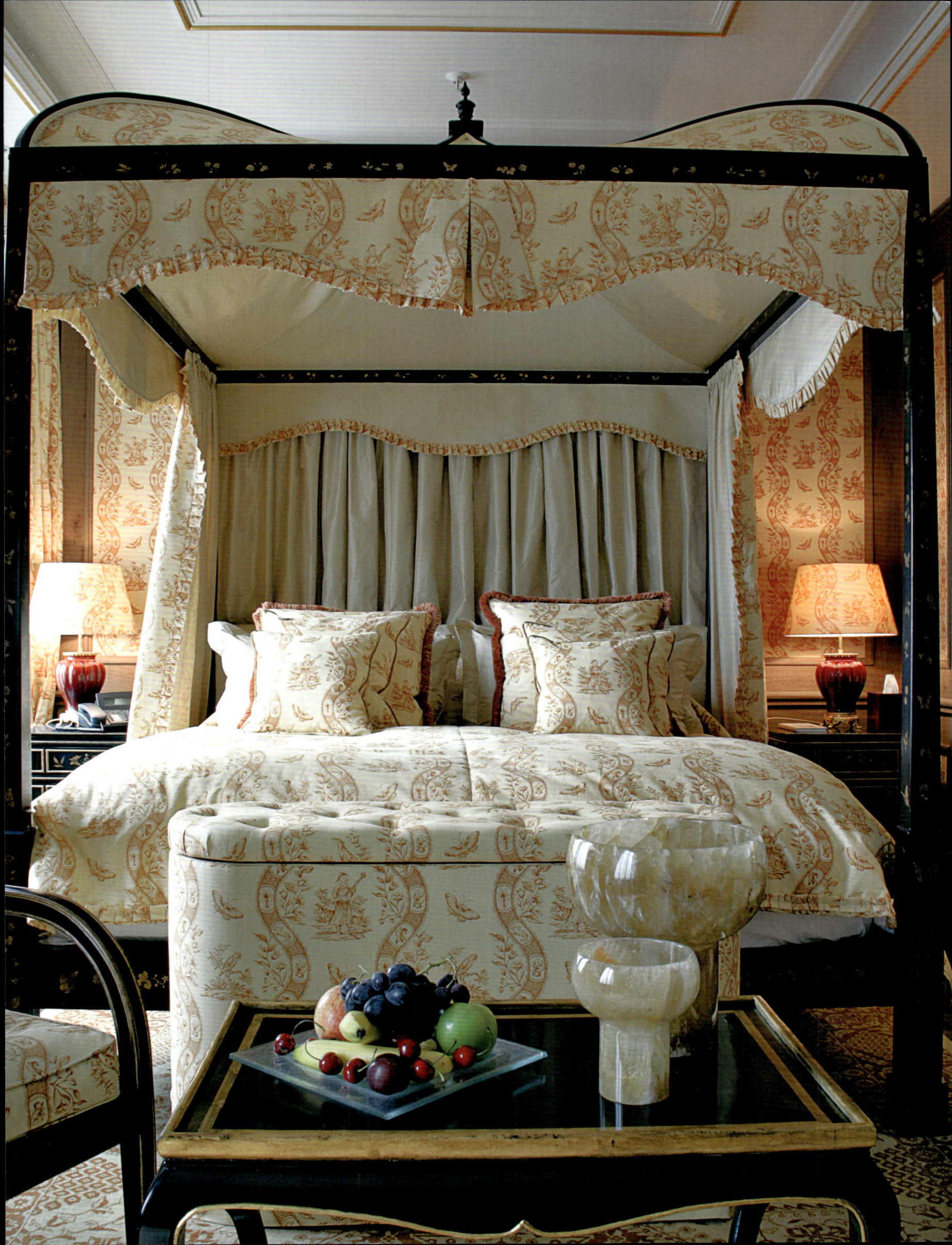

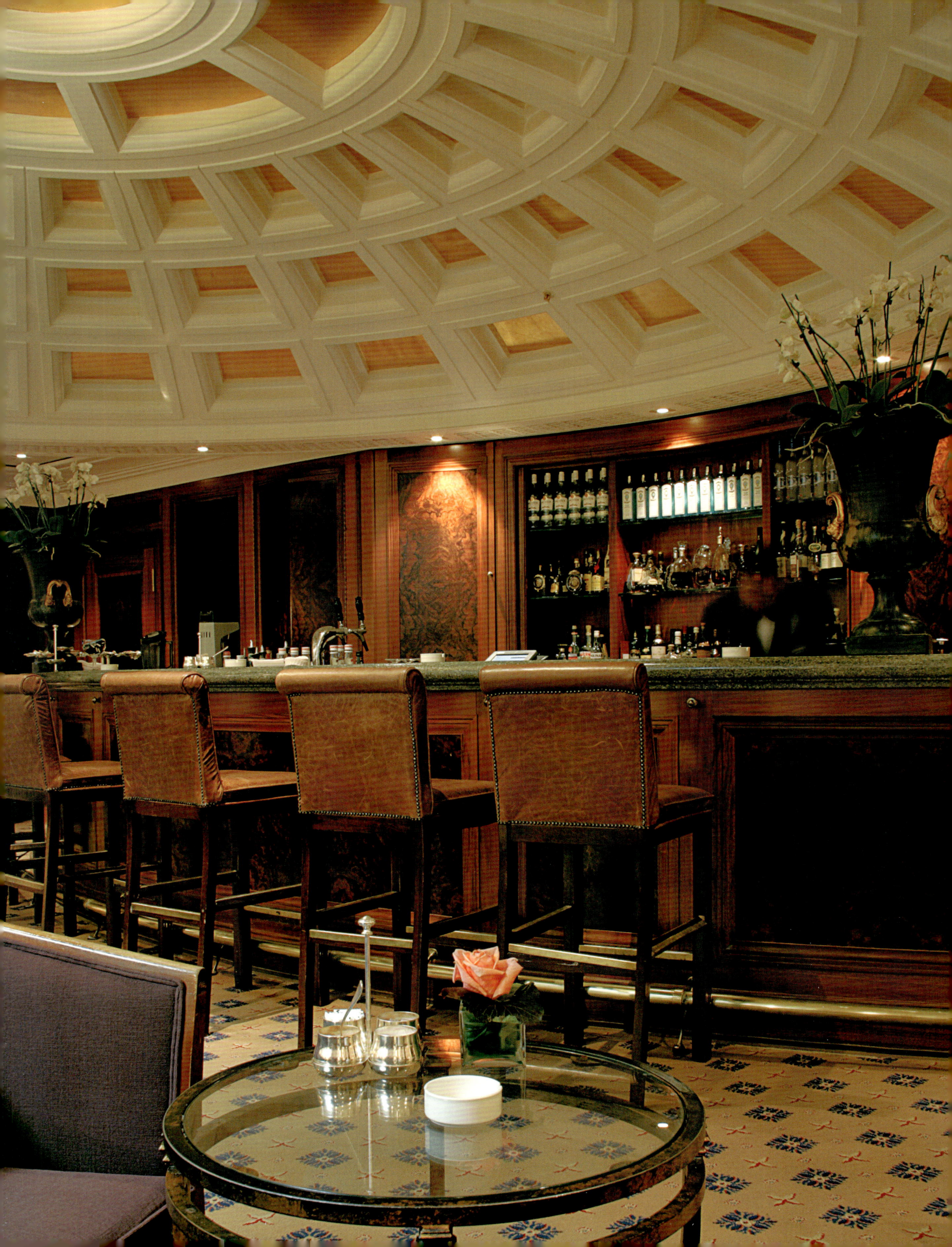

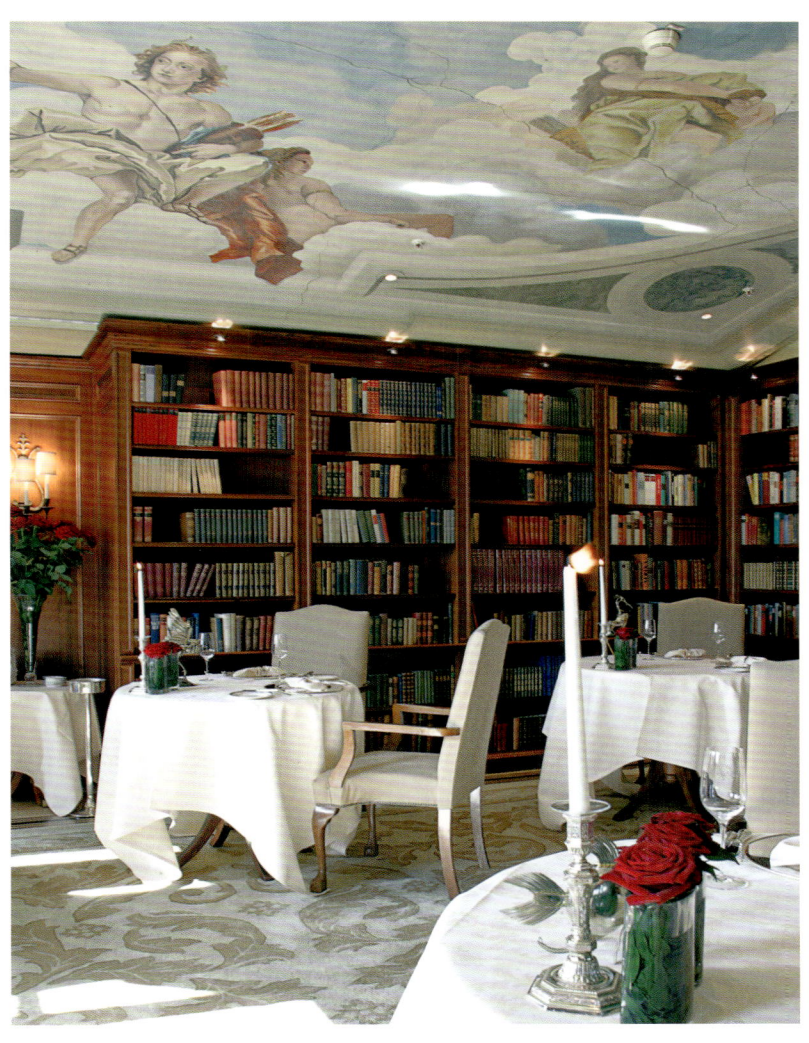

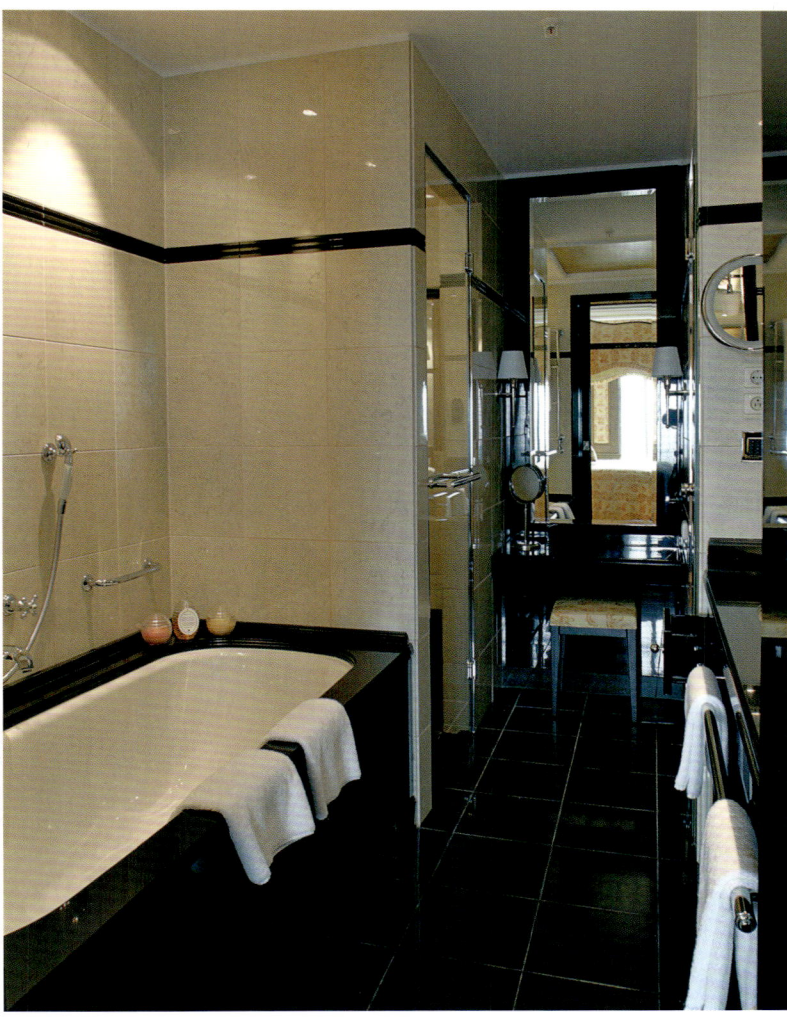

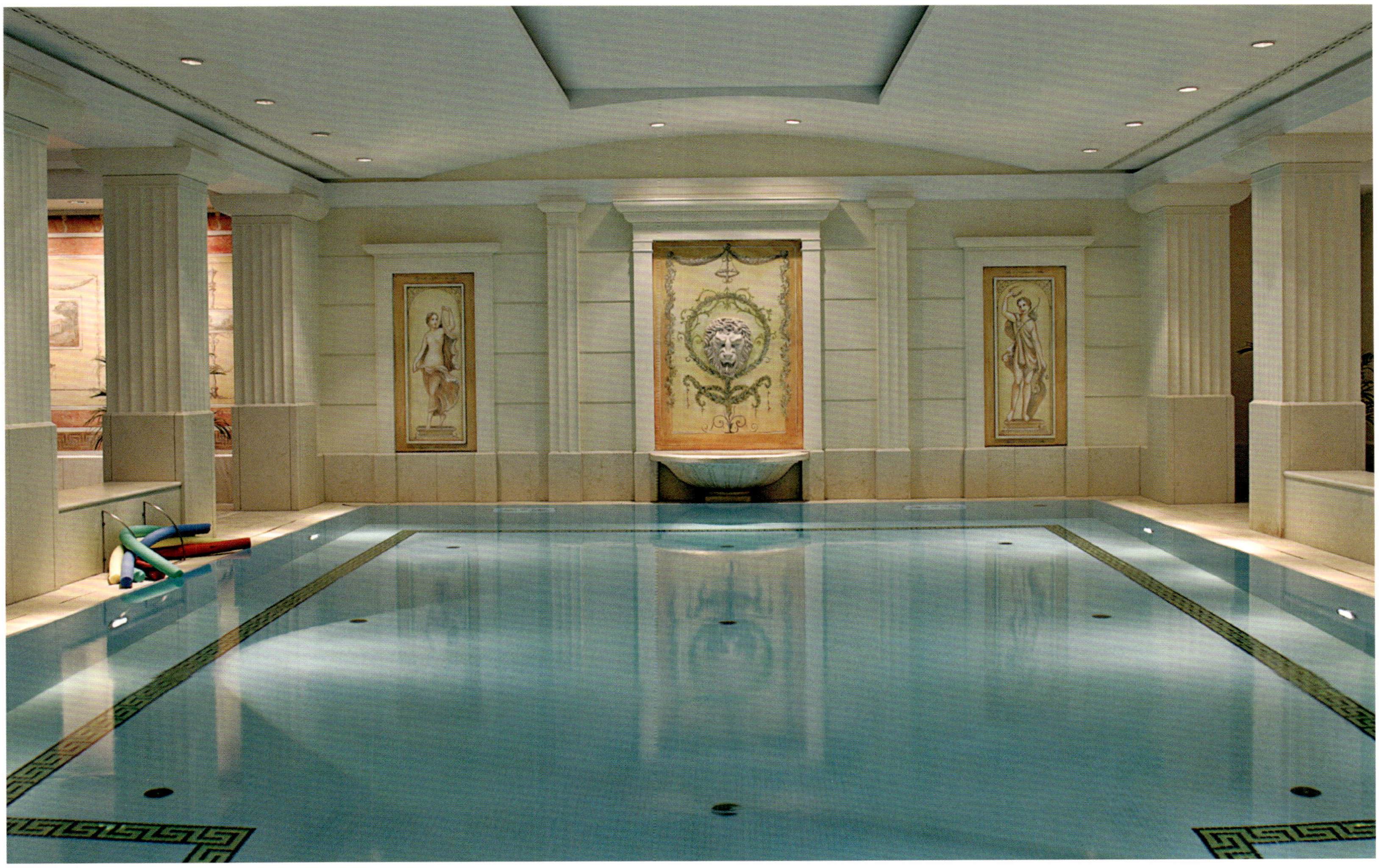

10178 Berlin
Germany
Phone: +49 30 93 62 80 0
Fax: +49 30 93 62 88 0
www.lux-eleven.com

Rooms: 72 apartments and 1 penthouse
Facilities: Restaurant, bar, Aveda hair spa
Services: Suntrainer
Located: In the heart of the city near Hackescher Markt
Public transportation: S-Bahn, Underground Alexanderplatz
Style: Urban minimalistic

The concept of the 72-suite apartment house on Rosa-Luxemburg-Straße in Berlin plays with opposites: cold and warm, soft and rough. For example, the ubiquitous unprocessed concrete is combined with soft carpets. Lux Eleven offers a place to stay to city nomads, to whom a stylish interior including DSL connection is more important than the turndown service in the evening. For architect Claudio Silvestrin, who also designs the Giorgio Armani shops, minimalism is more than just a style; it is practically a philosophy of life.

Das Konzept des 72-Suiten-Apartmenthauses an der Rosa-Luxemburg-Straße in Berlin Mitte spielt mit Gegensätzen: kalt und warm, weich und rau. Zum Beispiel wird der überall präsente unbearbeitete Beton mit weichen Teppichen kombiniert. Es will Stadtnomaden eine Bleibe bieten, denen ein stylisches Interieur samt DSL-Anschluss wichtiger ist als der Turn-down-Service am Abend. Minimalismus ist dabei für Architekt Claudio Silvestrin, der auch für Giorgio Armani Läden entwirft, mehr als nur ein Stil, er wird geradezu zur Lebenseinstellung.

Le concept de cette résidence de 72 suites dans la rue Rosa Luxemburg, au centre de Berlin, est de jouer avec les opposés : chaud et froid, doux et rugueux. Par exemple, l'aspect du ciment brut, qui prévaut partout, a été combiné avec des tapis veloutés. Il convient particulièrement aux nomades urbains, pour lesquels un intérieur tendance, avec connexion DSL, est plus important qu'un service jour et nuit. Pour l'architecte Claudio Silvestrin, qui conçoit également les boutiques Giorgio Armani, le minimalisme est plus qu'un simple style, une véritable philosophie.

El concepto de este conjunto de 72 apartamentos, situado en la calle Rosa Luxemburg en el centro de Berlín, se basa en un juego de contrastes: frío y caliente, suave y áspero. Buen ejemplo de ello es la combinación entre el siempre presente hormigón en bruto y suaves alfombras. El objetivo del hotel es ofrecer alojamiento a aquellos nómadas de la ciudad para los que los interiores con estilo y una conexión DSL son más importantes que encontrar la cama hecha y un bombon en la almohada por la noche. Para el arquitecto Claudio Silvestrin, que también diseña tiendas para Giorgio Armani, el minimalismo es más que un simple estilo, es una forma de entender la vida.

L'idea che ha dato vita a questo complesso di 72 appartamenti situato sulla Rosa-Luxemburg-Straße, nel centro di Berlino, è quella dell'opposizione tra contrari: freddo e caldo, duro e morbido. Lo rivela la calcolata combinazione tra il cemento grezzo, cui spetta la parte del leone, e soffici tappeti. Un vero e proprio rifugio per quei nomadi urbani che considerano lo stile degli interni e la connessione DSL più importanti che non trovare, alla sera, il letto rifatto e un biscotto cioccolatino sul cuscino. Perché per l'architetto Claudio Silvestrin – che progetta negozi anche per Giorgio Armani – più che una questione di stile il minimalismo è una scelta di vita.

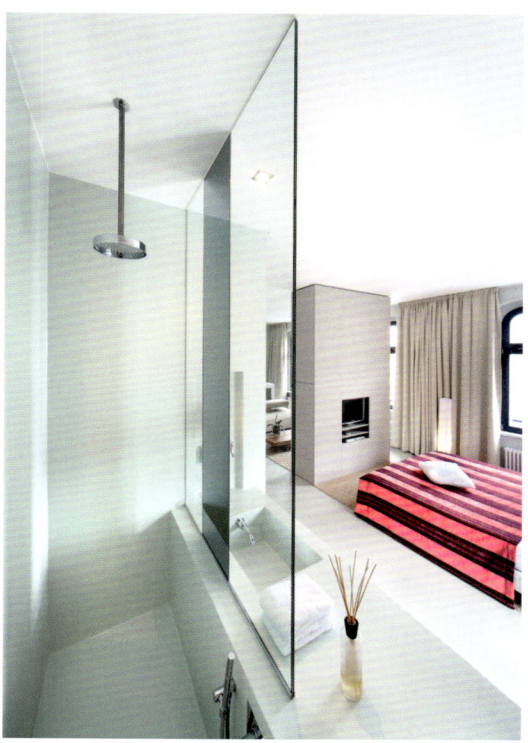
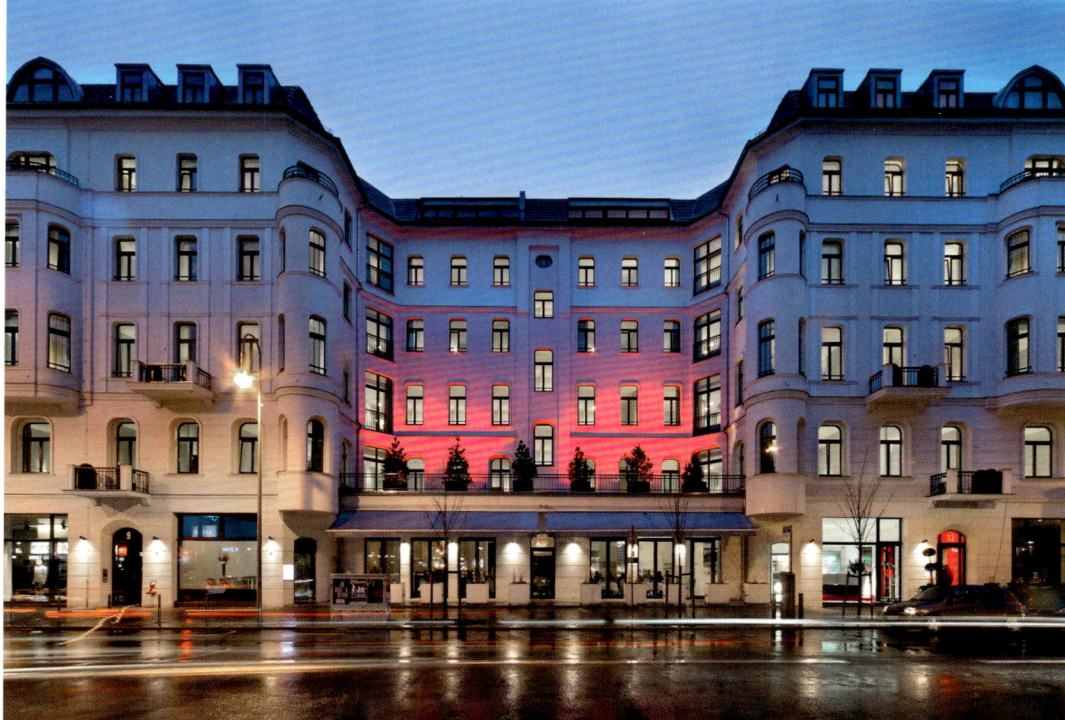

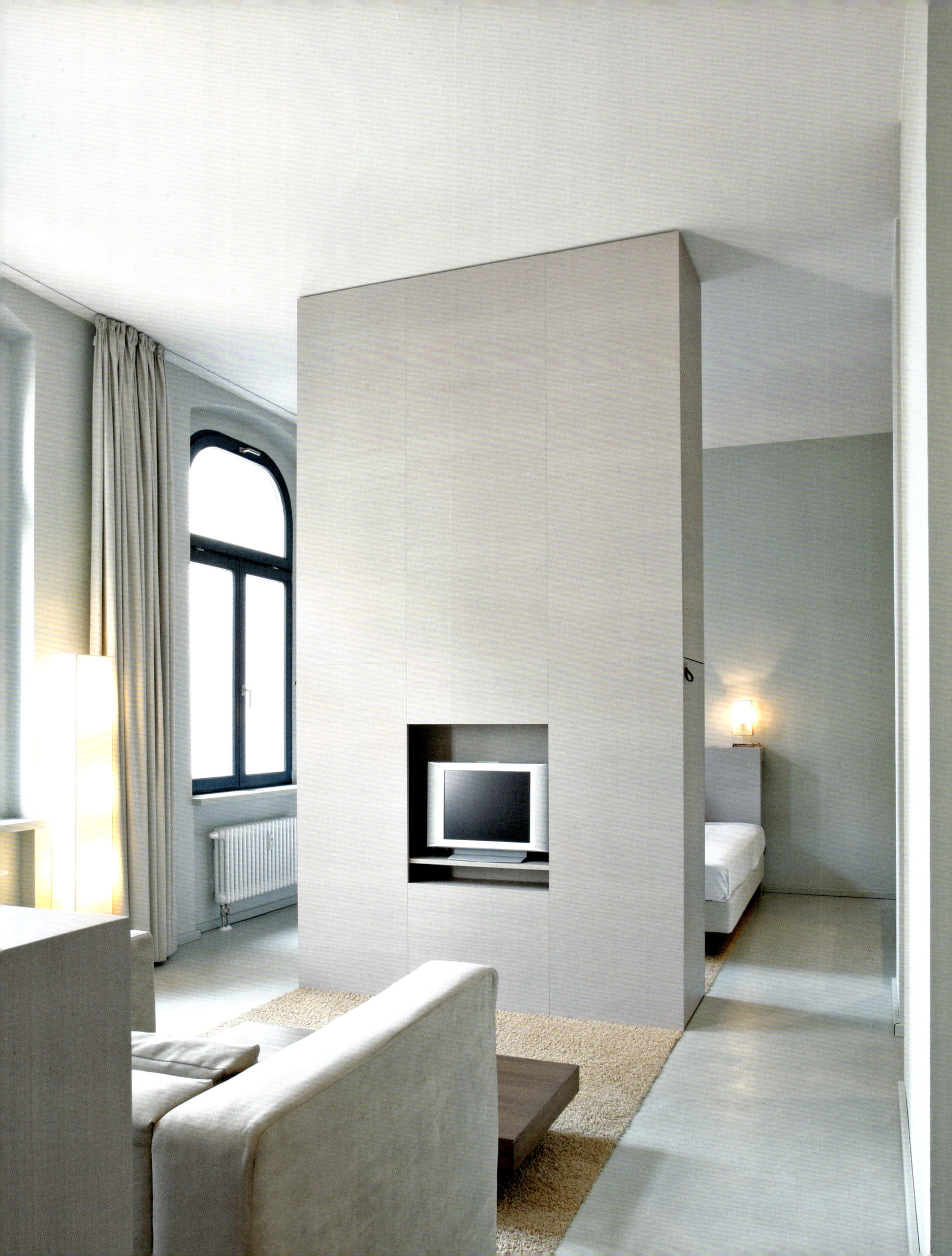

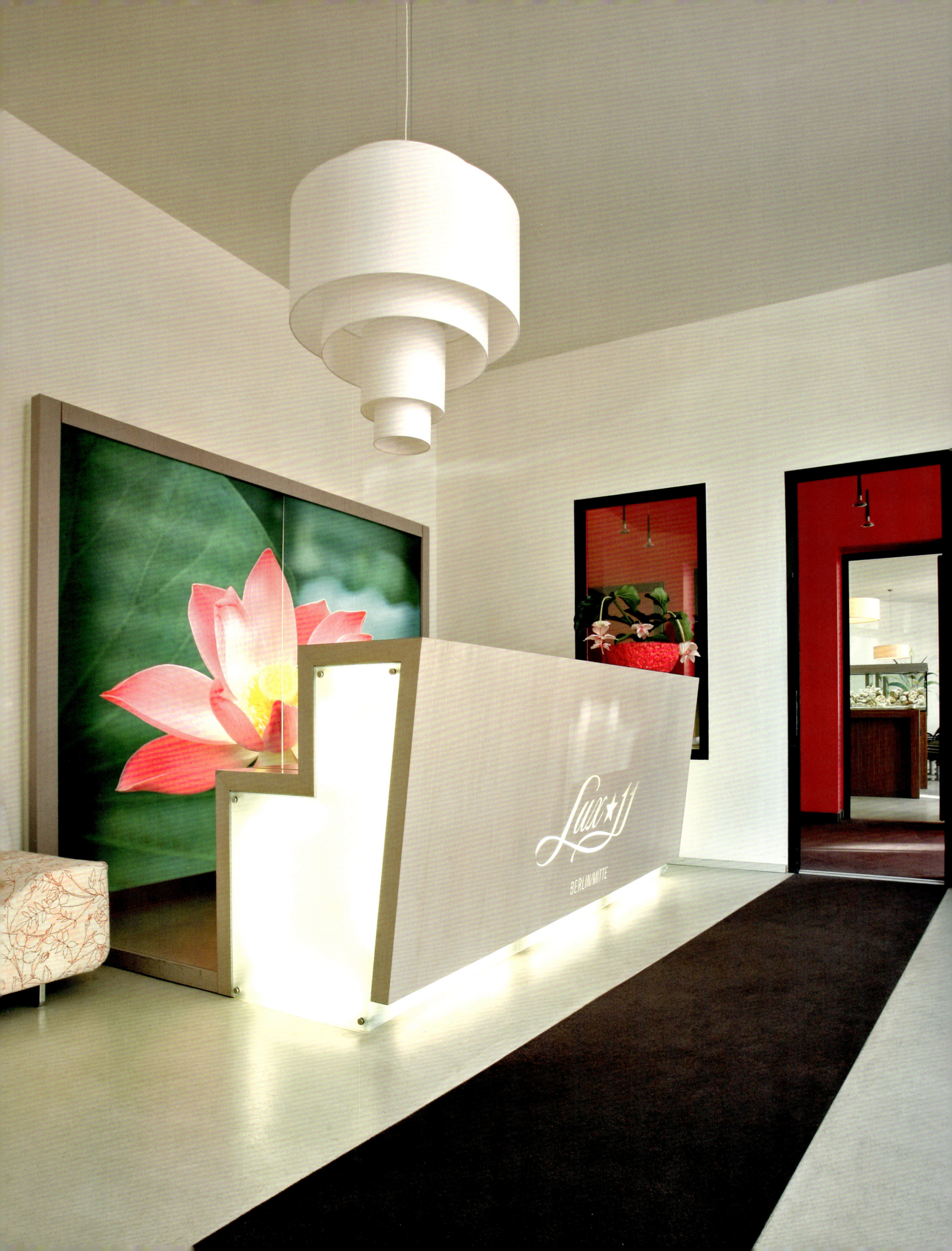

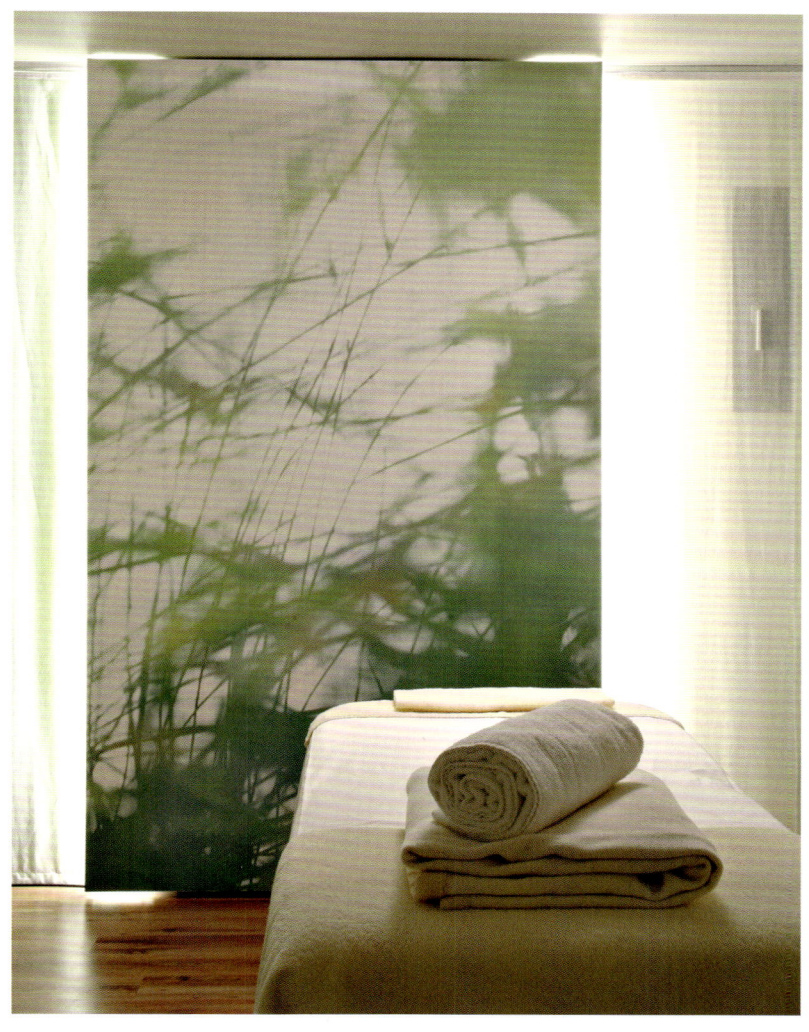
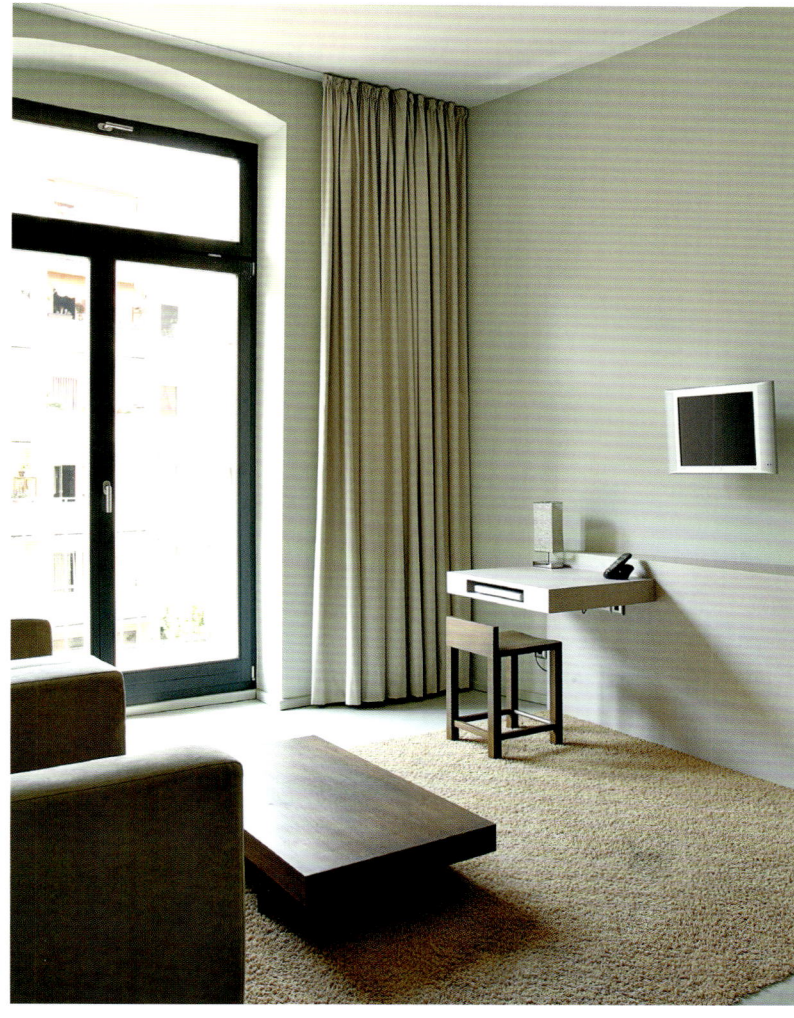
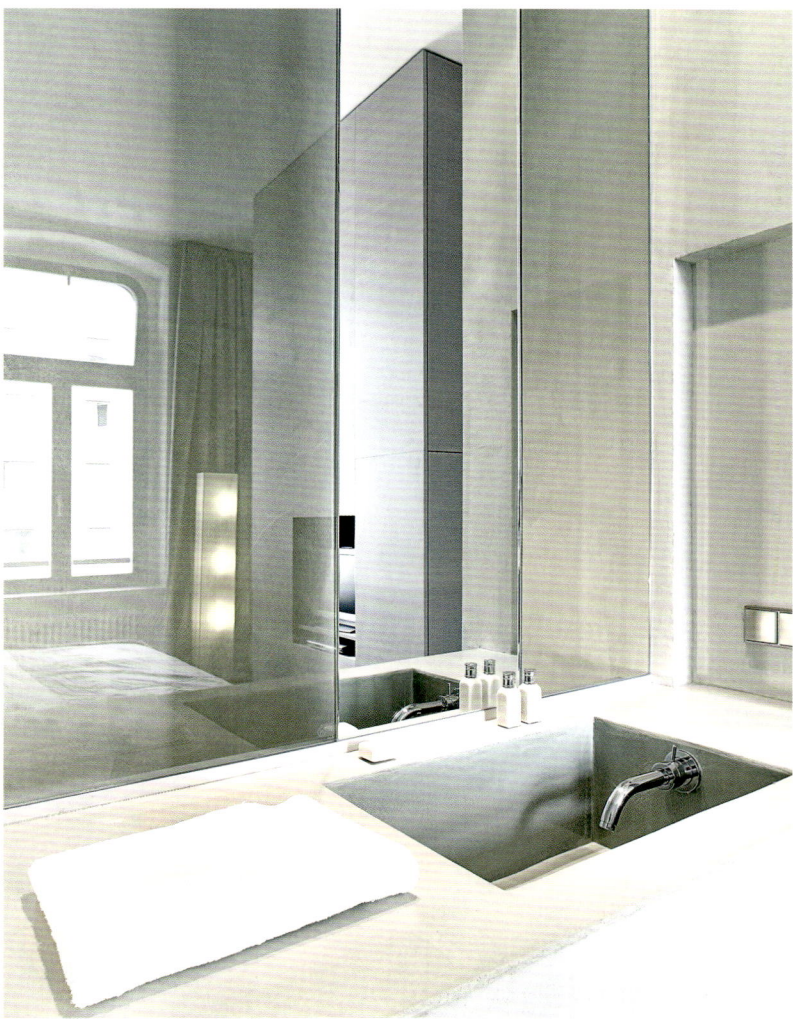
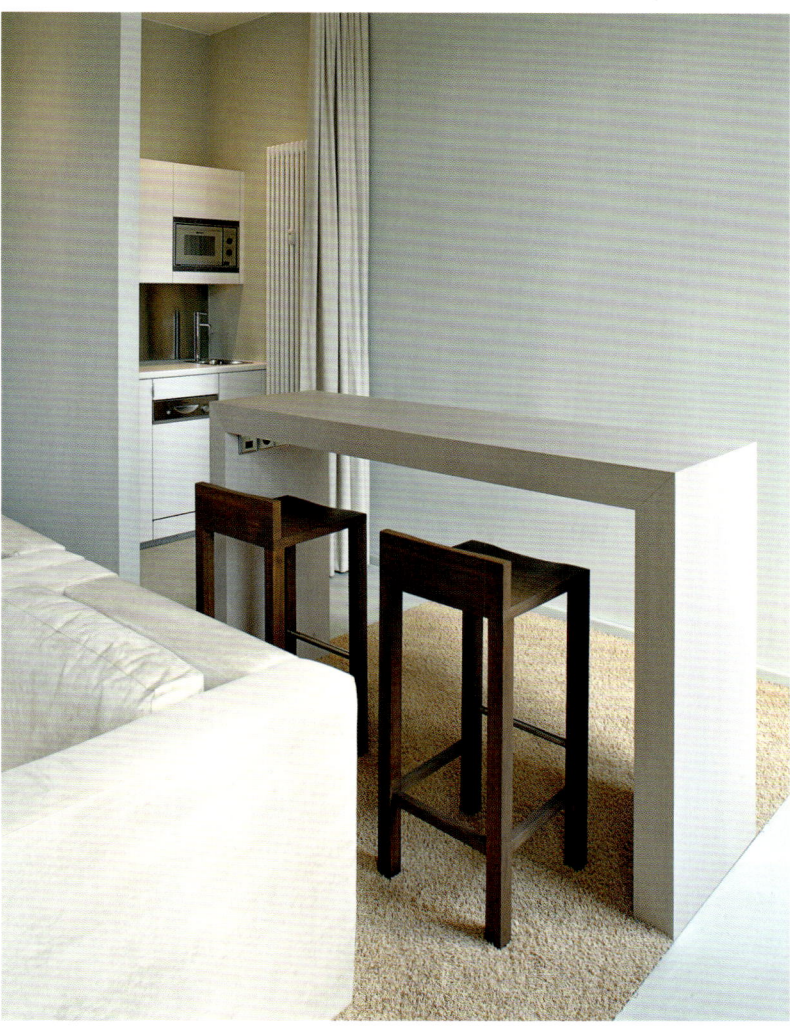

10623 Berlin
Germany
Phone: +49 30 81 00 66 0
Fax: +49 30 81 00 66 66 6
www.loock-hotels.com

Rooms: 77 rooms including 4 studios and 1 penthouse
Facilities: Restaurant, member bar, spa
Services: 24 h concierge and room service, WiFi, laundry, private cooking
Located: In the center of West Berlin, next to Kurfürstendamm
Public transportation: S-Bahn, Undergound Savignyplatz; bus Bleibtreustraße
Style: Design and fashion

The architect office GRAFT's design of a 77-room hotel became a pilgrimage site for those interested in design after its opening in 2004. The Q!, located near the Kurfürstendamm, offers the guest a singular space experience. All forms seem to flow; walls, ceilings and floors compose a continuum. All pieces of furniture including bathtubs are integrated into this concept of flow. The highlight in the spa is the sand room. There, you can rest in warm sand, accompanied by soft sound effects, and find unexpected deep relaxation.

Zum Wallfahrtsort für Design-Interessierte wurde das vom Architekturbüro GRAFT entworfene 77-Zimmer-Hotel gleich nach seiner Eröffnung 2004. Das in der Nähe des Kurfürstendamms gelegene Q! bietet dem Gast ein einzigartiges Raumerlebnis. Alle Formen scheinen zu fließen; Wände, Decken, Fußböden bilden ein Kontinuum. Sämtliche Möbelstücke, sogar die Badewannen, sind in dieses fließende Konzept integriert. Highlight im Spa ist der Sandraum. Eingebettet in warmen Sand, begleitet von sanften Soundeffekten, stellt sich eine ungeahnte Tiefenentspannung ein.

Cet hôtel de 77 chambres, conçu par les architectes de GRAFT, est devenu un lieu de pèlerinage pour les fans de design dès son ouverture en 2004. L'hôtel Q!, situé près du Kurfürstendamm, propose à ses clients une expérience spatiale assez singulière. Toutes les formes semblent flotter, les plafonds, les murs, les sols forment une vraie continuité. Tous les meubles, même les baignoires, sont intégrés dans ce concept flottant. Le joyau du spa est la « salle de sable » : être plongé dans du sable chaud, accompagné d'effets sonores doux, apporte une sensation inattendue de relaxation intense.

En 2004 abrió sus puertas el hotel diseñado por el estudio de arquitectura GRAFT, convirtiéndose desde el primer momento en un lugar de peregrinación para los adeptos al diseño. El Q! se encuentra en las inmediaciones de la avenida Kurfürstendamm y ofrece al huésped una experiencia de espacio única. Todas las formas parecen fluir; paredes, techos y suelos forman un continuo. Todos los muebles, e incluso las bañeras, están integrados en el concepto. En el spa destaca la habitación de arena. Su templada arena y sus suaves efectos de sonidos invitan a relajarse profundamente de una manera insospechada.

Fin dalla sua apertura nel 2004 questo albergo da 76 stanze, progettato dallo studio di architettura GRAFT, è diventato un luogo di pellegrinaggio per gli appassionati di design. Il Q!, situato nelle vicinanze del viale Kurfürstendamm, offre ai suoi ospiti un'originalissima concezione dello spazio. Forme e linee sembrano fluire, pareti, soffitti e pavimenti si fondono in un continuum ininterrotto. I mobili, incluse le vasche da bagno, sono tutti integrati in questa visione liquida e fluida. La proposta più allettante dello spa è il stanza di sabbia, una sala ricoperta di sabbia tiepida in cui distendersi e, accompagnati da delicati effetti sonori, godere di un profondo senso di relax.

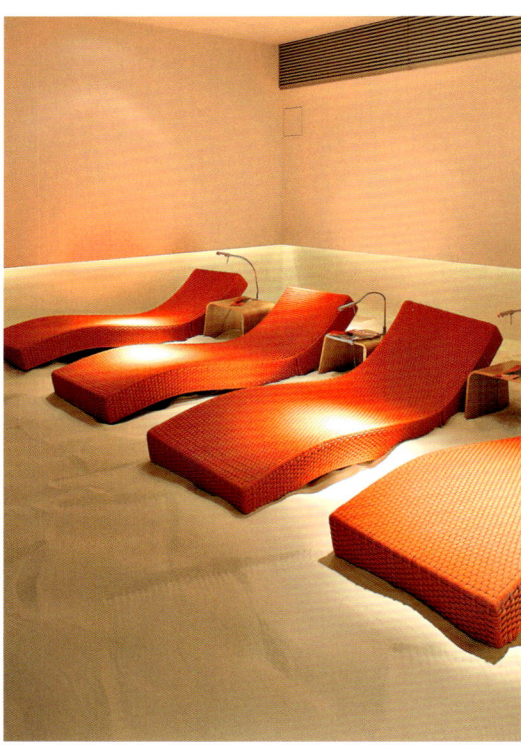
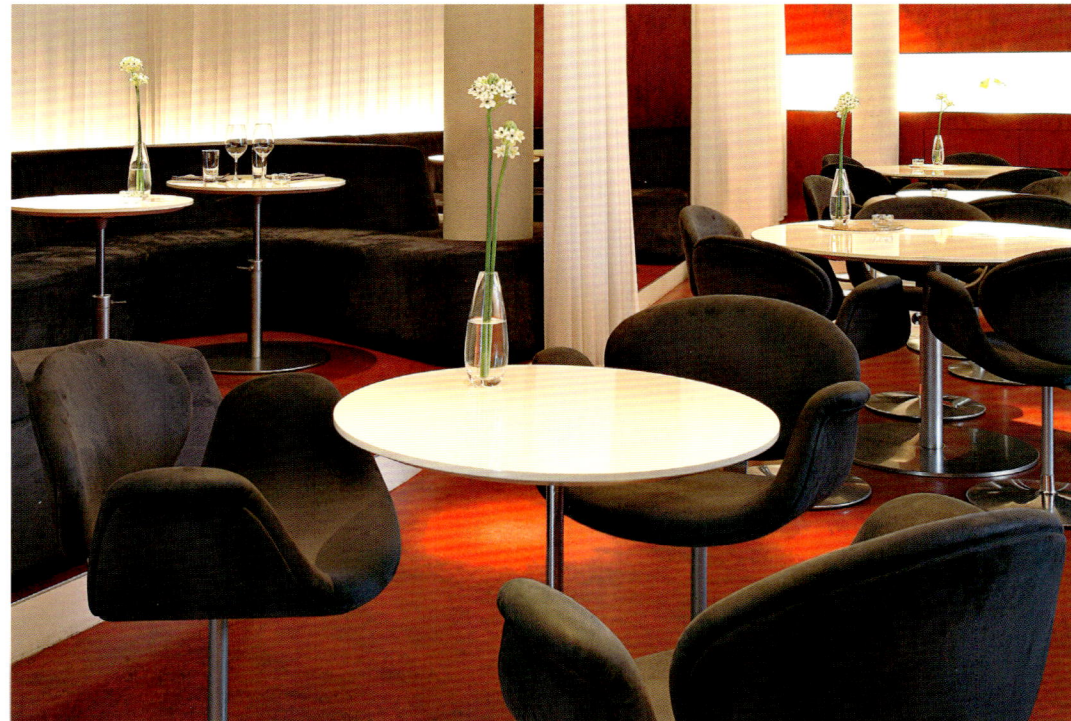

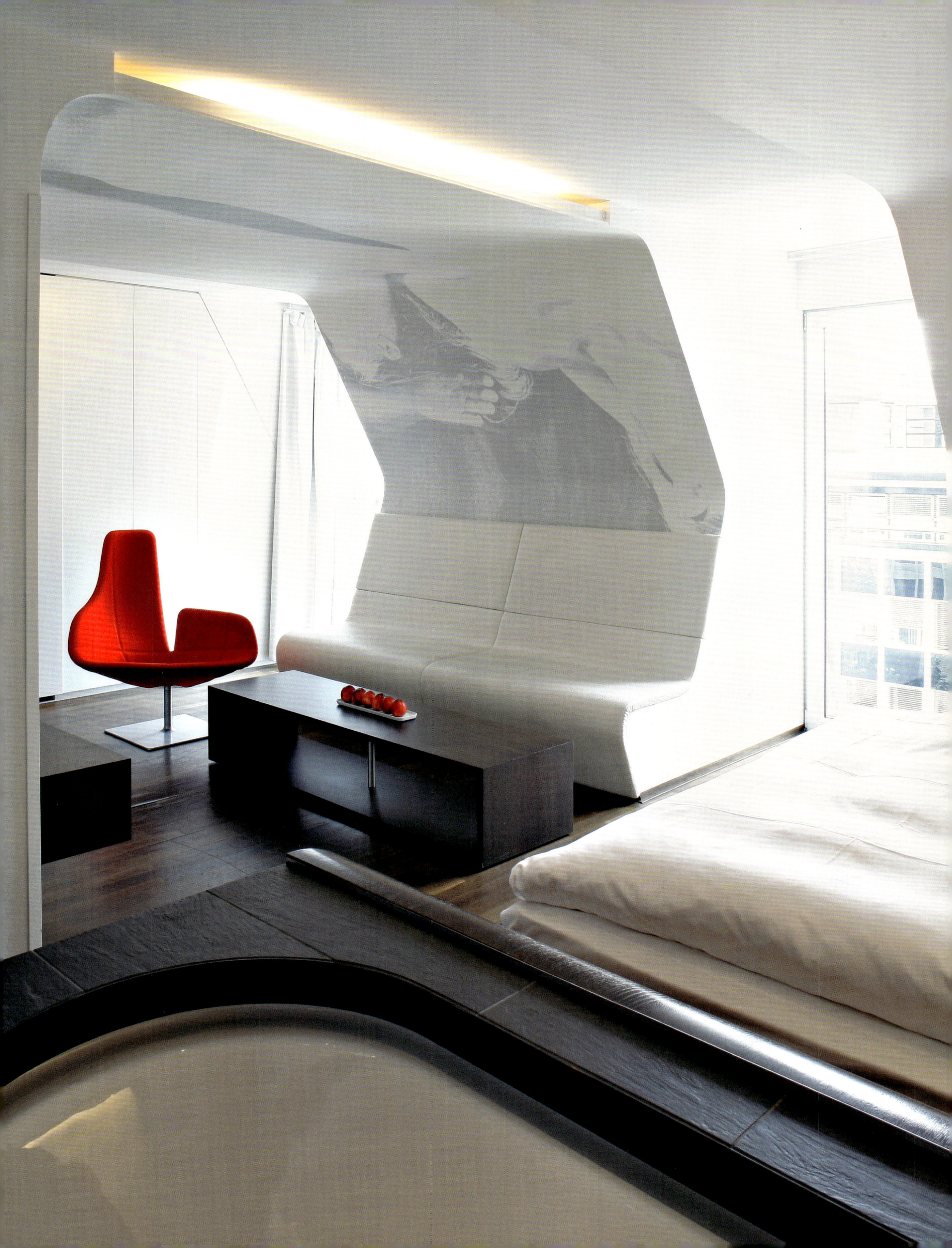

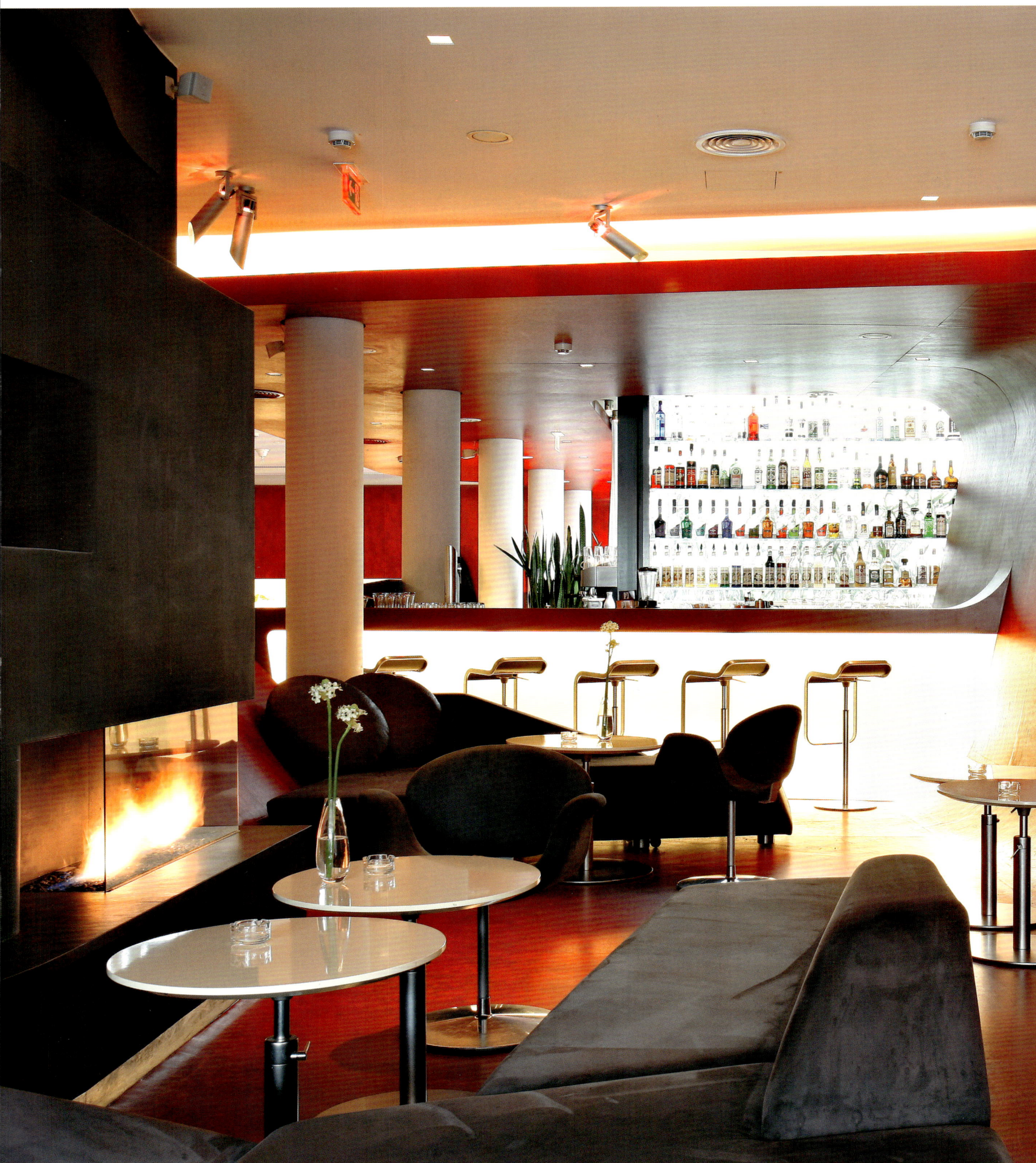

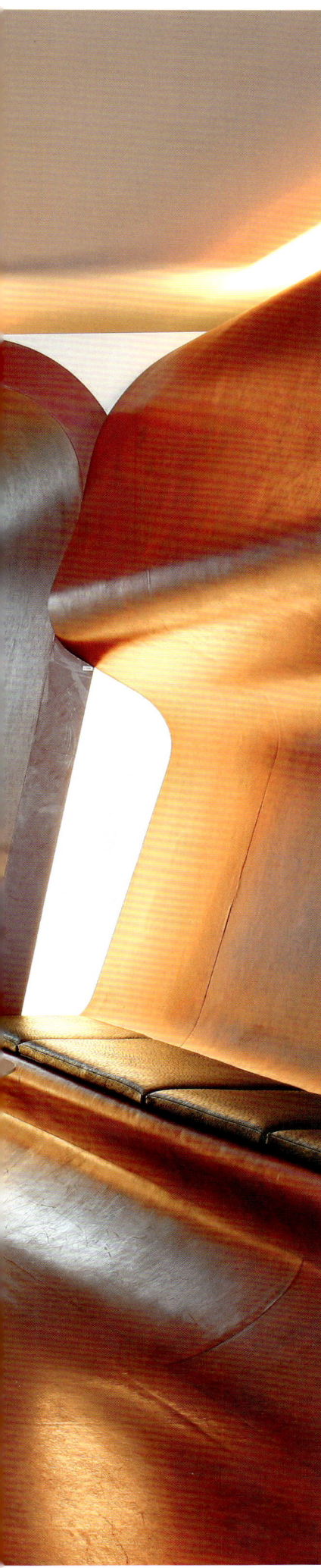

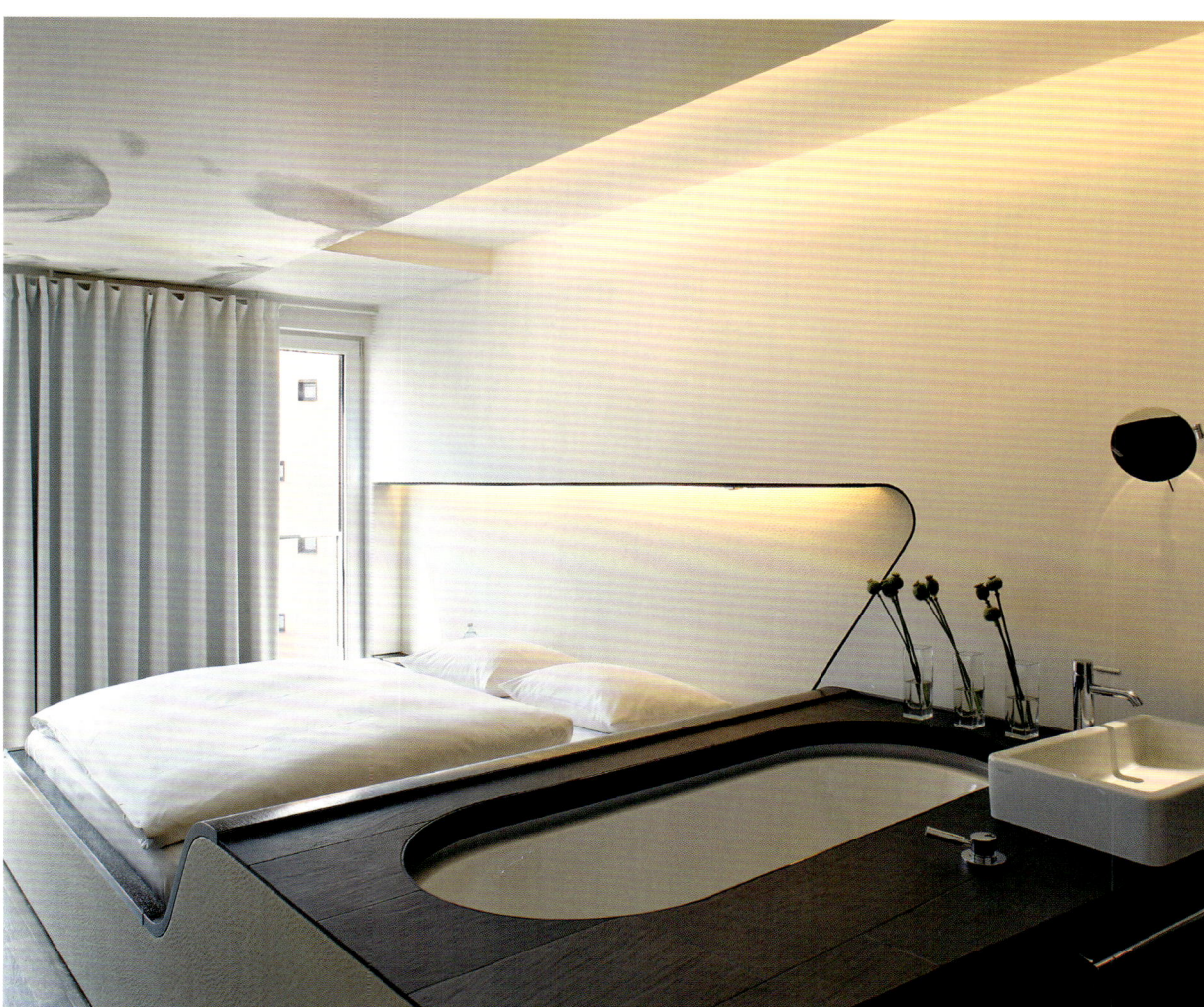

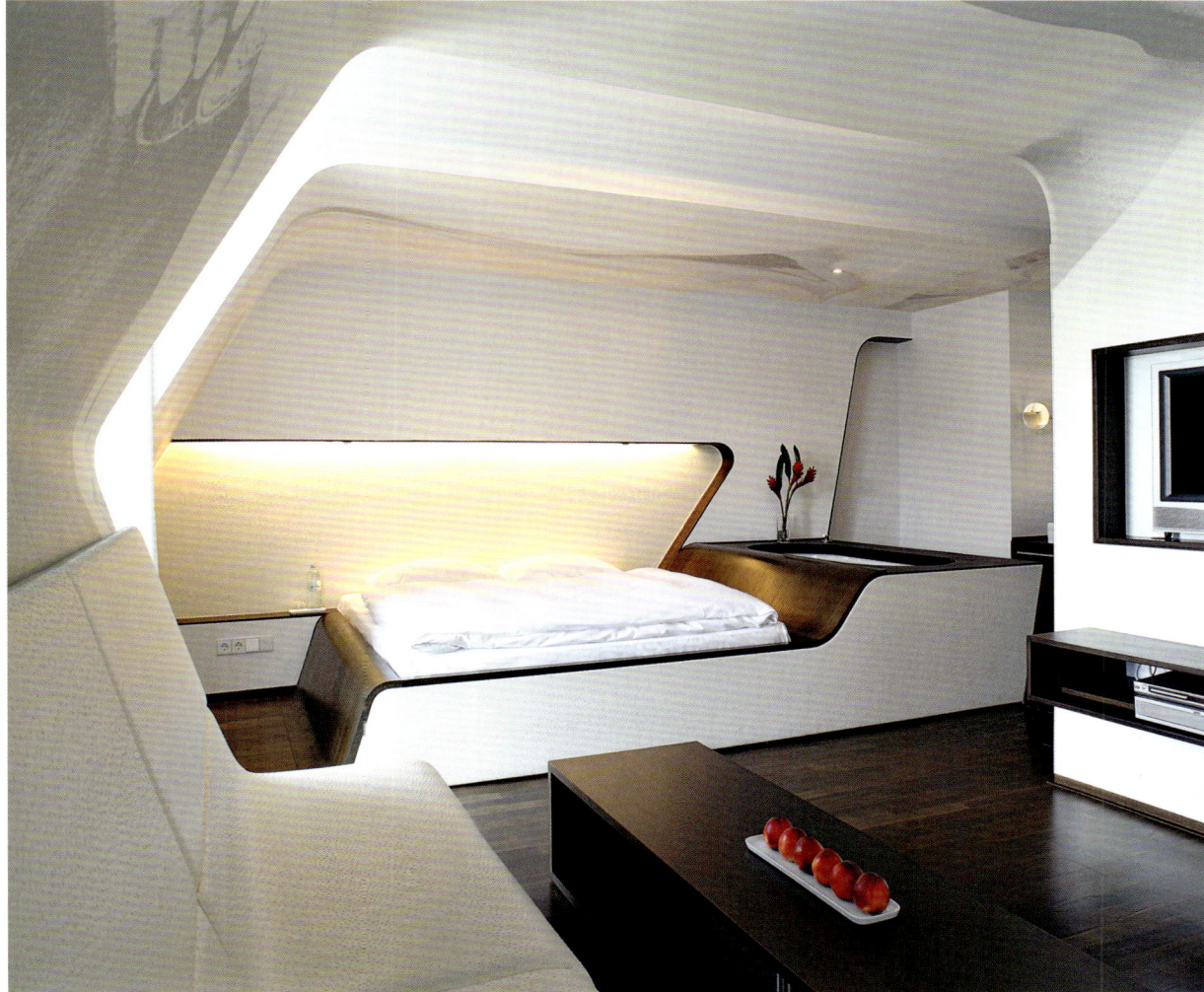

Drehbahn 49
20354 Hamburg
Germany
Tel.: +49 40 30 99 90
Fax: +49 40 30 99 93 99
www.side-hamburg.de

Price category: €
Rooms: 168 rooms and 10 suites
Facilities: fusion bar + restaurant, sky lounge with 8th floor terrace overlooking Hamburg, spa
Services: 24 h room service, laundry service, free newspapers, parking garage, concierge
Located: In the heart of Hamburg near the Opera House and Gänsemarkt
Public transportation: Dammtor train station; Underground U2 Gänsemarkt;
bus 4 and 5 Stephansplatz
Style: Modern puristic

The one and only five star superior design hotel in Hamburg is just five minutes on foot away from the city center and Binnenalster. Although its facade of glass and natural stone are rather plain in effect, the hotel's excellent design with aesthetically balanced lines render the facade quite winning, while the inner rooms and lighting are unsurpassed. Matteo Thun designed the puristic interior, the New York director and light designer Robert Wilson drafted the illumination. But not only the design is first class, the service leaves nothing to be desired.

Nur fünf Gehminuten von Stadtzentrum und Binnenalster entfernt liegt das erste und einzige Fünf-Sterne-Superior-Designhotel Hamburgs. Obwohl es mit seiner Fassade aus Glas und Naturstein von außen eher schlicht wirkt, besticht das Hotel durch sein herausragendes Designkonzept, das in der ästhetischen Ausgewogenheit seiner Fassade, der Innenräume und der Lichtführung seinesgleichen sucht. Das puristische Interieur gestaltete Matteo Thun, für die Illumination zeichnet der New Yorker Regisseur und Lichtdesigner Robert Wilson verantwortlich. Aber nicht nur die Gestaltung ist erstklassig, auch der Service lässt keine Wünsche offen.

L'unique hôtel design superieur à cinq étoiles d'Hambourg n'est qu'à cinq minutes à pied du centre ville et du Binnenalster. La magnifique architecture de l'hôtel, aux lignes esthétiquement équilibrées, confère énormément de charme à sa façade de verre et de pierre naturelle, d'aspect plutôt sobre, tandis que les pièces intérieures et l'éclairage sont d'une beauté sans rivale. Matteo Thun a dessiné l'intérieur puriste, le metteur en scène et plasticien newyorkais Robert Wilson l'éclairage. Et outre le design de première classe, le service ne laisse rien à désirer non plus.

A tan sólo cinco minutos a pie del centro de la ciudad y del lago Binnenalster se encuentra el primer y único hotel de diseño de cinco estrellas superiór en Hamburgo. Vista desde fuera, su fachada de cristal y piedra resulta más bien sobria. Sin embargo, el diseño del hotel sigue un concepto único y muy seductor, basado en el equilibrio estético entre la fachada, los espacios interiores y la iluminación. Matteo Thun fue el encargado de acondicionar el interior de manera purista y la iluminación corrió a cargo de Robert Wilson, director y diseñador de iluminación neoyorquino. Pero el hotel no destaca sólo por su decoración exclusiva, el servicio también satisface todos los deseos de los huéspedes.

A soli cinque minuti a piedi dal centro e dal lago Binnenalster si trova il primo e unico albergo di design a cinque stelle superiore di Amburgo. Benché dall'esterno, con la sua facciata in vetro e pietra naturale, appaia piuttosto semplice, l'hotel spicca per la straordinaria concezione del suo design, che in quanto a equilibrio estetico della facciata, degli interni e dei giochi di luce non ha eguali. L'interno, in stile purista, è stato progettato da Matteo Thun, mentre l'illuminazione porta la firma del regista ed esperto newyorkese Robert Wilson. Ma non solo il design di questo hotel è di prima classe, anche il servizio esaudirà ogni vostro desiderio.

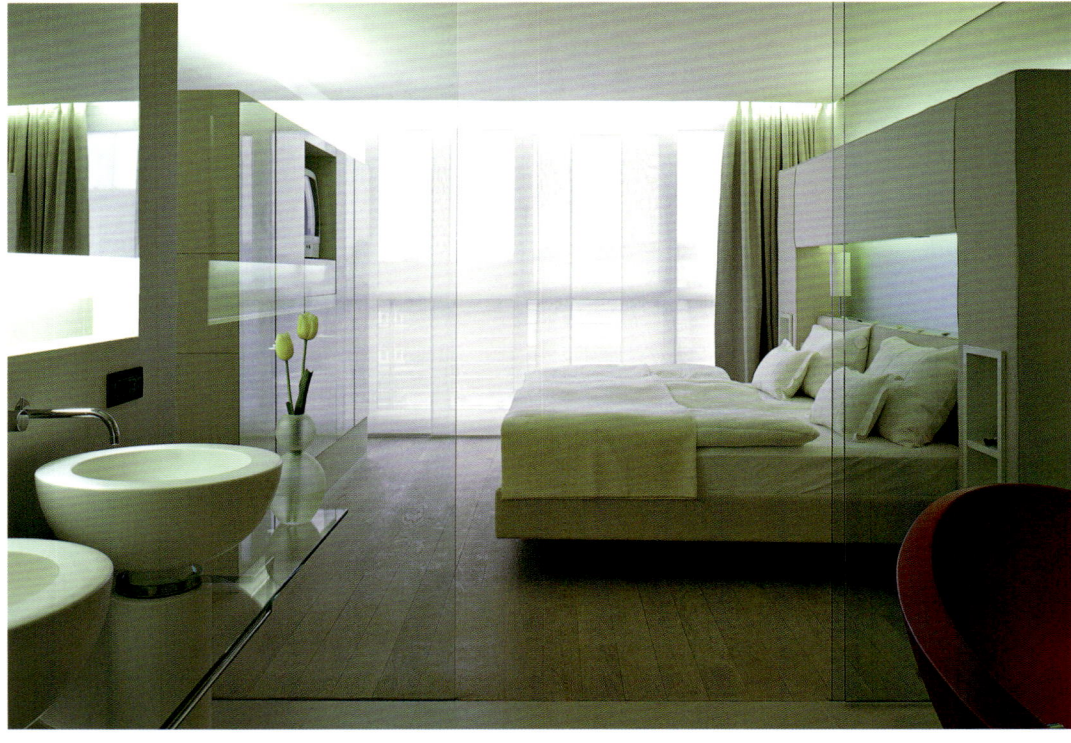
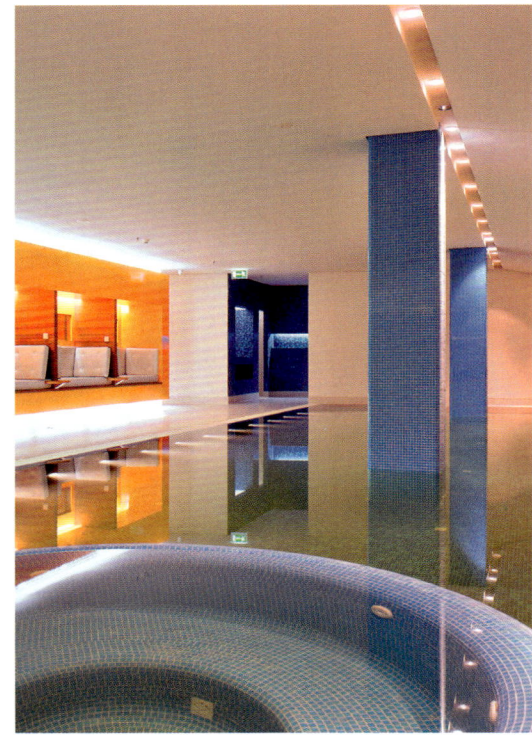

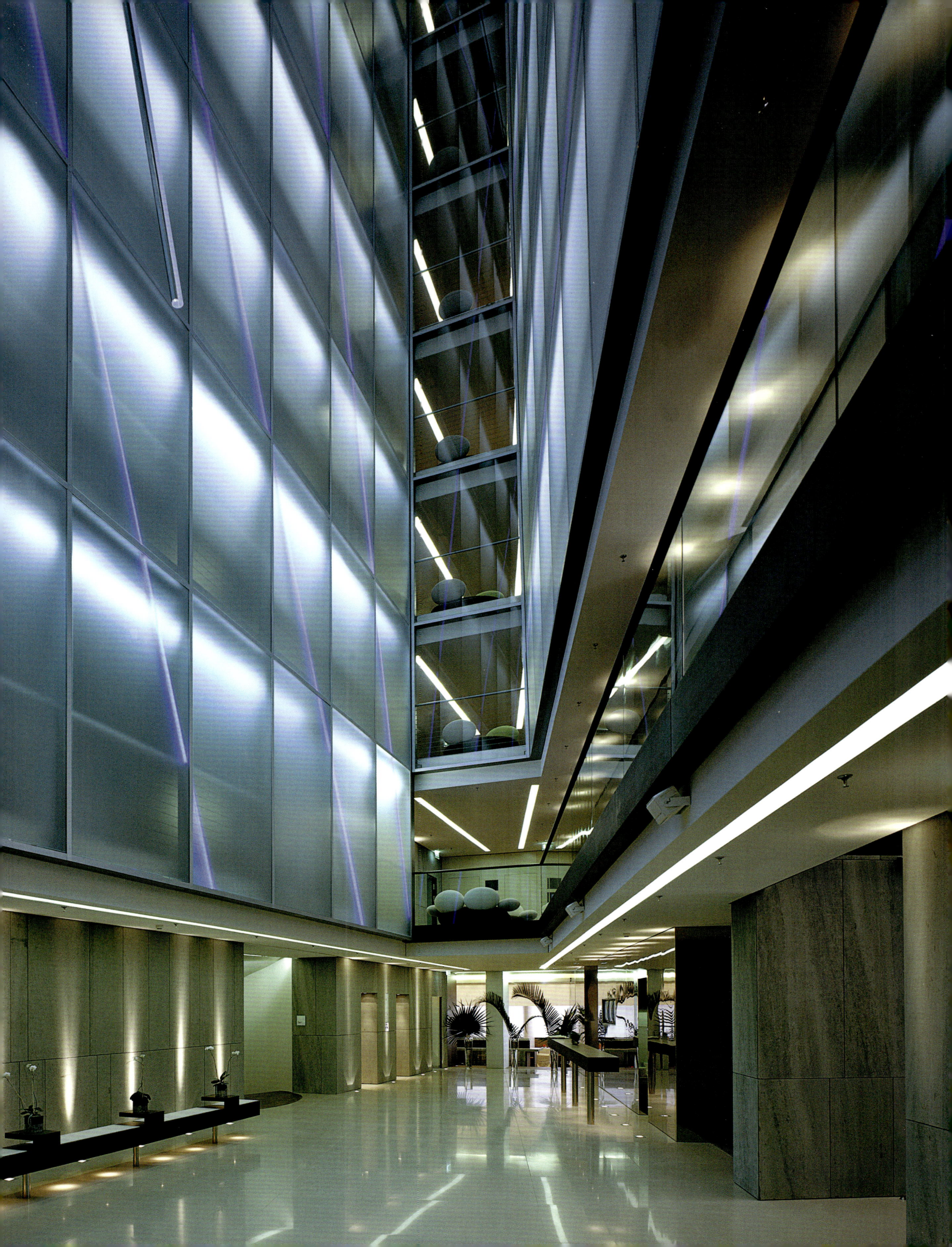

Goldman 25hours Hotel

Frankfurt, Germany

Hanauer Landstraße 127
60314 Frankfurt
Germany
Phone: +49 69 40 58 68 90
Fax: +49 69 40 58 68 98 90
www.25hours-hotels.com

Price category: €
Rooms: 49 rooms
Facilities: Restaurant, bar, lounge
Services: Free WiFi, jogging corner, iPod sound system
Located: In the Frankfurt East End, situated among design furniture stores, creative agencies and insider clubs
Public transportation: S-Bahn Osthafenplatz, Underground Ostbahnhof
Style: Eclectic design, vintage aesthetic with fancy details

Artistic, communicative and a bit kitsch describe the hotel in the trendy East End Quarter of the metropolis on the Main where understatement is an unknown word. Ardi Goldman, a visionary of Frankfurt's nightlife, conceived the reincarnation of the dignified Henninger Hof as a jovial designer hotel. Between the French restaurant and the living room with ironically meant laced covers, there is constant coming and going, greeting and taking leave. And in the rooms designed from rockingly colorful to ascetic, the big city nomads sink back in their favorite personal worlds.

Künstlerisch, kommunikativ und ein bisschen kitschig – für das Hotel im trendigen Ostend-Viertel der Mainmetropole ist Understatement ein Fremdwort. Ardi Goldman, Visionär des Frankfurter Nachtlebens, konzipierte die Reinkarnation des gediegenen Henninger Hofes zum fröhlichen Designhotel. Zwischen französischem Restaurant, Bar und Wohnzimmer mit ironisch gemeinten Spitzendeckchen, herrscht ein ständiges Kommen und Gehen, Begrüßen und Verabschieden. Und in den von rockig-bunt bis asketisch gestalteten Zimmern versinken die Großstadt-Nomaden in ihre persönlichen Lieblingswelten.

Artistique, communicatif et un peu kitsch : pour cet hôtel du quartier tendance d'Ostend, minimalisme est un mot étranger. Ardi Goldman, un visionnaire de la vie noctambule de Francfort, a conçu la réincarnation du très chic Henninger Hofes en un joyeux hôtel de designer. Entre le restaurant français, le bar et le lounge aux plafonds décorés, et leurs touches ironiques, règne un constant va-et-vient de bonjours et d'adieux. Et dans les chambres qui vont du coloré rock and roll au design ascétique, les nomades urbains se plongent dans leur univers favori.

Artístico, comunicativo y con un leve toque kitsch. El flamante hotel ubicado en el barrio de moda Ostend de la metrópolis del Meno es de todo menos austero. Ardi Goldman, visionario de la vida nocturna en Francfort, concibió la transformación del aplomado Henninger Hof en el alegre hotel de diseño que hoy es. Tanto en el restaurante francés, como en el bar o en el salón con sus irónicos mantelitos de encaje, reina un incesante ir y venir, lleno de constantes saludos y despedidas. En sus habitaciones, con estilos que van de lo roquero-colorido hasta lo ascético, los nómadas de la metrópolis podrán sumergirse en el universo que más les atraiga.

Artistico, comunicativo e un po' kitsch – per quest'albergo situato a Ostend, quartiere alla moda della metropoli sul Meno, "understatement" è una parola sconosciuta. Ardi Goldman, visionario della vita notturna di Francoforte, è l'artefice della felice reincarnazione dell'accurato Henninger Hof in un design hotel. Tra il ristorante francese, il bar e il salotto con tanto di ironici centrini regna un continuo andare e venire, salutare e congedarsi. E in camere che spaziano da colori sgargianti ad arredi ascetici, i nomadi della grande città sprofondano in uno splendido mondo tutto loro.

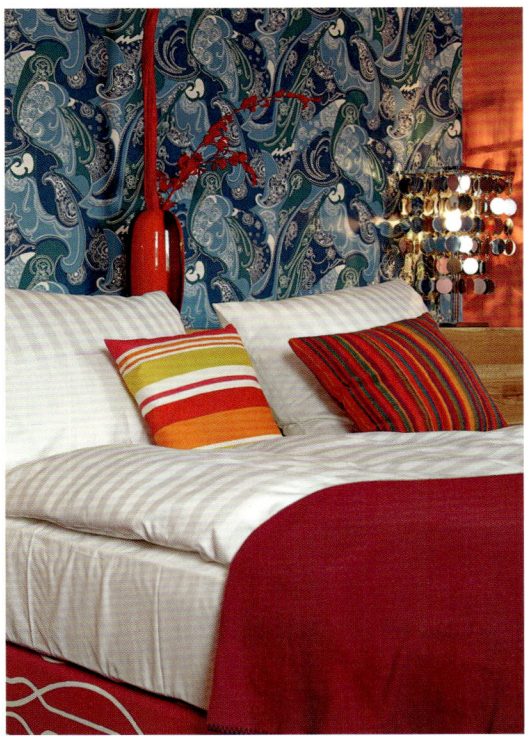
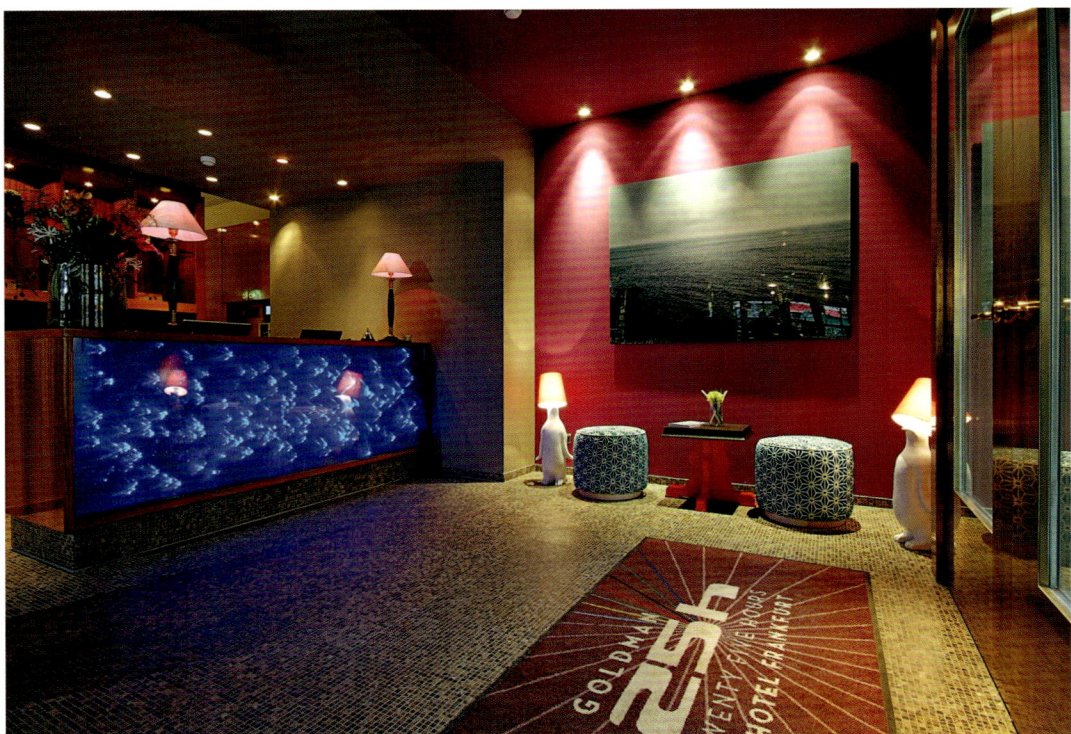

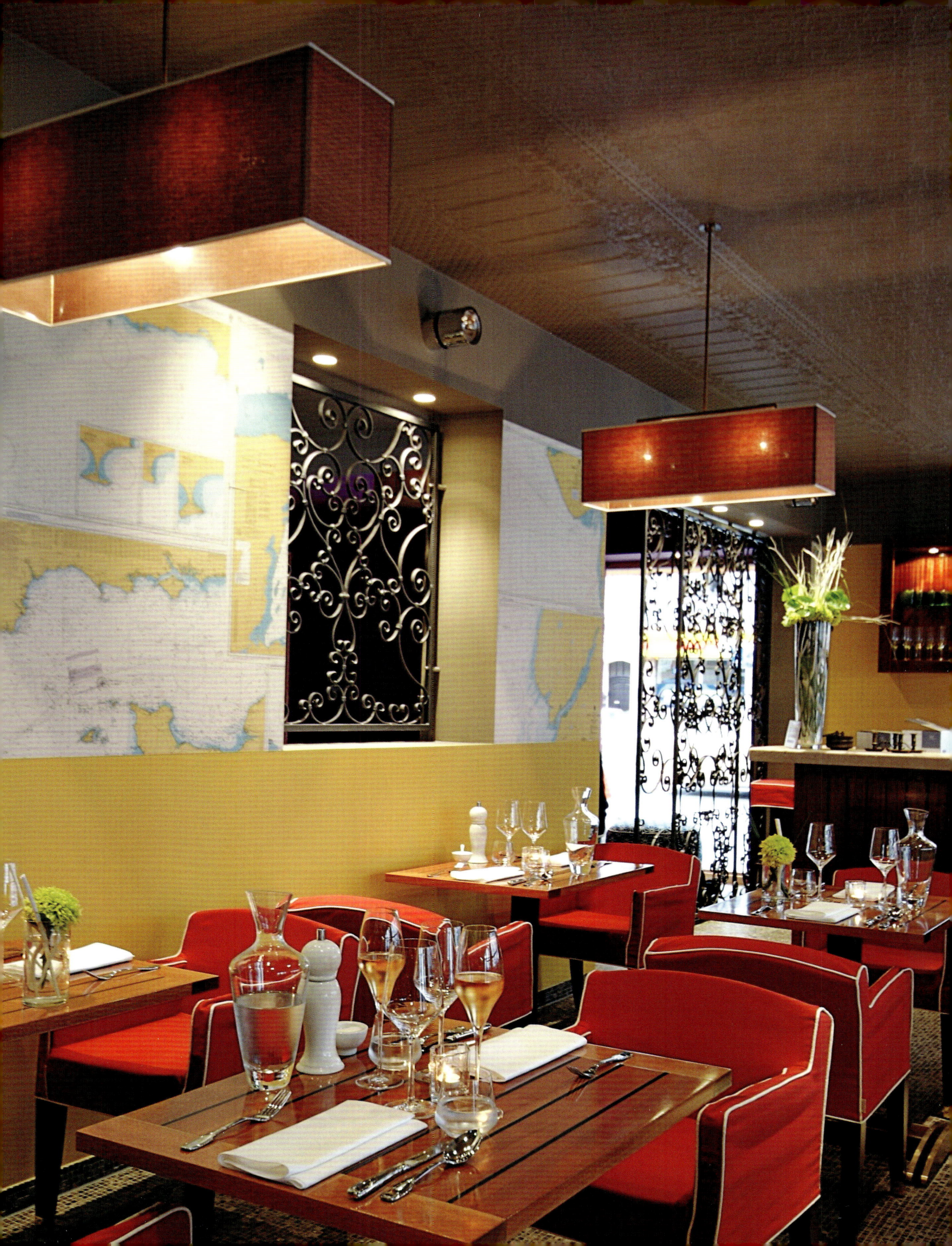

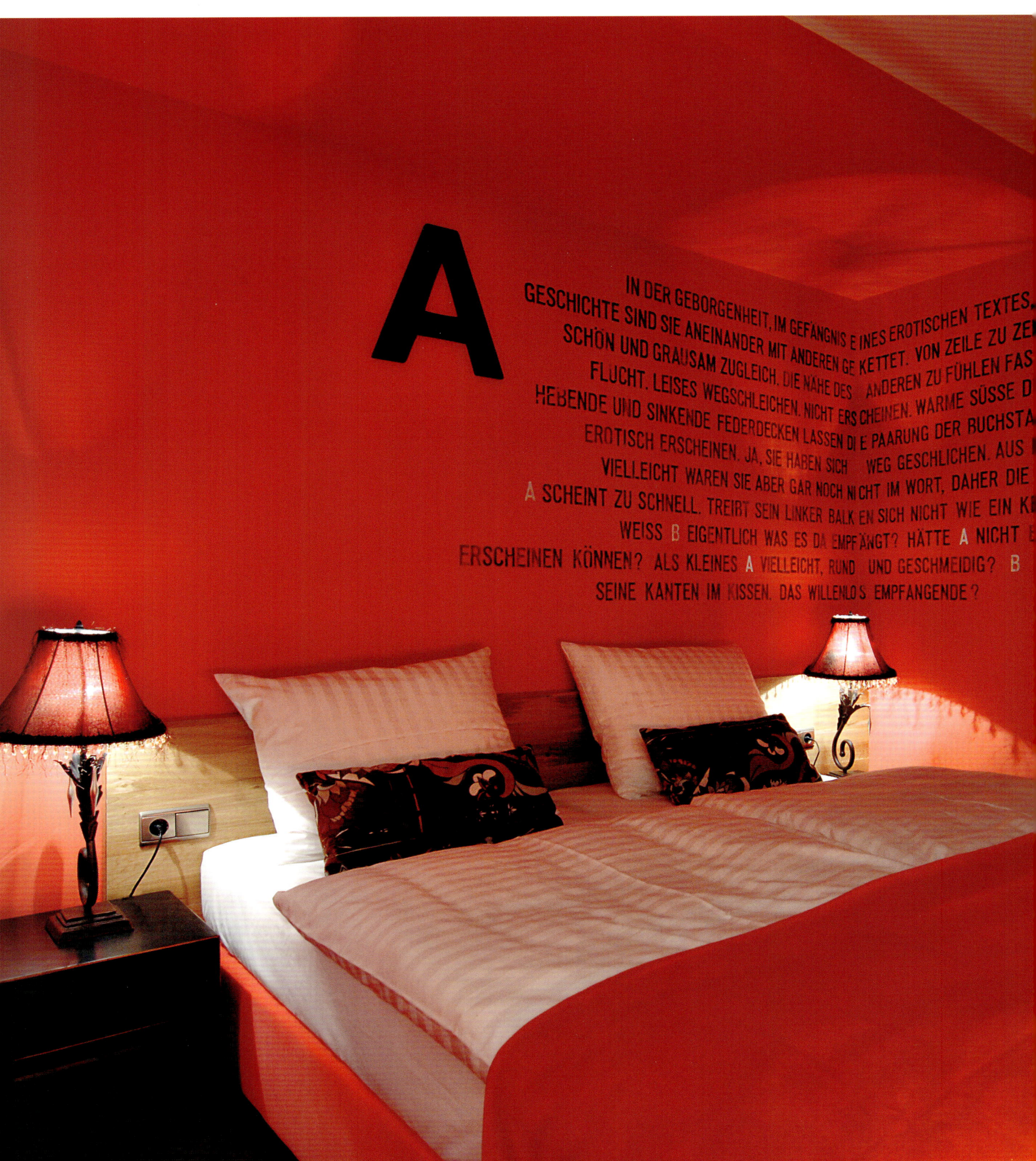

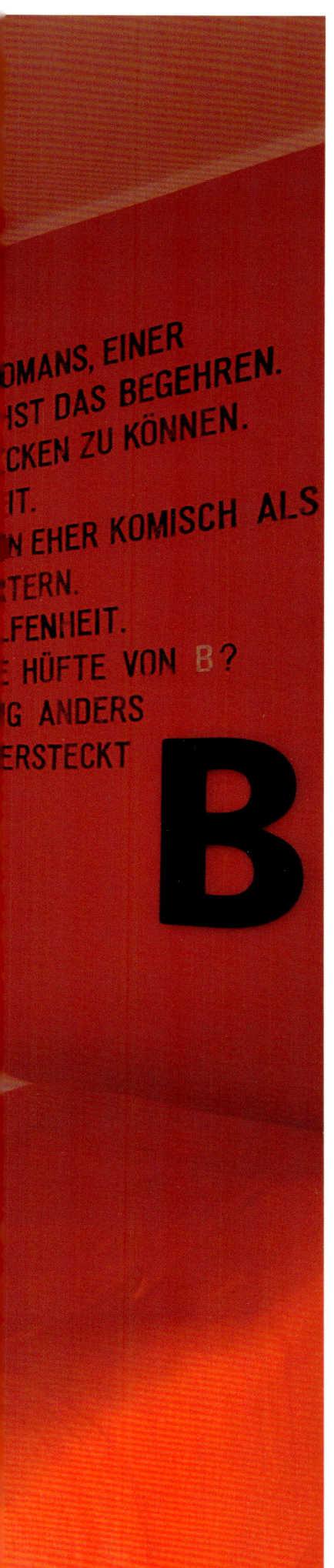

OMANS, EINER
IST DAS BEGEHREN.
CKEN ZU KÖNNEN.
IT.
N EHER KOMISCH ALS
RTERN.
LFENHEIT.
E HÜFTE VON B?
G ANDERS
ERSTECKT

B

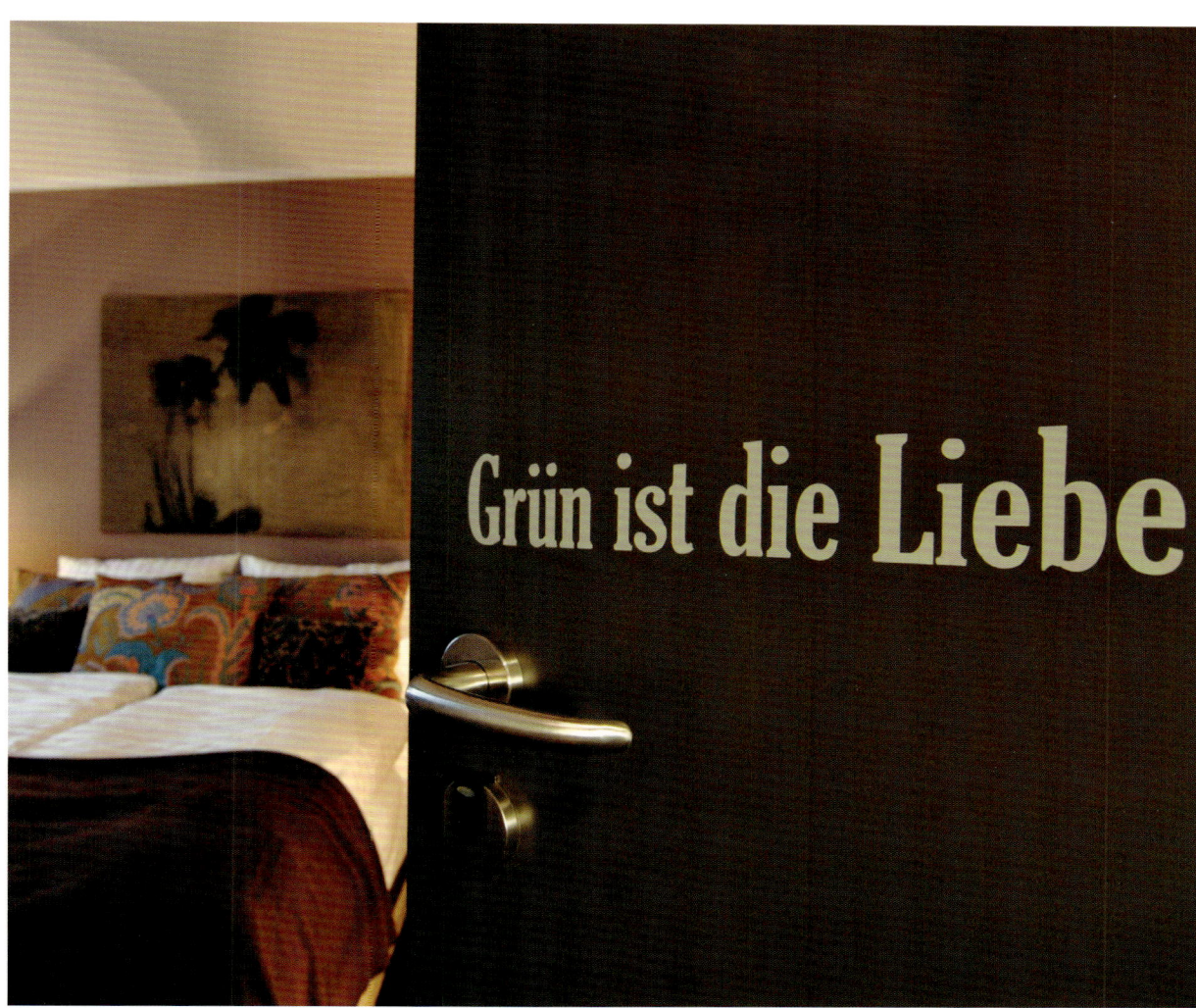

Grün ist die Liebe

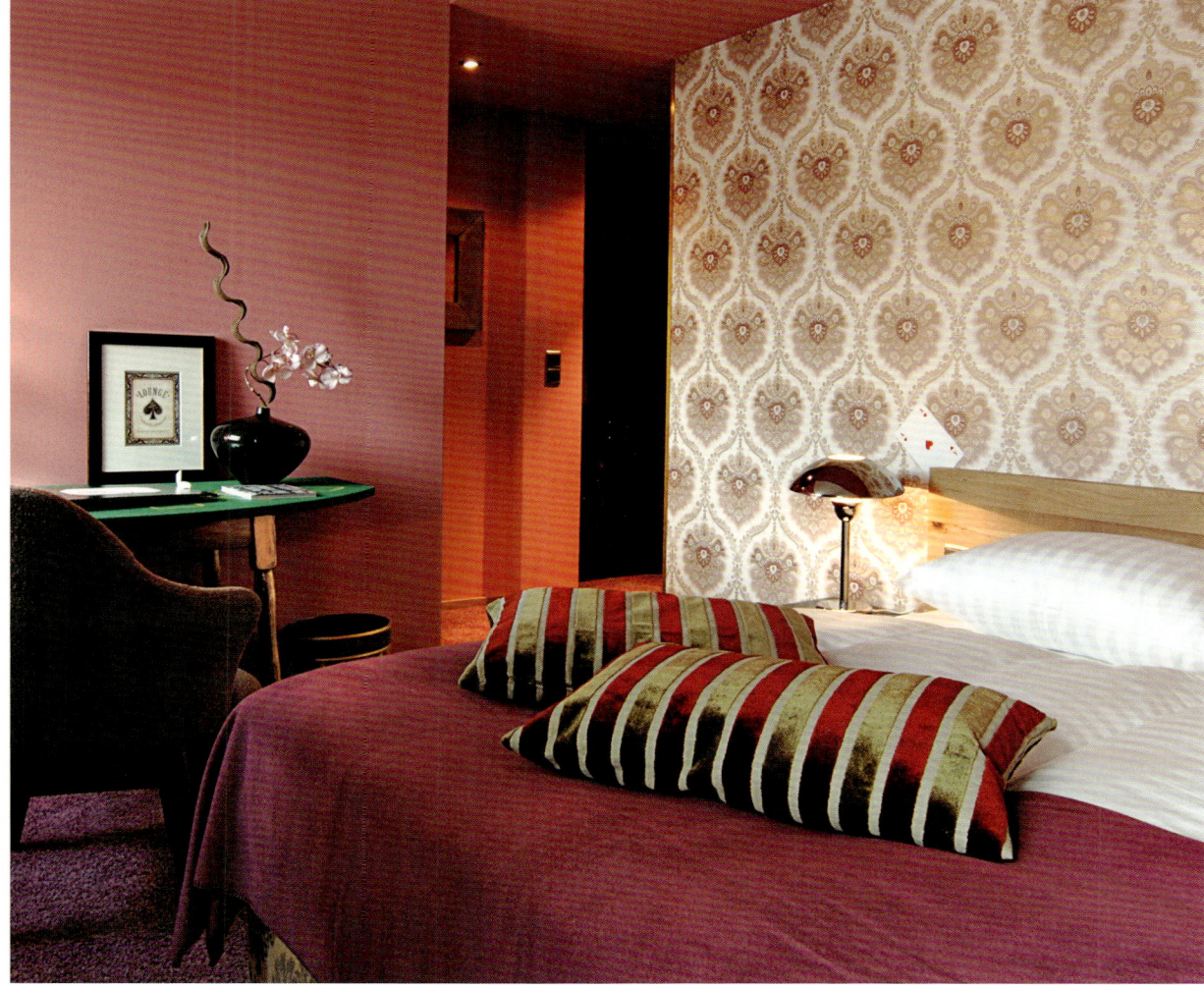

Villa Kennedy

Frankfurt, Germany

Kennedyallee 70
60596 Frankfurt
Germany
Phone: +49 69 71 71 20
Fax: +49 69 71 71 22 43 0
www.roccofortecollection.com

Price category: €€€
Rooms: 134 rooms, 28 suites, 1 presidential suite
Facilities: JFK Bar, Gusto Restaurant, Villa Spa, gym, 9 meeting rooms including a ball room
Services: Villa Spa has a 15 m indoor pool and treatment rooms
Located: Within walking distance from the Main river and close to the financial district
Public transportation: Tram Stresemannallee and Gartenstraße
Style: Classic elegance, traditional and innovative

In the brief time since its opening in 2006 Sir Rocco Forte's Villa Kennedy has become the noblest address of the Main metropolis. The heart of the 163 room hotel (including 29 suites) is the historical Villa Speyer that was built for a Frankfurt banker family in 1904. The three new wings are grouped around a quiet green inner court with restaurant terrace. Precious materials and discreet elegance are the by-word for the interior design. Relaxation is offered by the award-winning spa with its 50-feet pool.

In der kurzen Zeit seit ihrer Eröffnung 2006 ist Sir Rocco Fortes Villa Kennedy zur nobelsten Adresse der Mainmetropole avanciert. Kernstück des 163-Zimmer-Hotels (inklusive der 29 Suiten) ist die historische Villa Speyer, die 1904 für eine Frankfurter Bankiersfamilie erbaut wurde. Drei neue Flügelanbauten gruppieren sich um einen ruhigen grünen Innenhof mit Restaurant-Terrasse. Edle Materialen und zurückhaltende Eleganz prägen den Interieur-Stil. Entspannung bietet der preisgekrönte Spa mit seinem 15-Meter-Pool.

La Villa Kennedy de Sir Rocco Fortes est devenue l'une des adresses les plus chics de la métropole du Main, malgré le peu de temps qui s'est écoulé depuis son ouverture en 2006. Le cœur de cet hôtel de 163 chambres (dont 29 suites) est la Villa Speyer, construite en 1904 pour une famille de banquiers de Francfort. Trois nouvelles ailes sont regroupées autour d'une cour intérieure verte paisible, avec un restaurant en terrasse. Des matériaux nobles et une élégance discrète dominent à l'intérieur. Le spa primé, avec sa piscine de 15 mètres de long, permet de se relaxer.

En el corto periodo desde su apertura en 2006, la Villa Kennedy de Sir Rocco Forte, se ha convertido en una de las direcciones más exclusivas de la metrópolis alemana del Meno. El núcleo del hotel de 163 habitaciones (incluidas 29 suites) es la histórica Villa Speyer, construida en 1904 para una familia de banqueros de Francfort. Las tres nuevas alas del edificio se agrupan en torno a un patio interior muy tranquilo lleno de vegetación, con restaurante y terraza. El estilo del interior viene marcado por los materiales de lujo y ofrece una imagen discreta y elegante. Para relajarse, nada mejor que el premiado spa con su piscina de 15 metros.

Già nel breve periodo trascorso dall'anno della sua apertura, il 2006 la Villa Kennedy di Sir Rocco Forte è diventata l'indirizzo più esclusivo della città sul Meno. Il nucleo di questo hotel da 163 stanze (tra cui 29 suite) è la storica Villa Speyer, fatta costruire nel 1904 da una famiglia di banchieri francofortesi. Le tre nuove ali dell'edificio si dispongono attorno a un verde e tranquillo cortile, in cui trova spazio anche un ristorante all'aperto. Lo stile degli interni è caratterizzato dalla presenza di materiali pregiati, che conferiscono all'insieme un'eleganza riservata. Il relax è assicurato da uno spa molto rinomato, che è dotato, tra l'altro, di una piscina da 15 metri.

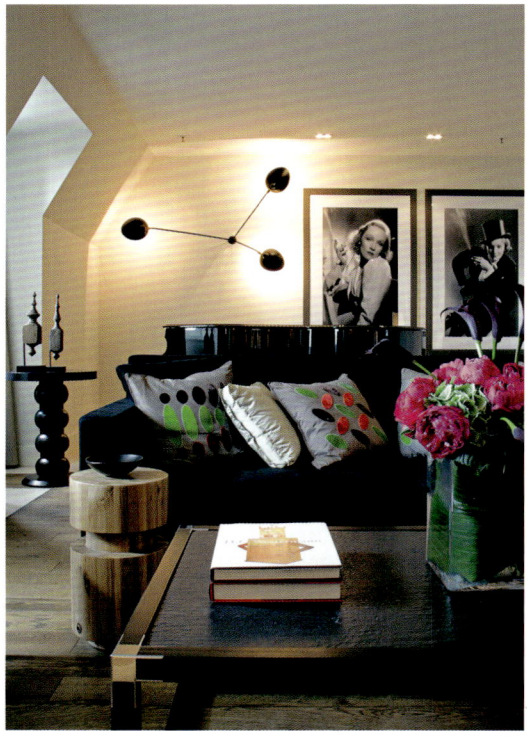
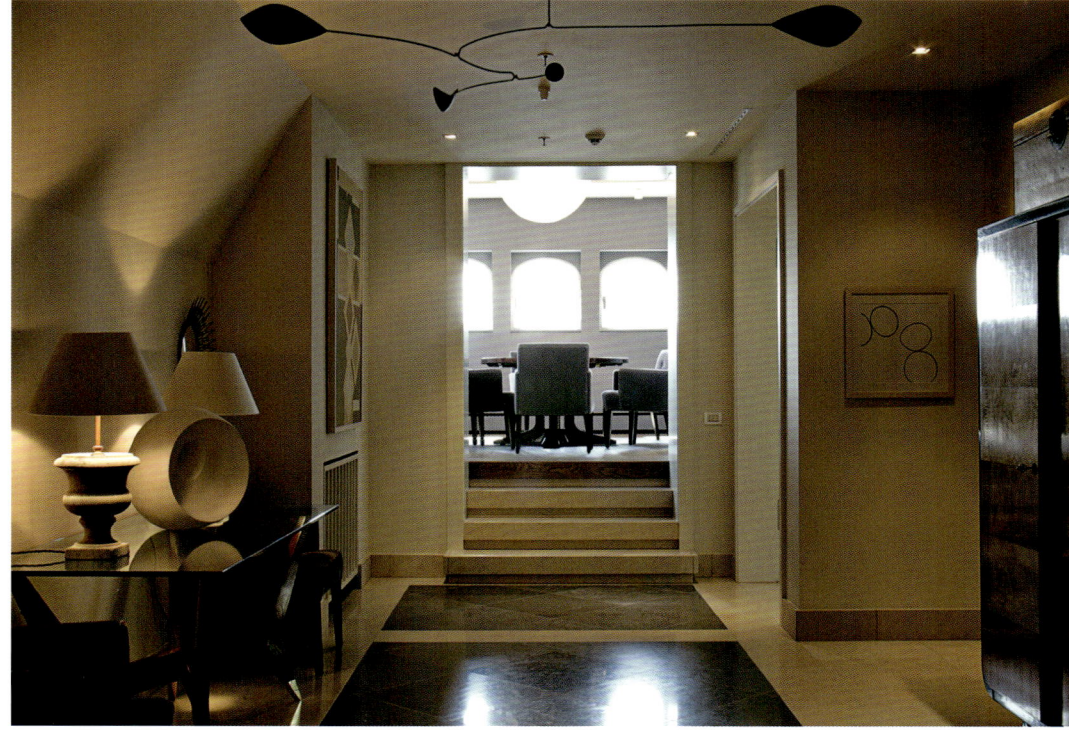

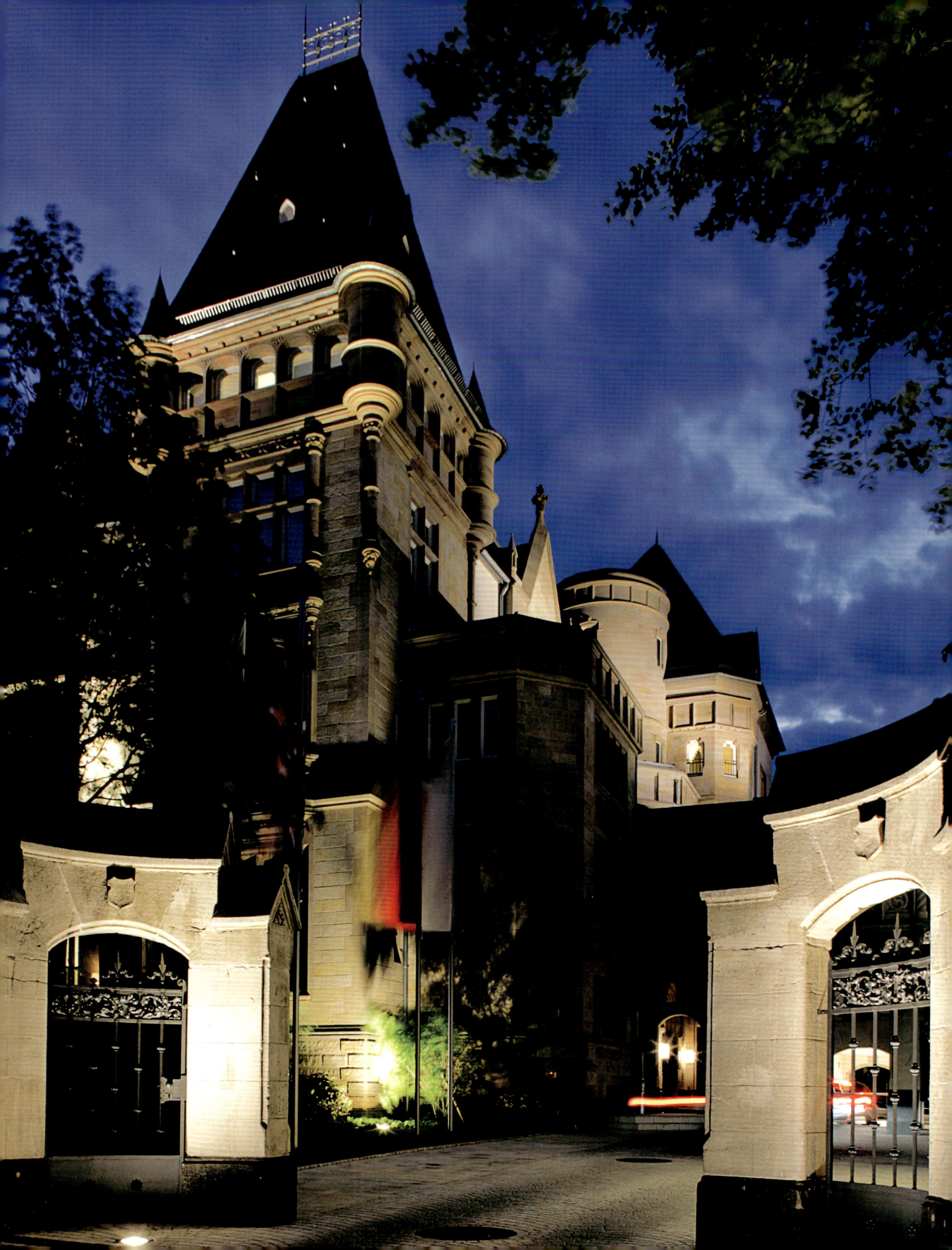

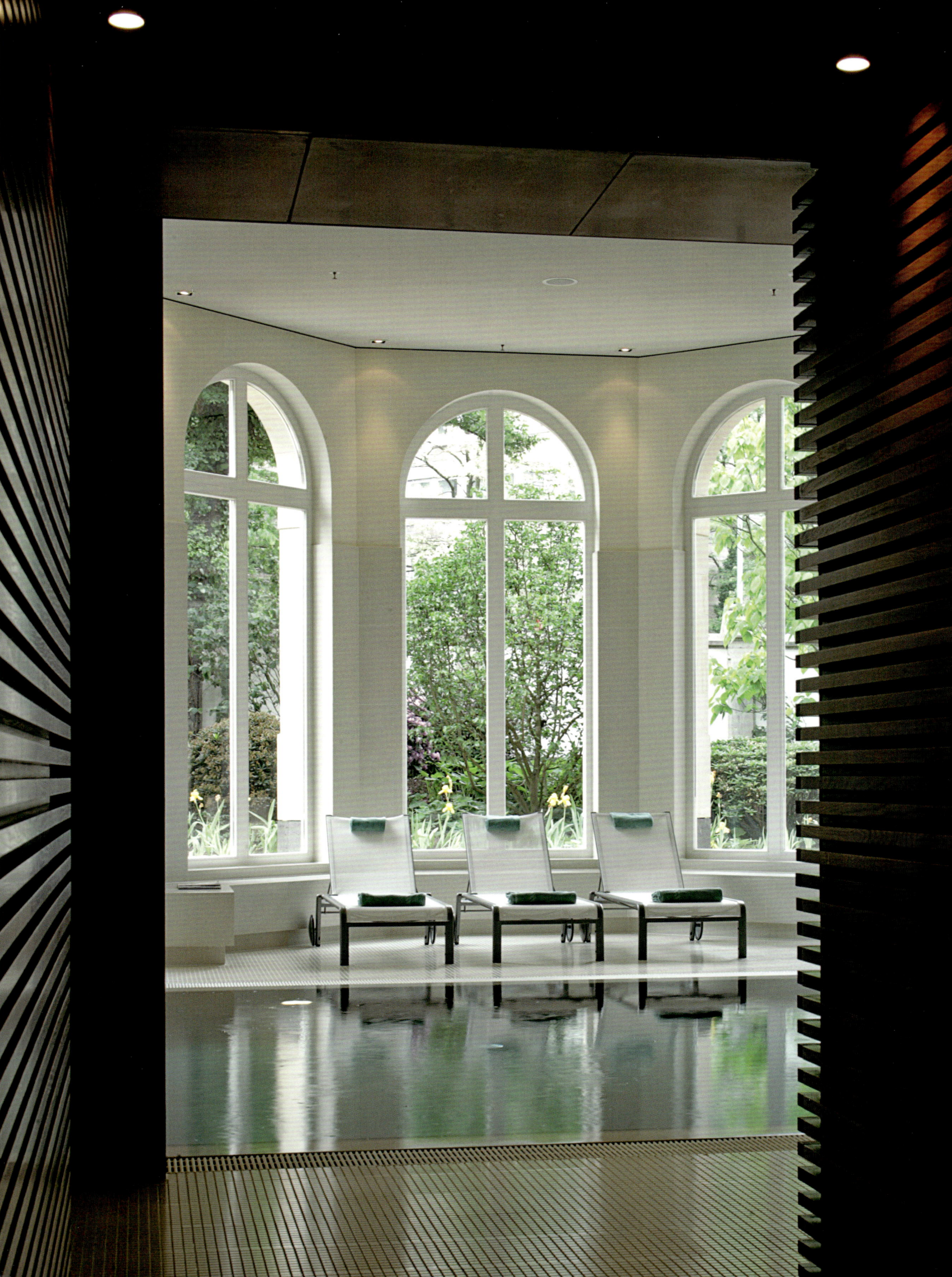

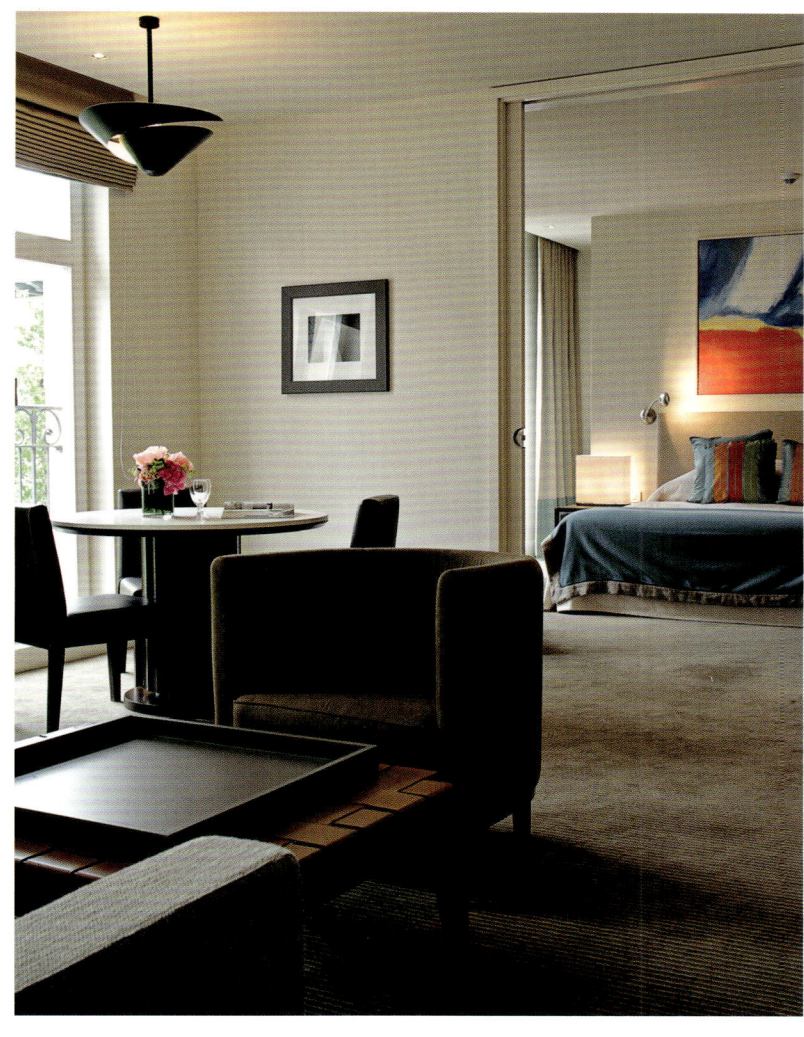
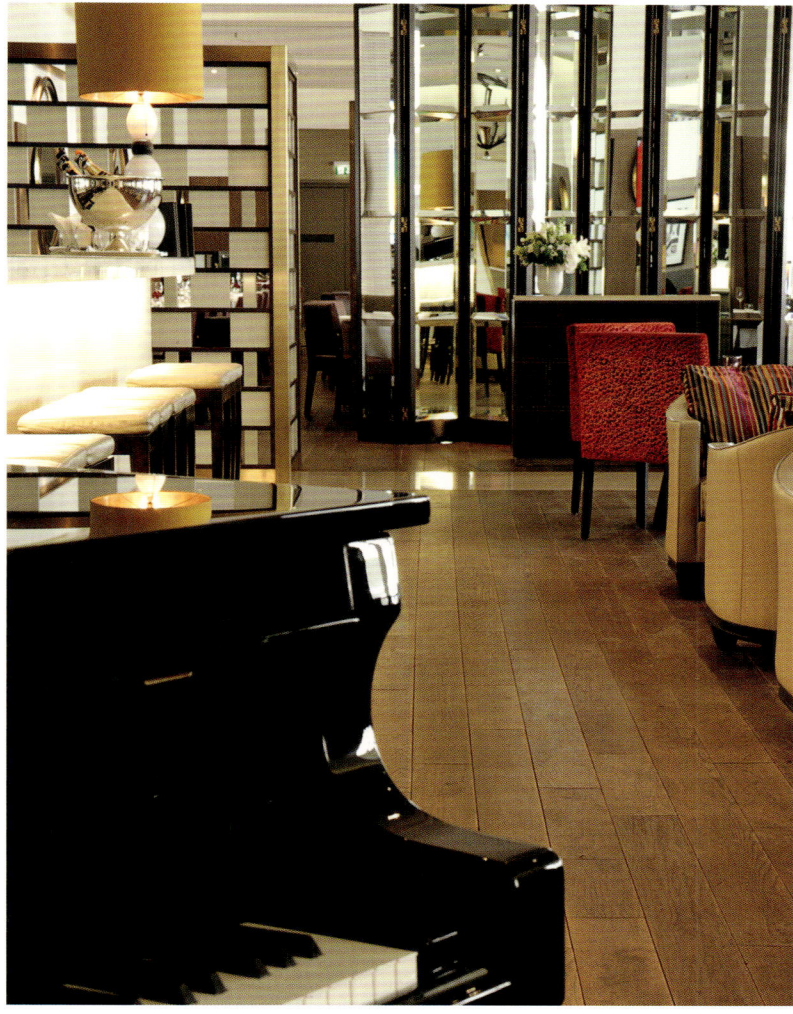
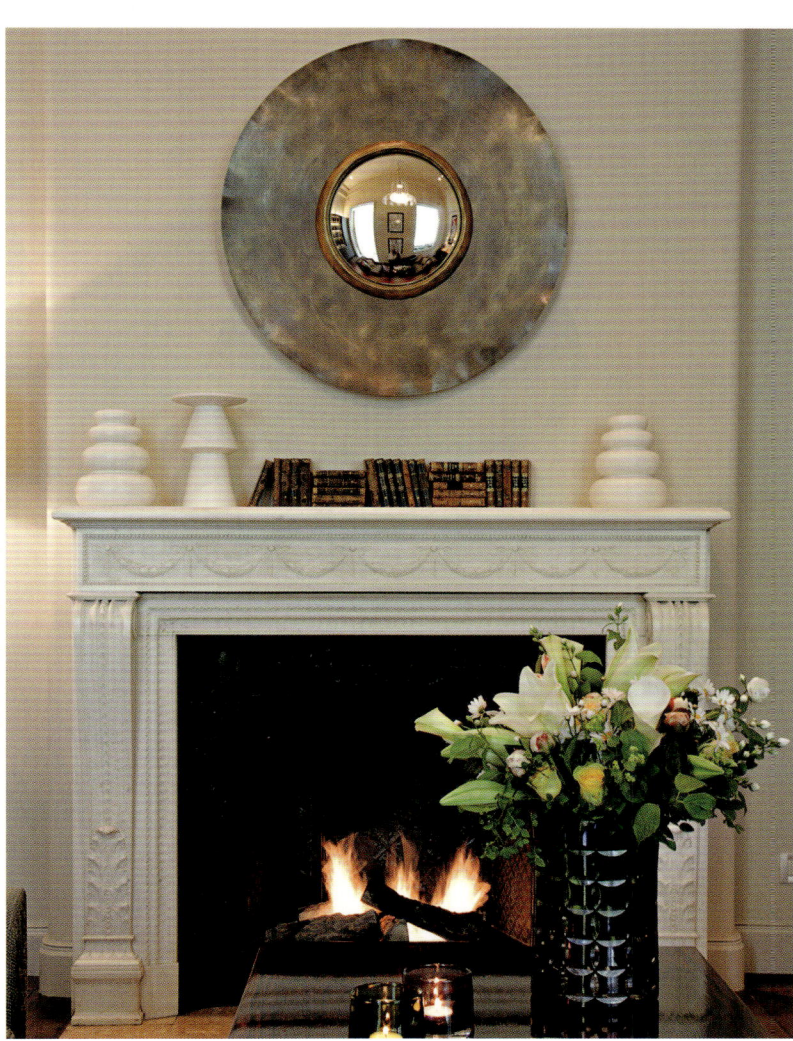
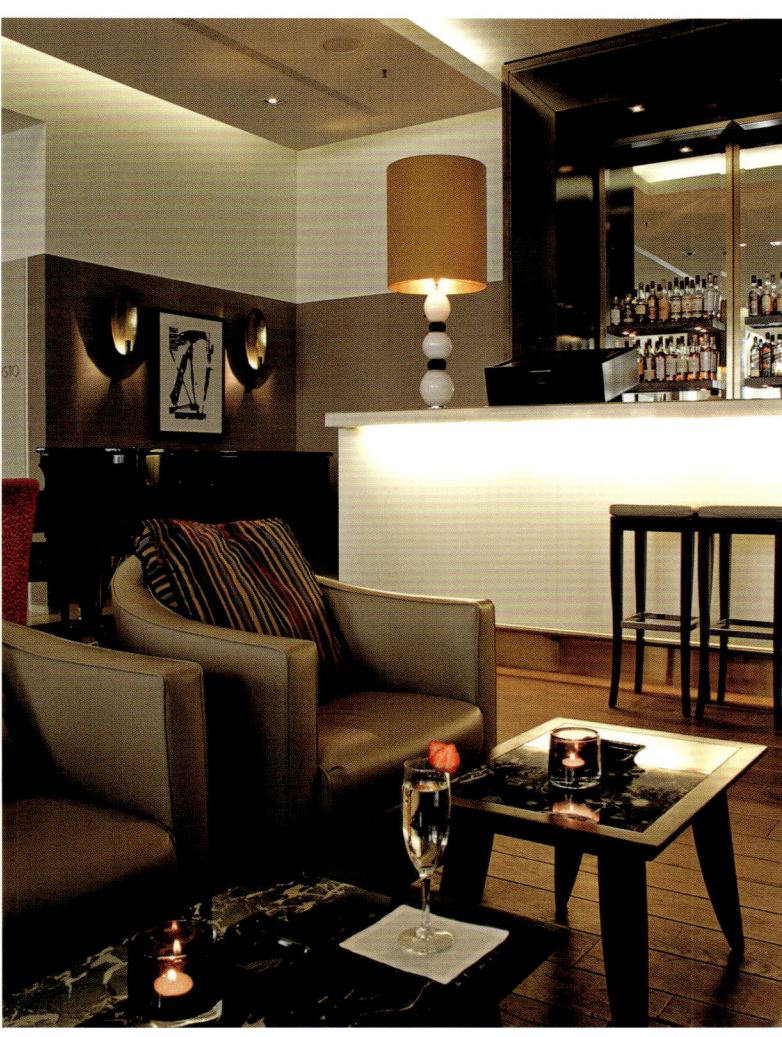

50674 Cologne
Germany
Phone: +49 2 21 20 71 50
Fax: +49 2 21 23 91 37
www.hotel-chelsea.de

Rooms: 35 rooms and 3 suites
Facilities: Café Central
Services: Free WiFi, 24 h room service
Located: In the city center
Public transportation: S-Bahn, Rudolfplatz
Style: Contemporary design

The roof is folded back, the balconies upside down and the windows seem to be falling from the building. Its deconstructivist design assembly makes the hotel in the city of Cologne a total piece of art. Behind the plain facade of the '50s the house trumps in with a sizeable collection that has come from "contributions" by famous artists. Joseph Kosuth installed a neon sculpture in the lobby, Rosemarie Trockel and A. R. Penck decorated the rooms. And Martin Kippenberger who issued the credo "Lodgings for art" in the '80s paid for his stays of several weeks with large-format pictures.

Das Dach ist aufgeklappt, die Balkone stehen Kopf und die Fenster scheinen aus dem Gebäude herauszupurzeln. Sein dekonstruktivistischer Aufbau macht das Hotel in der Kölner City zum Gesamtkunstwerk. Hinter der schlichten 50er-Jahre-Fassade trumpft das Haus mit einer beachtlichen Sammlung auf, entstanden durch die „Spenden" namhafter Künstler. Joseph Kosuth installierte eine Neon-Skulptur in der Lobby, Rosemarie Trockel und A. R. Penck dekorierten die Zimmer. Und Martin Kippenberger, der das Credo „Logis gegen Kunst" in den 80er Jahren ausgab, bezahlte seine wochenlangen Aufenthalte mit großformatigen Bildern.

Le toit est plié vers l'arrière, les balcons sont sens dessus-dessous et les fenêtres semblent tomber du bâtiment. Son design déconstructiviste fait de ce bâtiment, situé dans le centre ville de Cologne, une vraie œuvre d'art. Derrière sa façade banale qui date des années 50, l'établissement triomphe avec une collection d'art respectable, accumulée au fil des « contributions » de célèbres artistes. Joseph Kosuth a installé une sculpture au néon à la réception, Rosemarie Trockel et A. R. Penck ont décoré les chambres. Et Martin Kippenberger, qui a lancé le slogan « logis contre l'art » durant les années 80, a payé ses séjours de plusieurs semaines en nature, sous forme de grands tableaux.

El techo está abierto, los balcones cabeza abajo y las ventanas parecen salirse del edificio. La arquitectura deconstructivista de este hotel en el centro de Colonia lo convierte en una verdadera obra de arte. Detrás de su fachada sobria de los años 50, este establecimiento sorprende con una imponente colección, ganada a través de las "donaciones" de artistas prestigiosos. Joseph Kosuth instaló una escultura de neón en el vestíbulo, Rosemarie Trockel y A. R. Penck decoraron las habitaciones y Martin Kippenberger, quien en los años 80 prodigó el dogma del "alojamiento a cambio de arte", pagó sus estancias de varias semanas con lienzos de gran formato.

Il tetto è aperto, i balconi sono sotto sopra e le finestre sembrano schizzare fuori dall'edificio. La struttura decostruttivista fa di questo hotel nel centro di Colonia un'opera d'arte in ogni suo dettaglio. Dietro una sobria facciata anni '50 l'albergo stupisce gli ospiti con una ragguardevole collezione nata dalle "offerte" di rinomati artisti. Joseph Kosuth ha installato una scultura al neon nella lobby, Rosemarie Trockel e A. R. Penck hanno decorato le camere. E Martin Kippenberger, che negli anni '80 rese famoso il credo della "logica contro l'arte", pagò i suoi soggiorni di varie settimane in questo albergo con dipinti in formato gigante.

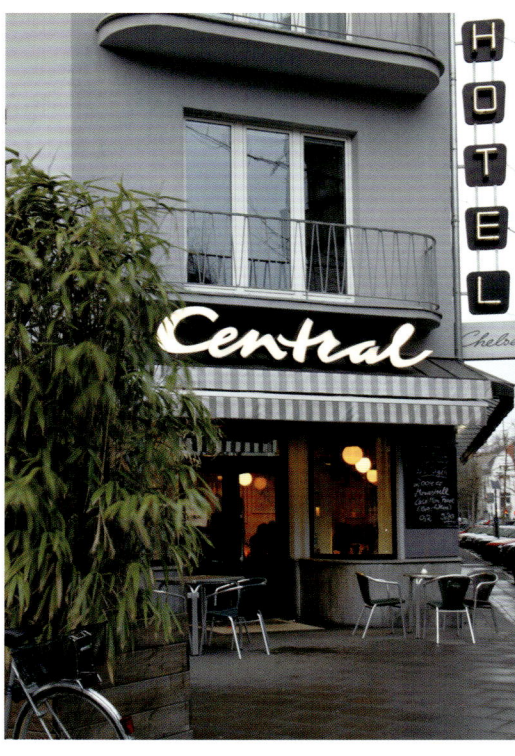
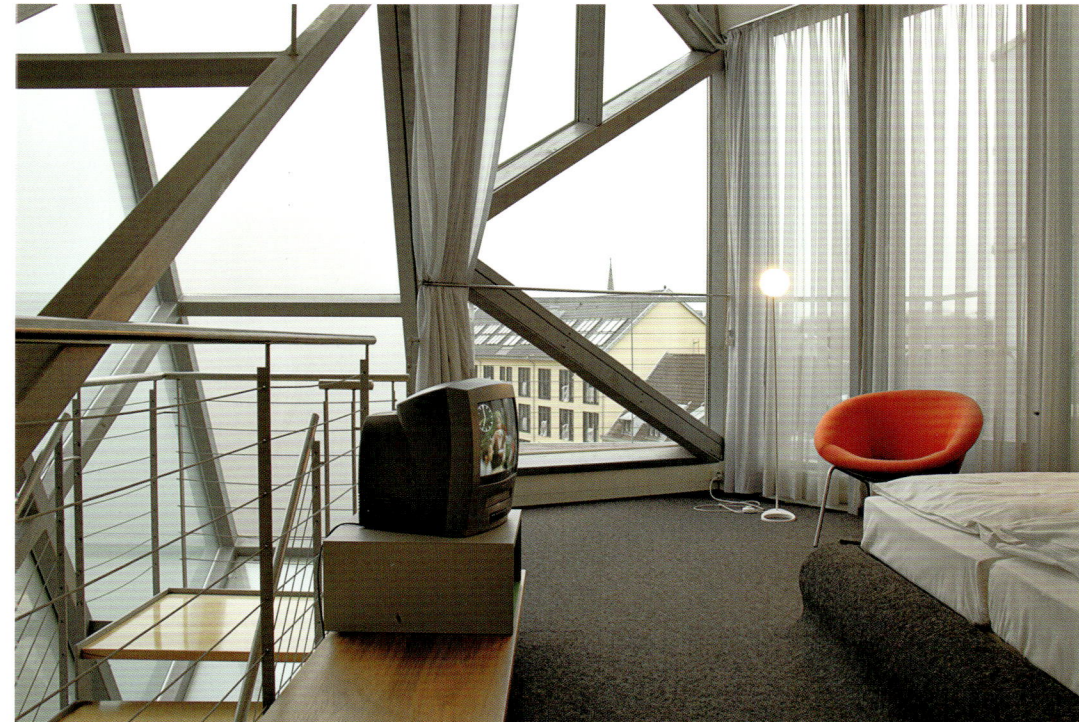

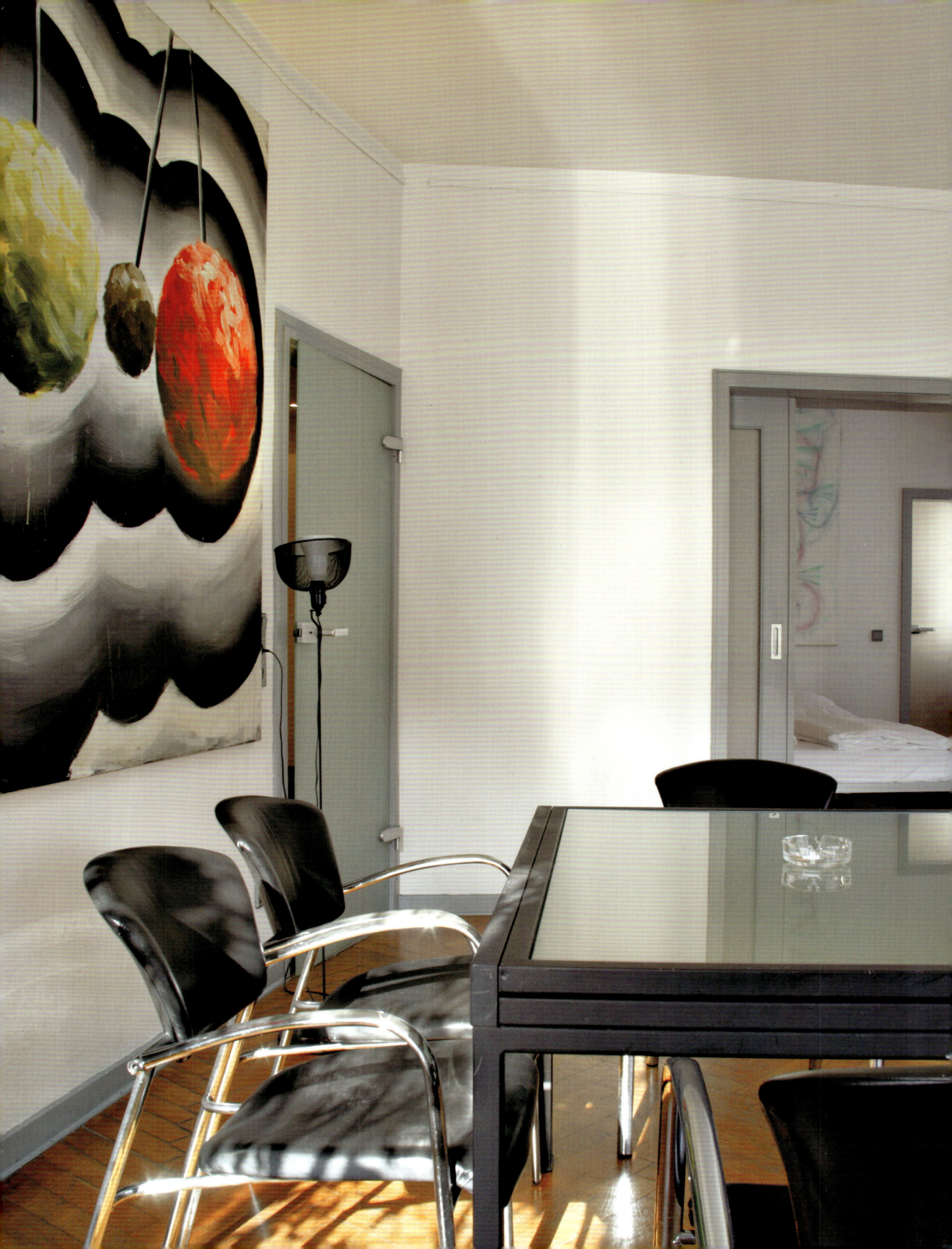

Schloss Auel

Lohmar-Wahlscheid, Germany

Haus Auel 1
53797 Lohmar
Germany
Phone: +49 2206 60 03 0
Fax: +49 2206 60 03 22 2
www.schlossauel.de

Price category: €
Rooms: 3 single rooms, 12 double rooms, 6 junior suites
Facilities: Restaurant, clubhouse, rooms for conferences, weddings and banquet rooms for up to 100 people, own chapel in rococo style
Services: Babysitting
Located: 30 km from Cologne, situated on a 27-hole golf course
Public transportation: Bus, train station in Honrath and Overath
Style: Classic elegance

For centuries the palace near Cologne has belonged to noble families; since 1818 the Barons of la Valette St. George have owned it. The former water castle was first documented in 1391, then under Peter van Auel. Its three-winged shape originates from the baroque period. The grand park has been strolled through by such illustrious guest as Tsar Alexander I, Emperor Wilhelm II and Napoleon, who dwelt here while inspecting the Rhine Army. You can also book the comfortable suite with canopy bed, costly antiques, brocade plaids, and cozy wing chairs.

Seit Jahrhunderten gehört das Anwesen bei Köln adligen Familien, seit 1818 den Freiherren von la Valette St. George. Erstmals tauchte die ehemalige Wasserburg 1391 in einer Urkunde auf, damals unter Peter van Auel. Seine dreiflüglige Form stammt aus der Barockzeit. Durch die Parkanlage wandelten schon illustre Gäste wie Zar Alexander I., Kaiser Wilhelm II und Napoleon, der hier 1811 nächtigte, als er die Rheinarmee inspizierte. Auch die komfortable Suite mit Baldachinbett, kostbaren Antiquitäten, Brokat-Plaids und Ohrensesseln kann man buchen.

Pendant des siècles, cette propriété près de Cologne a appartenu à des familles nobles, et depuis 1818 ce sont les Barons de la Valette St. George qui en sont propriétaires. Cet ancien château entouré d'eau apparaît pour la première fois dans un document de 1391, sous Pierre van Auel. Sa forme à trois ailes date de la période baroque. Parmi les hôtes illustres qui ont foulé la pelouse du parc, le tsar Alexandre Ier, l'empereur Guillaume II et Napoléon lors de son inspection de l'Armée du Rhin en 1811. On peut aussi réserver une suite confortable avec un lit à baldaquins, des antiquités précieuses, des couvre-lits de brocart et de confortables bergères à oreilles.

La propiedad cerca de Colonia ha estado desde hace siglos en manos de familias aristócratas y, desde 1818, pertenece a los barones de la Valette St. George. El castillo, antiguamente rodeado de agua, fue mencionado por primera vez en un texto del año 1391, mientras se hallaba bajo el potentado de Peter van Auel. Su forma de tres naves proviene del período barroco. Por sus jardines pasearon visitantes tan ilustres como Alejandro I de Rusia, Guillermo II de Alemania o Napoleón, quien, en 1811, se hospedó en el castillo mientras estaba de viaje para pasar revista al ejército del Rin. Actualmente se puede reservar la confortable suite con cama de dosel, suntuosas antigüedades, mantas de brocado y sillones de orejeras.

Questa tenuta nei pressi di Colonia appartiene a famiglie aristocratiche da diversi secoli, e dal 1818 è proprietà dei baroni di la Valette St. George. La prima documentazione di quella che un tempo era una fortezza circondata dall'acqua risale al 1391, quando il proprietario era Peter van Auel. La sua struttura a tre ali è dell'epoca barocca. Attraverso il suo parco hanno camminato già molti illustri ospiti, come lo zar Alessandro I, l'imperatore Guglielmo II e Napoleone, che vi pernottò nel 1811 quando ispezionò l'esercito del Reno. Si puó prenotare la confortevole suite con letto a baldacchino, preziosi oggetti d'antiquariato, plaid in broccato e poltrone relax.

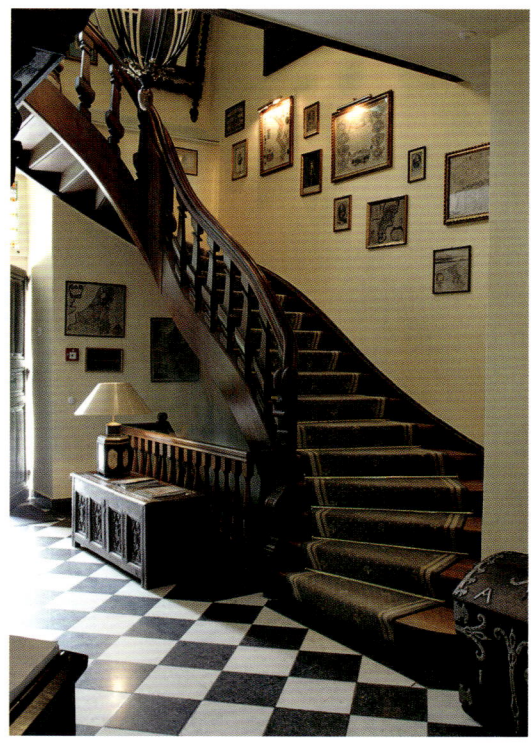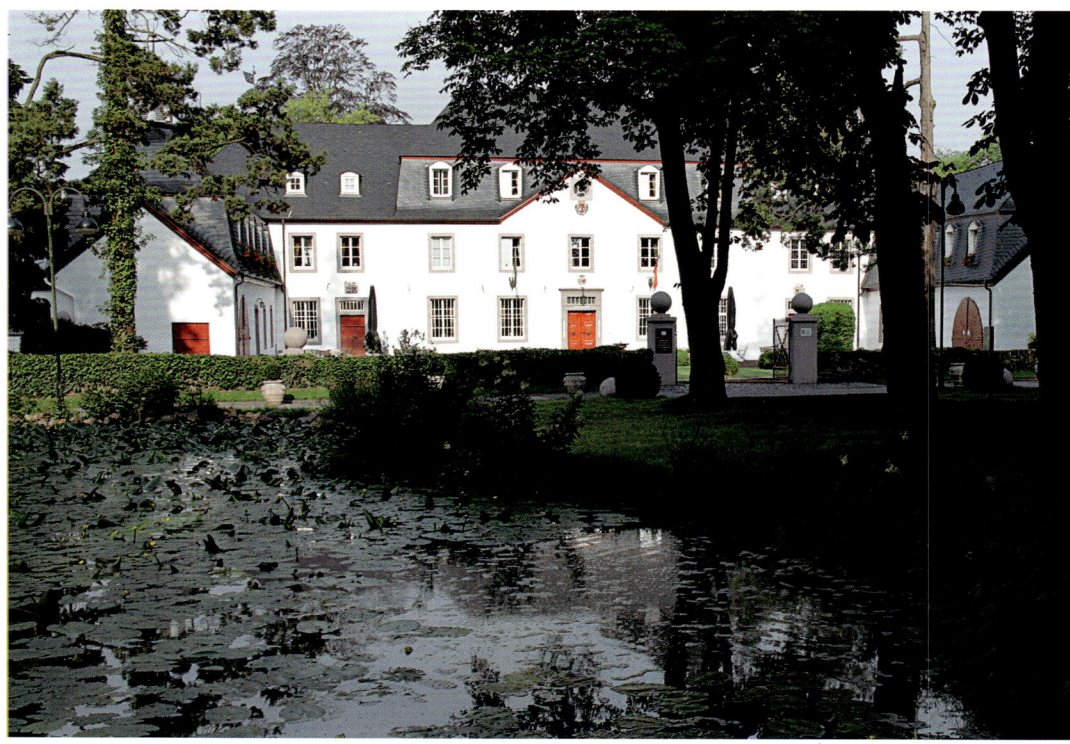

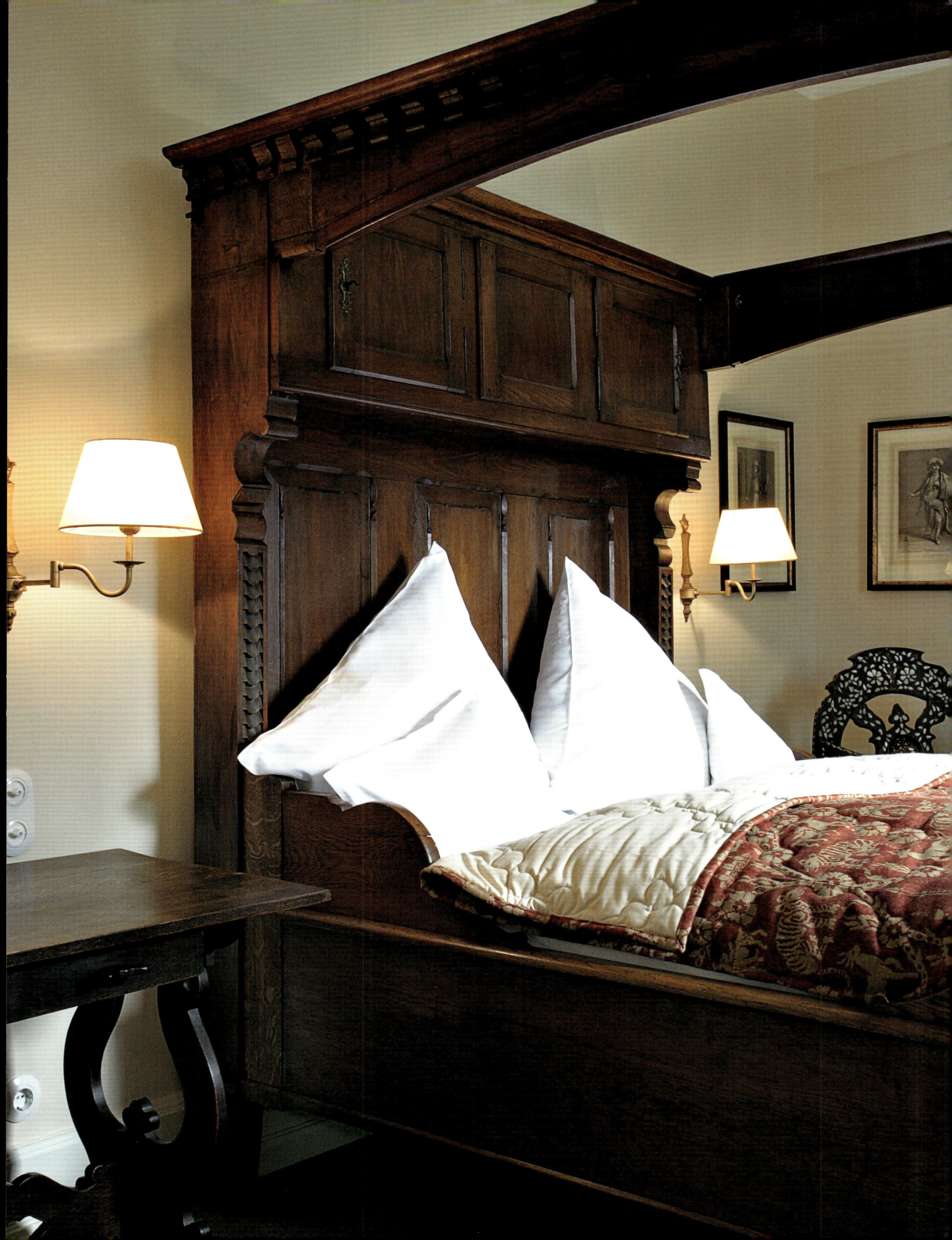

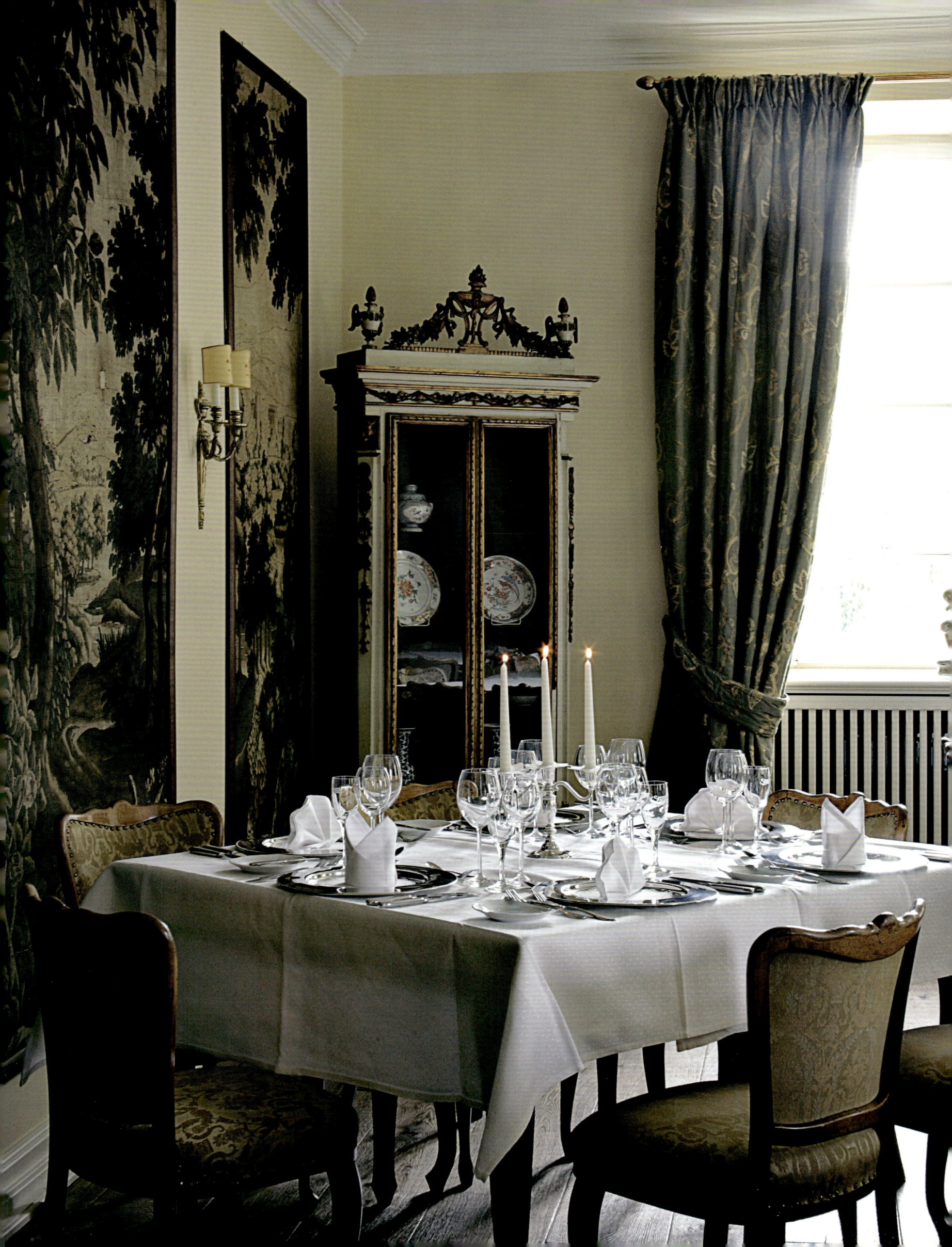

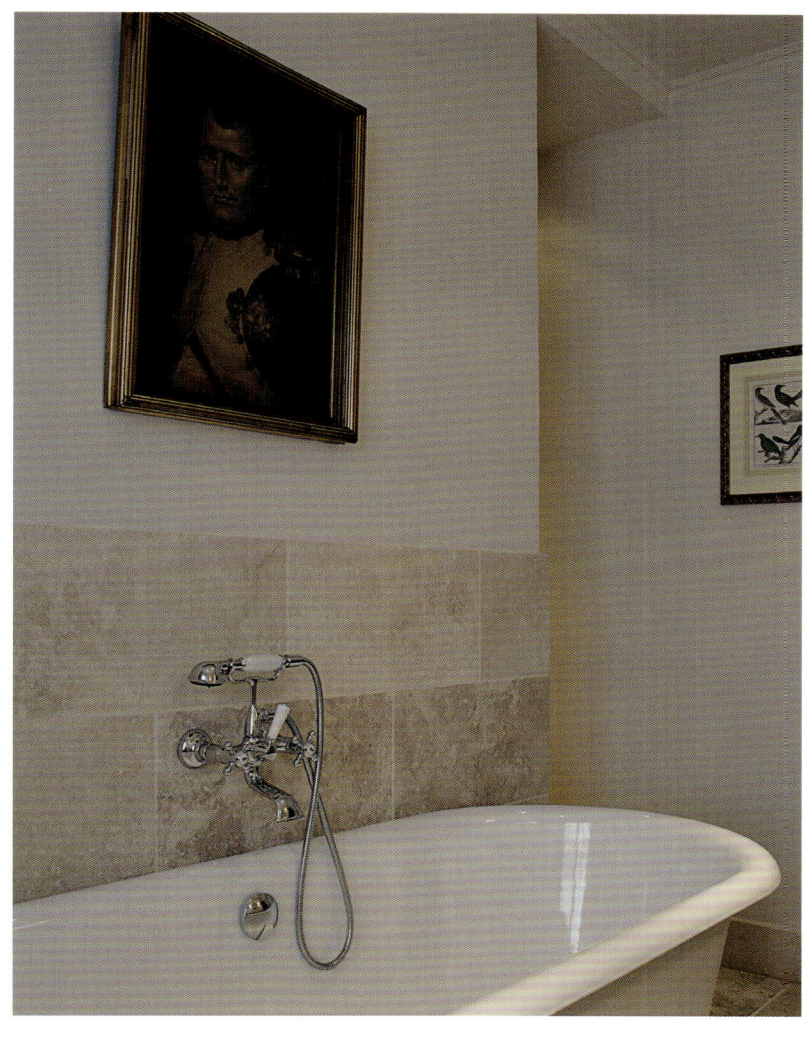

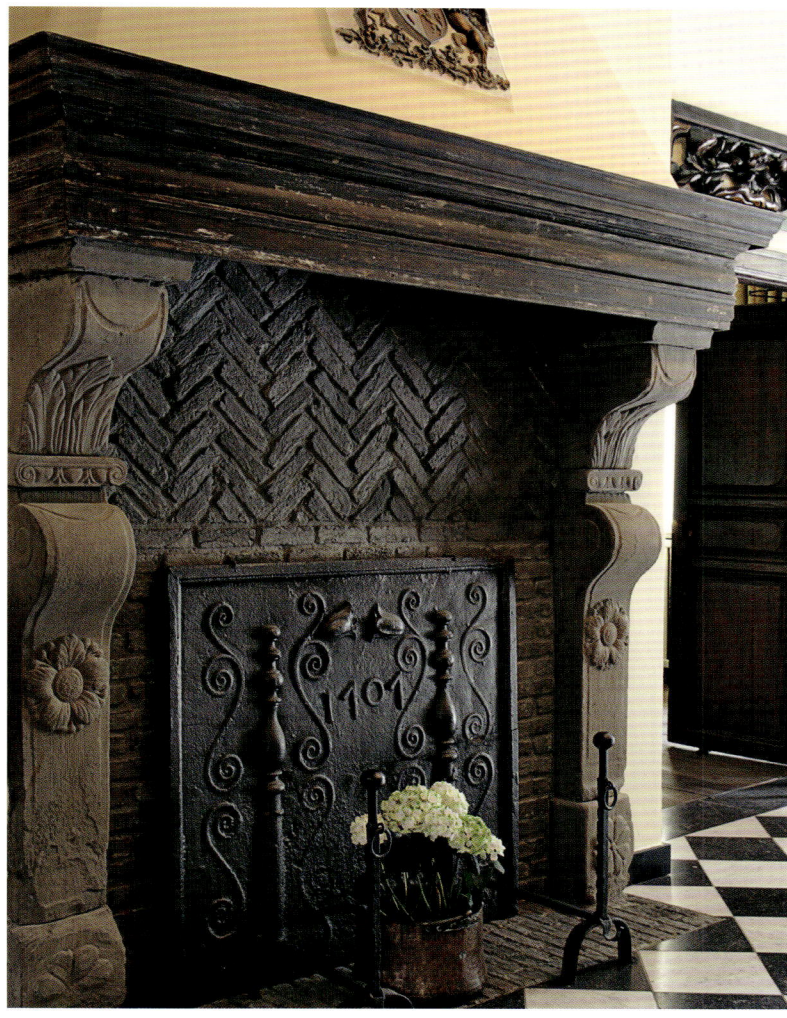

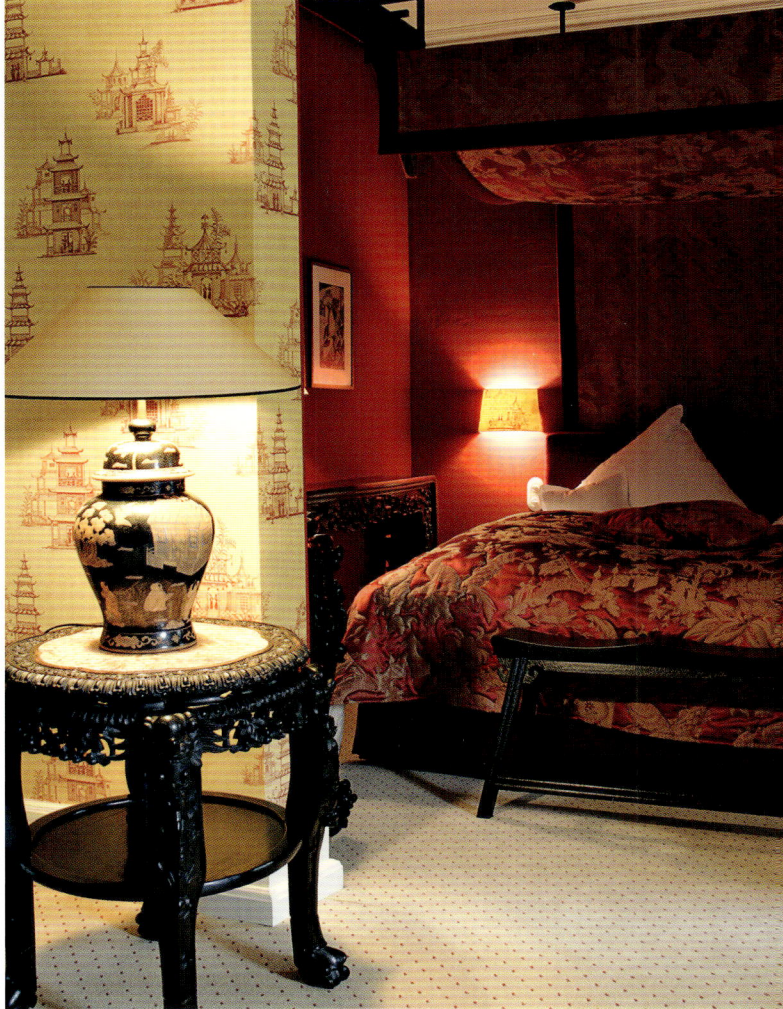

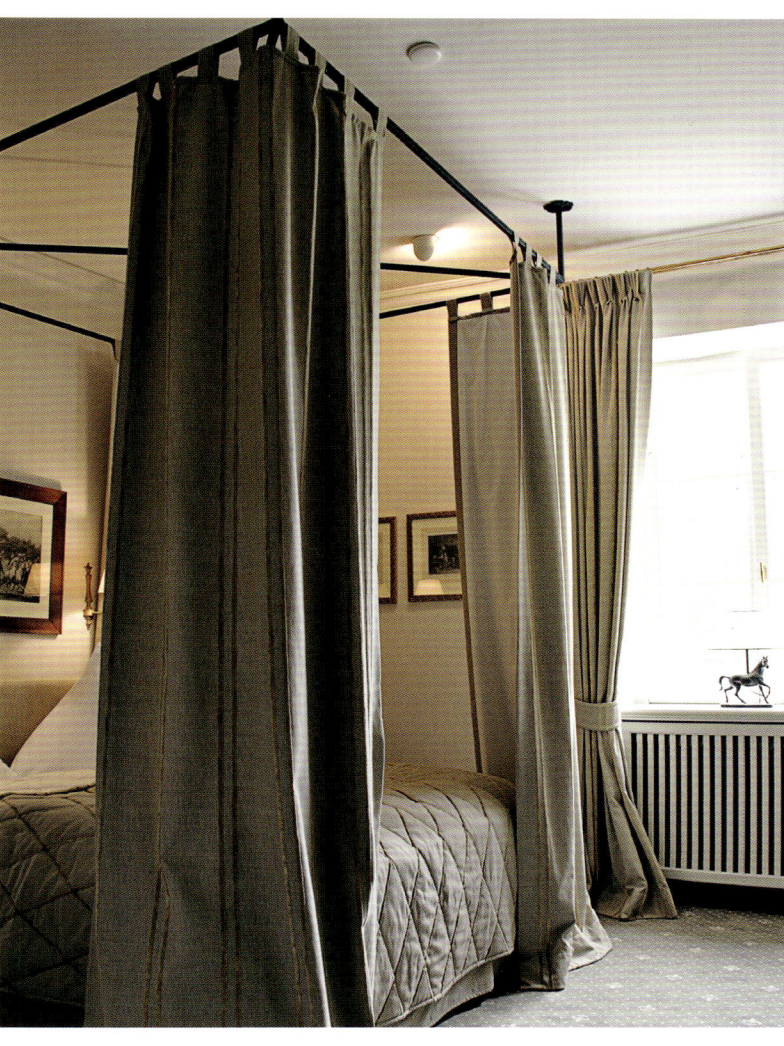

70182 Stuttgart
Germany
Phone: +49 711 237 77 70
Fax: +49 711 237 77 75
www.zauberlehrling.de

Rooms: 18 rooms including 4 suites and 1 penthouse
Facilities: Restaurant, private room
Services: Babysitting, cooking class, wine tasting, laundry service
Located: In the city center, next to the Old Castle
Public transportation: Underground 5, 6, 7; bus 43
Style: Design

There was a little magic involved when Karen and Axel Heldmann opened their Hotel Zauberlehrling in Stuttgart's old "Bohnenviertel," for nowhere else do so many-artistic styles come together distributed among the 17 rooms. The Thulamela in Zen-style promises recovery, guests experience the rich warmth of terracotta in the Barolo room. Cozy loungers invite you for a dream in the Chalet Suite, but in 1001 Nights Suite gold and candlelight will rob you of your senses. Travelers can bathe on the terrace of the Sunrise Suite or gaze at the stars.

Ein bisschen Magie war schon mit im Spiel als Karen und Axel Heldmann ihr Hotel Zauberlehrling in Stuttgarts altem Bohnenviertel eröffneten. Denn nirgendwo sonst treffen derart viele Stilwelten verteilt auf 17 Zimmer zusammen. Das Thulamela im Zen-Stil verheißt Erholung, die satte Wärme von Terracotta erleben Gäste im Barolo-Zimmer. Kuschelliegen laden in der Chalet-Suite zum Träumen ein, in 1001-Nacht-Suite betören Gold und Kerzenschein die Sinne. Und auf der Terrasse der Sunrise-Suite können Reisende sogar Baden und dabei in die Sterne schauen.

Une touche de magie est entrée en jeu quand Karen et Axel Heldmann ont ouvert l'hôtel Zauberlehrling dans le vieux Bohnenviertel de Stuttgart. On ne retrouve nulle part ailleurs autant de styles internationaux réunis que cans cet hôtel de 17 chambres. Thulamela au style zen promet de la relaxation, et les clients apprécient toute la chaleur de la terre cuite dans la chambre portant le nom de Barolo. Dans la suite Chalet, des canapés moelleux invitent à rêver, et dans la 1001 Nuits l'or et la lumière des chandelles ensorcellent les sens. Sur la terrasse de la suite Sunrise, les voyageurs peuvent même contempler les étoiles en se baignant.

Un cierto toque de magia acompañó a Karen y Axel Heldmann cuando inauguraron su hotel Zauberlehrling en el antiguo Bohnenviertel de Stuttgart. En ningún otro lugar se concentran tantos universos estilísticos en tan sólo 17 habitaciones. Thulamela, diseñada al estilo zen, promete descanso. La calidez generosa de la terracota se percibe en la habitación Barolo. Unos asientos de cojines invitan a soñar en la suite Chalet. En la suite Las Mil y una Noches el resplandor dorado y la luz de las velas cautivan los sentidos. En la terraza de la suite Sunrise, los viajeros pueden darse el placer de bañarse mientras contemplan las estrellas.

Un tocco di magia Karen e Axel Heldmann lo diedero già solo con l'apertura del loro hotel Zauberlehrling, nel cosiddetto Bohnenviertel, il vecchio quartiere dei fagioli di Stoccarda. In nessun altro posto, infatti, si incontrano così tanti universi stilistici rappresentati in 17 camere. Quella denominata Thulamela, con il suo stile zen, promette relax, nella stanza chiamata Barolo gli ospiti sono avvolti da un caldo colore terracotta, nella suite Chalet le comode sdraio invitano a sognare, mentre nella suite Le mille e una notte si resta ammaliati dall'oro e dal lume delle candele. E sulla terrazza della suite Sunrise gli ospiti possono persino fare il bagno guardando le stelle.

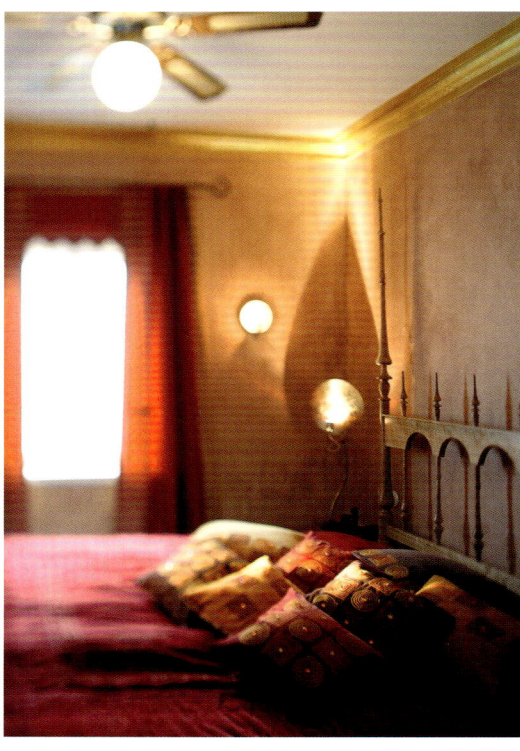
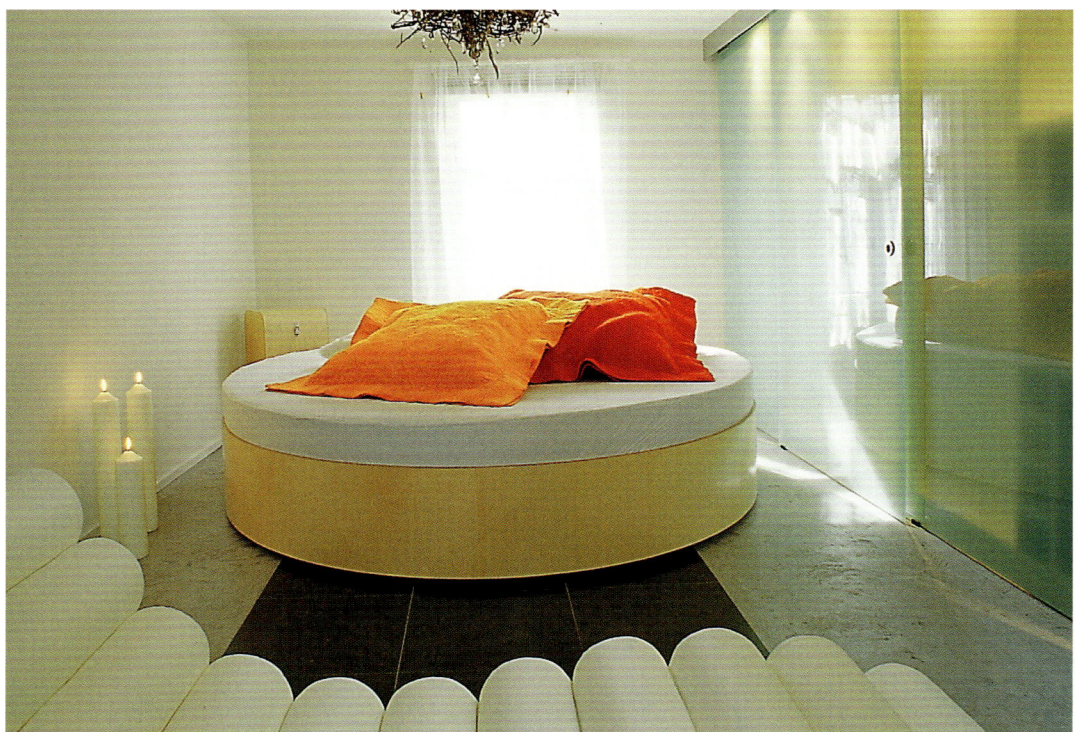

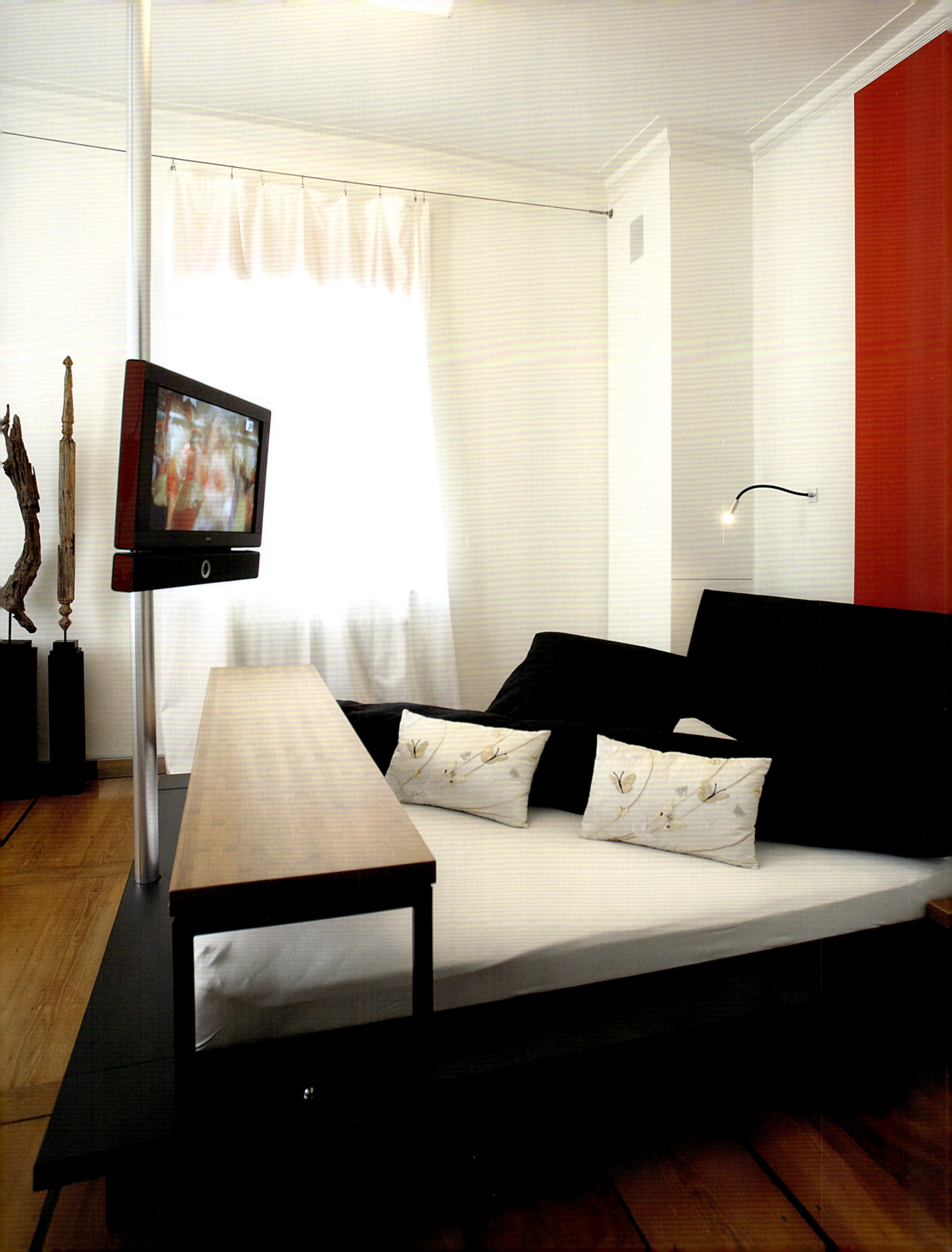

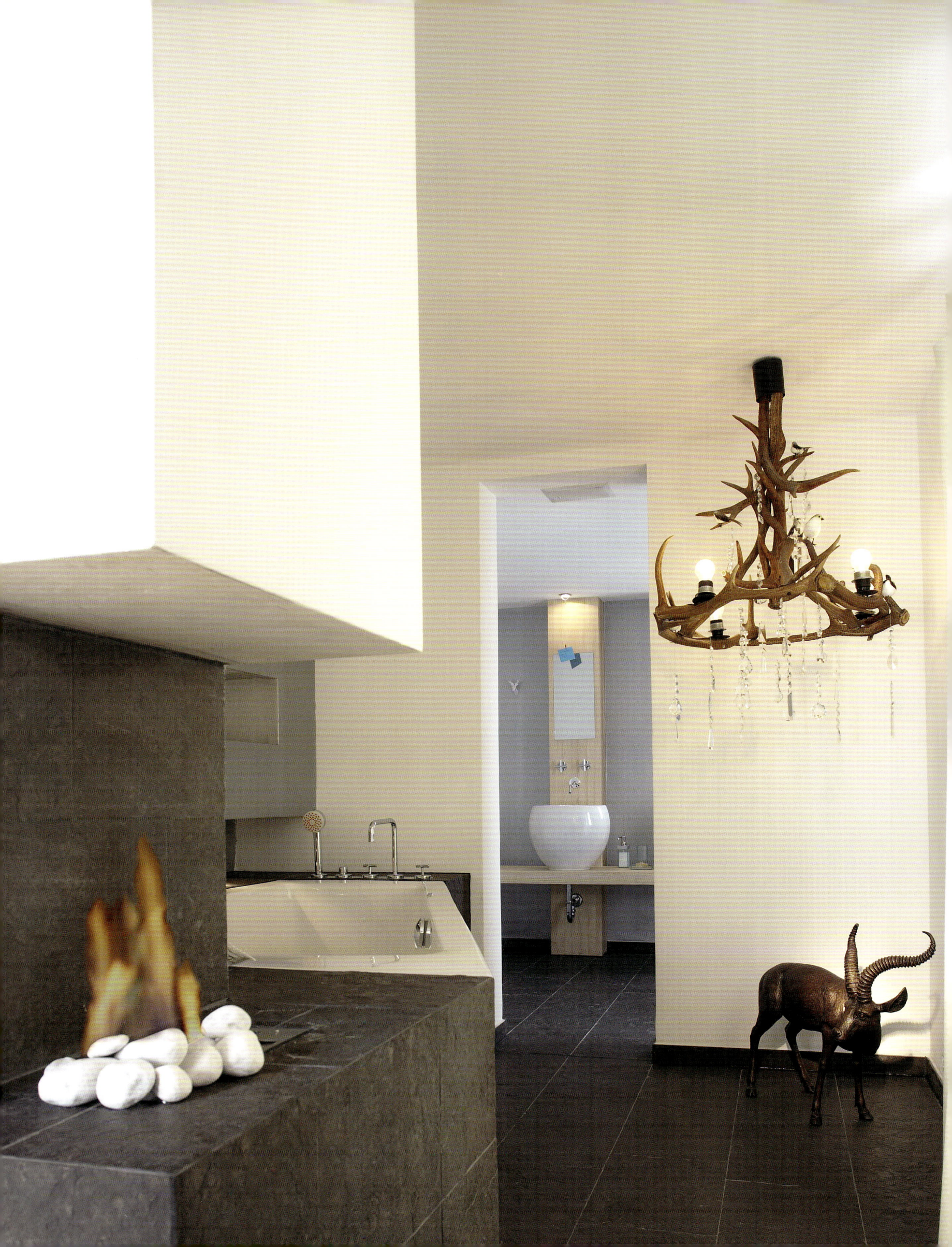

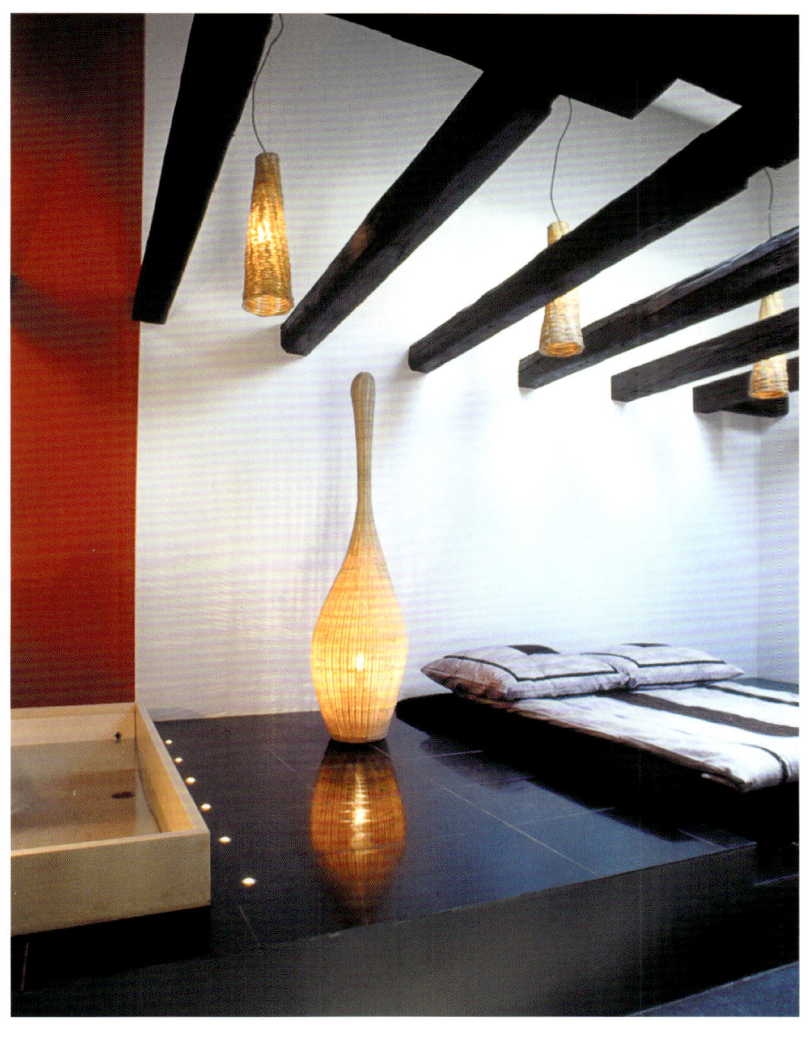
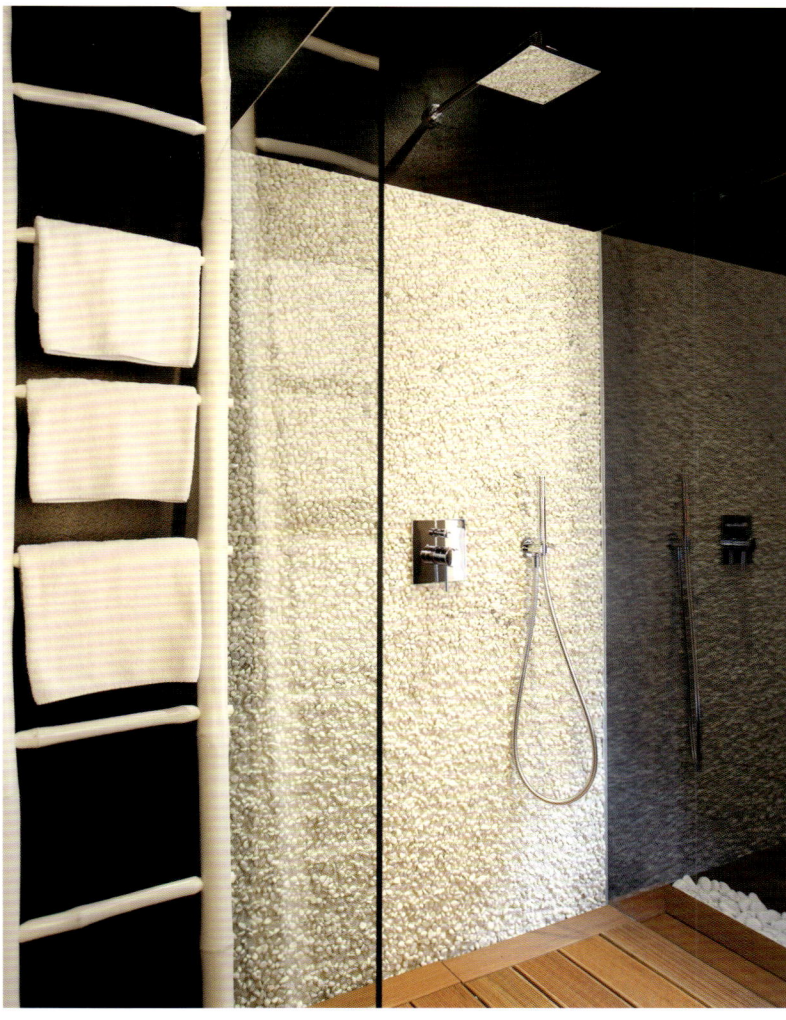
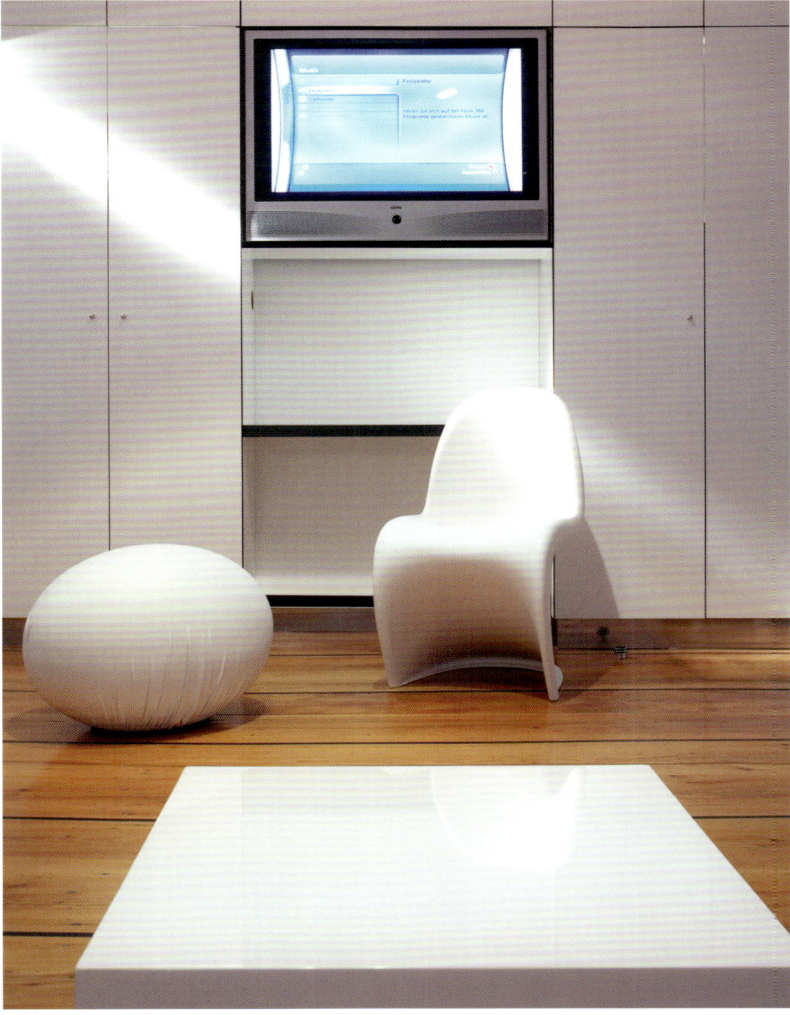
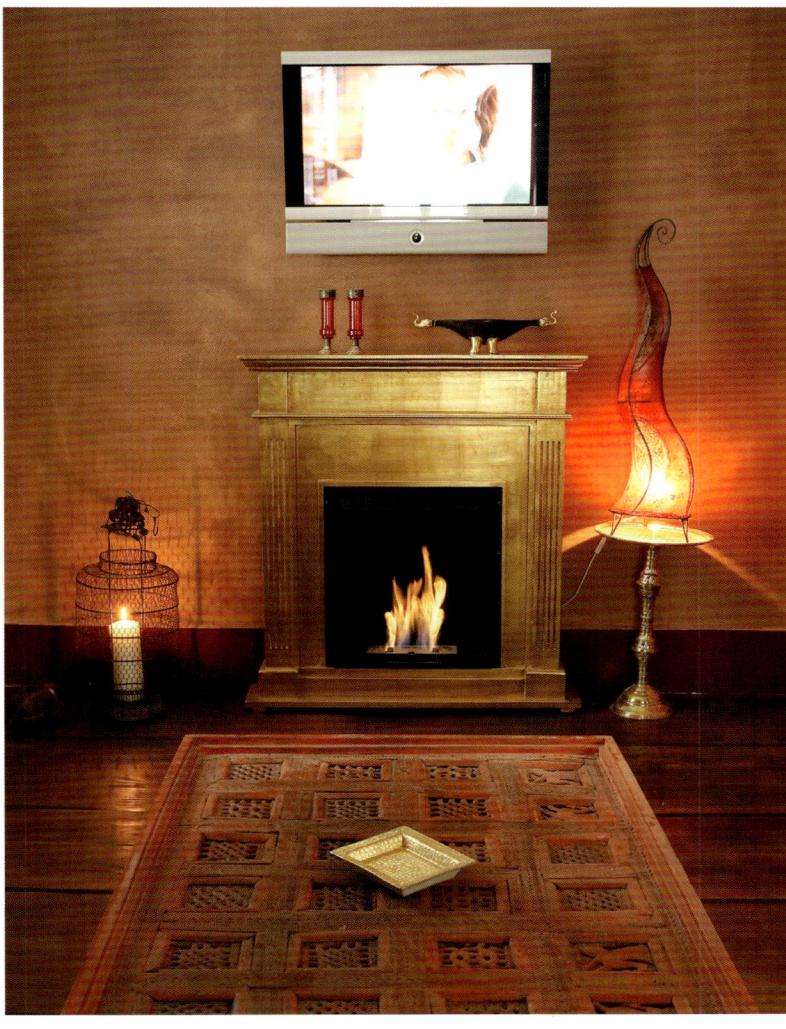

80802 Munich
Germany
Phone: +49 89 33 03 55 50
Fax: +49 89 33 03 55 55 5
www.hotel-la-maison.com

Rooms: 31 rooms
Facilities: Bar, restaurant
Services: Babysitting, leave-and-go service
Located: In the center of the Schwabing near the Englischer Garten
Public transportation: Underground U6, U3 Münchner Freiheit
Style: Design boutique hotel

Even the name of the 31-room hotel in the heart of Altschwabing signifies the owners' French inspiration. This house near the English Garden was opened in the summer of 2006 and features a new opulent style with baroque furniture and costly tapestries reminding you a bit of the Schwabing boheme. The color scheme is typical French interior style: grey, pink and light rose dominate. The studio with its own small library and view of the English Garden is especially beautiful.

Schon der Name des 31-Zimmer-Hotels im Herzen Altschwabings signalisiert, dass sich die Besitzer von Frankreich inspirieren ließen. Das im Sommer 2006 eröffnete Haus in der Nähe des Englischen Gartens zeigt mit seinen barocken Möbeln und kostbaren Tapeten eine neue Opulenz, die ein wenig an die Schwabinger Boheme erinnert. Die Farben orientieren sich am französischen Interieurstil: grau, lila und zartrosa dominieren. Besonders schön: das Studio mit eigener kleiner Bibliothek und Blick in den Englischen Garten.

Même le nom de cet hôtel de 31 chambres au cœur du quartier Altschwabing signale que le propriétaire a été inspiré par la France. Cet établissement, qui a ouvert en 2006 et est proche du Jardin anglais, affiche des meubles baroques et de précieuses tapisseries, une nouvelle opulence pour évoquer à la bohème de ce quartier. L'agencement des couleurs est aussi d'inspiration française : gris, lavande et rose pâle dominent. Notre coup de cœur, le studio avec sa propre petite bibliothèque et une vue sur le Jardin anglais.

El mismo nombre del hotel de 31 habitaciones en el corazón del barrio Altschwabing deja claro que Francia ha sido la fuente de inspiración de los dueños. La casa, situada cerca del Jardín Inglés, abrió sus puertas en verano de 2006 y muestra, mediante sus muebles barrocos y sus valiosos tapices, una nueva opulencia que recuerda vagamente a la bohemia de Schwabing de finales del siglo XIX. Los colores siguen el modelo del estilo interiorista francés: dominan el gris, el lila y el rosa pálido. Especialmente bonito es el estudio, con una pequeña biblioteca propia y vistas al Jardín Inglés.

Il nome stesso di questo albergo da 31 stanze, situato nel cuore del quartiere Altschwabing, rivela che il proprietario ha cercato ispirazione nello stile francese. Con i suoi mobili barocchi e le sue preziose tappezzerie, la casa, che è stata inaugurata nell'estate del 2006 nelle vicinanze dell'Englischer Garten, sembra accennare a un'opulenza di tipo nuovo, una specie di bohème nello stile di Schwabing. I colori si richiamano allo stile degli interni francesi; predominano il grigio, il lilla e il rosa pastello. Di particolare bellezza è lo studio, che dispone di una piccola biblioteca privata e gode di una bella vista sull'Englischer Garten.

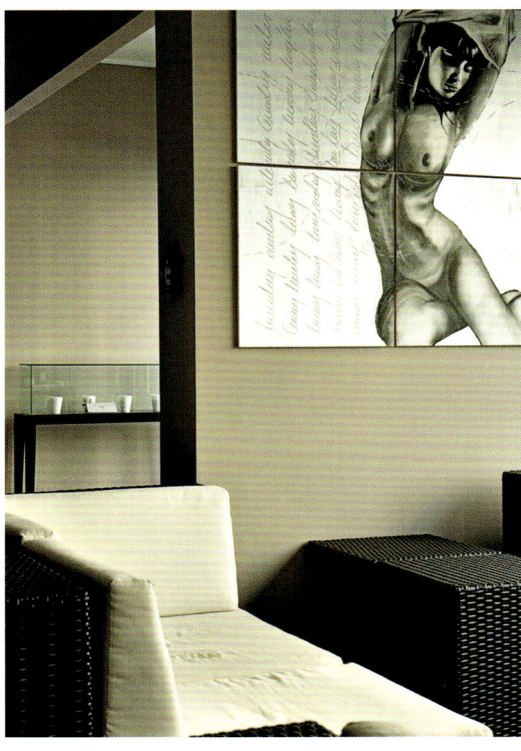
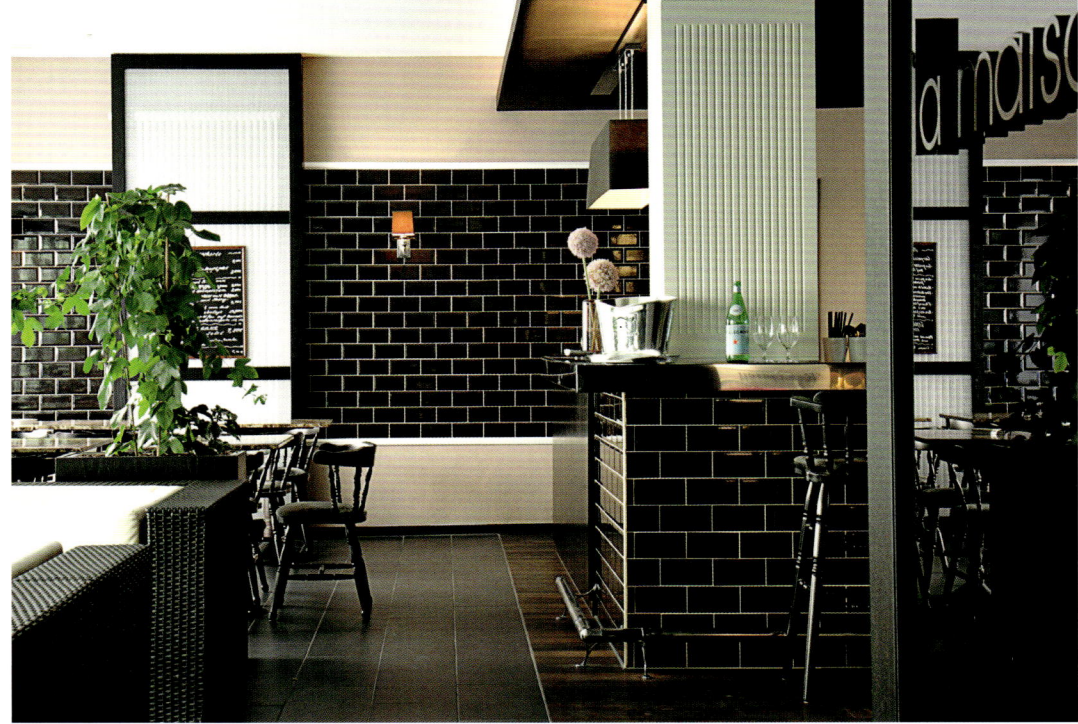

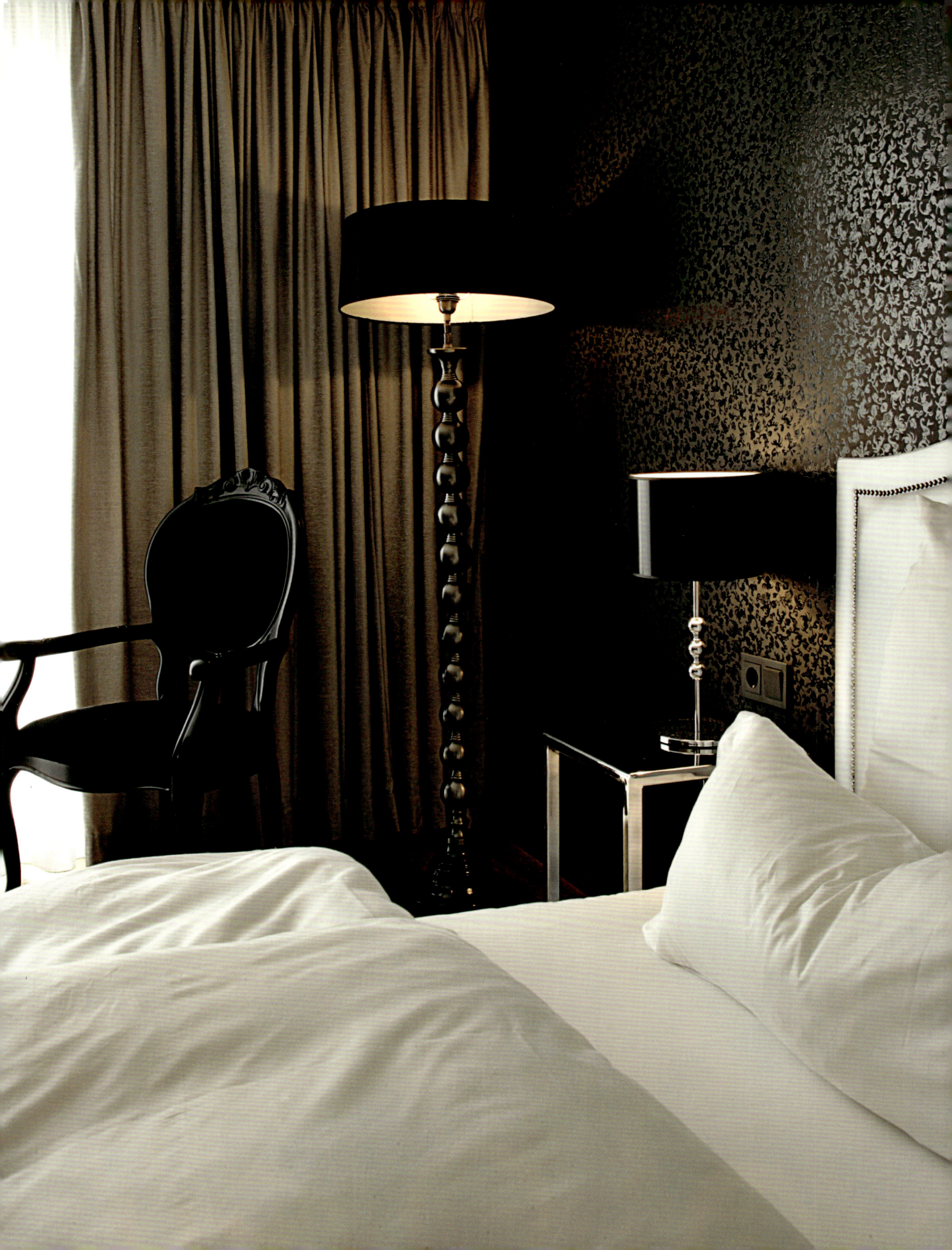

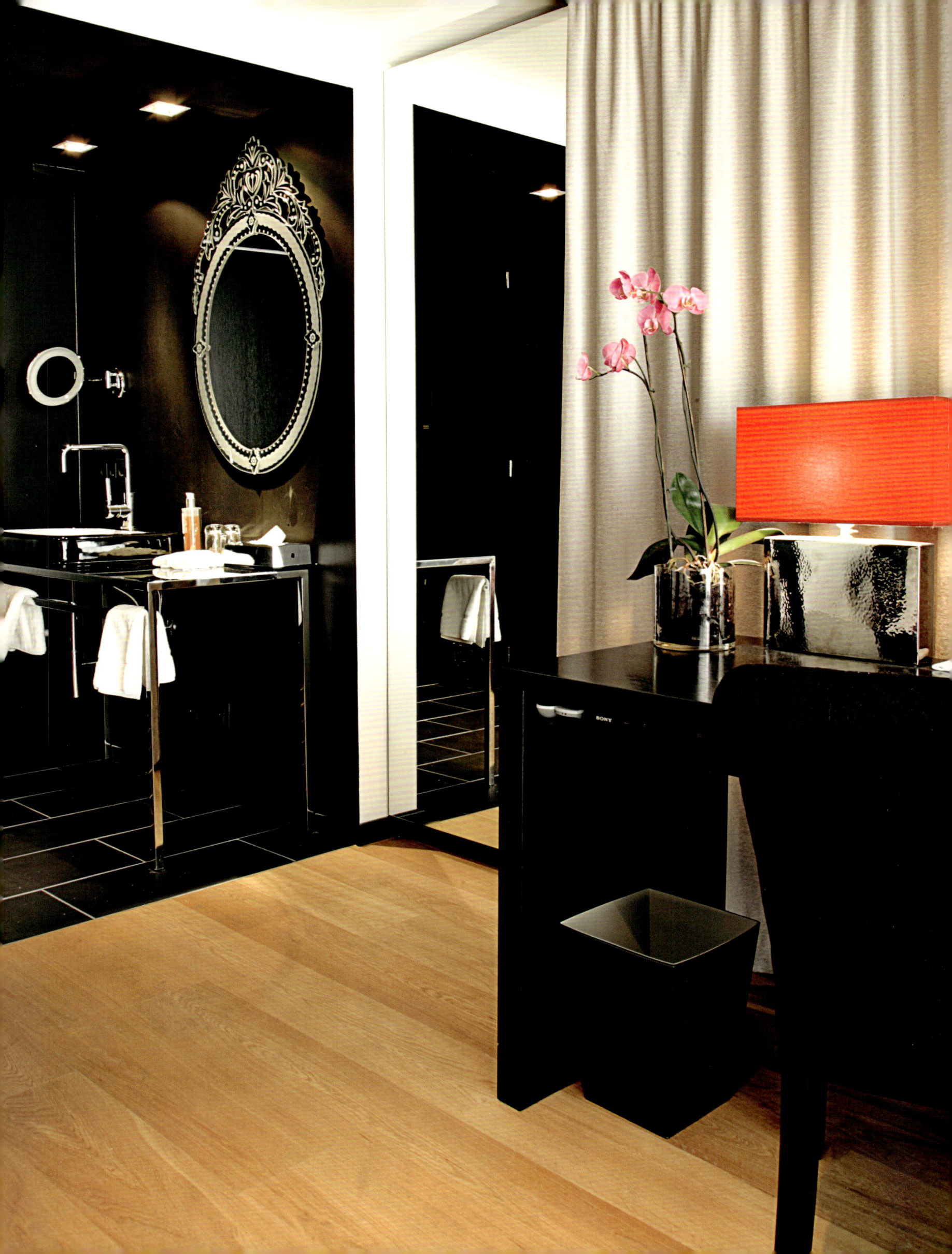

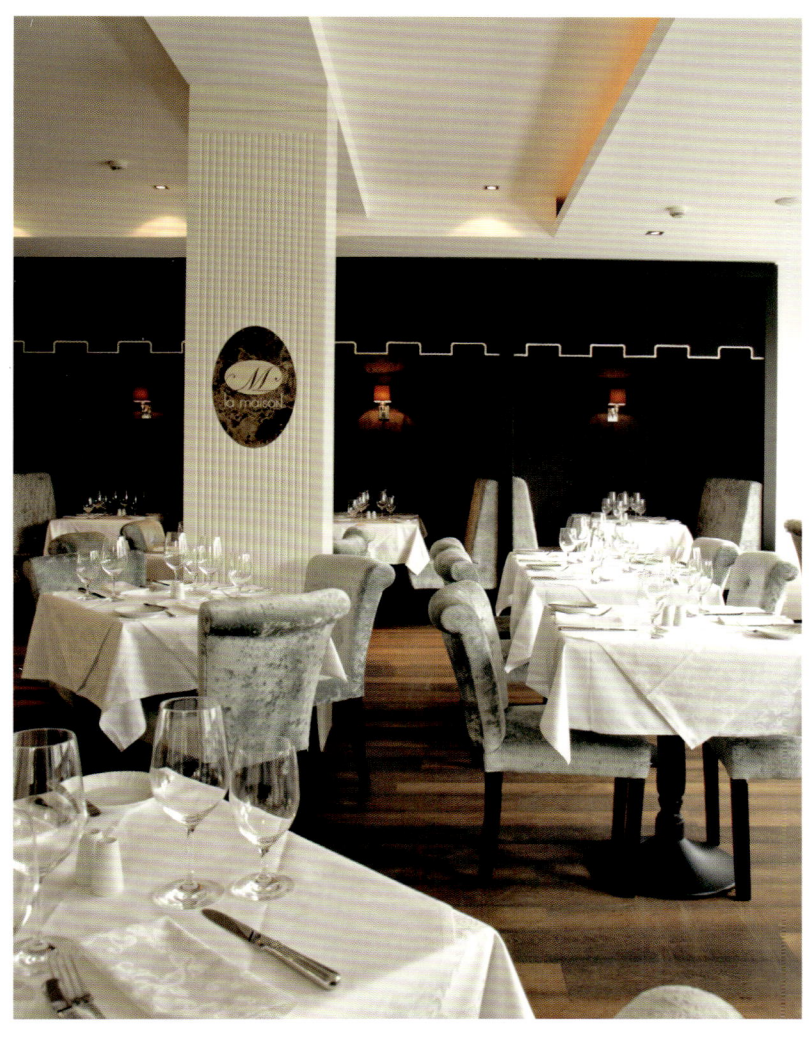

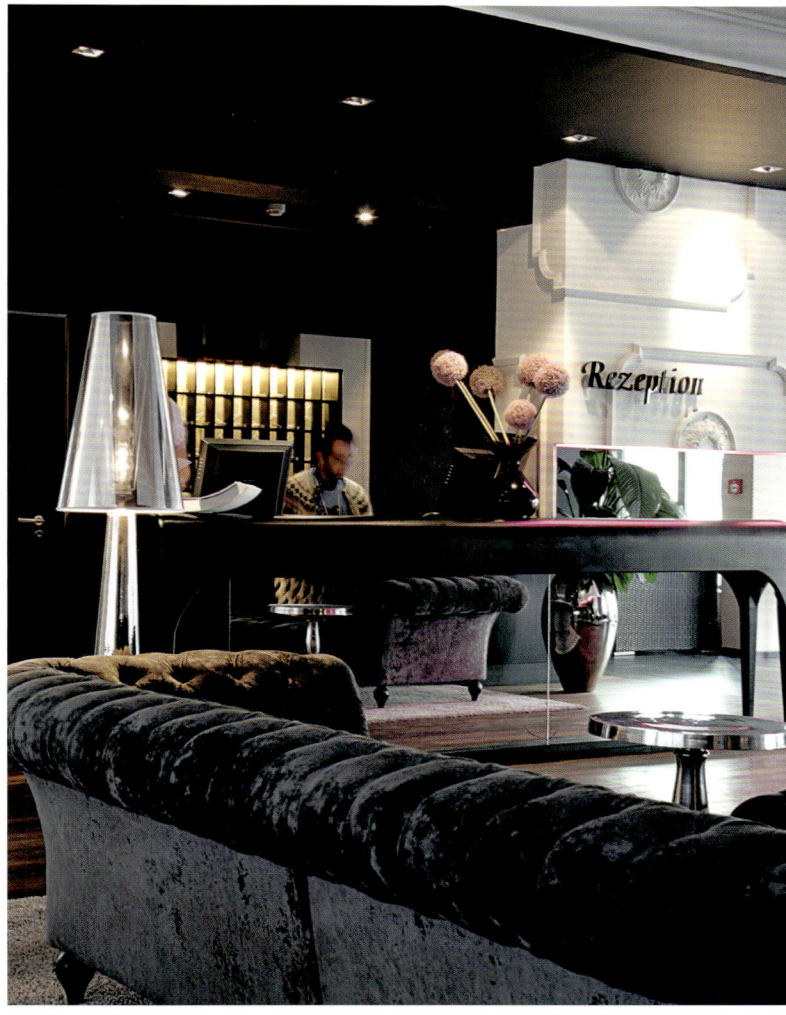

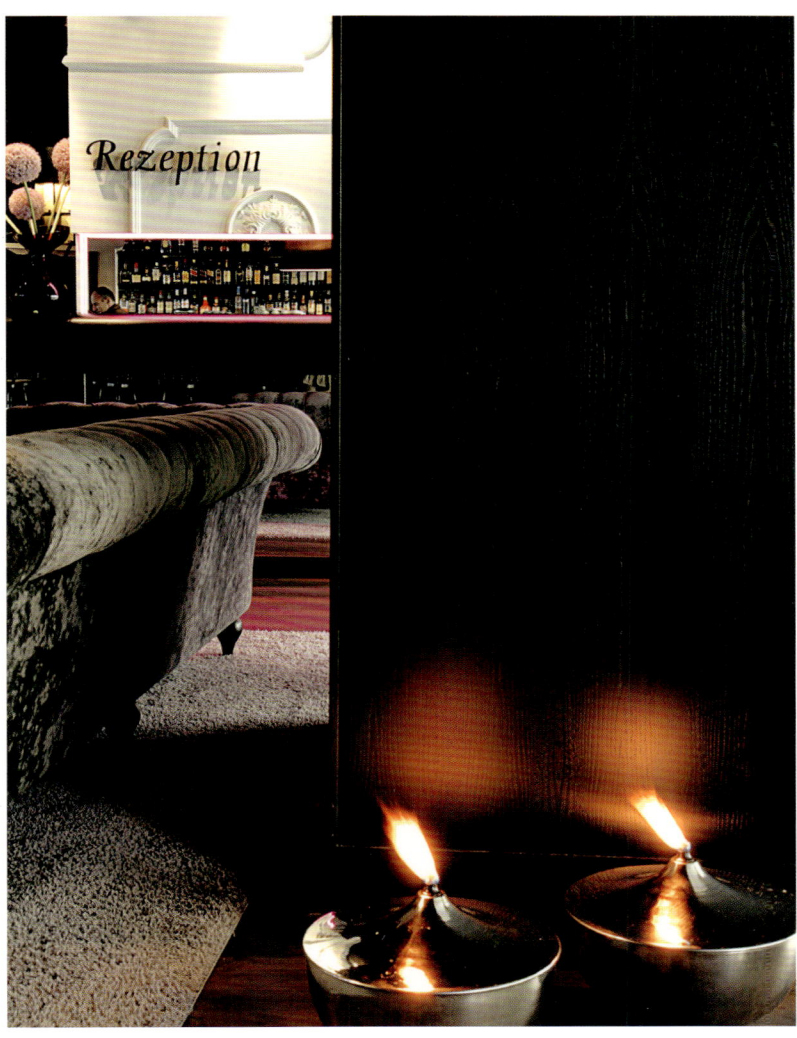

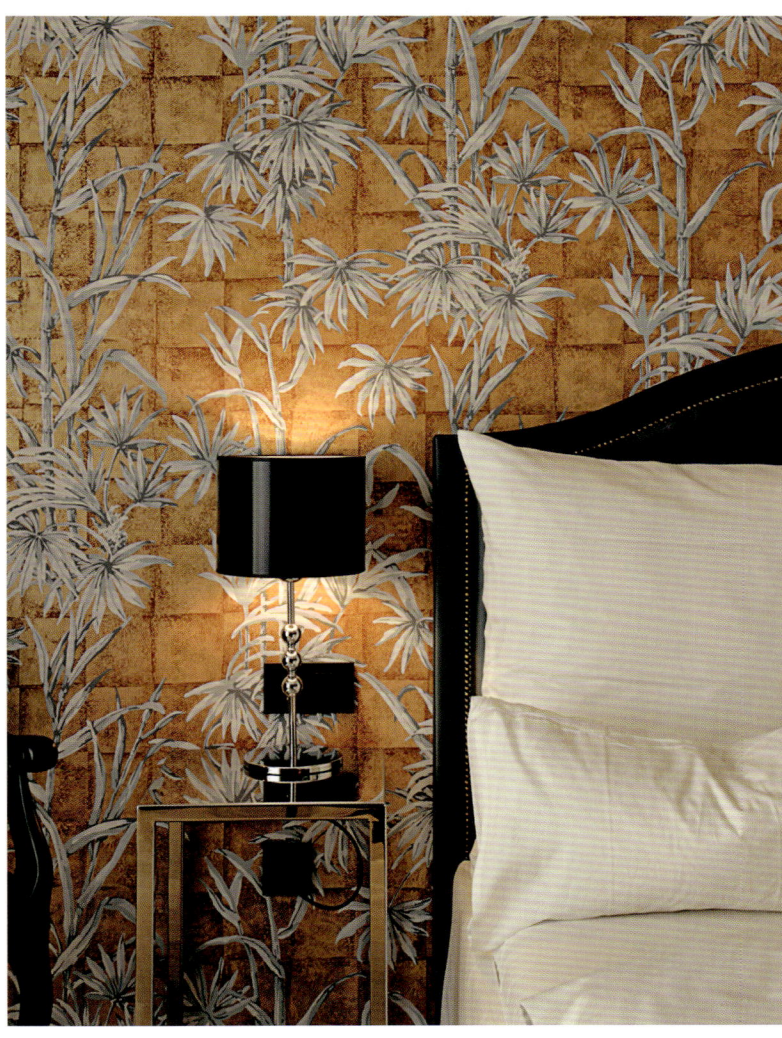

Bayerischer Hof

Munich, Germany

Promenadeplatz 2–6
80333 Munich
Germany
Phone: +49 89 21 20 0
Fax: +49 89 21 20 90 6
www.bayerischerhof.de

Price category: €€€
Rooms: 373 rooms including 60 suites
Facilities: 6 bars, 4 restaurants, 40 conference rooms, Blue Spa with pool, fitness room, beauty center, sauna, in-house theater, night club with international live jazz program
Services: 24 h concierge, WiFi, facilities for the disabled, business center
Located: In the city center
Public transportation: S-Bahn, Underground Marienplatz
Style: Classic elegance

Social life in Munich would be unthinkable without the splendid hotel on Promenade Square. Here is the place to meet and celebrate a glittering ball or hear a sophisticated jazz concert. The hotel was opened in 1841 at King Ludwig I's behest to worthily house the growing number of guests at his ever more pompous court. Even today the luxury hotel with 373 rooms counts as one of Germany's best booked hotels. The Blue Spa designed by Andrée Putman has catapulted the traditional house into a new league. From the roof terrace there is a splendid view of Munich's landmark, the Frauenkirche.

Ohne das prachtvolle Hotel am Promenadeplatz ist das gesellschaftliche Leben in München undenkbar. Hier trifft man sich, feiert rauschende Bälle, hört anspruchsvolle Jazz-Konzerte. Auf Wunsch König Ludwig I. wurde das Hotel 1841 eröffnet, weil der eine komfortable Herberge für seine Gäste brauchte. Bis heute gehört das luxuriöse 373-Zimmer-Hotel zu den bestgebuchten Deutschlands. Der von Andrée Putman gestaltete Blue Spa katapultierte das Traditionshaus in eine neue Liga. Von der Dachterrasse eröffnet sich ein Traumblick auf Münchens Wahrzeichen, die Frauenkirche.

Sans cet hôtel magnifique sur la Promenadeplatz, la vie sociale de Munich serait impensable. On s'y rencontre, on y participe à des bals fastueux et on y écoute de formidables concerts de jazz. Sur la demande du Roi Louis Ier, qui souhaitait disposer d'un logement confortable pour ses invités, l'hôtel a été ouvert en 1841. Même aujourd'hui, ce luxeux hôtel de 373 chambres est un des hôtels les plus fréquentés d'Allemagne. Le Blue Spa créé par Andrée Putman a catapulté cet établissement traditionnel dans une nouvelle catégorie. Depuis la terrasse du toit, une vue de rêve s'offre sur l'emblème de Munich, la Cathédrale Notre-Dame.

La vida social en Munich es impensable sin el majestuoso hotel de la Promenadeplatz. Es lugar de encuentro, de celebración de grandes bailes y exigentes conciertos de Jazz. El hotel abrió sus puertas en 1841 a petición del Rey Ludwig I, ya que el regente necesitaba un alojamiento confortable para sus invitados. El lujoso hotel de 373 habitaciones se mantiene hasta hoy como uno de los de mayor ocupación de toda Alemania. El Blue Spa creado por Andrée Putman convirtió esta tradicional casa en un establecimiento de primer nivel. Desde la azotea se puede disfrutar de un panorama de ensueño y admirar el símbolo de Munich, la catedral Frauenkirche.

Senza questo glorioso hotel sulla Promenadeplatz la vita sociale di Monaco sarebbe impensabile. Qui ci si incontra, si tengono fastosi balli e ricevimenti e si ascoltano concerti jazz di prima qualità. L'hotel fu inaugurato nel 1841 su espresso desiderio di re Ludovico I, che aveva bisogno di un luogo dove alloggiare i propri ospiti con tutti i comfort. Fino a oggi questo lussuoso hotel da 373 stanze non ha mai smesso di essere uno dei più prenotati dell'intera Germania. Il Blue Spa realizzato da Andrée Putman ha saputo conciliare tradizione e modernità. Inoltre dalla terrazza posta sul tetto si gode una vista d'incanto sul simbolo stesso di Monaco, il Frauenkirche, il duomo dedicato alla Madonna.

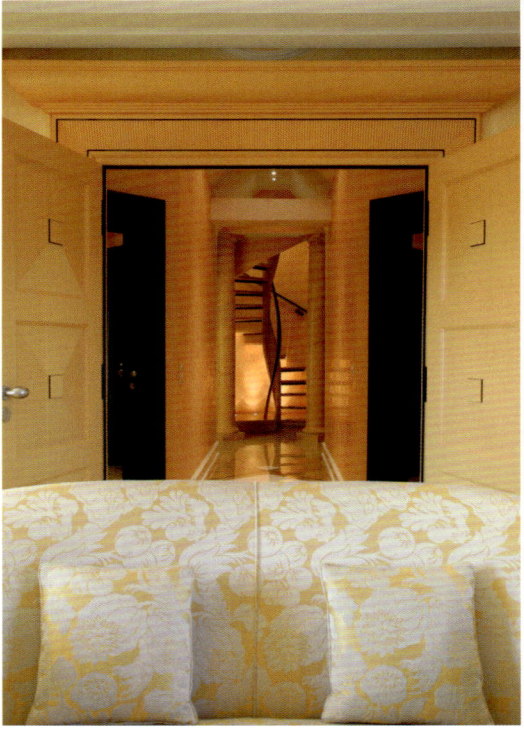
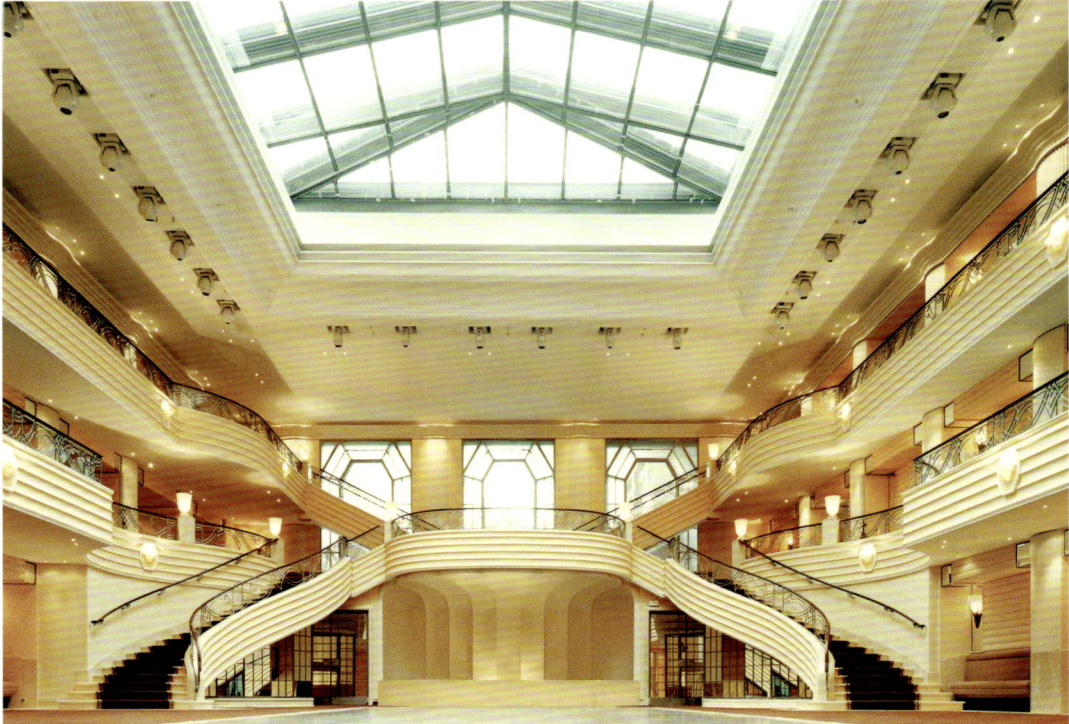

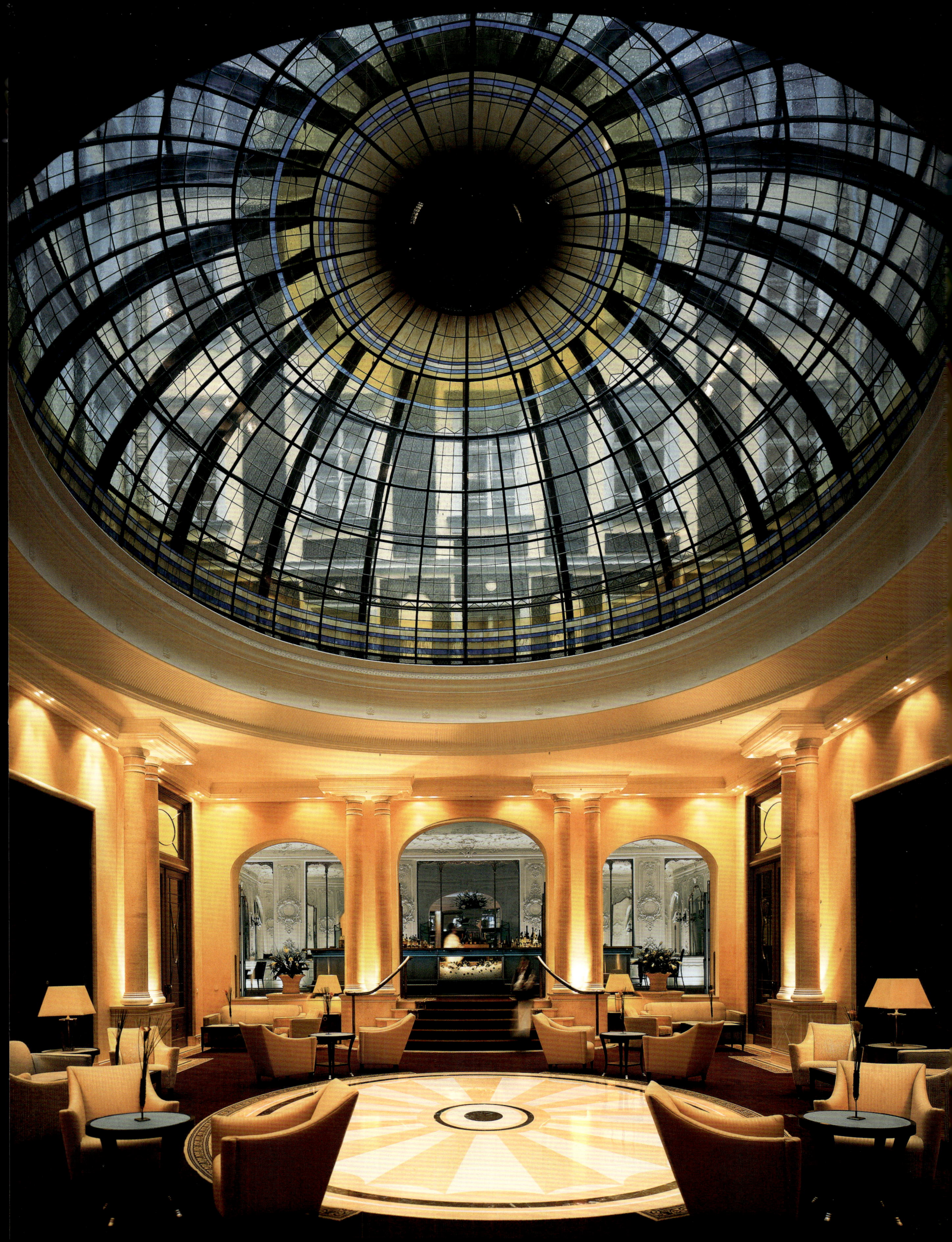

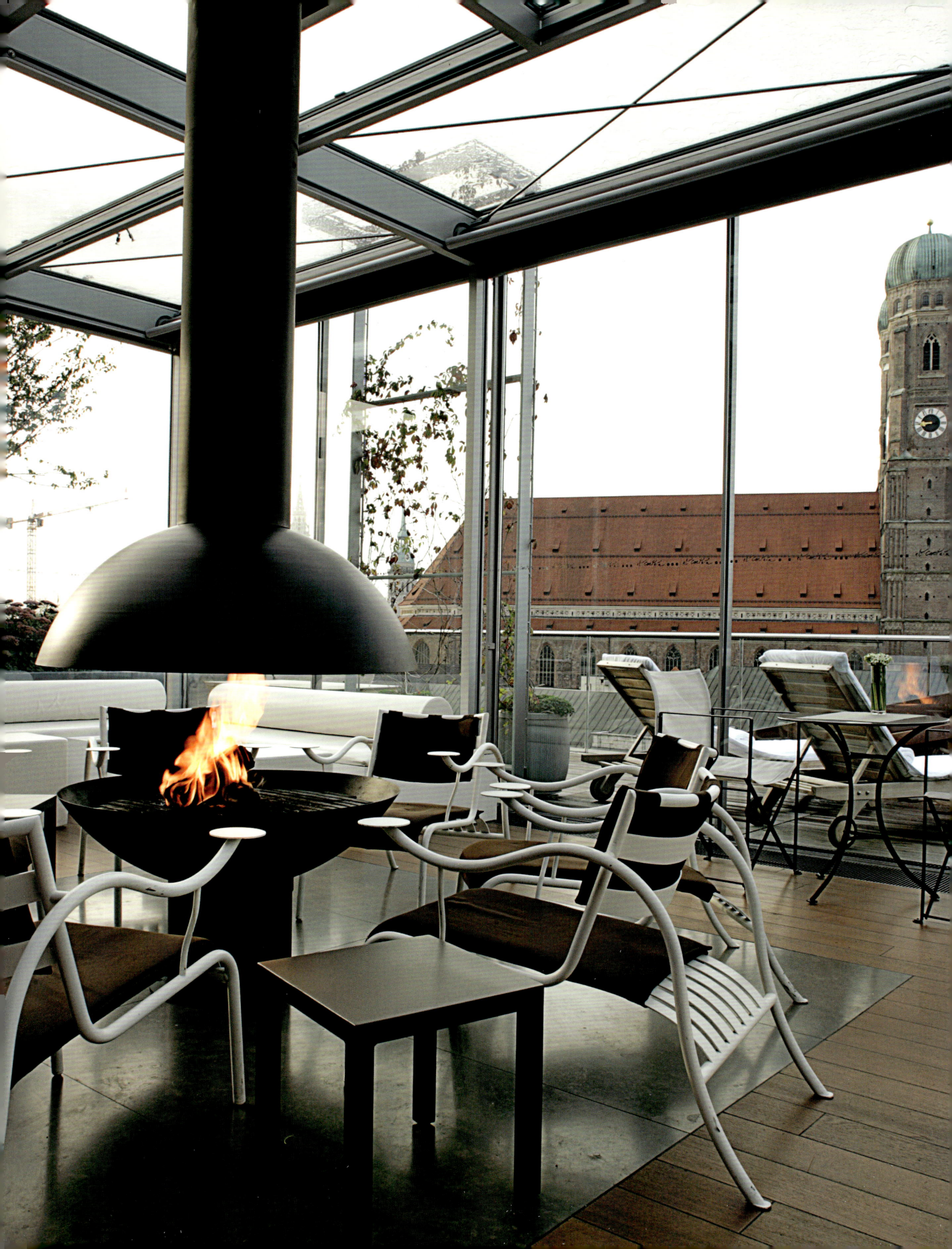

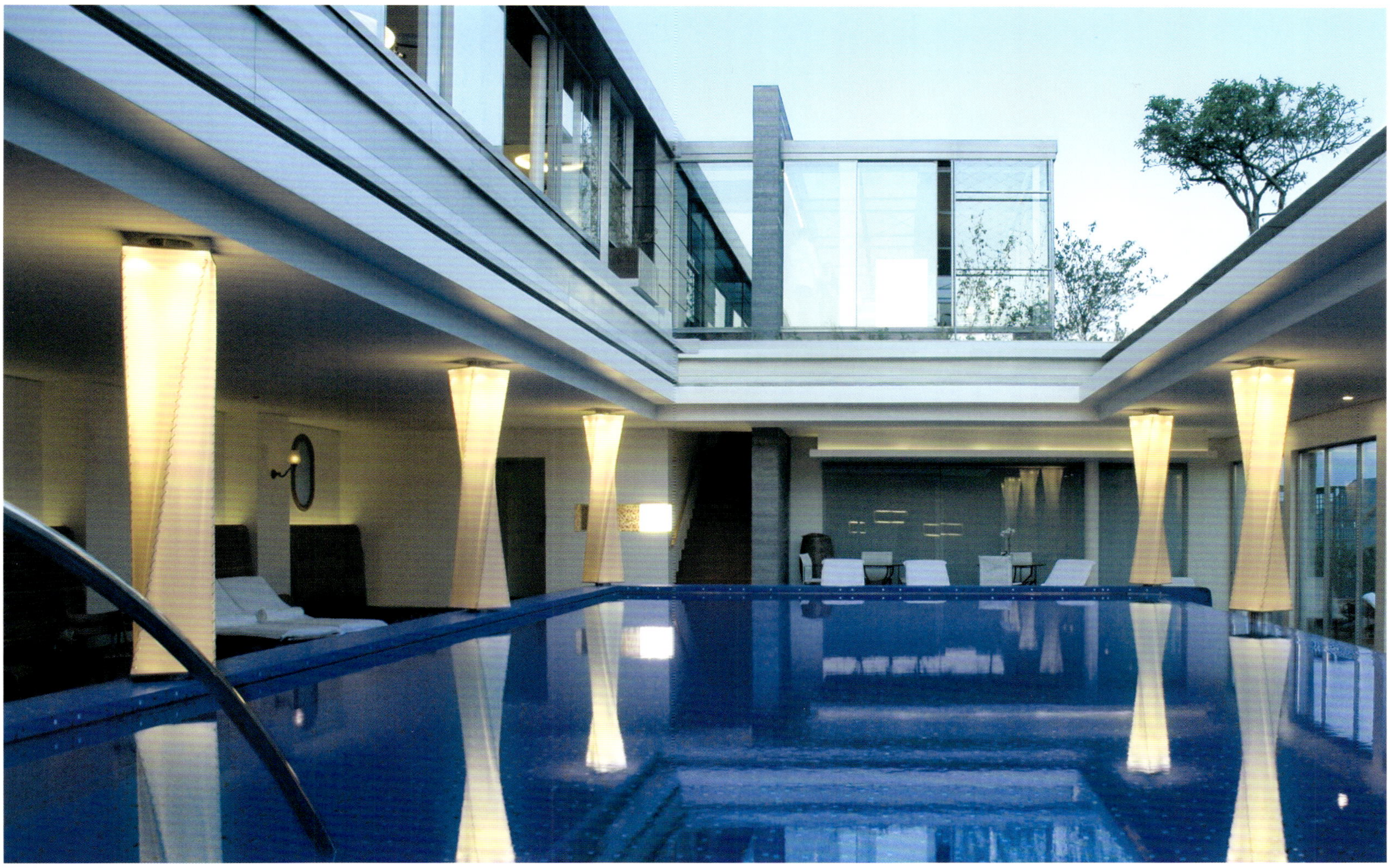

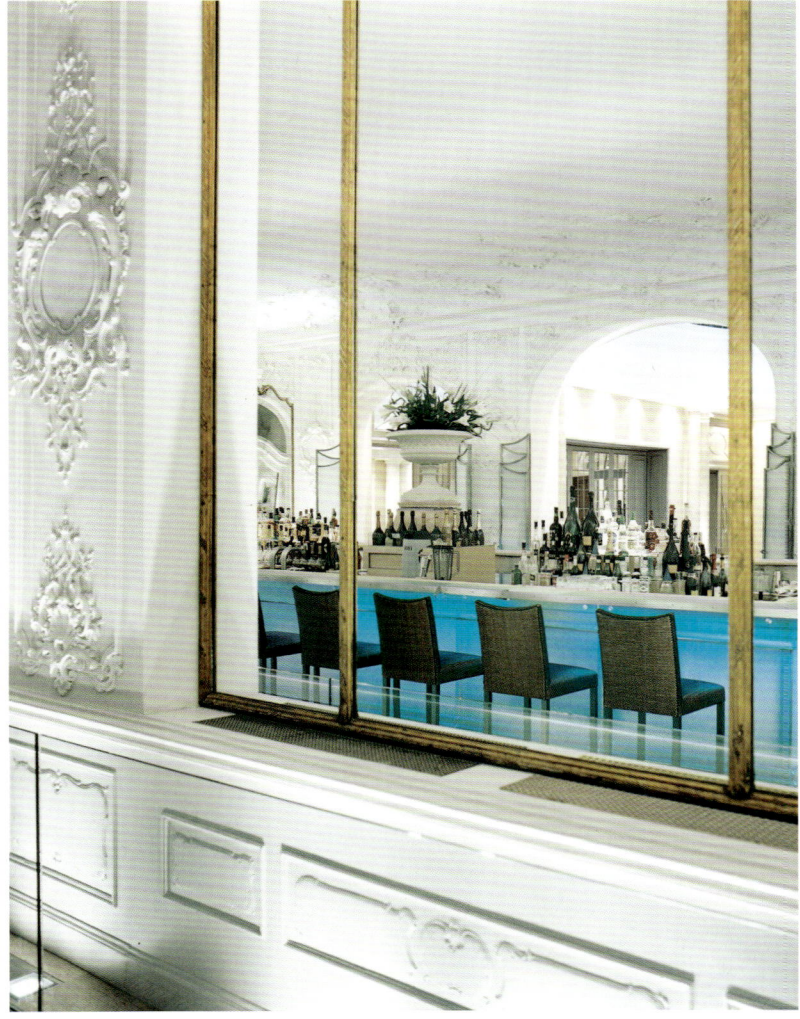

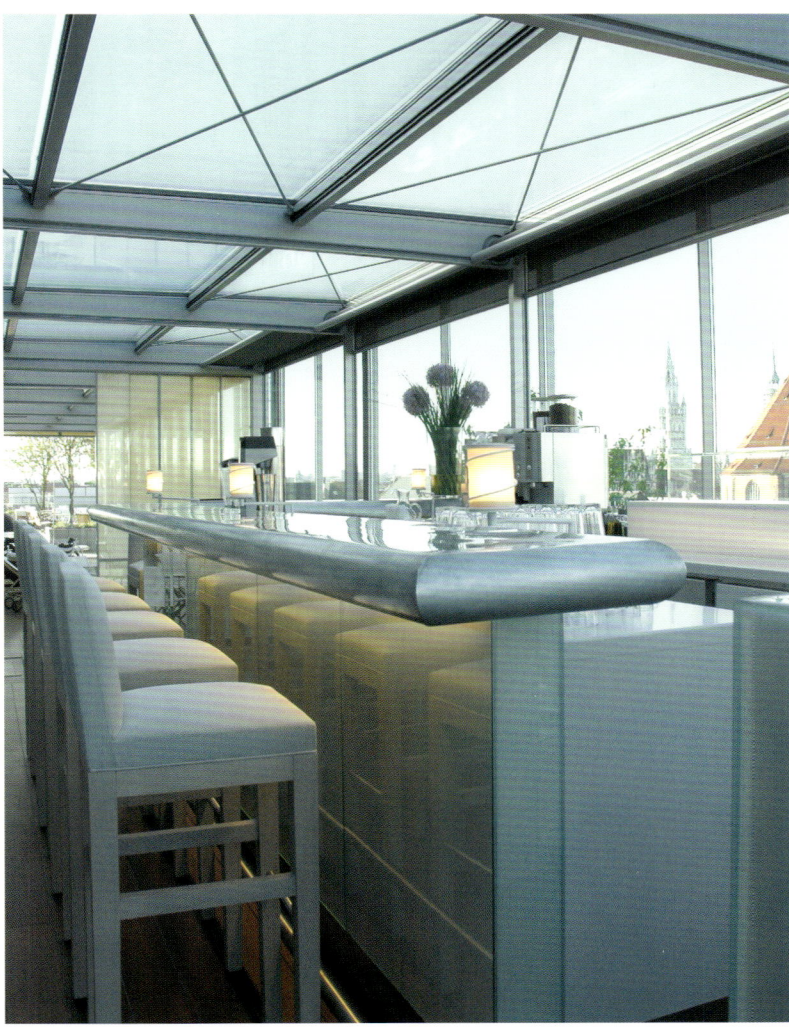

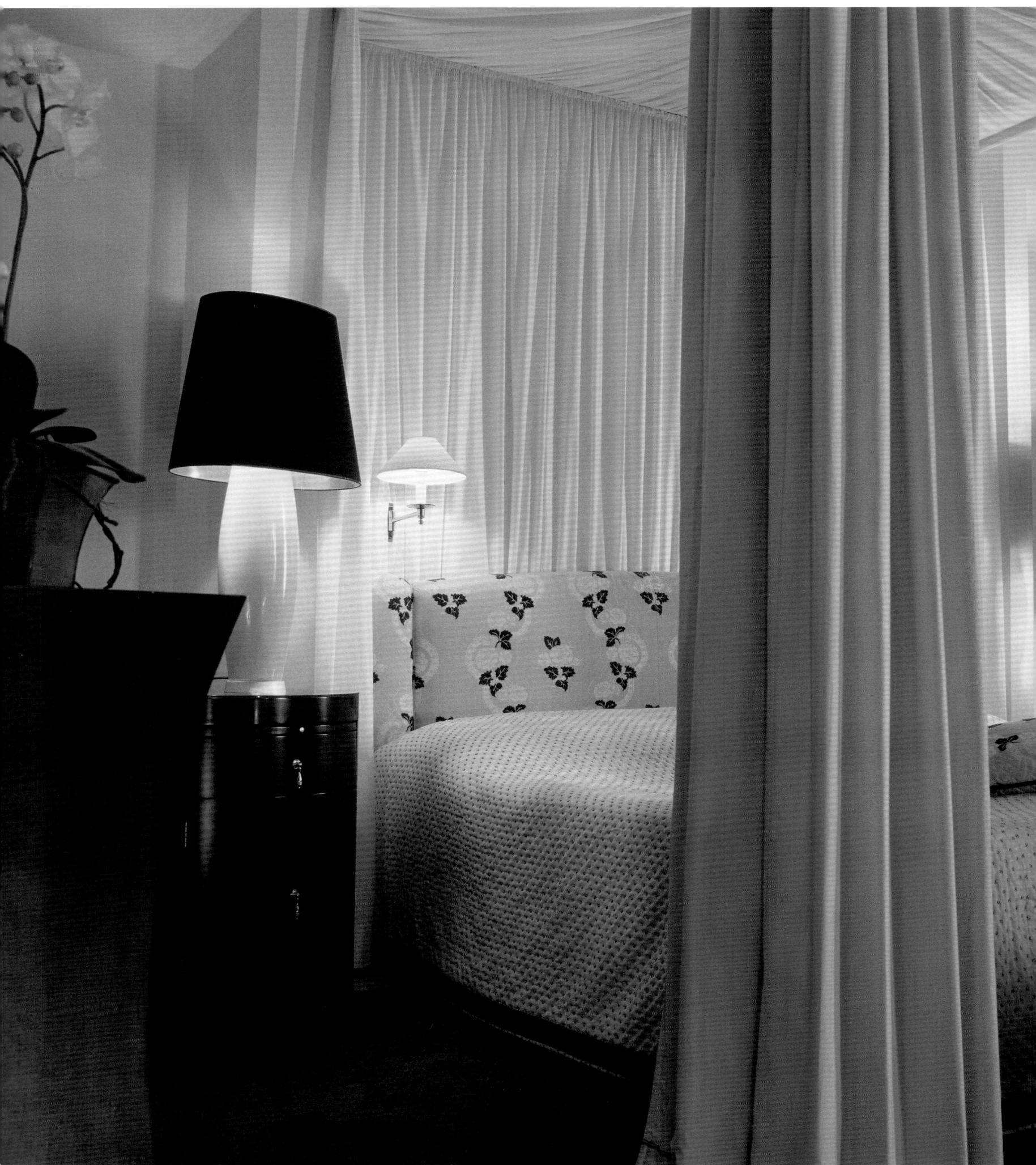

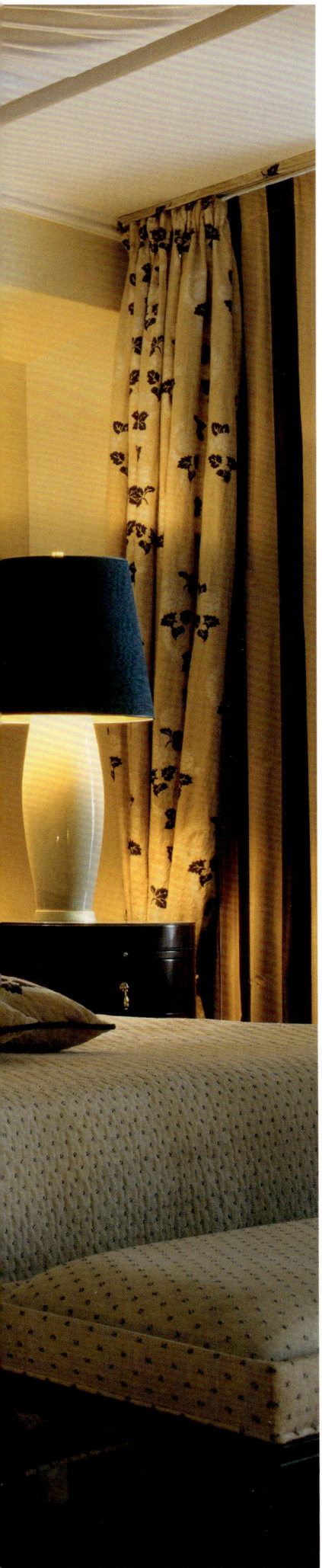

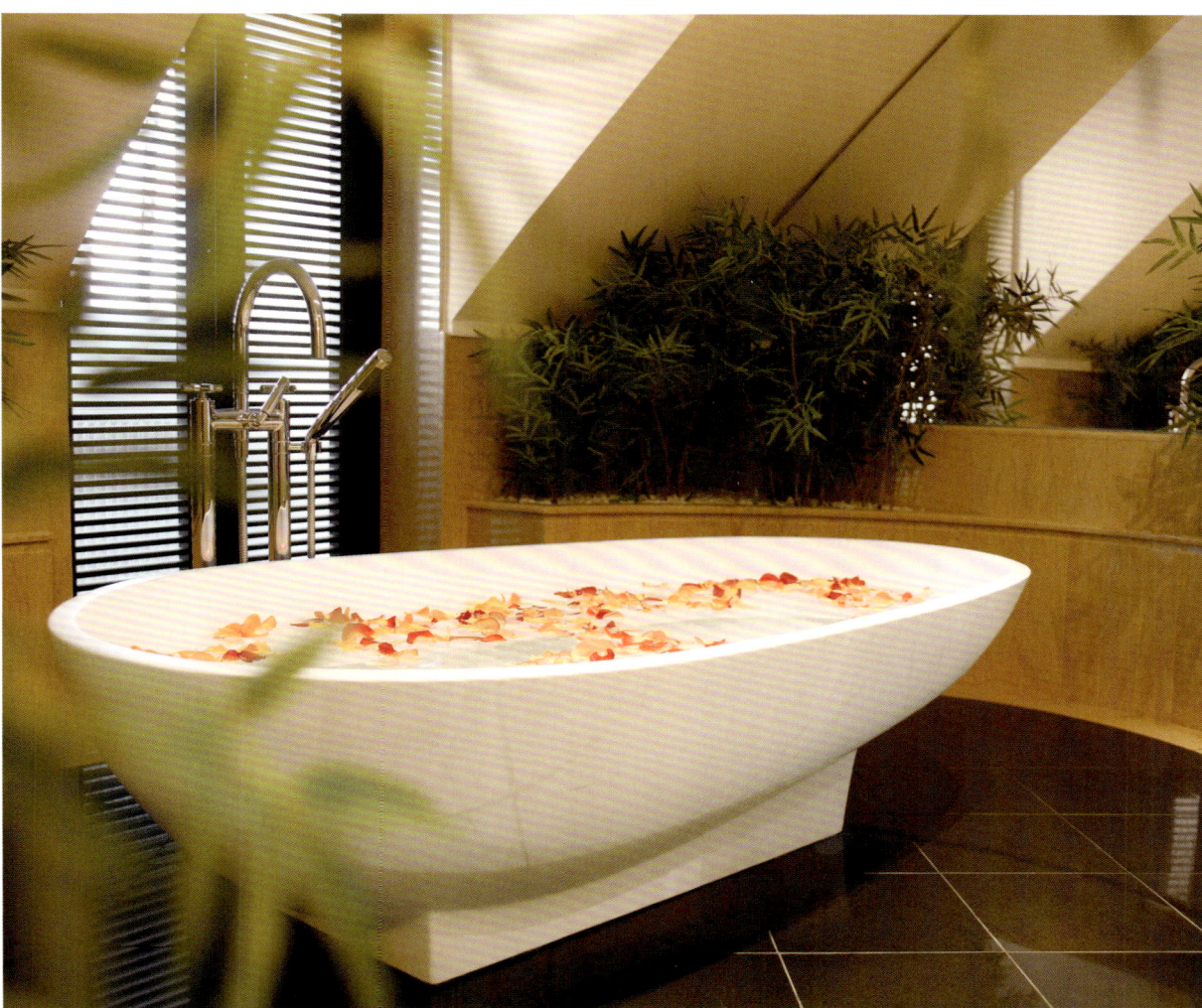

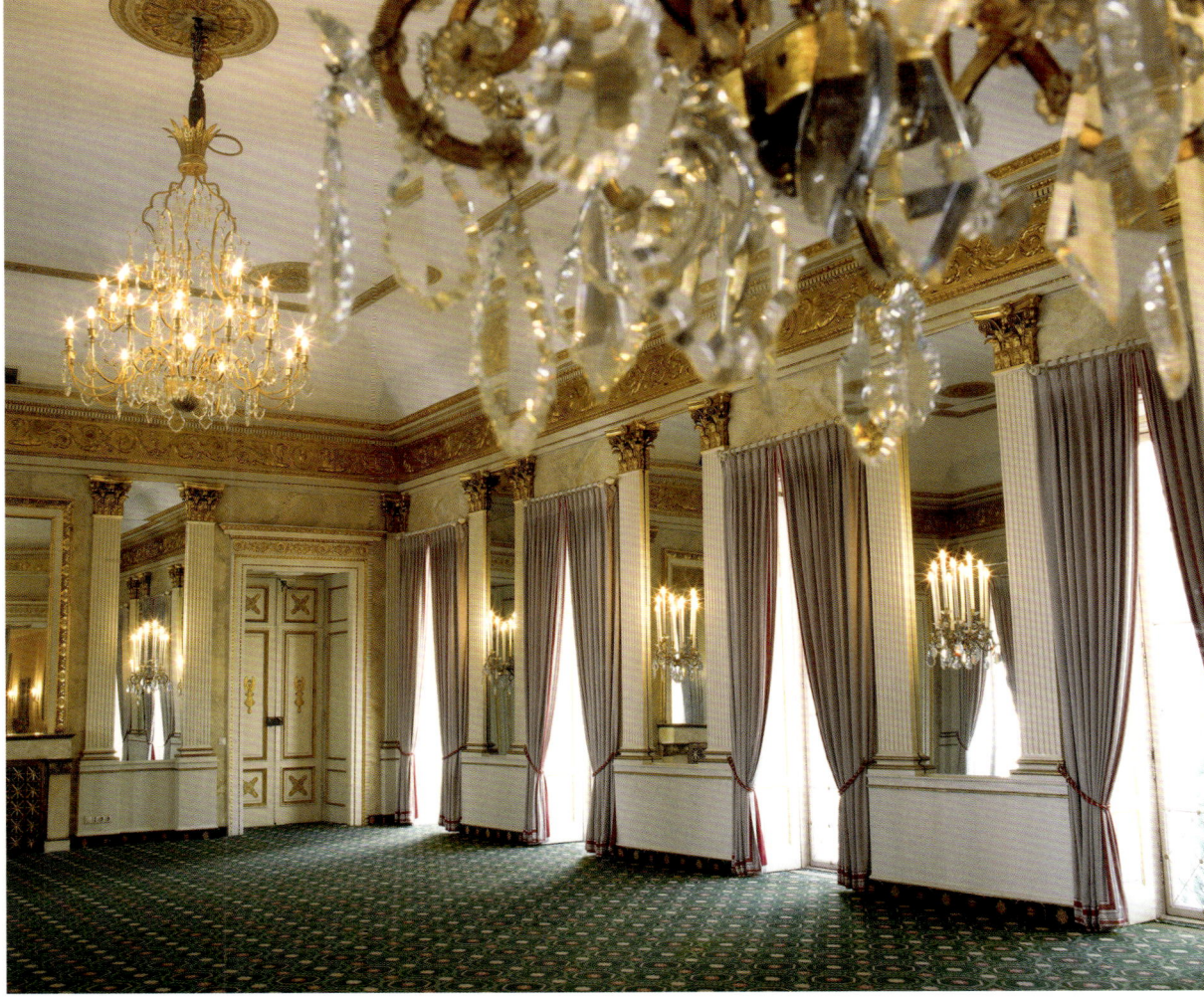

andel's Hotel & Suites Prague

Prague, Czech Republic

Stroupeznickeho 21
15000 Andel City
Czech Republic
Phone: +420 296 889 688
Fax: +420 296 889 999
www.andelssuites.com

Price category: €€
Rooms: 290 rooms including 8 suites and 51 apartments
Facilities: Oscar's bar/brasserie, Delight breakfast restaurant, fitness center
Services: WiFi, concierge, underground parking
Located: Near the historical center of Prague
Public transportation: Metro, tram, bus
Style: Design hotel

This hotel with 231 rooms, eight suites and 51 apartments is situated in the business district of the same name in the Czech metropolis and was designed by London architects Jestico + Whiles. Ceiling-high windows let in a lot of natural light while the clear lines of the modern furniture and warm colors of the textiles render a cheery atmosphere. The generous baths with floor heating are streaming a decent luxury. A fitness center as well as sauna, solarium, steam bath and beauty parlour will refresh any guest exhausted from sightseeing or business appointments.

Im gleichnamigen Geschäftsviertel gelegen, bringt dieses von den Londoner Architekten Jestico + Whiles entworfene Hotel mit seinen 231 Zimmern, acht Suiten und 51 Appartments zeitgenössisches Design in die tschechische Metropole. Raumhohe Fenster sorgen für viel natürliches Licht, die klaren Linien der modernen Möbel und die warmen Farben der Textilien für eine angenehme Atmosphäre. Großzügige Bäder mit Fußbodenheizung verströmen dezenten Luxus. Ein Fitnessraum sowie eine Sauna, ein Solarium, ein Dampfbad und ein Schönheitssalon bringen von Sightseeing oder Geschäftsterminen erschöpfte Gäste wieder ins Gleichgewicht.

Situé dans le quartier des affaires du même nom, l'hôtel de 231 chambres, huit suites et 51 appartements conçu par les architectes londoniens Jestico + Whiles, apporte une touche de design intemporel dans la capitale tchèque. Des hautes fenêtres garantissent un maximum de lumière naturelle, les lignes claires des meubles modernes ainsi que les couleurs chaudes des matériaux contribuent à créer une atmosphère chaleureuse. De vastes salles de bains avec chauffage par le sol dégagent un luxe discret. Une salle de fitness, ainsi qu'un sauna, un solarium, un hammam et un institut de beauté remettent en forme les clients épuisés par les visites de la ville ou les rendez-vous d'affaires.

Situado en el barrio comercial del mismo nombre, el hotel diseñado por los arquitectos londinenses Jestico + Whiles aporta con sus 231 habitaciones, ocho suites y 51 apartamentos un toque de diseño moderno a la metrópolis checa. Los enormes ventanales que cubren totalmente las paredes proporcionan una suave luz natural, las claras líneas de los modernos muebles y los tejidos de colores cálidos generan una atmósfera muy agradable. Grandes baños con suelo radiante ofrecen un lujo discreto. Los huéspedes agotados tras una dura jornada de visitas turísticas o citas comerciales pueden relajarse y reponerse en la sala de fitness, como en la sauna, en el solarium, en el baño turco o y en el instituto de belleza.

Situato nell'omonimo quartiere d'affari, questo hotel progettato dagli architetti londinesi Jestico + Whiles, con le sue 231 stanze, otto suite e 51 appartamenti, ha saputo portare il design contemporaneo nella metropoli ceca. Finestre alte fino al soffitto lasciano entrare una bella luce naturale, mentre le linee pulite dei mobili moderni e i colori caldi dei tessuti rendono l'atmosfera intima e piacevole. Dagli splendidi bagni con riscaldamento a pavimento sembra emanare un lusso discreto. Il locale fitness, la sauna, il solarium, il bagno turco e l'istituto di bellezza sapranno restituire il loro equilibrio naturale agli ospiti stremati dalle visite alla città o da appuntamenti di lavoro.

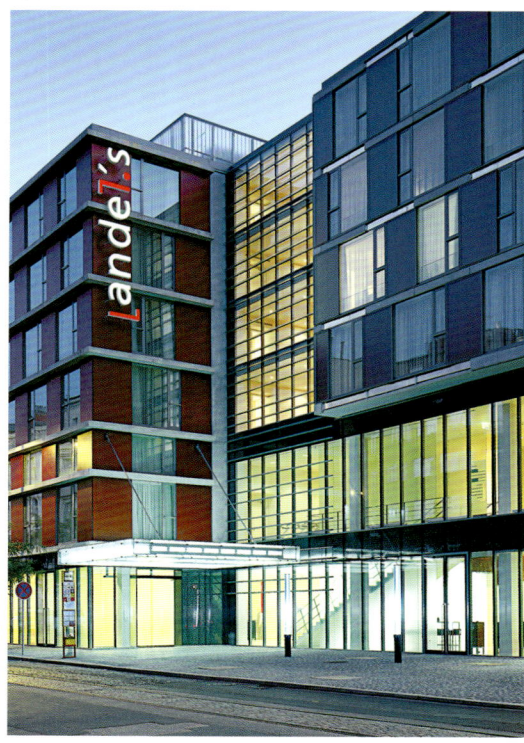 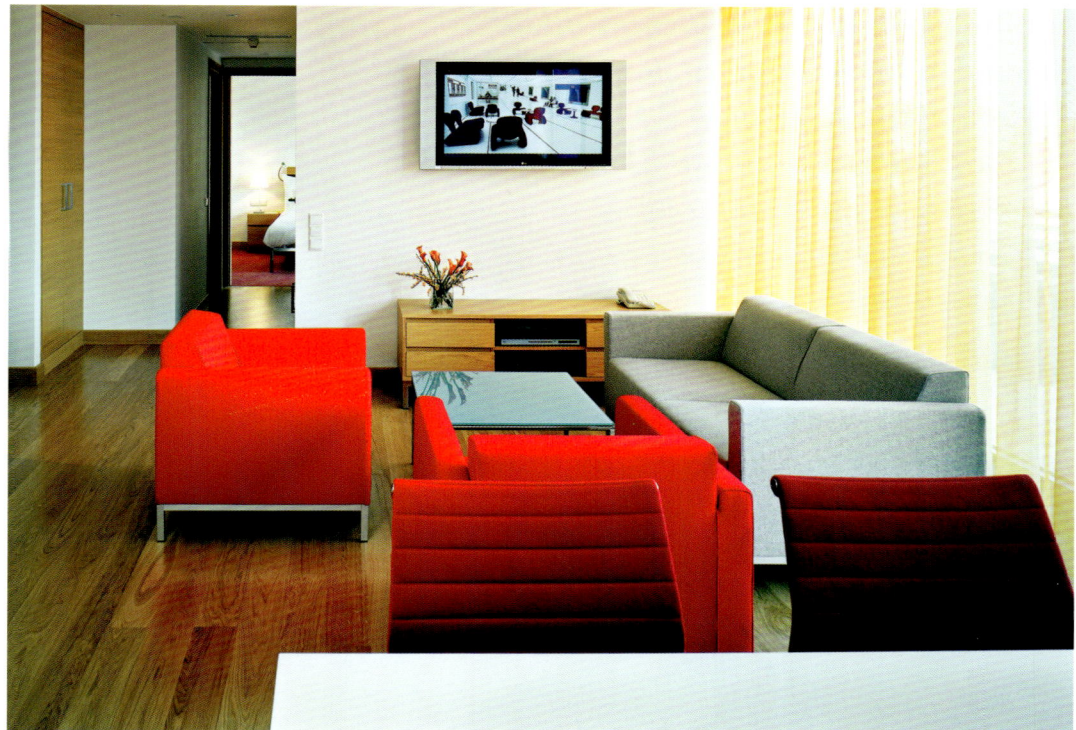

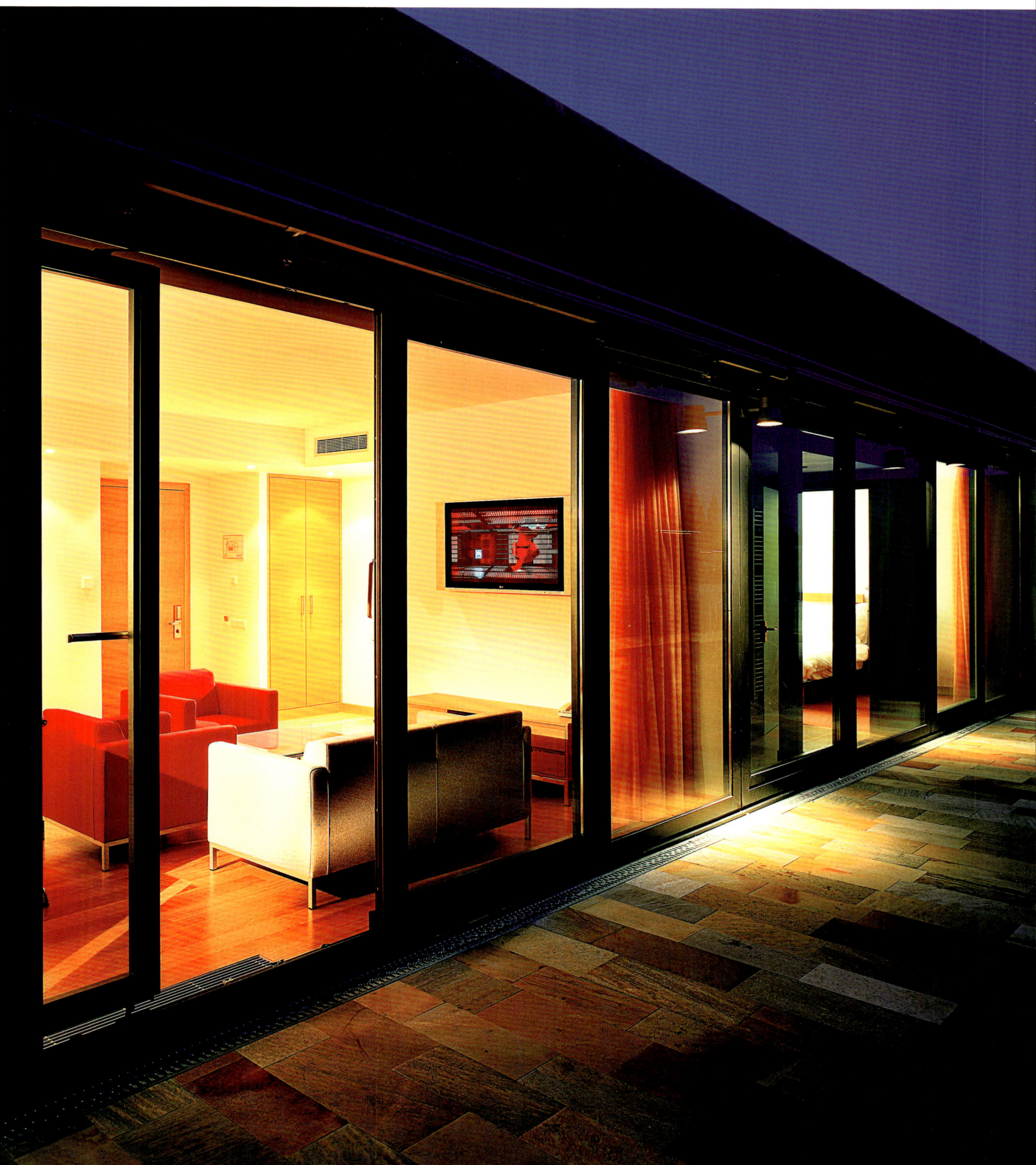

Hotel Josef

Prague, Czech Republic

Rybna 20
11000 Prague
Czech Republic
Phone: +420 221 700 901
Fax: +420 221 700 999
www.hoteljosef.com

Price category: €€
Rooms: 109 rooms
Facilities: Garden, conference room, business center, gymnasium, sauna, massage room, garage
Services: Concierge, guest relations
Located: In the city center, 5 min from the Old Town Square
Public transportation: Metro B and C, Tram 26 and 5
Style: Elegant and pure

This hotel near the former Jewish quarter embodies the clean chic concept in its purest form: Eva Jiricna lines up 109 classic yet modern rooms with light materials as well as glass baths in two houses facing an inner court. Armchairs, pillows or ceilings bear their house's colors proudly in the play off between the Orange House and the Pink House. Even the bar with an illuminated counter and the restaurant with hue-glazing focus on understatement. An iPod station or massage perfects the chill-out feeling.

Nahe des früheren jüdischen Viertels gelegen verkörpert dieses Hotel Clean Chic in seiner reinsten Form: Eva Jiricna hat in zwei Gebäuden mit Blick auf einen Innenhof 109 Zimmer untergebracht – klassisch-modern, mit hellen Materialien sowie gläsernen Bädern. Sessel, Kissen oder Decken bringen Farbe ins Spiel und ordnen den Raum dem „Orange House" oder dem „Pink House" zu. Auch die Bar mit beleuchtetem Tresen und das Restaurant mit riesiger Fensterfront setzen auf Understatement. Das Chill-out-Feeling perfekt machen iPod-Stationen und Massagen.

Situé tout près de l'ancien quartier juif, cet hôtel incarne le « clean chic » dans sa forme la plus pure : Eva Jiricna a réparti 109 chambres dans deux bâtiments en jouant sur les couleurs, au-dessus d'une cour intérieure, dans un style classique-moderne caractérisé par des matériaux légers et des baignoires de verre. Les fauteuils, les coussins ou les toits portent fièrement les couleurs de l'établissement, rappelant l'interaction entre le Orange House et le Pink House. Même le bar avec son comptoir illuminé et le restaurant acec sa vaste façade de verre ont une élégance plutôt symbole d'exigence que d'extravagance. Grâce aux stations iPod et aux massages, la sensation de détente est parfaite.

Ubicado cerca del antiguo barrio judío, este hotel encarna el estilo minimalista "clean chic" en su forma más pura. En dos edificios con vistas a un patio interior, Eva Jiricna dispuso 109 habitaciones clásicas pero a la última, con materiales de tonos claros y cuartos de baño de cristal. Butacas, cojines y tapices añaden un toque de color y condicionan los nombres de habitaciones como la Orange House o la Pink House. Asimismo, se apuesta por la elegancia discreta, como atestiguan el bar de barra iluminada y el restaurante con una inmensa cristalera. Además, las distintas estaciones de conexión para el iPod y los masajes que se ofrecen contribuyen a crear un ambiente de relax perfecto.

Situato nei pressi del vecchio quartiere ebraico, questo hotel è la perfetta incarnazione del concetto di "clean chic": distribuendoli in due edifici con vista su un cortile interno, Eva Jiricna ha realizzato 109 stanze in stile classico-moderno, con materiali chiari e bagni di vetro. Poltrone, cuscini e coperte sono un trionfo di colori, in base ai quali le camere sono attribuite alla Orange House o alla Pink House. Anche il bar con bancone illuminato e il ristorante con la sua gigantesca vetrata panoramica puntano sull'understatement. iPod stations e massaggi creano il perfetto "chill-out feeling".

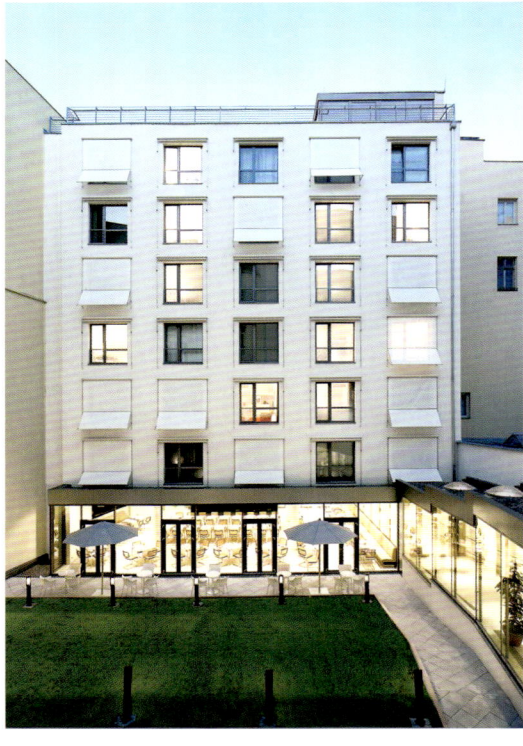
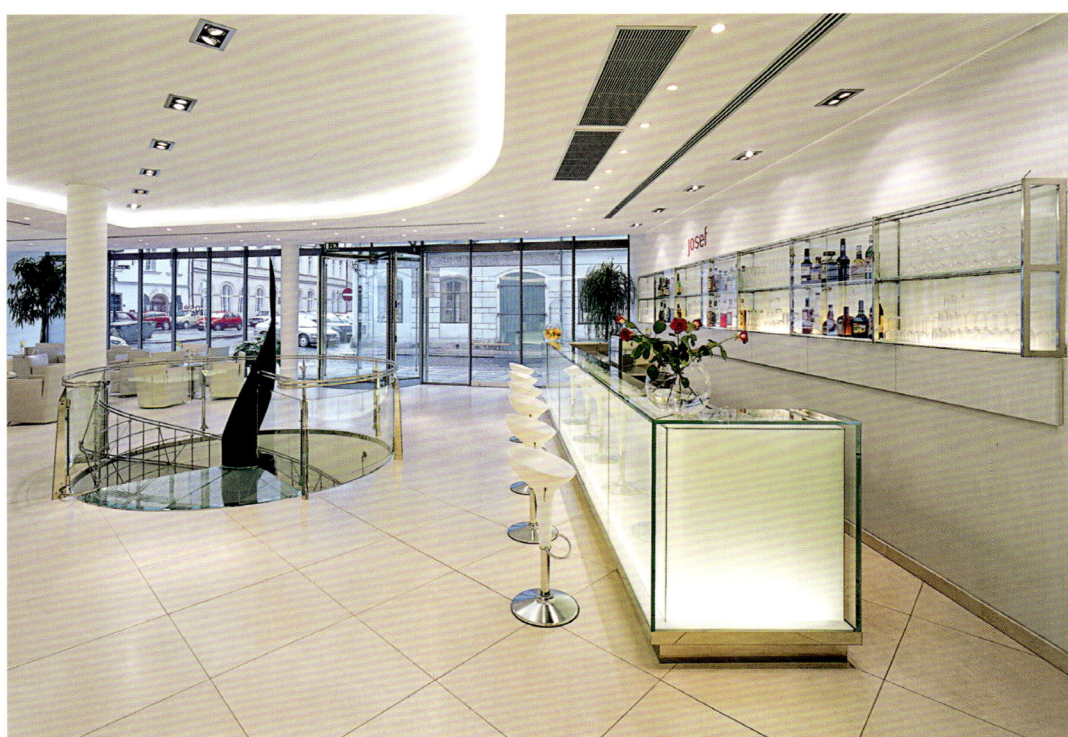

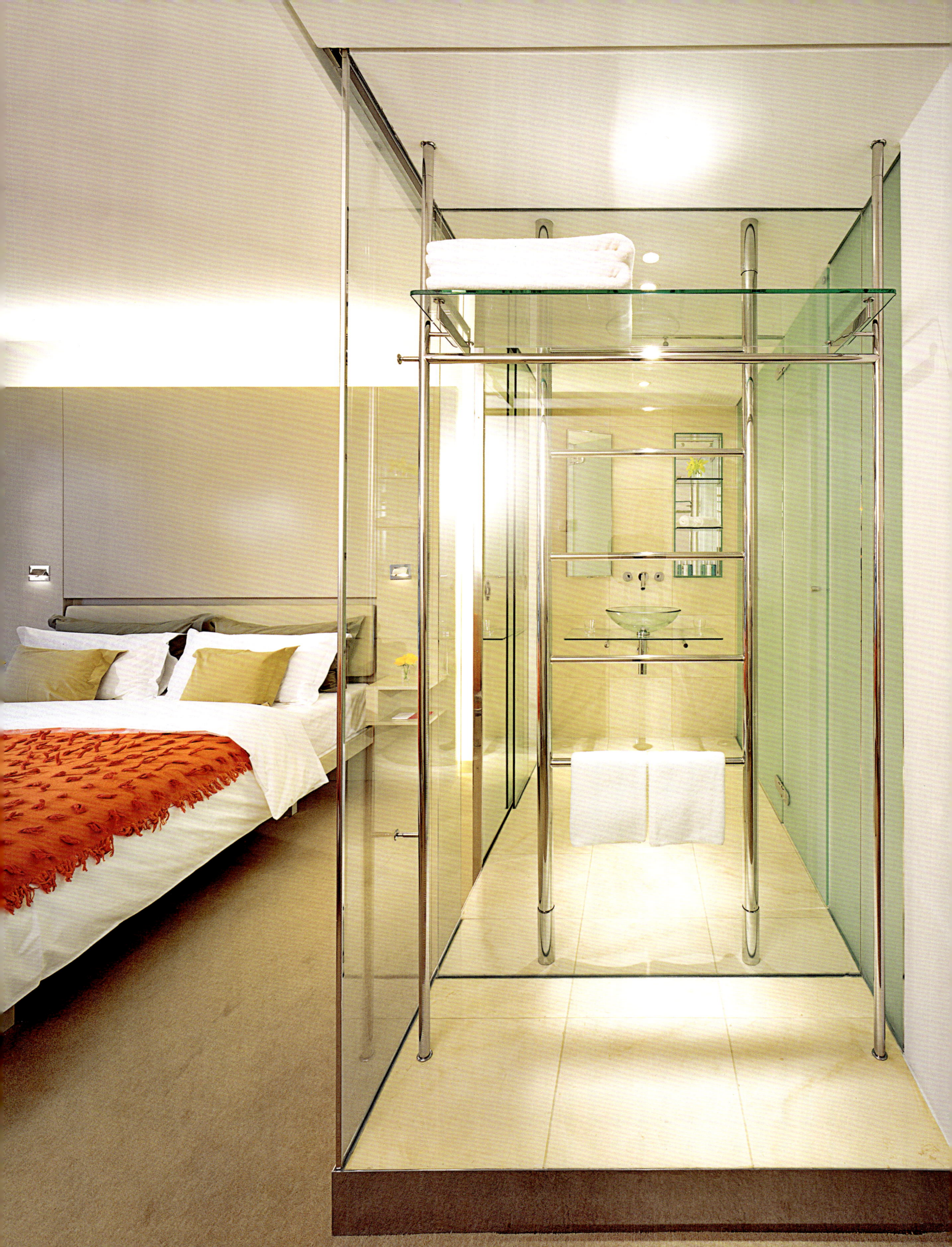

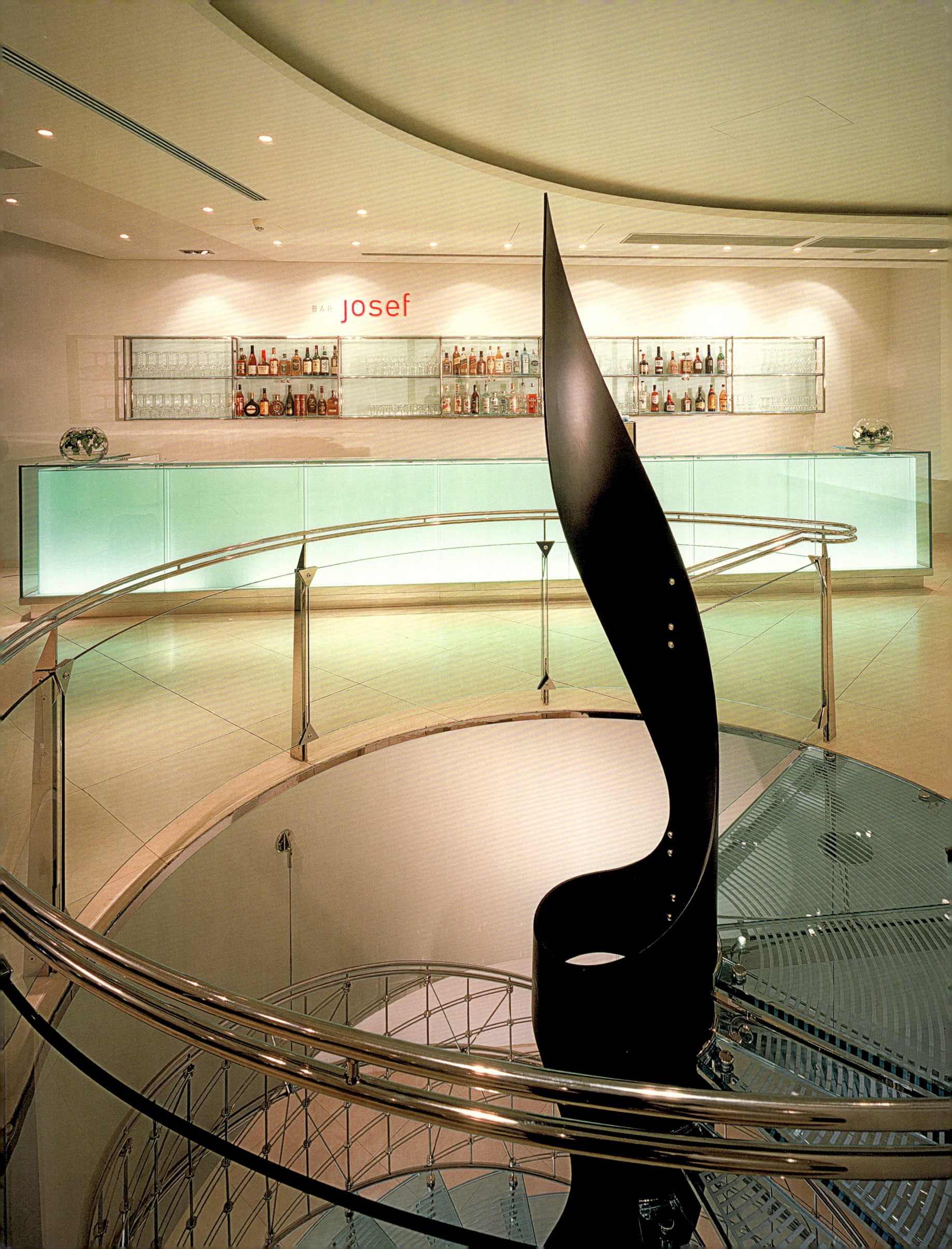

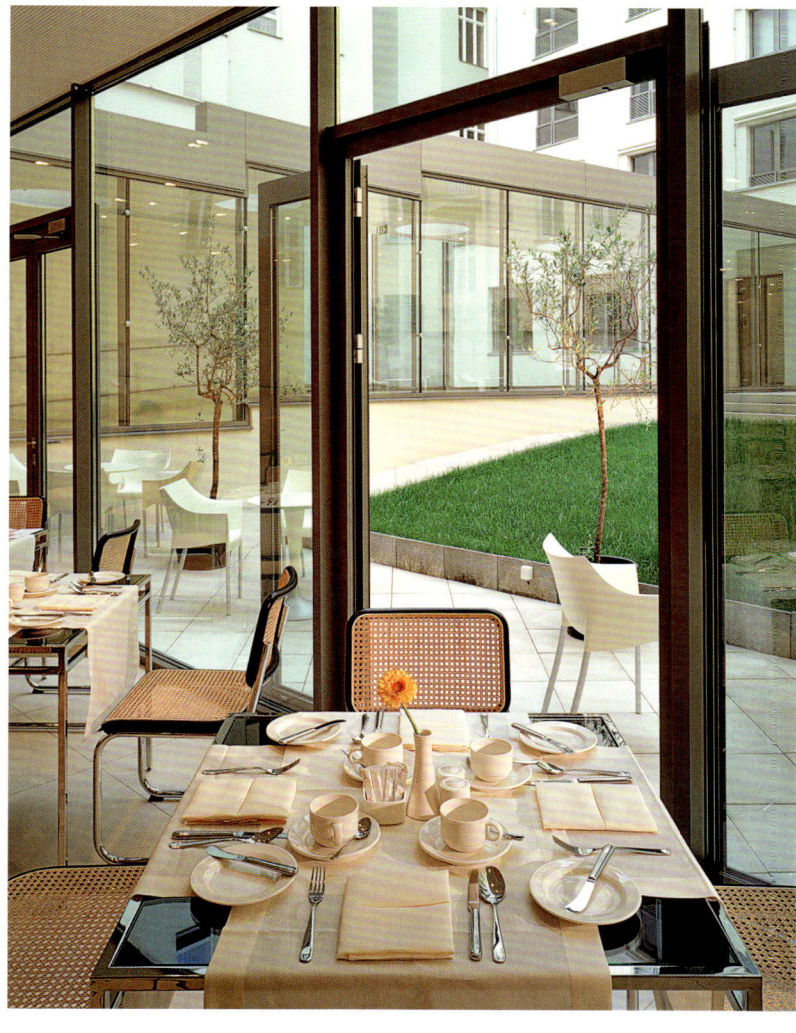

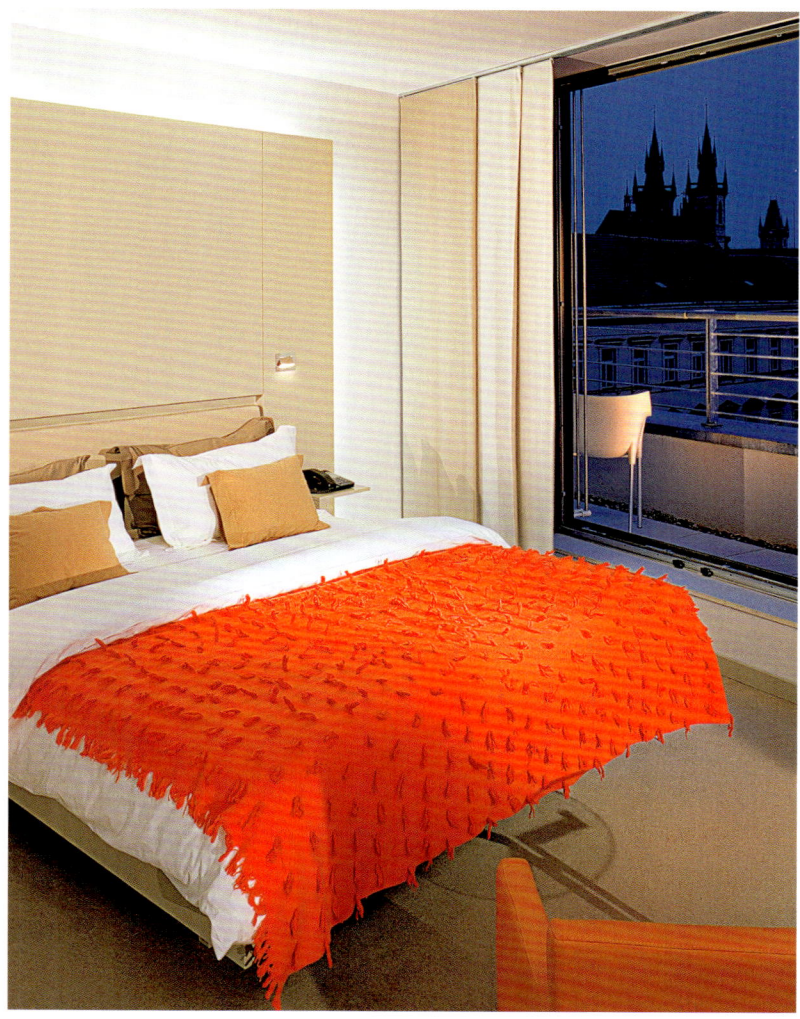

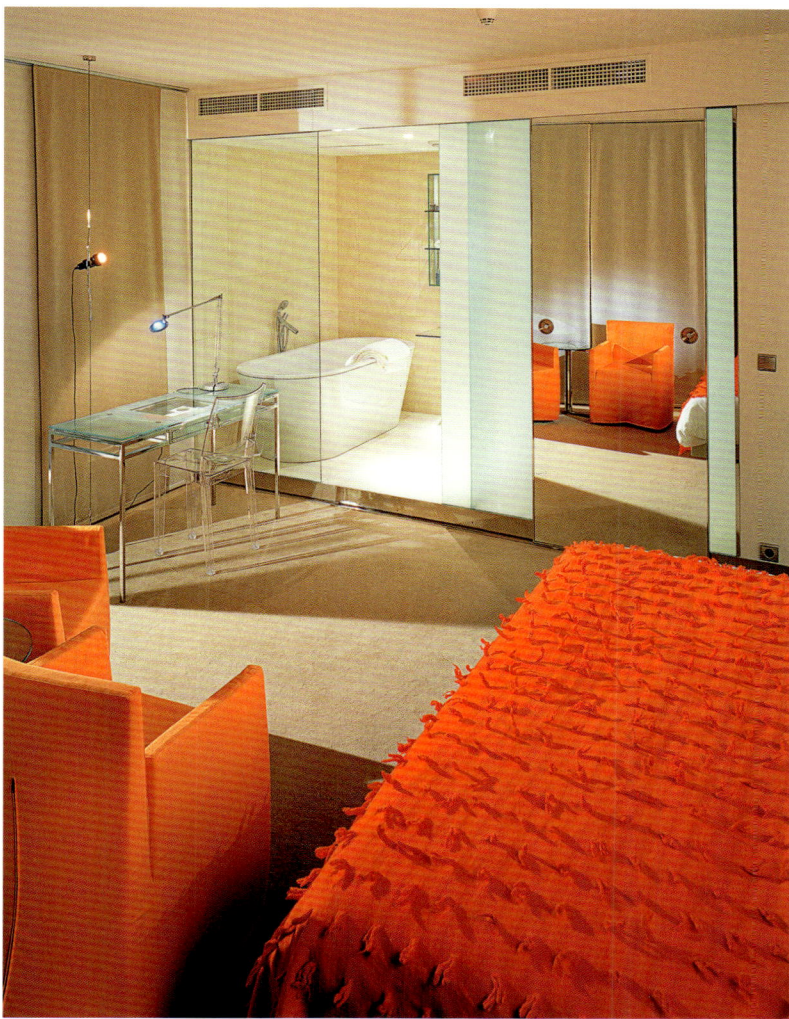

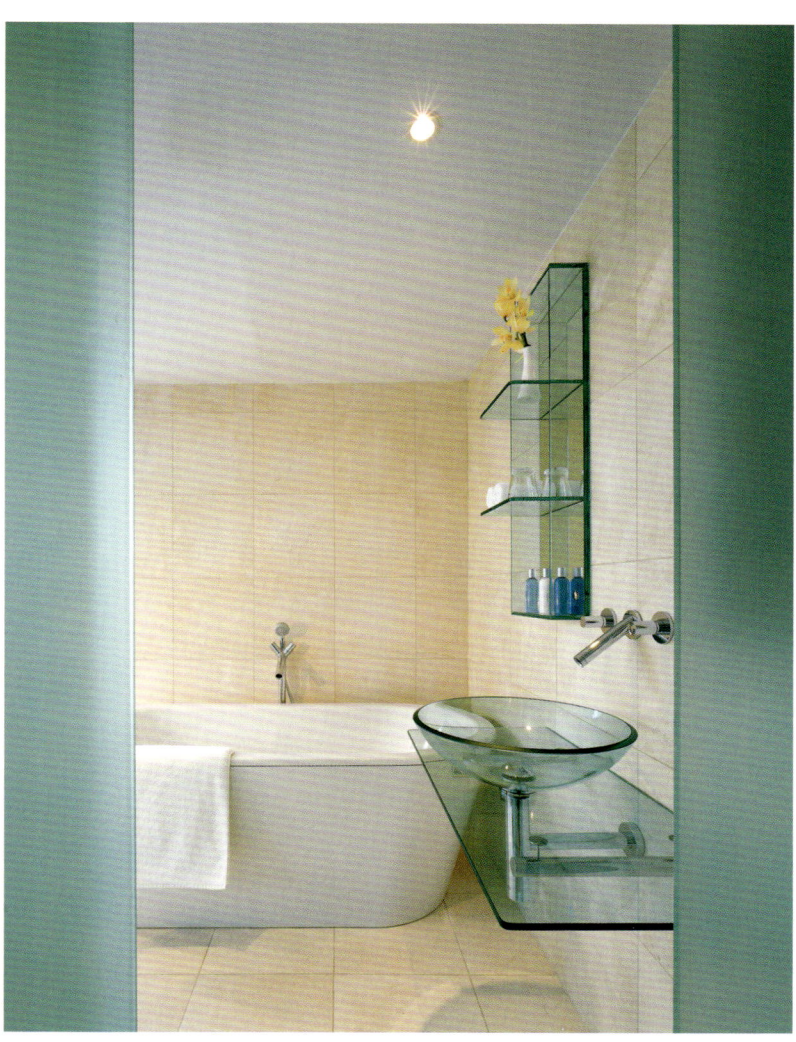

Hastalska 14
11000 Prague
Czech Republic
Phone: +420 225 300 111
Fax: +420 225 300 110
www.maximilianhotel.com

Price category: €€
Rooms: 70 rooms and 1 suite
Facilities: Zen Asian wellness, conference room, library
Services: Guest relations, drawing room, garage
Located: In the center of Prague, 5 min from the Old Town Square
Public transportation: Metro B and C, Tram 26 and 5
Style: Art deco

There is an air of Pierre Chareau's La maison de Verre and the drafts of Eileen Grey, Luke Pearson or Tom Lloyd: the Maximilian combines art deco, modern design and contemporary construction to succeed as an entirety. The onyx wall in the lobby is the opener followed by 71 rooms thought-out in detail and a restaurant with a glass ceiling supported by steel girders. Clear lines also dominate in the spa with a touch of Asia—and in the Wellness Floating Center you can drift away from everyday life.

Man fühlt sich an Pierre Chareaus La Maison de Verre erinnert und an Entwürfe von Eileen Grey, Luke Pearson oder Tom Lloyd: Das Maximilian verbindet Art déco, modernistisches Design und zeitgemäßes Bauen zu einem gelungenen Ganzen. Die Lobby mit ihrer Onyxwand ist der Auftakt – gefolgt von 71 bis ins Detail durchdachten Zimmern und einem Restaurant, dessen Glasdecke von schmalen Stahlträgern gestützt wird. Klare Linien herrschen auch im asiatisch angehauchten Spa – und im Wellness Floating Center kann man dem Alltag entschweben.

Il rappelle La Maison de Verre de Pierre Chareau et les créations d'Eileen Grey, Luke Pearson ou Tom Lloyd : le Maximilian combine l'art déco, le design moderniste et la construction contemporaine. Le hall avec son mur d'onyx en est le prélude, suivi par 71 chambres pensées jusque dans les détails et d'un restaurant dans lequel le plafond de verre est soutenu par des poutrelles d'acier. Des lignes claires et des touches asiatiques règnent également au spa, et dans le Wellness Floating Center, vous pouvez vous échapper de la routine quotidienne

El hotel Maximilian evoca La Maison de Verre de Pierre Chareaus y los esbozos de Eileen Grey, Luke Pearson y Tom Lloyd. Este edificio fusiona el art-déco, el diseño modernista y la arquitectura contemporánea de manera armónica. El vestíbulo con la pared de ónice constituye el preludio al que siguen 71 habitaciones pensadas hasta el último detalle y un restaurante, cuyo techo de cristal soporta unas delgadas vigas de acero. Las líneas bien definidas también marcan el estilo de un spa con cierto aire oriental y en el Wellness Floating Center uno puede escapar de lo cotidiano.

Viene da pensare alla Maison de Verre di Pierre Chareau e a disegni di Eileen Grey, Luke Pearson o Tom Lloyd: il Maximilian unisce art déco, design modernista e architettura contemporanea in una combinazione perfettamente riuscita. La lobby, con la sua parete in onice, ne è il preludio – cui seguono 71 camere curate fino nel dettaglio e un ristorante con il soffitto di vetro sostenuto da sottili supporti in alluminio. Le linee semplici predominano anche nello Spa dagli effluvi asiatici – e nel Wellness Floating Center potrete farvi trasportare piacevolmente lontano dalla vita di tutti i giorni.

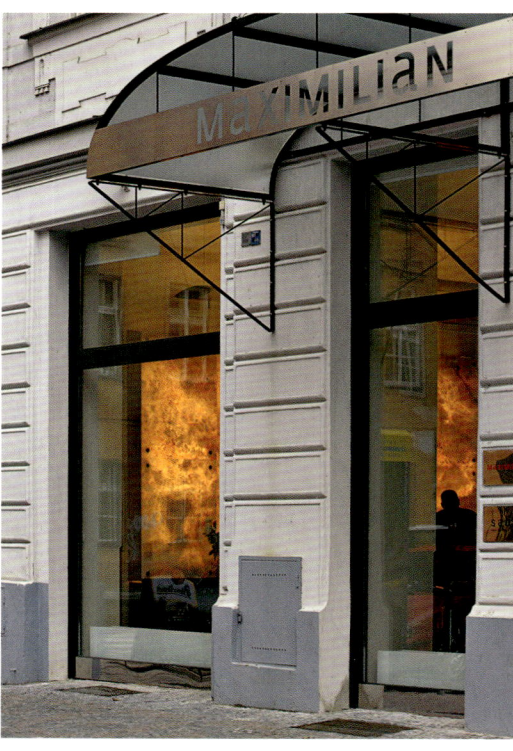 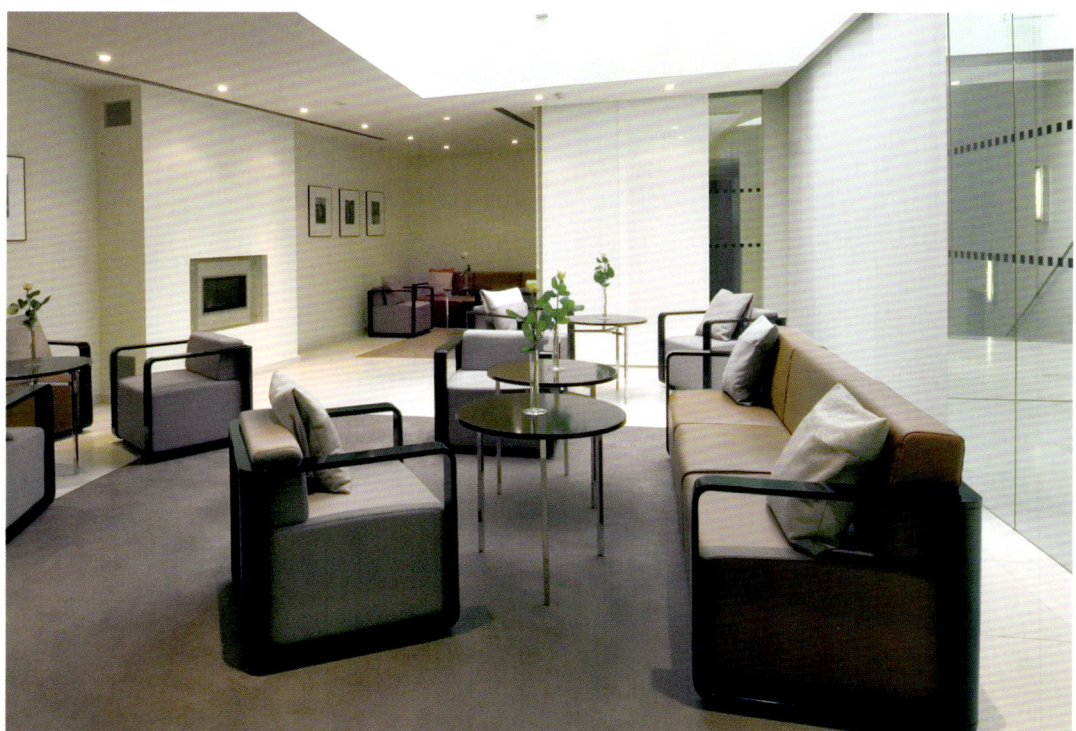

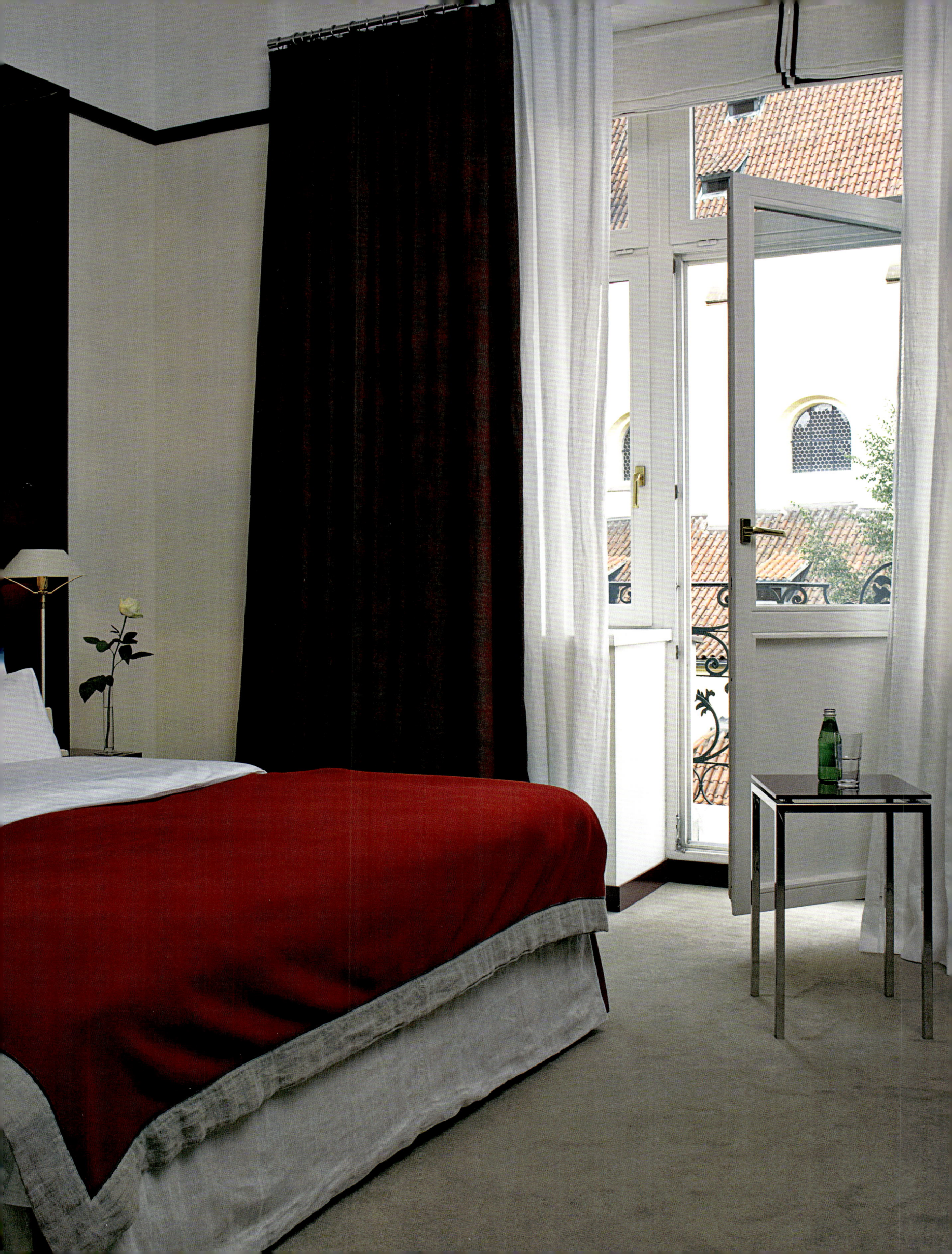

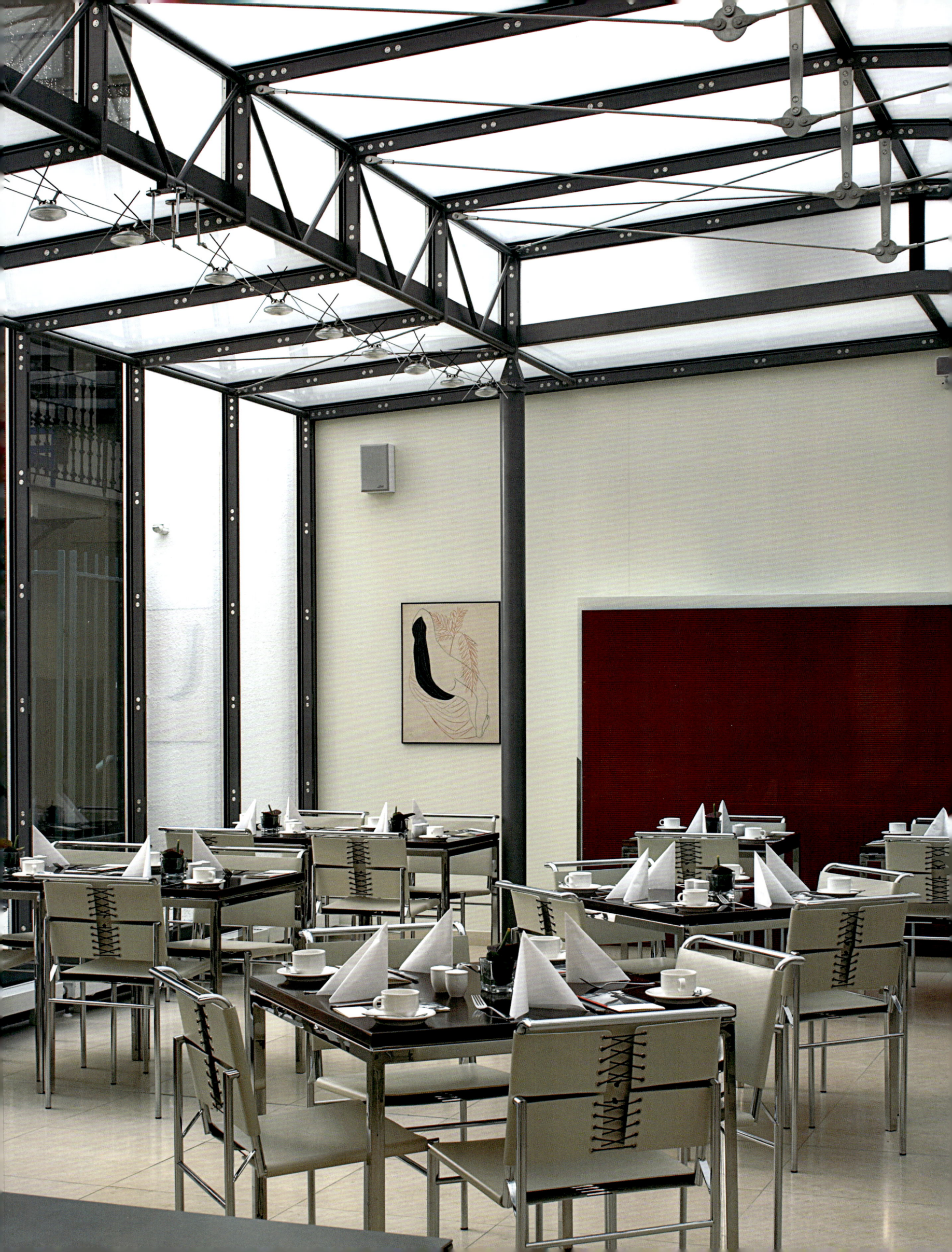

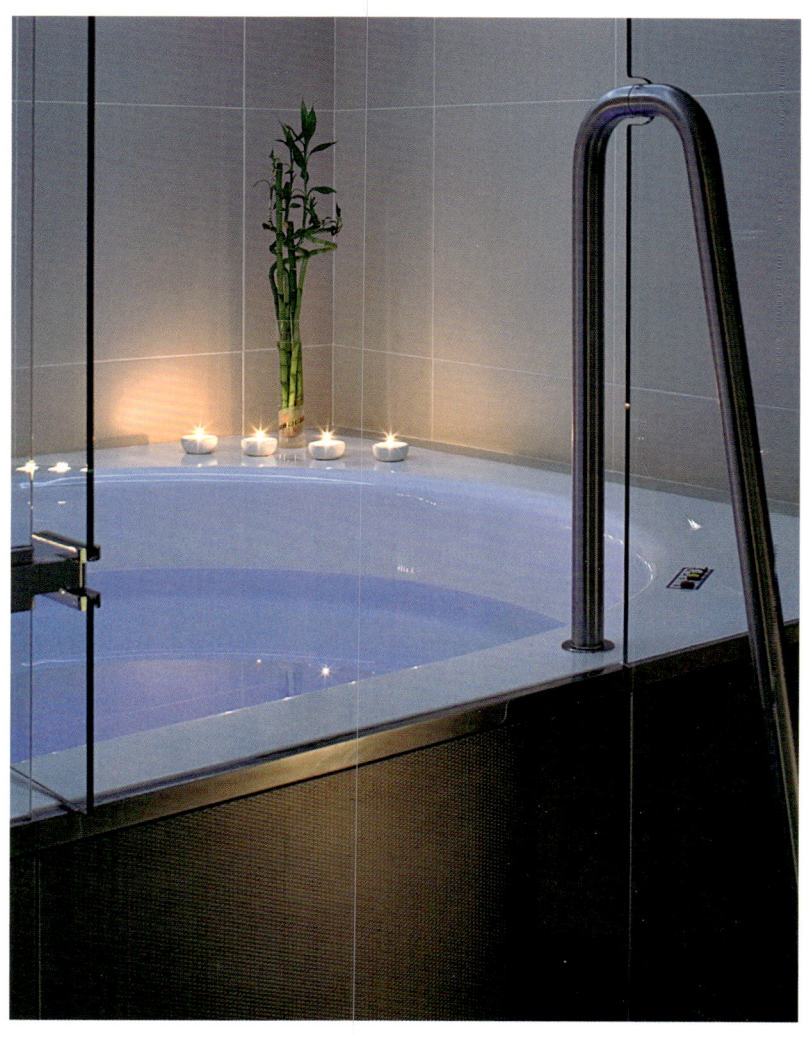
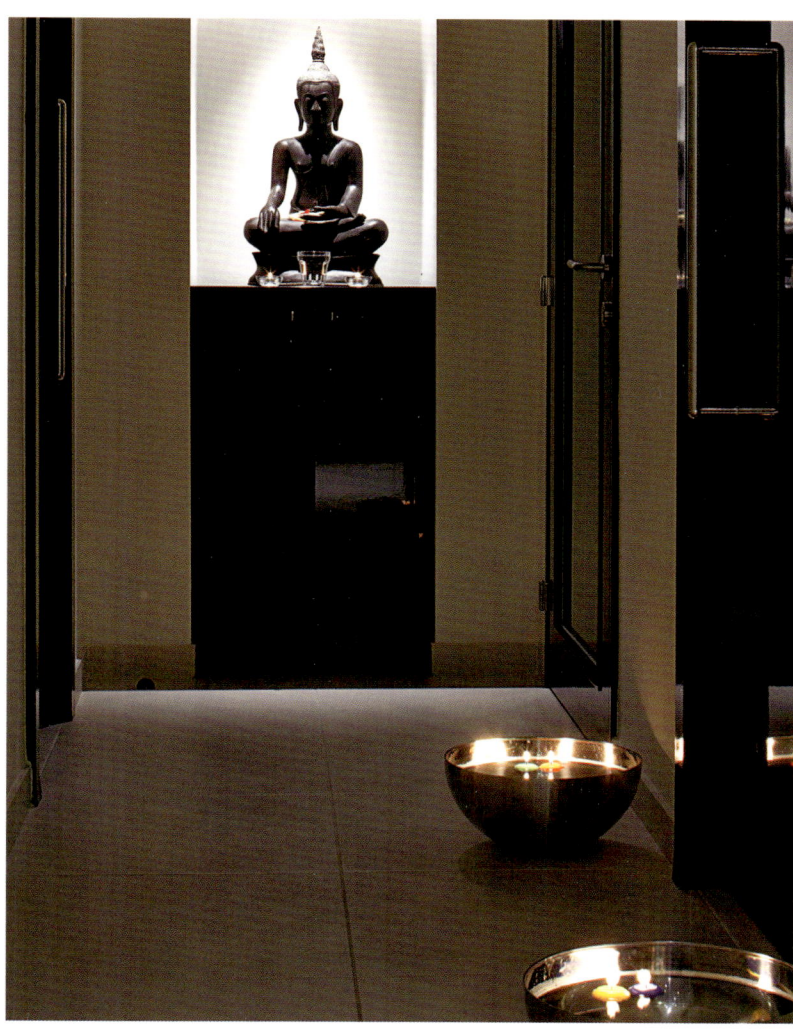

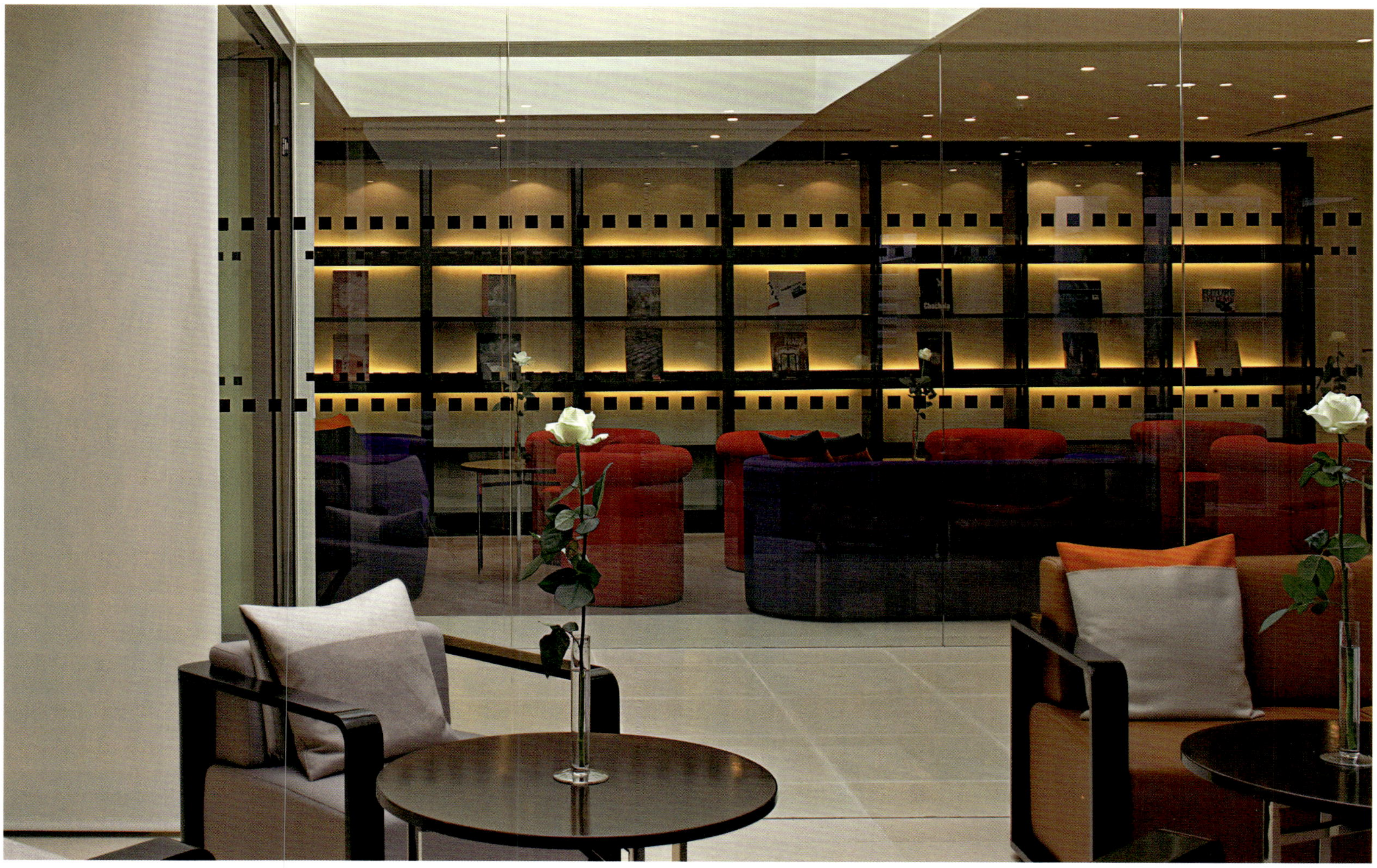

Lánchíd utca 19
1013 Budapest
Hungary
Phone: +36 1 419 1900
Fax: +36 1 419 1919
www.lanchid19hotel.hu

Price category: €
Rooms: 48 rooms including 3 suites
Facilities: Restaurant, bar, 3 meeting rooms
Services: Laundry, cultural program organization, change, business services
Located: In the city center, by the Danube
Public transportation: Bus 16, 105; tram 19, 41; funiculaire Budavári Sikló
Style: Modern

In a street characterized by 19th-century buildings, this hotel designed in contemporary style stands out like a sparkling jewel. Its glass facades that open up like an accordion are illuminated in the dark by large-format pictures. The 48 rooms and suites are furnished in minimalist style that really brings out the effect of their designer furniture. Plasma TVs and internet access are, of course, part of their equipment. The spacious lobby reaches over several levels lined by galleries.

In einem Straßenzug, den Gebäude aus dem 19. Jahrhundert prägen, sticht dieses in zeitgenössischem Design gestaltete Hotel wie ein funkelndes Juwel heraus. Seine Glasfassaden, die sich nach Akkordeon-Prinzip öffnen lassen, werden bei Dunkelheit von großflächigen Bildern illuminiert. Die 48 Zimmer und Suiten sind in minimalistischem Stil eingerichtet, der ihre Designermöbel wirkungsvoll zur Geltung bringt. Plasma-Fernseher und Internetzugang gehören in diesem Haus selbstverständlich zur Ausstattung. Die spacige Lobby erstreckt sich über mehrere, von Galerien gesäumten Ebenen.

Dans une rue où règnent les bâtiments du XIXème siècle, cet hôtel au design contemporain resplendit comme un joyau. Ses façades de verre qui s'ouvrent en accordéon sont illuminées pendant la nuit par d'immenses images d'art. Les 48 chambres et suites sont décorées dans un style minimaliste, qui met en valeur les meubles de designer. Des téléviseurs plasma et un accès internet font naturellement partie de l'équipement. Le hall de réception spacieux s'étend sur plusieurs niveaux doublés de couloirs.

En una calle caracterizada por sus edificios del siglo XIX, este hotel de diseño moderno destaca como una brillante joya. Sus fachadas de cristal, las cuales se abren siguiendo el mismo principio de un acordeón, se iluminan al caer la noche con enormes imágenes. Las 48 habitaciones y suites están decoradas en estilo minimalista, marcado especialmente por sus muebles de diseño. Los televisores de plasma y el acceso a Internet forman, por supuesto, parte del equipamiento. El vestíbulo tiene un look futurista y ocupa varios pisos, con galerías que recorren todo el perímetro.

In un tratto di via caratterizzato da edifici del XIX secolo, questo albergo dal design contemporaneo risalta come un gioiello scintillante. Con il buio le sue facciate, composte da pannelli in vetro disposti a fisarmonica, si illuminano in riquadri di grandi dimensioni. Le 48 tra stanze e suite sono arredate in uno stile minimalista, che sa mettere in risalto i mobili di design dell'arredamento. Naturalmente, della dotazione della casa fanno parte televisori al plasma e accesso a Internet. La spaziosa lobby è ricavata in uno spazio interno che si apre su più piani.

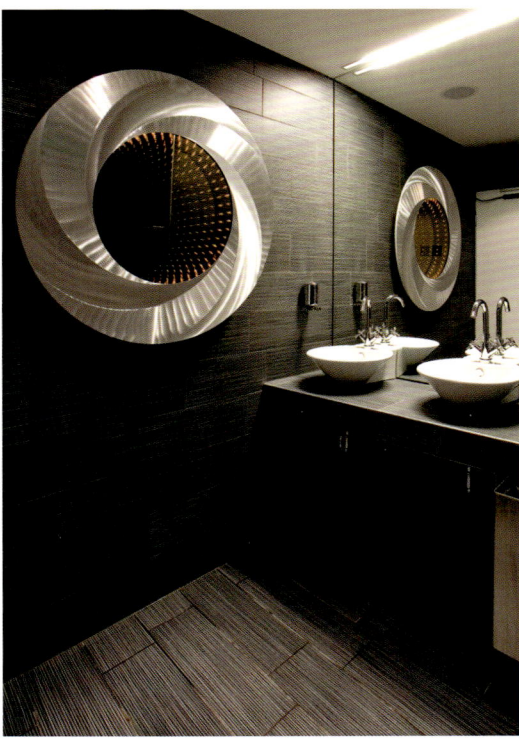
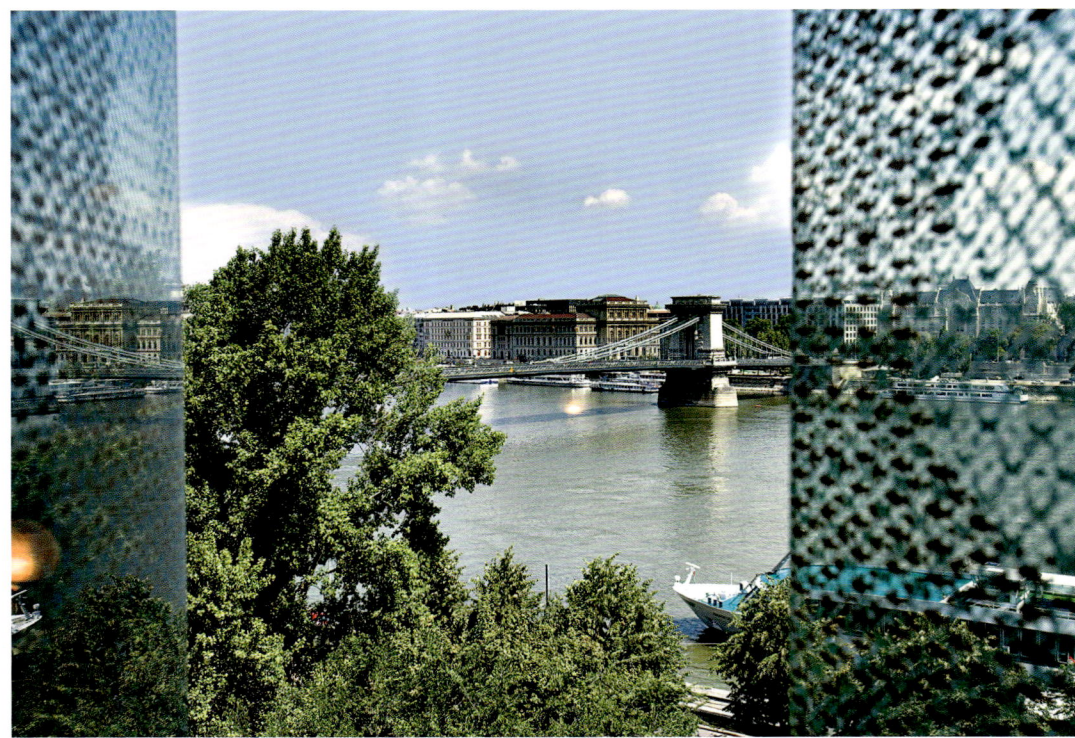

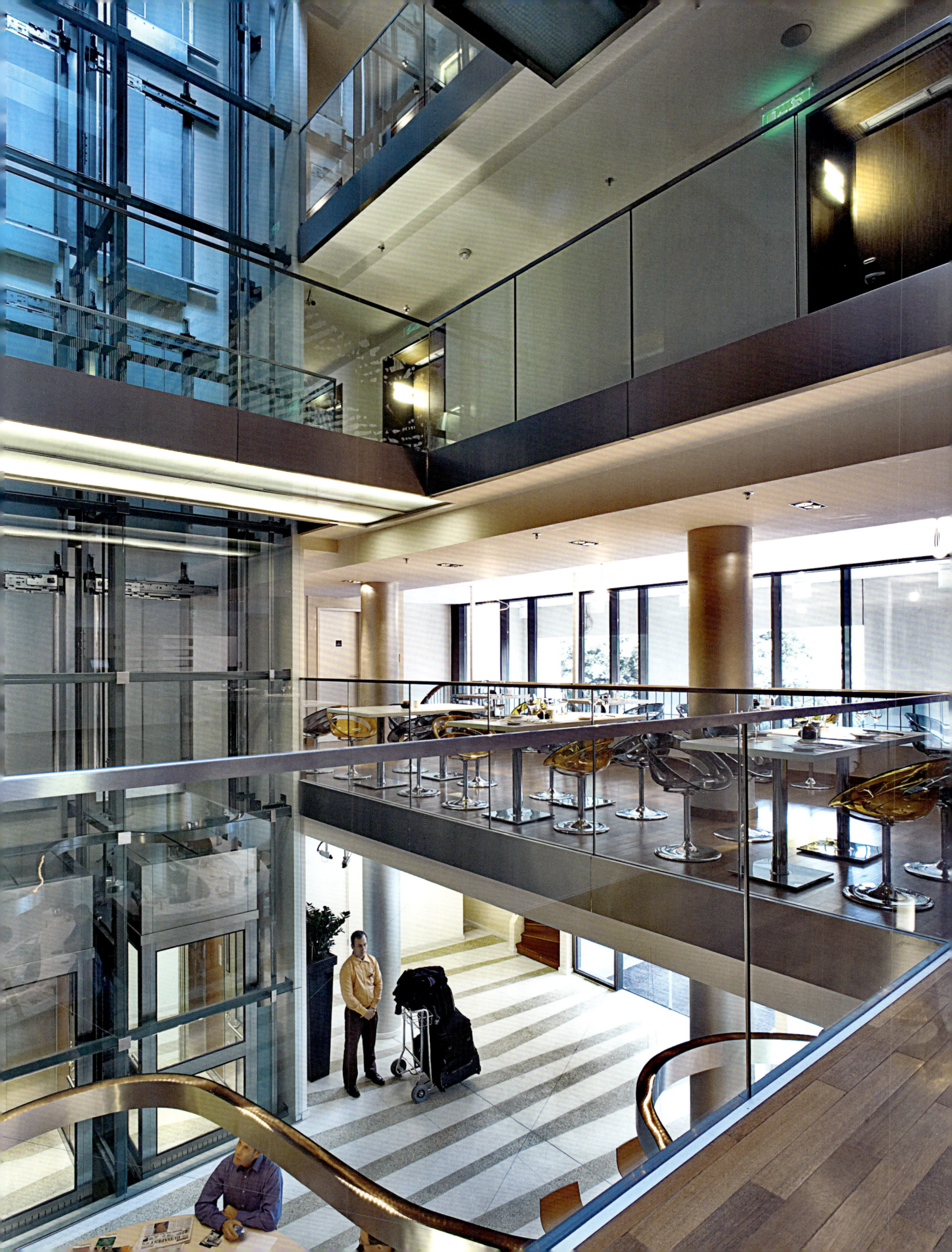

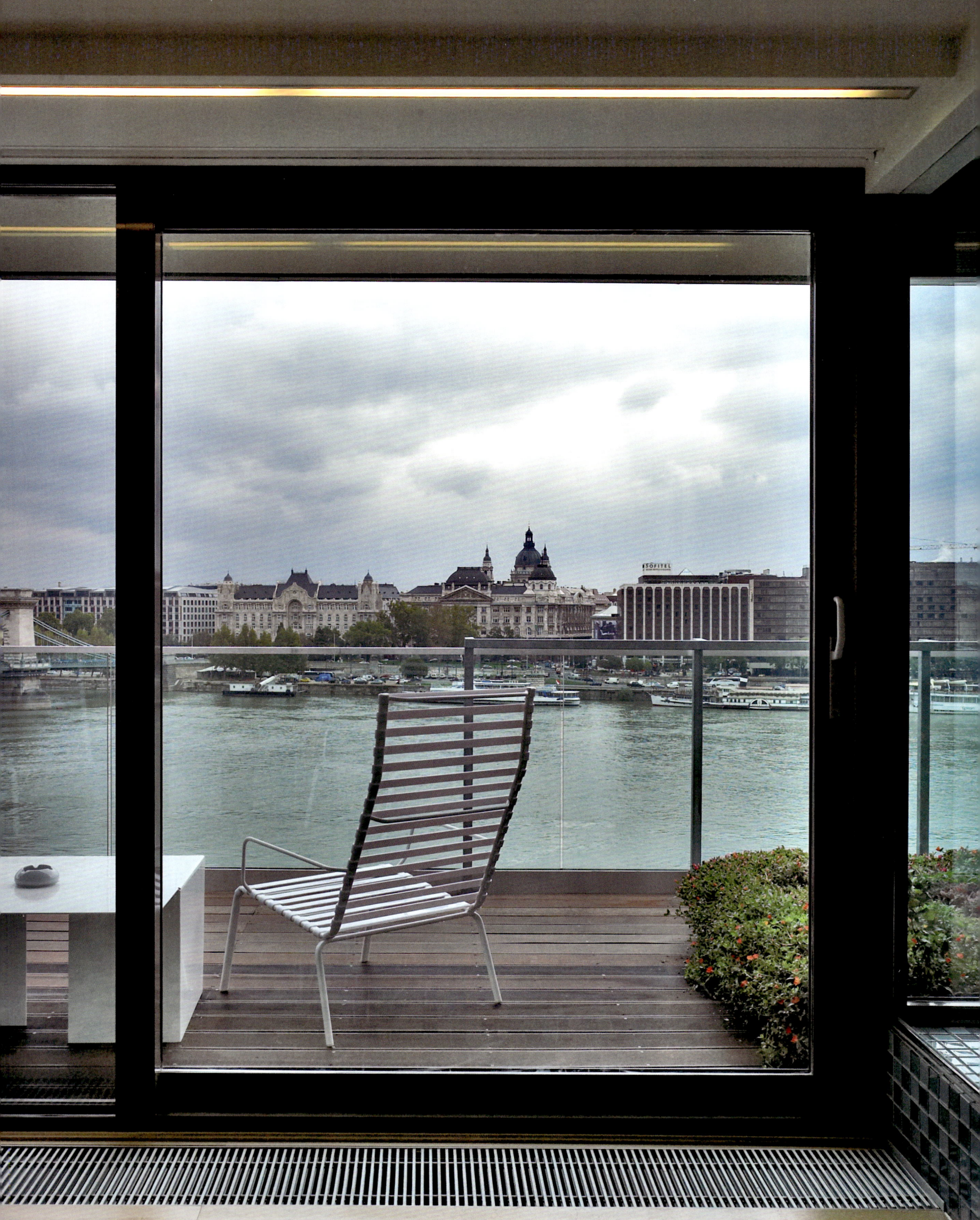

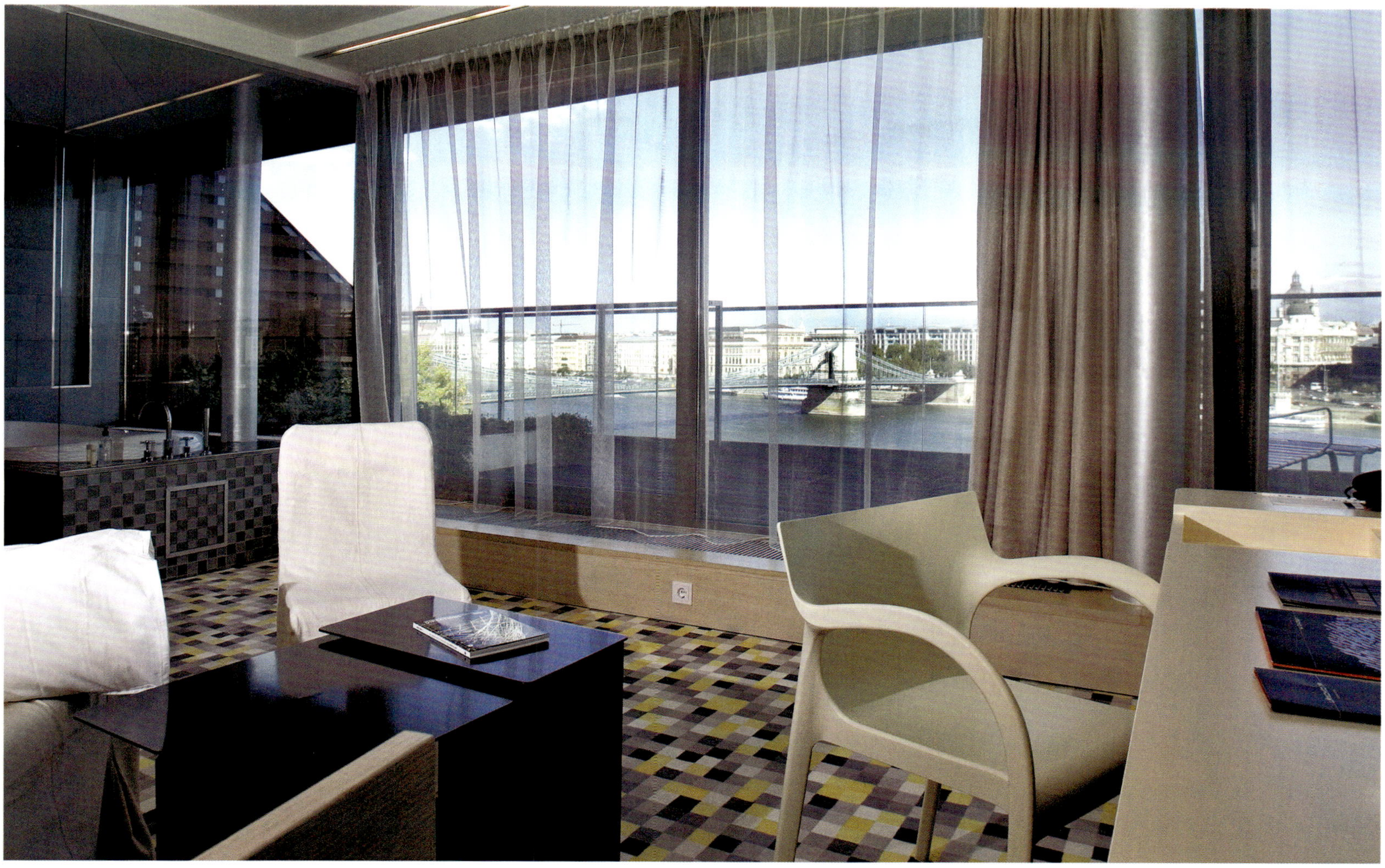

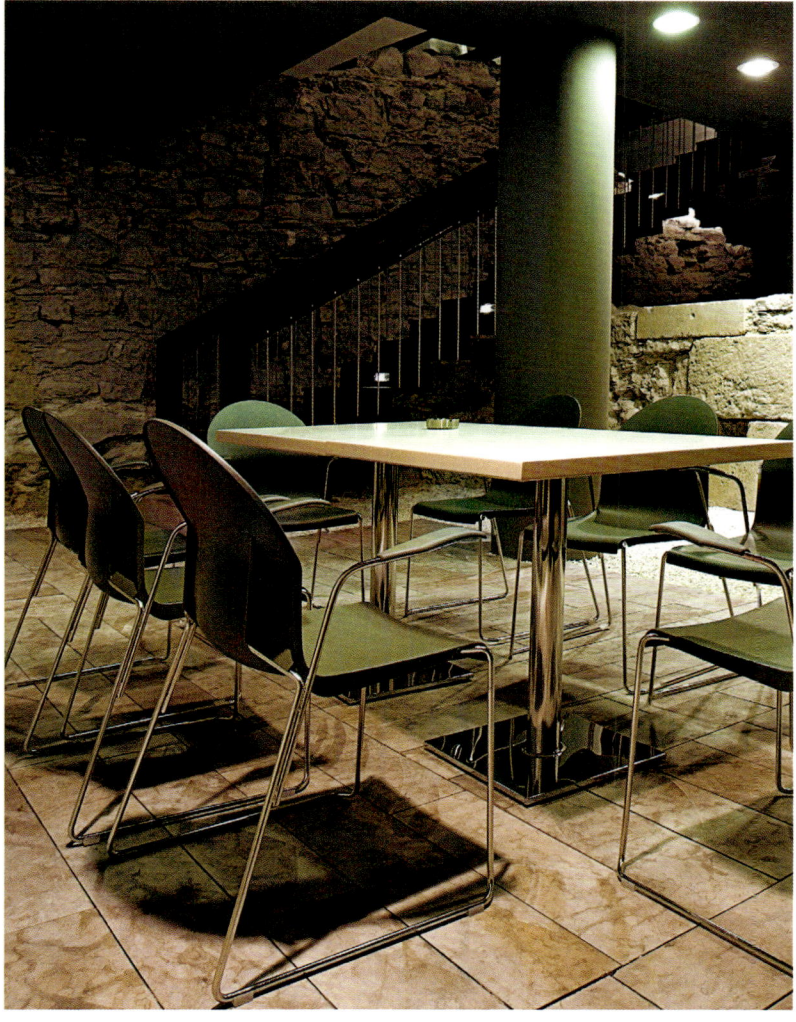

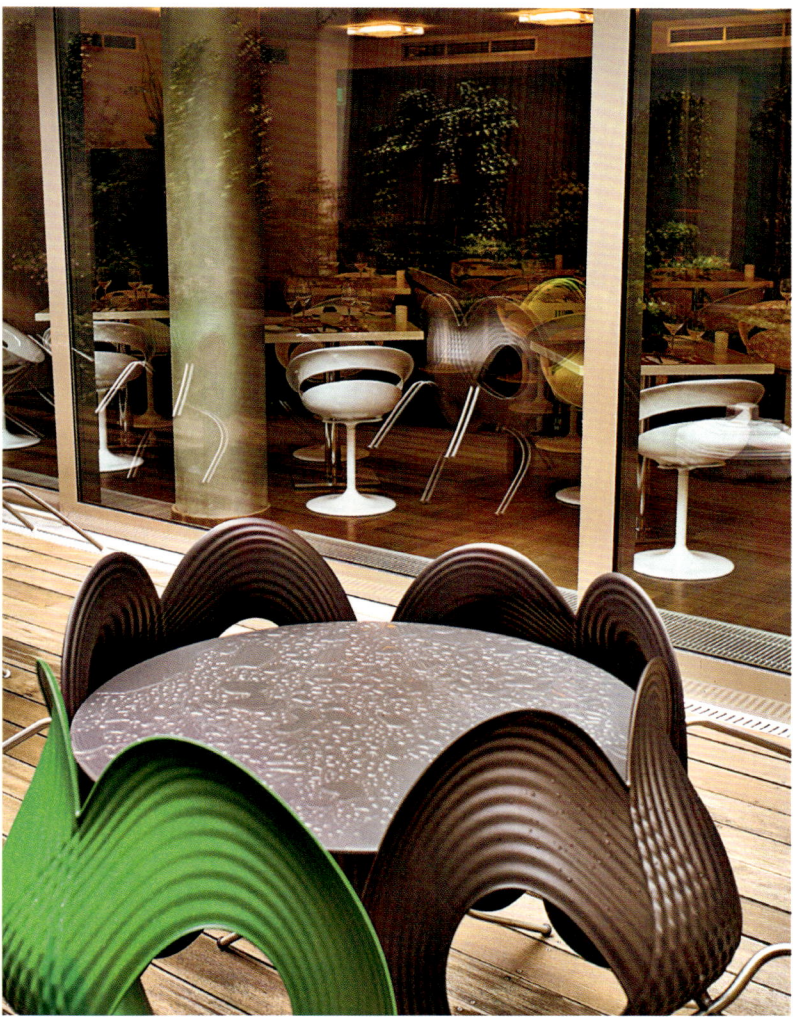

Ski & Golfresort Kitzhof

Kitzbühel, Austria

Schwarzseestraße 8–10
6370 Kitzbühel
Austria
Phone: +43 5356 632 110
Fax: +43 5356 632 1115
www.hotel-kitzhof.com

Price category: €
Rooms: 63 single rooms, 93 double rooms and 8 suites
Facilities: Kitz Lounge with bar and open fireplace, restaurant Weißer Hirsch with garden, à la carte restaurant Kaminstube, wine cellar, Kitz Spa
Services: Babysitting upon request
Located: 5 min walk from Kitzbühel center
Public transportation: 100 m from bus stop
Style: Innovative design with much old wood, glass, felt and modern furniture.

In the noble ski resort of Kitzbühel, the 164 room hotel sets a pleasantly fresh accent. It is situated directly on the city park only five minutes away from the center of town with its the famous Tyrolean houses and noble shops. The rooms have a cozy atmosphere with lots of wood and warm colors. There was no place for the Alpine chic that dominates elsewhere. From the terrace you can enjoy the inspiring view of the snow-covered peak of the Kitzbüheler Horn. The newly opened spa will help you relax.

Im Nobel-Skiort Kitzbühel setzt das 164-Zimmer-Hotel einen angenehmen, frischen Akzent. Es liegt direkt am Stadtpark, zum Ortskern mit seinen berühmten Tiroler Häusern und den Edel-Shops sind es nur fünf Minuten. Die Zimmer haben eine behagliche Atmosphäre mit viel Holz und warmen Farben. Auf den vielerorts grassierenden rustikalen Alpen-Chic wurde bewusst verzichtet. Von der Terrasse genießt man einen Traumblick auf die schneebedeckten Gipfel des Kitzbüheler Horns. Für Entspannung sorgt der neueröffnete Spa.

L'hôtel de 164 chambres apporte une note de fraîcheur et de confort à la station de ski huppée de Kitzbühel. Il est situé au sein-même du parc de la ville, à seulement cinq minutes du centre avec ses célèbres maisons tyroliennes et ses boutiques nobles. Les chambres ont une atmosphère douillette, avec beaucoup de bois et des couleurs chaudes. Le chic alpin rustique très répandu dans la région a été volontairement oublié ici. Depuis la terrasse, on peut profiter d'une vue de rêve sur les sommets enneigés du massif de Kitzbühel. Le spa récemment ouvert permet de se relaxer.

En la noble ciudad de Kitzbühel, famosa por su estación de esquí, el hotel de 164 habitaciones aporta un toque agradable y fresco. Se encuentra al lado del parque de la ciudad, a sólo cinco minutos del centro, con sus famosas casitas tirolesas y sus tiendas de lujo. Las habitaciones tienen una atmósfera muy agradable, con mucha madera y colores cálidos. Se prescindió conscientemente del rústico estilo chic alpino, muy común en esta zona. Desde la terraza se puede disfrutar de una maravillosa vista de las cimas nevadas del monte Kitzbühler Horn. El nuevo spa ofrece relajación a los huéspedes.

Questo hotel da 164 camere ha introdotto nella prestigiosa località sciistica di Kitzbühel un piacevole tocco di freschezza. Posto ai margini del parco civico, l'albergo dista soli cinque minuti dal centro cittadino con le sue famose case in stile tirolese e i raffinati negozi. L'atmosfera delle stanze, in cui predominano il legno e i colori caldi, è pensata per mettere gli ospiti a proprio agio, mentre si è volutamente rinunciato allo stile alpino rustico-chic che abbruttisce molte località di montagna. Dalla terrazza dell'albergo si può godere di una vista fantastica sulla cima innevata del Corno di Kitzbühel. Uno spa inaugurato di recente garantisce un perfetto relax.

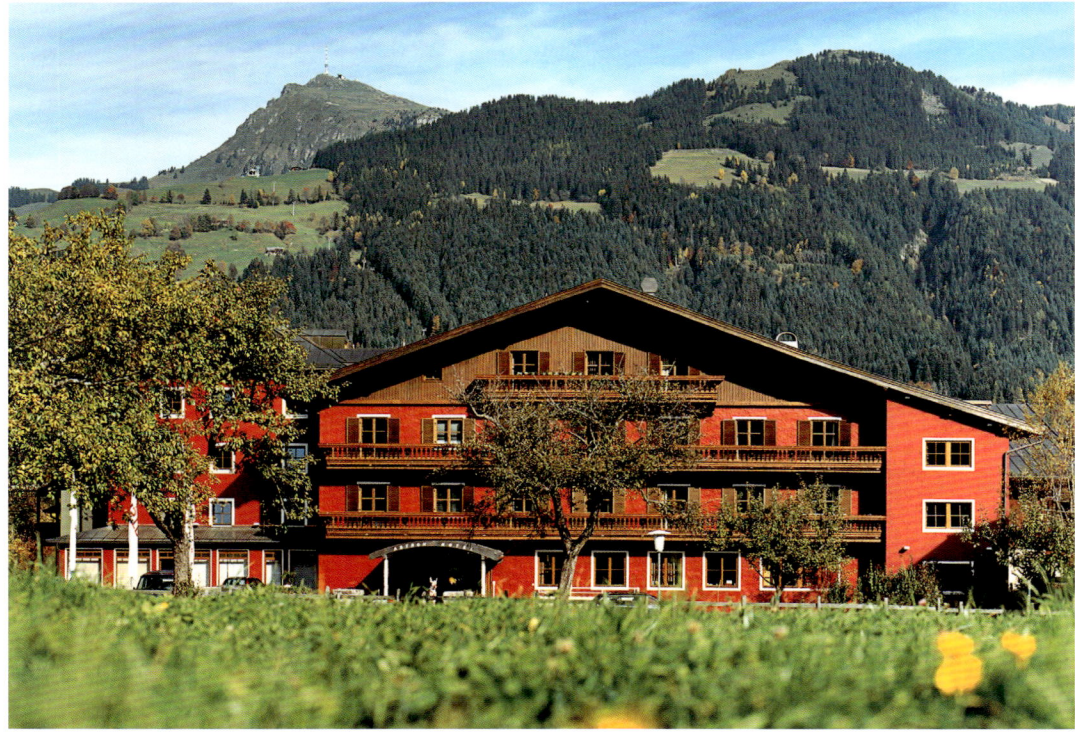
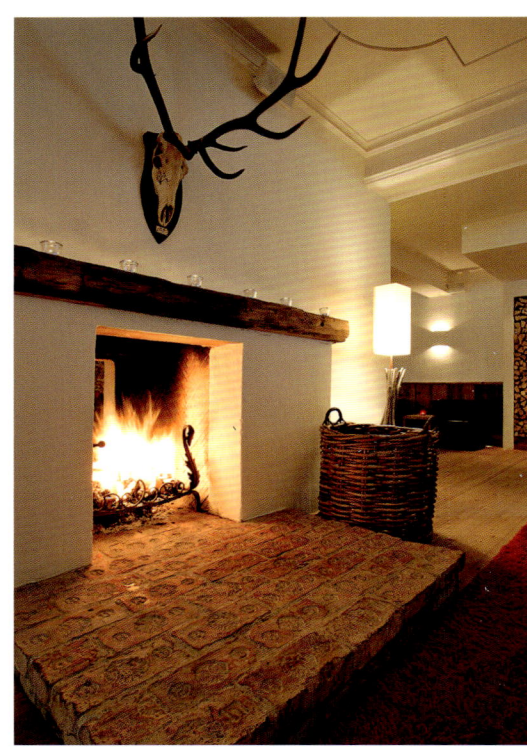

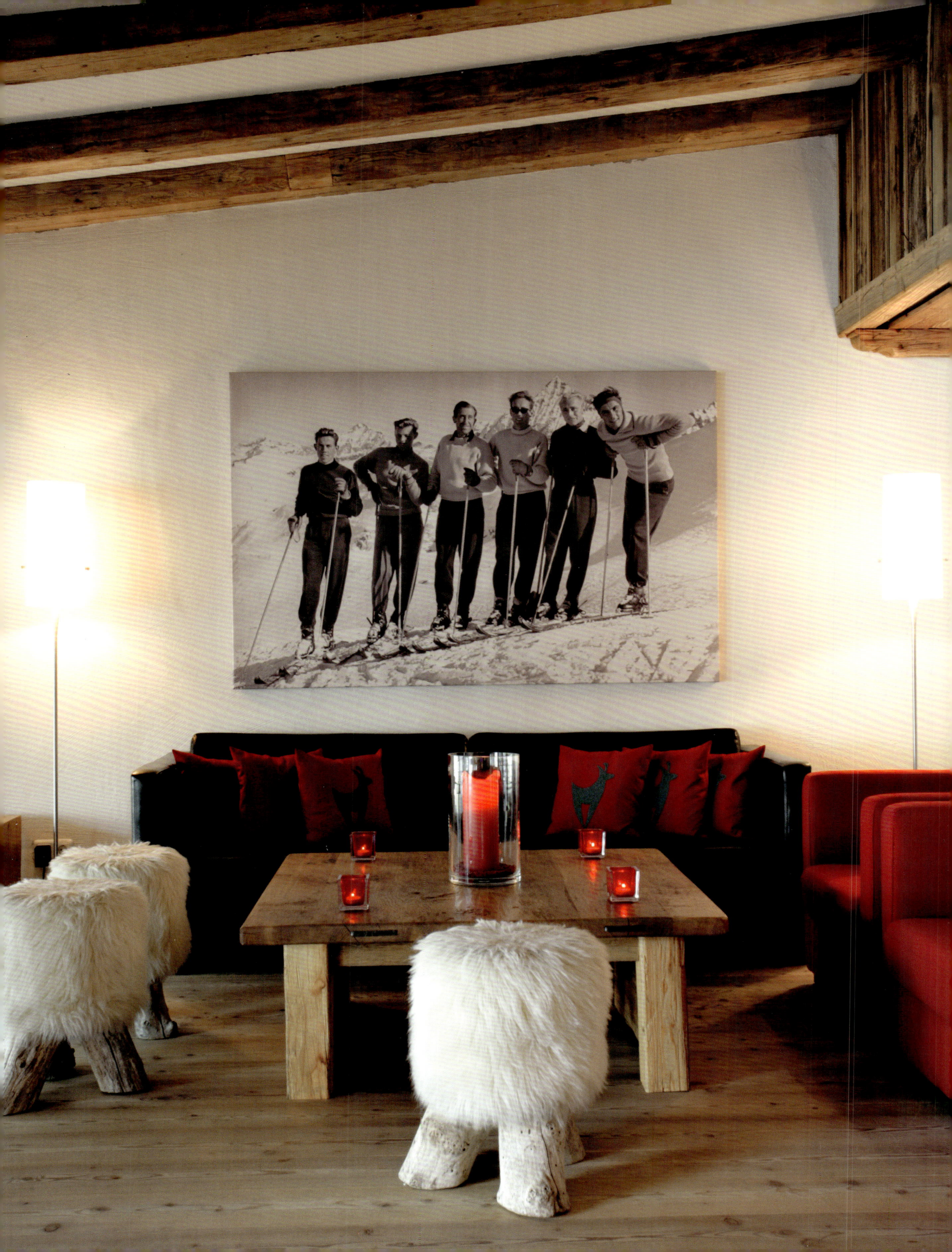

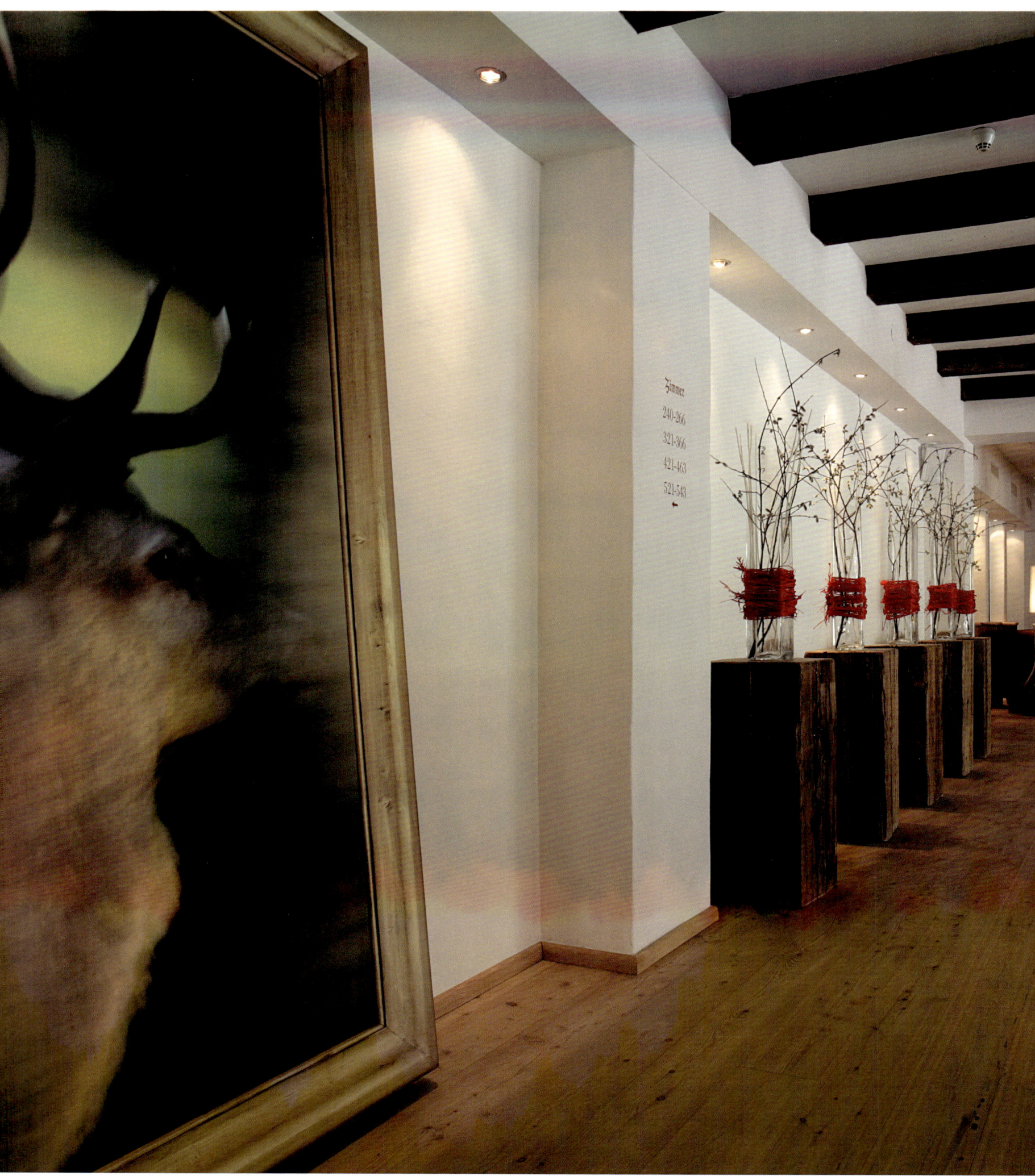

Zimmer
240-266
321-366
421-463
521-543

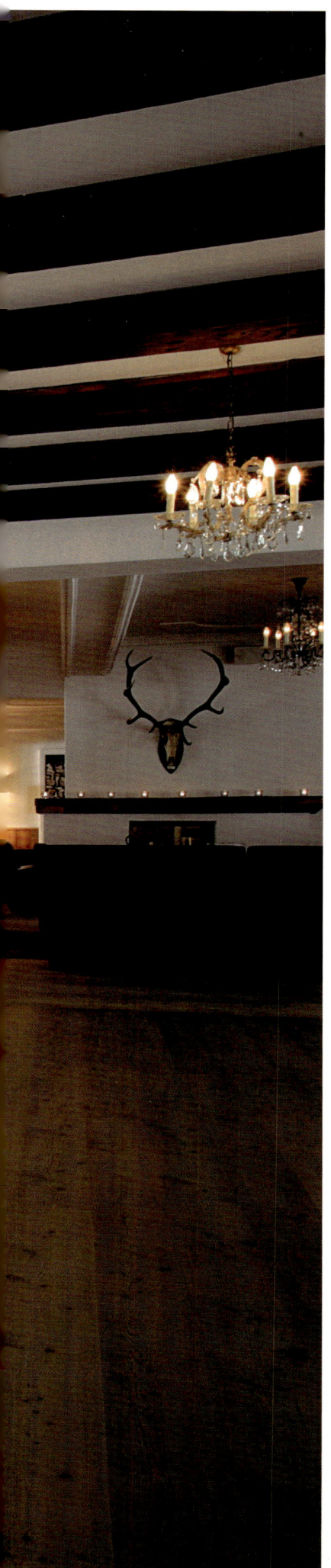

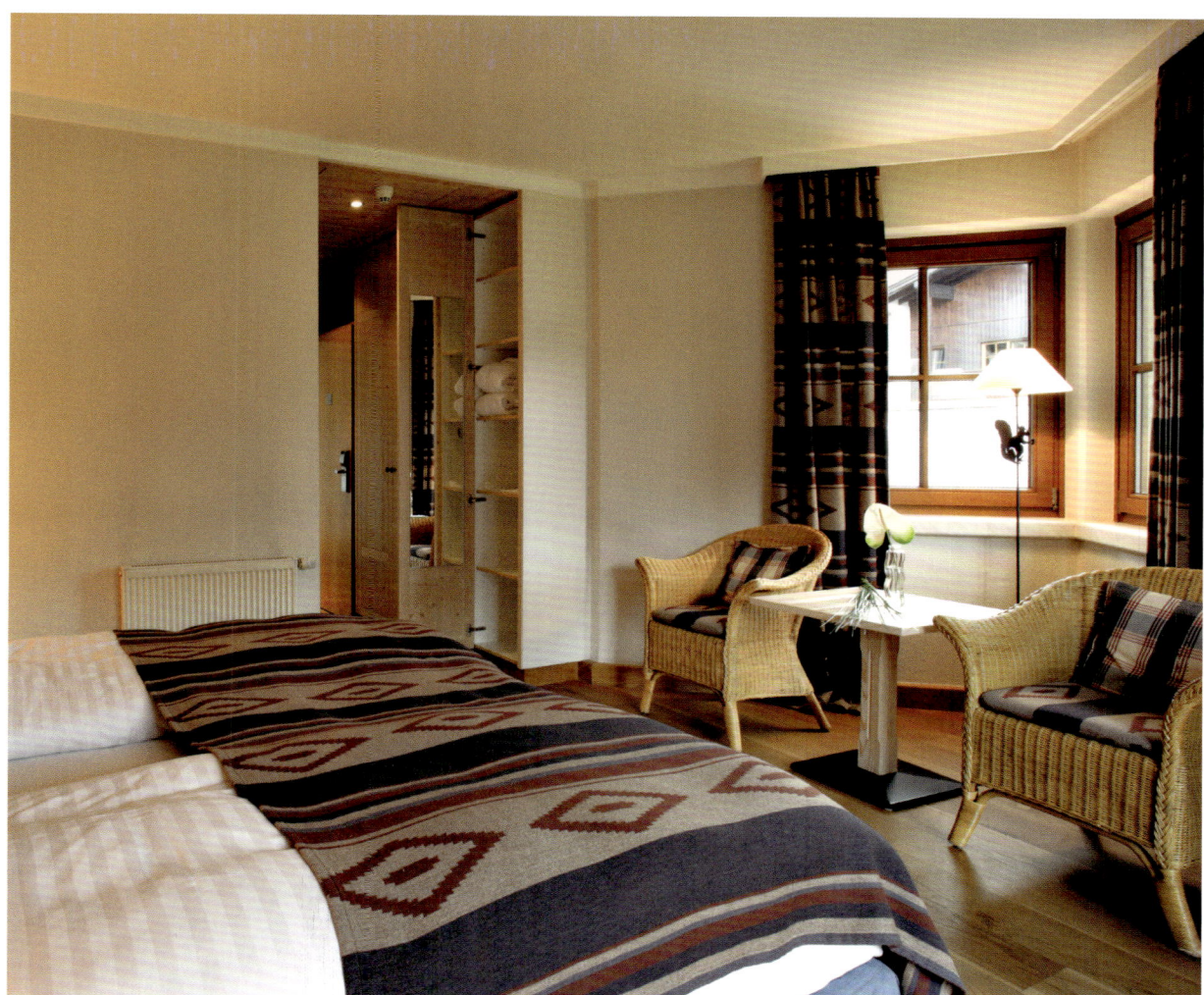

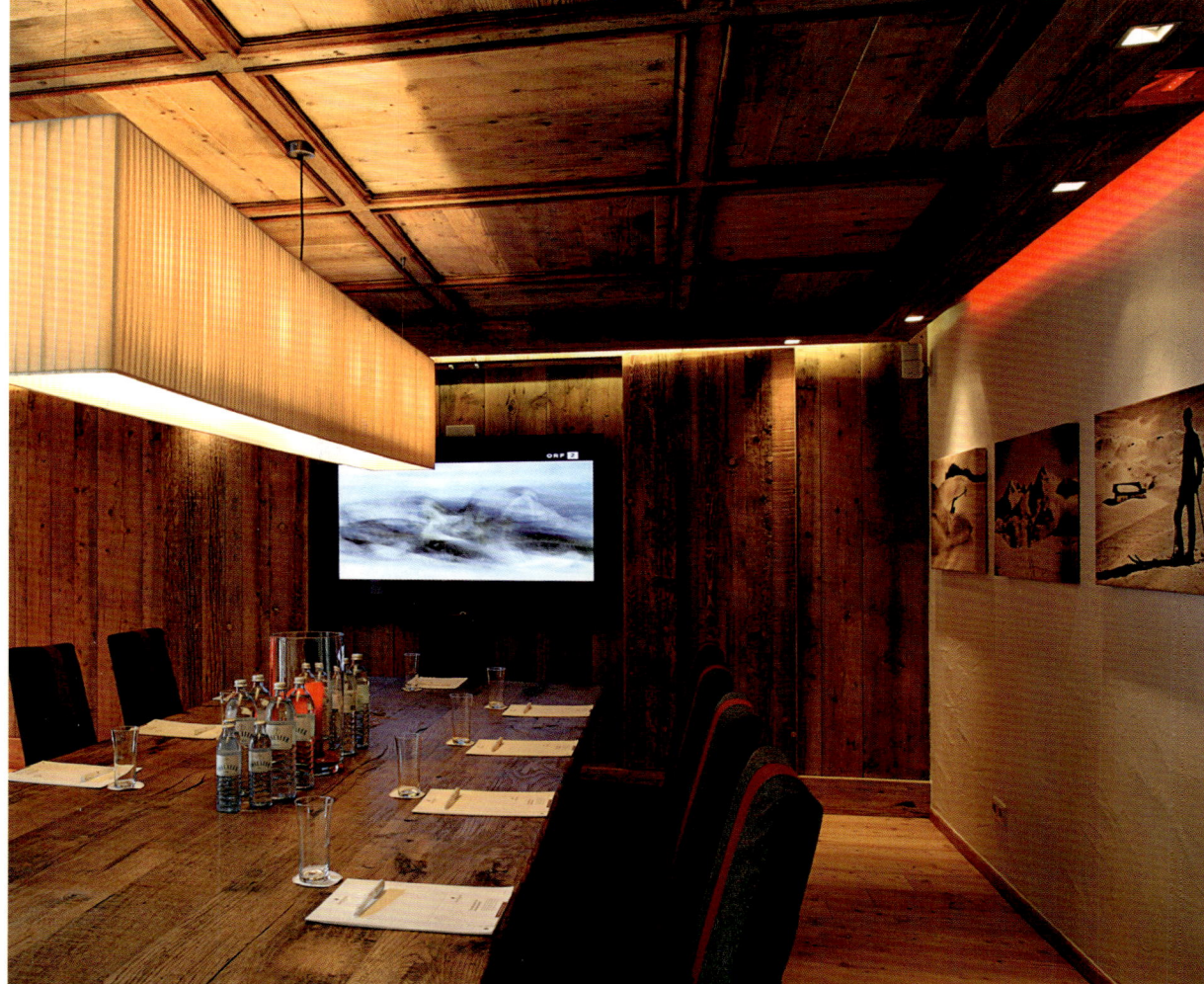

Schloss-Straße 19
5322 Hof bei Salzburg
Austria
Phone: +43 6229 2253 1500
Fax: +43 6229 2253 1557
www.schlossfuschlresort.at

Price category: €€€
Rooms: 110 rooms, 39 suites and 6 lake cottages
Facilities: Bar, restaurant, gourmet restaurant Imperial, Vinothek, spa, shop, fishery, classic cars
Services: Babysitting, room service, butler on request
Located: 20 km to the Salzburg city center
Public transportation: Bus, train
Style: Historic building

After total renovation in 2006, the luxurious palace hotel can only be seen as a total work of art. The location on a peninsula at Lake Fuschl is right out of a dream. The interior of the 110 rooms and suites is sumptuous and noble with all their carefully restored antiques. 170 works of art by old masters worthy of places in museums as well as a collection of really rare classic cars underscore the hotel's top class. One of the highlights is the Sissi Suite in the listed tower with a 360 degree panoramic view of the lake and the mountains.

Nach kompletter Renovierung im Jahr 2006 präsentiert sich das luxuriöse Schlosshotel als Gesamtkunstwerk. Traumhaft ist die Lage auf einer Halbinsel am Fuschlsee. Kostbar und edel ist das Interieur der 110 Zimmer und Suiten, die mit sorgsam restaurierten Antiquitäten eingerichtet wurden. 170 Kunstwerke Alter Meister von musealem Rang wie auch eine Oldtimer-Sammlung mit wahren Raritäten unterstreichen die Extraklasse. Eines der Highlights ist die Sissi-Suite im denkmalgeschützten Turm mit 360-Grad-Panoramablick auf See und Berge.

Après une rénovation complète en 2006, ce palace hôtel luxueux se présente comme une œuvre d'art totale. Il bénéficie d'un splendide emplacement sur un promontoire au-dessus du lac de Fuschl. L'intérieur des 110 chambres et suites est opulent et élégant, et décoré d'antiquités soigneusement restaurées. 170 œuvres d'art de vieux maîtres dignes des plus grands musées, ainsi qu'une collection de voitures anciennes comportant de vraies raretés, soulignent la classe de l'hôtel. Un de ses joyaux est la suite Sissi dans la tour classée, qui offre une vue panoramique à 360 degrés sur le lac et les montagnes.

Tras una completa renovación en 2006, el lujoso hotel-palacio se presenta como una auténtica obra de arte. Su ubicación, en una península del lago Fuschl, es maravillosa. El interior de las 110 habitaciones y suites es exquisito y refinado, con abundantes antigüedades cuidadosamente restauradas. La clase superior del hotel viene reforzada por 170 obras de arte firmadas por antiguos maestros y dignas de cualquier museo, así como por una colección de coches de época que incluye auténticas rarezas. En la torre, monumento histórico protegido, se encuentra una de las atracciones principales del hotel, la suite Sissi, con una vista panorámica de 360 grados del lago y las montañas.

Dopo la completa ristrutturazione del 2006, questo lussuoso hotel situato in un castello è diventato una vera e propria opera d'arte. Incantevole è già la sua posizione, una penisola che si inoltra nel lago Fuschl. Preziosi e raffinati gli interni delle 110 tra camere e suite, arredate con pezzi d'antiquariato accuratamente restaurati. L'eccellenza della casa è sottolineata dalla presenza di 170 opere d'arte di maestri del passato, degne di figurare in un museo, e di una collezione auto d'epoca che comprende autentiche rarità. Uno dei punti di forza messi a disposizione del cliente è la suite Sissi, situata in una torre sottoposta a tutela monumentale e dalla quale si gode di una vista a 360° sul lago e sulle montagne.

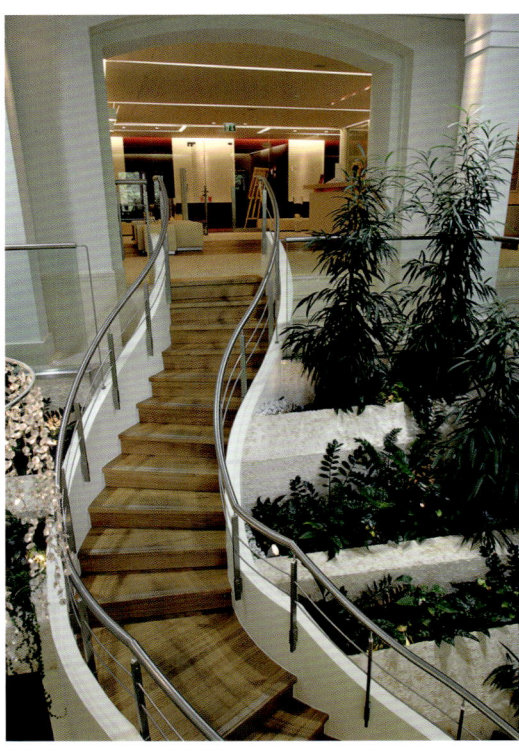
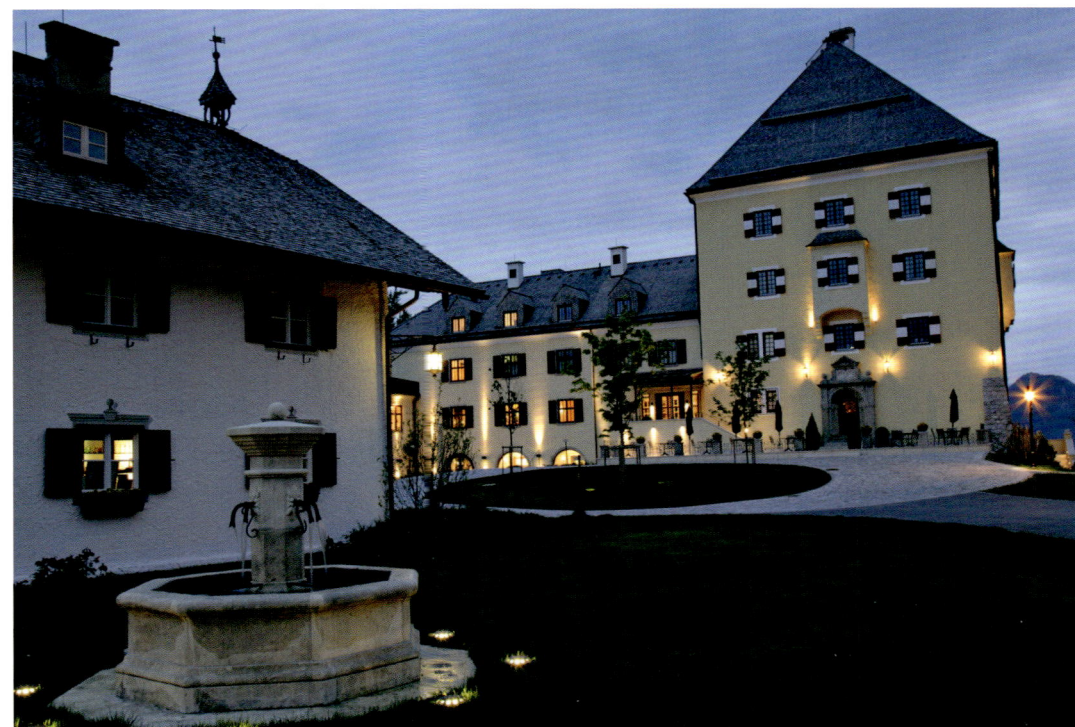

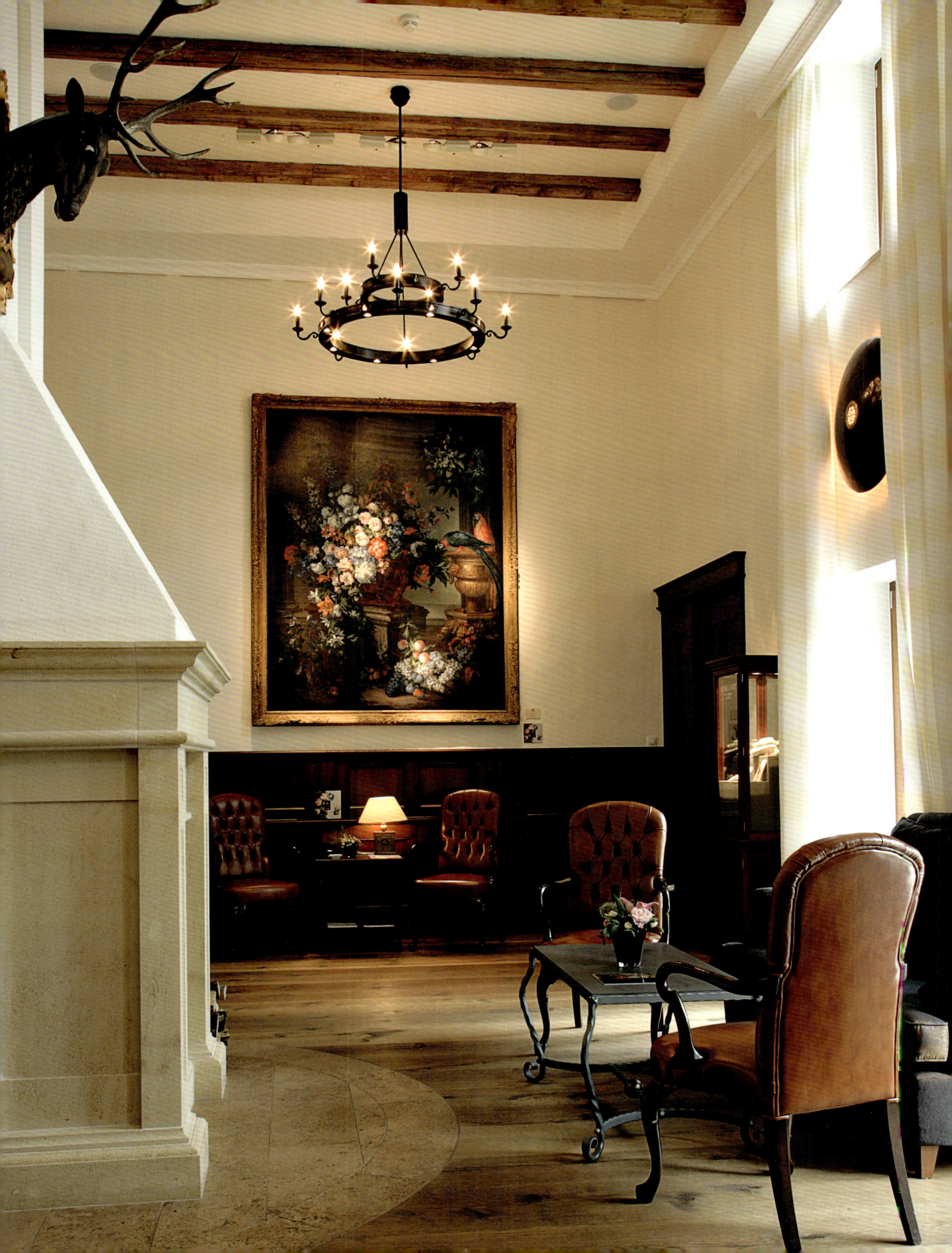

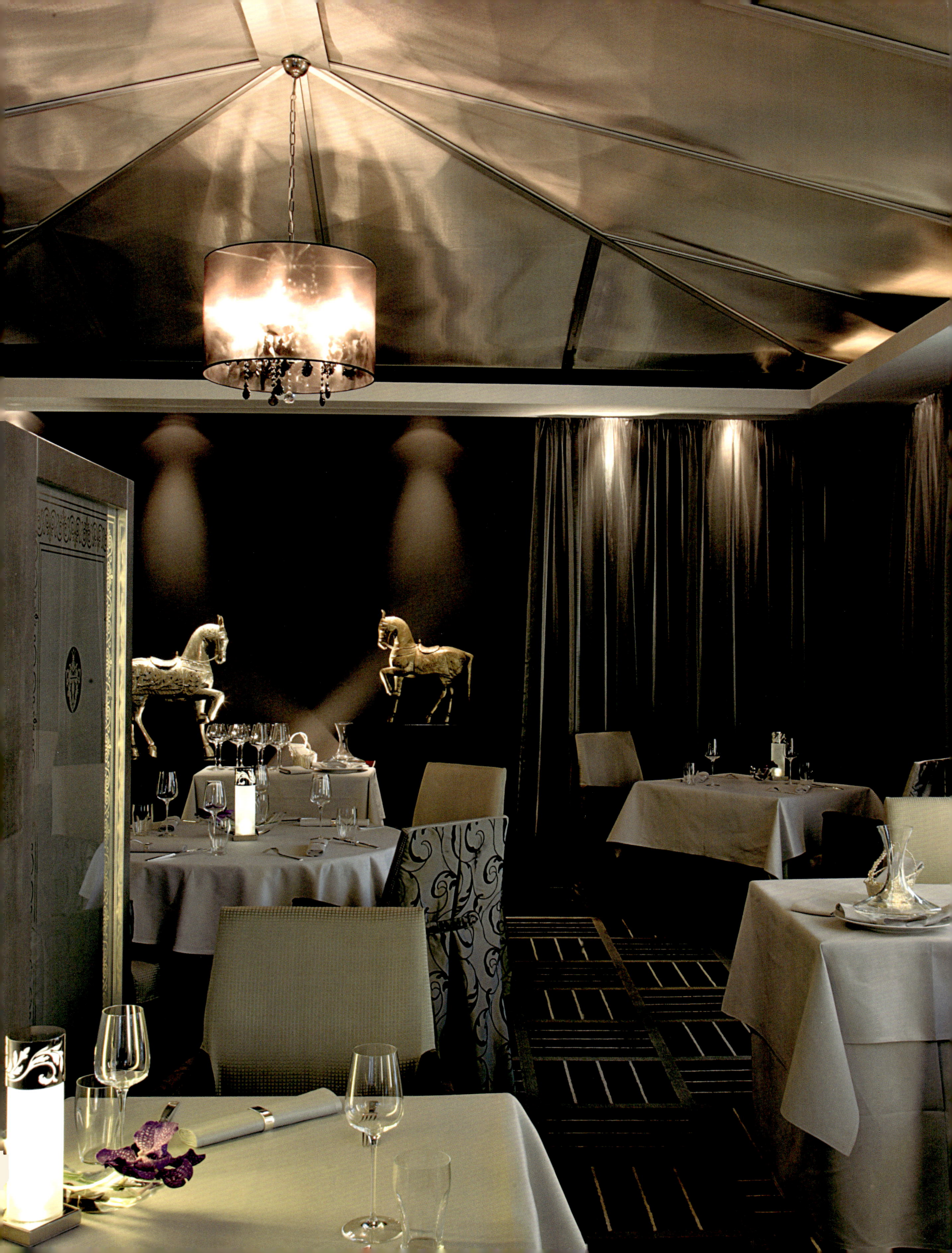

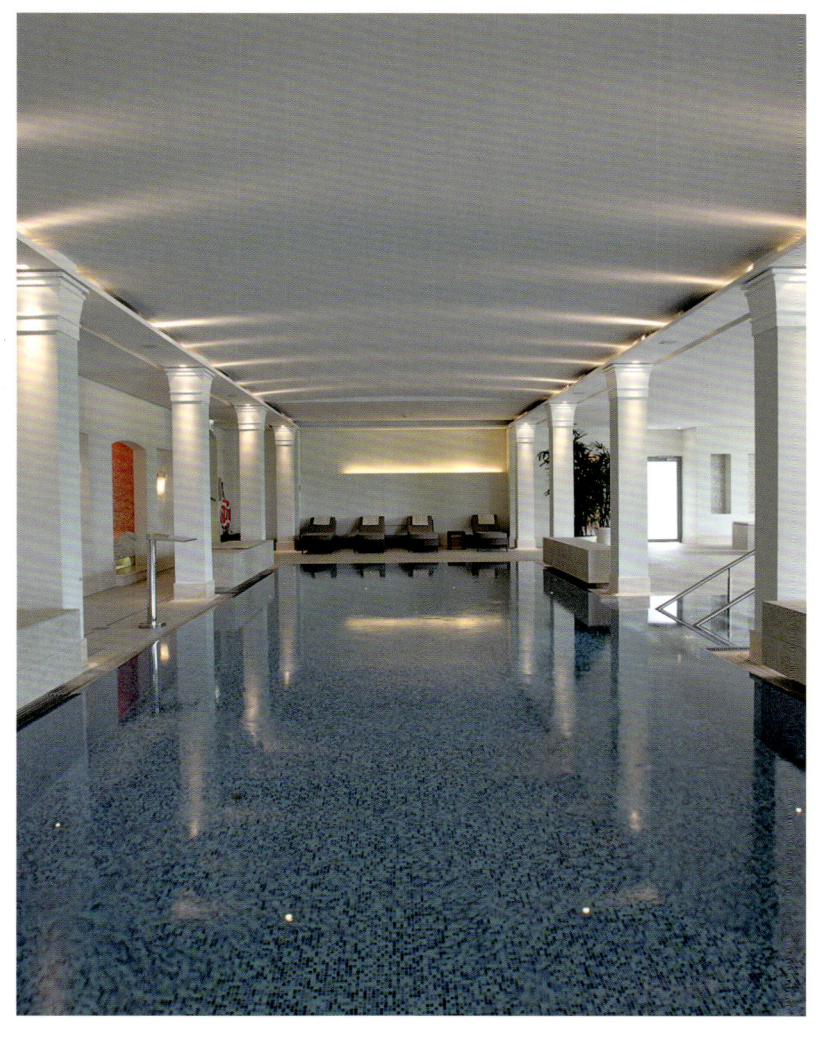

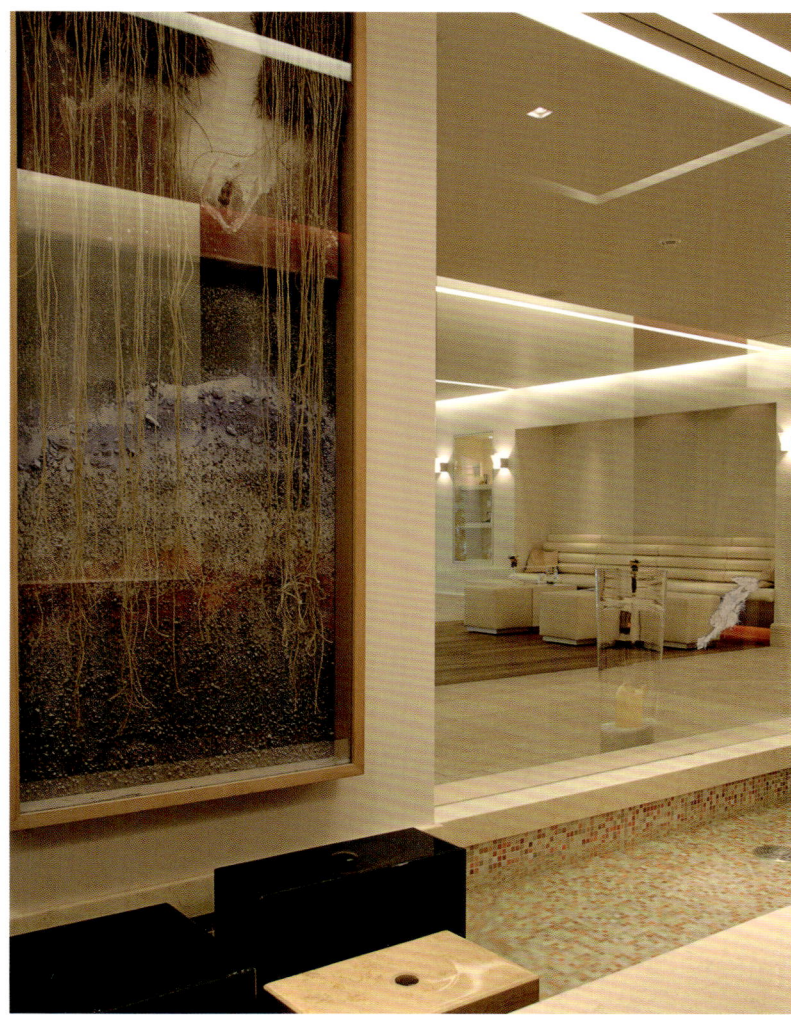

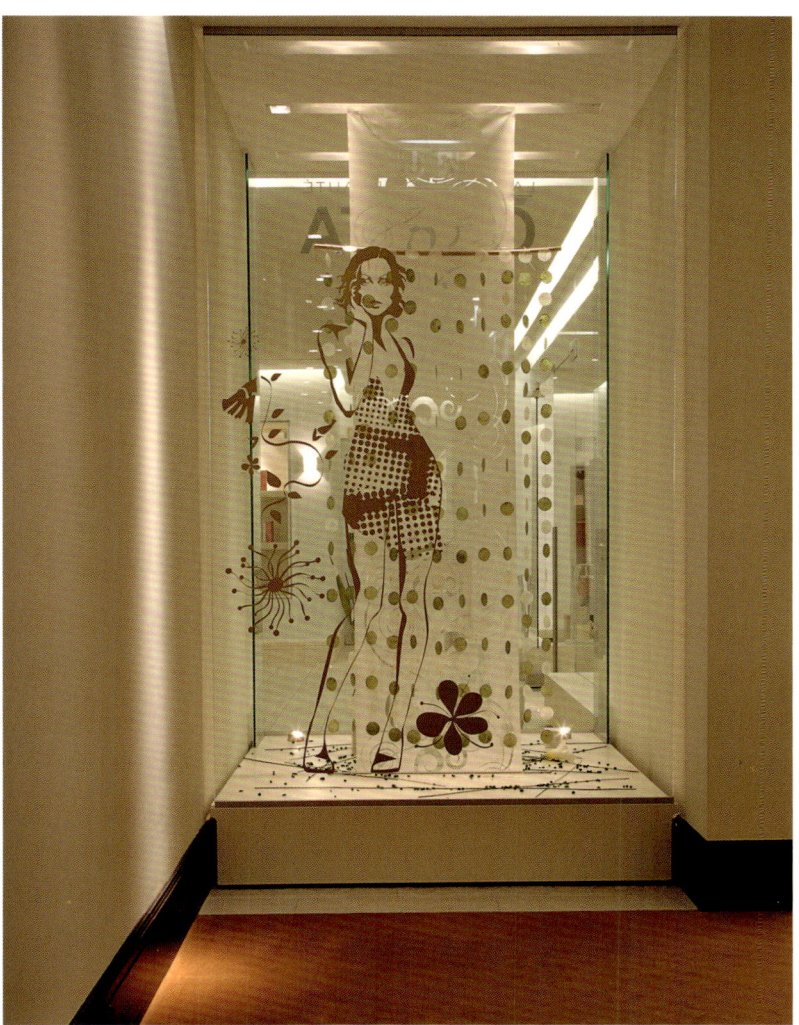

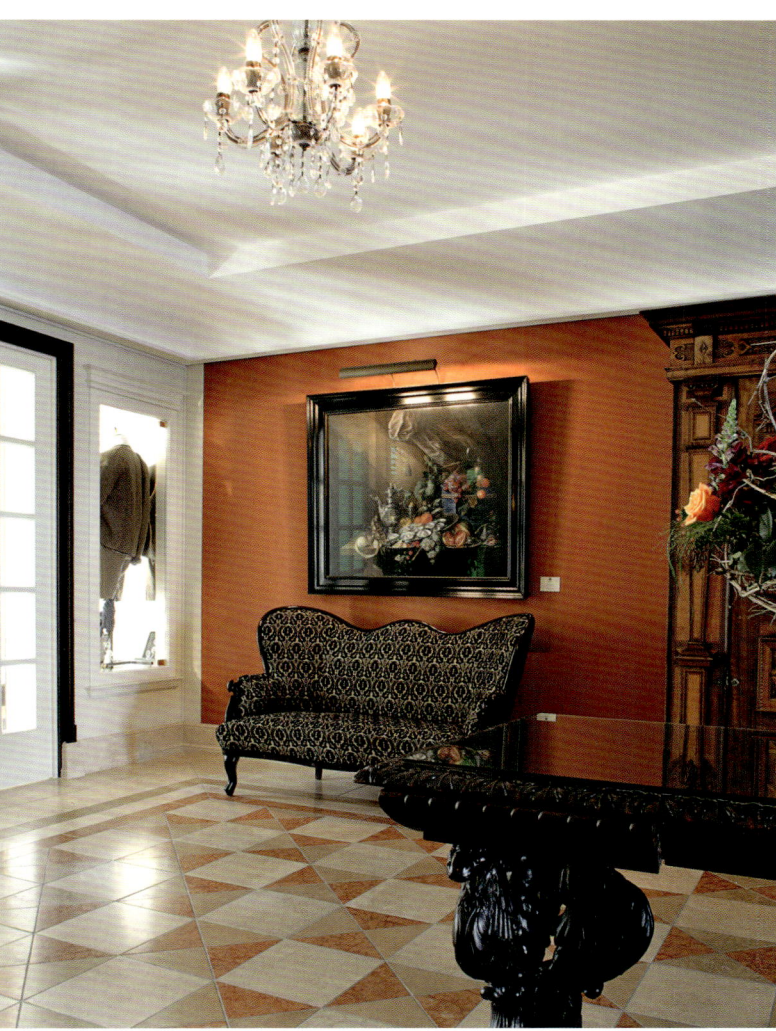

Palais Coburg Residenz

Vienna, Austria

Coburgbastei 4
1010 Wien
Austria
Phone: +43 1 518 180
Fax: +43 1 518 181 00
www.palais-coburg.com

Price category: €€€€
Rooms: 35 fully equipped suites
Facilities: Gourmet restaurant, wine bistro & bar, 6 wine cellars, spa, sun terrace, fitness room
Services: 24 h room service, limousine service, babysitting, private dining and sightseeing
Located: In the city center, 1st district
Public transportation: Underground U4 Stadtpark, U1, U3 Stephansplatz;
tram 1, 2 Weihburggasse
Style: Luxury hotel in a city palace

The grand splendor of imperial Austria is mirrored by the palace in the heart of the old city of Vienna built by Duke Ferdinand of Saxe-Coburg & Gotha from 1840 to 1845. The gold-leafed plaster moulding, splendid paintings and pompous stairway have been carefully restored and contrasted by modern structural details. There are 35 generously sized suites designed in different styles to live in, from the elegant Imperial Suites to modern loft suites. The wine cellar stocked with 60,000 items is a real sensation.

Die ganze Pracht des alten Österreichs darf sich in dem 1840 bis 1845 von Herzog Ferdinand von Sachsen-Coburg und Gotha erbauten Palais im Herzen der Wiener Altstadt entfalten. Die vergoldeten Stuckaturen, prunkvollen Gemälde und repräsentativen Treppenaufgänge wurden sorgfältig restauriert und mit modernen Baudetails kontrastiert. Wohnen kann man in 35 großzügigen Suiten, die in unterschiedlichen Stilrichtungen gestaltet sind, von den eleganten Imperialsuiten bis zu den modernen Loftsuiten. Als sensationell gilt der Weinkeller mit seinen 60 000 Positionen.

Toute la gloire de la vieille Autriche s'expose dans ce palace situé au cœur de la vieille ville de Vienne, qui a été construit entre 1840 et 1845 par Le duc Ferdinand de Saxe-Coburg et Gotha. Les stucs plaquées or, les tableaux pompeux et les escaliers représentatives ont été très soigneusement rénovés et contrastent avec les détails de construction modernes. On peut séjourner dans l'une des 35 confortables suites, qui ont été créées dans différents styles, des élégantes Suites Impériales aux modernes suites loft. La cave à vins et ses 60.000 bouteilles jouissent d'une formidable réputation.

Toda la majestuosidad de la antigua Austria se muestra en este palacio, construido por Fernando de Sajonia-Coburgo-Gotha en el corazón del casco histórico vienés entre 1840 y 1845. Los estucados dorados, las fastuosas pinturas y las características escaleras; todo fue cuidadosamente restaurado y contrastado con detalles arquitectónicos modernos. El hotel dispone de 35 suites muy amplias, decoradas en los estilos más diversos, desde las elegantes suites imperiales hasta las modernas suites en el ático. La bodega, con sus más de 60.000 referencias, goza de gran renombre.

Tutto lo splendore della vecchia Austria rivive in questo palazzo nel cuore del centro storico di Vienna, costruito tra il 1840 e il 1845 da Ferdinando II di Sassonia-Coburgo-Gotha. Gli stucchi dorati, i fastosi dipinti e le caratteristiche scalinate sono stati accuratamente restaurati e inseriti in un calcolato contrasto con la modernità degli altri dettagli architettonici. Gli ospiti possono risiedere in 35 magnifiche suite arredate in stili diversi, dalle eleganti suite imperiali fino alle più moderne suite collocate nei loft. Eccezionale la cantina, che offre 60.000 bottiglie.

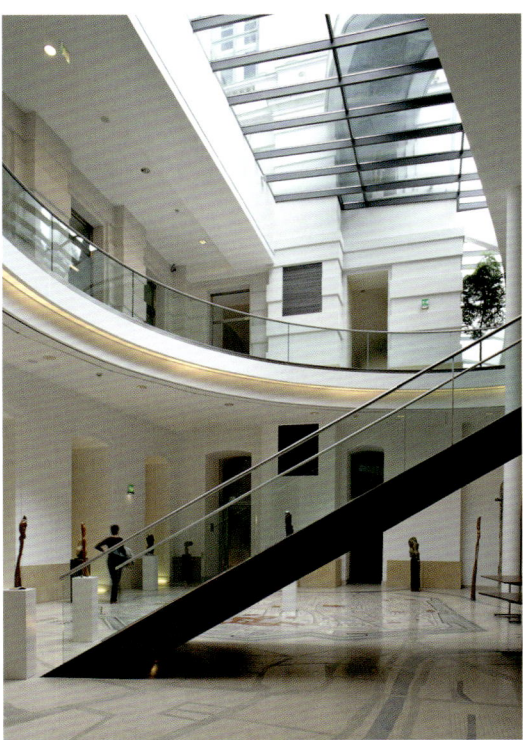
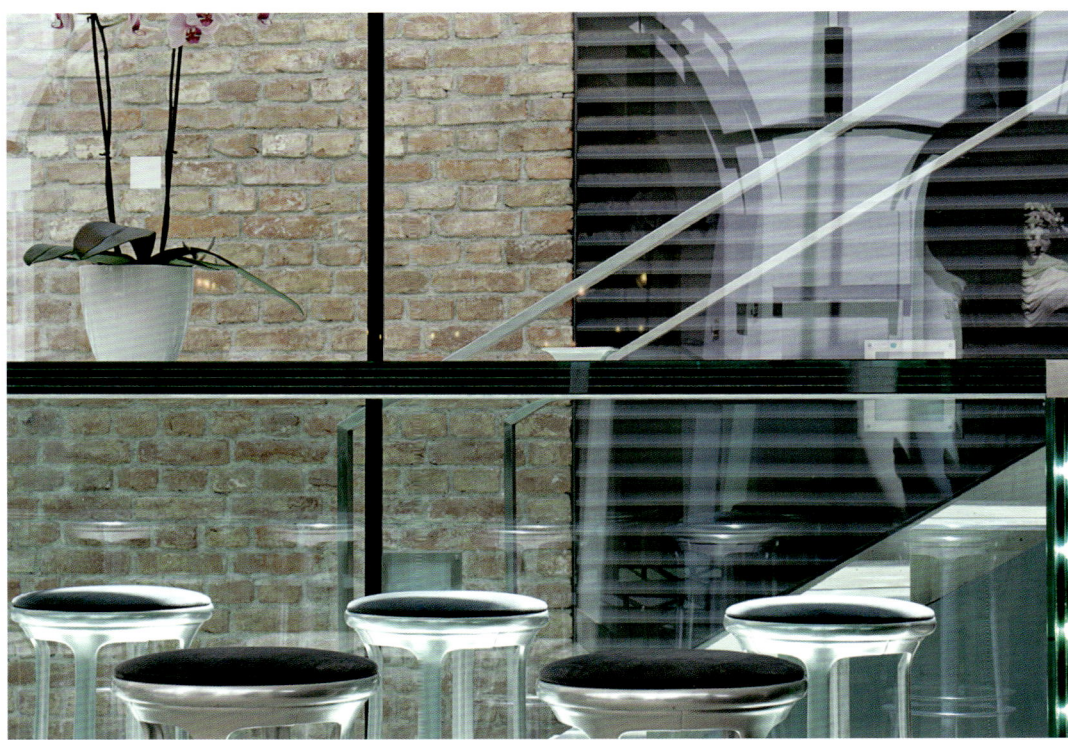

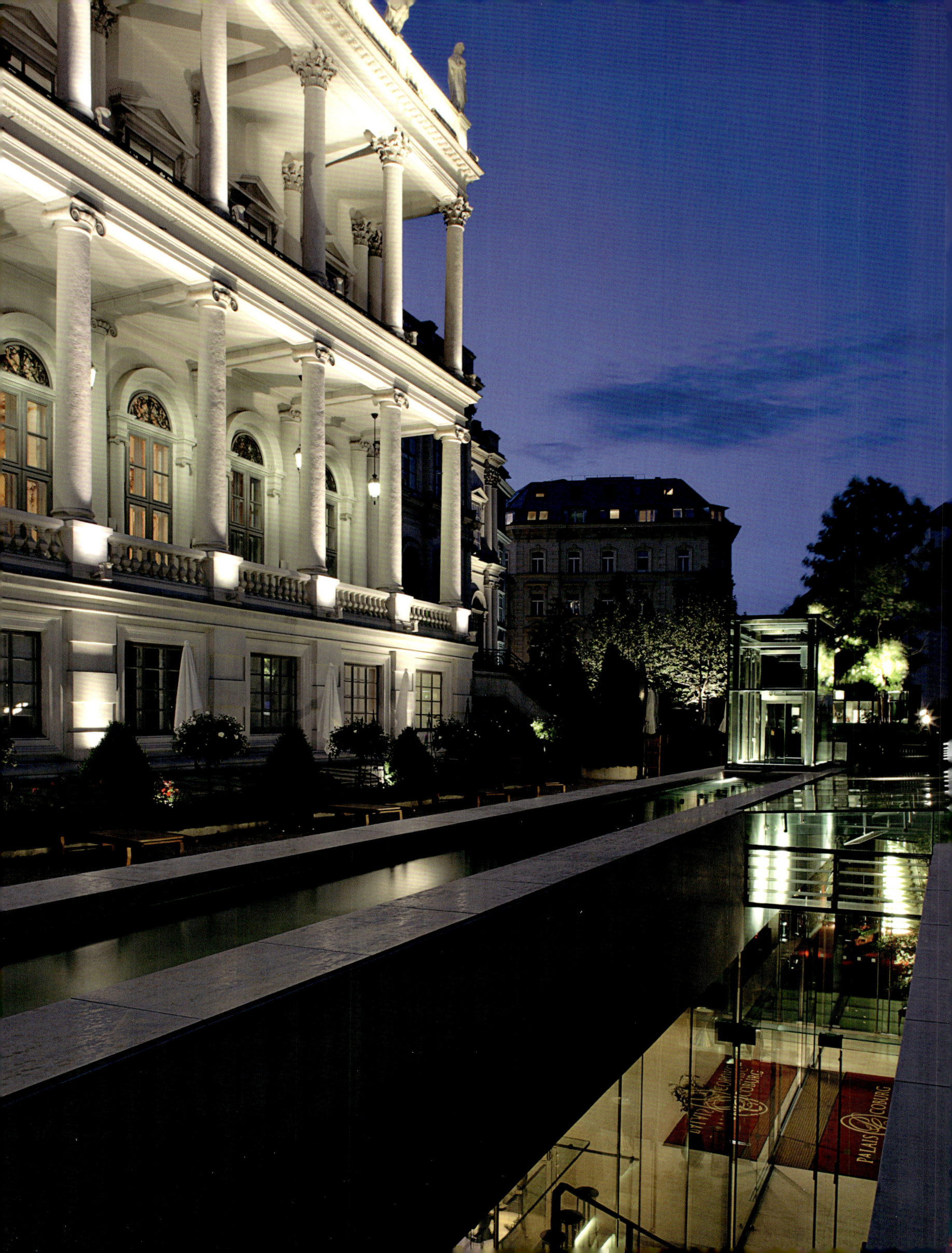

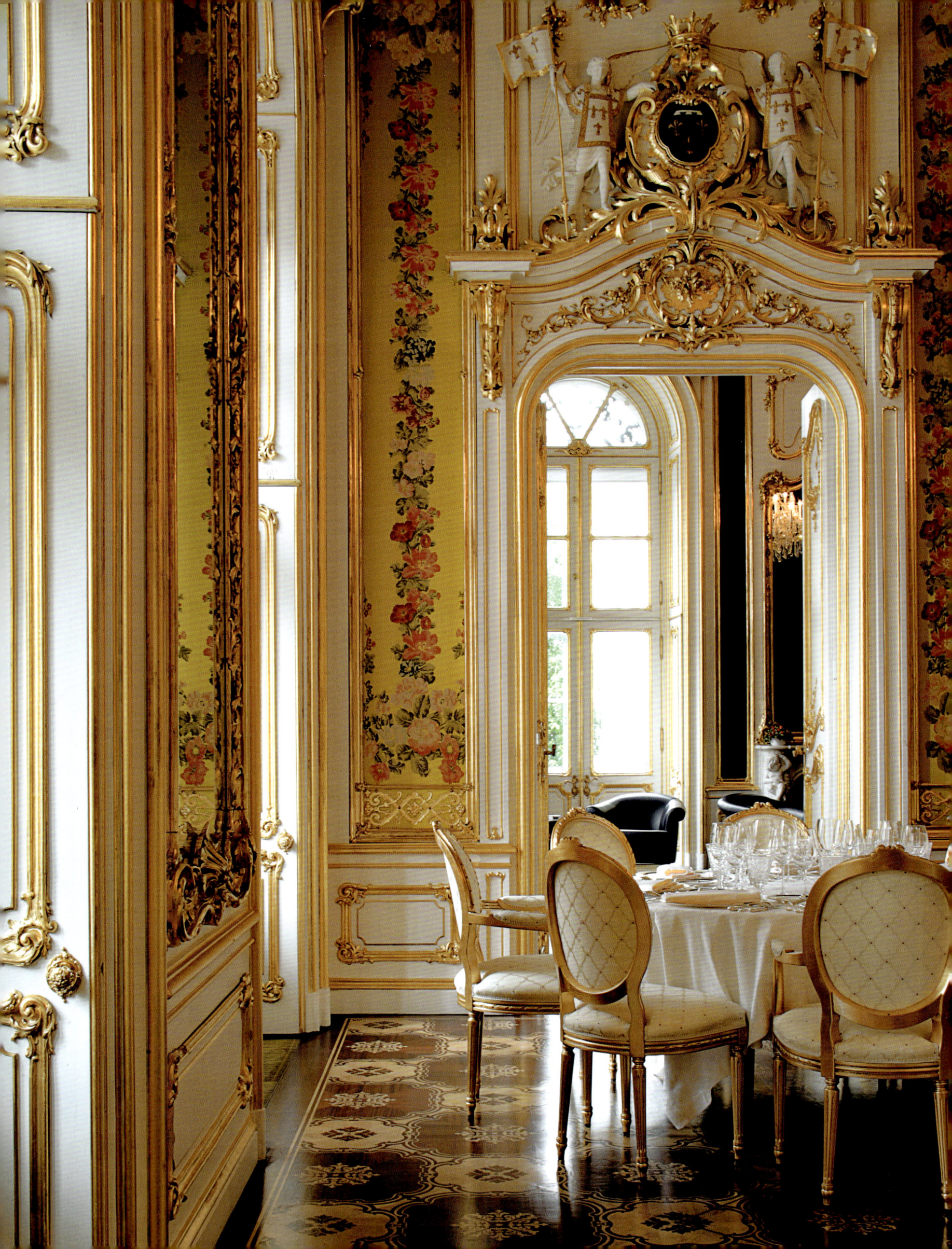

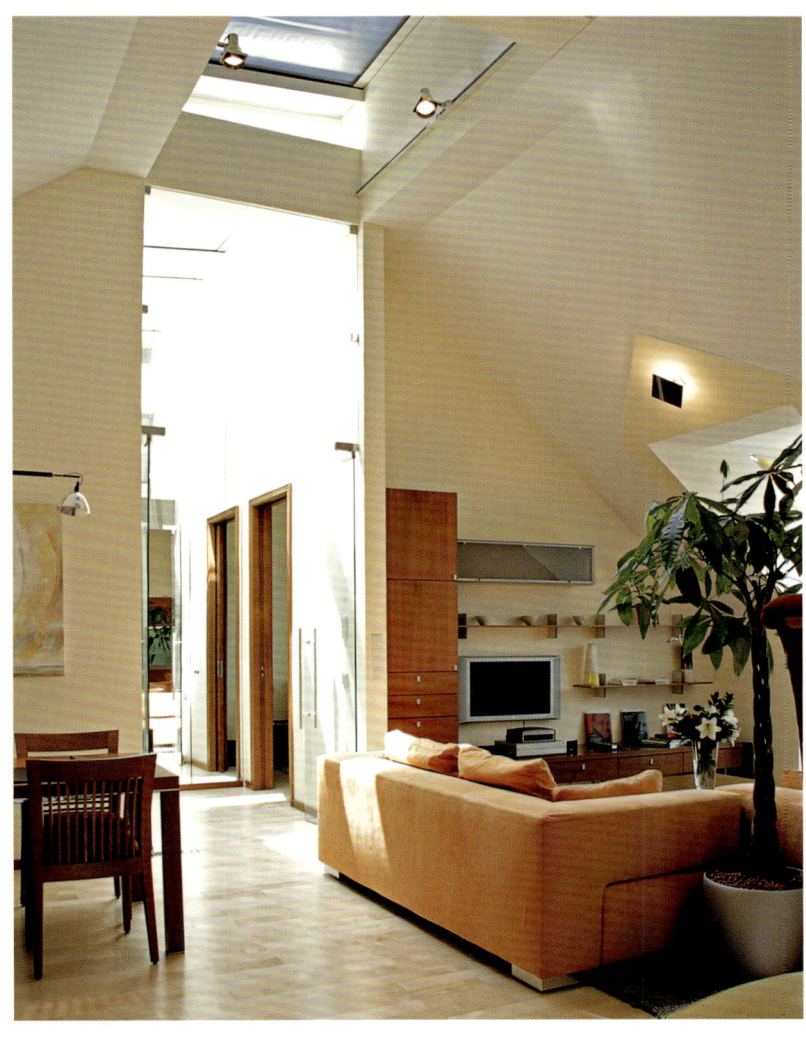
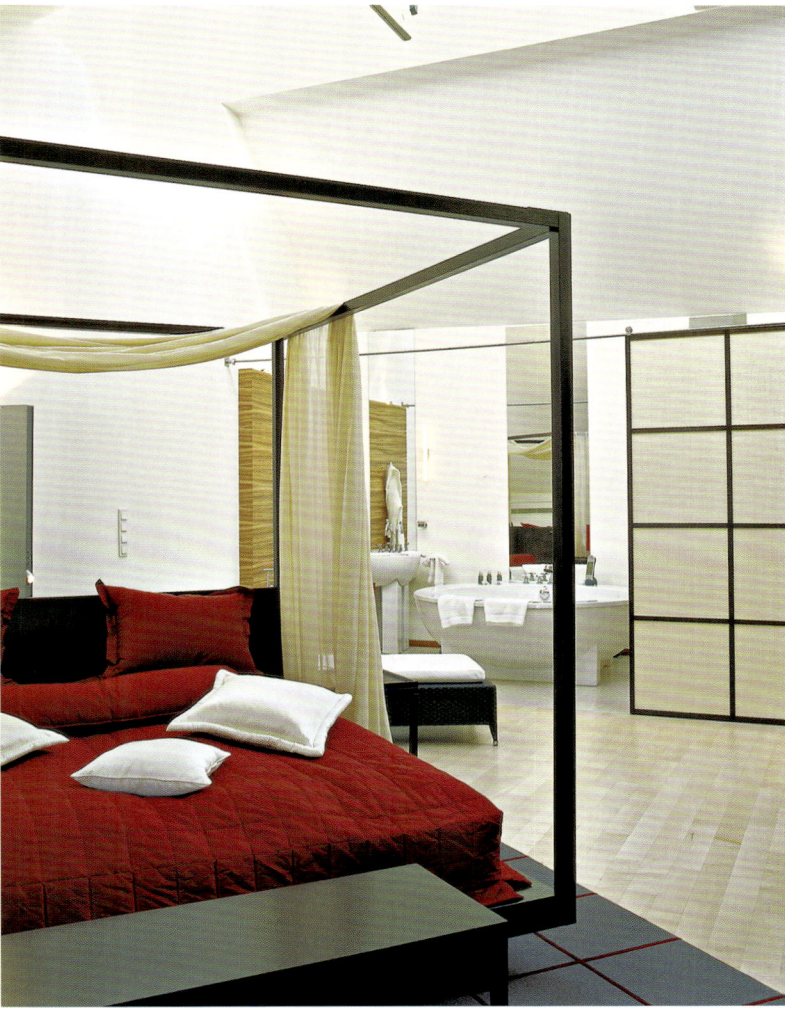
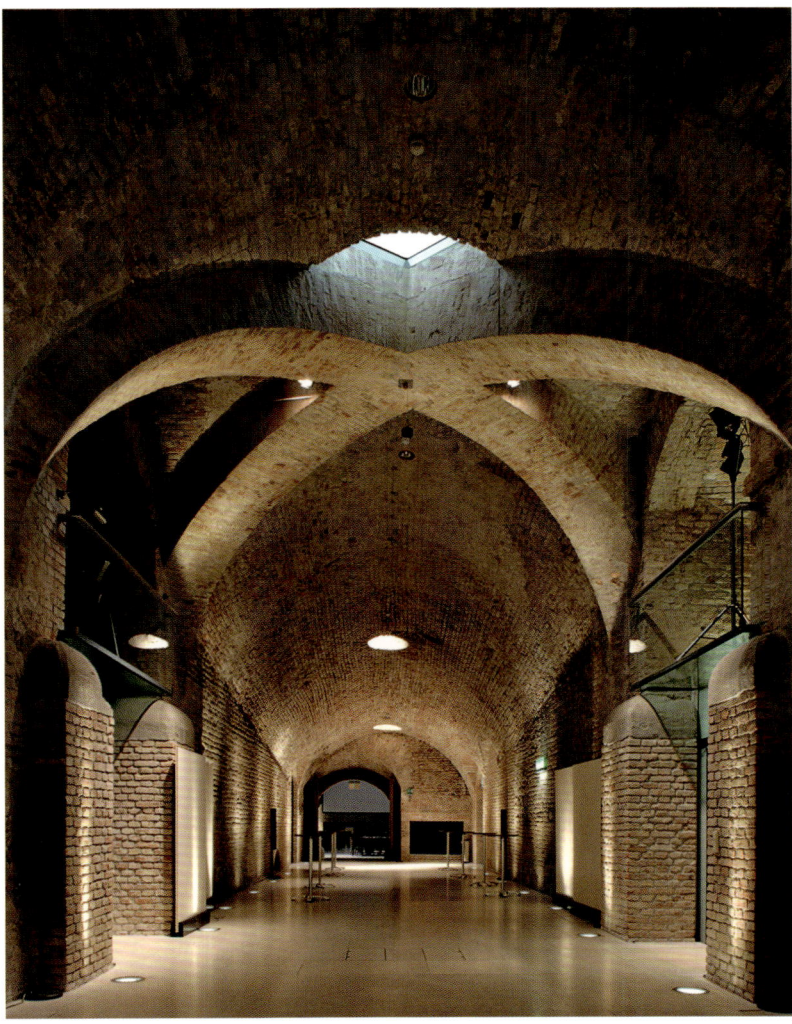
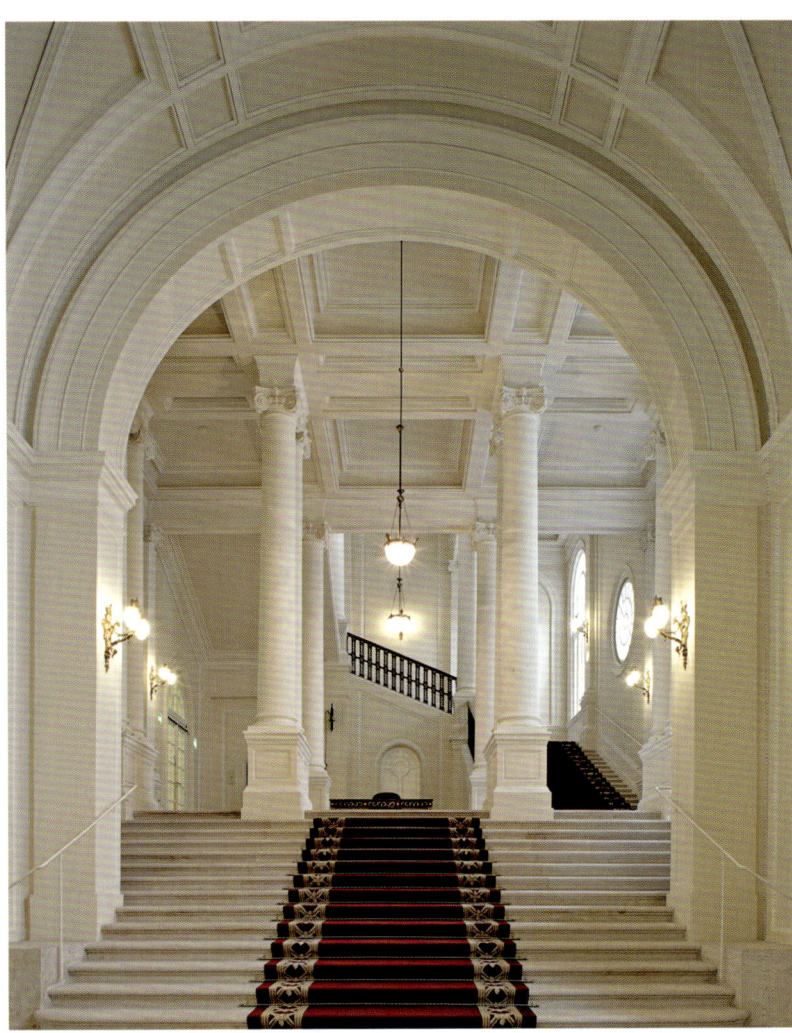

Tschuggen Grand Hotel

Arosa, Switzerland

Sonnenbergstrasse
7050 Arosa
Switzerland
Phone: +41 81 378 99 99
Fax: +41 81 378 99 90
www.tschuggen.ch

Price category: €€€
Rooms: 98 rooms, 32 suites and junior suites
Facilities: 5 restaurants, 3 conference rooms, shopping arcade, Bergoase spa
Services: Babysitting and kids club, personal trainer, 24 h concierge, hairdresser, ski rental and school on property, business center and secretarial service
Located: 1.5 km from the center of Arosa
Public transportation: Transfer from airport and train station arranged by the hotel on request
Style: Contemporary design

During the day they seem like over-sized sails that sun beams dance on; in the night stylized Christmas trees setting sparkling dots in the mountain world. The glass and steel sculptures crown Mario Botta's "mountain oasis"—a 54,000 square-foot spa orchestrated over the depths of four subterranean levels like a symphony of resonating rock, granite, wood, and water. A glass bridge connects this wellness landscape to the Tschuggen Grand Hotel and its 130 colorful rooms each with picturesque panoramas over Arosa.

Tagsüber wirken sie wie überdimensionale Segel, auf denen Sonnenstrahlen tanzen; nachts wie stilisierte Weihnachtsbäume, die Glanzpunkte in die Bergwelt setzen: Die Glas-Stahl-Skulpturen, die Mario Bottas „Bergoase" krönen – ein 5 000 Quadratmeter großes Spa, das sich über vier unterirdische Ebenen erstreckt und eine Sinfonie aus Fels, Granit, Holz und Wasser ist. Eine gläserne Brücke verbindet die Wellness-Landschaft mit dem Tschuggen Grand Hotel, dessen 130 Zimmer farbenfroh gestaltet sind und Bilderbuchpanoramen über Arosa eröffnen.

Pendant la journée, elles ressemblent à des voiles surdimensionnées sur lesquelles dansent les rayons de soleil, et pendant la nuit à des sapins de Noël stérilisés, qui mettent en valeur le cadre montagnard : les sculptures de verre et d'acier qui couronnent Mario Bottas « oasis de montagne » : un spa de 5.000 mètres carré sur quatre strates terrestres, comme une symphonie de pierre, de granit, de bois et d'eau. Un pont de verre relie ce cadre de bien-être avec le Tschuggen Grand Hotel et ses 130 chambres colorées qui offrent un panorama sur le cadre très pittoresque d'Arosa.

Durante el día parecen colosales velas sobre las que bailan los rayos de luz, por la noche, alargados árboles de navidad que añaden puntos brillantes al entorno montañoso: así son las esculturas de acero y cristal que coronan el "oasis de montaña" de Mario Botta. Un spa de 5.000 metros cuadrados repartido en cuatro plantas subterráneas constituye una auténtica sinfonía de roca, granito, madera y agua. Un pequeño puente de cristal conecta la zona del spa con el Tschuggen Grand Hotel, cuyas 130 coloridas habitaciones ofrecen vistas panorámicas de ensueño sobre Arosa.

Di giorno sembrano enormi vele su cui danzano i raggi del sole, di notte alberi di Natale stilizzati che creano delle fonti luminose nell'ambiente di montagna: sono le sculture in vetro e acciaio che coronano l'"oasi montana" di Mario Botta – uno spa di 5.000 metri quadrati che si sviluppa su quattro piani sotterranei ed è una sinfonia di roccia, granito, legno e acqua. Un ponte di vetro collega la zona Wellness con il Tschuggen Grand Hotel, le cui 130 camere sfoggiano colori vivaci e offrono vedute panoramiche di Arosa degne di un libro illustrato.

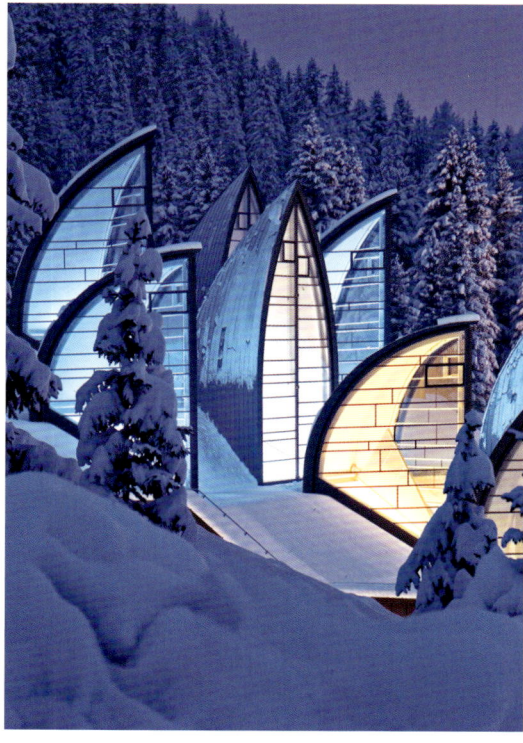
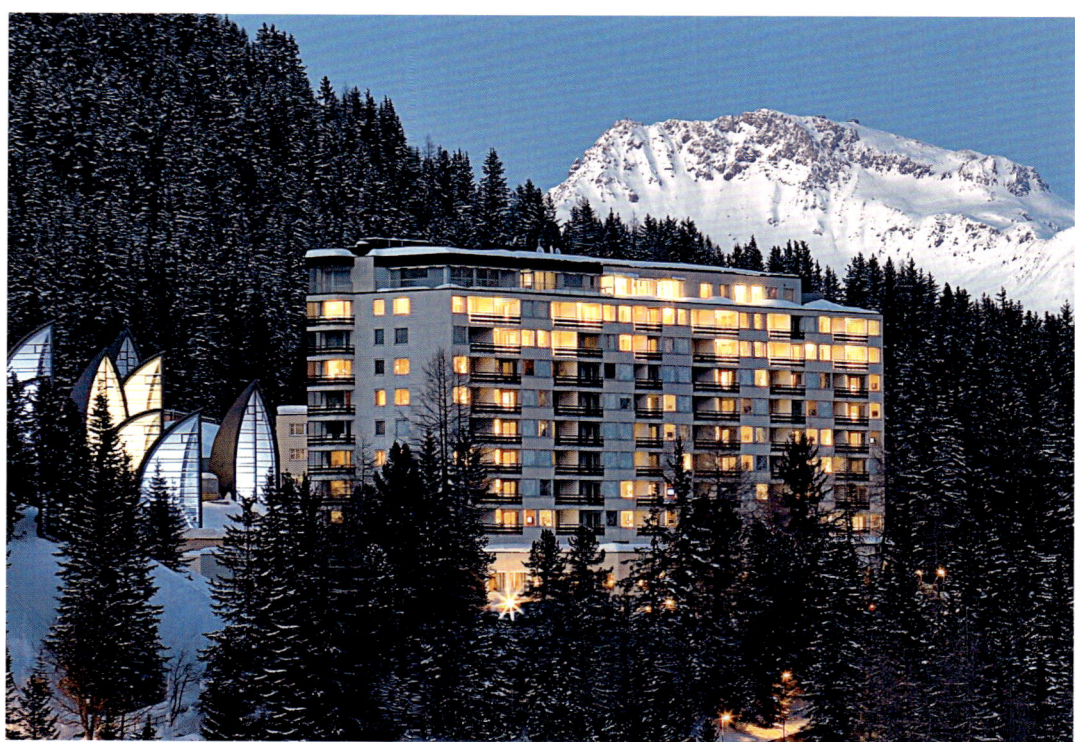

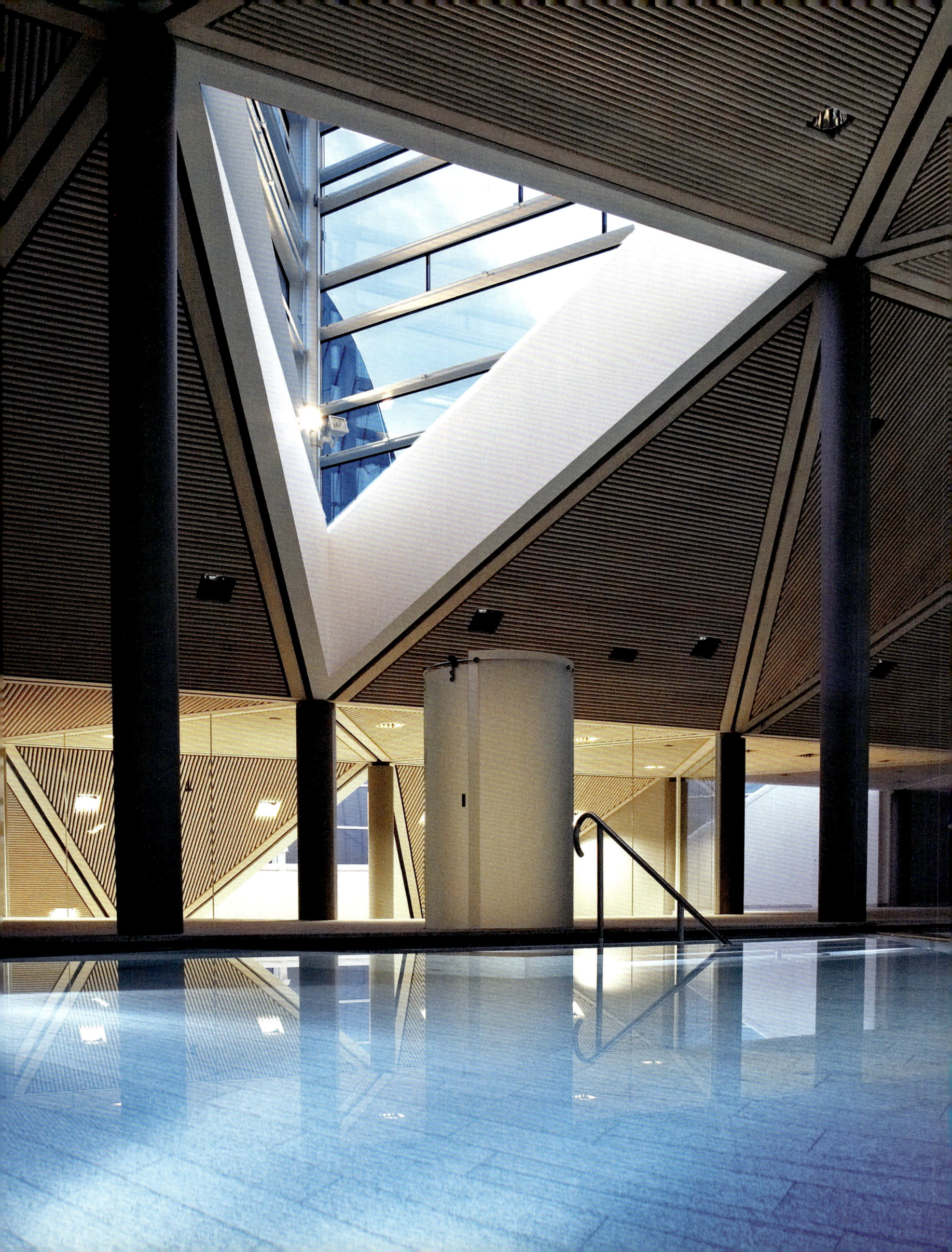

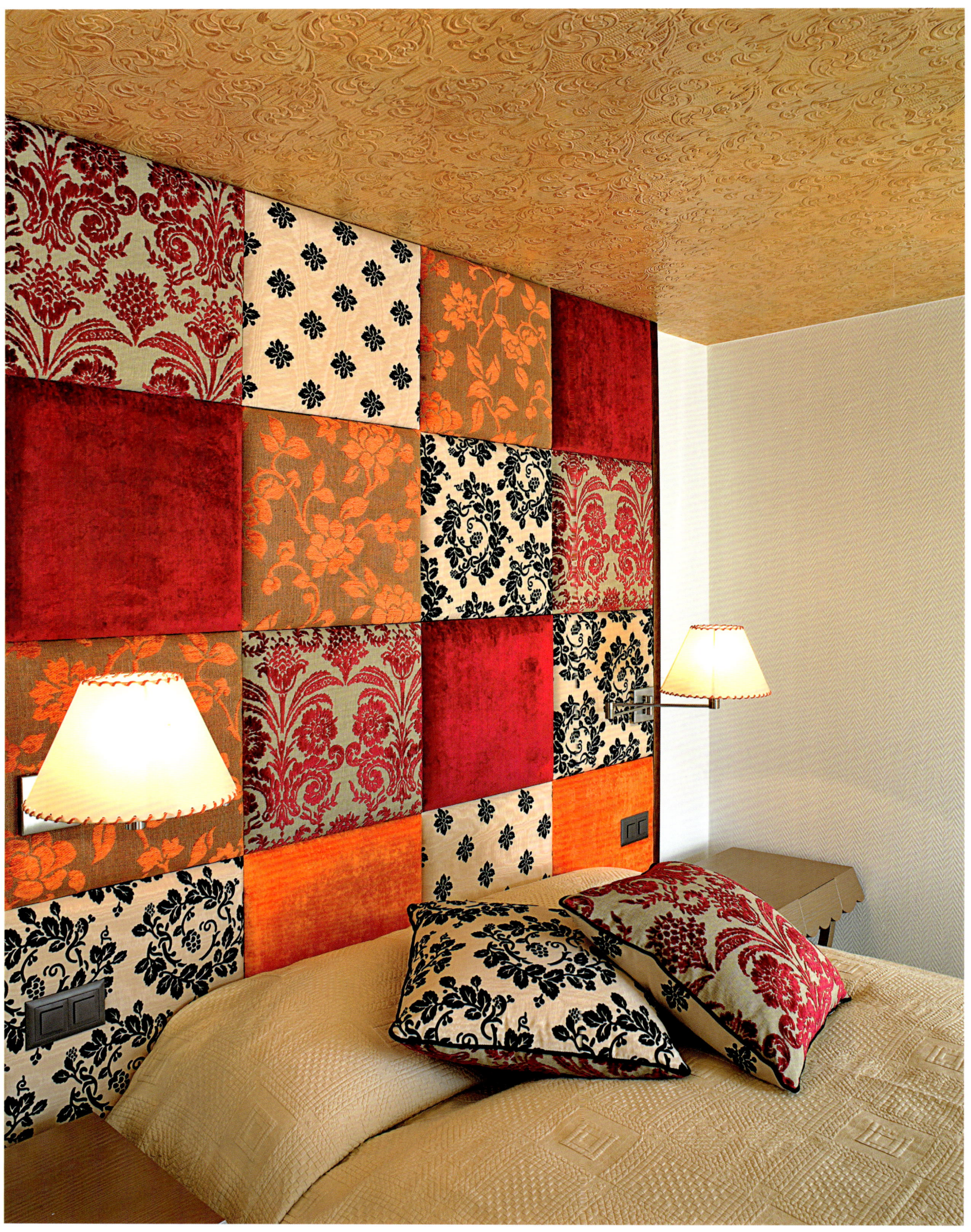

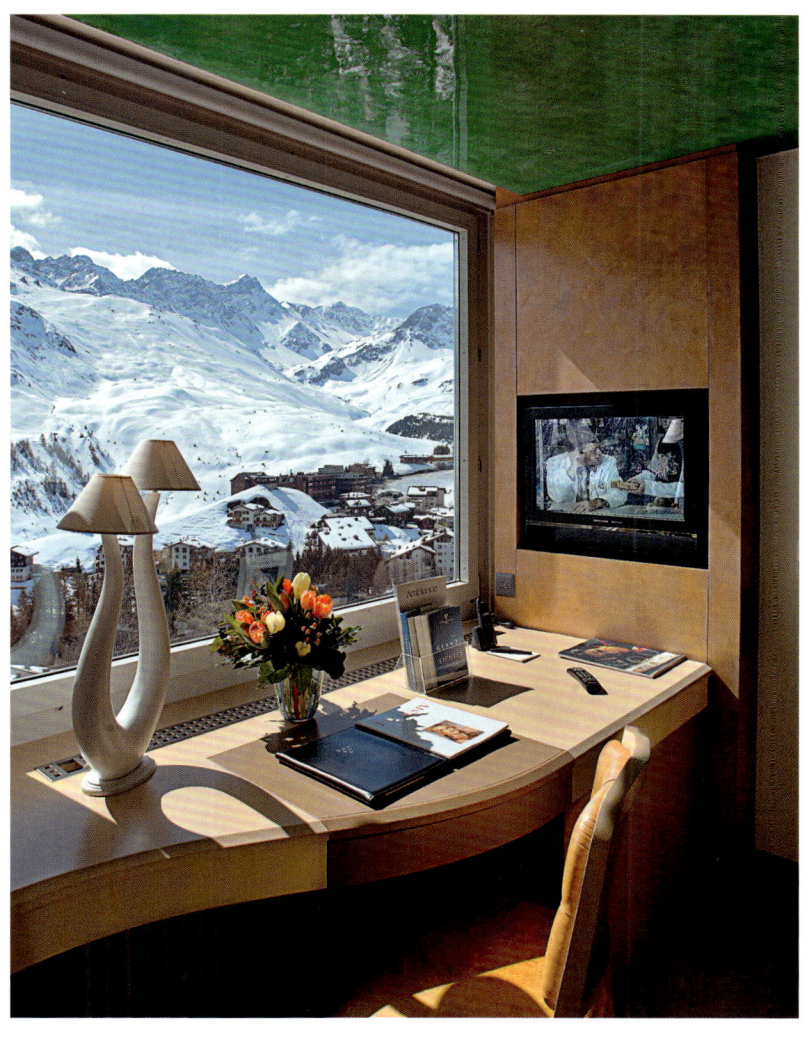
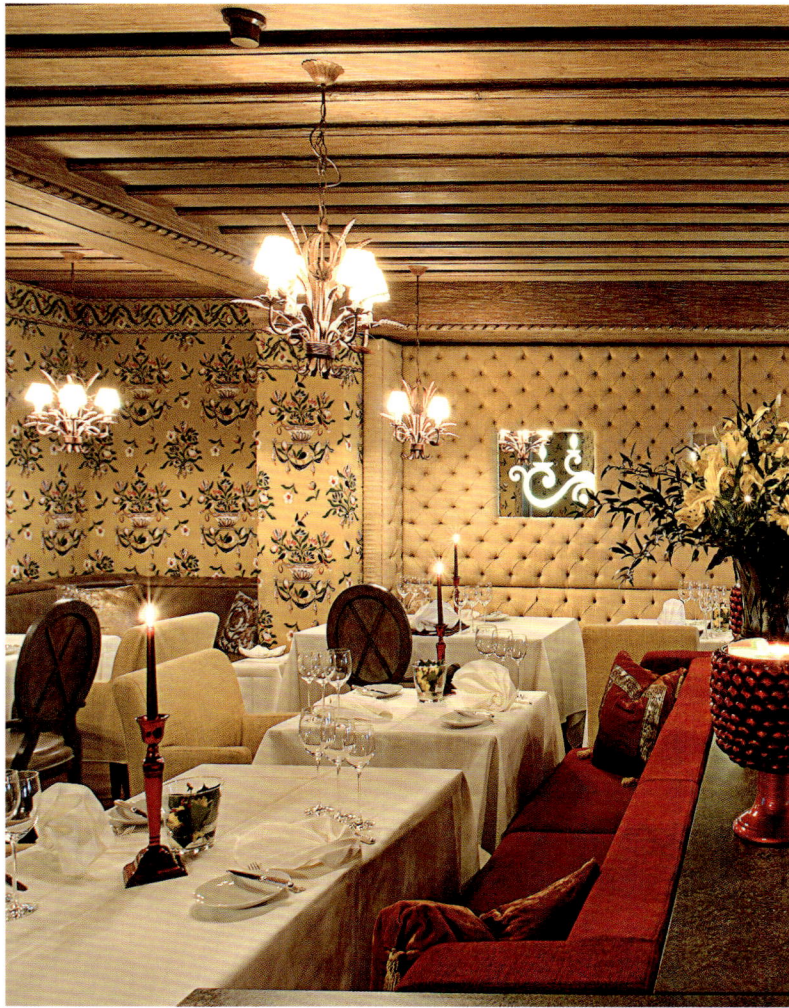
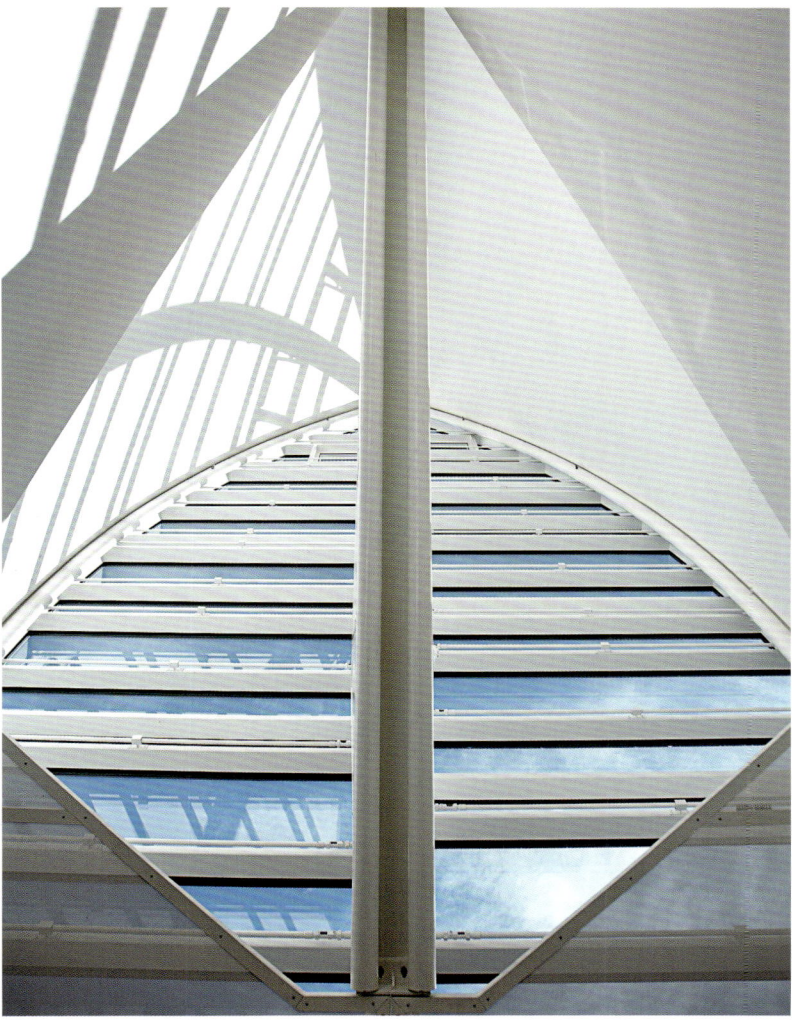
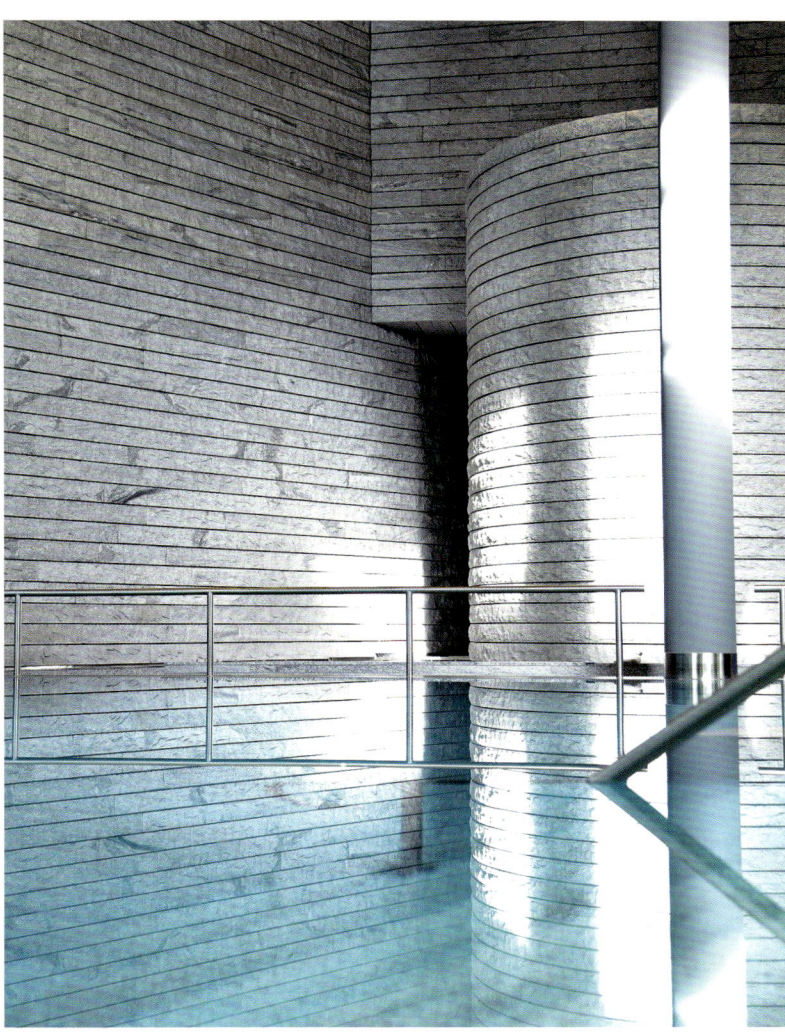

Victoria-Jungfrau Grand Hotel & Spa

Interlaken, Switzerland

Höheweg 41
3800 Interlaken
Switzerland
Phone: +41 33 828 28 28
Fax: +42 33 828 28 80
www.victoria-jungfrau.ch

Price category: €€€
Rooms: 212 rooms including 100 suites
Facilities: 3 restaurants, 3 bars, spa
Services: Babysitting, free WiFi
Located: 45 min from Bern airport, 2.5 h from Zurich airport, 3 h from Geneva airport
Style: Classic elegance

The Victoria-Jungfrau that first opened in 1865 has long since become the grand Lady of Swiss Luxury hotels—glamorous, elegant and obviously regularly picking up the trends from Paris, London or Rome to stylishly blend them with Swiss tradition. The timeless modern design instantly makes any of the 212 rooms your favorite place (such as the very chic Bel Air Junior suites with dark parquet and refined lighting). The 59,000 square-foot spa combines wellness methods from the East and West, and the best *foie gras* in the country is served in the restaurant "La Terrasse."

Das 1865 eröffnete Victoria-Jungfrau ist heute die Lady der Schweizer Luxushotellerie – glamourös, elegant und offensichtlich regelmäßig in Paris, London oder Rom unterwegs, um die Trends aus den Metropolen stilvoll mit eidgenössischen Traditionen zu verbinden. Zeitlos modernes Design macht die 212 Zimmer zu Lieblingsplätzen (sehr chic: die Bel Air Junior Suiten mit dunklem Parkett und raffiniertem Licht), das 5 500 Quadratmeter große Spa vereint Wellnessmethoden aus Ost und West, und im „La Terrasse" wird die beste Foie Gras des Landes serviert.

Le Victoria-Jungfrau, qui a ouvert en 1865, est devenue la Grande Dame de l'hôtellerie de luxe suisse : glamour, élégante et bien sûr régulièrement à Paris, Londres ou Rome, pour capter les tendances et les marier élégamment à la tradition confédérale. Un design moderne intemporel fait de l'hôtel de 212 chambres un lieu de prédilection immédiat (comble du chic : la Junior Suite Bel Air avec son parquet sombre et son éclairage raffiné), le spa de 5.500 mètres carré allie bien-être d'Extrême-Orient et d'Occident, et au restaurant « La Terrasse », le meilleur foie gras du pays est servi.

El hotel Victoria-Jungfrau, que abrió sus puertas en 1865, es hoy la gran dama de la hostelería de lujo en Suiza. Esta gran dama, glamorosa, elegante y desde luego siempre informada sobre las últimas modas de París, Londres y Roma, fusiona de manera sublime las últimas tendencias de las metrópolis con lo tradicional del país. Un diseño moderno a prueba del tiempo convierte las 212 habitaciones en estancias de referencia (lo más chic: sus suites junior Bel Air, con parqué de madera oscuro y sofisticada iluminación). El espacioso spa de 5.500 metros cuadrados ofrece un wellness que mezcla estilos orientales y occidentales. En el restaurante "La Terrasse" se sirve el mejor *foie gras* del país alpino.

Aperto nel 1865, oggi il Victoria-Jungfrau è la regina degli alberghi di lusso della Svizzera – affascinante, elegante e chiaramente in costante contatto con Parigi, Londra o Roma per unire in grande stile la moda delle metropoli alle tradizioni elvetiche. Un classico design moderno fa di ciascuna delle 212 camere un adorabile angolino privato (molto chic le suite Bel Air Junior, con parquet scuro e un'elegante illuminazione), lo Spa di 5.500 metri quadrati è una fusione di benessere dell'Ovest e dell'Estremo Oriente, e nel ristorante "La Terrasse" viene servito il miglior *foie gras* del Paese.

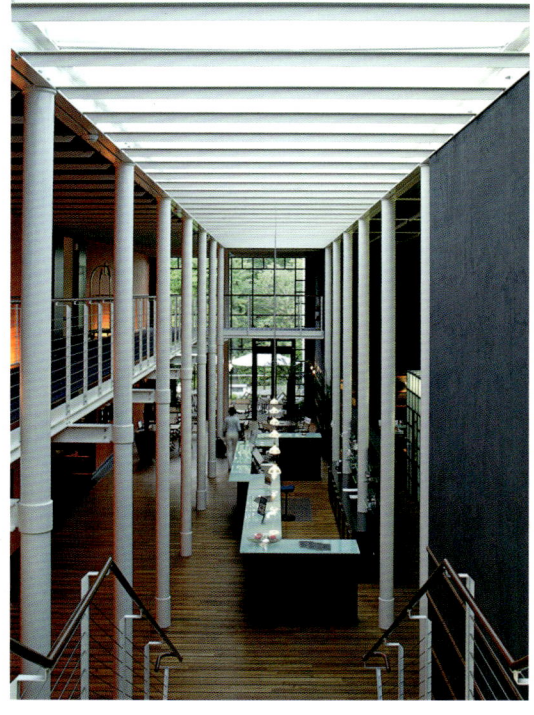
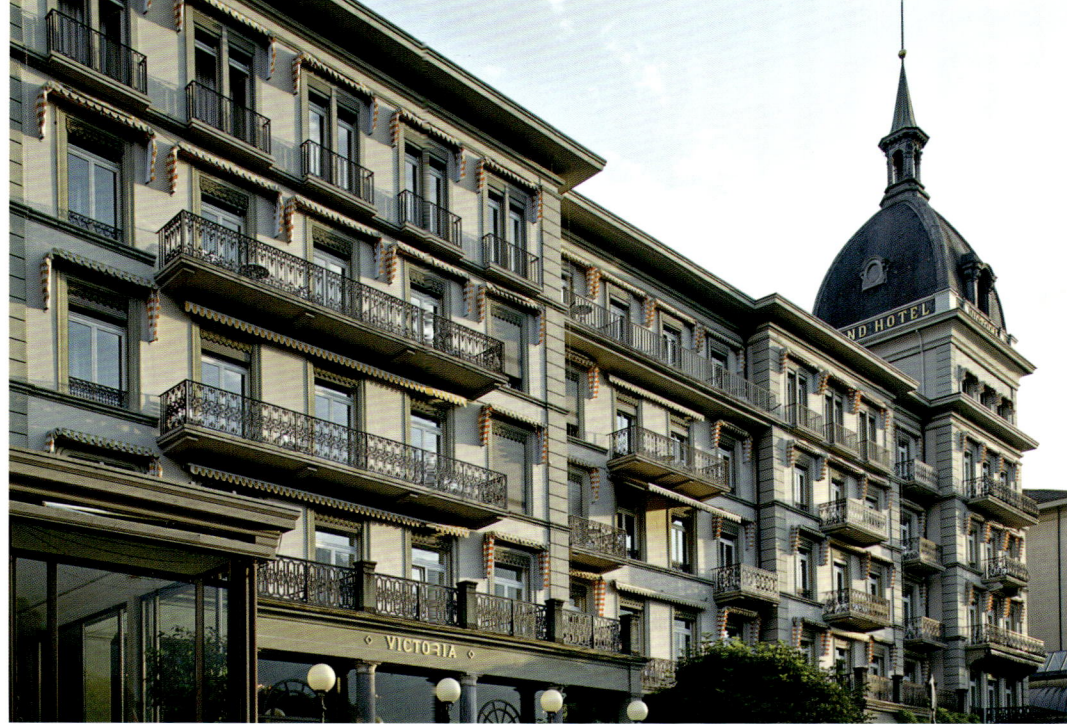

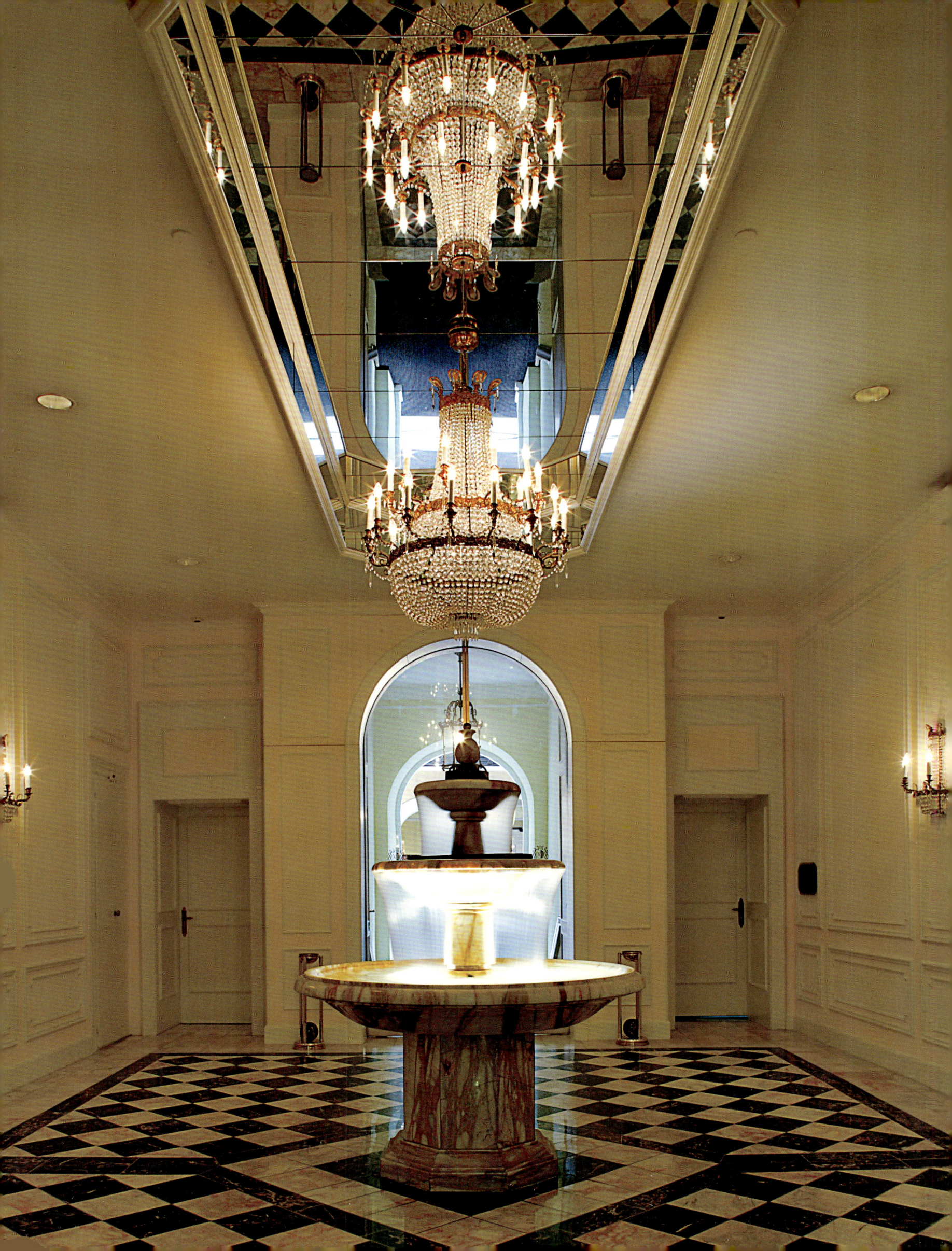

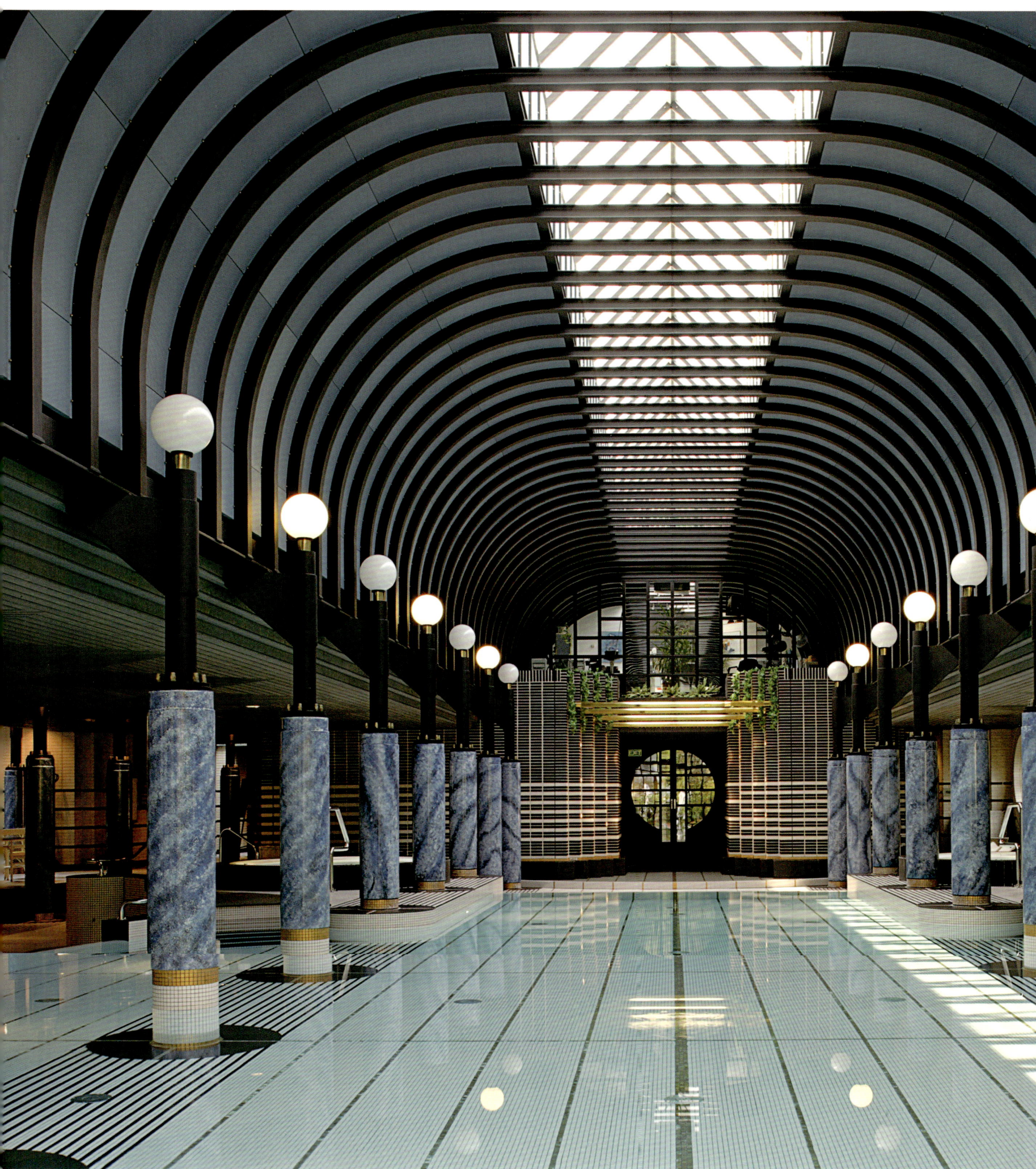

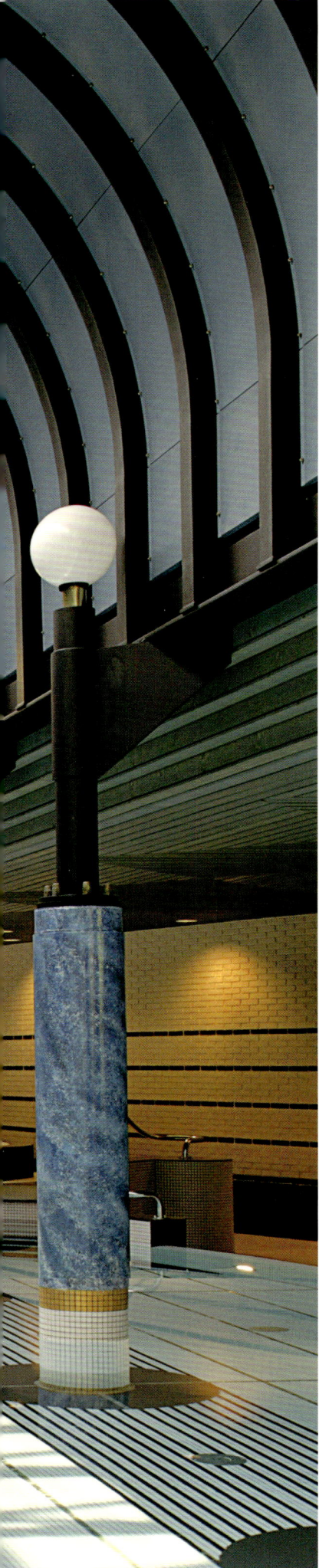

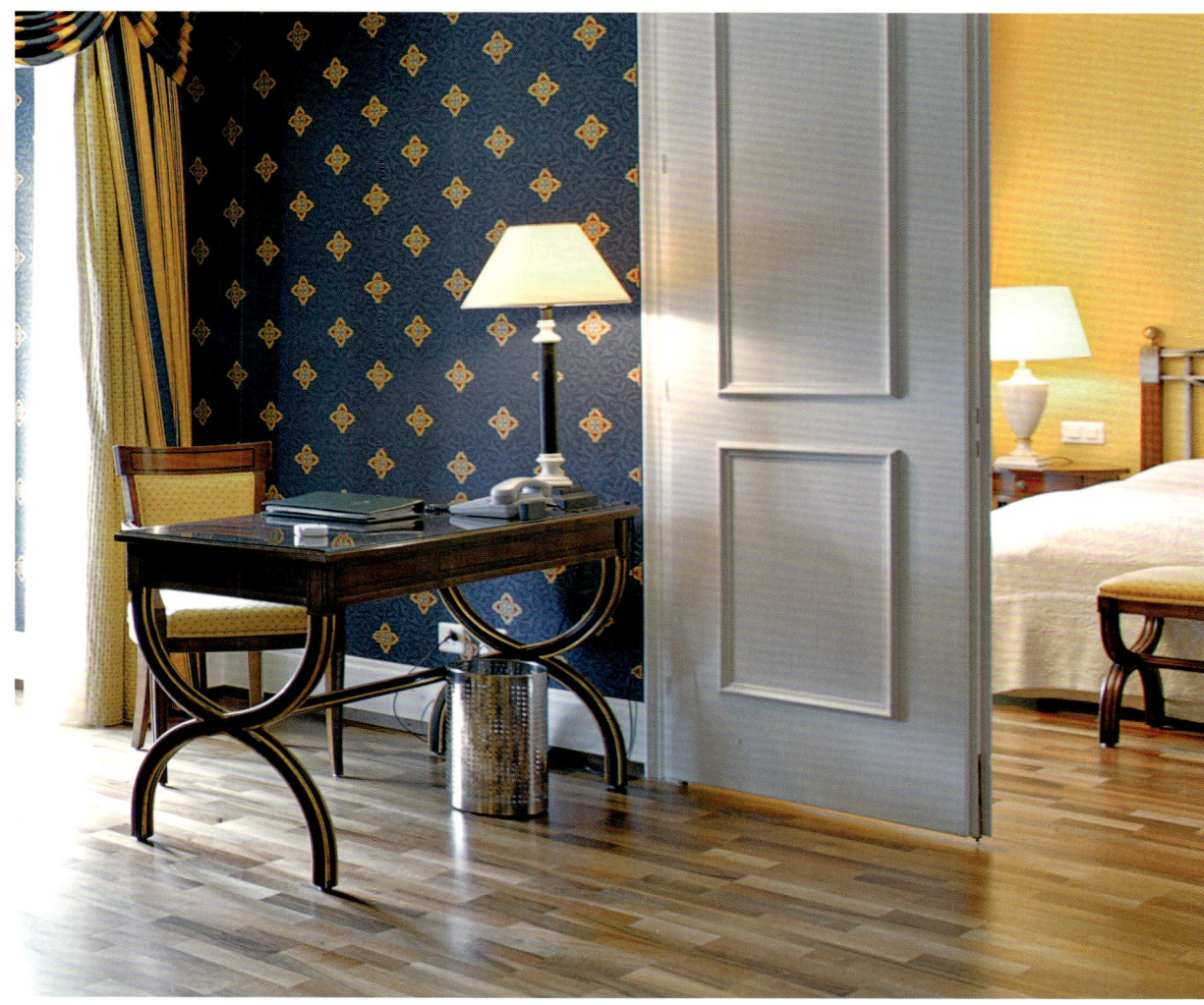

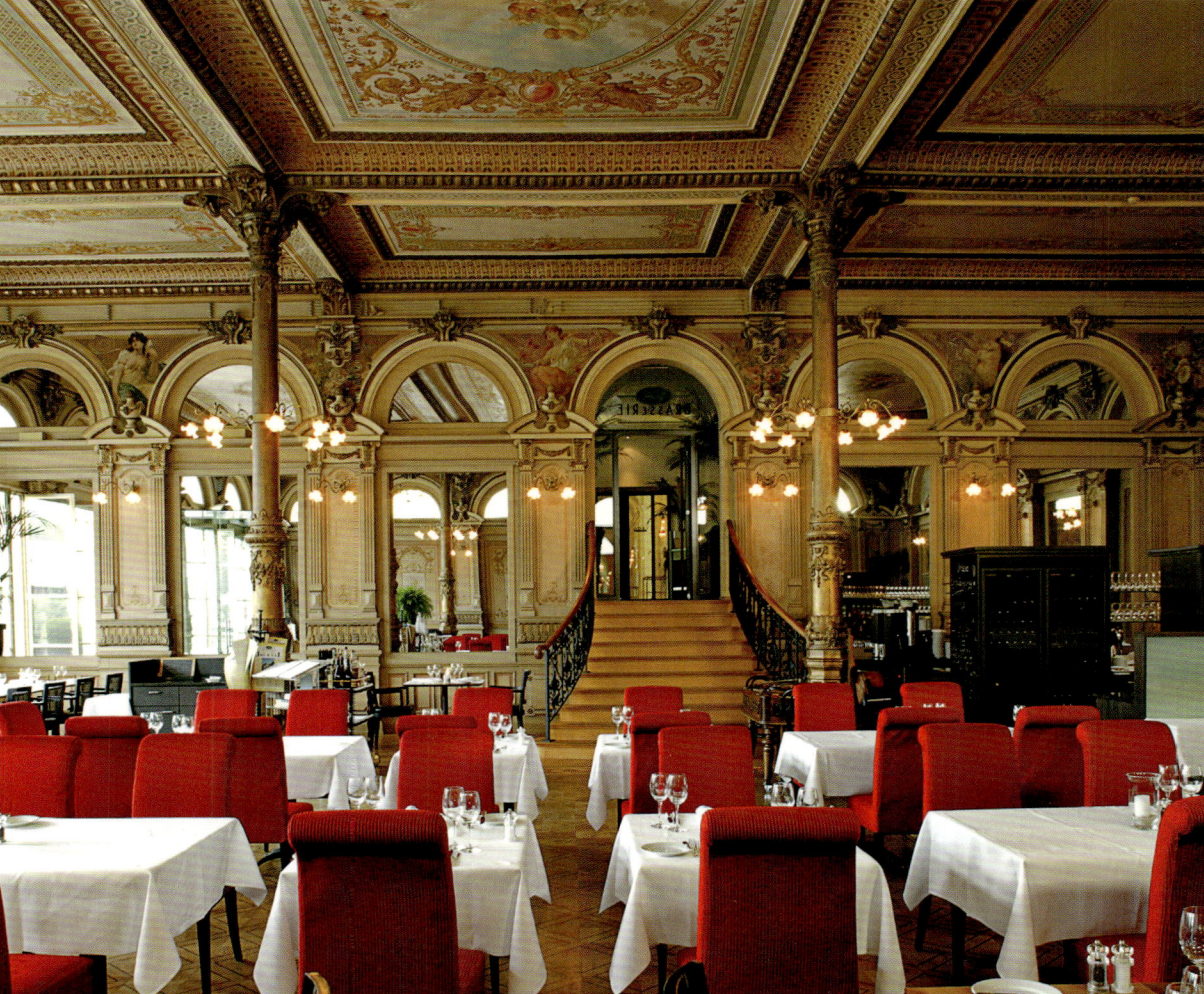

Badrutt's Palace Hotel

St. Moritz, Switzerland

Via Serlas 27
7500 St. Moritz
Switzerland
Phone: +41 81 837 10 00
Fax: +41 81 837 29 99
www.badruttspalace.com

Price category: €€€
Rooms: 159 rooms including 38 suites
Facilities: 4 bars, 7 restaurants, beauty spa, boutiques, pool, tennis courts, kids club
Services: Butlers, guest relations, 24 h concierge and room service, airport transfers, WiFi
Located: In the center of St. Moritz overlooking the lake and the Swiss alps
Public transportation: 800 m from train station
Style: Classic elegance

Badrutt's Palace first cast its magic spell on St. Moritz as a fairy-tale palace in 1896. The palace with the prominent tower affords guests the choice of 159 singularly distinctive rooms—two suites are dedicated to Hans and Helen Badrutt who reigned over the hotel from 1898 till 1960. Their magic has always lured the prominence of nobility, politics and show business with their localities: the "Nobu" and the "Chesa Veglia" are true VIP lodges, and the "King's Club" is the most famous disco in Switzerland. Whoever fails to get past the doorman can meet the stars the next day in the famous "Renaissance Bar" with a little bit of luck.

Mit dem Badrutt's Palace bekam St. Moritz 1896 sein Märchenschloss: Der Palast mit dem markanten Turm umfasst 159 Zimmer, von denen keines dem anderen gleicht – zwei Suiten sind Hans und Helen Badrutt gewidmet, die das Hotel von 1898 bis 1960 führten. Prominente aus Adel, Politik und Showbiz zieht das Haus auch mit seinen Lokalen an: Das „Nobu" und die „Chesa Veglia" sind wahre VIP-Logen, und der „King's Club" ist die berühmteste Disco der Schweiz. Wer am Türsteher nicht vorbeikommt, kann die Stars mit etwas Glück am nächsten Tag treffen – in der berühmten „Renaissance Bar".

En 1896, le Badrutt's Palace enchantait St. Moritz en dotant la station de son propre château de contes de fées : avec sa tour étonnante, il abrite 159 chambres, chacune différente des autres. Deux suites sont dédiées à Hans et Helen Badrutt, qui ont dirigé l'hôtel de 1898 à 1960. Sa magie a toujours séduit l'élite de la haute noblesse, de la politique et du show business avec ses établissements : le « Nobu » et le « Chesa Veglia » sont de vrais salons VIP, et le « King's Club » la discothèque la plus célèbre de Suisse. Ceux qui n'arrivent pas à dépasser le videur peuvent, avec un peu de chance, rencontrer les stars le lendemain au fameux « Renaissance Bar ».

En 1896, St. Moritz recibió su propio castillo de cuento de hadas: el Badrutt's Palace. Junto a su distintiva torre, este palacio cuenta con 159 habitaciones únicas y diferentes entre si. Dos de las suites están dedicadas a Hans y Helen Badrutt, quienes regentaron el hotel entre 1898 y 1960. También gracias a sus locales de encuentro, este establecimiento atrae a famosos de la aristocracia, la política y el mundo del espectáculo. El "Nobu" y el "Chesa Veglia" son verdaderas pasarelas de gente VIP y el "King's Club" es la discoteca más famosa de toda Suiza. Quien no consiga convencer al portero para entrar podrá ver, con un poco de suerte, a los famosos el día siguiente en el famoso "Renaissance Bar".

Costruito nel 1896, il Badrutt's Palace è il castello delle favole di St. Moritz. Il palazzo, con la sua prominente torre, comprende 159 camere, una diversa dall'altra – due suite sono dedicate ad Hans ed Helen Badrutt, che gestirono l'hotel dal 1898 al 1960. L'albergo attira famosi personaggi dell'aristocrazia, della politica e dello spettacolo anche grazie ai suoi locali: il "Nobu" e il "Chesa Veglia" sono veri e propri palcoscenici per VIP, e il "King's Club" è la discoteca più famosa della Svizzera. Se il buttafuori non vi farà entrare, con un po' di fortuna potrete vedere le star il giorno seguente a famoso "Renaissance Bar".

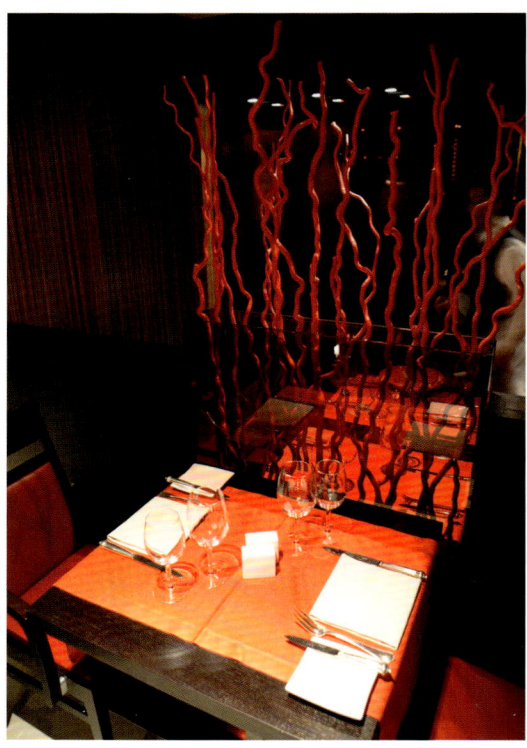 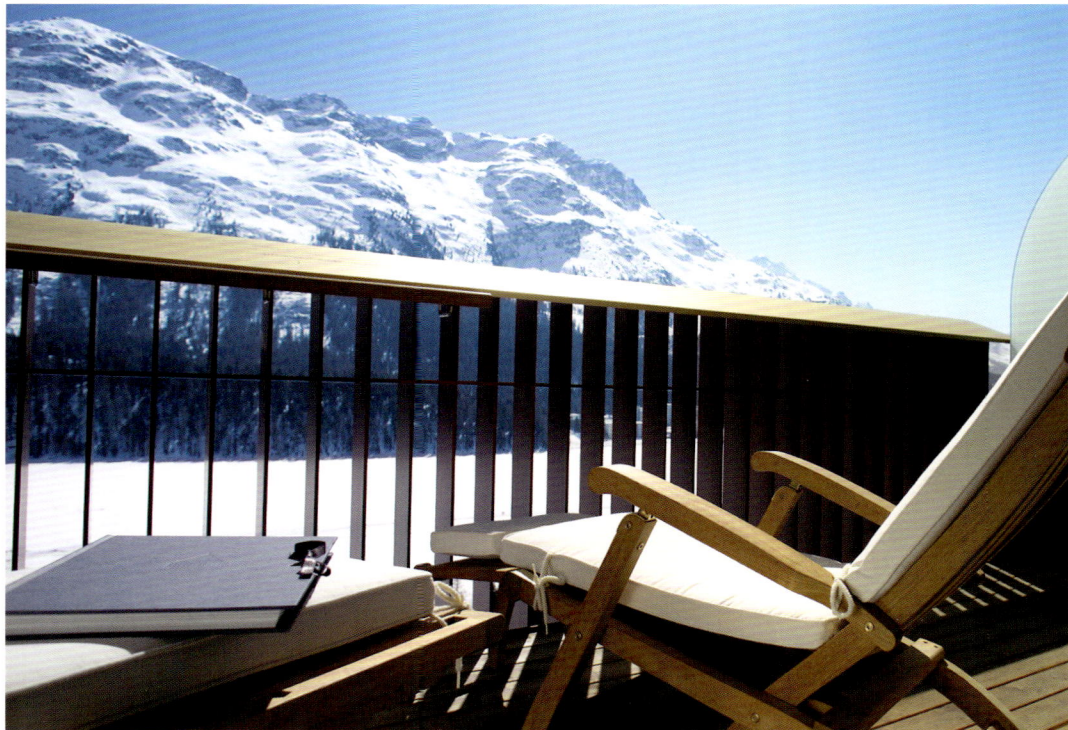

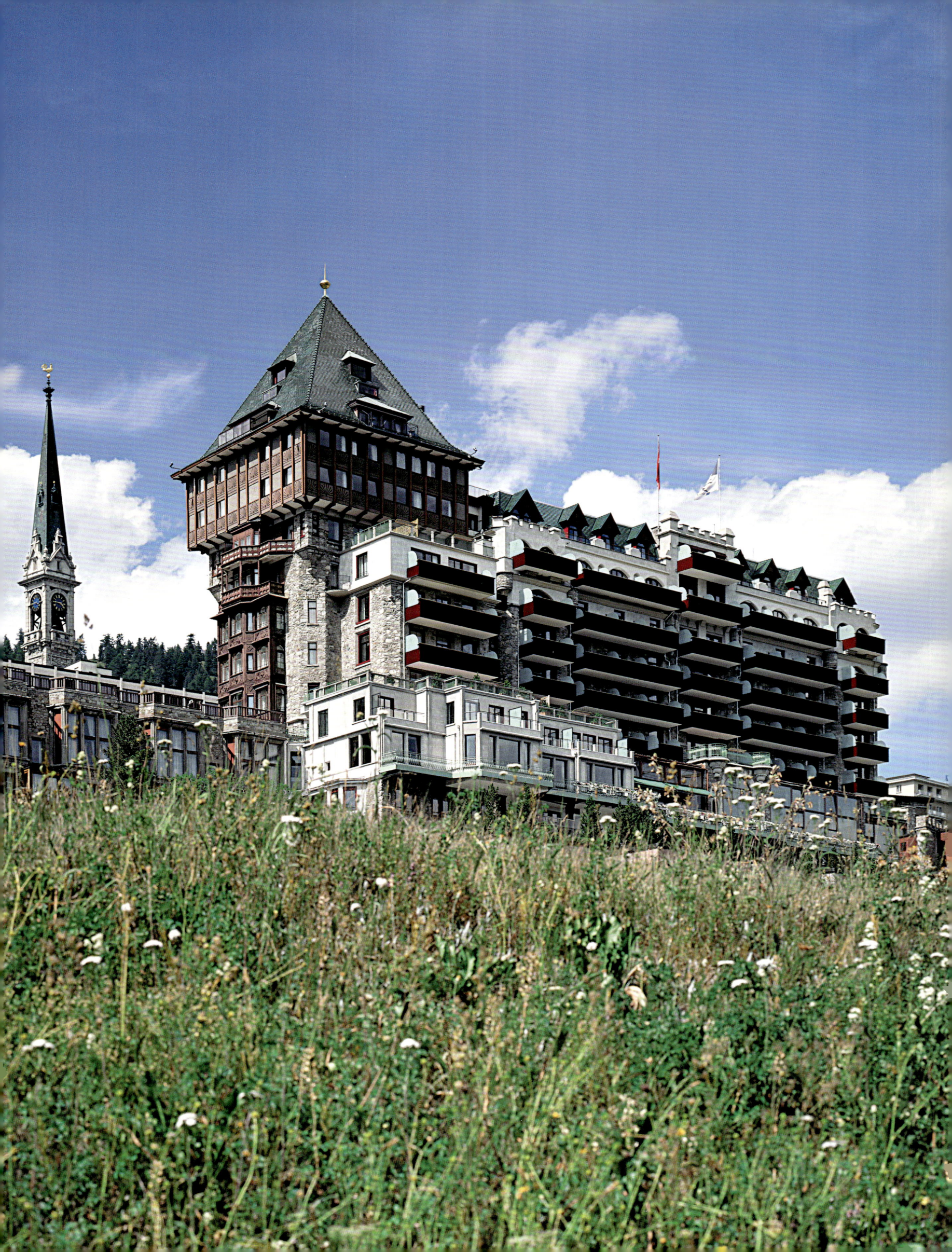

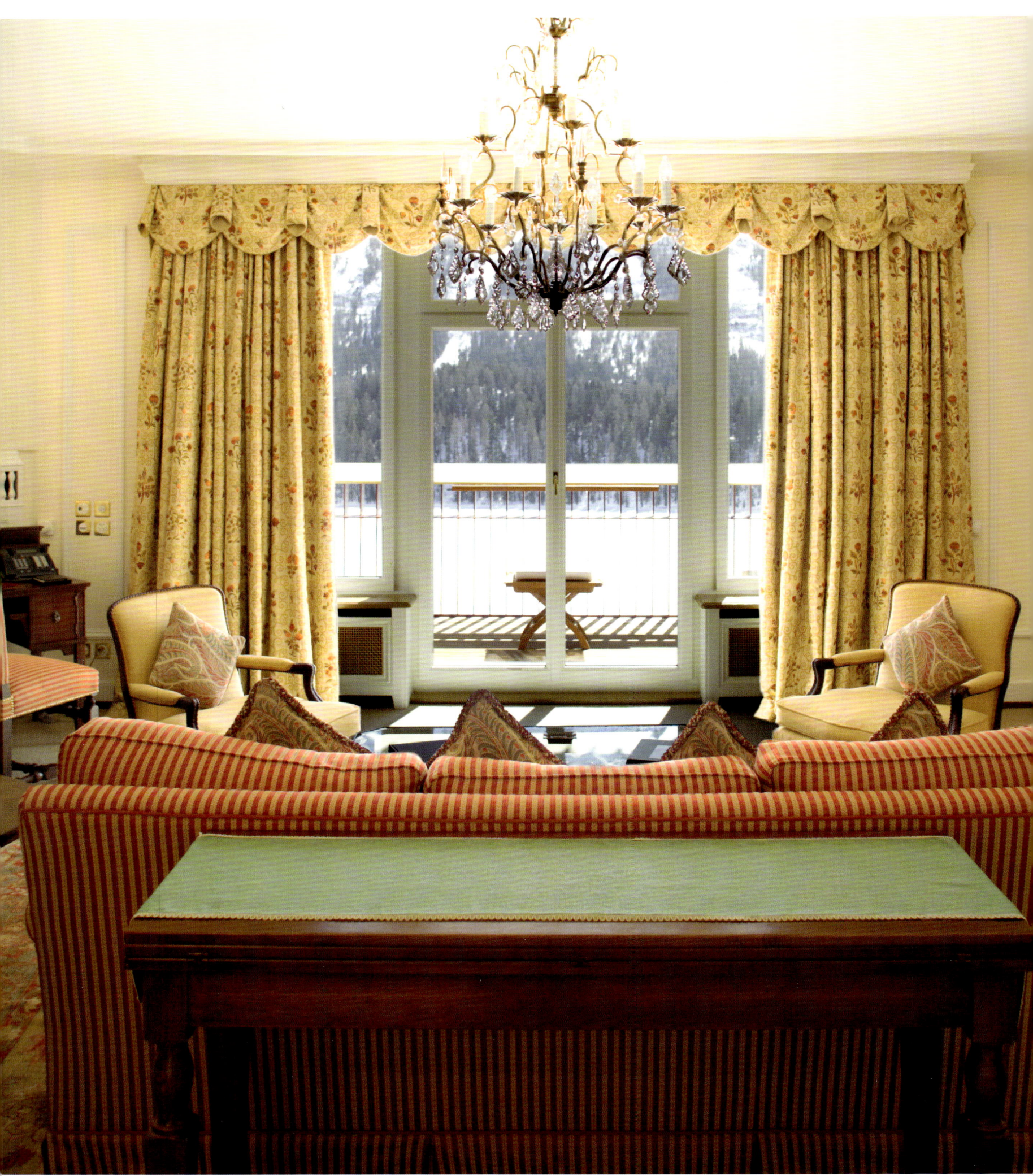

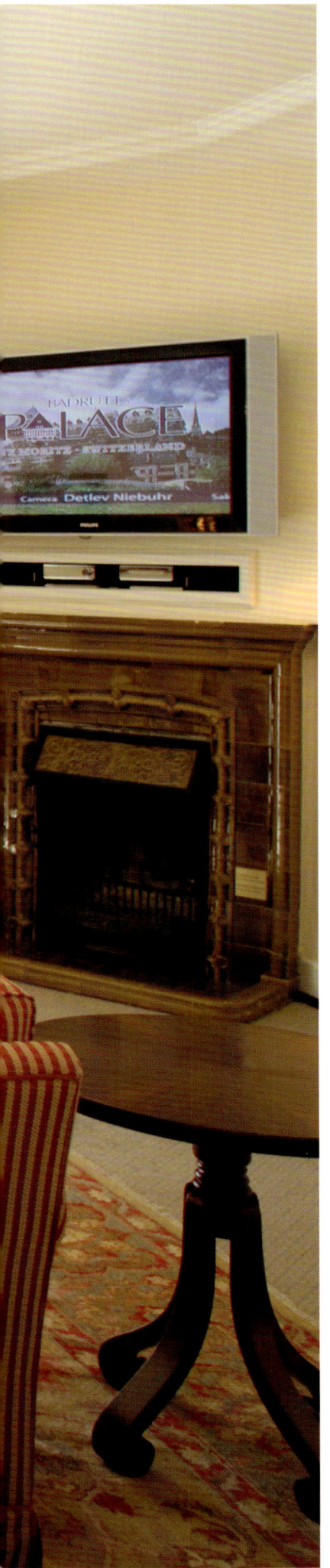

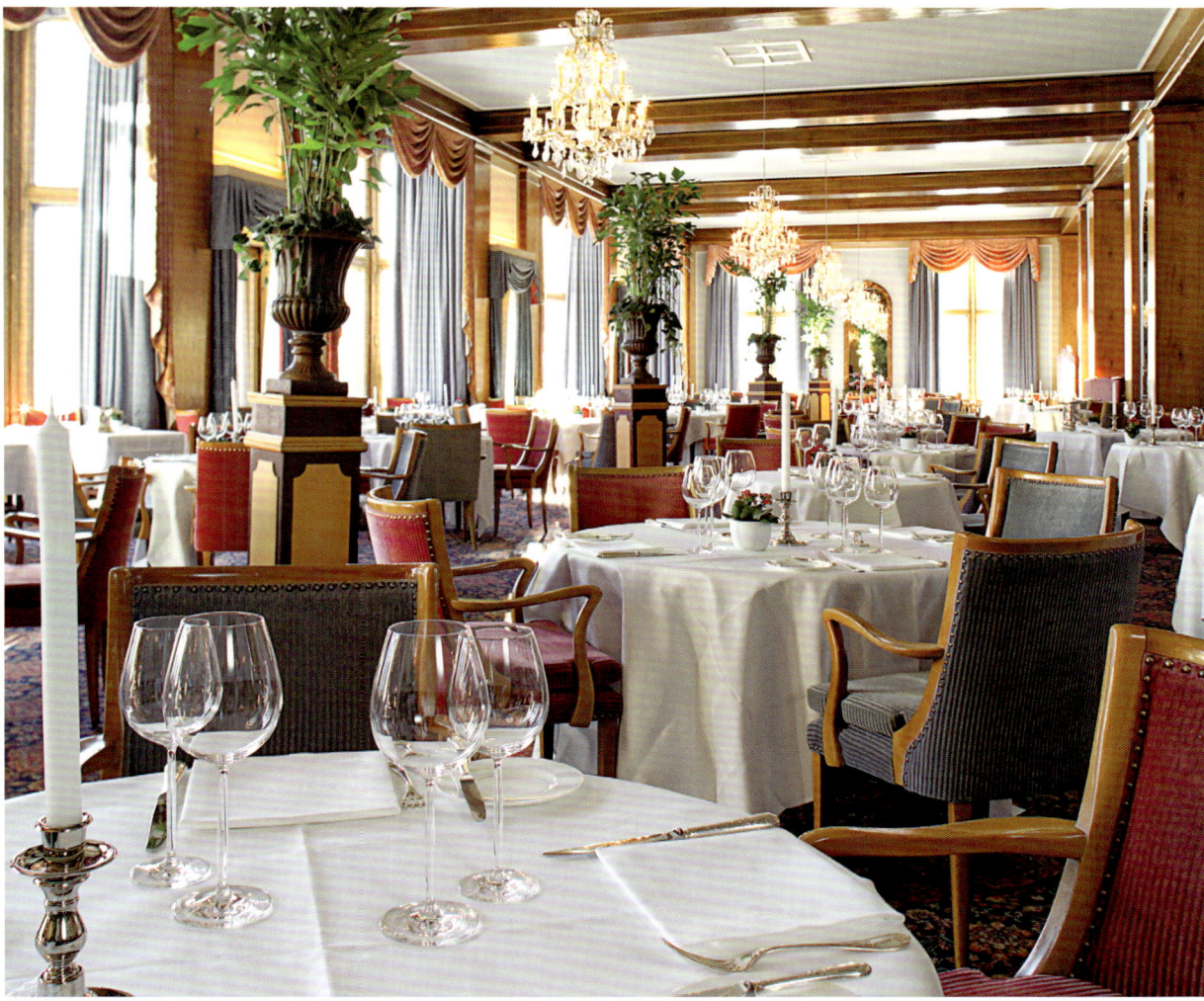

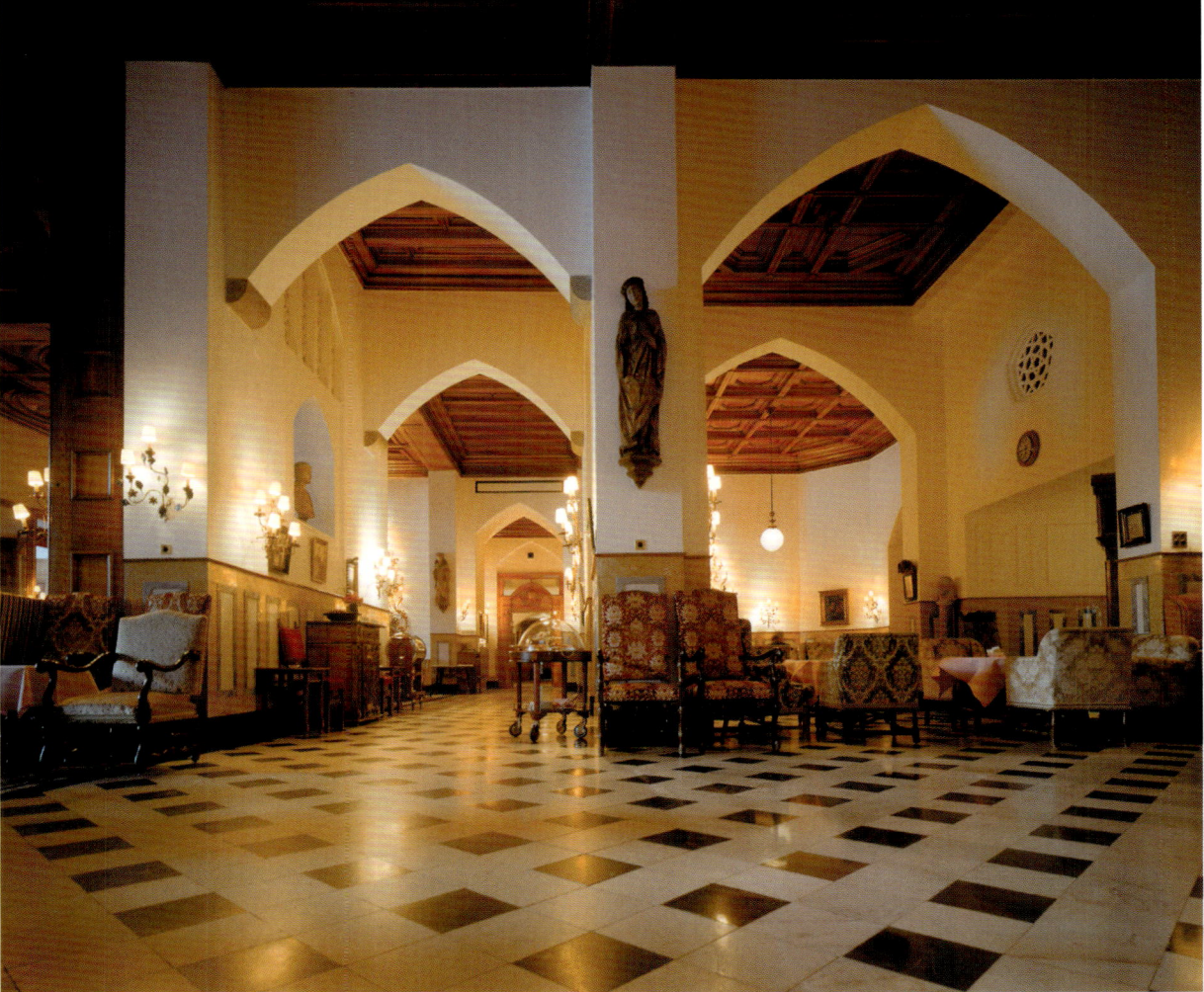

8004 Zurich
Switzerland
Phone: +41 43 243 42 43
Fax: +41 43 243 42 00
www.greulich.ch

Rooms: 201
Facilities: Spanish restaurant, Kreis 4 open air café, bar and cigar lounge, Birch Grove design garden, room for private events
Services: Room service, bicycle rent
Located: In the West side, close to the city center
Public transportation: Bus 31 and Tram 8 Bäckeranlage
Style: Modern design

The rich blue color and the curved form of the facade immediately clarify that the 18-room house in the Zurich city quarter of Aussersihl is a very extraordinary hotel. Inside it is discreet and concentrates on essentials. The rooms that are all situated in a flat addition are reached over a birch grove of 160 trees that are conducive to meditation especially in the summer when timbral sound is heard with every stirring of the air. The cuisine matches the total concept by obeying the principles of the slow food movement.

Die starkblaue Farbe und die geschwungene Form der Fassade machen sofort klar, dass es sich bei dem 18-Zimmer Haus im Zürcher Stadtteil Aussersihl um ein sehr außergewöhnliches Hotel handelt. Das Innere gibt sich zurückhaltend und konzentriert sich auf das Wesentliche. Die Zimmer, die sämtlich in einem flachen Anbau liegen, erreicht man durch einen zur Meditation einladenden Birkenhain mit 160 Bäumen, der im Sommer zum Klanggarten wird. Auch die Küche passt in das Gesamtkonzept, sie folgt den Prinzipien der Slow-Food-Bewegung.

Avec le bleu profond et la forme courbe de la façade, on s'aperçoit très vite que cette maison de 18 chambres dans le quartier d'Aussersihl, à Zurich, est un hôtel extraordinaire. L'intérieur est discret et concentré sur l'essentiel. Les chambres, qui sont toutes situées dans une extension, sont accessibles par un bosquet de bouleau qui invite à la méditation avec ses 160 arbres, particulièrement pendant l'été quand les sons des cuivres s'entendent dans tout le jardin. Même la cuisine s'inscrit dans le concept général, car elle obéit aux principes du mouvement Slow Food.

El color azul oscuro y la forma ondulada de su fachada no dejan lugar a dudas, esta casa de 18 habitaciones en el barrio de Aussersihl es un hotel muy especial. El interior es modesto, se concentra sólo en lo esencial. Todas las habitaciones se encuentran en un edificio contiguo bajo. Para llegar a ellas hay que atravesar un bosque de 160 abedules que invita a la meditación y que, en verano, se transforma en un jardín lleno de vida y sonidos. La cocina también se adapta al concepto de la casa siguiendo una filosofía totalmente opuesta a la de la comida rápida, la del movimiento de la comida lenta.

Il colore blu intenso e le linee curve della facciata affermano a chiare lettere che questo albergo da 18 stanze nel quartiere Aussersihl di Zurigo è fuori dal comune. Gli interni trasmettono un'impressione di riservatezza e sembrano concentrarsi sull'essenziale. Le camere si trovano tutte in una dependance di un solo piano, che si raggiunge attraverso un bosco di betulle con più di 160 piante; il percorso nel boschetto, che d'estate si trasforma in una specie di giardino dei suoni, è quanto di meglio si possa pensare per favorire la meditazione. Anche la cucina, improntata ai principi del movimento Slow Food, si integra bene nella concezione complessiva dell'hotel.

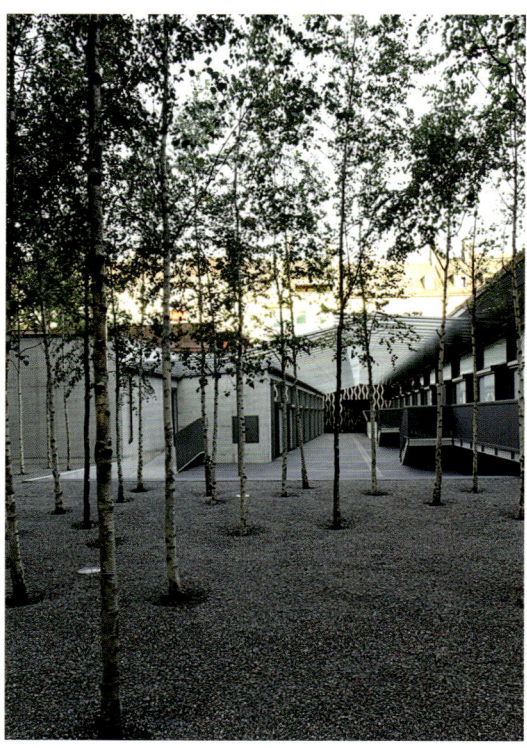
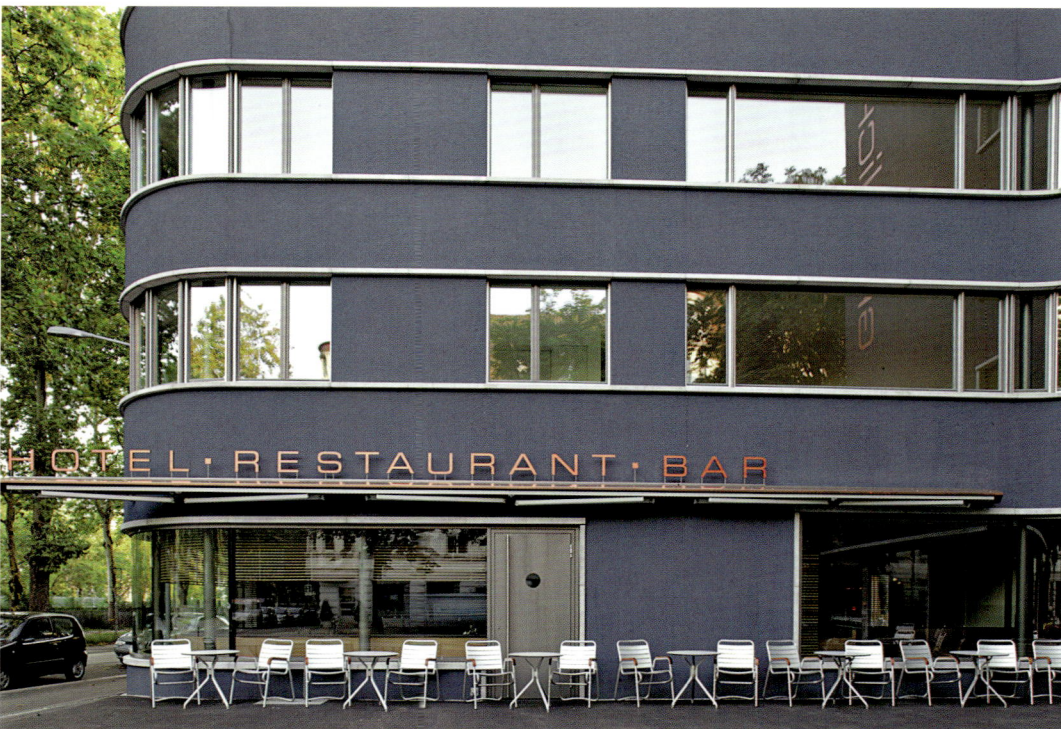

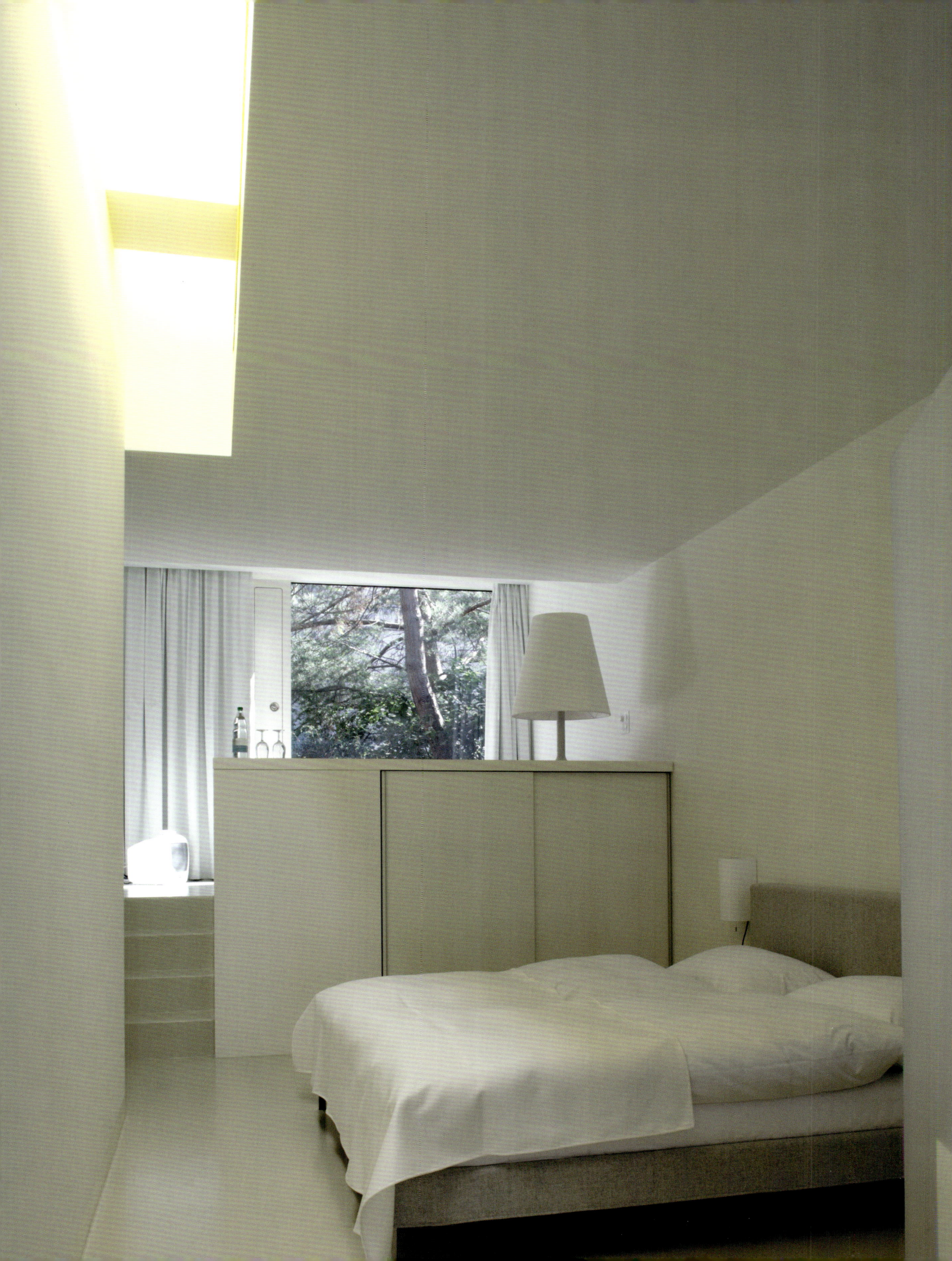

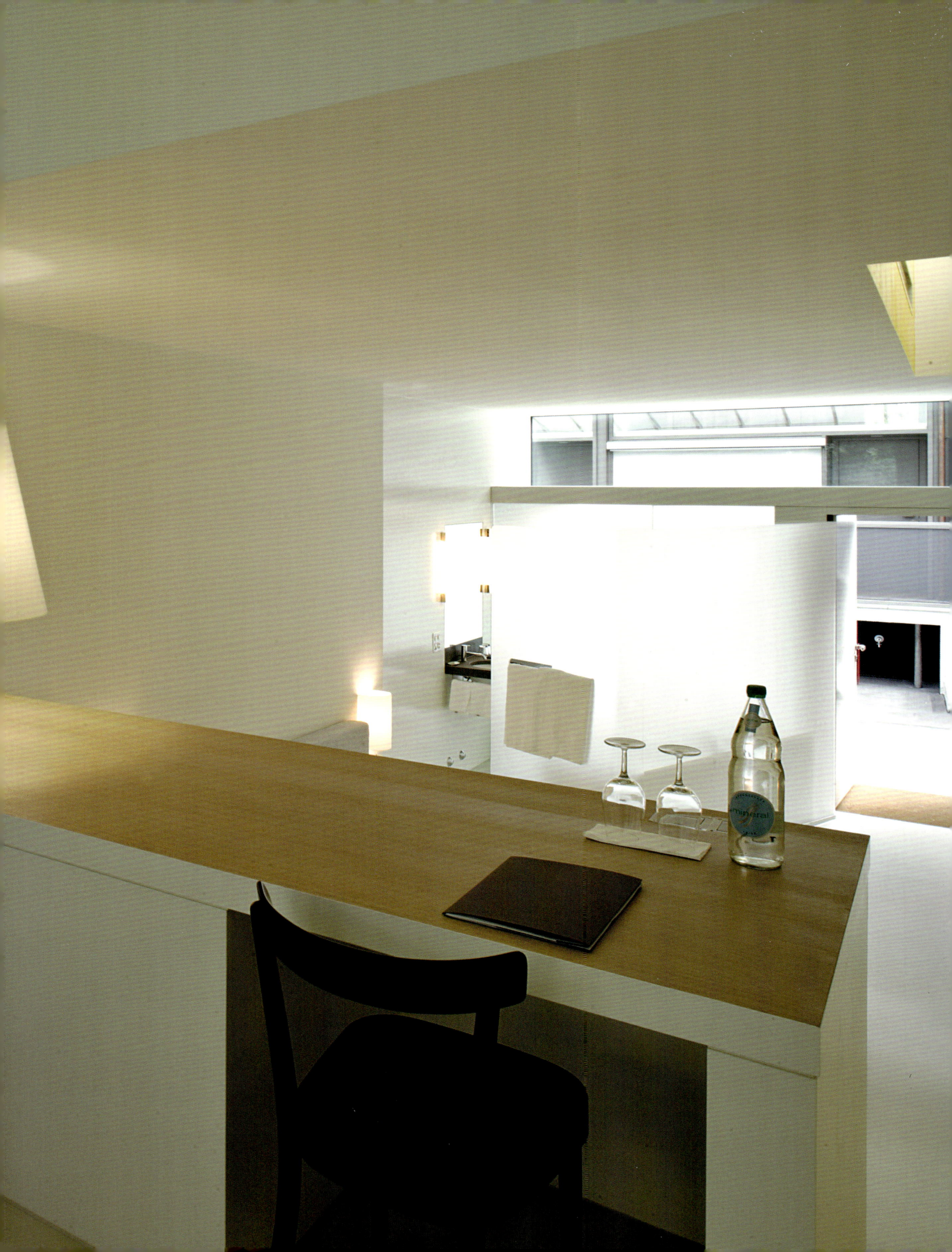

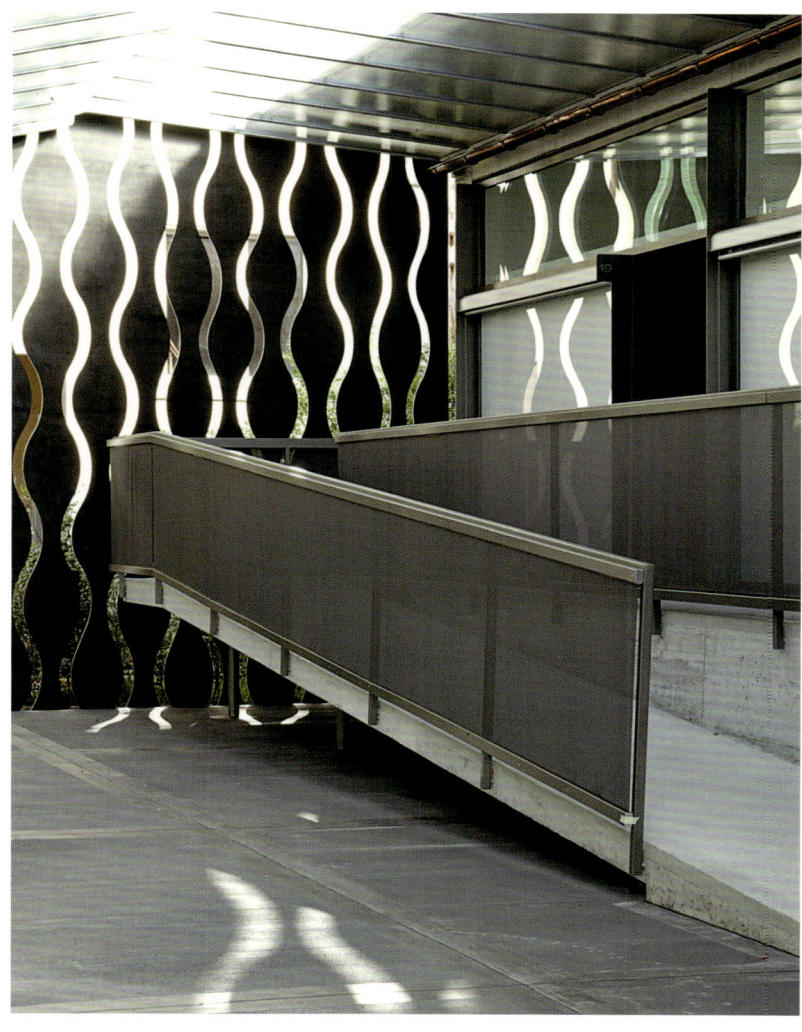
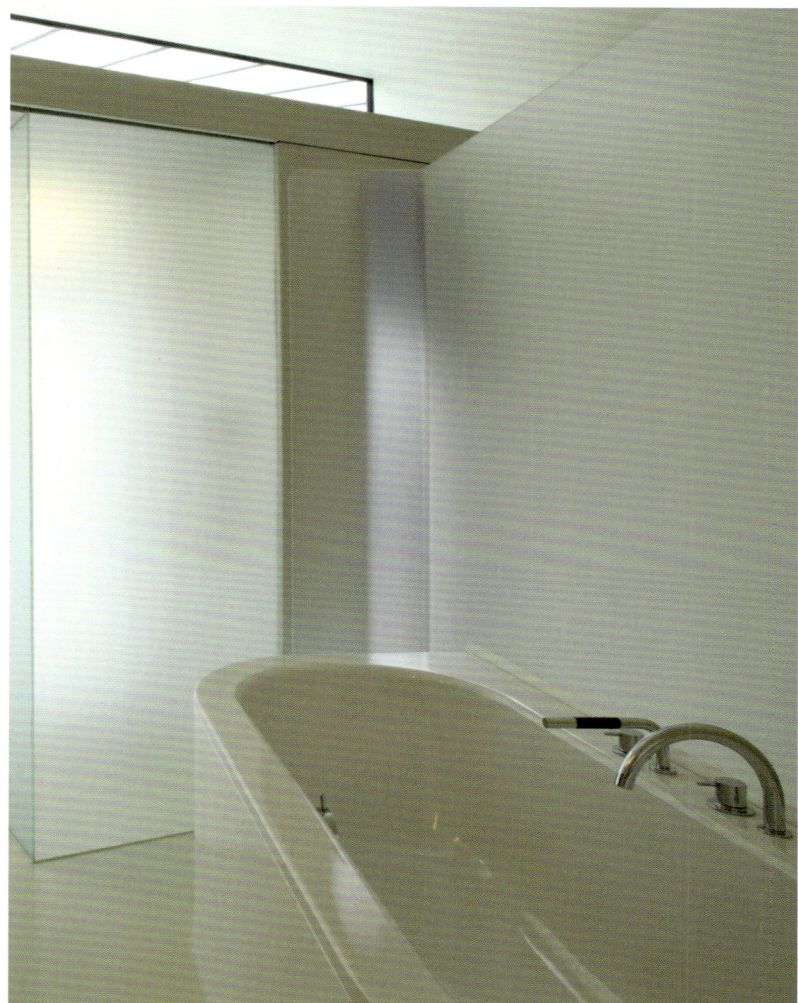
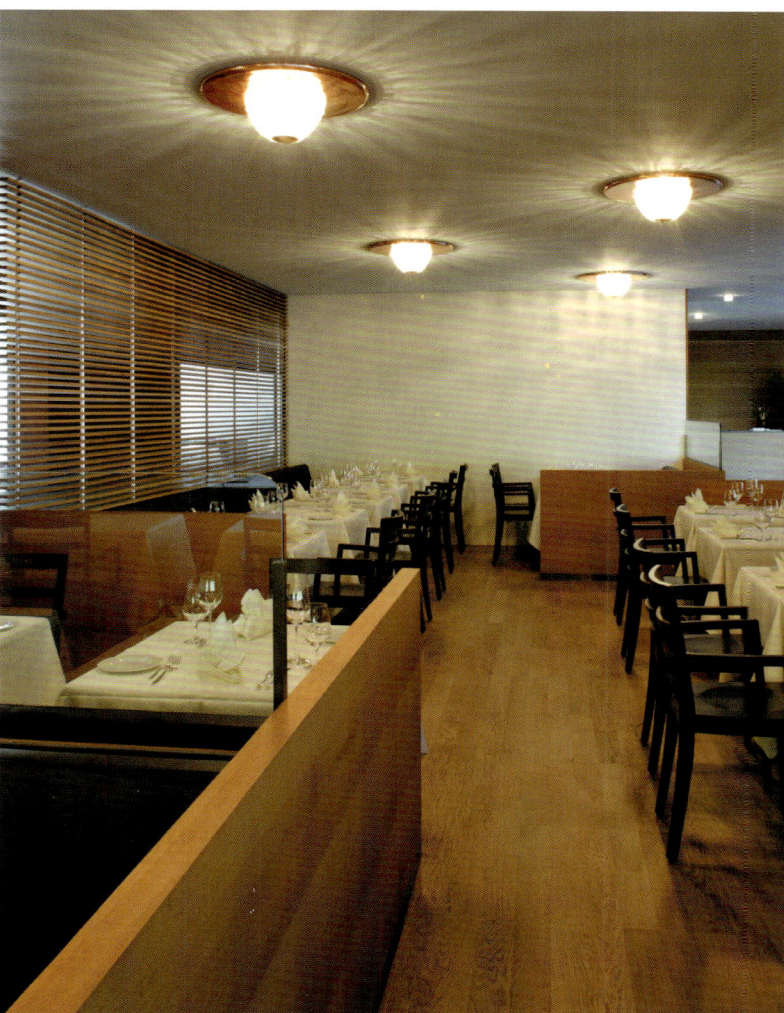
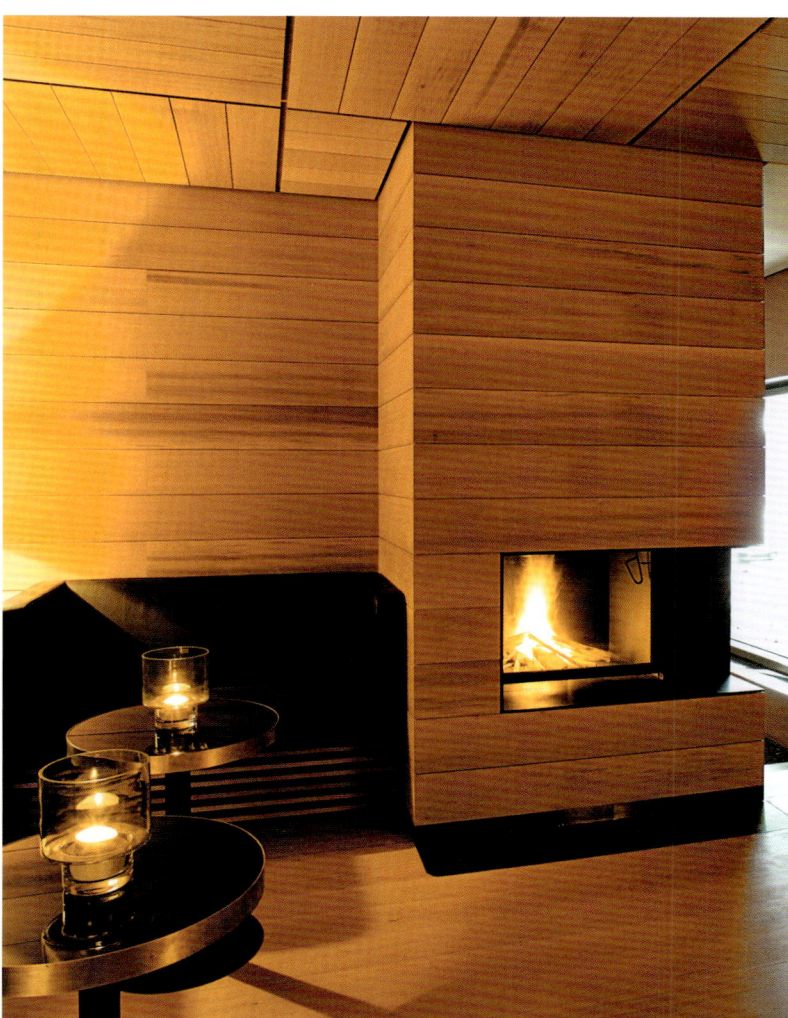

Widder Hotel

Zurich, Switzerland

Rennweg 7
8001 Zurich
Switzerland
Phone: +41 44 224 25 26
Fax: +41 44 224 24 24
www.widderhotel.ch

Price category: €€€
Rooms: 42 rooms and 7 suites
Facilities: Restaurant, bar, Wirtschaft zur Schtund, small technogym, library, business center, 8 conference rooms for up to 200 people
Services: 24 h room service, concierge, valet service, WiFi, interactive B&O screen TV and stereo
Located: In the heart of Zurich's Old Town, close to the Bahnofstrasse
Public transportation: 500 m from the main station; tram 6, 7, 11, 13 Rennweg
Style: Artfully fashioned

Eight stolid city houses from seven centuries in the middle of the old city of Zurich were remodeled to form the small but mighty luxury hotel. The Zurich architect Tilla Theus designed each of the 42 rooms and seven suites as something unique with modern furniture classics from Adolf Loos to Le Corbusier. The art exhibits are spectacular, among them a Poliakoff worth € 150,000. Robert Rauschenberg created an expressive late work especially for the penthouse suite. The "Library of Spirits" enjoys legendary fame with more than 250 single malt whiskies.

Acht behäbige Stadthäuser aus sieben Jahrhunderten mitten in der Zürcher Altstadt wurden zum kleinen, feinen Luxushotel umgebaut. Die Zürcher Architektin Tilla Theus gestaltete jedes der 42 Zimmer und sieben Suiten zu einem Unikat mit modernen Möbelklassikern von Adolf Loos bis Le Corbusier. Spektakulär sind die Kunstexponate, darunter ein € 150.000 teurer Poliakoff. Robert Rauschenberg schuf eigens für die Penthouse-Suite ein expressives Spätwerk. Einen legendären Ruf genießt die „Library of Spirits" mit mehr als 250 Single Malt Whiskys.

Au cœur de la vieille ville de Zurich, huit maisons de ville datant de sept siècles différents ont été transformées en un joli petit hôtel de luxe. Tilla Theus, une architecte de Zurich, a créé les 42 chambres et les 7 suites pour en faire une unité unique avec des classiques du mobilier moderne, d'Adolf Loos au Corbusier. Les œuvres d'art sont spectaculaires, avec notamment un Poliakoff d'une valeur de € 150.000. Robert Rauschenberg a spécialement créé une œuvre d'art tardive pour la suite penthouse. La « Library of Spirits », sa collection d'alcools comportant plus de 250 whiskies single malt, jouit d'une réputation mythique.

Este pequeño y refinado hotel de lujo, situado en pleno centro histórico de Zúrich, se alberga en ocho monumentales casas privadas construidas a lo largo de siete siglos diferentes. La arquitecta zuriquesa Tilla Theus ha decorado cada una de sus 42 habitaciones y siete suites, haciendo de ellas ejemplares únicos, con muebles clásicos de Adolf Loos o Le Corbusier. Las obras de arte son espectaculares y entre ellas destaca un Poliakoff de € 150.000. Asimismo, Robert Rauschenberg creó especialmente para la suite de lujo del ático una obra expresionista tardía. De gran fama es el bar "Library of Spirits" con sus más de 250 diferentes whiskys de malta.

Un piccolo hotel di qualità, collocato nel cuore del centro storico di Zurigo. Ristrutturando con grande creatività un complesso di otto case massicce risalenti agli ultimi sette secoli, l'architetto zurighese Tilla Theus ha saputo trasformare in un pezzo unico ognuna delle 42 camere e delle 7 suite della casa – camere e suite che sono arredate con classici mobili di modernariato, da Adolf Loos a Le Corbusier. Spettacolari le opere d'arte esposte, tra le quali spicca un Poliakoff, stimato sui € 150.000, e un espressivo Robert Rauschenberg ultimo periodo, appositamente creato per la suite Penthouse. Di fama leggendaria gode la "Library of Spirits", che raccoglie più di 250 whisky single malt.

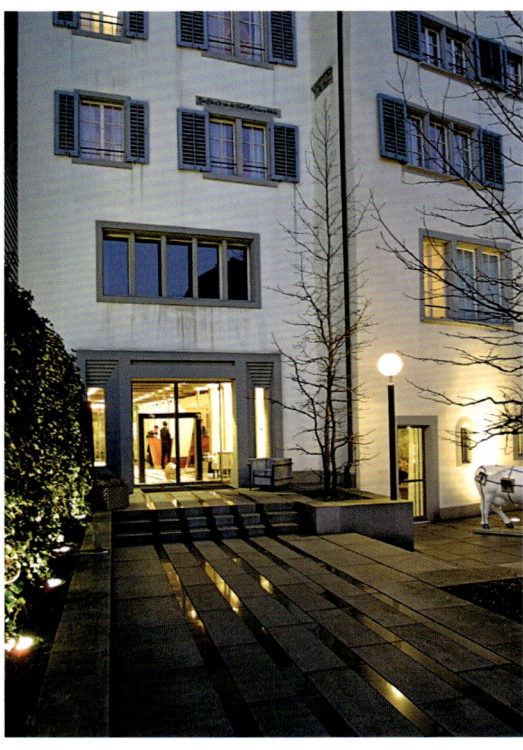 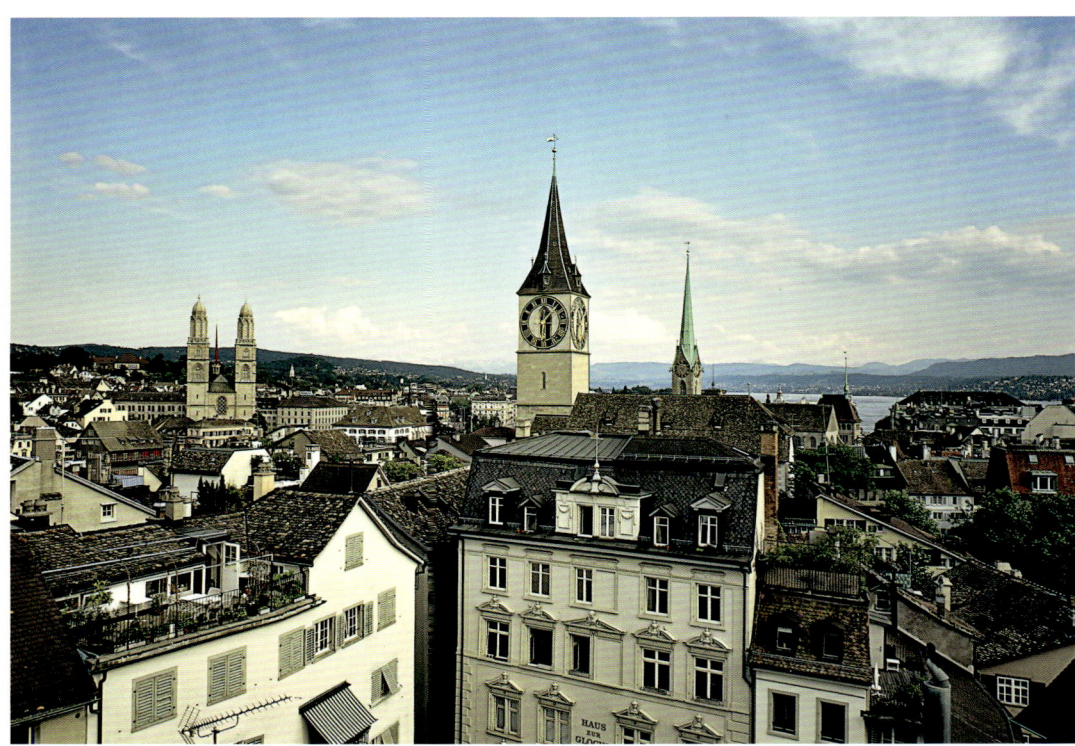

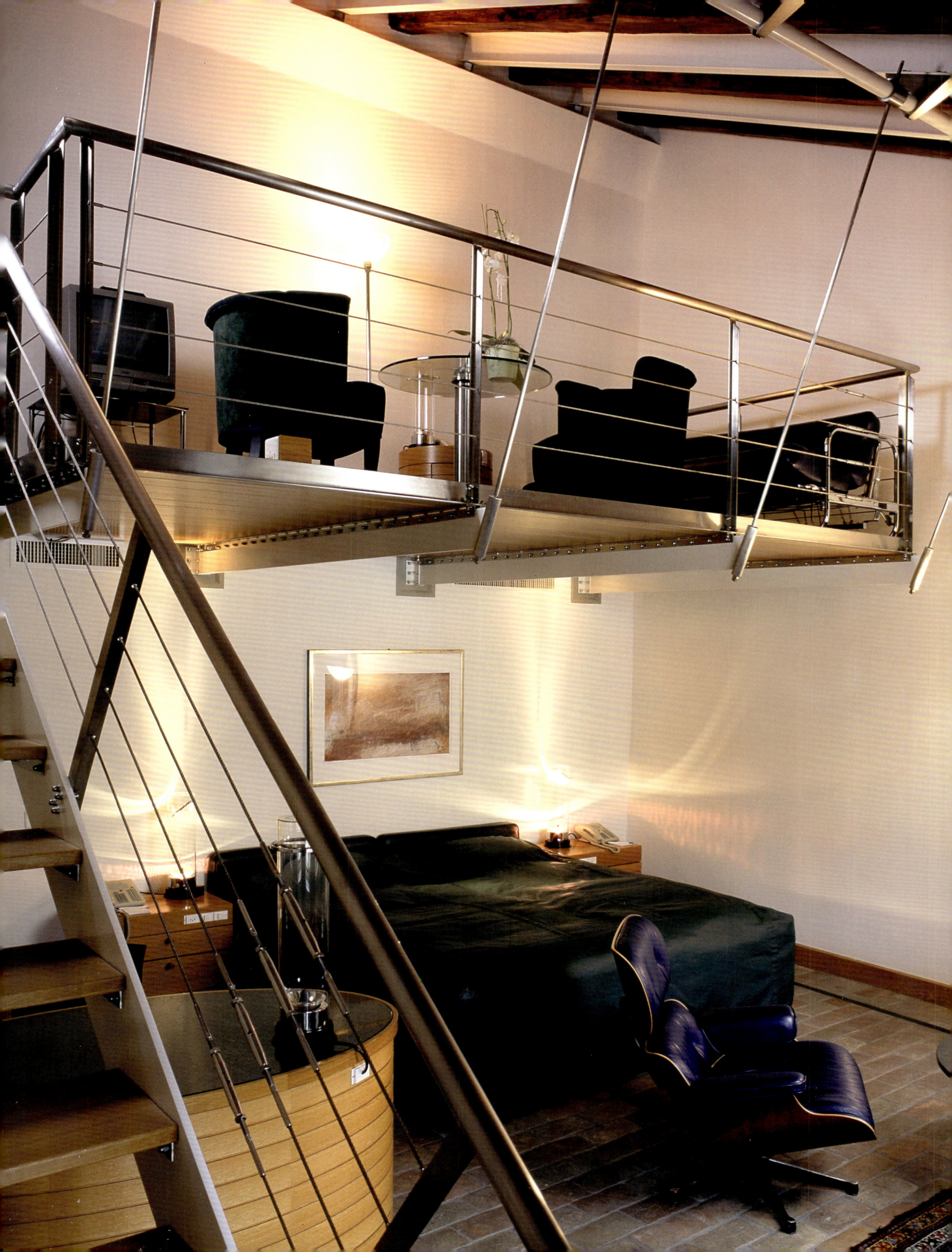

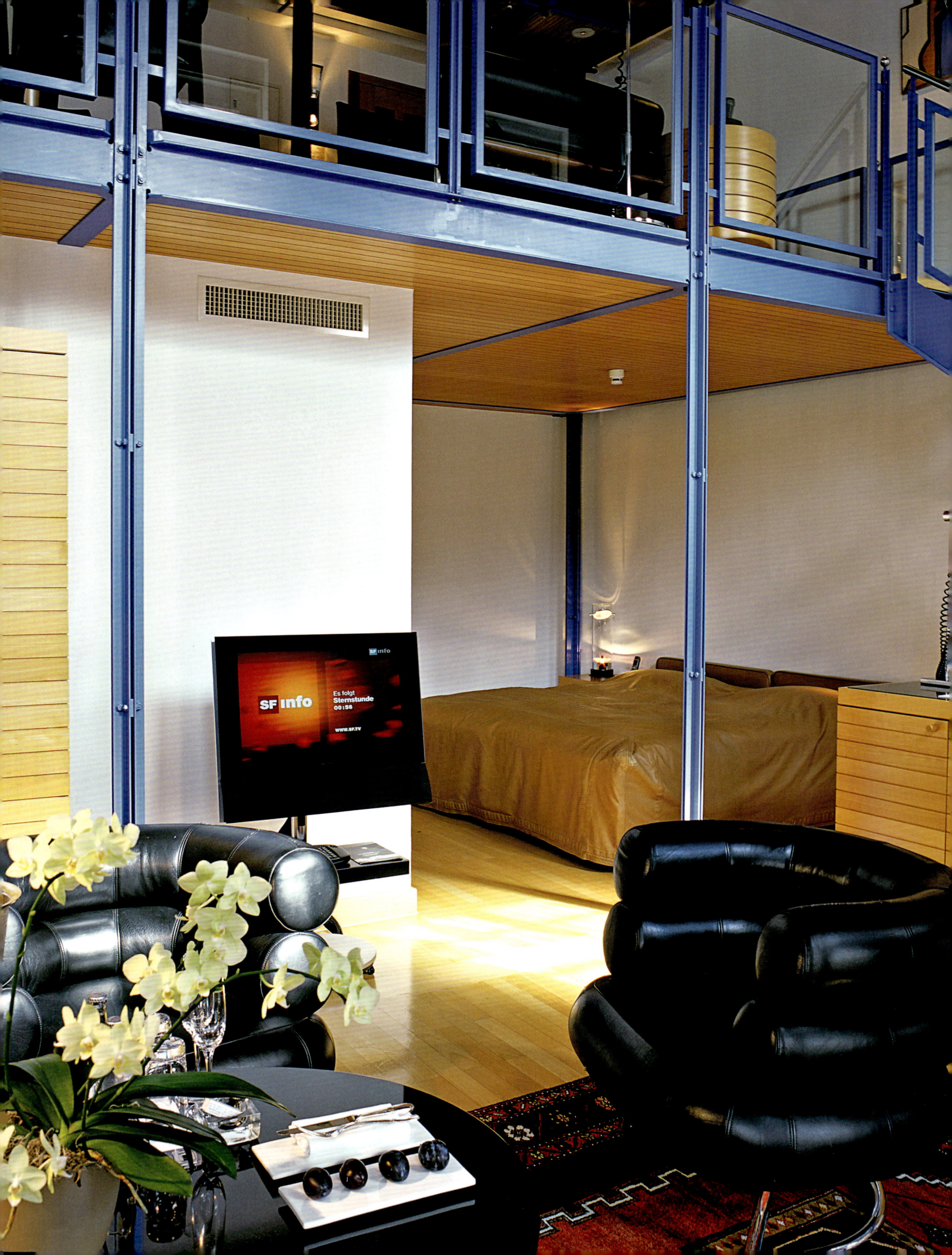

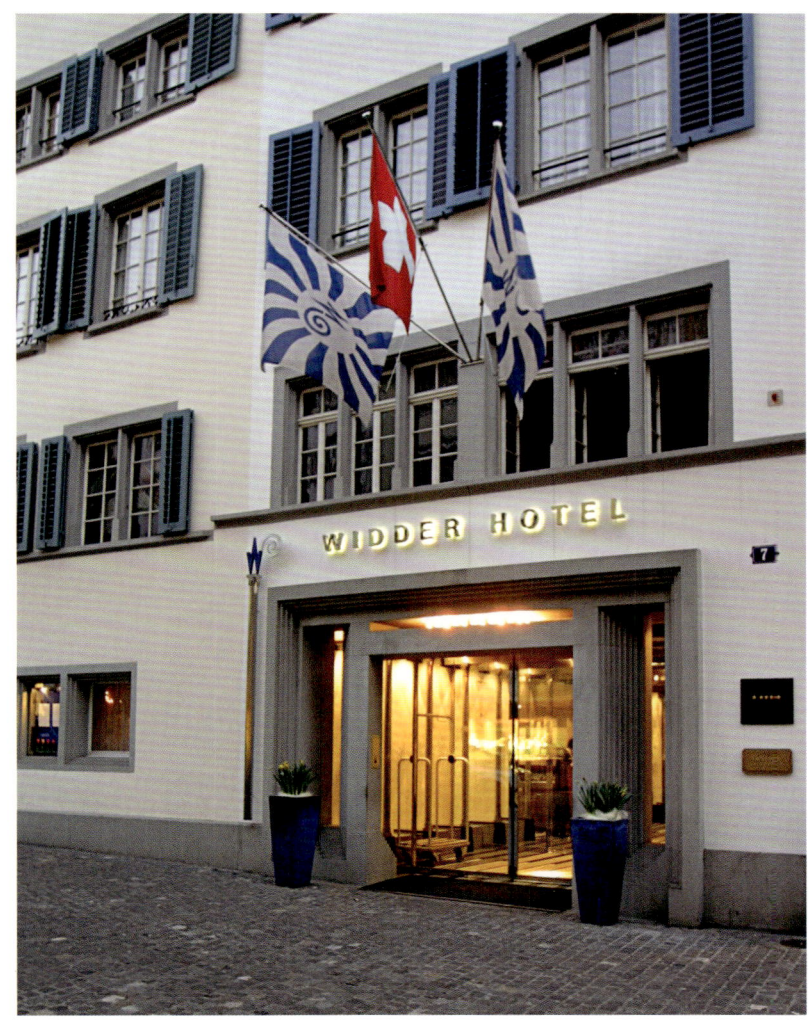

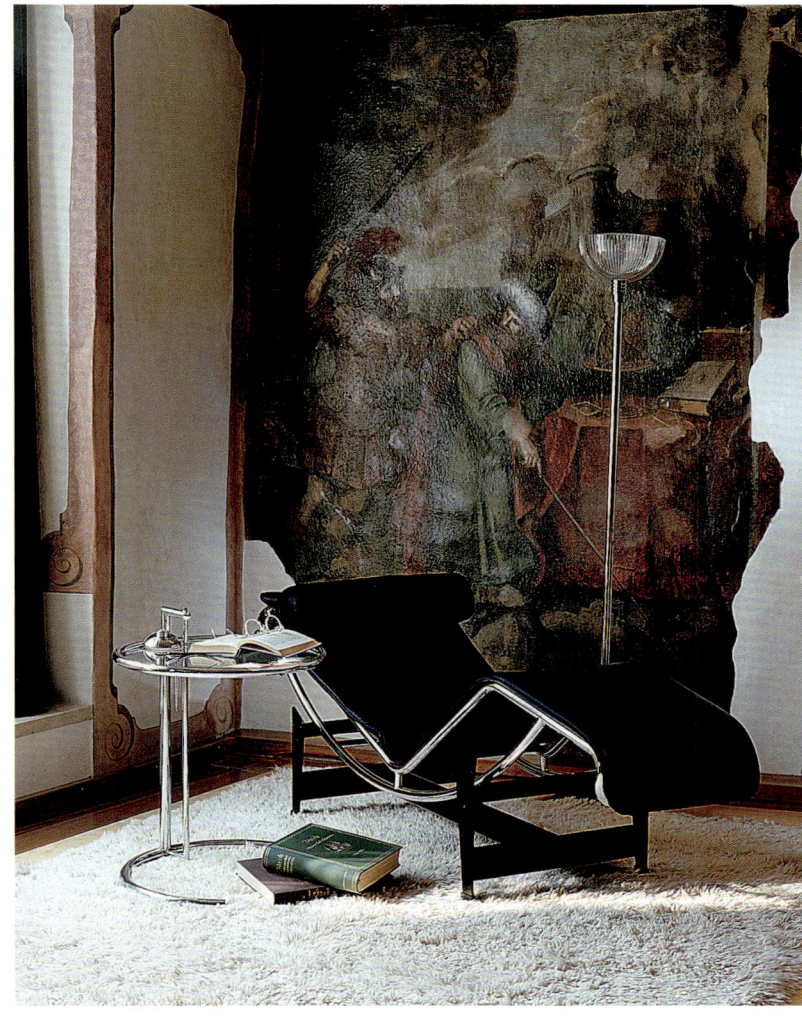

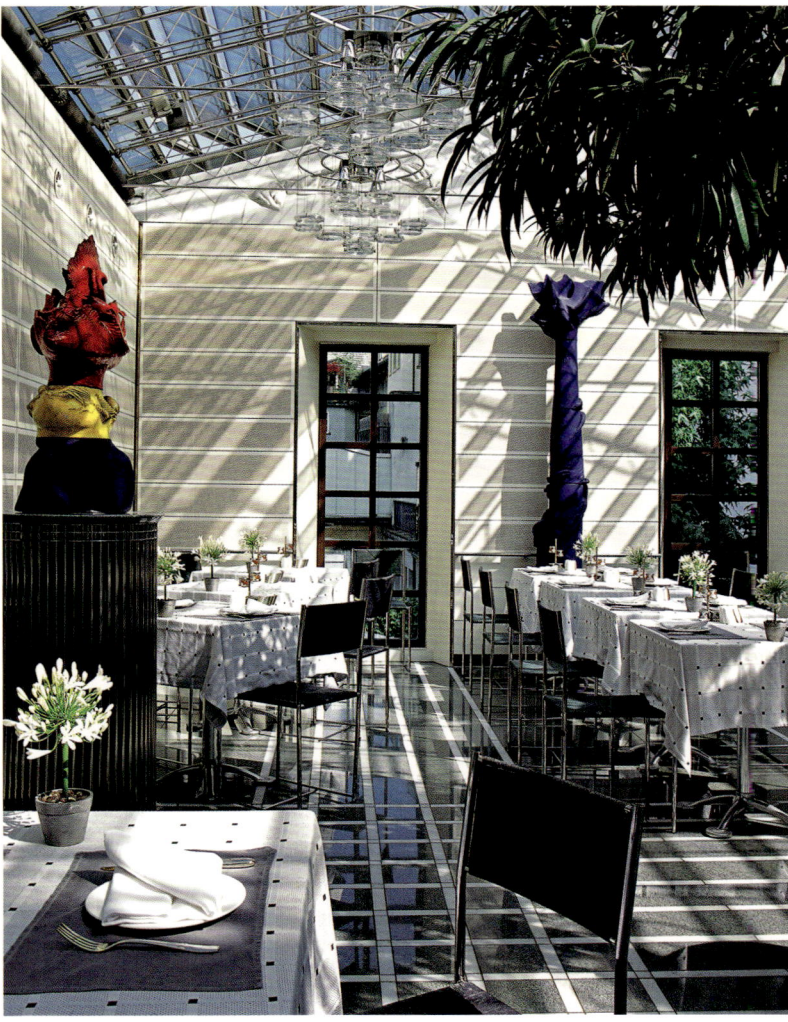

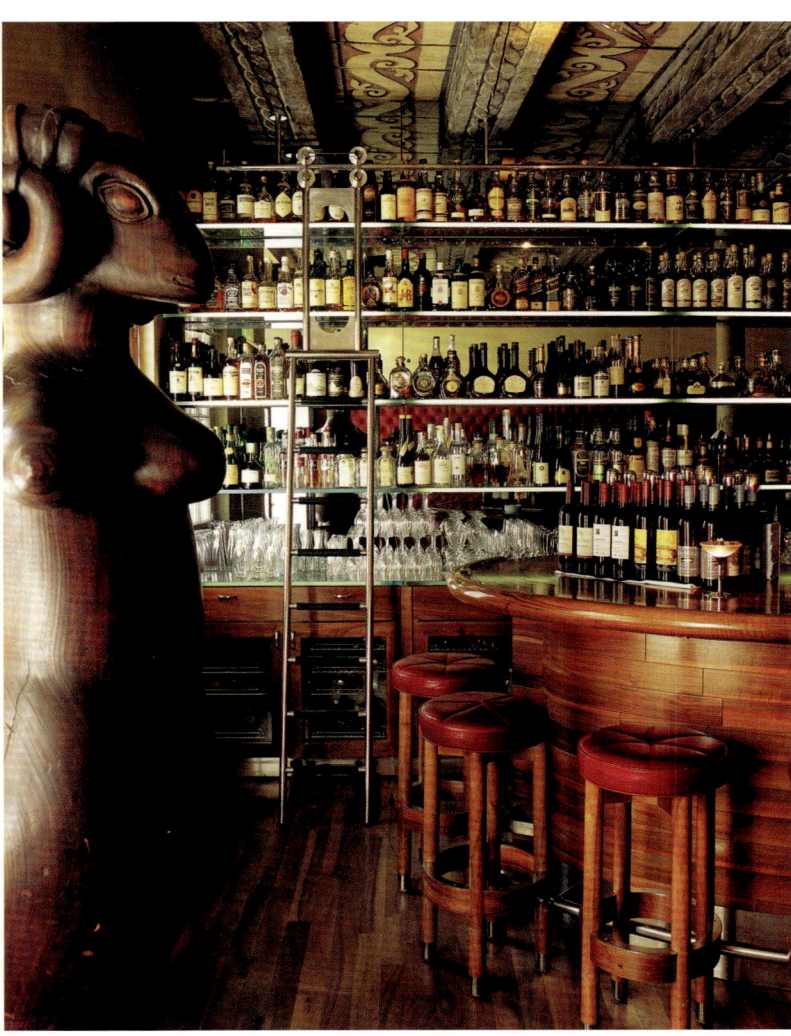

20137 Porto Vecchio, Corsica
France
Phone: +33 4 95 72 34 34
Fax: +33 4 95 72 34 35
www.casadelmar.fr

Rooms: 34 rooms and suites
Facilities: Gastronomic restaurant with 1 Michelin star, pool restaurant, lounge bar
Services: Spa Carita and Decleor, hair stylist, private beach, heated outdoor swimming pool, business center
Located: 6 km from Porto Vecchio center
Public transportation: 20 km to the Figari International Airport
Style: Design hotel

With a view over the bay of Porto Vecchio, the fragrance of the pines and the crystal clear light, at Casadelmar you experience the essence of Corsica more intensively than anywhere else on the island. The building of cedar, stone and glass is the epitome of harmony between nature and architecture: sea, sky and pool flow together, and all 34 rooms open out onto terraces. The interior is defined by clean lines, design classics as well as color accents. The spa soothes the soul, and the restaurant is pure Mediterranean inspiration—the unforgettable taste of summer.

Der Blick über die Bucht von Porto Vecchio, der Duft von Pinien und das kristallklare Licht: Im Casadelmar erlebt man die Essenz Korsikas so intensiv wie nirgendwo sonst auf der Insel. Der Bau aus Zedernholz, Stein und Glas ist der Inbegriff von Harmonie zwischen Natur und Architektur: Meer, Himmel und Pool fließen ineinander, und alle 34 Zimmer öffnen sich zu Terrassen. Das Innere bestimmen klare Linien, Designklassiker sowie Farbakzente. Das Spa ist Balsam für die Seele, und das Restaurant mediterran inspiriert – so schmeckt der Sommer.

Vue sur la Baie de Porto Vecchio, parfum des pins et lumière cristalline : nulle part ailleurs sur l'île on ne ressent mieux l'essence-même de la Corse qu'à Casadelmar. La structure du bâtiment, en cèdre, pierre et verre, est le symbole de l'harmonie entre la nature et l'architecture ; la mer, le ciel et la piscine semblent se fondre, et les 34 chambres s'ouvrent toutes sur des terrasses. L'intérieur est dominé par des lignes claires, des classiques du design et des touches de couleur. Le spa apporte du baume à l'âme et le restaurant est d'inspiration purement méditerranéenne : le goût inoubliable de l'été.

La vista sobre la bahía de Porto Vecchio, el aroma de los pinos y la luz cristalina; en el hotel casadelmar se percibe la esencia de Córcega como en ningún otro lugar de la isla. El edificio de cedro, piedra y cristal es el súmmum de la armonía entre naturaleza y arquitectura. El mar, el cielo y la piscina se fusionan entre si y sus 34 habitaciones se abren hacia terrazas exteriores. El interior está marcado por las líneas claras, los clásicos del diseño y las diferentes tonalidades cromáticas. El spa es como un bálsamo para el alma y el restaurante se inspira en la cocina mediterránea. Así sabe el verano.

La vista sulla baia di Porto Vecchio, il profumo dei pini e l'aria cristallina: Casadelmar permette di vivere l'essenza della Corsica nel modo più intenso di qualsiasi altro posto dell'isola. La struttura in legno di cedro, pietra e vetro è la quintessenza del perfetto equilibrio tra natura e architettura: mare, cielo e piscina formano un tutt'uno, e ciascuna delle 34 camere dell'albergo si apre su una terrazza. L'interno è dettato da linee semplici, classici pezzi di design e colori marcati. Lo Spa è un balsamo per l'anima, e il ristorante d'ispirazione mediterranea – questo è il sapore dell'estate.

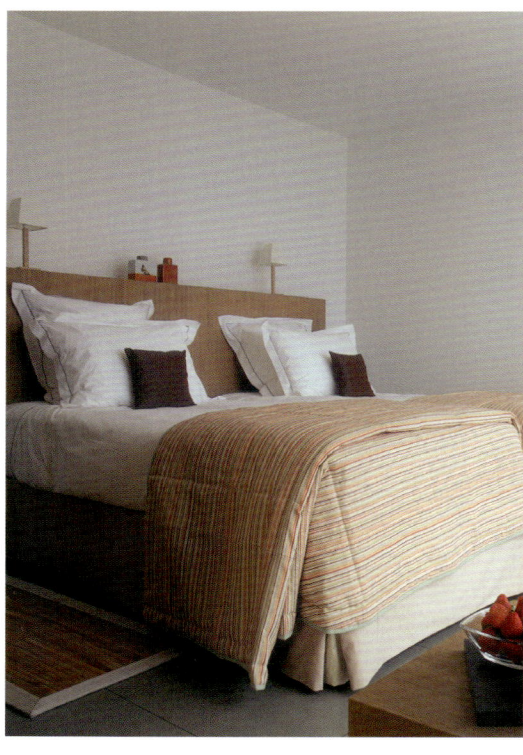
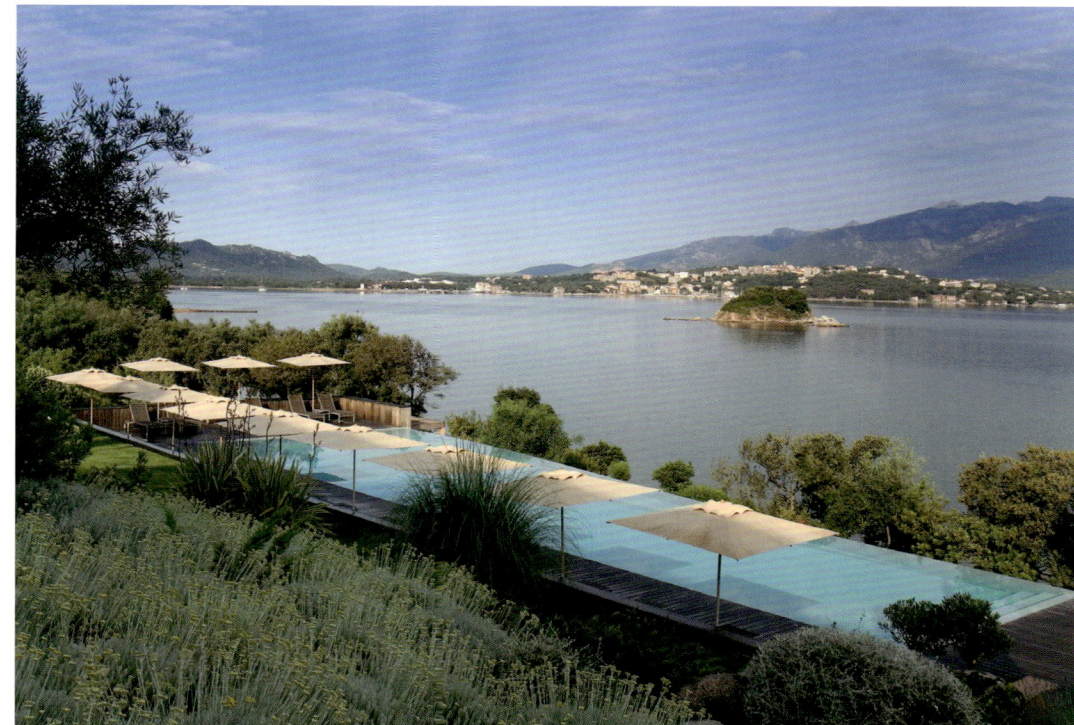

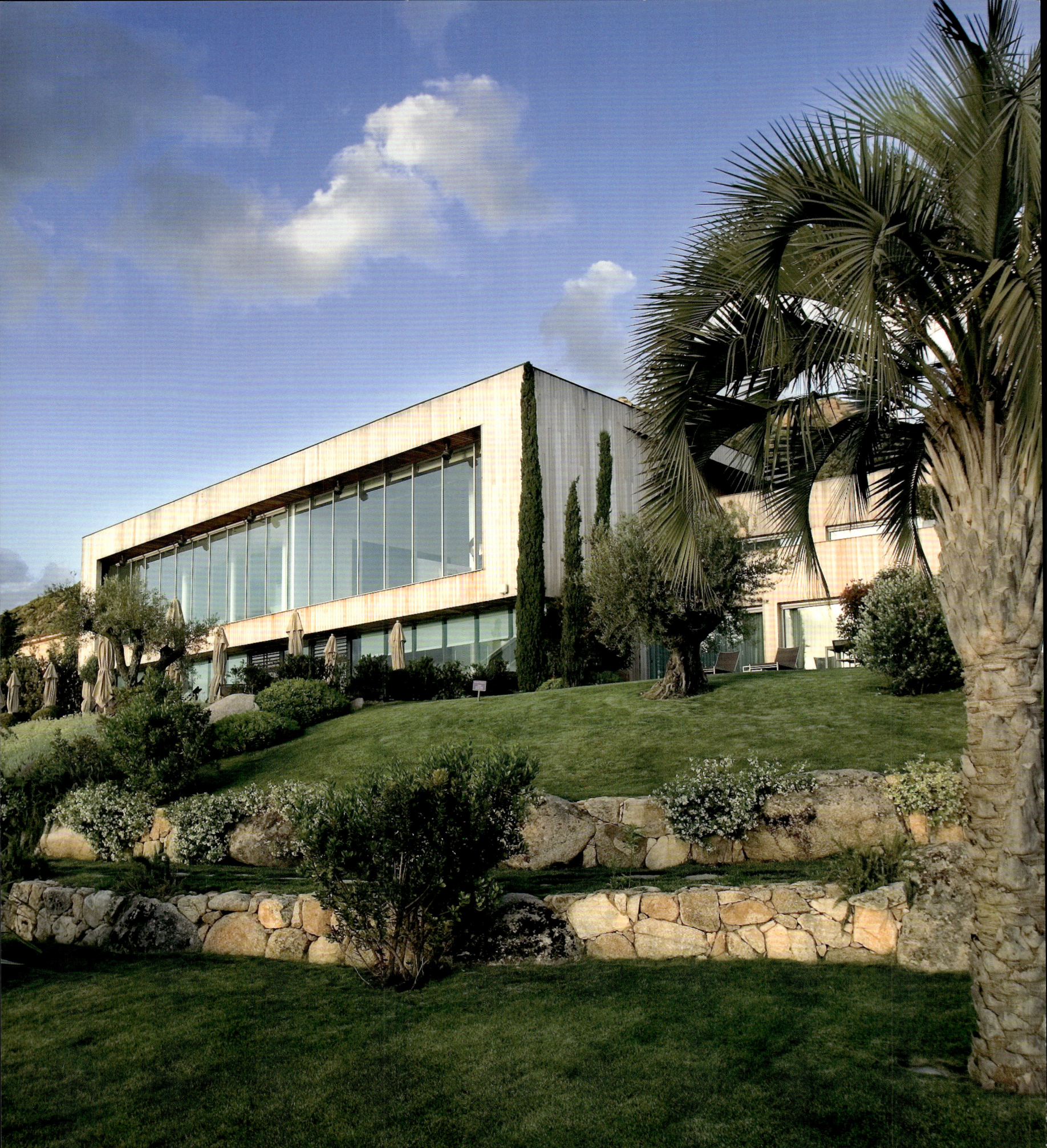

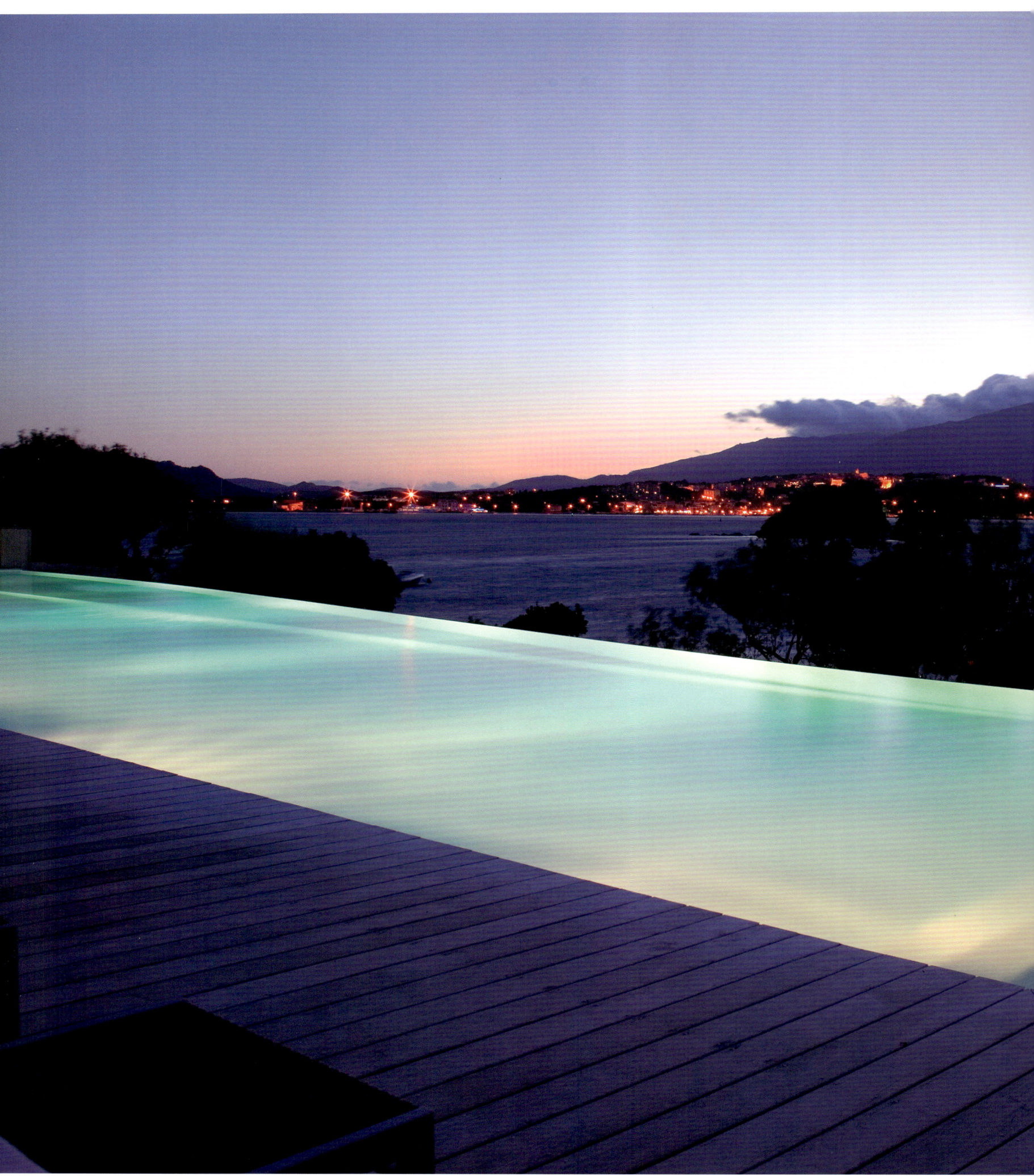

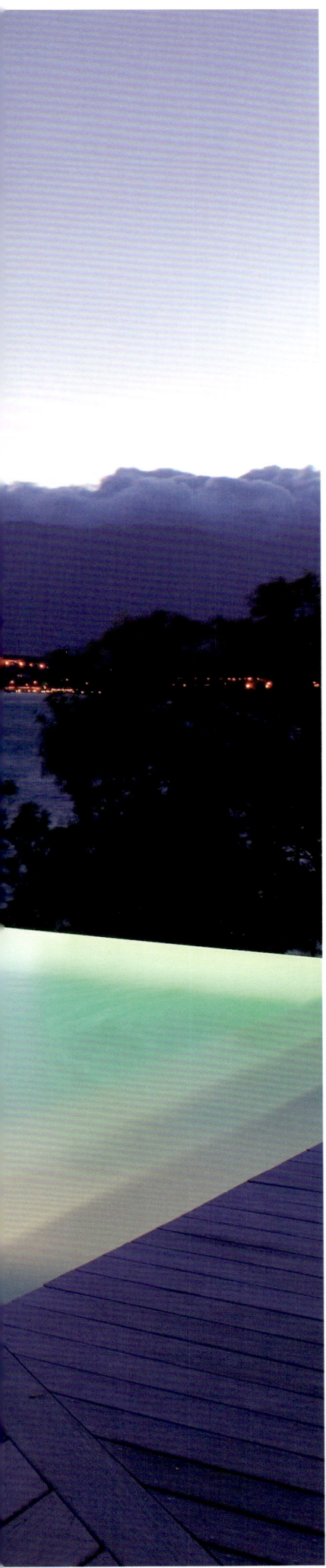

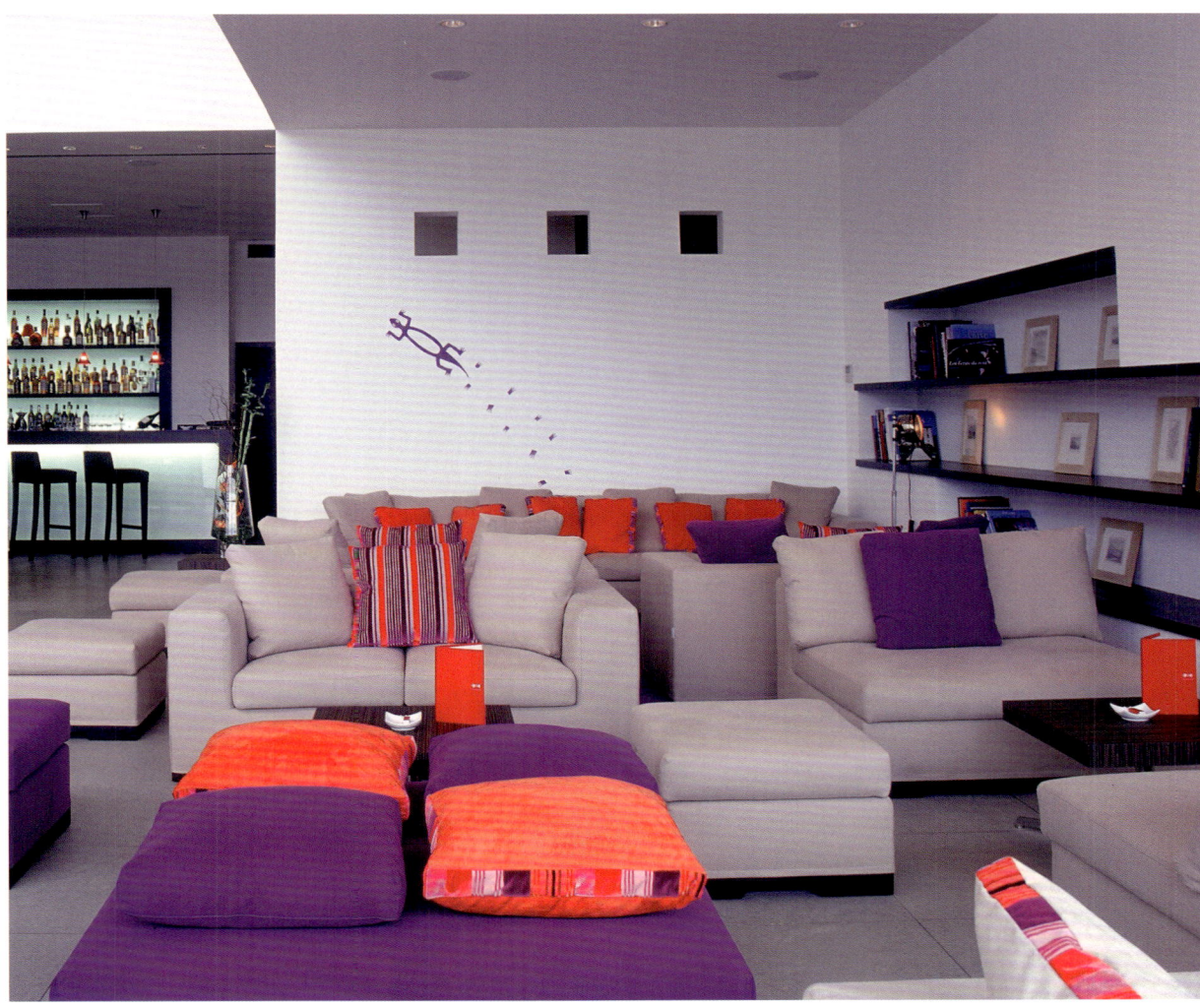

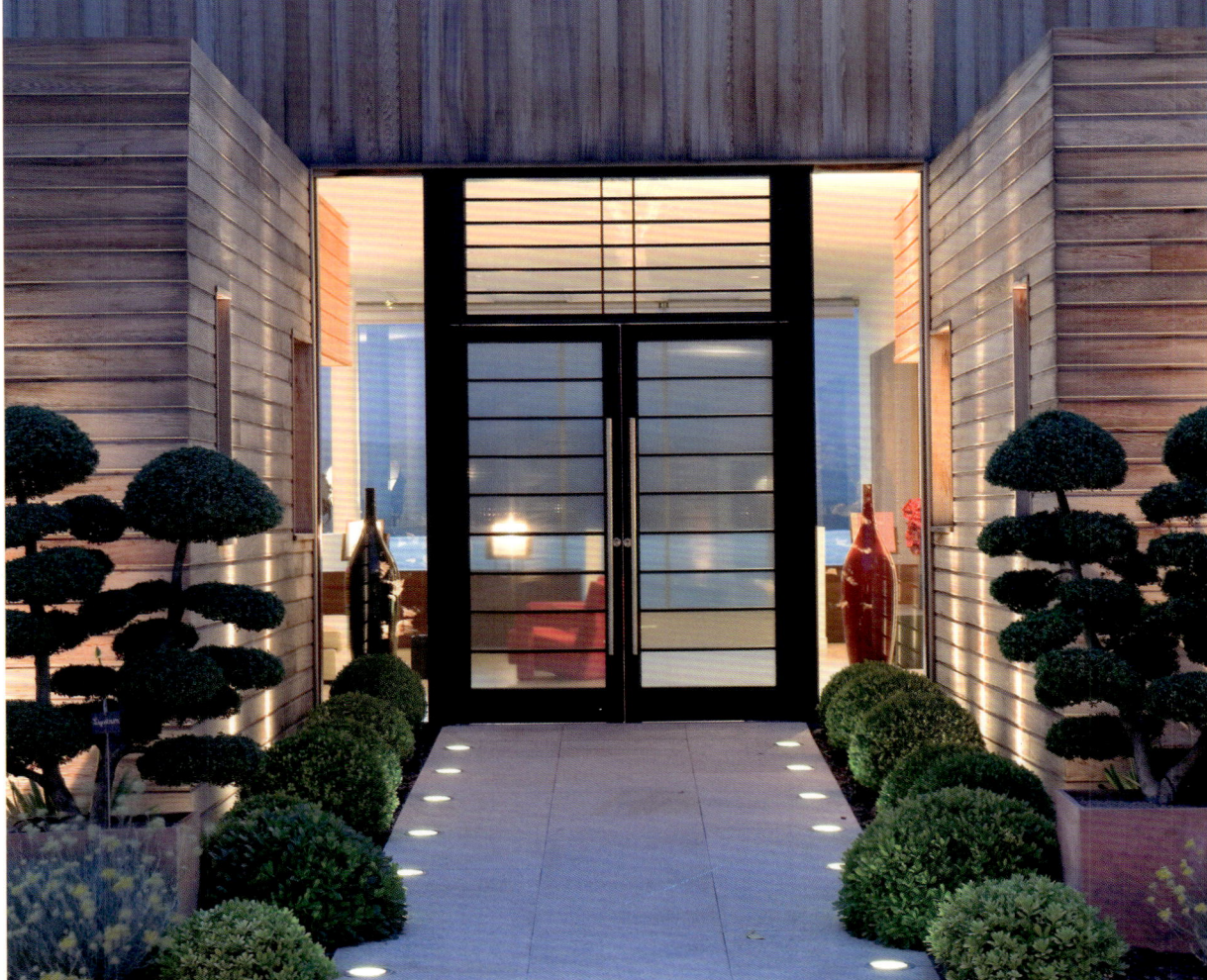

98000 Monaco
Monaco
Phone: +377 92 05 90 00
Fax: +377 92 05 91 67
www.columbushotels.com

Rooms: 181 rooms including 28 suites
Facilities: Bar restaurant La Brasserie, swimming pool
Services: "Toys for Big Boys," à la carte "men at play" itinerary; "Gracefully Shopping," a chauffeur-driven shopping to chic retail destinations in the principality
Located: On the left hand side of the Rock/Rocher
Public transportation: Bus
Style: Contemporary

Even if he has withdrawn a little in the meantime, the "speedy style" of hotel founder David Coulthard is still noticeable in the Columbus. Be it in the 181 rooms, in the domination of masculine materials like leather, natural stone and wood or in the bar that is one of the best star spotting places in Monaco. The neighboring Princess Grace Rosegarden promises a moment of rest, but it is only a few steps further to where the yacht harbor and heliport await—speed is everything.

Auch wenn er sich inzwischen etwas zurückgezogen hat: Der „Speedy Style" von Hotelgründer David Coulthard ist im Columbus noch immer spürbar. Sei es in den 181 Zimmern, in denen maskuline Materialien wie Leder, Naturstein und Holz dominieren, oder an der edlen Bar, die einer von Monacos besten Plätzen zum Starspotting ist. Einen Moment der Ruhe verspricht der benachbarte Prinzessin-Gracia-Rosengarten, doch nur wenige Schritte weiter warten bereits Jachthafen und Heliport – Geschwindigkeit ist eben alles.

Bien qu'il se soit calmé un peu dans l'intervalle, le style « speedé » de son fondateur, le pilote David Coulthard, se ressent toujours à l'hôtel Columbus, à la fois dans ses 181 chambres, dans lesquelles des matériaux masculins comme le cuir, la pierre naturelle et le bois dominent, ou dans le pub très chic, l'un des meilleurs endroits pour croiser une star à Monaco. Vous pouvez savourer un moment de calme au jardin Princesse Grace voisin, et à seulement quelques pas un port de plaisance et un héliport vous attendent : la vitesse fait tout.

Aunque con el tiempo, David Coulthard, fundador de este hotel, haya disminuido un tanto su actividad, su "estilo vertiginoso" sigue aún vigente en el Columbus. Ya sea en sus 181 habitaciones, donde predominan los materiales masculinos como el cuero, la piedra natural y la madera, o en el bar de ambiente distinguido, donde se reúnen las caras más célebres de Mónaco. El cercano jardín de rosas de la Princesa Grace promete momentos de sosiego, pero a tan sólo unos pasos de allí, aguardan el puerto de yates y el helipuerto. Al fin y al cabo, la velocidad lo es todo.

Anche se nel frattempo si è un po' ritirato dalla scena, David Coulthard, fondatore di diversi alberghi, fa ancora sentire il suo stile "Formula 1" nell'hotel Columbus. Vuoi nelle 181 camere, realizzate con materiali "mascolini" come cuoio, pietra naturale e legno, vuoi nell'elegante bar, uno dei posti migliori di Monaco per riuscire a vedere personaggi famosi. L'adiacente giardino di rose della Principessa Grace è garanzia di un momento di tranquillità, ma solo a pochi passi di distanza vi aspettano il porto turistico e l'eliporto. Qui la velocità è proprio tutto.

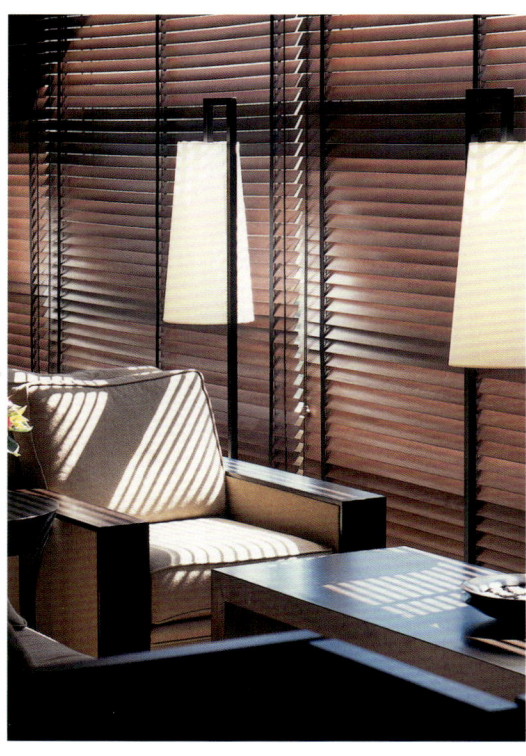
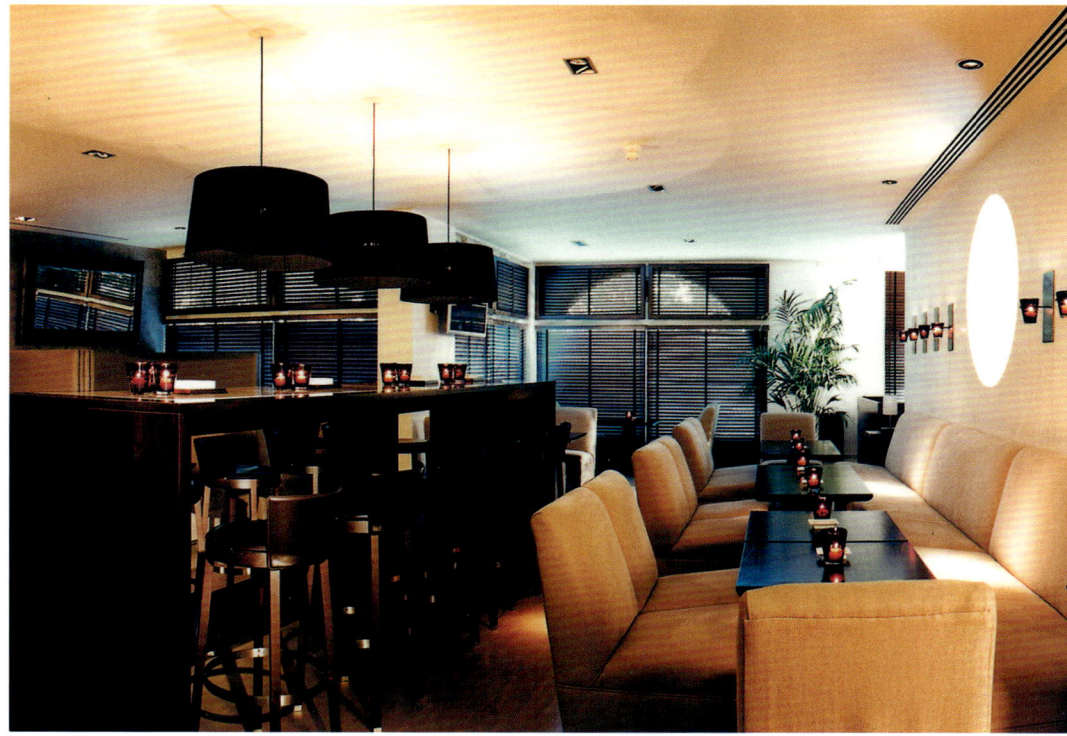

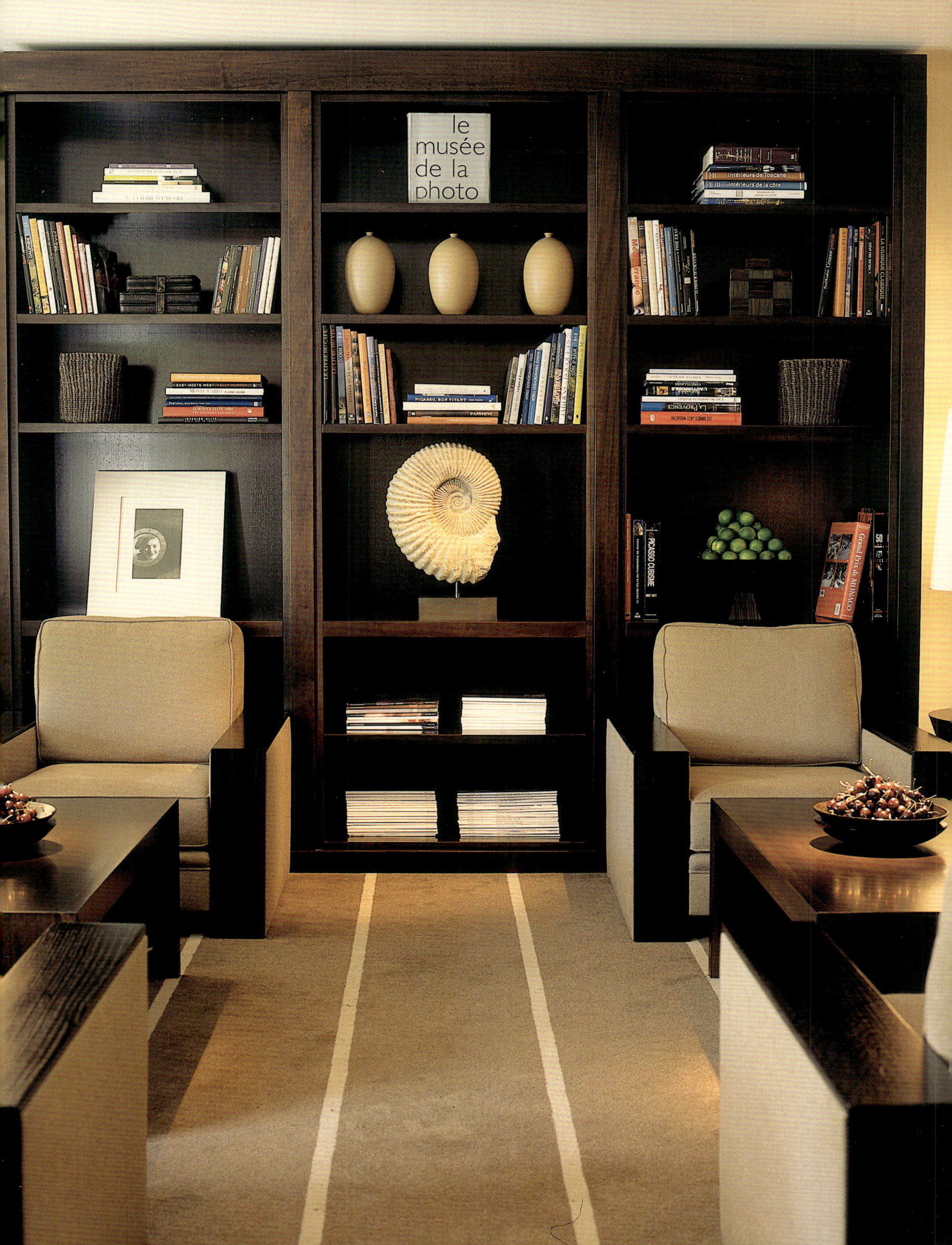

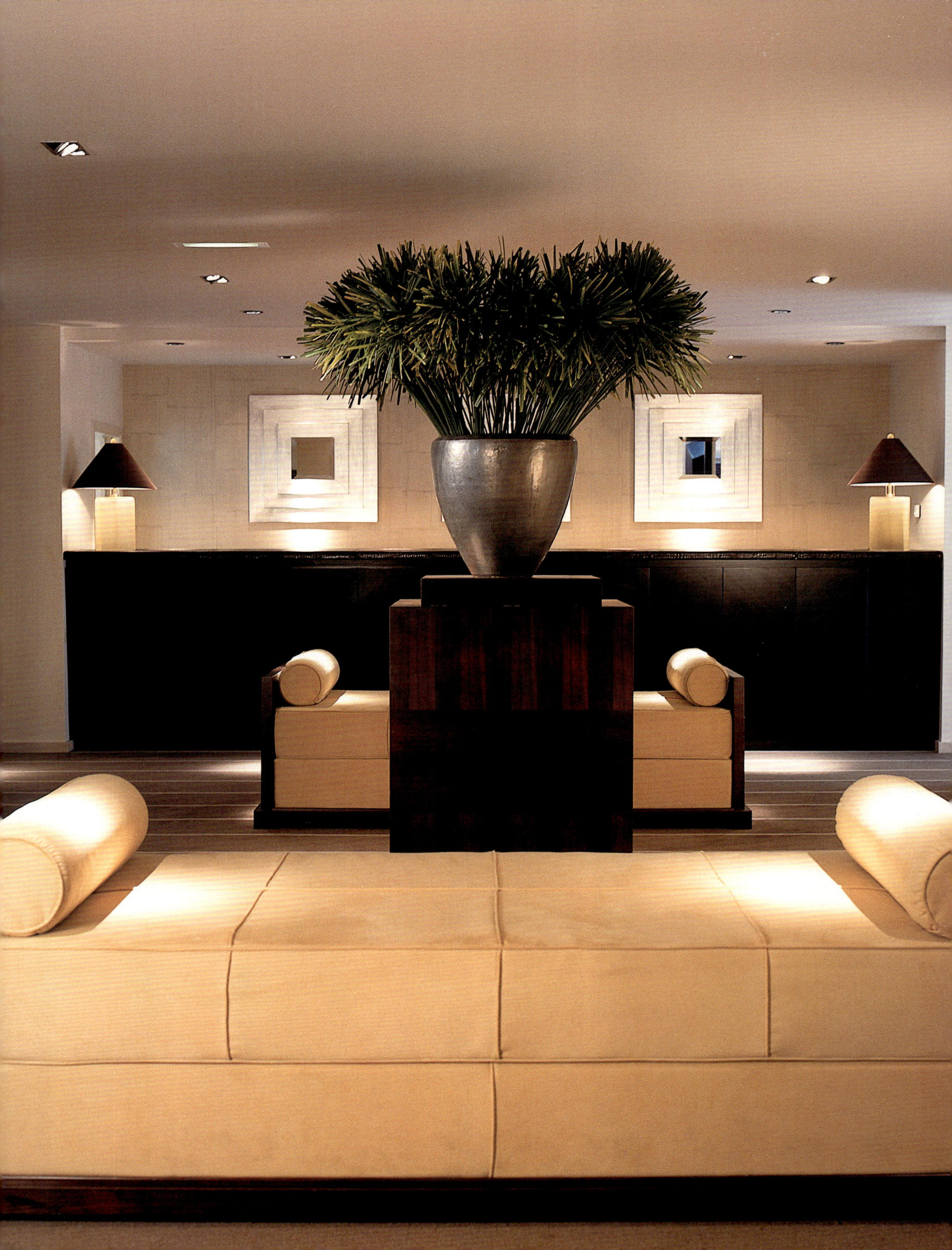

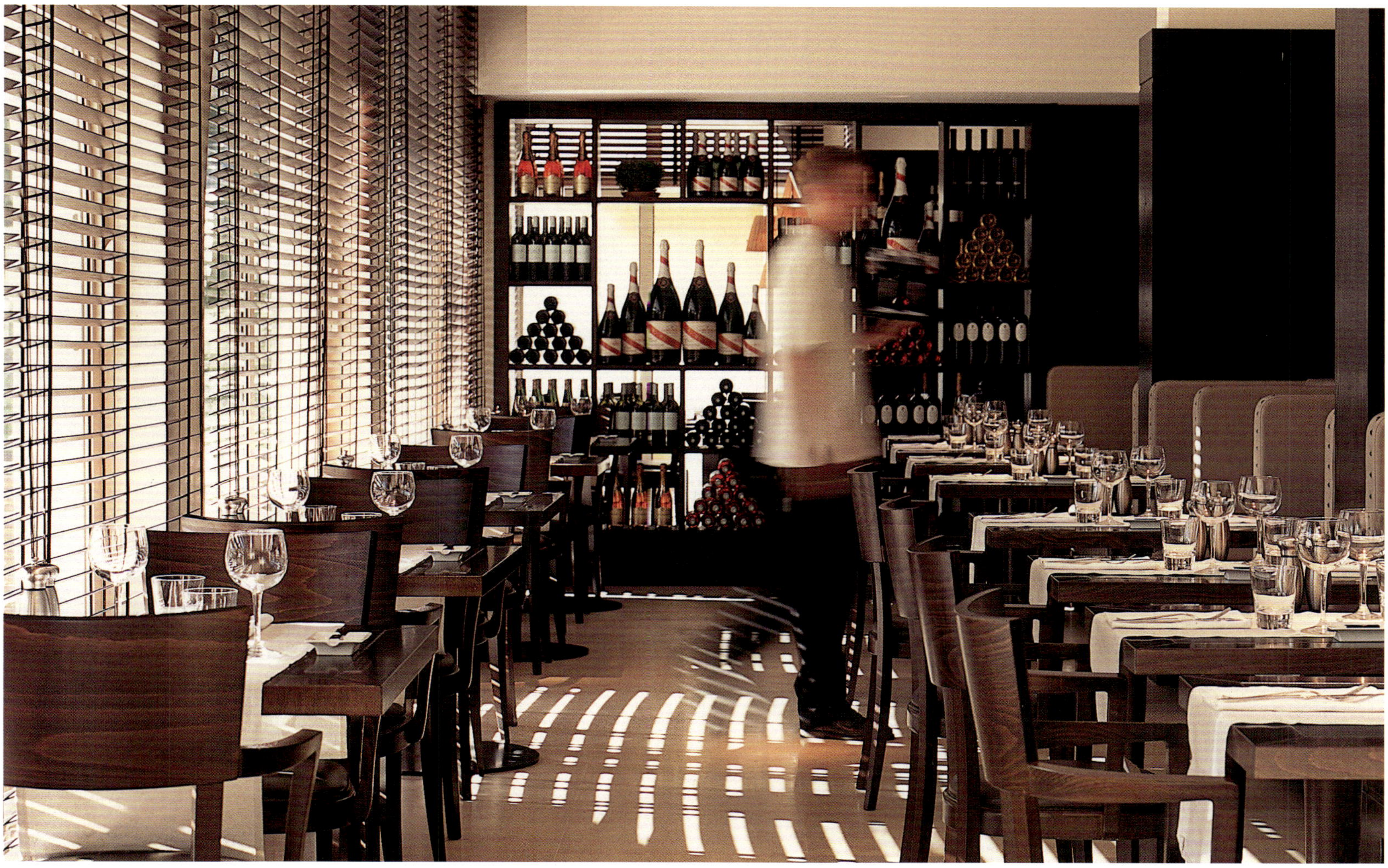

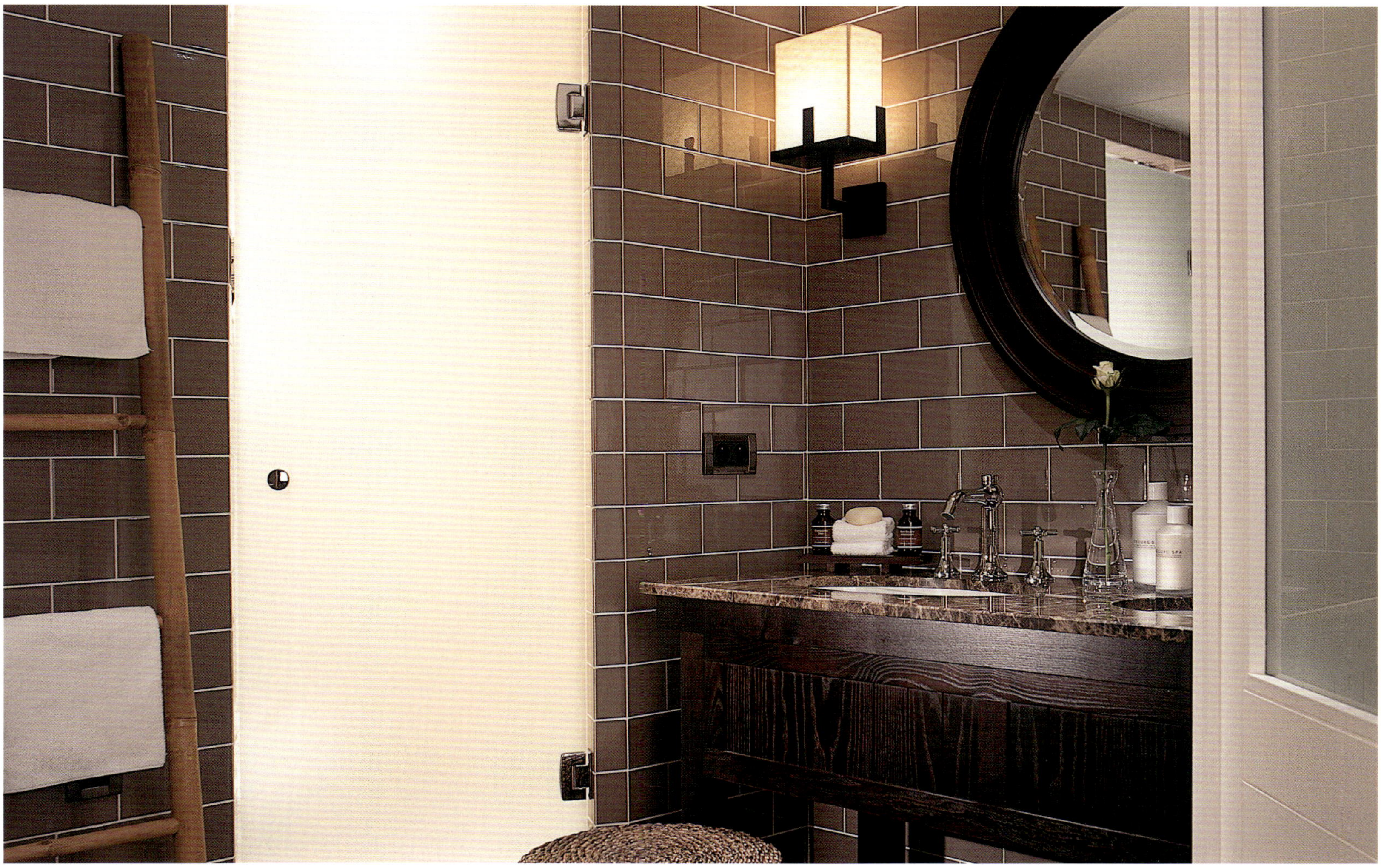

84000 Avignon
France
Phone: +33 4 90 27 55 55
Fax: +33 4 90 82 24 01
www.cloitre-saint-louis.com

Rooms: 80 rooms
Facilities: Restaurant, rooftop terrace, outdoor pool, garden, parking
Services: Satellite TV
Located: In the heart of Avignon
Public transportation: Bus, TGV train station
Style: Modern

Anyone wanting to live in the papal city of Avignon in true style is at the best address here: the Hôtel Cloître Saint Louis was built in the 16th century as Jesuit monastery—today it combines the old architecture effectively with a modern addition designed by Jean Nouvel. 80 rooms and suites with black leather furniture, red materials and mirrored baths set a cool contrast to the Mediterranean restaurant in the cloister vault, from where you have a view of the idyllic inner courtyard with its mighty plane trees. Small but great: the roof pool.

Wer in der Papststadt Avignon möglichst stilgetreu wohnen möchte, ist hier an der besten Adresse: Das Hôtel Cloître Saint Louis wurde im 16. Jahrhundert als Jesuitenkloster erbaut – heute kombiniert es die alte Architektur effektvoll mit einem modernen Anbau, den Jean Nouvel entwarf. 80 Zimmer und Suiten mit schwarzen Ledermöbeln, roten Stoffen und verspiegelten Bädern setzen kühle Kontraste zum mediterranen Restaurant im Kreuzgang, von wo aus man einen Blick in den idyllischen Innenhof mit seinen mächtigen Platanen hat. Klein aber fein: der Dachpool.

Celui qui veut vivre avec style dans la cité des Papes est ici à la bonne adresse : l'Hôtel Cloître Saint Louis a été construit au XVIème siècle comme un monastère jésuite, et aujourd'hui, il marie cette architecture ancienne avec une nouvelle extension moderne, dessinée par Jean Nouvel. 80 chambres et suites avec des meubles en cuir noir, des matériaux rouges et des salles de bains à miroirs offrent des contrastes rafraichissants avec le restaurant méditerranéen du cloître, où l'on a une vue sur la cour intérieure idyllique avec ses grands platanes. La piscine de toit est petite, mais très agréable.

Quien desee vivir con estilo en la ciudad papal de Aviñón encontrará aquí la mejor dirección. El Hôtel Cloître Saint Louis fue construido en el siglo XVI como convento de Jesuitas. Hoy en día combina de manera espectacular la arquitectura antigua con un nuevo edificio diseñado por Jean Nouvel. Sus 80 habitaciones y suites, con muebles tapizados en cuero negro, tejidos rojos y baños llenos de espejos, ofrecen un contraste frío en comparación con el restaurante mediterráneo del claustro, desde donde pueden contemplarse los enormes plataneros del idílico patio interior. La piscina en el tejado es pequeña pero formidable.

Chi volesse soggiornare nella città papale di Avignone con il massimo dello stile troverà qui ciò che fa per lui: nell'Hôtel Cloître Saint Louis, un ex convento di gesuiti risalente al XVI secolo, le originarie forme architettoniche si combinano con grande efficacia con la modernità della dependance progettata da Jean Nouvel. Le sue 80 fra camere e suite – arredate con mobili di pelle nera, stoffe rosse e bagni rivestiti di specchi – cerano un espressivo contrasto con il ristorante mediterraneo situato nel chiostro, dal quale si gode di una splendida vista sull'idilliaco cortile interno e sui suoi possenti platani. Piccola ma elegantissima la piscina sul tetto.

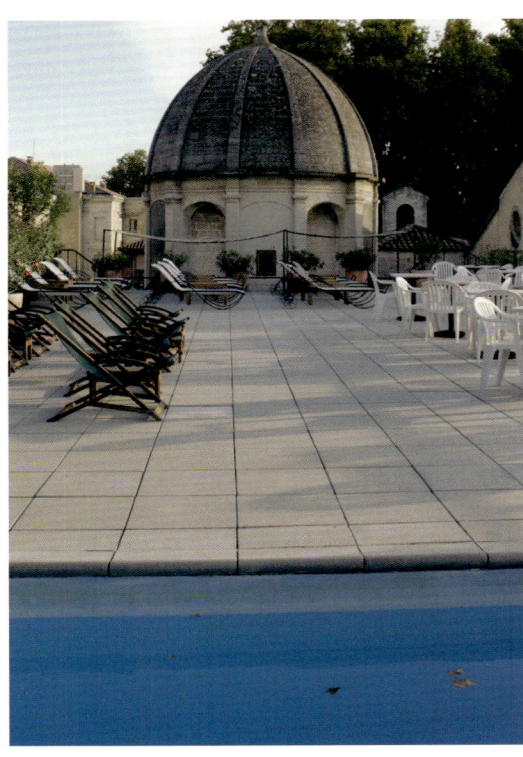
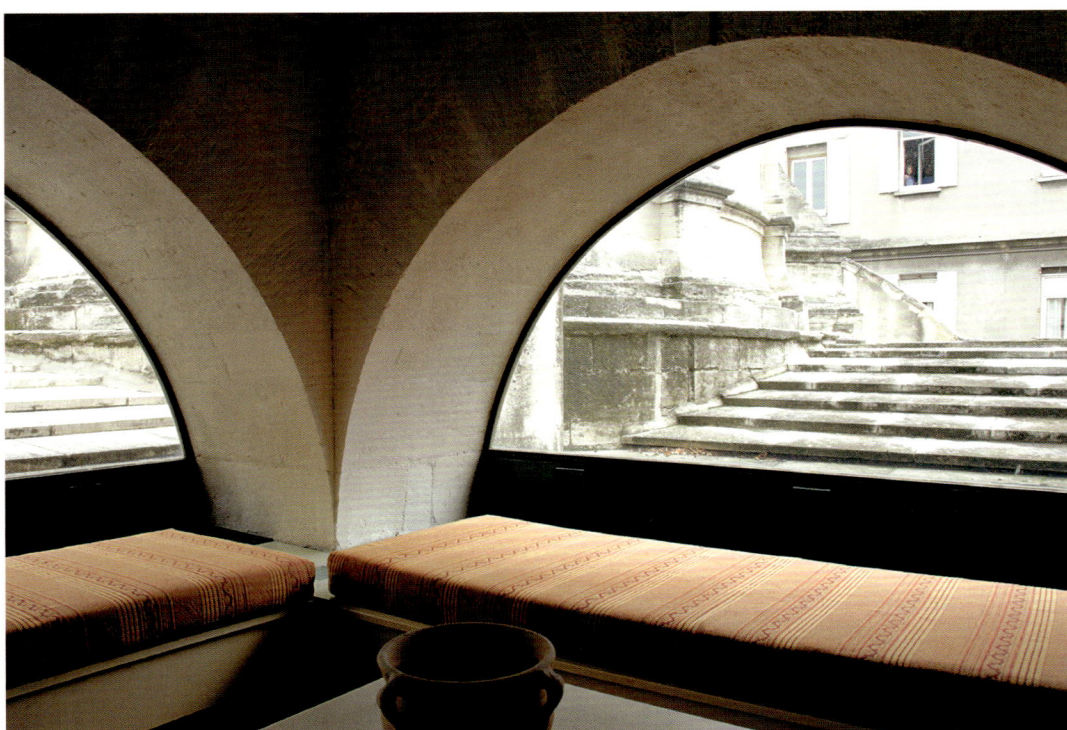

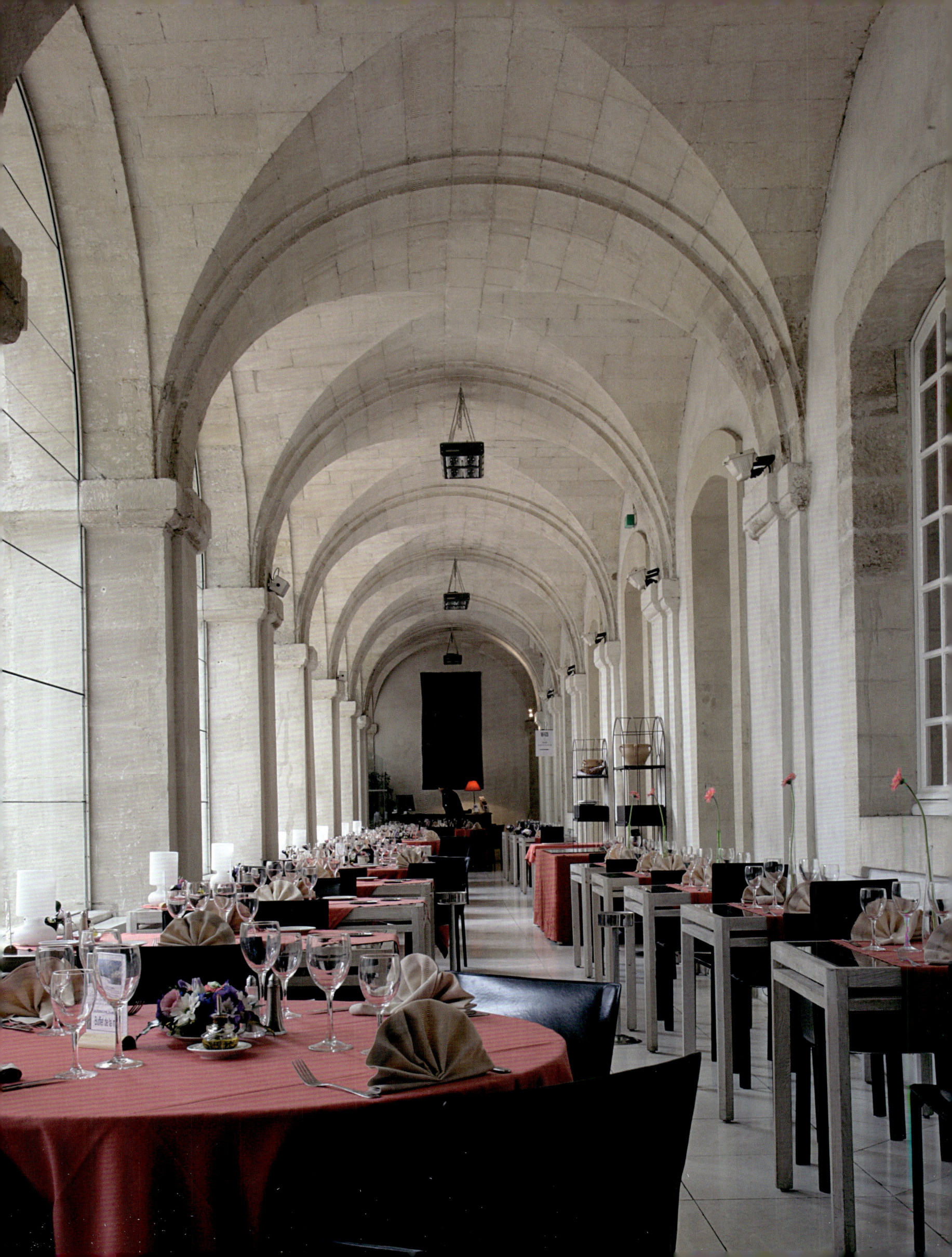

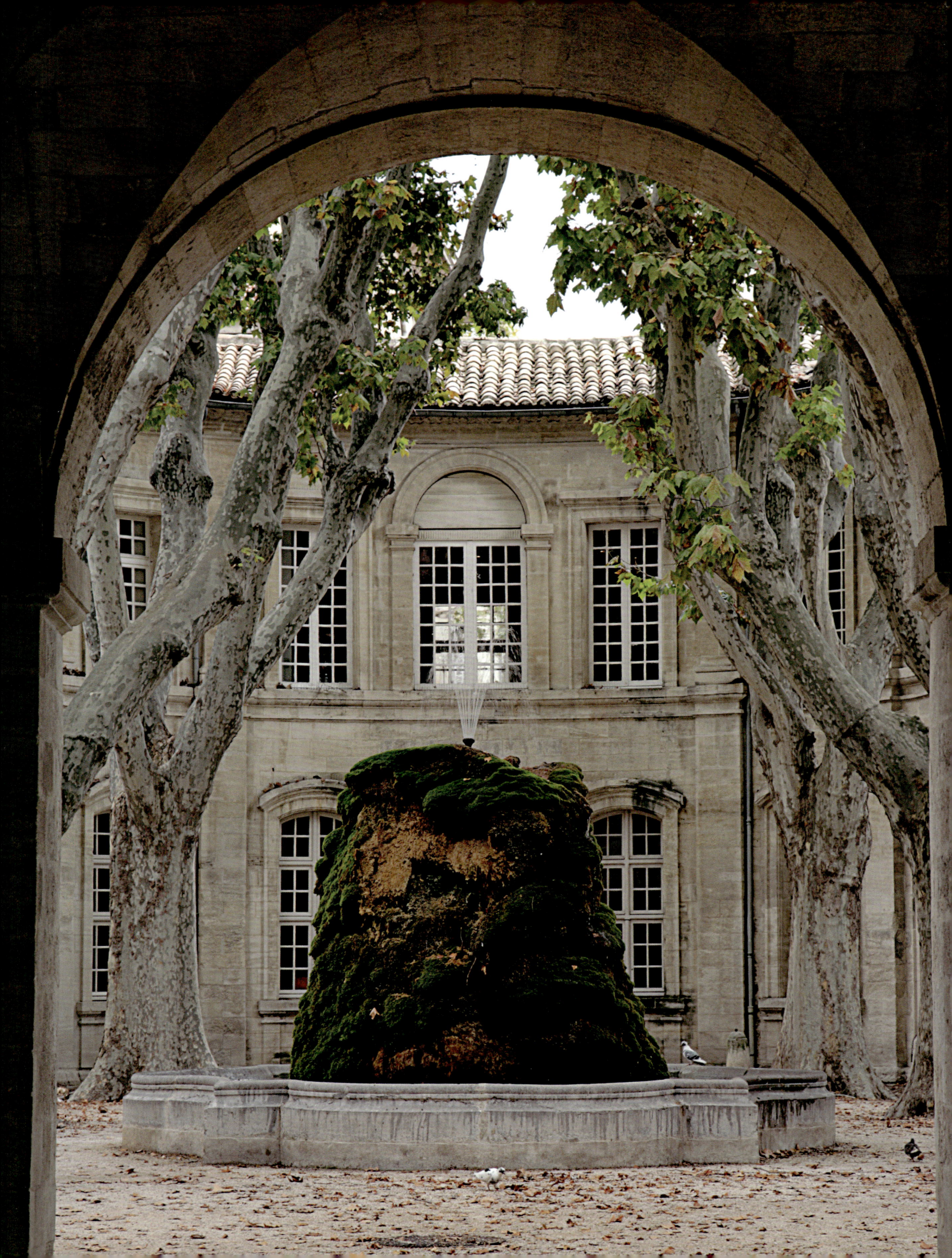

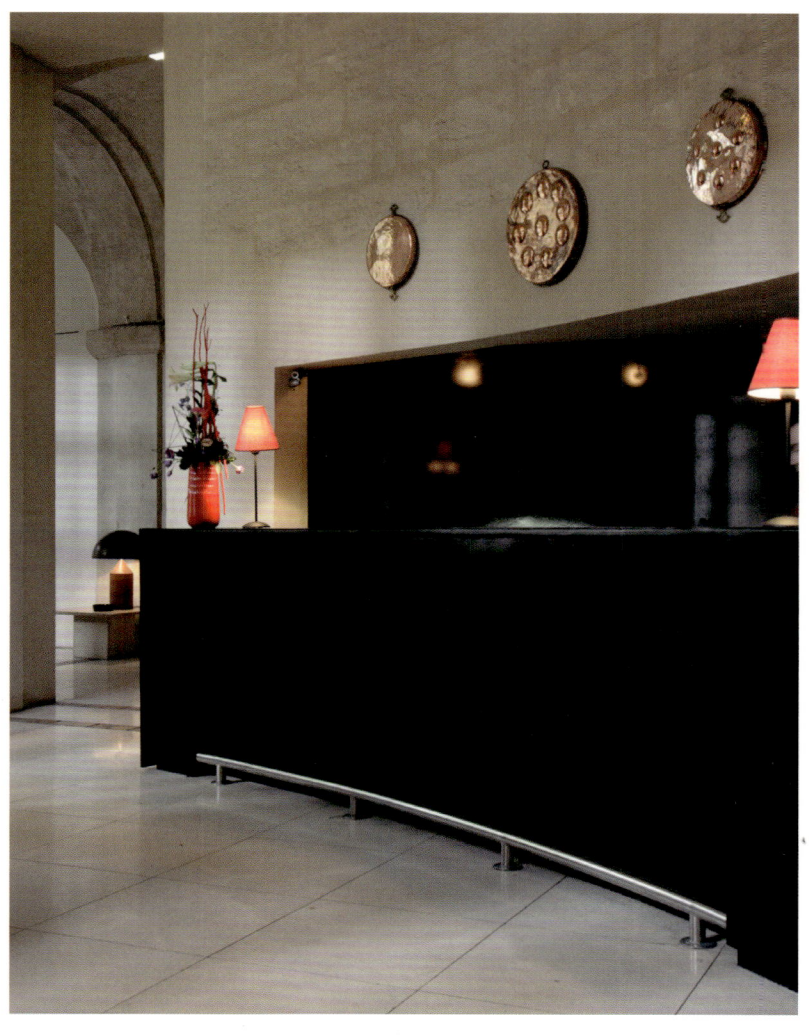
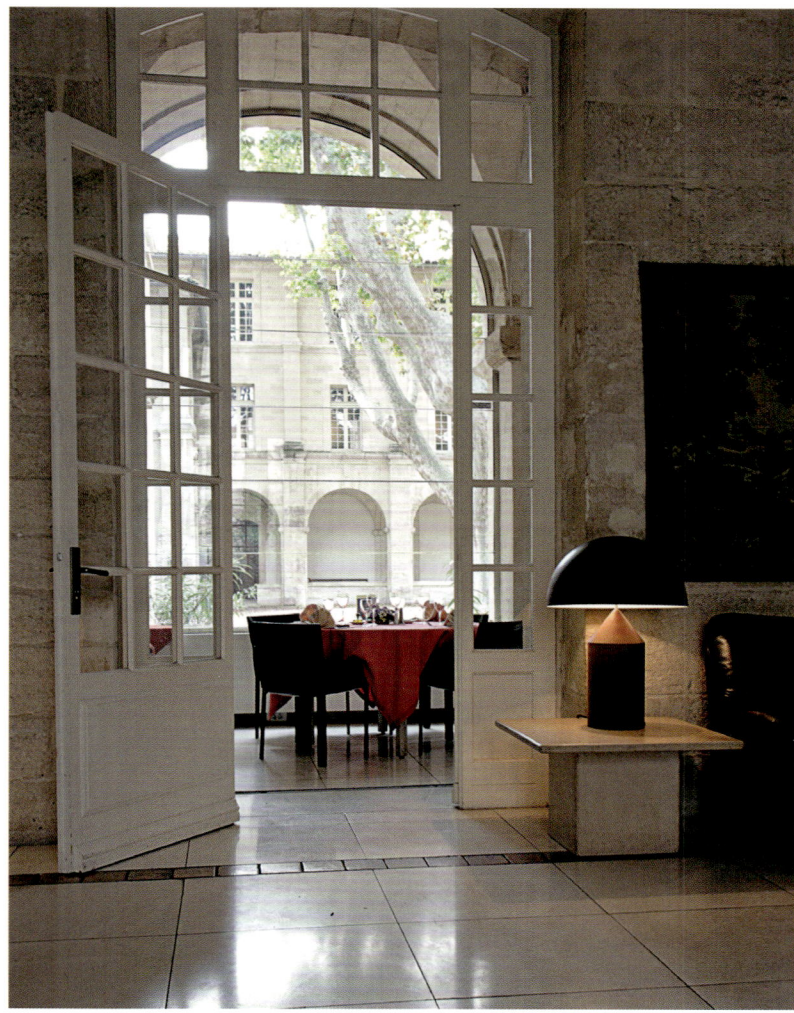
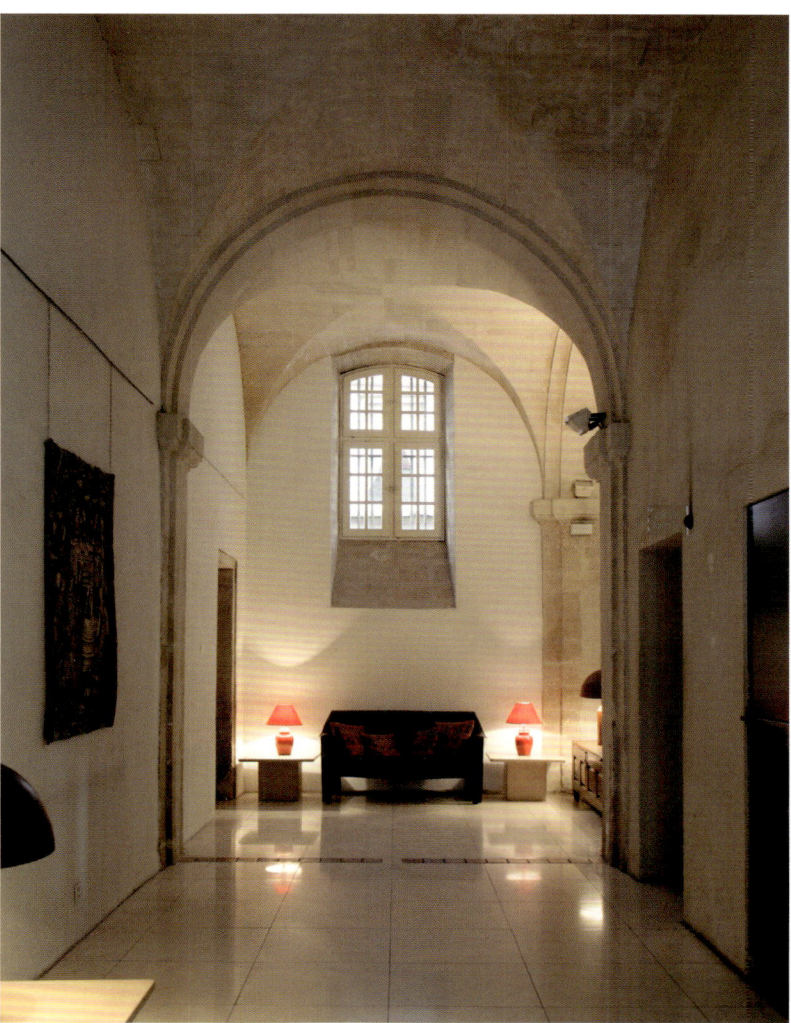
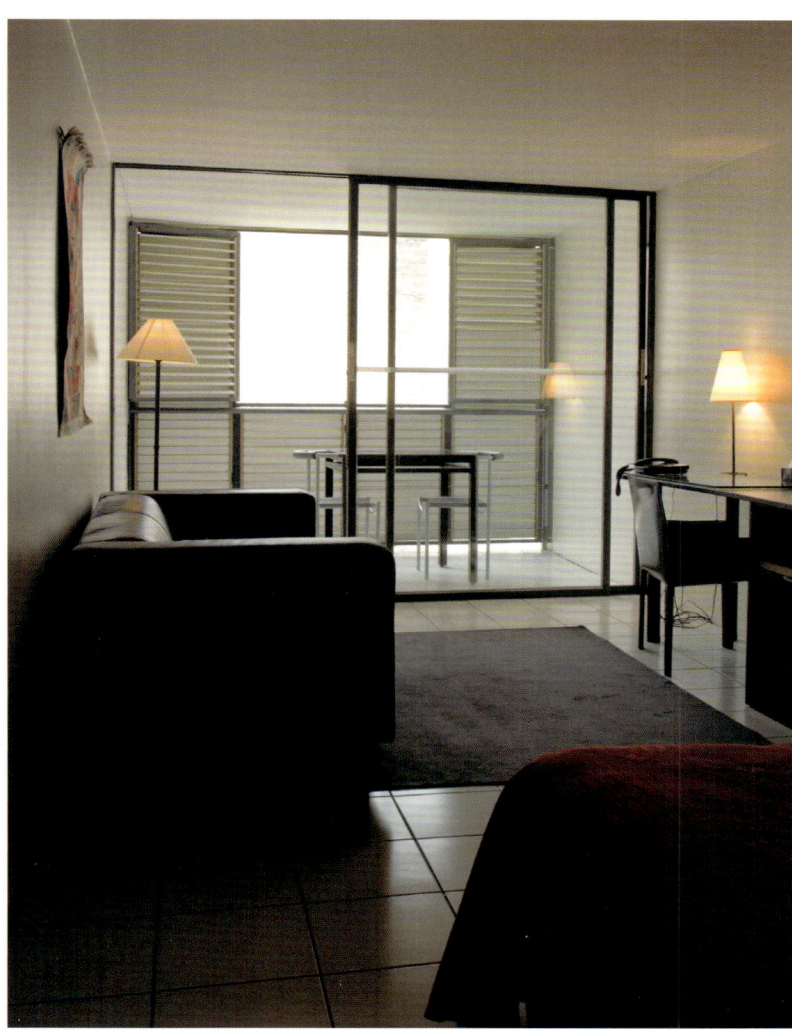

06130 Grasse
France
Phone: +33 4 97 01 10 00
Fax: +33 4 97 01 10 09
www.bastidestmathieu.com

Rooms: 6 rooms including 1 suite
Facilities: Bar, restaurant, beauty salon
Services: Golf, tennis
Located: In the country between Grasse, Mougins and Valbonne
Public transportation: 25 min from Nice International Airport
Style: Provencal

Who do you want to be on your holidays: Cole Porter Junior or James Baldwin, Brigitte Bardot or Empress Sissi? The seven rooms of the Bastide Saint Mathieu are named after such international stars and furnished correspondingly different: in sunny yellow, lavender blue, or poppy red, under old beams with slanted ceilings or fireplaces. But the country hotel turns totally French when it comes to boules or at the pool bordered by cypresses and in the restaurant where the aromatic cuisine of the south is on the menu.

Wer möchten Sie während Ihres Urlaubs sein: Cole Porter Junior oder James Baldwin, Brigitte Bardot oder Kaiserin Sissi? Nach den Namen solcher internationaler Stars sind die sieben Zimmer der Bastide Saint Mathieu benannt und entsprechend unterschiedlich eingerichtet; in Sonnengelb, Lavendelblau oder Klatschmohnrot, unter alten Balken, mit Schrägdecken oder Kaminen. Ganz französisch gibt sich das charmante Landhotel hingegen an der Boule-Bahn, am von Zypressen begrenzten Pool und im Restaurant, wo die aromatische Küche des Südens auf der Karte steht.

Qui aimeriez-vous être pendant vos vacances ? Cole Porter Junior ou James Baldwin, Brigitte Bardot ou Sissi l'Impératrice ? Ce sont les noms de stars qui ont été donnés aux sept suites de la Bastide Saint Mathieu, meublées différemment selon ces noms : en jaune soleil, en bleu lavande ou en rouge coquelicot, avec des plafonds aux poutres apparentes ou des cheminées. Et ce charmant hôtel de campagne s'inscrit dans la plus pure tradition française, avec son terrain de boules, sa piscine entourée de cyprès et son restaurant à la goûteuse cuisine provençale.

¿Quién le gustaría ser durante sus vacaciones? ¿Cole Porter Junior o James Baldwin, Brigitte Bardot o la emperatriz Sissi? Las siete habitaciones del hotel Bastide Saint Mathieu llevan los nombres de estrellas internacionales y su decoración varía de una a otra dependiendo del personaje al que estén dedicadas: del amarillo claro al azul lavanda o al rojo amapola, bajo vigas antiguas, con techos inclinados o con chimeneas. Por el contrario, el elegante hotel muestra su cara más francesa en la pista de petanca, en la piscina rodeada de cipreses y en el restaurante, en cuya carta se pueden encontrar los aromas de la cocina del sur.

Chi vorreste essere durante la vostre vacanze: Cole Porter Junior o James Baldwin, Brigitte Bardot o l'imperatrice Sissi? Le sette camere del Bastide Saint Mathieu portano il nome di star internazionali di questo calibro e sono arredate con lo stile e i colori più intonati a esse: troverete il giallo sole, il blu lavanda o il rosso papavero, incontrerete vecchie travi, solai spioventi e caminetti. Questo hotel di campagna pieno di charme rispetta in pieno lo stile francese; non possono quindi mancare la pista da bocce, una piscina delimitata da cipressi e un ristorante specializzato nell'aromatica cucina del sud.

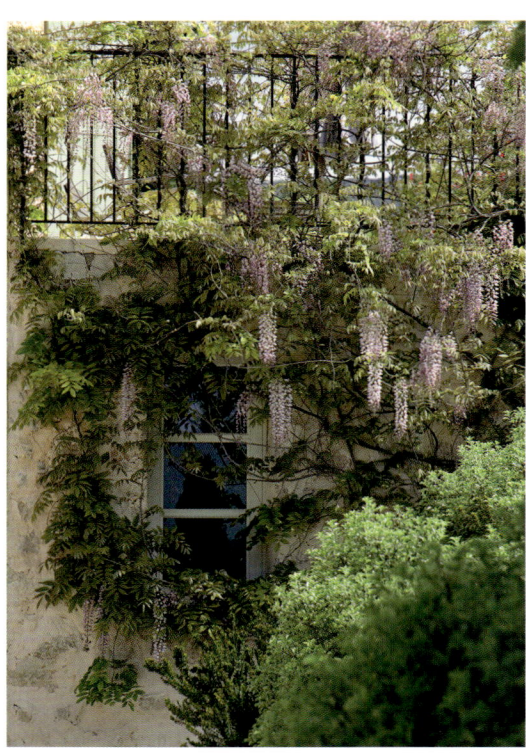
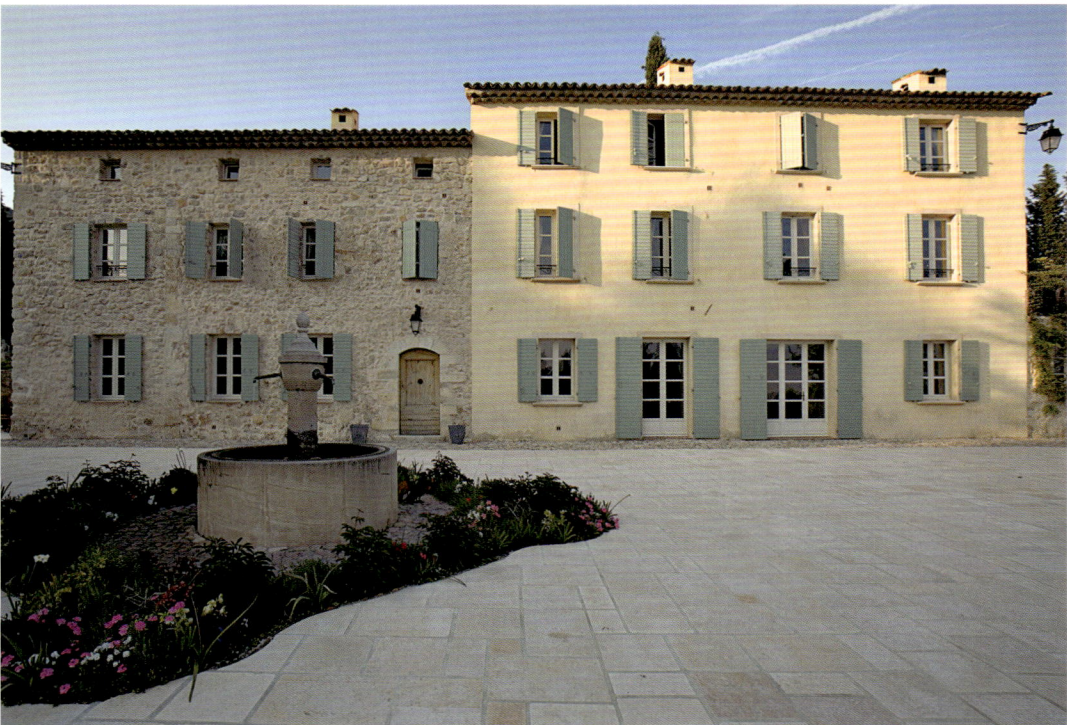

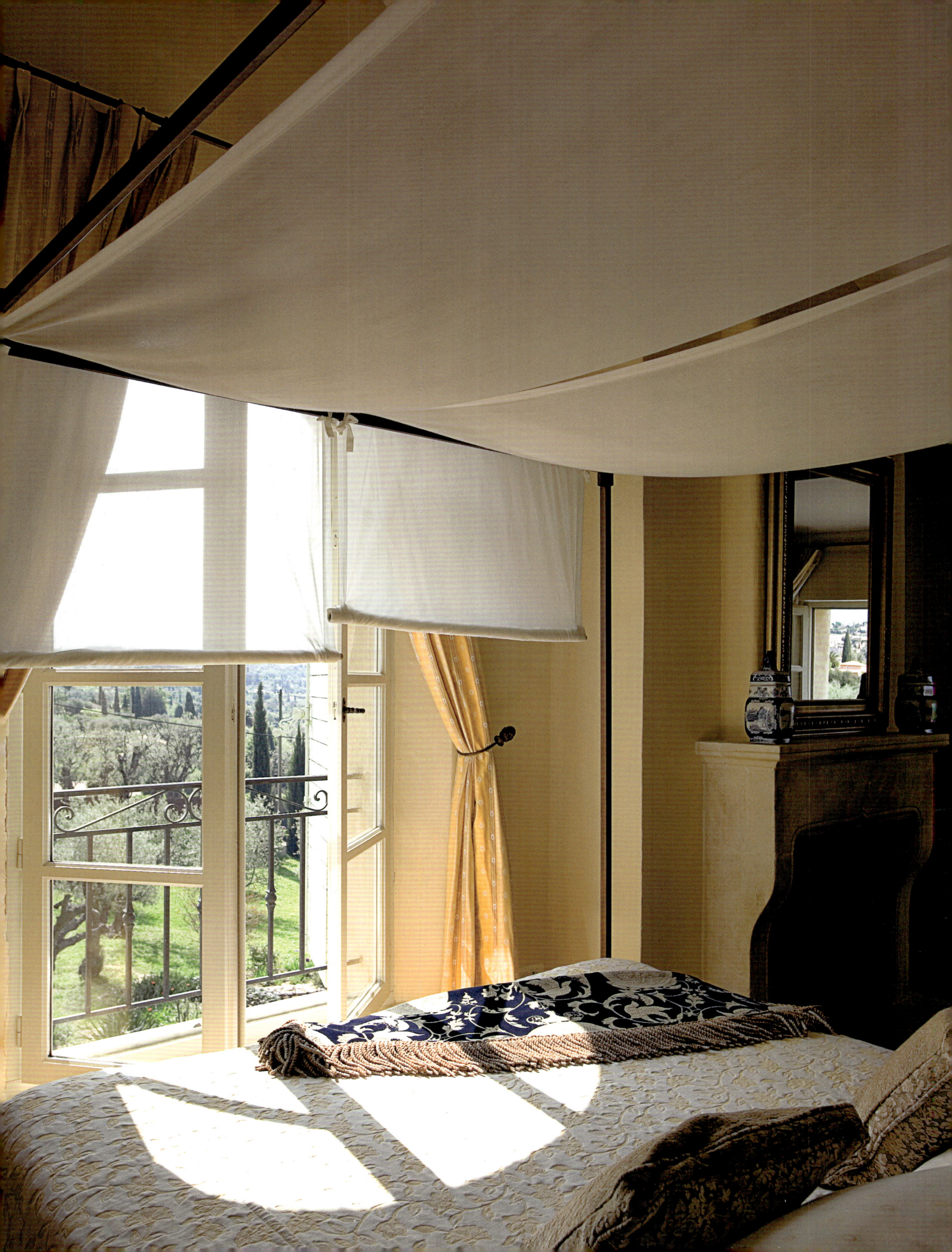

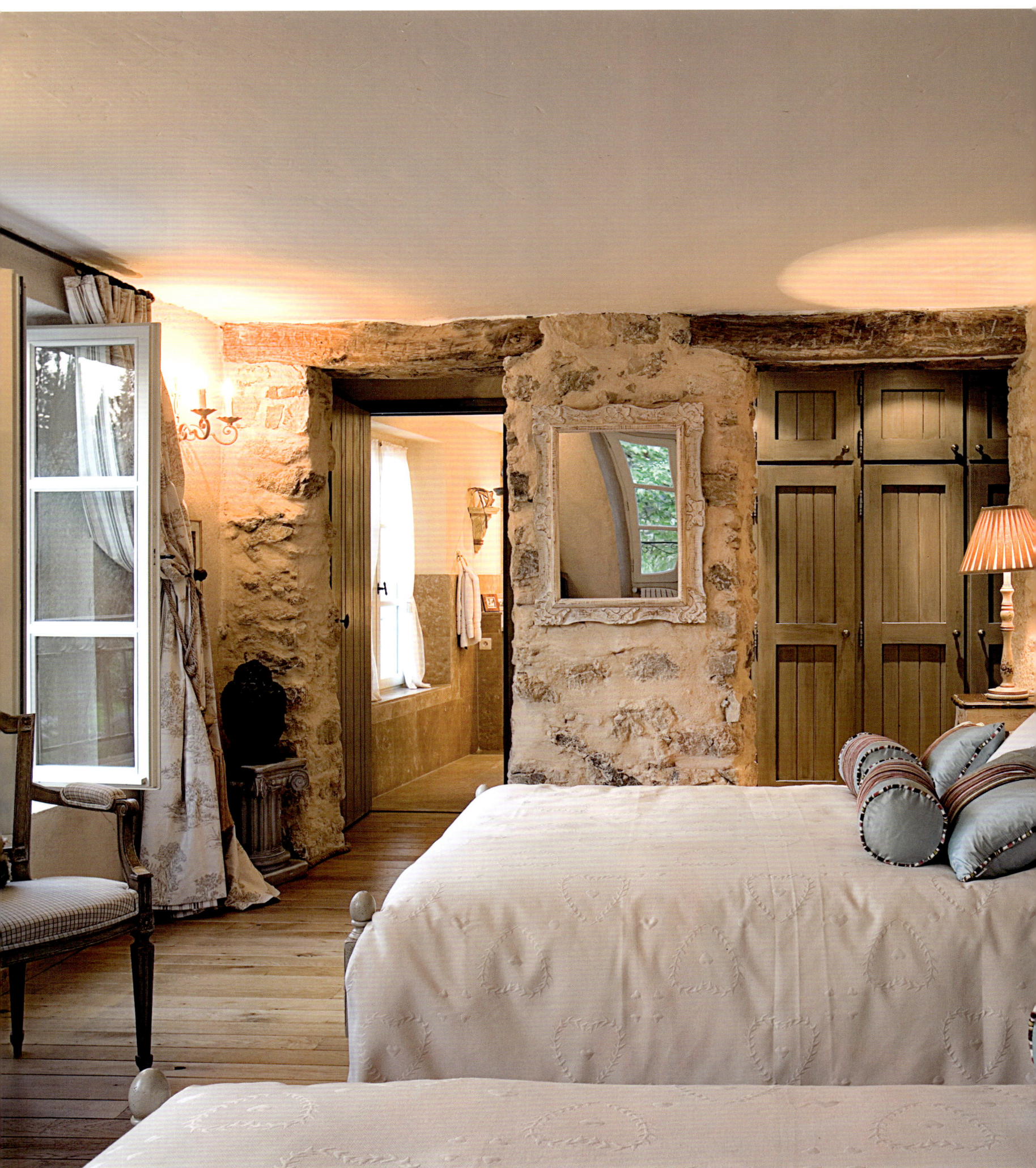

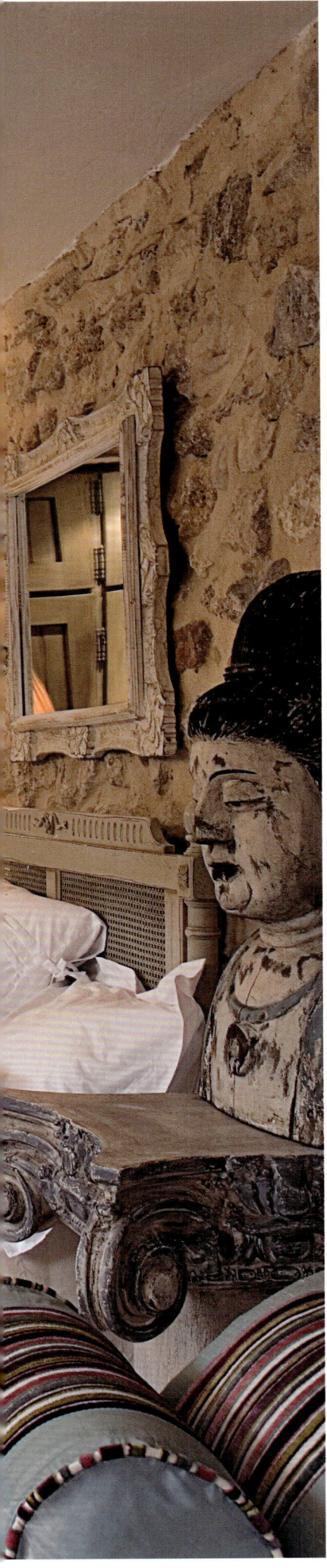

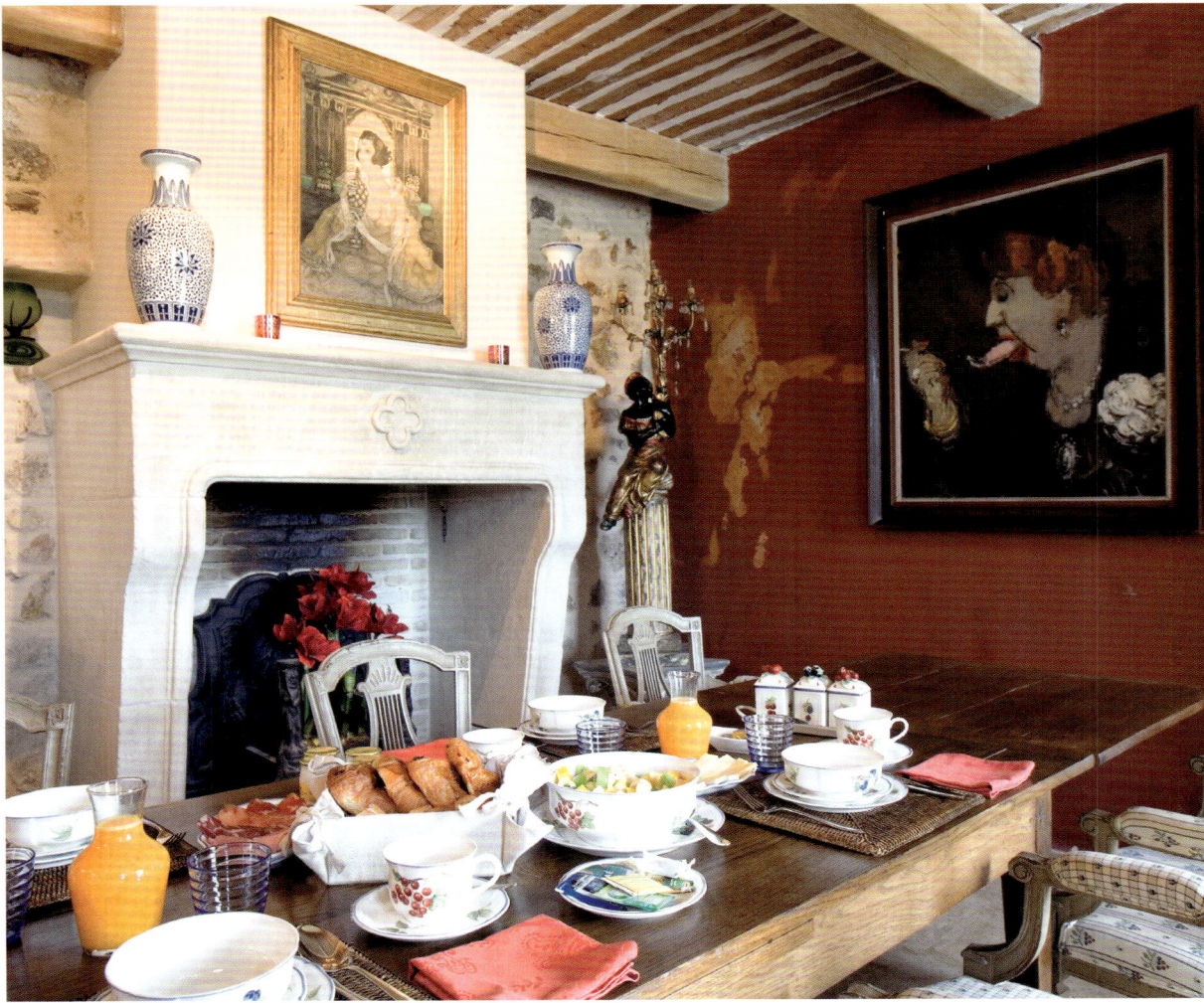

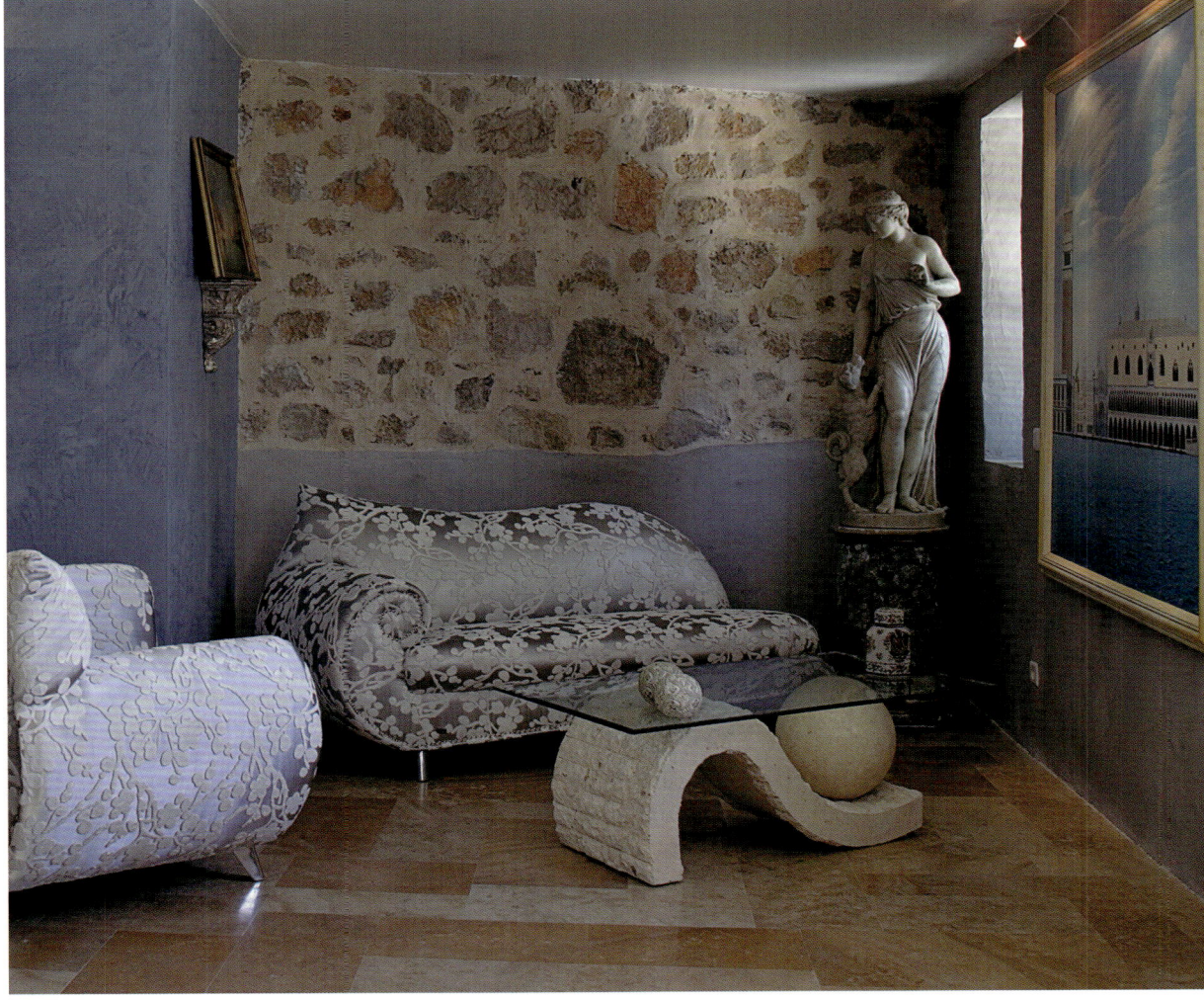

84560 Ménerbes
France
Phone: +33 4 90 72 30 20
Fax: +33 4 90 72 54 20
www.sibuethotels-spa.com

Rooms: 14 including 6 suites
Facilities: Bar, restaurant, Pure Altitude spa
Services: Room service
Located: In the heart of a vineland in the Luberon, overlooking the Vaucluse mountains
Style: Provencal

Formerly a farm house of the 18th century, La Bastide de Marie is a Provence picturesque hideaway surrounded by aromatic herb gardens, purple lavender field and knotty trees. The region brings all its charm into play in the rooms and suites with old stone walls and fireplaces, antiques and canopy beds, soft colors and warm light. A pleasure for all senses is promised in both the restaurant and in the magical spa with its own mountain plants beauty line Pure Altitude.

Ein ehemaliges Bauernhaus aus dem 18. Jahrhundert, umgeben von duftenden Kräutergärten, lilafarbenen Lavendelfeldern und knorrigen Bäumen: La Bastide de Marie ist ein provenzalisches Refugium wie aus dem Bilderbuch. In den Zimmern und Suiten lässt die Region ihren ganzen Charme spielen – mit alten Steinwänden und Kaminen, Antiquitäten und Himmelbetten, sanften Farben und warmem Licht. Genuss für alle Sinne versprechen auch das Restaurant sowie das zauberhafte Spa mit der hauseigenen Pflegelinie Pure Altitude mit Bergpflanzen.

Une ancienne ferme du XVIIIème siècle, entourée des parfums du jardin aromatique, de champs de lavandes et d'arbres noueux : la Bastide de Marie est un refuge pittoresque au cœur de la Provence. Tout le charme de la région agit dans les chambres et les suites, avec leurs vieux murs de pierre et leurs cheminées, leurs antiquités et leurs lits à baldaquin, leurs couleurs pastel et leur lumière chaude. Un plaisir de tous les sens vous est offert par le restaurant et par le fantastique spa qui propose sa propre ligne de soins aux plantes de montagne Pure Altitude.

Antiguamente un antiguo caserío del siglo XVIII, la Bastide de Marie es un pintoresco refugio provenzal rodeado de jardines de hierbas aromáticas, praderas de lavanda color lila y árboles nudosos. En las habitaciones y suites es donde la región muestra todo su encanto; con viejas paredes de piedra y chimeneas, antigüedades y camas con dosel, colores suaves y luz cálida. El restaurante y el encantador spa, con su propia línea de productos de belleza Pure Altitude procedentes de su cultivación de plantas de montaña, prometen placeres para todos los sentidos.

Anticamente una casa colonica del XVIII secolo, La Bastide de Marie è un pittoresco rifugio provenzale circondato da orti dagli aromi intensi, alberi nodosi e campi di lavanda dal delicato color lillà. Le sue camere e suite raccontano tutto lo charme di questa regione francese, fatto di caminetti e antiche pareti in pietra, pezzi d'antiquariato e letti a baldacchino, colori tenui e luci calde. Il ristorante e l'incantevole spa, che mette a disposizione del cliente l'originale linea di prodotti di bellezza Pure Altitude ricavati dalla propria coltivazione di piante di montagna, riserveranno benessere e piaceri a tutti i vostri sensi.

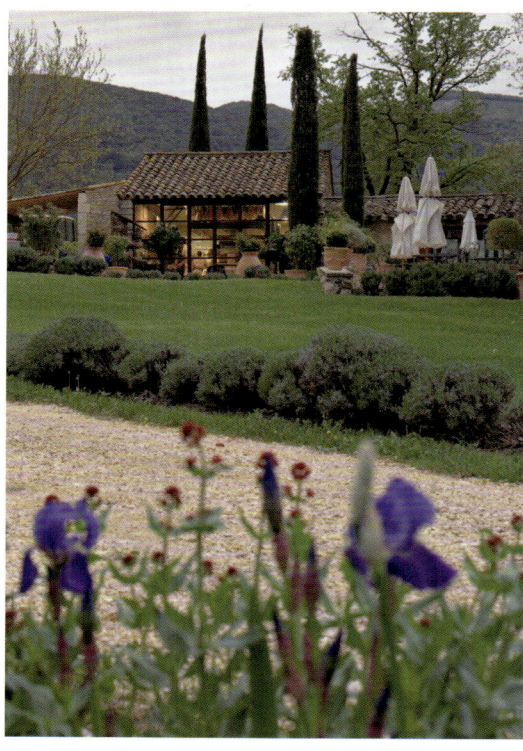
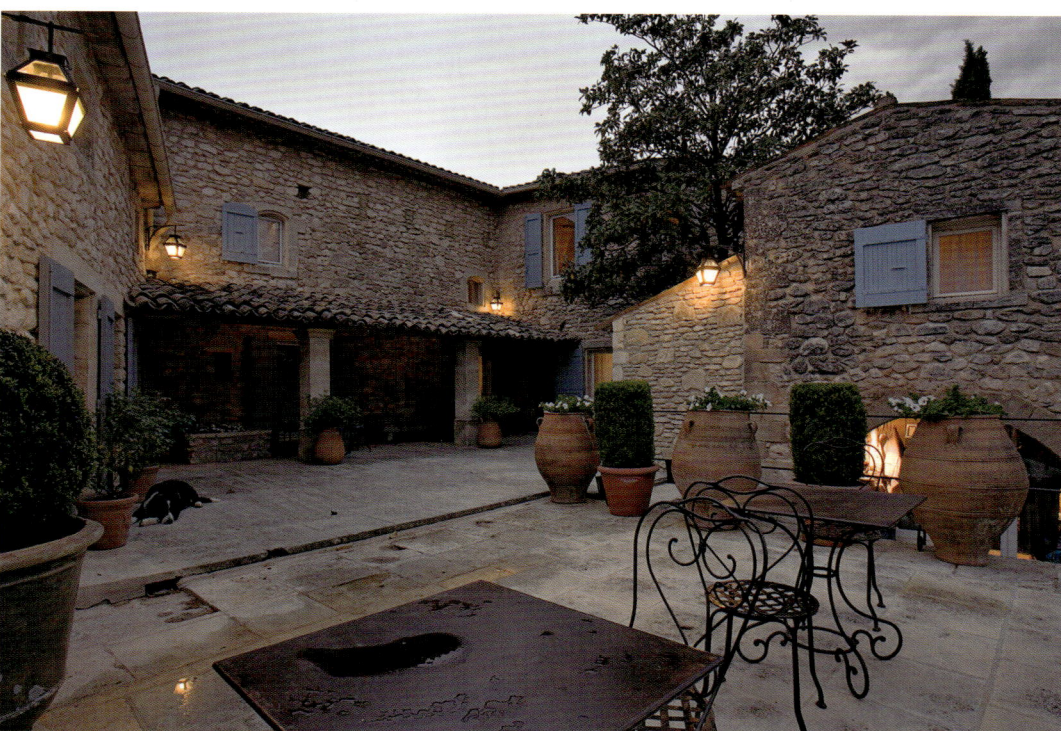

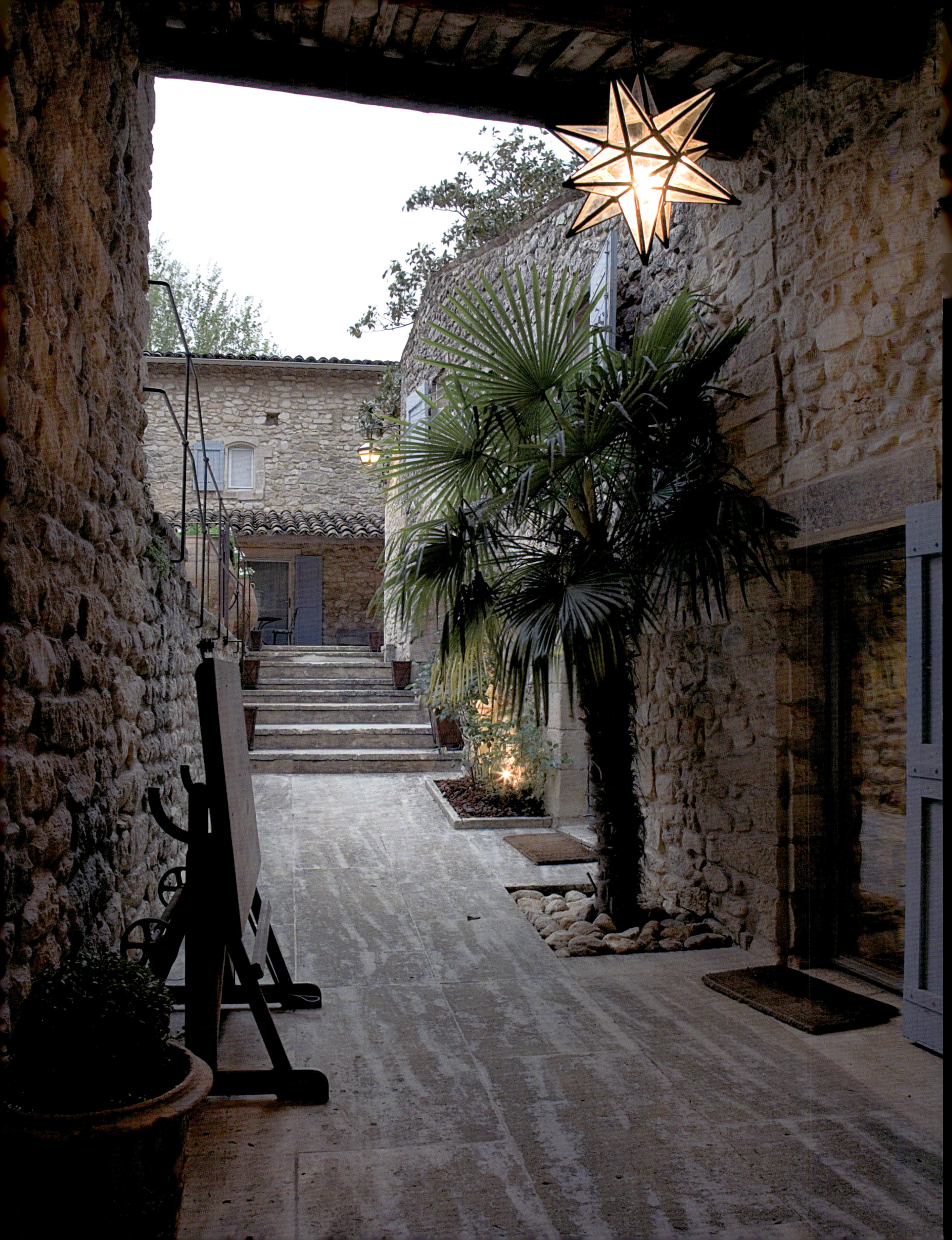

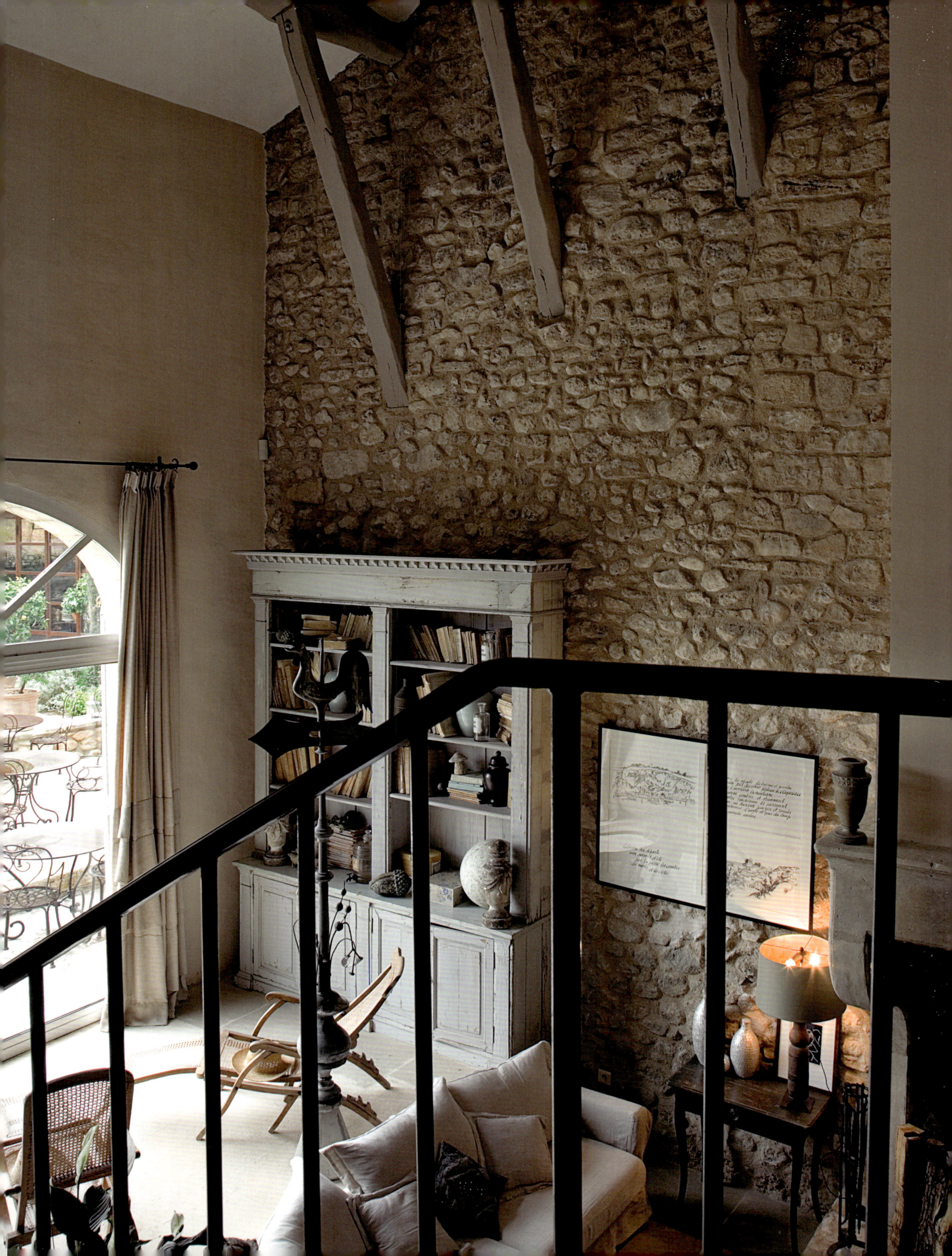

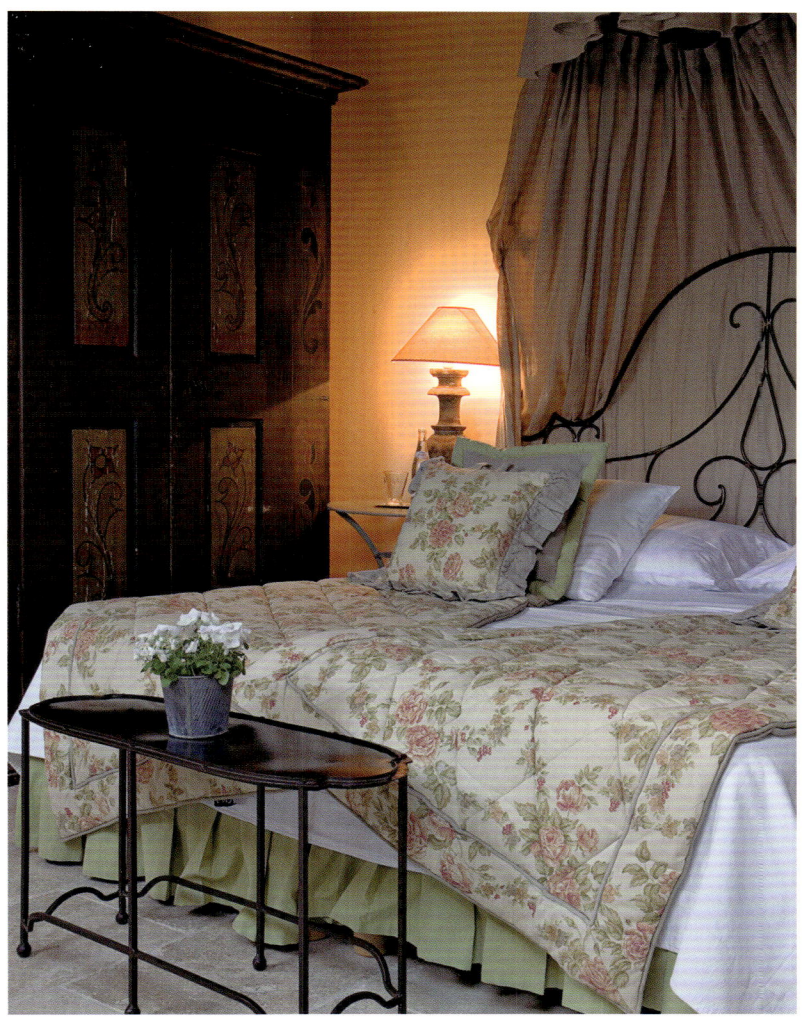
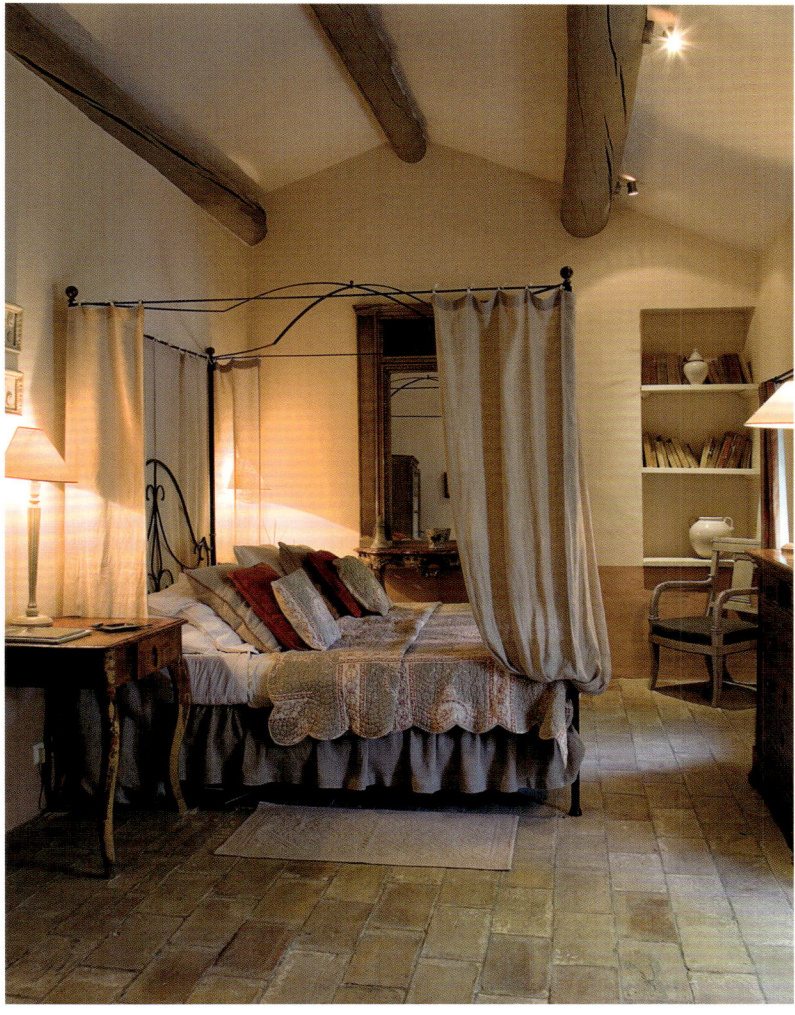
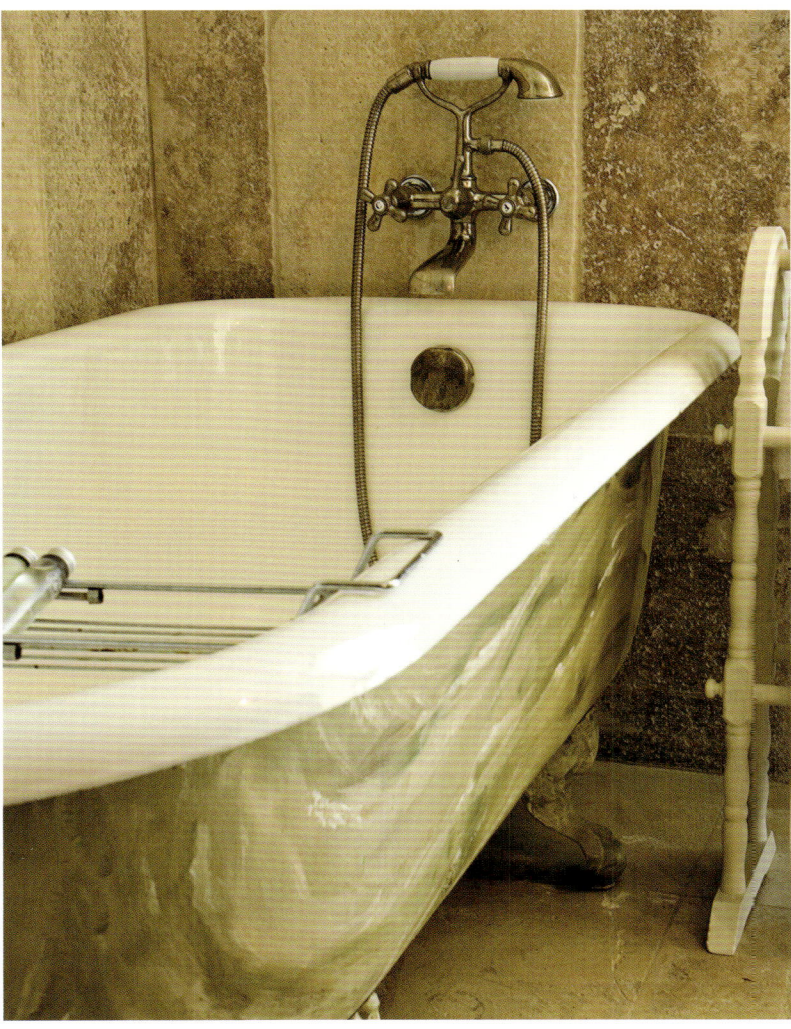
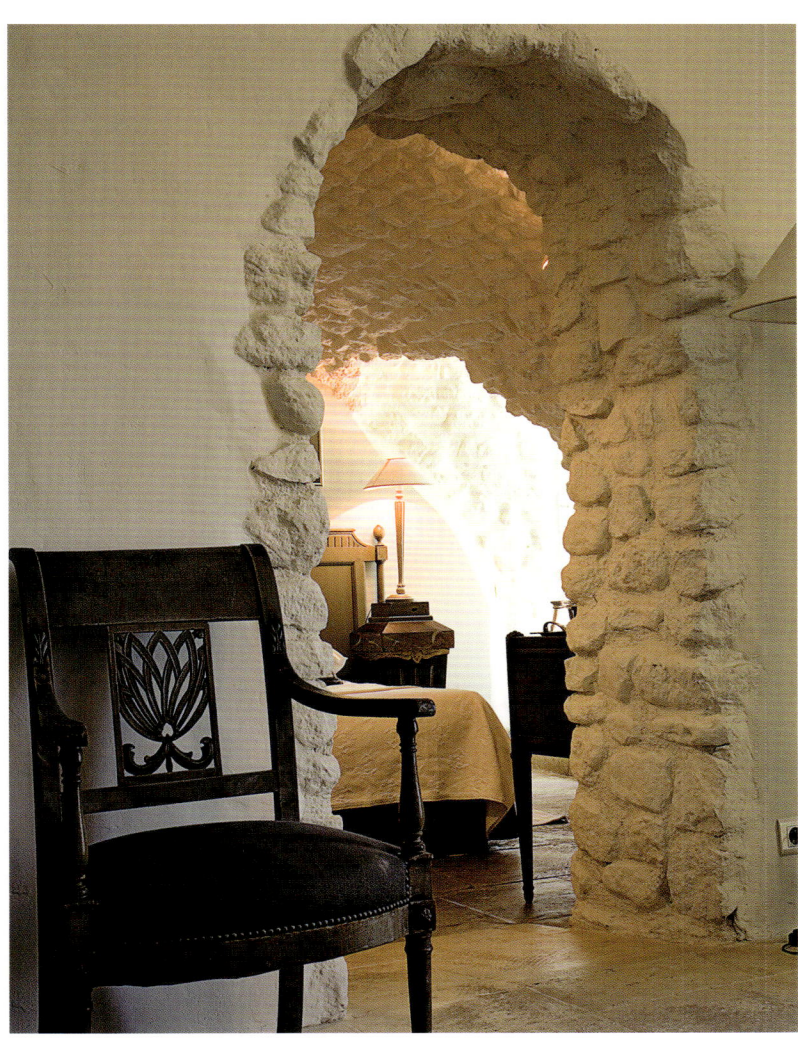

06000 Nice
France
Phone: +33 4 93 16 64 00
Fax: +33 4 93 88 35 68
www.hotel-negresco-nice.com

Rooms: 121 rooms and 24 suites
Facilities: Award-winning restaurant Le Chantecler, brasserie La Rotonde, bar Le Relais, private beach, luxury shops, fitness room, conference rooms
Services: Clé d'Or concierge service, golf, tennis, massage and hair salons
Located: On the Promenade des Anglais
Style: Enchanted

The Negresco thanks its fame to two personalities: Henri Negresco, once director of the casino of Nice who had the hotel built in 1912 as noble accommodation for his illustrious clientele, and Jeanne Augier, who owned it since 1957. She interpreted the palace with the pink-colored dome as a total work of art. None of the 145 rooms are the same, but each represents an epoch of French culture from Louis XIII to the modern. Suite 327 is fantastic—a thousand square feet and a panoramic view of the Baie des Anges.

Das Negresco verdankt seinen Ruhm zwei Persönlichkeiten: Henri Negresco, seinerzeit Direktor des Casinos von Nizza, der das Hotel 1912 als Nobelherberge für seine illustre Klientel bauen ließ, und Jeanne Augier, die es seit 1957 besitzt. Sie interpretierte den Palast mit der pinkfarbenen Kuppel als Gesamtkunstwerk: Keines der 145 Zimmer gleicht dem anderen, aber alle repräsentieren eine Epoche französischer Kultur; von Louis XIII bis zur Moderne. Fantastisch ist die Suite 327 – hundert Quadratmeter groß und mit Panoramablick auf die Baie des Anges.

Le Negresco peut remercier deux personnalités pour sa célébrité : Henri Negresco, ancien directeur du Casino de Nice, qui l'a fait construire en 1912 comme un lieu de séjour luxueux pour ses clients illustres, et Jeanne Augier, qui en est la propriétaire depuis 1957. Elle a interprété le palace au dôme rose comme une œuvre d'art total : aucune des 145 chambres n'est semblable à une autre, mais chacune représente une époque de la culture française, de Louis XIII jusqu'aujourd'hui. La suite 327 est fantastique : cent mètres carrés avec vue panoramique sur la Baie des Anges.

El Negresco le debe su fama a dos personajes: en primer lugar, a Henri Negresco, antiguo director del casino de Niza, quien lo construyó en 1912 como albergue de lujo para sus clientes ilustres; en segundo lugar, a Jeanne Augier, dueña desde 1957. Ella concibió el palacio de la cúpula rosada como una obra de arte total. Cada una de las 145 habitaciones es diferente, pero todas representan una época de la cultura francesa: desde Luís XIII hasta la modernidad. La suite 327, con sus 100 metros cuadrados y su vista panorámica sobre la bahía de Baie des Anges, es simplemente fantástica.

Il Negresco deve la sua fama a due personalità di spicco: Henri Negresco, ai suoi tempi direttore del Casinò di Nizza, che lo fece erigere nel 1912 come residenza esclusiva per la sua illustre clientela, e Jeanne Augier, che ne è la proprietaria dal 1957. Augier ha interpretato il palazzo dalle cupole rosa come un'unica opera d'arte: nessuna delle sue 145 camere assomiglia a un'altra, tutte riproducono lo stile di un'epoca diversa della cultura francese, da Luigi XIII al liberty. Fantastica la suite 327, che si estende su cento metri quadri e gode di vista panoramica sulla Baia degli Angeli.

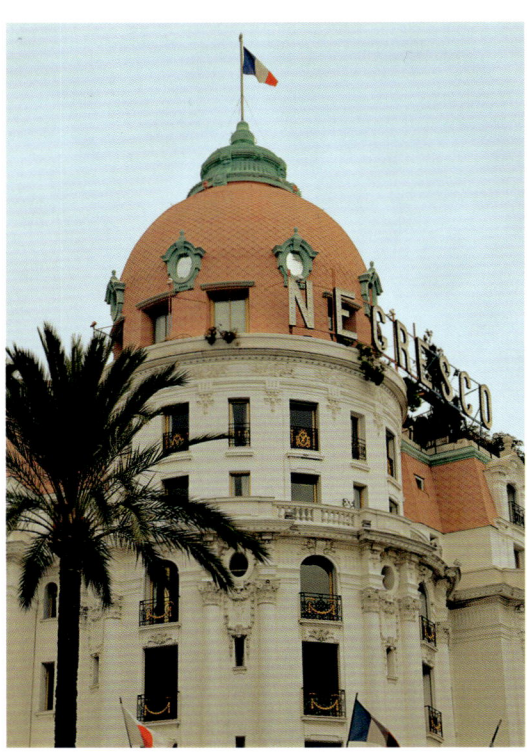 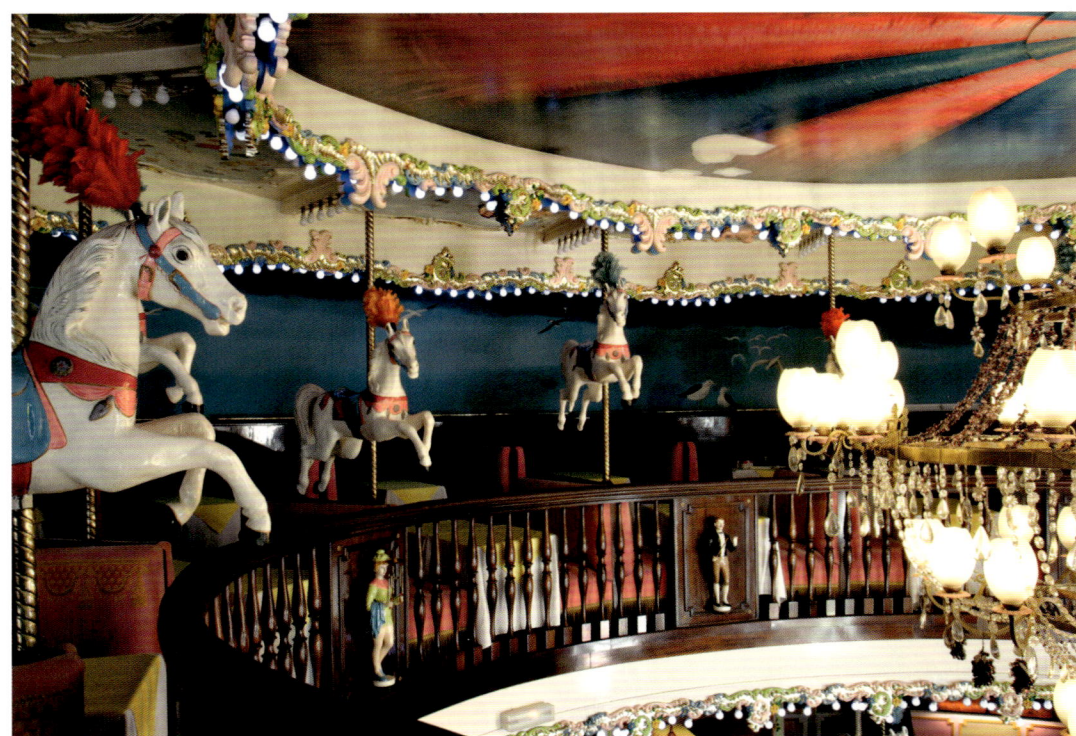

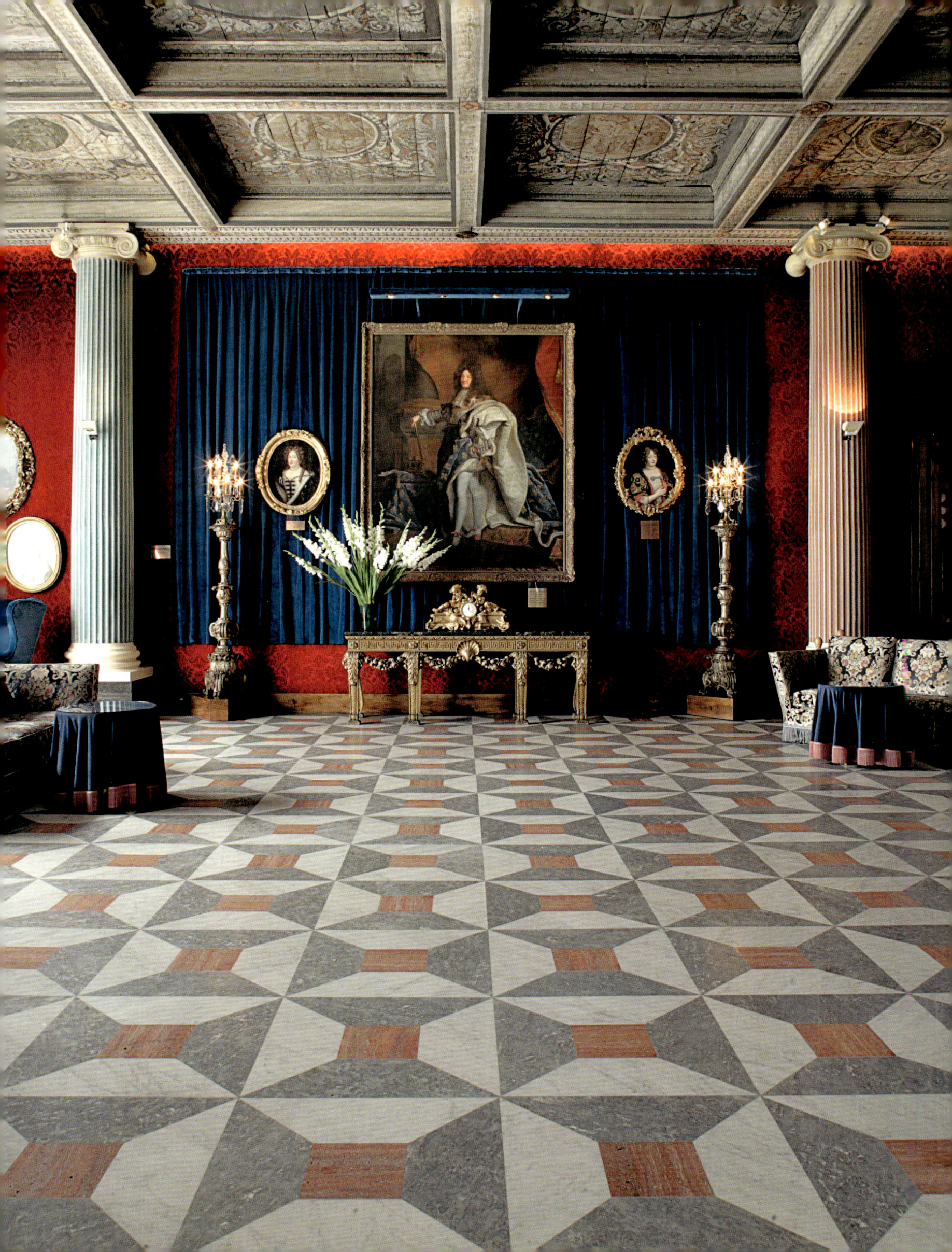

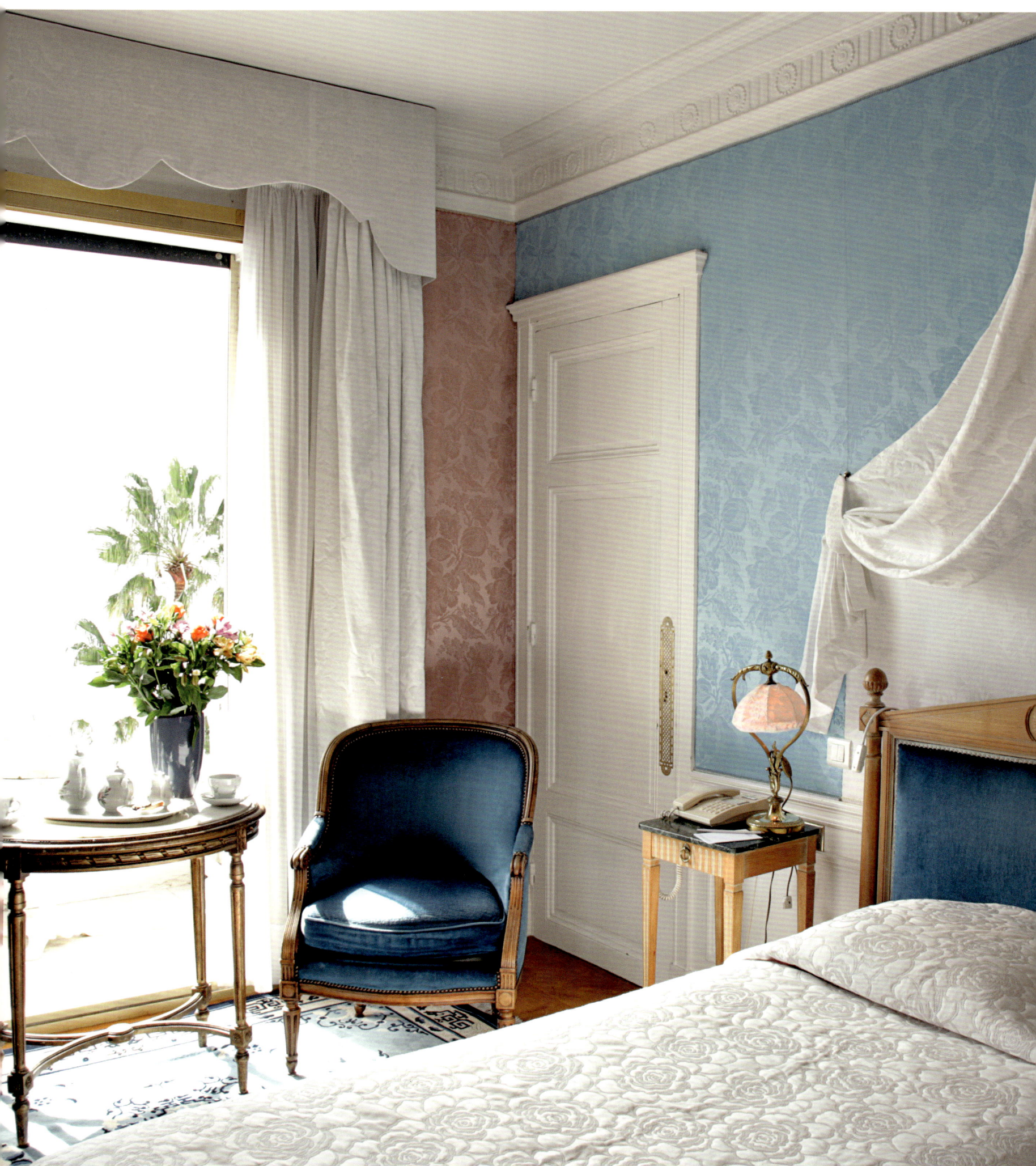

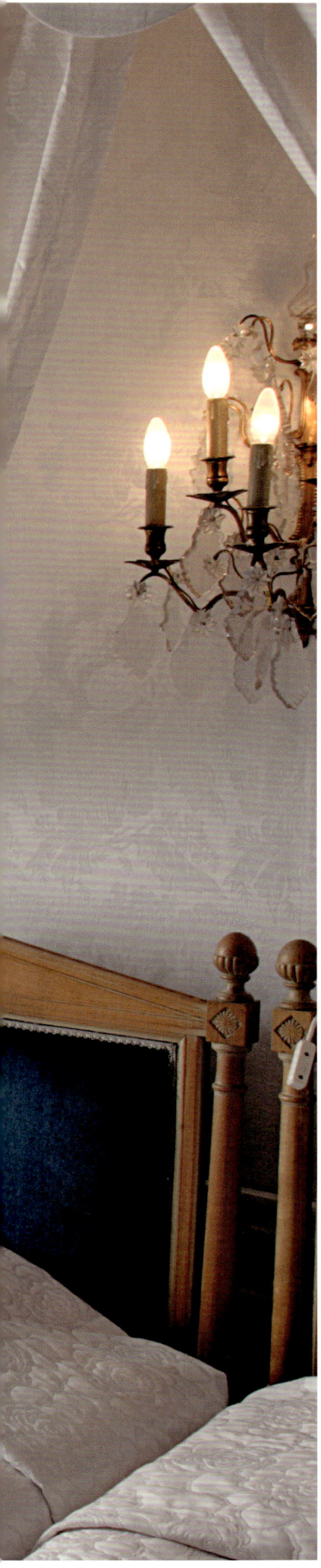

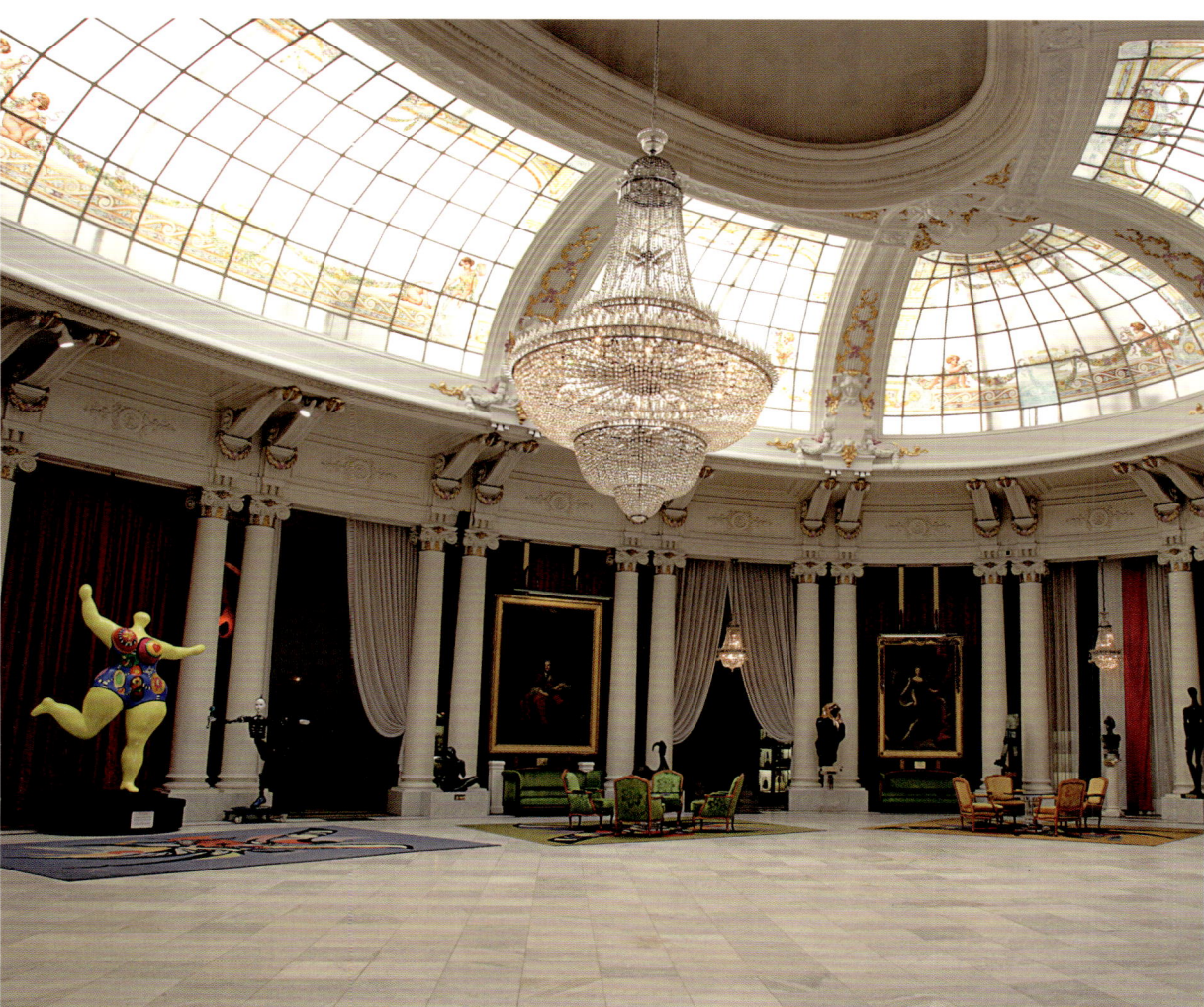

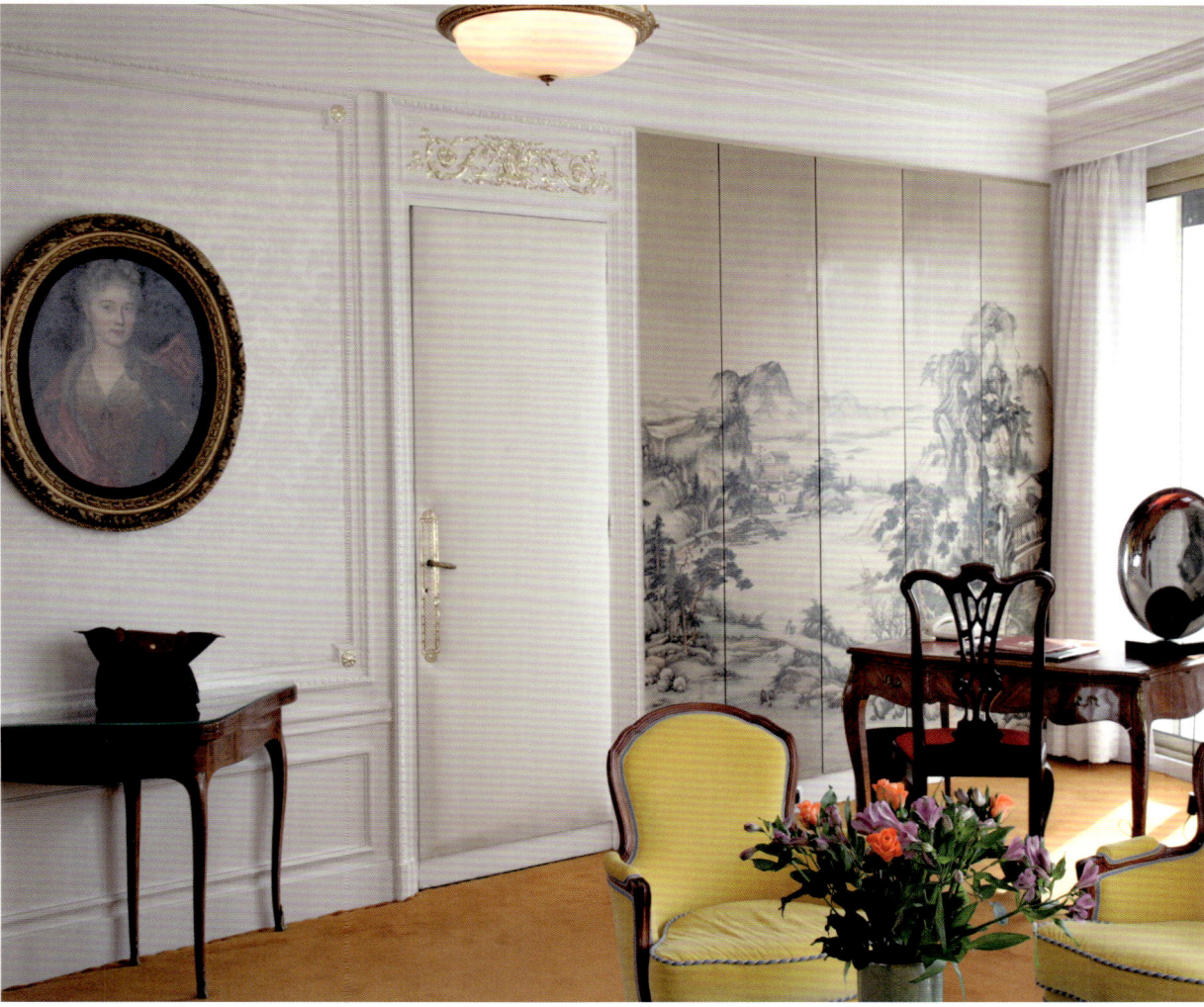

83990 Saint-Tropez
France
Phone: +33 4 98 12 56 50
Fax: +33 4 94 96 99 82
www.pastis-st-tropez.com

Rooms: 9 rooms
Facilities: Bar, heated pool, boules terrain, private parking, meeting room
Services: WiFi, DVD players in rooms, local and international newspapers
Located: A 5 min walk from the heart of the village and the port of St Tropez
Style: Contemporary-Provencal

King palms shade the sun beds by the pool, dove-colored shutters, a sweeping spiral staircase, deep bathtubs with iron feet and the legendary French Riviera at the front door: the hotel was once a Provençal house, now re-created and run by a couple from London, with their own upbeat, personal and eclectic style. Contemporary art and furniture, Chinese rugs, traditional French antiques and bed linens add to the relaxed luxury among the grand hotels of the coast. Anyway, there is no stuffy dress code here—although you can run into the young high society.

Königspalmen, die ihre Fächer über den Liegen am Pool ausbreiten, taubenblaue Fensterläden, weitläufige Wendeltreppen, Badewannen, die auf Eisenpfoten stehen und vor der Tür die legendäre französische Riviera: Das Hotel, einst ein provenzalisches Herrenhauses, ist nun renoviert und wird von einem Paar aus London in ihrem unverwechselbar unkonventionellen, persönlichen und vielseitigen Stil geleitet. Zeitgenössische Kunst und Möbel, chinesische Teppiche, traditionelle französische Antiquitäten und Bettwäsche gehören dabei zur Ausstattung. Entspanntes Understatement inmitten der glamourösen Grand Hotels der Küste. Einen Dresscode gibt es hier nicht – obwohl man hier die junge High Society treffen kann.

Des palmiers centenaires qui ombragent les transats à côté de la piscine, des volets gris clair, l'escalier en colimaçon, des baignoires profondes sur pieds et en face de l'entrée, la légendaire Côte d'Azur : cet hôtel qui était autrefois une vielle maison provençale, est rénovée et gérée par un couple de Londoniens avec leur style peu conventionnel, personnel et varié. l'art et des meubles contemporains, des tapis chinois, des antiquités et des dessus de lit provençaux sont omni-présents dans l'hôtel. Une sobriété très appréciable au millieu des grands hôtels glamours de la côte. Il n'y a pas de code vestimentaire, même si on peut rencontrer la jeunesse de la haute société.

Palmas reales dan sombra a las tumbonas de la piscina, contraventanas de color azul grisáceo pálido, escaleras de caracol, bañeras sostenidas por patas de hierro y la legendaria Costa Azul francesa delante de la puerta. El edificio, anteriormente una casa noble provenzal, fue reinventado y es dirigido por una pareja de Londres con su propio estilo, personal y ecléctico. Muebles y arte contemporáneos, alfombras Chinas, sabanas y objetos antiguos de la tradición francesa. Lujo desenfadado entre los grandes hoteles de la costa. Sin código de vestimenta y a pesar de esto aquí puedes encontrar los jóvenes de la alta sociedad.

Palme reali ombreggiano le sdraio attorno alla piscina; persiane di un delicato grigio azzurro; scale a chiocciola, vasche da bagno su zampe di ferro e, appena fuori dalla porta, la leggendaria Costa Azzurra francese. L'hotel, una residenza signorile in stile provenzale, è stato rinnovato ed è oggi diretto da una coppia di Londra con il suo stile eclettico e personale. Mobili e pezzi d'arte contemporanei, tappeti cinesi, lenzuola ed oggetti antichi della tradizione francese. Lusso rilassato nel bel mezzo dei Grand Hotel della costa. Non è in vigore nessun dress code, e nonostante ció qui potrete incontrare i giovani dell'alta società.

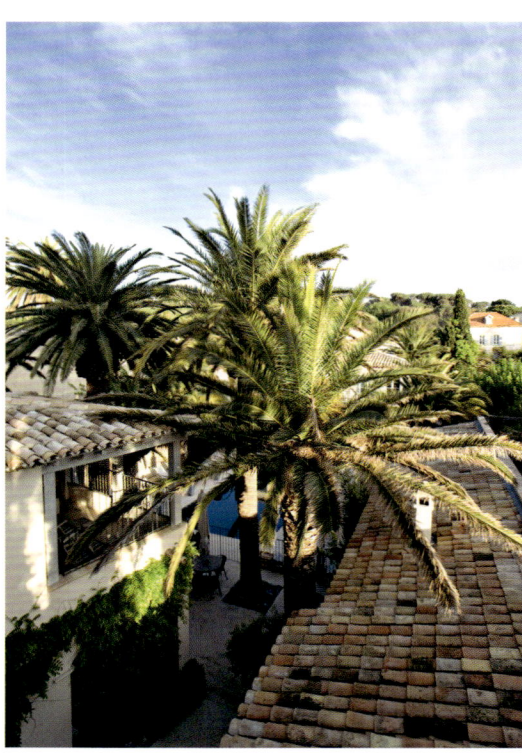
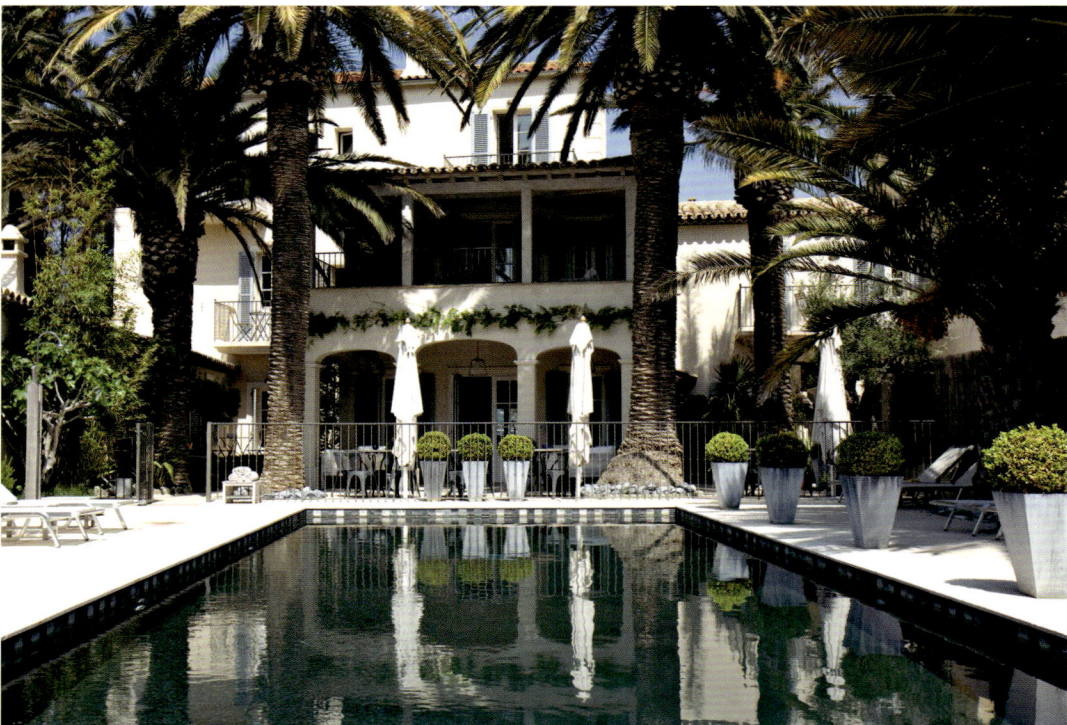

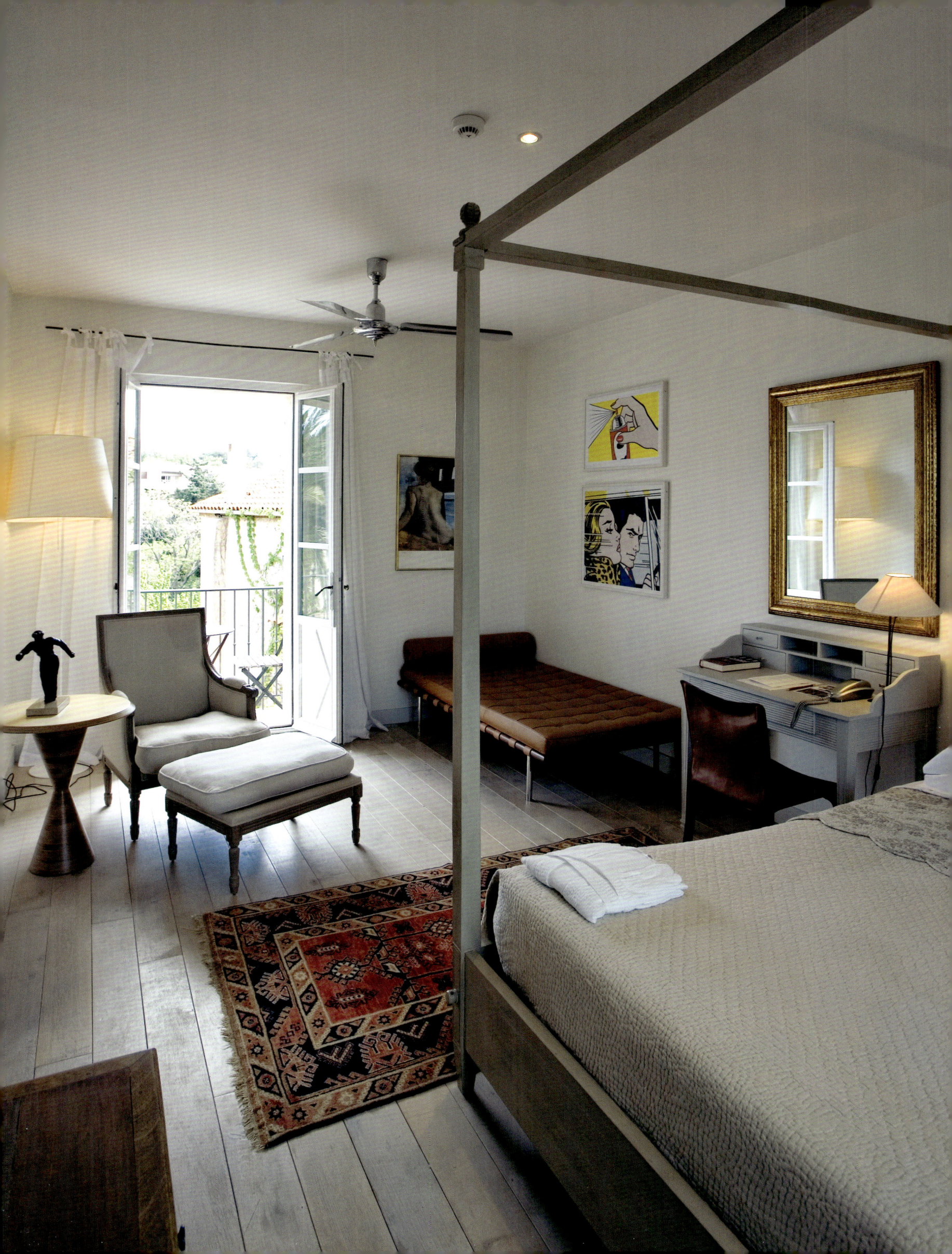

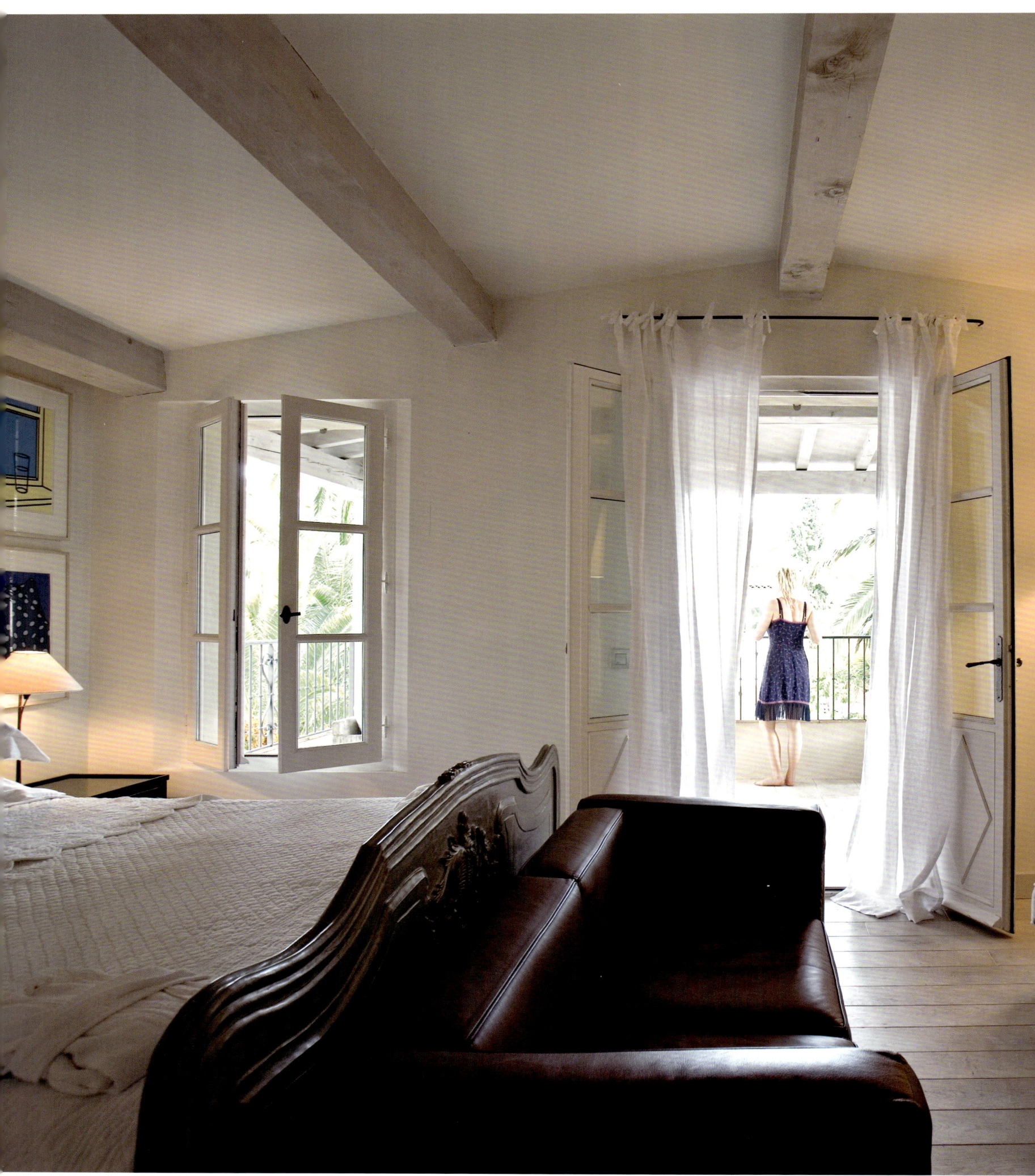

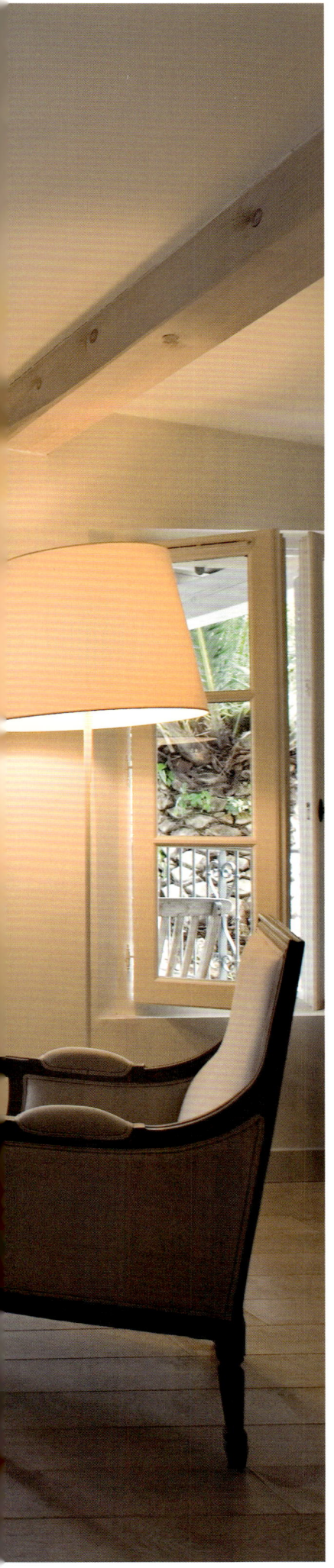

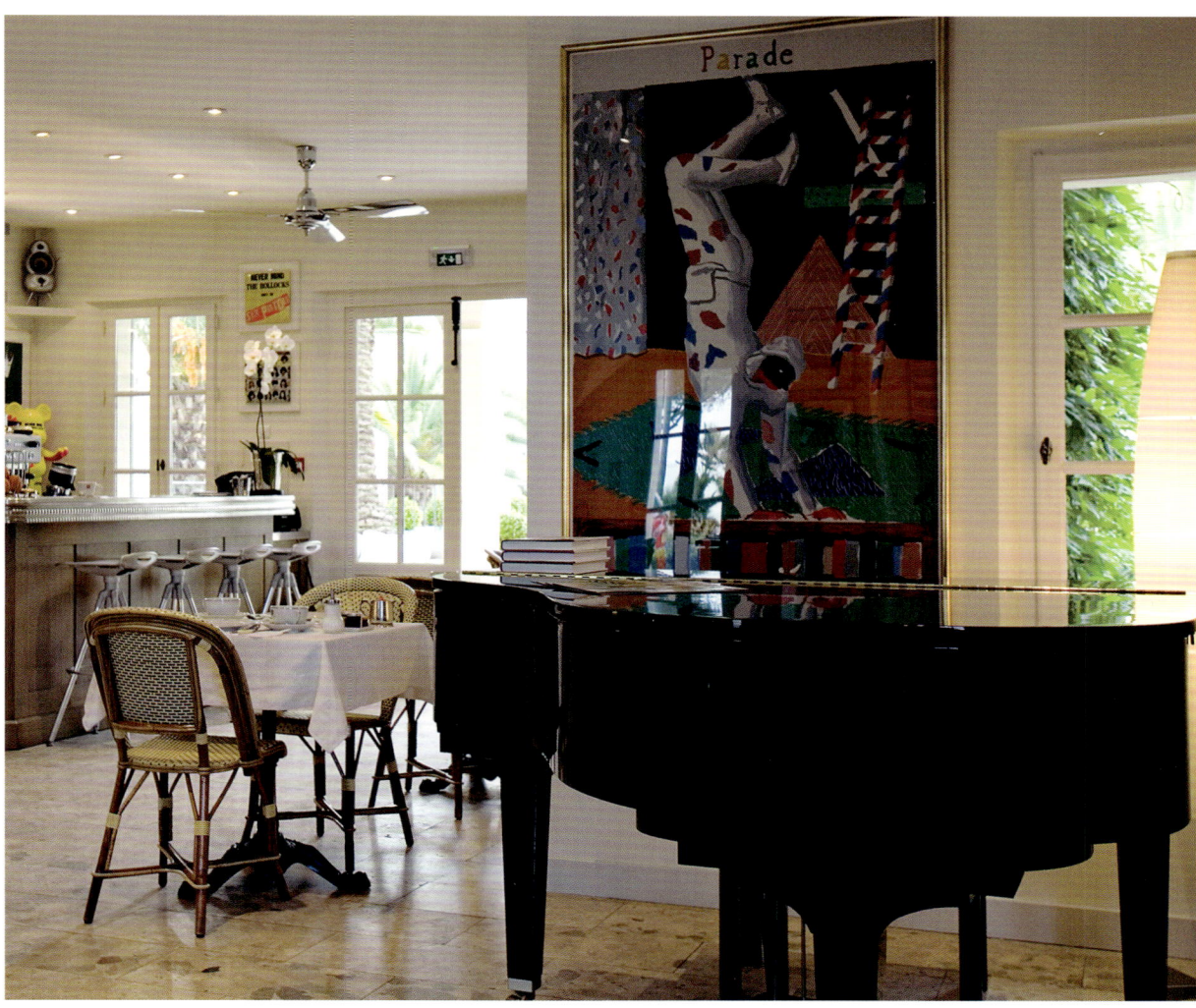

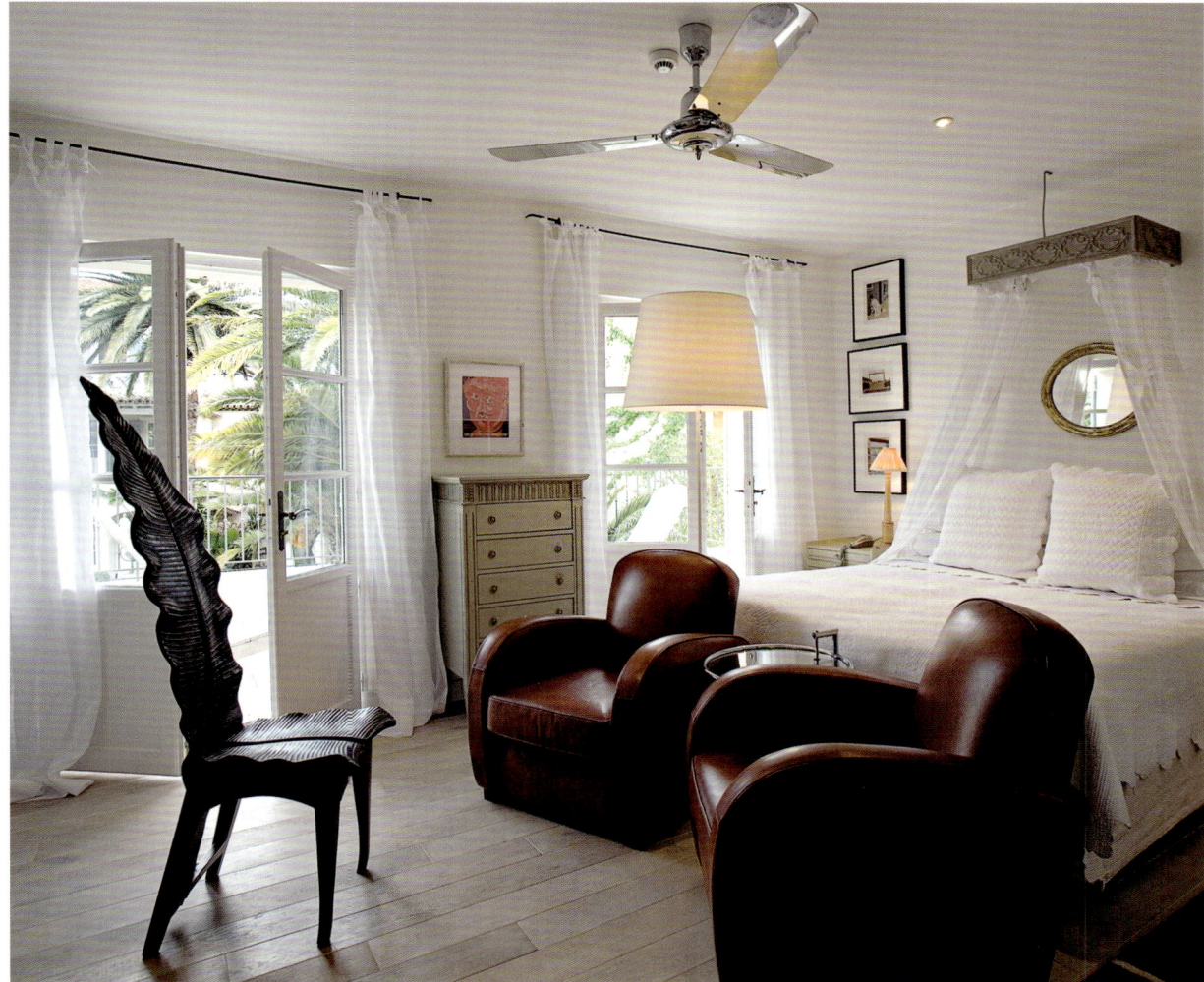

3, avenue Jean Monnet
06230 Saint-Jean-Cap-Ferrat
France
Phone: +33 4 93 76 31 00
Fax: +33 4 93 01 23 07
www.royal-riviera.com

Price category: €€€€
Rooms: 96 rooms
Facilities: Restaurant, bar, wellness center, private sandy beach
Services: Swimming lessons, nautical activities
Located: Facing the Mediterranean sea
Style: Classic

Anyone wanting to spend the winter stylishly under southern sun only had one choice at the beginning of the 20th century: Saint-Jean-Cap-Ferrat. The Prince of Wales recovered in the former fishing village, here is where Gustave Eiffel built his private villa, and in 1904 the Royal Riviera was built. Totally renovated now, it connects nostalgic glamour with modern luxury—in the lobby combining art deco and neo-classicism, in the 96 rooms kept in the colors of the South of France, as well as in the garden that is a Mediterranean oasis.

Wer den Winter stilvoll unter südlicher Sonne verbringen wollte, hatte zu Beginn des 20. Jahrhunderts nur eine Wahl: Saint-Jean-Cap-Ferrat. Im einstigen Fischerdorf erholte sich der Prince of Wales, hier baute Gustave Eiffel seine private Villa, und 1904 wurde das Royal Riviera errichtet. Rundum renoviert verbindet es heute nostalgischen Glamour mit modernem Luxus – in der Lobby, die Art déco und Neoklassizismus kombiniert, in den 96 Zimmern, die in den Farben Südfrankreichs gehalten sind, sowie im Garten, der eine mediterrane Oase ist.

Au début du XXème siècle, ceux qui voulaient passer un hiver chic sous le soleil du sud n'avaient qu'un seul choix : Saint-Jean-Cap-Ferrat. Le Prince de Galles venait se reposer dans ce lieu qui n'était encore qu'un village de pêcheurs, et Gustave Eiffel y fit construire son manoir privé. En 1904, le Royal Riviera était créé. Aujourd'hui totalement rénové, il marie glamour et luxe moderne ; à la réception par exemple, l'art déco et le néoclassique se mêlent. Dans les 96 chambres, les couleurs du sud de la France prédominent, tout comme dans le jardin, qui ressemble à une oasis méditerranéenne.

Para aquellos que, a comienzos del siglo XX, deseaban pasar el invierno bajo el sol del sur sólo había una posibilidad: Saint-Jean-Cap-Ferrat. A este antiguo pueblo pesquero acudía el príncipe de Gales a descansar, aquí es donde Gustave Eiffel se hizo construir su mansión privada y donde, en 1904, se levantó el hotel Royal Riviera. Renovado por completo, reúne hoy en día el glamour nostálgico con el lujo moderno: en el vestíbulo, el cual combina art-déco con neoclasicismo; en las 96 habitaciones, en las que se han mantenido los colores típicos del sur de Francia, y en el jardín, un auténtico oasis mediterráneo.

Agli inizi del XX secolo, chi voleva trascorrere l'inverno sotto il sole del Sud senza rinunciare allo stile aveva un'unica scelta: Saint-Jean-Cap-Ferrat. In questo che un tempo era un villaggio di pescatori veniva a riposarsi il Principe di Galles; qui Gustave Eiffel costruì la sua villa privata e sempre qui, nel 1904, venne edificato il Royal Riviera. Oggi, dopo una completa ristrutturazione, l'hotel coniuga un nostalgico glamour con un lusso moderno: nella lobby, in cui si combinano Art Déco e neoclassicismo, nelle 96 camere arredate nei colori della Francia meridionale e infine nel giardino, una vera e propria oasi mediterranea.

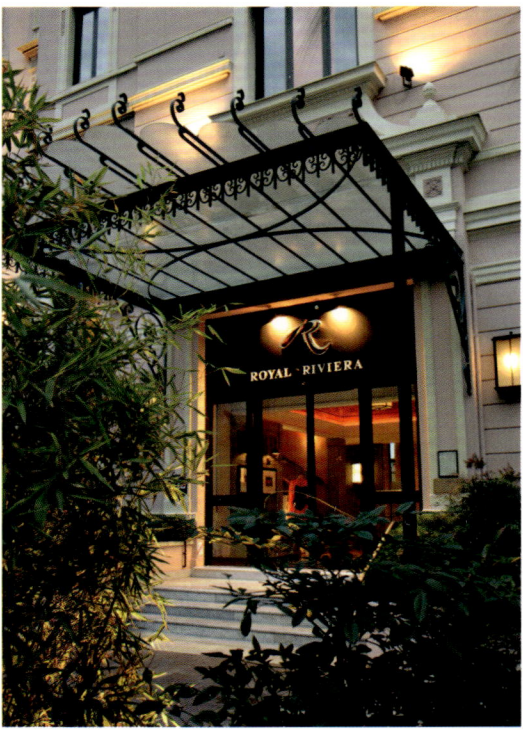
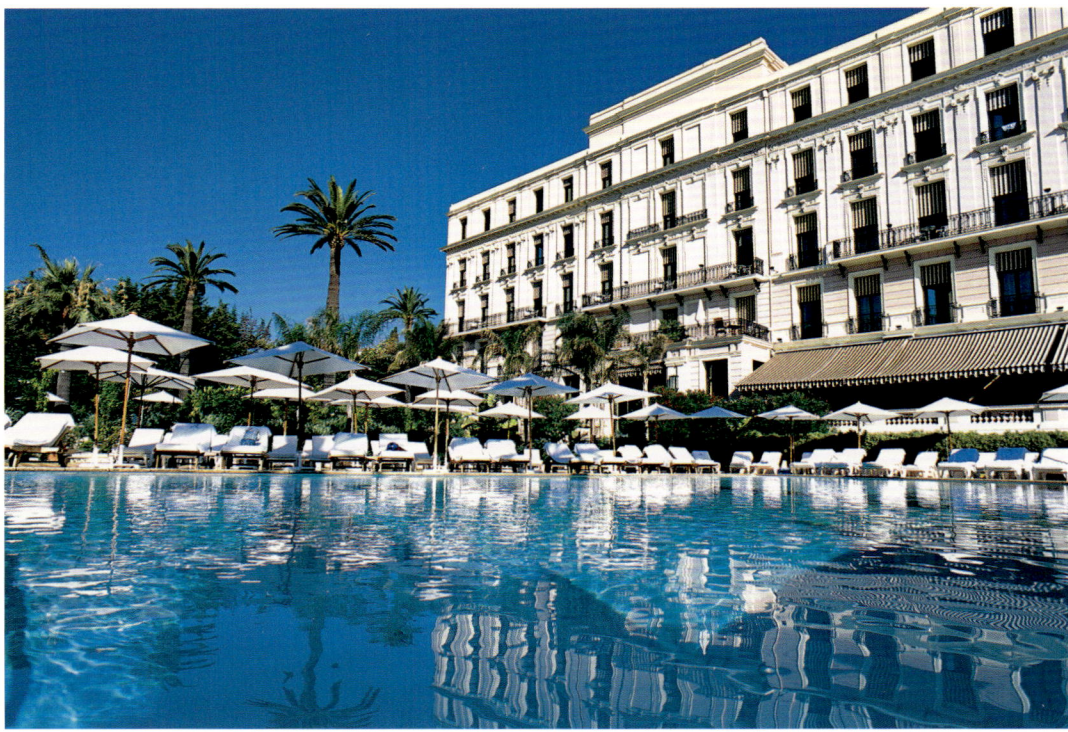

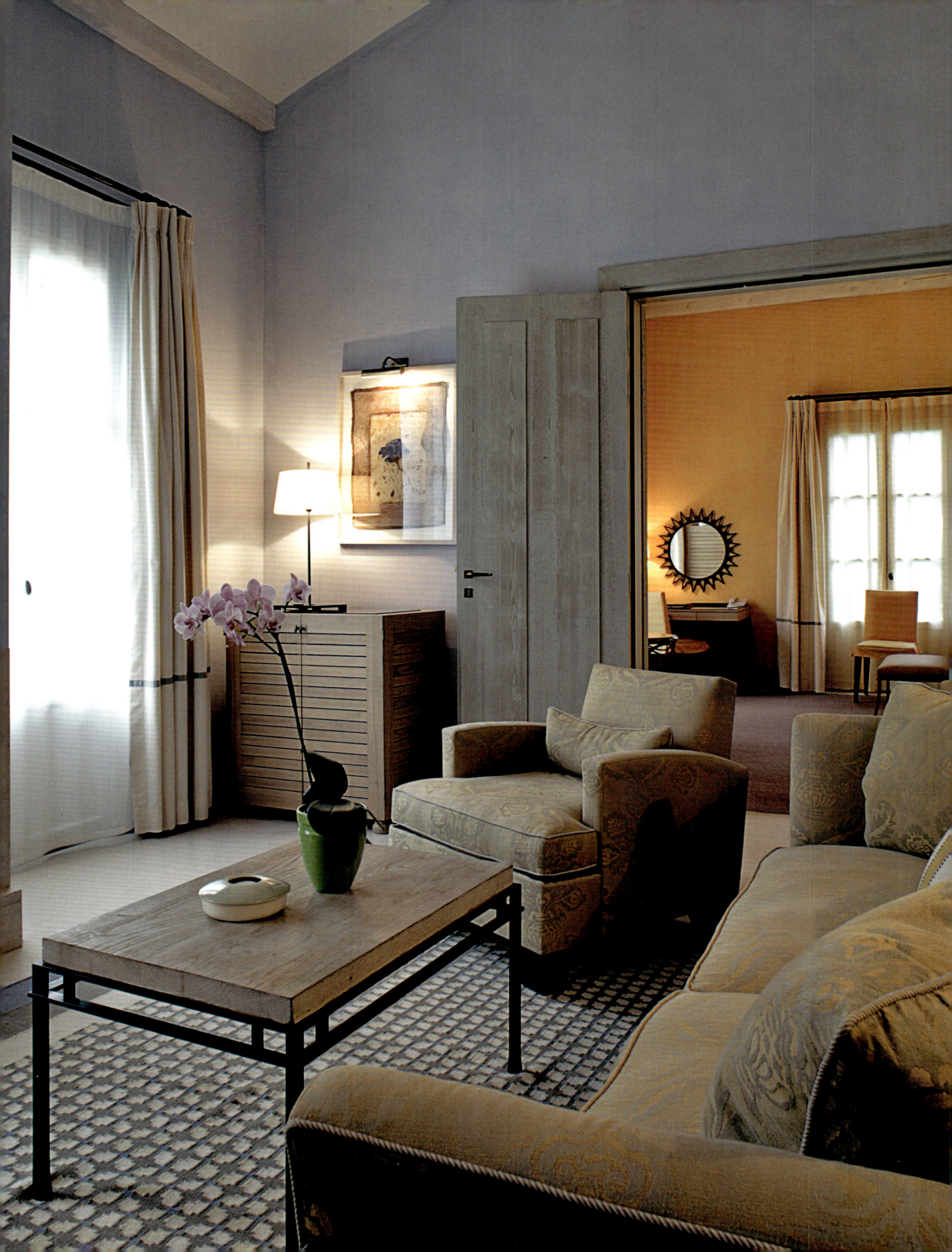

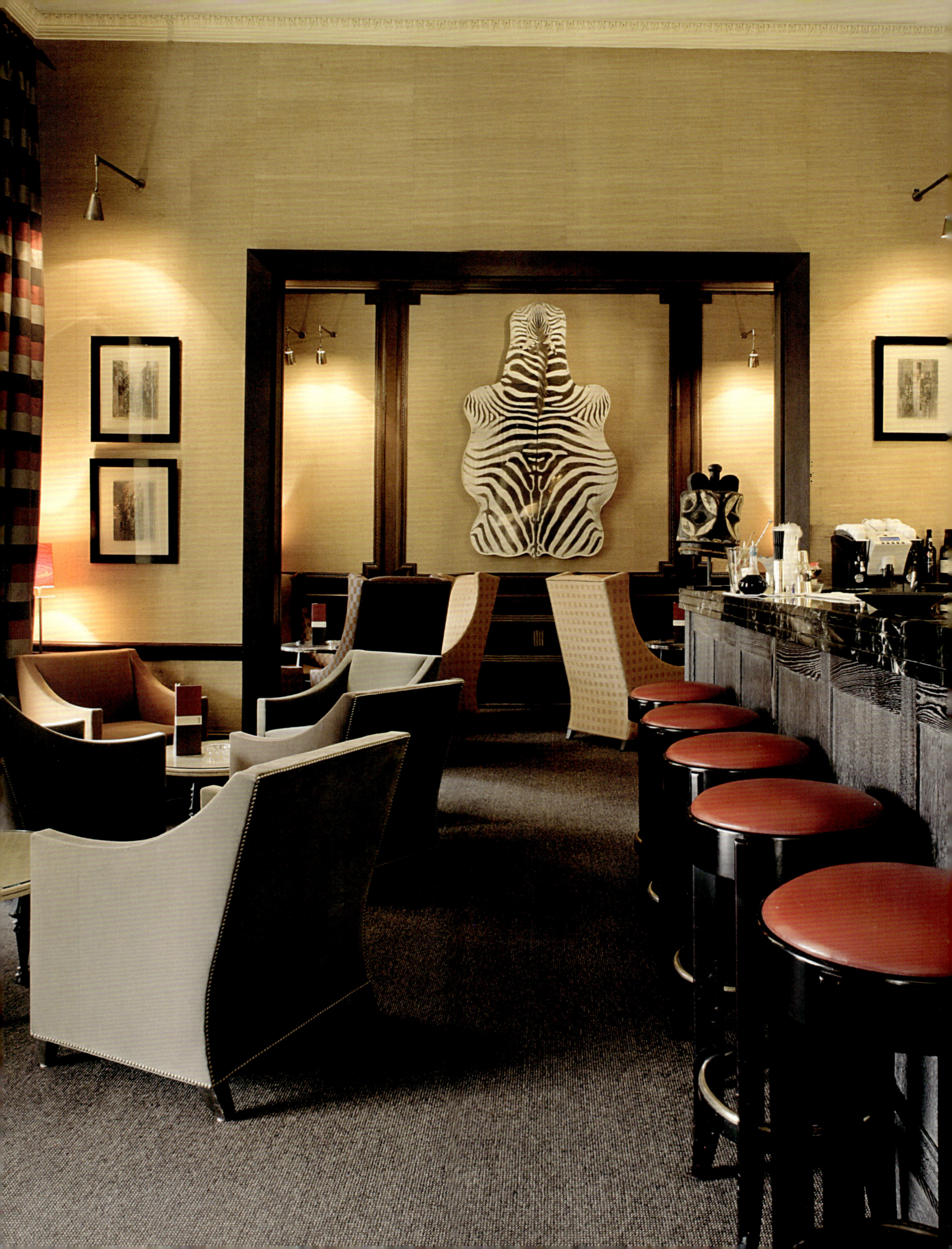

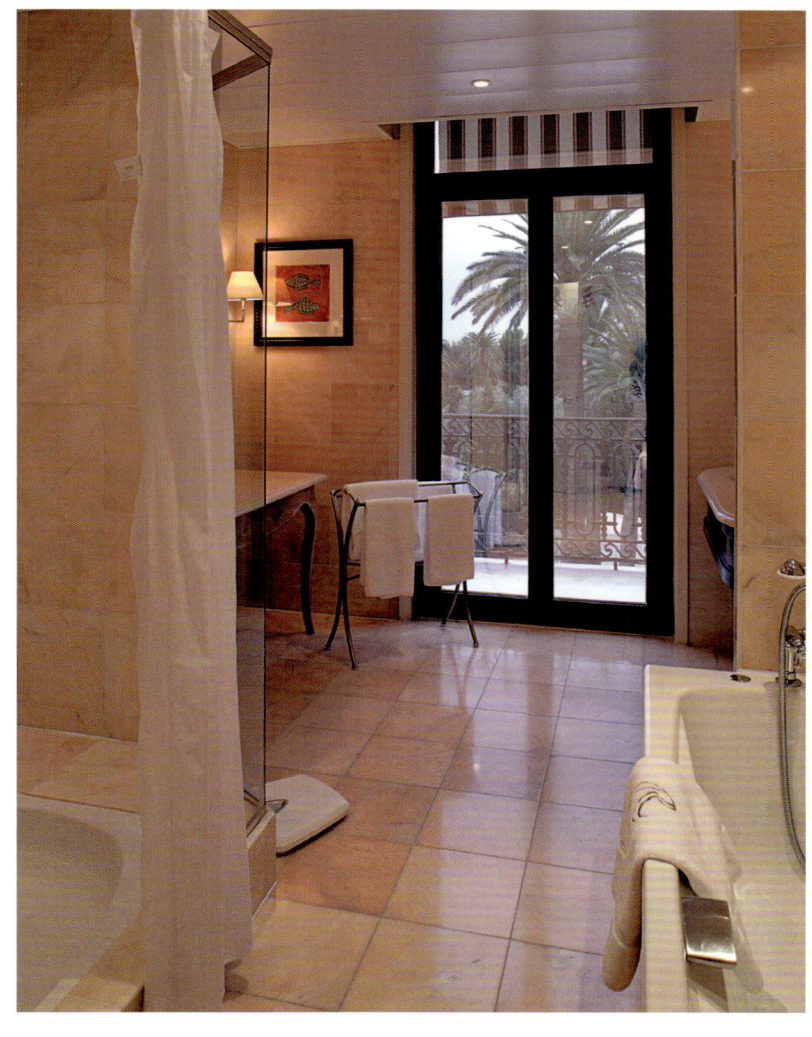

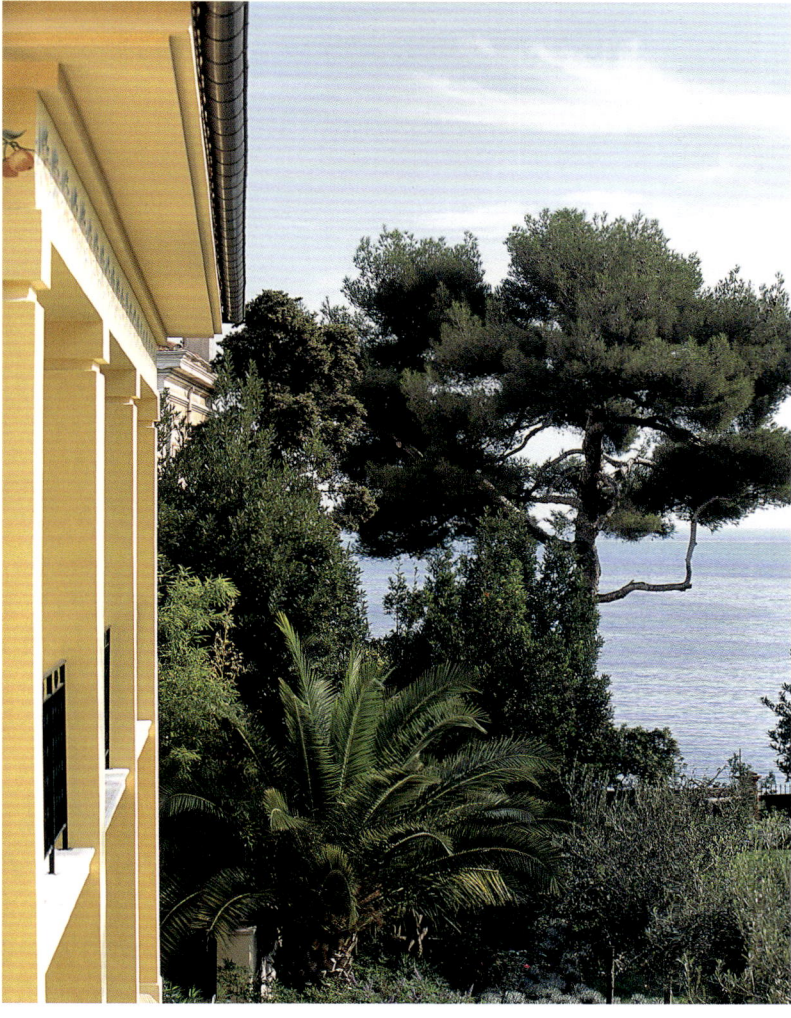

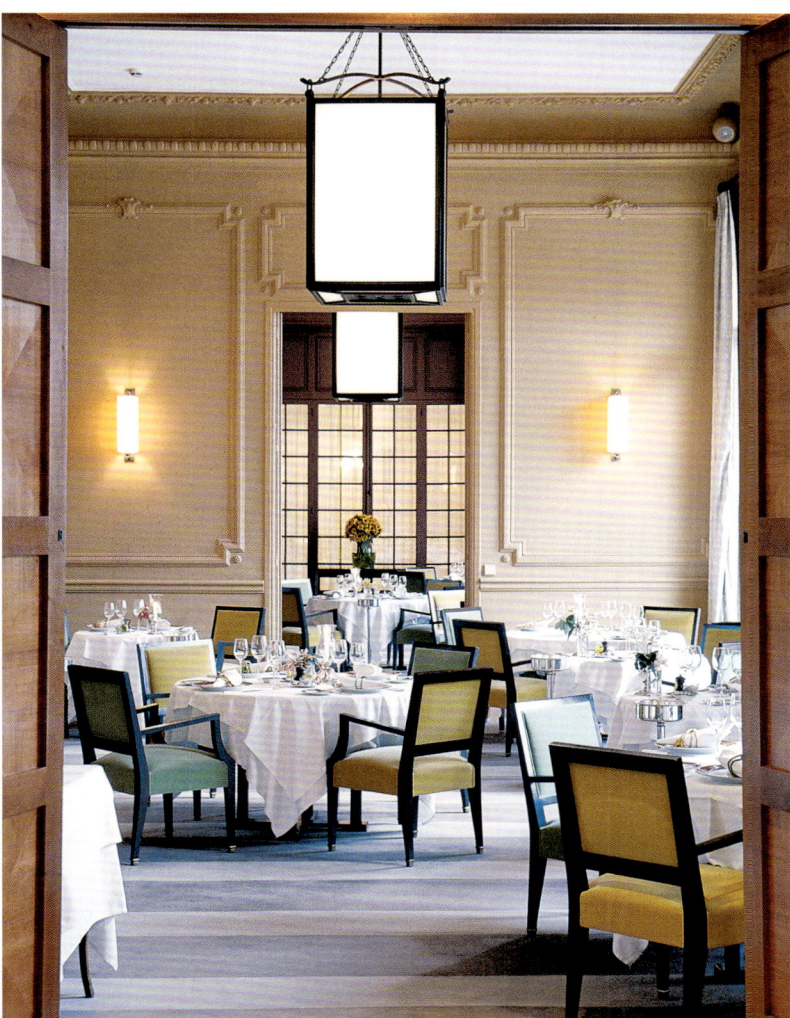

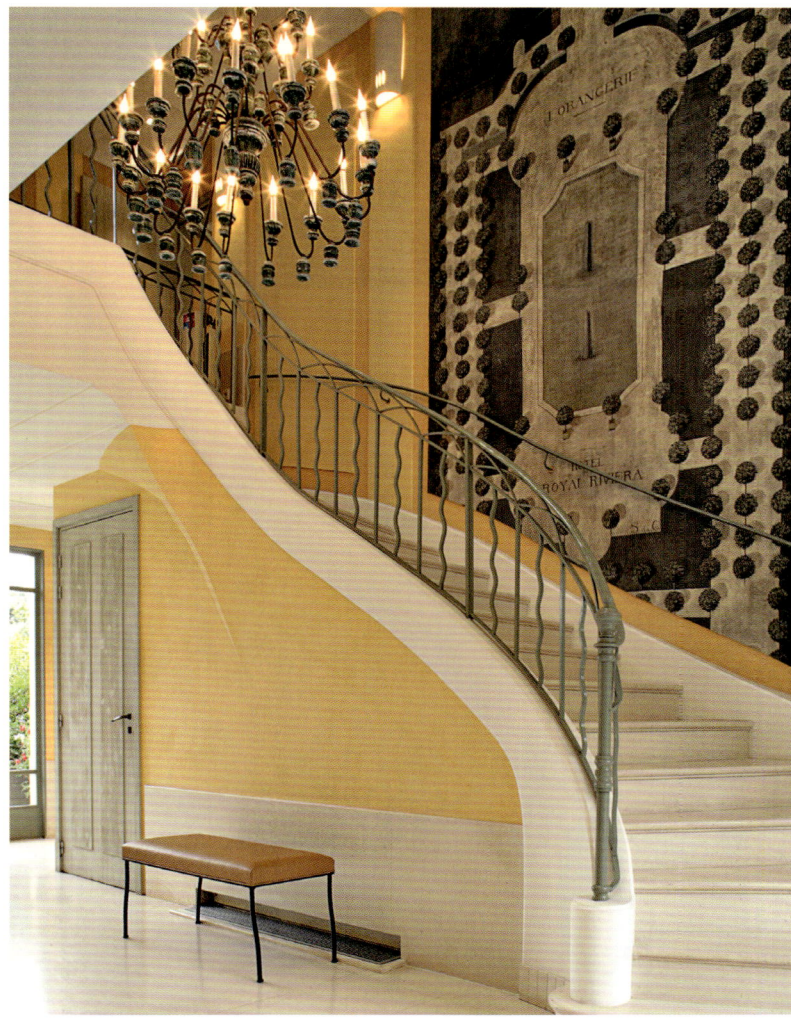

75007 Paris
France
Phone: +33 1 45 50 22 31
Fax: +33 1 45 51 52 36
www.lebellechasse.com

Rooms: 34 rooms
Facilities: Salon, bar
Services: WiFi
Located: A few steps from the Quai de Seine and the Musée d'Orsay
Public transportation: Metro 12 Solférino; RER C Musée d'Orsay
Style: Modern couture

It would like to allow its guest "a trip during a trip" in a hotel that mirrors the chic and charm of the Parisian boheme in all its facets. Fashion designer Christian Lacroix had the 34 rooms of the Bellechasse near the Musée d'Orsay dressed to seven different themes and every haute couture gown tailored. Filigreed butterflies, baroque portraits or whole solar systems adorn the walls and even the ceilings. Opulently mixed forms and colors make up an almost surreal dreamworld of fantasy.

„Eine Reise während der Reise" möchte er seinen Gästen ermöglichen – in einem Hotel, das den Chic und Charme der Pariser Boheme in all seinen Facetten widerspiegelt. Modeschöpfer Christian Lacroix hat die 34 Zimmer des Bellechasse nahe des Musée d'Orsay nach sieben unterschiedlichen Themen eingekleidet und jedes Haute-Couture-Gewand maßgeschneidert. Filigrane Schmetterlinge, barocke Portraits oder ganze Sonnensysteme schmücken Wände und sogar Decken. Opulent gemischte Formen und Farben bilden eine fantasievolle, fast surreale Traumwelt.

Il offre à ses clients « un voyage dans le voyage », dans un hôtel qui reflète le chic et le charme du bohème parisien sous toutes ses facettes. Le créateur de mode Christian Lacroix a habillé les 34 chambres du Bellechasse, près du Musée d'Orsay, selon différents thèmes, et chaque robe haute-couture a été faite sur mesure. Des papillons en filigrane, des portraits baroques ou le système solaire au grand complet décorent les murs et même les plafonds. Des formes et des couleurs richement mêlées créent un monde onirique imaginatif, presque surréel.

"Un viaje durante el viaje" es lo que procura ofrecer a sus huéspedes; en un hotel que refleja en todas sus facetas el chic y la elegancia de la bohemia parisina. El diseñador Christian Lacroix ha vestido las 34 habitaciones del hotel Bellechasse junto al Musée d'Orsay basándose en siete temas diferentes y ha confeccionado cada uno de sus modelos de alta costura a medida. Las paredes, e incluso los techos, están engalanados con delicadas mariposas, retratos barrocos o sistemas solares completos. Las formas y los colores, mezclados de manera opulenta, crean un mundo de ensueño lleno de fantasía, casi surrealista.

L'idea è di rendere possibile agli ospiti un vero e proprio "viaggio dentro il viaggio", ricreando in un hotel tutte le sfaccettature dell'eleganza e dello charme della boheme parigina. Lo stilista di moda Christian Lacroix ha arredato con tessuti haute couture le 34 camere del Bellechasse, situato nelle vicinanze del Musée d'Orsay, ispirandosi a sette diverse tematiche e tagliando su misura ogni pezzo. Farfalle in filigrana, ritratti barocchi e interi sistemi solari adornano le pareti e persino i soffitti. Forme e colori opulenti combinati con fantasia sanno dar vita a un mondo da sogno, che non mancherà di incantarvi.

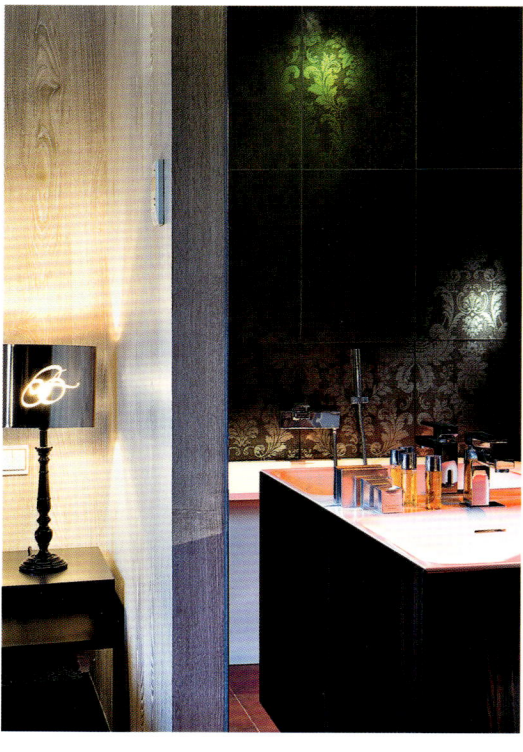
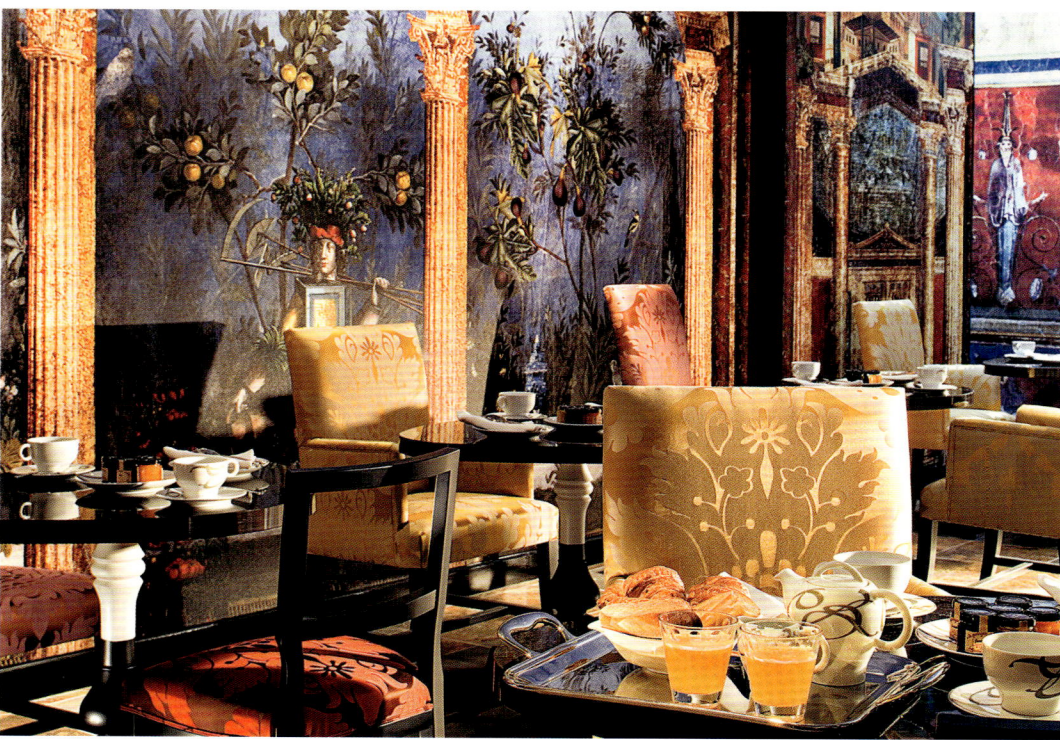

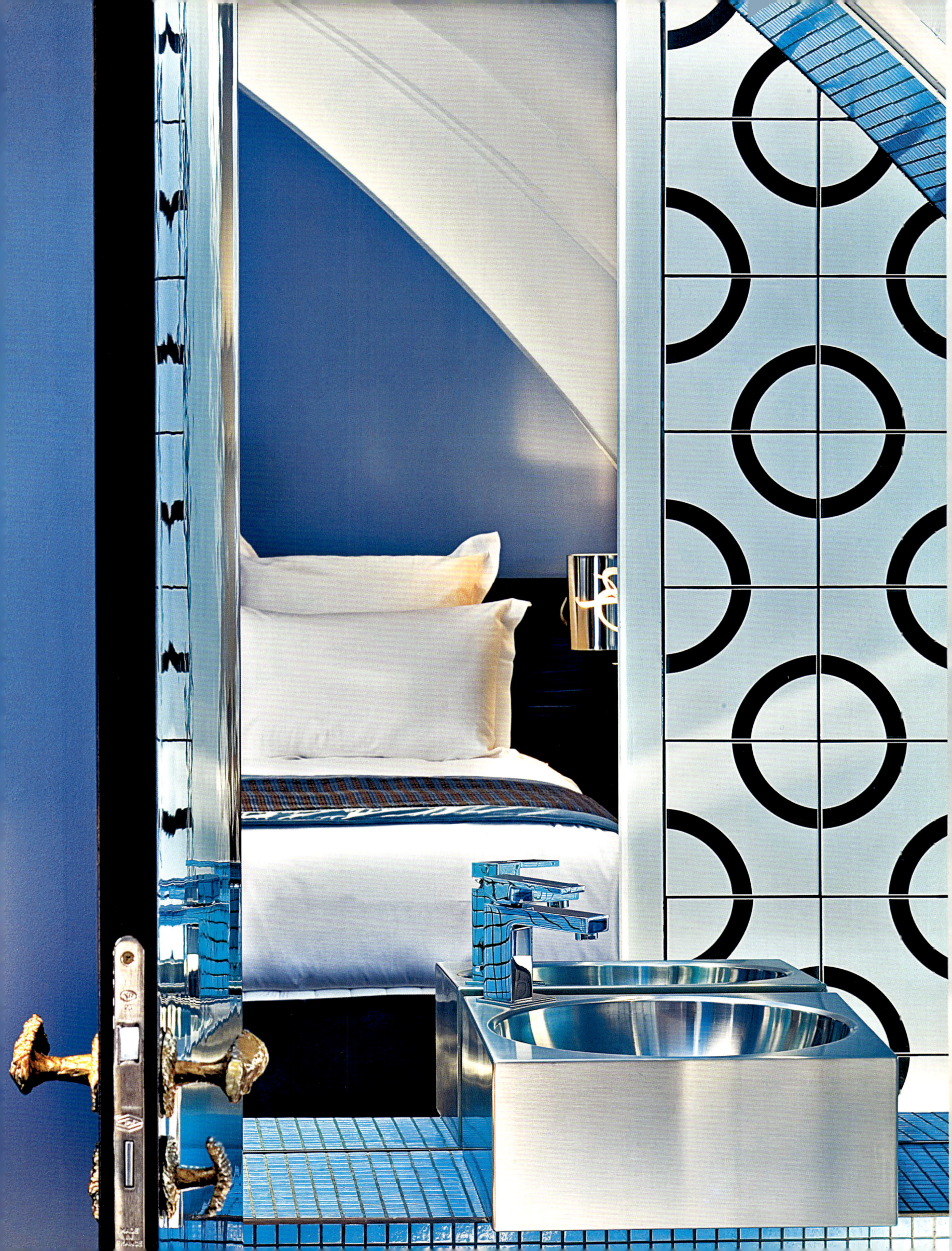

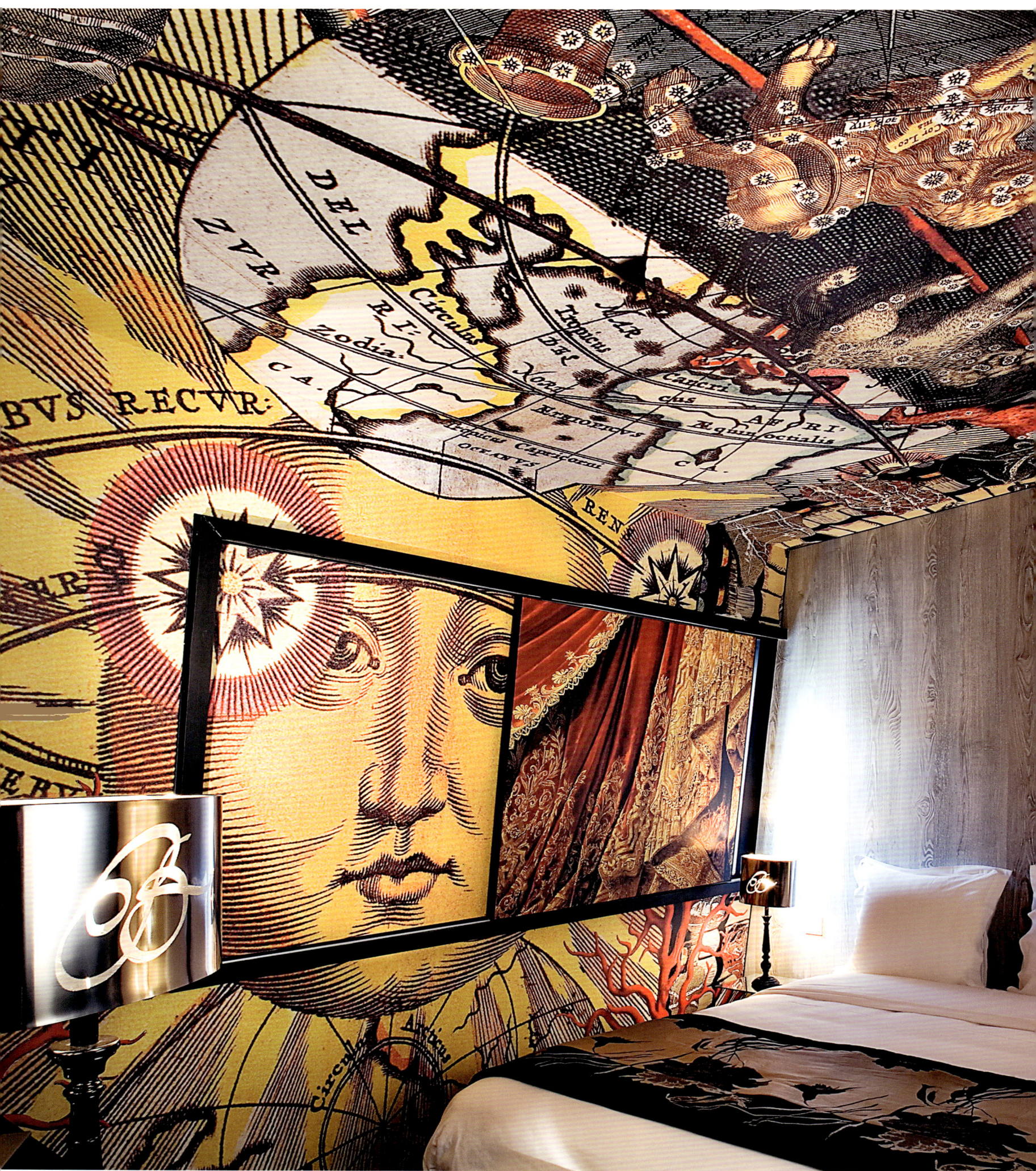

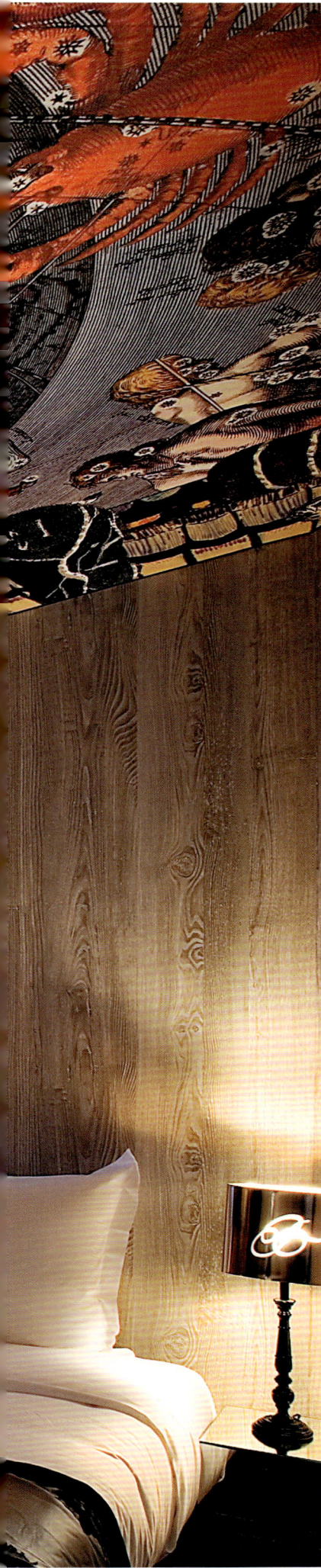

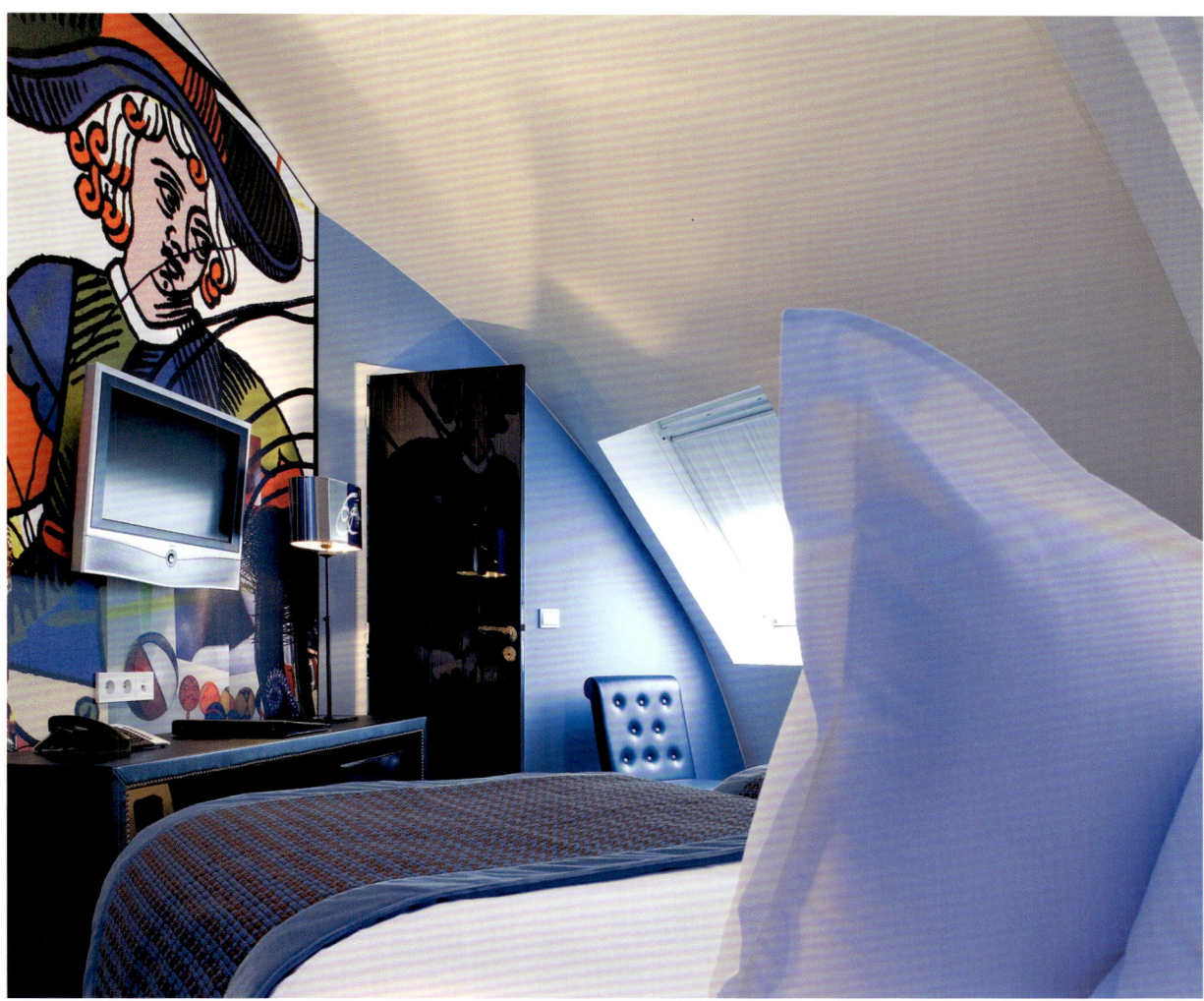

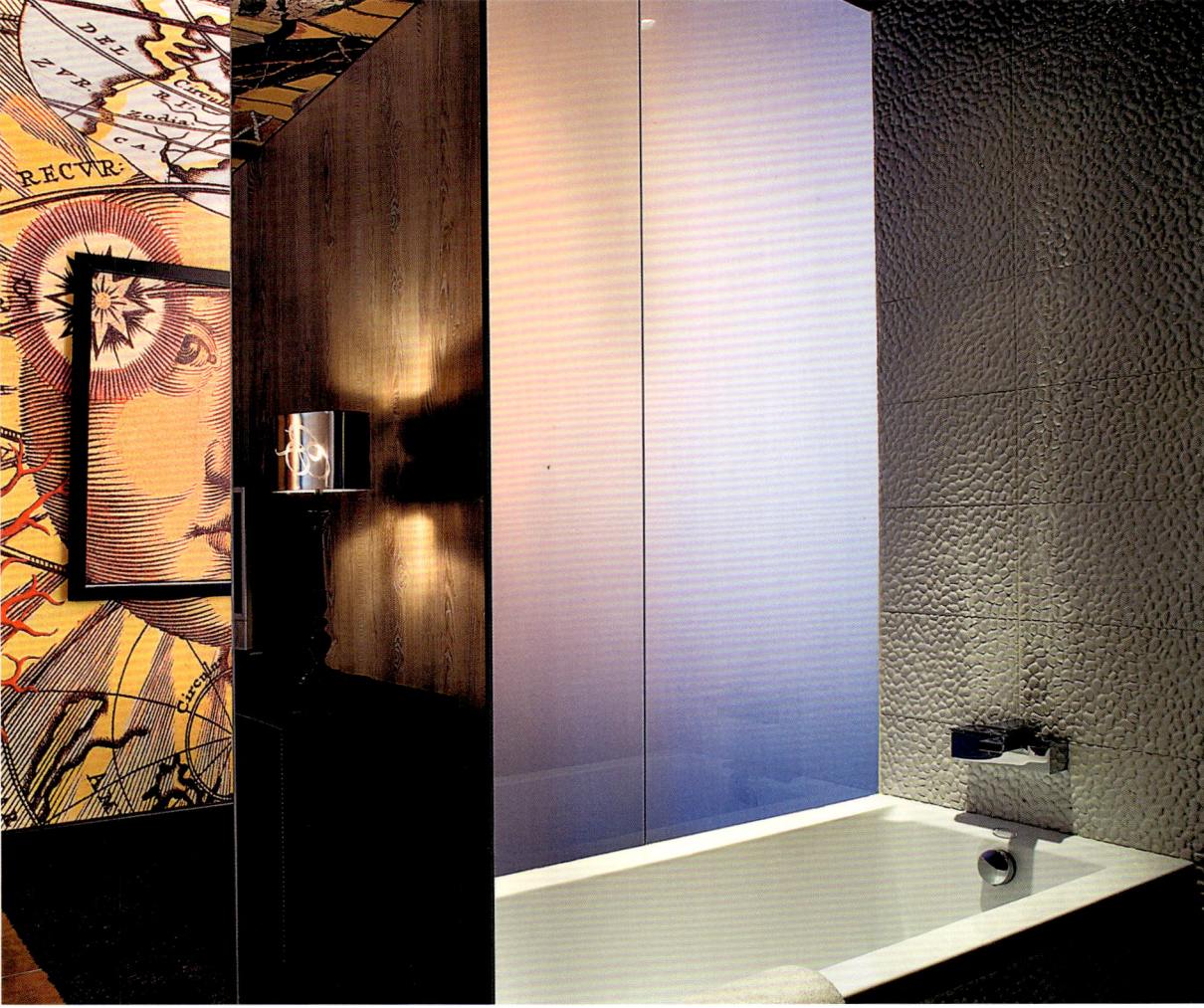

75116 Paris
France
Phone: +33 1 53 65 66 99
Fax: +33 1 53 65 66 88
www.dokhans-sofitel-paris.com

Rooms: 41 rooms and 4 suites
Facilities: Champagne-Bar
Services: Small dogs allowed, internet access
Located: Located between the Trocadéro and Arc de Triomphe
Public transportation: Metro 6, 9 Trocadéro and 2 Victor Hugo; RER A Etoile
Style: Neoclassic

Interior designer Frédéric Méchiche made a stylish boutique hotel with plenty of atmosphere out of the city palace in the noble 16th arrondissement of Paris. The 45 rooms and suites are elegant with narrow striped tapestries as well as classical furniture. In the intimate bar there is modern French cuisine besides the finest brands of champagne on the menu. An elevator that perfectly matches the glamorous world of travel is a real extra—it was made out of a wardrobe trunk by Louis Vuitton.

Aus einem Stadtpalais im edlen 16. Arrondissement von Paris hat Interior Designer Frédéric Méchiche ein stilvolles Boutiquehotel mit viel Atmosphäre gemacht: Die 45 Zimmer und Suiten sind elegant mit schmal gestreiften Tapeten sowie klassischen Möbeln ausgestattet, und in der intimen Bar stehen neben moderner französischer Küche feinste Champagnersorten auf der Karte. Ein besonderes Extra, das perfekt zur glamourösen Welt des Reisens passt, ist der Aufzug – er wurde aus einem Schrankkoffer von Louis Vuitton gefertigt.

D'un palace citadin du très chic seizième arrondissement de Paris, l'architecte d'intérieur Frédéric Méchiche a fait un bel hôtel-boutique, avec beaucoup d'atmosphère. Les 45 chambres et suites sont élégantes, tapissées de fines rayures et meublées de manière classique. Dans le bar à l'ambiance intime, la cuisine française la plus exquise figure à côté des meilleurs champagnes. L'ascenseur est un petit bijou, qui s'accorde parfaitement au monde glamour du voyage : il est fait d'une malle garde-robe Louis Vuitton.

El diseñador de interiores Frédéric Méchiche ha transformado un palacio del noble distrito 16 de la capital francesa en un elegante hotel boutique con mucha atmósfera. Sus 45 habitaciones y suites, con tapices de rayas finas y muebles clásicos, destilan elegancia. En la carta del bar se pueden encontrar, junto a la moderna cocina francesa, los más finos champañas. Un detalle especial que combina de maravilla con el glamoroso mundo de los viajes es el ascensor, hecho con un baúl armario de Louis Vuitton.

Da un palazzo dell'esclusivo 16 arrondissement di Parigi il designer di interni Frédéric Méchiche ha tratto questo boutique hotel dallo stile impeccabile e dalle sottili atmosfere: le 45 tra camere e suite sono elegantemente arredate con mobili classici e tappezzerie a righe sottili, e nel raccolto locale bar, accanto alla moderna cucina francese, è possibile trovare sul menù le più raffinate varietà di champagne. Un ulteriore tocco di classe, che si accorderà perfettamente con il glamour dei vostri viaggi, è rappresentato dall'ascensore ricavato da un baule di Louis Vuitton.

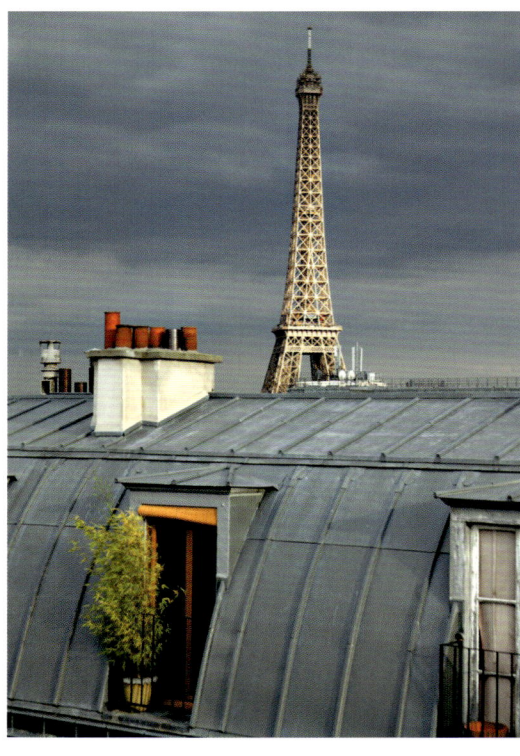
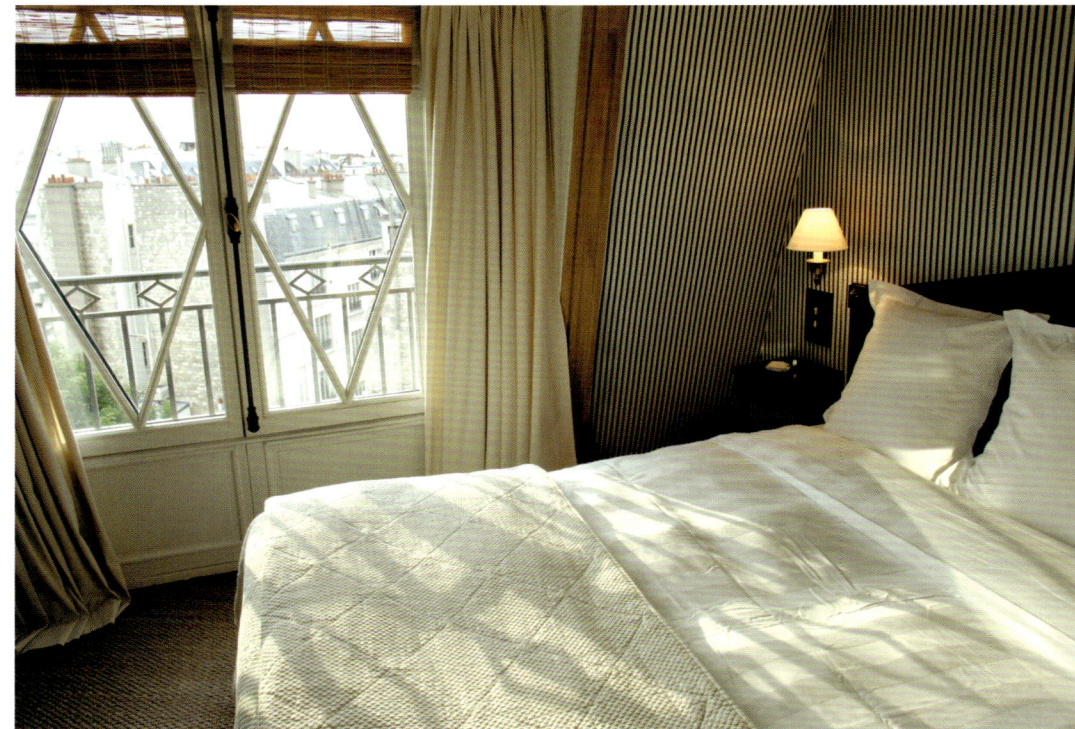

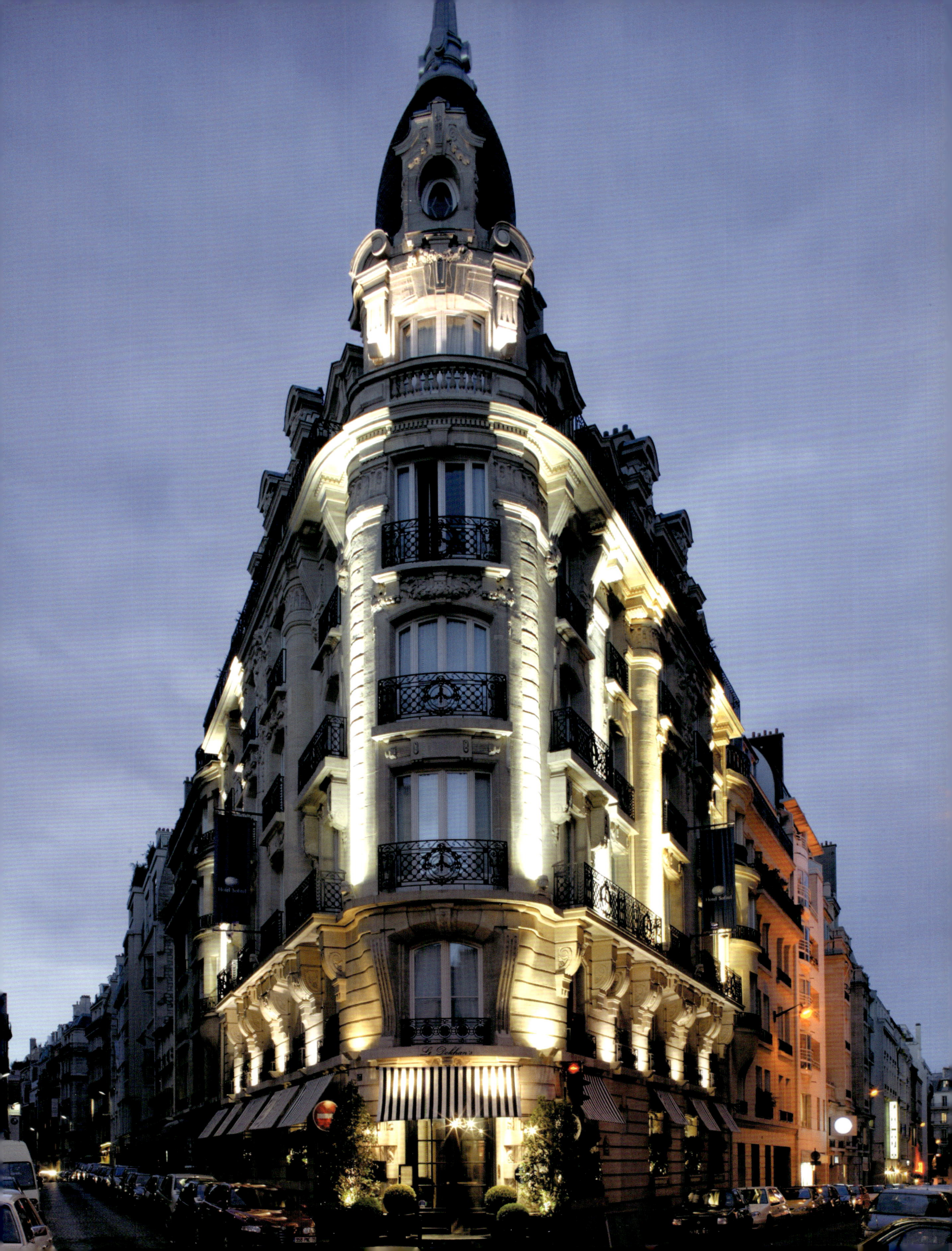

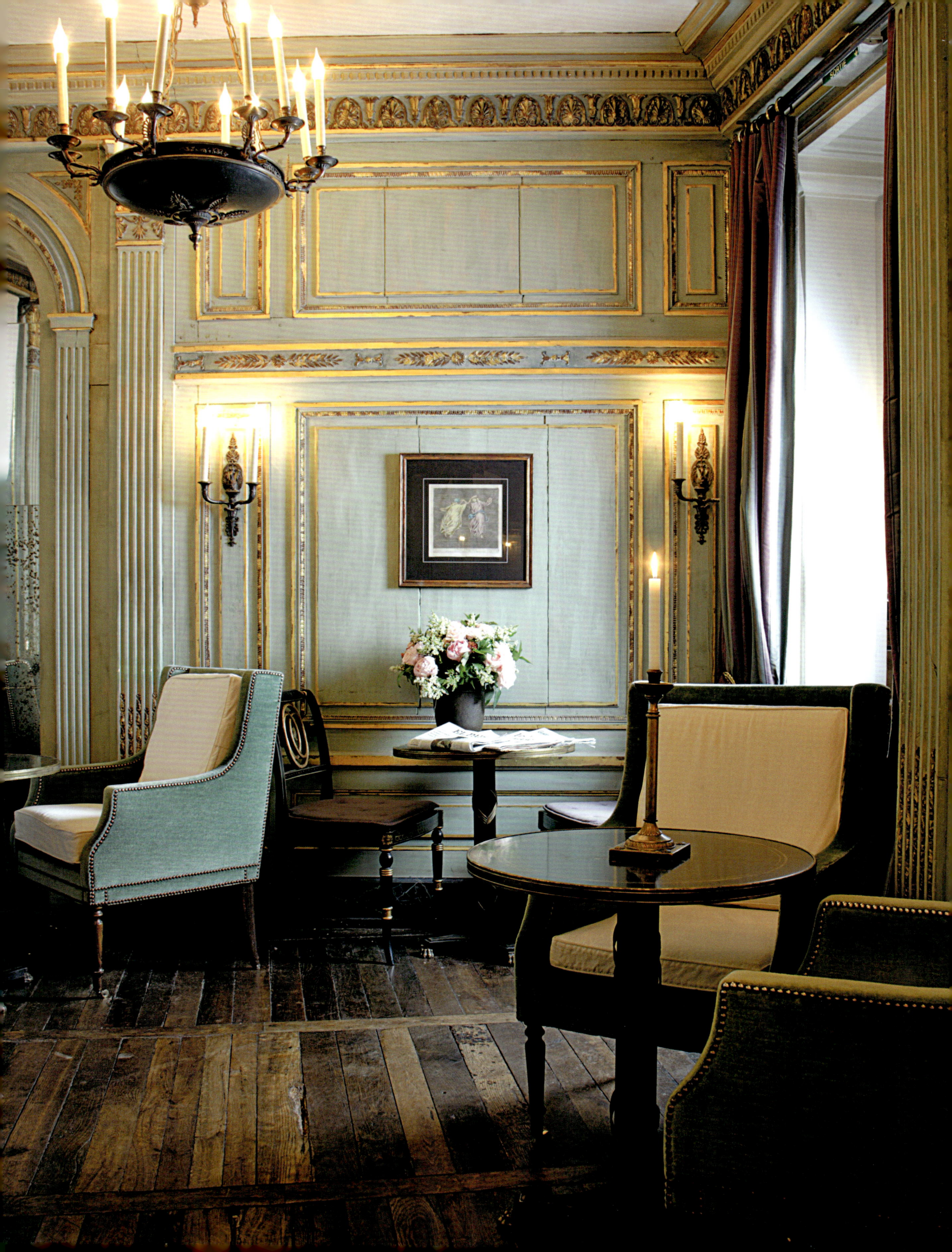

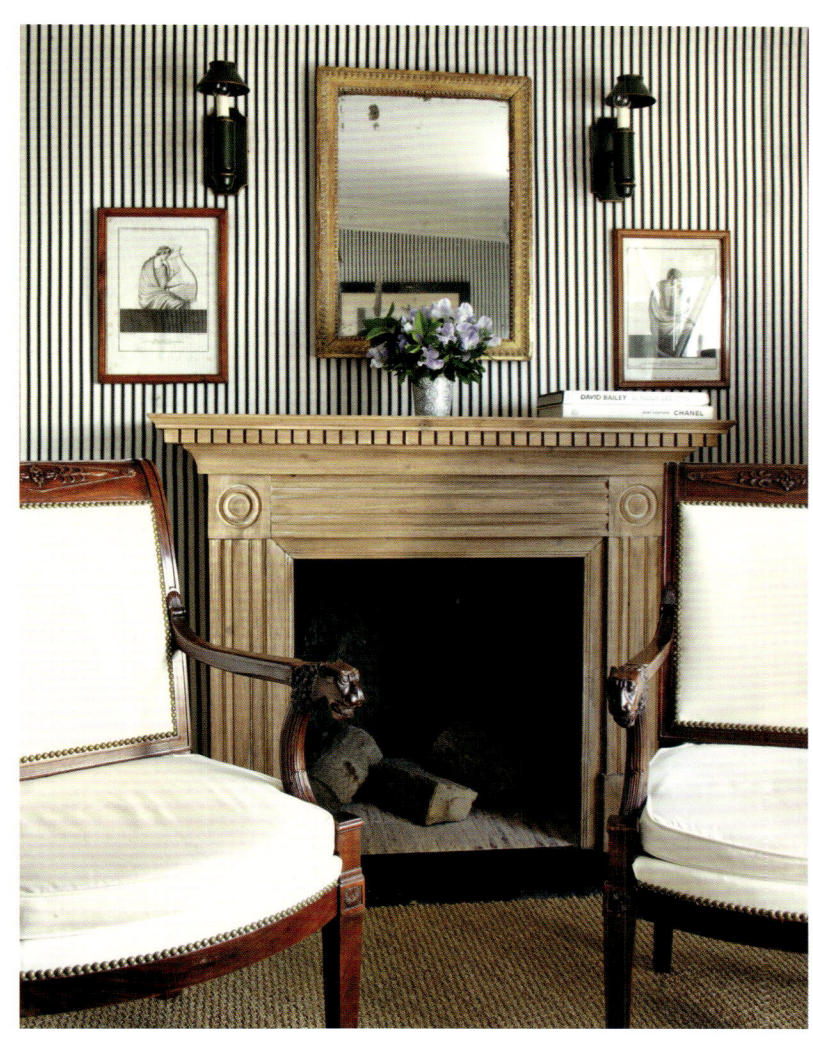
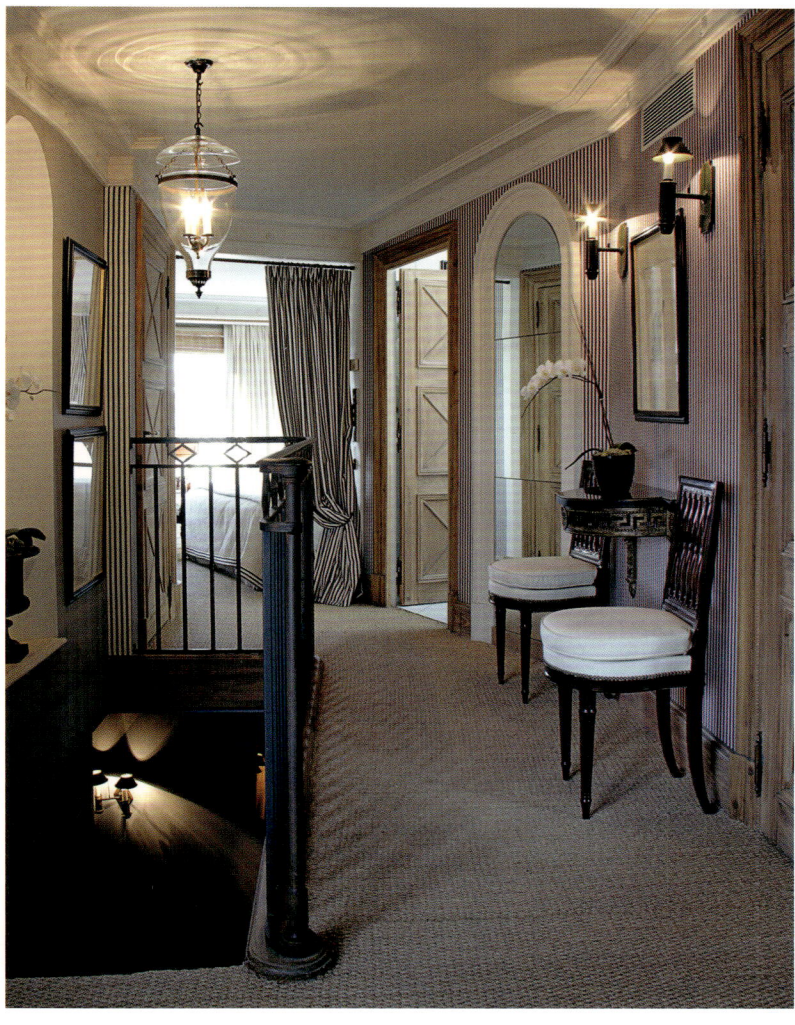
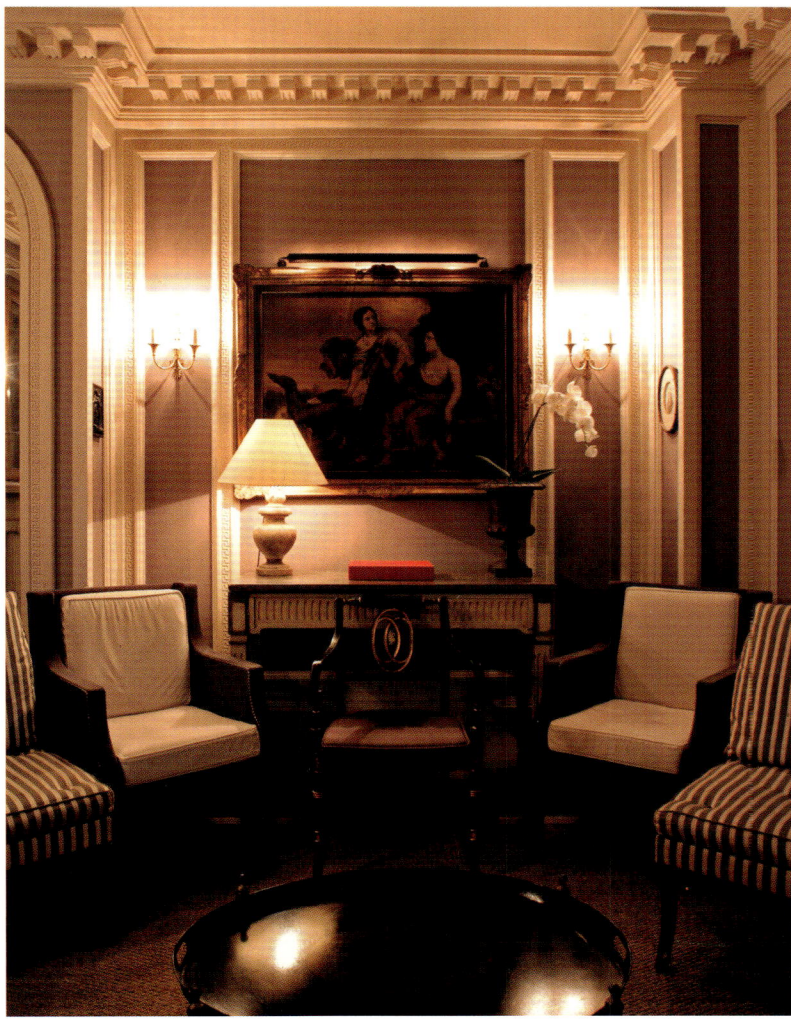
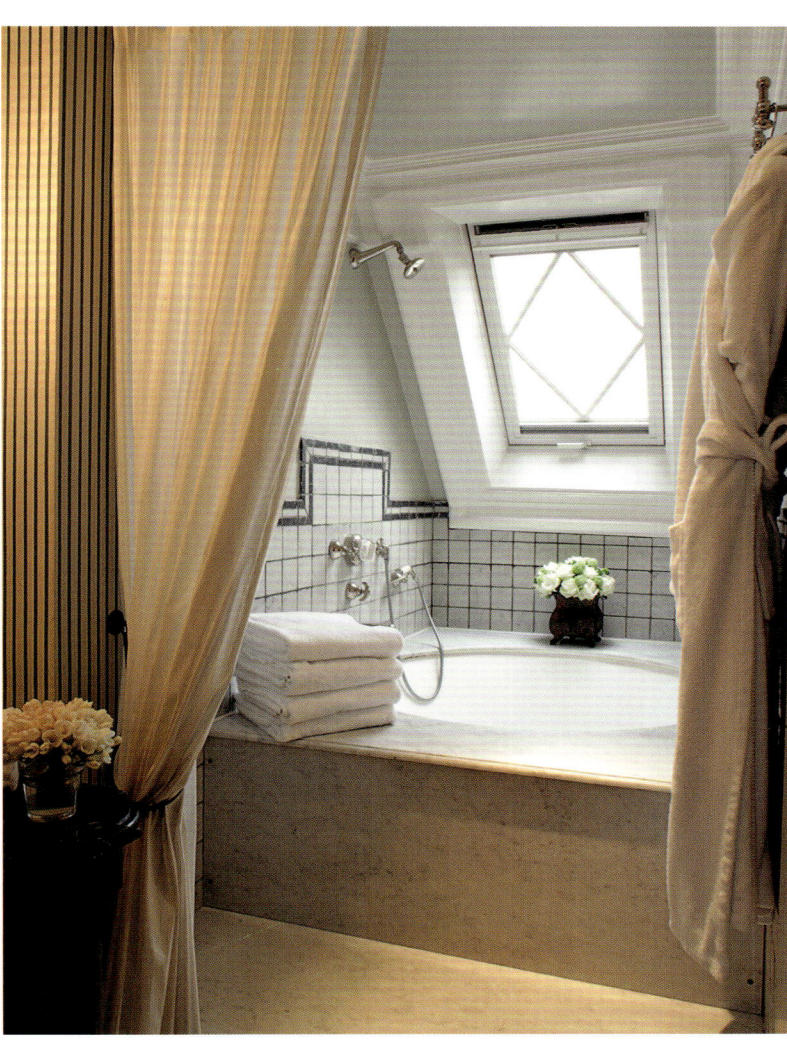

Hotel Keppler

Paris, France

10, rue Kepler
75016 Paris
France
Phone: +33 1 47 20 65 05
Fax: +33 1 47 23 02 29
www.keppler-paris-hotel.com

Price category: €€
Rooms: 39 rooms including 4 suites and 1 penthouse
Facilities: Bar, fitness room including steam room, sauna and gym
Services: Clé d'Or concierge service, WiFi, room service, laundry, facilities for the disabled, parking
Located: In a quiet street next to the Champs-Elysées
Public transportation: Metro 1 Georges V and 2 Charles de Gaulle – Etoile; RER A Etoile
Style: Modern

His talent for unusual color and material combinations have made him famous. The French designer Pierre-Yves Rochon once again evidenced his refined creativeness in this new city hotel. He placed pink colored sofas on black and white tiles, let honey yellow flower arabesques and zebra prints compete with checkered materials as well as leather desks with Turkish carpets, and clothed the walls in the baths in *toile de jouy dessins*. The penthouse suites are so generously designed with their own terraces that they seem more like lofts than hotel rooms. And he still found a place for a wellness oasis with sauna and steam bath.

Sein Talent für ungewöhnliche Farb- und Materialkombinationen machte ihn bekannt. Der französische Designer Pierre-Yves Rochon bewies in dem neuen Stadthotel einmal mehr seine kreative Finnesse: Er platziert pinkfarbene Sofas auf schwarz-weißen Fliesen, lässt honiggelbe Blumenarabesken und Zebra-Prints mit Karo-Stoffen konkurrieren sowie lederne Schreibtische mit türkischen Teppichen, und die Wände der Bäder kleiden Toile-de-Jouy-Dessins. Die Penthouse-Suiten mit eigenen Terrassen konzipierte er so großzügig, dass sie eher Lofts ähneln, als Hotelzimmern. Und für eine Wellness-Oase mit Sauna und Dampfbad fand er auch noch Platz.

Son talent pour les combinaisons inattendues de couleurs et de matériaux ont fait sa renommée ; le designer français Pierre-Yves Rochon a encore prouvé sa finesse créative avec ce nouvel hôtel citadin. Il a placé des canapés roses sur des sols carrelés noir et blanc, laissé les arabesques jaune miel et les imprimés zèbre rivaliser avec les matériaux à damier, tout comme les tables couvertes de cuir et les tapis turcs, et les murs des salles de bains décorés de motifs Toile de Jouy. Les suites sous les toits, disposant de leur propre terrasse, sont si vastes qu'elles rappellent plus un loft qu'une chambre d'hôtel. Et il a réussi à dégager assez d'espace pour créer une oasis de bien-être avec sauna et hammam.

Su talento para combinar colores y materiales de forma inusual le hizo famoso. El diseñador francés Pierre-Yves Rochon ha demostrado una vez más su especial creatividad en este hotel urbano, colocando sofás de color rosa sobre suelos de losas blancas y negras, arabescos de flores color miel y estampados de cebra junto a tejidos de cuadros, escritorios tapizados en cuero con alfombras turcas y diseños *Toile de Jouy* en las paredes de los baños. Las lujosas suites del ático, con sus terrazas propias, son tan espaciosas que recuerdan más a un loft que a una habitación de hotel. Rochon también encontró espacio para un oasis de wellness, con sauna y baño turco incluidos.

Con questo hotel il designer francese Pierre-Yves Rochon, famoso per il suo talento nell'usare inconsuete combinazioni di colori e materiali, ha dato prova una volta di più della sua fine creatività. Ha disposto divani rosa shocking su piastrelle bianconere, ha fatto contrastare zebrature e motivi floreali color miele con stoffe quadrettate, e scrivanie in pelle con tappeti turchi; dal canto loro le pareti dei bagni sono impreziosite con scene *Toile de Jouy*. Le Penthouse Suite con terrazza propria sono state pensate così in grande da assomigliare più a dei loft che a camere d'albergo. E non è mancato lo spazio per creare un'oasi di benessere con sauna e bagno turco.

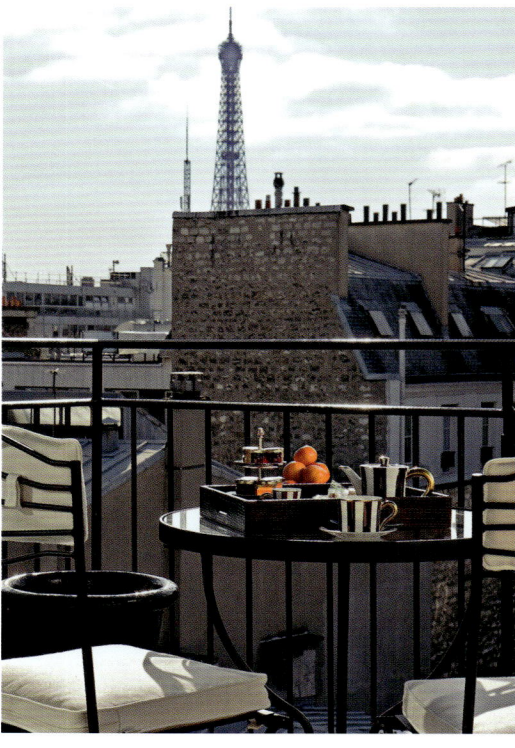
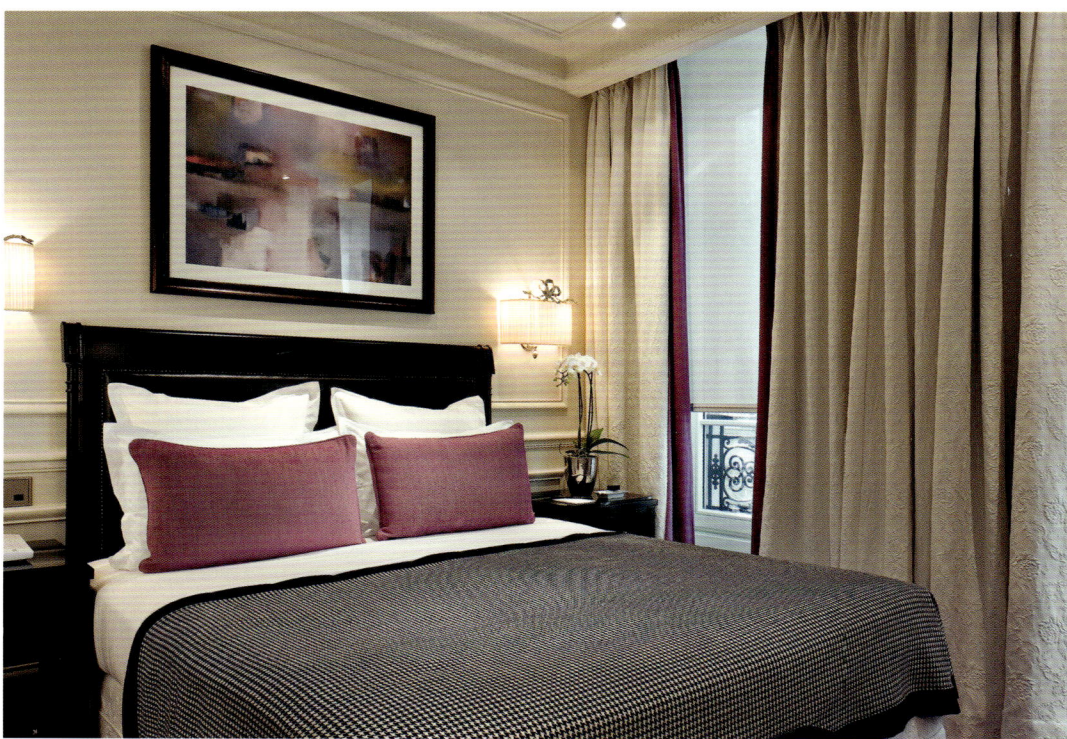

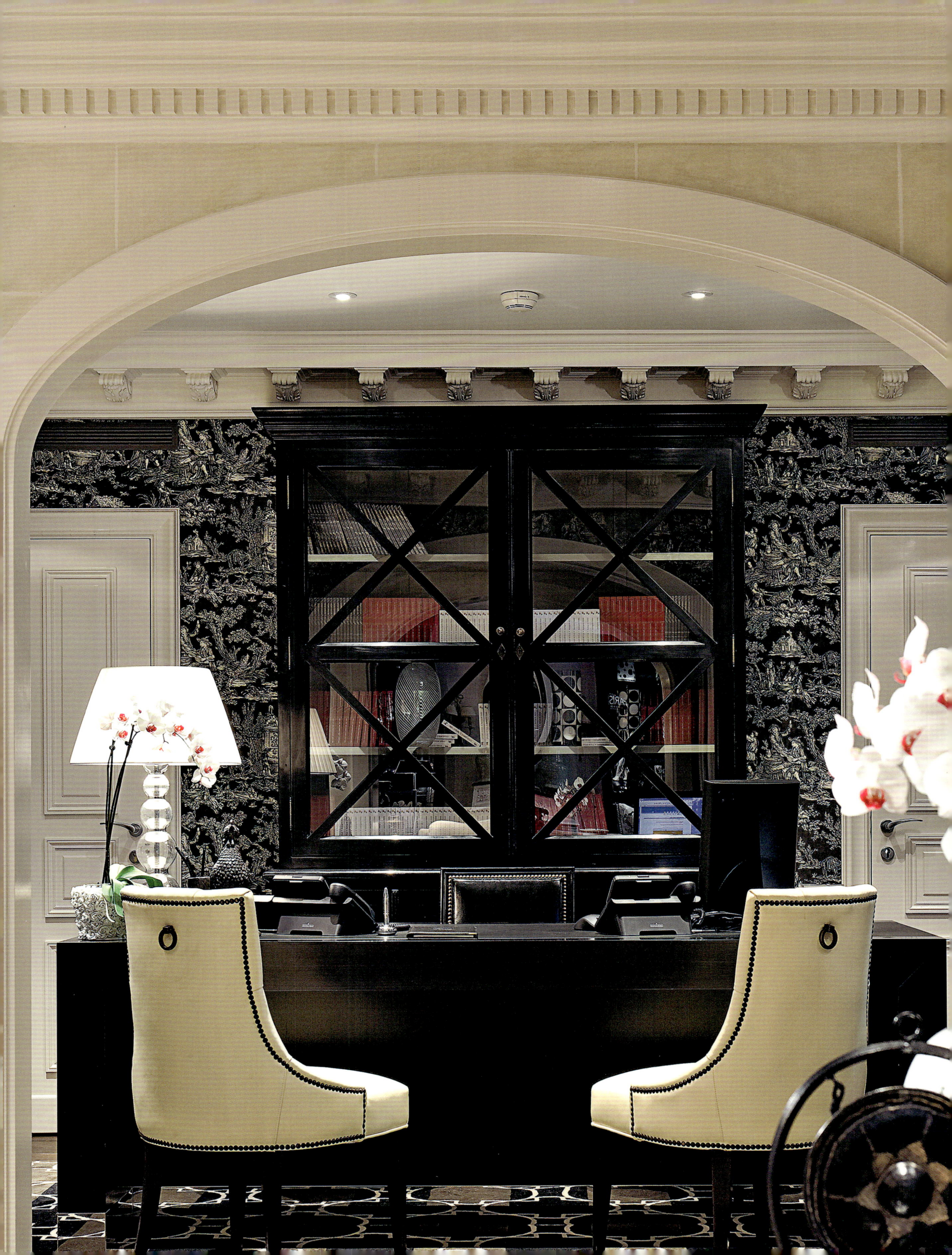

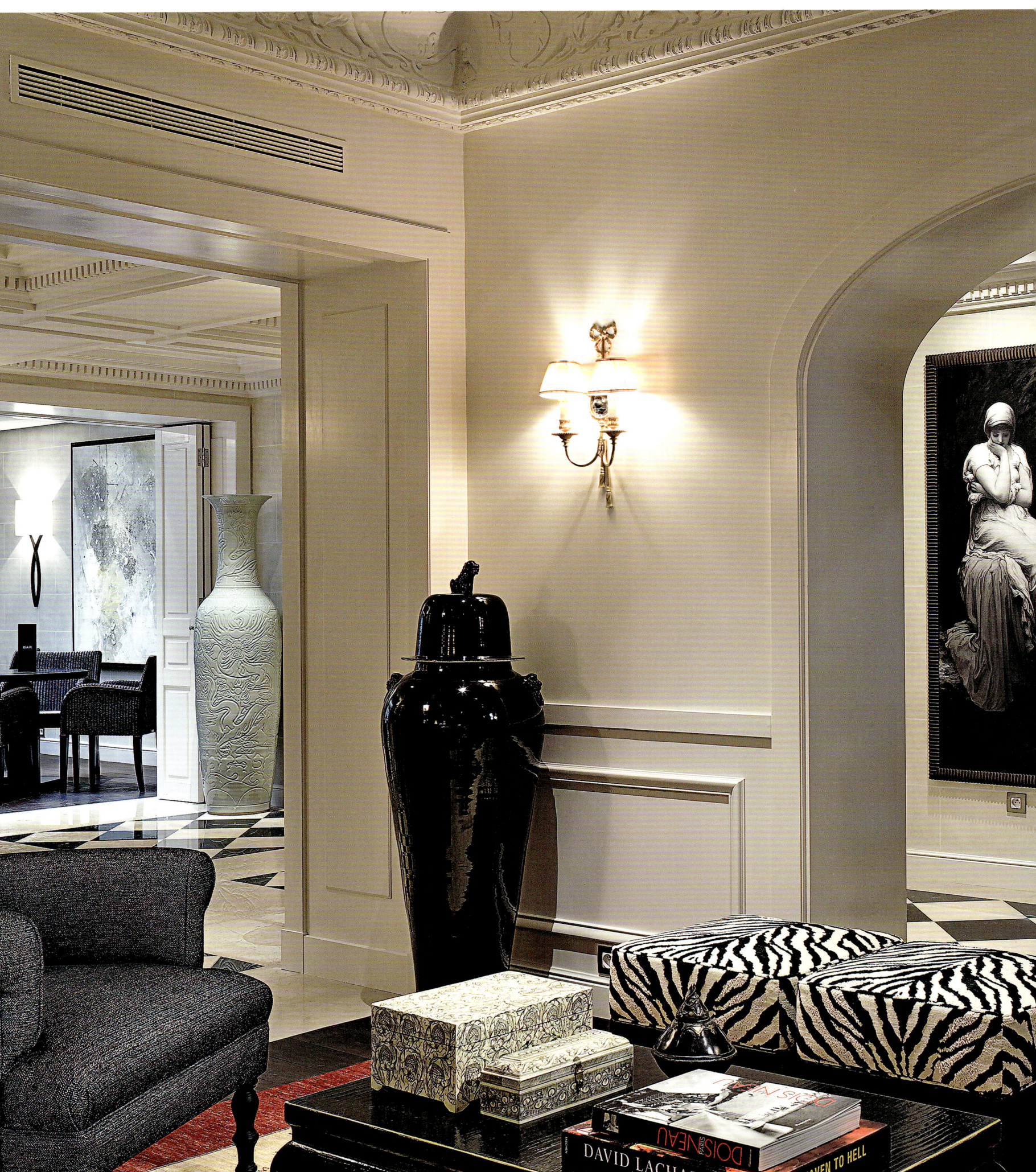

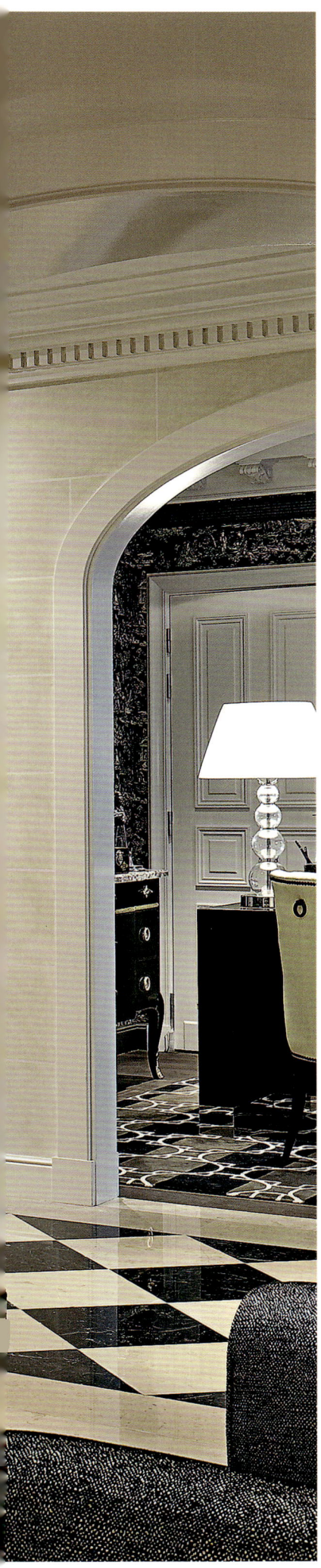

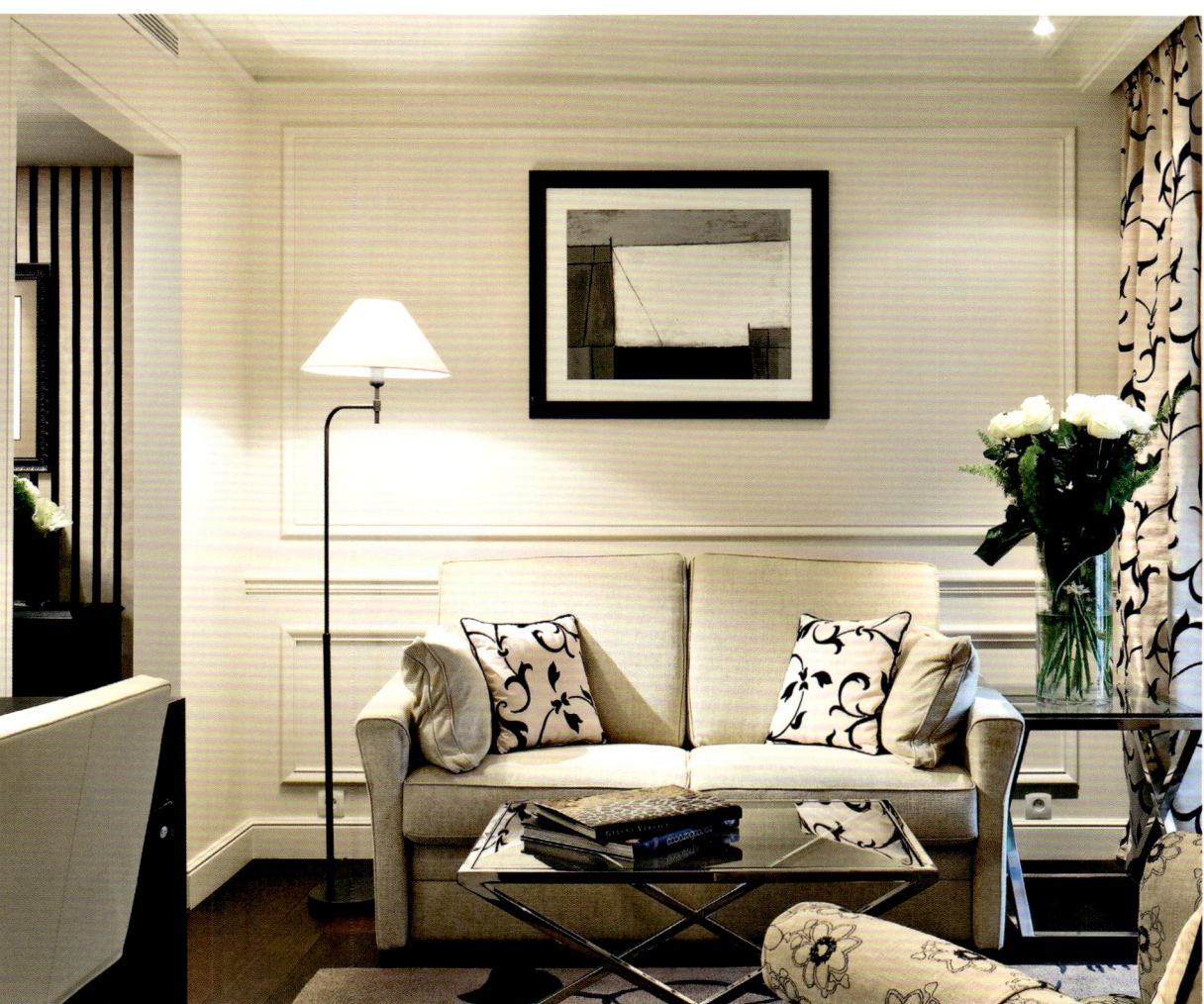

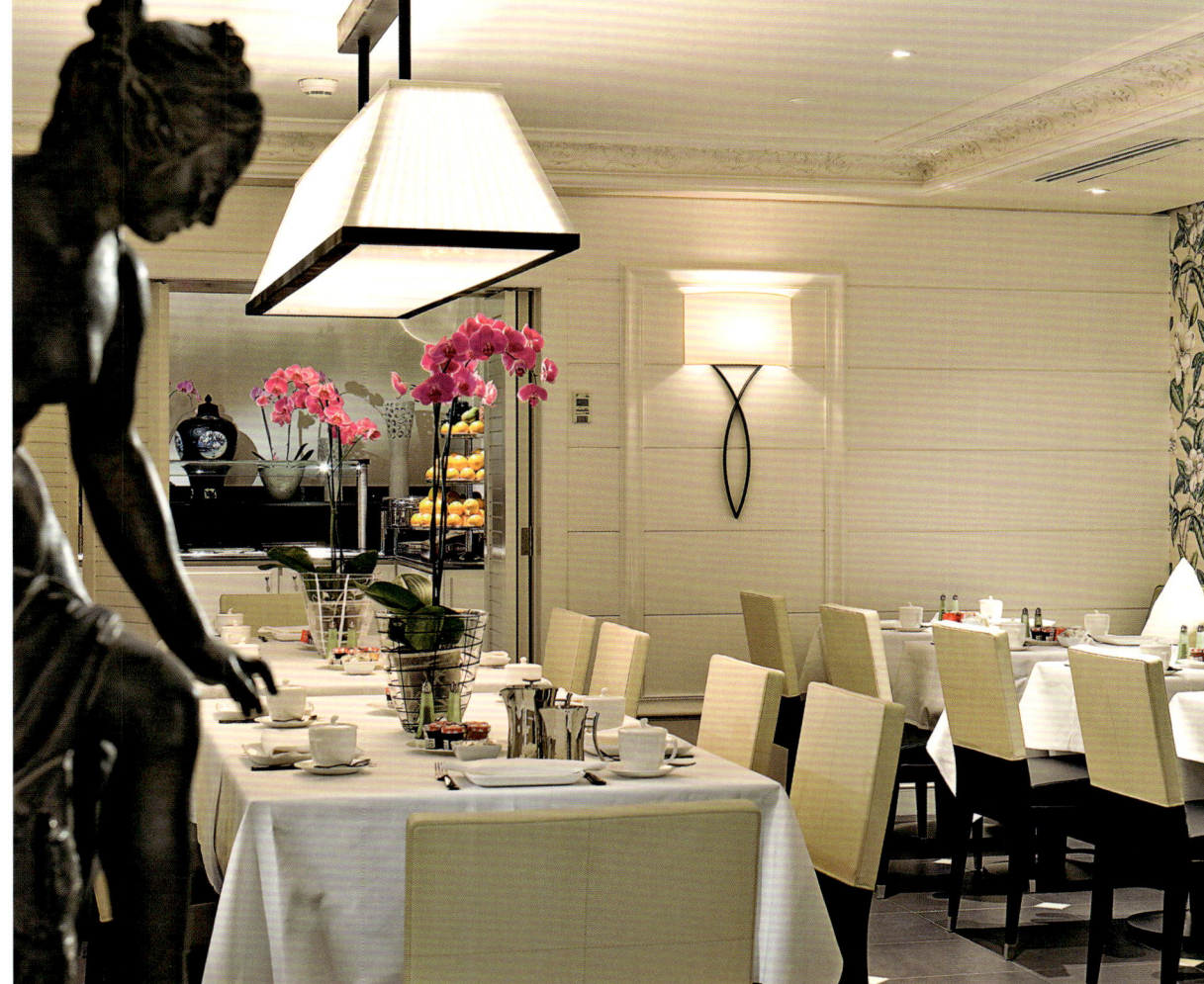

Hotel LUMEN Paris Louvre

Paris, France

15, rue des Pyramides
75001 Paris
France
Phone: +33 1 44 50 77 00
Fax: +33 1 44 50 77 10
www.hotel-lumenparis.com

Price category: €€
Rooms: 32 rooms including 1 family and 1 rooftop suite
Facilities: Restaurant, bar Le Passage Saint Roch, conference facilities
Services: Concierge service, room service, laundry
Located: In the heart of Paris between the Louvre, the Opéra and the Place Vendôme
Public transportation: Metro 14, 7 Pyramides and 1 Tuileries
Style: Contemporary and baroque

This new boutique hotel resides in a typical Haussmann building. Paris, the city of lights, inspired the architect Alain Daronian and the designer Claudio Colucci to this refined interplay of sun and artificial light: rays break in the crystal drops of the chandeliers, in the neo-baroque Plexiglas table legs and the silvery gleaming blinds. Anyone living in the Saint Roch room has a gallery view of the stained-glass window of the church of the same name. The location of the hotel could hardly be better: the Louvre, the Opera, Place Vendôme and the elegant shopping mile Rue Saint-Honoré are only a few minutes away.

Das neue Boutique-Hotel residiert in einem typischen Haussmann-Gebäude. Paris, die Stadt des Lichts, inspirierte den Architekten Alain Daronian und den Designer Claudio Colucci zu dem raffinierten Spiel mit Sonnen- und Kunstlicht: Strahlen brechen sich in den Kristalltropfen der Lüster, in den neo-barocken Plexiglas-Tischbeinen und den silbrig schimmernden Jalousien. Wer im Saint-Roch-Zimmer wohnt, hat einen Logenblick auf die Buntglasfenster der Kirche gleichen Namens. Die Lage des Hotel könnte kaum besser sein: Der Louvre, die Oper, Place Vendôme und die elegante Shoppingmeile Rue Saint-Honoré sind nur wenige Minuten entfernt.

Ce nouveau boutique hôtel est aménagé dans un immeuble typique de style Haussmann. Paris, la ville des lumières, a inspiré l'architecte Alain Daronian et le designer Claudio Colucci, pour un jeu intelligent entre le soleil et la lumière artificielle : les rayons passent dans les gouttes de cristal des lustres, les pieds des tables néobaroques en plexiglas et les stores argentés brillants. La chambre Saint Roch offre une vue sur les vitraux de l'église du même nom. La position de l'hôtel ne pourrait être plus idéale : le Louvre, l'Opéra, la Place Vendôme et les élégantes boutiques de la rue Saint-Honoré ne sont qu'à quelques pas.

El nuevo hotel boutique reside en un típico edificio del urbanista francés Haussmann. París, la ciudad de la luz, inspiró al arquitecto Alain Daronian y al diseñador Claudio Colucci para crear un refinado juego de luces naturales y artificiales: los haces de luz se dividen en los cristales de las lámparas del techo, en las patas de plexiglás de las mesas neobarrocas y en las persianas de brillos plateados. Aquel que se aloje en la habitación Saint Roch podrá apreciar, desde un lugar privilegiado, las cristaleras de colores de la iglesia que llevan el mismo nombre. La situación del hotel es simplemente inmejorable: el Louvre, la Ópera, la plaza Vendôme y la elegante zona de tiendas de la Rue Saint-Honoré están a pocos minutos.

Questo nuovo boutique hotel è ospitato da un tipico edificio stile Haussmann. Parigi, la città della luce, ha ispirato all'architetto Alain Daronian e al designer Claudio Colucci un gioco raffinato tra illuminazione solare e artificiale, con raggi di luce che si insinuano attraverso le gocce di cristallo dei lustri metallici, le gambe in plexiglas dei tavoli neobarocchi e le imposte dai riflessi d'argento. Chi risiede nella camera Saint Roch può godere di una vista da sogno sulle vetrate colorate dell'omonima chiesa. Del resto, la collocazione dell'albergo non potrebbe essere migliore: il Louvre, l'Opera, Place Vendôme e l'elegante Rue Saint-Honoré, paradiso dello shopping, si trovano a pochi passi di distanza.

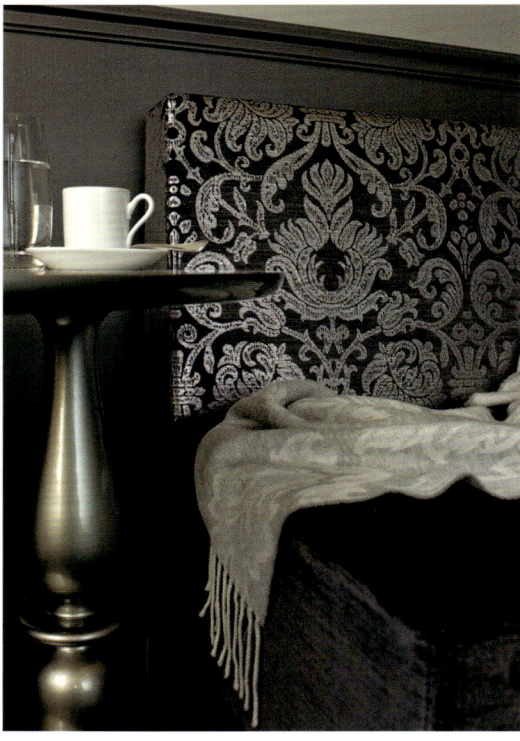
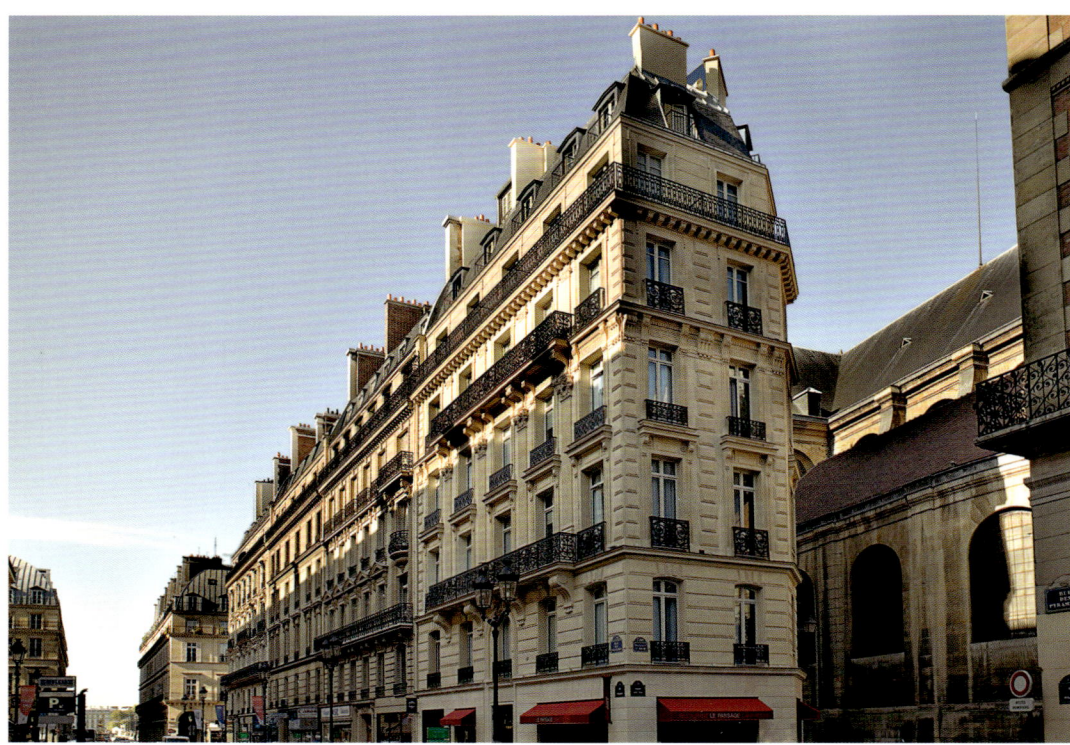

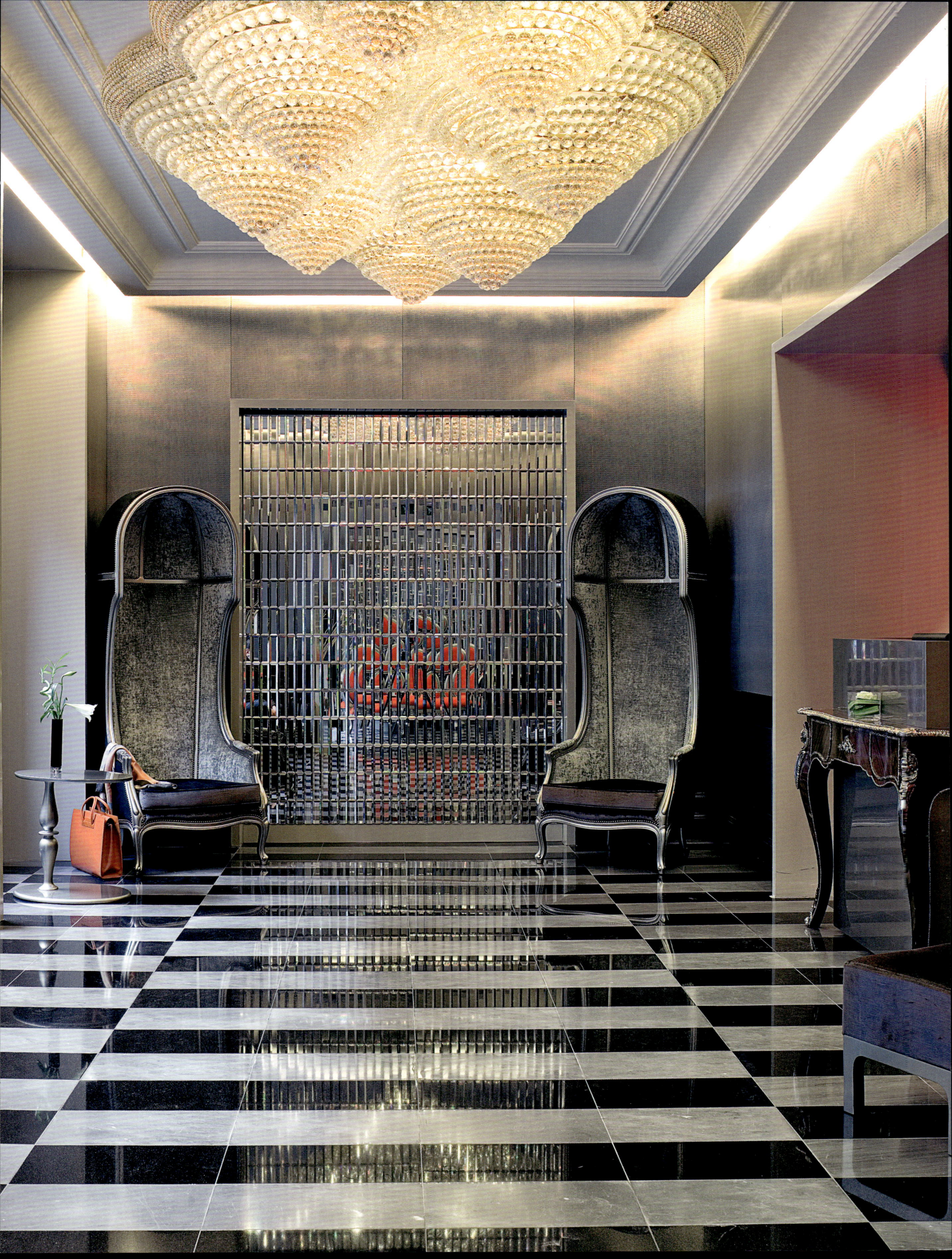

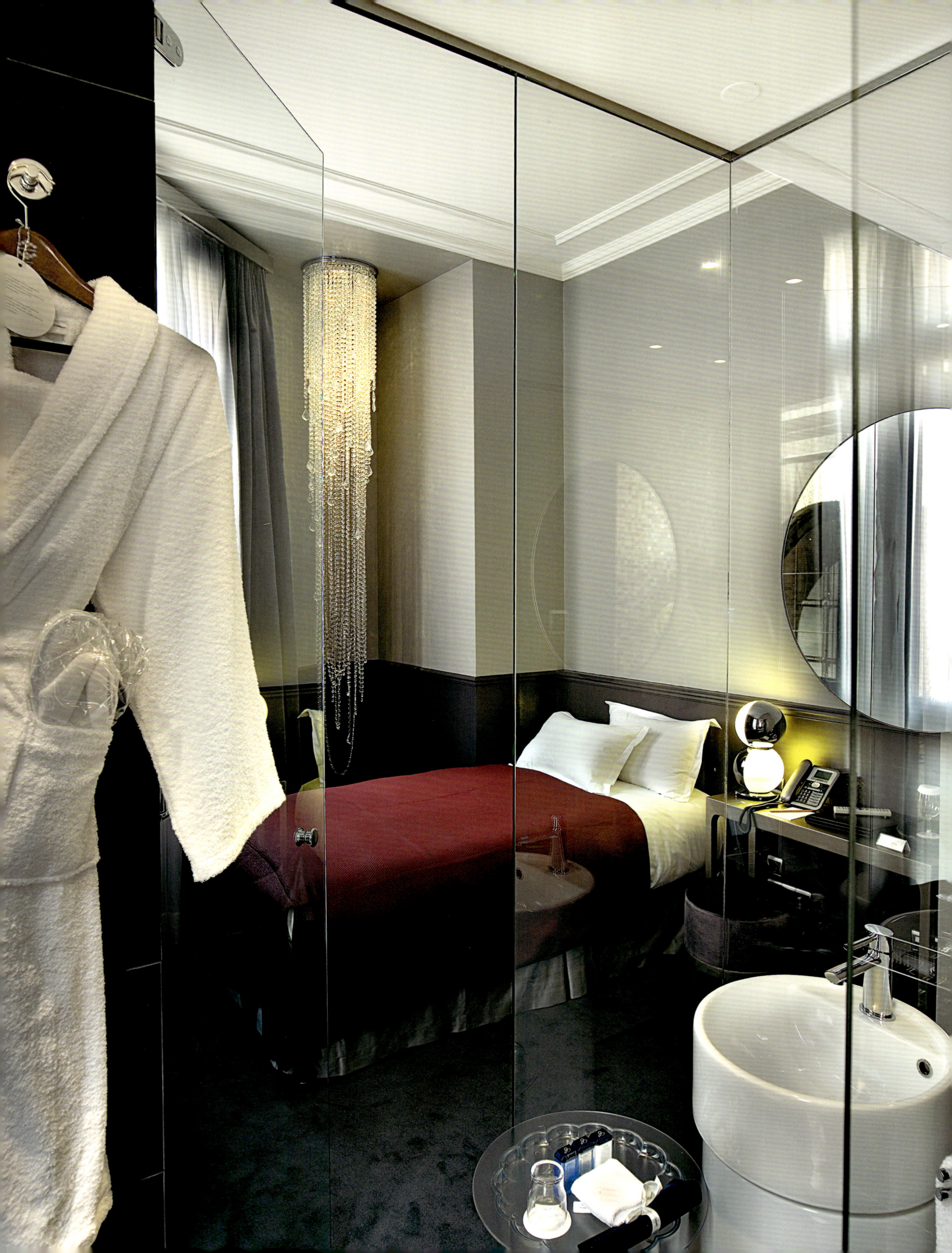

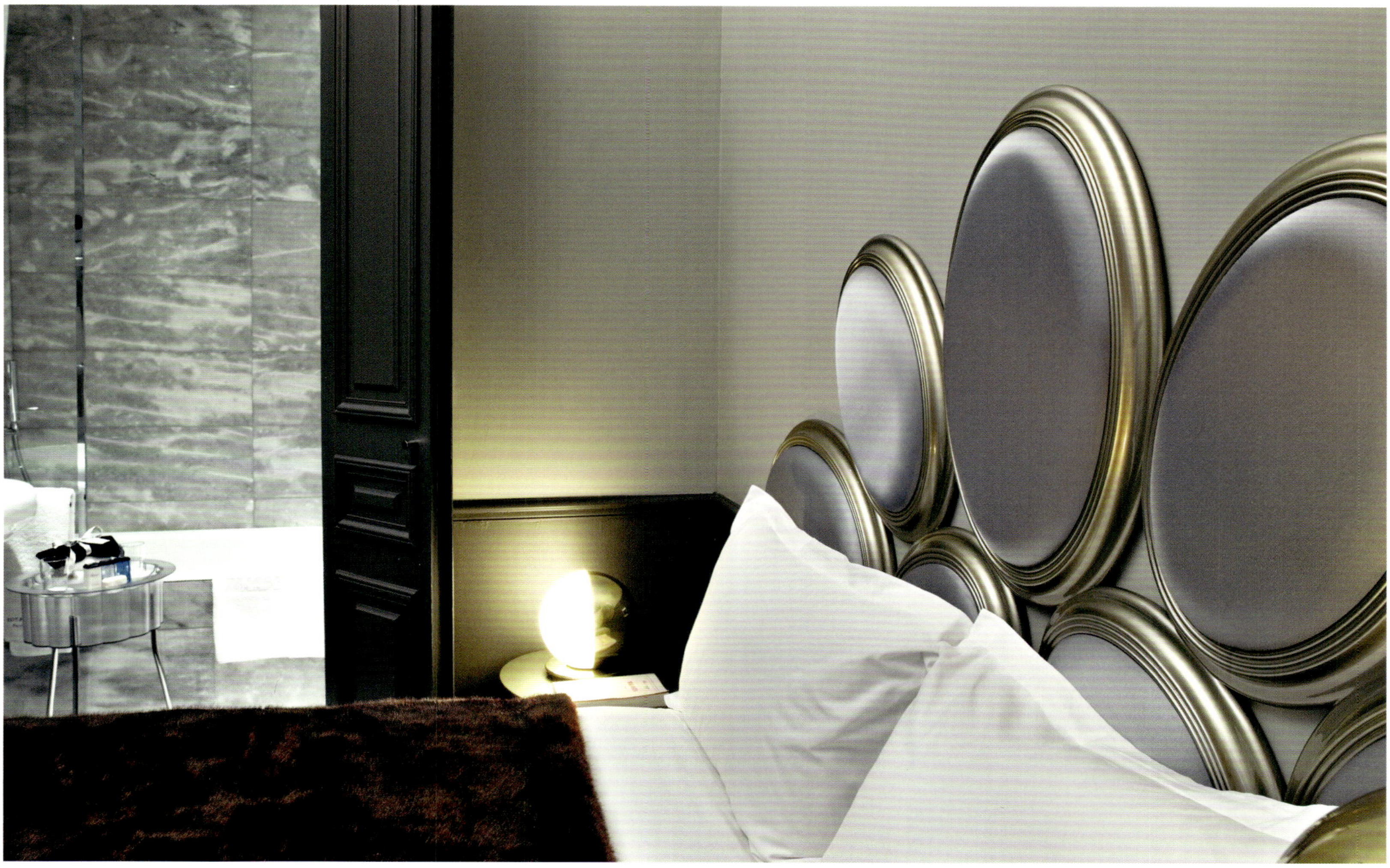

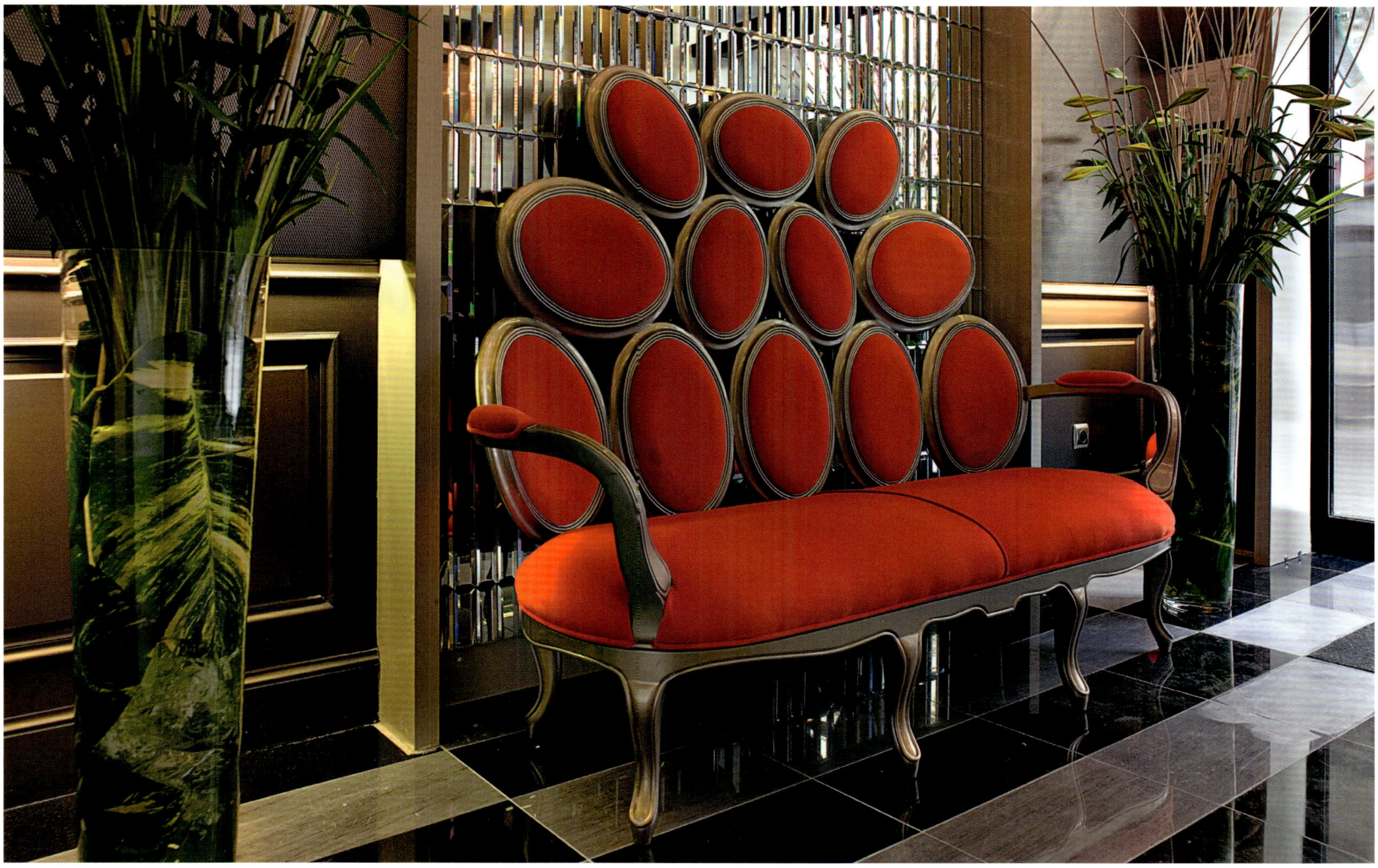

50123 Florence
Italy
Phone: +39 055 27 26 40 00
Fax: +39 055 27 26 44 44
www.lungarnohotels.com

Rooms: 43 rooms including 1 penthouse suite
Facilities: Bar, Sky Lounge on the panoramic terrace, fitness center
Located: In the center of Florence, next to Ponte Vecchio
Style: Contemporary design

The stylish hotel on the banks of the Arno belongs to the small but mighty hotel empire of the Ferragamo fashion dynasty. Located in the heart of the renaissance capital, its interior plays with '50s retro chic by setting ironic accents in a strong pink. The interior designer Michele Bönan created a finely-tarred balance between high-tech and soft forms. From the Sky Lounge you can enjoy a breathtaking view of the river and over the roofs of the Florentine skyline.

Das stylische Hotel am Ufer des Arno gehört zum kleinen, feinen Hotelimperium der Ferragamo-Modedynastie. Mitten in der Hauptstadt der Renaissance gelegen, spielt das Interieur mit einem hintergründigen Fifty-Retro-Chic, in dem ein starkes Pink ironische Akzente setzen darf. In den 43 Zimmern kreierte Interieur-Designer Michele Bönan eine fein austarierte Balance zwischen Hightech und soften Formen. Von der Sky-Lounge genießt man einen atemberaubenden Blick auf den Fluss und über die florentinische Dachlandschaft.

Cet hôtel élégant sur la berge de l'Arno appartient au petit empire hôtelier de la dynastie de la mode, la famille Ferragamo. Situé au milieu de la capitale Renaissance, l'intérieur joue avec un look chic rétro des années 50, dans lequel un rose vif vient poser des touches ironiques. Dans les 43 chambres, l'architecte d'intérieur Michele Bönan a créé un équilibre fin entre high tech et formes douces. Depuis le Sky Lounge, on peut profiter de la vue époustouflante sur la rivière et les toits de Florence.

El hotel de tendencias modernas a orillas del río Arno pertenece al pequeño, pero muy exquisito, imperio hotelero de la dinastía de la moda italiana Ferragamo. En medio de la capital del renacimiento, el interior de este hotel juega con furtivo chic retro de los años 50, en el cual un fucsia chillón pone notas irónicas al conjunto. En sus 43 habitaciones, el diseñador de interiores Michele Bönan creó un equilibrio bien armonizado entre el hightech y las formas suaves. Desde el Sky Lounge en la azotea, el huésped disfruta de una maravillosa vista sobre el río y los techos de Florencia.

L'elegante hotel sulla riva dell'Arno appartiene al piccolo e raffinato impero alberghiero della dinastia di esperti di moda Ferragamo. Nel cuore della capitale del Rinascimento, l'interno denota un vago fascino retrò anni '50, con ironici dettagli in un marcato colore rosa. Nelle 43 camere dell'albergo il designer d'interni Michele Bönan ha creato un perfetto equilibrio di alta tecnologia e morbide forme. Dalla Sky Lounge si gode di una vista mozzafiato sul fiume e sui tetti di Firenze.

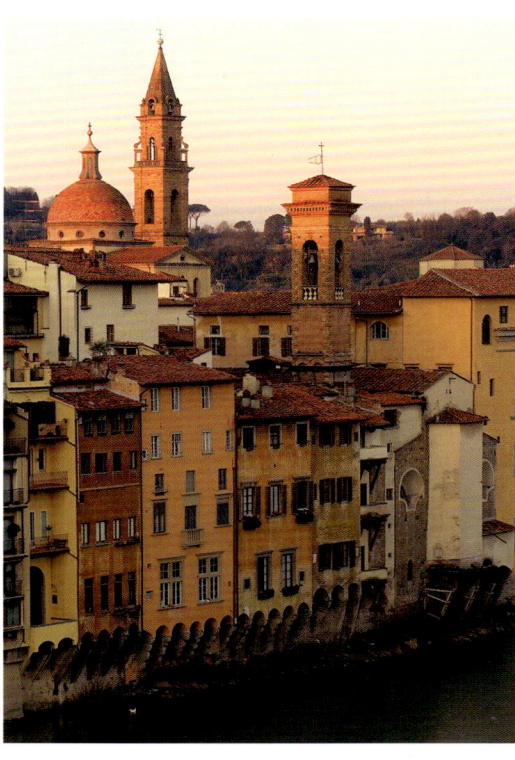 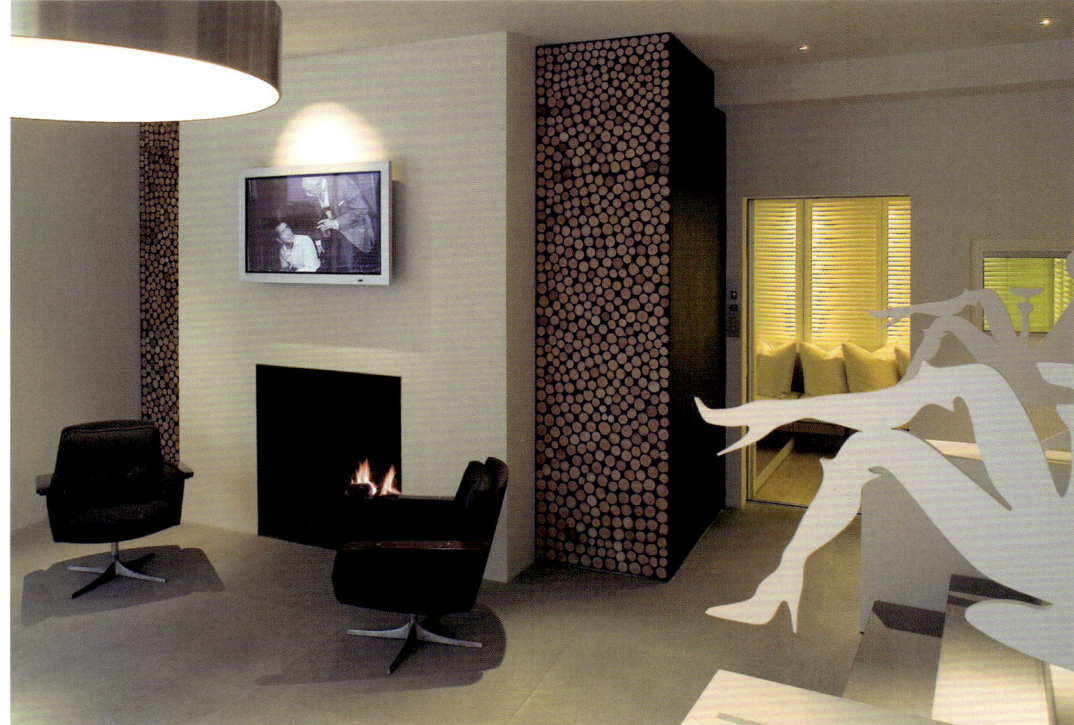

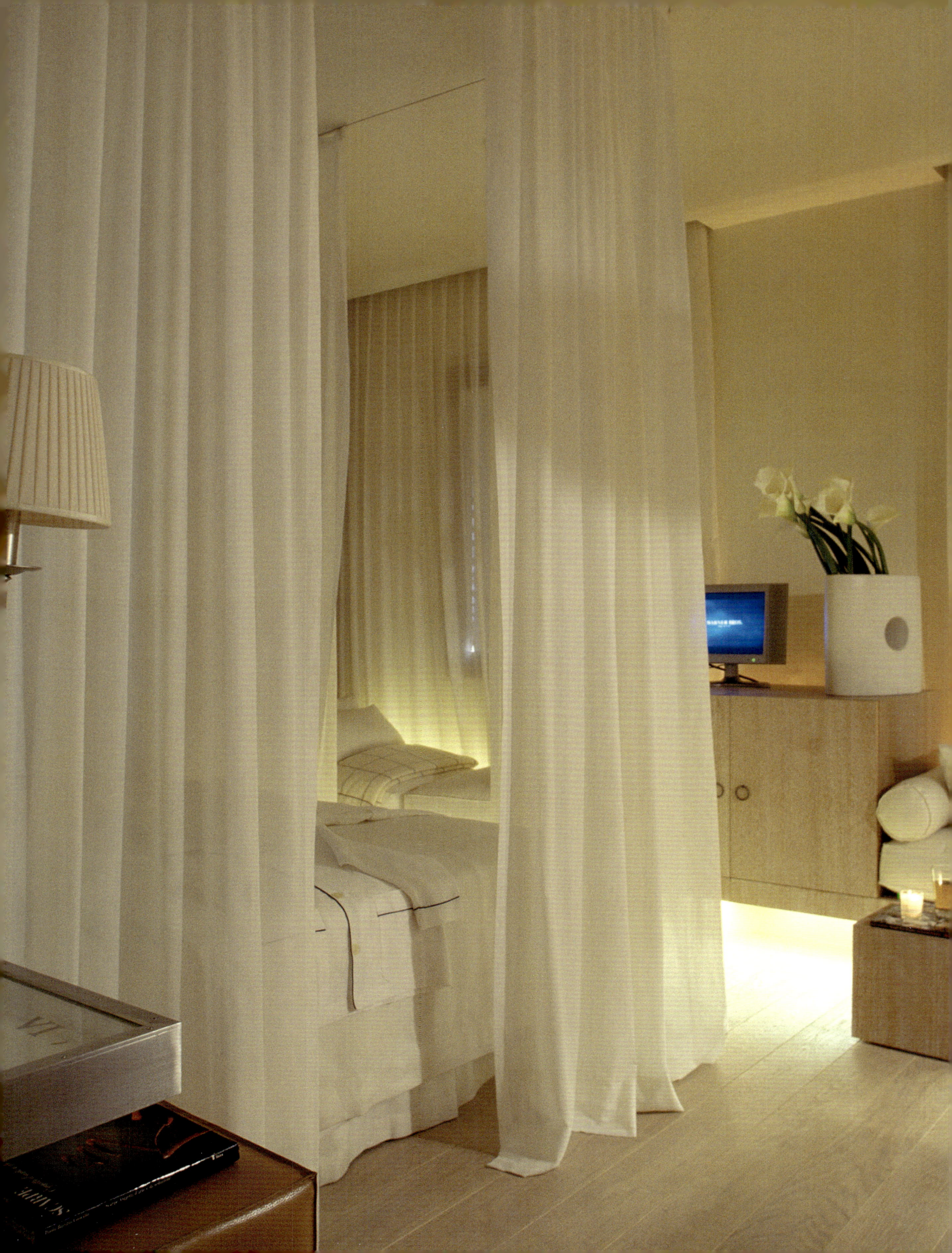

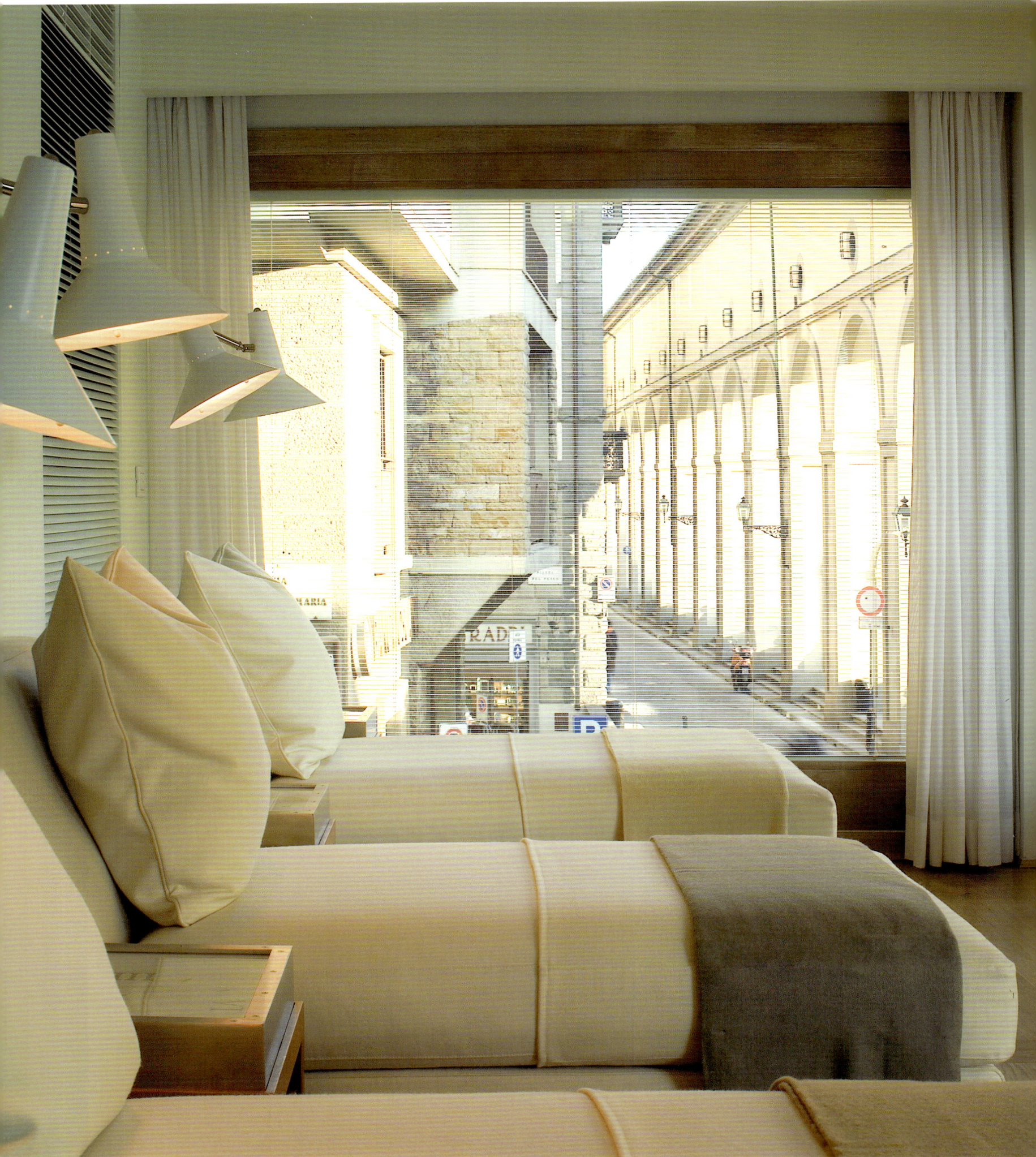

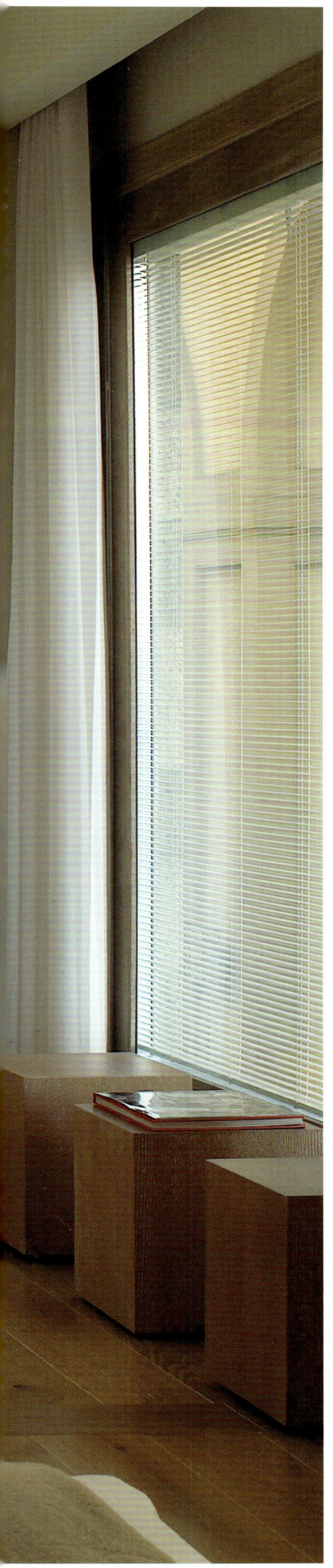

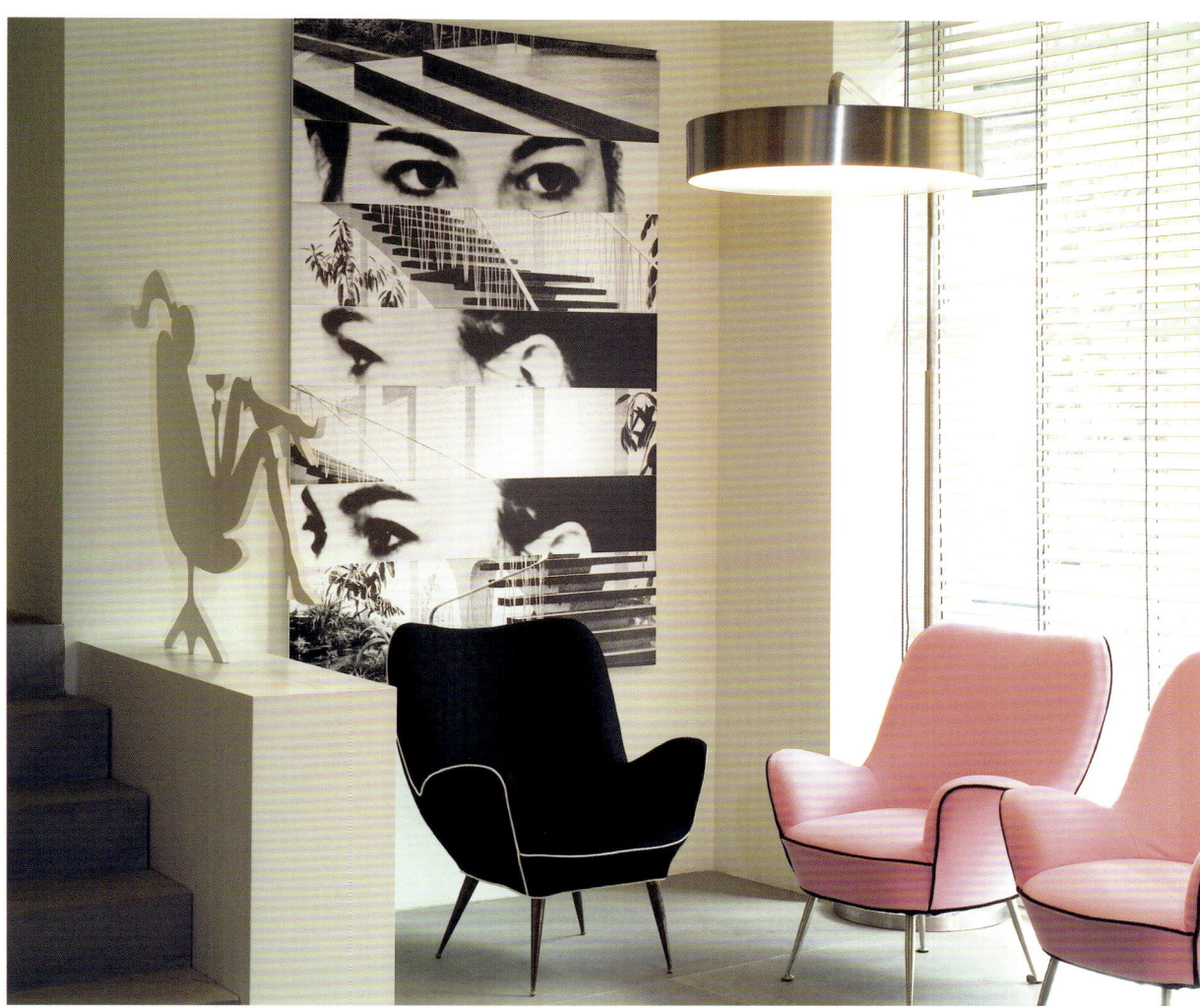

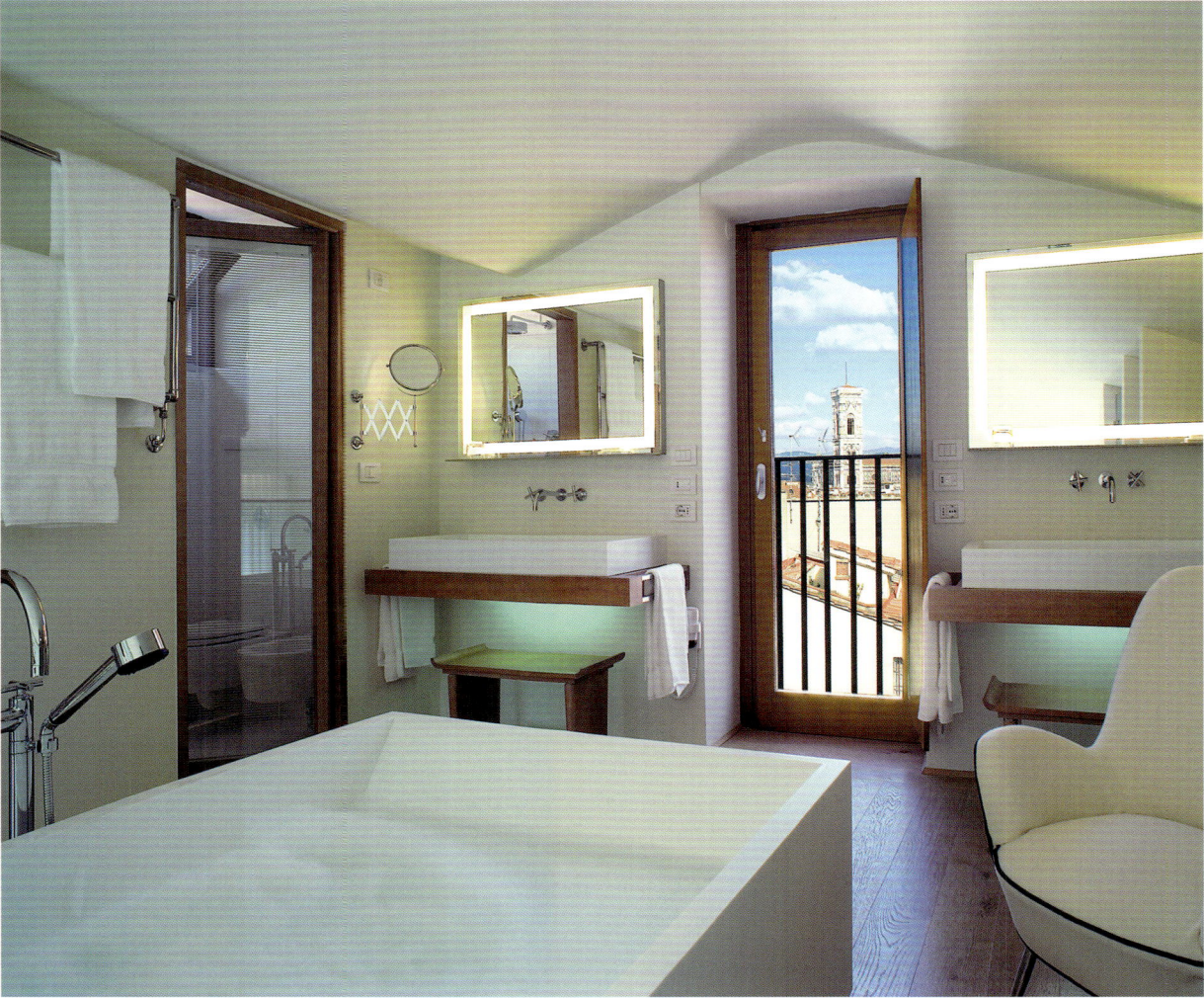

Granducato

Florence, Italy

Via Di Tomerello 1
50013 Campi Di Bisenzio
Italy
Phone: +39 05 58 80 51 11
Fax: +39 05 58 80 50 00
www.boscolohotels.com

Price category: €€€€
Rooms: 60 rooms and suites
Facilities: Restaurant, brasserie, garden, pool, fitness room, private chapel
Services: Conference rooms, shuttle service
Located: In green landscape, 9 km to the city center of Florence, 5 km to Prato
Style: Mixture of original architecture and modern furnishing

Palazzo Pitti, Ponte Vecchio, the Uffizi: Florence offers a number of sights. Unfortunately, you usually have to share these with thousands of other travelers. Whoever wants to escape the bustle ought to afford a stay at the Granducato. Just six miles away from the renaissance city, a refreshing quiet prevails at the aristocratic villa with the purple-walled suites in the midst of the Tuscan hills. The alternative program: dreaming of your own holiday home on a chaise longue at the pool and enjoying wild boar ragout in the restaurant "Locando Toscana."

Palazzo Pitti, Ponte Vecchio, die Uffizien: Florenz hat jede Menge Sehenswürdigkeiten zu bieten. Leider muss man sich diese meist mit Tausenden anderer Reisenden teilen. Wer dem Gewusel entkommen möchte, der sollte sich einen Aufenthalt im Granducato gönnen. Neun Kilometer von der Renaissance-Stadt entfernt, herrscht in der aristokratischen Villa mit purpurrot getünchten Suiten, inmitten toskanischer Hügel, erholsame Ruhe. Das Alternativprogramm: im Liegestuhl am Pool vom eigenen Ferienhaus träumen und abends im Restaurant „Locando Toscana" Wildscheinragout genießen.

Palazzo Pitti, Ponte Vecchio, Galerie des Offices : Florence a de nombreuses attractions à offrir. Malheureusement, il faut les partager avec des milliers d'autres touristes. Qui veut s'échapper de la routine devrait s'offrir un séjour au Granducato. A seulement neuf kilomètres de la ville Renaissance, le calme règne dans ce manoir aristocratique aux suites pourpres, au milieu des collines de Toscane. Un programme alternatif : rêvez de votre propre maison de vacances en vous reposant dans une chaise longue au bord de la piscine, et dégustez le soir un ragoût de sanglier au restaurant « Locando Toscana ».

El Palazzo Pitti, el Ponte Vecchio y la galería Uffizi: Florencia ofrece numerosas atracciones de interés. Por desgracia, en la mayoría de los casos, hay que compartirlas con otros mil viajeros. Aquel que quiera escapar de la multitud debería probar a deleitarse con una estancia en el hotel Granducato. Situada a nueve kilómetros de la ciudad renacentista, en esta mansión de suites rojo púrpura encallada entre suaves colinas toscanas se respira una gran tranquilidad. Como programa alternativo se puede también soñar tumbado en una hamaca junto a la piscina de una casa de verano privada y degustar por la noche un ragout de jabalí en el restaurante "Locanda Toscana".

Palazzo Pitti, il Ponte Vecchio, Gli Uffizi: Firenze ha un'infinità di attrattive da offrire. Che purtroppo il più delle volte bisogna condividere con migliaia di altri viaggiatori. Chi vuole sfuggire alla confusione dovrebbe concedersi un soggiorno nel Granducato. A nove chilometri dalla città rinascimentale, in una villa nobiliare con suite tinteggiate di rosso porpora situata nel cuore delle colline toscane, regna una tranquillità ristoratrice. Un programma alternativo: distesi su una sdraio a bordo piscina, sognare una propria casa delle vacanze e, la sera, godersi uno spezzatino di cinghiale nel ristorante "Locanda Toscana".

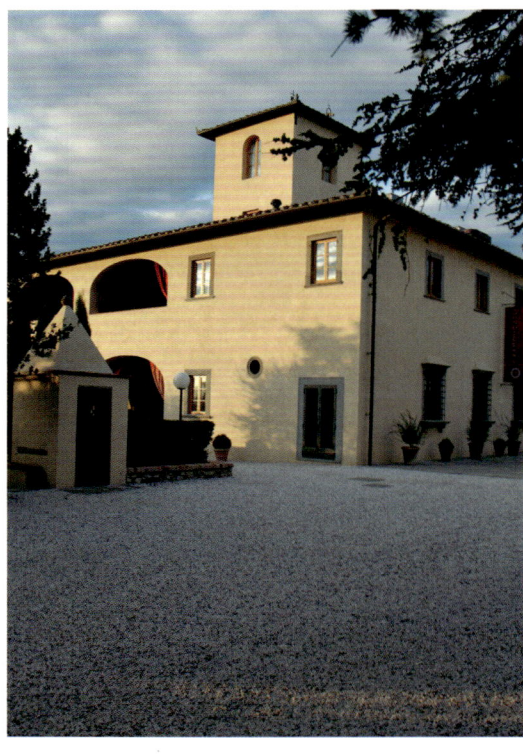 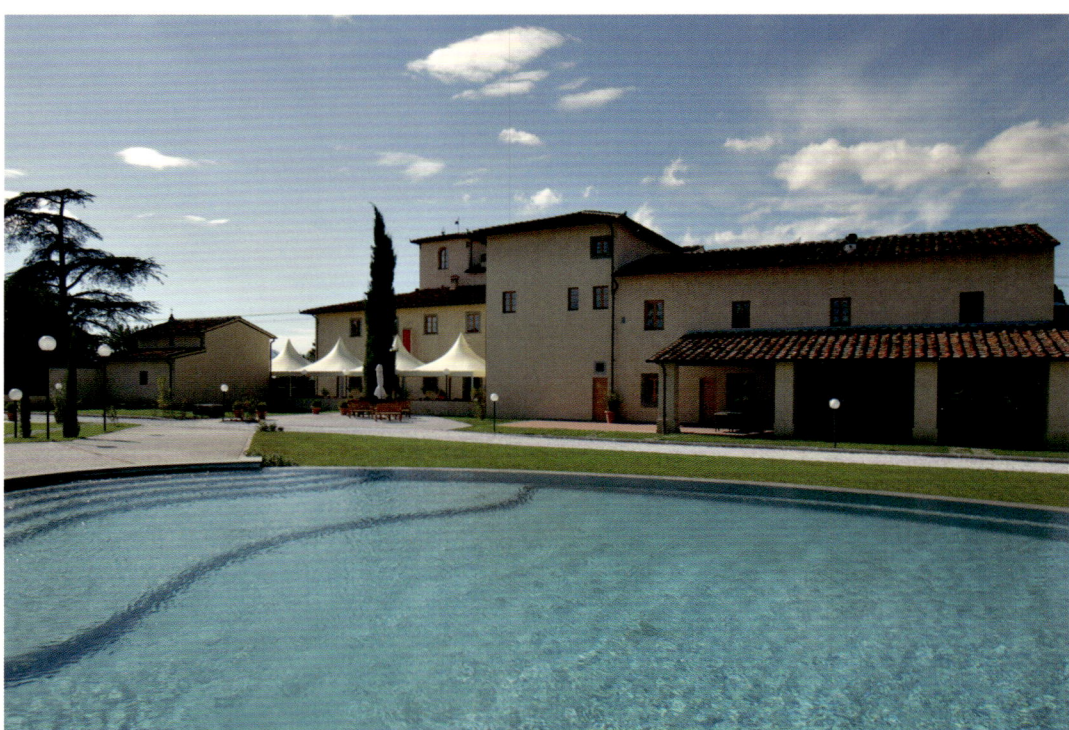

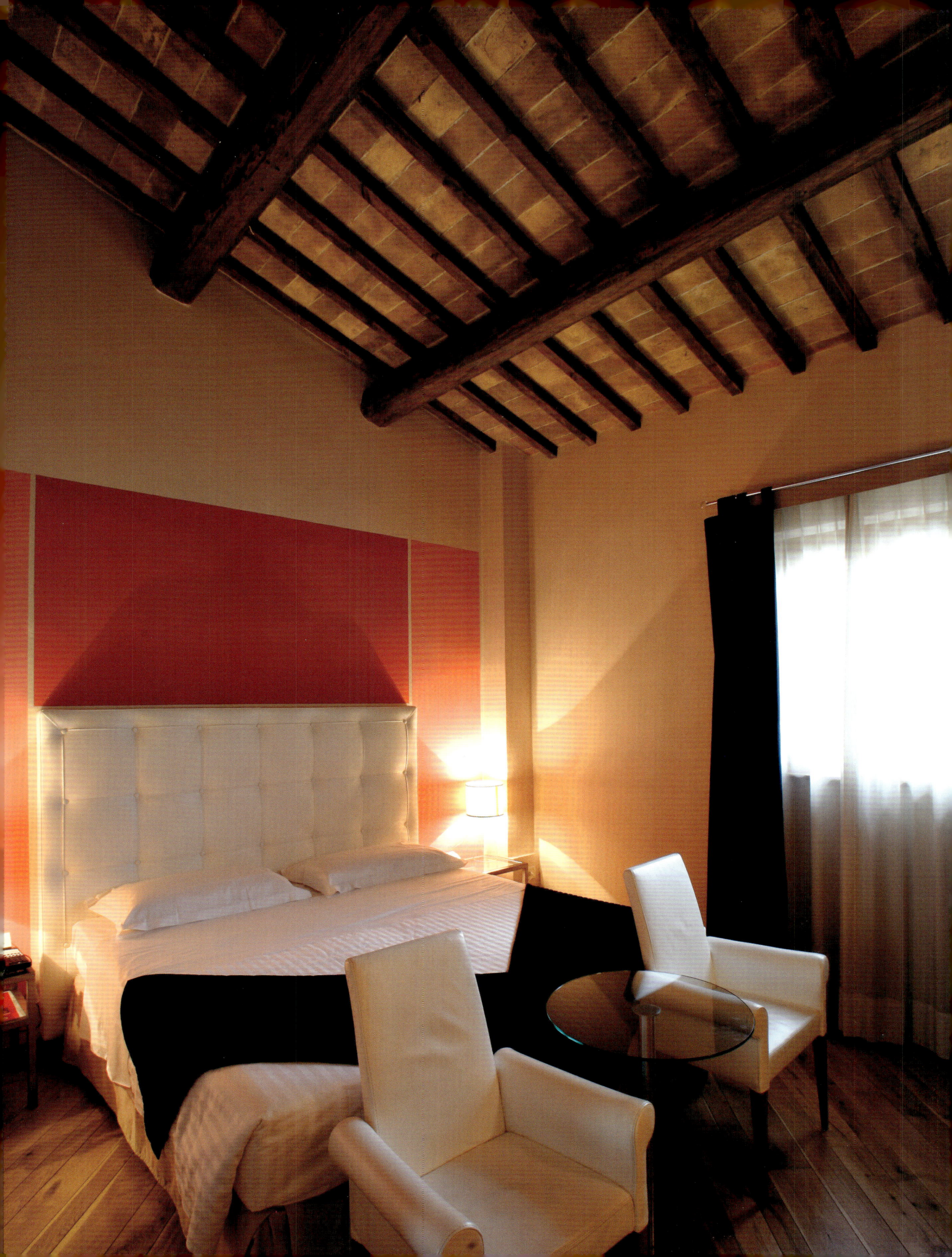

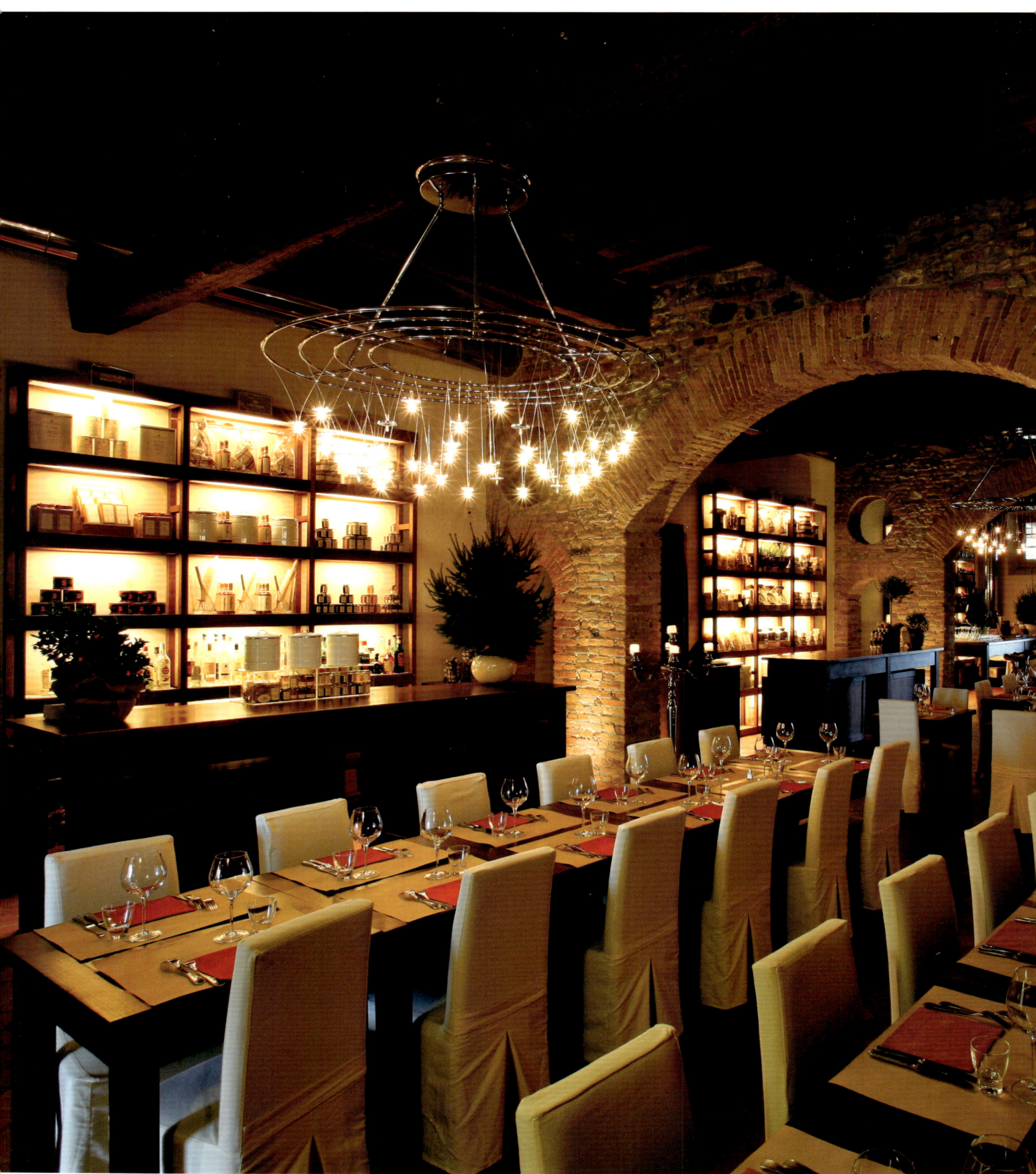

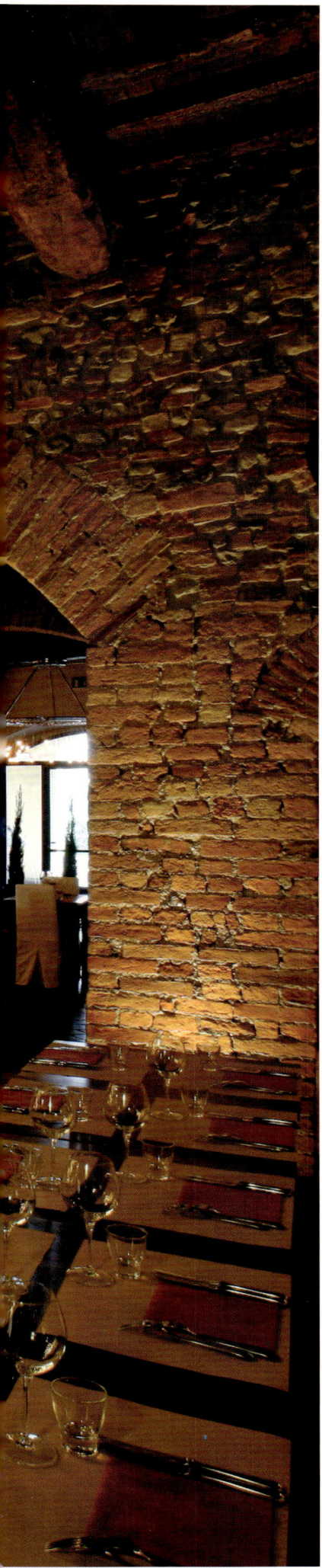

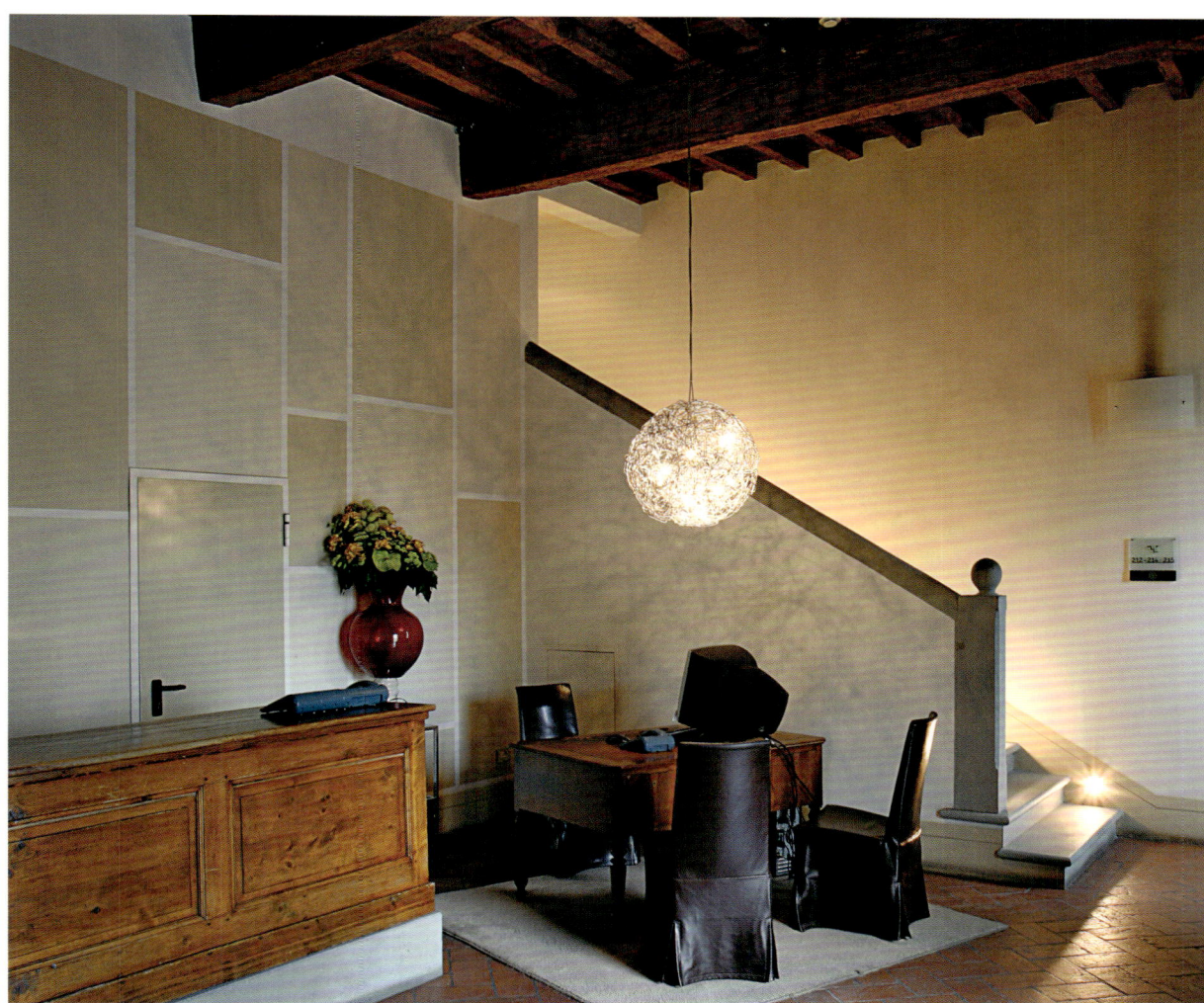

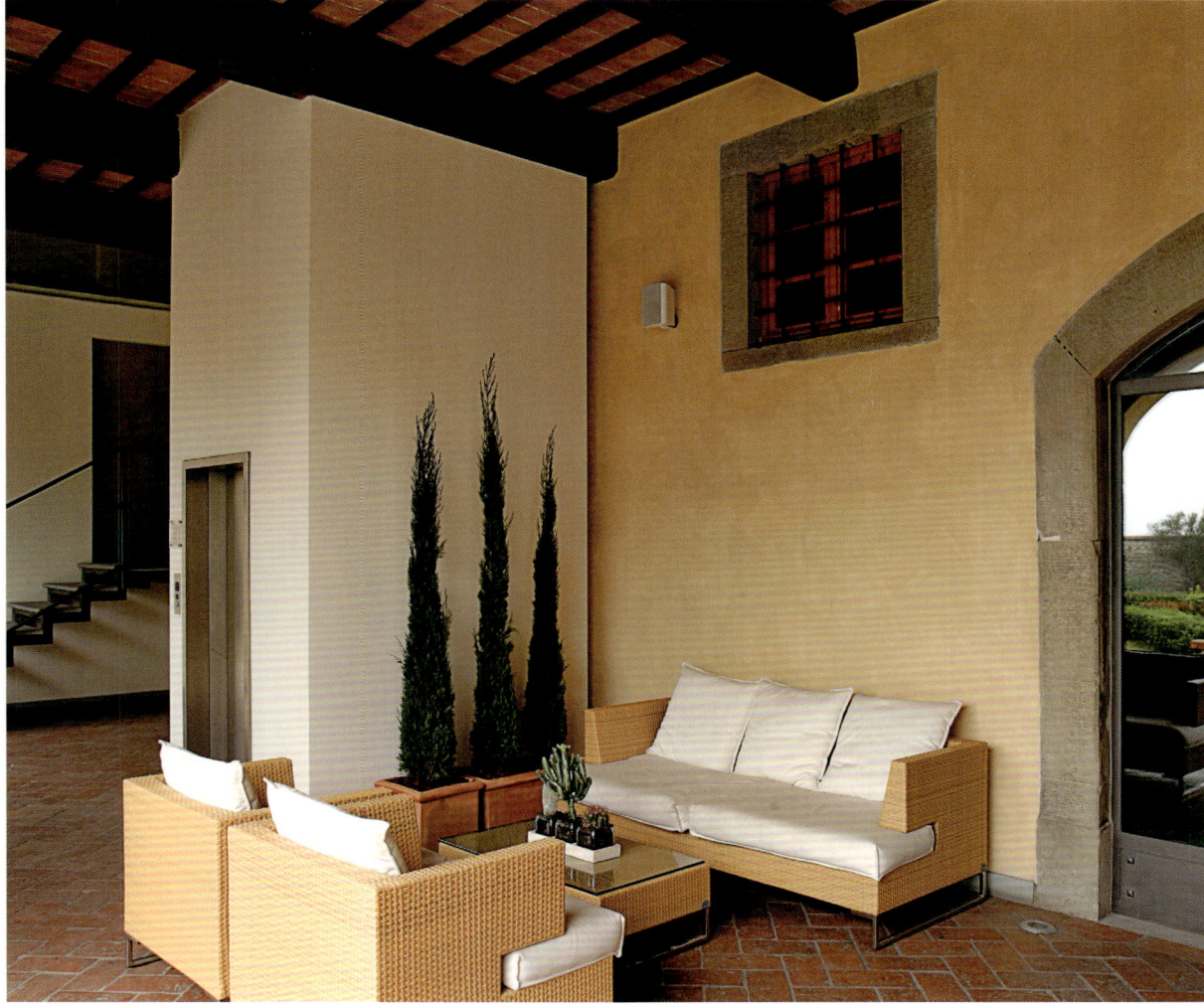

Grand Hotel a Villa Feltrinelli

Gargnano, Italy

Via Rimembranza 38–40
25084 Gargnano
Italy
Phone: +39 036 57 98 000
Fax: +39 036 57 98 001
www.villafeltrinelli.com

Price category: €€€€
Rooms: 21 suites
Facilities: Michelin star restaurant, bar, croquet lawn, heated outdoor pool
Services: WiFi, packing and un-packing service
Located: On the western shore of Lake Garda
Style: Liberty style villa

A superior hideaway can be found in the villa situated on the west shore of Lake Garda in the middle of the extensive park with rare centuries-old trees. The former summer residence of the Italian family of industrialists and publishers Feltrinelli was built in 1892 in liberty style. It was remodeled under strict monument protection regulations into the smallest grand hotel in the world with only 21 rooms and suites. Here the historical rooms have blossomed to opulent splendor. The suite in the boat house offers a special private sphere with its landing stage.

Ein Refugium der Superlative ist die am noblen Westufer des Gardasees inmitten eines weitläufigen Parks mit jahrhundertealtem kostbarem Baumbestand gelegene Villa. Das ehemalige Sommerdomizil der italienischen Industriellen- und Verlegerfamilie Feltrinelli, 1892 im Liberty-Stil erbaut, wurde unter strengen Auflagen des Denkmalschutzes mit nur 21 Zimmern und Suiten zum kleinsten Grandhotel der Welt. In den historischen Räumen darf sich opulente Pracht entfalten. Besondere Privatsphäre bietet die Suite im Bootshaus mit eigenem Bootssteg.

Ce refuge des superlatifs se trouve sur la berge ouest du Lac de Garde, au milieu d'un large parc planté de précieux arbres centenaires. L'ancienne résidence d'été construite dans le style Liberty en 1892, a appartenu aux Feltrinelli, famille italienne d'éditeurs et d'industriels. Elle a été soumise aux réglementations les plus strictes car elle est inscrite au registre des monuments historiques, et avec ses 21 chambres, c'est le plus petit Grand Hôtel du monde. Dans les chambres historiques, son opulente splendeur se dévoile. La suite située dans l'ancien hangar à bateaux dispose d'une certaine sphère d'intimité grâce à son propre ponton d'amarrage.

La mansión, situada en la distinguida orilla oeste del Lago de Garda y rodeada de un extenso parque lleno de valiosos árboles centenarios, es un refugio sin igual. El antiguo domicilio veraniego de la familia de industriales y editores Feltrinelli, construido en 1892 en estilo Liberty, está dotado solamente de 21 habitaciones, respetando así las estrictas normas de conservación del patrimonio histórico, lo que lo convierte en el hotel de lujo más pequeño del mundo. En las históricas salas se despliega toda la opulencia y la majestuosidad propias de una mansión del siglo XIX. Especial intimidad ofrece la suite en la casita de los botes, la cual dispone de su propio embarcadero.

Questa villa, situata sull'elegante riva occidentale del Lago di Garda e posta al centro di un ampio parco ricco di pregiati alberi secolari, è una sintesi di superlativi. Ex residenza estiva della famiglia di industriali ed editori italiani Feltrinelli, l'edificio fu costruito nel 1892 in stile liberty e divenne poi, nel pieno rispetto della normativa per la tutela dei beni architettonici, il più piccolo Grand Hotel del mondo, con sole 21 tra camere e suite. Alle sue stanze storiche ben si accorda una sontuosa magnificenza, mentre la suite nella rimessa per le barche, dotata di imbarcadero proprio, offre un'atmosfera di grande riservatezza.

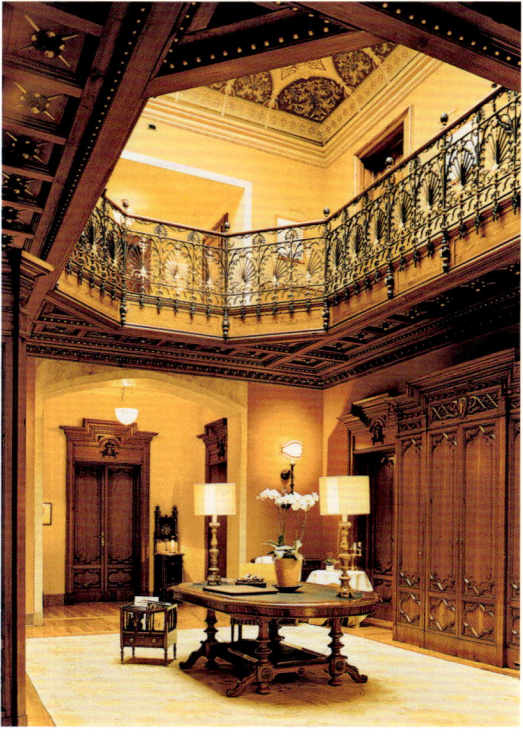
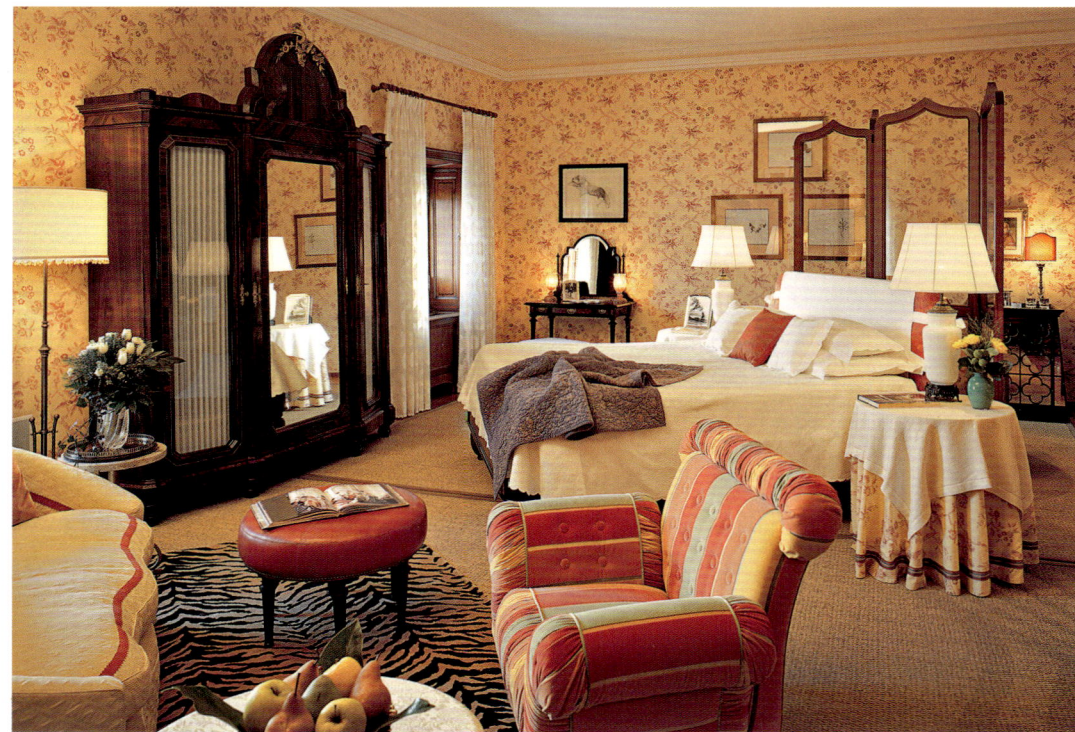

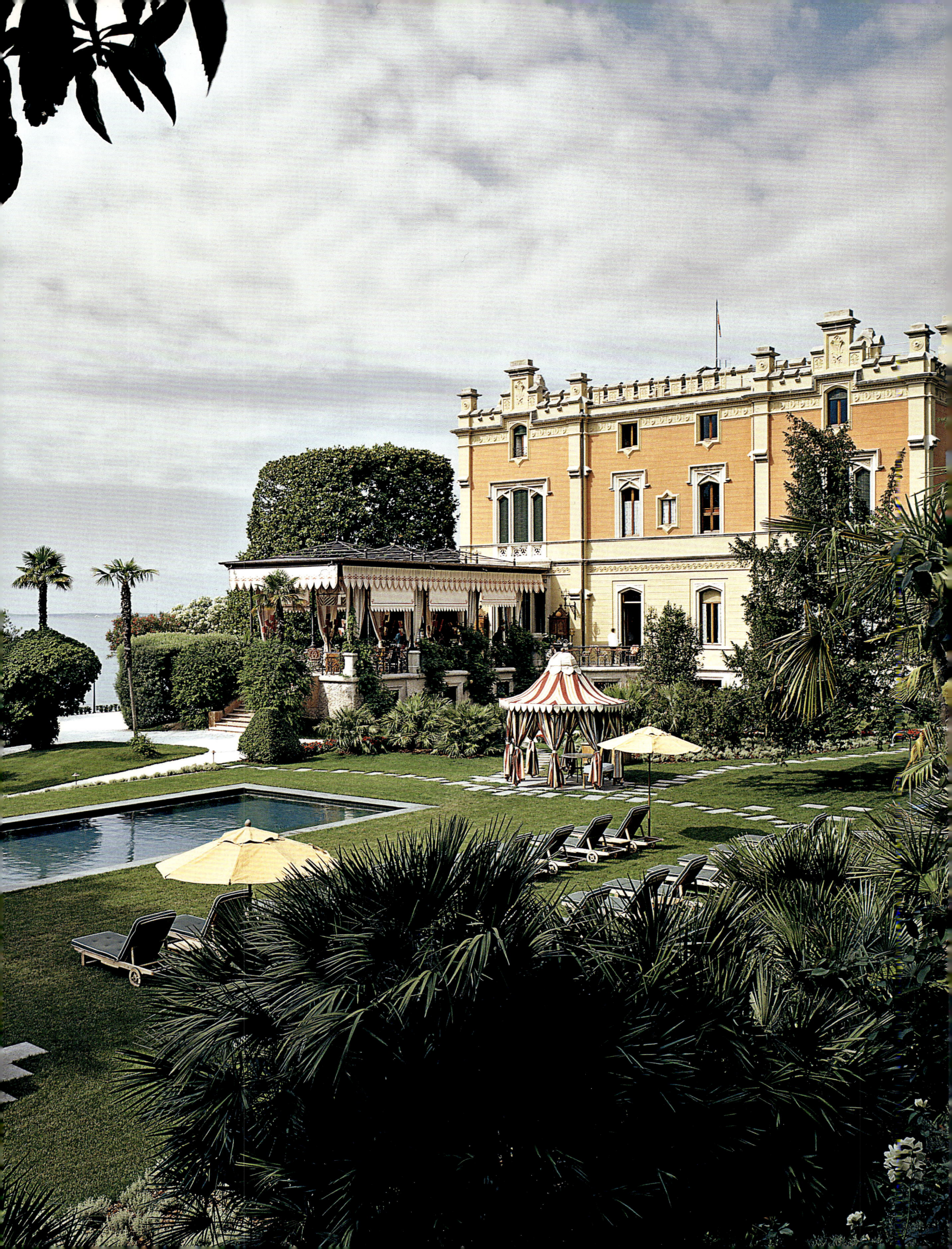

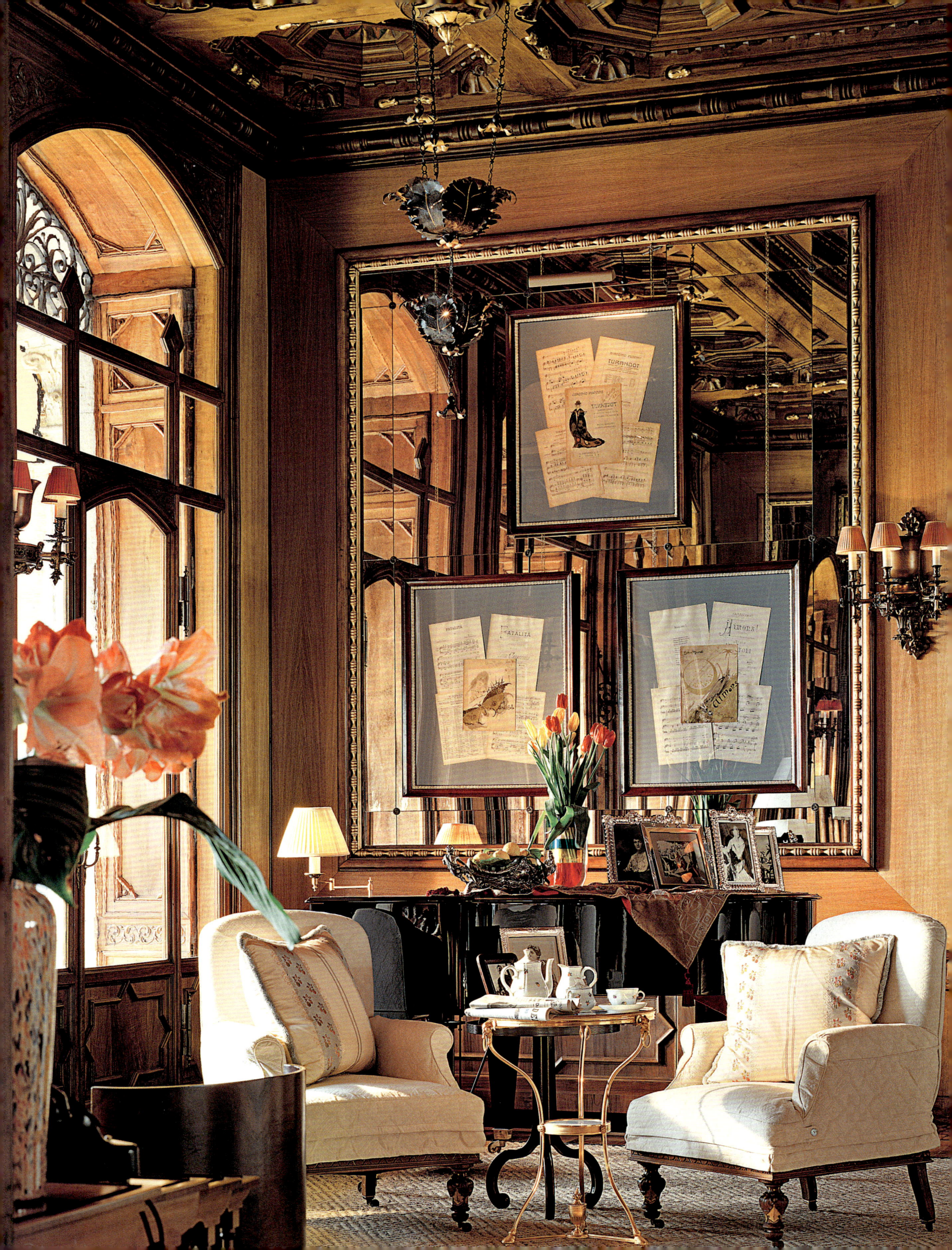

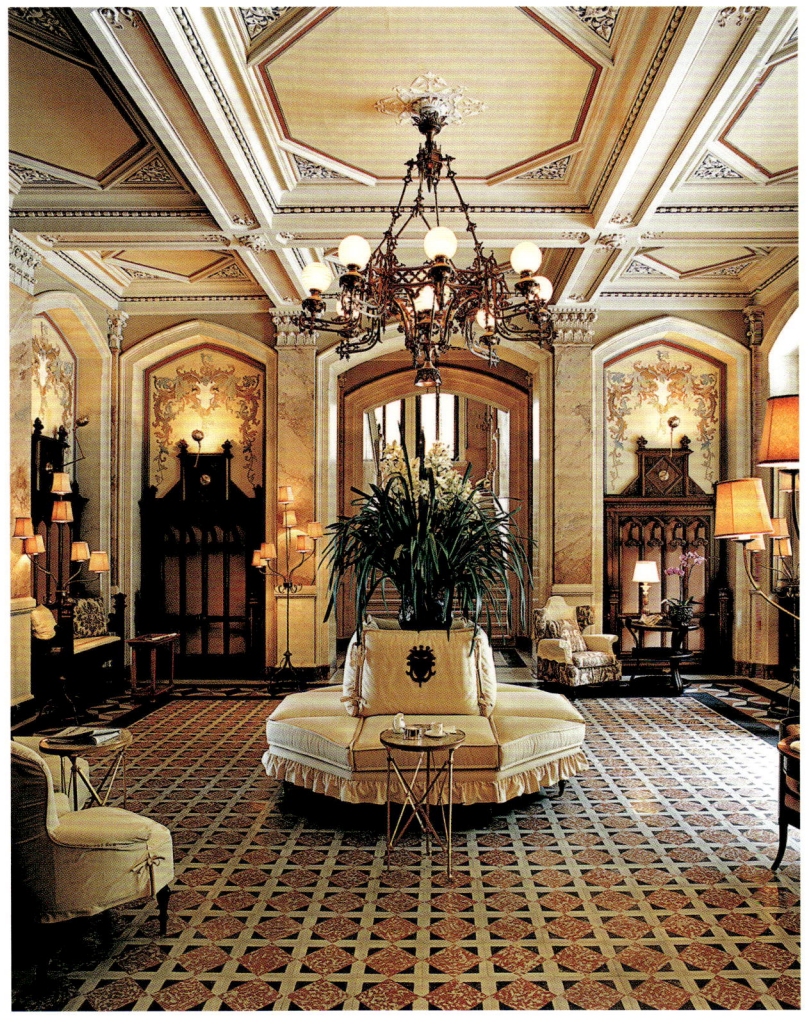
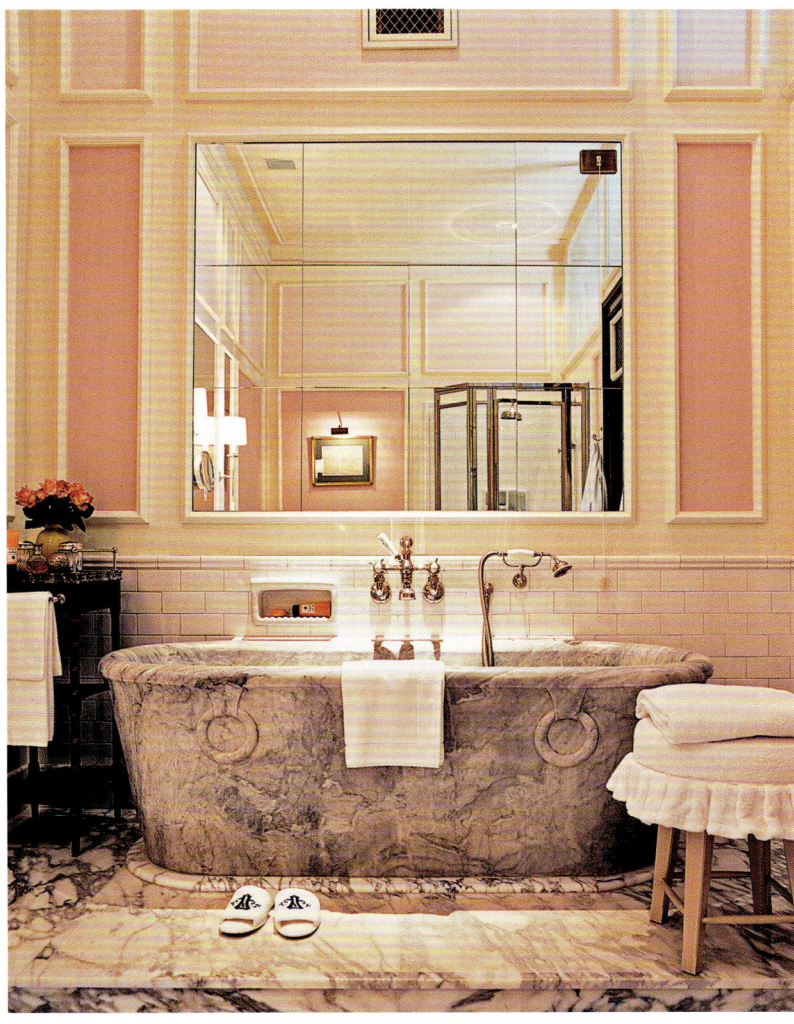
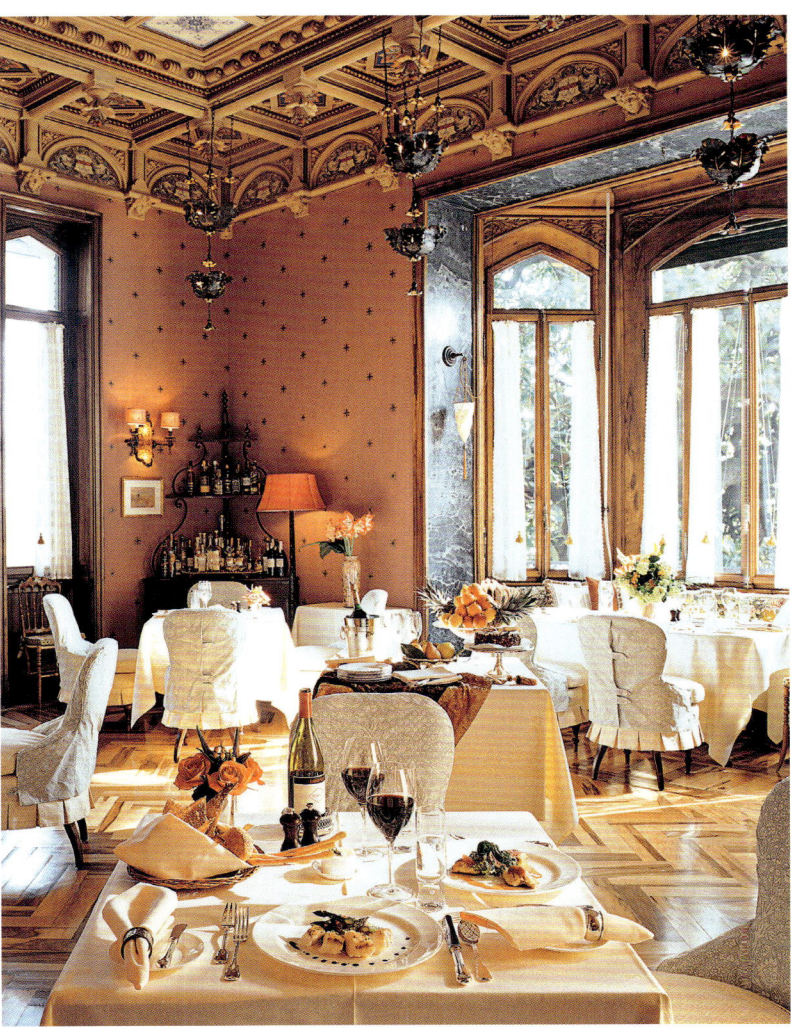
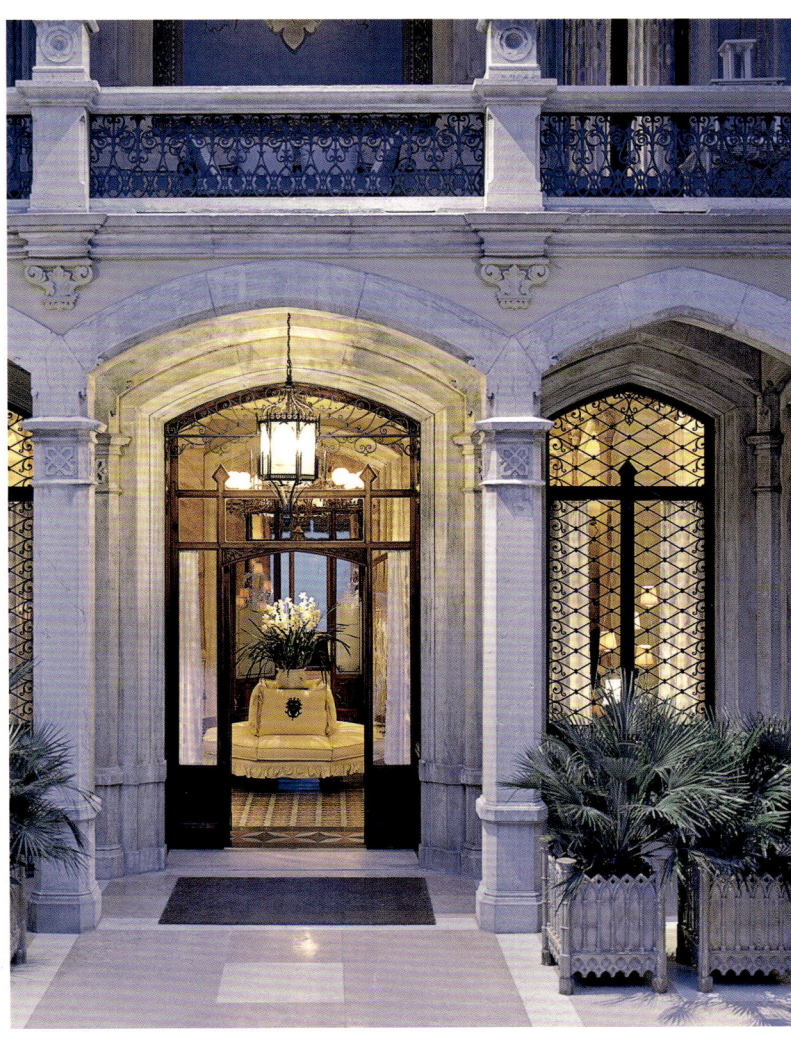

20121 Milan
Italy
Phone: +39 02 89 05 82 97
Fax: +39 02 89 05 82 99
www.townhousegalleria.it

Rooms: 24 rooms and suites
Facilities: Bar, restaurant La Sinfonia (only for guests)
Services: Exclusive butler service, events planning, shopping and art planning
Located: In the heart of Milan, inside the historical Galleria Vittorio Emanuele II
Public transportation: Metro 1, 3 Duomo
Style: Rustic elegance

What until now only seemed to be possible in Dubai, has been realized in Europe. The Town House Galleria is the first European seven star hotel. Even the location of the exclusive Galleria Vittorio Emanuele of 1876 in the very center of the fashion metropolis is spectacular. A personal butler knows the guests' preferences even upon arrival, reserves tickets for the Scala, and chooses bed linens and favorite dishes as they desire. Of course, in such a house the obligatory espresso machine is there in the 24 suites wainscoted in oak, not to mention leather-covered laptops.

Was bisher nur in Dubai möglich schien, wurde nun auch in Europa realisiert: das erste Sieben-Sterne-Hotel, die Town House Galleria. Schon die Lage in der exklusiven Galleria Vittorio Emanuele von 1876, mitten im Zentrum der Modemetropole, ist spektakulär. Ein persönlicher Butler kennt die Vorlieben der Gäste schon bei der Ankunft, reserviert Karten für die Scala und sucht Bettwäsche und Lieblingsspeisen wunschgemäß aus. Selbstverständlich stehen in so einem Haus italienische Espressokocher und lederbezogene Laptops in den 24 eichenvertäfelten Suiten bereit.

Ce qui semblait uniquement possible à Dubai, est maintenant devenu réalité en Europe : le premier hôtel sept étoiles, le Town House Galleria. Son seul emplacement, dans la splendide Galleria Vittorio Emmanuele datant de 1876, au centre de la métropole de la mode, est spectaculaire. Un majordome personnel connaît les préférences des clients, dès la réception ; il réserve des places pour la Scala et choisit le linge de lit et les plats préférés des clients. Dans un tel hôtel, il y a bien sûr des machines à espresso italiennes et des ordinateurs portables vêtus de cuir dans les 24 suites couvertes de lambris de chêne.

Lo que antes sólo parecía posible en Dubai, se ha hecho realidad ahora en Europa con el Town House Galleria, el primer hotel de siete estrellas en el continente. Espectacular por si sola ya es la ubicación del hotel en la galería Vittorio Emanuele, del año 1878, encallada en el corazón mismo de la metrópolis de la moda. Un mayordomo personal conoce las preferencias de los huéspedes de antemano y reserva entradas para la Scala o escoge las sábanas y platos favoritos según el gusto de cada huésped. Se sobreentiende que, en un hotel de esta índole, las cafeteras de expreso talianas y los portátiles forrados de cuero están disponibles en cada una de sus 24 suites revestidas de roble.

Quello che finora sembrava essere possibile solo a Dubai, adesso è stato realizzato anche in Europa: il primo albergo a sette stelle, il Town House Galleria. La sola posizione nell'esclusiva Galleria Vittorio Emanuele, del 1876, nel cuore della metropoli della moda, è già spettacolare. Un maggiordomo privato capisce le preferenze degli ospiti già al loro arrivo, prenota biglietti per la Scala e fornisce lenzuola e piatti secondo i loro desideri. Naturalmente, nelle 24 suite rivestite in legno di quercia di un edificio come questo non potevano mancare caffettiere italiane e portatili rivestiti in pelle.

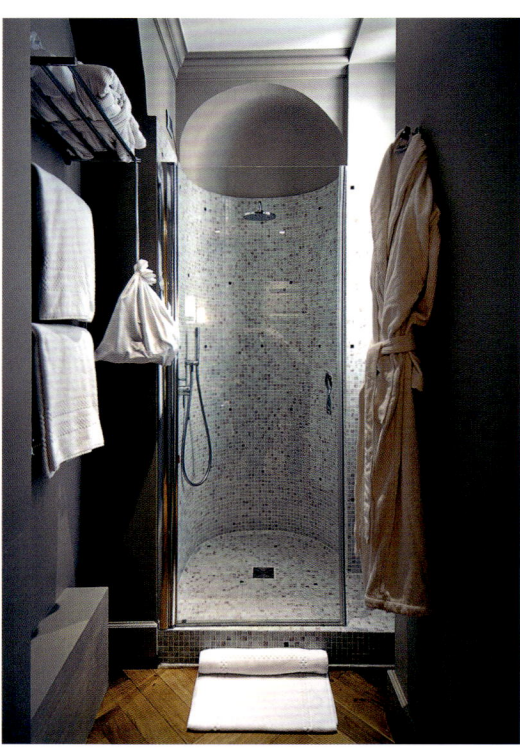
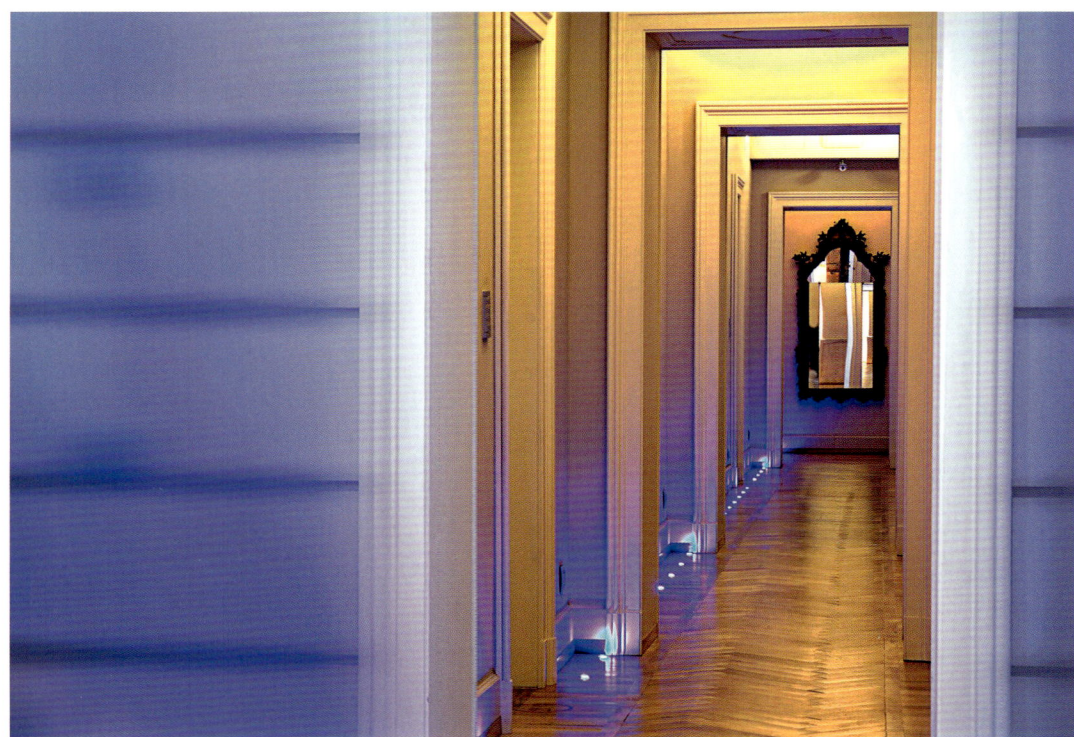

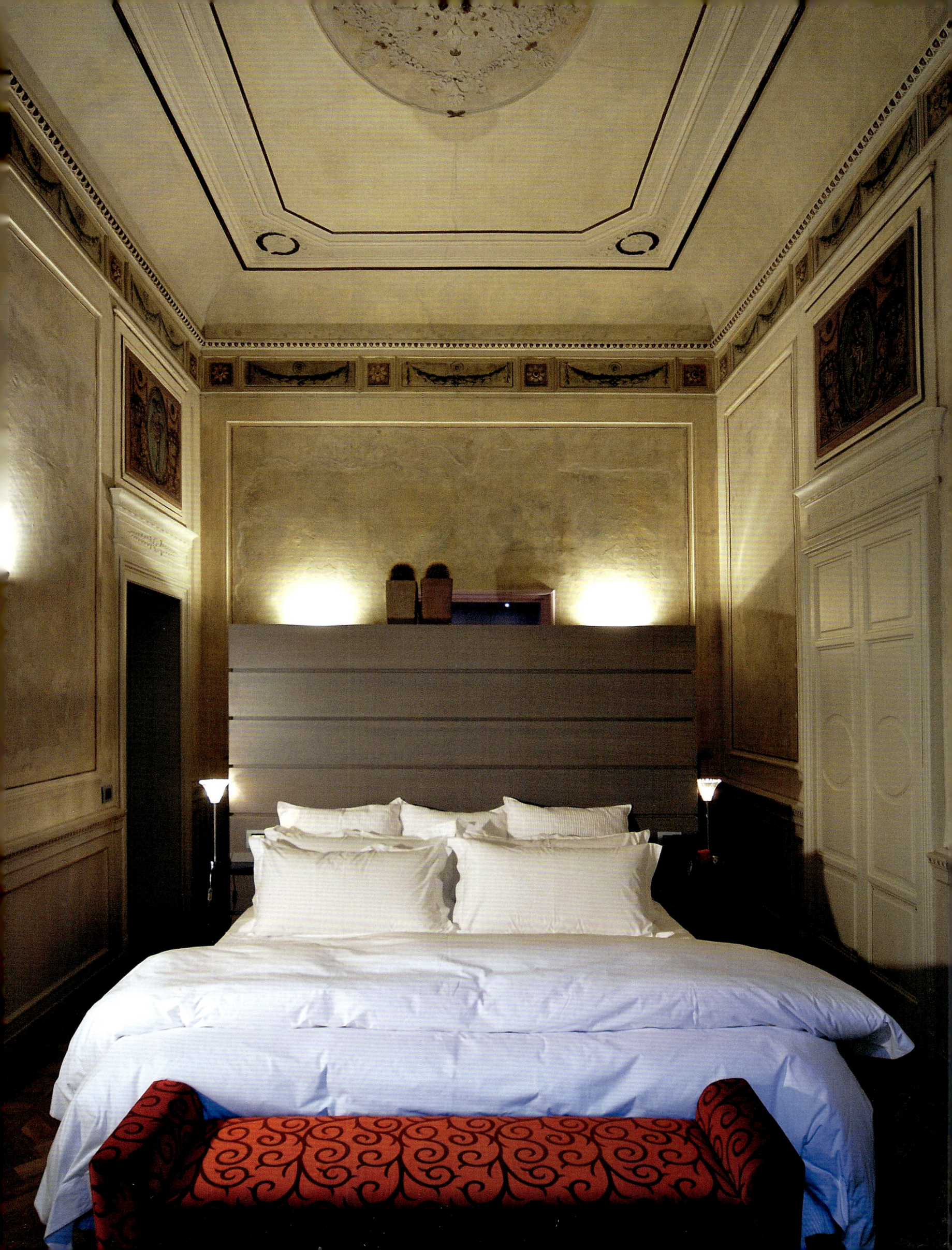

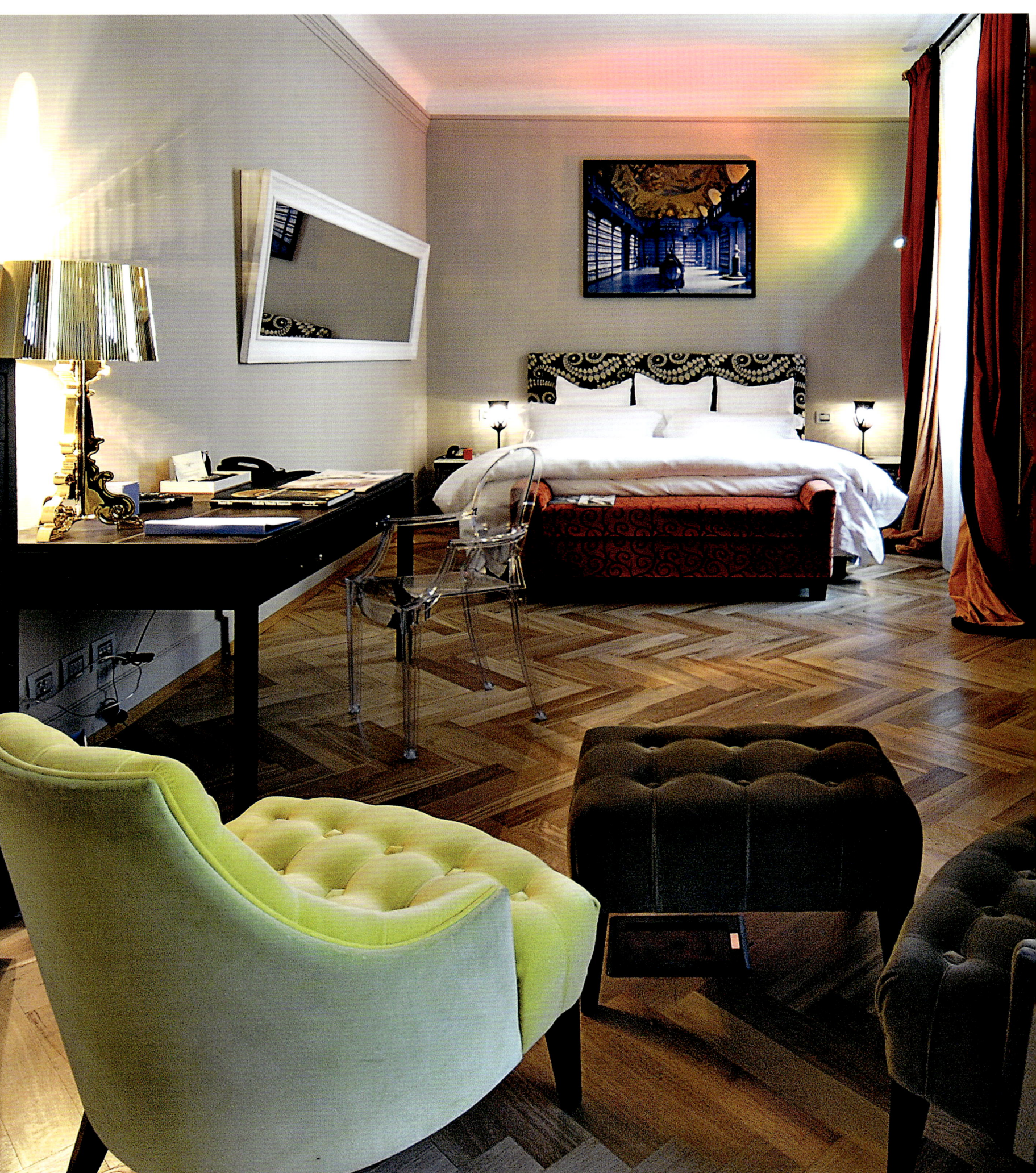

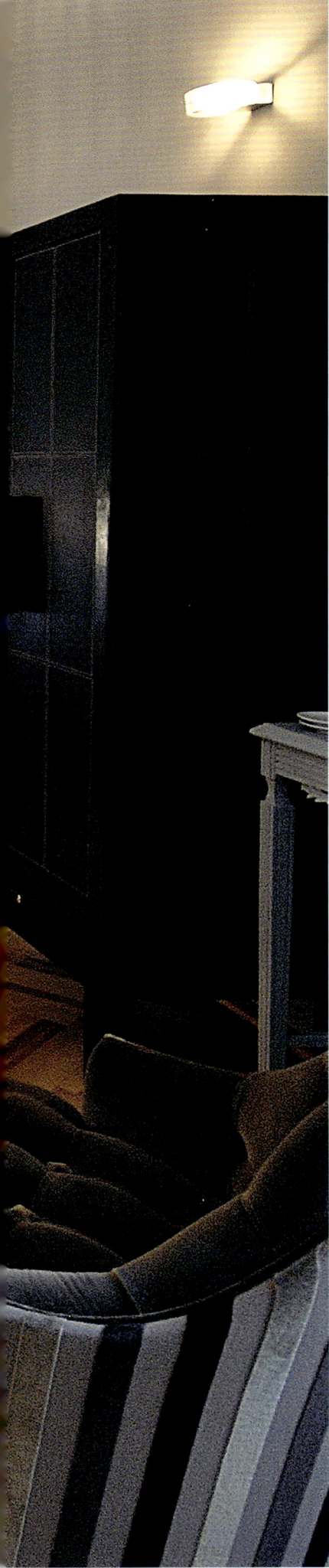
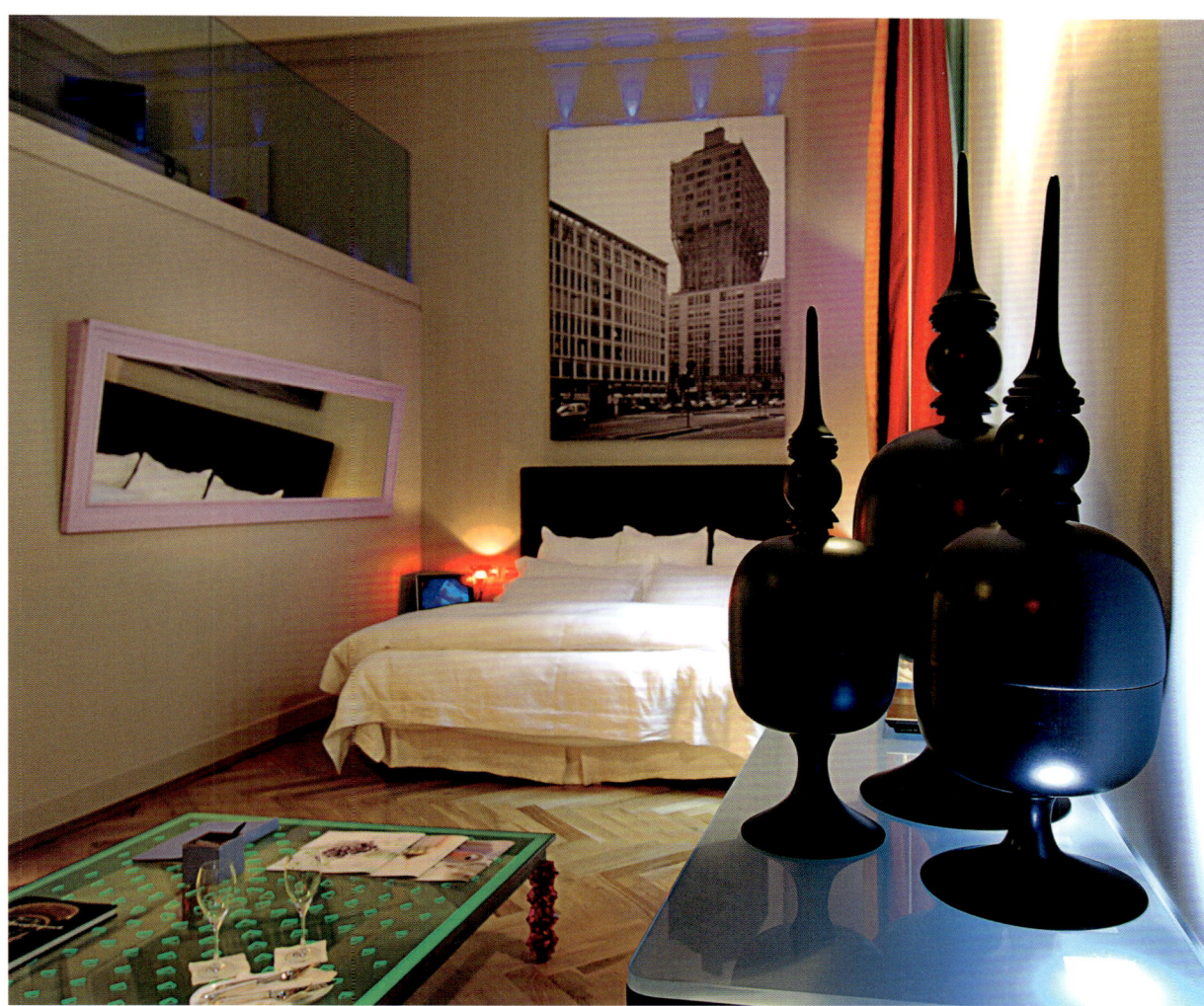
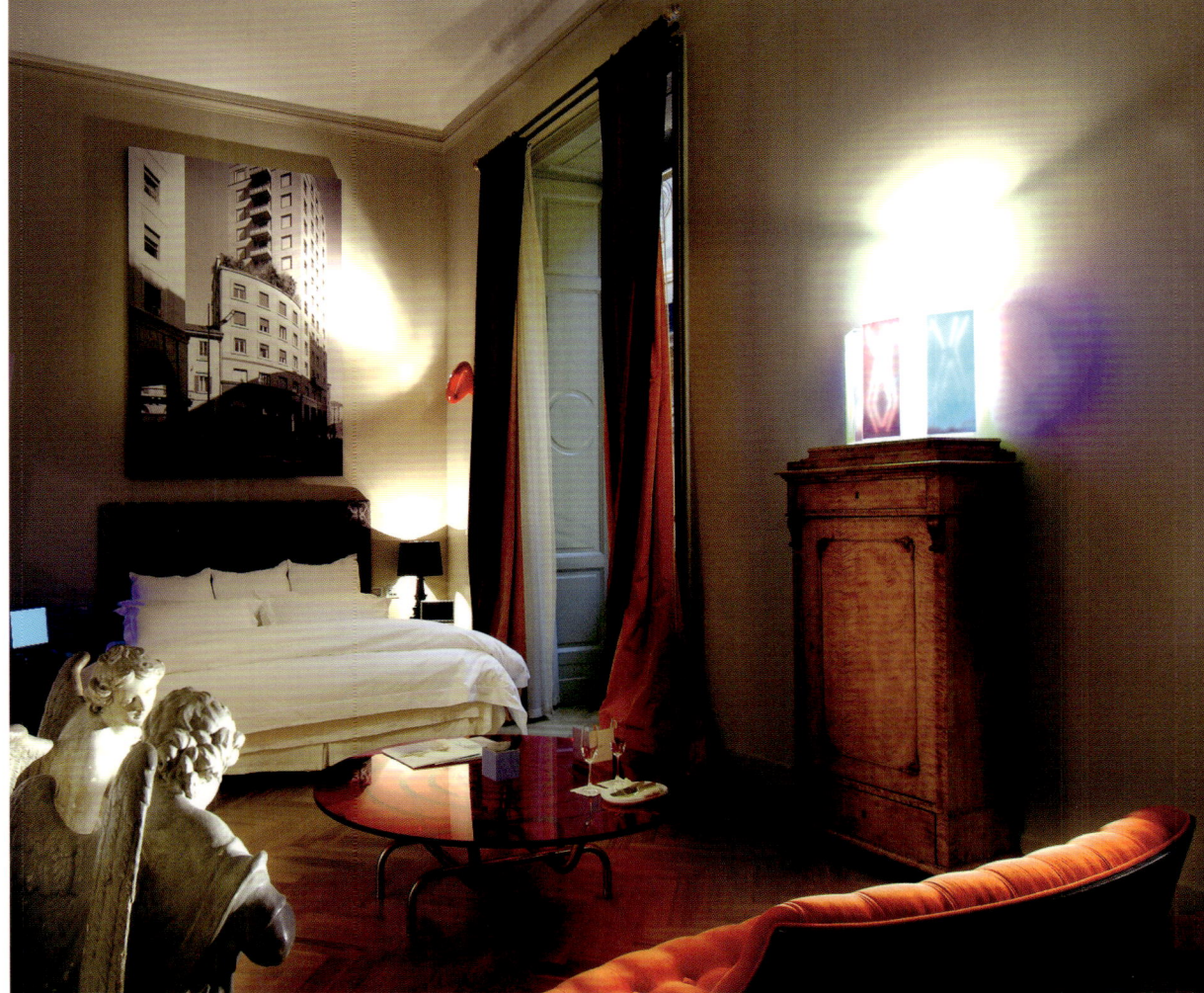

10126 Turin
Italy
Phone: +39 011 66 42 780
Fax: +39 011 66 42 004
www.lemeridien.com/turin

Rooms: 141 rooms and 1 suite
Facilities: Art+Cafe Bar and Restaurant, business center
Services: Babysitting, free parking, 24 h room service, fitness center, power-shower
Located: In the center of Lingotto
Public transportation: Bus 1, 18, 35 Porta Nuova
Style: Design

Why not jet off to Turin for a chocolate weekend? Turin is just as famous for sweet chocolate delights and truffles as for its baroque old city and historical cafés. But the Le Méridien Turin Art+Tech built by Renzo Piano is ultra-modern. The celebrated architect consequently integrated the refined modern rooms into the former Lingotto Fiat works that also houses the elegant shopping mile "8 Gallery." You can dine on red-and-white cushions in the airy "Art+Café." Watching the mountain panorama while jogging on the former test track on the roof is a must.

Warum nicht auf ein Schokoladen-Wochenende nach Turin düsen? Für die süßen Tafeln und Pralinés ist Turin ebenso berühmt wie für seine barocke Altstadt und die historischen Cafés. Ultramodern ist hingegen das Le Méridien Turin Art+Tech, gebaut von Renzo Piano. Der gefeierte Architekt hat das Haus mit konsequent modernen Zimmern raffiniert in das ehemalige Fiatwerk Lingotto integriert, das auch die elegante Einkaufsmeile „8 Gallery" beherbergt. Diniert wird auf rot-weißen Polstern im luftigen „Art+Café". Der Clou: das Bergpanorama beim Joggen auf der ehemaligen Teststrecke auf dem Dach.

Pourquoi ne pas prendre l'avion pour passer un weekend chocolat à Turin ? La ville est aussi connue pour ses tablettes de chocolat et ses pralinés que pour sa vieille cité baroque et ses cafés historiques. Par contraste, Le Méridien Turin Art+Tech, construit par Renzo Piano, est ultramoderne. L'architecte renommé a intelligemment intégré les chambres de style moderne dans l'ancienne usine Fiat Lingotto, qui abrite également l'élégant centre commercial « 8 Gallery ». Les repas se prennent sur les coussins rouges et blancs du spacieux « Art+Café ». Le must : la vue sur les montagnes depuis l'ancienne piste de course située sur le toit.

¿Por qué no pasar un dulce fin de semana en Turín? La ciudad es tan famosa por sus chocolates y bombones, como por su casco antiguo barroco y sus históricos cafés. El hotel Le Méridien Turin Art+Tech, erigido por Renzo Piano, constituye un contraste ultramoderno en esta ciudad. El celebrado arquitecto integró un edificio con habitaciones de estilo consecuentemente moderno en la antigua factoría Lingotto de Fiat, que alberga también la elegante calle comercial "8 Gallery". La cena se sirve en el airoso "Art+Café" sobre sedosos cojines de color rofo y blanco. Y lo mejor, el panorama montañoso que se puede observar mientras se hace footing en la antigua pista de pruebas sobre la azotea.

Perché non fare una puntatina a Torino per un fine settimana all'insegna della cioccolata? Questa città è famosa per le sue praline e tavolette di cioccolato così come per la sua città vecchia in stile barocco e i bar storici. Il Le Méridien Turin Art+Tech è invece un modernissimo hotel costruito da Renzo Piano. L'acclamato architetto ha meravigliosamente ricavato quest'albergo, dotato di camere ovviamente moderne, dall'ex stabilimento Fiat Lingotto, che ospita anche il centro commerciale "8 Gallery". La cena viene servita nell'arioso "Art+Café" tra sedie rosse e tovaglie bianche. Il non plus ultra: il panorama delle montagne che si gode facendo jogging sull'ex pista di collaudo del tetto.

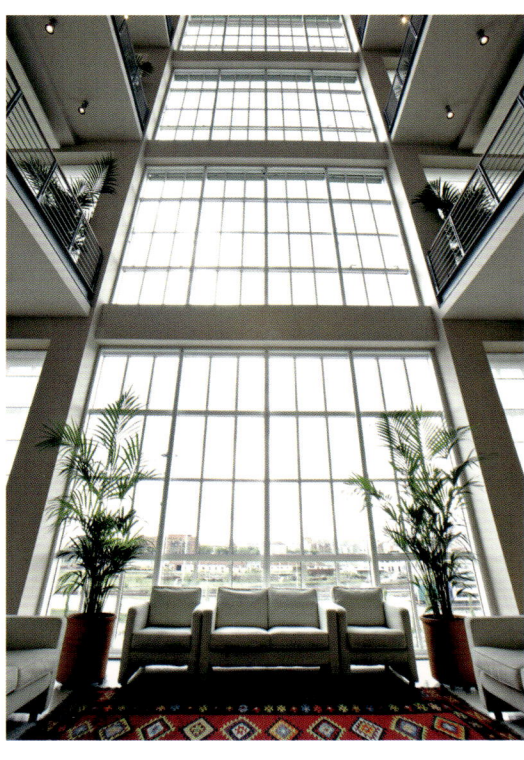
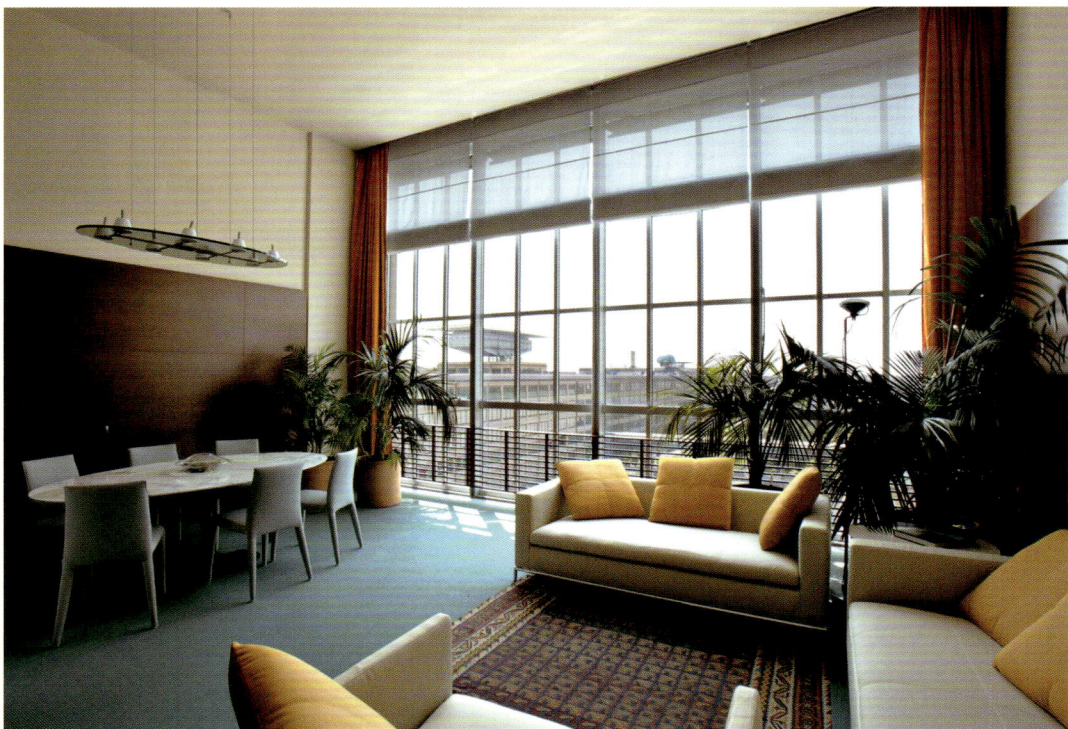

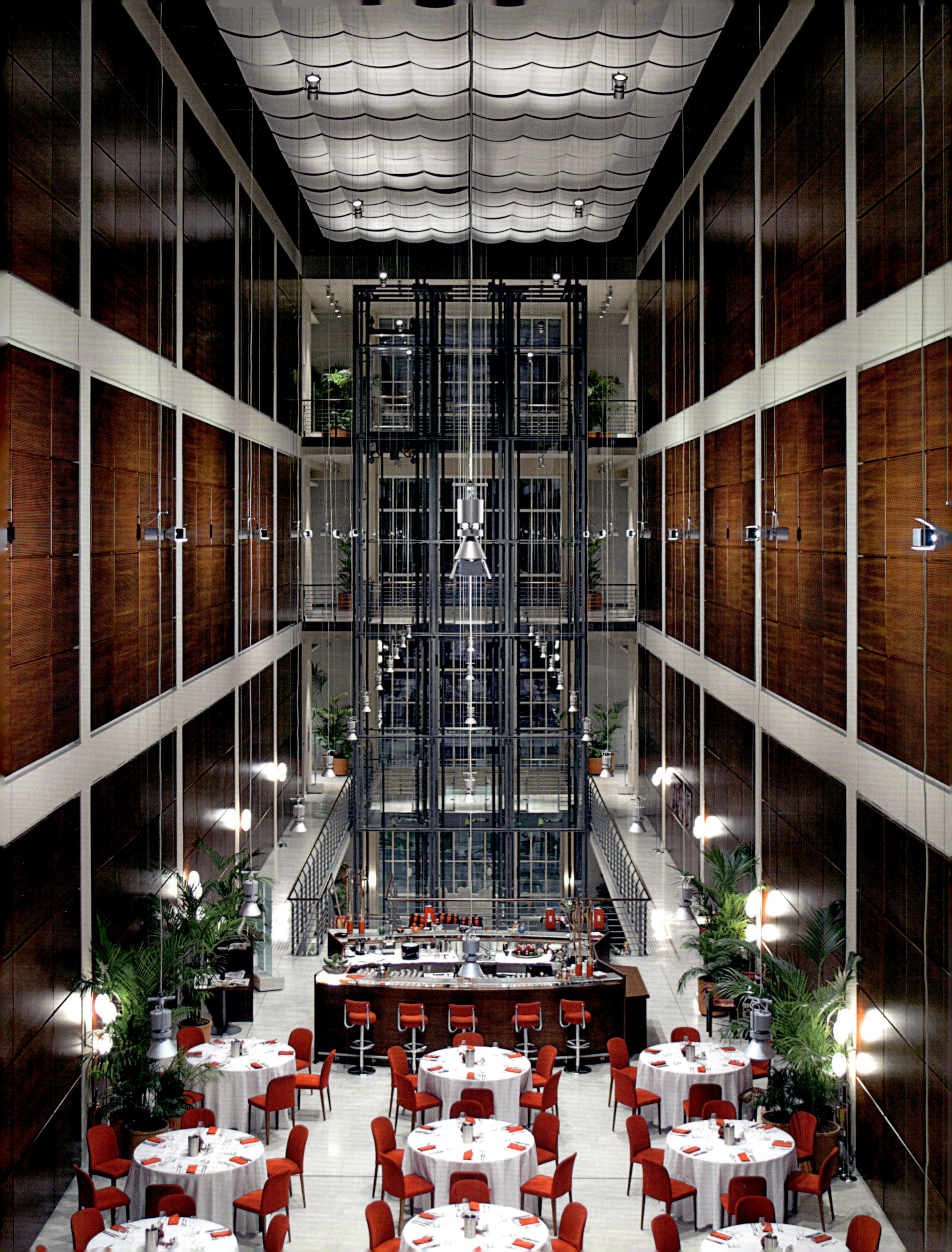

06100 Perugia
Italy
Phone: +39 075 57 32 541
Fax: +39 075 57 20 210
www.sinahotels.com

Rooms: 94 rooms including 31 suites
Facilities: Collins Bar, Collins Restaurant and panoramic Terraza Bellavista
Services: Dry-cleaning and laundry service, valet parking and private indoor garage
Located: On top of Perugia's highest hill overlooking the valley
Public transportation: Bus, mini-metro, train
Style: Classic

The cream-colored villa rises above the crest of a hill high over the old city lanes of Perugia. Illustricus guests like the British Queen Mother and Prince Albert of Monaco have walked its antique parquet floor. The stained-glass ceilings, silk tapestries and fireplace masonry are designed to match the elegant style of the belle époque. The natives and hotel guests meet for an aperitivo on the roof terrace. Far below in the cellar of the house, the ruins of the Etruscan period gleam through the glass arch of the pools.

Auf einer Hügelkuppe hoch über den Altstadtgassen von Perugia erhebt sich die noble, cremefarbene Villa. Über ihren original erhaltenen Paketboden sind schon so illustre Gäste wie die britische Königinmutter und Prinz Albert von Monaco geschritten. Auf den eleganten Stil der Belle Epoque abgestimmt sind auch die Buntglasdecken und Seidentapeten und gemauerten Kamine. Zum Aperitivo treffen sich Hotelgäste und Einheimische auf der Dachterrasse. Und ganz unten, im Keller des Hauses, schimmern Ruinen der Etruskerzeit durch den Glasboden des Pools.

Au sommet d'une colline, au-dessus des ruelles de la vieille ville de Pérouse, s'élève cette villa couleur crème. D'illustres clients comme la Reine Mère britannique et le Prince Albert de Monaco ont parcouru son antique parquet originel. Les plafonds de verre coloré, les papiers peints soyeux et les cheminées de pierre s'harmonisent avec le style élégant de la Belle Epoque. A l'heure de l'apéritif, clients de l'hôtel et locaux se rencontrent sur la terrasse de toit. Et juste en bas, dans la cave de l'hôtel, on peut contempler des ruines de l'ère étrusque à travers le sol de verre de la piscine.

En lo alto de la colina, muy por encima de los callejones del centro histórico de Perugia, se levanta esta noble mansión color crema. Sobre su parqué original han caminado visitantes tan ilustres como la reina de Inglaterra y el príncipe Alberto de Mónaco. En sintonía con el elegante estilo belle époque están también los techos de cristales multicolores, las tapicerías de seda y las chimeneas mazonadas. Los huéspedes y lugareños se reúnen en la azotea para tomar el aperitivo y, en las profundidades del sótano de este edificio, a través del fondo de cristal de la piscina, se divisan ruinas de origen etrusco.

Sul cocuzzolo di una collina che sovrasta le stradine del centro storico di Perugia si erge questa raffinata villa color crema. Sul suo pavimento di parquet, conservato allo stato originale, hanno già camminato personaggi illustri quali la regina madre d'Inghilterra e il principe Alberto di Monaco. In sintonia con lo stile belle èpoque sono anche i soffitti in vetro colorato, i tappeti di seta e i caminetti a muro. Per un aperitivo sulla terrazza del tetto si ritrovano tanto gli ospiti dell'albergo quanto la gente del luogo. E sotto, nella cantina della casa, attraverso il pavimento in vetro della piscina risplendono alcune rovine di epoca etrusca.

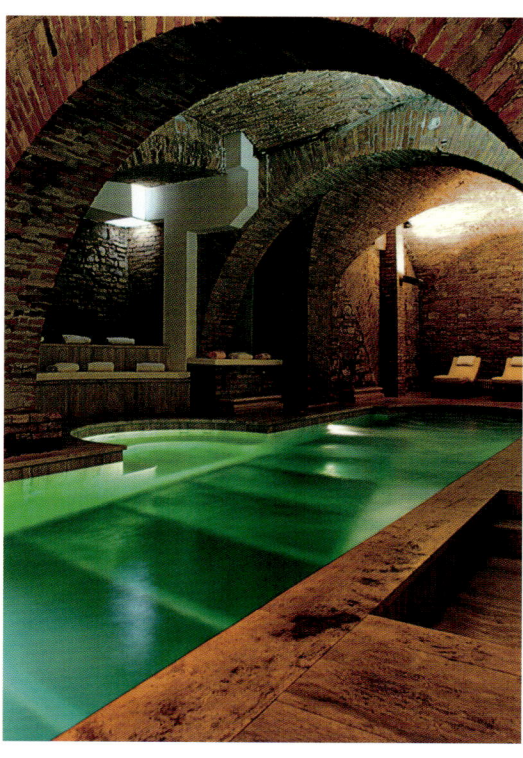
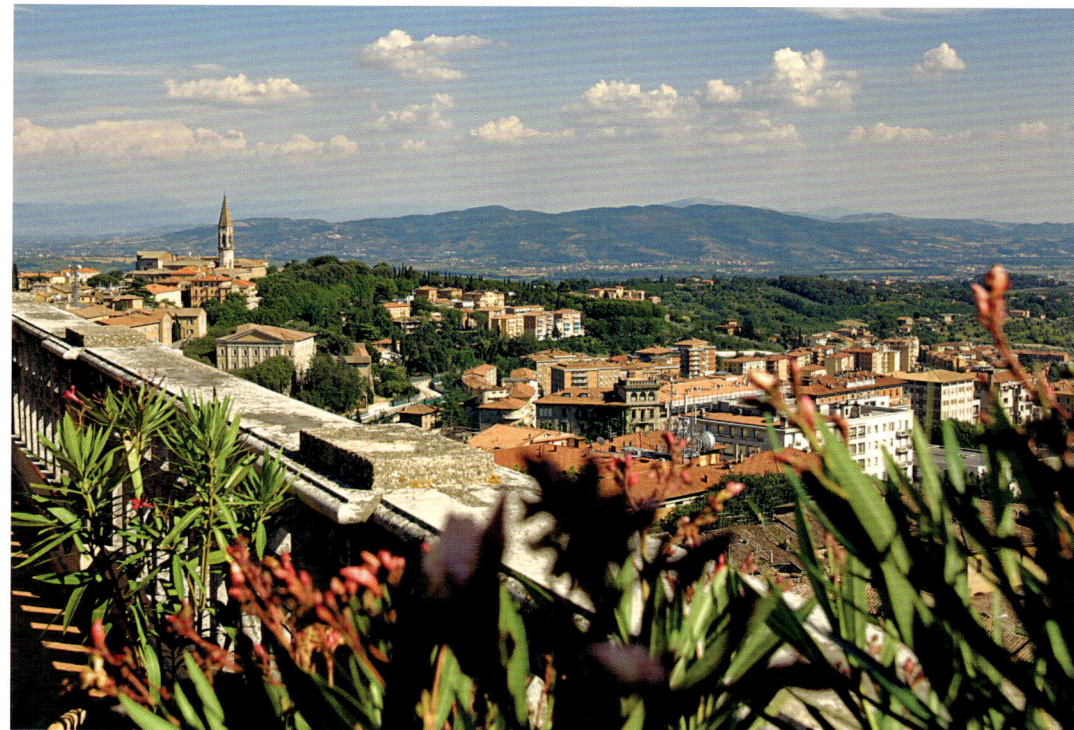

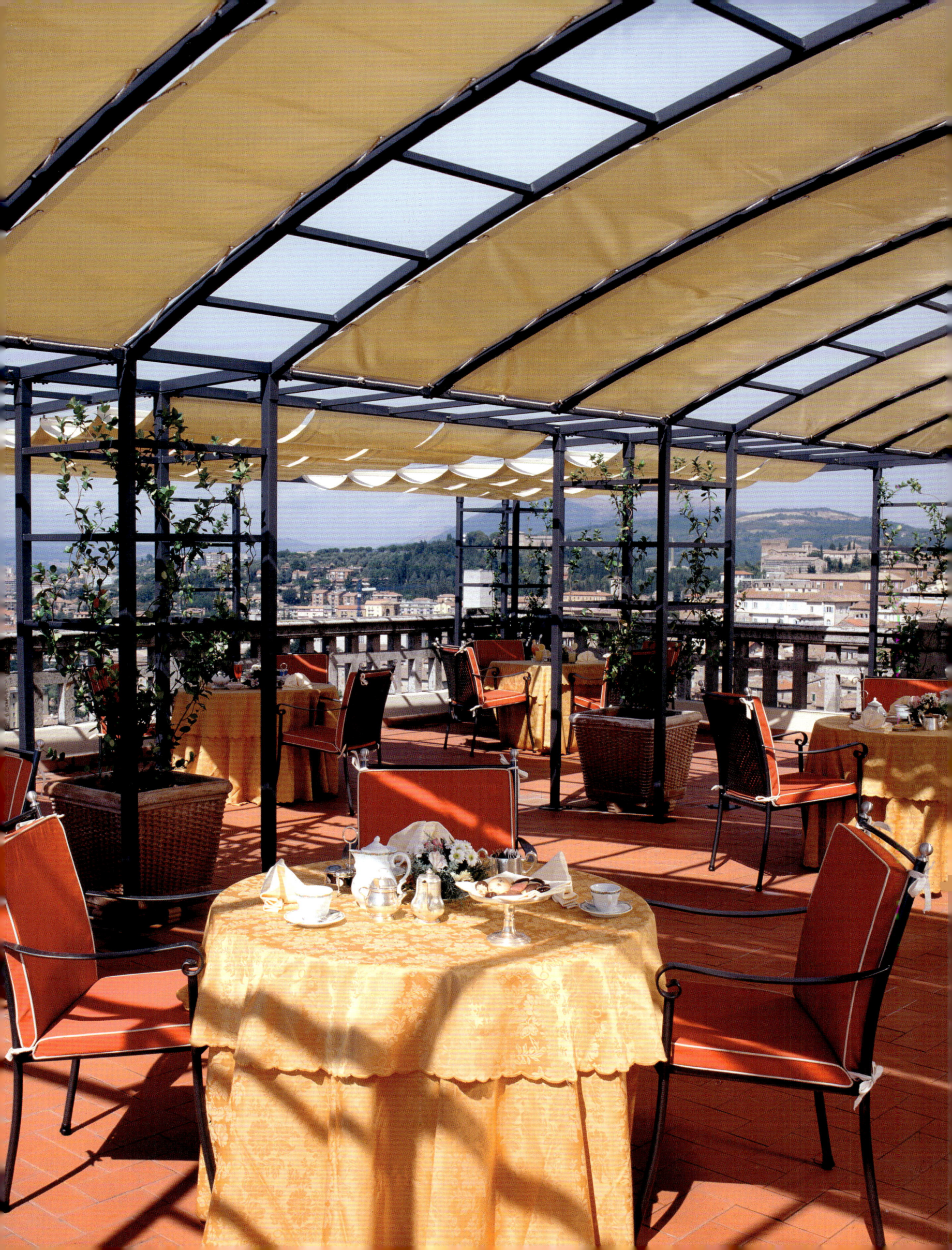

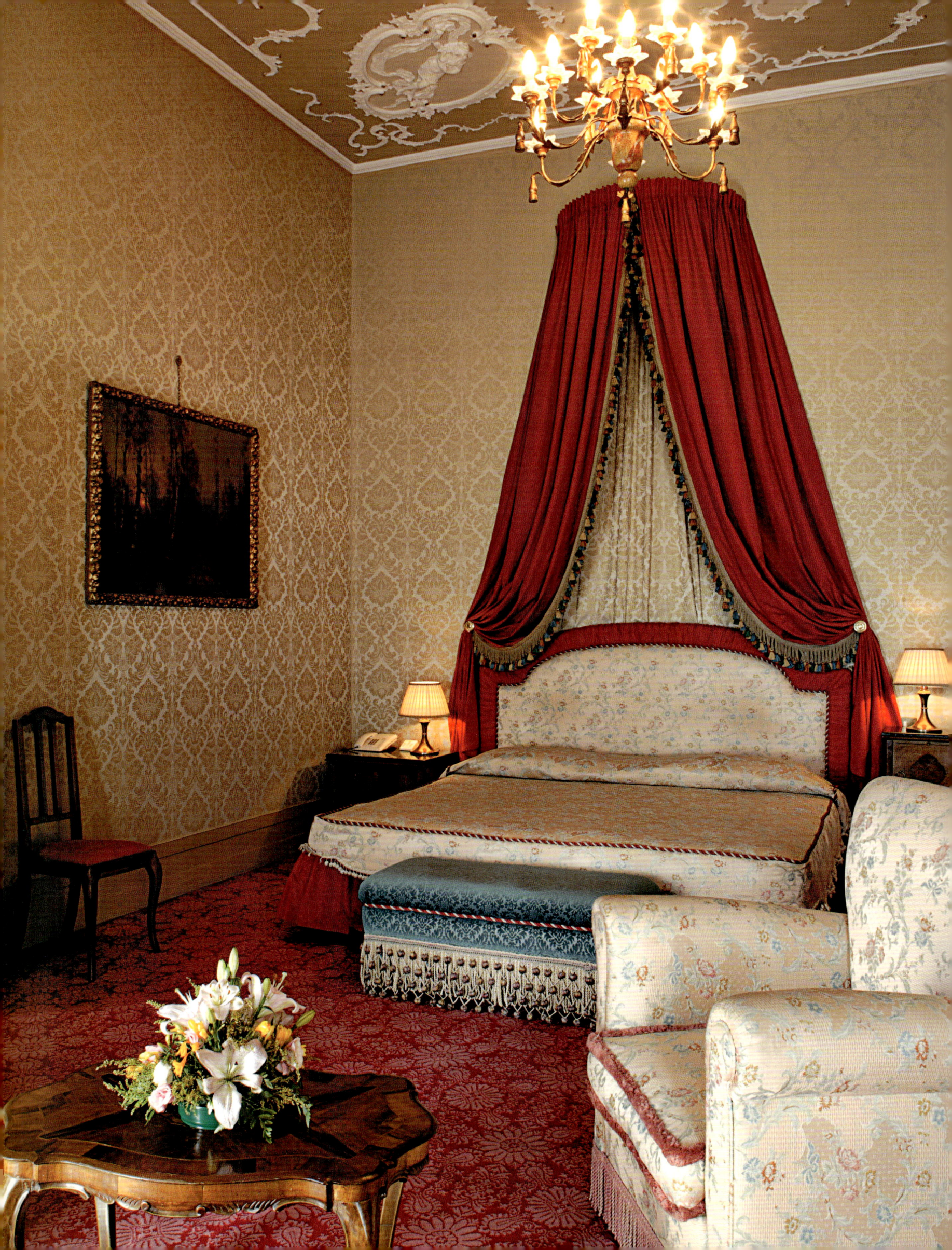

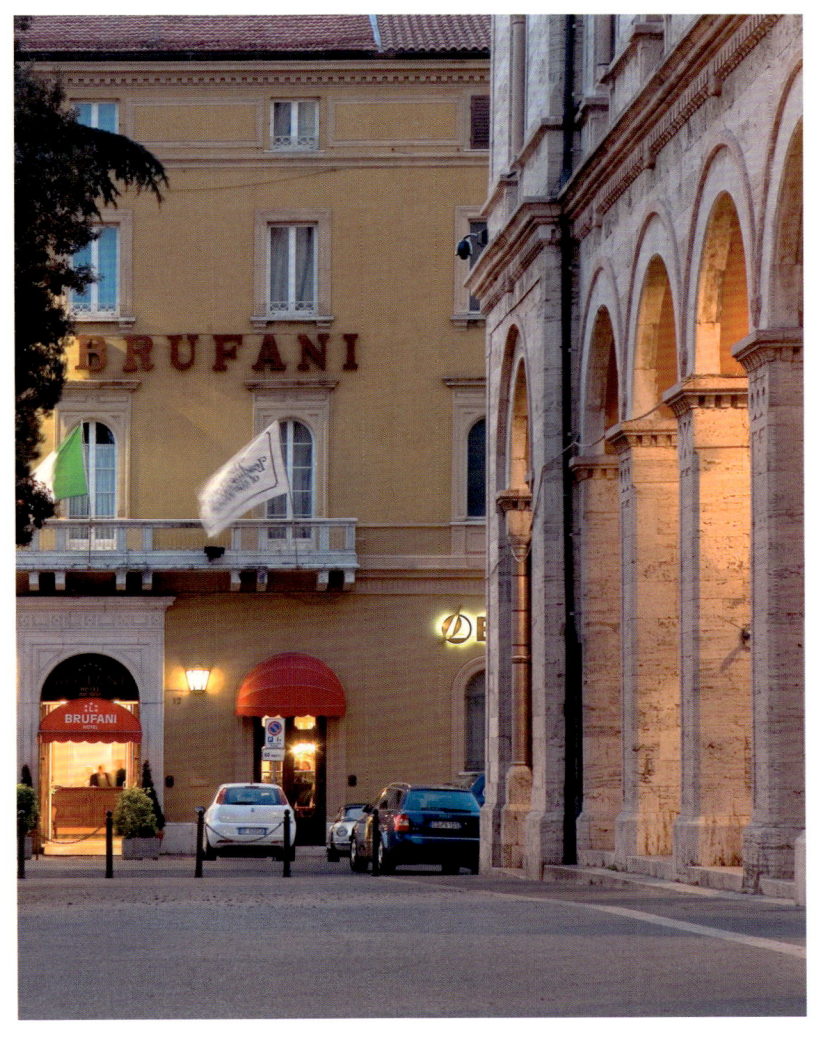

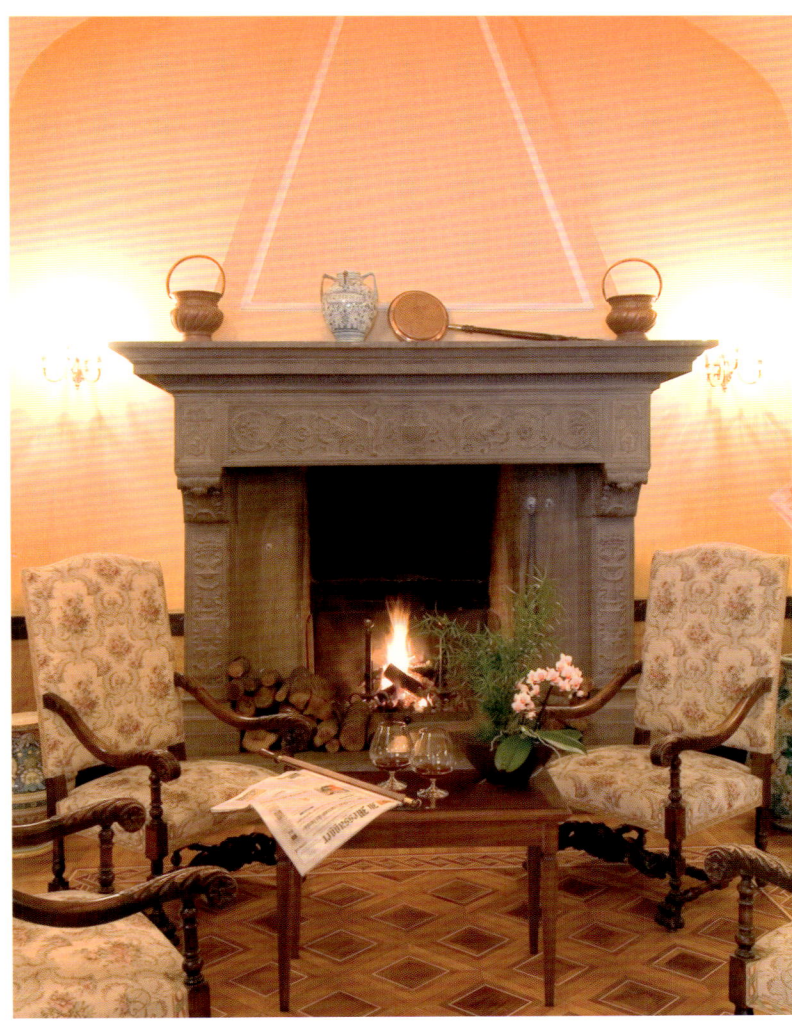

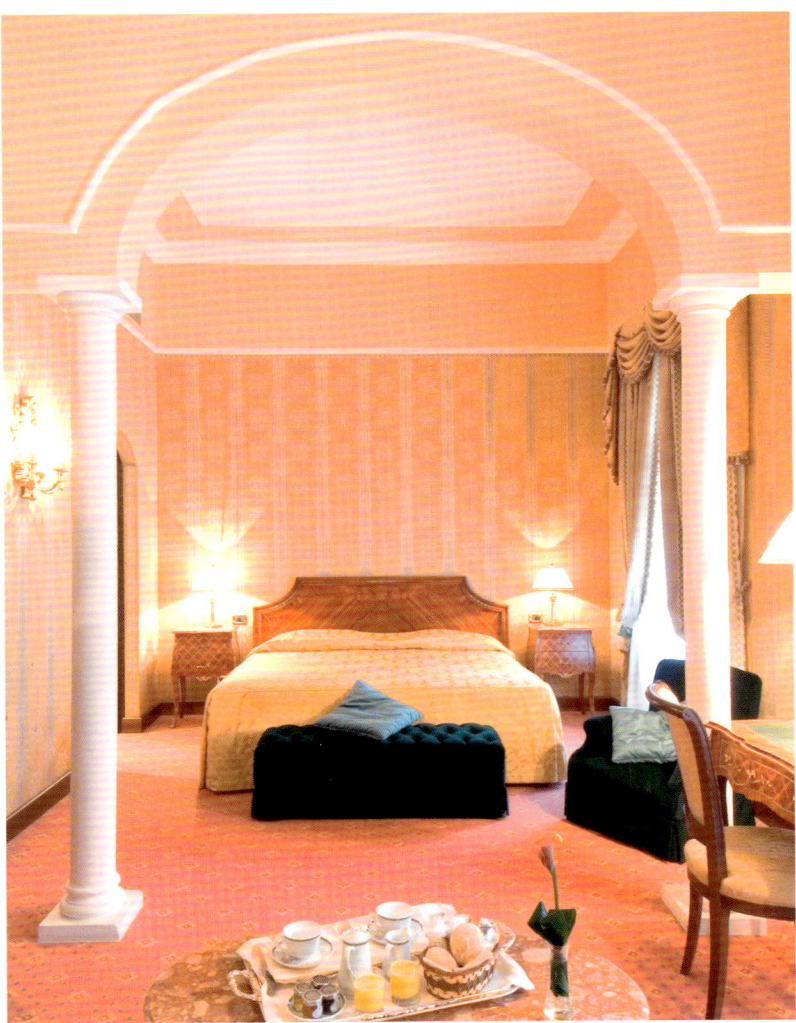

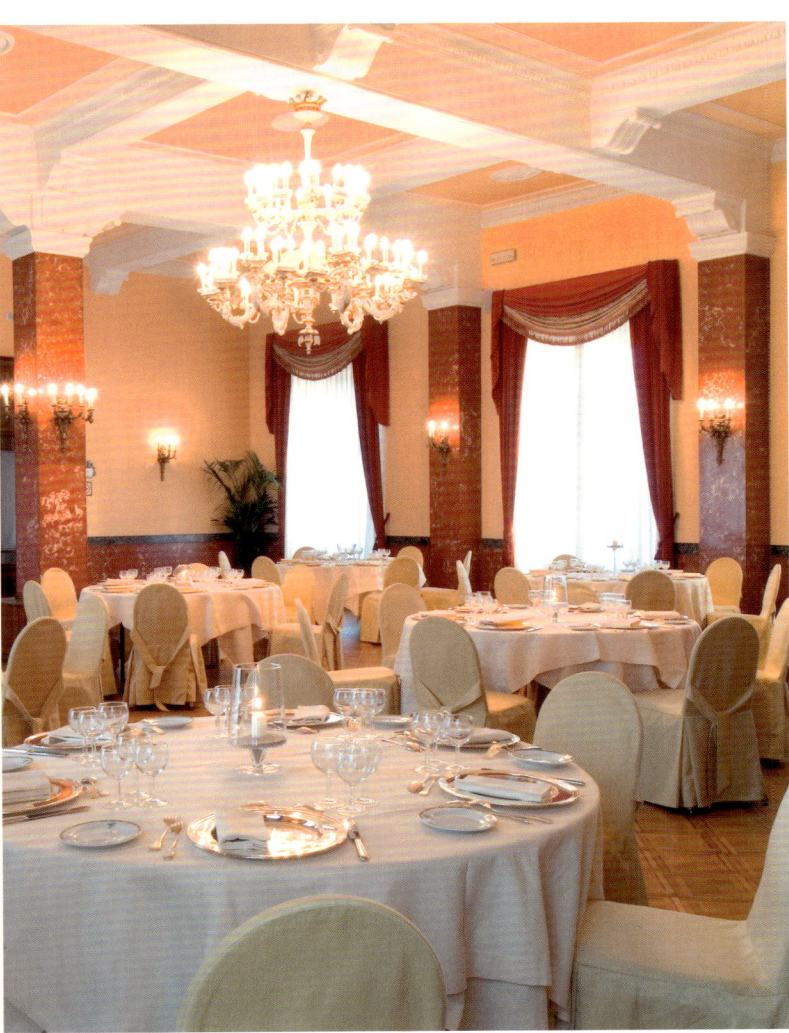

30124 Venice
Italy
Phone: +39 041 52 07 022
Fax: +39 041 52 07 557
www.bauerhotels.com

Rooms: 82 rooms including 38 suites and junior suites
Facilities: De Pisis gourmet restaurant, BBar and Bar Canale
Services: Babysitting, concierge, 24 h room service
Located: In the center of Venice, 50 m from St Mark square
Public transportation: Vaporetto 1, 2 San Marco Vallaresso
Style: Classic elegance

The Bauer has been a stately institution in the city set in a lagoon for generations. Behind the Byzantine-styled facade from the 18th century on the Canale Grande, you see the gleam of Murano glass chandeliers, Venetian brocade by the famous Rubelli manufactury, art deco furniture, and here and there contemporary works of art. The chic nostalgically furnished suites remind you of the days of Venice's doges. Afternoons are the perfect time for having a Bellini on the terrace with a fantastic view of the gondolas on the Canale Grande. Later, chef Giovanni Ciresa will spread the table at the "De Pisis" with traditional Italian delicacies.

Das Bauer ist seit Generationen eine Institution in der Lagunenstadt. Hinter der Fassade des 18. Jahrhunderts im byzantinischen Stil am Canale Grande, funkeln Murano-Glasleuchter, venezianische Brokate der berühmten Rubelli-Manufaktur, Art-déco-Möbel und hier und da ein zeitgenössisches Kunstwerk. Die nostalgisch-chic eingerichteten Suiten erinnern an die Herrschaftsjahre Venedigs. Nachmittags ist die perfekte Zeit für einen Bellini auf der Terrasse mit traumhaftem Blick auf die Gondolieri und den Canale Grande. Anschließend tischt Chef Giovanni Ciresa im „De Pisis" traditionelle italienische Köstlichkeiten auf.

Pendant des générations, le Bauer a été une institution dans cette ville sur la lagune. Sur le Grand Canal, derrière la façade byzantine du 18ème siècle, on trouve des lustres de Murano étincelants, des brocarts vénitiens de la fameuse manufacture Rubelli, des meubles Art déco, et ici et là une œuvre d'art contemporaine. Les suites meublées de manière nostalgique chic rappellent la vieille époque aristocratique de Venise. L'après-midi est le moment parfait pour siroter un Bellini sur la terrasse, au-dessus des gondoliers du Grand Canal. Plus tard, le chef Giovanni Ciresa vous concoctera des délices italiens traditionnels au « De Pisis ».

Desde hace generaciones, el hotel Bauer es una institución en la ciudad lacustre. Detrás de la soberbia fachada de estilo Bizantino del siglo XVIII que da al Canal Grande lucen arañas de cristal de cristal de Murano, brocados venecianos de la famosa manufactura Rubelli, muebles art-déco e incluso algunas obras de arte contemporáneo. Sus suites de decoración elegante y nostálgica recuerdan la época de auge de Venecia. La caída de la tarde es el momento idóneo para tomar un Bellini en la terraza y para observar a los gondoleros y el Gran Canal. A continuación, el chef del restaurante "De Pisis", Giovanni Ciresa, sirve delicias de la cocina italiana.

Il Bauer è un'istituzione nella città lagunare da diverse generazioni. Dietro la sontuosa facciata in stile bizantino del XVIII secolo affacciata sul Canal Grande brillano lampade di vetro di murano, broccati veneziani della famosa azienda Rubelli, mobili in stile art déco e qua e là un'opera d'arte contemporanea. Le suite arredate con tocco nostalgico rimandano al periodo della sovranità di Venezia. Il pomeriggio è il momento ideale per un Bellini sulla terrazza con fantastica vista sui gondolieri e sul Canal Grande. E a fine giornata, nel "De Pisis", lo chef Giovanni Ciresa mette in tavola specialità tradizionali della cucina italiana.

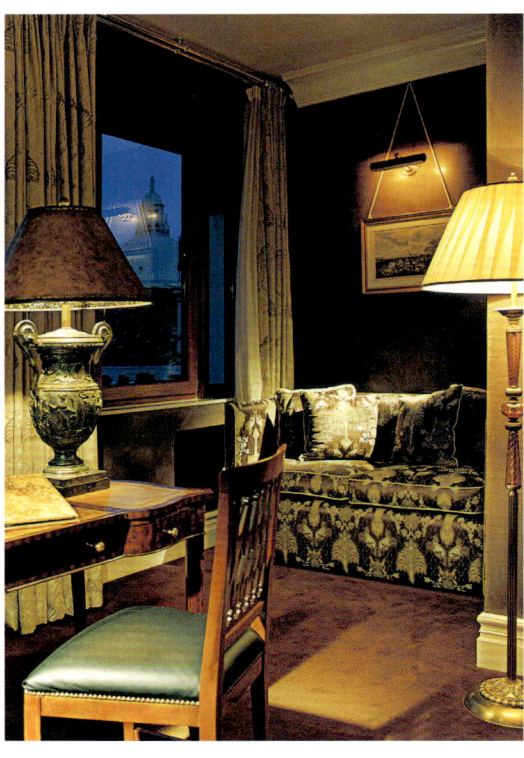
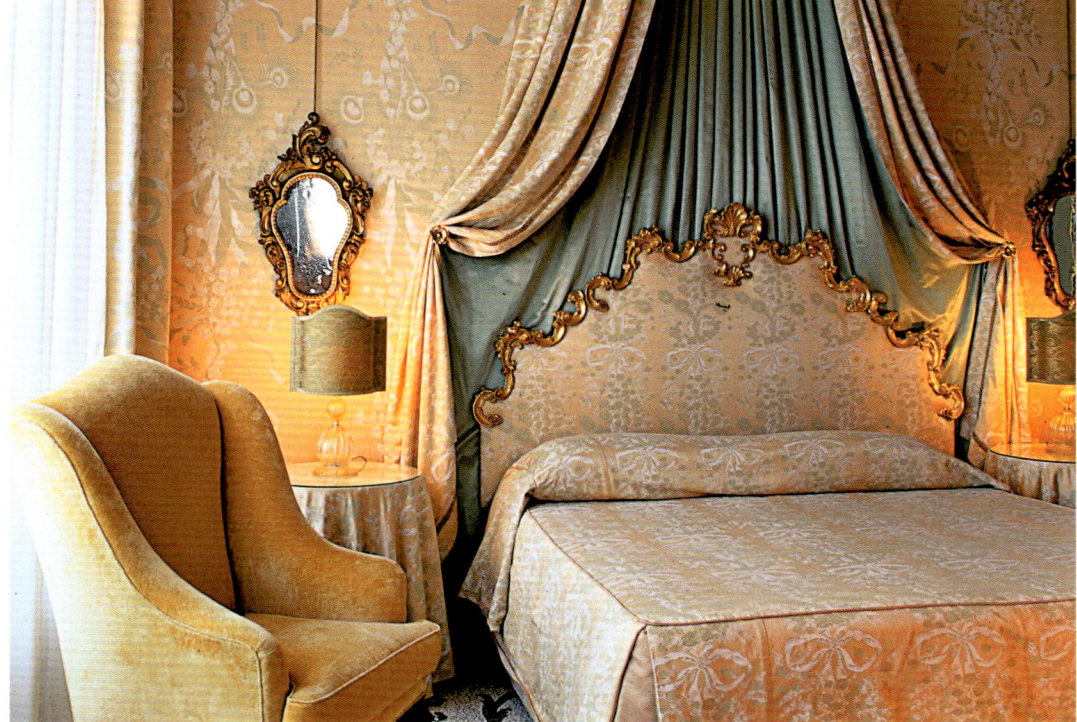

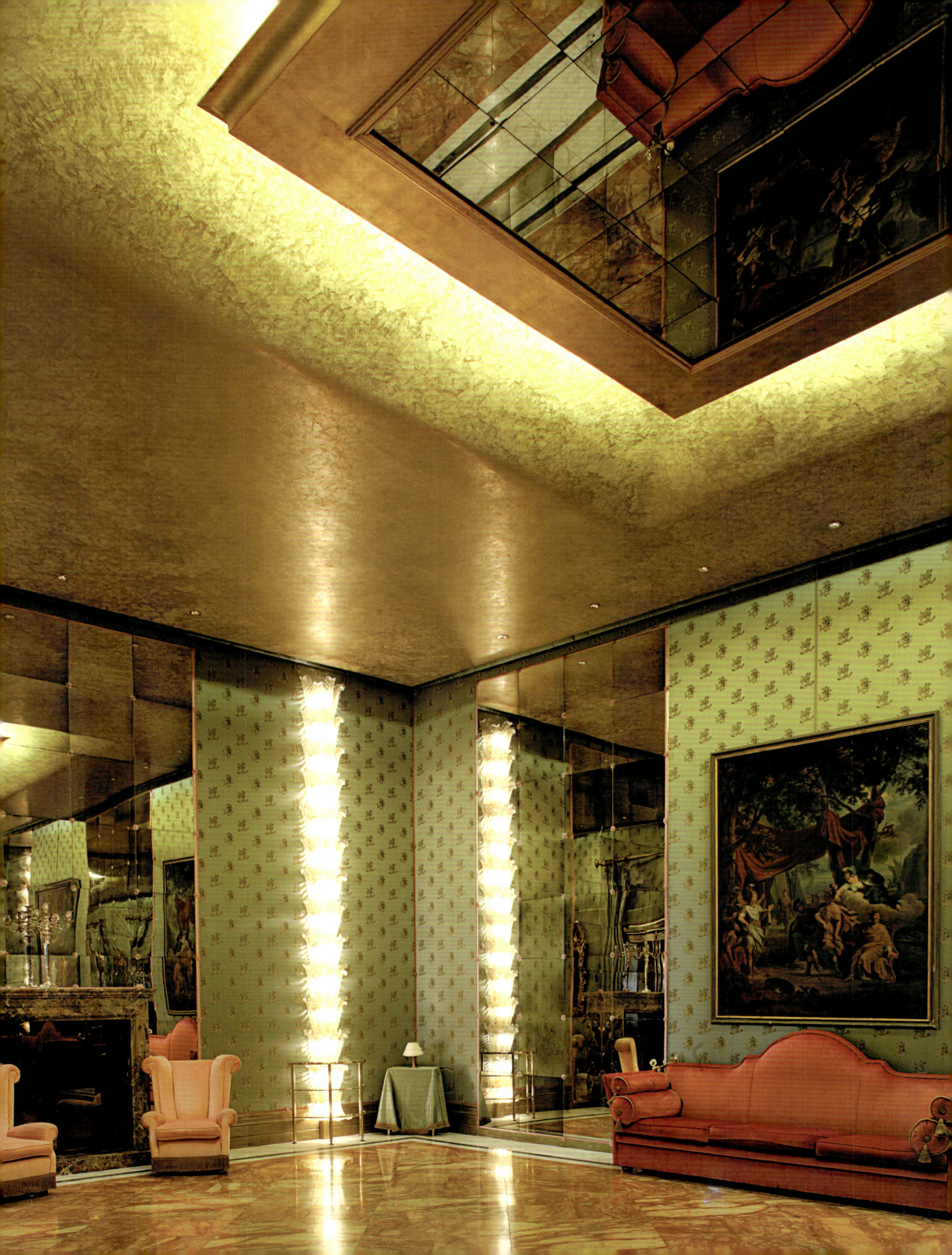

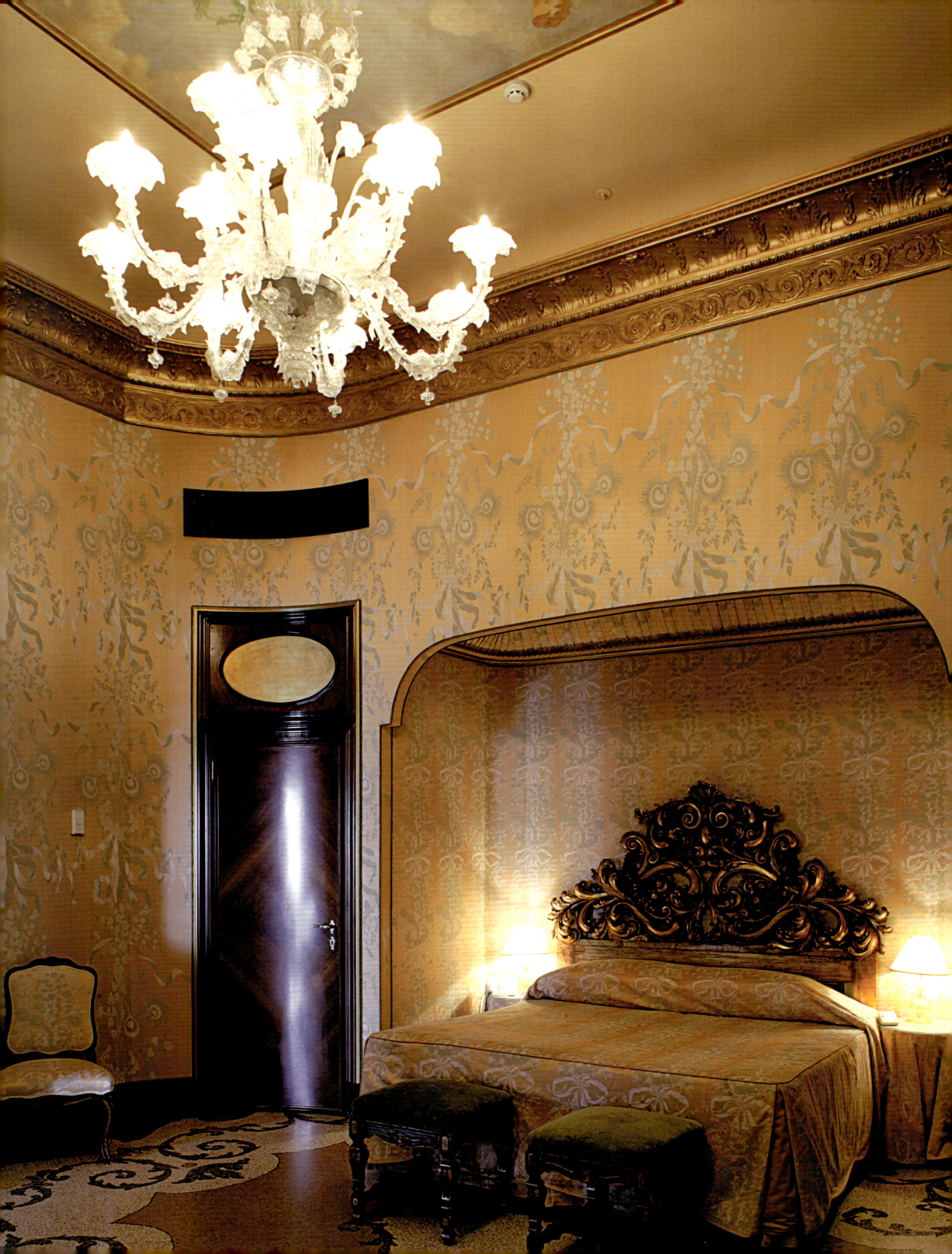

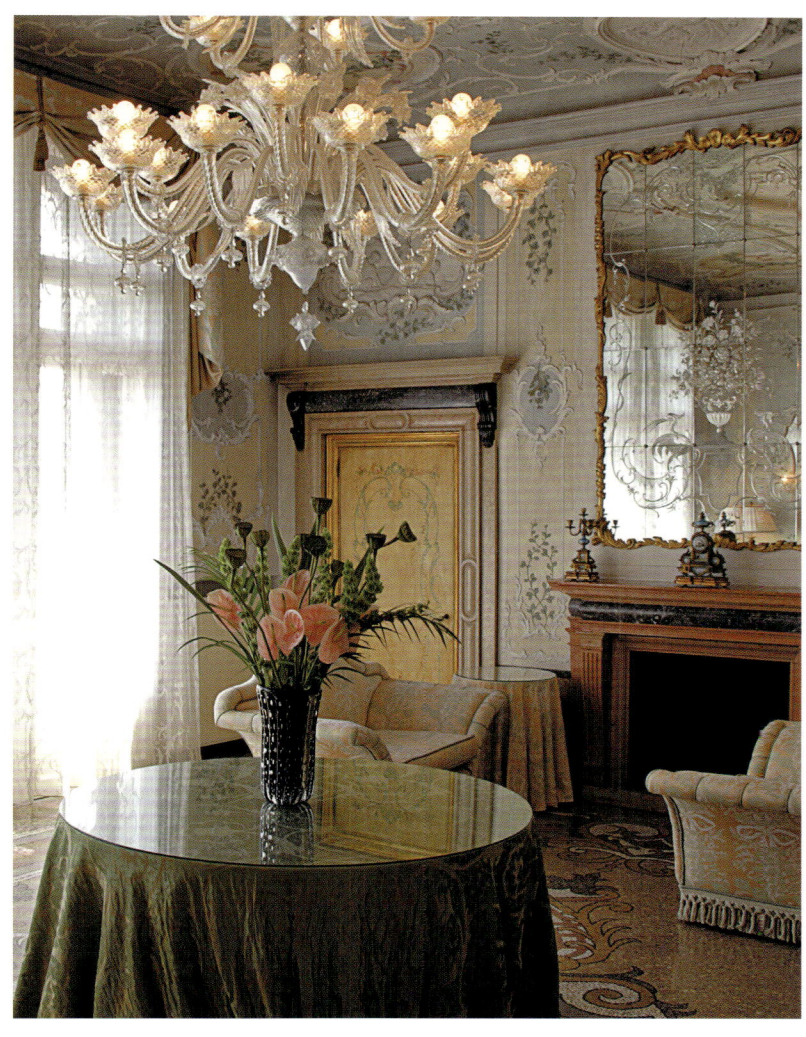

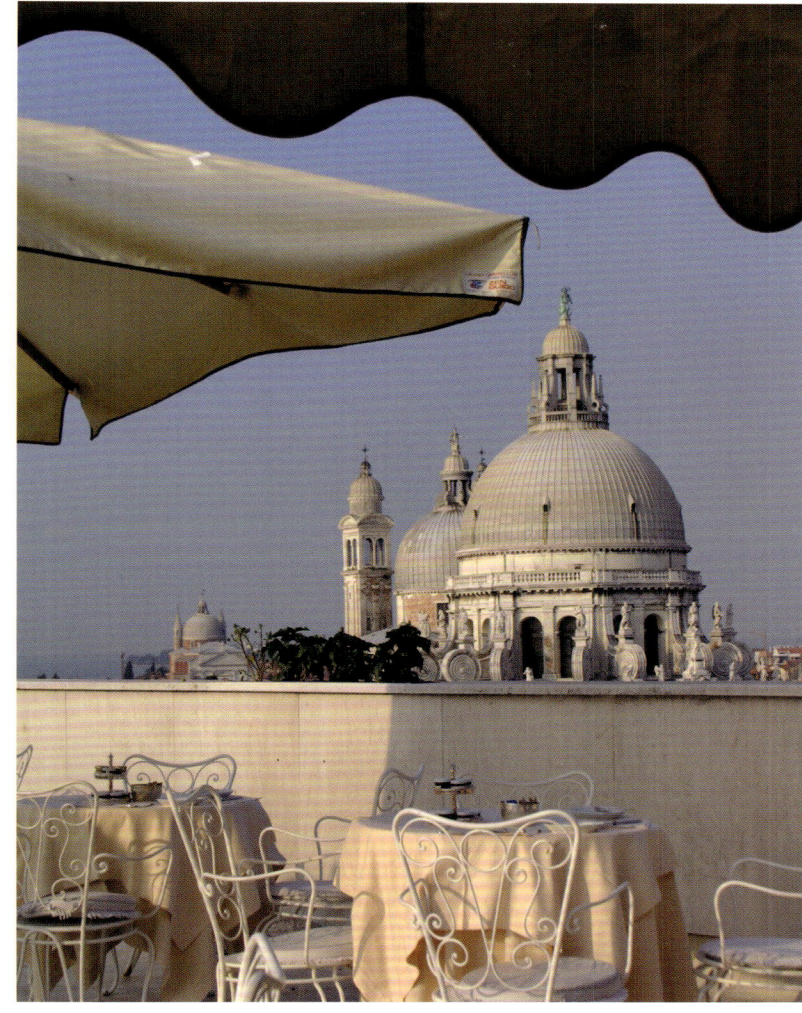

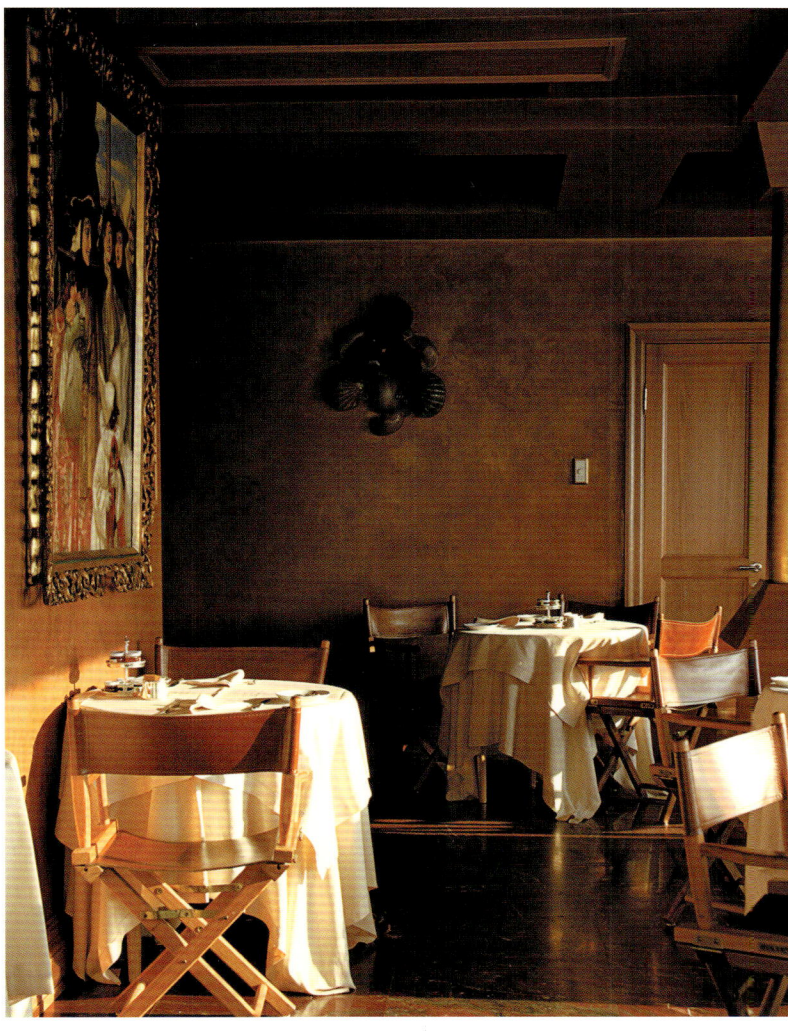

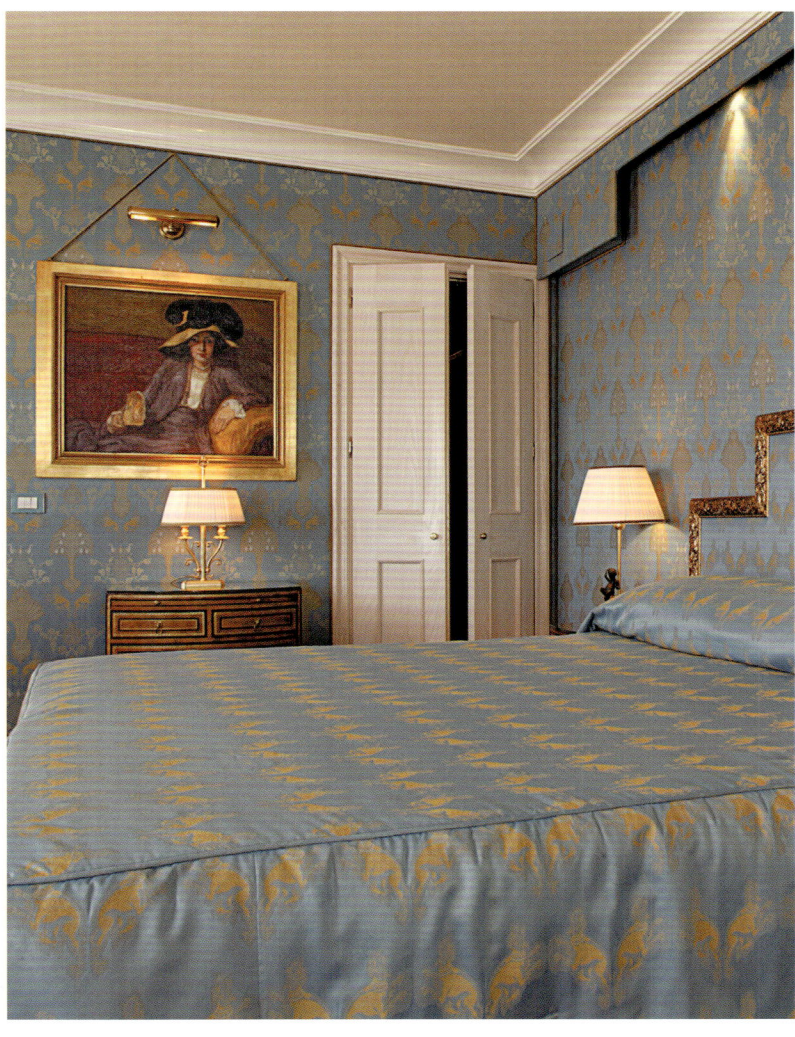

Byblos Art Hotel Villa Amista

Verona, Italy

Via Cedrare 78
37020 Corrubbio di S. Pietro
in Cariano (Verona)
Italy
Phone: +39 045 68 55 555
Fax: +39 045 68 55 500
www.byblosarthotel.com

Price category: €€€
Rooms: 60 rooms
Facilities: Gourmet restaurant, bar and spa
Located: Surrounded by a park in the Valpolicella area, 7 km to the center of Verona
Style: Contemporary design mixed with art

The garden view of the classical villa in Corrubbio near Verona might have been taken from a Fellini film. The path to the portal is bordered by flower beds and the splashing of a fountain. A considerable collection of contemporary art is distributed among the suites. The moon faces by Japanese Takashi Murakami smile from the ceiling and the lobby is framed by nudes by photographer Vanessa Beecroft. Designer furniture, wall paintings and Venetian chandeliers emphasize a fairytale flair. You can relax in the spa with Chenot methode hydrotherapy massages.

Die Gartenansicht der klassischen Villa in Corrubbio bei Verona könnte einem Fellini-Film entnommen sein: Den Weg zum Portal zieren Blumenrabatten und ein plätschernder Springbrunnen. Auf die Suiten verteilt sich eine beachtliche Sammlung zeitgenössischer Kunst: Die Mondgesichter des Japaners Takashi Murakami lächeln von der Decke und die Lobby rahmen Akte der Fotokünstlerin Vanessa Beecroft. Designermöbel, Wandbemalungen und venezianische Leuchter betonen das märchenhafte Flair. Entspannung bietet der Spa des Hauses mit Hydrotherapy-Massagen nach der Chenot-Methode.

La vue depuis le jardin de cette villa classique à Corrubbio, près de Vérone, pourrait avoir été prise dans un film de Fellini. Le chemin qui mène au portail est orné de parterres de fleurs et de jets d'eau. Une remarquable collection d'art contemporain est répartie entre les suites. Les faces de la lune, par le Japonais Takashi Murakami, sourient depuis le plafond et la réception sert de cadre à l'œuvre de la photographe Vanessa Beecroft. Des meubles de designer, des peintures murales et des chandeliers vénitiens en accentuent le charme féérique. Le spa de l'hôtel permet de se relaxer avec des massages d'hydrothérapie inspirés de la méthode Chenot.

La vista del jardín en la mansión clásica en Corrubbio, cerca de Verona, podría pertenecer a una de las tomas de una película típica de Fellini. Arriates y una fuente murmurante adornan el sendero hacia el portal. Una colección considerable de arte contemporánea queda distribuida por todas las suites: las caras de luna llena del japonés Takashi Murakami sonríen desde los techos y los desnudos de la artista Vanessa Beecroft enmarcan el vestíbulo. Los muebles de diseño, los frescos en las paredes y los candelabros venecianos acentúan el ambiente de cuento de hadas. El spa propio con el que cuenta la casa ofrece relajamiento a base de masajes de hidroterapia según el método Chenot.

La vista sul giardino di questa classica villa di Corrubbio sembra presa da un film di Fellini: la via che conduce all'ingresso è abbellita da composizioni floreali e da una fontana zampillante. Tra le suite è distribuita una ragguardevole collezione di opere d'arte contemporanea. Dal soffitto ammiccano i volti a luna piena del giapponese Takashi Murakami e la lobby è decorata con fotografie di nudi scattate dall'artista Vanessa Beecroft. Mobili di design, dipinti murali e lampade veneziane accentuano l'atmosfera da favola. Lo spa annesso offre momenti di relax con massaggi idroterapeutici secondo il metodo Chenot.

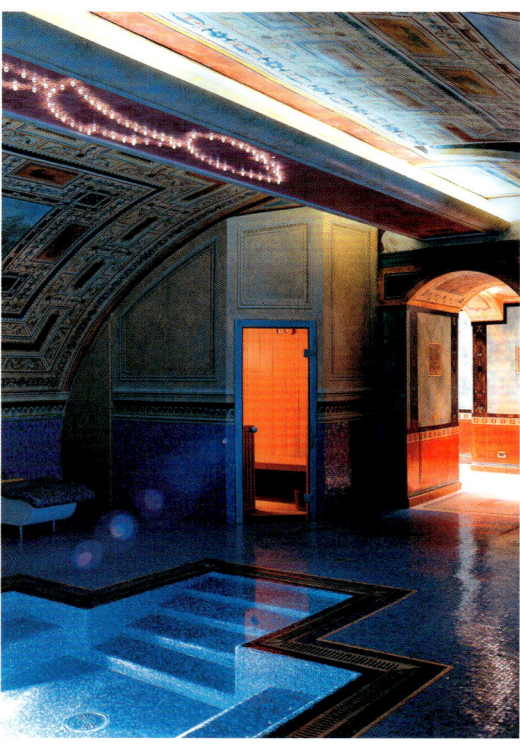 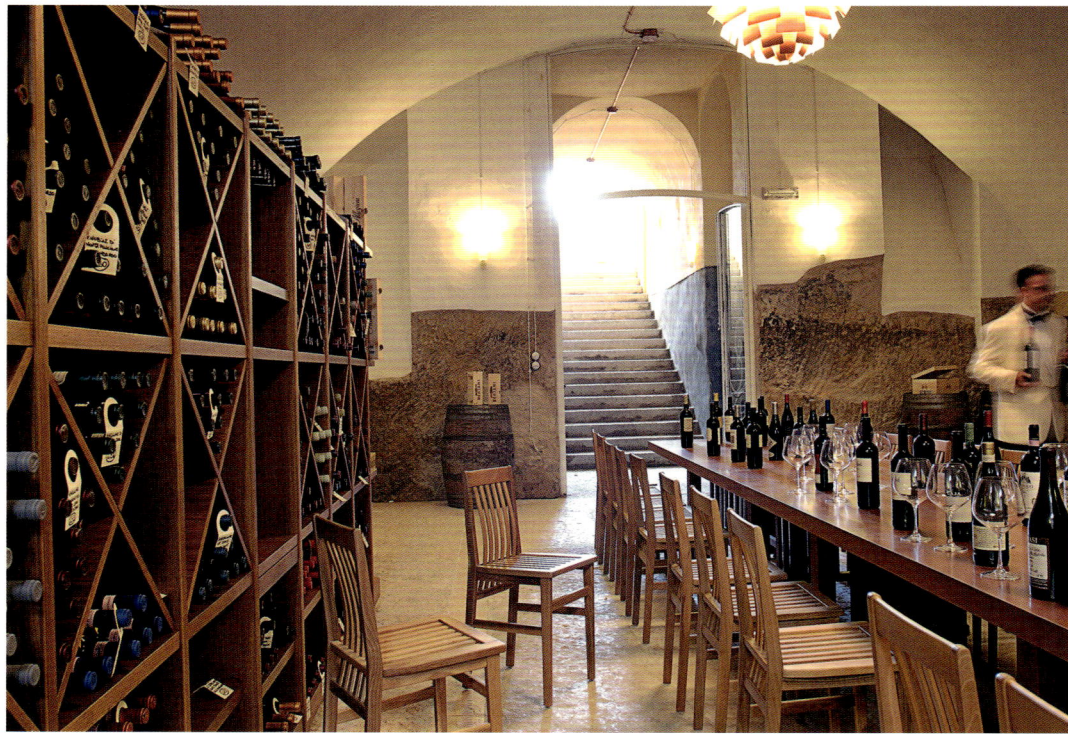

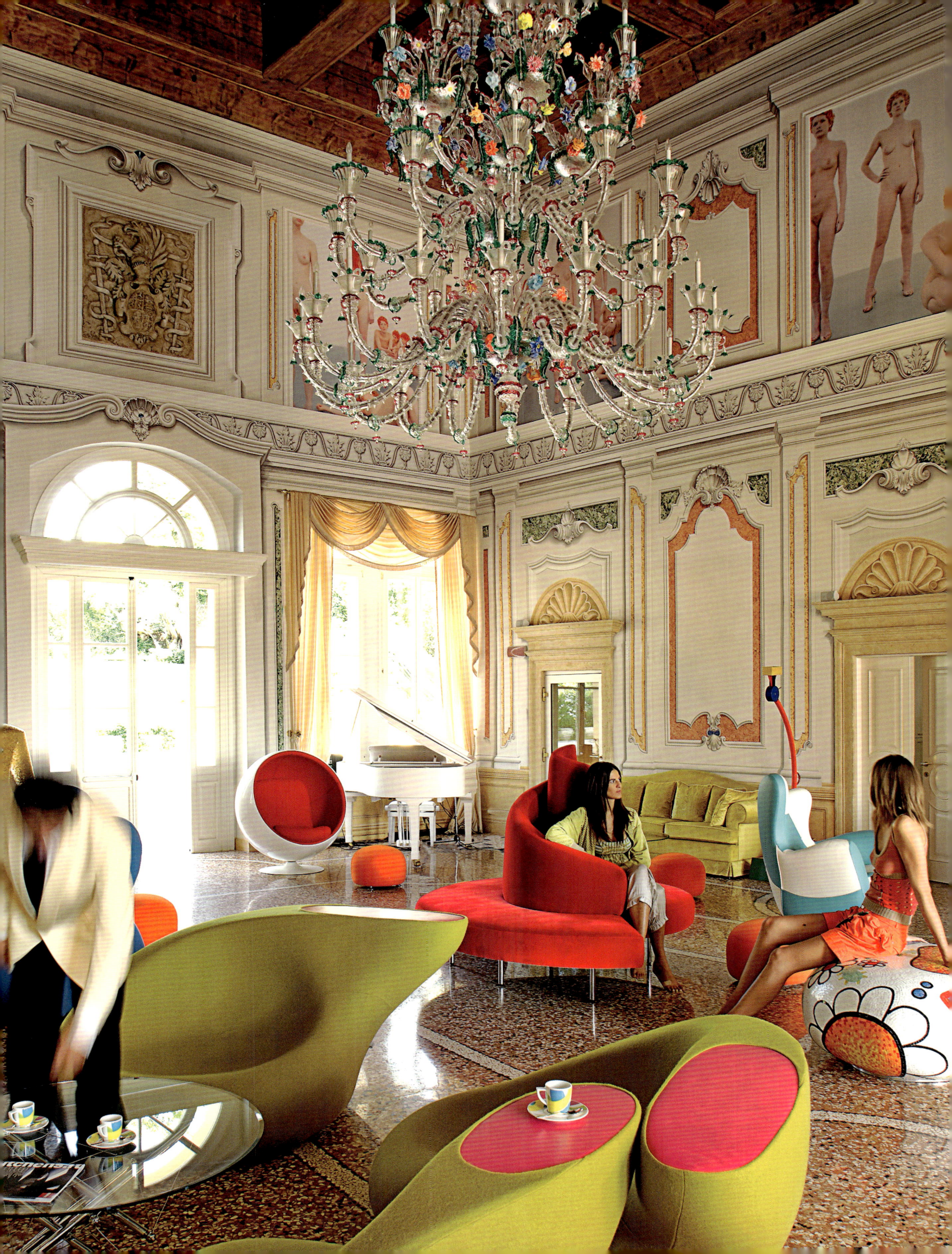

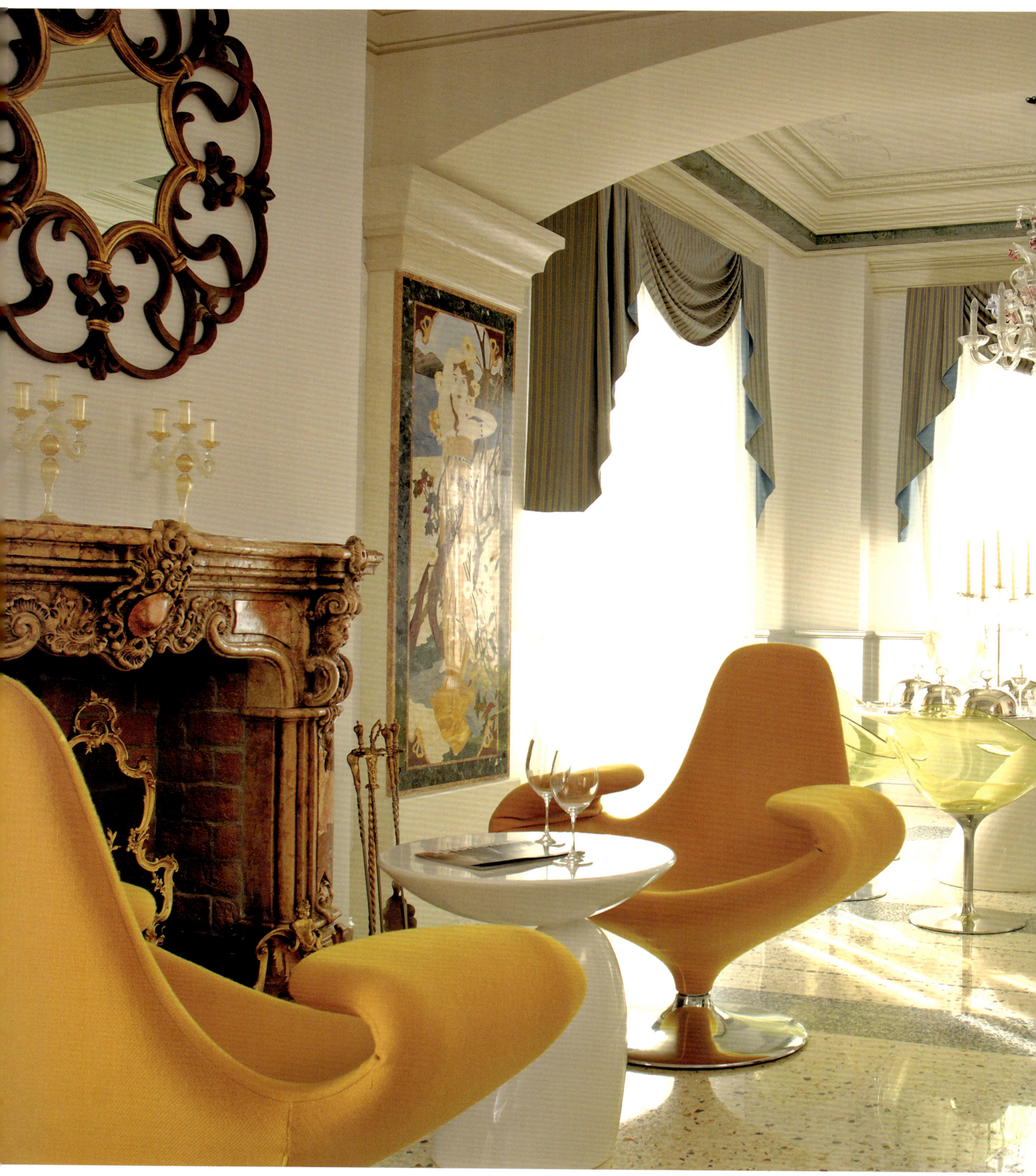

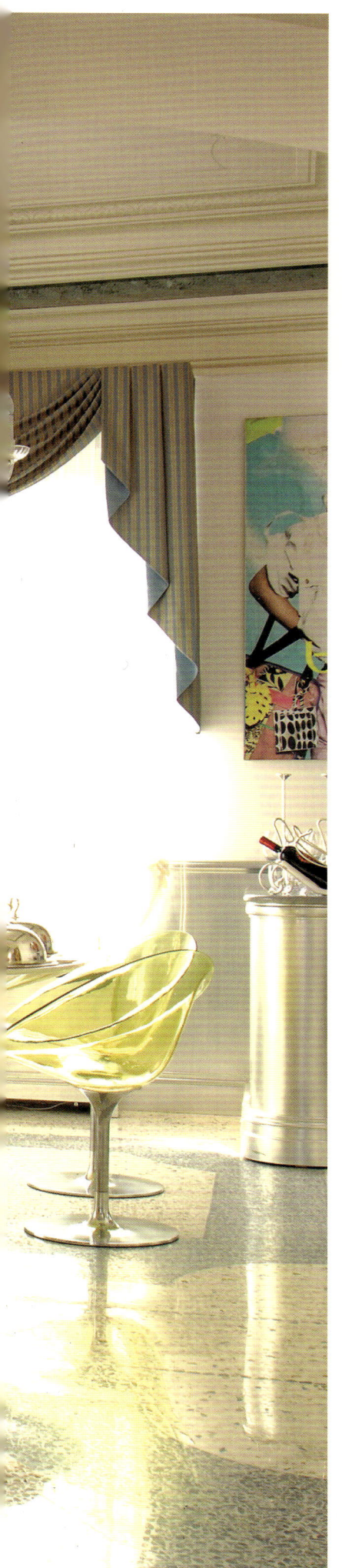

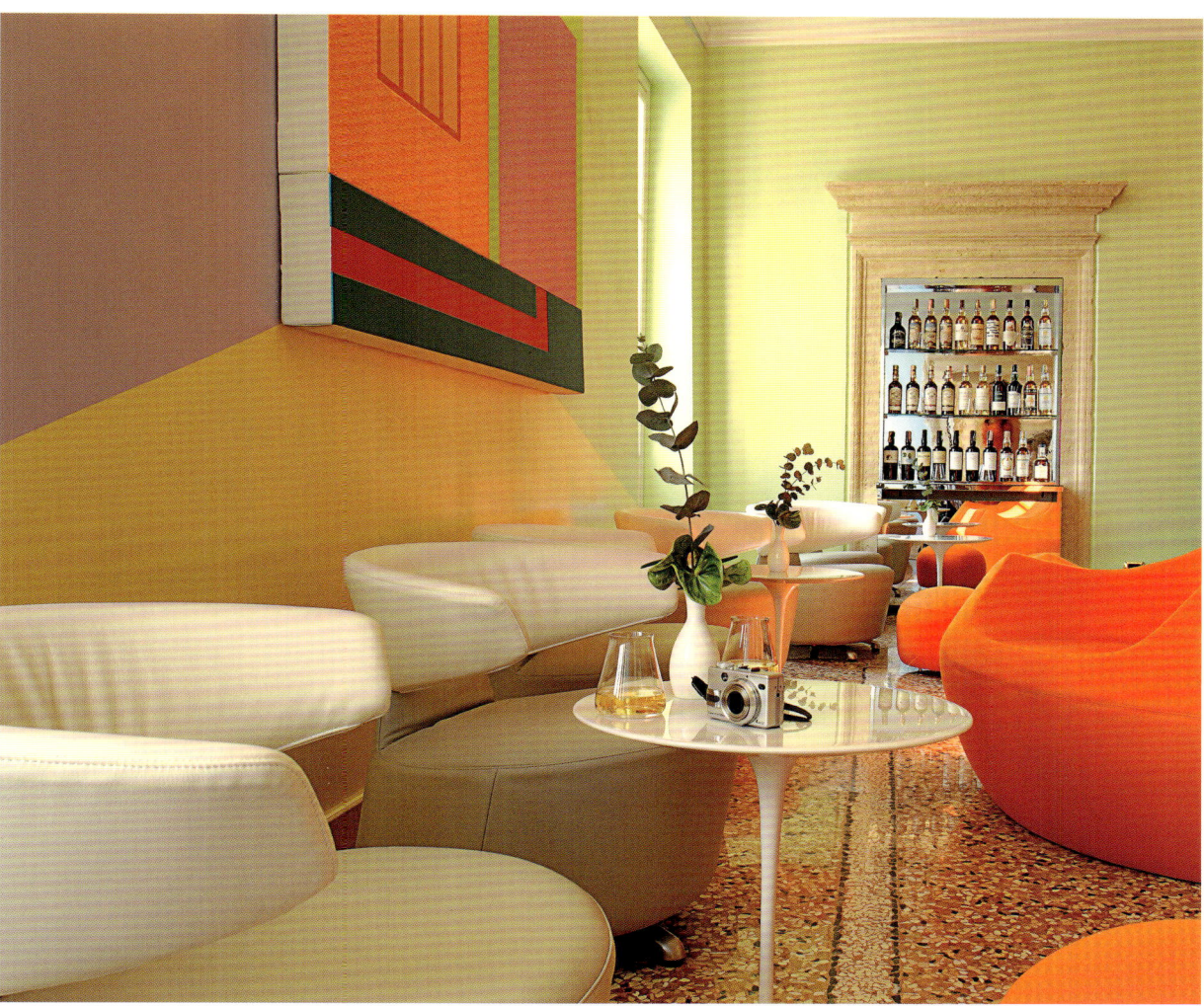

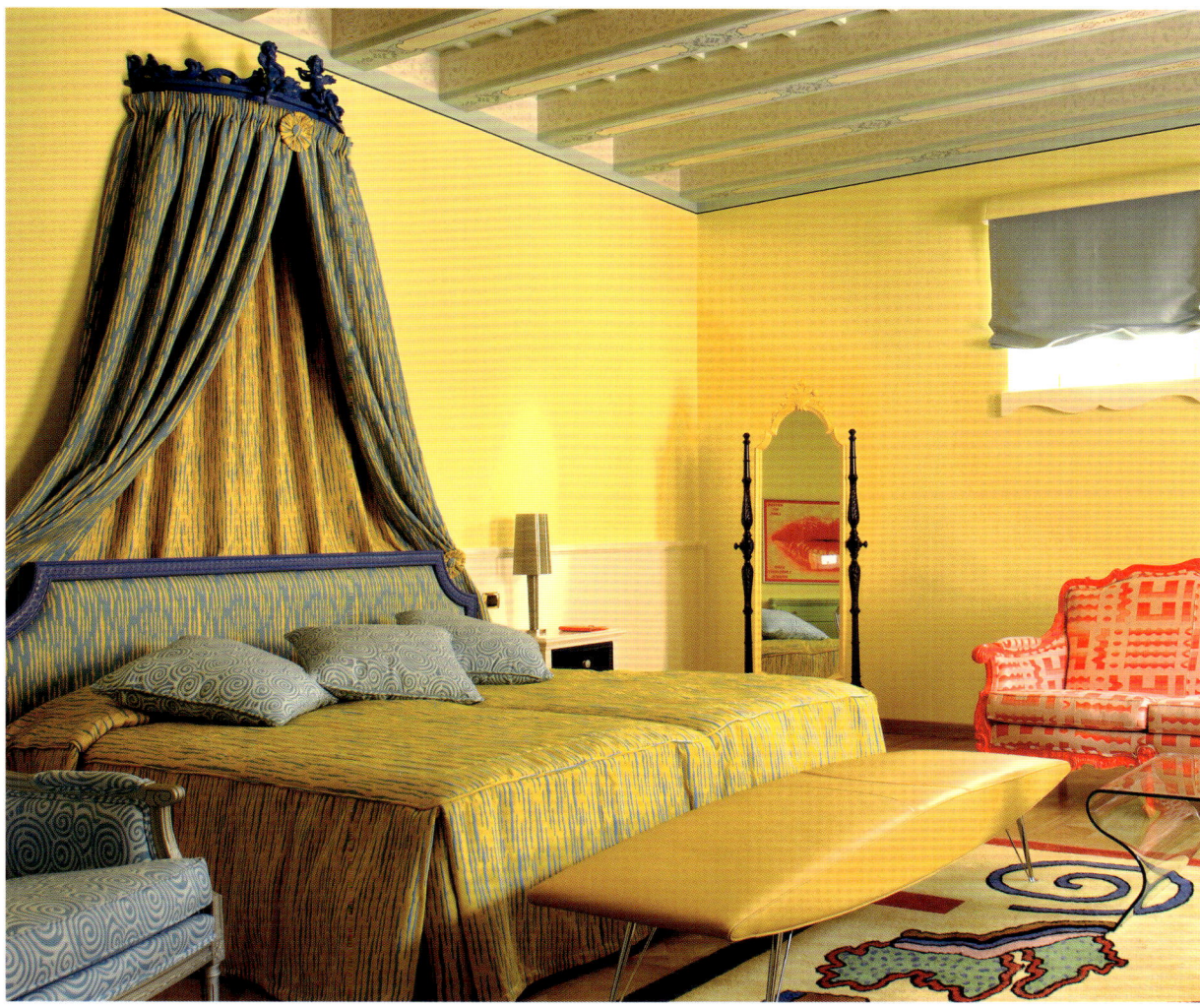

00185 Rome
Italy
Phone: +39 339 74 22 788
Fax: +39 06 23 32 45 562
www.casadellapalma.it

Rooms: 8 rooms and loft for 5 people
Facilities: Rooftop terrace, green inner courtyard
Services: Free city bikes, WiFi in all rooms
Located: In the San Lorenzo district
Public transportation: Tram Reti; bus Marrucini
Style: Romantic-industrial

Just take it easy and enjoy! Cruise around the alleys of the Eternal City on a scooter and stop for a chat with the barista at the café around the corner. The scooters reserved for guests of the Casa della Palma are available for you at any time to enjoy "La Dolce Vita." This recently renovated, citreous mansion in San Lorenzo, the university quarter of Rome, is surrounded by various inexpensive bistros and live music bars that are just waiting to be discovered. The rooms are equipped with new marble baths. During the hot Italian summer, the patio, lined with palm trees, is a refreshing oasis.

Das Leben leichter nehmen. Mit einem Scooter durch die Gassen der ewigen Stadt brausen und beim Barista an der Ecke Neuigkeiten austauschen. Der Gäste-Scooter im Casa della Palma ist startbereit, um La Dolce Vita zu genießen. Rund um die frisch renovierte zitronengelbe Villa in San Lorenzo, dem Universitätsviertel Roms, liegen zahlreiche preiswerte Bistros und Livemusik-Bars, die entdeckt werden wollen. Die Zimmer haben neue Marmorbäder. Eine erfrischende Oase im heißen italienischen Sommer ist der palmenbestandene Patio.

Vivre plus léger, foncer à travers les ruelles de la Ville éternelle avec le scooter et échanger des nouvelles avec le barista du coin. A l'hôtel Casa della Palma, le scooter spécial invités est prêt à partir. Direction la dolce vita. Tout autour de la villa jaune citron fraîchement rénovée, il y a de nombreux bistros et bars à musique live à découvrir sans dépenser trop d'argent, car nous sommes ici à San Lorenzo, dans le quartier universitaire de Rome. Les chambres sont équipées de salles de bains en marbre neuves. Enfin, l'oasis de fraîcheur que constituent le patio et ses palmiers, ne sera vraiment pas de trop durant le brûlant été italien.

Tomarse la vida un poco más a la ligera. Atravesar a gran velocidad sobre un ciclomotor las callejuelas de esta ciudad eterna y charlar con el camarero del café de la esquina. El scooter del hotel Casa della Palma siempre está a punto para dejar que los huéspedes disfruten con el de la dolce vita. En los alrededores del recién renovado palacio color limón en San Lorenzo, el barrio de la Universidad de Roma, hay una gran cantidad de bares asequibles y locales de música en vivo que esperan a ser descubiertos. Las habitaciones disponen de nuevos baños de mármol. El Patio de Palmeras es un verdadero oasis en el abrasador verano italiano.

Prendere la vita più alla leggera. Sfrecciare con uno scooter lungo le stradine della città eterna e scambiarsi le ultime novità con il barista del bar all'angolo. Gli scooter di Casa della Palma sono sempre pronti ad accompagnare gli ospiti nel pieno della dolce vita. Nei dintorni del recentemente rinnovato palazzo color limone di San Lorenzo, il quartiere universitario di Roma, si può fare sosta in numerosi bar economici e locali con musica dal vivo che non aspettano altro di essere scoperti. Le camere dispongono di nuovi bagni in marmo. E nella caldissima estate italiana, il patio pieno di palme è una vera e propria oasi rigenerante.

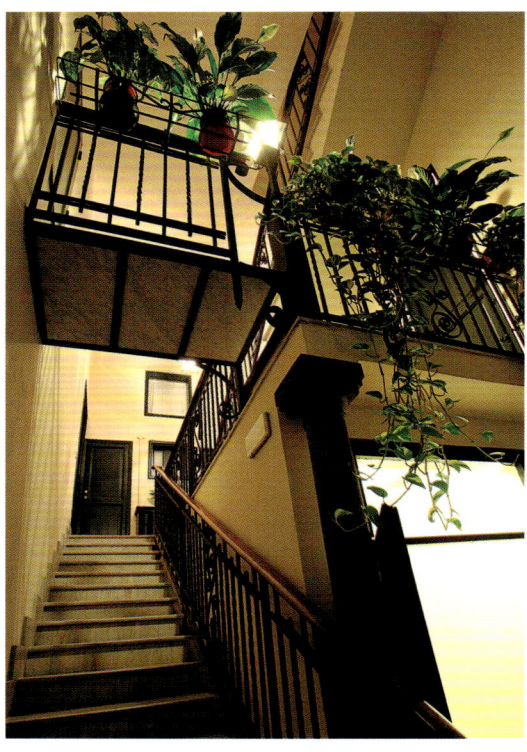
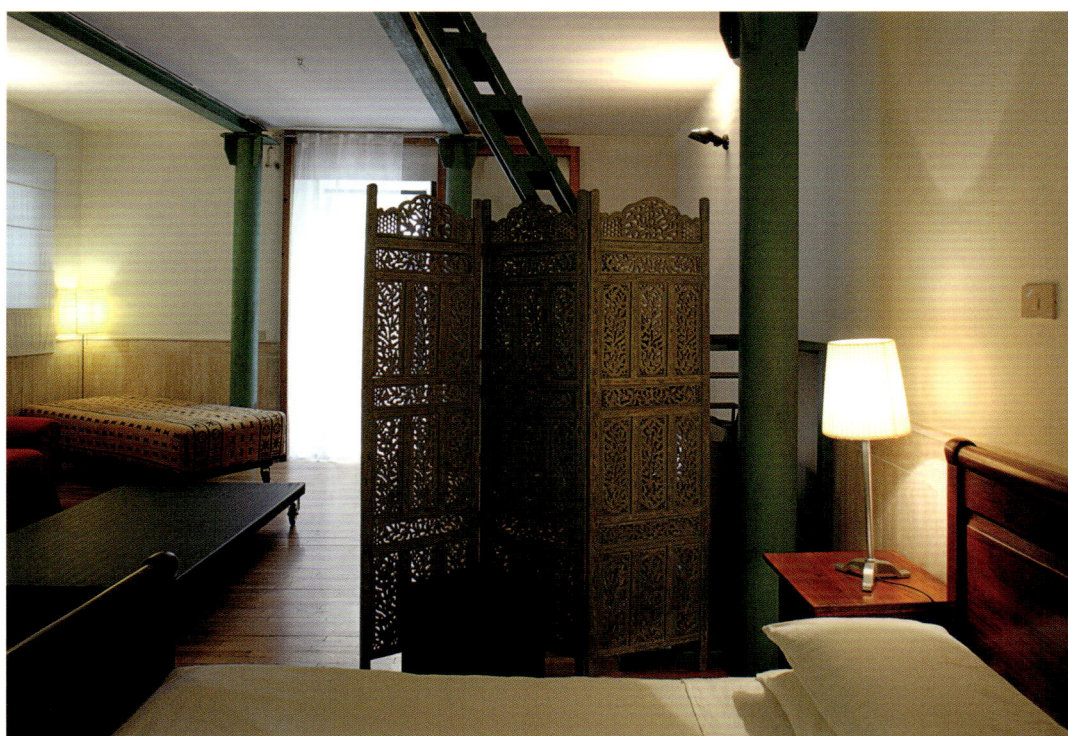

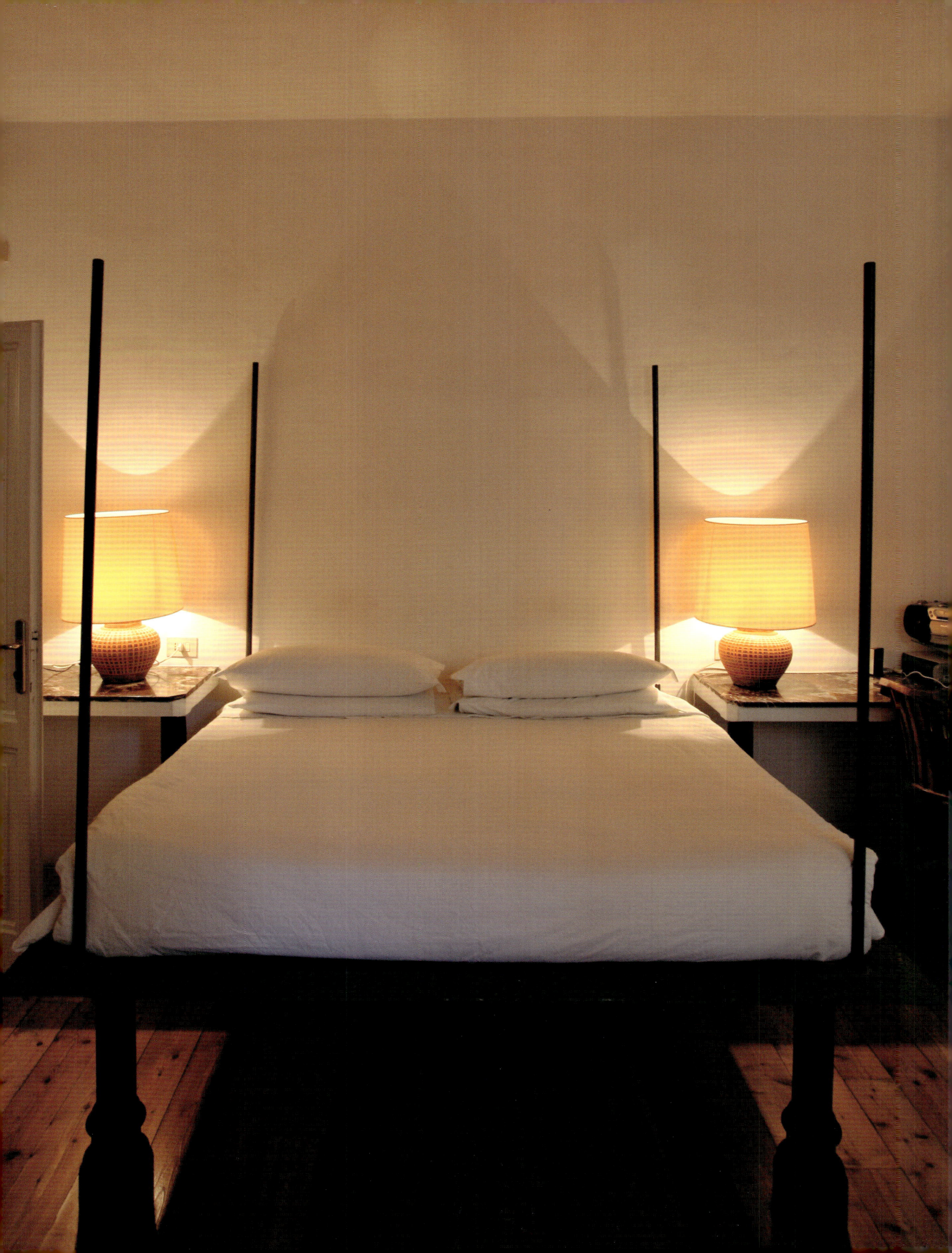

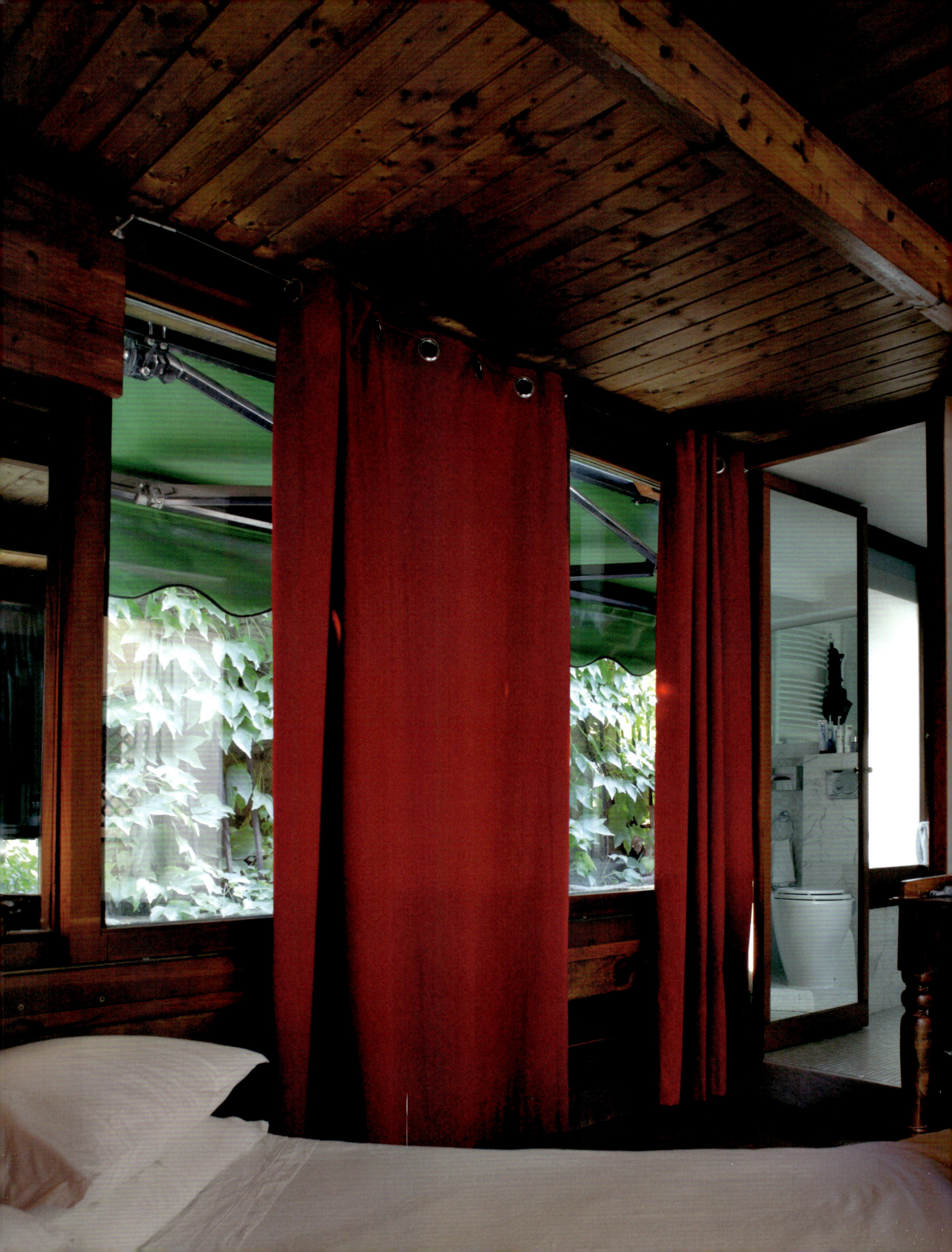

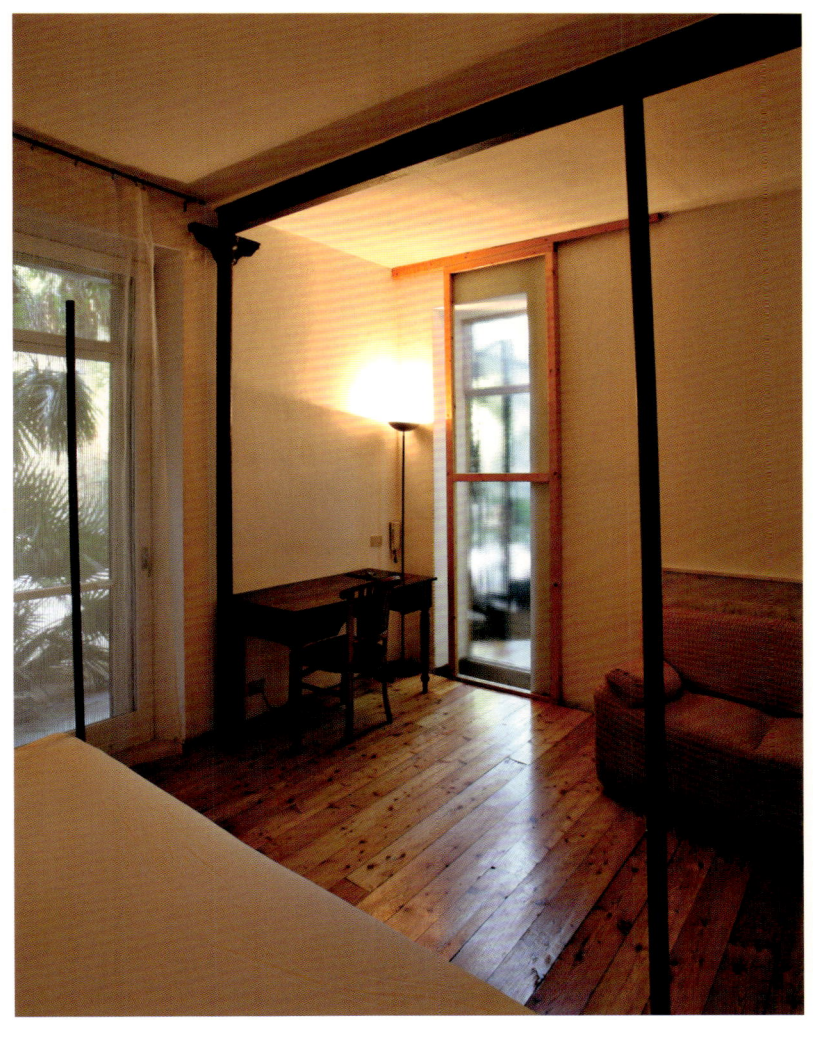
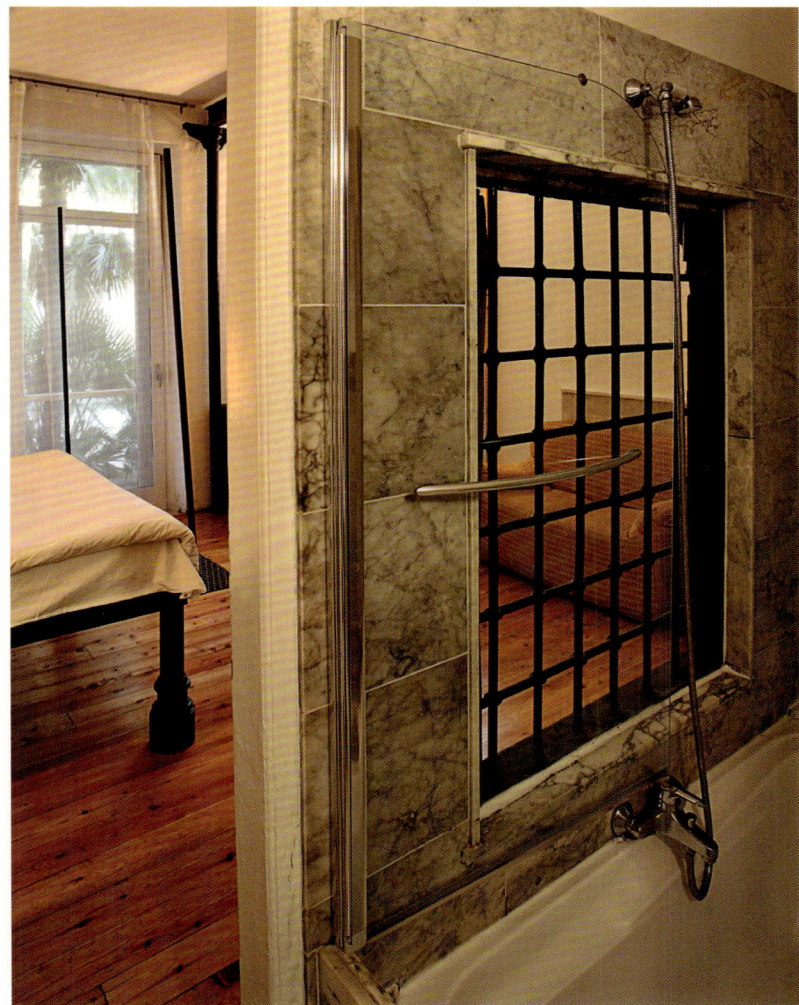
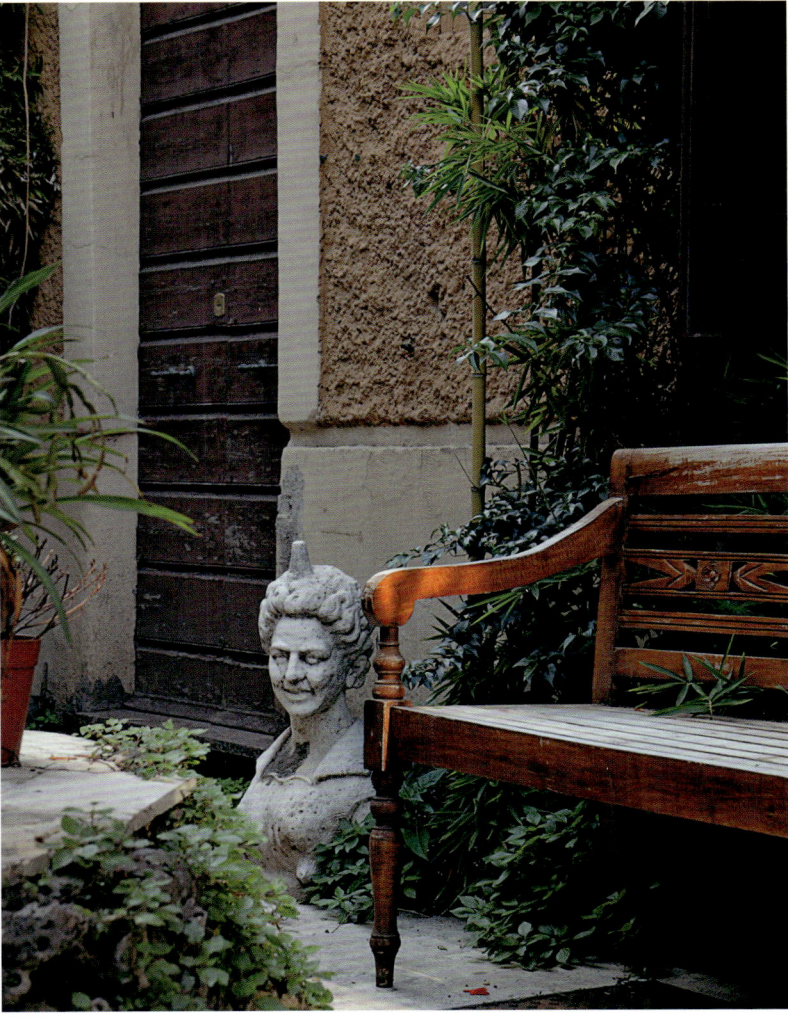
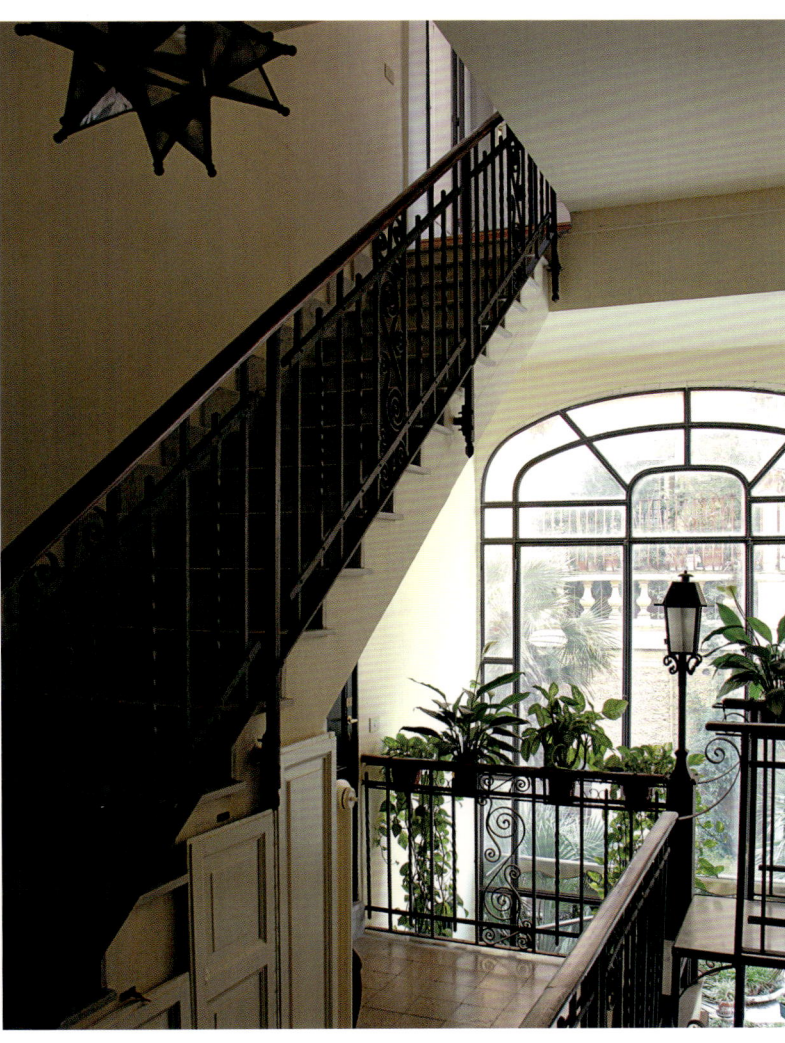

St George Roma

Rome, Italy

Via Giulia 62
00186 Rome
Italy
Phone: +39 06 68 66 11
Fax: +39 06 68 66 12 30
www.stgeorgehotel.it

Price category: €€€
Rooms: 64 rooms
Facilities: Restaurant I Sofà di Via Giulia, Terrazza Rosé roof terrace, wine bar, spa with Jacuzzi, sauna, personalized treatments and gym, library
Services: WiFi, concierge service, limousine service, butler on request
Located: In the historical center of Rome
Public transportation: Electric bus 116 Via Giulia
Style: Contemporary design

The St George Roma is to be found in Via Giulia, surrounded by craftsmen's workshops, antique dealers and historical mansions. This prestigious building was built five centuries ago by Donato Bramante to house the law courts. Today, architect Lorenzo Bellini has breathed new life into this monumental project, taking inspiration from the work of the Scandinavian designers Arne Jacobsen and Alvar Aalto. Now minimal chic, soft lighting and warm sand tones give the property a contemporary air. The roof terrace is home to Europe's first bar to be dedicated exclusively to prestigious rosé wines.

In der Via Gulia, gesäumt von Antiquitätenhändlern, Manufakturen und alten Palazzi, liegt das gediegene St George Roma. Der herrschaftliche Bau wurde vor über 500 Jahren von dem Architekturgenie Donato Bramante als Gericht konzipiert. Nun wagte sich der Architekt Lorenzo Bellini an das Mammutprojekt. Inspiriert haben ihn dabei vor allem die zwei skandinavischen Designer Arne Jacobsen und Alvar Aalto. Nun dominieren Minimal Chic, sanftes Licht und warme Sandtöne das Hotel. Auf dem Dach liegt Europas erste Bar, in der ausschließlich Rosé-Weine gereicht werden.

Le St George Roma est situé sur la Via Giulia, bordée de boutiques d'antiquaires, de manufactures et de vieux palazzi. Ce bâtiment a été construit il y a plus de 500 ans comme palais de justice par le génie de l'architecture Donato Bramante. De nos jours, c'est l'architecte Lorenzo Bellini qui a osé se lancer dans ce projet monumental. Il a été particulièrement inspiré par deux designers scandinaves, Arne Jacobsen et Alvar Aalto. Minimalisme, lumières douces et tons sable règnent à présent sur l'hôtel. Au-dessus du toit se trouve le premier bar d'Europe qui serve exclusivement du vin rosé.

Situado en la calle Via Gulia y rodeado de tiendas de antigüedades, manufacturas y palacios antiguos se encuentra el hotel St George Roma. Hace más de 500 años, el genio arquitectónico Donato Bramante concibió este ilustre edificio como corte tribunal. Ahora, el arquitecto Lorenzo Bellini se ha puesto al frente de este titánico proyecto. Inspirado sobre todo en los diseñadores escandinavos Arne Jacobsen y Alvar Aalto, el estilo minimalista, de luces tenues y matices color arena domina hoy este conjunto. En su azotea se encuentra el primer bar en toda Europa donde únicamente se sirve una exclusiva selección de vinos rosados.

In Via Giulia, circondato da botteghe di artigiani, negozi di antiquariato e palazzi storici, si trova il St George Roma. Il prestigioso edificio fu costruito più di cinque secoli fa come tribunale progettato dal geniale Donato Bramante. Oggi l'architetto Lorenzo Bellini ha ridato soffio vitale a questo monumentale progetto ispirandosi soprattutto a due designer scandinavi Arne Jacobsen e Alvar Aalto. Adesso nell'hotel suites dominano fascino minimalista, giochi di luce e calde tonalità color sabbia. All'ultimo piano si trova il primo bar d'Europa che propone esclusive degustazioni di selezionate etichette di vini rosé.

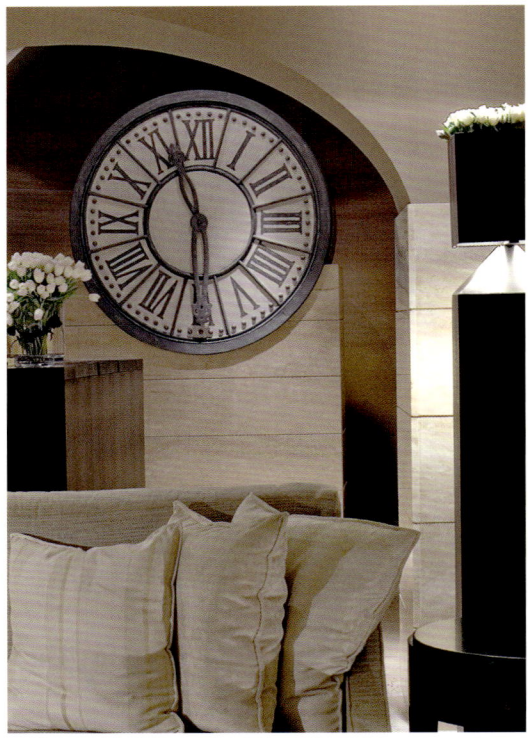
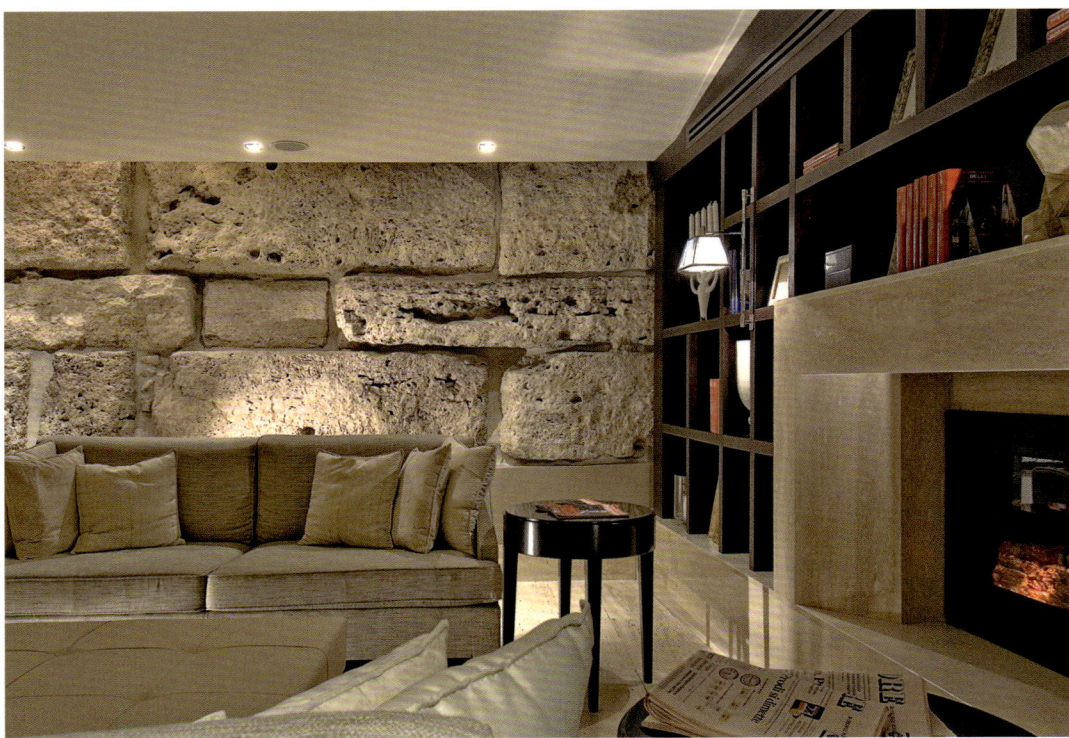

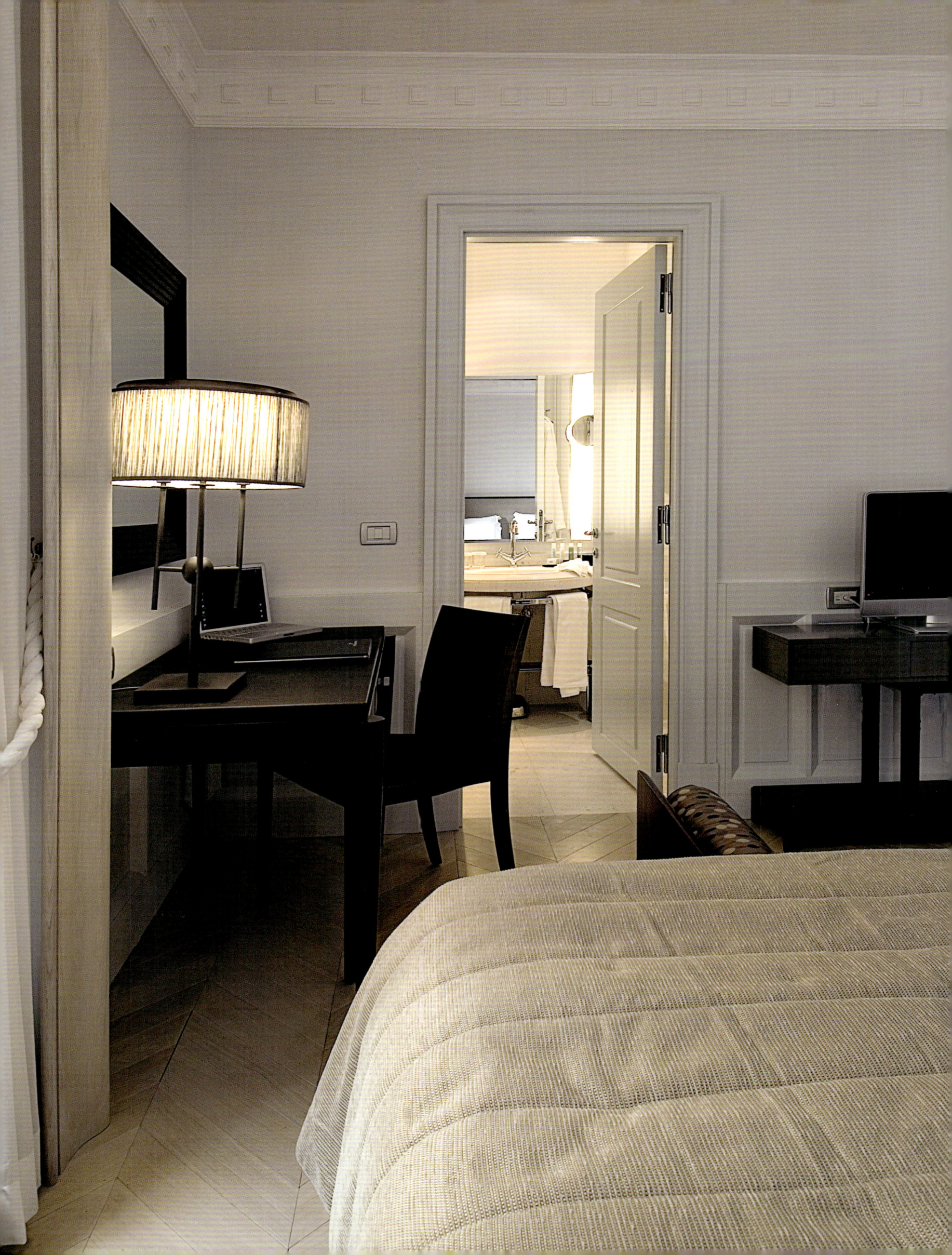

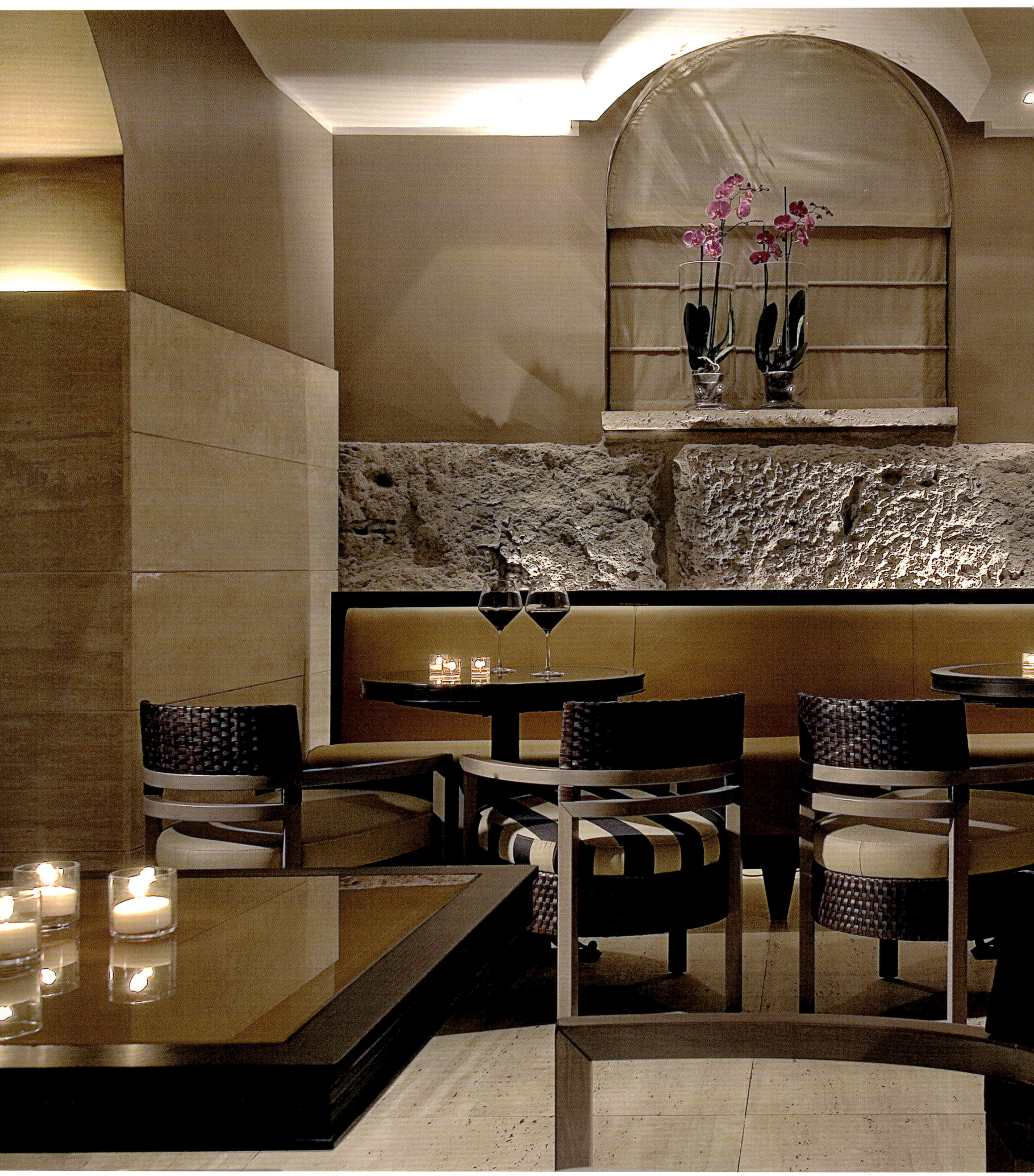

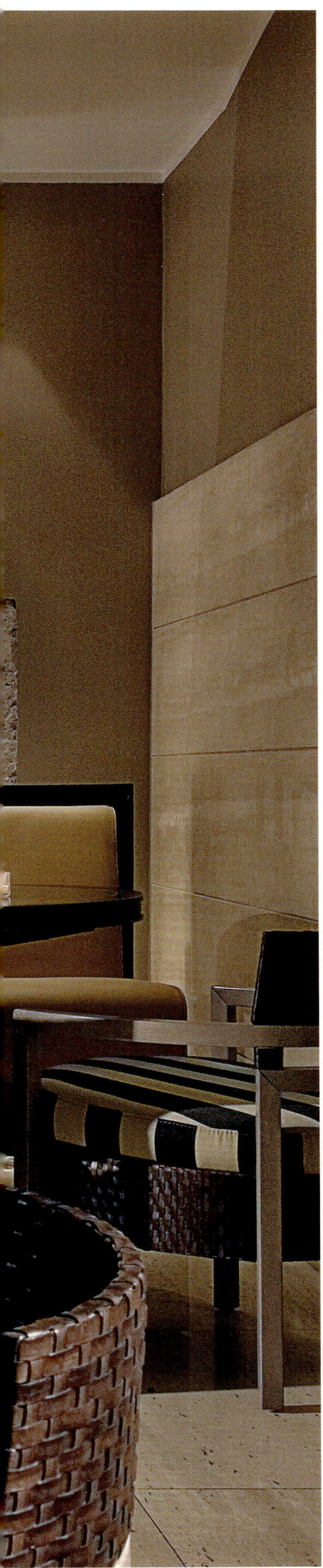

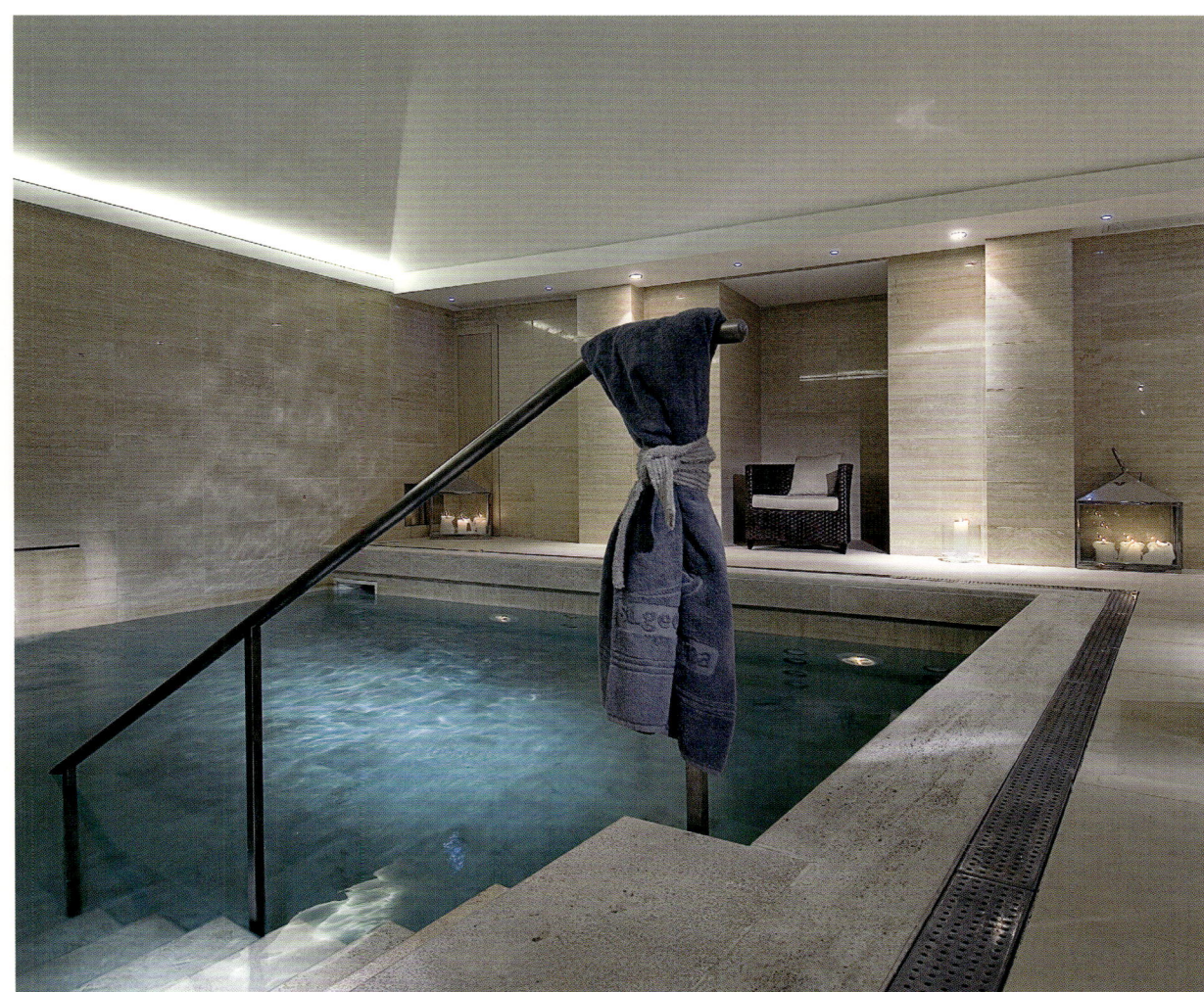

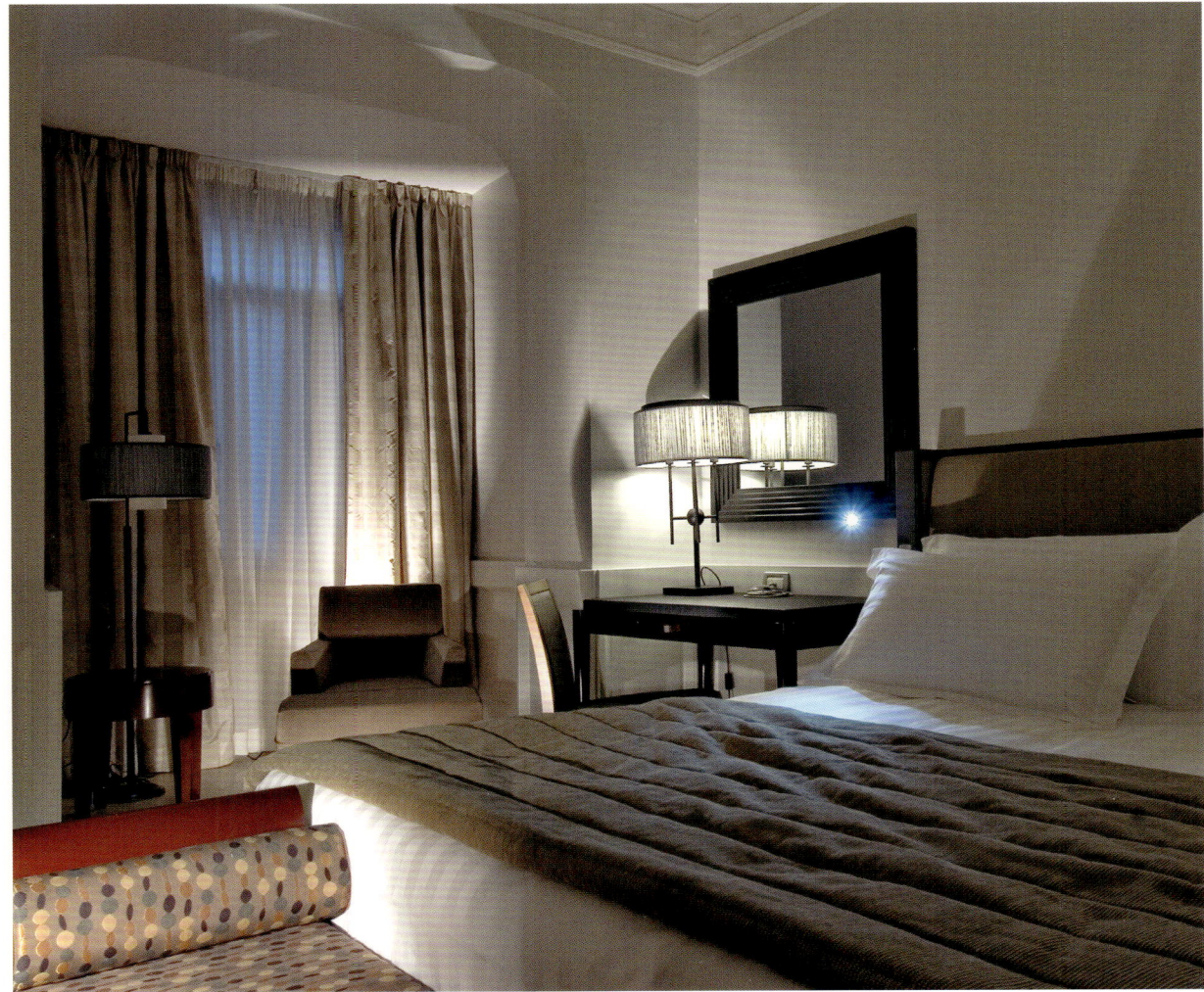

07012 Palma de Mallorca
Spain
Phone: +34 971 72 59 43
Fax: +34 971 72 59 46
www.hmjaimeiii.com

Rooms: 86 rooms and 2 junior suites
Facilities: Bar, restaurant, meeting rooms, spa
Services: Concierge, laundry, WiFi, room service
Located: In the center of Palma
Public transportation: Bus 11 Paseo Mallorca
Style: Avant-garde

From the sculpture "diving" through the lobby to the neon art announcing "to die for" in the stairwell: Hotel hm jaime III is dedicated to contemporary art with a library with exhibition catalogs even keeps the guests up to date on the international art scene. The 88 rooms were renovated in 2004 and even thought of three- and four-bed rooms for families and friends in the process. Anyone with sore feet after shopping can relax in the spa that is just as stylish and artful as the hotel.

Von der Skulptur, die durch die Luft der Lobby „taucht", bis zur Neon-Art, die im Treppenhaus „to die for" verkündet: Das Hotel hm jaime III hat sich der zeitgenössischen Kunst verschrieben – eine Bibliothek mit Ausstellungskatalogen hält die Gäste sogar über die internationale Szene auf dem Laufenden. Die 88 Zimmer wurden 2004 renoviert und man hat dabei auch an Drei- und Vierbett-Räume für Familien und Freunde gedacht. Wer nach dem Shoppen in Palmas Boutiquen müde Füße hat, entspannt im Spa, das ebenso stil- und kunstvoll gestaltet ist wie das Hotel.

Le ton est donné dès l'entrée et sa sculpture qui « plonge » à travers la réception, ou les œuvres d'art au néon dans l'escalier, « à mourir » : l'Hotel hm jaime III se consacre à l'art contemporain. Une bibliothèque de catalogues d'exposition informe les clients des nouveautés de la scène artistique internationale. Les 88 chambres ont été rénovées en 2004, et l'hôtel a été doté des chambres à trois et quatre lits pour accueillir les familles et les groupes d'amis. Si vos pieds sont fatigués après une virées shopping dans les boutiques de Palma, vous pouvez vous détendre au spa, aussi élégant et artistique que l'hôtel.

Desde la escultura que "bucea" en el aire del vestíbulo hasta el cartel de neón que proclama "to die for" sobre las escaleras, el Hotel hm jaime III muestra un claro compromiso con el arte contemporáneo. Su biblioteca de catálogos de exposiciones mantiene a los huéspedes al tanto sobre la escena internacional. Entre las 88 habitaciones reformadas en 2004 también se cuentan estancias de tres y cuatro camas para familias y grupos de amigos. El huésped que llegue cansado de sus compras por las tiendas de Palma podrá relajarse en el spa, donde prepondera el mismo estilo elegante y artístico presente en todo el hotel.

Dalla scultura che "nuota" nell'aria della lobby alla neon-art della scala che preannuncia ambienti irresistibilmente belli, "to die for", l'Hotel hm jaime III si è consacrato all'arte contemporanea – una biblioteca con cataloghi di mostre tiene aggiornati gli ospiti persino sul piano internazionale. Le 88 camere, rinnovate nel 2004, comprendono ora anche alcune stanze con tre o quattro letti pensate per famiglie e gruppi di amici. Se dopo aver fatto shopping nelle boutique di Palma sentite i piedi stanchi, potete andare a rilassarvi allo spa, realizzato con stile e arte tanto quanto l'hotel.

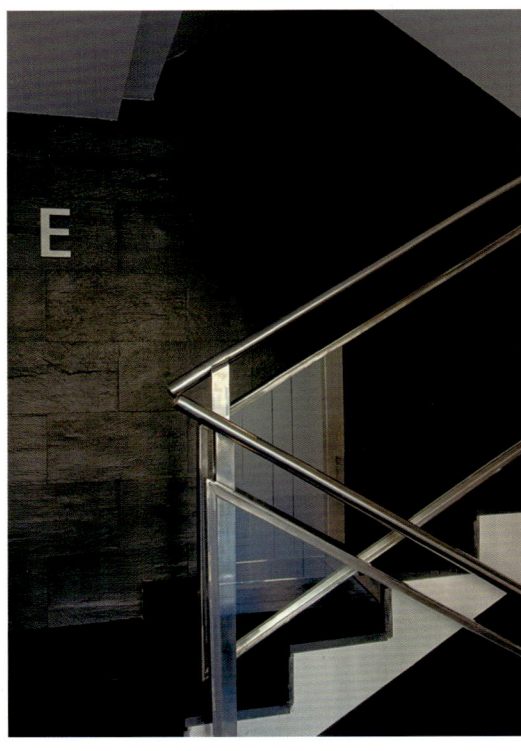
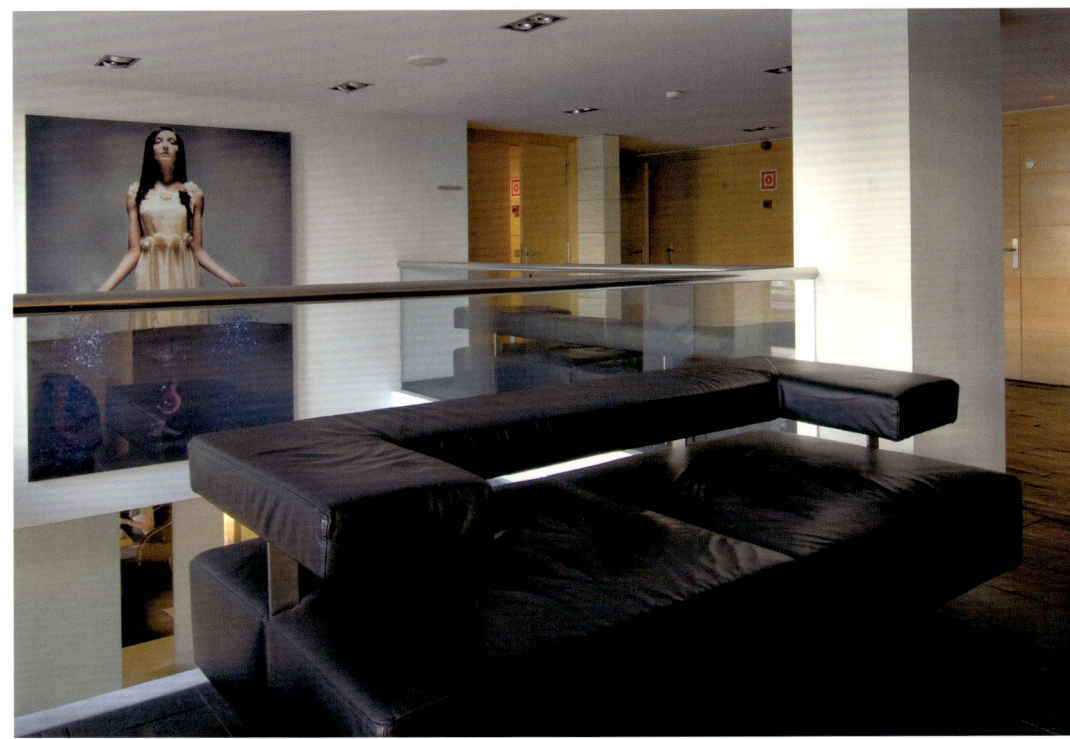

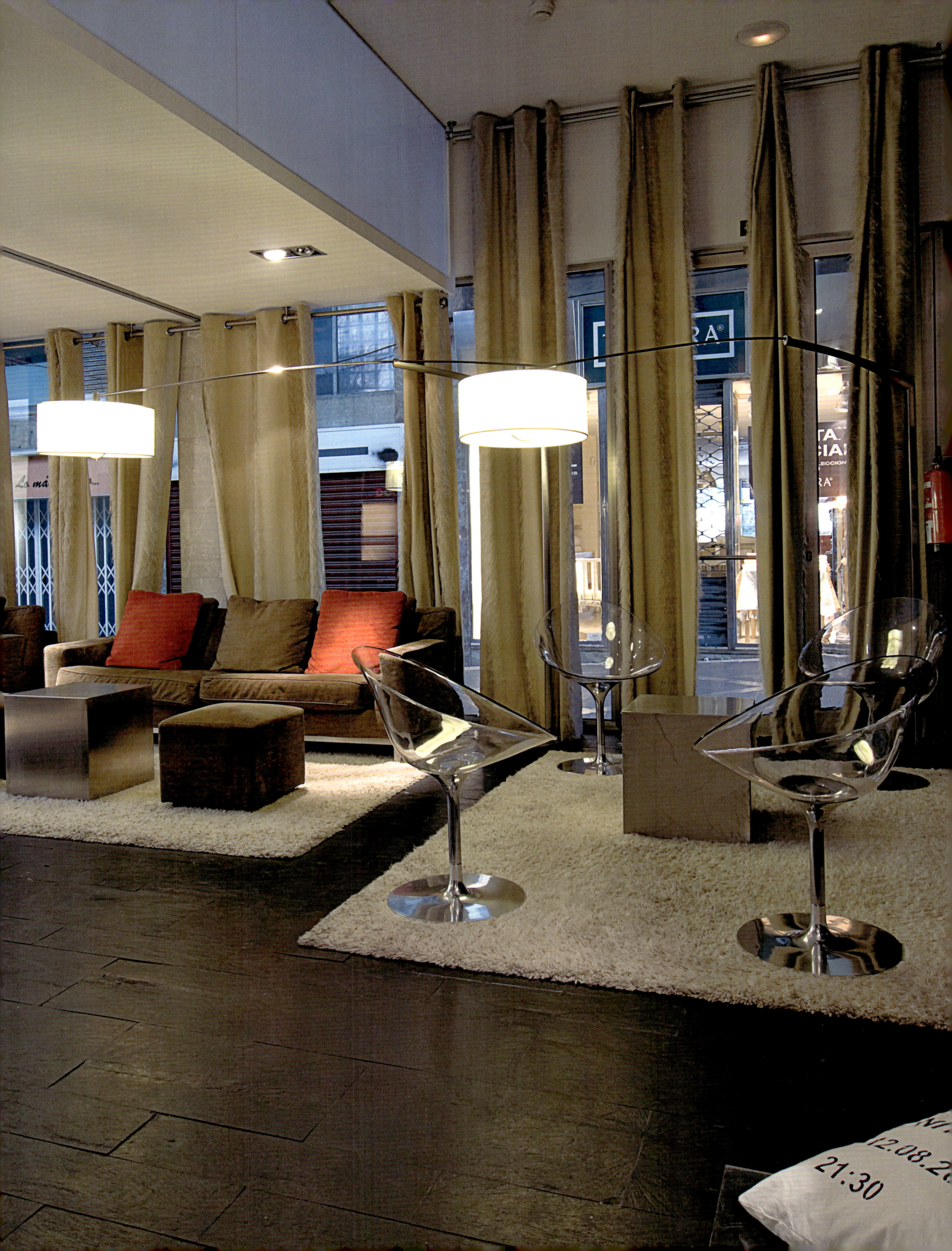

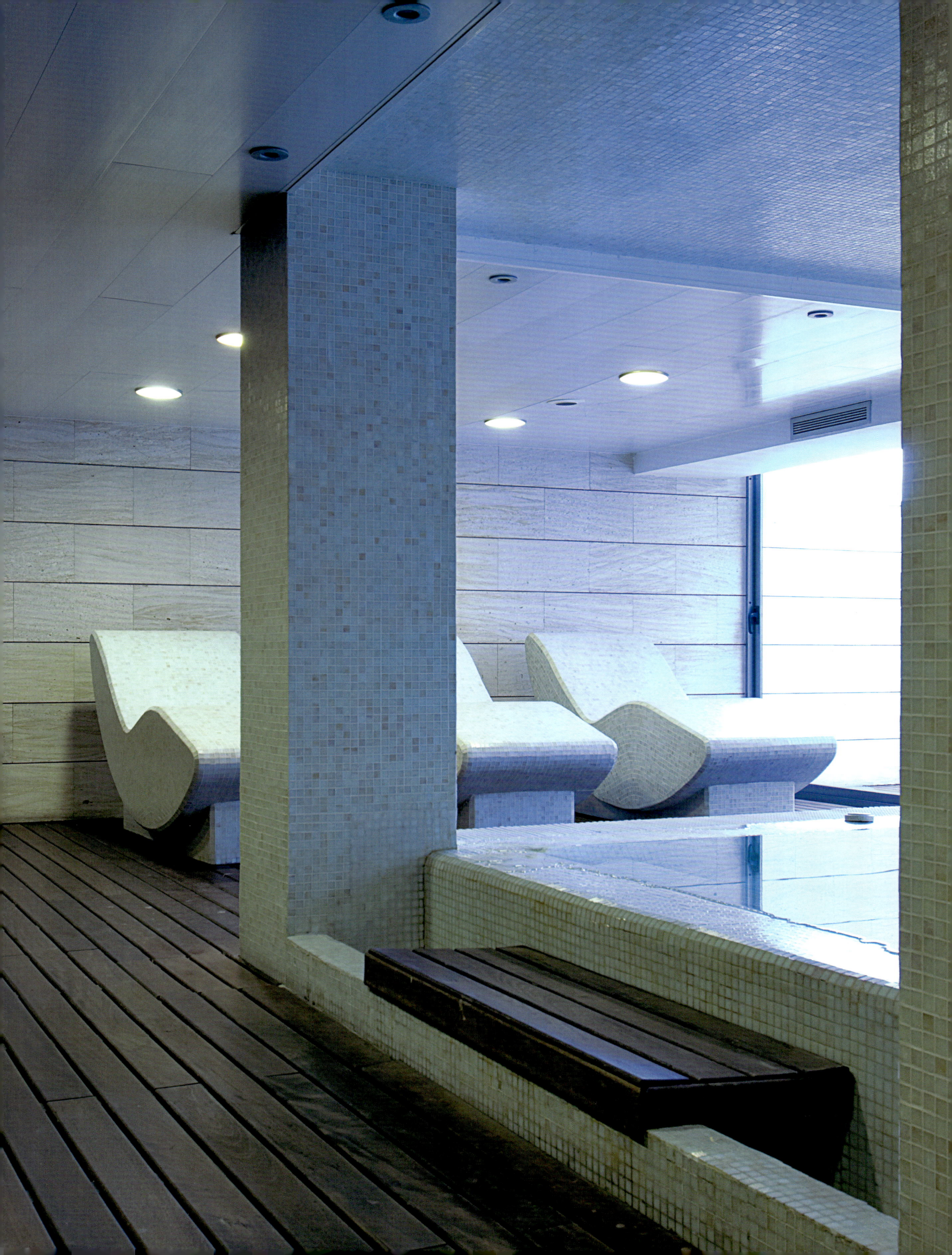

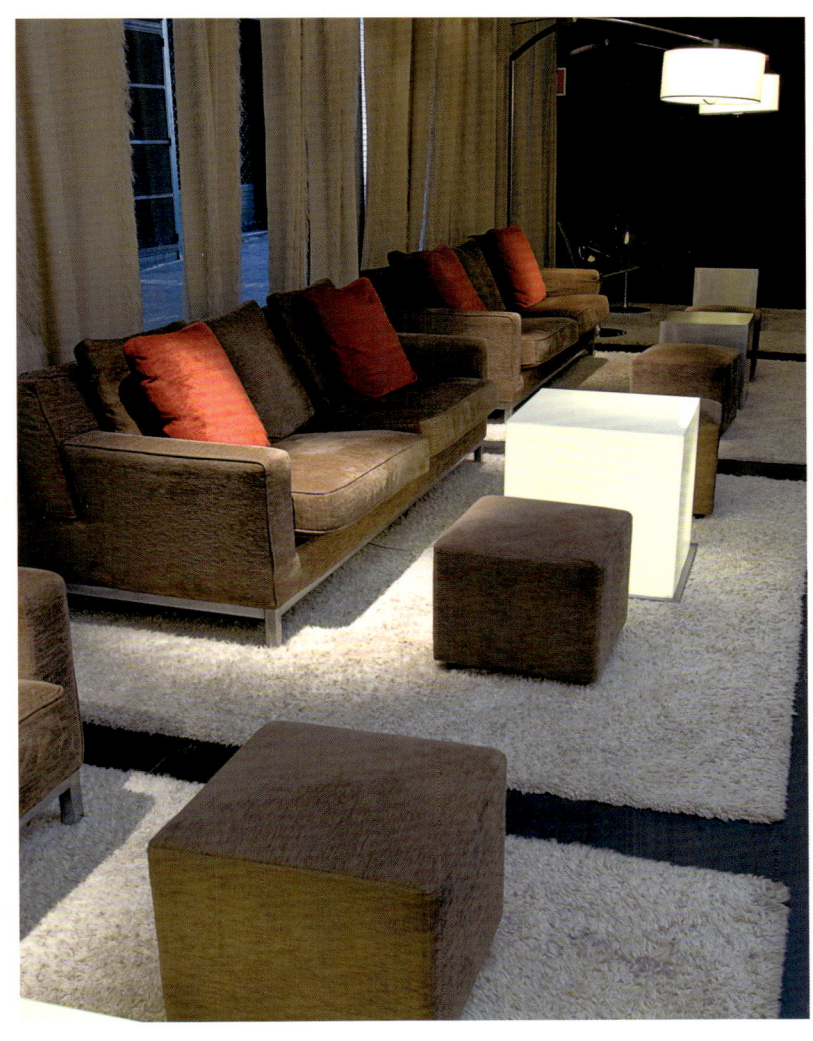
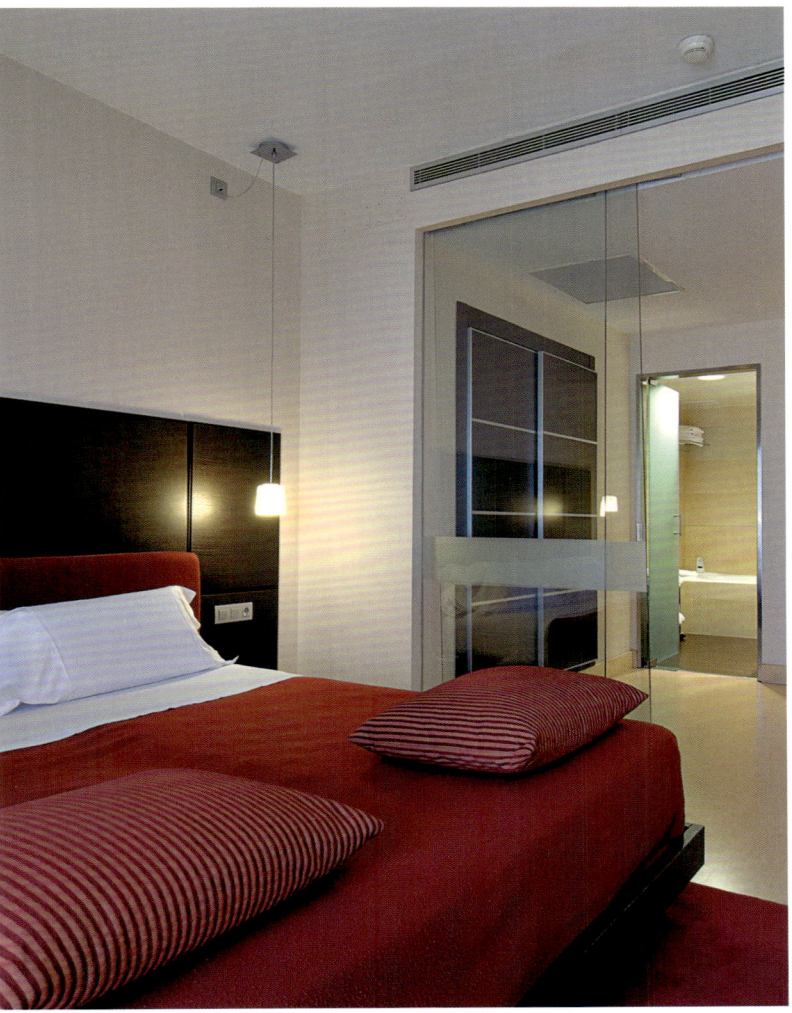
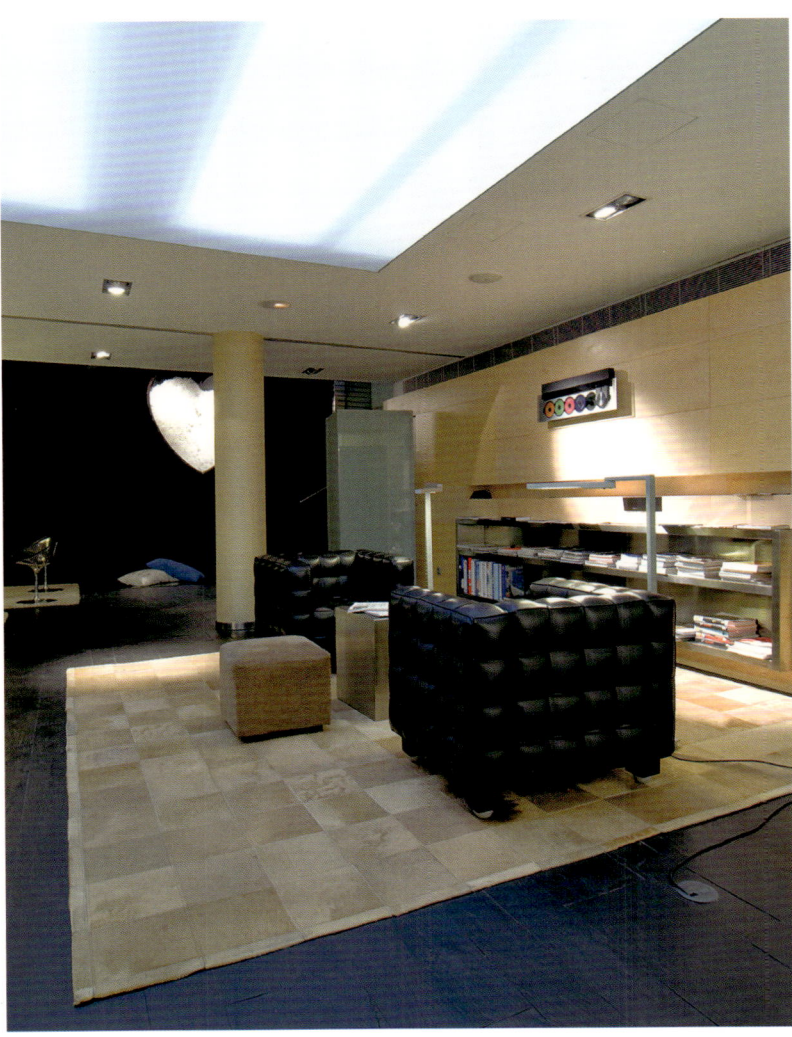
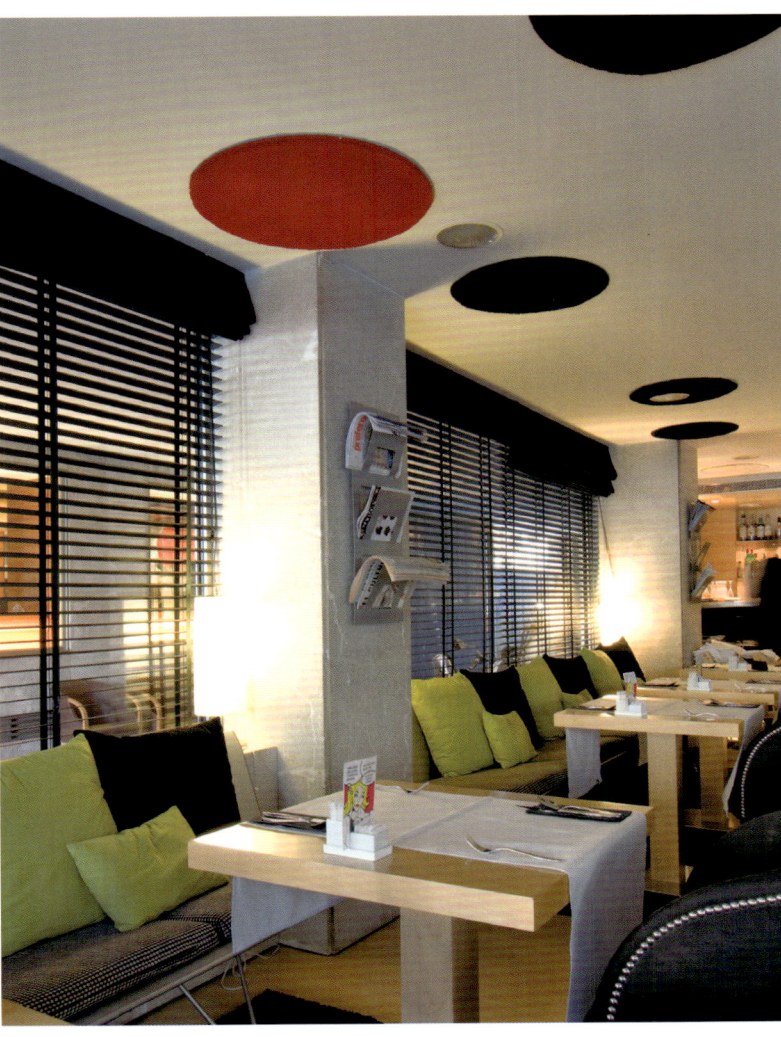

07012 Palma de Mallorca
Spain
Phone: +34 971 717 333
Fax: +34 971 717 372
www.hoteltres.com

Rooms: 38 rooms and 3 suites
Facilities: Bar/bistro, library, courtyard, conference room, roof terrace, plunge pool, sauna
Services: Room service
Located: In the old part of Palma, close to La Lonja
Public transportation: Bus 15 Plaza de la Reina
Style: Contemporary

On the roof terrace you almost forget you are in the midst of the hustle and bustle of Palma—up here Majorca's capital shows its most picturesque side. Anyone not wanting to share the rooftop pool with other guests ought to book the biggest suite with its own veranda and private jacuzzi. All 41 rooms of the Tres are quite modern in marble, glass and steel. The rustic style of the island is brought into play by the 16th-century palace that has been carefully restored. The perfect place for the evening: the patio where a palm tree reaches up into the sky like in a picture book.

Auf der Dachterrasse vergisst man fast, mitten im Trubel Palmas zu sein – von hier oben zeigt Mallorcas Hauptstadt ihre pittoreske Seite. Wer den Rooftop-Pool nicht mit anderen Gästen teilen möchte, sollte die größte Suite mit eigener Veranda und Privat-Jacuzzi buchen. Alle 41 Zimmer des Tres geben sich mit Marmor, Glas und Stahl modern – den rustikalen Stil der Insel bringt das Palais aus dem 16. Jahrhundert ins Spiel, das sorgsam restauriert wurde. Perfekter Platz für den Abend: der Patio, in dem eine Bilderbuchpalme in den Himmel ragt.

Sur la terrasse du toit, on oublie presque qu'on est au milieu de la turbulente Palma : d'ici la capitale de Majorque montre son aspect le plus pittoresque. Ceux qui ne veulent pas partager la piscine de toit avec les autres clients devront louer la plus grande suite avec sa propre véranda et son jacuzzi privé. Chacune des 41 chambres de l'hôtel Tres est plutôt moderne, avec du marbre, du verre et de l'acier : le style rustique de l'île interagit avec ce palais du XVIème siècle soigneusement rénové. Lieu parfait pour passer la soirée : le patio, dans lequel un palmier impressionnant semble toucher le ciel.

En su azotea, uno casi olvida que se encuentra en medio de la bulliciosa ciudad de Palma. Desde la altura de esta terraza, la capital de Mallorca muestra su lado más pintoresco. Aquel que no quiera compartir la piscina de la azotea puede también alquilar la suite mayor con terraza y jacuzzi propias. Cada una de las 41 habitaciones del hotel Tres presenta un estilo moderno marcado por el uso del mármol, del cristal y del acero. El palacio del siglo XVI, cuidadosamente restaurado, asimila el aire rústico de la isla. Su patio, con una palmera de película que se levanta hacia el cielo, es sin duda el lugar idóneo para la velada perfecta.

Sulla terrazza del tetto quasi ci si dimentica di essere nel cuore della confusione di Palma. Da lassù il capoluogo dell'Isola di Maiorca mostra il lato più pittoresco della sua essenza. Se non volete condividere con altri ospiti la piscina sul tetto, dovreste prenotare la suite più grande dotata di veranda e jacuzzi privata. Tutte le 41 camere hanno un aspetto moderno, suggerito da marmo, vetro e acciaio. Il cinquecentesco palazzo meticolosamente restaurato in cui è ospitato l'albergo denota invece uno stile rustico. Il patio, con una palma da cartolina che svetta verso il cielo, è il posto ideale in cui trascorrere la serata.

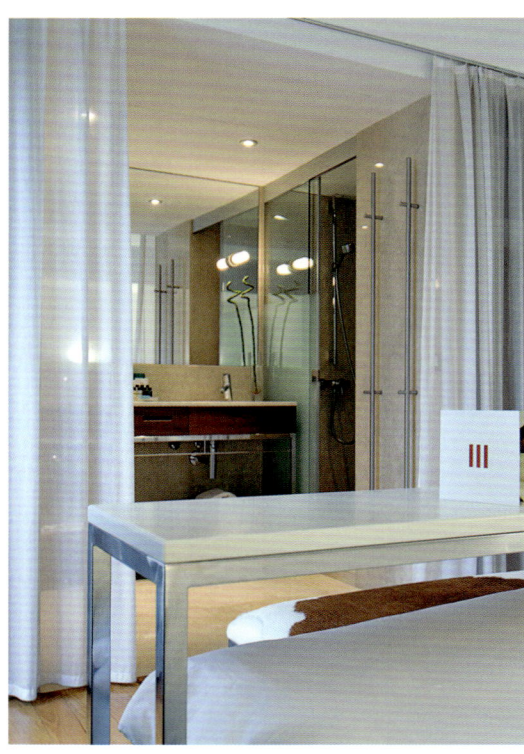
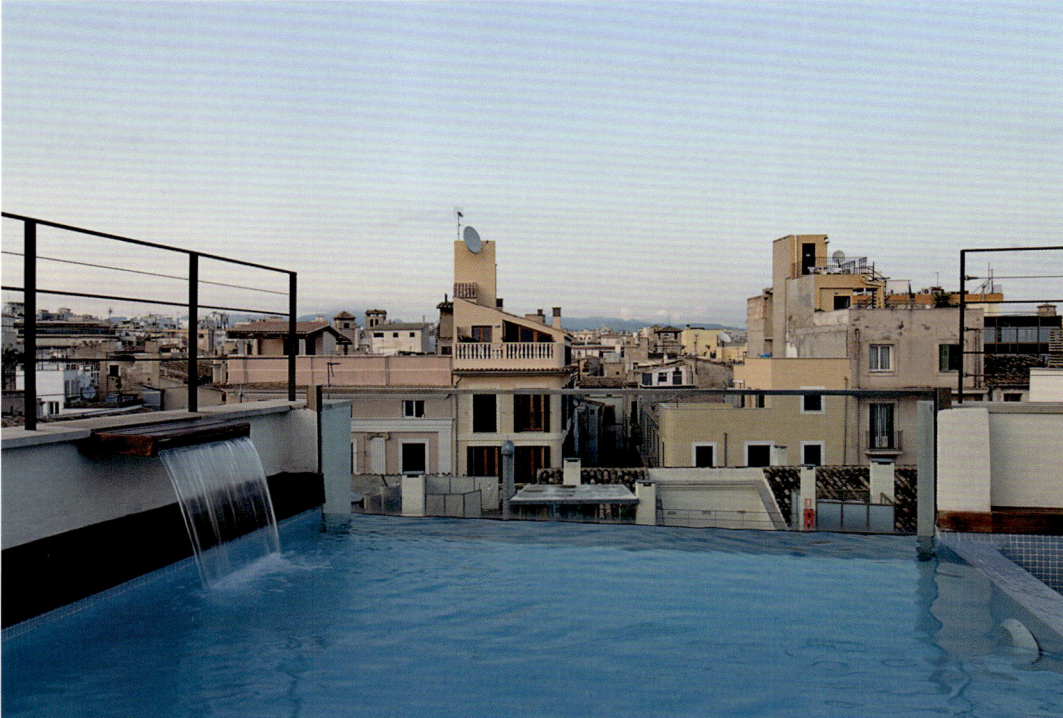

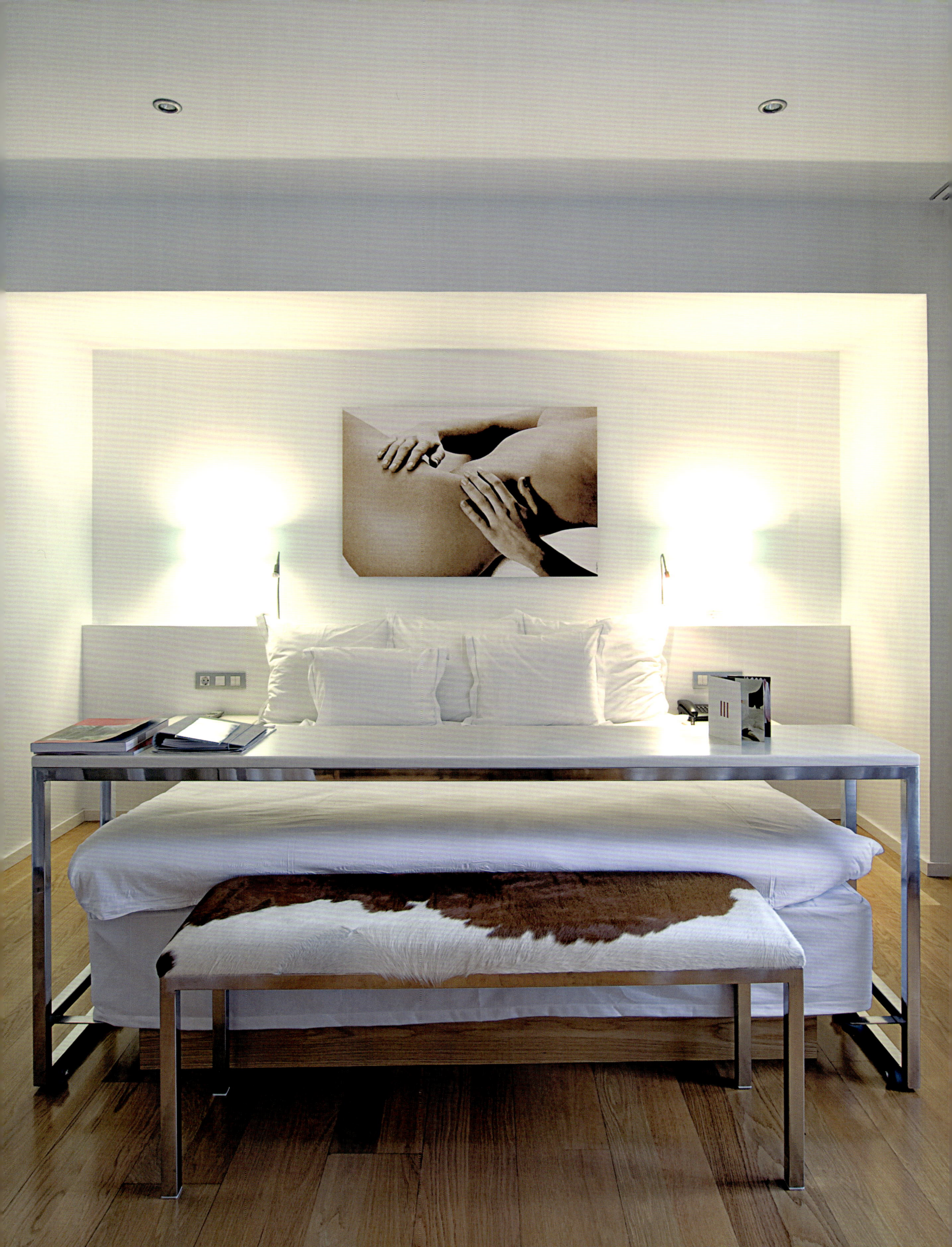

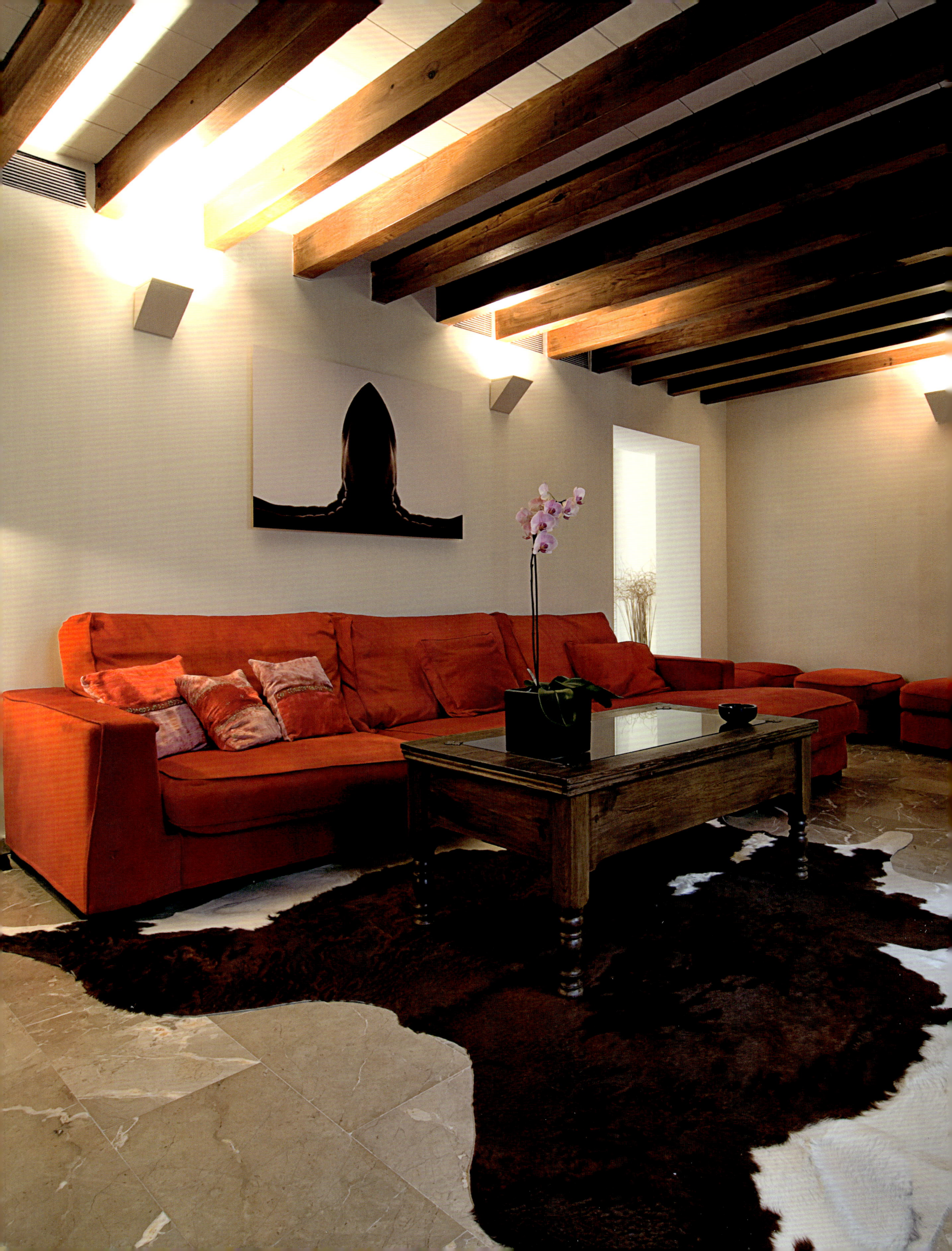

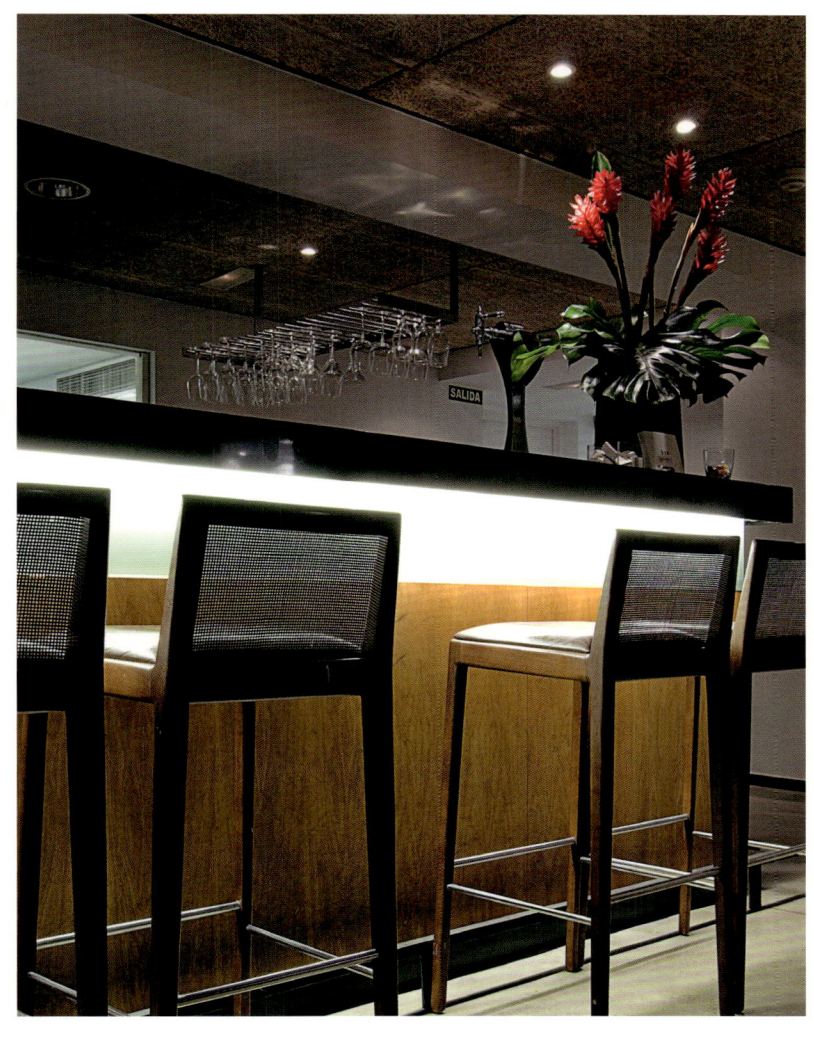
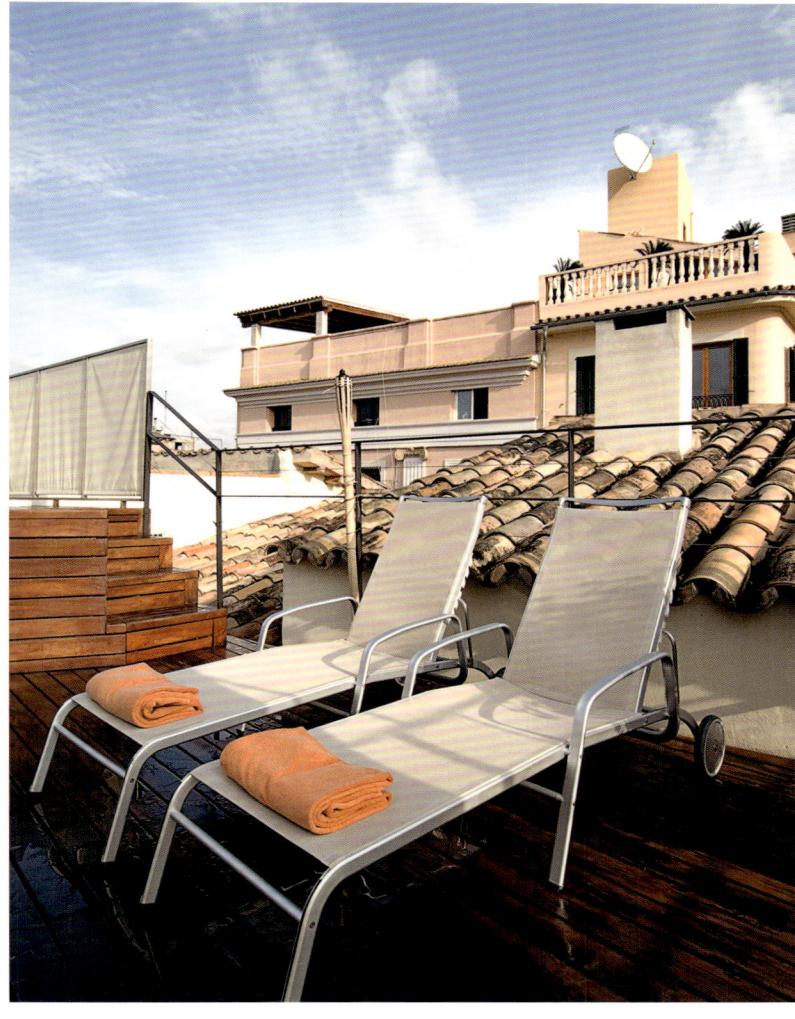
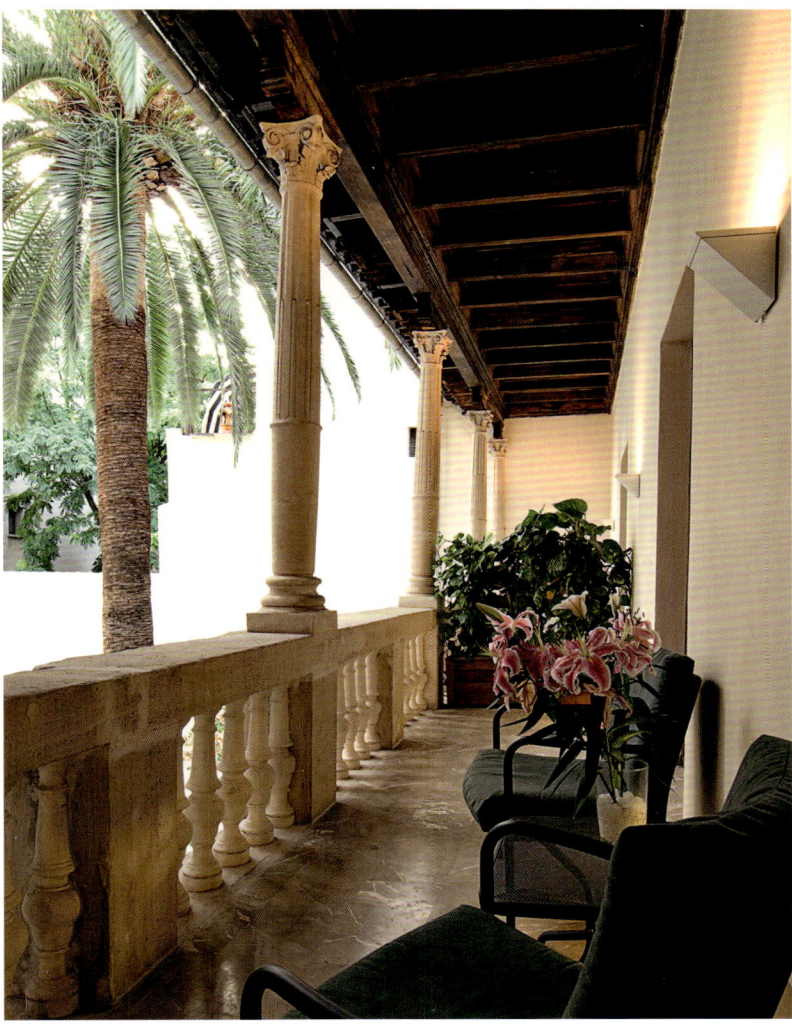
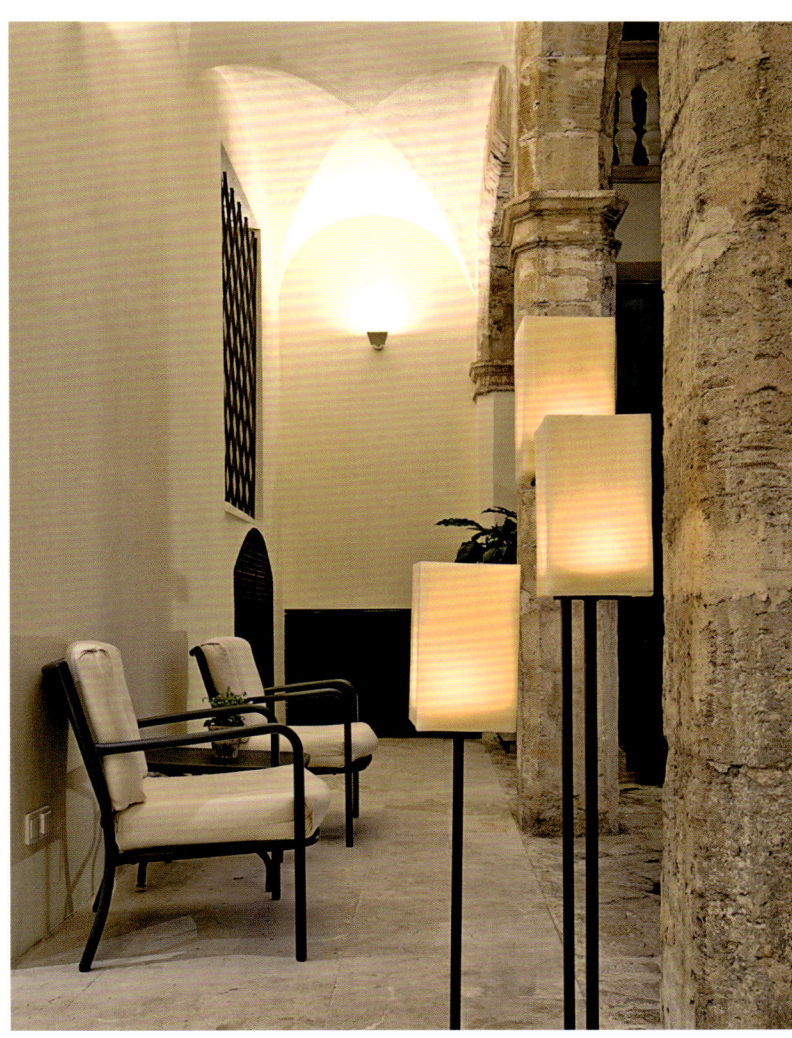

08037 Barcelona
Spain
Phone: +34 934 763 396
Fax: +34 934 763 394
www.987barcelonahotel.com

Rooms: 88 rooms
Facilities: 987 Lounge, restaurant
Services: Babysitting, room service, massage, free WiFi
Located: In the city center next to Paseo de Gracia and La Pedrera
Public transportation: Metro L3, L5 Diagonal, Metro L4 Verdaguer; bus, train RENFE Paseo de Gracia
Style: Design

Behind the ornate facades with bay windows, columns and balconies you would expect a traditional house, but the 987 Barcelona Hotel, which opened in the spring of 2007 is part of the city's avant-garde section. Its 88 rooms are furnished with dark wood lusciously accented in kiwi green, lemon yellow and azure blue, the bar is illuminated in pink, and the restaurant is extended by the wall-high photos. The modern design has not forgotten the building's history in any way—ornate plasterwork and antique mirrors adorn the walls and ceilings of especially majestic rooms.

Hinter der mit Erkern, Säulen und Balkonen verzierten Fassade hätte man eher ein traditionelles Haus vermutet – doch das im Frühjahr 2007 eröffnete 987 Barcelona Hotel zählt zur Avantgarde-Fraktion der Stadt. Seine 88 Zimmer sind mit dunklen Möbeln sowie Akzenten in Kiwigrün, Zitronengelb und Himmelblau gestaltet, die Bar ist in Pink illuminiert, und das Restaurant zieren raumhohe Fotos. Das moderne Design hat die Geschichte des Gebäudes aber nicht vergessen. Stuck und antike Spiegel schmücken in den besonders schönen Räumen Decken und Wände.

Sa façade décorée avec ses colonnes, ses baies vitrées et ses balcons peut faire penser à une maison traditionnelle. Cependant, le 987 Barcelona Hotel, qui a ouvert au printemps 2007, est considéré comme appartenant à l'avant-garde de la ville. Ses 88 chambres ont un mobilier sombre savoureusement agrémenté de notes vert kiwi, jaune citron et bleu ciel, le bar est éclairé en rose et le restaurant comporte d'immenses photos. Le design moderne n'a pour autant pas oublié d'intégrer l'histoire du bâtiment : les murs et les plafonds des chambres majestueuses sont ornés de stuc et de miroirs anciens.

Detrás de su fachada adornada con ventanas saledizas, columnas y balcones, uno esperaría encontrar una casa de estilo tradicional, pero el 987 Barcelona Hotel pertenece sin duda a la fracción más vanguardista de la ciudad. Sus 88 habitaciones están decoradas con muebles de madera oscura y toques de verde kivi, amarillo limón y azul celeste. El bar está iluminado en tonos fucsia y las paredes del restaurante se encuentran cubiertas por enormes fotografías que llegan hasta el techo. No obstante, el diseño moderno de este establecimiento no prescinde de la historia del edificio que lo alberga. Así, los techos y paredes de sus suntuosas estancias lucen molduras de estuco y espejos antiguos.

Dietro una facciata ornata da bovindi, colonne e balconi ci si sarebbe aspettati un ambiente in stile tradizionale – invece il 987 Barcelona Hotel, inaugurato nella primavera del 2007, fa parte del gruppo avanguardista della città. Le sue 88 camere sono arredate con mobili scuri e decorate nelle tonalità del verde kiwi, del giallo limone e dell'azzurro, il bar sfoggia un'illuminazione fucsia, e il ristorante è abbellito da foto alte quanto le pareti. Tuttavia, il design moderno non ha sacrificato la storia dell'edificio – soffitti e pareti delle sale più belle sono infatti ornati da stucchi e specchi antichi.

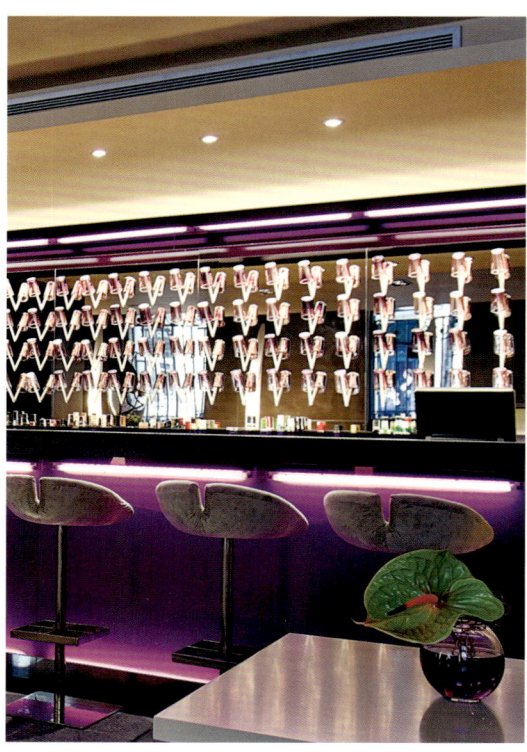
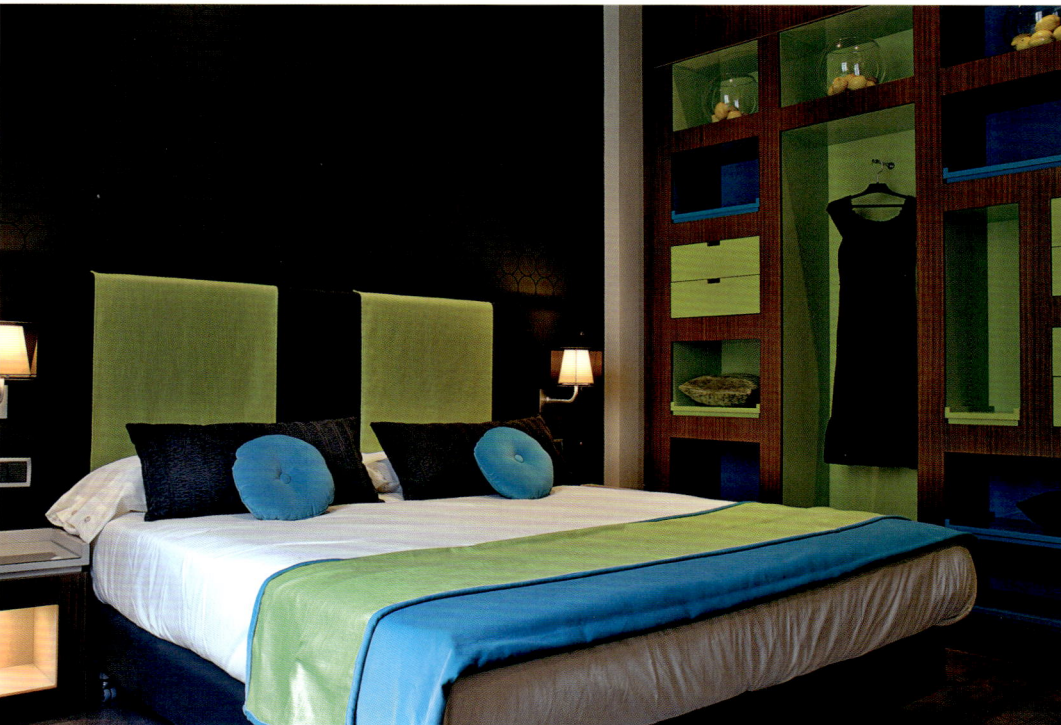

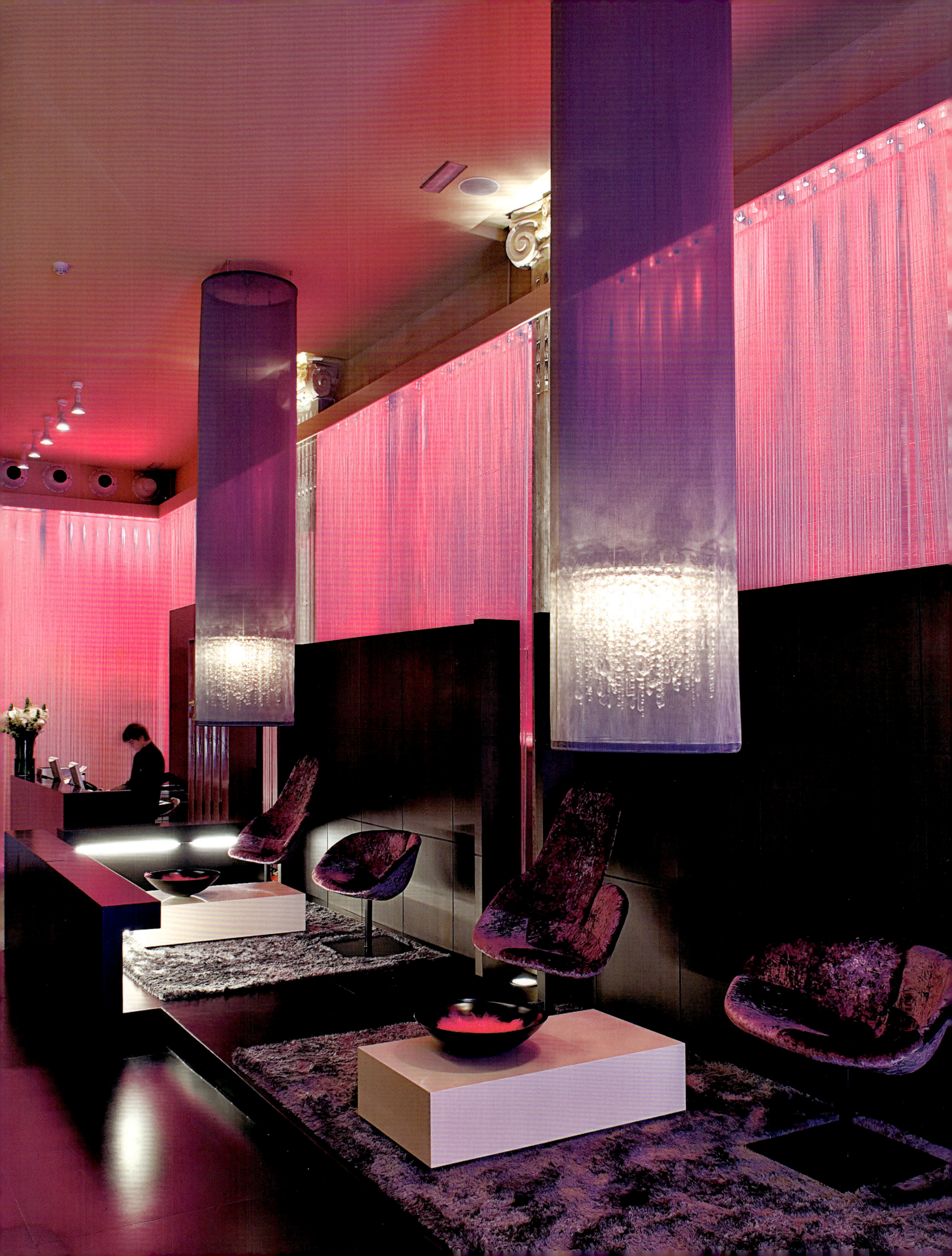

08008 Barcelona
Spain
Phone: +34 932 553 000
Fax: +34 932 553 002
www.hotelcasafuster.com

Rooms: 75 rooms and 21 suites
Facilities: Restaurant Galaxó, Café Vienés, rooftop pool, Jacuzzi
Services: 10 meeting rooms for up to 300 people
Located: At the highest point of Paseo de Gracia
Public transportation: Metro L3, L5 Diagonal
Style: Mixture of art deco and traditional furnishing

When Casa Fuster was christened in 1911 it was called the most elaborate private house in Barcelona—in the three years of continuous construction only the finest materials were used. This crowning of art nouveau architecture can still be admired in today's 96-room hotel, like in the "Café Vienés" with its ornate columns and high windows that open out directly onto the splendid Boulevard Paseo de Gracia. The beloved roof terrace with pool looks over another of the city's sights: the Sagrada Familia.

Als die Casa Fuster 1911 eingeweiht wurde, galt sie als das teuerste Privathaus Barcelonas – waren doch bei den drei Jahre andauernden Bauarbeiten nur edelste Materialien verwendet worden. Die fantasievolle Jugendstilarchitektur lässt sich im heutigen 96 Zimmer-Hotel noch immer bewundern: Zum Beispiel im „Café Vienés" mit seinen verzierten Säulen und hohen Fenstern, die direkt auf den Prachtboulevard Paseo de Gracia hinausgehen. Die beliebte Dachterrasse mit Pool blickt auf eine weitere Sehenswürdigkeit der Stadt: die Sagrada Familia.

Au moment de son inauguration en 1911, la Casa Fuster était considérée comme l'une des maisons privées les plus sophistiquées de Barcelone : pendant sa phase de construction, qui a duré trois ans, seules les matières premières les plus précieuses ont été utilisées. Ce triomphe de l'architecture art nouveau peut toujours s'admirer aujourd'hui dans l'hôtel de 96 chambres, tout comme au « Café Vienés » avec ses piliers magnifiquement décorés et ses hautes fenêtres qui donnent directement sur le splendide Paseo de Gracia. La terrasse de toit très appréciée, avec piscine, permet de contempler un autre site de la ville : la Sagrada Familia.

Cuando, en 1911, se inauguró la Casa Fuster fue considerada la residencia privada más valiosa de toda Barcelona. Las obras duraron tres años y sólo se utilizaron los materiales más nobles. En las 96 habitaciones de este hotel aún se puede admirar la arquitectura creativa de estilo modernista. Ejemplo de ello es el "Café Vienés", con sus pilares esculpidos y sus altas ventanas que dan al concurrido Paseo de Gracia. La conocida azotea con piscina también presente en este edificio abre la vista hacia otra valiosa atracción de la ciudad: la Sagrada Familia.

Quando Casa Fuster fu inaugurata, nel 1911, questa era la residenza privata più costosa di Barcellona – in effetti, nei tre anni di ininterrotti lavori di costruzione vennero utilizzati solamente i materiali più preziosi. Il fantasioso stile liberty dell'edificio si può ancora ammirare nelle 96 camere dell'odierno albergo, per esempio in quella denominata "Café Vienés", con le sue colonne decorate e le alte finestre che si affacciano direttamente sul magnifico viale Paseo de Gracia. L'amata terrazza sul tetto con piscina offre la vista su un'altra attrattiva della città: la Sagrada Familia.

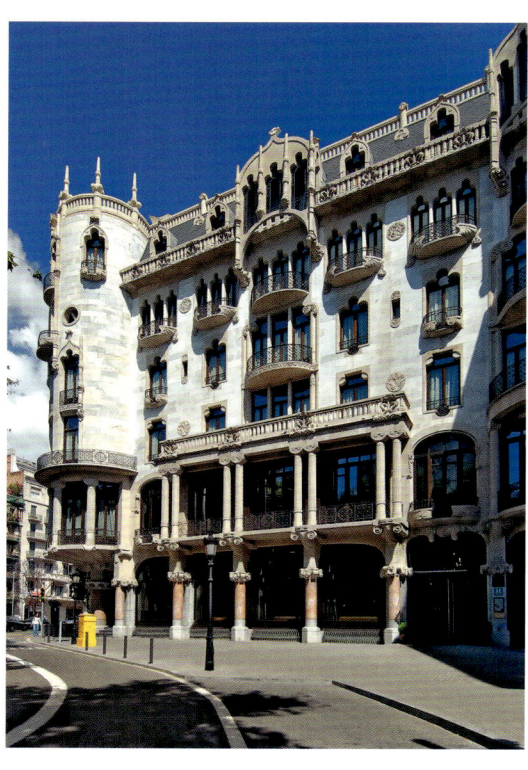
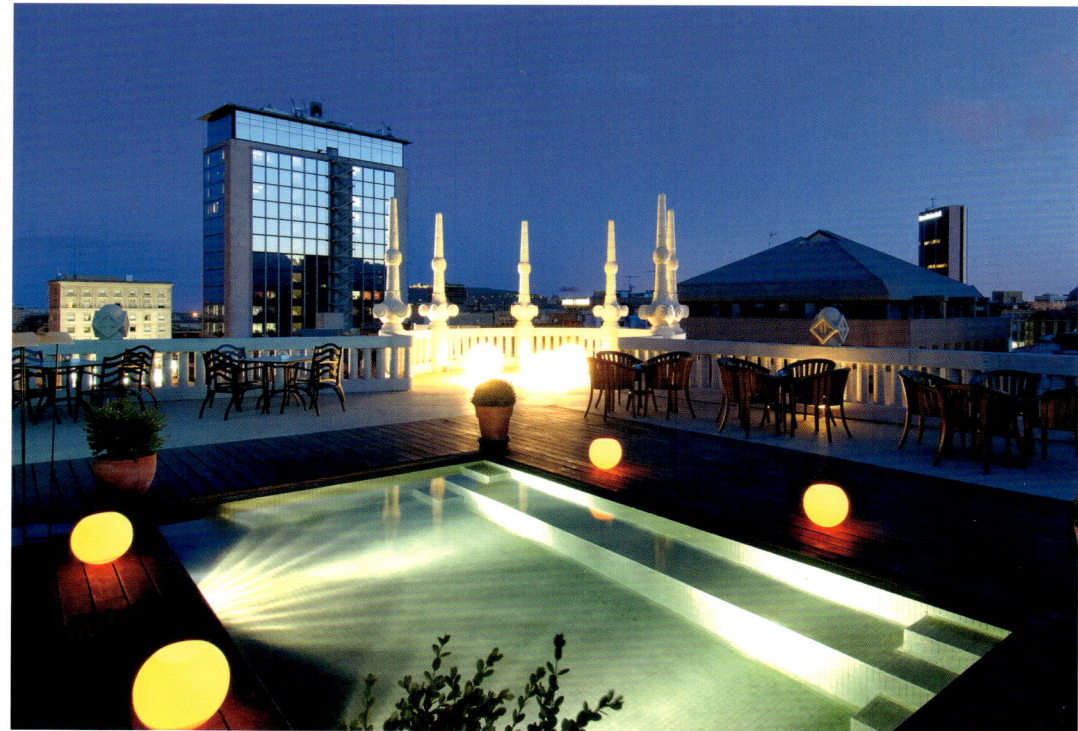

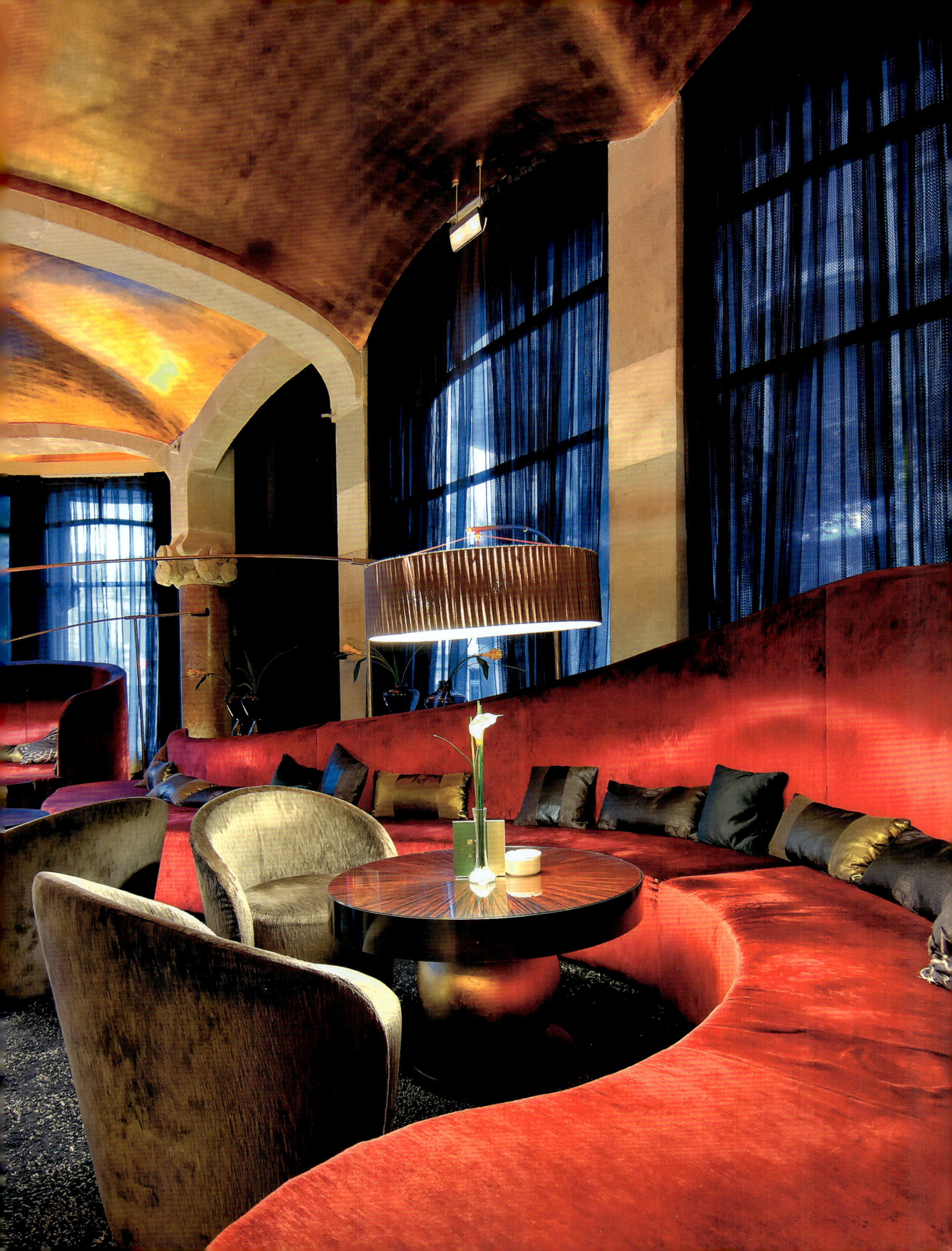

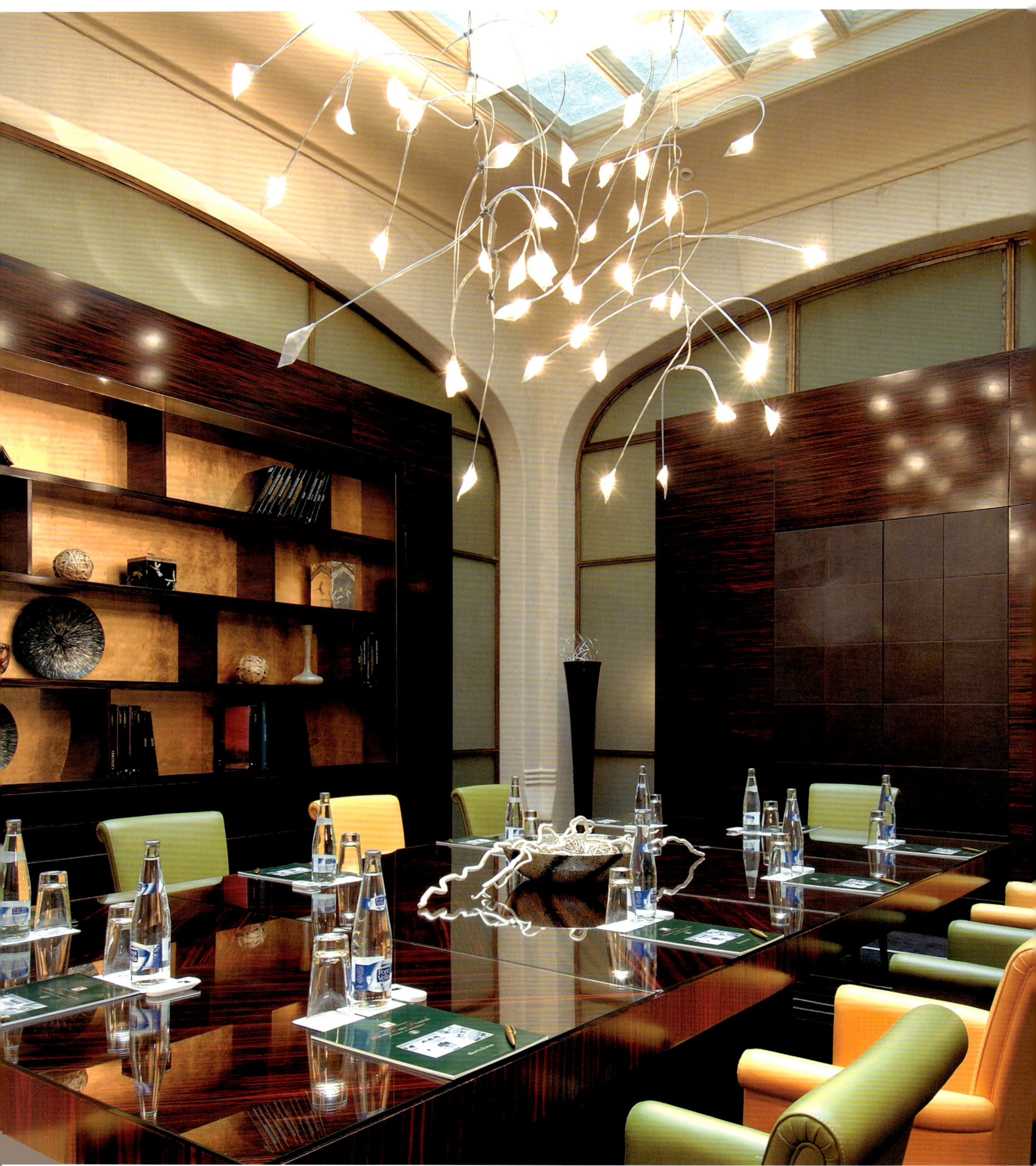

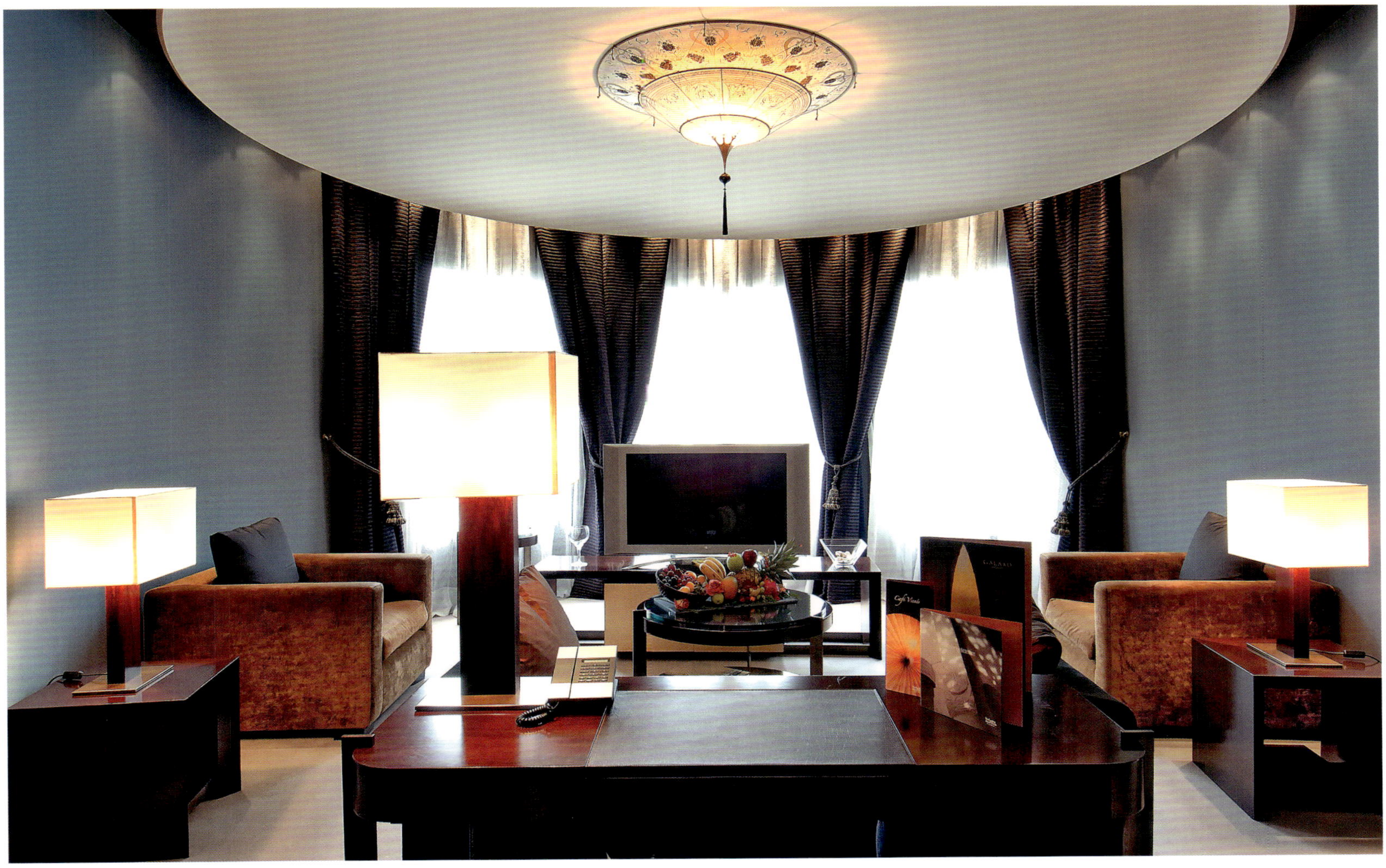

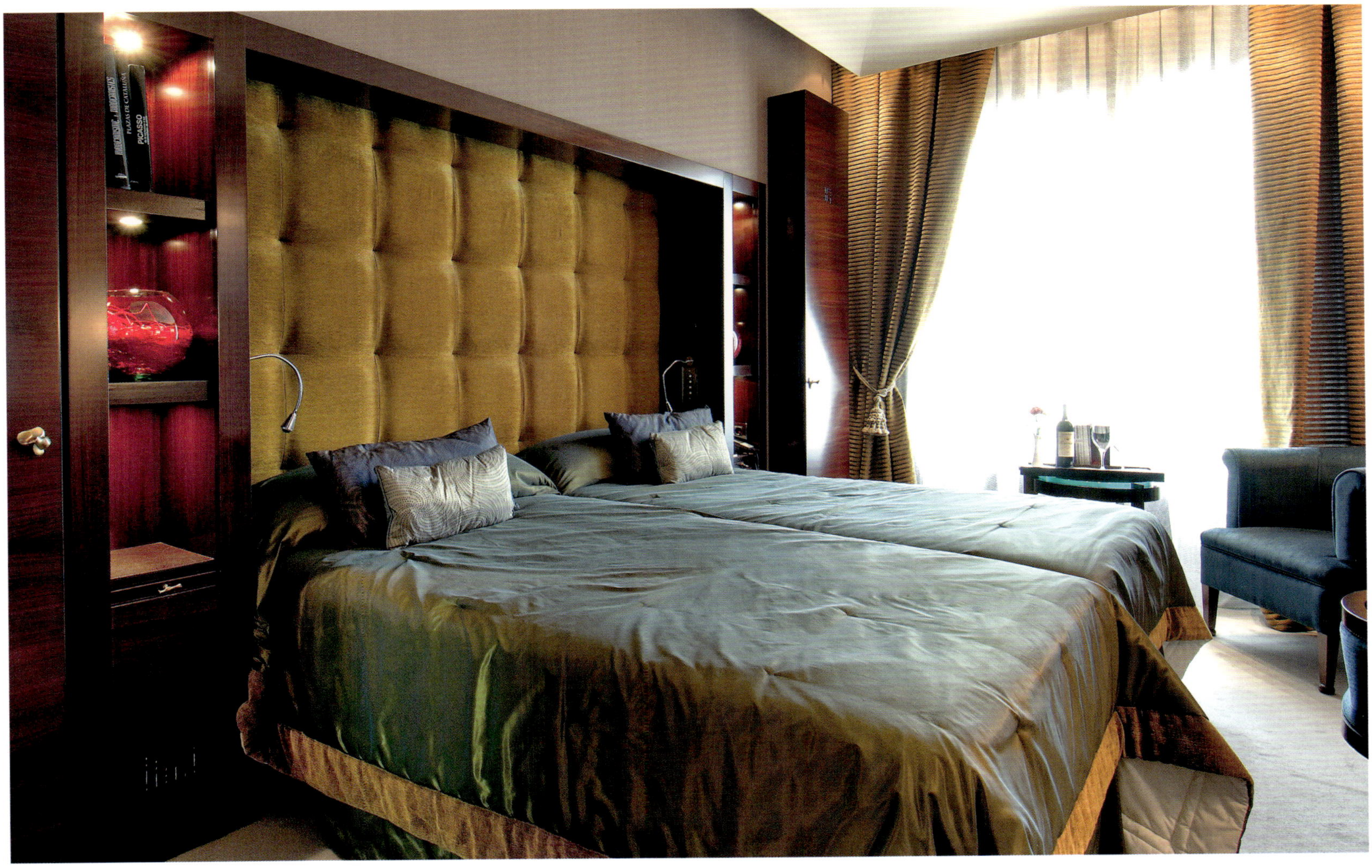

H1898

Barcelona, Spain

La Rambla, 109
08002 Barcelona
Spain
Phone: +34 935 529 552
Fax: +34 935 529 550
www.hotel1898.com

Price category: €€
Rooms: 169 rooms
Facilities: Bar and restaurant, outdoor bar and restaurant (closed in winter), spa, outdoor pool, sauna, steam room, solarium, library, gym, business center
Services: Room service, pillow menu, massages, garage
Located: On La Rambla, next to Plaza Cataluña
Public transportation: Metro L1, L3, train Cataluña
Style: Colonial and modern

In 2005 the headquarter of the "Compañía General de Tabacos de Filipinas" went up in a pipe dream knowing that its location directly on La Rambla made it suitable for something grander than managing tobacco and turned into a splendid hotel. It got its name H1898 from the year that Spain lost its lasts colonies, Cuba and the Philippines. The 169 rooms combine elegant design and exotic colonial style emphasized by the pictures of tropical plants in black-and-white that Maria Espeus flew especially to the Philippines to photograph. The Suites Coloniales are especially luxurious: each with a private terrace with pool and panoramic view of Barcelona.

Direkt an La Rambla gelegen, war dieses 2005 eröffnete Hotel früher die Zentrale der „Compañía General de Tabacos de Filipinas". Seinen Namen bekam das edle H1898 von dem Jahr, in dem mit Kuba und den Philippinen die letzten spanischen Kolonien unabhängig wurden. Die 169 Zimmer verbinden elegantes Design und exotischen Kolonialstil (für die Schwarz-Weiß-Fotos tropischer Pflanzen flog Maria Espeus extra auf die Philippinen). Besonders luxuriös sind die Suites Coloniales: Sie besitzen eine Privatterrasse mit Pool und Panoramablicken über Barcelona.

En 2005, la « Compañía General de Tabacos de Filipinas », située directement sur la Rambla, a su tirer profit de cet emplacement exceptionnel pour devenir un grand hôtel, au lieu de se contenter de s'occuper de tabac. Le H1898 tire son nom de l'année où Cuba et les Philippines, les dernières colonies espagnoles, ont obtenu leur indépendance. Les 169 chambres marient design élégant et style colonial exotique, mis en valeur par les photos noir et blanc de plantes tropicales pour lesquelles Maria Espeus est venue spécialement des Philippines. Les Suites Coloniales sont particulièrement luxueuses : elles disposent chacune d'une terrasse privée avec piscine et vue panoramique sur Barcelone.

Situado directamente en Las Ramblas, este hotel inaugurado en 2005, ubicó antiguamente la sede de la "Compañía General de Tabacos de Filipinas". Su egregio nombre H1898 evoca el año en el que Cuba y Filipinas, últimas colonias españolas, lograron su independencia. Sus 169 habitaciones combinan un diseño elegante con un exótico estilo colonial (para poder captar las imágenes de plantas tropicales en blanco y negro, Maria Espeus viajó hasta Filipinas). De un lujo extraordinario se presentan las suites Coloniales, cada una con una terraza privada con piscina y una vista panorámica de Barcelona.

Situato direttamente sulla Rambla, questo hotel aperto nel 2005 fu in passato la sede centrale della "Compañía General de Tabacos de Filipinas". Il raffinato H1898 prende il nome dall'anno in cui Cuba e le Filippine, le ultime colonie spagnole, furono rese indipendenti. Le sue 169 camere uniscono un elegante design a un esotico stile coloniale (per scattare le foto in bianco e nero di piante tropicali, Maria Espeus si è recata apposta nelle Filippine). Particolarmente lussuose le Suites Coloniales, dotate di terrazza privata con piscina e vedute panoramiche su Barcellona.

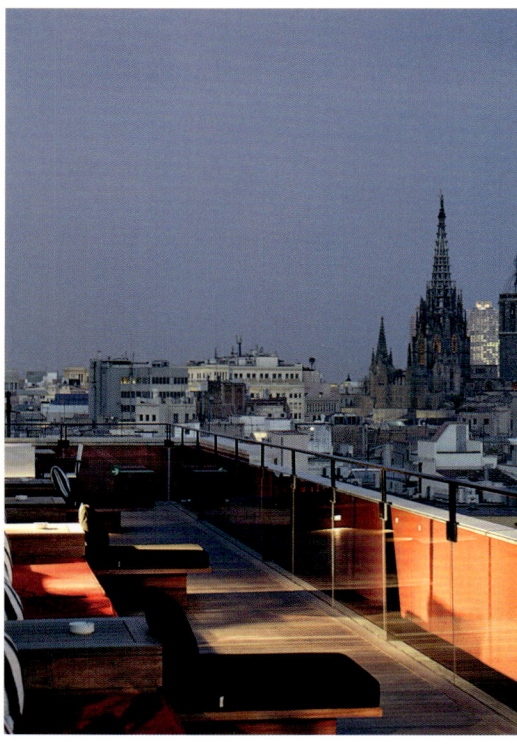 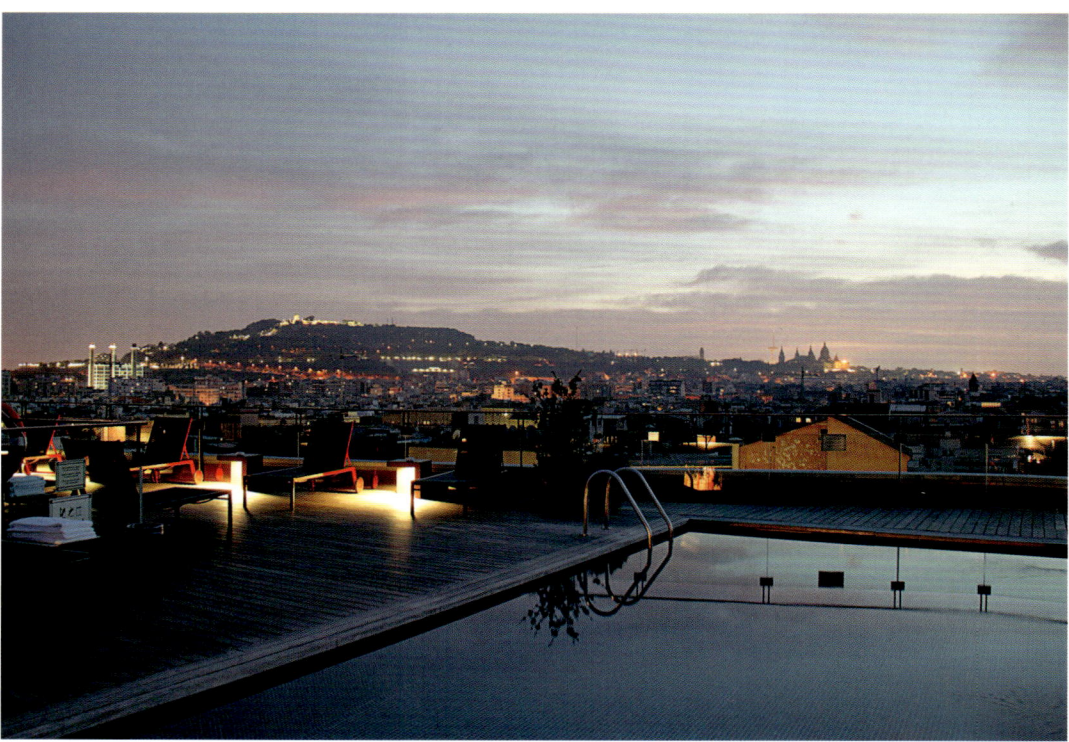

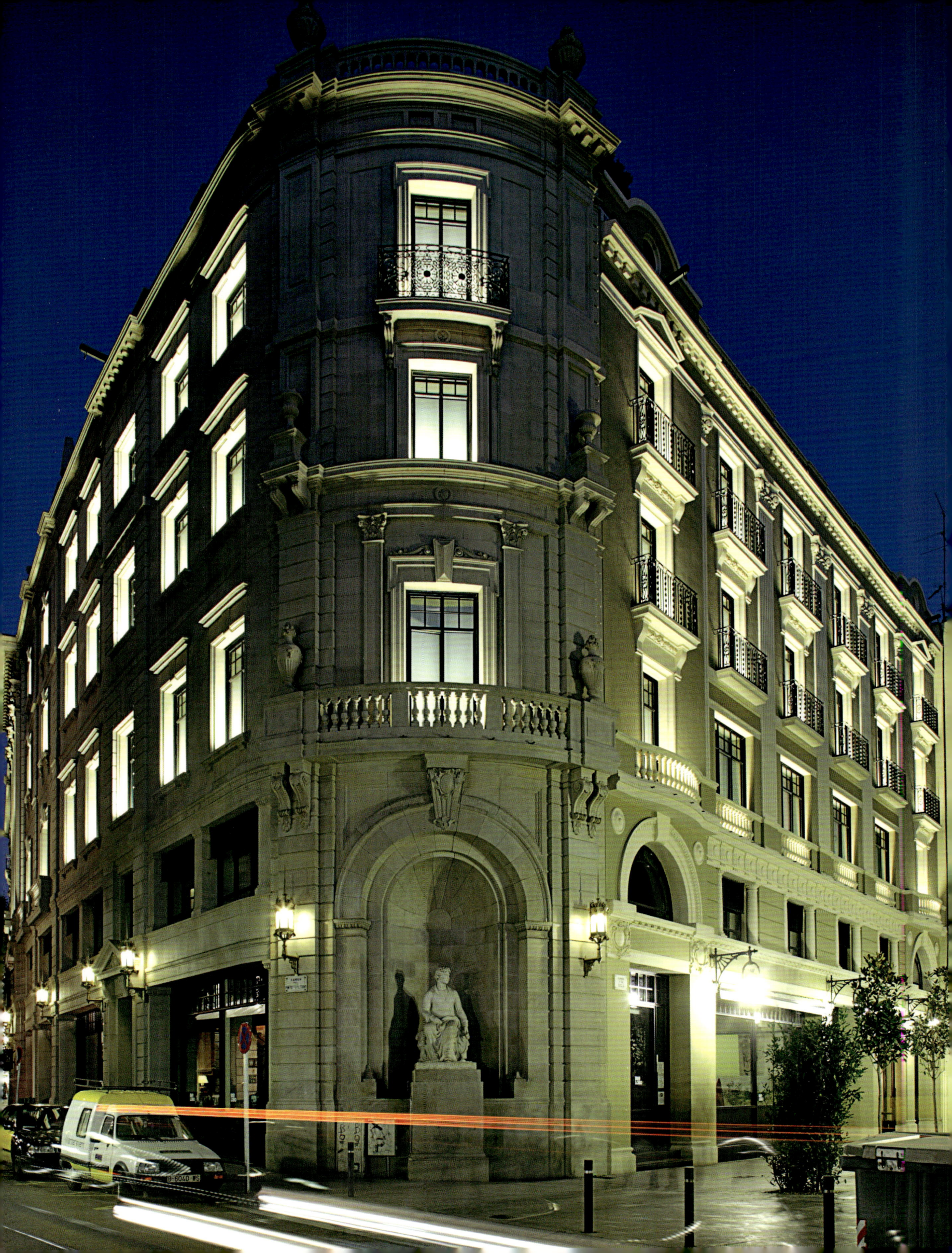

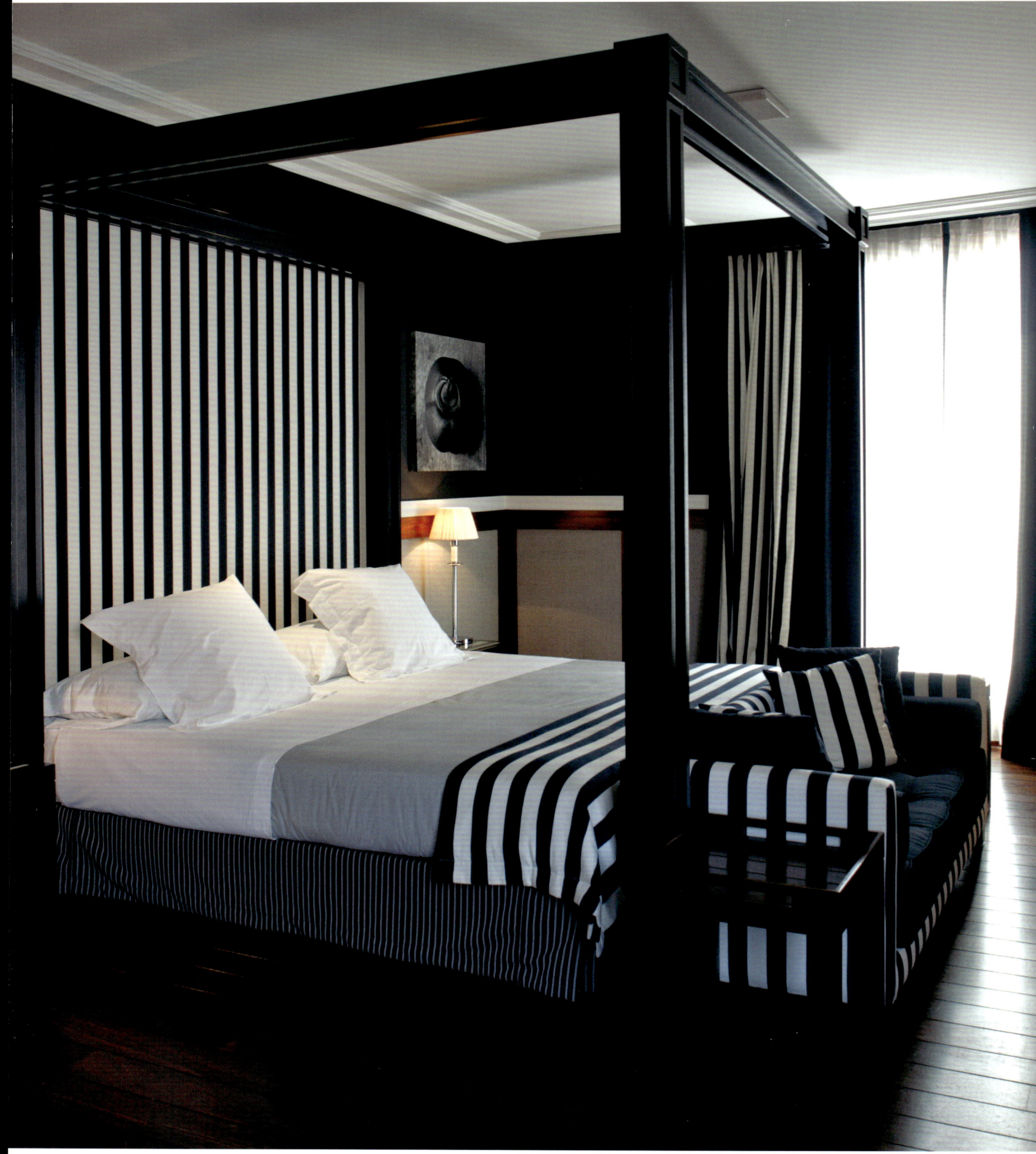

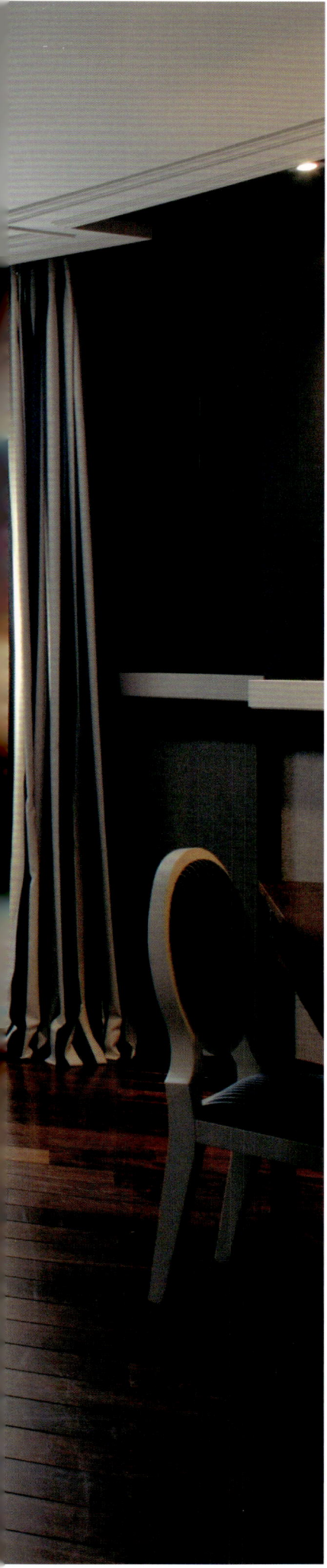

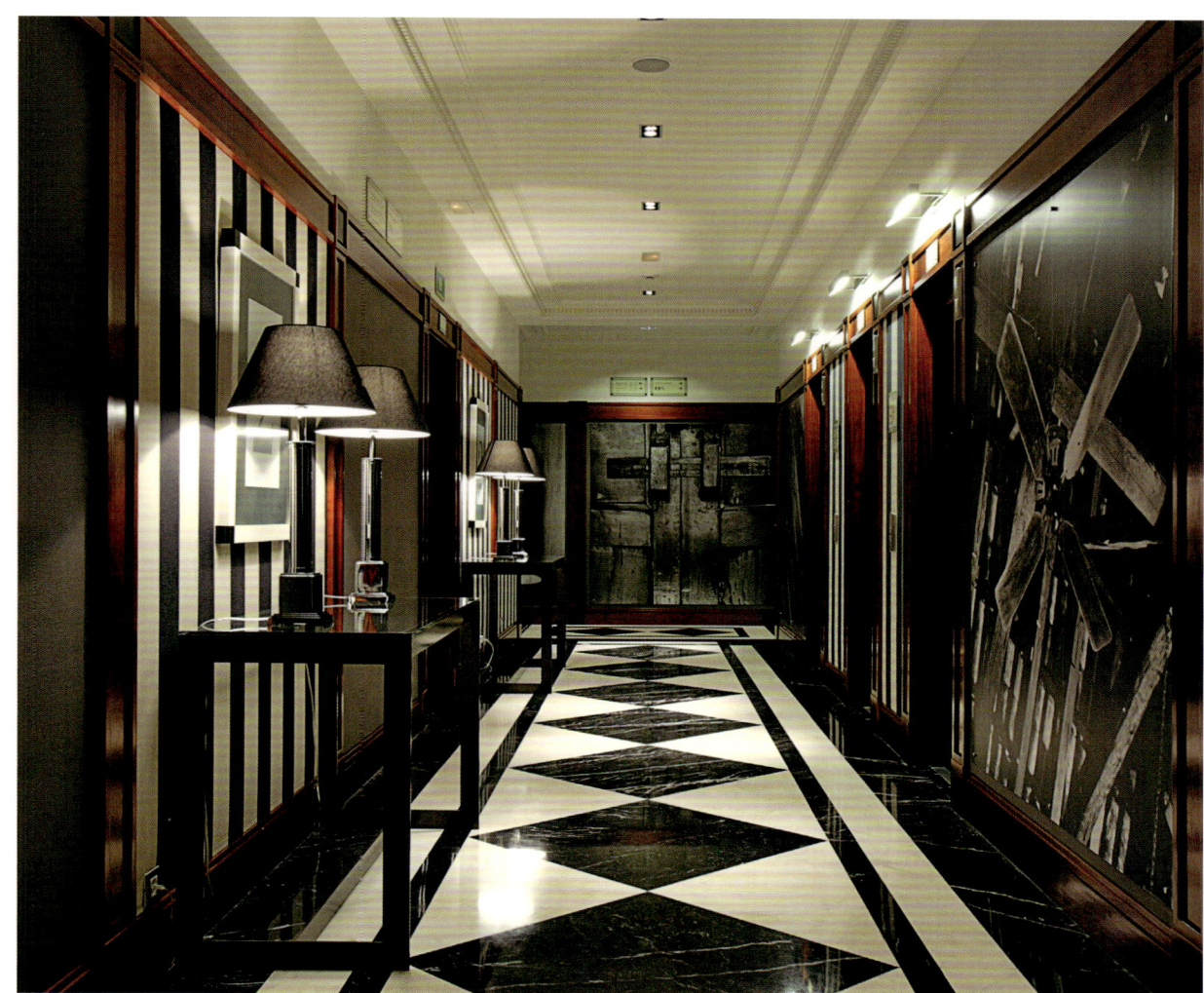

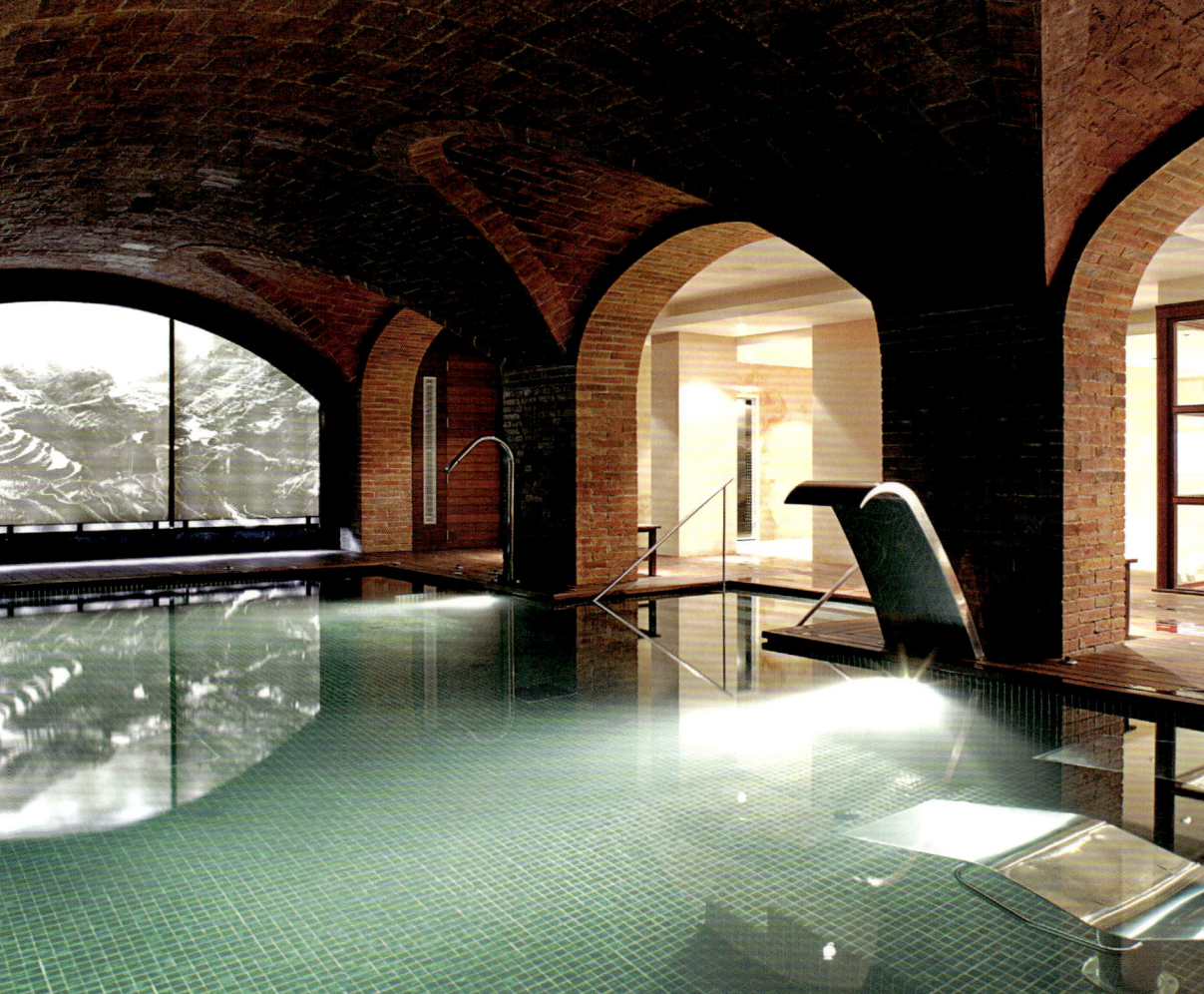

08015 Barcelona
Spain
Phone: +34 933 251 205
Fax: +34 934 242 965
www.markethotel.com.es

Rooms: 46 rooms
Facilities: Restaurant, meeting room for 100 people
Services: Free notebook available, free WiFi an all rooms for guests, bicycle renting
Located: Next to the San Antonio Market, between Plaza Cataluña and Plaza España
Public transportation: Metro L2 Sant Antoni, Metro L1 Urgell
Style: Modern

An Asian atmosphere in the middle of Catalonia, the Market Hotel surprises with Chinese cabinets and lanterns at the reception as well as 33 rooms kept in purest black and white. Bright red dots offer an effective contrast, and the suites open out onto their own terraces. The restaurant has been more loyal to European cuisine than to the Far East with fine Catalonian cuisine is served under the sparkling chandelier. A rare extra: in the lobby available are free mineral water and apples all day.

Asiatisches Ambiente mitten in Katalonien: Das Market Hotel überrascht mit chinesischen Schränken und Lampen an der Rezeption sowie 33 Zimmern, die puristisch in Schwarz-Weiß gehalten sind – knallrote Farbtupfer bilden effektvolle Kontraste, und die Suiten bieten sogar den Luxus einer eigenen Terrasse. Das Restaurant wendet sich aber eher europäischen denn fernöstlichen Genüssen zu: Unter einem funkelnden Kronleuchter wird gute katalanische Küche serviert. Seltenes Extra: In der Lobby stehen ganztags kostenfrei Mineralwasser und Äpfel bereit.

Une ambiance asiatique au cœur de la Catalogne : le Market Hotel surprend avec ses armoires et lampes chinoises à la réception, ainsi que dans les 33 chambres décorées en pur noir et blanc (des notes de couleur rouge vif créant un contraste marqué) et les suites disposant d'une terrasse privée. Le restaurant, plutôt que d'offrir des saveurs extrême-orientales, mise sur le style européen : on y sert une délicieuse cuisine catalane sous un lustre étincelant. Petit plus rare, de l'eau minérale et des pommes sont gracieusement mises à disposition dans le hall de réception.

Un ambiente asiático en plena Cataluña. El Market Hotel sorprende con armarios y lámparas de estilo chino en su recepción y con 33 habitaciones de una atmósfera purista marcada por el blanco y el negro, donde las pequeñas salpicaduras de rojo carmesí crean contrastes espectaculares. Las suites brindan incluso el lujo de una terraza propia. El restaurante, sin embargo, se orienta más bien hacia los paladares europeos que a los de extremo oriente. Debajo de una resplandeciente araña de cristal se sirven platos de la alta cocina catalana. Y un detalle poco común: el vestíbulo ofrece a sus huéspedes agua y manzanas gratuitas.

Un ambiente asiatico nel cuore della Catalogna. Le Market Hotel sorprende gli ospiti tanto con i mobili e le lampade cinesi della reception quanto con le sue 33 camere, consacrate alle puristiche tonalità del bianco e del nero – i particolari rosso fuoco creano un bellissimo contrasto, e le suite offrono persino il lusso di una terrazza privata. Il ristorante, tuttavia, è orientato verso le specialità europee più che verso quelle dell'Estremo Oriente: sotto uno scintillante lampadario a corona si servono piatti di cucina catalana. Un raro extra: nella lobby sono a disposizione tutto il giorno acqua minerale e mele gratuite.

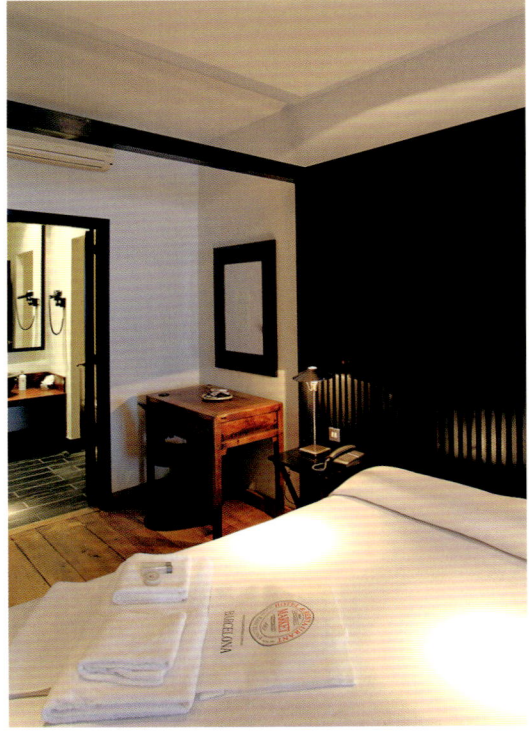
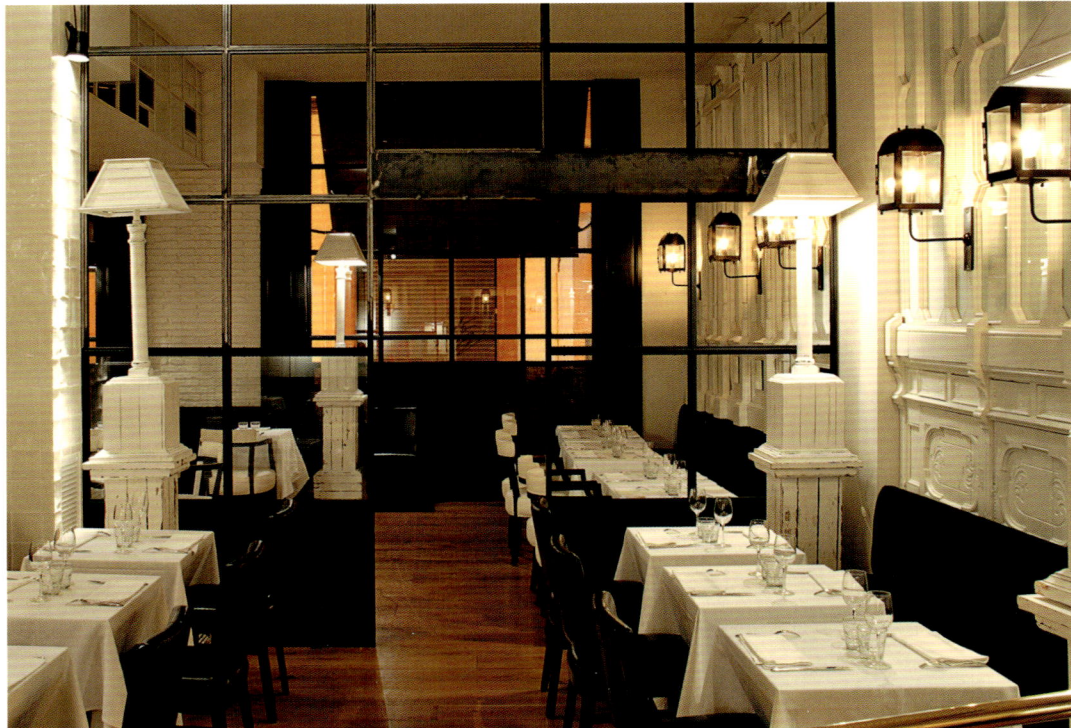

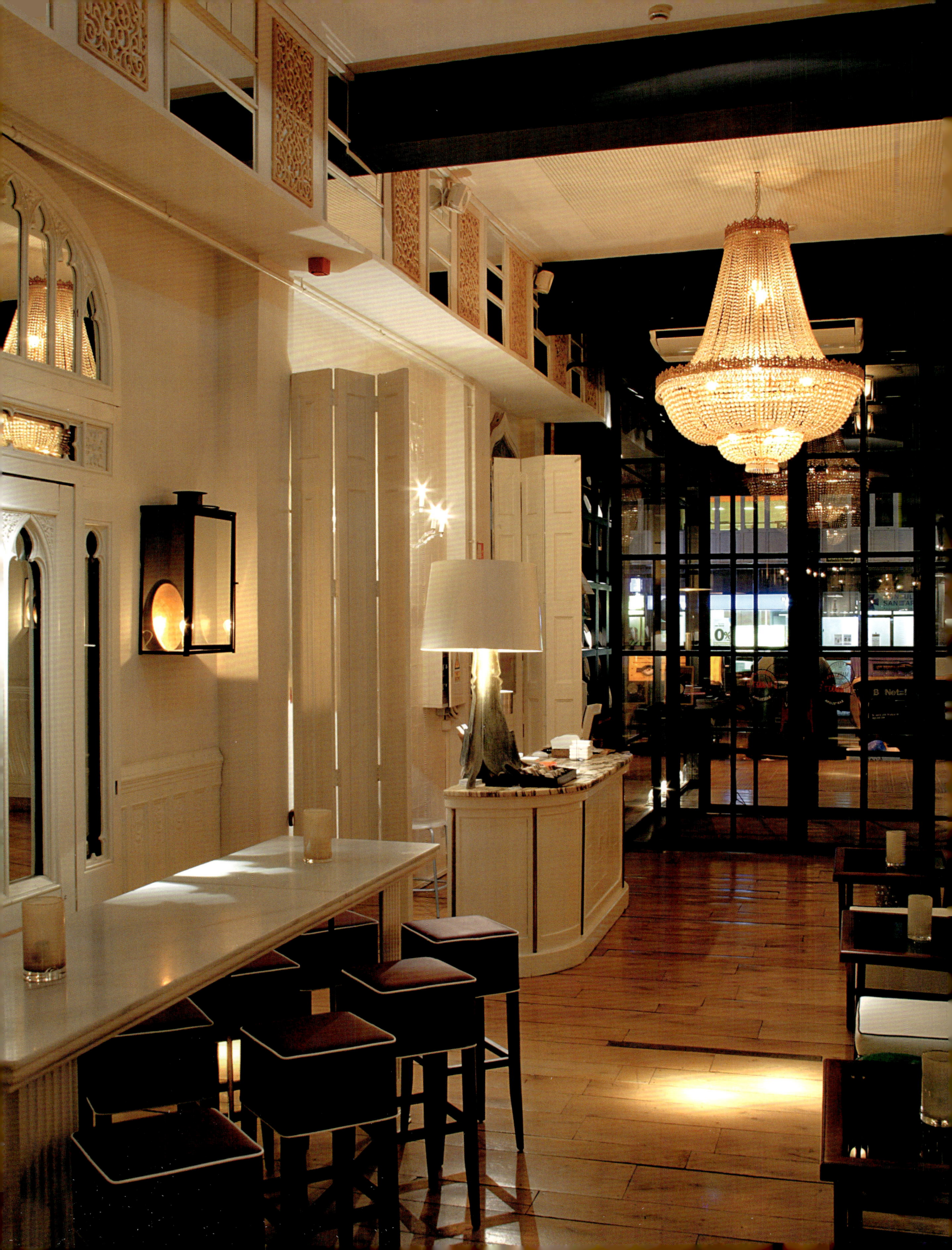

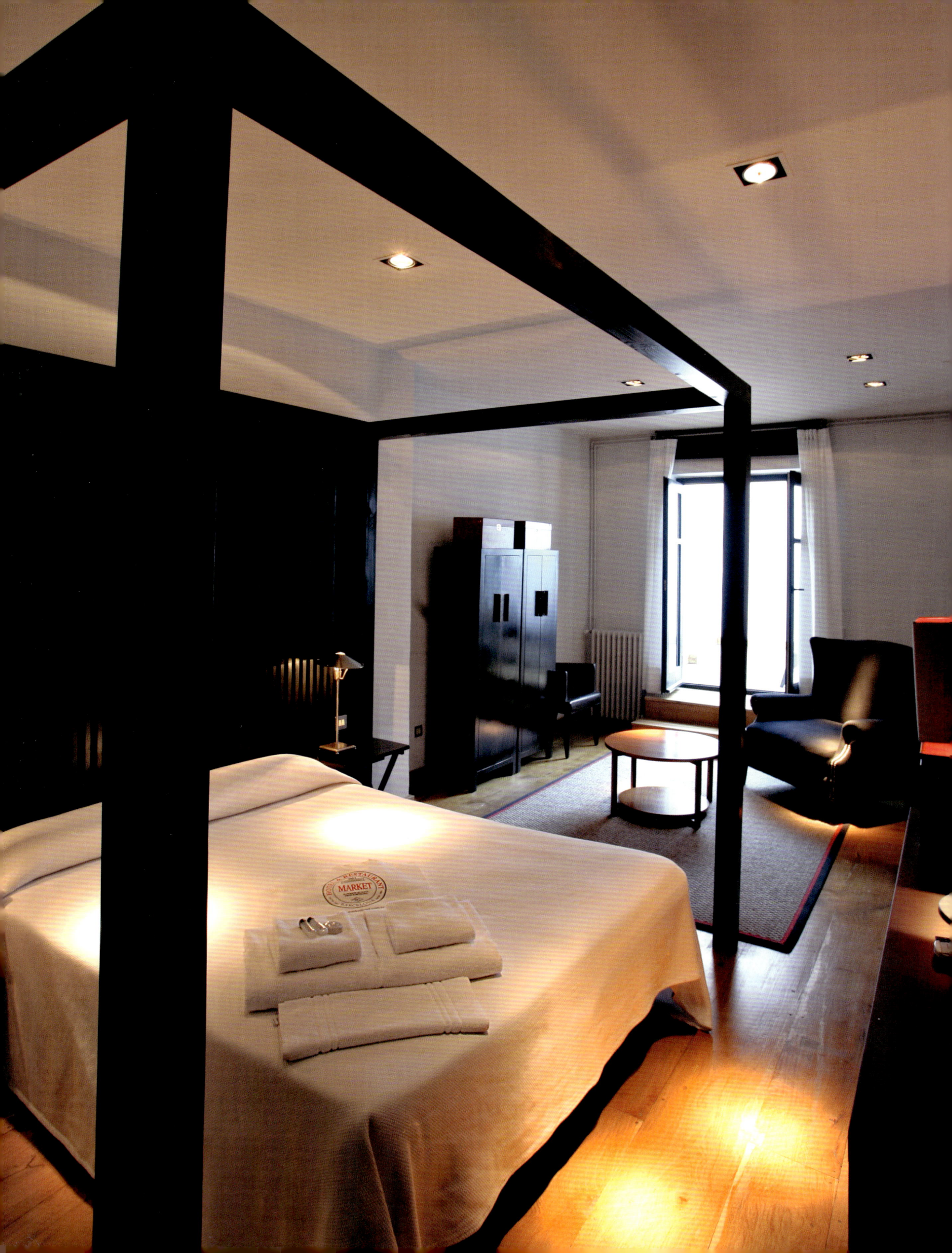

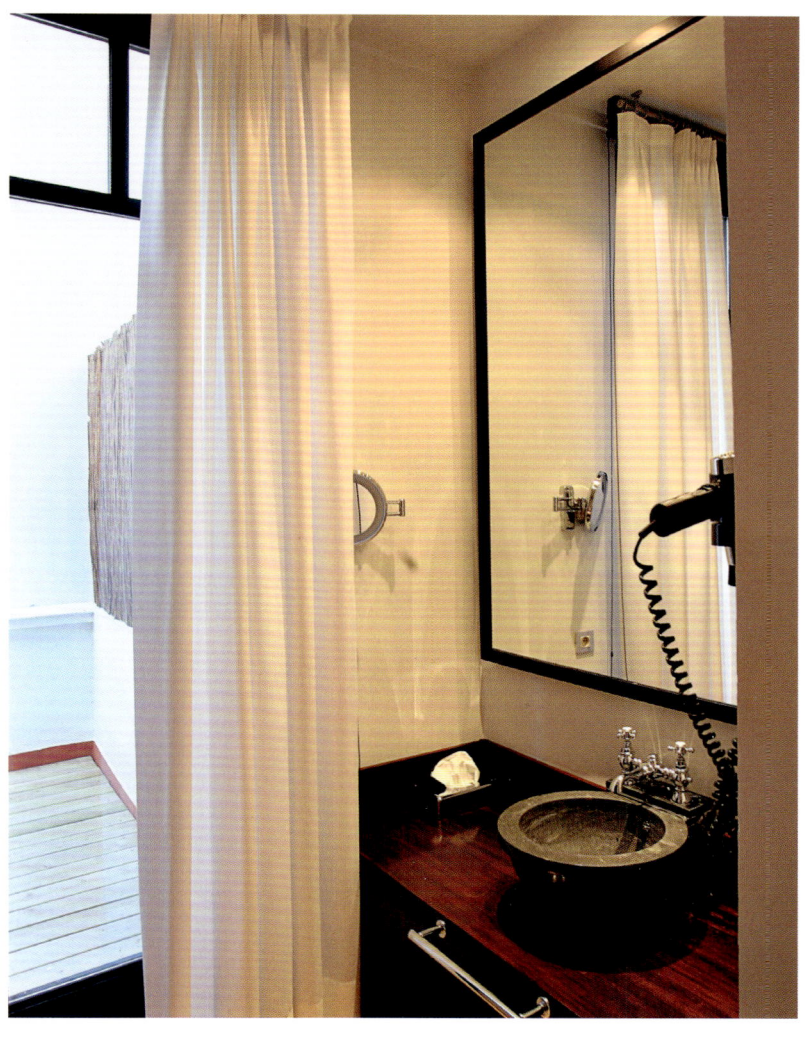
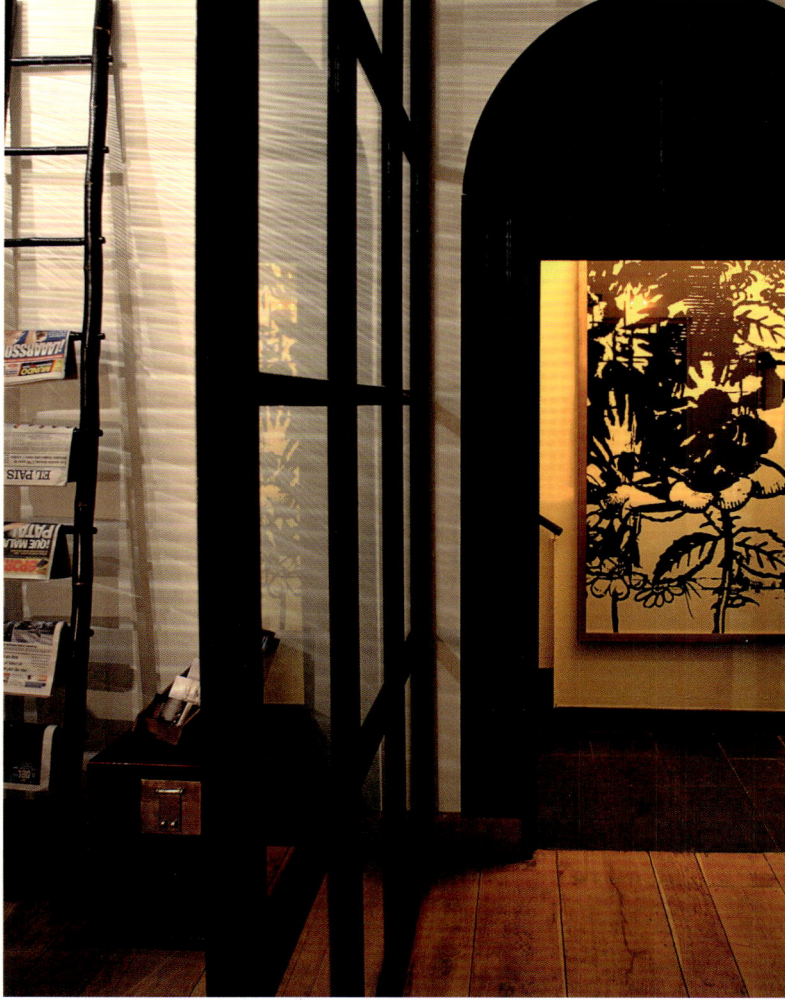
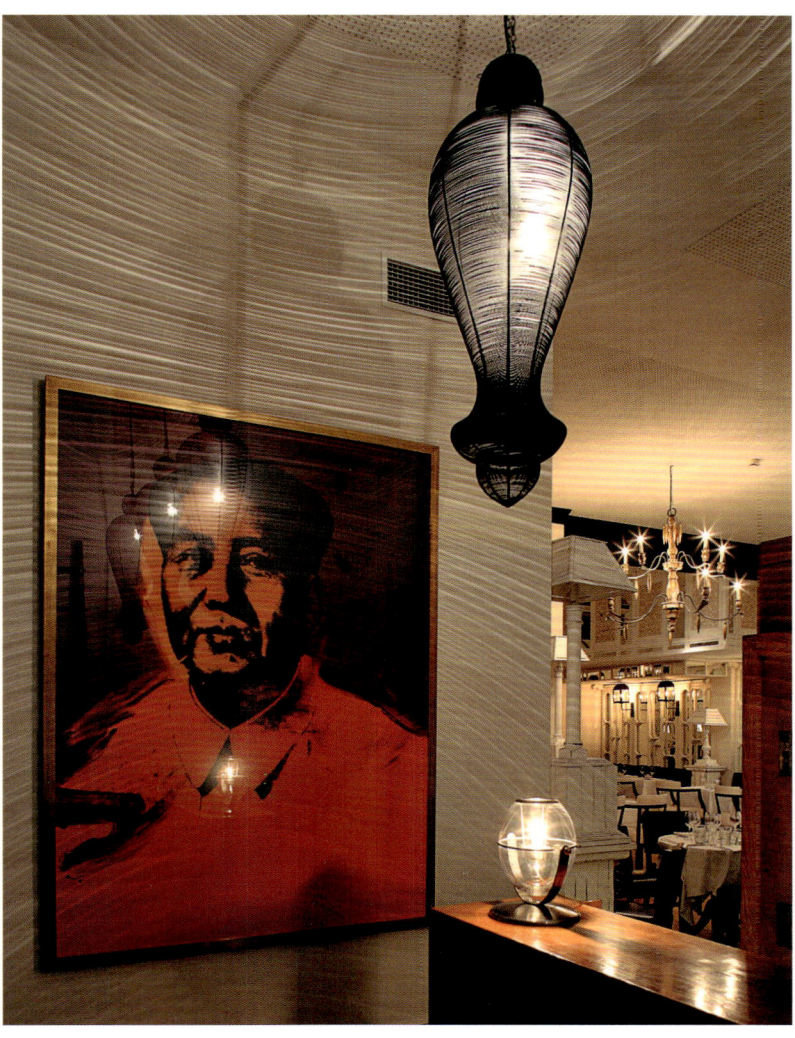
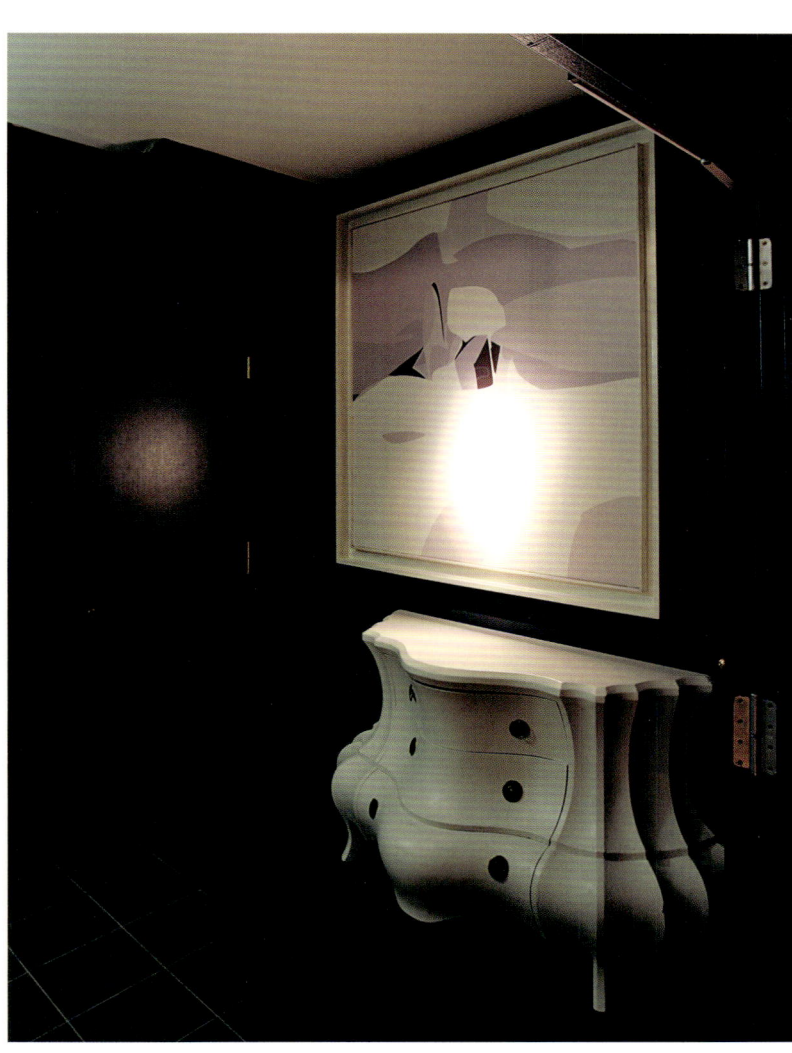

Hotel Soho Barcelona

Barcelona, Spain

Gran Vía, 543–545
08011 Barcelona
Spain
Phone: +34 935 529 610
Fax: +34 935 529 611
www.hotelsohobarcelona.com

Price category: €
Rooms: 51 rooms
Facilities: Lounge, terrace, outdoor pool
Services: Conference room for up to 20 people
Located: Next to Plaza Cataluña, Paseo de Gracia, La Rambla, the Gothic district and the Cathedral
Public transportation: Metro L1 Urgell and Universitat, Metro L2 Universitat
Style: Contemporary design

Barcelona is so infected by "design fever" that creating a really new and really good design hotel is a challenge, but Alfredo Arribas managed it for the Soho quite sovereignly. With only 51 rooms the house on the Gran Vía stays intimate and small-scaled, but urban and cosmopolitan at the same time. Light spots in yellow, orange or red tones yield a lounge-like club flair while glass walls with a moire pattern geometrically captivate you, as the lamps in the lobby evoke homage to Verner Panton, the cult designer of the '60s.

Im vom Designfieber infizierten Barcelona ein wirklich neues und wirklich gutes Designhotel zu gestalten, ist eine Herausforderung – Alfredo Arribas hat sie mit dem Soho souverän gemeistert. Mit nur 51 Zimmern gibt sich das Haus an der Gran Vía intim und minimalistisch, aber zugleich urban und kosmopolitisch. Lichtspots in Gelb-, Orange- oder Rottönen sorgen für loungiges Club-Flair, im Moiré-Stil gehaltene Glaswände haben geometrische Wirkung und die Lampen in der Lobby sind eine Hommage an Verner Panton, den Kultdesigner der 60er-Jahre.

Créer un hôtel de designer vraiment réussi dans une Barcelone gagnée par la fièvre du design représente une vraie gageure, qu'Alfredo Arribas a relevée superbement avec le Soho. Avec seulement 51 chambres, cet établissement situé sur la Gran Vía, n'est pas seulement intime mais aussi pittoresque, urbain tout en étant cosmopolite. Les spots de couleur jaune, orange ou rouge créent une atmosphère lounge, sur les façades de verre moiré aux effets géométriques et les lampes dans le hall sont un hommage à Verner Panton, le designer culte des années 60.

En la Barcelona de hoy, sacudida por la fiebre del diseño, crear un hotel de moda que resulte realmente innovador llega a ser todo un reto. Alfredo Arribas, con su Soho, ha logrado hacer frente a este cometido. El hotel de la Gran Vía dispone de tan sólo 51 habitaciones y se presenta como un espacio íntimo y minimalista, pero no por ello menos urbano o cosmopolita. Los espacios de luz en tonos amarillo, naranja y rojo proporcionan un ambiente relajado con un ligero sabor a club, las paredes de cristal con dibujos geométricos de efecto moiré y las lámparas en el vestíbulo son un homenaje a Verner Panton, el diseñador de culto de los años 60.

Realizzare un design hotel veramente nuovo e veramente bello in una città contagiata dalla febbre del design come Barcellona è una vera e propria sfida – che Alfredo Arribas è riuscito a vincere in modo magistrale con il Soho. Mettendo a disposizione solo 51 camere, questo albergo situato sulla Gran Vía offre una sistemazione intima e minimalista, ma allo stesso tempo di tipo urbano e cosmopolita. Punti luce nelle tonalità del giallo, dell'arancione e del rosso creano un'atmosfera da lounge, le pareti di vetro presentano motivi geometrici moiré e le lampade nella lobby sono un omaggio a Verner Panton, grandissimo designer degli anni '60.

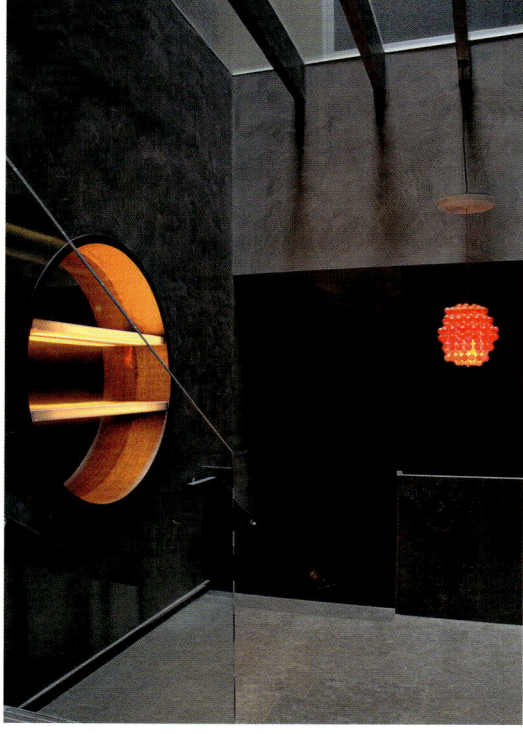
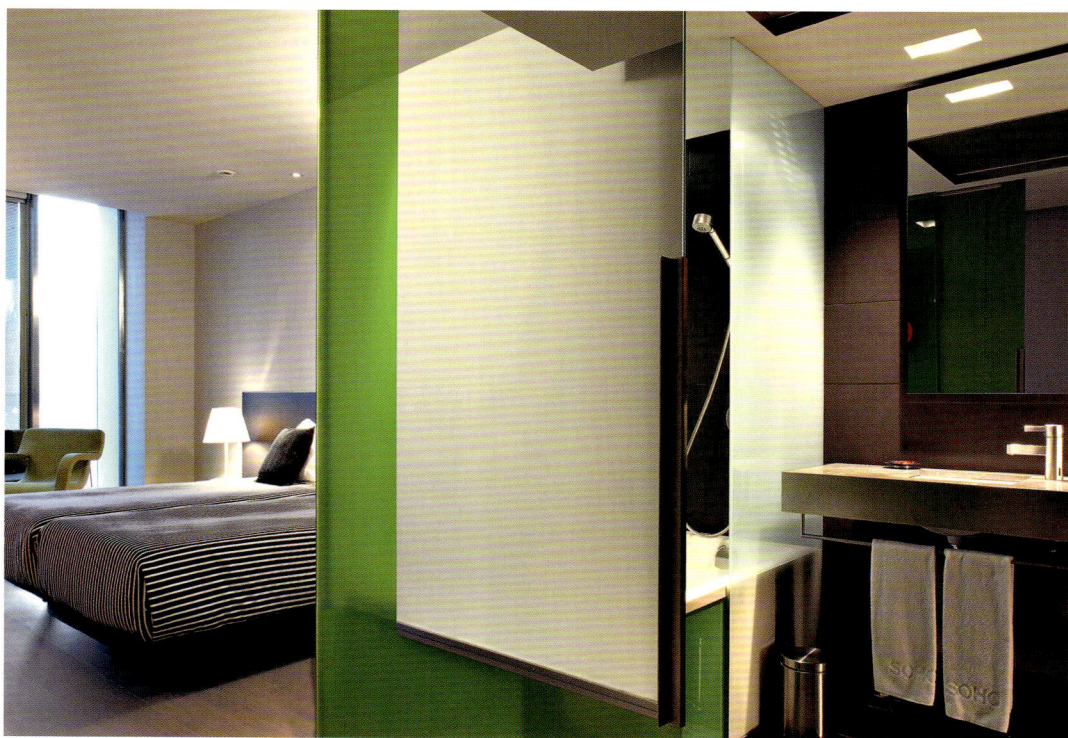

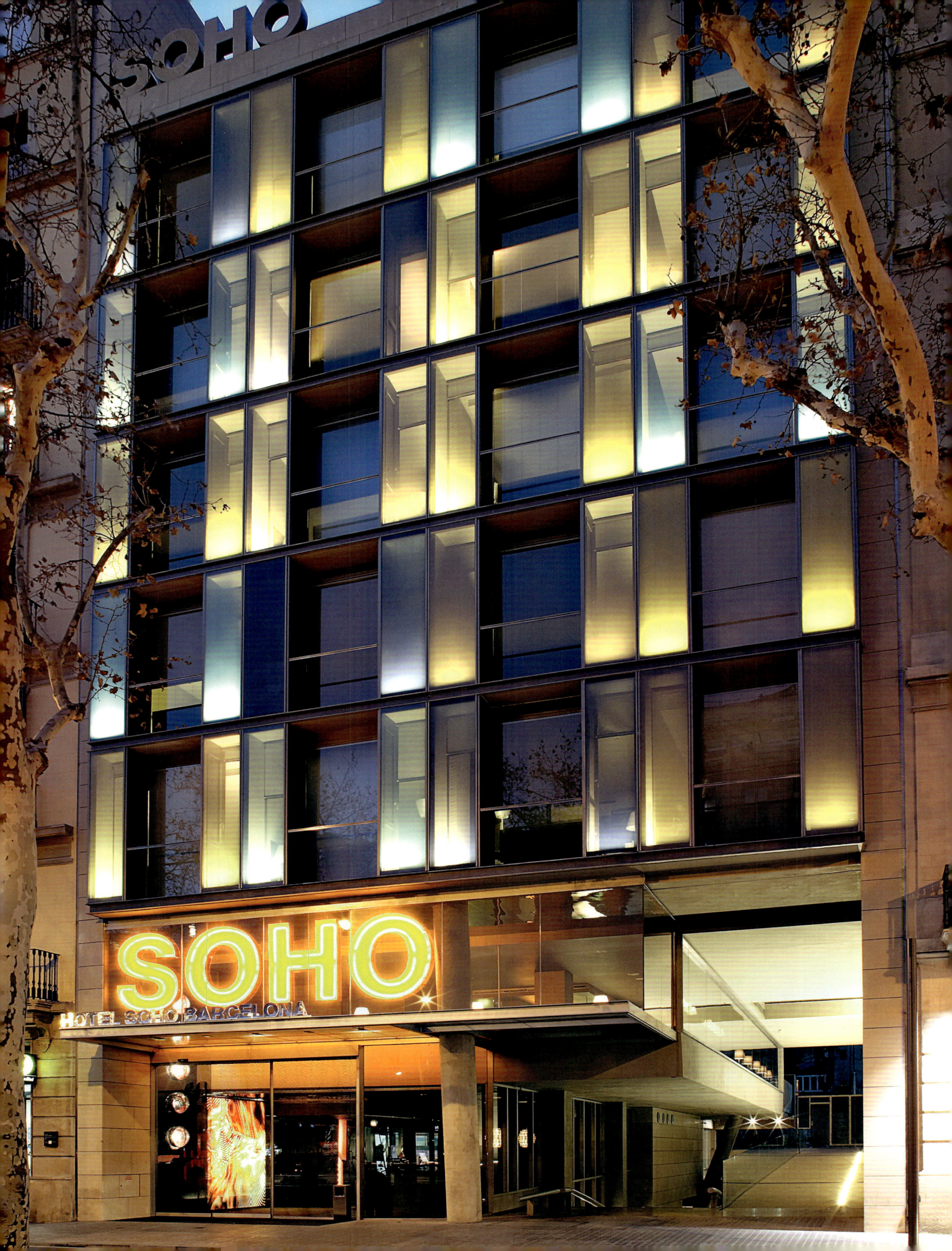

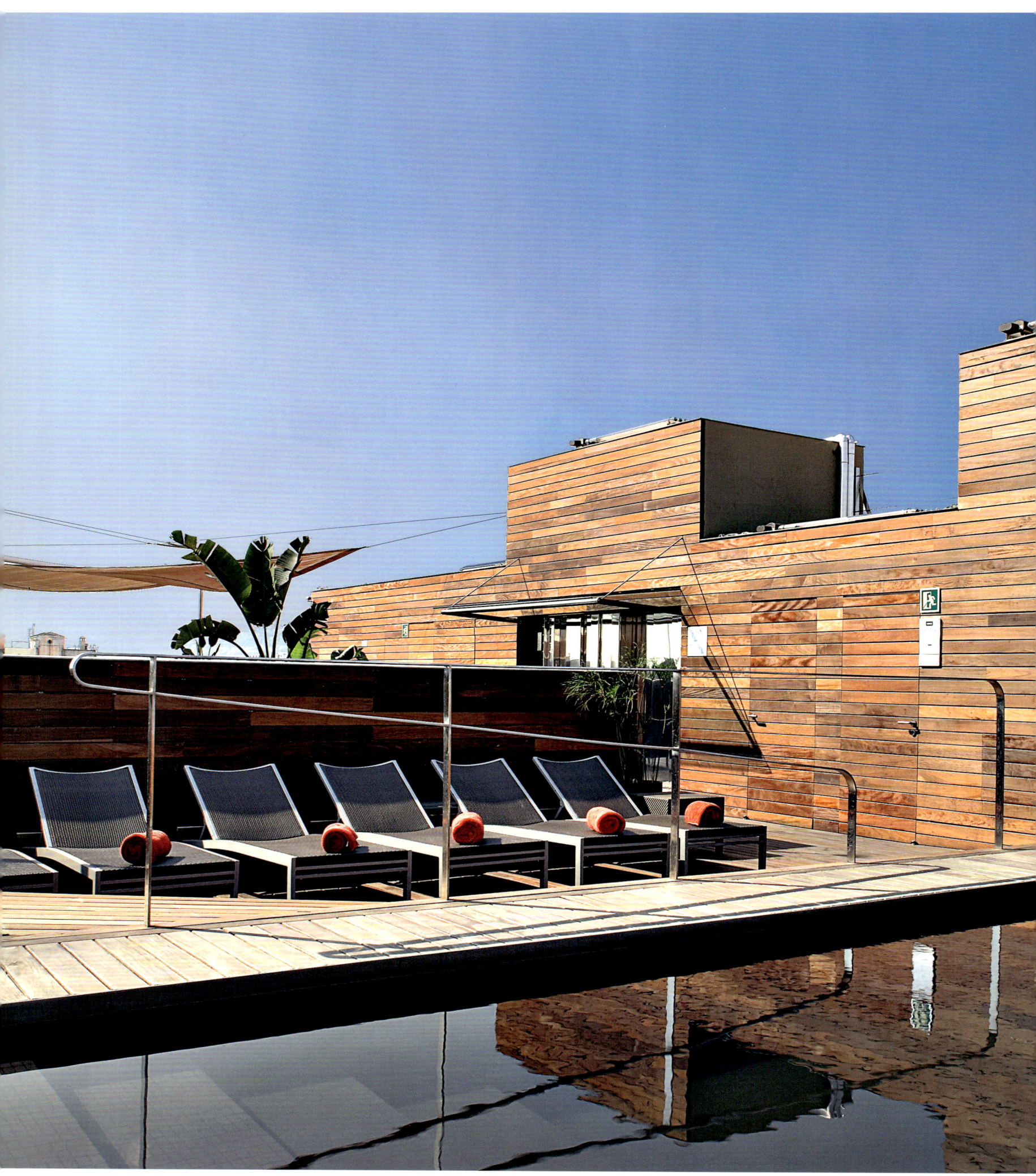

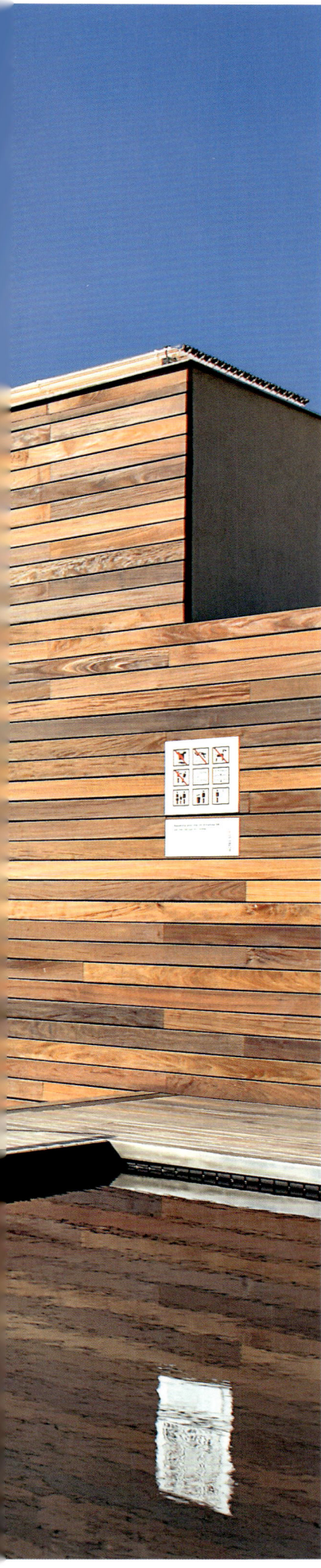

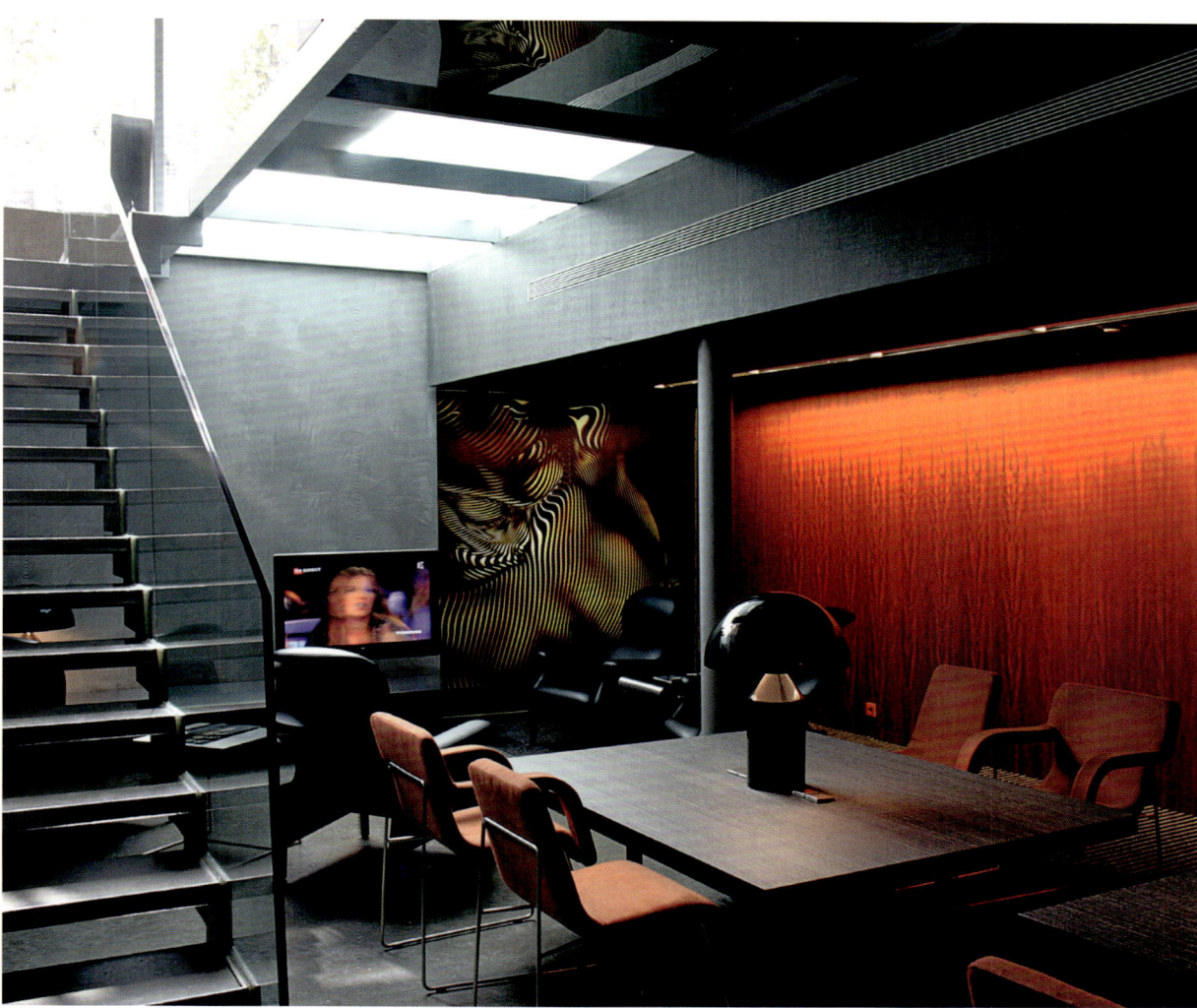

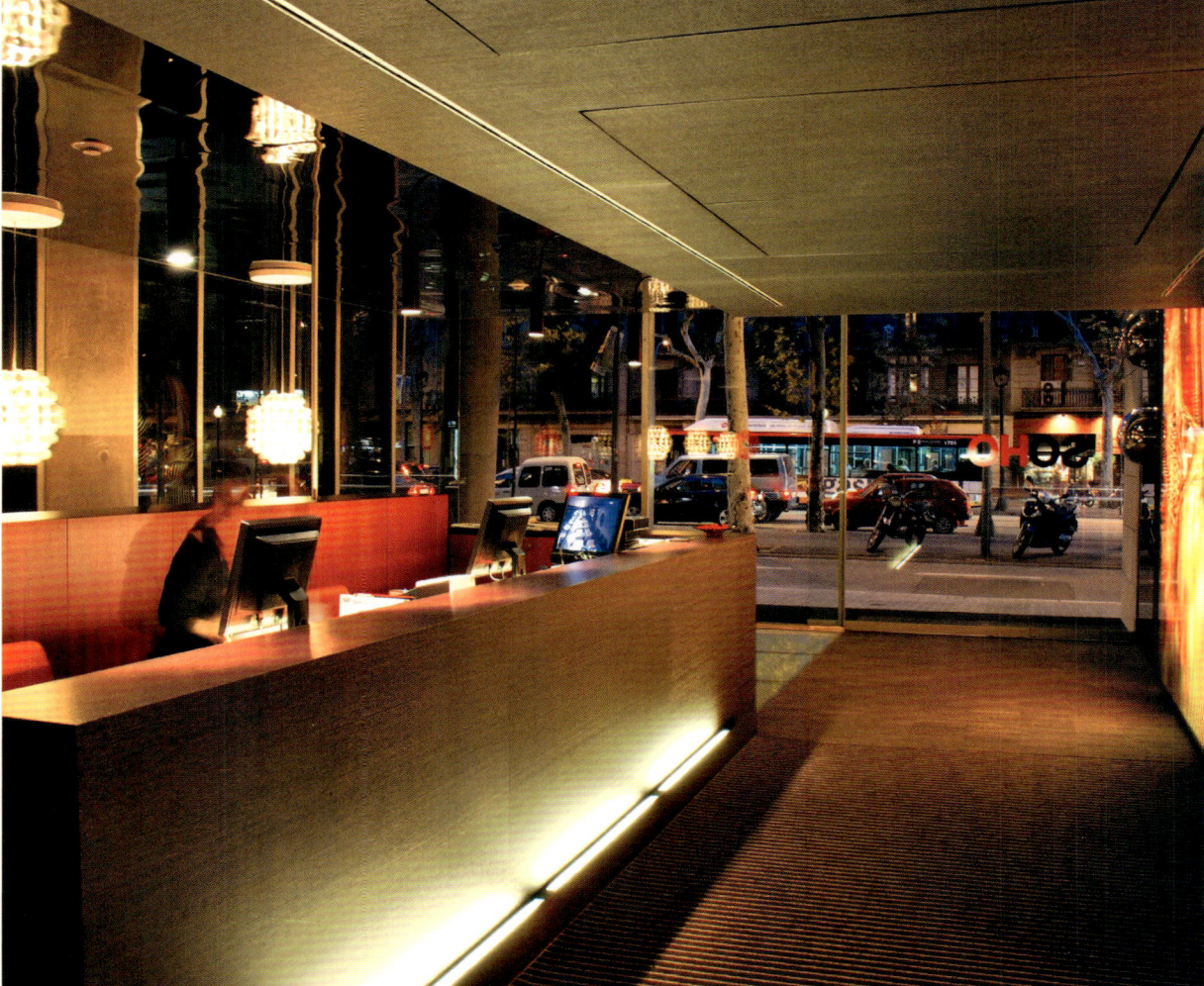

Solarillo de Gracia, 1
18002 Granada
Spain
Phone: +34 958 535 790
Fax: +34 958 536 968
www.hospes.com

Price category: €€
Rooms: 42 rooms including 5 suites
Facilities: Senzone restaurant, Bodyna spa, massage & treatments, pool, Jacuzzi, sauna and Turkish bath
Services: Meeting rooms for up to 60 people
Located: In the historic and business center of Granada
Style: Modern and 19th century contrasts

You usually do not call a hotel a "beauty," but this is one: sophisticated, stylish, and sensuous. Combining the listed 19th-century palace with a new building behind an alabaster wall is sheer breathtaking; the interior design is a luxurious understatement. Gleaming white and grey nuances, modern and antique accessories like frescos, plaster molding or coffered ceilings make treasured hideaways of the 42 hotel rooms. Just one visit to the spa will make you never want to leave again.

Es kommt selten vor, dass man ein Hotel als „Schönheit" bezeichnet – doch dieses ist eine: sophisticated, stilvoll, sinnlich. Die Kombination aus einem denkmalgeschützten Palast des 19. Jahrhunderts und einem Neubau hinter einer Alabasterwand ist schlicht atemberaubend, das Interior Design luxuriöses Understatement. Schimmernde Weiß- und Grau-Nuancen, moderne Materialien und alte Accessoires wie Fresken, Stuck oder Kassettendecken machen aus den 42 Hotelzimmern Hideaways. Und wer einmal im Spa war, möchte vor allem eines: nie wieder weg.

La beauté est rarement le premier mot employé pour décrire un hôtel, mais c'est celui qui s'impose d'emblée pour cet établissement à la fois sophistiqué, élégant et sensuel. Le mariage d'un palais du XIXème siècle classé monument historique et d'un bâtiment neuf situé derrière un mur d'albâtre est tout simplement époustouflant, et l'intérieur affiche une simplicité luxueuse. Du blanc étincelant et des nuances grises, des matériaux modernes et des détails anciens comme des fresques, du stuc ou des plafonds à caissons font des 42 chambres de véritables refuges. Et si vous essayez le spa, vous ne voudrez plus jamais en partir.

Rara vez se califica un hotel de "auténtica belleza" y esta es, sin duda, una de las excepciones. Sofisticado, elegante, sensual. La combinación entre el palacio del siglo XIX, declarado patrimonio nacional, y las instalaciones renovadas tras la pared de alabastro simplemente quita el aliento. El diseño interior está marcado por un lujo discreto. Matices en blanco y gris de un tenue resplandor, materiales modernos y accesorios antiguos, como frescos, estucos o casetones, convierten sus 42 estancias en verdaderos refugios. Y aquel que visite su spa alguna vez, no querrá sino quedarse para siempre.

Capita raramente di definire un albergo "bellezza", ma qui è proprio il caso di farlo: il Palacio de los Patos è un hotel sofisticato, sensuale e di classe. La combinazione di un palazzo del XIX secolo, patrimonio culturale della città di Granada, e di un edificio di nuova costruzione dietro alla parete di alabastro è semplicemente mozzafiato, e il design degli interni un lussuoso understatement. Le lucenti tonalità del bianco e del grigio, i moderni materiali e i dettagli antichi, come gli affreschi, gli stucchi o i soffitti a cassettoni, fanno delle 42 camere di questo albergo dei veri e propri angoli di privacy. E se provate lo spa, vorrete rimanere per sempre.

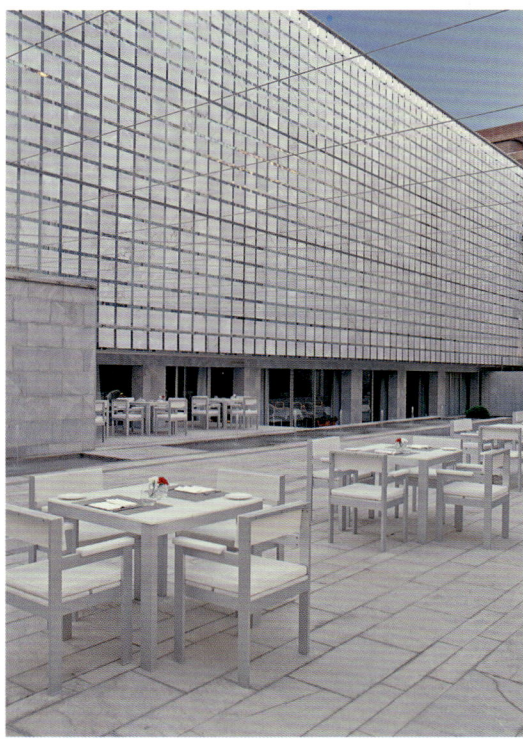

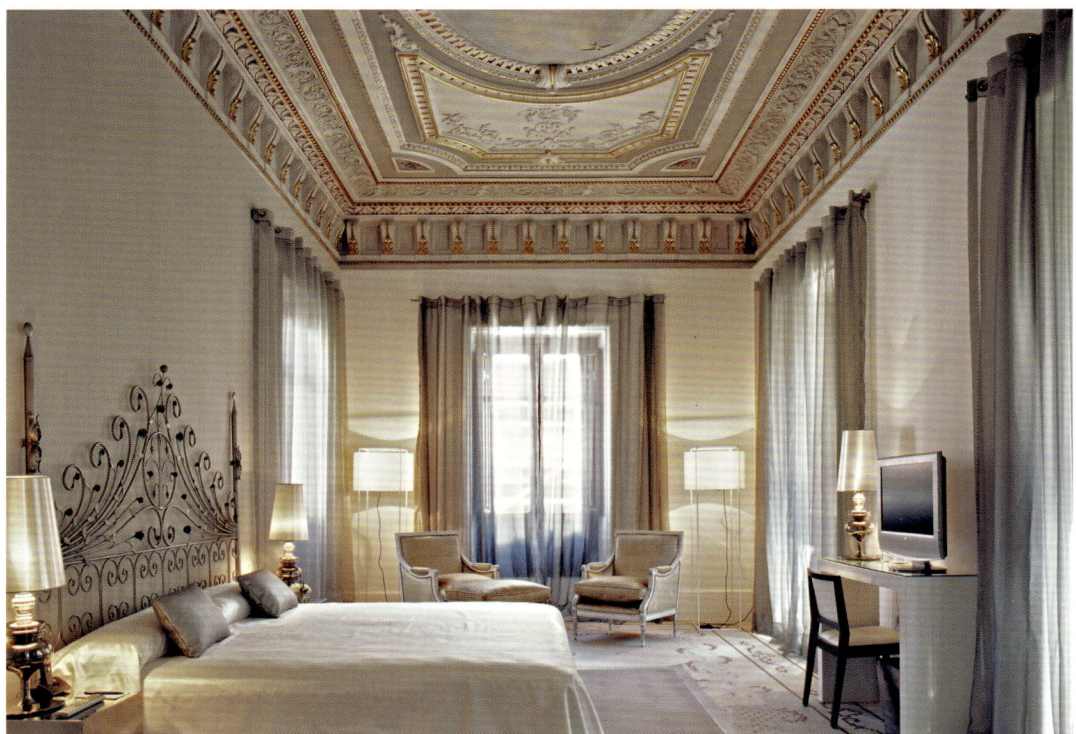

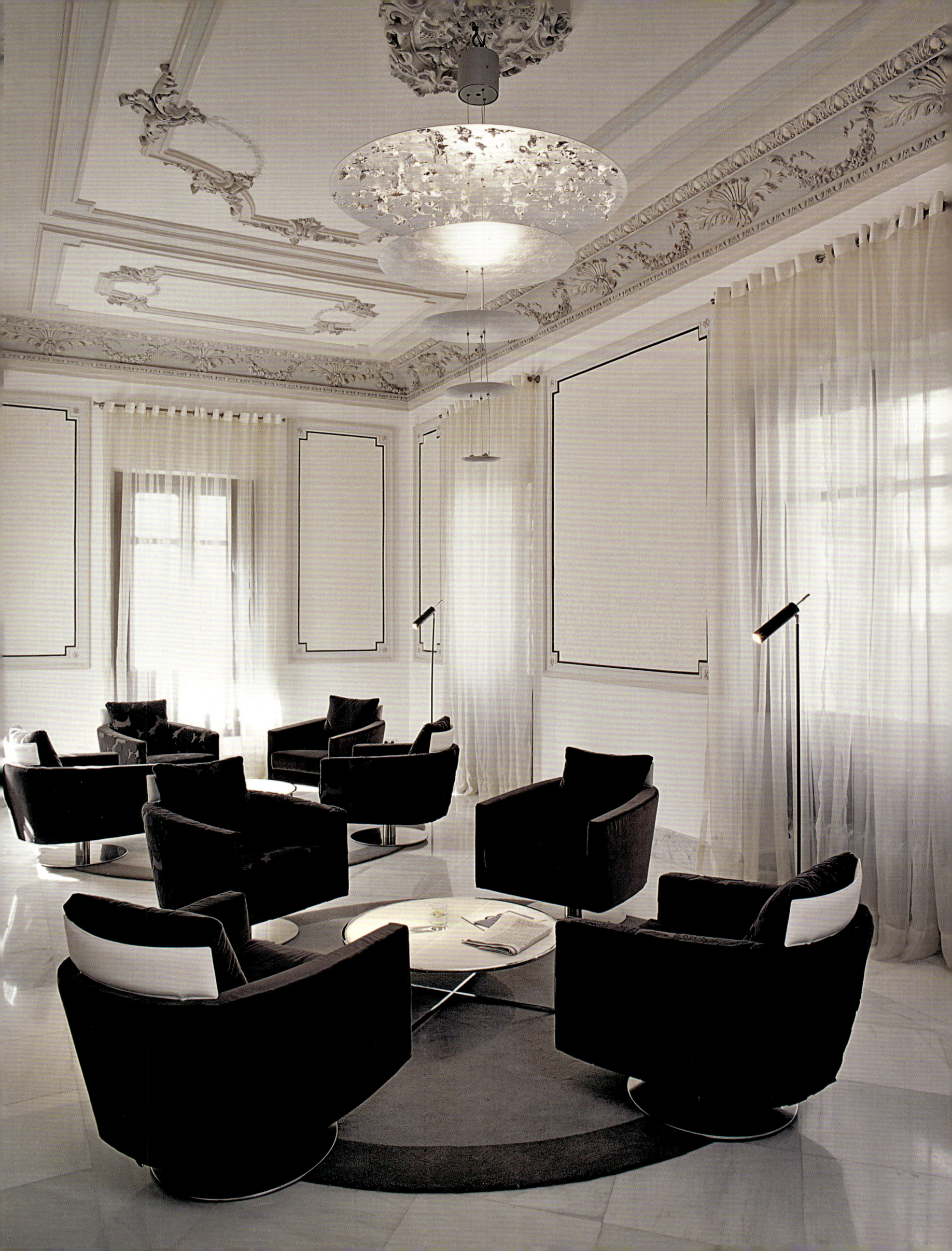

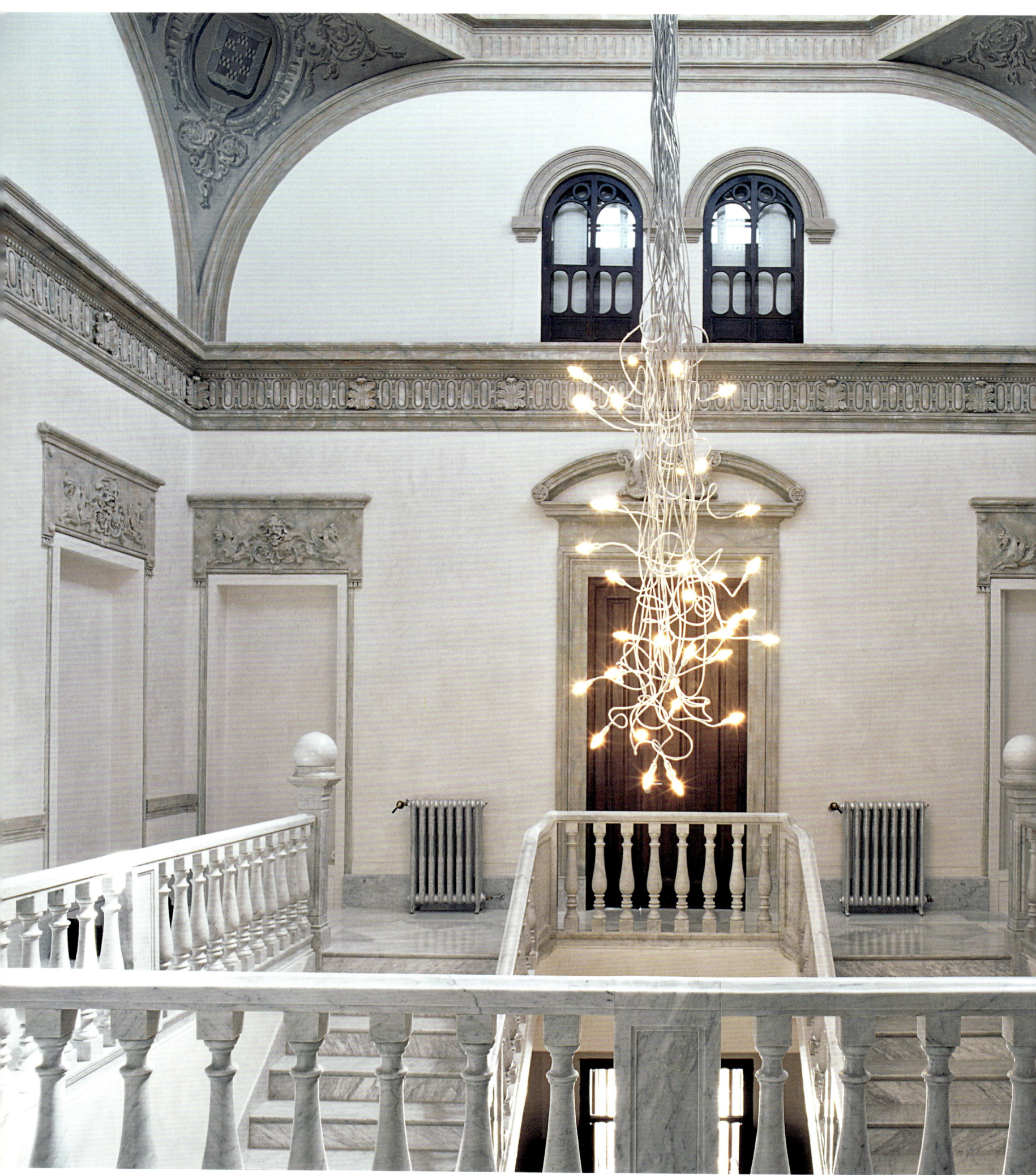

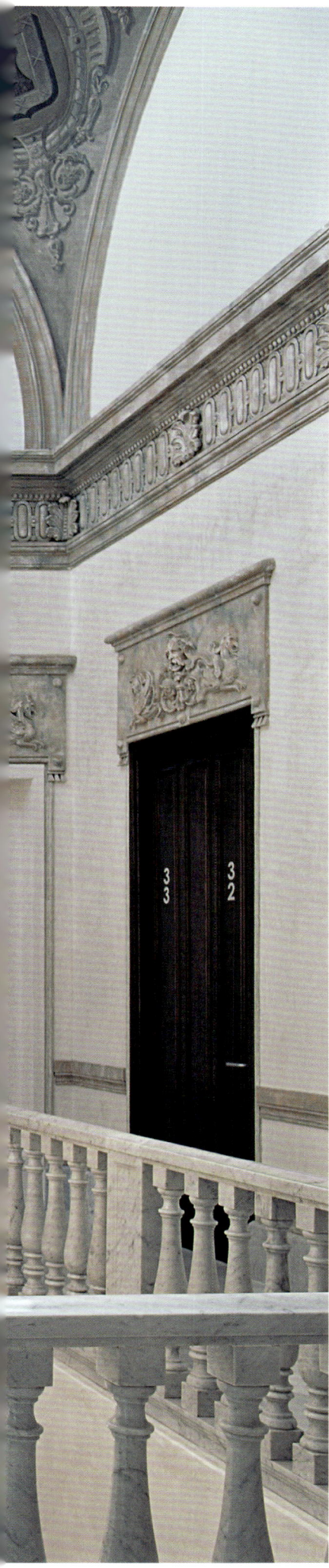

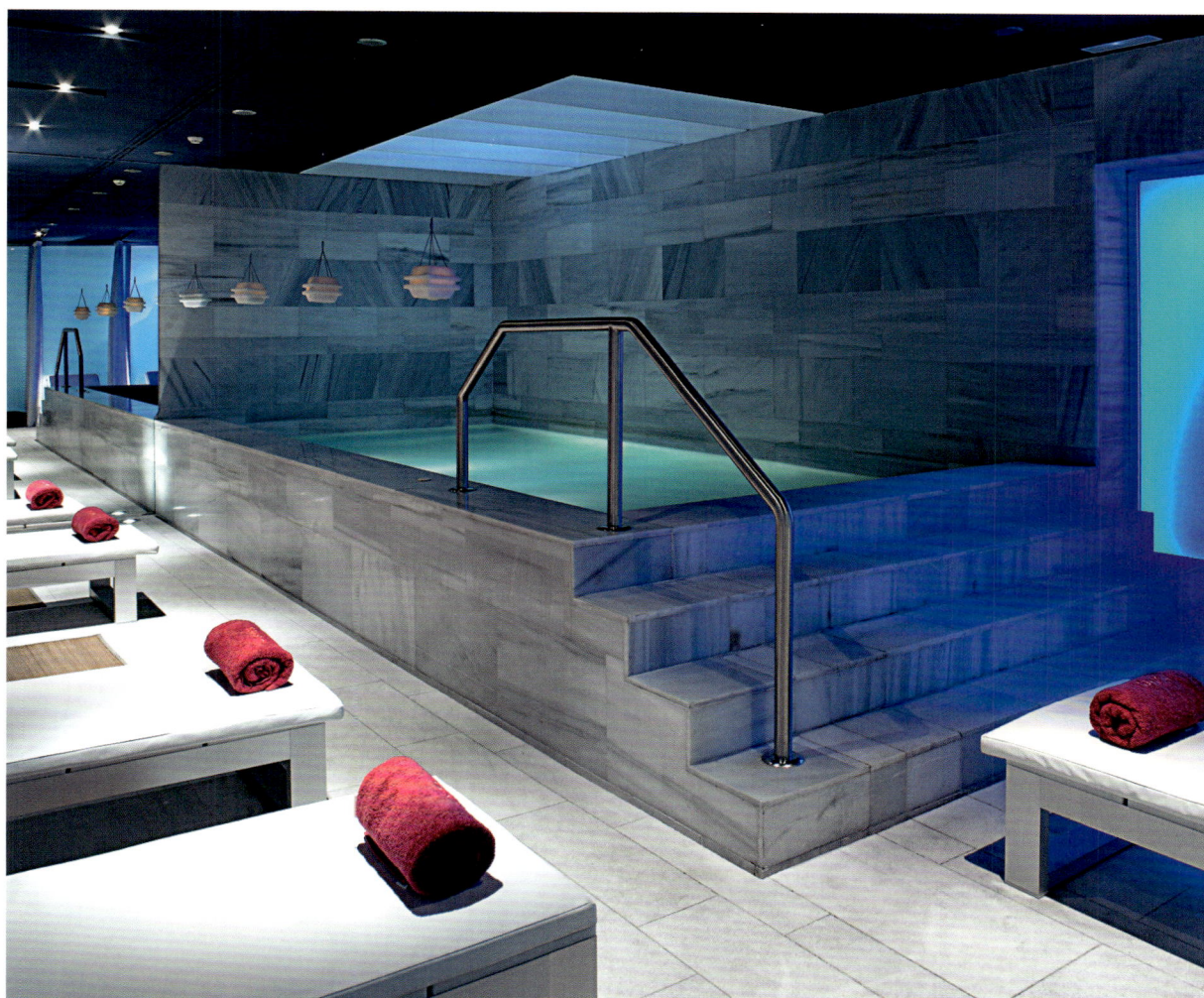

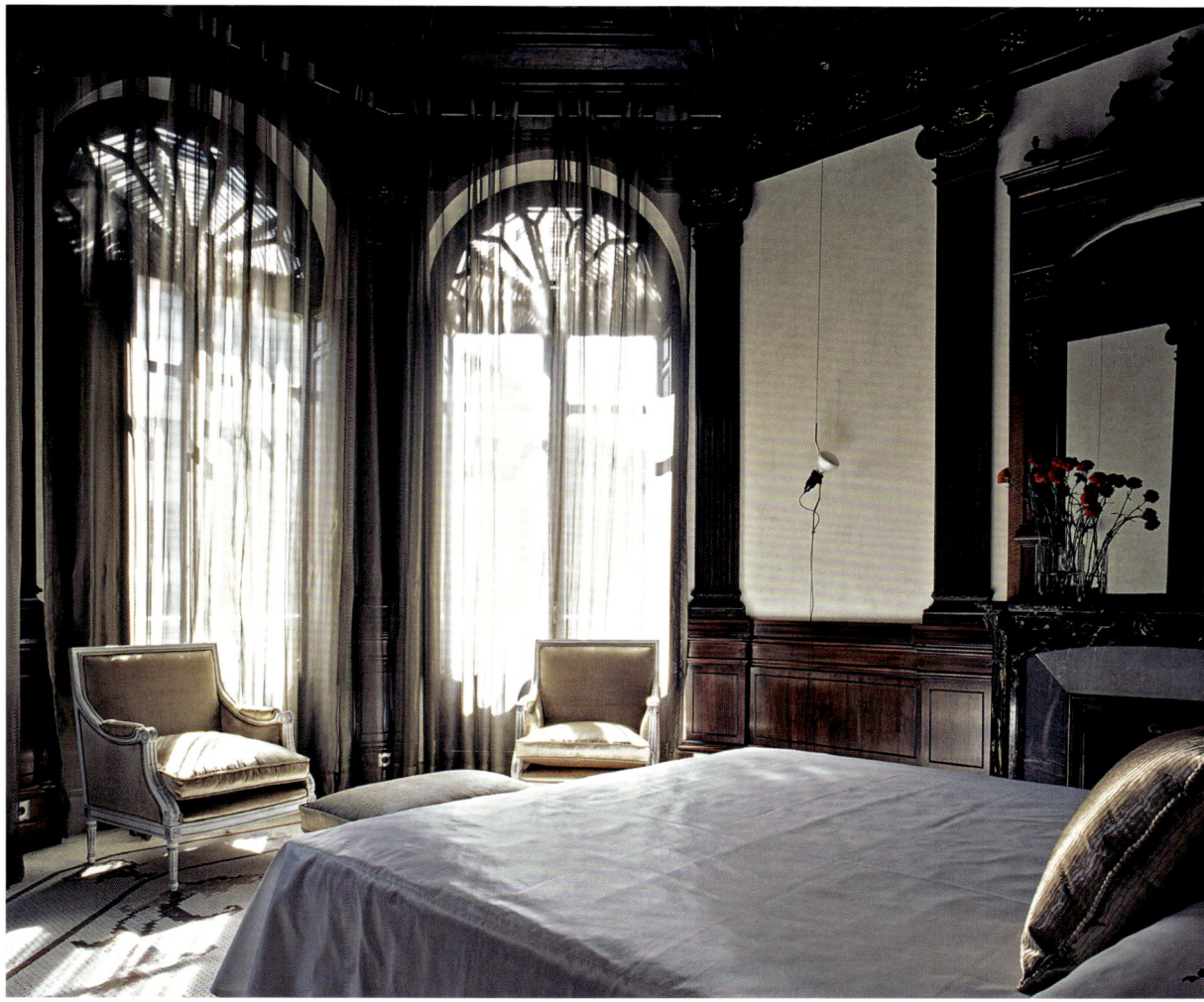

28013 Madrid
Spain
Phone: +34 915 237 980
Fax: +34 915 237 981
www.hoteldelasletras.com

Rooms: 102 rooms including 3 suites
Facilities: Restaurant, lounge, fitness & spa, solarium, library
Services: Meeting rooms for up to 150 people
Located: In the city center next to the Puerta del Sol and Mayor Square
Public transportation: Metro Gran Vía, Sevilla
Style: Modern

The name is a commitment: quotes from famous authors adorn the walls in all 102 rooms in De las Letras. And should one of the muses haunting among the worthy assortment of books from the library shelves spur a guest on to literary ambition, they have endless virtual space for publishing poems on their website. The literary spirited hotel came to life in a belle époque building from 1917. The staircase laden in handsome carving and mosaic inspired the designer Virgina Figueras to mate them with modern interiors and crown it with the roof terrace looking far out over Madrid.

Der Name verpflichtet: Im De las Letras zieren Zitate berühmter Autoren die Wände aller 102 Zimmer, die hauseigene Bibliothek ist gut sortiert, und Gäste mit schriftstellerischen Ambitionen können auf der Website eigene Gedichte veröffentlichen. Entstanden ist das literarisch inspirierte Hotel in einem Belle-Époque-Gebäude von 1917. Designerin Virginia Figueras hat alte Elemente wie das traumhafte Treppenhaus mit Holzschnitzereien und Mosaiken mit modernen Interieurs verbunden und mit einer Dachterrasse gekrönt, die weit über Madrid blickt.

Son nom donne le ton : au De las Letras, des citations d'auteurs célèbres décorent les murs de chacune des 102 chambres, et si les muses qui hantent la bibliothèque bien fournie inspirent quelque ambition littéraire aux clients, ils disposent d'un espace virtuel pour publier leur œuvre sur le site web de l'établissement. Cet hôtel littéralement inspiré a pris vis dans un immeuble Belle Epoque datant de 1917. Son designer, Virginia Figueras, a marié des éléments anciens, comme un merveilleux escalier sculpté en bois et décoré de mosaïques, avec un intérieur moderne et a couvert le tout d'un toit terrasse offrant une vue sur tout Madrid.

Su nombre obliga a ello: en el Hotel de las Letras, diversas citas de autores célebres adornan las paredes de sus 102 habitaciones. Este establecimiento posee una biblioteca propia bien dotada y los huéspedes con aspiraciones de poeta pueden publicar sus propias obras en la página Web del hotel. Un edificio belle-époque del año 1917 alberga hoy este hotel inspirado en la literatura. La diseñadora Virginia Figueras armonizó elementos antiguos, como la maravillosa escalinata de madera tallada y mosaicos, con interiores modernos y coronó su obra con una azotea que ofrece una espléndida vista sobre Madrid.

Il nome dice tutto: nel De las Letras le pareti di tutte le 102 camere sono decorate da citazioni di autori famosi, la biblioteca dell'albergo vanta un ottimo assortimento di libri, e gli ospiti con ambizioni letterarie possono pubblicare le proprie poesie sulla pagina web dell'albergo. Culla di questo hotel ispirato al mondo della letteratura è un edificio in stile belle époque del 1917. La designer Virginia Figueras ha unito elementi antichi – come la meravigliosa scalinata, abbellita da intagli in legno e mosaici – a interni moderni, coronando il tutto con una terrazza sul tetto con vista su tutta Madrid.

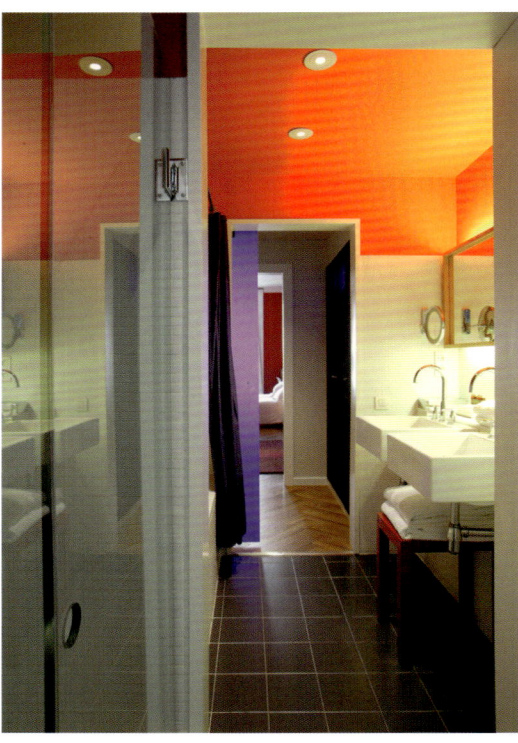
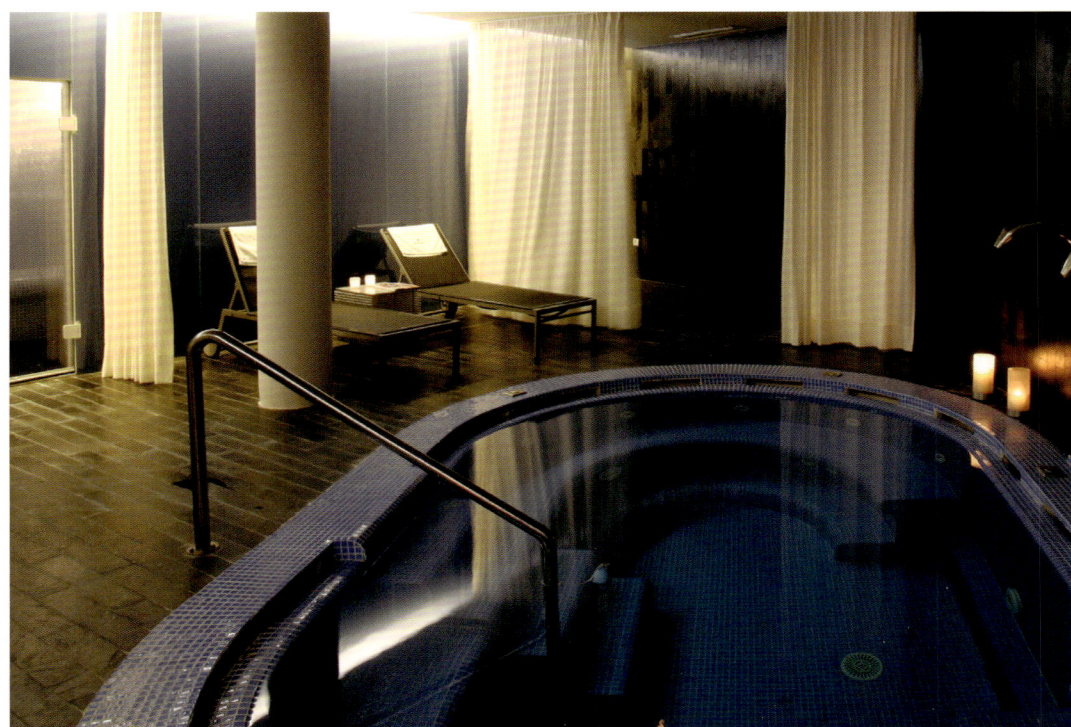

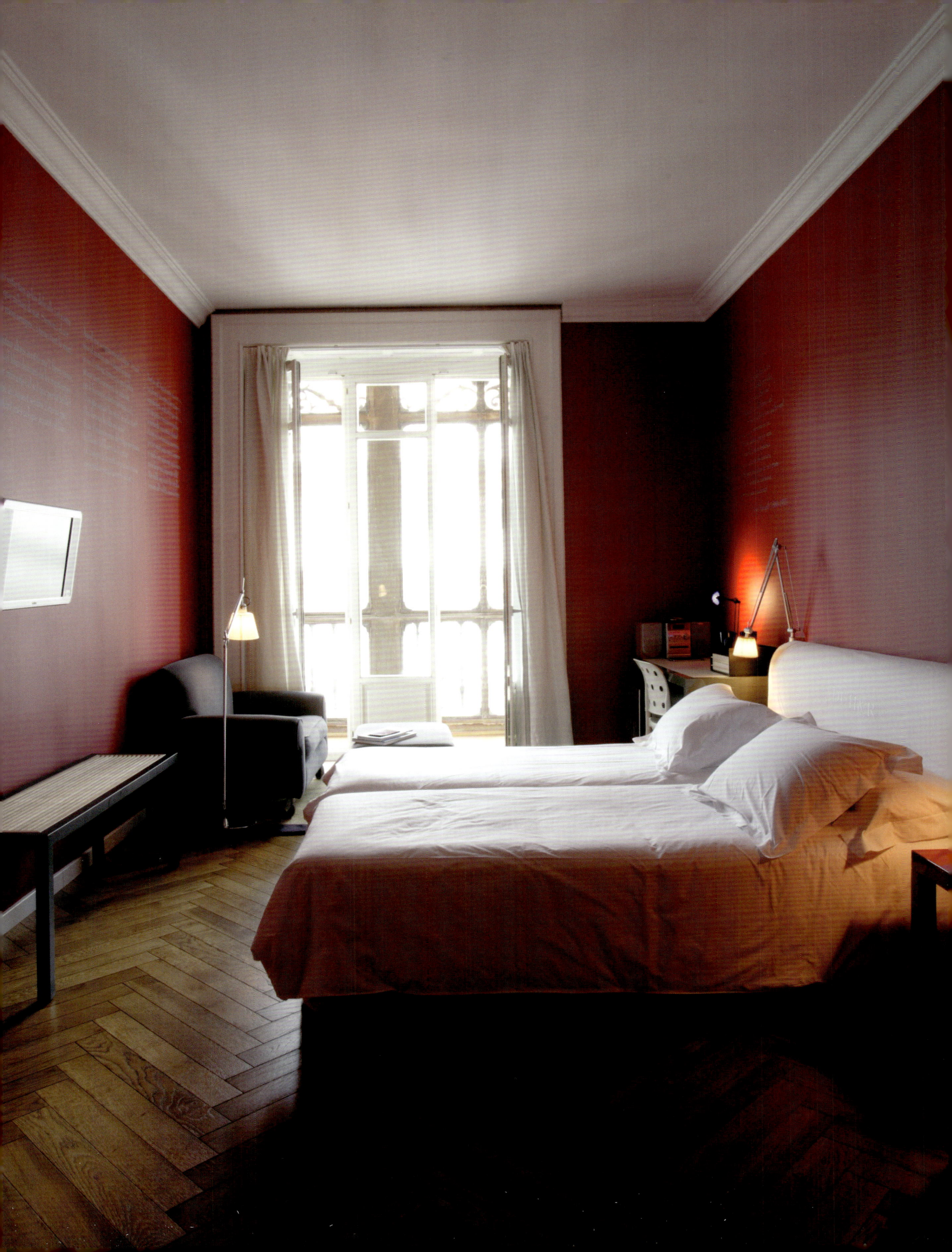

Hotel Puerta América

Madrid, Spain

Avenida de América, 41
28002 Madrid
Spain
Phone: +34 917 445 400
Fax: +34 917 445 401
www.hotelpuertamerica.com

Price category: €€€
Rooms: 315 rooms
Facilities: Restaurant, bars and café, garden, indoor, 16 meeting rooms, swimming pool, sauna, business center
Services: Babysitting
Located: 8 km to Madrid-Barajas airport, in a business and commercial area of Madrid
Public transportation: Metro Cartagena
Style: Contemporary design

19 of the best architects of the world draft one single hotel: it sounds like an unattainable dream, but became reality in Madrid. For three years the greats of the trade literally came and went each trying his best to out-do the other in designing the 315 rooms on twelve floors. From Zaha Hadid's organic forms, Lord Norman Fosters' sexy material mix of leather, wood and alabaster, to Jean Nouvel's Hollywood-like ceiling paintings, the Puerta América trumps with the best of international design. Even the subterranean garage makes an artistic drive out of parking.

19 der besten Architekten der Welt entwerfen ein einziges Hotel – was wie eine unerfüllbare Wunschvorstellung klingt, wurde in Madrid Wirklichkeit. Drei Jahre lang gaben sich hier die Größen des Fachs buchstäblich die Klinke in die Hand und gestalteten 315 Zimmer auf zwölf Etagen. Vom Zaha Hadids organischen Formen über Lord Norman Fosters sexy Materialmix aus Leder, Holz und Alabaster bis zu Jean Nouvels hollywoodesken Deckengemälden präsentiert das Puerta América ein „Best of" des internationalen Designs – selbst die Tiefgarage ist ein Kunstwerk.

19 des meilleurs architectes au monde construisant un hôtel étonnant : ce qui semble un rêve impossible est devenu réalité à Madrid. Pendant trois ans, les meilleurs de la profession se sont littéralement donné la main pour créer 315 chambres réparties sur douze étages. Des formes organiques de Zaha Hadid et des mélanges sexys de cuir, de bois et d'albâtre de Lord Norman Foster aux peintures de plafond hollywoodiennes de Jean Nouvel, le Puerta América présente le meilleur du design international : même le parking souterrain est une vraie œuvre d'art.

Diecinueve de los mejores arquitectos del mundo han colaborado para diseñar este hotel, lo que parecía un sueño imposible, pasó a ser realidad en Madrid. Los grandes del sector trabajaron codo con codo durante tres años para crear 315 habitaciones repartidas en doce plantas. Desde las orgánicas formas de Zaha Hadid, pasando por la sugerente mezcla de materiales en cuero, madera y alabastro de Lord Norman Foster, hasta los frescos al estilo de Hollywood de Jean Nouvel, el hotel Puerta América presenta una selección de lo mejor del diseño internacional. Hasta el garaje subterráneo es una verdadera obra de arte.

Diciannove dei migliori architetti del mondo per il progetto di un solo albergo – sembra un sogno irrealizzabile, e invece a Madrid è diventato realtà. Per tre anni i grandi del settore si sono letteralmente passati il testimone realizzando 315 camere distribuite su dodici piani. Dalle forme organiche di Zaha Hadid alla sensuale combinazione di materiali come pelle, legno e alabastro proposta da Lord Norman Foster fino ai dipinti hollywoodiani sul soffitto ideati da Jean Nouvel, il Puerta América presenta il "best of" del design internazionale – lo stesso garage sotterraneo è un'opera d'arte.

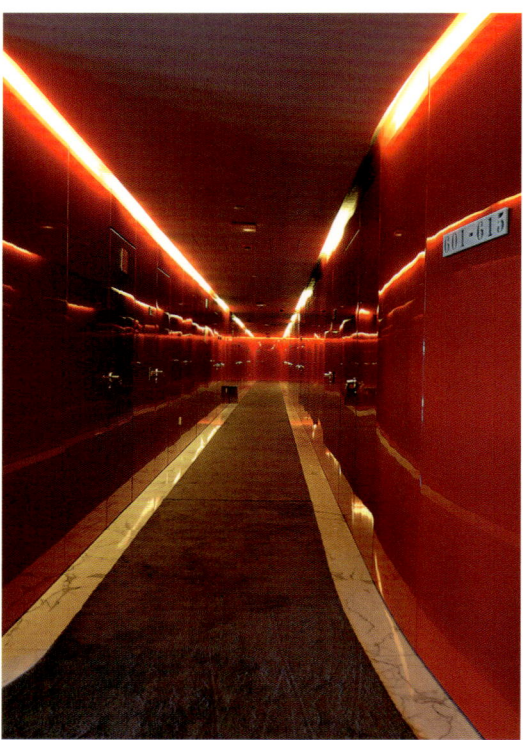 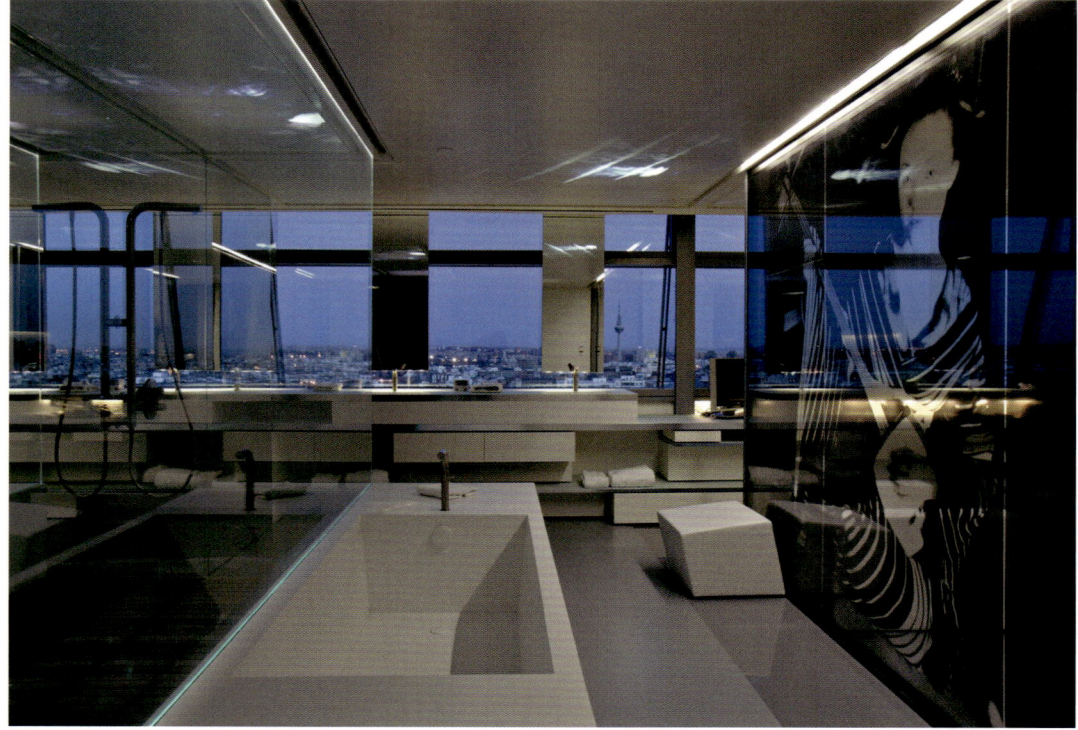

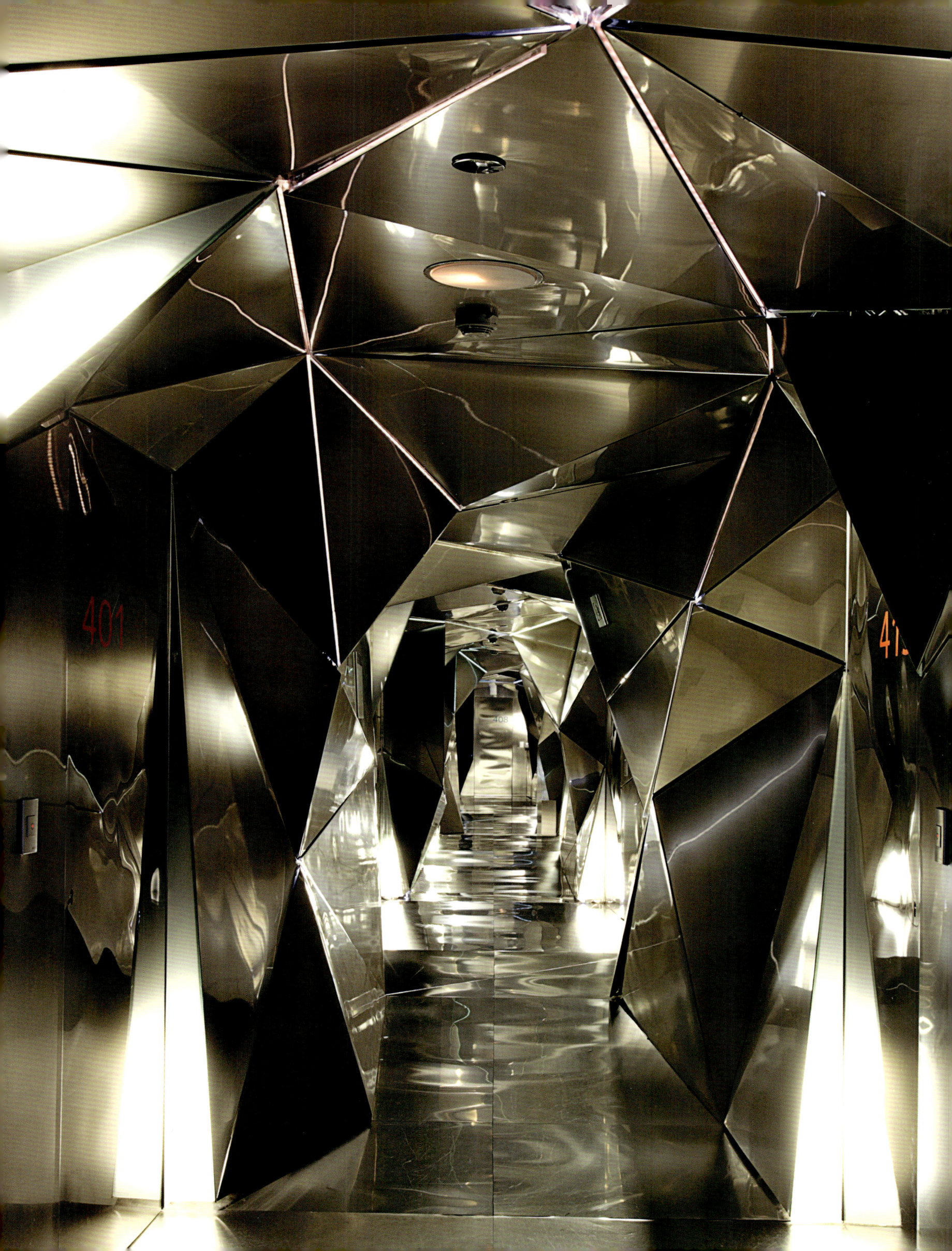

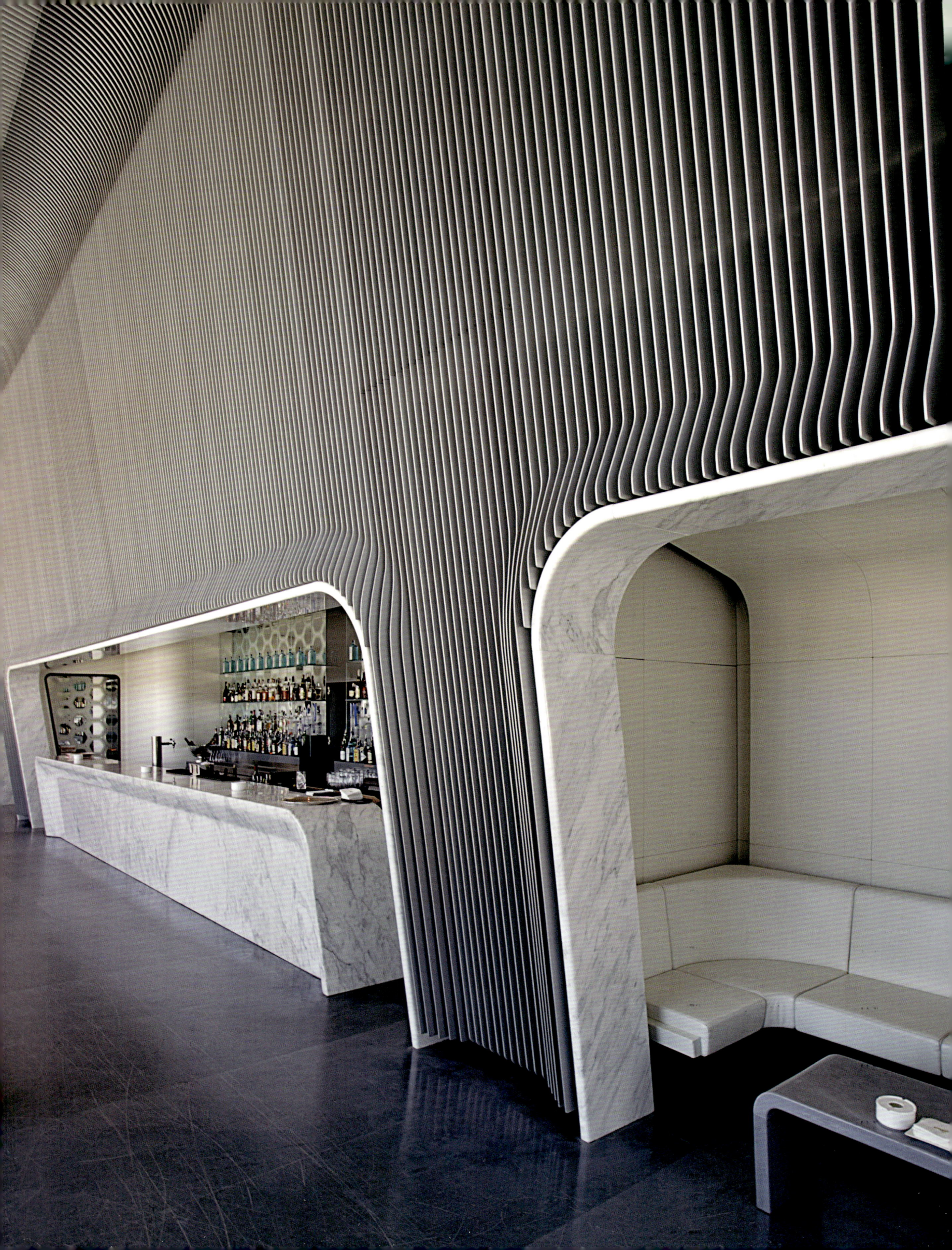

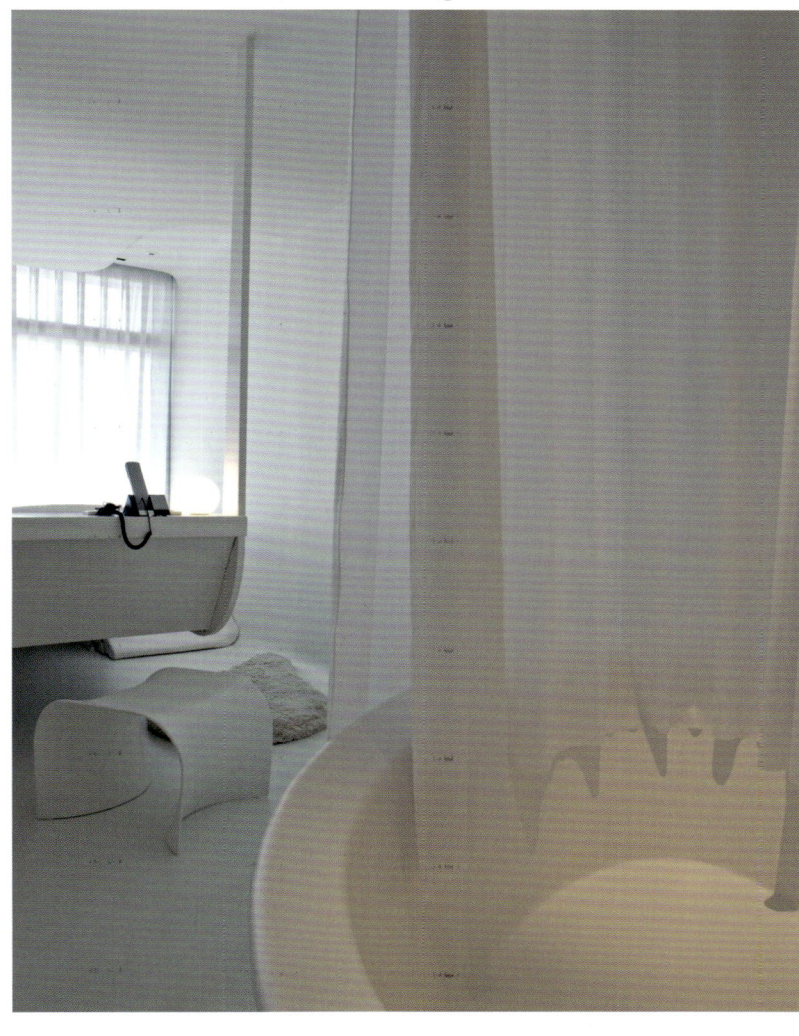
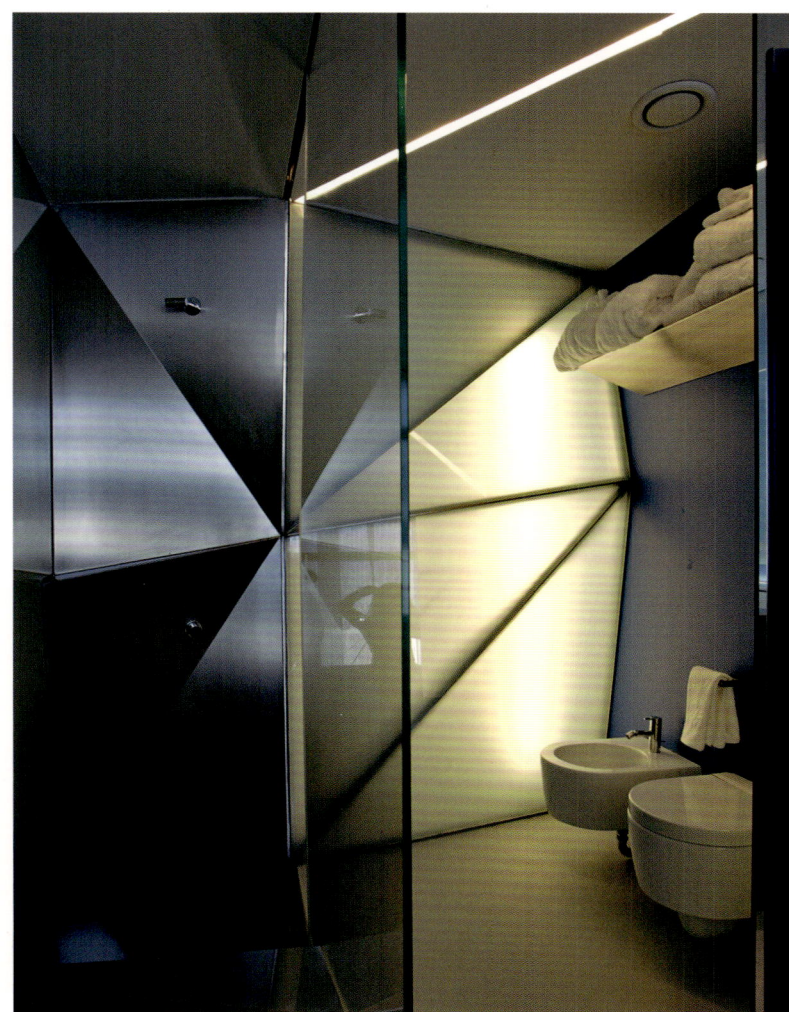
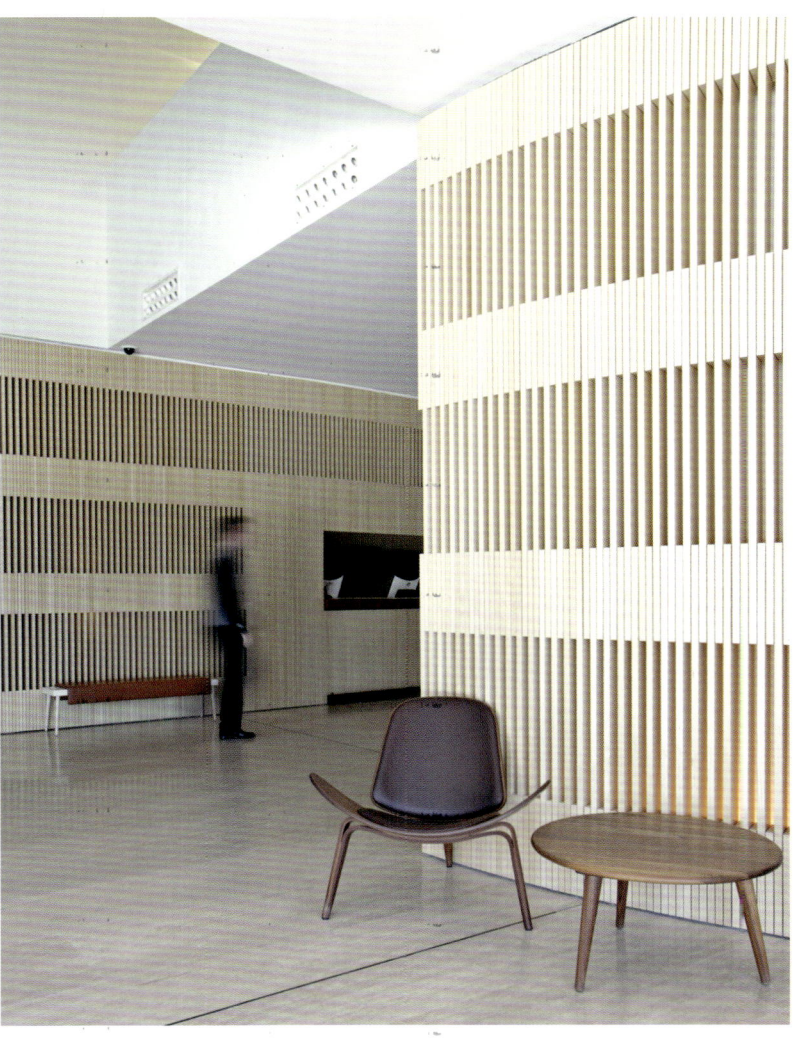
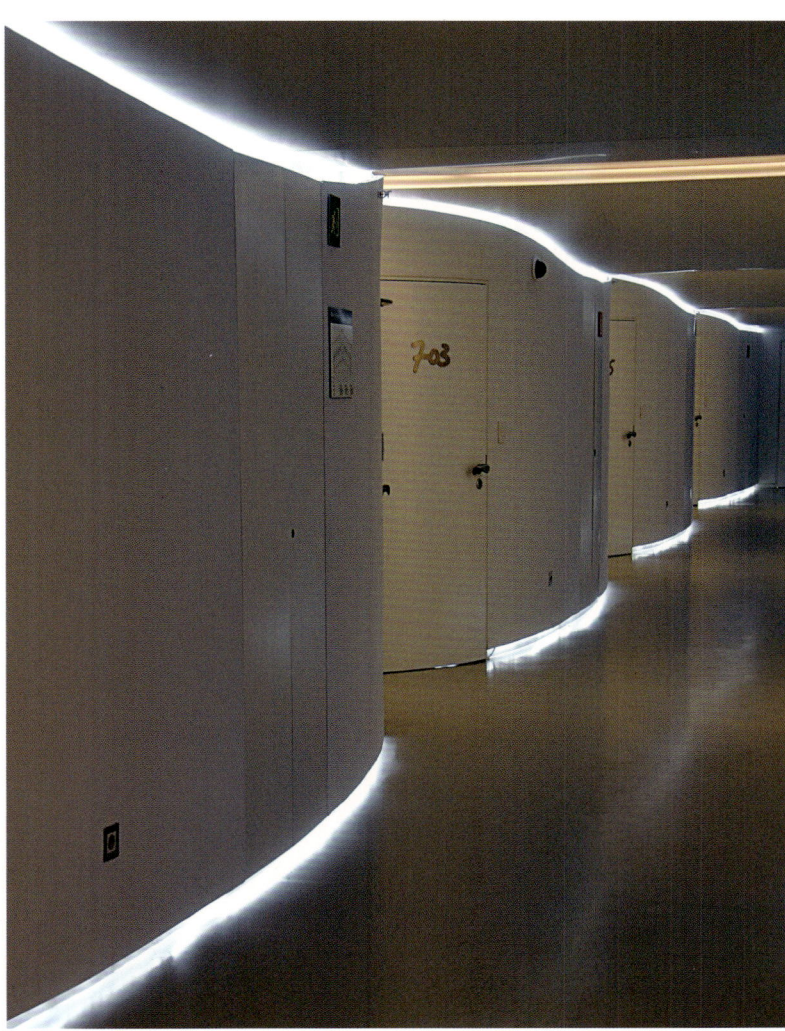

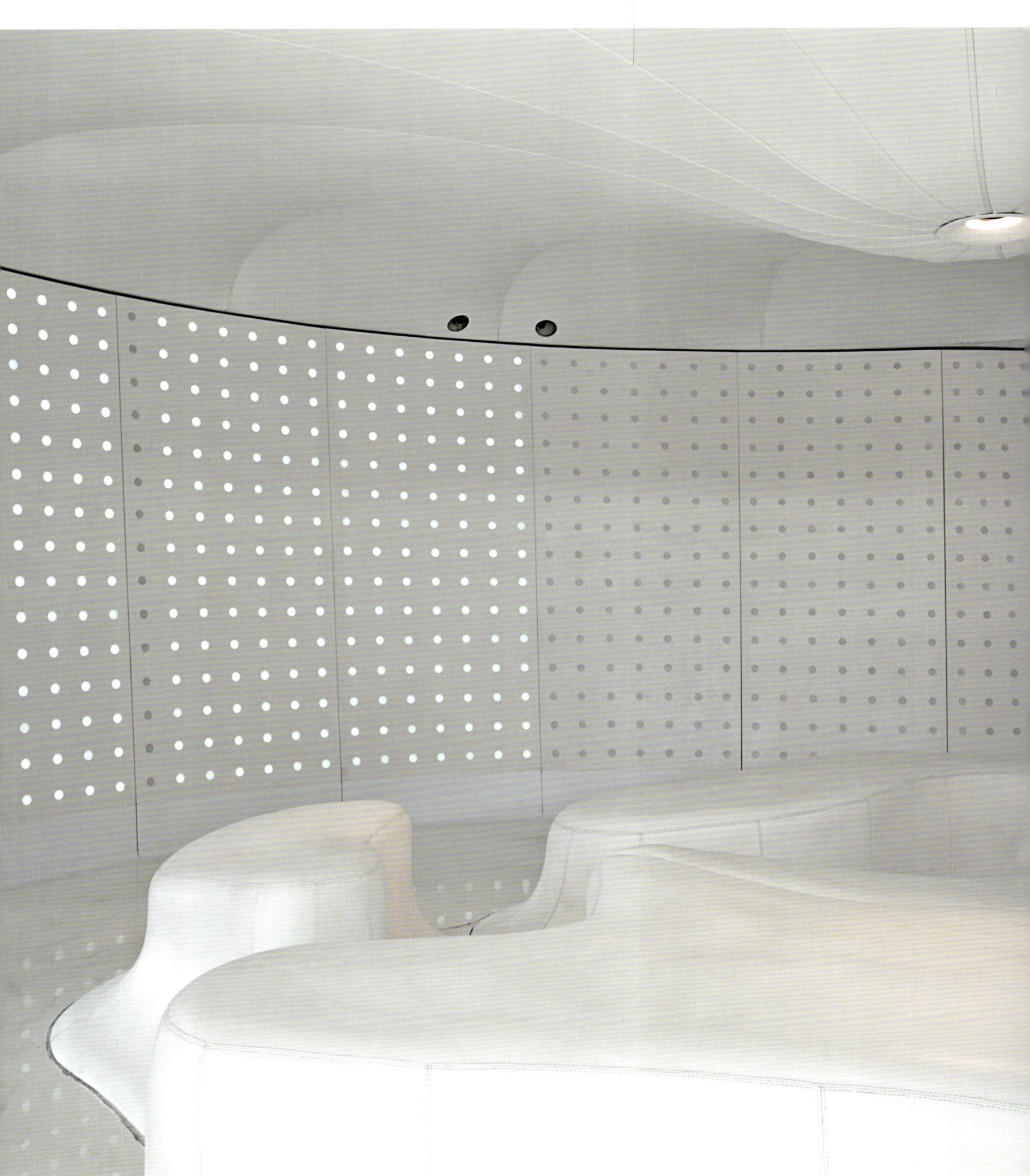

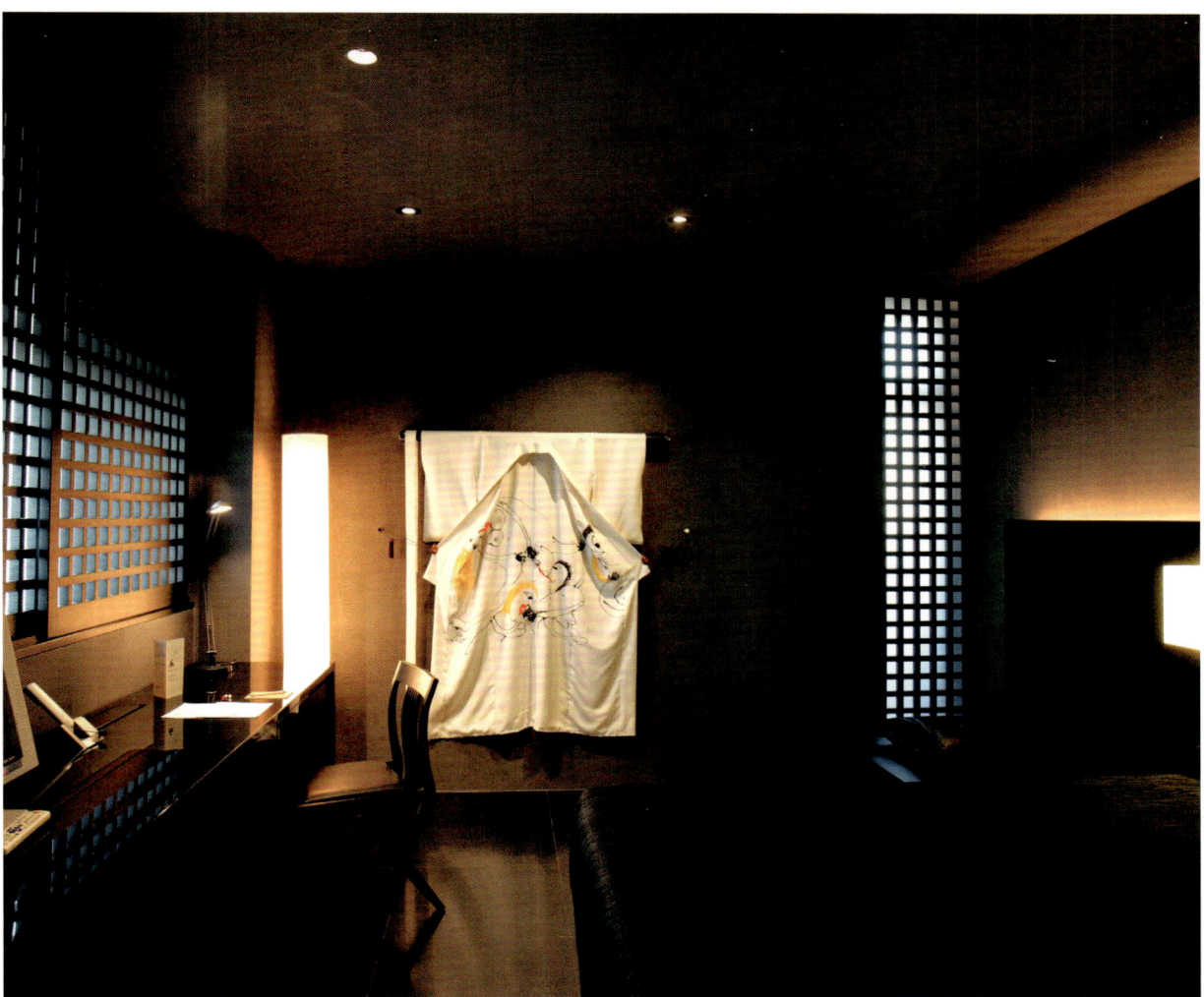

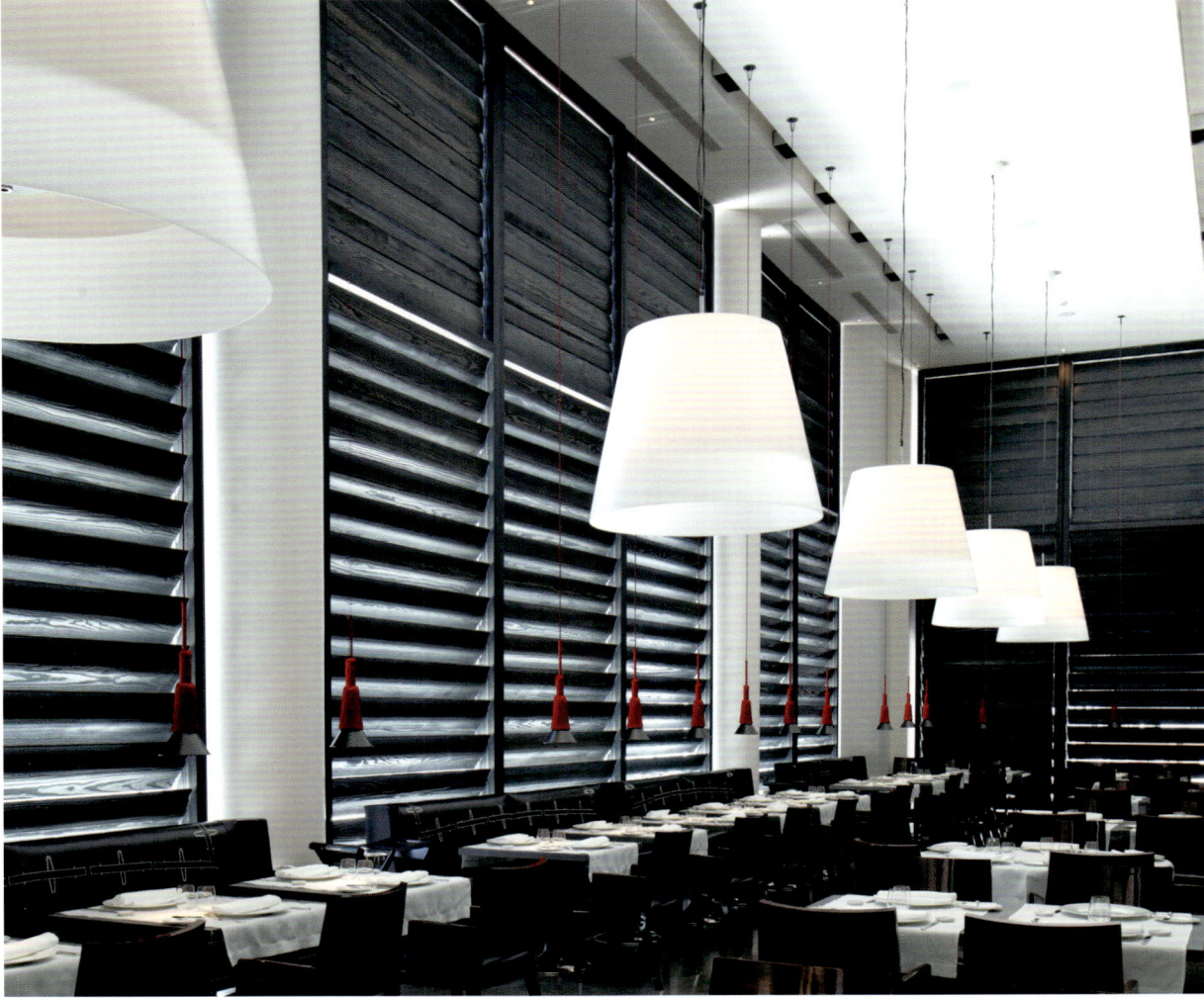

Hotel Urban

Madrid, Spain

Carrera de San Jerónimo, 34
28014 Madrid
Spain
Phone: +34 917 877 770
Fax: +34 917 877 799
www.derbyhotels.com

Price category: €€€
Rooms: 96 rooms
Facilities: Gourmet restaurant Europa Decó and La Terraza, the GlassBar, rooftop pool, solarium, art collection, gym
Services: Meeting rooms
Located: In the cultural center of Madrid, next to the shopping and business district
Public transportation: Metro Sevilla
Style: Art deco

Once the palace of the Duque de Ribas stood here, today an ultra-modern construction of steel and glass enclose one of the noblest hotels of Madrid. The design of the 96 rooms is an exclusive trip around the world with tropical wood, green marble from Guatemala, antique portraits from China and totems from Papua New Guinea. Not only hotel guests slurp down fresh oysters on Philippe Starck's Ghost Chairs in the "GlassBar," but also trend-conscious Madrilenians—the Urban is considered to be one of the city's hot spots.

Einst stand hier der Palast des Duque de Ribas, heute birgt ein ultramoderner Bau aus Stahl und Glas eines der edelsten Hotels von Madrid. Das Design der 96 Zimmer ist eine exklusive Reise um die Welt – die Hölzer stammen aus den Tropen, der grüne Marmor aus Guatemala, die antiken Portraits aus China und die Totems aus Papua-Neuguinea. In der „GlassBar" mit Philippe Starcks Ghost Chairs schlürfen nicht nur Hotelgäste frische Austern, sondern auch trendbewusste Madrileños – das Urban gilt als neuer Szenetreff der Stadt.

Le Palais des Ducs de Ribas se situait autrefois ici, mais c'est aujourd'hui un bâtiment ultramoderne de verre et d'acier, considéré comme l'un des hôtels les plus chics de Madrid. Le design des 96 chambres représente un voyage unique à travers le monde : le bois utilisé provient des tropiques, le marbre vert du Guatemala, les portraits antiques de Chine et les totems sont originaires de Papouasie-Nouvelle Guinée. Les clients de l'hôtel mais aussi tous les Madrileños branchés dégustent des huîtres fraîches au « GlassBar » sur des Ghost Chairs de Philippe Starck : l'Urban est considéré comme le nouveau lieu de rencontre à la mode.

En otra época se erguía en este lugar el palacio del Duque de Ribas. Hoy en día, un edificio ultramoderno de acero y cristal alberga aquí uno de los hoteles más nobles de Madrid. El diseño de sus 96 habitaciones es un exclusivo viaje por el mundo, las maderas provienen de los trópicos, el mármol verde de Guatemala, los retratos antiguos de China y los tótem de Papúa Nueva Guinea. Entre las Ghost Chairs de Philippe Starck en el "GlassBar", no sólo huéspedes, sino también los madrileños más a la moda deleitan sus paladares con ostras frescas. El Hotel Urban se ha convertido en un nuevo y obligado punto de encuentro en la ciudad.

Un tempo qui sorgeva il palazzo del Duque de Ribas, oggi questa modernissima struttura in vetro e acciaio ospita uno dei più raffinati alberghi di Madrid. Il design delle sue 96 camere è un esclusivo viaggio intorno al mondo – il legno utilizzato proviene dai tropici, il marmo verde dal Guatemala, i ritratti antichi dalla Cina e i totem dalla Papua Nuova Guinea. Nel "GlassBar", con le sue Ghost Chairs disegnate da Philippe Starck, vedrete non solo gli ospiti dell'albergo intenti a succhiare ostriche, ma anche i madrileños più attenti alla moda – l'Urban è il nuovo posto 'in' della città.

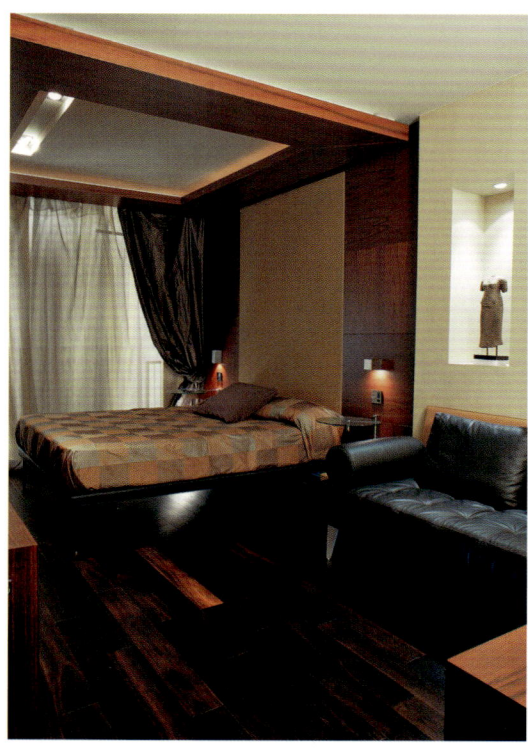
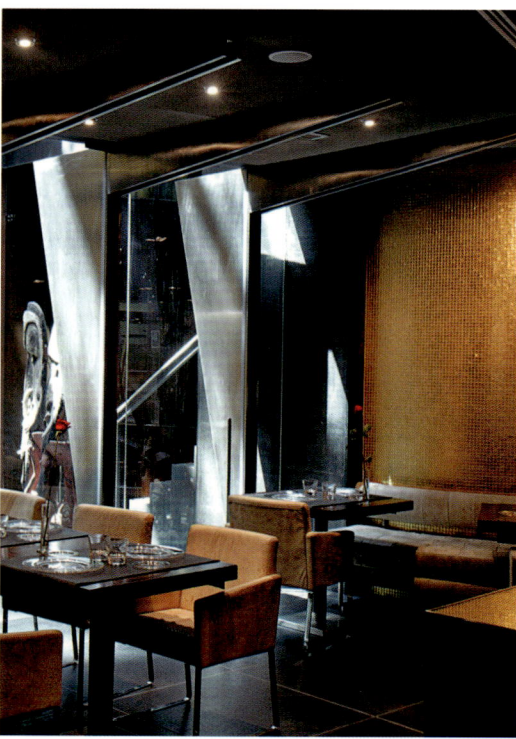
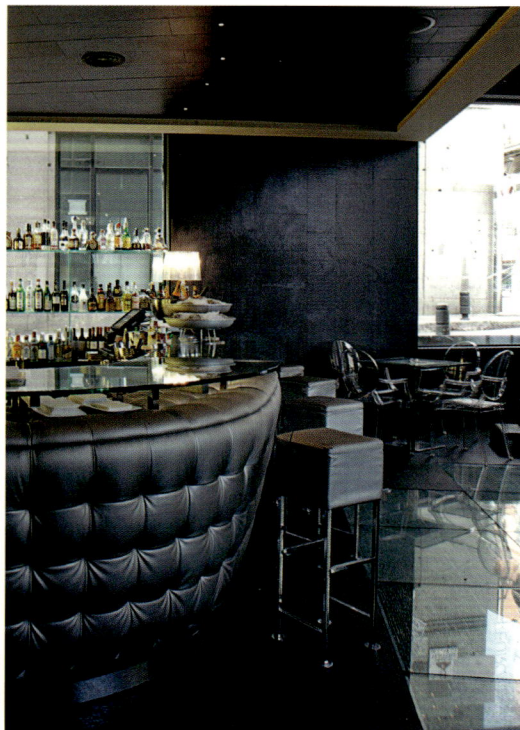

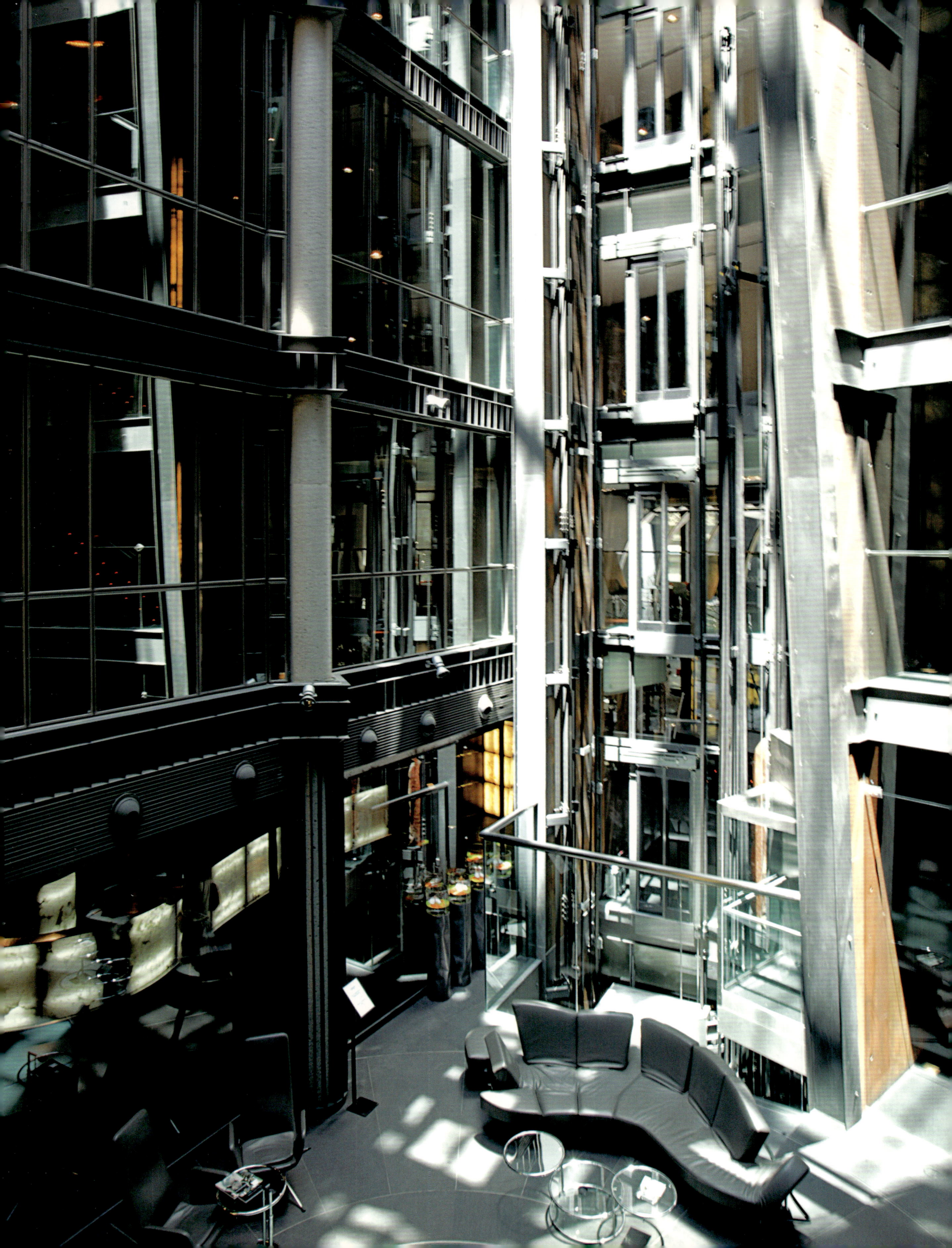

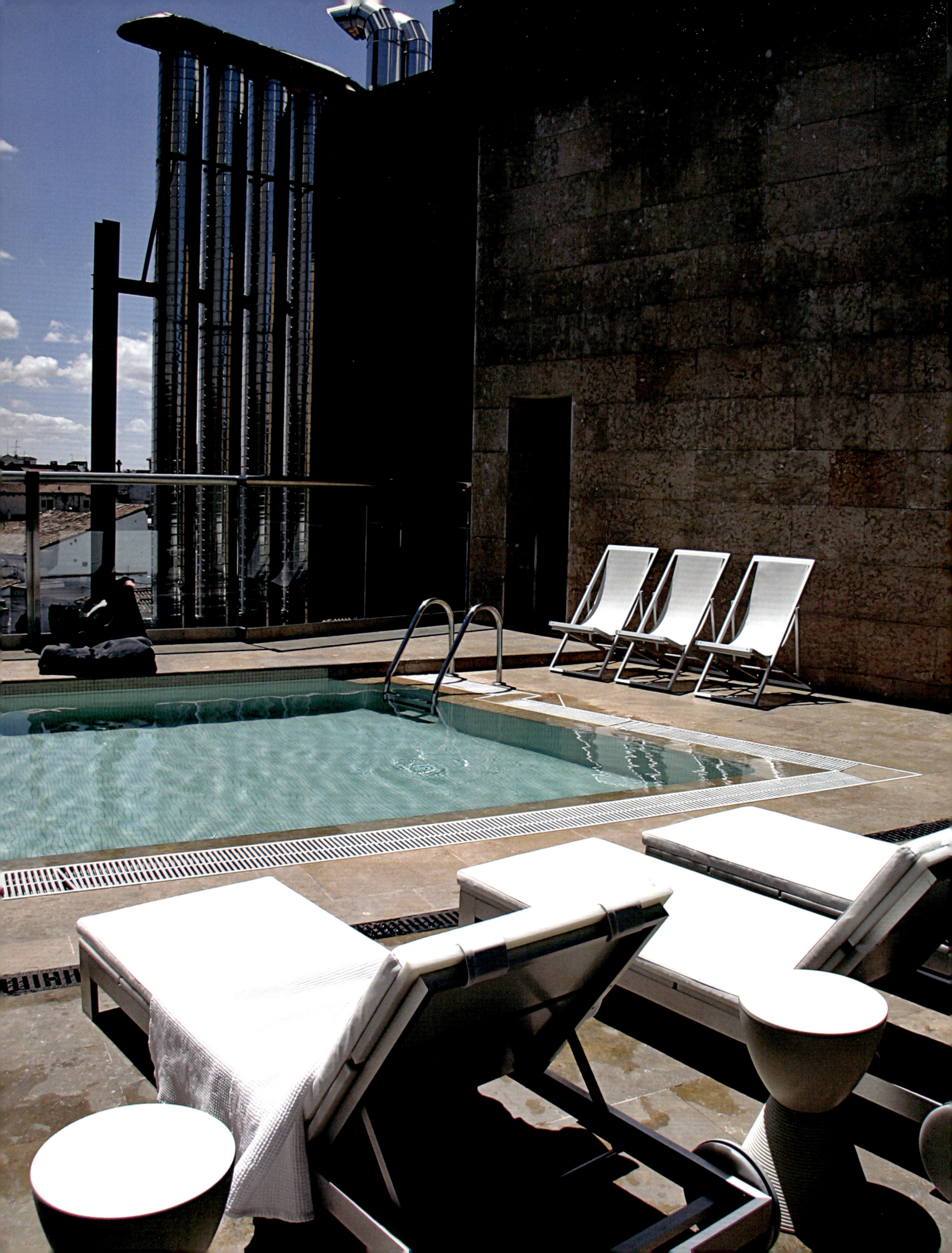

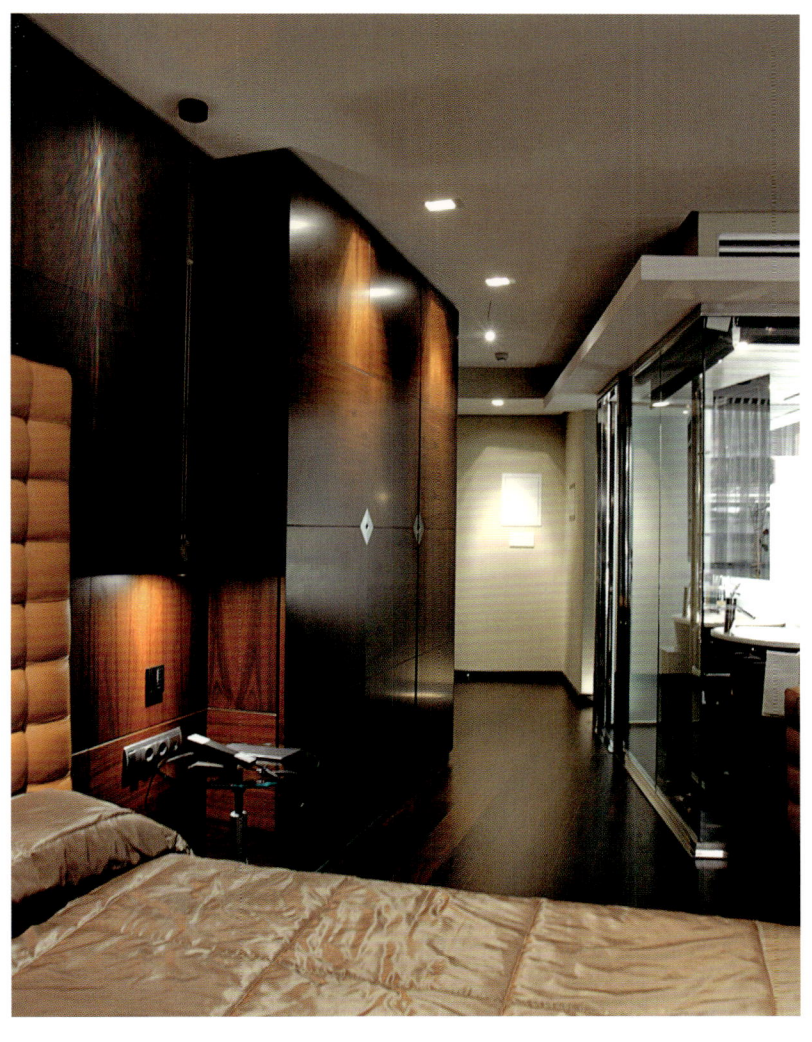
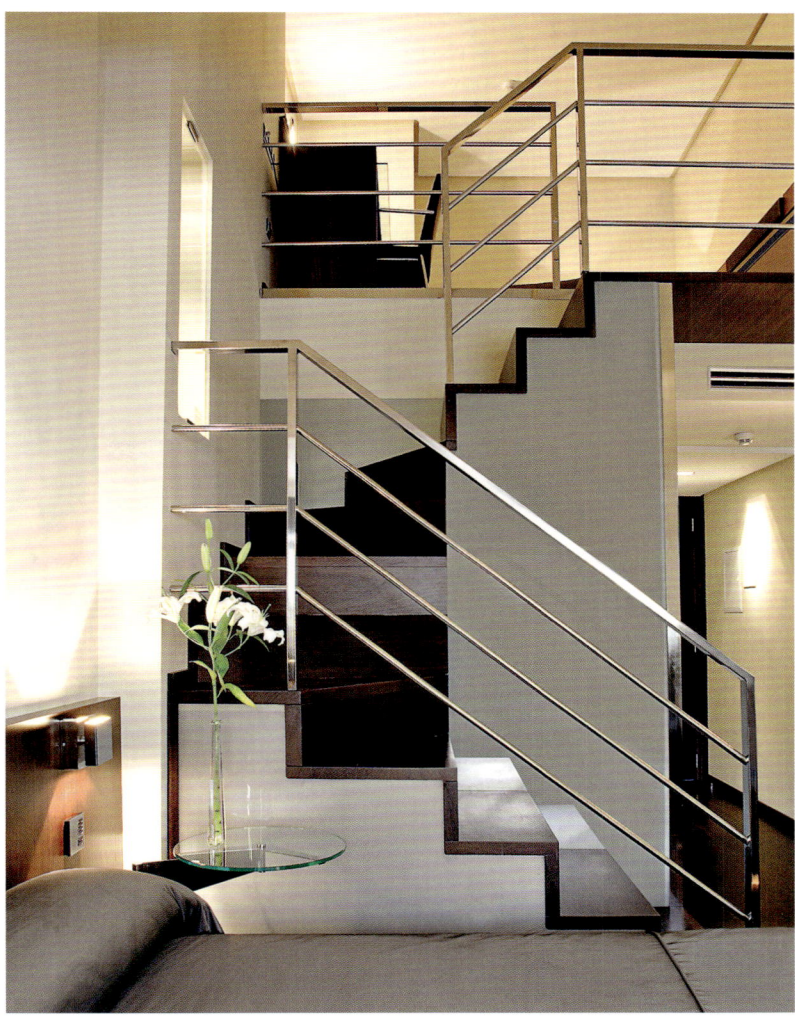
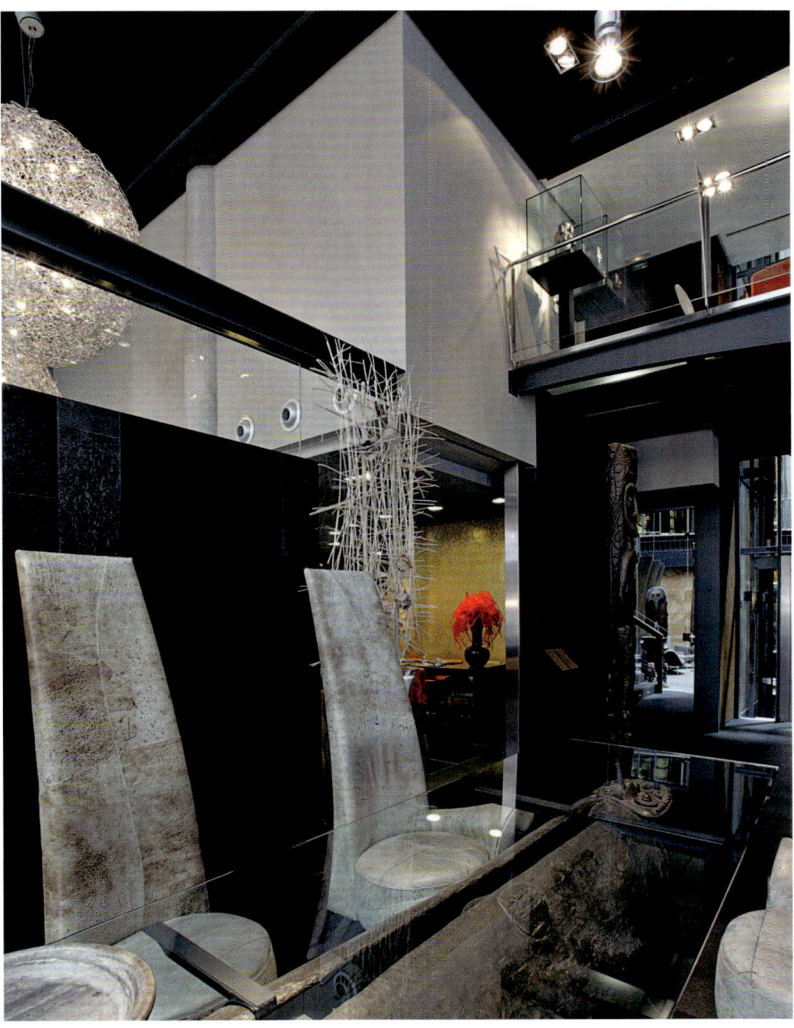
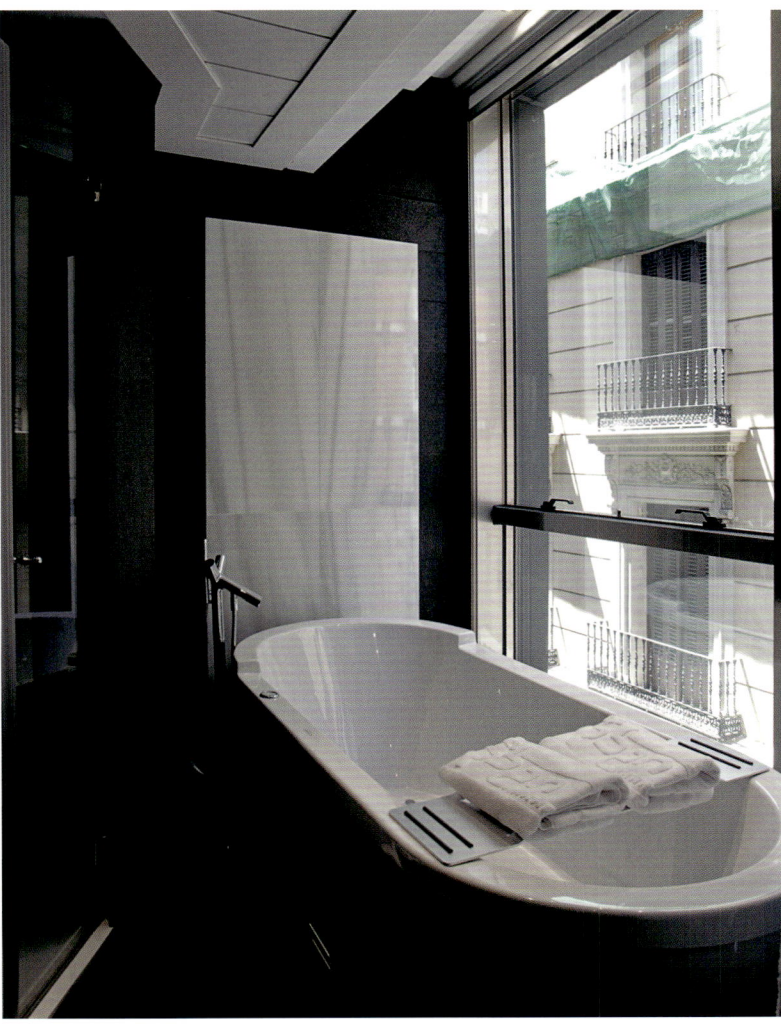

4159 Porto
Portugal
Phone: +351 226 086 600
Fax: +351 226 091 467
www.hotelportopalacio.com

Rooms: 251 rooms and suites
Facilities: 2 restaurants, 2 bars, business center, health club and spa, pool
Services: Babysitting, hair stylist, concierge, parking, laundry
Located: In the city center
Public transportation: Bus
Style: Modern luxury

Velvet soft sofas, silk curtains, floor heating in a marble bath and leather accessories all go to achieve the five star comfort of the hotel in the heart of Porto, one of the UNESCO world heritage cities. The opulent breakfast buffet boasts of over one hundred different delectables. Italian and Portuguese specialties are conjured up before your very eyes in the open "show kitchen" of the top restaurant "Le Coin." The view of the scenic bay is best from the VIP Lounge. And the famous Port wine cellars are only a few miles away.

Samtweiche Sofas, Seidengardinen, Fußbodenheizung im Marmorbad, Lederaccessoires – das Hotel im Herzen von Porto, einer UNESCO-Weltkulturerbestadt, setzt auf Fünf-Sterne-Komfort. Das opulente Frühstücksbüffet bietet über Hundert verschiedene Köstlichkeiten. Im Spitzenrestaurant „Le Coin" mit offener „Schauküche" werden italienische und portugiesische Spezialitäten serviert. Der Blick auf die traumhafte Bucht ist von der VIP-Lounge am besten. Und die berühmten Portwein-kellereien sind nur wenige Kilometer entfernt.

Des canapés de velours doux, des rideaux en soie, un chauffage par le sol sous la salle de bain en marbre, des accessoires en cuir : l'hôtel est au cœur de Porto, ville classée au patrimoine culturel mondial de l'UNESCO, et offre un confort cinq étoiles. L'opulent buffet du petit-déjeuner offre plus d'une centaine de délices, et dans le restaurant « Le Coin » des spécialités italiennes et portugaises sont préparées devant vous dans la cuisine ouverte. La vue sur la splendide baie est plus belle depuis le salon VIP. Et les célèbres caves à porto ne sont qu'à quelques kilomètres.

Sofás aterciopelados, cortinas de seda, mármol radiante en los suelos de los cuartos de baño, accesorios de cuero … Este hotel en el mismísimo corazón de Oporto, declarado patrimonio cultural de la humanidad por la UNESCO, apuesta por un confort de cinco estrellas. El copioso buffet del desayuno nos tienta con más de cien delicias diferentes. En el restaurante "Le Coin", con una cocina abierta de primera categoría, se sirven especialidades italianas y portuguesas. La vista sobre la espectacular bahía desde el salón VIP es espléndida y las famosas bodegas de oporto se encuentran a tan sólo unos pocos kilómetros.

Divani morbidi come il velluto, tende di seta, riscaldamento radiante a pavimento nei bagni di marmo, accessori in pelle – l'albergo nel cuore di Oporto, città annove-rata dall'UNESCO nel patrimonio culturale mondiale, punta sul comfort a cinque stelle. L'opulento buffet della prima colazione offre più di cento diverse prelibatezze. Nel superbo ristorante "Le Coin", dotato di cucina aperta a vista, si servono specialità italiane e portoghesi. Il panorama della favolosa baia si gode al meglio dalla cosiddetta VIP lounge. E le famose cantine che offrono vino di porto non sono che a pochi chilometri di distanza.

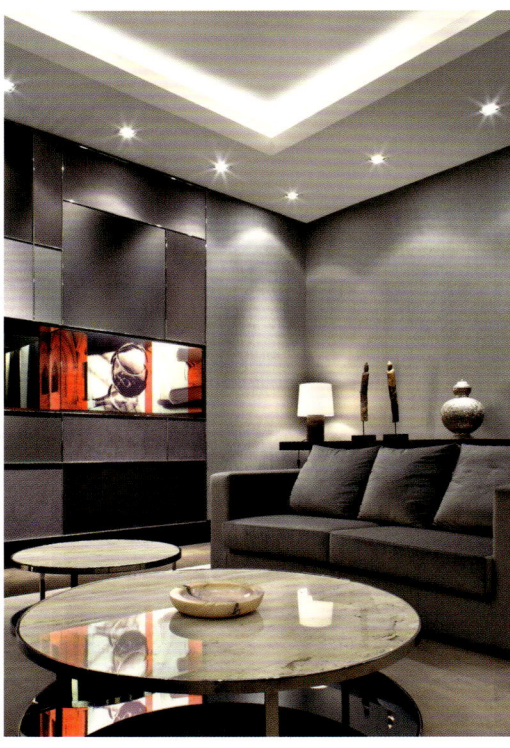
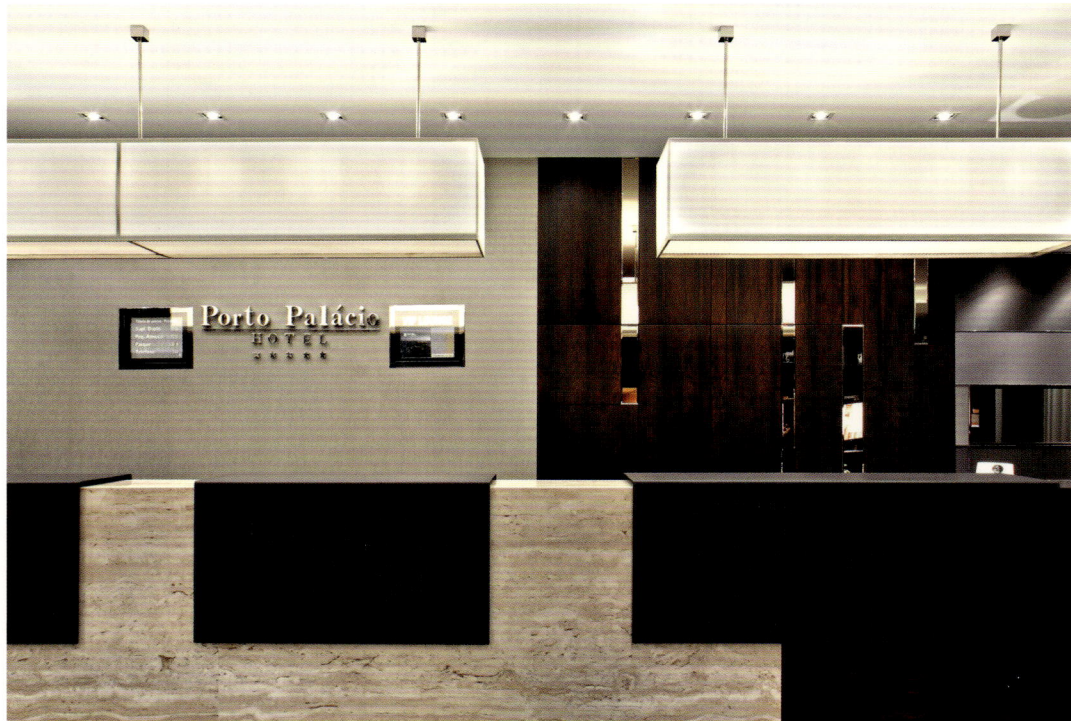

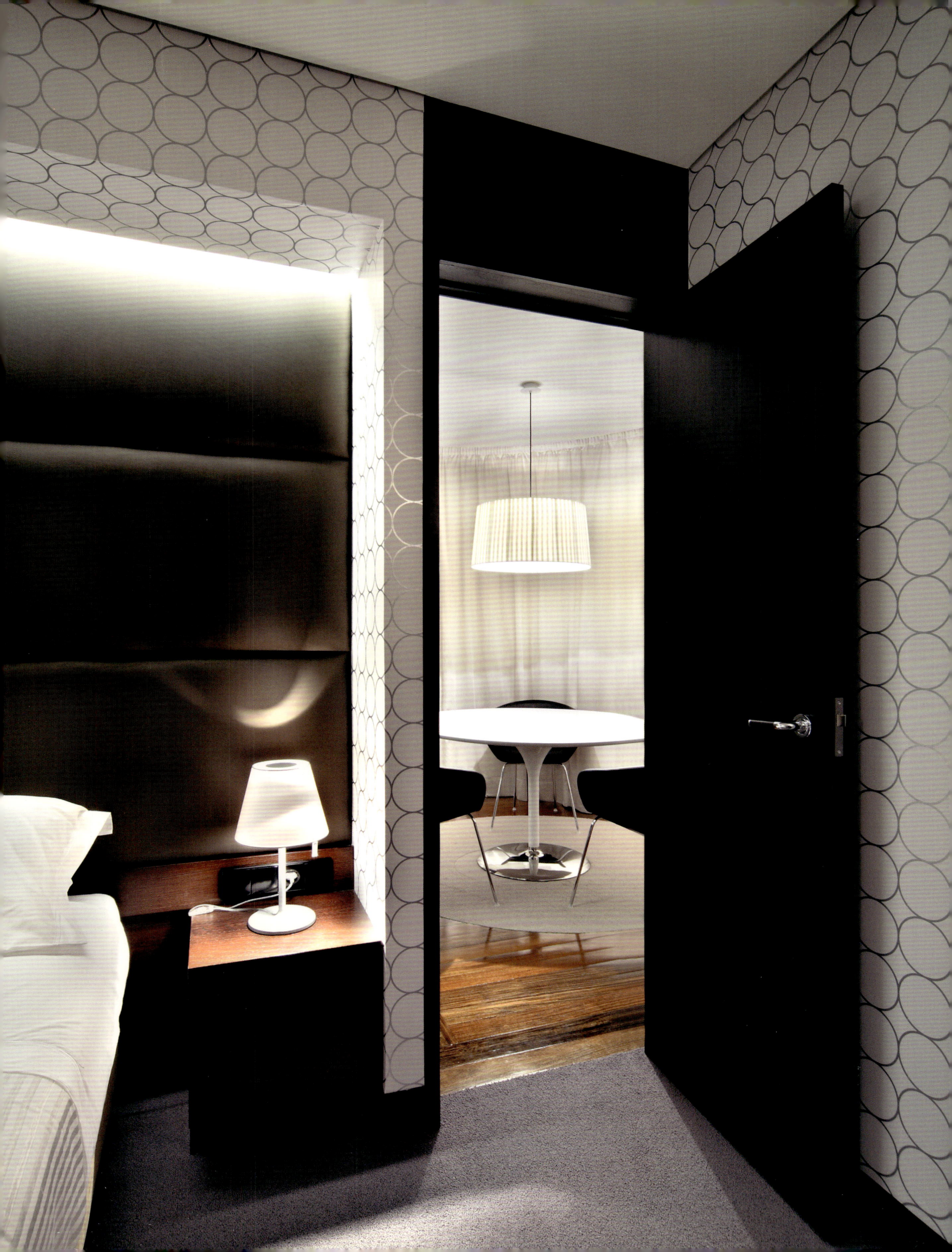

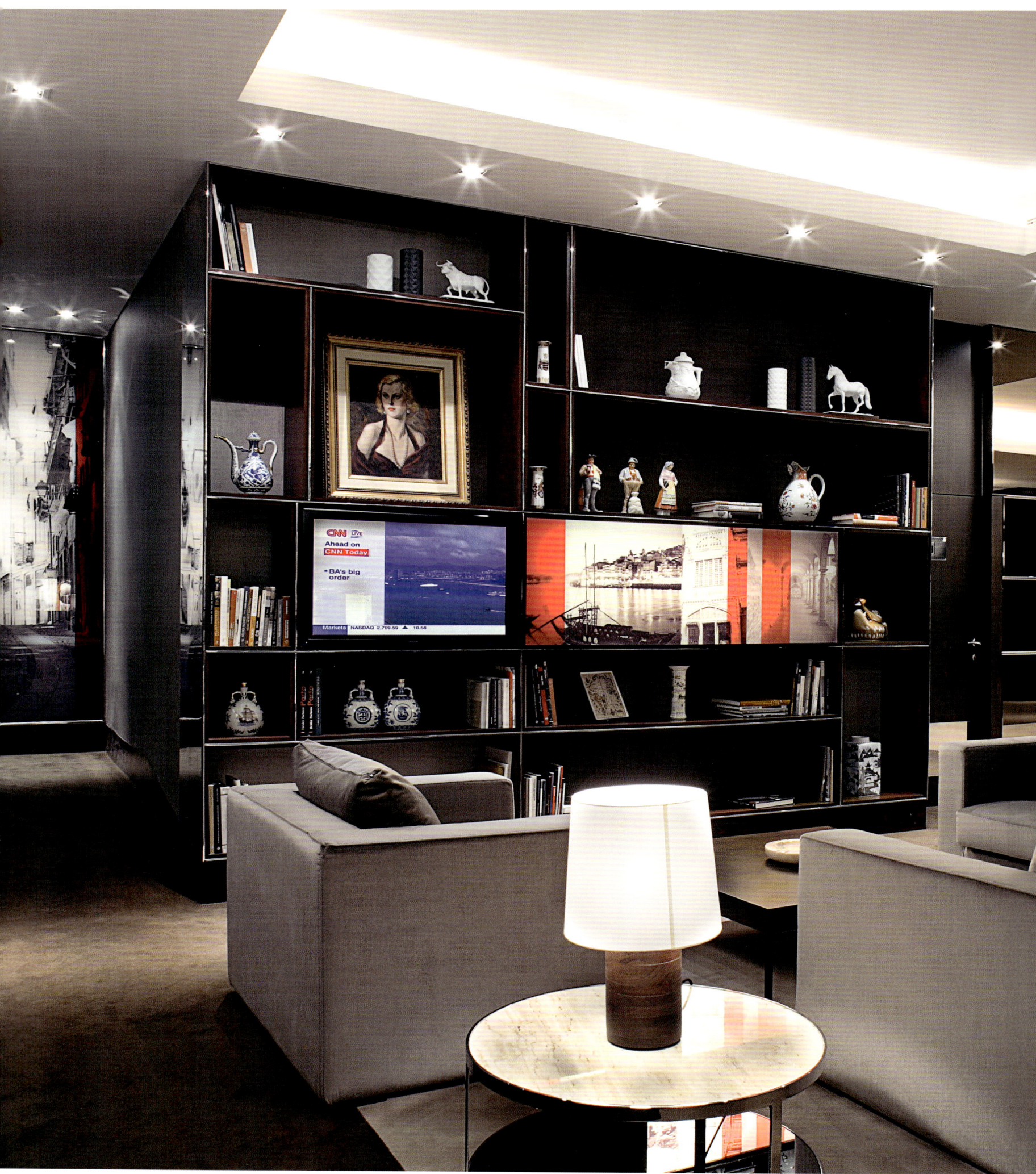

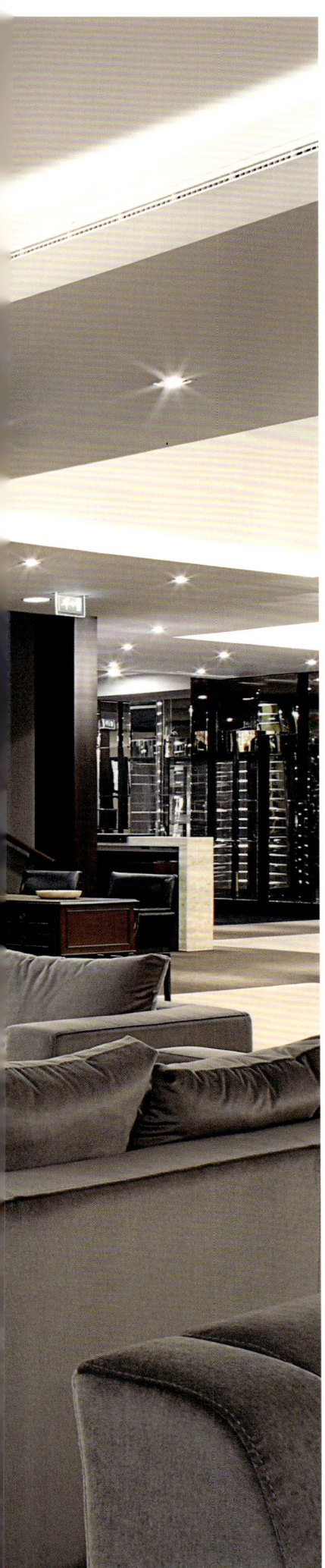

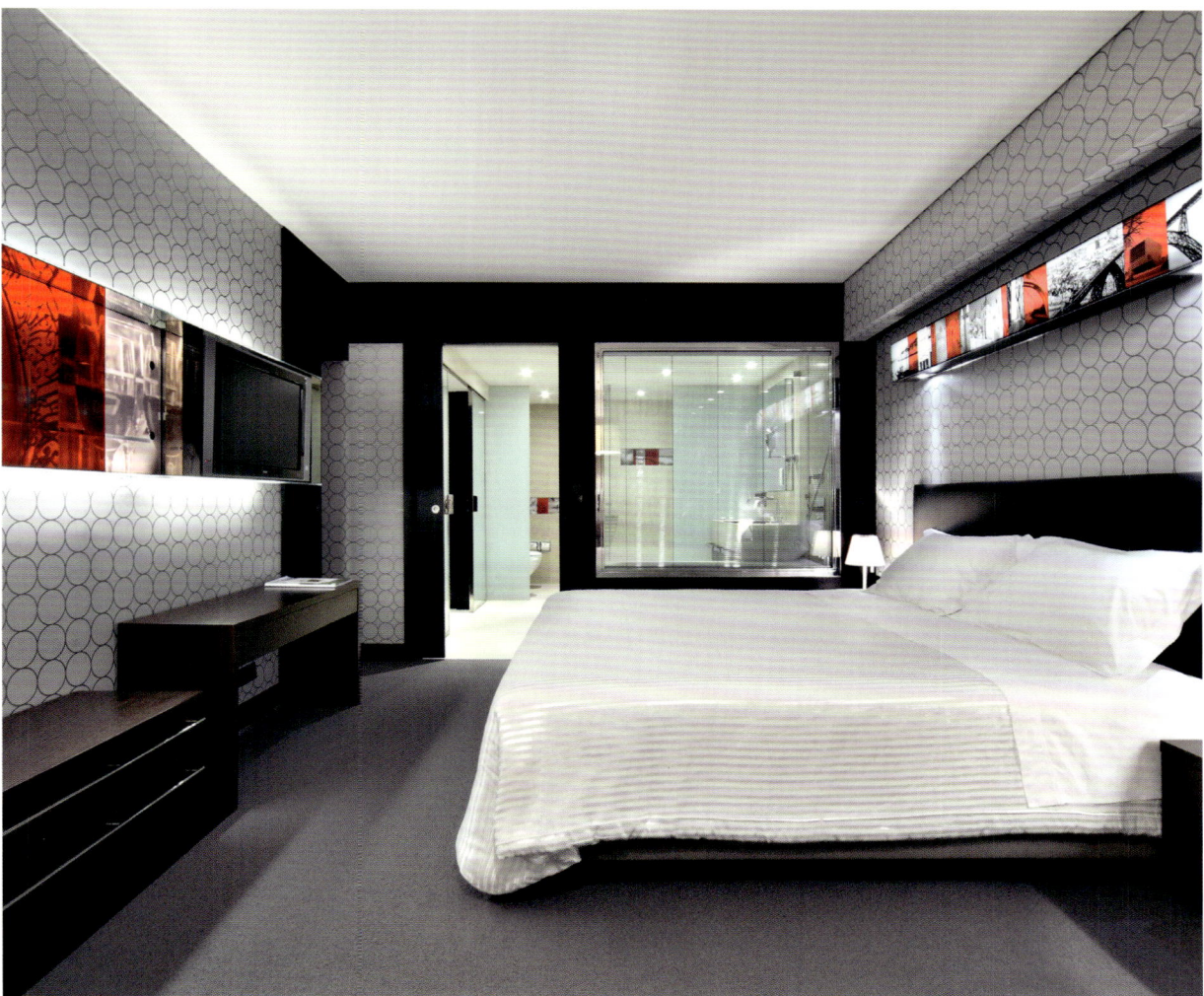

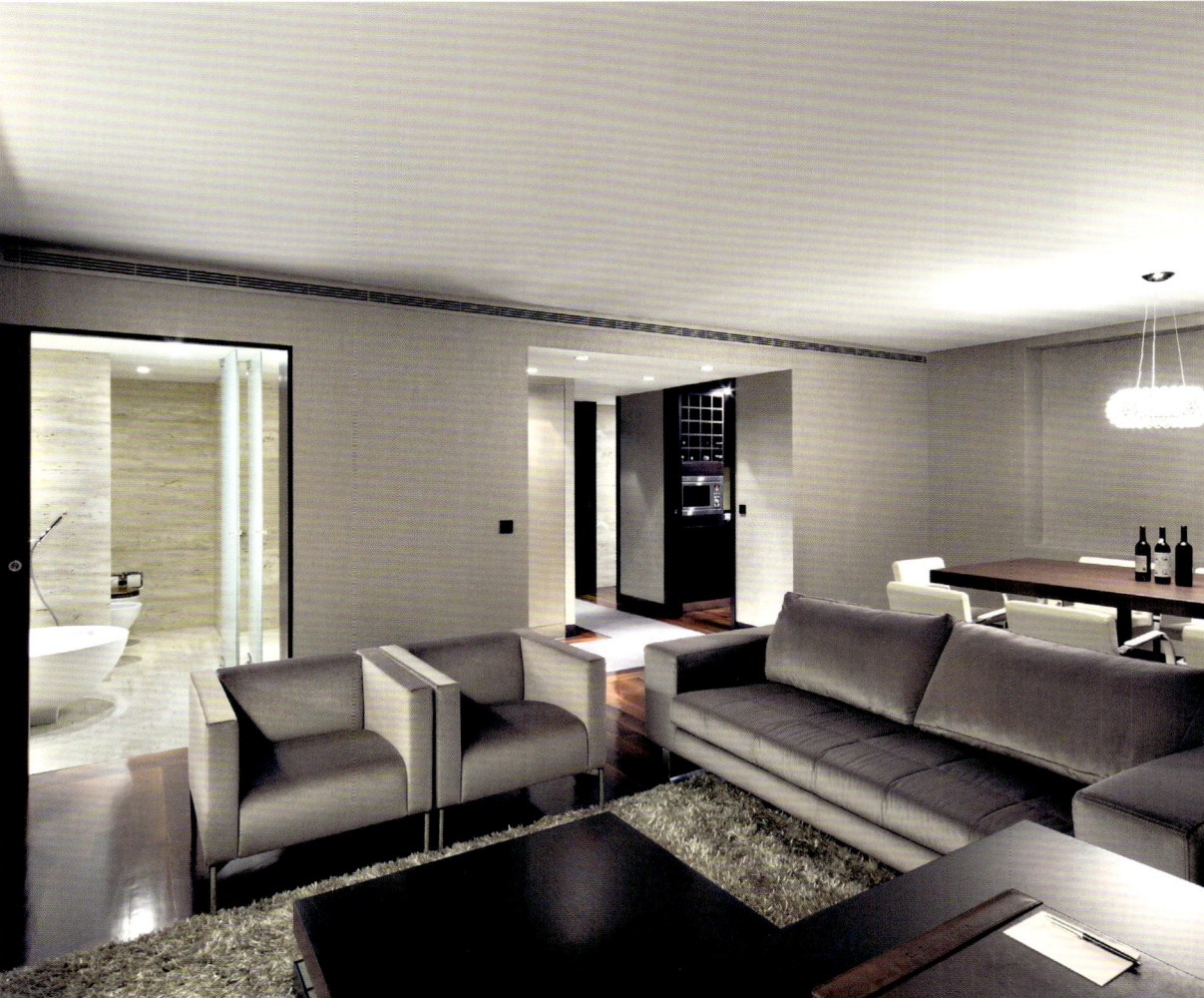

1400-211 Lisbon
Portugal
Phone: +351 21 360 09 00
Fax: +351 21 360 09 08
www.almeidahotels.com

Rooms: 61 rooms and 4 suites
Facilities: Bar, sun deck
Services: Room service, valet parking
Located: In picturesque Belém, Lisbon's historic monument and museum district, a few steps from the Tagus riverfront
Public transportation: Belém train station
Style: Urban resort in a traditional building

Behind the traditional facade of the unusual hotel in the museum quarter of Belém, across from the impressive monastery Mosteiro dos Jerónimos, you are surprised by generous rooms, minimalistic furniture, marble baths, and a soft color scale of coffee brown to vanilla yellow. Nowhere does a glaring light or sharp corner bother you. The entire interior is harmoniously combined. Guests should not miss the opportunity of enjoying the rare wine only served in the maroon "Bussaco Bar" that shares the same name.

Hinter der traditionellen Fassade dieses ungewöhnlichen Hotels im Museumsviertel Belém, gegenüber dem eindrucksvollen Kloster Mosteiro dos Jerónimos, überraschen großzügige Räume, minimalistische Möbel, Marmorbäder und eine weiche Farbscala von Kaffeebraun bis Vanillegelb. Nirgendwo stören grelles Licht oder spitze Kanten. Das gesamte Interieur ist harmonisch aufeinander abgestimmt. Gäste sollten die Gelegenheit nutzen, in der karminroten „Bussaco Bar" einen der seltenen gleichnamigen Weine zu genießen, die nur hier ausgeschenkt werden.

Derrière la façade traditionnelle de cet hôtel original du quartier des musées de Belém, en face de l'impressionnant Mosteiro dos Jerónimos, les larges chambres surprennent, avec leurs meubles minimalistes, leurs baignoires en marbre et leur palette de couleurs douces, du brun café au jaune vanille. Tout l'intérieur est en totale harmonie. Dans le « Bussaco Bar » rouge carmin, les clients peuvent avoir le privilège de déguster le vin rare uniquement servi ici et qui porte le nom de l'établissement.

Detrás de la fachada tradicional de este singular hotel, situado justo enfrente del impresionante monasterio de dos Jerónimos en el barrio de los museos llamado Belém, sorprenden unas habitaciones espaciosas, unos muebles minimalistas, unos cuartos de baño de mármol y una sucesión de tonalidades suaves que van del color café a la vainilla. En este espacio no caben las incómodas luces deslumbrantes ni los ángulos puntiagudos. Todos los elementos en su interior están perfectamente armonizados. Los huéspedes deberían aprovechar su estancia para disfrutar en el "Bussaco Bar" de uno de los peculiares vinos tintos que se ofrecen aquí bajo ese mismo nombre.

Dietro la facciata in stile tradizionale di questo singolare albergo nel quartiere dei musei di Belém, di fronte al maestoso Mosteiro dos Jerónimos, vi attendono ampi spazi, arredi minimalisti, bagni in marmo e una morbida scala di colori che spazia dalle tonalità del caffellatte a quelle della vaniglia. Un'armonia mai spezzata da colori chiassosi o forme spigolose. Tutto l'interno è una perfetta sinfonia di elementi. Nel "Bussaco Bar" color cremisi, gli ospiti dovrebbero cogliere l'occasione di assaporare uno degli omonimi vini, rare etichette offerte soltanto in questo posto.

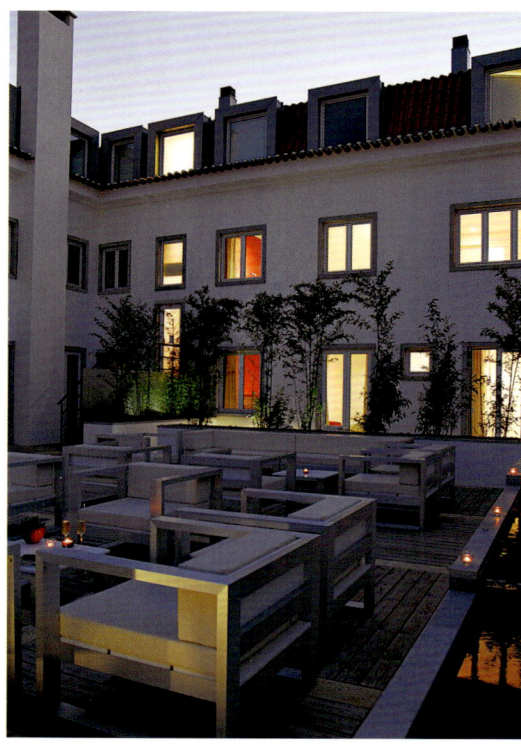 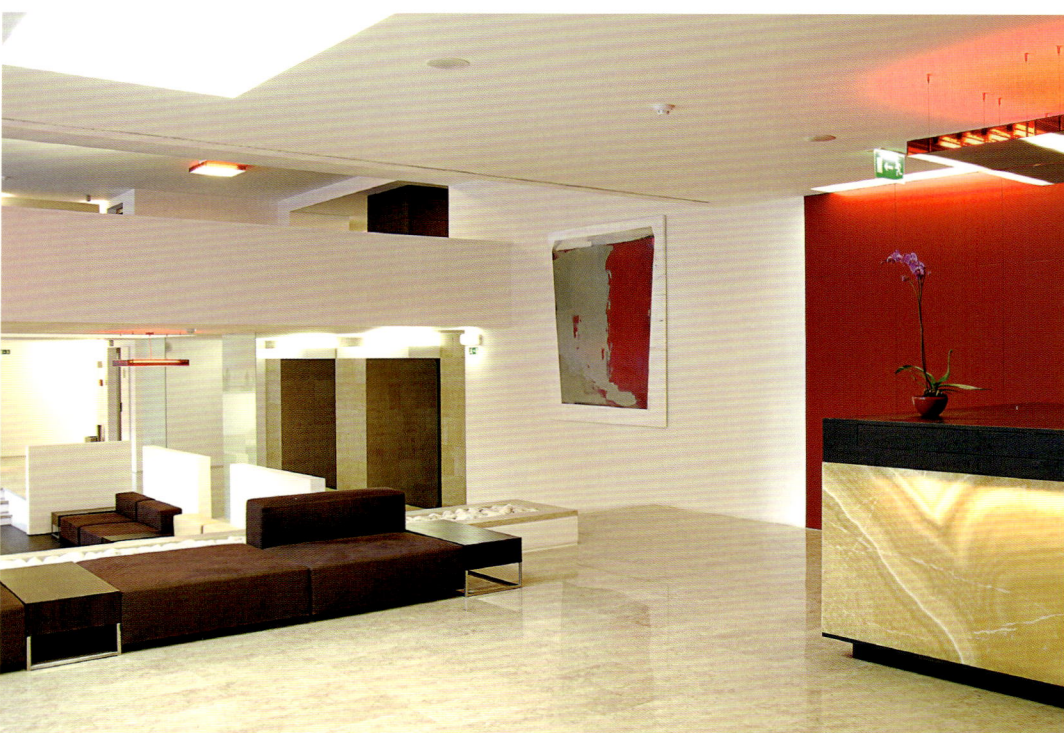

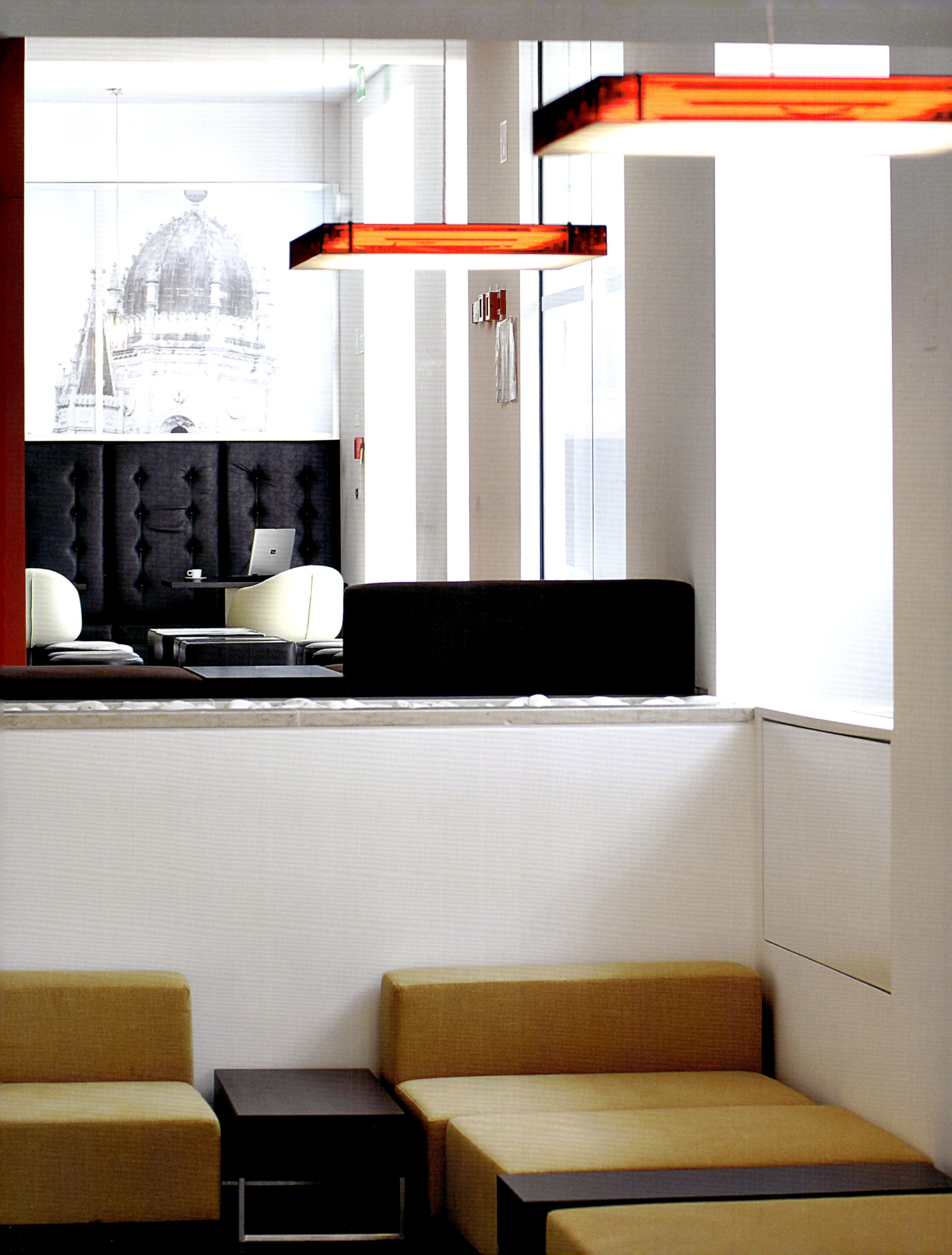

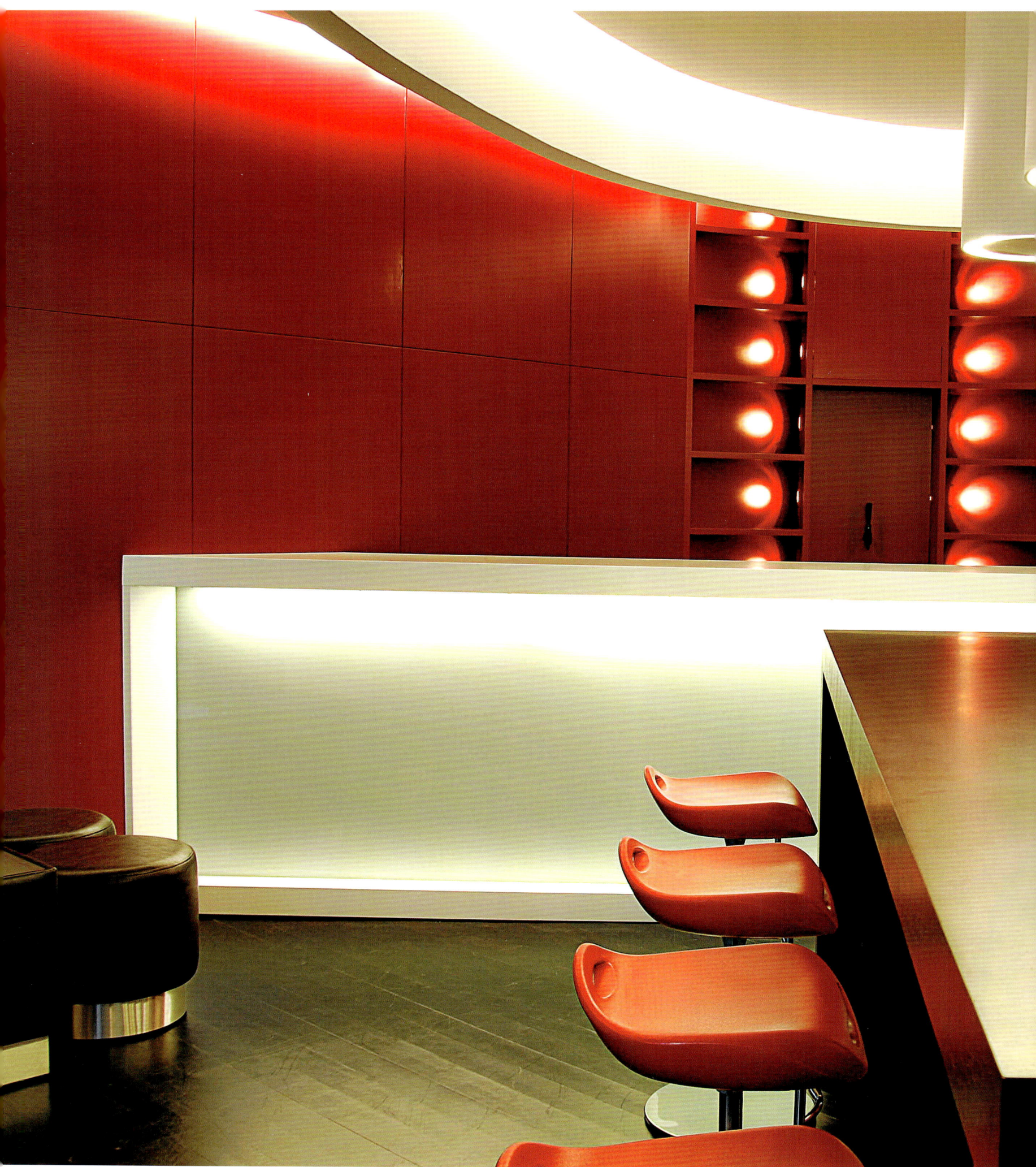

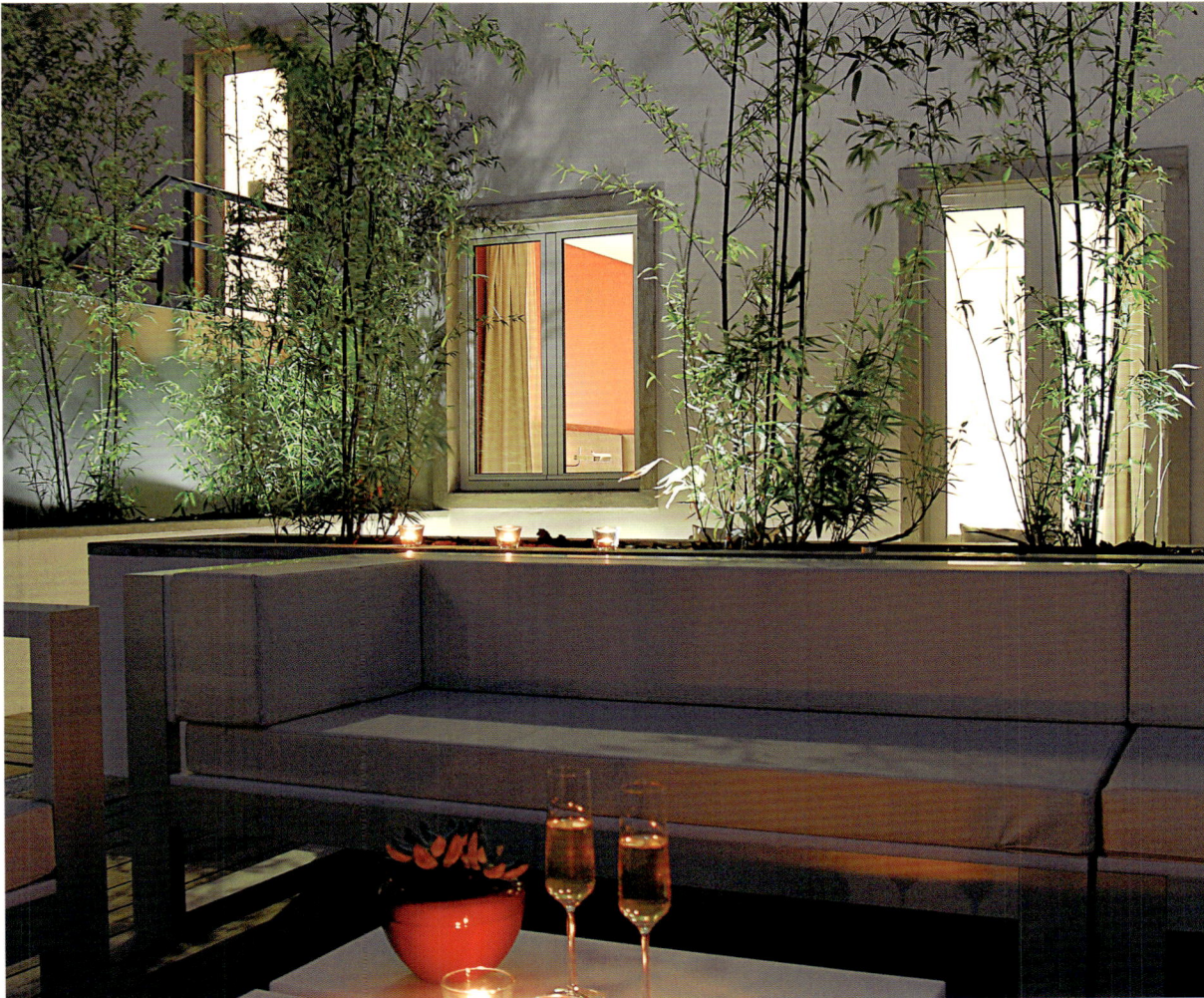

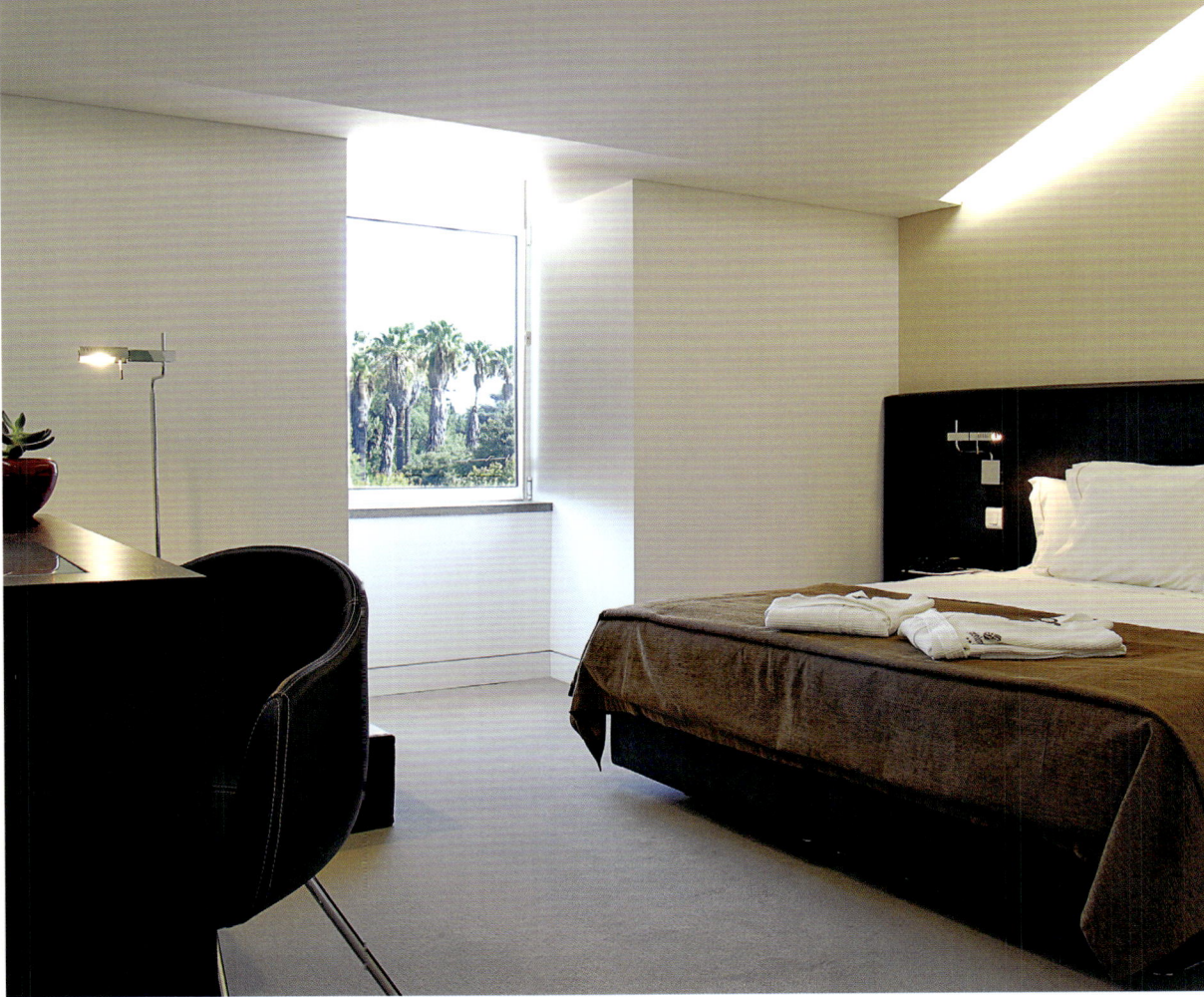

Fresh Hotel

Athens, Greece

26 Sophocleous & Klisthenous St.
10552 Athens
Greece
Phone: +30 210 524 8511
Fax: +30 210 524 8517
www.freshhotel.gr

Price category: €
Rooms: 133 rooms
Facilities: Orange Bar, Magenta Restaurant, Air Lounge pool bar, conference facilities
Services: WiFi
Located: In the city center, only a few min from Syntagma square and the old market place
Public transportation: Metro Monastiraki; bus Omonia
Style: Modern

Anyone checking-in in the ice cream colored lobby is already getting the taste of a fresh hotel experience: sunflowers dancing in curved vases on the counter, blossom shaped chandeliers beaming from the ceiling, and soft lounge music overplaying anything standard. The minimal furnishings or the suites soothe the senses like balsam—especially after a tour through exuberant old city and market place near the hotel. You can best review the impressions of the day in the "Air Lounge" on the roof terrace next to the pool. The cocktails are excellent, and the view of the Acropolis is free.

Wer an der eiscremefarbenen Lobby eincheckt, ist schon mittendrin im erfrischenden Hotelerlebnis: Auf der Theke tanzen Sonnenblumen in geschwungenen Vasen, von der Decke strahlt ein blütenförmiger Leuchter und den Alltag übertönt sanfte Lounge-Musik. Balsam für die Sinne sind auch die reduziert eingerichteten Suiten – besonders nach einer Tour durch die quirlige Altstadt und die Markthalle nahe dem Hotel. Die Eindrücke des Tages lässt man am besten in der „Air Lounge" auf der Dachterrasse neben dem Pool Revue passieren. Die Cocktails sind exzellent – und der Blick auf die Akropolis gratis.

Lorsqu'on s'enregistre à la réception couleur pastel, on est déjà au cœur d'une expérience hôtelière rafraîchissante : des tournesols dansent dans des vases sur le comptoir, des lustres aux formes florales pendent du plafond et les bruits de la vie quotidienne sont couverts par de la musique douce. Le mobilier sobre des suites est un baume pour les sens, surtout après un tour à travers la vieille ville très animée et le marché couvert tout près de l'hôtel. Les meilleurs endroits pour se remémorer les impressions du jour sont l'« Air Lounge » ou la piscine sur la terrasse du toit. Les cocktails sont excellents, et la vue sur l'Acropole est gratuite.

Ya al llegar a su vestíbulo, bañado en los colores propios de un helado, el viajero se sumerge en la refrescante aventura que proporciona este hotel. En su entrada hay girasoles que se mecen en jarrones curvados, un candelabro en forma de flor resplandece en el techo y una suave música lounge envuelve la atmósfera. Un verdadero bálsamo para los sentidos son también sus suites de composición minimalista, sobre todo, después de una excursión por el ajetreado centro histórico y el mercado situados cerca del hotel. El bar "Air Lounge", junto a la piscina en la azotea, es el lugar idóneo para evocar de nuevo las impresiones del día. Los cócteles son excelentes y la vista sobre la acrópolis incluso gratuita.

Basta fare il check-in nella lobby dai vivaci colori gelato per calarsi immediatamente nella rinfrescante atmosfera di questo albergo: sul banco ci sono vasi arcuati pieni di girasoli danzanti, dal soffitto pende un raggiante lampadario a forma di fiore, e una morbida musica lounge lascia scivolare via i rumori della vita di tutti i giorni. Anche le suite dagli arredi minimalisti sono balsamo per i sensi – specialmente dopo una visita nel vivacissimo centro storico o al mercato coperto situato vicino all'albergo. Per ripercorre le impressioni della giornata non c'è luogo migliore dell'"Air Lounge", il bar sulla terrazza del tetto con tanto di piscina. I cocktail sono eccellenti e la vista sull'acropoli gratuita.

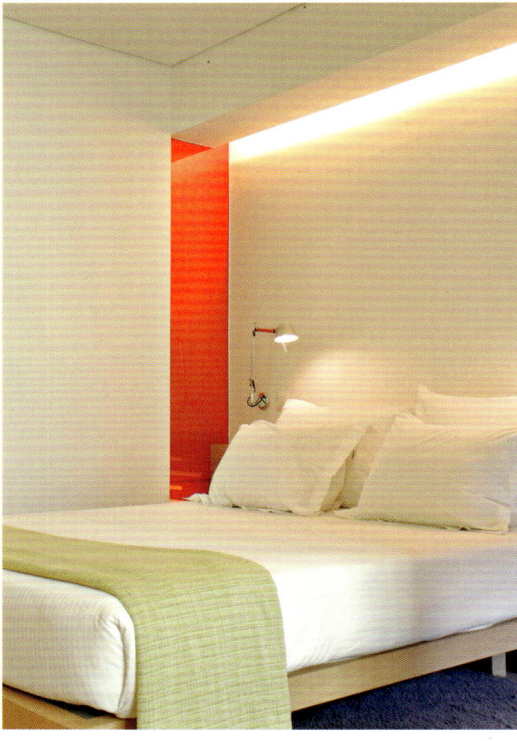
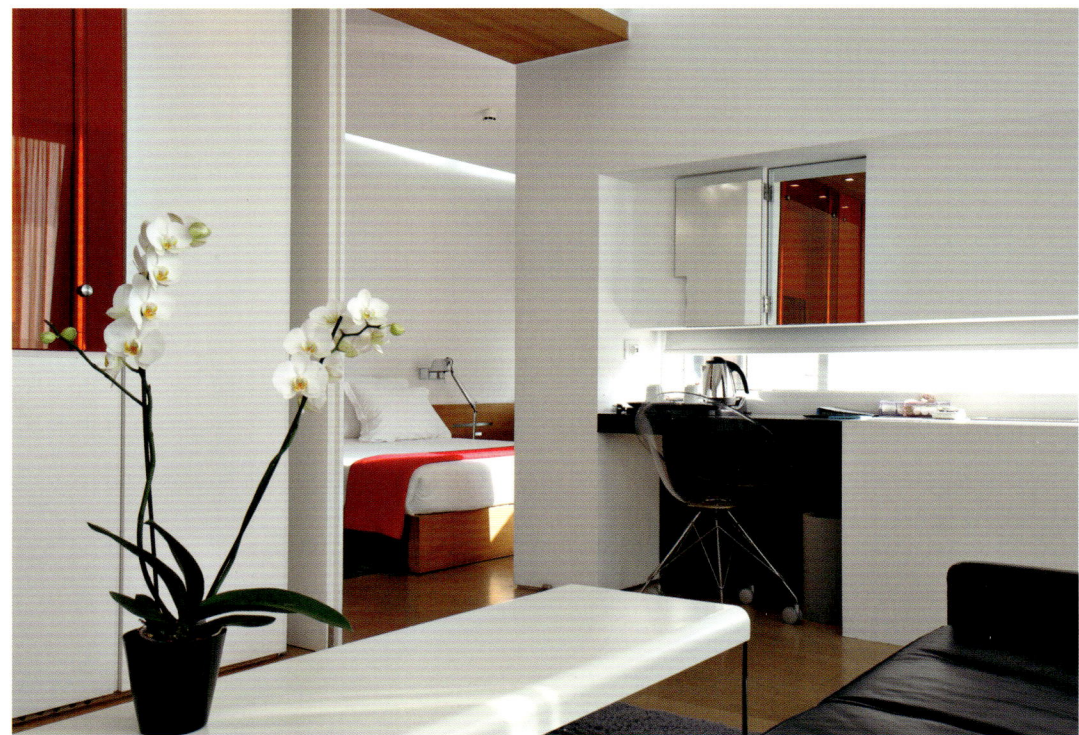

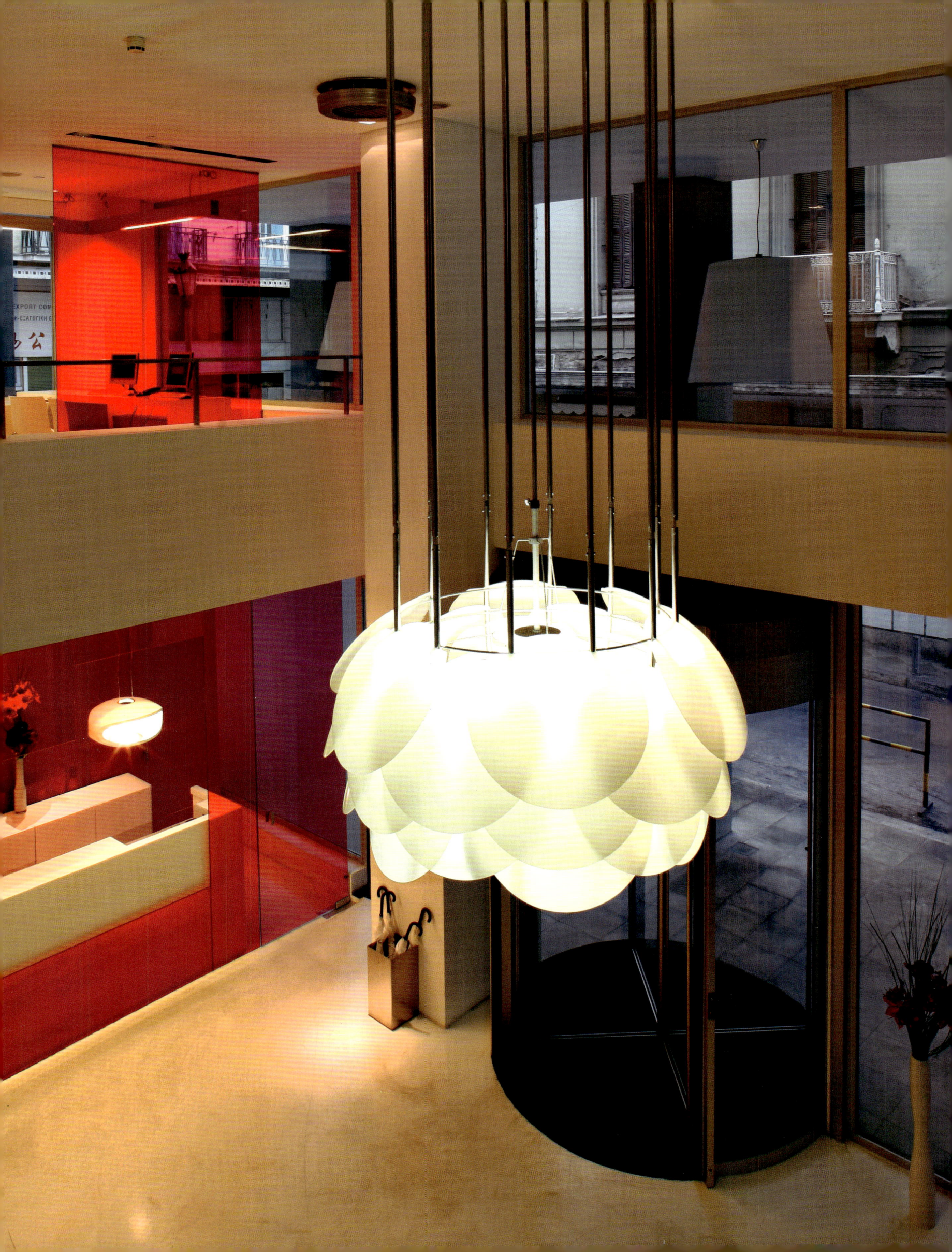

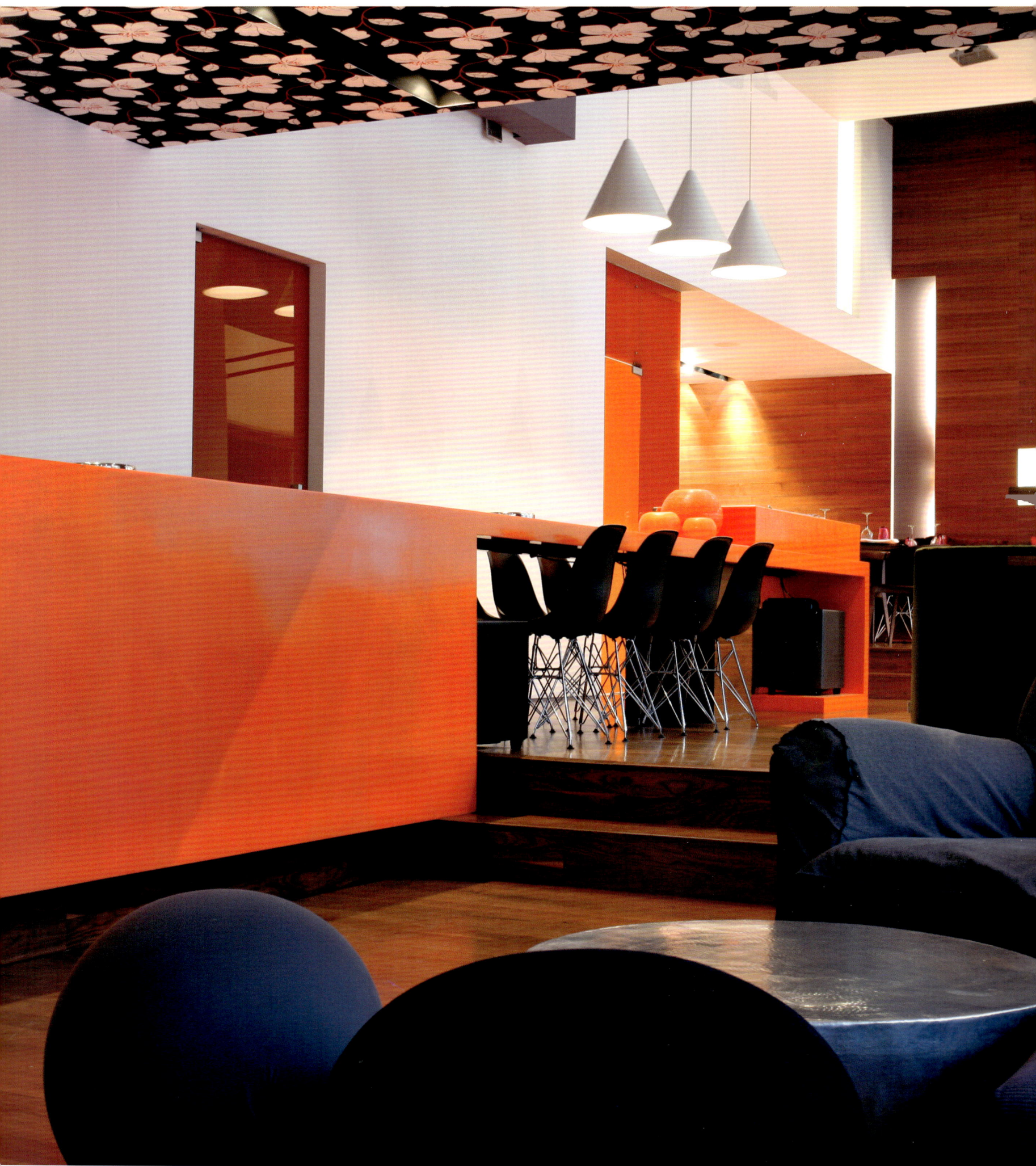

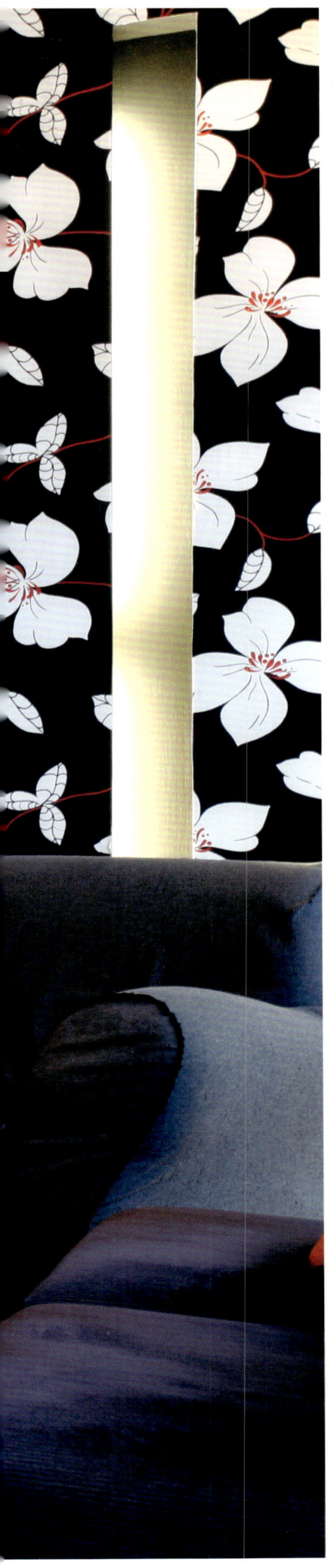

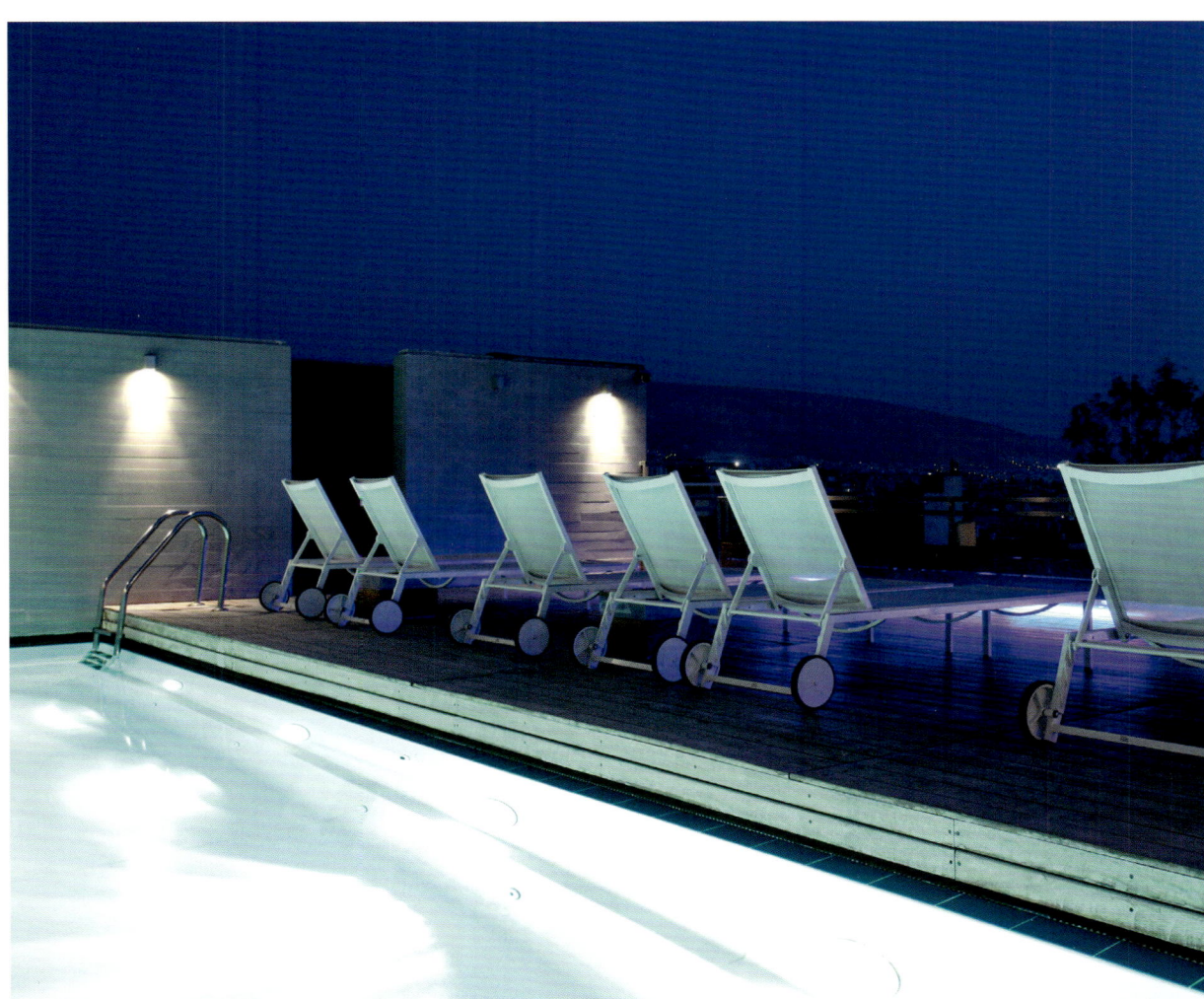

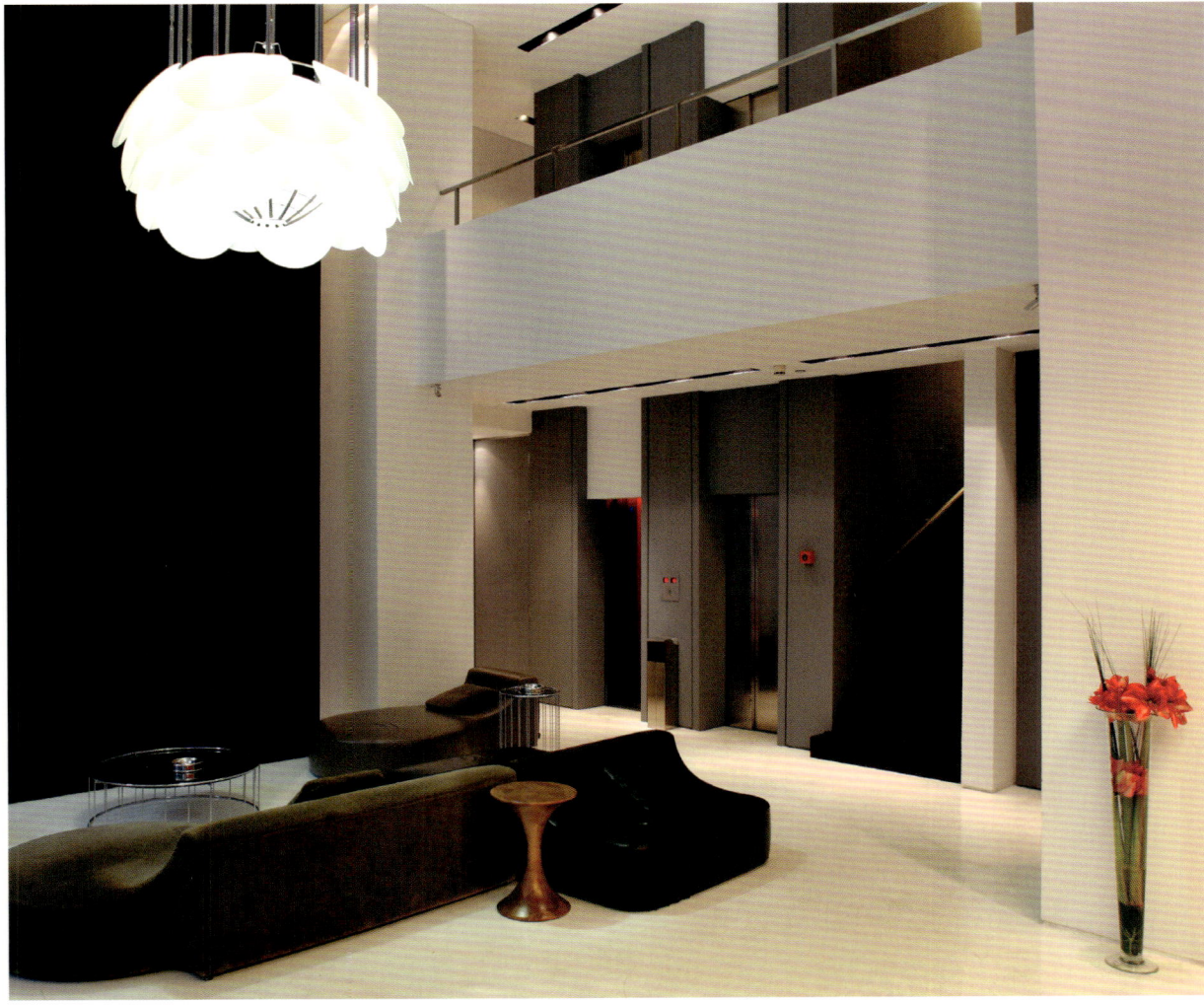

48 Charilaou Trikoupi St.
14562 Kifissia
Greece
Phone: +30 210 628 4400
Fax: +30 210 628 4499
www.semiramisathens.com
www.yeshotels.gr

Price category: €€
Rooms: 42 rooms, 5 bungalows and 4 penthouse suites
Facilities: Bar, pool restaurant, 3 meeting rooms, gym with sauna, spa
Services: Babysitting, free WiFi, face and body treatments, concierge, personal trainer
Located: In Kifissia, 10 min from the Olympic stadium
Public transportation: Metro Kifissia
Style: Design

No one less than top designer Karim Rashid vented his fury here: for his first hotel project the native Egyptian brewed lurid pink with pastel tones, lounge chairs of squeezy foamed rubber with light boxes of acrylic glass, and colored concrete with rubber floors. A teak swimming deck frames the pool in the shape of a lava lamp. The futuristic designer's stroke of genius is mastered in chic, green Kifissia suburb. Even art fans get their share with the works of international artists like Jeff Koons adorning the lobby's walls.

Kein geringerer als Top-Designer Karim Rashid hat sich hier ausgetobt: Für sein erstes Hotelprojekt kombinierte der gebürtige Ägypter grelles Pink mit Pastelltönen, Lounge-Sessel aus knautschigem Schaumstoff mit Lichtboxen aus Acrylglas, und farbigen Beton mit Böden aus Gummi. Den Pool in Form einer Lavaleuchte rahmt ein Badedeck aus Teak. Der Geniestreich im schicken grünen Vorort Kifissia ist dem Zukunftsgestalter gelungen. Auch Kunstinteressierte kommen auf ihre Kosten: In der Lobby werden Arbeiten internationaler Künstler wie Jeff Koons präsentiert.

Le grand Karim Rashid en personne s'est déchaîné ici : pour son premier projet hôtelier, le designer d'origine égyptienne a marié le rose vif et les tons pastel, des chaises longues en mousse de caoutchouc déformée avec des caissons lumineux en verre acrylique, et un ciment coloré avec des sols en caoutchouc. La piscine en forme de lampe lava embrasse la terrasse en bois de teck. Cette touche de génie dans le quartier verte et chic Kifissa est un coup de maître pour le designer futuriste. Même les amateurs d'art seront comblés : les œuvres d'artistes contemporains internationaux comme Jeff Koons sont exposés à la réception.

El encargado de dar forma a este hotel fue, nada menos, que el célebre diseñador Karim Rashid. En el que sería su primer proyecto hotelero, el egipcio combinó el fucsia chillón con tonos pasteles, los sillones de espuma con cubos de vidrio acrílico iluminados y las paredes de hormigón tintado con suelos de goma. Una plataforma de madera de teca enmarca la piscina de formas sinuosas. En el elegante y verde barrio de Kifissia, este visionario perpetró su genial hazaña. También los adeptos al arte disfrutarán de su estancia en este hotel, en su vestíbulo se exponen obras de artistas de prestigio internacional como Jeff Koons.

In questo hotel si è sbizzarrito niente meno che il grandissimo designer Karim Rashid: per realizzare il suo primo albergo, l'architetto egiziano ha combinato un rosa sgargiante con colori pastello, eleganti poltrone in materiale espanso sgualcito con light box in vetro acrilico, e calcestruzzo colorato con pavimenti in gomma. La piscina a forma di lava lamp è circondata da un pavimento in legno di teck. Si tratta di un vero e proprio colpo di genio che al forgiatore di nuove tendenze è riuscito alla perfezione nel verde ed elegante quartiere di Kifissia. Anche gli amanti dell'arte saranno soddisfatti: nella lobby vengono presentati lavori di artisti di fama internazionale come Jeff Koons.

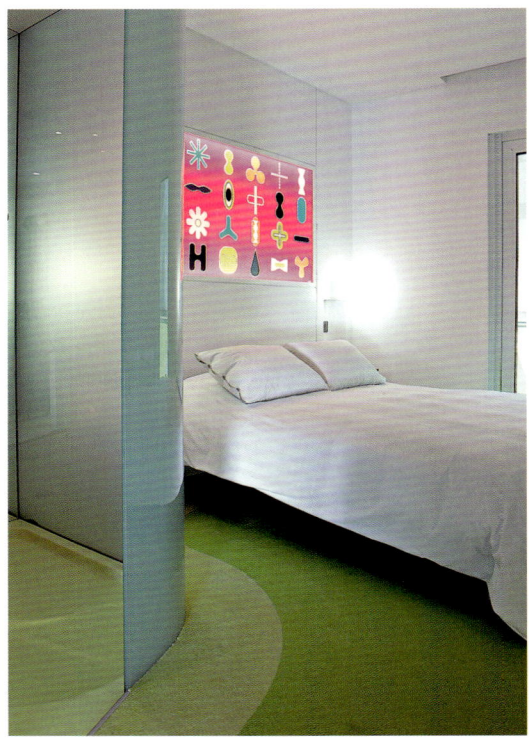
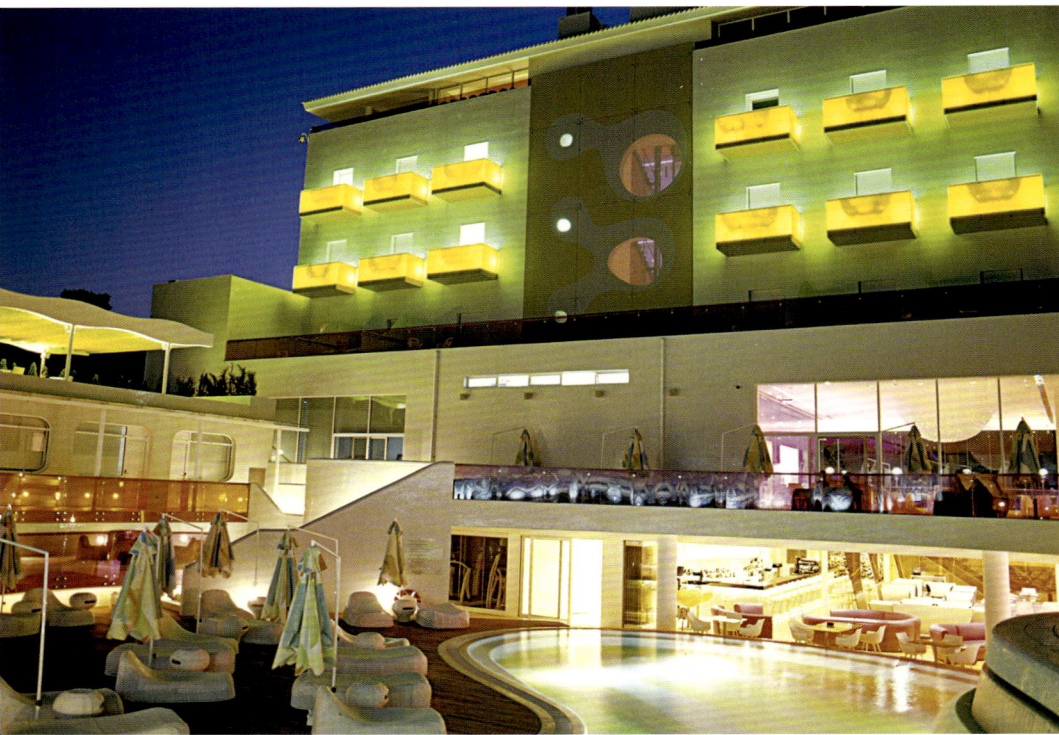

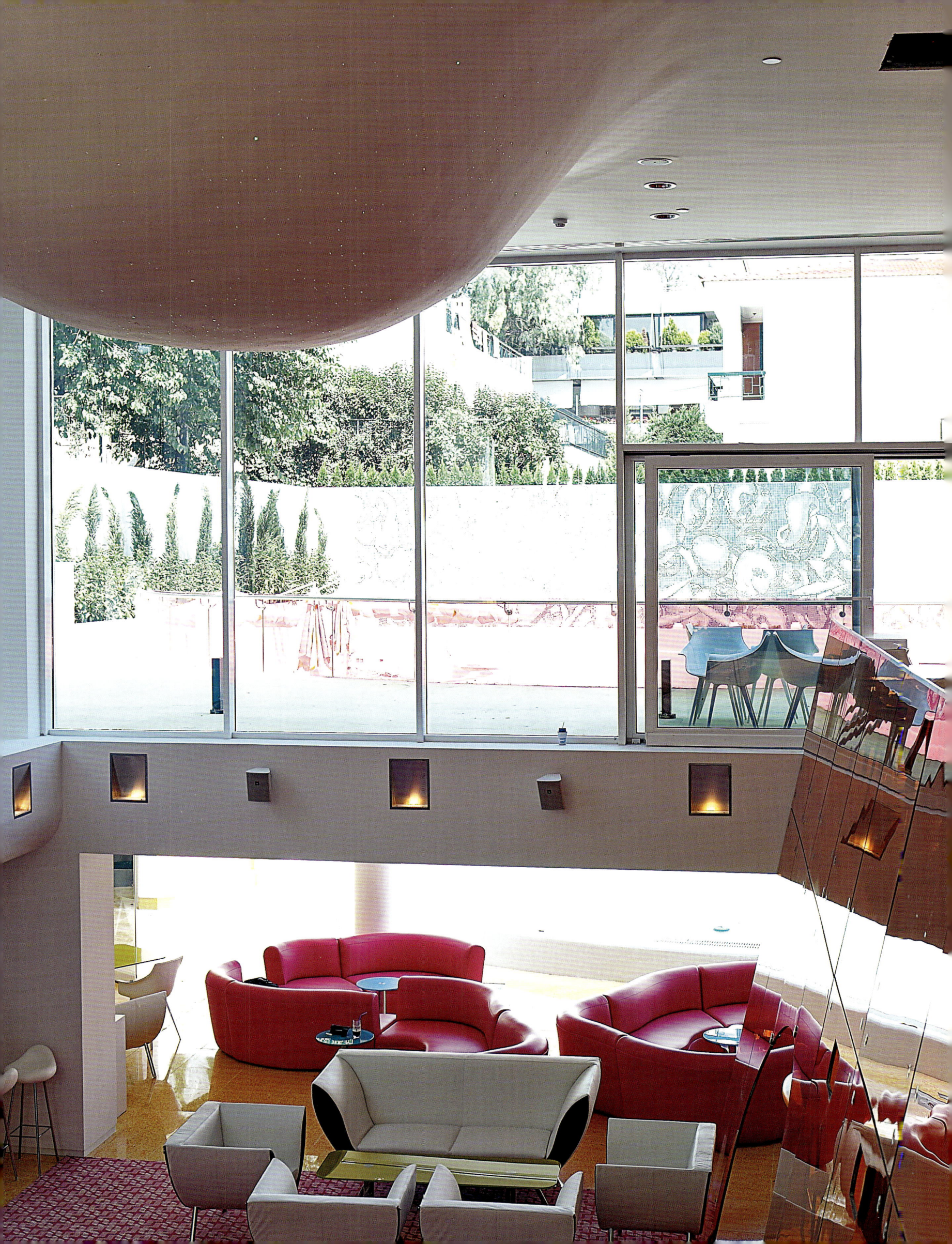

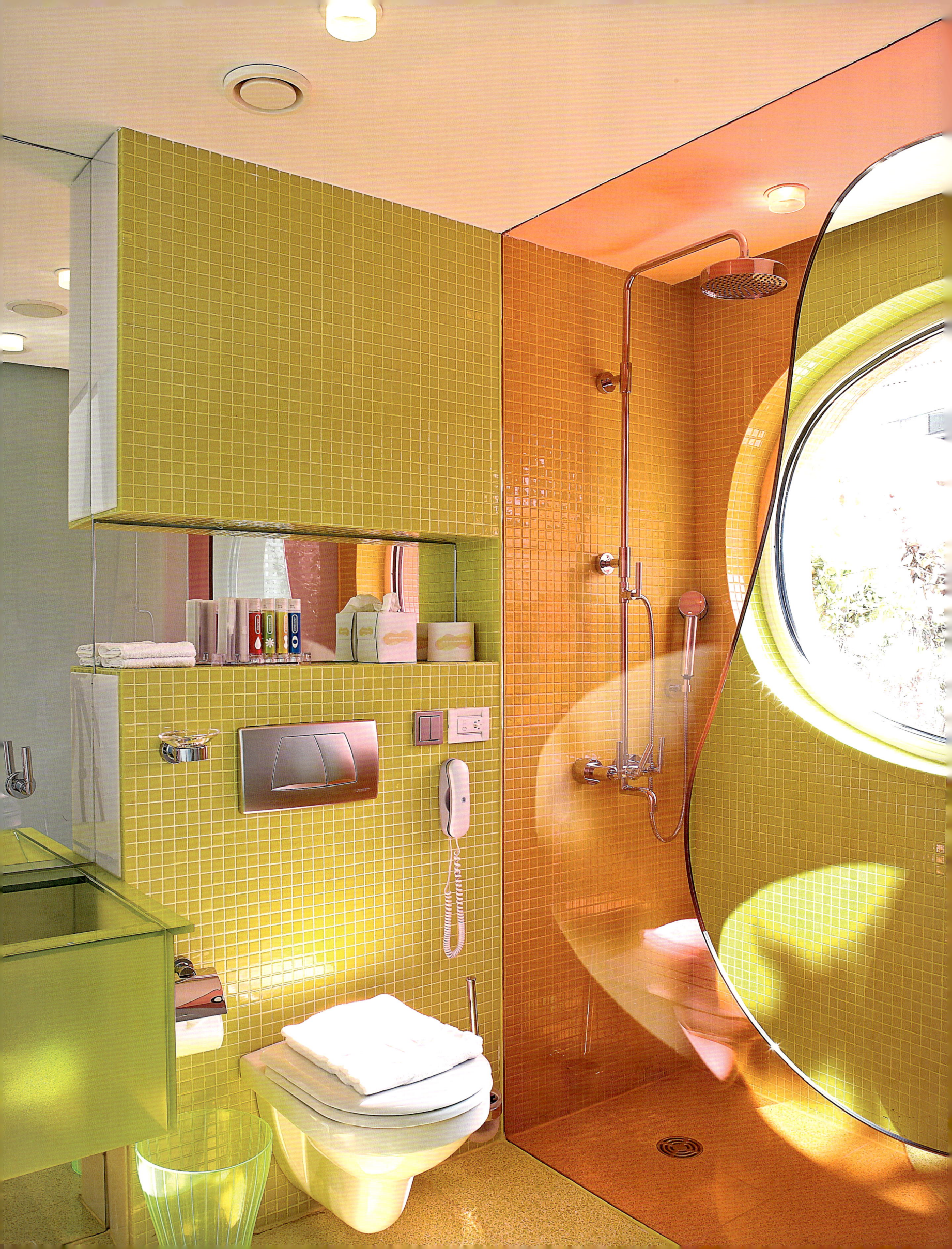

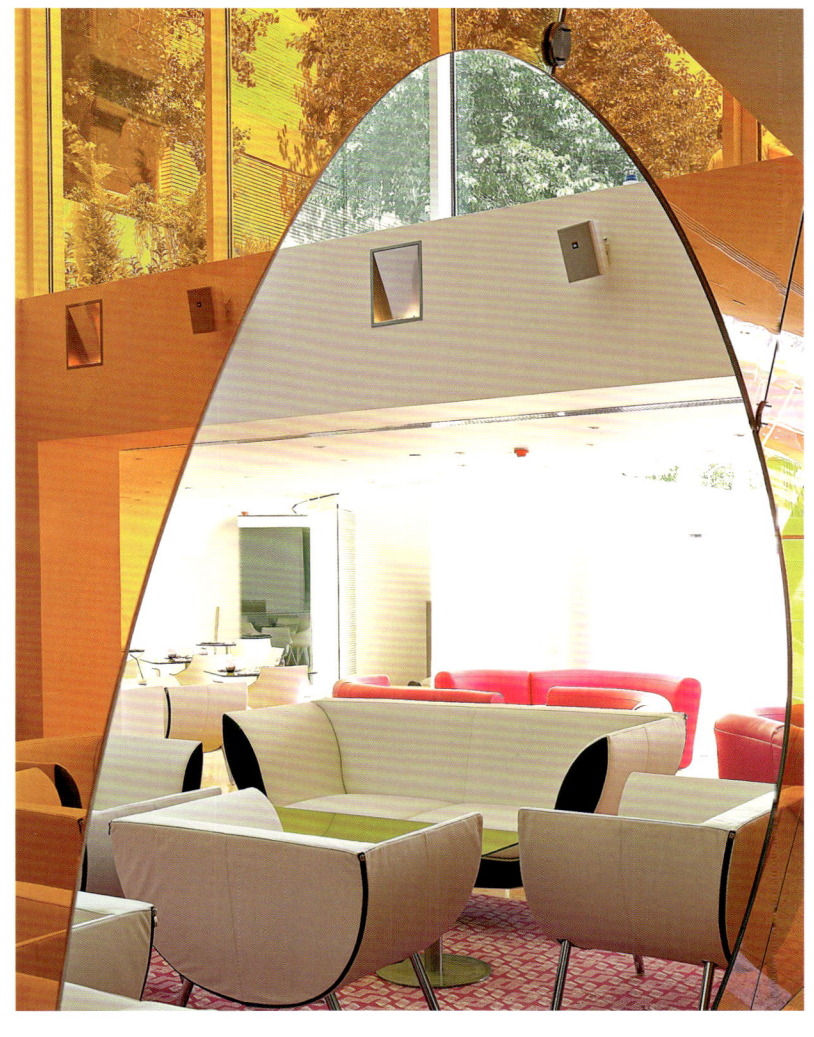
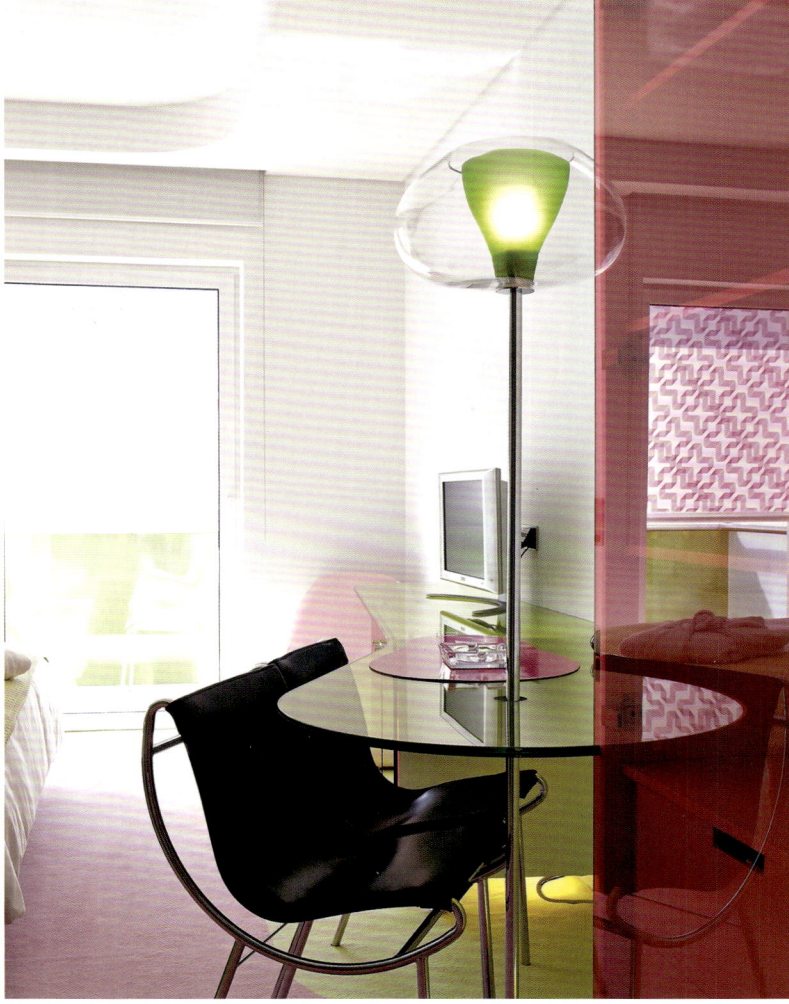
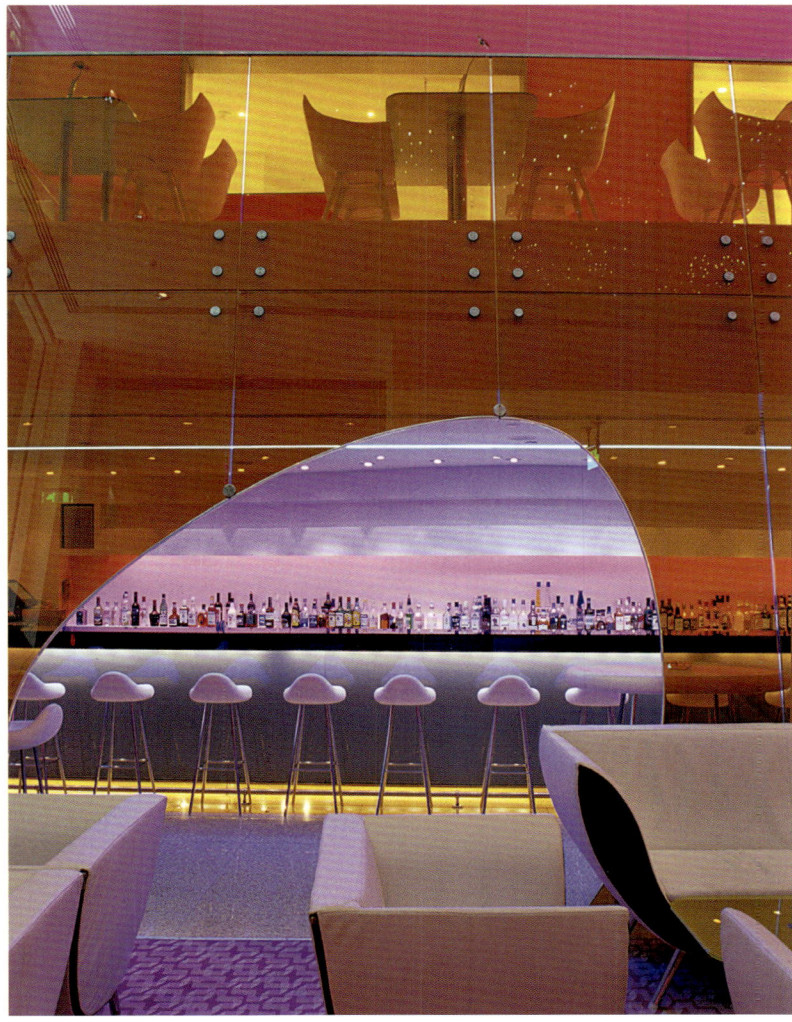
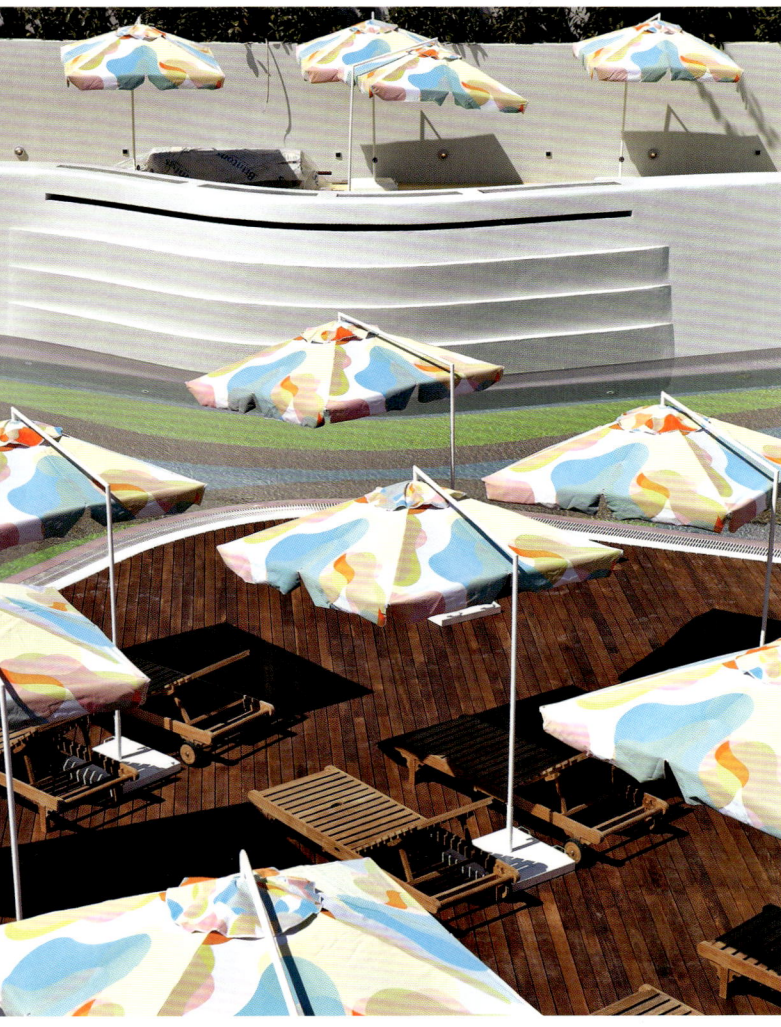

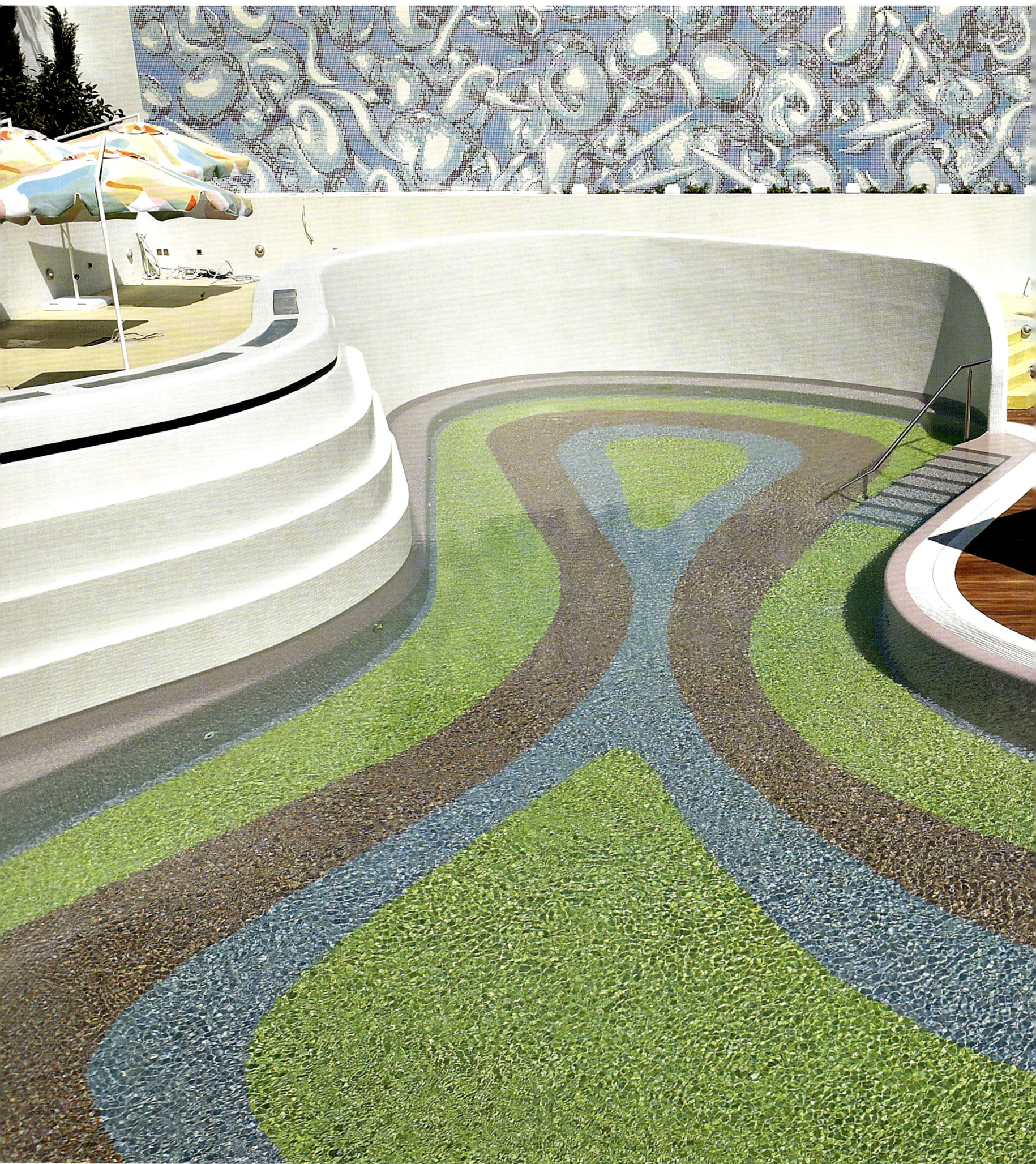

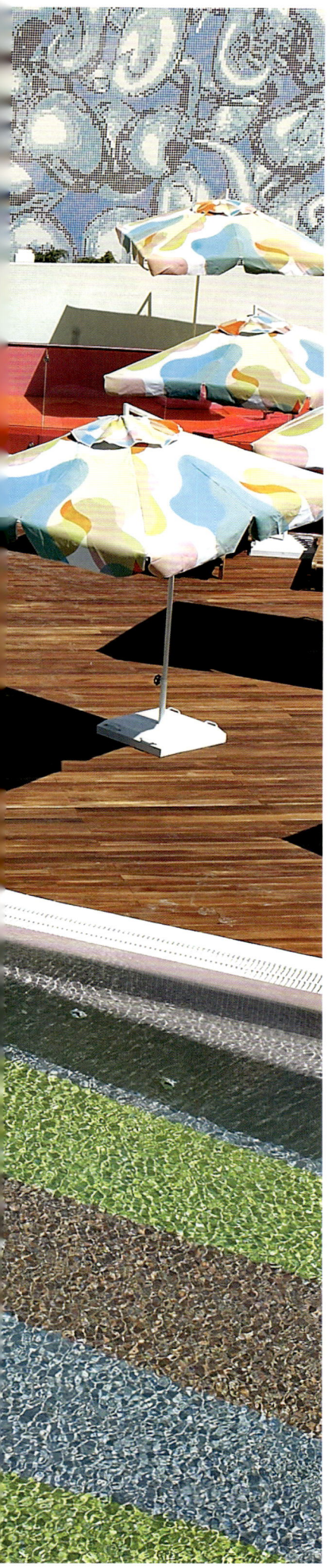

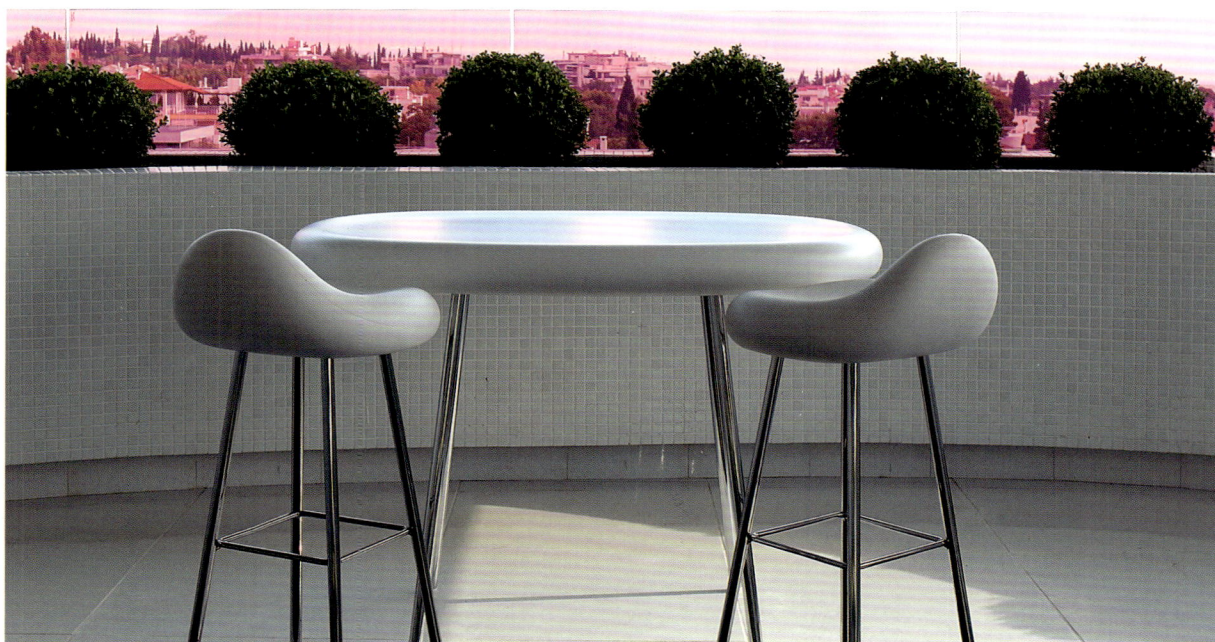

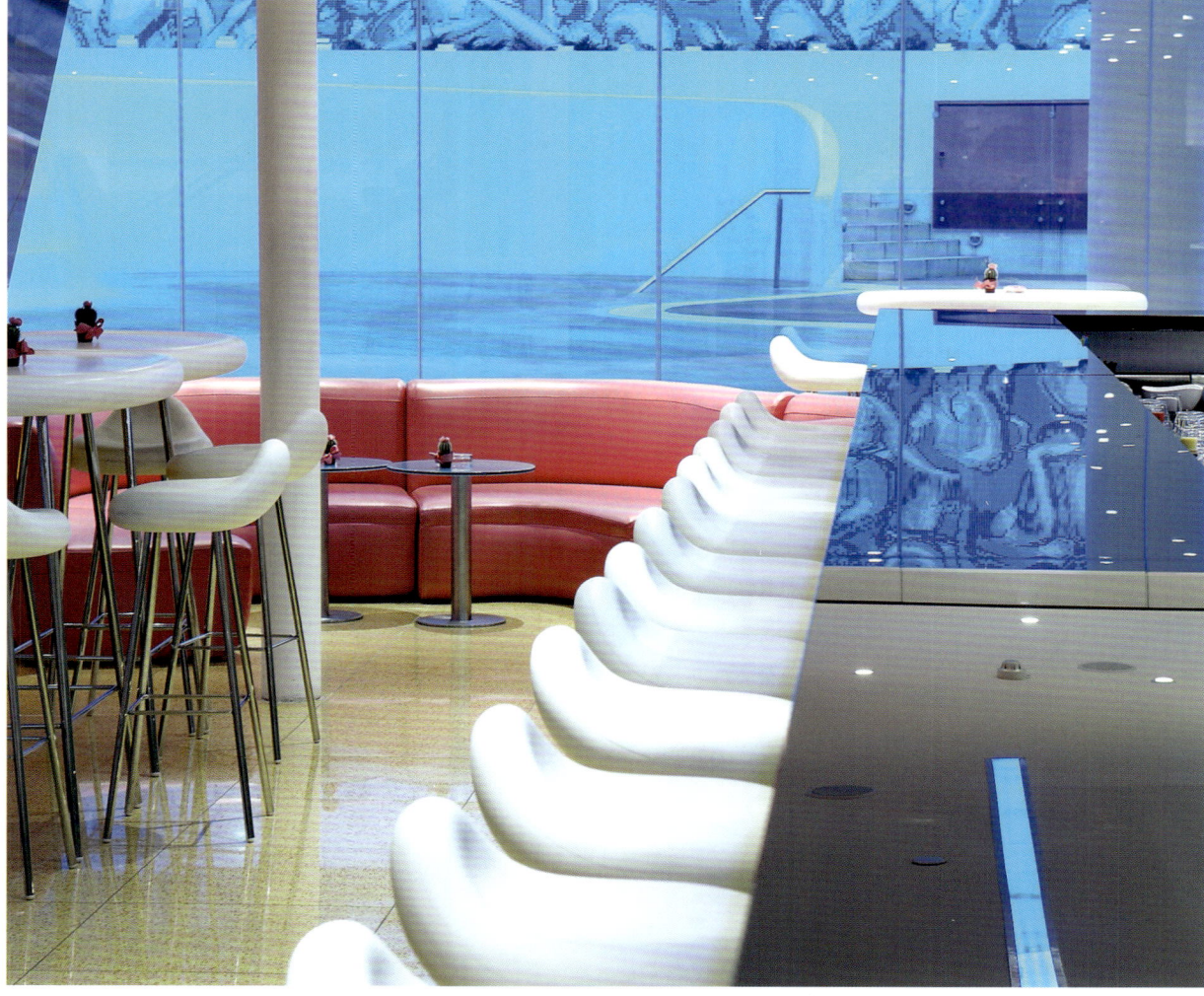

Greece
Phone: +30 228 902 6690
Fax: +30 228 902 6689
www.mykonosgrace.com

Facilities: Poolside cocktail bar and restaurant, gym and spa, library
Services: TV lounge, parking, free baby cots for up to 4 years old
Located: North of Mykonos town, 1.5 km from the new port, 300 m to the beach
Public transportation: Bus 300 m from the hotel
Style: Hip luxury

Whitewashed walls, azure blue mosaic tiles with straight-lined designer furniture—the island's traditional building elements are fused to an oasis of wellness in the boutique hotel north of the city of Mykonos on the sheltered beach of Agios Stefanos. Now and then in this temple above the sea with beauty salon and gym, sun worshipers are refreshed with ice-cooled bathing towels and frozen fruit juices. From the private Jacuzzi gleaming in front of some suites, the sight of the sun going down is enough to fulfill holiday bliss.

Weißgetünchte Mauern, azurblaue Mosaikfliesen, dazu gradlinige Designermöbel – in dem Boutique-Hotel nördlich der Stadt Mykonos am geschützten Strand Agios Stefanos vereinen sich traditionelle Bauelemente der Insel und modernstes Design zu einer Wohlfühl-Oase. Ab und zu werden in diesem Tempel über dem Meer mit Beauty-Salon und Gym, Sonnenanbeter mit eisgekühlten Badetüchern und gefrorenen Fruchtsäften überrascht. Vom privaten Whirlpool aus, der vor einigen Suiten glitzert, reicht zum Ferienglück allerdings der Blick auf die untergehende Sonne.

Murs blancs, mosaïques bleu azur, et meubles de designer aux lignes simples : dans cet hôtel-boutique au nord de la ville de Mykonos, situé sur la plage protégée d'Agios Stefanos, les éléments de construction traditionnels de l'île se mélangent et forment une oasis de bien-être. De temps en temps, ce temple au-dessus de la mer, comprenant un salon de beauté et une salle de gym, surprend les adorateurs du soleil avec des serviettes fraîches et des jus de fruits glacés. Mais tout ce dont on a besoin pour des vacances parfaites, c'est de voir le coucher de soleil depuis les bains à remous privés qui brillent devant certaines des suites.

Murallas encaladas de blanco, suelos con pequeñas baldosas de un color azul intenso y angulosos muebles de diseño. En el hotel boutique al norte de la ciudad de Mikonos, en la playa protegida de Agios Stefanos, los elementos de construcción tradicionales se funden con el diseño moderno para crear un verdadero oasis de bienestar. En este templo sobre el mar, con salón de belleza y gimnasio, los amantes del sol quedan a menudo sorprendidos por las toallas refrigeradas y los zumos helados. Basta contemplar la puesta de sol desde el jacuzzi privado que algunas suites ostentan para encontrar la felicidad absoluta.

Muri bianchi, piastrelle a mosaico azzurre, e mobili di design dalle linee rette – nel boutique hotel situato a nord della città di Mykonos, sulla spiaggia riparata di Agios Stefanos, elementi architettonici tradizionali dell'isola si fondono con un design ultra-moderno a creare un'oasi del benessere. Di tanto in tanto, questo tempio sul mare con tanto di palestra e salone di bellezza sorprende gli amanti del sole con asciugamani gelidi e succhi di frutta ghiacciati. Ma basta anche solo la vista del tramonto dalla vasca a idromassaggio privata che scintilla davanti ad alcune suite per sentirsi completamente appagati dalla propria vacanza.

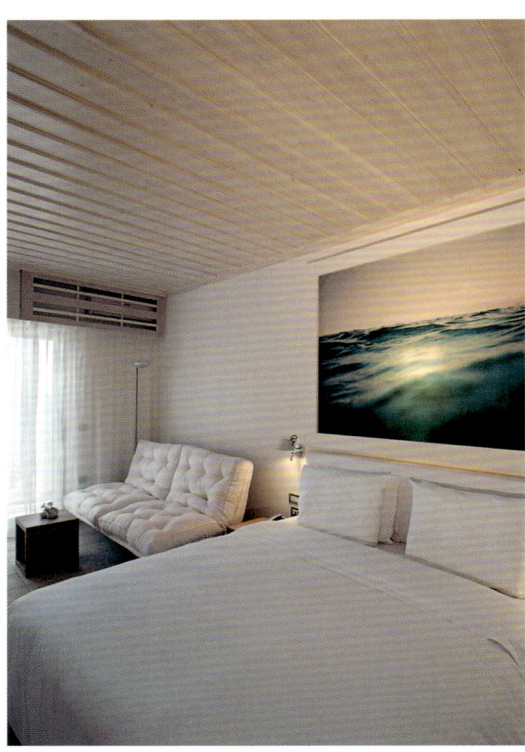
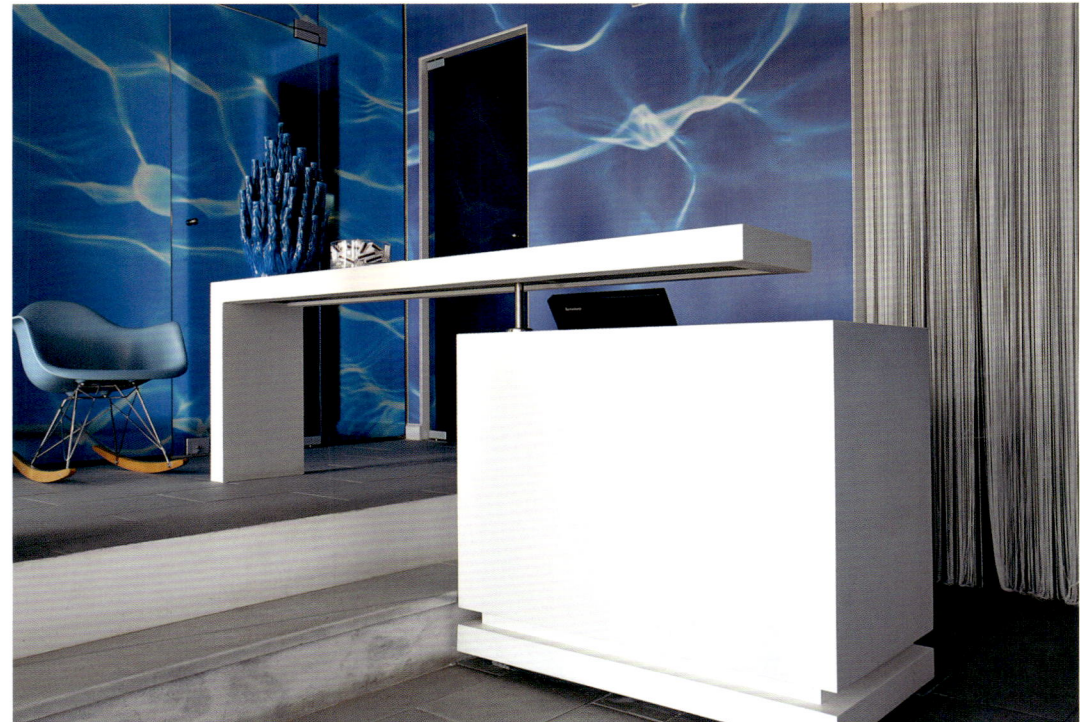

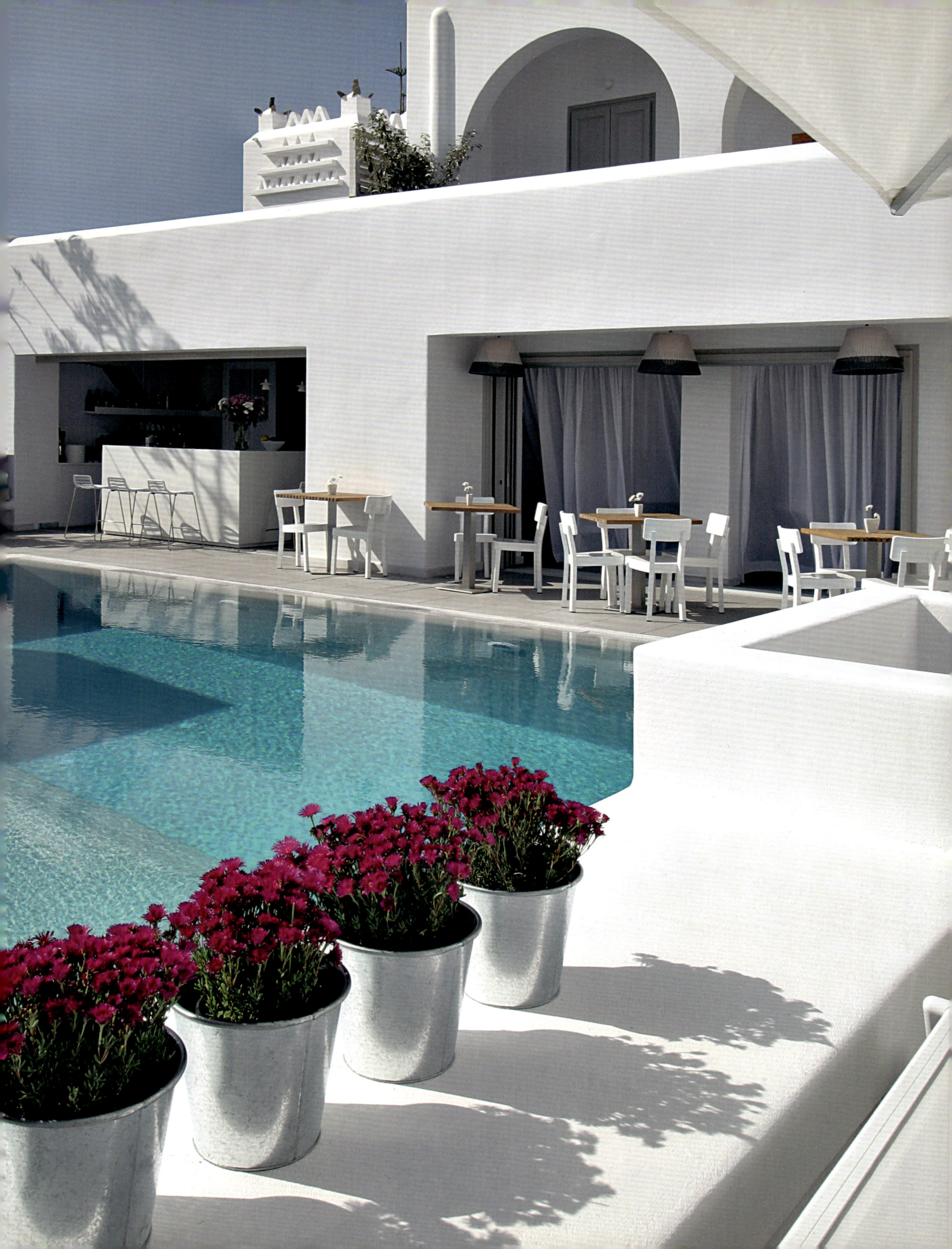

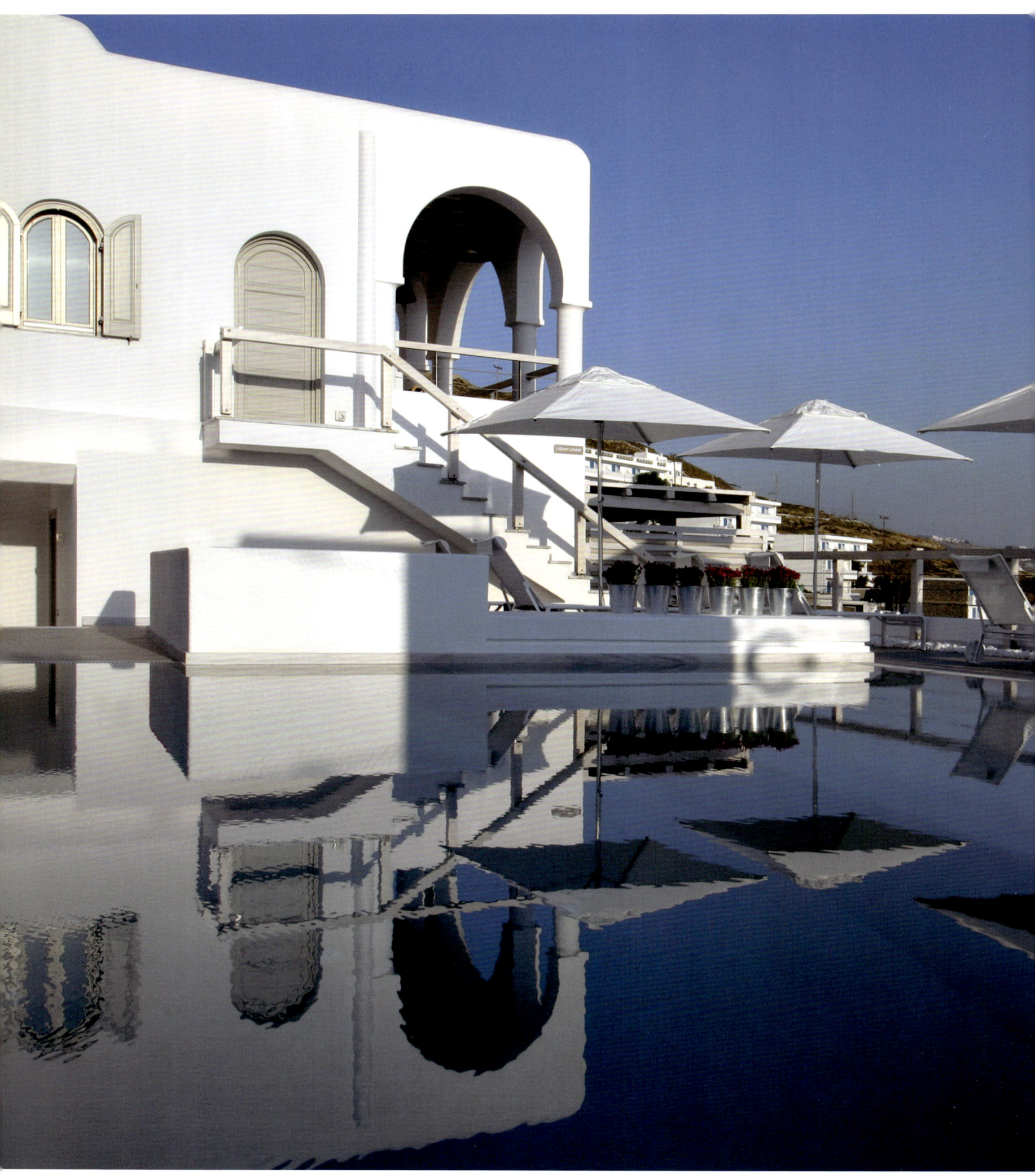

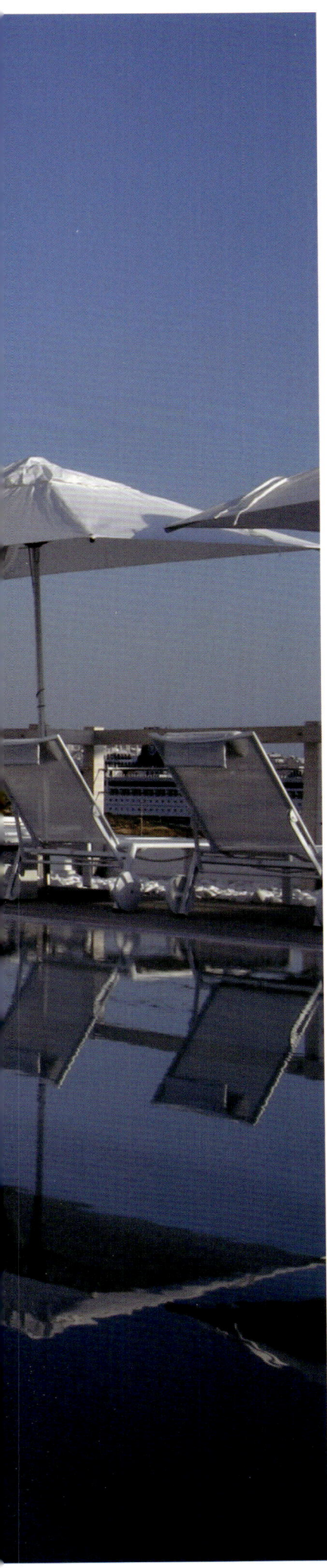

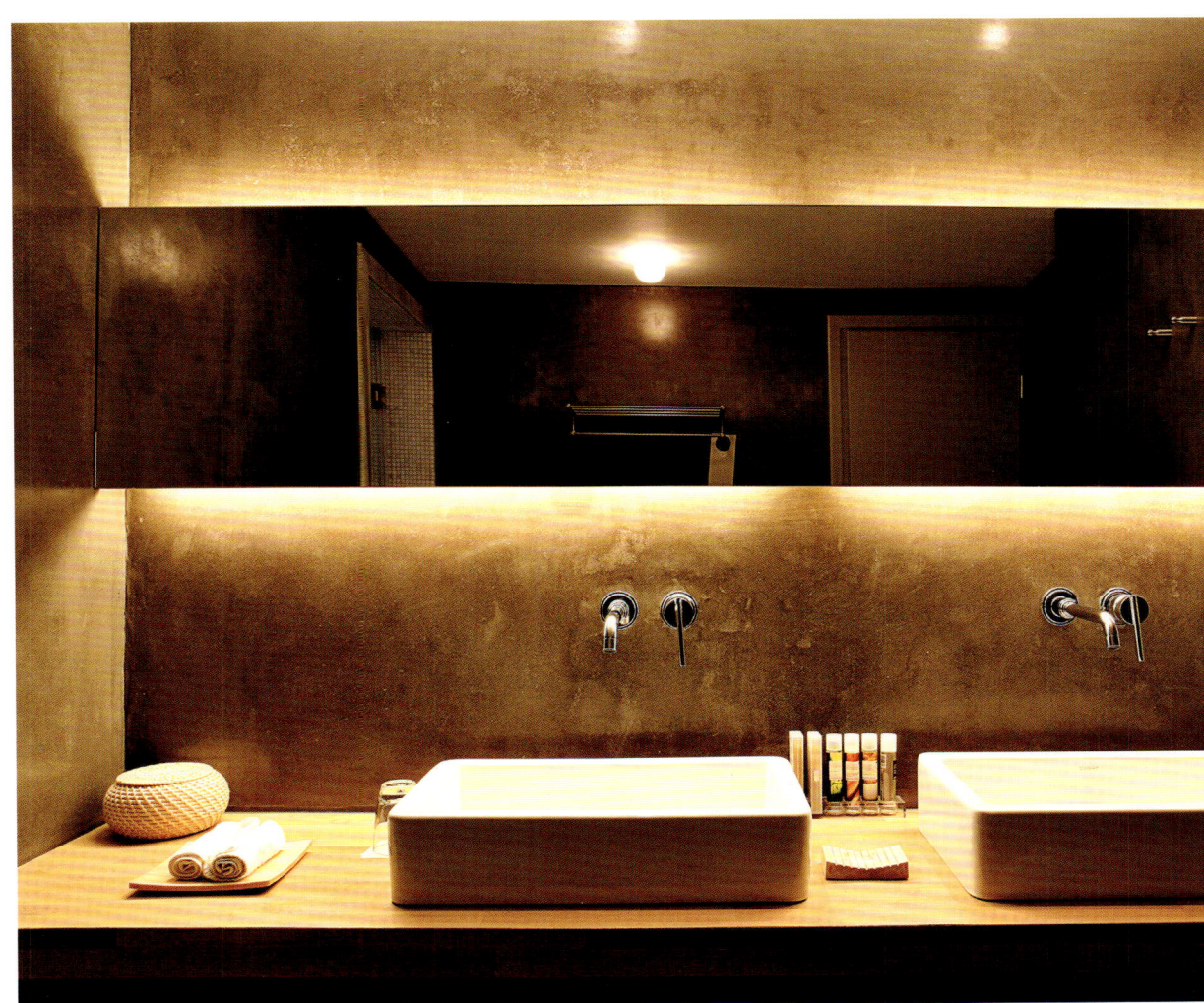

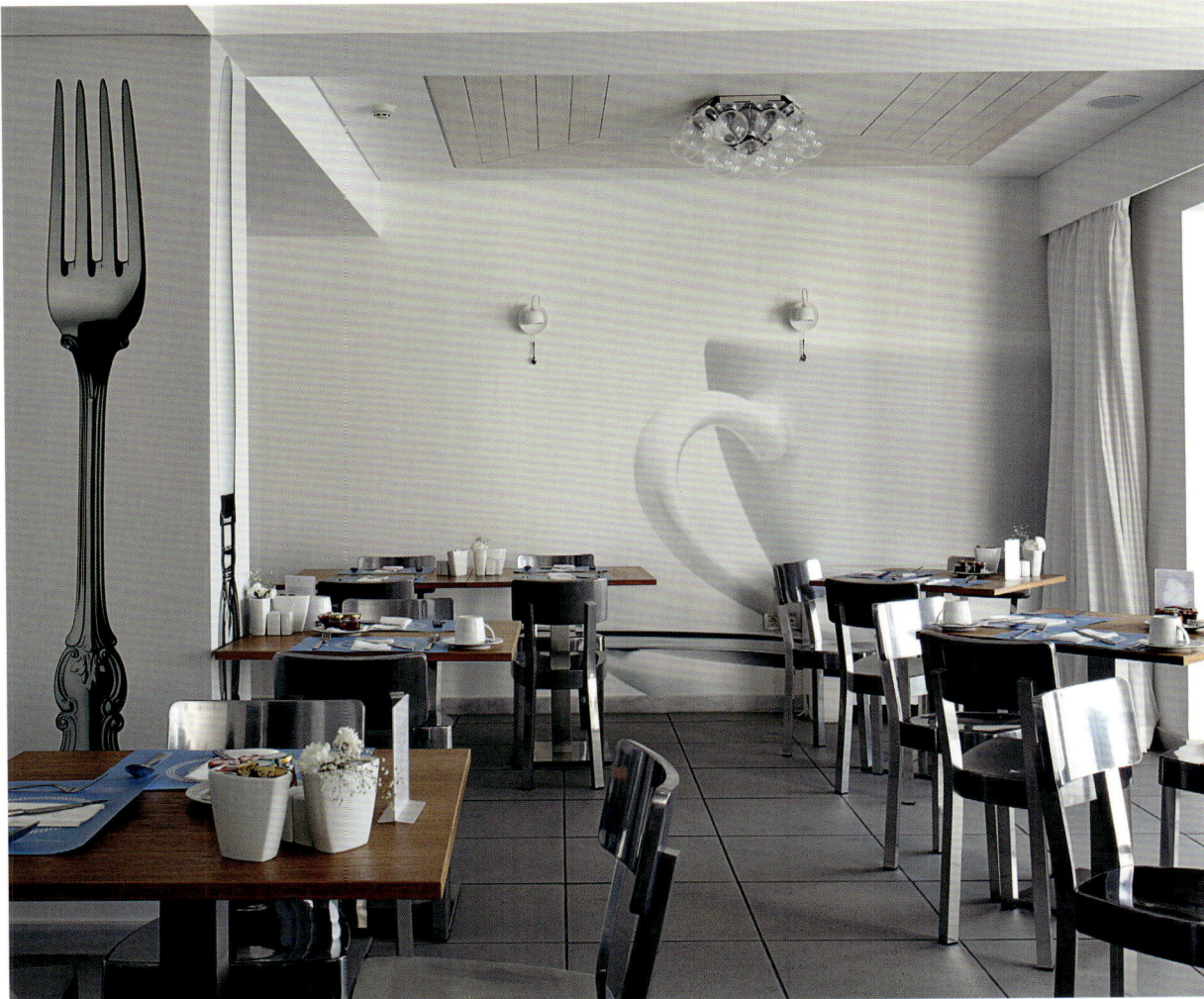

Oia
84702 Santorini
Greece
Phone: +30 228 607 1308
Fax: +30 228 607 1309
www.perivolas.gr

Price category: €€€
Rooms: 20 suites
Facilities: Bar, restaurant, pool, spa
Services: Concierge, transfers, room service, parking
Located: On the cliff overlooking the Caldera
Public transportation: Bus
Style: Mediterranean

Vacationers feel like being in their own Garden of Eden in this individual hideaway high up on a cliff overlooking the Aegean Sea. You only leave the deck chair on your private veranda to take a refreshing dip in the infinity pool. The bright white bungalow complex is extended over a former wine terrace only a stone's throw from Oia, the most beautiful village of the island. Costis Psychas, the owner, had the spacious suites worked out of the volcanic stone with no worry about straight lines or symmetry, and furnished the rooms with island antiques and fine craftsmanship.

Wie im eigenen Garten Eden fühlen sich Urlauber in dem individuellen Hideaway hoch oben auf einem Felsvorsprung über der Ägäis. Den Liegestuhl auf der Privat-veranda verlässt man nur, um sich im Infinity-Pool zu erfrischen. Die blendend weiße Bungalowanlage breitet sich über ehemalige Weinterrassen aus, einen Katzen-sprung entfernt von Oia, dem schönsten Dorf der Insel. Costis Psychas, der Inhaber, ließ die geräumigen Suiten nach Inseltradition aus dem Vulkanstein heraus-arbeiteten, verzichtete auf gerade Linien und Symmetrie und möblierte die Räume mit Insel-Antiquitäten und edlem Kunsthandwerk.

Les vacanciers se sentent comme dans leur propre jardin dans ce refuge individuel, situé sur une saillie rocheuse au-dessus de la mer Egée. Le seul moment où l'on quitte sa chaise longue dans la véranda privative, c'est pour se rafraîchir dans la piscine à débordement. Le complexe de bungalows d'un blanc éblouissant s'étend sur des anciens vignobles en terrasse, à un saut de puce d'Oia, le plus beau village de l'île. Costis Psychas, le propriétaire, a fait construire les spacieuses suites en pierre volcanique dans la plus pure tradition de l'île, et a renoncé à la symétrie et aux lignes claire pour faire meubler les chambres de manière plus traditionnelle avec des antiquités locales et de beau artisanat d'art.

En este retiro individual, muy en lo alto de un saliente sobre el mar Egeo, los visitantes se sienten como en su propio jardín del Edén. El único motivo para dejar la tumbona de la terraza privada es para refrescarse en la piscina de bordes fundidos con el horizonte. El complejo de bungaloes, de un blanco deslumbrante, se extiende sobre una antigua terraza donde se cultivan vides a un paso de Oia, el pueblo más bonito de la isla. Siguiendo la tradición de la isla, Costis Psychas, el dueño del hotel hizo construir las amplias suites con piedra volcánica, prescindió de las líneas rectas y la simetría y amuebló las habitaciones con antigüedades de la isla y una exquisita artesanía.

I clienti che risiedono nei resort individuali arroccati su uno spuntone di roccia sopra il Mar Egeo si sentono come immersi in un personale giardino dell'Eden. Qui si può passare dalle sedie a sdraio della veranda privata a un tuffo rinfrescante nella infinity pool. I bungalow di un bianco accecante sono sgranati sopra un ex vigneto a quattro passi da Oia, il più bel villaggio dell'isola. Costis Psychas, il proprietario, ha ristrutturato le spaziose suite servendosi di pietra lavica (nel pieno rispetto delle tradizioni isolane), ha rinunciato alle linee rette e alle simmetrie, e ha arredato gli interni con pezzi di antiquariato dell'isola e preziose opere d'arte.

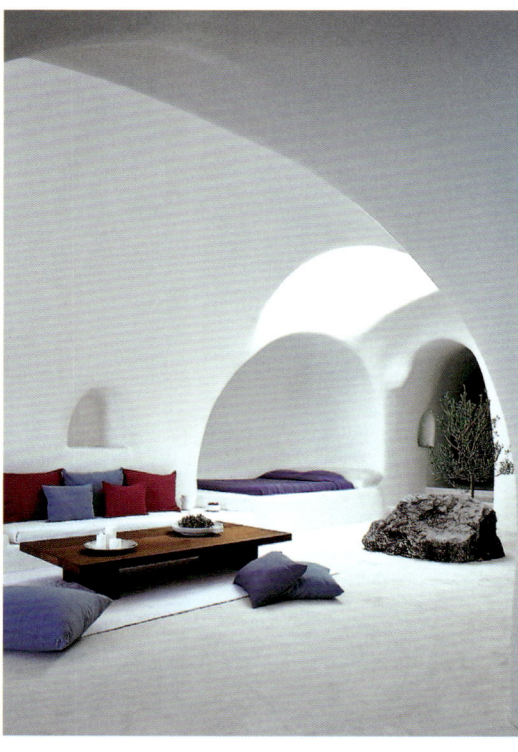
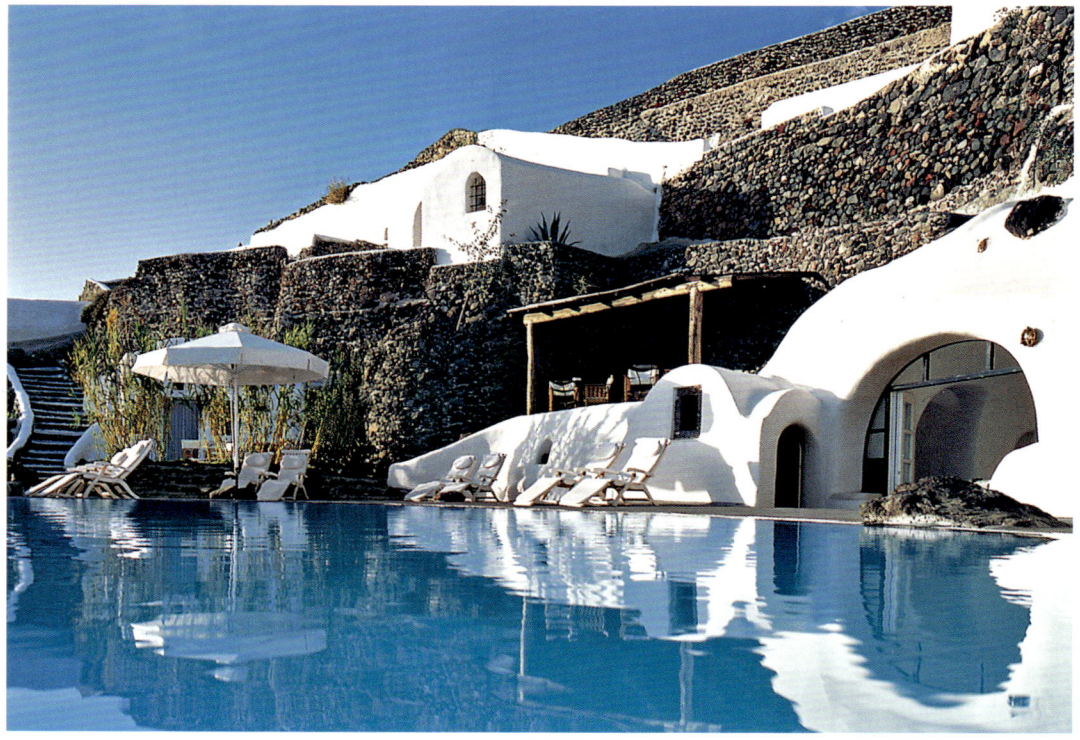

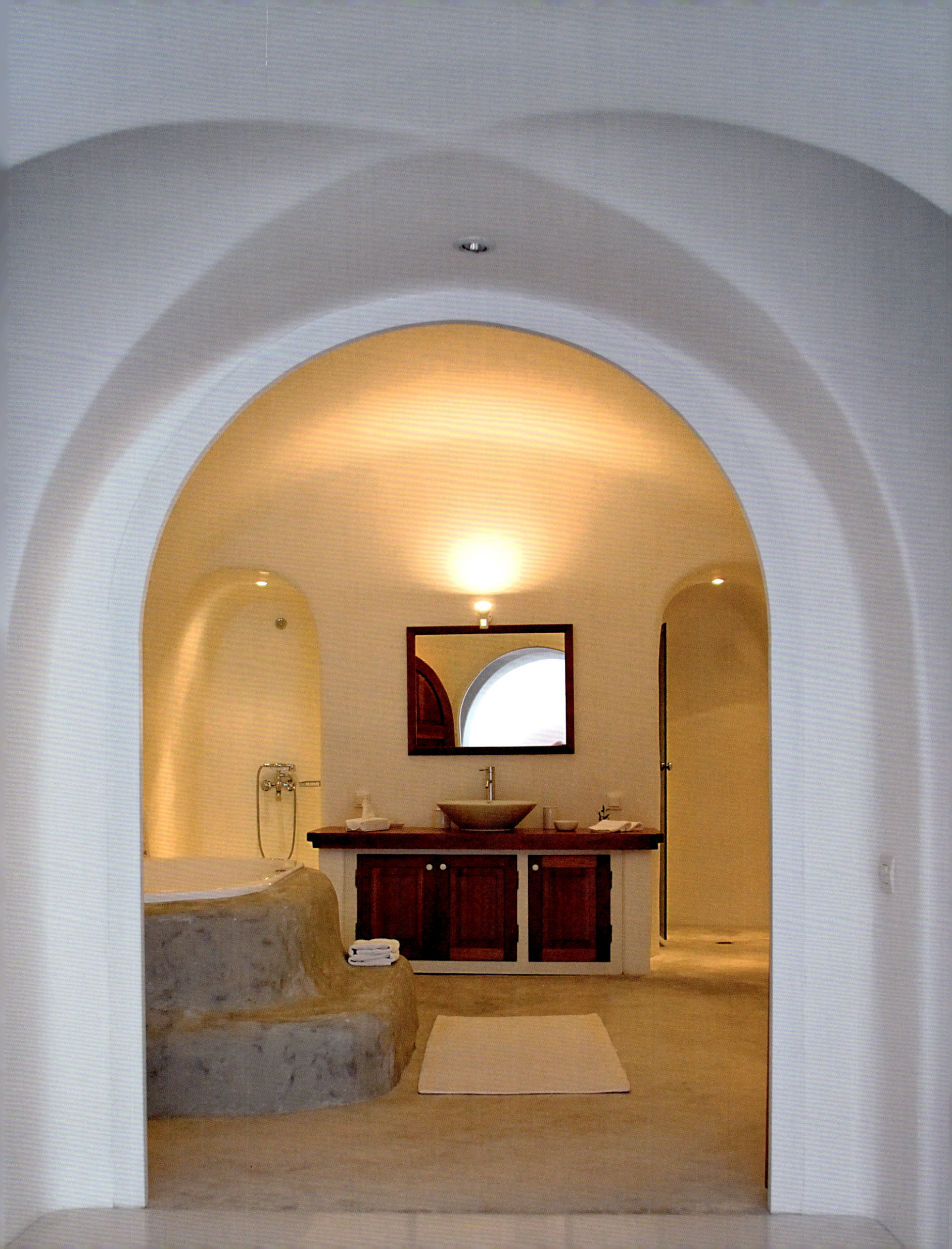

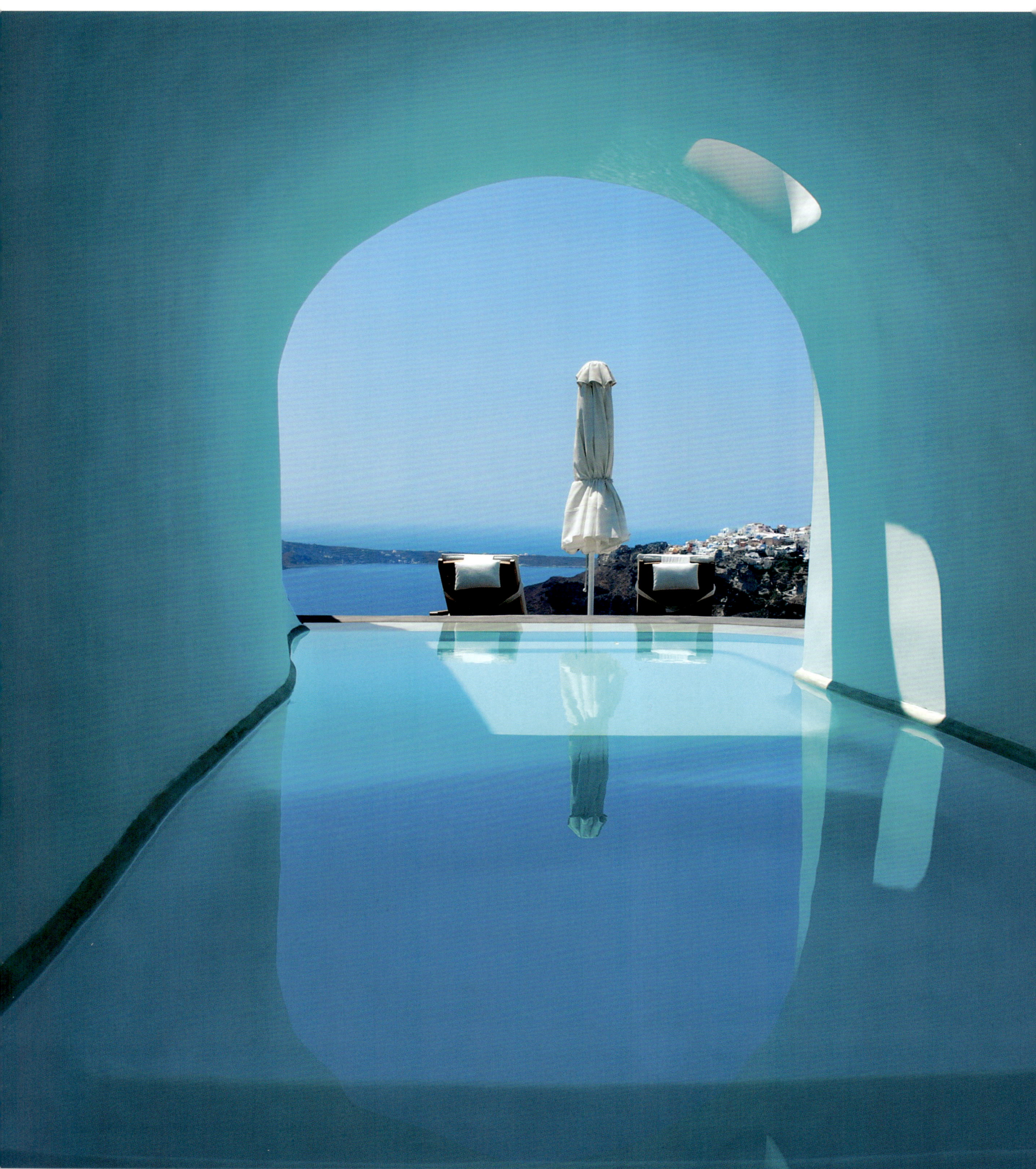

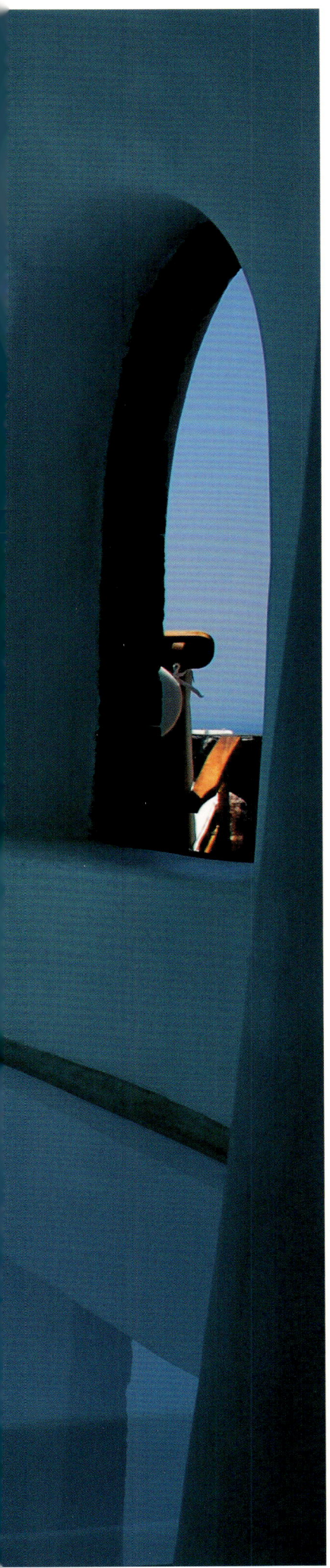

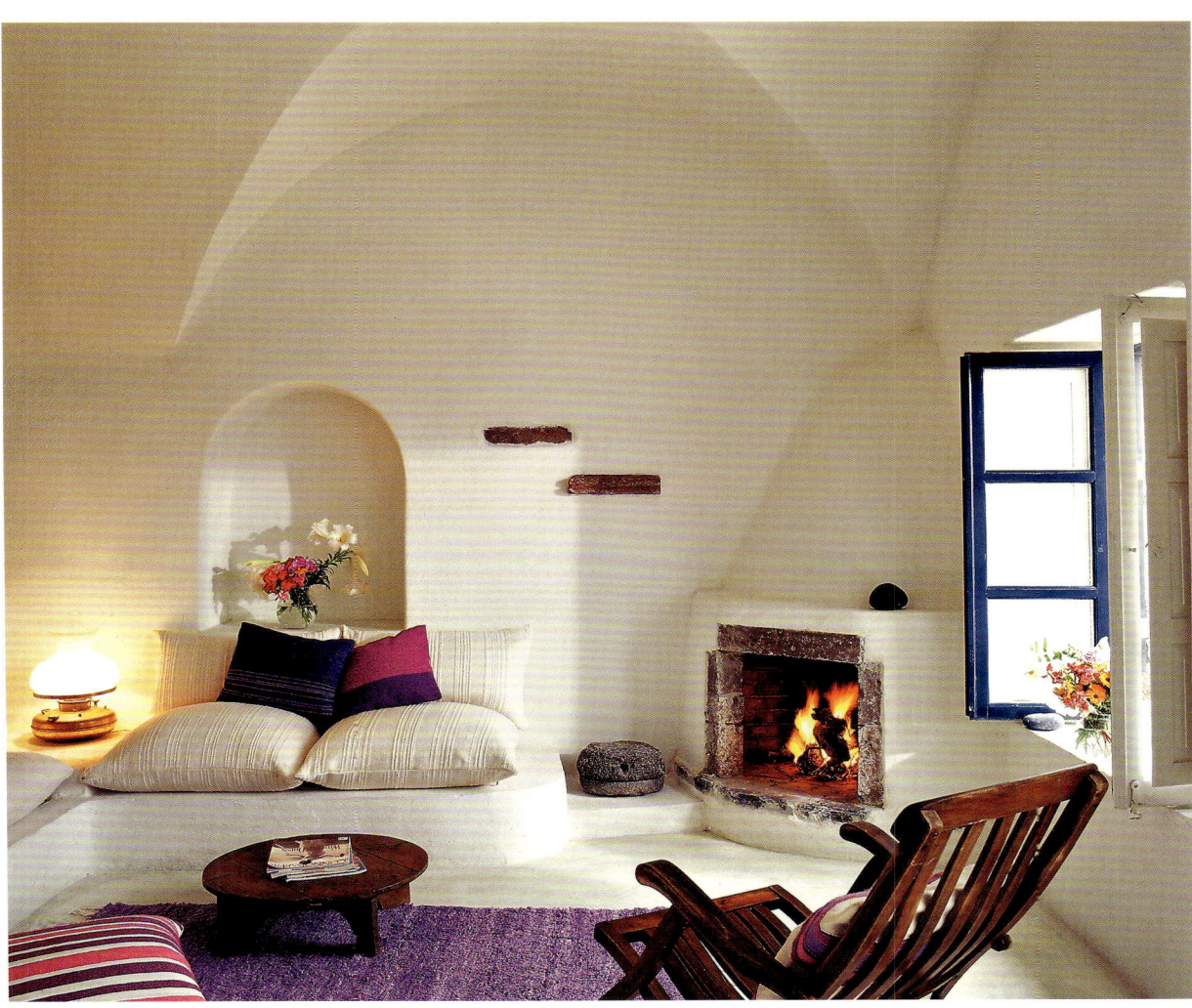

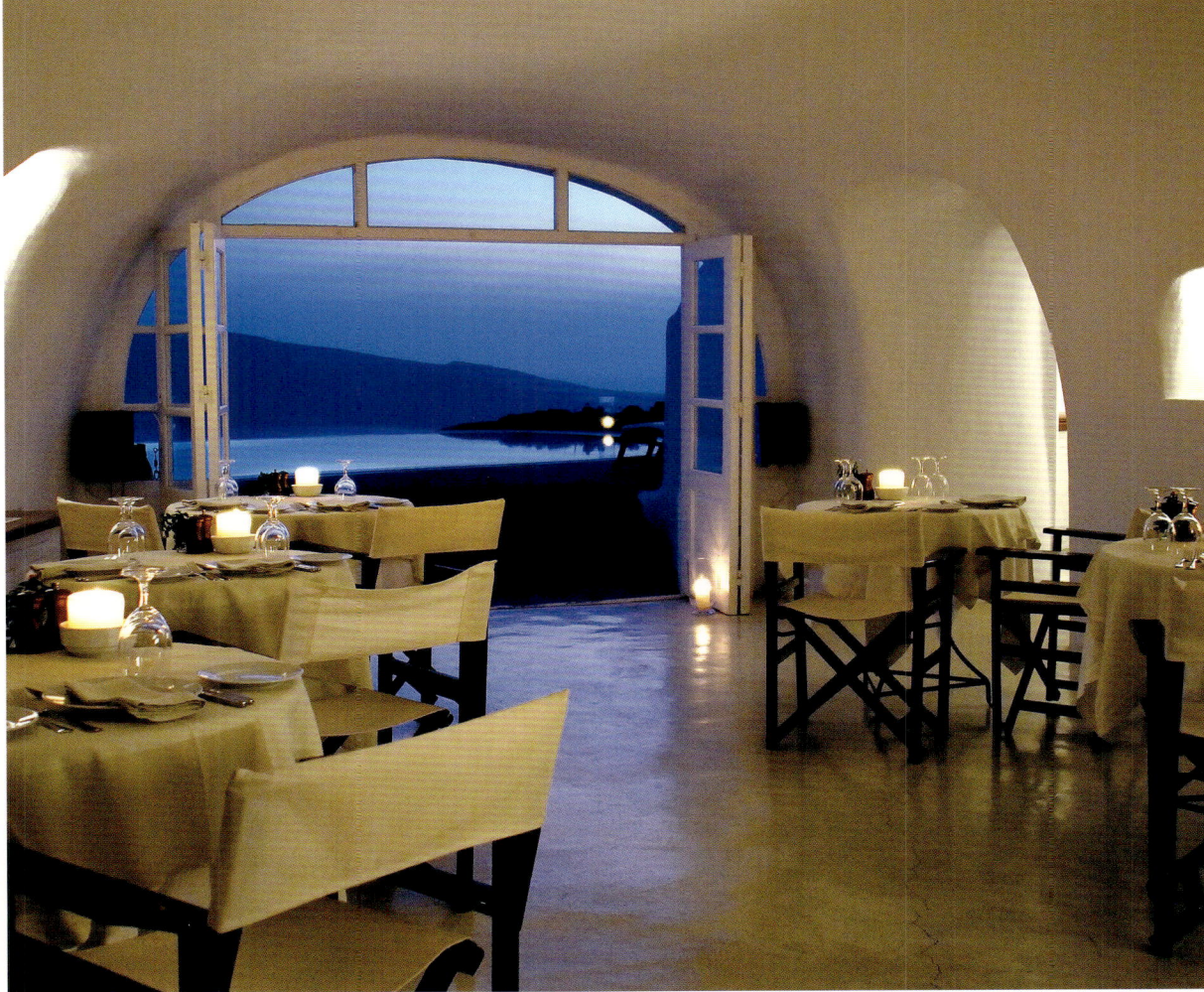

Kanlica, Istanbul
Turkey
Phone: +90 216 413 9300
Fax: +90 216 413 9355
www.ajiahotel.com

Rooms: 16 rooms including 6 suites
Facilities: Restaurant, bar, garden
Services: Babysitting, boat at disposal, room service, pressing-ironing
Located: On the shore of the Bosphorus
Style: Contemporary design

This white villa on the shore of the Bosphorus was one of those summer residences that the high society of the Ottoman Empire built in the 19th century. Today there is a small luxurious hotel with only 16 rooms including suites and consequentially contemporary design behind the neoclassical facade. The Deluxe Bosphorus Suite is particularly impressive with its seven ceiling-high windows and a grand view of the sea. The three mezzanine suites have opulent baths by Philippe Starck. The bustling center of Istanbul is only half an hour away.

Die weiße Villa am Ufer des Bosporus war einer dieser Sommersitze, wie sie sich die osmanische Elite im 19. Jahrhundert baute. Hinter der neoklassizistischen Fassade befindet sich heute ein kleines luxuriöses Hotel mit nur 16 Zimmern inklusive der Suiten und einem konsequent zeitgenössischen Design. Besonders eindrucksvoll ist die Deluxe Bosphorus Suite mit ihren sieben raumhohen Fenstern und einer grandiosen Sicht aufs Meer. Die drei Mezzanin-Suiten verfügen über großzügige Philippe-Starck-Bäder. Das quirlige Zentrum Istanbuls erreicht man in einer halben Stunde.

La villa blanche sur la berge du Bosphore est une des résidences de villégiature construites par l'élite ottomane du XIXème siècle. Derrière sa façade néoclassique se trouve un petit hôtel luxueux de seulement 16 chambres et suites, au design résolument contemporain. La suite Deluxe Bosphorus est particulièrement impressionnante, avec ses sept hautes fenêtres et sa large vue sur la mer. Les trois suites mezzanine disposent de généreuses baignoires concevoir par Philippe Starck. Le centre animé d'Istanbul est à seulement une demi-heure.

La mansión blanca a orillas del Bósforo era una de esas residencias veraniegas construidas por la élite otomana en el siglo XIX. Tras la fachada neoclásica se alberga hoy un pequeño y lujoso hotel de cuidado diseño contemporáneo con sólo 16 habitaciones, incluyendo las suites. Especialmente impresionante es la suite Deluxe Bósforo, con sus siete enormes ventanales abarcando toda la superficie de la pared y sus espectaculares vistas al mar. Las tres suites Mezzanin disponen de grandes baños de Philippe Starck. El bullicioso centro de Estambul está a media hora del hotel.

In origine questa villa bianca sulle rive del Bosforo era una delle residenze estive che l'élite osmanica si fece erigere nel corso del XIX secolo. Dietro una facciata in stile neoclassico si nasconde oggi un piccolo hotel lussuoso con sole 16 stanze (suite incluse) realizzate in un design contemporaneo pulito e coerente. Particolarmente affascinante la suite Deluxe Bosphorus, con le sue sette finestre alte fino al soffitto e una splendida vista sul mare. Le tre suite del mezzanino dispongono di meravigliosi bagni Philippe Starck. E in una mezz'ora ci si trova nel pieno dell'effervescente vita del centro di Istanbul.

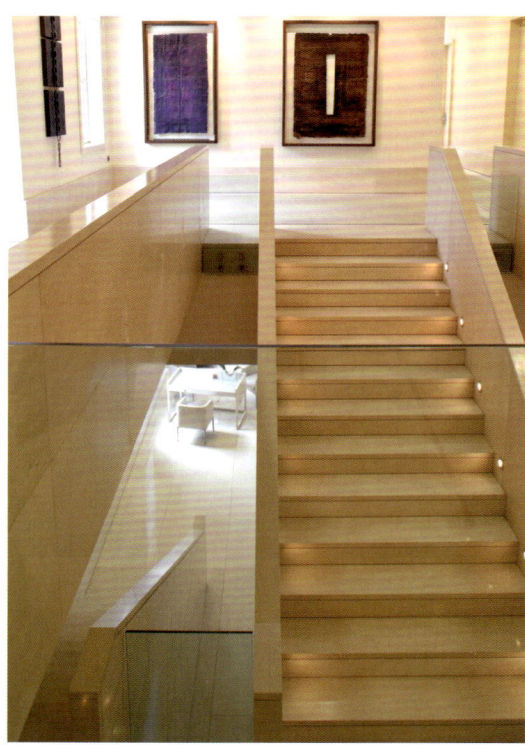
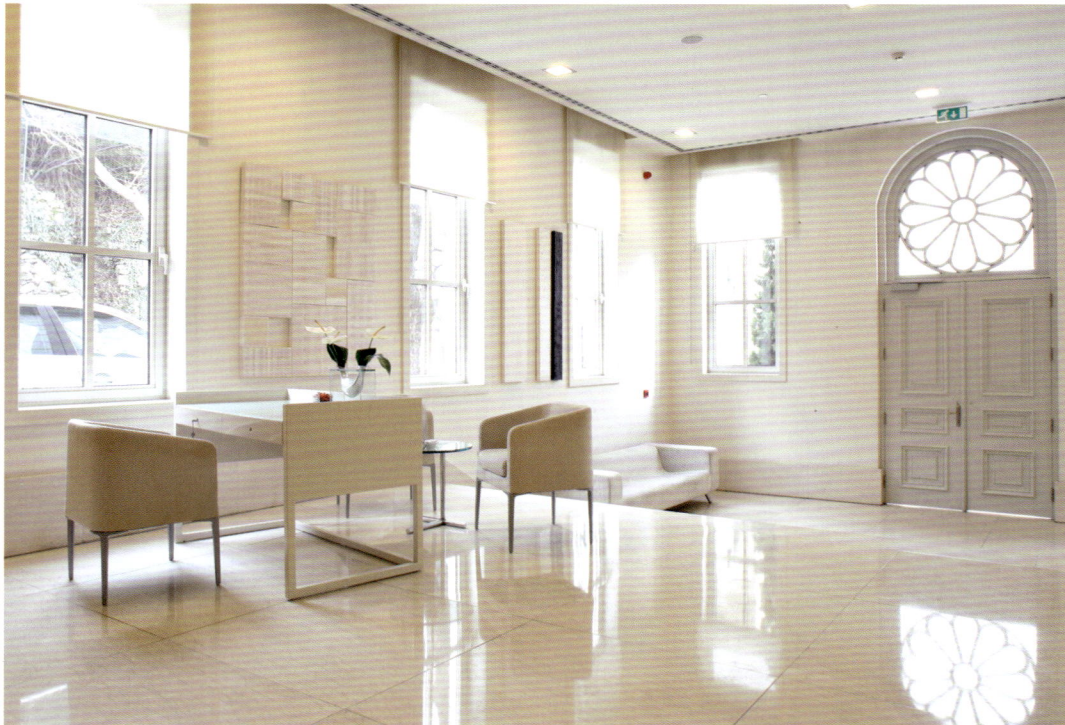

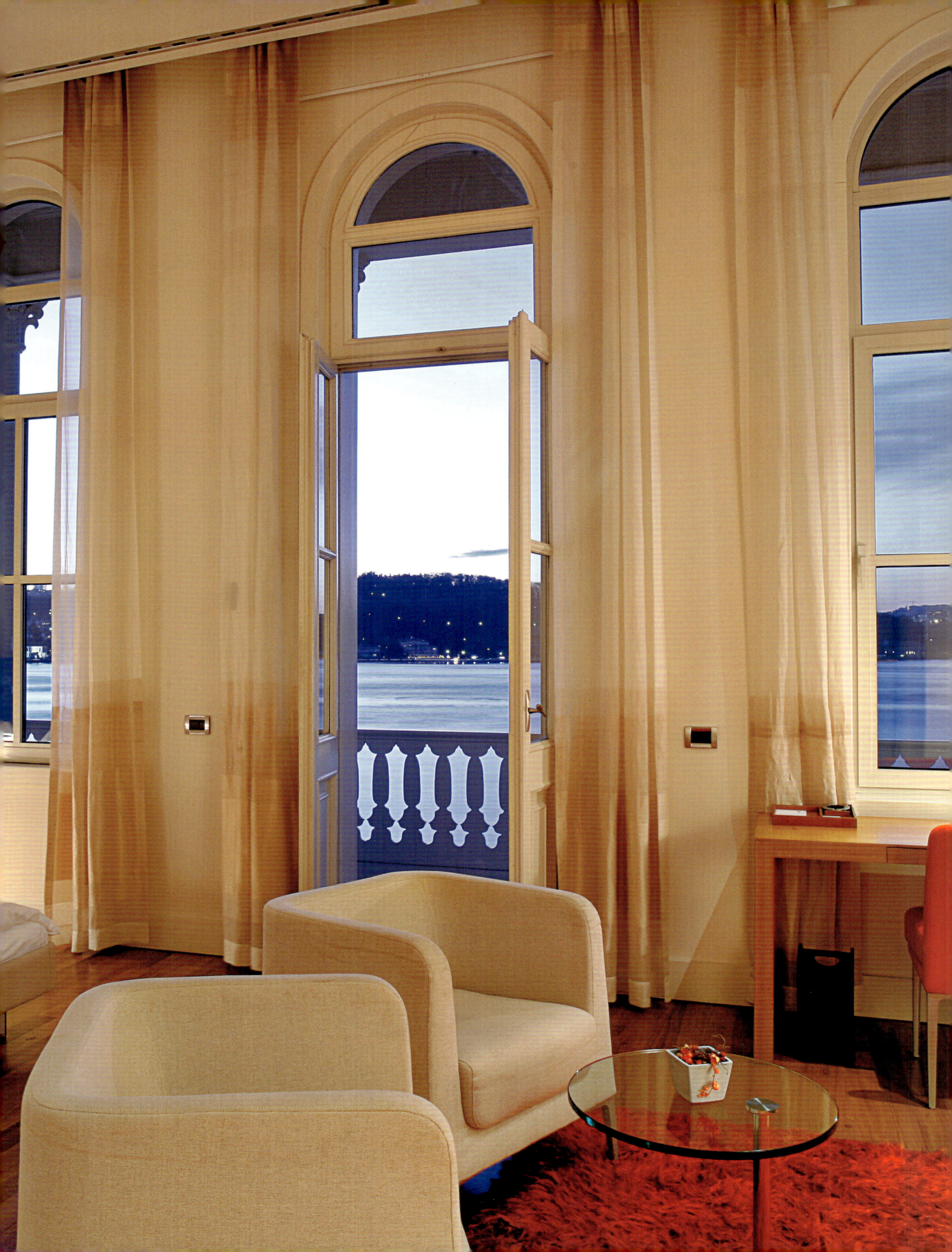

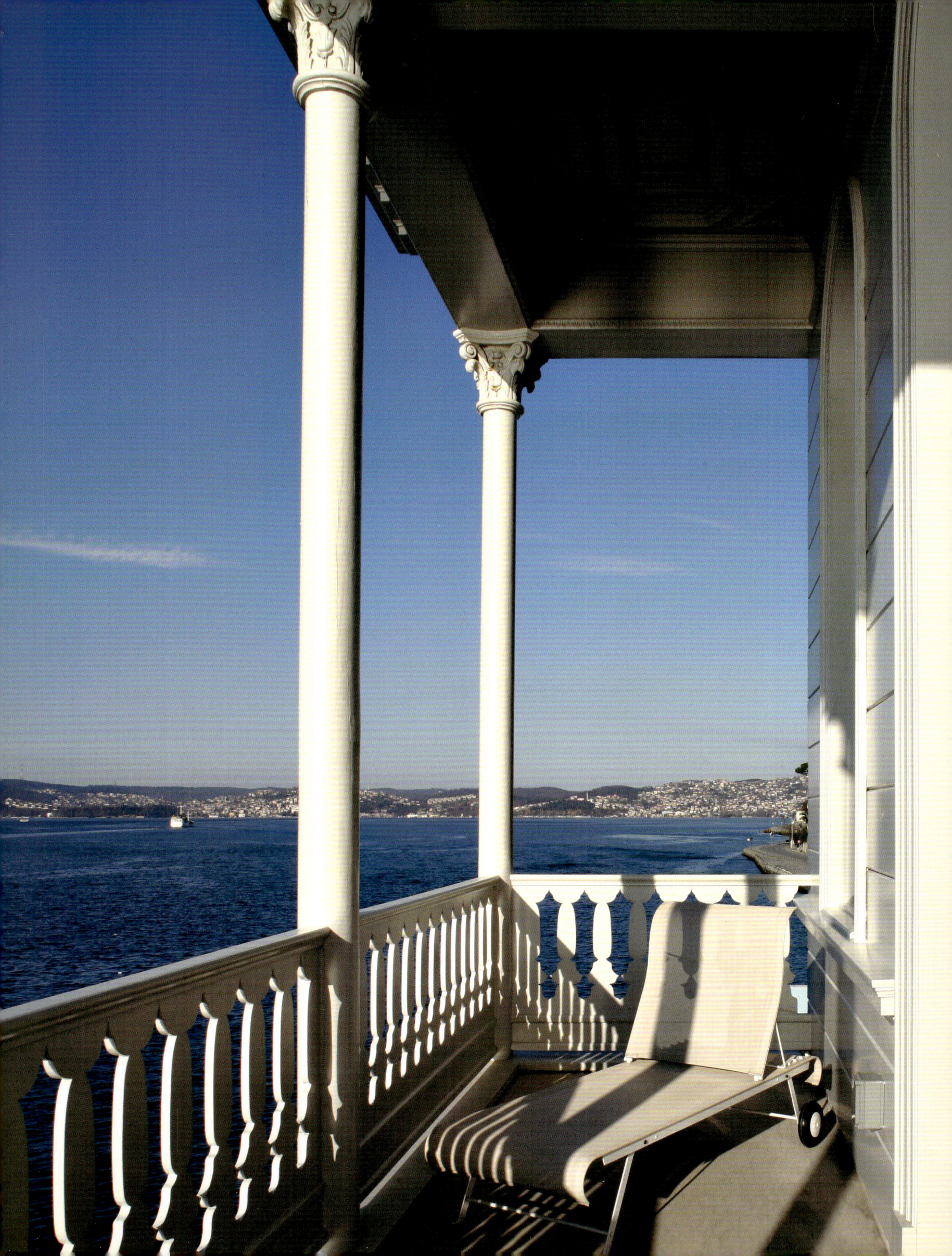

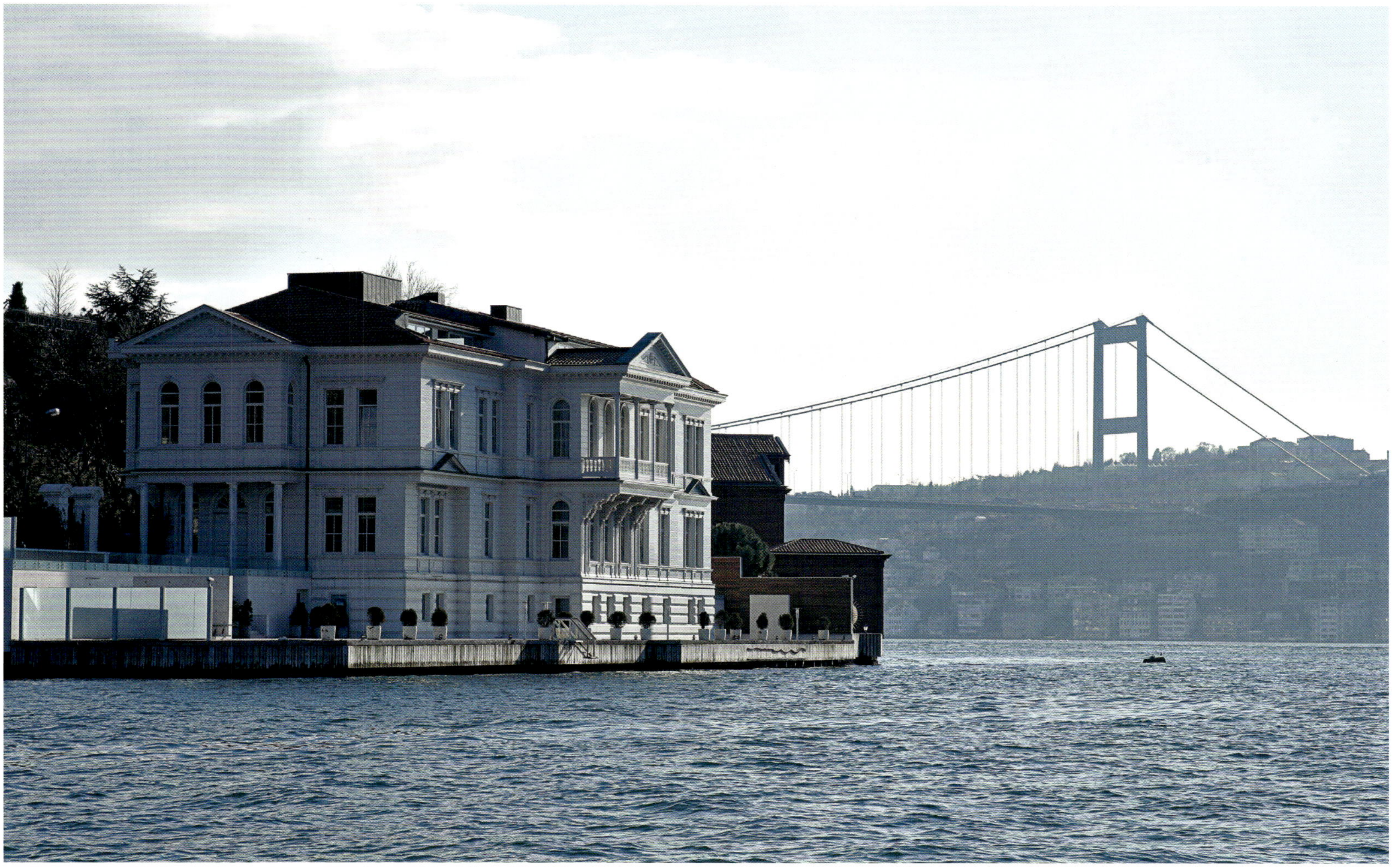

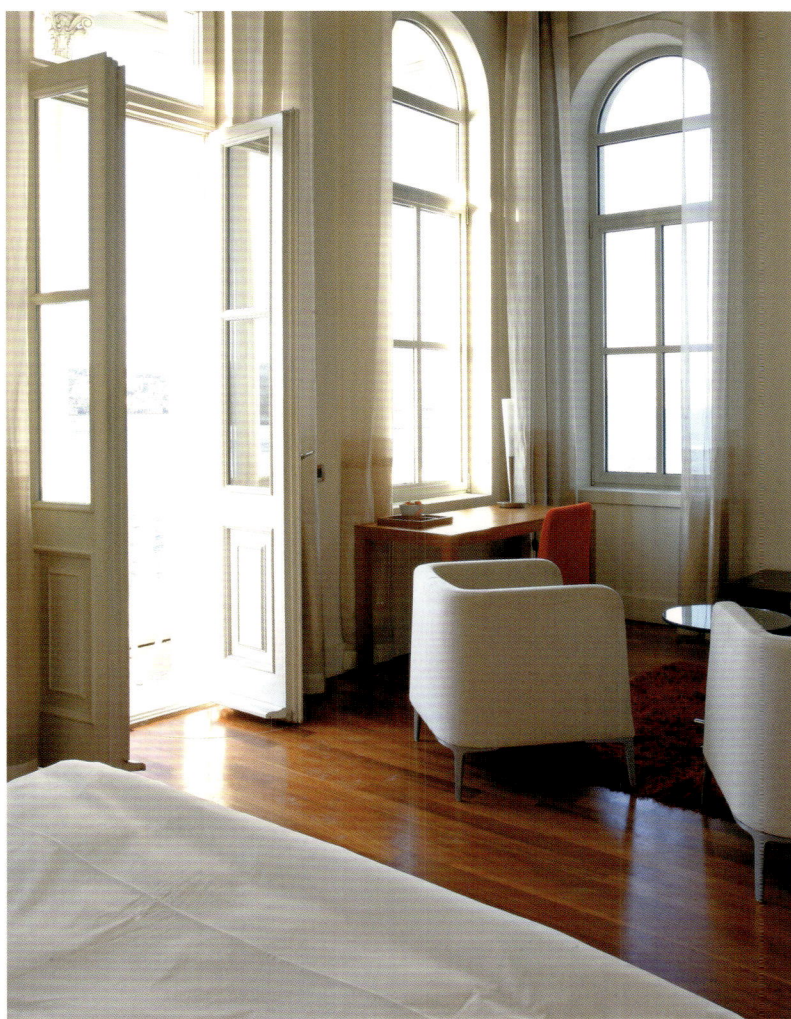

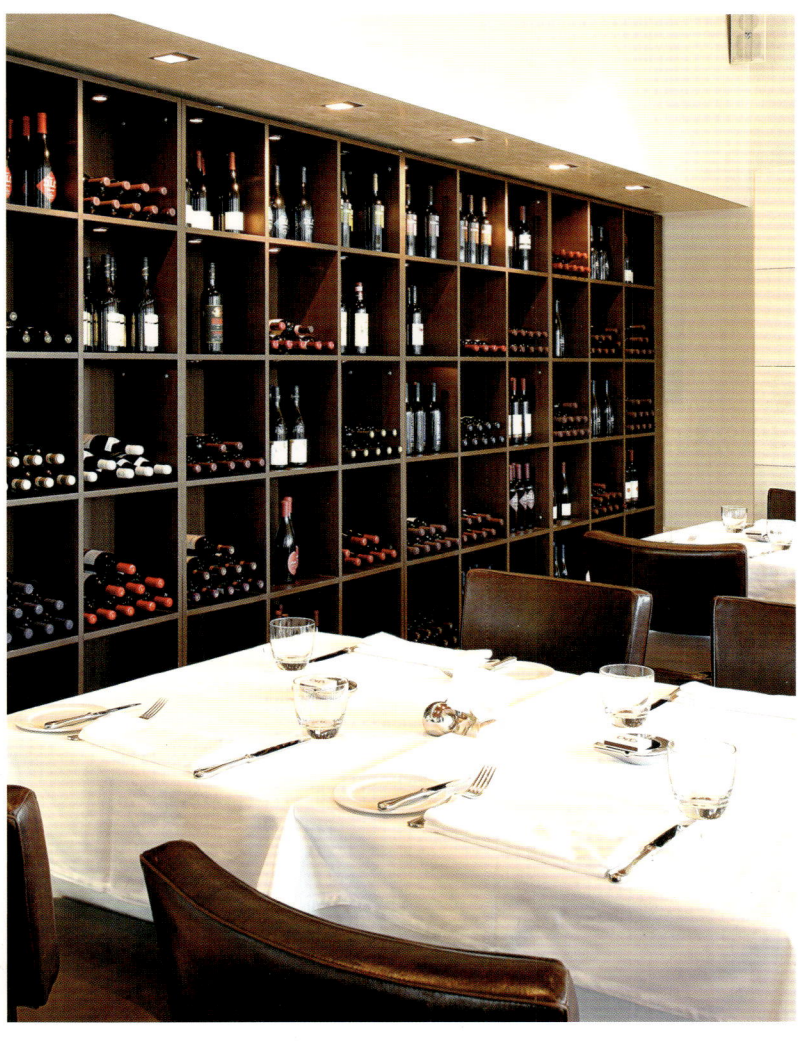

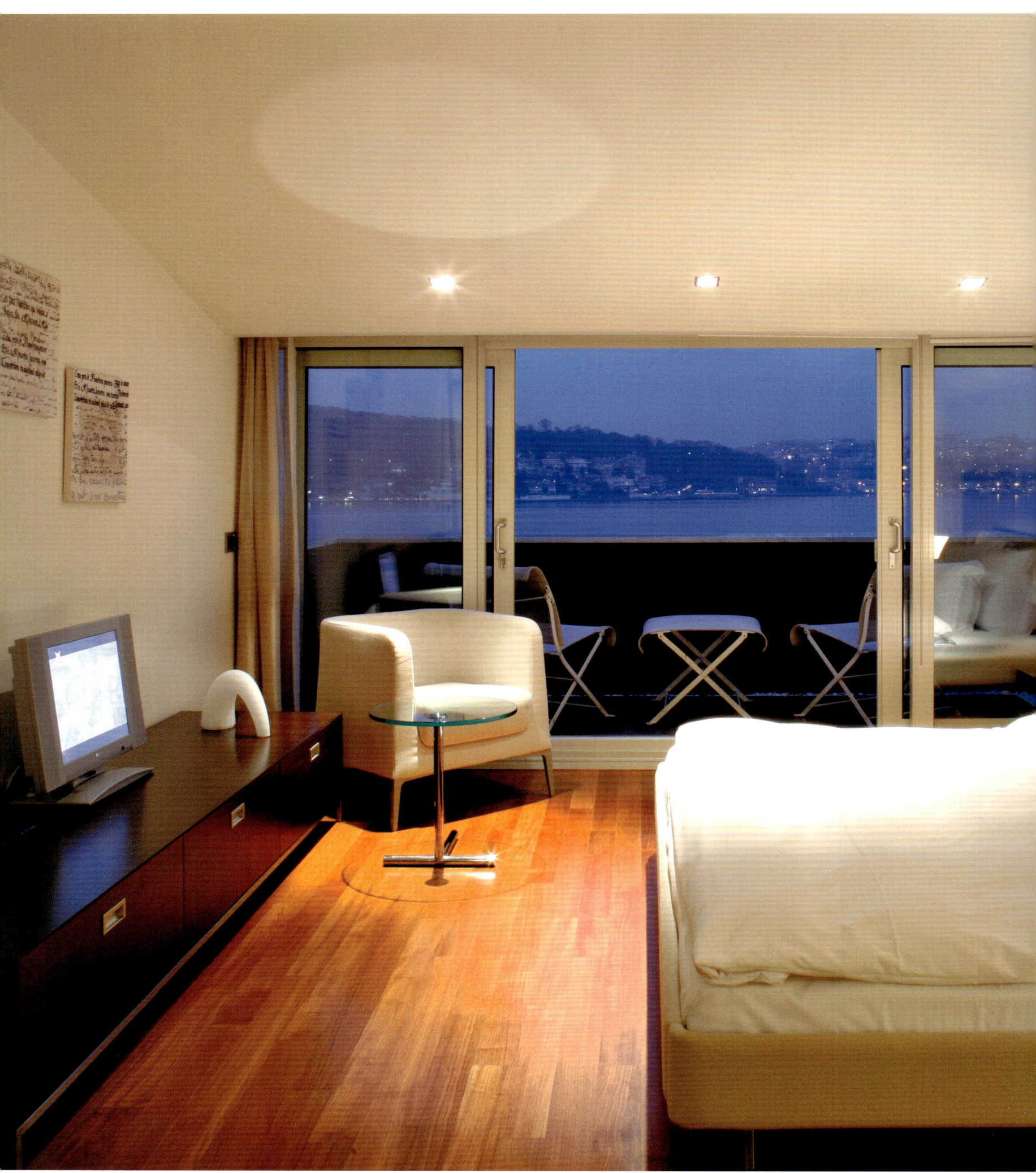

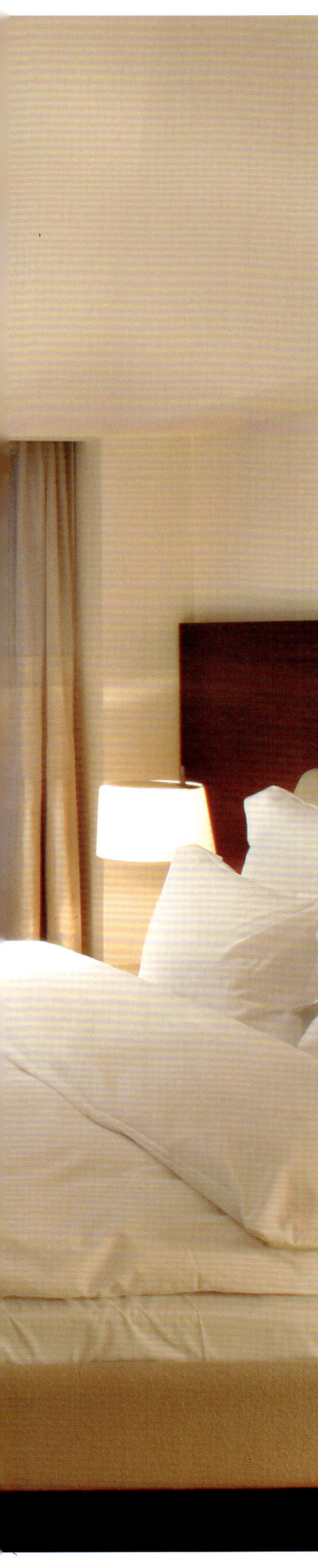

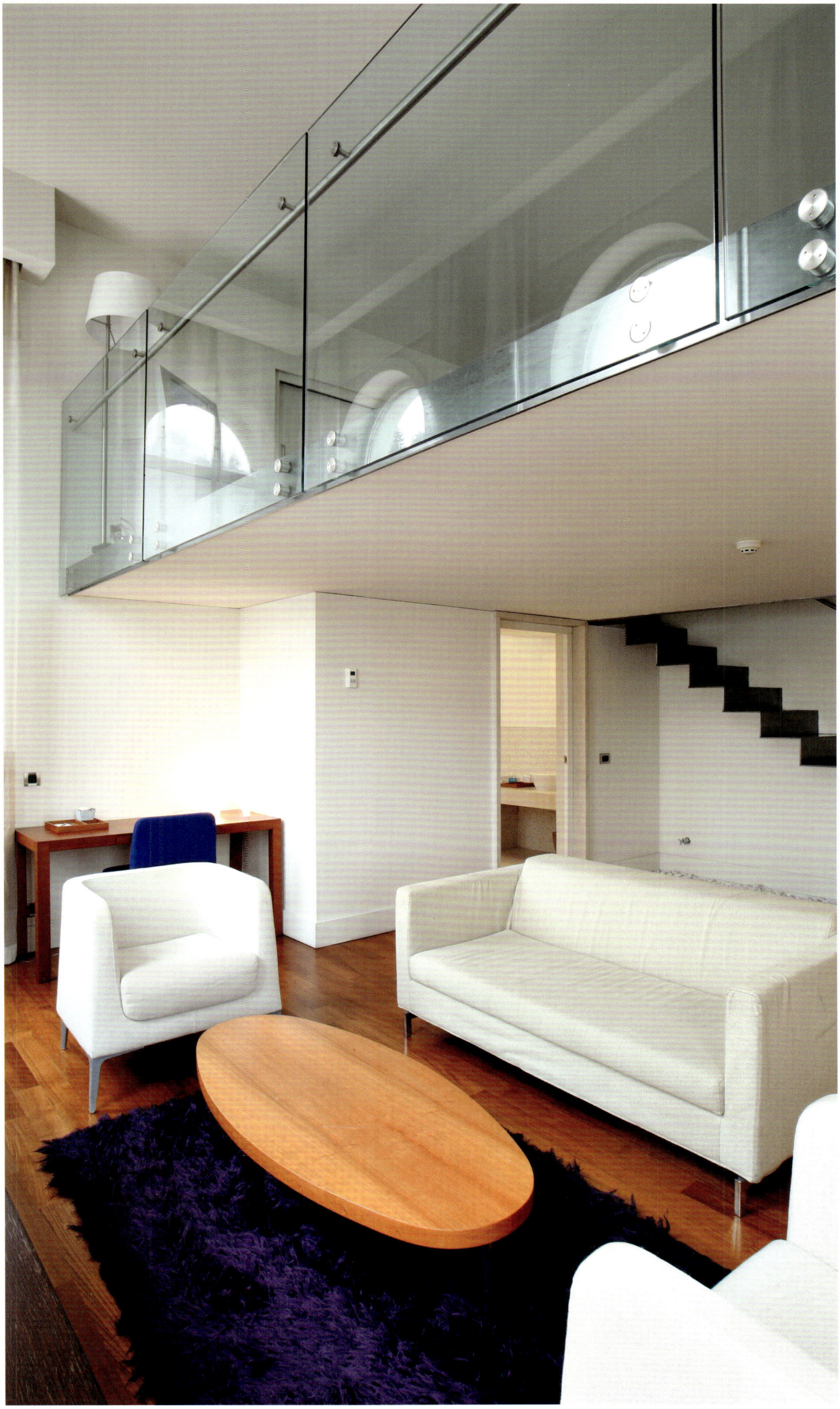

Turkey
Phone: +90 216 422 8000
Fax: +90 216 422 8008
www.sumahan.com

Facilities: 2 Restaurants, wellness center, meeting room
Services: Babysitting, fitness and massage service, 24 h room service, library, accessible for the disabled, dry cleaning, laundry service
Located: On the Asian shore of the Bosphorus
Public transportation: Public ferry and bus
Style: Modern

A former 19th-century distillery was remodeled by the Turkish-American architect couple Mrs. Nedret and Mr. Mark Butler to an unconventional gem of a hotel. The location on the more neglected Asian shore of the Bosphorus proves to have a particular advantage. From the lobby, you can have a unique view of the minarets and domes of the old city of Istanbul as well as of the Ataturk Bridge that spans the busy strait. Almost all 20 rooms and suites have an open fireplace, while the seven loft suites also have their own gardens.

Eine ehemalige Destillerie aus dem 19. Jahrhundert bauten das türkisch-amerikanische Architektenpaar Nedret und Mark Butler zu einem eigenwilligen Hotelkleinod um. Die Lage am eher vernachlässigten asiatischen Ufer des Bosporus erweist sich als besonderer Vorteil: Von der Lobby genießt man einen einzigartigen Blick auf die Minarette und Kuppeln der Istanbuler Altstadt wie auch auf die Atatürk-Brücke, welche die vielbefahrene Wasserstraße überspannt. Fast alle 20 Zimmer und Suiten haben einen offenen Kamin, die sieben Loft-Suiten zusätzlich einen eigenen Garten.

Une ancienne distillerie du XIXème siècle a été convertie en un bijou d'hôtel par le couple d'architectes américano-turc Nedret and Marc Butler. Son emplacement sur la rive asiatique, souvent délaissée, du Bosphore, a démontré un avantage particulier : depuis la réception, on peut profiter d'une vue unique sur les minarets et les dômes de la vieille ville d'Istanbul, ainsi que sur le Pont Atatürk, qui s'étend au-dessus de la voie d'eau très fréquentée. Presque toutes les 20 chambres et suites possèdent une cheminée, et les sept suites loft disposent de leur propre jardin.

La pareja de arquitectos turco-americana Nedret y Mark Butler ha transformado una antigua destilería del siglo XIX en una original joya hotelera. La ubicación en la algo más descuidada orilla asiática del Bósforo resulta ser una gran ventaja. Desde el vestíbulo se puede disfrutar de una vista única de los minaretes y las cúpulas del centro histórico de Estambul, como también del puerte de Atatürk, el cual cruza la muy transitada vía fluvial. Casi la totalidad de las 20 habitaciones disponen de chimenea, las siete suites loft tienen además su propio jardín.

La coppia di architetti turco-americani Nedret e Mark Butler ha saputo trasformare un'ex distilleria del XIX secolo in questo hotel che, a ragione, può essere definito un pezzo unico. La collocazione dell'albergo – che si trova sulla riva asiatica del Bosforo, piuttosto trascurata – si è tradotta in un vantaggio non da poco: dalla lobby si può godere di una vista straordinaria sulle cupole e i minareti del centro storico di Istanbul e sul ponte Atatürk, che collega tra loro le due sponde di questa trafficata via fluviale. Quasi tutte le 20 camere o suite hanno un caminetto con fuoco a vista, mentre le suite collocate nei sette loft dispongono anche di un giardino proprio.

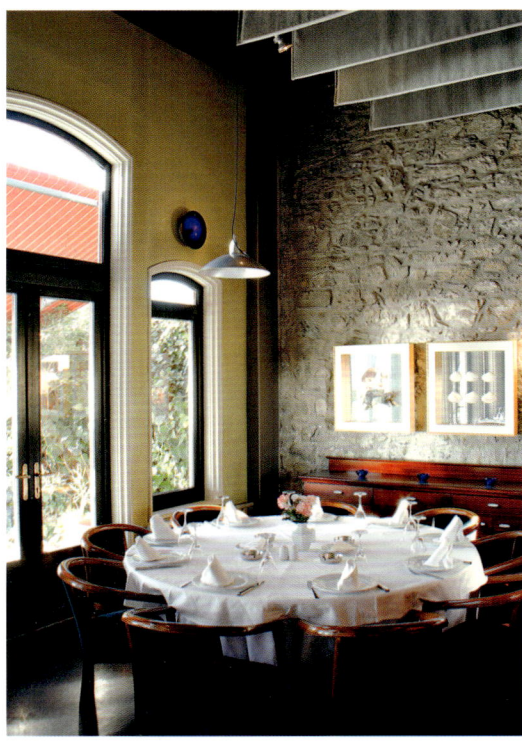
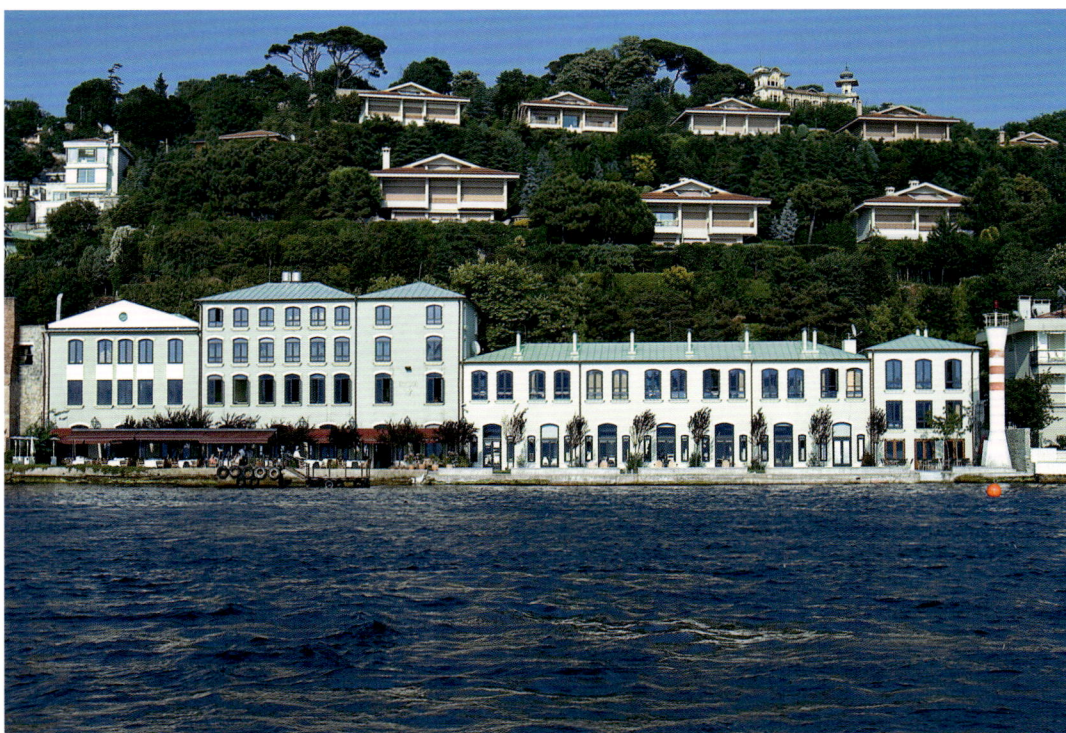

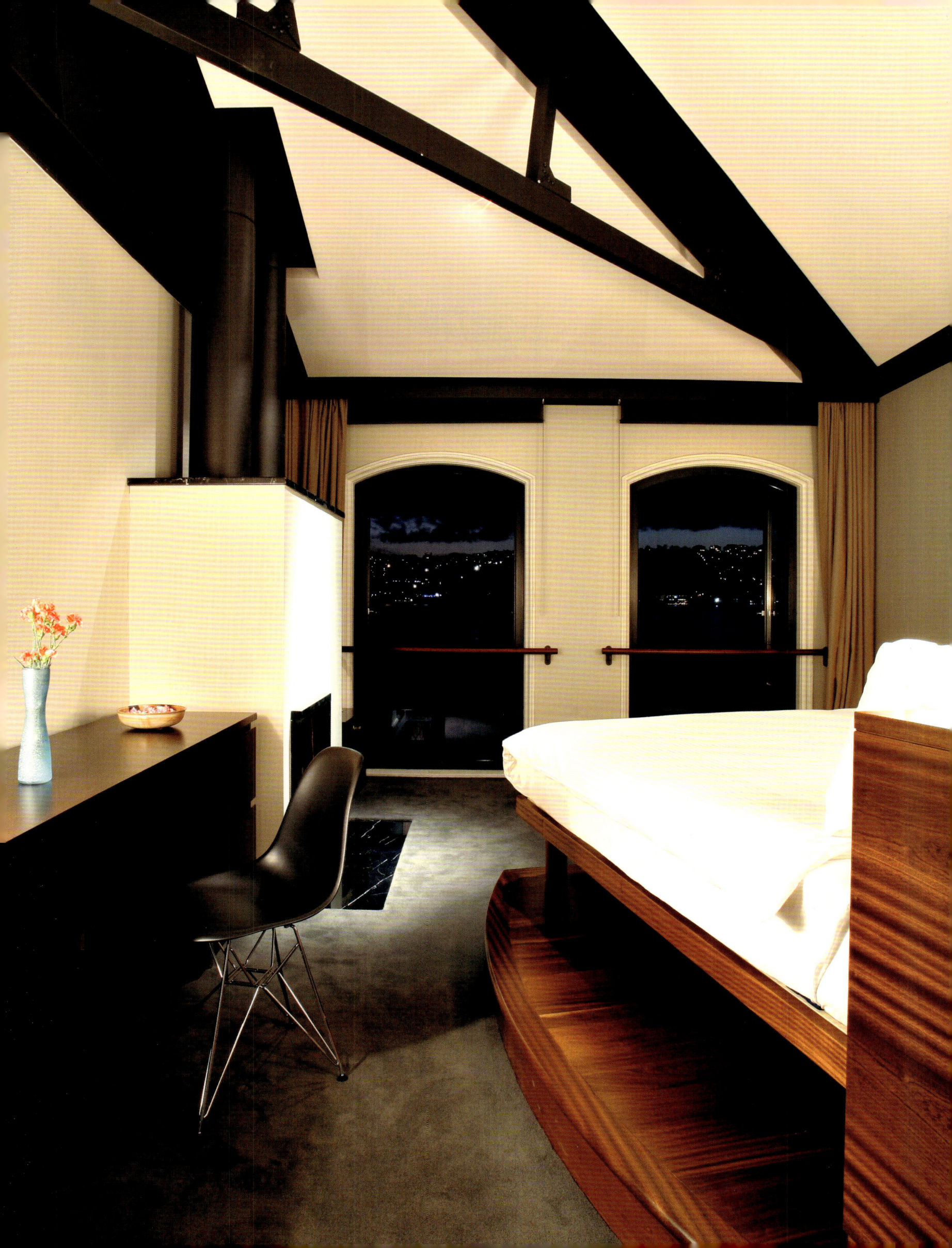

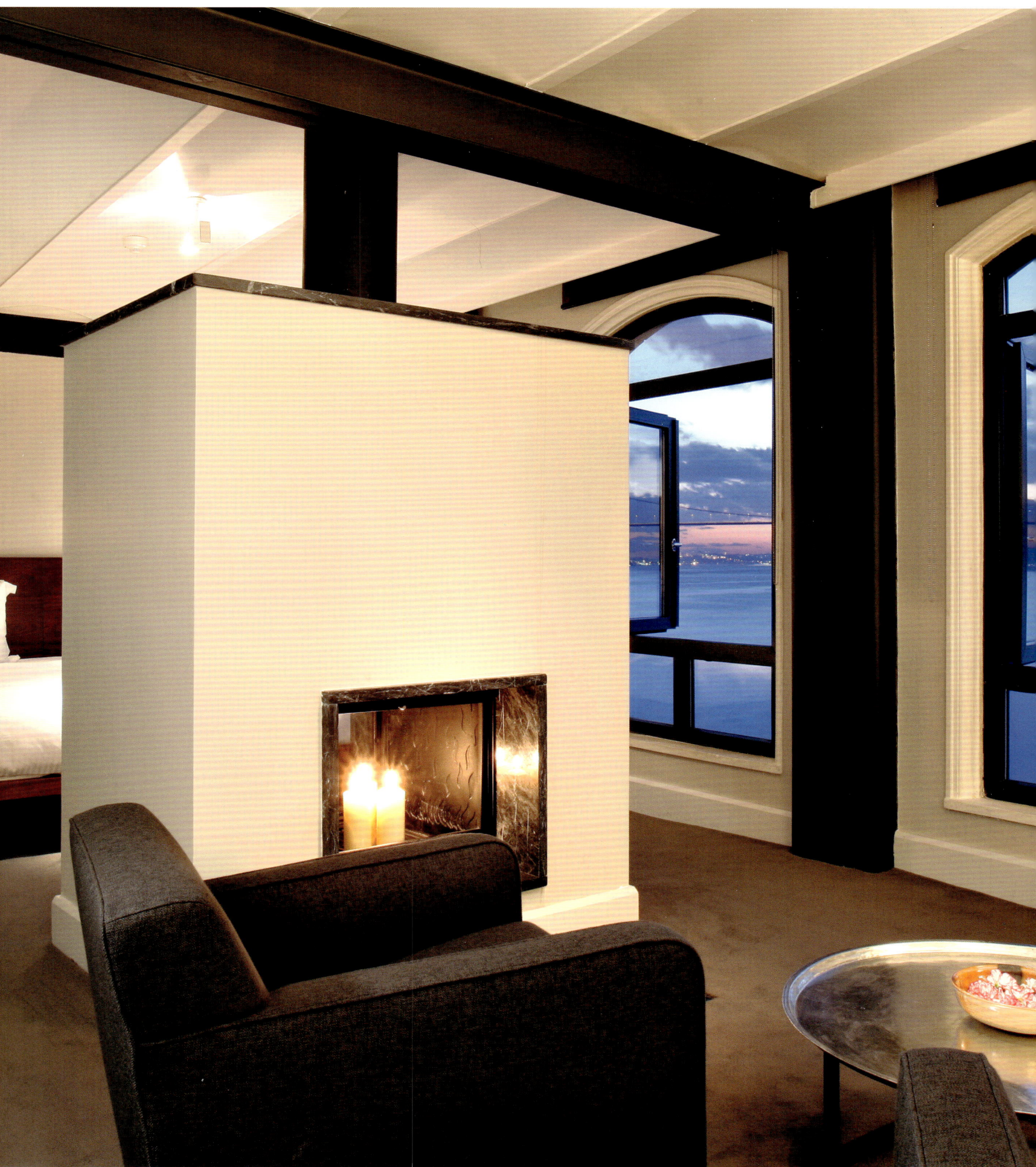

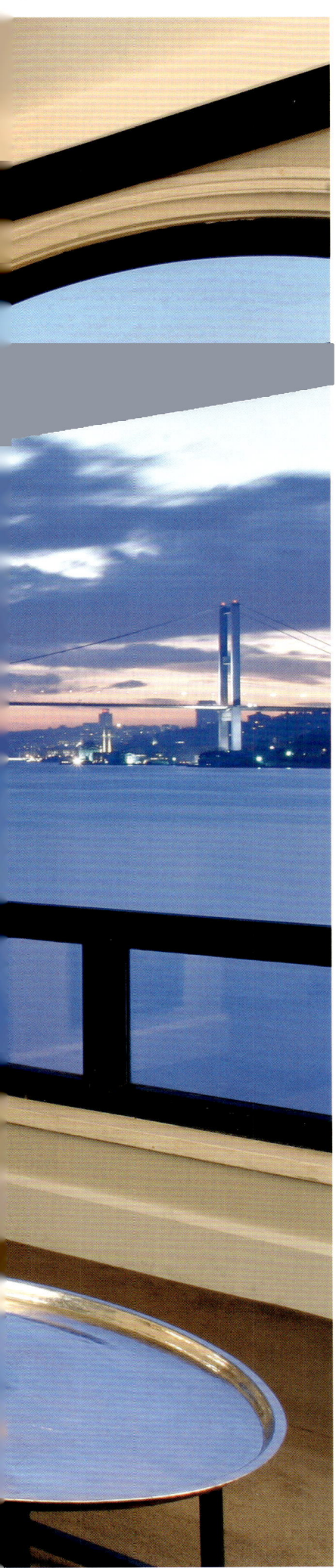

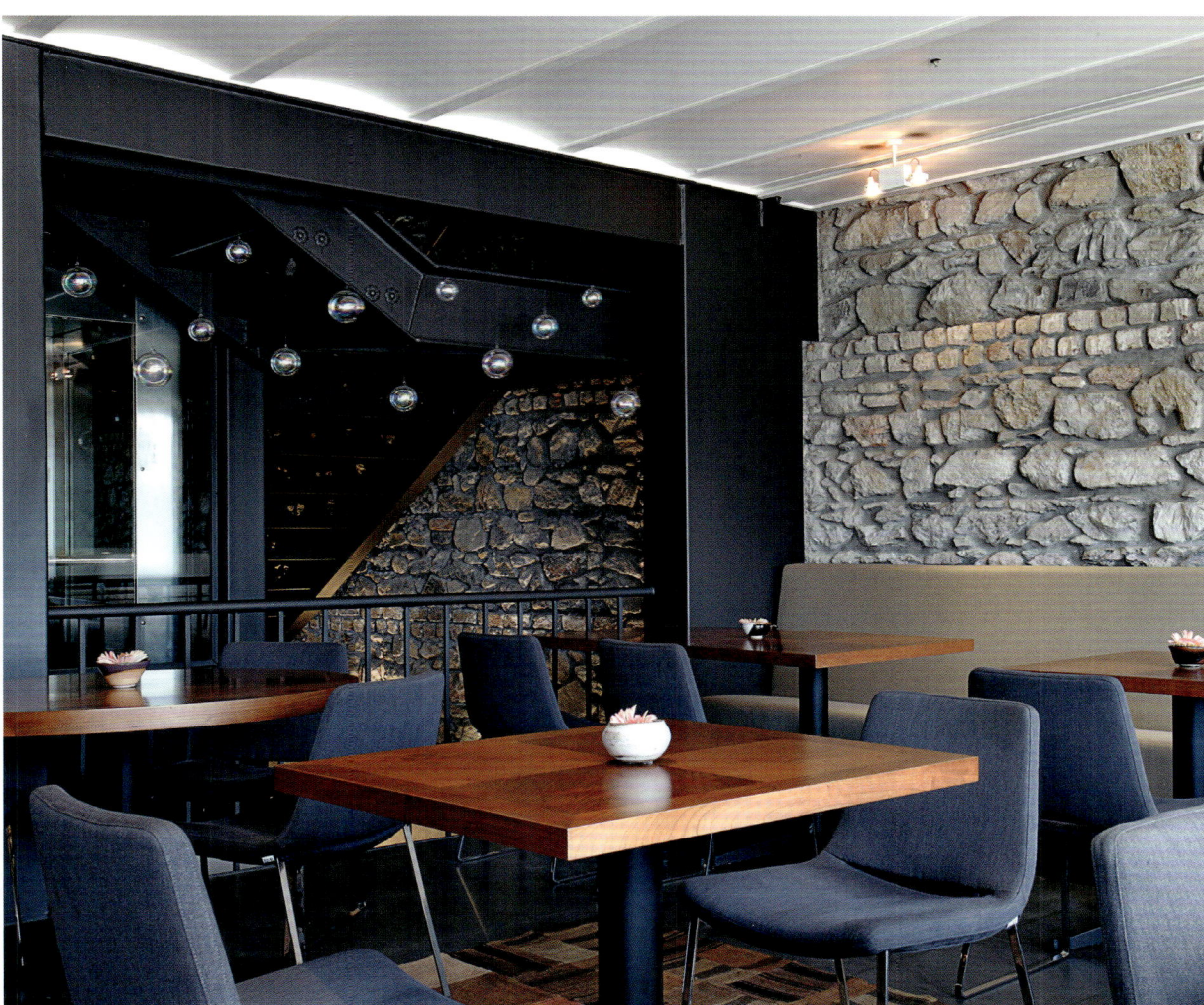

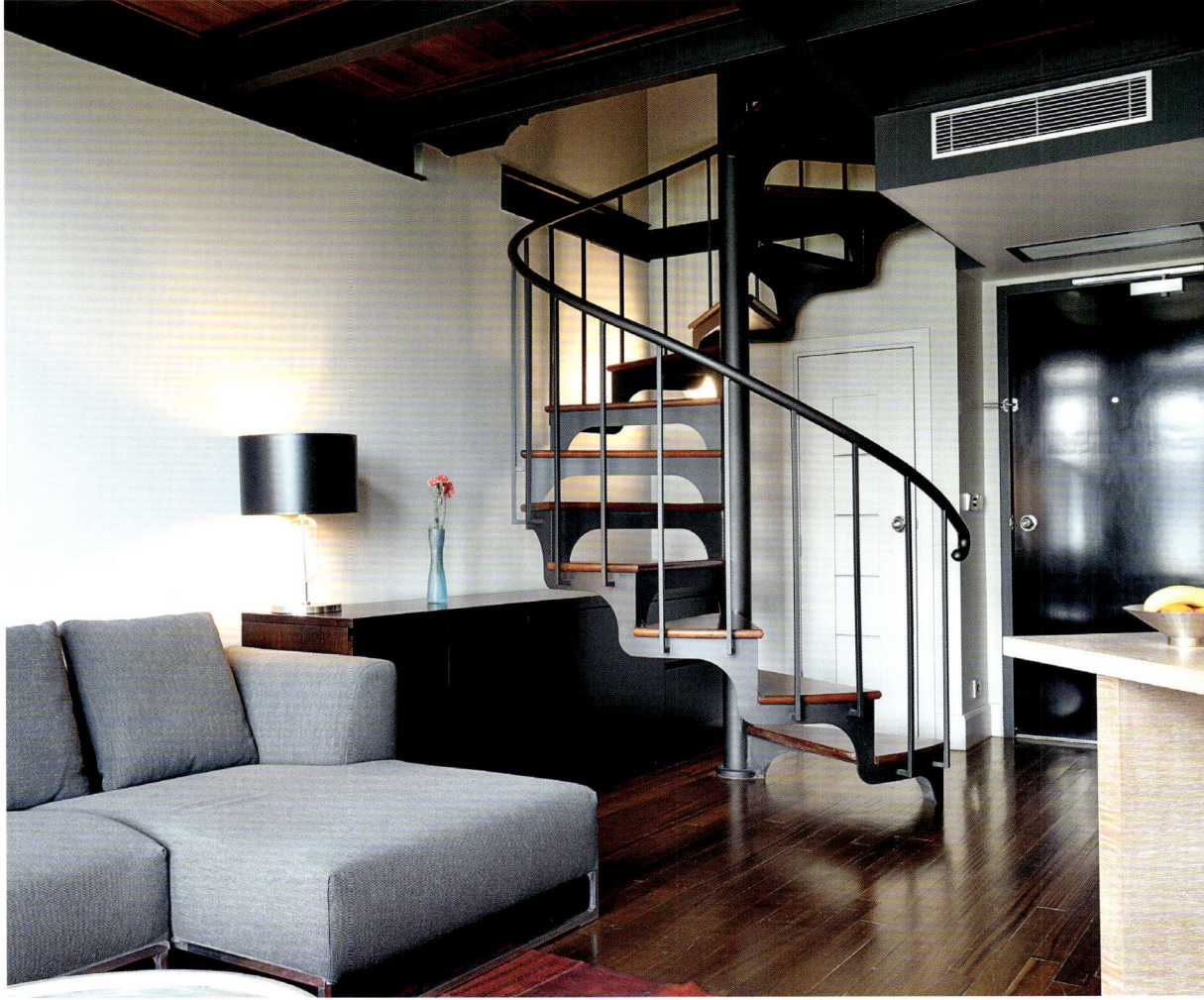

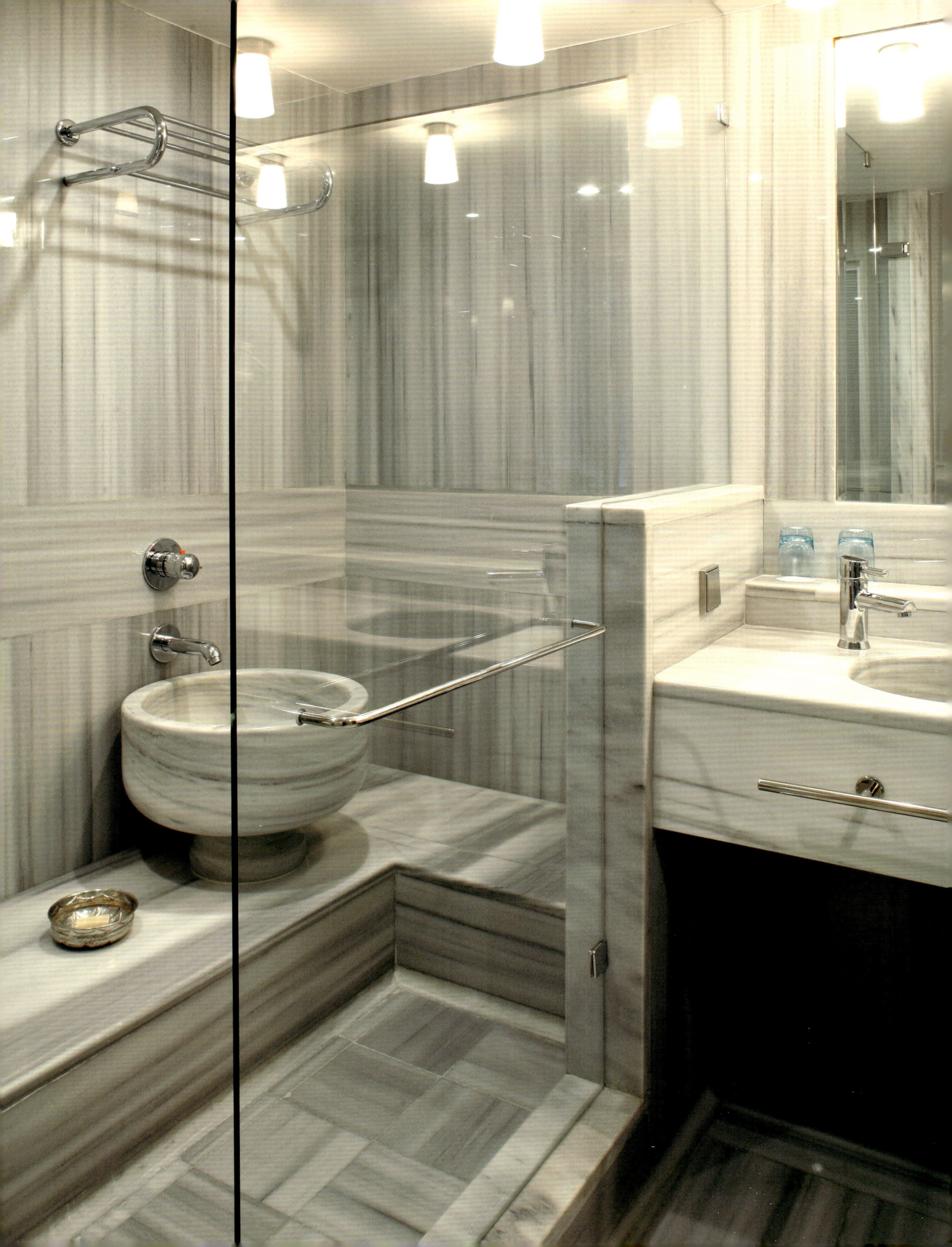

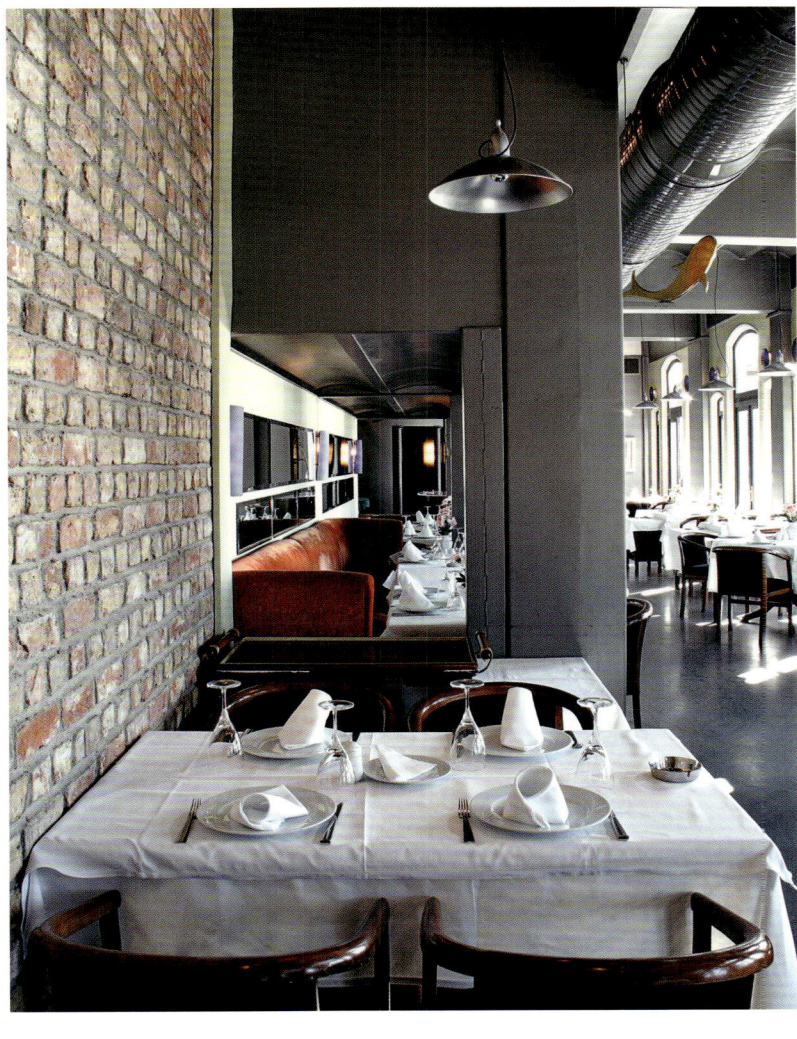

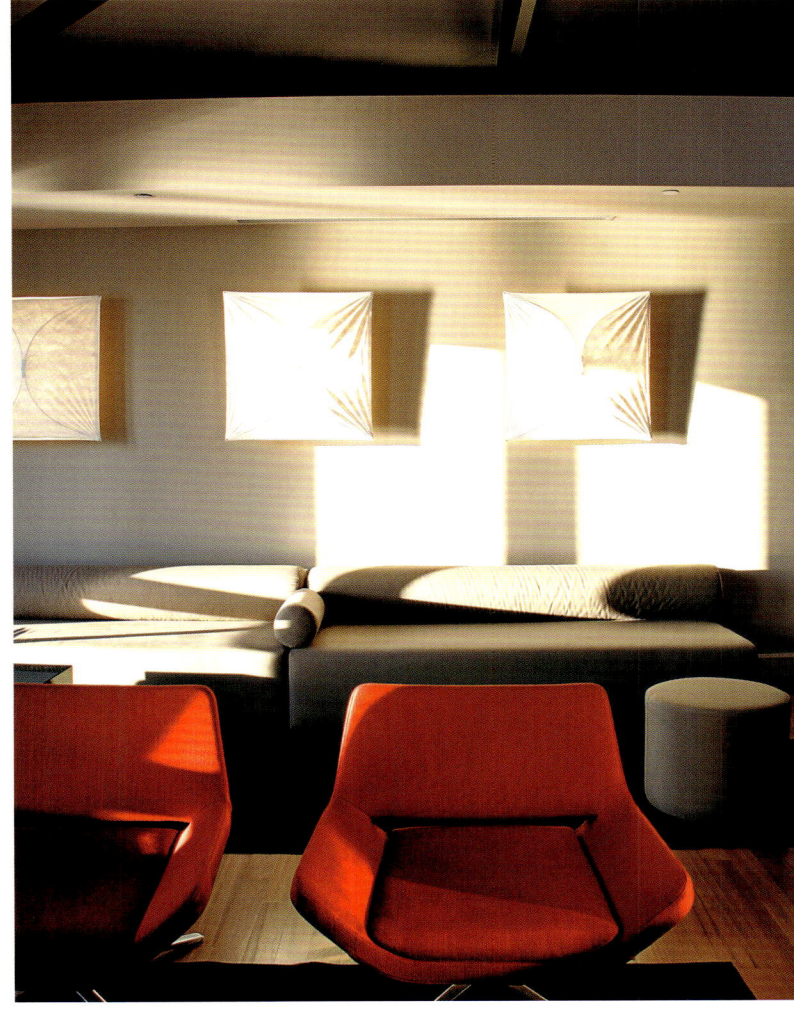

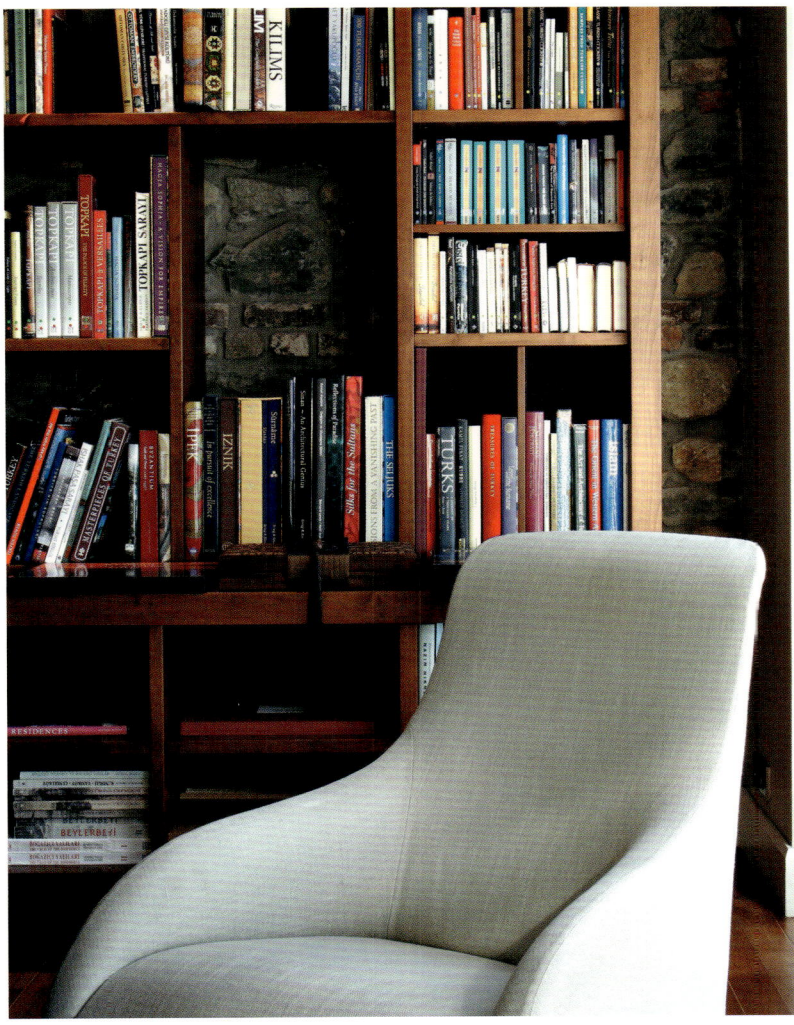

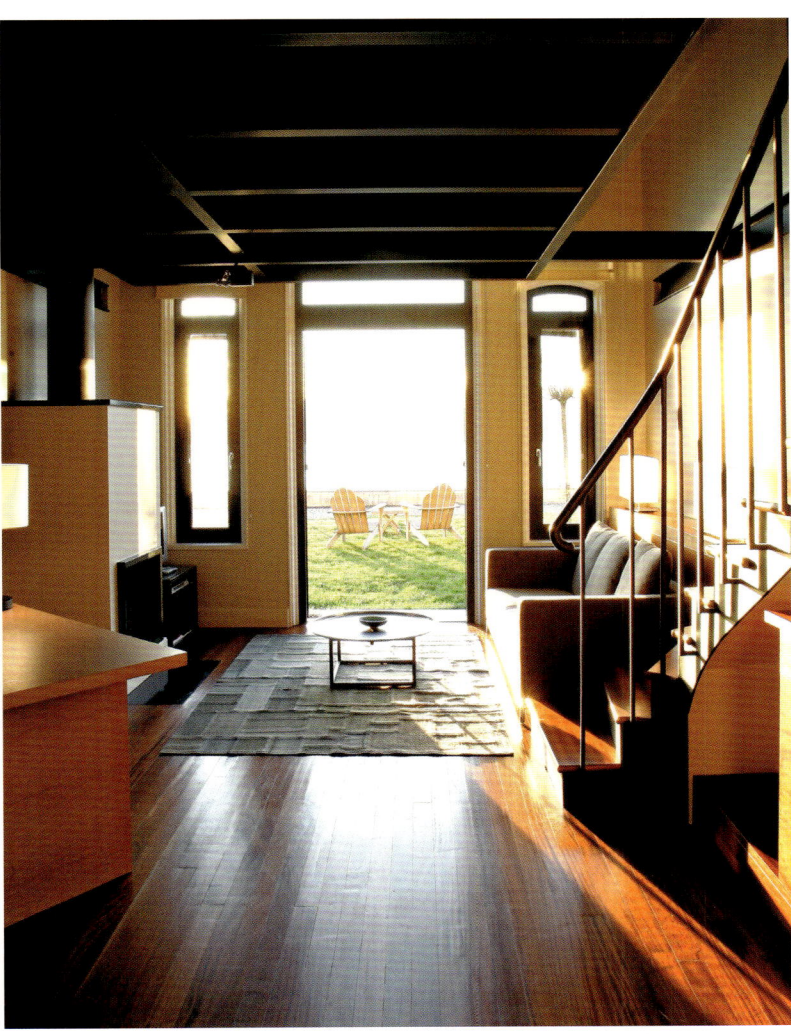

Index

Russia

Moscow

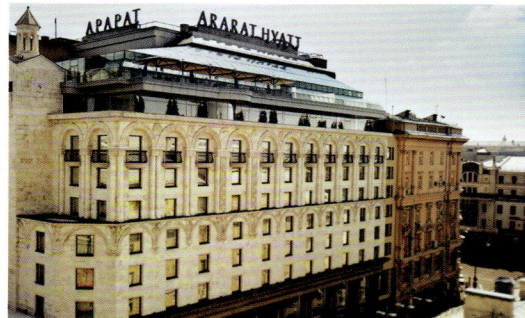

Ararat Park Hyatt Moscow

Neglinnaya Street 4 | Moscow 109012
Phone: +74 9 57 83 12 34   Fax: +74 9 57 83 12 35
www.moscow.park.hyatt.com

Price category: €€€€
Rooms: 220 including 17 suites
Facilities: Café, restaurant, bar with panoramic views over the city, spa, library
Services: Business services, WiFi, 24 h room service
Style: Timeless, world-class, residential-style hotel

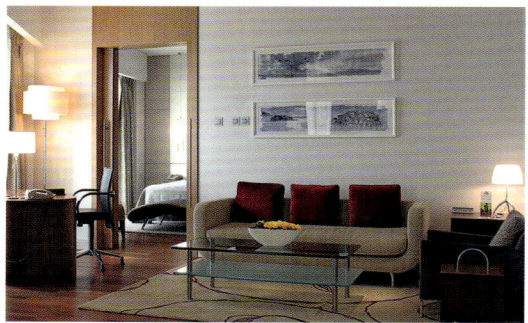

Swissôtel Krasnye Holmy

Kosmodamianskaya Embankment. 52, Bld. 6 | Moscow 115054
Phone: +74 9 57 87 98 00   Fax: +74 9 57 87 98 98
www.swissotel.com/moscow

Price category: €€€€
Rooms: 233 rooms including 27 suites with the latest state-of-the-art technology
Facilities: 2 restaurants, 3 bars, 11 conference rooms, spa
Services: Parking, concierge, business center
Style: Modern, dynamic and contemporary style

Estonia

Tallinn

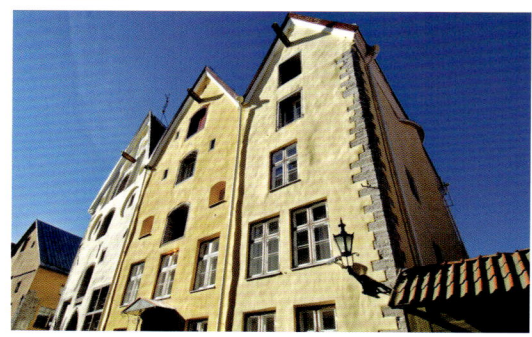

The Three Sisters Hotel

Pikk, 71; Tolli, 2 | 10123 Tallinn
Phone: +372 630 6300   Fax: +372 630 6301
www.threesistershotel.com

Price category: €€€
Rooms: 23 rooms and suites
Facilities: Restaurant, wine bar, summer wine garden, conference rooms for private events
Services: Free airport shuttle on request, 24 h room service, complimentary newspapers, daily laundry and dry cleaning, free WiFi in public areas
Style: Historical boutique hotel with modern flavor

Sweden

Stockholm

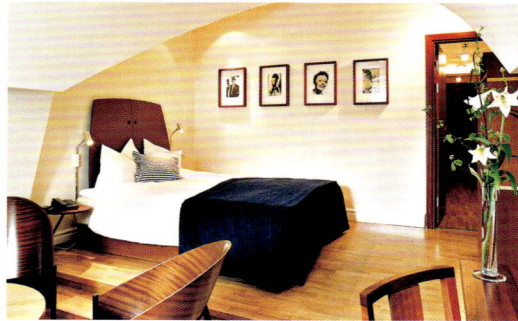

Berns Hotel

Näckströmsgatan 8 | Stockholm 11147
Phone: +46 8 566 322 00   Fax: +46 8 566 322 01
www.berns.se

Price category: €€
Rooms: 65 rooms
Facilities: Bar, 2 restaurants, nightclub, theater, concert hall
Services: Extensive concierge service, room service
Style: Boutique hotel

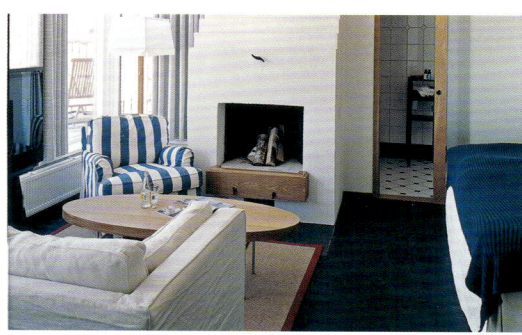

Hotel J

Ellensviksvagen 1, Nacka Strand | Stockholm 13127
Phone: +46 8 601 300 0   Fax: +46 8 601 300 9
www.hotelj.com

Price category: €€
Rooms: 45 rooms including 5 suites
Facilities: Seafood restaurant, bar/lounge, sauna, boutique, drugstore, convention center
Services: Concierge, 24 h room service, dry cleaning, babysitting, massage service
Style: Contemporary marine

Denmark

Copenhagen

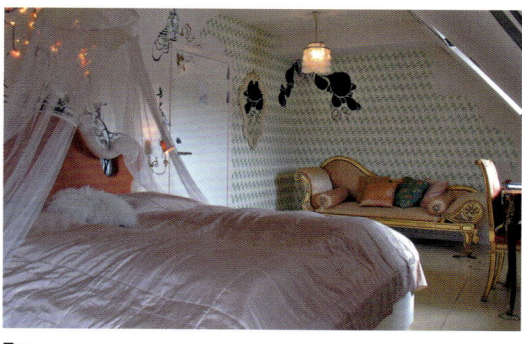

Fox

Jarmers Plads 3 | 1551 Copenhagen
Phone: +45 33 13 30 00   Fax: +45 33 14 30 33
www.hotelfox.dk

Price category: €
Rooms: 61 rooms
Facilities: Bar and restaurant Intoxica, Tiki bar, roof terrace
Services: Free WiFi, flatscreen TVs, international newspapers and magazines, room service
Style: Creative, art

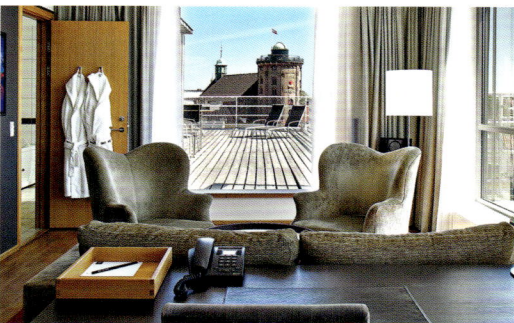

First Hotel Skt. Petri

Krystalgade 22 | 1172 Copenhagen
Phone: +45 33 45 91 00   Fax: +45 33 45 91 10
www.hotelsktpetri.com

Price category: €€
Rooms: 268 rooms and suites including 1 penthouse
Facilities: Bar, restaurant, café, fitness suite, courtyard terrace
Services: Concierge, valet parking, massage, private yoga, 24 h roomservice, air-conditioning, broadband internet access, a two-lined telephone, TV, minibar, safe
Style: Modern Scandinavian

Ireland

Galway

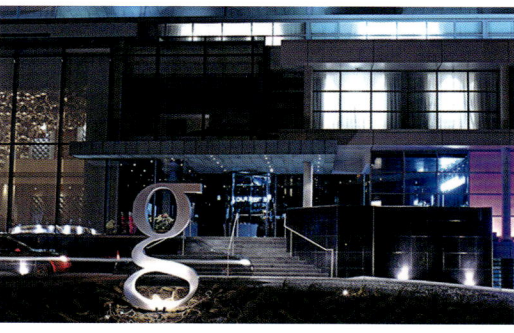

g Hotel

Wellpark Retail Park | Galway
Phone: +353 91 865 200   Fax: +353 91 865 203
www.theghotel.ie

Price category: €€
Rooms: 101 rooms including 2 Speciality Suites and the Presidential Suite
Facilities: Designed lounger areas, ESPA at the g
Services: Complimentary valet parking, babysitting, Eye Cinema next door
Style: Hollywood glamour

Dublin

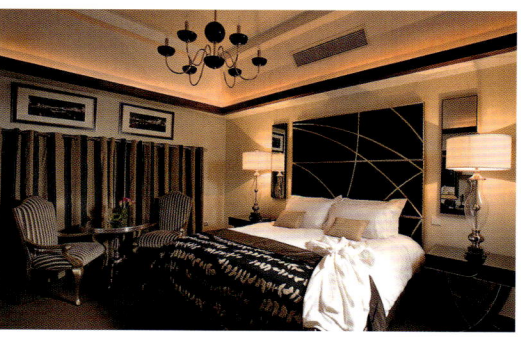

Dylan

Eastmoreland Place | Dublin 4
Phone: +353 1 660 3000   Fax: +353 1 660 3005
www.dylan.ie

Price category: €€€
Rooms: 44 rooms including 5 suites
Facilities: Dylanbar, Still Restaurant, The Library, private dining room
Services: Concierge, 24 h room service, valet parking
Style: Relaxing haven with breathtaking views

Navan

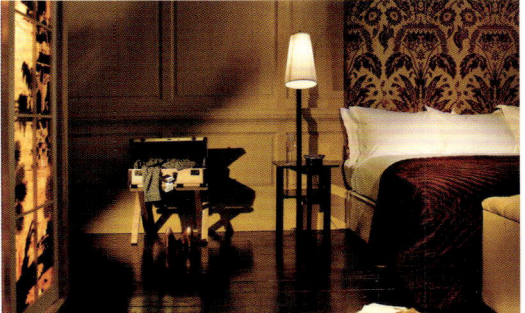

Bellinter House

Navan, Co. Meath
Phone: +353 46 903 0900   Fax: +353 46 903 1367
www.bellinterhouse.com

Price category: €€
Rooms: 34 rooms
Facilities: Bar, restaurant, spa, leisure facilities
Services: Babysitting, room service, on property fishing
Style: Classic contemporary

United Kingdom

Brighton

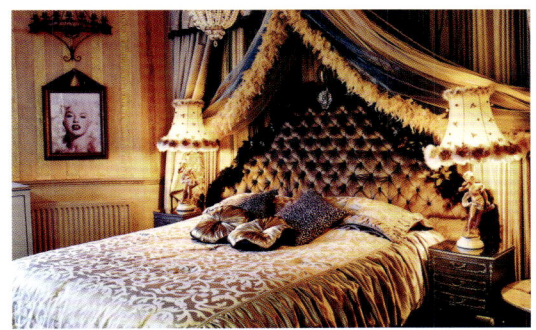

Hotel Pelirocco

10 Regency Square | Brighton BN1 2FG
Phone: +44 1273 327 055   Fax: +44 1273 733 845
www.hotelpelirocco.co.uk

Price category: €€
Rooms: 19 rooms
Facilities: PlayStation bar, ever changing photographic and art gallery, 14 people conference room
Services: PlayStation in every room, Durex Play Time room service menu offering sexy goodies
Style: Art deco

Chandler's Cross

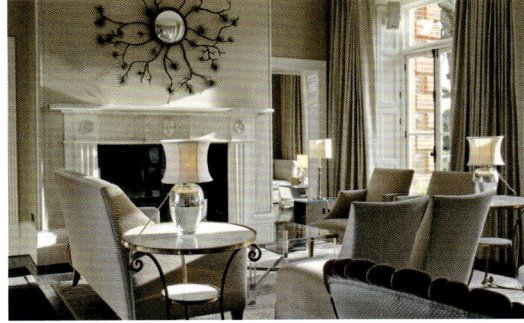

The Grove

Chandler's Cross | Hertfordshire WD3 4TG
Phone: +44 1923 807 807   Fax: +44 1923 221 008
www.thegrove.co.uk

Price category: €€€
Rooms: 227 rooms and suites
Facilities: 3 restaurants, 2 bars, 4 drawing rooms, spa, 18-hole golf course, kids club, park and woodland, urban beach, private dining facilities
Services: Babysitting, room service, dry cleaning, concierge, valet parking, helipad
Style: Groovy Grand

Malmesbury

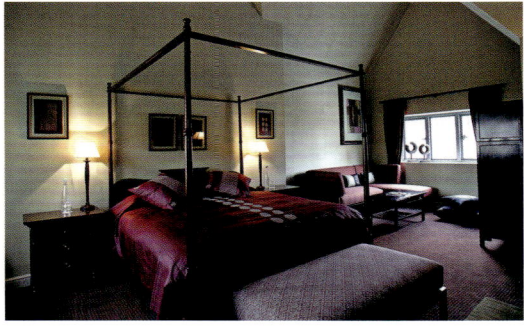

Whatley Manor

Easton Grey | Malmesbury SN16 0RB
Phone: +44 1666 822 888   Fax: +44 1666 826 120
www.whatleymanor.com

Price category: €€€
Rooms: 23 rooms including 8 suites
Facilities: Michelin star restaurant The Dining Room, the brasserie Le Mazot, Aquarias spa, La Prairie "Art of Beauty" center, conference suite, cinema for guests
Services: 24 h room service, valet parking, spa treatments (exclusive use available)
Style: Traditional with a contemporary theme

Cotswolds

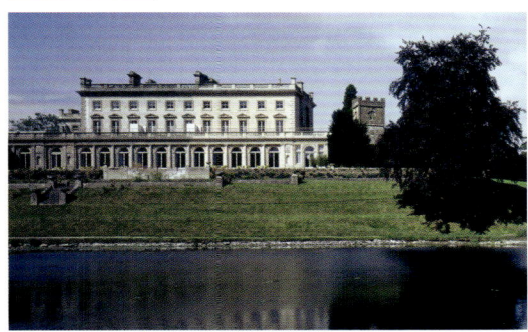

Cowley Manor

Cowley | Gloucestershire GL53 9NL
Phone: +44 1242 870 900   Fax: +44 1242 870 901
www.cowleymanor.com

Price category: €€
Rooms: 30 suites
Facilities: Restaurant, terrace and indoor dining, bar, spa, 55 acres of private gardens
Services: 24 h room service, babysitting available, horse riding, winery visits
Style: Contemporary chic

London

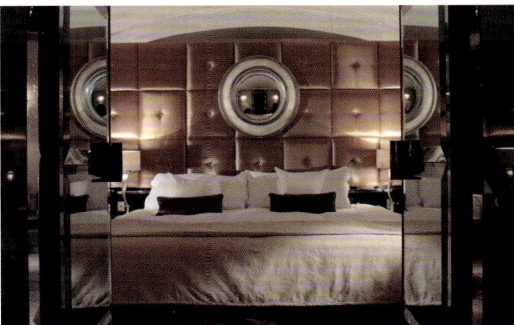

The Berkeley

Wilton Place, Knightsbridge | London SW1X 7RL
Phone: +44 20 7235 6000   Fax: +44 20 7235 4330
www.the-berkeley.com

Price category: €€€
Rooms: 214 rooms including 65 suites
Facilities: The Blue Bar, Marcus Wareing's 3 Michelin stars Pétrus restaurant, Gordon Ramsay's Boxwood Café, rooftop swimming pool and spa
Services: Babysitting, concierge, spa, personal shoppers
Style: Contemporary Chic

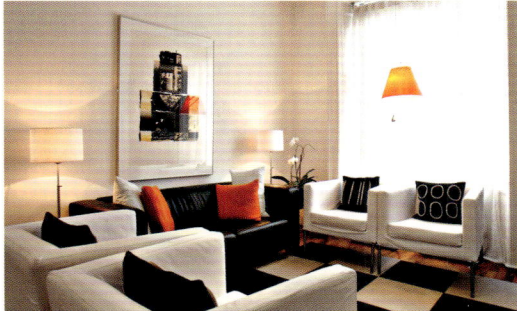

B+B Belgravia

64–66 Ebury Street | London SW1W 9QD
Phone: +44 20 7259 8570   Fax: +44 20 7259 8591
www.bb-belgravia.com

Price category: €
Rooms: 17 rooms including 2 family rooms
Facilities: Guest lounge, breakfast room, private garden
Services: Concierge guest service
Style: Cool and contemporary

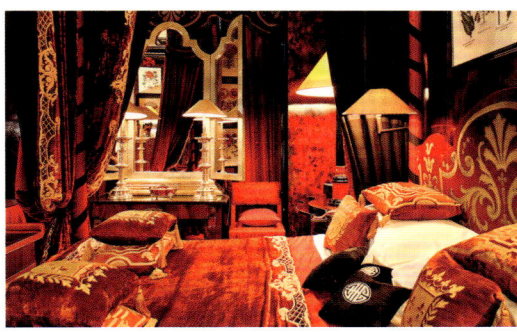

Blakes Hotel

33 Roland Gardens | London SW3PF
Phone: +44 20 7370 6701   Fax: +44 20 7373 0442
www.anouskahempeldesign.com

Price category: €€€€
Rooms: 50 rooms and suites
Facilities: Restaurant, health club, conference rooms
Services: 24 h room service, concierge service, babysitting, laundry, car rental
Style: Sophisticated and contemporary

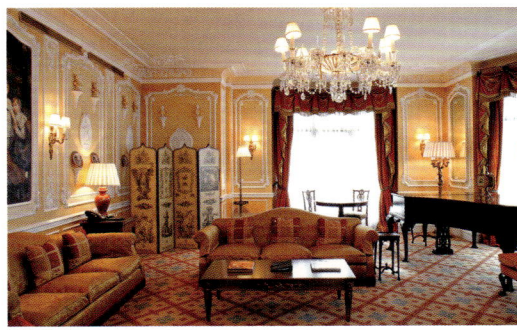

Claridge's

Brook Street, Mayfair | London W1K 4HR
Phone: +44 20 7629 8860   Fax: +44 20 7499 2210
www.claridges.co.uk

Price category: €€€€
Rooms: 203 rooms
Facilities: Claridge's Bar, The Fumoir, Gordon Ramsay at Claridge's, The Foyer and The Reading Room Restaurant, Claridge's Beauty and Fitness
Services: 24 h room service, concierge, babysitting upon request
Style: Traditional

London

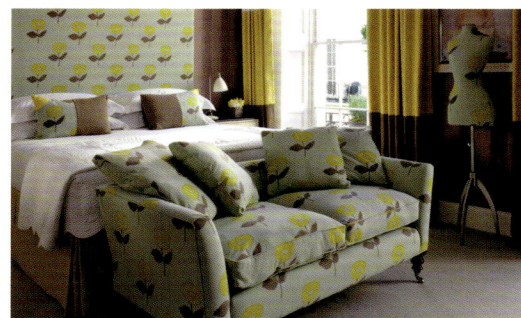

Haymarket Hotel

1 Suffolk Place | London SW1Y 4BP
Phone: +44 20 7470 4000   Fax: +44 20 7470 4004
www.firmdale.com

Price category: €€€
Rooms: 50 rooms and suites
Facilities: Brumus Bar & Restaurant, exclusive 2–5 bedroom townhouse, conservatory, library, 18-m indoor swimming pool, several private event spaces
Services: Concierge
Style: Interiors by Kit Kemp

Leeds

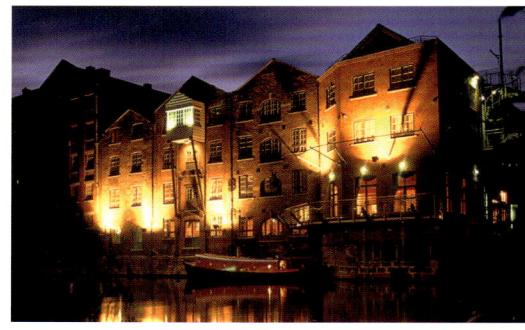

42 The Calls

42 The Calls | Leeds LS2 7EW
Phone: +44 113 244 0099   Fax: +44 113 234 4100
www.42thecalls.co.uk

Price category: €€
Rooms: 41 rooms and suites
Facilities: Brasserie 44 (next door)
Services: 24 h room service, fishing rods in rooms overlooking the river, WiFi, private bar, Molton Brown toiletries, plasma TVs with satellite channels
Style: Designed in a 18th-century corn mill

Edinburgh

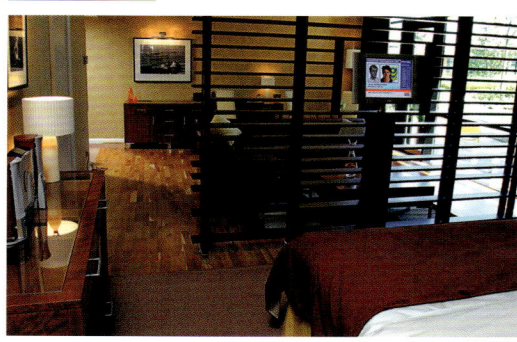

The Glasshouse

2 Greenside Place | Edinburgh EH1 3AA
Phone: +44 131 525 8200   Fax: +44 131 525 8205
www.theetoncollection.com/glasshouse

Price category: €€
Rooms: 47 rooms and 18 suites
Facilities: Rooftop garden, The Snug honesty bar
Services: 24 h room service, 24 h concierge, babysitting, in-room spa treatment, WiFi
Style: Contemporary boutique hotel

Netherlands

Amsterdam

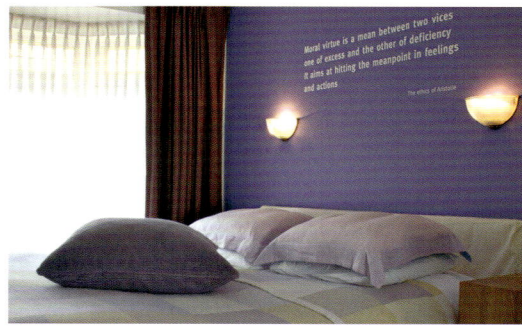

Hotel de Filosoof

Anna van den Vondelstraat 6 | 1054 GZ Amsterdam
Phone: +31 20 683 3013   Fax: +31 20 685 3750
www.hoteldefilosoof.nl

Price category: €€
Rooms: 38 rooms and suites
Facilities: Bar Symposium, meeting rooms, health club
Services: Parking, personal computer, WiFi, free newspapers
Style: Modern-art

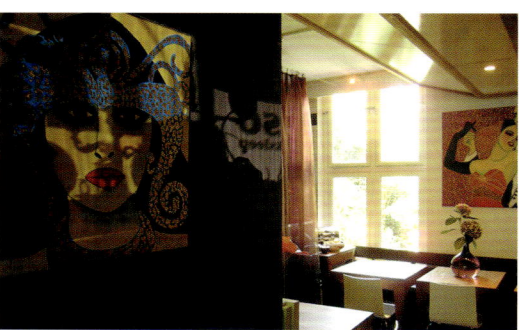

misc eatdrinksleep

Kolveniersburgwal 20 | 1012 CV Amsterdam
Phone: +31 20 330 6241   Fax: +31 20 330 6242
www.misceatdrinksleep.com

Price category: €
Rooms: 6 rooms
Facilities: Bar, restaurant
Services: Boat tour, taxi service, concierge, complimentary non-alcoholic drink & snack bar
Style: Boutique hotel

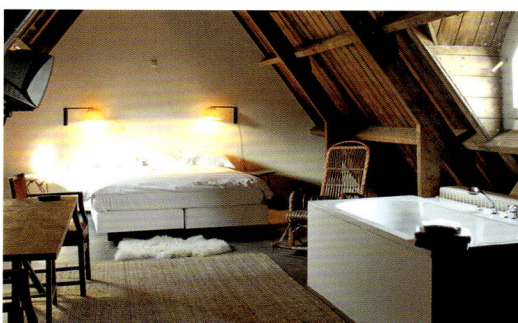

Lloyd Hotel

Oostelijke Handelskade 34 | 1019 BN Amsterdam
Phone: +31 20 561 3636   Fax: +31 20 561 3600
www.lloydhotel.com

Price category: €€
Rooms: 117 rooms
Facilities: Bar, restaurant, library, shop, "Cultural Embassy"
Services: Lloyd Time on Mondays, 24 h room service, WiFi
Style: Urban, quirky and boho-chic

Rotterdam

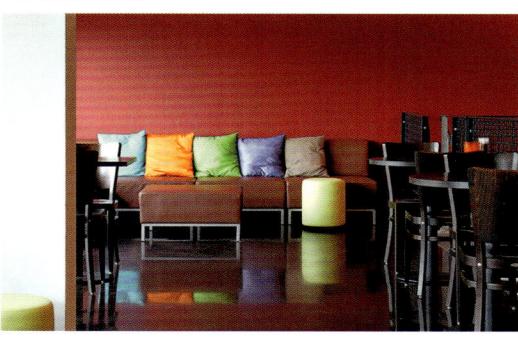

Stroom

Lloydstraat 1 | 3024 EA Rotterdam
Phone: +31 10 221 4060   Fax: +31 10 221 4061
www.stroomrotterdam.nl

Price category: €
Rooms: 18 studios
Facilities: Bar, restaurant, 3 meeting rooms, VIP zone
Services: Free internet
Style: Design hotel

Maastricht

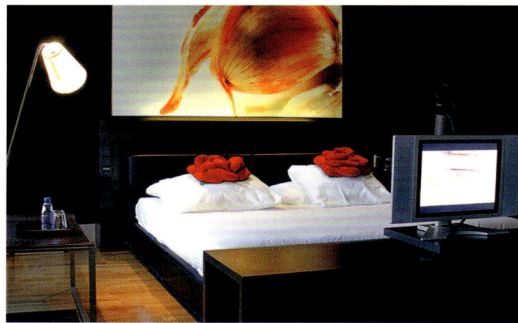

Eden Designhotel Maastricht

Stationsstraat 40 | 6221 BR Maastricht
Phone: +31 43 328 2525   Fax: +31 43 328 2526
www.edencityhotels.com

Price category: €
Rooms: 73 rooms
Facilities: Cocktail bar, trendy sandwich bar Simply Bread, beauty lounge, fitness room
Services: Room service, free newspapers and magazines, WiFi
Style: Design

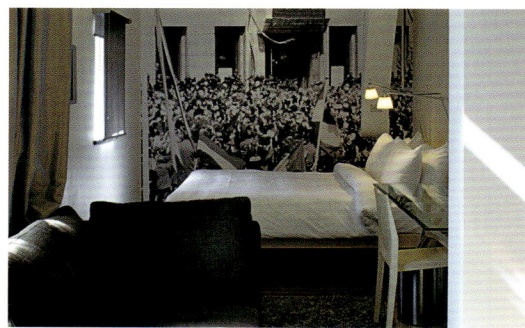

Kruisherenhotel Maastricht

Kruiserengang 19–23 | 6211 NW Maastricht
Phone: +31 43 329 2020   Fax: +31 43 323 3030
www.chateauhotels.nl

Price category: €€
Rooms: 32 rooms and 28 suites
Facilities: Winebar Rouge & Blanc, Kruiserenrestaurant, lounge corners, library, garden
Services: 24 h room service, laundry service, shoe shine, limousine service, valet parking, babysitting, dog walking, bicycles and Vespas available
Style: Design hotel

Belgium

Antwerp

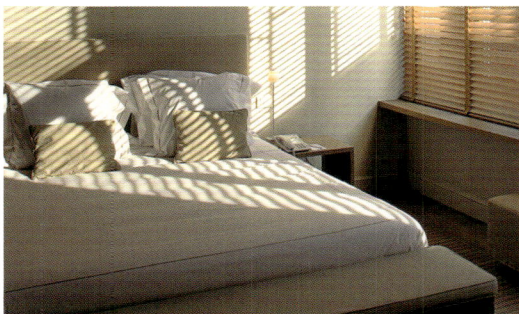

Hotel Julien

Korte Nieuwstraat 24 | 2000 Antwerp
Phone: +32 3 229 06 00   Fax: +32 3 233 35 70
www.hotel-julien.com

Price category: €€
Rooms: 11 rooms
Facilities: Breakfast room, library, lounge/bar, special designed porcelain for Hotel Julien
Services: Free WiFi, laundry and dry cleaning, babysitting, DVD and CD library, 24 h front desk, non-smoking rooms, choice of newspapers and magazines
Style: Contemporary design

Brussels

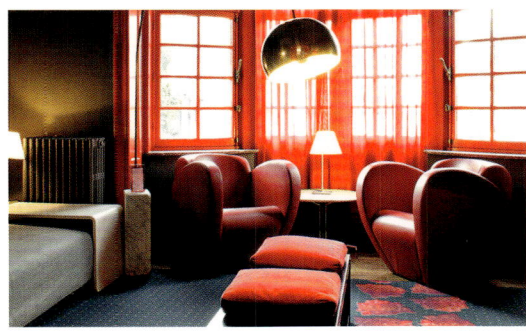

Monty Small Design Hotel

101, boulevard Brand Whitlock | 1200 Brussels
Phone: +32 2 734 56 36   Fax: +32 2 734 50 05
www.monty-hotel.be

Price category: €
Rooms: 18 rooms
Facilities: Bar, table d'hotes breakfast, business desk, garden
Services: Babysitting, free WiFi, bicycle rental, 24 h reception, luggage storage
Style: Design and contemporary

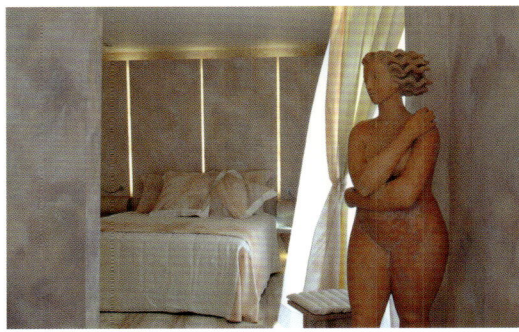

Royal Windsor

5, rue Duquesnoy | 1000 Brussels
Phone: +32 2 505 55 55   Fax: +32 2 505 55 00
www.royalwindsorbrussels.com

Price category: €€
Rooms: 266 rooms including 16 suites and 1 Royal Suite
Facilities: Chutney's Bar and Restaurant, nightclub, free fitness center and sauna, business center with internet access
Services: Babysitting on request, laundry and dry-cleaning
Style: Elegant and sophisticated

Germany

Berlin

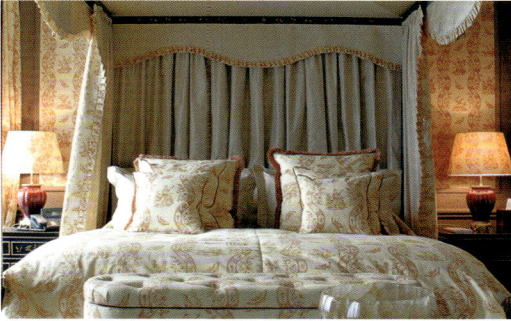

Adlon Kempinski

Unter den Linden 77 | 10117 Berlin
Phone: +49 30 22 61 0   Fax: +49 30 22 61 22 22
www.hotel-adlon.de

Price category: €€€
Rooms: 304 rooms and 78 suites
Facilities: Bar, 2 restaurants, terrace, spa
Services: Concierge, limousine service, butler, WiFi
Style: Classic-elegant

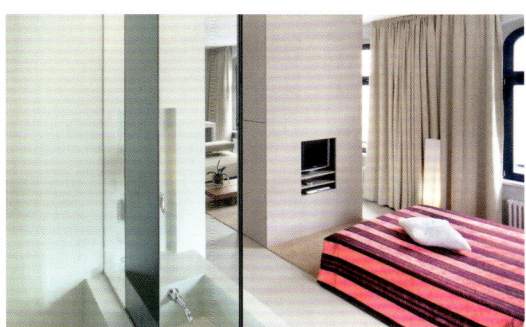

Lux Eleven

Rosa-Luxemburg-Straße 9–13 | 10178 Berlin
Phone: +49 30 93 62 80 0   Fax: +49 30 93 62 88 0
www.lux-eleven.com

Price category: €
Rooms: 72 apartments and 1 penthouse
Facilities: Restaurant, bar, Aveda hair spa
Services: Suntrainer
Style: Urban minimalistic

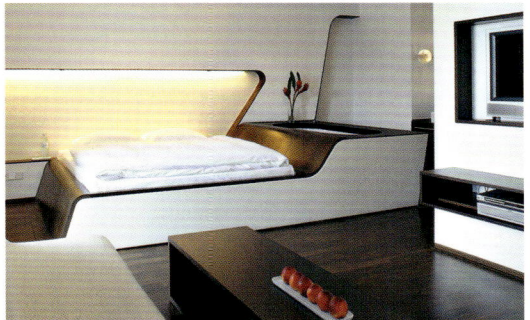

Q!

Knesebeckstraße 67 | 10623 Berlin
Phone: +49 30 81 00 66 0   Fax: +49 30 81 00 66 66 6
www.loock-hotels.com

Price category: €€
Rooms: 77 rooms including 4 studios and 1 penthouse
Facilities: Restaurant, member bar, spa
Services: 24 h concierge and room service, WiFi, laundry, private cooking
Style: Design and fashion

Hamburg

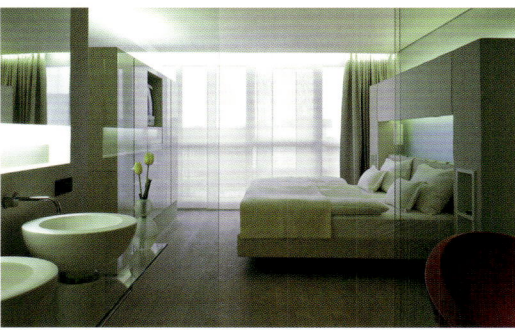

SIDE

Drehbahn 49 | 20354 Hamburg
Phone: +49 40 30 99 90   Fax: +49 40 30 99 93 99
www.side-hamburg.de

Price category: €
Rooms: 168 rooms and 10 suites
Facilities: fusion bar + restaurant, sky lounge with 8th floor terrace overlooking Hamburg, spa
Services: 24 h room service, laundry service, free newspapers, parking garage, concierge
Style: Modern puristic

Frankfurt

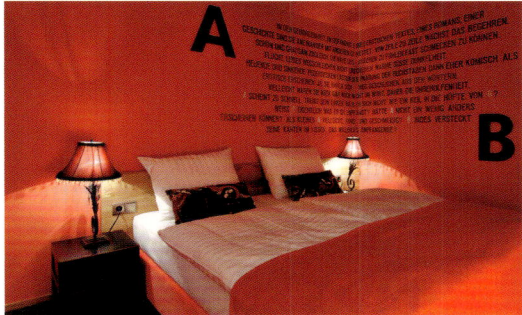

Goldman 25hours Hotel

Hanauer Landstraße 127 | 60314 Frankfurt
Phone: +49 69 40 58 68 90 Fax: +49 69 40 58 68 98 90
www.25hours-hotels.com

Price category: €
Rooms: 49 rooms
Facilities: Restaurant, bar, lounge
Services: Free WiFi, jogging corner, iPod sound system
Style: Eclectic design, vintage aesthetic with fancy details

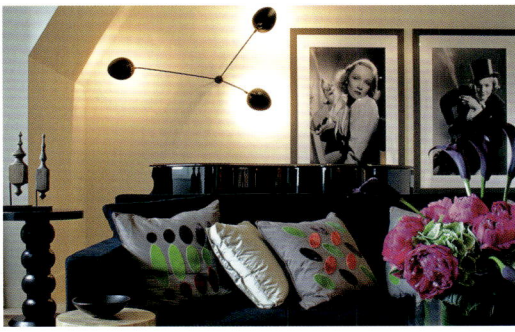

Villa Kennedy

Kennedyallee 70 | 60596 Frankfurt
Phone: +49 69 71 71 20   Fax: +49 69 71 71 22 43 0
www.roccofortecollection.com

Price category: €€€
Rooms: 134 rooms, 28 suites, 1 presidential suite
Facilities: JFK Bar, Gusto Restaurant, Villa Spa, gym, 9 meeting rooms including a ball room
Services: Villa Spa has a 15 m indoor pool and treatment rooms
Style: Classic elegance, traditional and innovative

Cologne

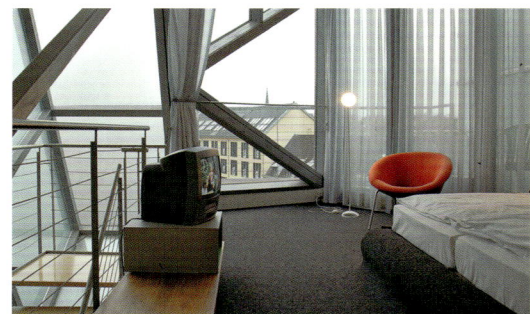

Chelsea

Jülicher Straße 1 | 50674 Cologne
Phone: +49 221 20 71 50   Fax: +49 2 21 23 91 37
www.hotel-chelsea.de

Price category: €
Rooms: 35 rooms and 3 suites
Facilities: Café Central
Services: Free WiFi, 24 h room service
Style: Contemporary design

Lohmar

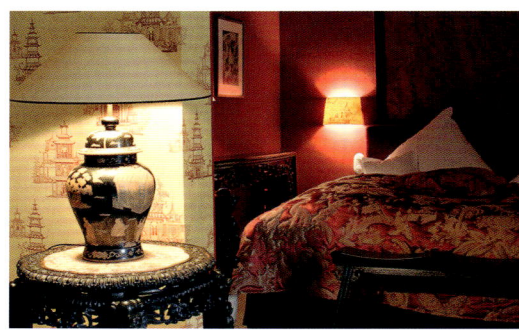

Schloss Auel

Haus Auel 1 | 53797 Lohmar
Phone: +49 2206 60 03 0   Fax: +49 2206 60 03 22 2
www.schlossauel.de

Price category: €
Rooms: 3 single rooms, 12 double rooms, 6 junior suites
Facilities: Restaurant, clubhouse, rooms for conferences, weddings and banquet rooms for up to 100 people, own chapel in rococo style
Services: Babysitting
Style: Classic elegance

Stuttgart

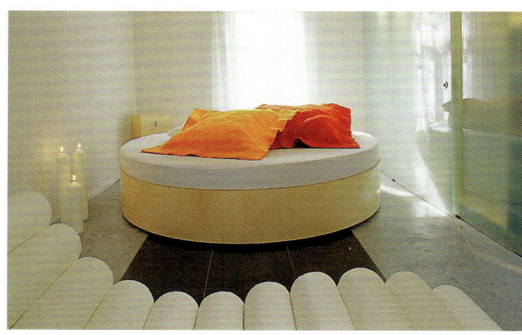

Der Zauberlehrling

Rosenstraße 38 | 70182 Stuttgart
Phone: +49 711 237 77 70   Fax: +49 711 237 77 75
www.zauberlehrling.de

Price category: €€
Rooms: 18 rooms including 4 suites and 1 penthouse
Facilities: Restaurant, private room
Services: Babysitting, cooking class, wine tasting, laundry service
Style: Design

Munich

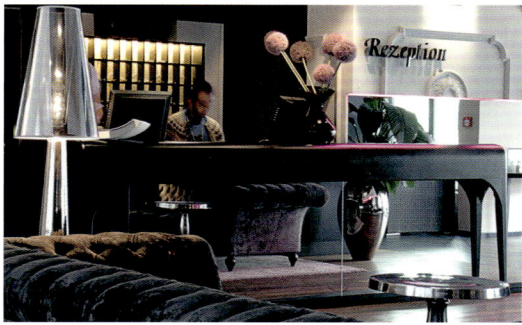

Hotel La Maison

Occamstraße 24 | 80802 Munich
Phone: +49 89 33 03 55 50   Fax: +49 89 33 03 55 55 5
www.hotel-la-maison.com

Price category: €
Rooms: 31 rooms
Facilities: Bar, restaurant
Services: Babysitting, leave-and-go service
Style: Design boutique hotel

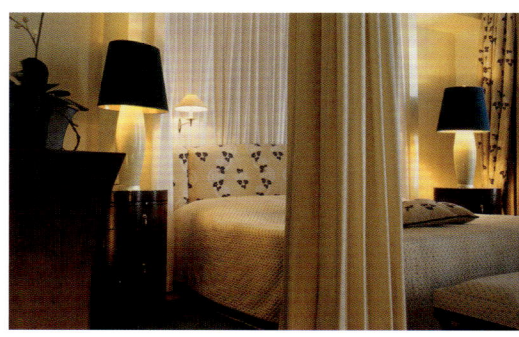

Bayerischer Hof

Promenadeplatz 2–6 | 80333 Munich
Phone: +49 89 21 20 0   Fax: +49 89 21 20 90 6
www.bayerischerhof.de

Price category: €€€
Rooms: 373 rooms including 60 suites
Facilities: 6 bars, 4 restaurants, 40 conference rooms, Blue Spa with pool, fitness room, beauty center, sauna, in-house theater, night club with international live jazz program
Services: 24 h concierge, WiFi, facilities for the disabled, business center
Style: Classic elegance

Czech Republic

Prague

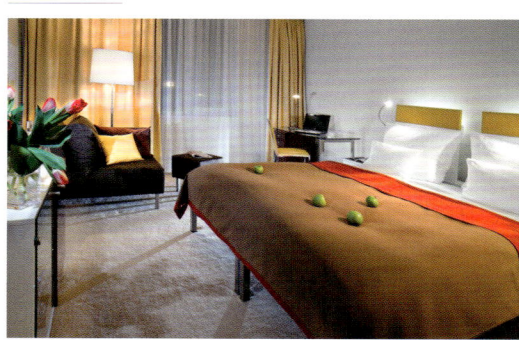

andel's Hotel & Suites Prague

Stroupeznickeho 21 | 15000 Andel City
Phone: +420 296 889 688   Fax: +420 296 889 999
www.andelssuites.com

Price category: €€
Rooms: 290 rooms including 8 suites and 51 apartments
Facilities: Oscar's bar/brasserie, Delight breakfast restaurant, fitness center
Services: WiFi, concierge, underground parking
Style: Design hotel

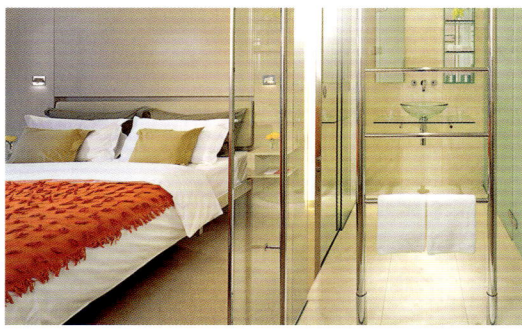

Hotel Josef

Rybna 20 | 11000 Prague
Phone: +420 221 700 901   Fax: +420 221 700 999
www.hoteljosef.com

Price category: €€
Rooms: 109 rooms
Facilities: Garden, conference room, business center, gymnasium, sauna, massage room, garage
Services: Concierge, guest relations
Style: Elegant and pure

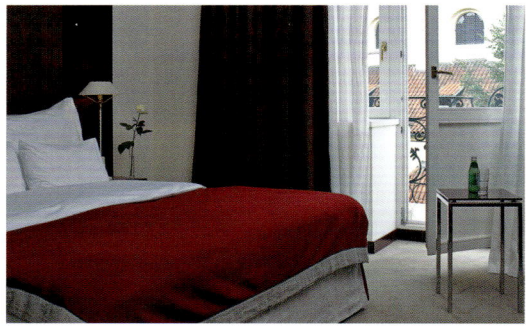

Maximilian

Hastalska 14 | 11000 Prague
Phone: +420 225 300 111   Fax: +420 225 300 110
www.maximilianhotel.com

Price category: €€
Rooms: 70 rooms and 1 suite
Facilities: Zen Asian wellness, conference room, library
Services: Guest relations, drawing room, garage
Style: Art deco

Hungary

Budapest

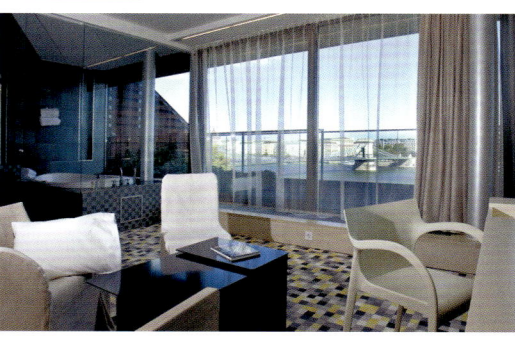

Lánchíd 19

Lánchíd utca 19 | 1013 Budapest
Phone: +36 1 419 1900   Fax: +36 1 419 1919
www.lanchid19hotel.hu

Price category: €
Rooms: 48 rooms including 3 suites
Facilities: Restaurant, bar, 3 meeting rooms
Services: Laundry, cultural program organization, change, business services
Style: Modern

Austria

Kitzbühel

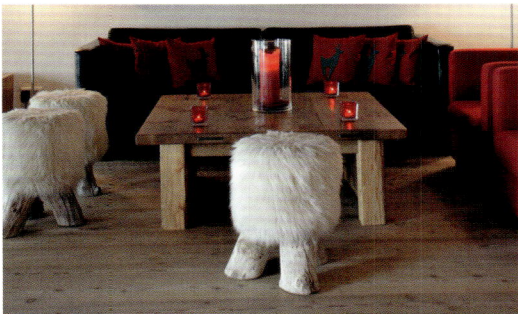

Ski & Golfresort Kitzhof

Schwarzseestraße 8–10 | 6370 Kitzbühel
Phone: +43 5356 632 110   Fax: +43 5356 632 1115
www.hotel-kitzhof.com

Price category: €
Rooms: 63 single rooms, 93 double rooms and 8 suites
Facilities: Kitz Lounge with bar and open fireplace, restaurant Weißer Hirsch with garden, à la carte restaurant Kaminstube, wine cellar, Kitz Spa
Services: Babysitting upon request
Style: Innovative design with much old wood, glass, felt and modern furniture

Salzburg

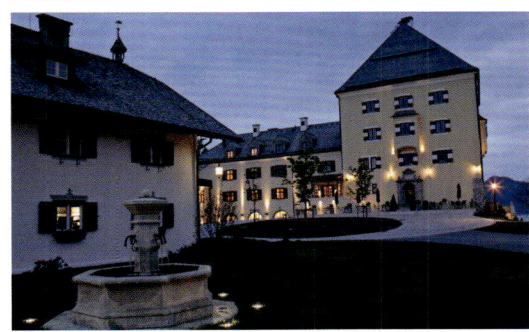

Hotel Schloss Fuschl

Schloss-Straße 19 | 5322 Hof bei Salzburg
Phone: +43 6229 2253 1500   Fax: +43 6229 2253 1557
www.schlossfuschlresort.at

Price category: €€€
Rooms: 110 rooms, 39 suites and 6 lake cottages
Facilities: Bar, restaurant, gourmet restaurant Imperial, Vinothek, spa, shop, fishery, classic cars
Services: Babysitting, room service, butler on request
Style: Historic building

Vienna

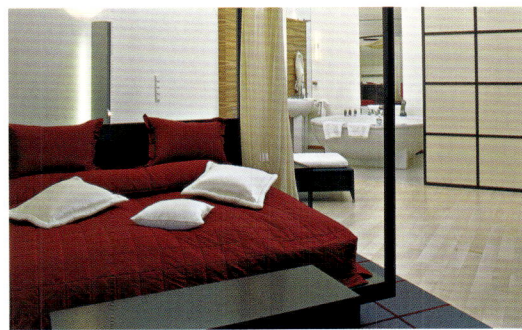

Palais Coburg Residenz

Coburgbastei 4 | 1010 Wien
Phone: +43 1 518 180   Fax: +43 1 518 181 00
www.palais-coburg.com

Price category: €€€€
Rooms: 35 fully equipped suites
Facilities: Gourmet restaurant, wine bistro & bar, 6 wine cellars, spa, sun terrace, fitness room
Services: 24 h room service, limousine service, babysitting, private dining and sightseeing
Style: Luxury hotel in a city palace

Switzerland

Arosa

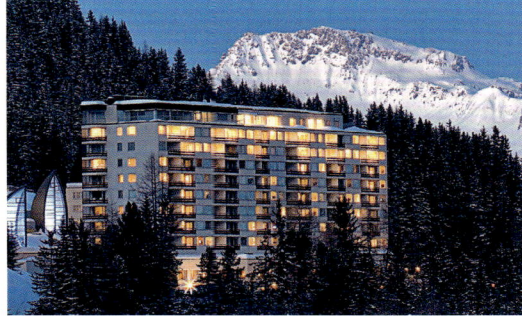

Tschuggen Grand Hotel

Sonnenbergstrasse | 7050 Arosa
Phone: +41 81 378 99 99   Fax: +41 81 378 99 90
www.tschuggen.ch

Price category: €€€
Rooms: 98 rooms, 32 suites and junior suites
Facilities: 5 restaurants, 3 conference rooms, shopping arcade, Bergoase spa
Services: Babysitting and kids club, personal trainer, 24 h concierge, hairdresser, ski rental and school on property, business center and secretarial service
Style: Contemporary design

Interlaken

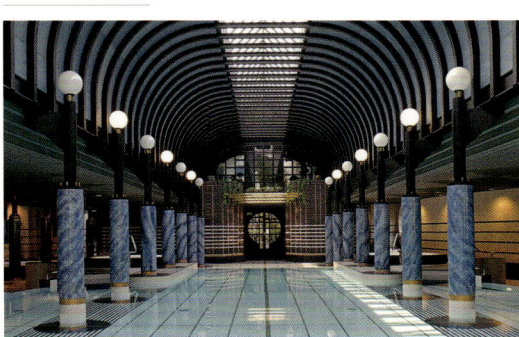

Victoria-Jungfrau Grand Hotel & Spa

Höheweg 41 | 3800 Interlaken
Phone: +41 33 828 28 28   Fax: +42 33 828 28 80
www.victoria-jungfrau.ch

Price category: €€€
Rooms: 212 rooms including 100 suites
Facilities: 3 restaurants, 3 bars, spa
Services: Babysitting, free WiFi
Style: Classic elegance

St. Moritz

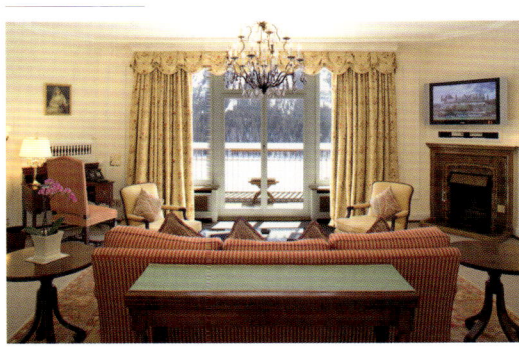

Badrutt's Palace Hotel

Via Serlas 27 | 7500 St. Moritz
Phone: +41 81 837 10 00   Fax: +41 81 837 29 99
www.badruttspalace.com

Price category: €€€
Rooms: 159 rooms including 38 suites
Facilities: 4 bars, 7 restaurants, beauty spa, boutiques, pool, tennis courts, kids club
Services: Butlers, guest relations, 24 h concierge and room service, airport transfers, WiFi
Style: Classic elegance

Zurich

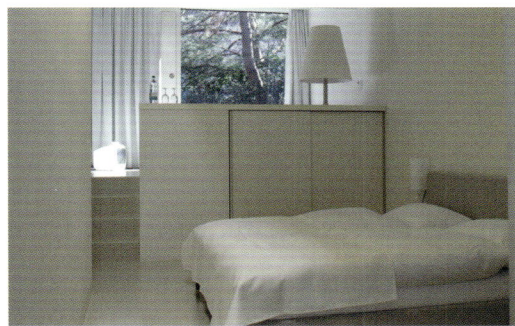

Greulich

Herman-Greulich-Strasse 56 | 8004 Zurich
Phone: +41 43 243 42 43   Fax: +41 43 243 42 00
www.greulich.ch

Price category: €
Rooms: 201
Facilities: Spanish restaurant, Kreis 4 open air café, bar and cigar lounge, Birch Grove design garden, room for private events
Services: Room service, bicycle rent
Style: Modern design

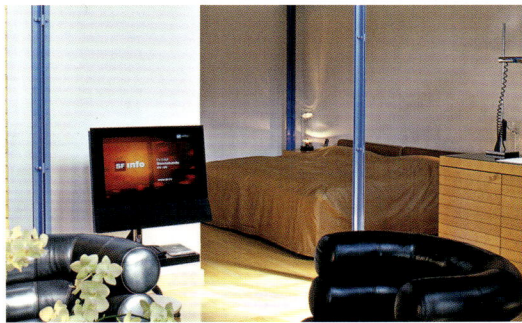

Widder Hotel

Rennweg 7 | 8001 Zurich
Phone: +41 44 224 25 26   Fax: +41 44 224 24 24
www.widderhotel.ch

Price category: €€€
Rooms: 42 rooms and 7 suites
Facilities: Restaurant, bar, Wirtschaft zur Schtund, small technogym, library, business center, 8 conference rooms for up to 200 people
Services: 24 h room service, concierge, valet service, WiFi, interactive B&O screen TV and stereo
Style: Artfully fashioned

France & Monaco

Corsica

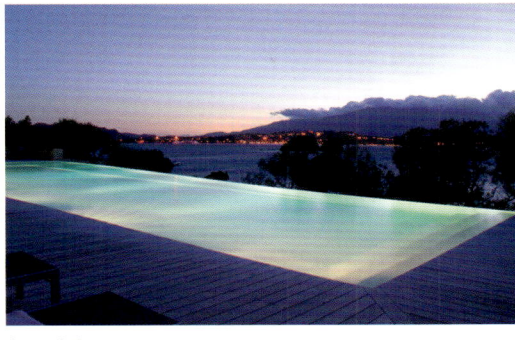

Casadelmar

Route de Palombaggia | 20137 Porto Vecchio
Phone: +33 4 95 72 34 34   Fax: +33 4 95 72 34 35
www.casadelmar.fr

Price category: €€€€
Rooms: 34 rooms and suites
Facilities: Gastronomic restaurant with 1 Michelin star, pool restaurant, lounge bar
Services: Spa Carita and Decleor, hair stylist, private beach, heated outdoor swimming pool, business center
Style: Design hotel

Monaco

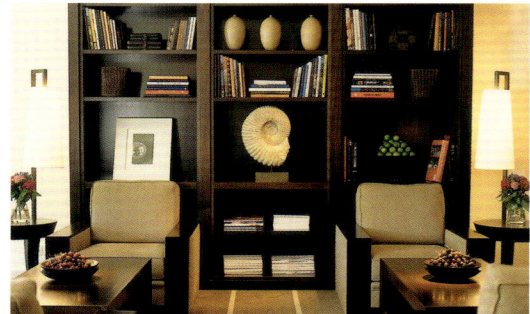

Columbus Monaco

23, avenue des Papalins | 98000 Monaco
Phone: +377 92 05 90 00   Fax: +377 92 05 91 67
www.columbushotels.com

Price category: €€
Rooms: 181 rooms including 28 suites
Facilities: Bar restaurant La Brasserie, swimming pool
Services: "Toys for Big Boys," à la carte "men at play" itinerary;
"Gracefully Shopping," a chauffeur-driven shopping to chic retail
destinations in the principality
Style: Contemporary

Avignon

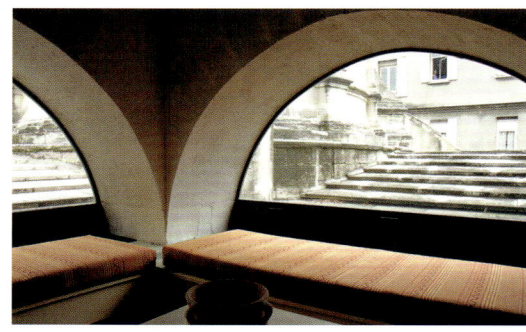

Hôtel Cloître Saint Louis

20, rue du Portail Boquier | 84000 Avignon
Phone: +33 4 90 27 55 55   Fax: +33 4 90 82 24 01
www.cloitre-saint-louis.com

Price category: €€
Rooms: 80 rooms
Facilities: Restaurant, rooftop terrace, outdoor pool,garden, parking
Services: Satellite TV
Style: Modern

Grasse

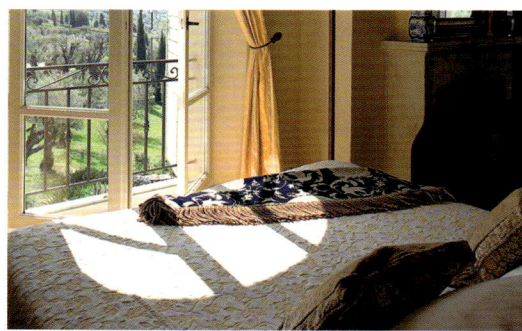

Bastide Saint Mathieu

35, chemin de Blumenthal | 06130 Grasse
Phone: +33 4 97 01 10 00   Fax: +33 4 97 01 10 09
www.bastidestmathieu.com

Price category: €€€
Rooms: 6 rooms including 1 suite
Facilities: Bar, restaurant, beauty salon
Services: Golf, tennis
Style: Provencal

Ménerbes

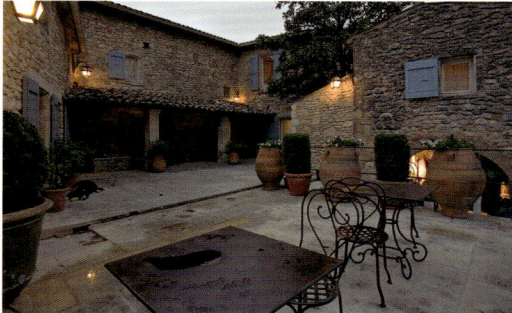

La Bastide de Marie

Route de Bonnieux | 84560 Ménerbes
Phone: +33 4 90 72 30 20   Fax: +33 4 90 72 54 20
www.sibuethotels-spa.com

Price category: €€€
Rooms: 14 including 6 suites
Facilities: Bar, restaurant, Pure Altitude spa
Services: Room service
Style: Provencal

Nice

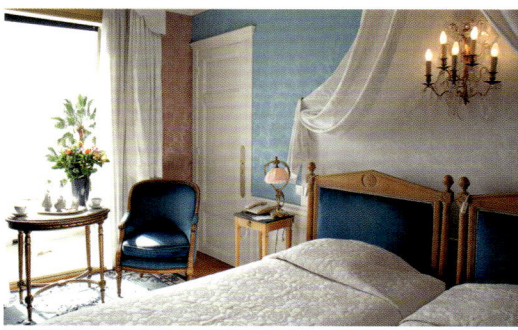

Negresco

37, promenade des Anglais | 06000 Nice
Phone: +33 4 93 16 64 00   Fax: +33 4 93 88 35 68
www.hotel-negresco-nice.com

Price category: €€€€
Rooms: 121 rooms and 24 suites
Facilities: Award-winning restaurant Le Chantecler, brasserie
La Rotonde, bar Le Relais, private beach, luxury shops, fitness
room, conference rooms
Services: Clé d'Or concierge service, golf, tennis, massage and hair
salons
Style: Enchanted

Saint-Tropez

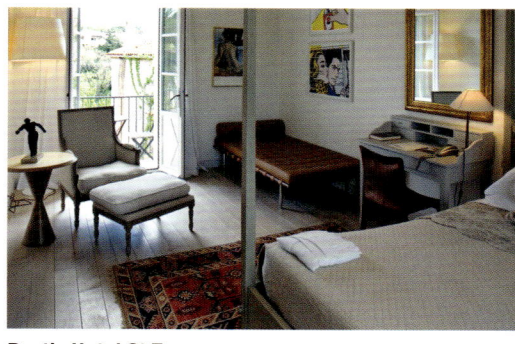

Pastis Hotel St Tropez

61, avenue du Général Leclerc | 83990 Saint-Tropez
Phone: +33 4 98 12 56 50   Fax: +33 4 94 96 99 82
www.pastis-st-tropez.com

Price category: €€€
Rooms: 9 rooms
Facilities: Bar, heated pool, boules terrain, private parking, meeting
room
Services: WiFi, DVD players in rooms, local and international
newspapers
Style: Contemporary-Provencal

Cap Ferrat

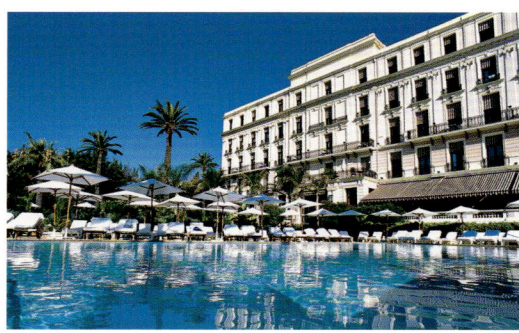

Royal Riviera

3, avenue Jean Monnet | 06230 Saint-Jean-Cap-Ferrat
Phone: +33 4 93 76 31 00   Fax: +33 4 93 01 23 07
www.royal-riviera.com

Price category: €€€€
Rooms: 96 rooms
Facilities: Restaurant, bar, wellness center, private sandy beach
Services: Swimming lessons, nautical activities
Style: Classic

Paris

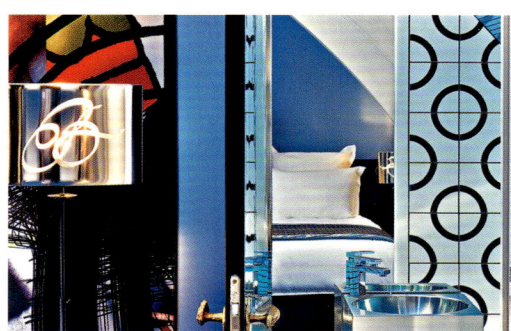

Hotel Le Bellechasse

8, rue de Bellechasse | 75007 Paris
Phone: +33 1 45 50 22 31   Fax: +33 1 45 51 52 36
www.lebellechasse.com

Price category: €€€
Rooms: 34 rooms
Facilities: Salon, bar
Services: WiFi
Style: Modern couture

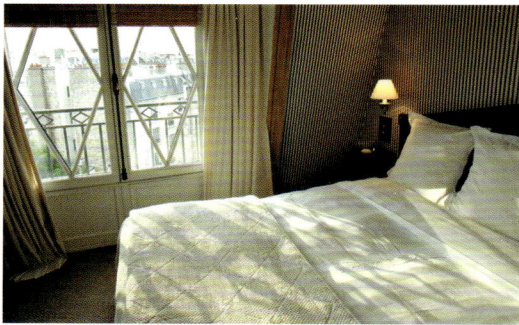

Sofitel Trocadéro Dokhan's

117, rue Lauriston | 75116 Paris
Phone: +33 1 53 65 66 99   Fax: +33 1 53 65 66 88
www.dokhans-sofitel-paris.com

Price category: €€
Rooms: 41 rooms and 4 suites
Facilities: Champagne-Bar
Services: Small dogs allowed, internet access
Style: Neoclassic

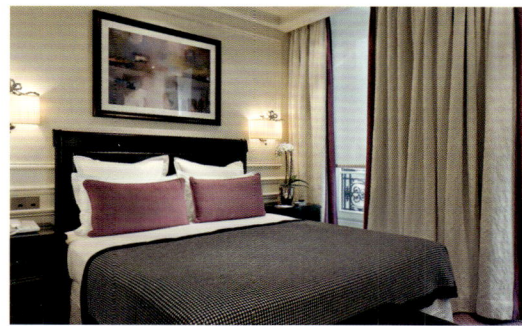

Hotel Keppler

10, rue Keppler | 75016 Paris
Phone: +33 1 47 20 65 05   Fax: +33 1 47 23 02 29
www.keppler-paris-hotel.com

Price category: €€
Rooms: 39 rooms including 4 suites and 1 penthouse
Facilities: Bar, fitness room including steam room, sauna and gym
Services: Clé d'Or concierge service, WiFi, room service, laundry, facilities for the disabled, parking
Style: Modern

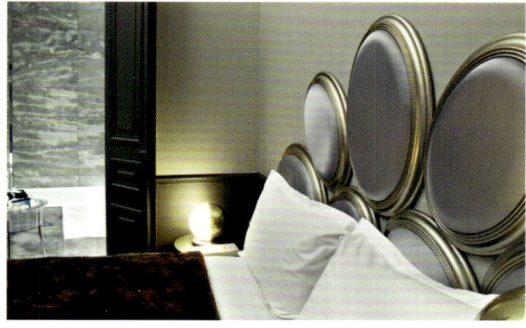

Hotel LUMEN Paris Louvre

15, rue des Pyramides | 75001 Paris
Phone: +33 1 44 50 77 00   Fax: +33 1 44 50 77 10
www.hotel-lumenparis.com

Price category: €€
Rooms: 32 rooms including 1 family and 1 rooftop suite
Facilities: Restaurant, bar Le Passage Saint Roch, conference facilities
Services: Concierge service, room service, laundry
Style: Contemporary and baroque

Italy

Florence

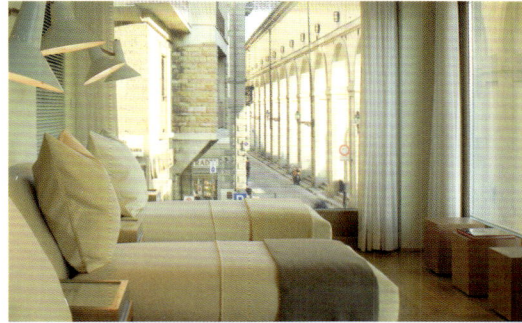

Continentale

Vicolo dell'Oro 6r | 50123 Florence
Phone: +39 055 27 26 40 00   Fax: +39 055 27 26 44 44
www.lungarnohotels.com

Price category: €€€
Rooms: 43 rooms including 1 penthouse suite
Facilities: Bar, Sky Lounge on the panoramic terrace, fitness center
Style: Contemporary design

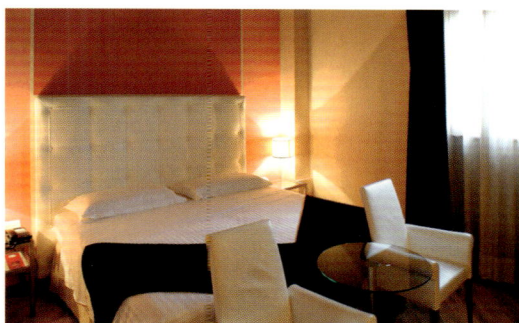

Granducato

Via Di Tomerello 1 | 50013 Campi Di Bisenzio
Phone: +39 05 58 80 51 11   Fax: +39 05 58 80 50 00
www.boscolohotels.com

Price category: €€€€
Rooms: 60 rooms and suites
Facilities: Restaurant, brasserie, garden, pool, fitness room, private chapel
Services: Conference rooms, shuttle service
Style: Mixture of original architecture and modern furnishing

Gargnano

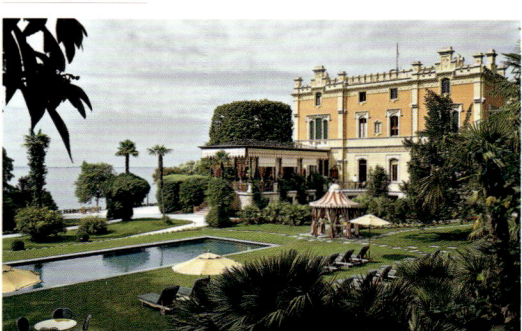

Grand Hotel a Villa Feltrinelli

Via Rimembranza 38–40 | 25084 Gargnano
Phone: +39 036 57 98 000   Fax: +39 036 57 98 001
www.villafeltrinelli.com

Price category: €€€€
Rooms: 21 suites
Facilities: Michelin star restaurant, bar, croquet lawn, heated outdoor pool
Services: WiFi, packing and un-packing service
Style: Liberty style villa

Milan

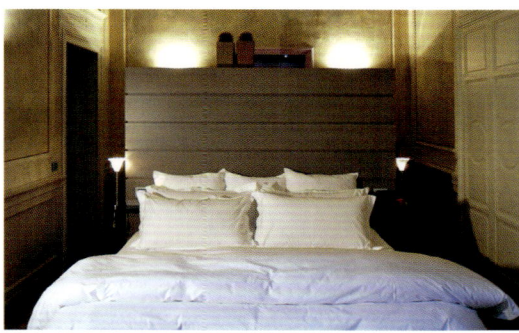

Town House Galleria

Via Silvio Pellico 8 | 20121 Milan
Phone: +39 02 89 05 82 97   Fax: +39 02 89 05 82 99
www.townhousegalleria.it

Price category: €€€€
Rooms: 24 rooms and suites
Facilities: Bar, restaurant La Sinfonia (only for guests)
Services: Exclusive butler service, events planning, shopping and art planning
Style: Rustic elegance

Turin

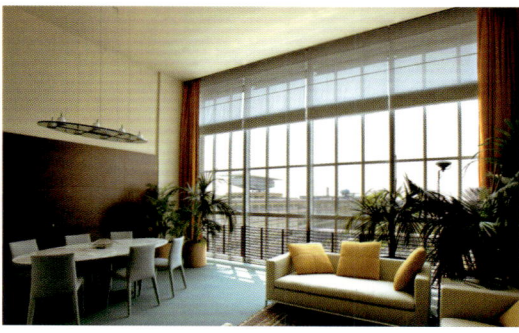

Le Méridien Turin Art+Tech

Via Nizza 230 | 10126 Turin
Phone: +39 011 66 42 780   Fax: +39 011 66 42 004
www.lemeridien.com/turin

Price category: €€
Rooms: 141 rooms and 1 suite
Facilities: Art+Cafe Bar and Restaurant, business center
Services: Babysitting, free parking, 24 h room service, fitness center, power-shower
Style: Design

Perugia

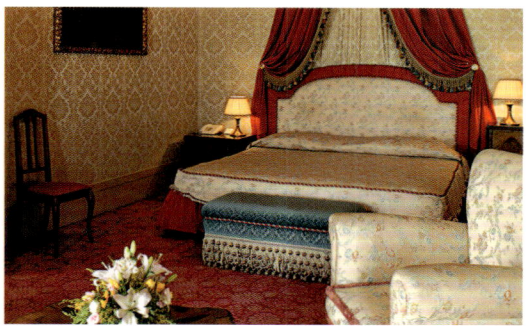

Brufani Palace

Piazza Italia 12 | 06100 Perugia
Phone: +39 075 57 32 541   Fax: +39 075 57 20 210
www.sinahotels.com

Price category: €€
Rooms: 94 rooms including 31 suites
Facilities: Collins Bar, Collins Restaurant and panoramic Terraza Bellavista
Services: Dry-cleaning and laundry service, valet parking and private indoor garage
Style: Classic

Venice

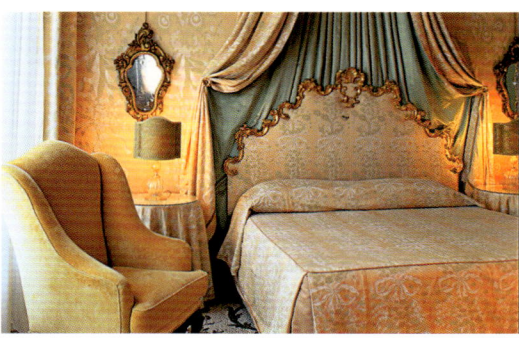

Bauer il Palazzo

San Marco 1459 | 30124 Venice
Phone: +39 041 52 07 022   Fax: +39 041 52 07 557
www.bauerhotels.com

Price category: €€€
Rooms: 82 rooms including 38 suites and junior suites
Facilities: De Pisis gourmet restaurant, BBar and Bar Canale
Services: Babysitting, concierge, 24 h room service
Style: Classic elegance

Verona

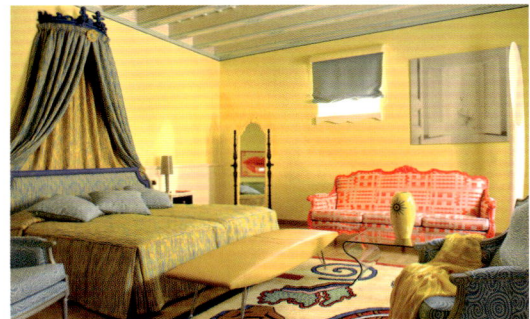

Byblos Art Hotel Villa Amista

Via Cedrare 78 | 37020 Corrubbio di S. Pietro in Cariano (Verona)
Phone: +39 045 68 55 555   Fax: +39 045 68 55 500
www.byblosarthotel.com

Price category: €€€
Rooms: 60 rooms
Facilities: Gourmet restaurant, bar and spa
Style: Contemporary design mixed with art

Rome

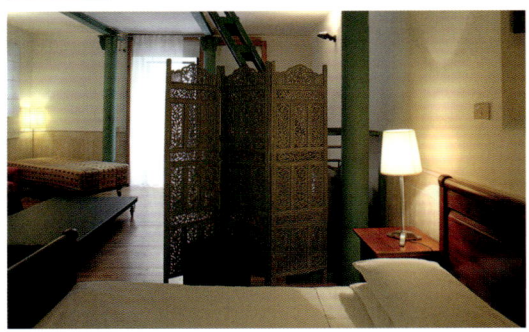

Casa della Palma

Via dei Sabelli 98 | 00185 Rome
Phone: +39 339 74 22 788   Fax: +39 06 23 32 45 562
www.casadellapalma.it

Price category: €
Rooms: 8 rooms and loft for 5 people
Facilities: Rooftop terrace, green inner courtyard
Services: Free city bikes, WiFi in all rooms
Style: Romantic-industrial

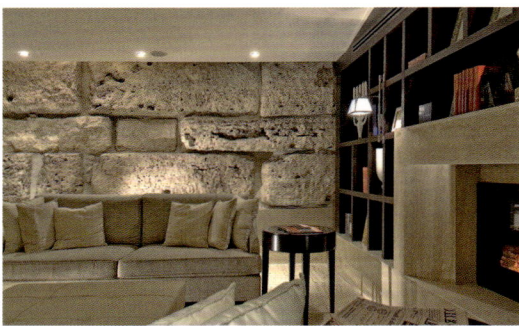

St George Roma

Via Giulia 62 | 00186 Rome
Phone: +39 06 68 66 11   Fax: +39 06 68 66 12 30
www.stgeorgehotel.it

Price category: €€€
Rooms: 64 rooms
Facilities: Restaurant I Sofà di Via Giulia, Terrazza Rosé roof terrace, wine bar, spa with Jacuzzi, sauna, personalized treatments and gym, library
Services: WiFi, concierge service, limousine service, butler on request
Style: Contemporary design

Spain

Mallorca

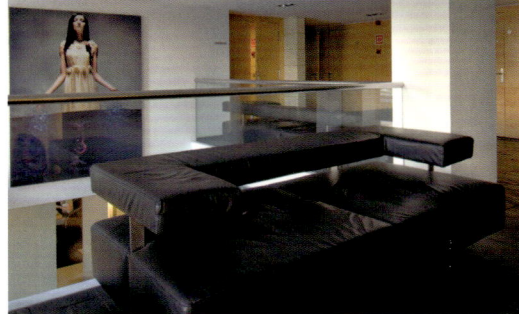

Hotel hm jaime III

Paseo Mallorca, 14 b | 07012 Palma de Mallorca
Phone: +34 971 72 59 43   Fax: +34 971 72 59 46
www.hmjaimeiii.com

Price category: €€
Rooms: 86 rooms and 2 junior suites
Facilities: Bar, restaurant, meeting rooms, spa
Services: Concierge, laundry, WiFi, room service
Style: Avant-garde

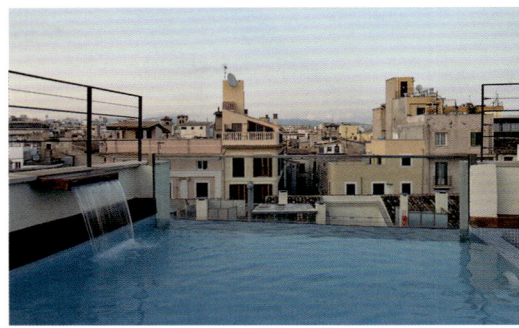

Tres

Calle Apuntadores, 3 | 07012 Palma de Mallorca
Phone: +34 971 717 333   Fax: +34 971 717 372
www.hoteltres.com

Price category: €€
Rooms: 38 rooms and 3 suites
Facilities: Bar/bistro, library, courtyard, conference room, roof terrace, plunge pool, sauna
Services: Room service
Style: Contemporary

Barcelona

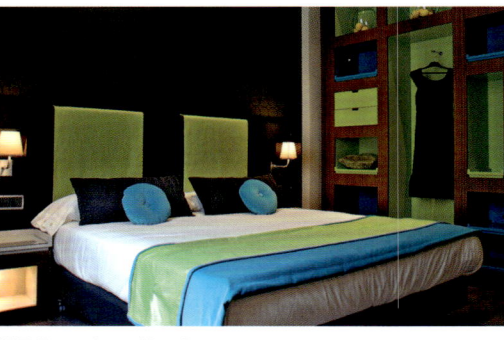

987 Barcelona Hotel

Calle Mallorca, 288 | 08037 Barcelona
Phone: +34 934 763 396   Fax: +34 934 763 394
www.987barcelonahotel.com

Price category: €
Rooms: 88 rooms
Facilities: 987 Lounge, restaurant
Services: Babysitting, room service, massage, free WiFi
Style: Design

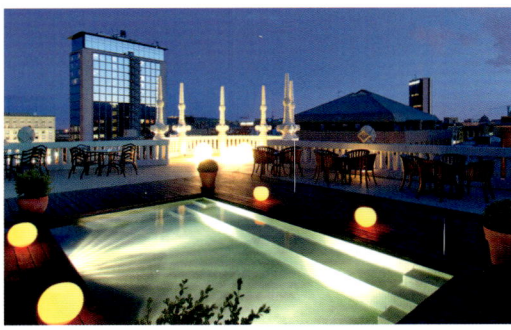

Casa Fuster

Passeo de Gracia, 132 | 08008 Barcelona
Phone: +34 932 553 000   Fax: +34 932 553 002
www.hotelcasafuster.com

Price category: €€€
Rooms: 75 rooms and 21 suites
Facilities: Restaurant Galaxó, Café Vienés, rooftop pool, Jacuzzi
Services: 10 meeting rooms for up to 300 people
Style: Mixture of art deco and traditional furnishing

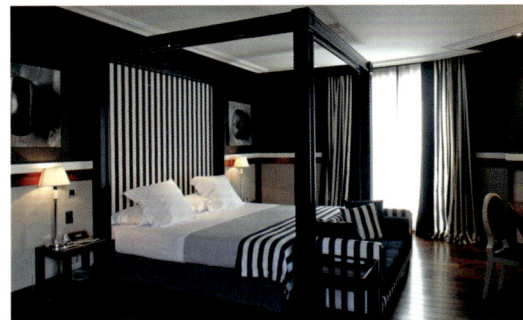

H1898

La Rambla, 109 | 08002 Barcelona
Phone: +34 935 529 552   Fax: +34 935 529 550
www.hotel1898.com

Price category: €€
Rooms: 169 rooms
Facilities: Bar and restaurant, outdoor bar and restaurant (closed in winter), spa, outdoor pool, sauna, steam room, solarium, library, gym, business center
Services: Room service, pillow menu, massages, garage
Style: Colonial and modern

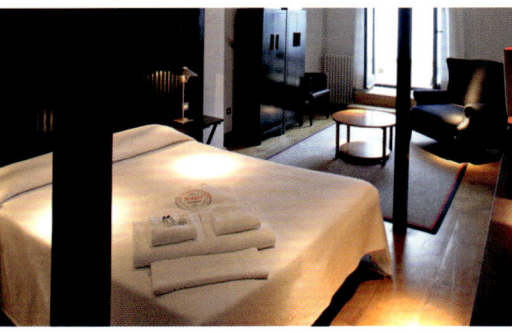

Market Hotel

Passaje Sant Antoni Abat, 10 | 08015 Barcelona
Phone: +34 933 251 205   Fax: +34 934 242 965
www.markethotel.com.es

Price category: €
Rooms: 46 rooms
Facilities: Restaurant, meeting room for 100 people
Services: Free notebook available, free WiFi an all rooms for guests, bicycle renting
Style: Modern

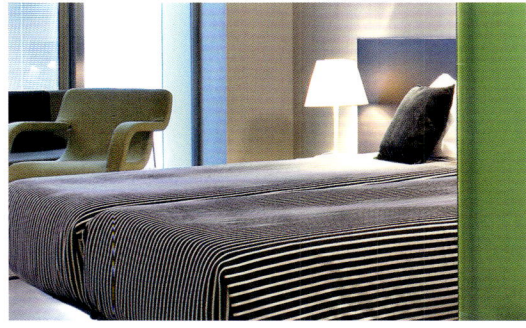

Hotel Soho Barcelona

Gran Vía, 543–545 | 08011 Barcelona
Phone: +34 935 529 610   Fax: +34 935 529 611
www.hotelsohobarcelona.com

Price category: €
Rooms: 51 rooms
Facilities: Lounge, terrace, outdoor pool
Services: Conference room for up to 20 people
Style: Contemporary design

Granada

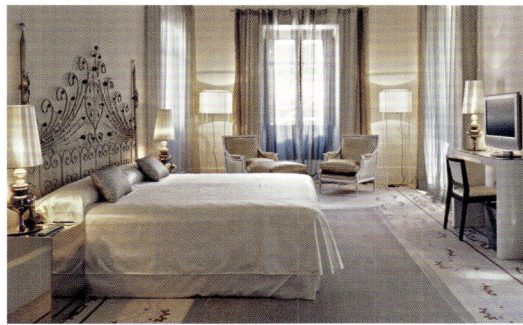

Palacio de los Patos

Solarillo de Gracia, 1 | 18002 Granada
Phone: +34 958 535 790   Fax: +34 958 536 968
www.hospes.com

Price category: €€
Rooms: 42 rooms including 5 suites
Facilities: Senzone restaurant, Bodyna spa, massage & treatments, pool, Jacuzzi, sauna and Turkish bath
Services: Meeting rooms for up to 60 people
Style: Modern and 19th century contrasts

Madrid

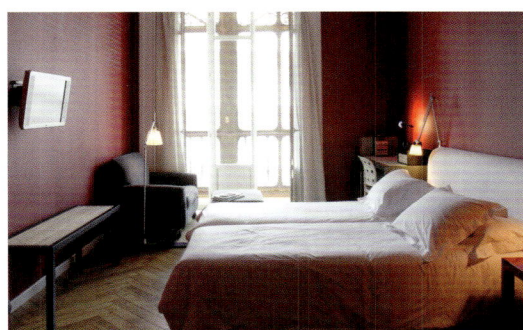

Hotel de las Letras H&R

Gran Vía, 1 | 28013 Madrid
Phone: +34 915 237 980   Fax: +34 915 237 981
www.hoteldelasletras.com

Price category: €€
Rooms: 102 rooms including 3 suites
Facilities: Restaurant, lounge, fitness & spa, solarium, library
Services: Meeting rooms for up to 150 people
Style: Modern

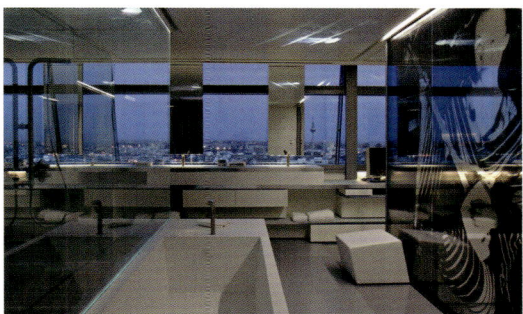

Hotel Puerta América

Avenida de América, 41 | 28002 Madrid
Phone: +34 917 445 400   Fax: +34 917 445 401
www.hotelpuertamerica.com

Price category: €€€
Rooms: 315 rooms
Facilities: Restaurant, bars and café, garden, indoor, 16 meeting rooms, swimming pool, sauna, business center
Services: Babysitting
Style: Contemporary design

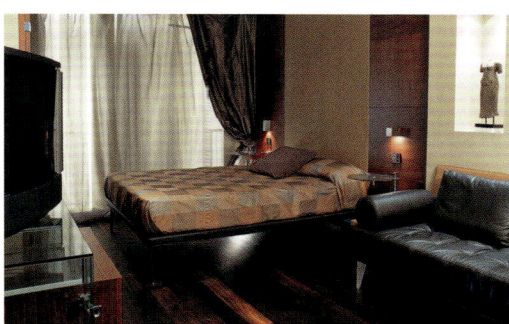

Hotel Urban

Carrera de San Jerónimo, 34 | 28014 Madrid
Phone: +34 917 877 770   Fax: +34 917 877 799
www.derbyhotels.com

Price category: €€€
Rooms: 96 rooms
Facilities: Gourmet restaurant Europa Decó and La Terraza, the GlassBar, rooftop pool, solarium, art collection, gym
Services: Meeting rooms
Style: Art deco

Portugal

Porto

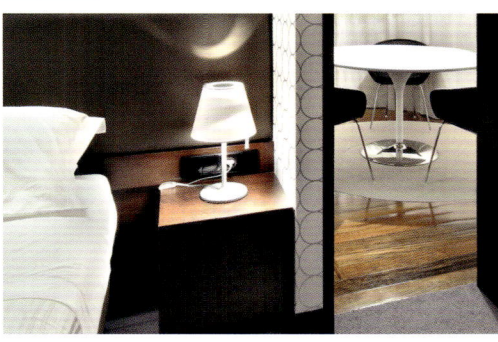

Porto Palacio Hotel

Ave da Boavista 1269 | 4159 Porto
Phone: +351 226 086 600   Fax: +351 226 091 467
www.hotelportopalacio.com

Price category: €€€
Rooms: 251 rooms and suites
Facilities: 2 restaurants, 2 bars, business center, health club and spa, pool
Services: Babysitting, hair stylist, concierge, parking, laundry
Style: Modern luxury

Lisbon

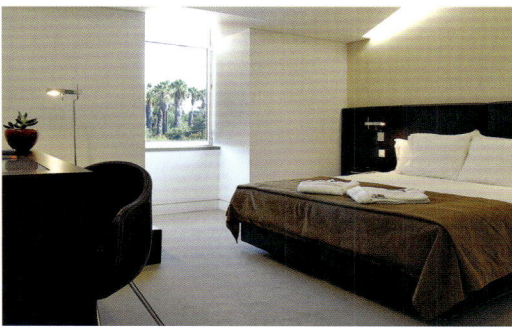

Jerónimos 8

Rua dos Jerónimos 8 | 1400-211 Lisbon
Phone: +351 21 360 09 00   Fax: +351 21 360 09 08
www.almeidahotels.com

Price category: €
Rooms: 61 rooms and 4 suites
Facilities: Bar, sun deck
Services: Room service, valet parking
Style: Urban resort in traditional building

Greece

Athens

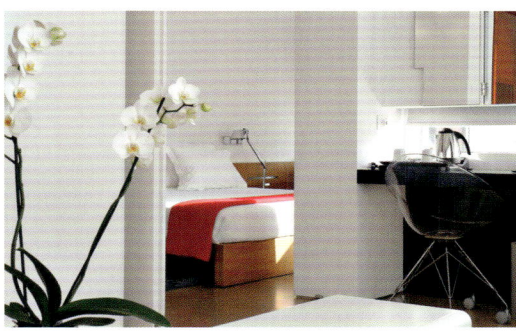

Fresh Hotel

26 Sophocleous & Klisthenous St. | 10552 Athens
Phone: +30 210 524 8511   Fax: +30 210 524 8517
www.freshhotel.gr

Price category: €
Rooms: 133 rooms
Facilities: Orange Bar, Magenta Restaurant, Air Lounge pool bar, conference facilities
Services: WiFi
Style: Modern

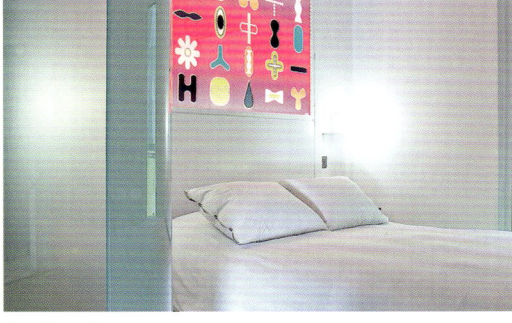

Semiramis

48 Charilaou Trikoupi St. | 14562 Kifissia
Phone: +30 210 628 4400   Fax: +30 210 628 4499
www.semiramisathens.com

Price category: €€
Rooms: 42 rooms, 5 bungalows and 4 penthouse suites
Facilities: Bar, pool restaurant, 3 meeting rooms, gym with sauna, spa
Services: Babysitting, free WiFi, face and body treatments, concierge, personal trainer
Style: Design

Mykonos

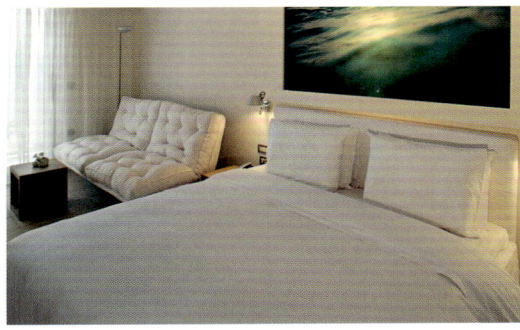

Mykonos Grace Hotel
Agios Stefanos | 84600 Mykonos
Phone: +30 228 902 6690   Fax: +30 228 902 6689
www.mykonosgrace.com

Price category: €€
Rooms: 16 rooms and 15 suites
Facilities: Poolside cocktail bar and restaurant, gym and spa, library
Services: TV lounge, parking, free baby cots for up to 4 years old
Style: Hip luxury

Santorini

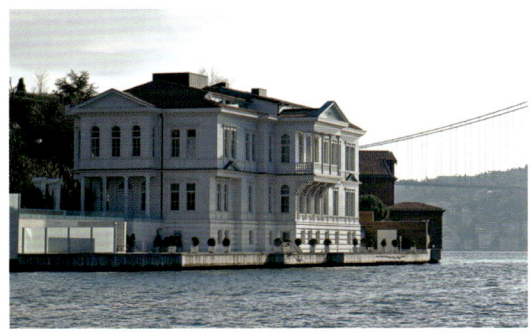

Perivolas
Oia | 84702 Santorini
Phone: +30 228 607 1308   Fax: +30 228 607 1309
www.perivolas.gr

Price category: €€€
Rooms: 20 suites
Facilities: Bar, restaurant, pool, spa
Services: Concierge, transfers, room service, parking
Style: Mediterranean

Turkey

Istanbul

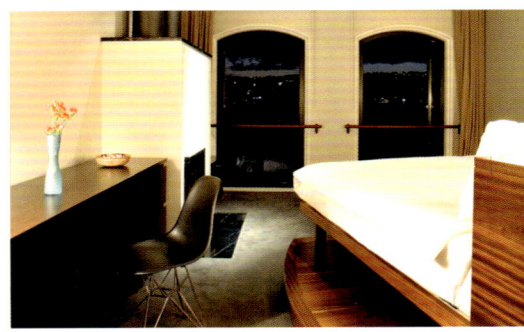

Ajia Hotel
Çubuklu Caddesi 27 | Kanlica, Istanbul
Phone: +90 216 413 9300   Fax: +90 216 413 9355
www.ajiahotel.com

Price category: €€€€
Rooms: 16 rooms including 6 suites
Facilities: Restaurant, bar, garden
Services: Babysitting, boat at disposal, room service, pressing-ironing
Style: Contemporary design

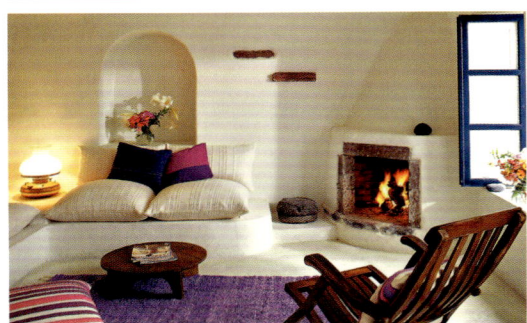

Sumahan
Kuleli Caddesi 51 | 34684 Istanbul
Phone: +90 216 422 8000   Fax: +90 216 422 8008
www.sumahan.com

Price category: €€
Rooms: 13 rooms and 7 suites
Facilities: 2 Restaurants, wellness center, meeting room
Services: Babysitting, fitness and massage service, 24 h room service, library, accessible for the disabled, dry cleaning, laundry service
Style: Modern

Price orientation
€ = < 200 EUR
€€ = 201 – 350 EUR
€€€ = 351 – 550 EUR
€€€€ = > 551 EUR

Photo Credits

William Abramowicz	Perivolas	368 (right), 371
Markus Bachmann	Fresh Hotel	354
James Balston	g Hotel	Cover, 40
Roland Bauer	The Grove	54
	Hotel de Filosoof	94
	misc eatdrinksleep	98 (left), 99
	Lloyd Hotel	100
	Stroom	104
	Eden Designhotel	106
	Kruisherenhotel	110
	Monty Small Design Hotel	120
	Adlon Kempinski	128
	Villa Kennedy	146
	Chelsea	150
	Schloss Auel	152
	Hotel La Maison	160
	Bayerischer Hof	164 (left), 166
	Ski & Golfresort Kitzhof	186
	Hotel Schloss Fuschl	190
	Palais Coburg Residenz	194
	Victoria-Jungfrau	202
	Greulich	210
	Hôtel Cloître Saint Louis	226
	La Bastide de Marie	234
	Negresco	238
	Royal Riviera	246
	Sofitel Trocadéro Dokhan's	254
Rachel Bonnewell	misc eatdrinksleep	98 (right)
Courtesy 42 The Calls	42 The Calls	88
Courtesy 987 Barcelona Hotel	987 Barcelona Hotel	312
Courtesy andel's hotel Prague	andel's Hotel & Suites Prague	170
Courtesy Ararat Park Hyatt Moscow	Ararat Park Hyatt Moscow	16
Courtesy Badrutt's Palace Hotel	Badrutt's Palace Hotel	206
Courtesy Bayerischer Hof	Bayerischer Hof	164
Courtesy Hotel Bauer	Bauer il Palazzo	288
Courtesy Bellinter House	Bellinter House	48
Courtesy Berns Hotel	Berns Hotel	26
Courtesy Byblos Art Hotel Villa Amista	Byblos Art Hotel Villa Amista	292
Courtesy Casa Fuster	Casa Fuster	314
Courtesy Columbus Monaco	Columbus Monaco	222

Courtesy Cowley Manor	Cowley Manor	64
Courtesy Design Hotels	Semiramis	358
Courtesy Dylan Hotel Dublin	Dylan	44
Courtesy Firmdale Hotels	Haymarket Hotel	84
Courtesy First Hotel Skt. Petri	First Hotel Skt. Petri	36
Courtesy Hospes Hoteles	Palacio de los Patos	330
Courtesy Hotel Brufani Palace	Brufani Palace	284
Courtesy Claridge's	Claridge's	81
Courtesy Hotel J	Hotel J	28
Courtesy Hotel Josef	Hotel Josef	174
Courtesy Hotel Keppler	Hotel Keppler	258
Courtesy Hotel Le Bellechasse	Hotel Le Bellechasse	250
Courtesy Hotel Le Méridien Art+Tech	Le Méridien Turin Art+Tech	282
Courtesy Hotel Lumen	Hotel LUMEN Paris Louvre	262
Courtesy Hotel Pelirocco	Hotel Pelirocco	52
Courtesy Hotel Soho Barcelona	Hotel Soho Barcelona	326
Courtesy Hotel St George Roma	St George Roma	300
Courtesy Jerónimos 8 Hotel	Jerónimos 8	350
Courtesy Lungarno Hotels	Continentale	266
Courtesy Maximilian Hotel	Maximilian	178
Courtesy Mykonos Grace Hotel	Mykonos Grace Hotel	364
Courtesy of 25hours Hotel Company	Goldman 25hours Hotel	142
Courtesy The Berkeley	The Berkeley	68
Courtesy The Glasshouse	The Glasshouse	92

Courtesy The Three Sisters Hotel	The Three Sisters Hotel	22
Courtesy Town House Galleria	Town House Galleria	278
Courtesy Tschuggen Grand Hotel	Tschuggen Grand Hotel	198
Courtesy Villa Feltrinelli	Grand Hotel a Villa Feltrinelli	274
Courtesy Whatley Manor	Whatley Manor	58
Courtesy Widder Hotel	Widder Hotel	215, 217 (bottom)
Serge Detalle	Casadelmar	218
diephotodesigner.de	Lux Eleven	132
Bernd Eidenmuller	Der Zauberlehrling	156
Katharina Feuer	Swissôtel Krasnye Holmy	20
Klaus Frahm	SIDE	Back cover, 140
Jean-Pierre Gabriel	Royal Windsor	124
Gavin Jackson	B+B Belgravia	72
	Blakes Hotel	74
	Claridge's	80, 82, 83
	Q!	136
	Ajia Hotel	372
	Sumahan	378
Rudolph Klein	Lánchíd 19	183, 184, 185 (bottom right)
Christoph Kranach	Fox	32
Martin Nicholas Kunz	Hotel Julien	116
	Widder Hotel	214, 216, 217 (top)
	Bastide Saint Mathieu	230
	Pastis Hotel St Tropez	242
	Granducato	270
	Casa della Palma	296
Martin Nicholas Kunz, Michelle Gallindo	Market Hotel	322
	Hotel de las Letras H&R	334
	Hotel Puerta América	336
	Hotel Urban	342
Ken Schluchtmann	Porto Palacio Hotel	346
Attila Szabó	Lánchíd 19	182, 185
Jörg Tietje	Hotel hm jaime III	304
	Tres	308
Timos Tsoukalas	Perivolas	368 (left), 369, 370

Imprint

Produced by fusion publishing gmbh, stuttgart . los angeles

Editorial team:

Martin Nicholas Kunz (Editor)

Nathalie Grolimund, Viviana Guastalla (Editorial Coordination)

Kristen Kress (Layout)

Stefanie Bisping, Bärbel Holzberg, Camilla Péus,
Anna Streubert (Texts)

Alphagriese Fachübersetzungen, Düsseldorf (Translations)
Dr. William Hester (English), Stéphanie Laloix (French)

Sylvia Lyschik, Bruno Plaza (Spanish translations)
Romina Russo, Frederica Benetti (Italian translations)

fusion publishing gmbh (prepress)

Everbest Printing Co.Ltd – www.everbest.com (imaging)

Published by teNeues Publishing Group

teNeues Verlag GmbH & Co. KG
Am Selder 37, 47906 Kempen, Germany
Tel.: 0049-(0)2152-916-0, Fax: 0049-(0)2152-916-111
E–mail: books@teneues.de

Press department: arehn@teneues.de
Tel.: 0049-(0)2152-916-202

teNeues Publishing Company
16 West 22nd Street, New York, NY 10010, USA
Tel.: 001-212-627-9090, Fax: 001-212-627-9511

teNeues Publishing UK Ltd.
P. O. Box 402, West Byfleet, KT14 7ZF, Great Britain
Tel.: 0044-1932-403509, Fax: 0044-1932-403514

teNeues France S.A.R.L.
93, rue Bannier, 45000 Orléans, France
Tel.: 0033-2-38541071, Fax: 0033-2-38625340

www.teneues.com

© 2008 teNeues Verlag GmbH + Co. KG, Kempen

ISBN: 978-3-8327-9235-0

Printed in Italy

Bibliographic information published by Die Deutsche
Bibliothek. Die Deutsche Bibliothek lists this publication in the
Deutsche Nationalbibliografie; detailed bibliographic data is
available in the Internet at http://dnb.ddb.de.